LYRICAL HERITAGE

LYRICAL HERITAGE

The National Library of Poetry

Melisa S. Mitchell, Editor

Lyrical Heritage

Library of Congress
Cataloging in Publication Data

ISBN 1-57553-157-7

Proudly manufactured in The United States of America by
Watermark Press
One Poetry Plaza
Owings Mills, MD 21117

Editor's Note

As artists undertake any creative endeavor, they draw on all of their experiences, including every piece of art they have ever witnessed. One might say that a poet draws on our collective *Lyrical Heritage*, a wellspring of previously created works which, during our creative journey through life, we have read, studied, analyzed and contemplated, taking from each something which would enrich our lives. Due to this link between present and past artistic endeavors, lyrical poetry, one of the first types of verse, serves as the foundation for modern poetry. Beginning with the Doric poets, like Sappho, Alcaeus and, later, Anacreon, lyrics were the prominent form of poetry throughout the ages. In Medieval Europe, the troubadours used lyrical verse in their ballads. Later, during the Renaissance, the sonnet became the most finished type of lyrical verse. The Romantic poets, including Robert Burns, William Blake, Percy Bysshe Shelley, John Keats, and Victor Hugo, used predominantly lyrical forms as well, becoming some of the most influential poets whose work is still part of the modern literary canon.

The earliest lyric poetry distinguished itself from narrative poetry and verse drama by its being used to express the poet's thoughts and feelings. This expressive element is certainly present in modern poetry. In this anthology, you will see that each poet has crafted a tool through which he or she sings the song of his or her life, emotions, and thoughts. The language in each is sometimes reflective of the language used in the original lyrical verse, sometimes more crafted to suit the individual needs of the poet. Whatever stylistic technique each uses, the poets represented here have created works that express their life experiences, whether general or specific, beneficial or destructive, personal or observational, descriptive or expository. A few have done this particularly well, like Robbin Thrush in her poem, "la belle dame sans merci" (p. 362).

The poet describes the dandelion, the fertile weed which "chokes all chance / of life existing around it." Personification and feminization of the plant help to fully illustrate its ability to propagate itself so prolifically. The dandelion, "our magnificent and conniving / slut of weeds," is compared to Ishtar, the Mesopotamian goddess of war and eros. This is an apt comparison, as Ishtar is also the goddess of contradictory forces, particularly of fertility and death. Though dandelions are attractive, brightly-colored or downy-white flowers, they also can harm the grass in which they grow. Additionally, the lion and the dove are sacred to Ishtar. The lion is present in the name of the weed, and the dove in its feathery, white appearance when it has gone to seed. The lines "lone-blossomed-ancient-mask" and "marked by her she-wolf scent" evoke the ancient ritualistic practices traditionally associated with goddess-worship. This further demonstrates the parallel drawn between the fertility goddess and the fertile, invasive flowers.

Another unique poem which uses interesting comparisons as an expository method is David Keene's "Duck Soup" (p. 334). This work makes a simultaneously comical and powerful statement about our society and its perhaps foreboding and inhuman future.

Every word in the poem is loaded with meaning and deliberation — each word carries its weight of significance. The descriptions of the people mentioned demonstrate this well: "TV talk show transvestites," "empowered soured politicians," "Low fat sexual lions," "Robot sentries with computer enhanced libidos." These totems of our society are put into their respective places, and are presented in a way that is representative of today's computer and information age, where we are all constantly bombarded with images and data, particularly in the media. The descriptions are also brief and broken up in such a way that it almost seems as though the poet is holding a television remote control. Each brief description shows what is seen as the poet toggles from channel to channel, pausing only long enough for the image to register in his brain. It is important to note, though, that none of these images is pleasant; and each is more inhuman than the last. Politicians point the finger at others to direct blame and suspicion away from themselves; television talk shows exploit people who have had difficult lives, putting them oftentimes at the center of public ridicule; "robot sentries" ensure our safety in family values; and billboards and flashing traffic lights insist that they are trustworthy.

The final stanza effectively summarizes the earlier description. The jester, commenting on the king's golf game, asks if he has "tried reducing [his] carbon intake?" As carbon exists in all life-forms, for the king to reduce the amount of carbon in his body would decrease his organic nature. This being the computer age, the jester could "write up a program" for such a thing, and the king, by decreasing his organic nature, would then reduce his humanness. This expository poem effectively illustrates the movement of life toward automation and, thus, toward being less human. This change renders us incapable of having the necessary sympathy and compassion in such a time when it is perhaps most important.

In another very interesting and creative work, "The Philosophy of Camaraderie" (p. 186), Monica Jackson presents an everyday scene with a new twist. A conversation in the "coliseum din" of a restaurant — perhaps a diner or a cafeteria of some kind — is compared to an interaction in ancient Greece. The two people presented seem to not know each other well, but are having a conversation over a meal. The speaker is comfortable with the man opposite her, but she also seems a bit intimidated by him, calling him a philosopher and referring to him as Aristotle. She describes the sun filtering through his hair creating "the dance of auburn nymphs in the sunlight behind / him." While she likens her companion to Aristotle, she seems to compare herself to Socrates. Though she never names the ancient philosopher outright, the allusion to Socrates is made toward the end of the poem when her "cup of hemlock seemed to grow cold."

Additionally, the two speak of "the greatness of platonic / encounters like this one and [their] own personal Greek / tragedies." A platonic encounter is one which transcends physical desire, but is also one which is characteristic of Plato or his philosophy. This can, as a result, be read in several different ways. On one hand, Plato's most famous works are written in the form of dialogues between Socrates and himself. The interaction in the poem is also a dialogue, and is thus platonic in its structural similarities to his works. Also, the interchange between the Socratic figure and the Aristotelian figure is one which, at least the persona feels, goes beyond the physical into something more profound and spiritually based. When the Aristotelian figure then says, "'You have a pretty face,'" the persona is disappointed by her having misread the situation, and pushes aside her cold cup of hemlock. Hemlock is a poison, and she thus rejects some sort of death — perhaps an emotional or spiritual one, which she would surely suffer at the hands of this person who is not what the speaker thought him to be. For Socrates himself, though, the hemlock which he drank as punishment for his alleged corruption of Grecian youth became a symbol of his patriotism and loyalty to the state. Although he felt that he was not guilty, he believed that each citizen is bound by conscience to obey the laws of the state, so he did not attempt to escape prison, but dutifully drank his poison and accepted his undue punishment. By pushing away the hemlock, the persona is realizing that her fealty to her companion is not based on something that she values — ultimately she is nothing more to him than "a pretty face." She rejects him, but sees that he is much more confident with his own ideas and theories than she is with hers. Her philosophies have become more of a useless burden to her, not possessing any degree of truth.

> . . . he strolled away,
> with his confident toga wrapped around him
> more tightly than any unshakable theories
> I albatrossed around myself.

The albatross, considered by sailors to be a good omen, is an enormous bird with a wing-span of up to twelve feet. The image of the persona with her theories "albatrossed" around herself evokes the image of the mariner from Coleridge's "Rime of the Ancient Mariner." After killing an albatross while at sea, the persona in this tale is vilified by his crew and made to carry the immense bird around his shoulders. Thus, the persona in this poem is burdened by the weight of her own unwieldy ideas. Additionally, Aristotle's philosophies and ideas were based almost exclusively in the sciences, whereas Socrates was more concerned with virtue and human conduct. The latter had no formal doctrine, established no school and wrote nothing. Despite his brilliant intellectualism, his ideas seem abstract and subjective. This supports the persona's assertion that the Aristotelian figure was more confident with his thoughts — they are all, at least metaphorically speaking, based in concrete fact and mathematical equations. This poem is an excellent illustration of how a brief personal experience can greatly influence one's thoughts.

Another poem which demonstrates the effects of interpersonal relationships in a touching and impressive way is Kimberly Lewis' "Mama Was Right" (p. 1). The poet renders a tragic situation in which a woman is married to a neglectful, adulterous alcoholic.

> Holy union committed her to foreign lipstick shades
> on his shirts, and nights spent in alcoholic solitude;
> Sunrise brought to her the cleanliness of a new day
> and the dread of another filthy evening

Each day brought new hope, but each night brought the same thing: "the snap! of kitchen cheese-traps, / the slow red change of clock numbers in the dark," while her husband "pocketed colored balls — stacking more of her quarters on the altar of a green table." Not only was he spending her quarters on games of pool and on the "ever-flowing anesthetic of draft," but he was also spending her time. The moments he was away added up to the ticking by of the quarters of hours of her life. Finally, "Giving birth brought only warnings of eviction." It is possible that when she gave birth, he threatened to make her leave their home. More likely, though, is that once she gave birth to their child, she began to threaten *him* with eviction, either his or her own. This is supported by her leaving in the second stanza.

> *The last night he hung her heart on a barroom coatrack,*
> *she quit lying to the phone.*
> *She took her bundled doll and trudged*
> *twenty-six miles of swallowed pride,*
> *and snuggled into an almost forgotten faded photograph*
> *that was mama's house.*

The woman finally swallows her pride, admits that "Mama Was Right," and goes back to the place that has become little more than a vague memory of the past. She returns to her girlhood comforts, like "her old frilly room" and "her teddy," because after all, "wasn't she once a child?" She and her own child, sleeping in her old room and "sharing her teddy," have escaped from their situation, and have "slept from hell to heaven." The two of them sleep from the sadness and misery of night into the hope and promise of the next day, as well as from one life into a new one. As for her husband, he had lost the game, both literally and figuratively speaking, for "he'd pocketed the eight ball too early."

Kimberly Lewis creates a sympathetic character without using extravagant and complicated language and description. Through the detailed illustration of the poem's setting, the characters, their relationships, and their problems, Kimberly creates a tremendously dynamic piece employing relatively simple poetic language. As a result, the judges have awarded her the Grand Prize.

There are many other poems in this volume which tell stories from the poets' lives, demonstrate a series of thoughts, or illustrate their emotional landscapes. Among them are the following noteworthy works: Bo Buchanan's "Zoom Lens" (p. 121), a poem which eloquently expresses the persona's horror and frustration at the inhumanity and voyeurism present in our society; Patricia Johnson's "Going Home to Mother" (p. 283), which tells of the struggle of an adult who returns home; Jana Palaski's "Anima Enema" (p. 446), which follows one person's thoughts as they grapple to deal with life; Annette Rasmussen's "Reclamation" (p. 441), the story of a woman trying to reclaim poetry, and herself, after she has sacrificed them both; Jim Sheridan's "Florida" (p. 195), a description of the American tropical paradise through the eyes of both its inhabitants and the persona; Ryan Schuchart's "Biting Pyramids" (p. 478), an interesting journey through the persona's inner landscape; and Chad White's "And this is all that's come of it, Sarah" (p. 459), beautifully illustrating the life of a couple whose passion has faded.

Each poem in *Lyrical Heritage* speaks from a singular life. As a result, not every poem will speak to every reader. Nonetheless, it is important to remember that each poem is a valid form of expression for the poet who created it. Please carefully read the works in this volume, as each is written from a perspective which offers a wealth of emotion and experience from which we all can learn. The poets in this anthology tell the stories of their lives through their verse, and because of the individuality of each, each poem takes on a life of its own. I congratulate everyone featured in this book on their poetic accomplishments.

I would like to thank the staff members from The National Library of Poetry, without whom this book would not have been possible. Judges, editors, associate editors, customer service representatives, data entry personnel, graphic artists, office administrators and administrative services staff have all made invaluable contributions to this effort. I am *grateful* to them for their contributions and support.

Melisa S. Mitchell
Editor

Cover Art: Tracy Hetzel

Grand Prize Winner

Kimberly Lewis / Columbus MS

Second Prize Winners

Bo Buchanan / Lancaster PA
Monica Jackson / Landis NC
Patricia Johnson / Scottsdale AZ
David Keene / Springfield MO
Jana Palaski / Erie PA

Annette Rasmussen / Kansas City MO
Ryan Schuchart / San Antonio TX
Jim Sheridan / Sandy Hook CT
Robbin Thrush / Winter Park FL
Chad White / Houston TX

Third Prize Winners

David Aikman / Springfield IL
David Bailey / Great Falls VA
Poet Batchelder / Swampscott MA
Thomas Beaird / St. Louis MO
Ronald Beattie / Albuquerque NM
Mary-Ann Bebko / Yellow Springs OH
Keith Boggess / Baducah KY
Deborah Bone / Phoenix AZ
Autumn Breaud / Burleston TX
Richard Brooks / Beaufort SC
Albert Cevallos / Washington DC
Hedwig Chappelle / New York NY
Louis Choi / San Francisco CA
Judith Colonna / New York NY
April Cox / Pomona CA
Leriget de la Plante / Parker CO
Sallie Dewberry / Birmingham AL
Francis Dispo / Peru NY
Joe Domino / Liberty MO
Daniel Dowell / Bremen KY
Gilbert Estrada / Downey CA
Poet Farrell / Briarwood NY
Brian Field / Norwalk CT
Mark Gatti / Kenmore NY
Marjorie Havens / Wells ME
Candace Herr / Pitman NJ
Greg Hester / Springfield TN
Rebecca Holtzman / Bloomington IN
Russell Jackson / Seattle WA
Kay Kocour / Morgan TX

Nancy Koven / Cherry Hill NJ
Balaji Krishna / Gainsville FL
Orrin Loftin / Great Falls MT
Jane Mason / Honolulu HI
Sandy McLain / Lubbock TX
Jennifer Miller / North Attleboro MA
Djordje Minic / Kildeer IL
Minoee Modi / Ithaca NY
Marian Ocampo-Diaz / Houston TX
Gregory Orloff / Santa Monica CA
Micah Palmer / Channelview TX
Claudia Patrick / Tulsa OK
Georges Pinel / San Diego CA
Angela Pulley / Auburn AL
William Schutter / Port Jervis NY
Ira Shull / Shirley MA
Shirley Spina / Santa Rosa CA
Eva Szabo / Waban MA
Matt Thompson / Milton MA
Timothy Tiess / South Windham ME
Amy Traub / Shaker Heights OH
Heather Ubelhor / Riverside CA
Sabrina Valentini / Baltimore MD
Raul Vallejo / Adelphi MD
Christina Watkins / Englewood CO
Bill West / Reston VA
Kelly Whitaker / Newport News VA
Gus Wilhelmy / Chicago IL
Donald Young / Willow Street PA

Congratulations also to all semi-finalists.

Grand Prize Winner

Mama Was Right
by Kimberly Lewis

Holy union committed her to foreign lipstick shades
on his shirts, and nights spent in alcoholic solitude;
Sunrise brought to her the cleanness of a new day
and the dread of another filthy evening
Her entertainment was the snap! of kitchen cheese-traps,
the slow red change of clock numbers in the dark;
His entertainment was the ever-flowing anesthetic of draft
as he pocketed colored balls – stacking more of her quarters
on the altar of a green table.
Giving birth brought only warnings of eviction.

The last night he hung her heart on a barroom coatrack,
she quit lying to the phone.
She took her bundled doll and trudged
twenty-six miles of swallowed pride,
and snuggled into an almost forgotten faded photograph
that was mama's house.
In her old frilly room (wasn't she once a child?)
they slept from hell to heaven, sharing her teddy.
(he'd pocketed the eight ball too early in the game)

Seeds

Naked
I stand alone
a windswept seed
no leaves, no roots
flying, floating, fleeing
no bearing, no course.
Sailing, soaring, seeking
a warm place to grow
light, hope, truth and peace
rhythmic patterns
dance in harmony.
I embrace the child
liberate the genie
paint my dreams
release the tigers
free the doves
follow the clouds
today, tomorrow, always
soar with eagles

Richard J. Lapenna

My Mother

Strong, yet vulnerable;
Disciplined, yet down to earth;
Clean, yet appropriately disheveled;
Protective, yet allowing;
Strict, yet forgiving;
Graceful, yet aloof;
Spiritual, yet sinfully beautiful;
Lover of life, yet
    killer of plants.

Cheryl Darnell

Peacemaker

With all the turbulence in the world
It's hard growing up as a girl.
The violence makes you outraged
Life is like turning a page.

People always fighting with each other
Instead of trying to stick together.
People look at other's faces.
Then turn against certain races.

The echo of discrimination
Spreading day after day
Pursuing in many ways.

So if there was an event
That really could prevent
Would it be the cure.
To keep us secure.

The feral minds of today
Should take a break to get away
It's your choice
Take a step towards a brighter day.

Shazeena Mohamed

The Wind Is Cold

The wind is cold
But I am bold
So I will sleigh
All his day.

When I am done,
I had some fun
But the warm fire
Is all my desire.

Michele Smith

I'm Alone, I'm Without

I'm alone, I'm without.
I'm a puppet without strings.
I'm a voice without compassion.
I'm a object without shape.
I'm a chastity belt without a buckle,
I'm a clown without a chuckle.
I'm old-fashion with a burning passion.
I'm a rambling brook without a stream.
I'm in love without love.
I'm alone, I'm without,
I'm alone, I'm without . . . you!

Kathy S. Britt

Early Morning Surprise

From my window
I looked out
and all about
Everything was white.
A pure delight!

Softly falling,
White on black,
all out-back
A fairy wonderland.
Breathless I stand!

Thank you, O Lord,
For this lovely sight:
the beautiful white
Of falling snow
Covering all below!

Elizabeth Flohr

Where Are We?

Where in the mind, there is a struggle,
you touch the world in deep embrace.
And nights are hard to understand,
Because the lights too Bright to face.
Yet deep inside a tortured soul,
A madness rages unforetold.
Many rooms locked with keys,
Betray the mind that can't be free.
As time escape's and makes its way,
when pain is near it will not say.
For pain engulfs the body clear,
There is no peace, for me, in here.
Stuck in a web not made by man,
But worn, no less, I understand
In life a struggle, makes us strong,
But where are we, that don't belong?

Amalia Noel

A Teardrop

For Allan Robinson
A teardrop on my cheek
is all it seems to be

A teardrop on my cheek
shed for you and me

A teardrop lost and lonely
lonely as I am for you

A teardrop slowly sliding, falling
as I fell for you

A teardrop being wiped away
as easily as I was from you

Dorian L. Hill

"Melina"

She came to clean
The very first time.
Face to face we gazed,
Fierce spirits now ready to shine.

For magic light
Was what they saw.
Ruby lips transpired me,
High above the floor.

That floor she cleaned
And all else too.
Unwittingly dancing and swaying;
Shafts of sun turned blue.

And then she came forward
To get her wages paid.
A wife and mother working;
Venus turned a maid.

Oh Beauty! As she left me,
That job so well done.
An inner being spent,
Shaken, and wrung, and spun.

Anthony F. Marceda

Untitled

His soul is love
His voice is calm
His lips refresh my soul
He is all I need in times of trouble
He is all I need to have, to hold

His eyes bring light
His hands caress
His laughter soothes me so
He keeps me warm when life is cold
He is with me where e'er I go.

Kris Douglas

Untitled

The late winter storm;
A fresh spire of columbine
Rising in the snow

Maria Katakozinos

Untitled

In the corner of the room,
Sits a women filled with gloom,
Her thought's are pure,
Yet her mind is unsure,
She cries for things long past.

Why you ask?
No one really knows,

Does she in fact?
I cannot say to tell you the truth,
Her dress,
Long and white,
Is tattered and torn,
From being over worn,
Blood stains on the dress,
What an unsightly mess!
Black tears run down her face,
She watches you from a far,
No words uttered, or spoken,
Watching Watching,
Watching you in your foolishness.

Susan R. Dudra

3

Ho "Boy-Yo"

Another cat here!!
Oh "Boy-Yo," oh "Boy-Yo,"
Gonna have a fight,
Oh "Boy-Yo,"
Love that scraping.

Don't like you.
Never have.

Spray my bush !!!
Oh "Boy-Yo," oh "Boy-Yo,"
Gonna have a fight,
Oh "Boy-Yo."
Gonna have a scrap.

Shirley Griffith

Spring Hope

If spring would last forever,
How lovely it would be!
New birth, new joy, new life
and faith eternally.

If spring would last forever,
The flowers' bursts of bloom,
Green grass, green trees, green leaves
Would chase away the gloom.

If spring would last forever
There'd be a constant hope
Of sunny days and summer breeze,
And wishful ways to cope.

But spring can't last forever,
No matter what the worth
Because that would be heaven,
But we are here on earth!

Marie Di Giorgio

True Love

How do you tell him you love him
When around his heart is a wall?
There's no way around it,
This obstacle is ten feet tall.
Words don't mean anything,
Nothing seems real.
This is a result of
Telling yourself not to feel.
You know in your heart
This love is true —
Yet all of these forces
Are working against you.
All that is left
Is to sit patiently and wait.
And hope that in the future,
It won't be too late.

Marguerite Barrett

My Best Friend

My Mother is my best friend
My love for her will never end
She made me what I am today
And that way I shall try to stay
She made me honest, kind and true
And brought me happiness when
   I was blue
And until my life will end
My mother will always be
   my best friend.

Marion Frederick Kordecki

My Brother's Pain

Oh! Lord hear my cry
the world has tore me
down, and brought me sorrow.

The pain of yesterday
only brought fear for tomorrow.

The tears in my heart
Weren't meant for me,
they are for all who cared for me.

Because they wouldn't
understand what I was
about to do.

Alone in my cell.
I have thought it all
through but I haven't
the time to cry out.

Oh! Lord finally my pain
will be silenced.

Paula Wells

Life

For all being
   Life's just
     Make more being
For man
   It's not sufficing
Creationist, evolutionist
Smart or fool, hard or cool
All have said
   Life's better than death

Enjoyment of giving
   Would fulfill living
Honest not cheating
Giving not taking
Humble not haughty
   That's what makes life
     So good for being
Birth till death
   On such a short path
Don't waste a moment
   On this one way path.

Mike Ershaghi

A Me In Me

Leave me where I seem to be
as long as there's
a me in me.
Don't stretch me out
beyond my time;
a senseless hulk
with life divine.
For life should only
be for me.
A hulk that's kept from dissolution
because of pumps and odds solutions;
is not to be if I can't be
the one who knows
The me in me.
If there is knowledge to be gained
by keeping life in useless frame
I'll be your goat
I'll not seek free.
But know that I believe, you see,
I'm only here while there's me in me.

Miles Gordon

Throbbing Of My Heart

There are sounds within my solitude
Though the silence paves the way
While no other voices can be heard
I hear these every day

My mind goes back to years gone by
Especially when I sleep
Then even in the still of night
The sounds always repeat

At first it use to trouble me
They gave me quite a start
Until last night I realized
It was the throbbing of my heart

Donald D. Conley

Children Of Abraham

We are the children of Abraham
Up Jacob's ladder we do climb
Over this Earth we do roam
Until God call His children home

Along life's pathway we often stumble
But let's be good kind and humble
And every day we will sing this song
Until God calls His children home

Frank Walker

Untitled

Far up
The valley floor it comes,
So weird and cold.
The whistle of a train —
And dies.

Patricia A. Wert

Untitled

I find no content or happiness
In being all alone,
But circumstances, good and bad,
Have left me on my own.
To work things out all by myself
Is hard I must admit.
I could use someone to share my love,
But I can't seem to commit.
I try too hard to find myself
Someone who's right for me,
Because I see no use in striving
For something that should not be.
Someday I hope I'll meet someone
Who will turn my heart around,
But until that someone comes along
I'll keep my feet here on the ground.

Jason Nitschke

All You Had

   Try to fight with all you had.
Last you seen was faces sad.
   Slip into unconscious state.
No one to predict your fate.
   You understand what's going on.
Slowly falling from your dawn.
   You try, but you can't move at all.
You see your body start to fall.
   Blinding light is shone upon.
See the beauty, now you're gone.

Liz Bosanko

Body Sleep-Talking

Slowly your
Eyes
Seduce me with
your smile
and flows from
your touch
to my Ears
that hear
your heart
talking to me while
kissing
my lips
in
our minds
as we sleep.

Toy Latarsha Parker

Mother

Yours the hand that held me tight.
When first I learned to walk.
Your kind eyes that smiled on me,
Encouraged me to talk.

Yours the lips that kissed away.
Each tear that hurt would bring.
Your songs have made me dream of bells,
The sweetest that could ring.

Your praise, now that I am older
And life success seems near,
Is still the sweetest praise
I hope, on earth, to hear!

Josephine E. Phillips

Dead

The sun comes
    through the open window
To the place
    where he is lying.
It is him,
    but not him.
It seems as if I could
    reach out
And touch his shoulder
    and he would awaken.

But the snow has fallen;
    the sky is dark,
And he must sleep
    the sleep of angels.

Mary Ann Overson

Cigarette Boy

And I flipped him a quarter and said,
"Good luck little cigarette boy."
I knew good and well that
He was not partial to cigarettes
Nor had he been related with them
In any way,
But, at the time, the
Name seemed fitting.
The boy paused for a second,
And only blankly, confusedly
Into my eyes wanting, apparently,
An explanation.
I gave him the quarter, though.

Jeremy C. Garland

Song Of Myself

I rejoice myself, I sing myself,
And for all I know you shall know,
For every piece belonging to me as
will belong to you.

I stop to welcome my soul,
I gaze afar and spot a
glimmer of light from the
water in this warm serene night.

My body feels light I have been
here, in this moment, all my life,
I am only growing, learning, waiting,
for life to start anew.

These eyes see beauty,
These ears hear music,
A soft melody, as
my soul dances on.

I close my eyes to hear laughter,
I feel the love near,
I run to find it,
My body floats away.

Juanita R. Marino

"The Mask Of Life"

We run around, and wish our
    lives away,
        While life slips by.
        The end of the day.
Never knowing we lost the fun.
    Growing, never stopping for
The sun.
Then the shadow of time
    Unveils our faces
O' what love is in this case
    For now the precious cover
    is gone.
Powder, blush, won't be our
    con.
A sweet tender smile.
Will be your trial, in no denial.
    Memory's will behold,
Everything you've been told.
To share with those, before doors close.

Barbara Phillips

God Given

Shut are their Eyes,
in peaceful Dreams
still, within they sing
fine Songs of thanksgiving
to their native Montana Land

Jutta H. Fernandez

My True Love

My true love lies in the ground
Whence soon I shall be
As death's dark knight is stalking me
My true love lies in the ground
He waits just for me
Death draws near and soon we'll rest
My true love and me

Marie Seitz Schultz

To Tell You

So many words to tell you,
About the love I feel,
Many memories,
That time will not erase,
Many uncertainties hanging at air,
For the fear of life.

I immerse in the insecurity of,
This Love,
Alive,
Like madness,
Searching for a route,
Not knowing that happiness
Died before and went at sunset,
Flying at the Wings of sweet madness.

Melinha Marini

Wings Of Dawn

A hectic world
It seems to me
A mostly cold
And evil thing

I see a light
The blackness gone
Up, toward the sky
The wings of dawn

A blanket of warmth
Surrounds me now
If only the world
Could see just how

The blanket slowly
Covers all
But by then, good
Shall be on call

So, as you see
It's plain to thee
The wings of dawn
Will set you free.

Candida M. Jadin

One Of God's Children

I may not look like you.
I cannot walk in your shoes.
My speech may have a certain ring.
But I know the song I sing.

My beliefs may seem strange.
Yet, my heart beats the same.
When I'm cut my blood is red,
I am as I was born and bred.

My eyes my be the shape of almonds.
My hair may look homespun.
My skin is still soft to feel;
I am, and I am real.

My heritage traces to far off lands,
Where the sea rushes upon the sands.
My ancestors were Kings and Queens.
I am one of their offsprings.

You look and me and all you see,
Is what you think I ought to be.
But whenever I look at you,
I see one of God's children too.

Angela G. Phelps-White

To See Her

I am drawn to her
by some electro-magnetic force
maybe it is her smile
that is the source

She is a vision of beauty
seen throughout the world
where ever she is
the banners are unfurled

She moves with such
grace and elegance
on a frozen cloud
she keeps me entrance

Though the spotlight shines on her
she already glows
a radiant beam
where ever she goes

Philip Reilly

Poverty

Here lies the tragedy of many nations;
Not that me are poor;
All men know something of poverty.
Not that men are wicket;
Who can claim to be good?
Not that men are ignorant;
Who can boast that he is wise?
But that men are strangers!

Van A. Jenkins

Winter

Somewhere in the distance,
wind nips a child's nose.
It howls through the cracks
of the building he calls home.
His small hands are frozen
as his mother holds him close.
If only she had a blanket
or just some warmer clothes,
she could warm his body
and keep it sheltered from the cold.
He can't even cry now.
It's as if his tears are froze.
Outside, the wind keeps blowing
as the snow drifts grow.
Soon the child will leave her.
His brilliant eyes will close.
Just like the millions before him,
this child too will go —
gathered up by the hands of winter
to be buried in the snow.

Shawn Jones

Untitled

Alone on a sandy beach
  I sat.
God-fed and wind swept
Figuratively a part of the
Universe, myself inept.
"Can there be more in less
Or less in more?" I asked.
The tide lapped at my feet,
It returned the sand to the
  Sea,
And left an empty seashell
That could not answer me.

Bonnie A. Lynch

"Missing You"

As I look outside
I'm reminded of you.
Free as a spirit and
Gone like a breeze.
I mourn for you.
My heart aches for you.
As I look around
I wonder where are you?
Are you there, or here?
But you will always be
In my soul, heart, and body.
We are one.
We are tied through time, space,
And thing called life.
I miss you deeply.

Jennifer Nelson

Freedom

Like the magic of
A trickling stream,

The Healing of the mind
And heavenly things,

As a Heavenly light
Grows into sunshine.

Your eyes reflect
Like gems from it sparkles.

And the freedom of
The crystal blue sky
Touches your heart.

And its peace is like a
Dove, so sweet, so silent.

And the stars shine
in a distance with
a Heavenly touch.

And as we journey beyond
Space, our minds grow in time,
And the Heavens open.

Richard D. Bacon

He Is The One!

He is the one,
the holy one,
the one who shed his blood,
the one that takes our sins
away, our blessed holy one.
He has an eye, for you and I,
he wants to set us free,
so we can live eternally,
in heaven safe we'll be!

Danita Gunter

Waterfalls

Waterfalls
Are one of
The
Earth's most beautiful
Resources

Flowing on like
A parent's
Love
Lingering never
Stopping

Jonathan Christy

Soul Mate

Timeless
Your essence;
Your face unchanged
While mine grows gray and lined
In the mirror of life.
Your's remains still;
Captured by the
Dimension I know of
Not yet
Your's stopped
By the chasm of
Eternal separation.
In dreams only
Our conversation picks up
Where it left off and
Words can still tell
How much I did not
Want you to go.

Barbara Ste. James

Silence

In the quiet of the evening
  When the thoughts of mind are nil
You can hear the sound of silence
  That's so tranquil and so still

If you listen more intently
  In a while you'll come to know
That it speaks a different language
  Like the sound of falling snow

Though we find we cannot touch it
  There's a depth you can't deny
That tends to captivate the listener
  Like a touching last good-bye

We are beckoned, like Ulysses
  To that peaceful inner space
Where all burdens pains and sorrows
  Disappear without a trace

We know not what beholds us
  But we feel that we have heard
The infinity of life itself
  And it spoke without a word

Stanley M. McCoy

Reflections On The Windshield

U.F.O. clouds
descend upon the orange horizon,
waves of soft violet foam
wash away the day,
as night speeds down
death's highway.

Stars glisten
above the dome,
songs full of soul,
good conversation,
tires roll
past a thousand empty minds

Couldn't help but wonder . . .
if we'd arrive
to see another day
drive by.

Tracy Lynn Monaco

Human Frailty

Do I possess a weakness;
Is there fault in my stand?
Is my mind imperfect,
with some impairment at hand?
Do I seem irresponsible?
Does culpability stop here?
Not really! I'm a mother.

Legora M. Norwood

Untitled

Oh God, how easy life would be . . .
    If there was only you and me.
"Do you really think so?"
    "Would that really make you free?"

"There was a time, under the sun
    when there was only one . . .
and still, he cost the life
    of my one and only Son."

"Not me, the fault is with another."
    "Not me!" He pointed at the other
And throughout time
    each one blames his brother.

"So love one another
    and do what you want done.
And as you do you will
    surely glorify my Son."

David Ruleman

Suzy Q

I knew a fair maiden named Sue
Who had eyes that were sparkling blue.
Her hair was quite long
And Teutonically blond,
But her roots were a much darker hue.

Michael Klikier

The Storm

The quiet before the storm
Breaks with sudden thunder
As the wind starts to roll
And the earth begins to shudder.

The waves begin to splash
As white water starts to spray
The bell begins to toll
For the life that ends today.

As cat with mouse
Playtime begins
As food to mouth
Playtime ends.

The fury of nature reverberates
Until the storm passes over
And the turbulence abates
Peaceful now
The storm is over.

Nathan Cook

The Things I Have

The music of the wind
    The gleam of stars
The gold of the sun
    The velvet of night
The light of day
    All that is mine
        and thine.

Marta Broido

The War

Saddam Hussein stood by the gate,
while his army burned Kuwait.

The people there began to cry,
"Help us please, before we die!"

The U.S.A. could not stand by
the gate and let them die.

The President said, "Grab your guns,
we will make their army run!"

We did, and now our soldiers are home.
They all deserve a medal of their own.

Kayla Nelson

What Is Love?

Love is not a conscious action
or softly spoken word
Love is like the sweetest song
that I've ever heard
Love's not something to be explained
and love you cannot force
A feeling that will last forever
well, that's love of course
Some will love just to be in love
for others it is real
I cannot tell why it's you I love
it's just the way I feel!

L. Alan Smith

SOMEDAY: *the me i am*

Someday . . .
someone will love me.
Appreciate the me
I'm more then willing to give.
They'll glow in the warmth.
Enjoy the humor.
Understand the me I am.

Someday . . .
someone will love me.
Have a need for the me
I'm only capable of giving.
They'll wait out my silence.
Sense my distress.
Understand the me I am.

Someday . . .
if only someday.
Someone would only,
some could only.
Try and understand . . .
understand the me I am.

Robert Malgren

"Weeping Willow"

The Weeping Willow feels so sad
Just why I cannot tell
But weeping is his job in life
To weep means all is well.

For if he did not weep at all
God's plan would go awry
For Willows not to weep would mean
The earth was going dry.

So weep on, little Willow
Keep order in the line.
The more you weep, the more we'll know
That everything is fine.

Mary L. Crow

Gift From Above

Here some birds flying,
soaring alone.
Also a pair
in the sky was shown.
A hope and a comfort
of birds not alone;
of birds alive
with an air bound home,
Birds without strife,
together they flew;
This great gift in life,
companion, they knew.

Lorisa Willis

Release

I fled from spring and hurried on
To meet the summer's fire.
I felt the heat
I saw defeat
But never lost desire.

Though summer's yield was modest gain
Inflation claimed it all.
There was a raise
A slow down phase
Then life was in a stall.

The autumn brought its bag of games
With Indian summer's trick or treat.
But Jack brought frost
And flowers lost
The taste was bittersweet.

The snow that covers sleeping earth
Now blankets us in peace.
The blooms are gone
We've said so long.
For we have found release.

E. June Mathews

Spring

Spring has sprung,
phones have rung,
with people calling for fun
Eating outside all day
will give you much more time to play.
You'll have lots of fun
while you run on this nice warm day.

Spring has come,
winter has gone,
Leaves are out
and bugs aren't in.
People don't want to lay,
instead they want to play,
So everyone is out all day

Sean Wayne Sturdivant

Untitled

It is forever unknown to me
what man is supposed to be
For he who is supposed to see
the difference the world may be
for he who sees the colors of others
but not really what it means
Cannot begin to comprehend
the difference in men.

Annie Briggs

"The Old Homeplace"

Back in the hills of Arkansas
Where I grew up as a child,
The summers were hot and sticky
The winters were short and mild.

Two tall trees still grow there
Where my old homeplace stood,
I can picture my mom in the kitchen
Filling the old cookstove with wood.

Across the open breezeway
The bedrooms were neatly kept,
When the nighttime befell us
Sometimes three in a bed we slept.

Out on the long porch my daddy sat
With his foot propped up on the rail
And over in the corner half asleep
An old hound dog thumped his tail.

Jessie R. Berry

Fleeting Chance

Her flowered dress was billowed
As the wind caught it anew
And I wished I'd had more time to spare
And gifts worth so much more

But a box of melting chocolates
Dampened by the surf's wet spray
Was all I had to offer her
As time sped quickly by

So suddenly fate deals a hand
And we must act upon it . . .
My routine break was now a part
Of all my life could hold

No words would come . . .
No arm would beckon her to stay
And like the sea upon the shore
She left and was no more.

Jean R. Sweigart

It's April In Indiana

Spring peeked in some days ago.
A lovely promise!

Last night
    lightning flashed;
    thunder boomed;
    rain hammered down;
    temperatures dropped!

At dawn, the trees, and all
    look like crystal sculptures.
Beautiful, fickle April.

Kathleen K. Cummins

Planners

Some use
Their

        Hammers

Before

Their

        Brain

Plan
        Errs.

Ronald Perron

Winter Snow

The ground is softly white
And the snow lies so cold.
As I looked out the window
It makes me feel so bold.

The winter atmosphere is harsh
With cold blustery wind blowing.
Yet underneath the cold wet snow
Are plants waiting to start growing.

The sun shining on the snow
Looks so bright and glistening.
You always liked to see it
And, honey, I hope you're listening.

I'm sure you have no snow
In heaven where you're living.
Sometimes it almost seems
That beside me you are sitting.

Some day I'll join you there
And we'll walk in sunlight warm.
The air will touch us lightly
With such soft angelic charm.

Frances E. Tolson

Fleeting Moments

Looking upward to the sky,
white clouds floating by.
Shining blue, with a gentle hue.
Oh! What a beautiful sight,
so gentle and so light.
Like a loving smile and a gentle touch,
by someone you love so very much.

Depthana Cunning

Spring

The most beautiful time is Spring!
The leaves are budding,
And the sun is bright.
When the sun sets,
It is the most exciting sight!
All of the purples,
The pinks, and the oranges,
As one, coming together to form
The sunset.
The birds are chirping from
Their nests, to one another,
I can bet.
You see, they are happy,
Because the darkness that
Hovered for some time,
For now is gone,
And they are rejoicing
With their song!
Like I said, the most
Beautiful time is . . . SPRING!

Kyong Schmidt

Cajun Joe Tells About "Snapping Turtle"

Now, de snapping turtle have no teeth,
    But him jaws be sharp like knife,
        And all day long he look around
        And try to grab a bite.

Ole snapping turtle doze on log,
    Look peaceful, soak up sun . . .
        But jest you try 'n pick him up
        And quick, he got your thumb!

Elizabeth Cron

Freedom

Thought I heard you call my name
as I slept upon the floor,
just inside my cabin's door

Thought I heard you whisper loud
as I dreamed of walkin' proud.
thought I heard you call again,
softly floatin' on the wind
as it brushed against my pain

In the heat of the day
as beneath this load I sway
share croppin' for the man,
thought I heard you call my name

On these mean and brutal streets,
where crack is king, and habits are fed
before babies eat,
in a junkie as he groaned
thought I heard you loudly moan

Freedom.
Is this where you've called me to?

Effie McKinney

To Love And Embrace You

To love and embrace you
Is all I want to do
To love and embrace you
To put my arms around you
To love and embrace you
Through each passing day
Would make my life complete
More than words can say
I've found a man
One who understands
My heart and soul like no one else can
If there was one thing I'd want to do
It's to love and embrace you
My whole life through

Mary L. Bannister

Can't Get My Mine Off A Little Man

Can't get my mine off a little man.
Only five years old.
Lost his life one day.
By another child, not very old.

Can't believe he's not here.
To grow up big and strong.
Was he so perfect in God's eyes.
That heaven had to be his home.

Can't get my mine off a little man.
He looked like someone so dear.
A small grand child that I love so.
It would be hard to let him go.

Can't get my mine off a little man.
Whom had to go in such a bad way.
Another child killed him.
That's what makes it so sad.

When a child kills a child.
And sends him to heaven.
Will the other child go to heaven too?
Although he took another child's life.

Beverly Townsend

Memories

At dawn
the sea lies calm.
The sea slowly
progresses up upward
throughout the day
and washes its
memories of the past
along the shore.

Darkness falls,
a storm arises,
waves form.
The sea is
aggravated
by the light of the moon.
The water violently
drags the memories
back into its depths
to be locked away
forever,
where they belong.

Margaret Goulet

Be With Me!

My life at times is trying
so often I get confused
I can feel my willpower dying
all my hopes I begin to lose.

When it seems I've reached my lowest
Please let me turn to you
to give me strength to go on
and help me fight my daily battles too.

I need your love to guide me
through all life has to deal
As long as you're beside me
my dreams can be fulfilled.

I'm asking you to help me
to always be my best
to help me get back up again
when I fall, Lord, I request.

Give me some self confidence
to help me see things through
and always keep reminding me
We can make it, Me and You.

Cherie Davidson

The Sky My Sky

I walk too the barn
I sat down on a chop table
The sky is clear an the sun
is out. I hear the birds
sing in the tree
I hear the animal in the
barn talk
The sky just turning dark
My sky is clear an I say
goodnight too my sky

Clarence Dickerman Jr.

Untitled

Families scatter like leaves
   but not blown by the wind
Every heart clings to their home
We find ourselves together —
   rooted in God's love.

Yolonda Clements

Words

They are only sounds and patterns,
But oh how they matter.
They can soothe, cut or maim.
They are even used to blame,
Or put you to shame.
They are only sounds and patterns,
But oh how they matter.
They can make you shatter.
They can wrench your soul
And take their toll!

Sandra Fossen

"Statement"

"Who taught You"
Who taught you to hate your
skin color
Who taught you to hate your rare
Who taught you that your skin
color makes a difference
Who taught you your words
don't mean anything
Who taught you not to like
you nose
Who taught you not to like
What you are
Who taught you that your nobody
Who taught you wrong,

Carolyn Tenedine

Winter Is Here

Disappointment rolls around when
April is far away
the season now is
cold and aggressive
the lands possessions
have gone to sleep
for winter is now here
there is an attitude
a cockiness in
the cold bitter air
a white blanket
covers the land
no leaves on the trees
no grass on the ground
winter has been found.

Jehnice Pimentel

"My Backyard"

My backyard is mainly green,
It is filled with lots of trees
I can see it smiling because
I keep it clean
It is where my family
and I drink tea,
Where bees and birds sing
their songs,
Where butterflies and dragonflies
like to roam,
My backyard is where we play
our games,
It is where I write stories
and poems.
Because it is where I can be alone,
I hope my backyard stays the same,
So I have a place to see and hear
beautiful things.

Melissa Ross

Walls Apart, Worlds Away

Take me away through the stars
Away from the pain inside
Across the sun
Through the solar divide
If I push hard enough
I'll escape mother earth's call
Far into the night
Far from it all

Jupiter is rising up
Saturn is calling my name
Pluto thanks me for playing the game

South bound star collision course
Parallel universal kiss
Warp through time and space
Is what I miss
Second wind's gravitational pull
Keeps me around
Universal rush is
What keeps me down...

Demosthenes Plomaritis

Another Planet

I believe there is another planet,
Where peace reigns over all.
Where love lives forever,
And happiness stands tall.

On this planet,
Nobody fights.
There are no bombs,
Or rocket filled nights.

On this planet,
You can love and be free.
Living out,
Your favorite fantasy.

On this planet,
Everyone is color blind.
And all have achieved,
A greater state of mind.

Where it is at,
Nobody knows.
It probably hangs,
Where the wind blows.

Lonnie Dween Rucker II

Untitled

Shadows — mind
spinning thoughts
many blind

Secret doors — mind
one for ever
locked behind

Orbit — mind
crowded head
rewind — rewind.

J. J. Runkle

Angels

Airborne and free
Not afraid to fly
Go to great heights
Everlasting life
Light and graceful
Soar with amazing grace

Barbara Jean Styles

Where Are They

Where are they
Who fill our hearts,
with that sense of love?

Where are they
Who make our hearts,
flutter like a dove?

Where are they
Who know us well,
in all of its meaning?

Where are they
Who make us laugh,
leave us smiling, gleaming?

Where are they
We love so much?
We know we're far apart.

Where are they?
Where have they gone?
They who hold our hearts.

Emily Sattazahn

The Between Time

"October" with all its color and beauty
The time to think and wonder,

The sun is warm and the wind is cold
but still we love you "October",

The trees will giving
up its leaves, to make
blanket on the ground,

Soon winter will be here
and the snow will fall and
show its beauty too,

And before you can turn,
Why it spring again,

Oh! October, October with
all your beauty,
why don't you stay awhile.

Edna Stewart

A Poem

A Poem is a poem.
But I think a poem is something
nice, generous, courageous.
   Some people think a poem is a joke,
or they just want to write about death,
Pestilence and murder!!!
When you think poem, what do you see?
Decide for yourself.

Matt Bisbee

"The Party"

As I lay my head to sleep I
Start thinking of you and me,
I remember the first time I saw
You at that party
It was you, me, Carol, and Marty
When Carol introduced me to you
I knew from the start,
That you and me would always
Be together,
Never to part.

Katherine Arias

Down The White Hall

Trembling
Rage deep within
Ache to scream
Pain to feel
Enigmatic to the eye
Burning inside
Screaming
Beating
No one hears me
When I scream
No one cares
When I hurt
No one dares
Come close
Fingers point
Harpies chant
 SNAP<

Crimson Flows
Down the White Hall

Carly R. Stuart

Thoughts

I close my eyes to be alone
I see the faces of people
I have and have not known

They tell me stories
Of deeds done and loves lost
Of bridges burned and lines crossed

They don't tell me of battles to come
What chances to take
Or even when to run

At twilight if sleep doesn't come
The chorus begins their recital
Like hymns in a book
It's the same old songs
I know them all now
So I even sing along

Do not judge me now for what I've done
My thoughts condemn more than anyone

Michael Williams

All's Well

The evening sun was descending
As the quiet of night was sitting in.
In all this evening splendor
You could see where God had been.

The trees bathed in moonlight
Were black against the sky.
This an occurrence every day
Not controlled by you or I.

Again the sun will rise
And another day will dawn.
Another cycle will be finished
As we move to carry on.

Betty Butler

The Chicken

The chicken hatches from the egg
and pecks scratches on the ground
All it does is run around
And squawk its little head
It's covered with feathers
And pokey feet
And beady eyes
With a long yellow beak
So now you know
Friend or foe
That a chicken
Can't be beat

Chad McClurg

White Velvet

When the snow is like white velvet
On the branches of a tree
When the snow is like white velvet
He'll come marching home to me
When the snow is like white velvet
And all fighting did subside
When the snow is like white velvet
I'll become his loving bride

Now the snow is like white velvet
As it flutters to the ground
The snow is like white velvet
The color of my gown
Yes the snow is like white velvet
But the sky above is gray
The snow flakes are all crying
My loved one died today

Caroline E. Stahl

A Rose

The wind caressed a red, red rose
And gently made it sway
I watched the fragile petals fall
As if to steal away.

To me it was a sad, sad sight
Of beauty torn apart
Like tender drops of blood that fell
From His Immaculate Heart.

If God would grant my secret wish
And give to me the power
I'd gather all the petals lost
and return to Him — His flower.

Edward J. Dempsey

Tears

What does my tears have
that make you wonder about me?
You have no knowledge of why they come
or where they go after you witness them
falling from my eyes.
For you have not known
the map I have traveled
to find the dry places in my soul.
These tears are not mine
Even though they come out of me.
They have their own minds.
They go where they please.
Even a tear desires to be free.
So why trouble me about this mystery.

James McClain

Thorns

While following your path in life,
Remember what the eagle has to say:
For every man who walks along
Must feel the thorns along the way.

And when your soul stumbles,
Remember that every man is weak.
Listen to the heron cry
For life is not so often bleak.

When the brown bear needs a hand,
Guide her with a word and smile.
Help her along her chosen way,
Walk with her a while.

Such love will cause the sun to shine,
While the thorns that sharply grow
Will fade away into memory
When the stag runs in the snow.

Christopher Harris

Homework

Homework does not make the world spin,
Though some teachers think so.
Homework is something we are buried in,
That we all know.

Teachers need to hold back,
Please cut us a little slack!
We really do need to sleep at night,
Not in school, where it causes a fight.

Please give us a little time
To enjoy our lives,
One day at a time.
All this homework give me hives.

We need to have a little fun,
Before you kill us one by one.
Please just give us one more day,
So we can do it the right way!

Homework does not make the world spin,
Though some teachers think so.
Homework is something we are buried in,
That we all know.

Brandi Feddersen

Wisdom

School, school the place for fools
And that's no place for me.
With books, books
And angry looks
From teachers who don't agree

That talking in class
Will help you pass
Or make your grades more than a "D"

Why should I stuff and cram
For some silly exam
To boost my grade to an "A?"

Why golly heck
It's making a wreck
Out of my poor mom so old and gray

She just fusses and worries
And hustles and hurries
Me off into the cold early morn

To school, school
The place for fools
Oh, why was I ever born!

Audley A. O'Connor

Mid-Term

Weariness pervades my soul.
It winds
like untamed grapevines
to reach
every sinew and fiber
of my being . . .
distorting sense and reality,
dulling mind and spirit.

Its tendrils wrap around my heart,
compressing, numbing
this fragile vessel.
I press on with heavy limbs
  and frail emotions —
pulled,
   pushed,
     and turned
by voice and by touch
to grow toward the light.

Even a bruised vine bears fruit
if it finds the sun.

Anita K. Rowe

Familiar Pain

I see and read what's on your mind
before you even speak
I understand your motives,
I'm shelter that you seek.
My talent is to comfort you,
to love you anyway.
I do accept you totally,
you're free to talk and stay.
My ears are tuned to hear you clear,
no judging will be done.
The sound from your lips will be safe,
no need for you to run.
My eyes already see you clear,
don't fear what they reveal.
To me it is familiar
all you say and feel.
I traveled once this road you're on,
I recognize your pain.
After all your fears have passed,
I hope you trust again.

Hannelore Grantham

"Come Back"

Each weary day and lonely night
I think of you and pray
That you will soon come back to me
And never go away
I miss you every moment love
I call to you and cry
But only empty echoes fill the hours
  passing by
The sky is gray all morning and
  throughout the afternoon
And there is nothing beautiful about
  the stars or moon
Whatever else that happens that my
  heart may be denied
I just want you to come back to me
  and never leave my side

Susan Roth-Weitzel

"Flowerpicker"

Flowerpicker
Better think second about stealing iris
Cuffed and Humiliated
You sit in back of authority
Name given
Sunday driver
Flower Picker
2:00 a.m.
Trashcan with wheels
Heavy duty shovel
Determined
60 bulbs
Replanted
Flower picker
Roots and fresh stems
All laid out and sorted
All watered
All cared for
All stolen

Christopher Yanez

My Wife

A glass of wine, a cup of tea
Graceful as your love can be
A glass of wine, a cup of tea
Balanced with a smile to me

A glass of wine, a cup of tea
Many would not much agree
Claiming impropriety

But to one who knows her well
Loves her more than most can tell
A glass of wine, a cup of tea
Describes her more than most can see

For she's not conventional
Things simply must be rational
To her mind and heart - that's all

So now perhaps you'll understand
Why to me my wife's so grand
As she climbs the stairs to be
With tea and wine and lucky me

Jake Hammerslag

Those Days That We Once Knew

Those days that we once knew
Have flown and gone.
We've only memories
To carry on.
The melody of love,
Once new and bright,
Has grown on through the years
To our delight.
Those years of work and fun:
The children, sweet and small,
Have come and gone again.
We've loved them all.
Grandchildren with their charms
And faces sweet
Have come to fill our arms
Make life complete.
They'll have the visions now,
The dreams that we once knew,
To make their lives grow strong
With love that's true.

Margaret Mills Muntz

A Dream Of Her

In my dreams,
She walks through the mist.
On top of water,
A tender kiss.
Of beauty untold,
Of a love beyond imagination.
Delicate is her touch,
Eyes full of passion.
Holding her close,
I know she's the one.
Our hearts brought together,
Intertwined by love.
She whispers softly,
That she loves me,
I smile contently,
As I wake from my dream.

Thomas Lambert

"Just Say Yes To Jesus"

Just say yes to Jesus
In everything you do!
Just say yes to Jesus
Cause Jesus knows what's best for you

He knows before you think a thought
Or before a word is spoken
He sees you when the tear drops fall
From a heart that's broken!

Just say yes to Jesus
Tho it may be hard to do
And do his will, instead of yours
His love will see you through

So trust in him and cling to him
Let this your motto be
"I will say yes to Jesus"
In all he asks of me

And then one day when he calls to you
And life on earth is thru
And you ask to be with him forever
He'll say yes to you!

Mary Margaret Drebobl

Can You

I need to find a love
A feeling that cannot steal
A love that understands
Something ravishing to feel

Can you lead me to the man
The one they say is love
The one who's name is Jesus
The son of Heaven above

I need to find this man
The one they call the King
I need to find the man
To whom the angels sing

Can you accept this glory
That this man died for you
Now you know forever
That only pure love is true

So can you find this man
The one they say is love
The one who's name is Jesus
The son of Heaven above

Leti Villegas

Untitled

Your kiss is
unlike any other
your arms hold me
like no one elses could
your eyes could easily
captivate and control
this love I feel for you
though the words
have not been spoken
some things
need not be said
my silence is
an expression of my fear.

Debby Seefeldt

Life's Real Treasure

The seasons like life's mysteries
Where spring like youth will bloom
The middle years and harvest time
All predate times of gloom

Our latter years like winter winds
That hearken the slowing stage
That comes to every human being
The ravages we call old age

This is the time, youth fear the most
Yet is our greatest pleasure
We appreciate our family more
For this is life's real treasure

Clint Davis

My Grandmother

She is blue, calm, serene, and
dignified and wise in the ways of life.

She is a cool, clearwater stream,
pure, honest and refreshing.
She is a wolf, protective of her
pack, with a motherly warmth.

She reminds me of silks, soft
and smooth that blows in the wind.

She fly's on the wings of the
angels in heaven who keep her safe.

She walks gracefully and slowly,
with her floats an air of class.
She is the last note of a symphony,
the final sound of beauty.

Jennifer L. Taber

Hate And Horror

When your head
is in the sand
you're not allowed.
To join the band.
But if horror
is what you seek
lift your head
and take a peek
Look around
you will see
all the hate
that's not for thee
So put your head
Back in the sand
For you don't want
to join the band

June E. Pancherovich

The Journey

Midst a sea of emotions
Sails a vessel,
A human being.

A vessel driven
By the waves of the sea
And
The winds of doctrines and beliefs.

On a course not set
By the waves
Nor
By the winds,
But
By the hand which directs the sail
To the vessel's
Final
Destination.

Michael J. Burch

Olympics

With my heart pounding
Excitement building
Perspiration shining on my skin
A quivering in my stomach

I thought it was real
I believed, each time
I thought that gold medal would be mine

Too quickly, I jumped into each race
Unknowing, the end was soon in sight
Only to be bumped out early

I dropped the torch
A few scorched places
Mostly around my heart

The flame is dying
No more sparks are flying
Chilly winds blow at my back

All that left when the crown departed
One lonely heart
I'm back where I started

Eileen Boyle

"Submarine Year 1943"

She was in the states in
forty three.
Jan. Feb. March makes three
overhaul over and ready for sea.
She's out again to make us free
one year has passed and a
lot has been done.
We've done our duty without the sun.
We're going back, "so they say"
after this run
to the USA.

Charles E. Hurd

Feelings

The mysterious love
That shadows hide
Is everywhere
But who can find
When all you see is beauty
Beauty inside
Find more to someone
Someone inside
Not just beauty, but intelligence
Must abide.

Melinda Pelkey

A Dream . . .

The highway
A cold black ribbon
Going nowhere
    Everywhere.
A pick-up truck full
Of corpses
Rotting green
Around a real
Cowboy
    And an indian
Without the snuff-can ring
In his pocket
Picked me up
    The hitchhiker
And added me
To the load.

    Kevin Crone

Flowery Notes

Though it was time to sit myself down
  and write a not to you,
What to say, can't really think, cause
  there's really nothing new.
Can't even think of a single joke
  something to make you smile.
So guess you know I'm thinking of you
  across the many miles.
Hope very soon that we can sit and talk
  together for hours.
Till then dear friend enjoy my poem
  and also the pretty flowers.

    L. Buckalew

Christ Is Risen! Alleluia!

Flowers blooming bright, birds singing
To the Lord their sweetest praise
Give to us an inspiration
As we hymns of glory raise.
Christ is risen! Alleluia!
Death's dread reign fore'er is o'er,
Christ has burst His three days prison,
He's alive forevermore.

Once He died from sin to save us,
Suffered silent and alone,
Faith in him who so much gave us
Brings us to our heavenly home,
Now we, too, shall live forever,
Death and grave have lost their string.
Alleluia! Alleluia!
Let the Easter praises ring.

    Margery C. Meyer

Winter Riddle

Feels light,
bright at night

It is cold,
but ever so bold

You can play in it
with a sled,
Then something might
hit your head.

What is it?

    Sarah Budde

Untitled

My sorrow is flesh
My burden to bear
Not to be loved
Not be desired
Alone with my reflection
Repulsed by the image
Trying to improve
My mind confused
My spirit lost
Longing for the impossible
Hoping for a miracle
Totally in vain
Will it never end?
Tired of wanting
Tired of needing
Feeling a failure
Never succeeding —

    Nicole Miller

Gibran

Gentle friend
With olive fire-eyes,
I never could disguise,
My special love for you;
The silken tigered fur,
The deep, resounding purr,
The catapulting jungle-stride,
Still racing past
The days we laughed,
The nights we cried;
Why must I give up something now
While still not knowing why — or how?
Or can I gather up my sorrow,
Knowing you are there tomorrow?
Will I say, "Remember when . . ."
For all the places we have been?
I can for you,
My sweet and gentle friend.

    Gwen L. Smith-Russell

Voices

Voices, voices
I hear voices in my head,
screaming, screams,
screams of the dying
and of the dead.
  A million voices,
  a thousand years,
  the secrets of the dead,
  singing-screaming-singing
  surging through and in my head.
Seeking rest, seeking peace,
but with a thousand
million voices, screaming
in-and-through my head.
  Running from, running too
  a million-thousand voices
  surging through my head.
Needing Hate, Fearing Love
voices screaming through my head.
  Voices screaming through my Voice.

    Brian Morgan

Statue Of Liberty

Our Statue of Liberty
A wonderful lady is she
with her hands held high to you and I
she's a lady of dignity
Our Statue of Liberty
With a torch in her hands held high
she's a lady who lights up the sky
She's our lady she's one lady
She's our lady of Liberty
Million climb her stairs
Million stop and stare
to see our lady of land and sea
Our Lady of Liberty

    Dorothy Ferruzzi

Reflection

You behind the mirror
Only you know who I am and
What I am
You behind the mirror

I have seen so many faces of
you and have so much to ask
Only you I can see only you
I can trust the real me
You behind the mirror

When will you give me back
Not my reflection by my face
My thoughts myself
You behind the mirror

If I loss you in the mirror
Who would I be with out you
You behind the mirror

    Carol Thomas Mantenuti

Wind

Can you feel the breeze?
The wind is passing by,
going we know not where.
Stirring leaves, swaying flowers,
rustling skirts and tangling hair.
It journeys here, quietly
hustling evening, on the run
Going to rest behind the sun.

    Mary Graliker

"He Has No Trust"

Behold he put no trust in his heart
lay down now put me in side of you.
Who is he that will strike hands with
me. For he has hid his heart from
understanding my love for you. Well he
as a shadow. Even that change
the night into day the light is
short because of darkness. If I
wait at the grave is mine home.
I've made my bed in the darkness.
My eyes are also dim by reason of
sorrow and where is now my hope.
As for my hope who shall see it. They
shall go down to bars of the pit. When
our rest together is in the dust you
are not a stranger to me. Be hold I
cry of worry but I'm not heard. I
cry out again but it is no answer. And
my fiends forgetting me.
When I was behinds a lock door.

    Marsha Bell

Blank White Walls

Gone. Nothing left.
No sadness. No happiness.
Just blank white walls.

Energy fades into the darkness.
Light brings empty smiles.
Feelings of a program.

Why a world full of deception?
No heaven. No hell.
Mindless bodies roam.

Gone. Nothing left.
No love. No hate.
Just blank white walls.

Pamela Helms

Christmas

Christmas is the time
of Jesus's birth
When God sent his Son
down to our Earth
Angels and Shepherds,
Wise men too,
Came to see Jesus,
So tiny and new
The wise men brought gold
Frankincense and Myrrh
That day a rejoicing
came over our Earth
So while we are shopping
And making a fuss
Let's not forget Jesus
God's present to us.

Amanda Nicole Largent

Reverie

I passed seven days
in sleep.

For in sleep, I was free
to dream.

For in dream, I was free
to love.

For in love, I was free
to act.

For in act, I was free
to commit.

For in commitment, I was free
to endure.

For in endurance, I was free
to survive.............

Madeleine De Nitto-Hodges

"The Gift"

A gift is such a special thing.
It might be some flowers,
Or a beautiful ring.
It might be a card,
That touches your heart.
It always reminds us,
When we are apart.
It's not the value,
Of the gift that we bring;
But the love we share,
That's the most precious thing.

Myra Ledet

Over The Edge

Dusty trails of toil and trouble,
Love and hate my life crumbles.
I walk the cliff above the shore.
The fear of falling is no more.
I've walked the line much too long,
Over the edge I know it's wrong.
There I hang grasping tight,
Calling for a little help.
All this pain and suffering
Never should be felt.
I stare into the mirror
And there's no one there to find.
No matter what I do,
No one seems to mind.
I know someday I'll reappear
Upon this world so cold,
But for now I'm left invisible
With no one there to hold.

Shasta Curtis

Love

Life is not my own
Just a heart beat away
not mind
dream away
who need this
I know I don't
How long can my heart take this
I am mix up what's real
I know I am
This love God is making me crazy
I want to know he is mine
His eyes, voice, hair, gives him away
I will win. I don't take no
Love I want you
pure and simple
Love I wait on you
I love you. My inter thoughts
Good looking man
No one has taking my heart like you
pray for your wishes love

Claudia Marie Beebe

No Hurry

Quiet is the atmosphere before the
storm of snow.
Serene is the still after.
The sun now quickly melts
what nature
blew on us in a flurry.

Solitude is the behavior of a child in
wrong doing, and hence, when forgiven,
the sound of laughter;
as you take that child in
open arms.
Forgetting what made you fury.

Thus the sun is put on yours, and the
child's face...
Nature and you now walk slowly...
    No hurry!!!

Deb Newman

"Again"

Sitting
Waiting
Anticipating

So high
I wait
My fate

My stomach tightens
My palms sweat
Mark, get set . . .

I lean forward
Then I slide
What a ride!

I race
I roar
I soar

Sitting
Waiting
Anticipating

Joanie Lang

Desert

Coyotes call and cactus prick
in dusty Desert winds;
Flat mesas, rolling tumbleweed,
the highway heat offends.

Roadrunners rise from fences hid,
and fossils from the floor
Of canyons where once rivers ran
to tell its ancient lore.

Sudden storms dig deep arroyos
through mountains cool and green;
A lonely mesa rises high
with Indian Pueblo scene.

Such startling colors changing too
red rock and sand dunes white;
A river runs where none should be;
red sunsets welcome night.

Kathryn Nelson Montoya

Only Today

For I only have today,
to do as God commands.
I only have this hour,
To follow the Savior's plan.

Tomorrow is not promised,
for today is all I have,
to unfold my visions, and
make my dreams come true.

One moment in time,
is all that I've been given,
to be all I can be,
To enjoy life's treasures,
and fulfill my destiny.

For I only have today,
to do the Master's will.
Tomorrow is not promised,
I can not stand still!!!!

Evangelist Acquinetta T. Davis

Passing Seasons

Summer haunts me.
Your face is etched on
every passing cloud.
You are the gentle breeze.

Winter's icy sun lays open
the gates of my soul.
As snow falls,
you vanish from my dreams.

Spring rain melts the loneliness
Of winter.
Fading softy in the mist,
your image trembles in my mind.

Though you may end
as only a pale green mist
Drifting the fall fields.
You remain in
my heart.

Michael W. Leone

The Prayer

I sat beside my bed
I bowed my head and
shut my eyes and
said no lies.

I looked outside into
the night and with my
sight I gazed into the
Heavens up above.

I thought about our
savior and asked him
for a favor to take his
part and come into my
heart.

Dominique Marie Sandoval

Make Calvary Real To Me

Oh, that I might be more like thee,
Lord make Calvary real to me.
Burn within this heart I pray
the grief you bore for me that day.

With a broken heart you bore the pain
that even I could heaven again.
The shame you bore for all to see;
Yes, Lord make Calvary real to me.

Light within my heart a flame
and make me worthy of thy name.
Let me feel your power today
and make Calvary real to me.

Lillie Sparkman

Flowers

I love to see the
pretty flowers when
they are in full bloom
they make the would
a better place and
drive away the gloom
the lily is a pretty
flower fresh as the
morning dew but
the tulip is just
as pretty as any I
even grew.

Mamie Guntes

Alone

Always alone and no one to see
    Day in and Day out
Just the walls and me

Always alone and no one to see
    So many faces — So many just leave

Always alone and time goes by
    One deep breath, One long sigh

Now it is dark and the day is done
    Tomorrow I'll be back, One Last Run

Always alone and no one to see
    Imagine how you'd feel
        With only one key.

Pamela S. Smith

Words

There's so many words I
Would like to express to
You, but when were together
I just can't say them.

Words that say how much
I care about you.

Words that say you make
me feel special.

Words I can say when you're
not around.

Words that nobody knows
    but me.

Because every time I see
Your face I just melt
Away, anytime you come
Around, I guess that I
    can't say those words.

Karen Leah Pearson

A Hug

What! You want a hug
Oh No not me . . .
I'm too grown up,
can't you see?

When I was a child
Alone at night . . .
Yeh, sure, then it was right.

Or when I fell and scraped a knee
My mom would come over and hug me.

Gram and Gramp, too, was fine
when they hugged me one more time.

But now, that I'm an adult
A hug? Oh no, that I'll not.

Well, Ok, I'll be nice
you may hug me once . . .
Oh . . ., Go on . . . do it twice.

Dee Cuff

I Wish

I wish I was a candle,
to fill your life with light,
I wish I was a blanket
to keep you warm at night,
I wish I was a dove,
to help you through life's flight,

I wish I was a tissue,
to wipe away your tears,
I wish I was a teddy bear,
to hug away your fears,
I wish I was a day,
to slow down the years,

I wishes my wishes would come true,
I wish I was all those things,
Then I could always be there for you,
to carry you on gentle wings

Amy Sue Daisy Pray

Untitled

I see by the light
Of the candle that burns
A life with a plan
And not many turns

Looking ahead
Don't look behind
On a platform of life
The path's all you'll find

As I reach the end
Only then it will show
So much is out there
I'll never know

Glenn D. Mueller

Unsung Melody

If you were the melody
And I were the rhyme,
We would blend together perfectly
In some other place and time.

Our passion would set the tempo.
Our hearts would pound the beat.
We would climb the scale together
Making the song complete.

But we are as fate has made us
In this time and in this place,
So our song will go unsung —
A tragedy, a waste.

Jeannie M. Mullins

Empty Space

The shots fractured the air
There was nowhere to run
Life gasped and
Left and empty space

Man softly smiled as he
Stroked the trophy heads
It's only life and
Life was his to take

The shots fractured the air
There was nowhere to run
Earth gasped and
Left an empty space

Charlotte Terwilliger

My True Valentine!

Through all the good times
and all the bad
Through all the happy times
and all the sad.
You've been there for me through thick
and through thin, I want you
to know how happy I've been.
Because of you I have smiled.
Because of you I've gone the miles.
You're everything I've ever dreamed of,
A man of sincerity, romance, and love
In my eyes those are the qualities
you are made of.
There's only one man who has my
heart, only one man who has my
Soul, there's only one man I'll ever
love, for you my heart is whole.
You are the one I want to be with
forever and a lifetime
You are the one who I want to be
My True Valentine

Tracey Cassady

Untitled

Loneliness my old friend
I knew you would be back.
Should we seal it with a kiss,
this melancholy pact?

Tell me you've come to stay
Only to leave me once again.
Please don't say goodbye
You're my oldest, dearest friend.

Surround me with your darkness,
Caress me with your emptiness,
Touch my heart like only you can
My pain, my pleasure, my life,
My only friend.

Lori E. Coale

Darkness

Dark is the world around me
Where am I, How can this be
Slowly I walk with my hands before me
frightened by what I cannot see
Colorless is the life I lead
Damp and gloomy is all I foresee
Darkness by day
Darkness by night.

Diana L. Jandreau

Nothing Will Never Happen

The night is filled
With owls and bats.
None speak English
Or Dutch
Or Spanish
Or German.
None of them are different
With bifocals or contacts
And silver jewelry.
They are not going
To a beach party or dance.
Only a tiny few
Sitting on their branches
Will whisper
In coherent phonics.

Melissa Birkhofer

1

The waves crash forth
From the incoming sea,
Violet they crash
Tranquil they seem.
Starting way out
In between the lands that be,
Trying to penetrate ours
Something within our scene.
All we want to claim
Is to be like a wave.
Accepting of other beings
Wanting the world to be
Just as you remember,
Something you have seen.
Nature and people
Merging into one.

Tiffany Wright

Heaven's Call

Someday I will soar on high
With angels passing by
Jesus will be there
A peace in the air.
Joy from the throne
No more sorrows there
No more tears
No more fears.
God is on His throne
Blessings overflow
Grace abounds,
Jesus is there.
Anxiety and pain cannot dwell there
O won't you give your life to Christ
And come soar with me?
Love, Joy, Happiness and Peace
Can all be yours for free
Call on Jesus name.

Melissa R. Just

Memorabilia

If when we part, what I wish you do
Is pack it all, the memories too.
The days and nights of sweet desire,
are causing pain that's hot like fire.

Don't leave behind one tiny trace.
I need so God to forget your face.
I need to close the suitcase tight,
to ship it off, far in the night.

Check every corner, every drawer.
And pick up every thread.
For memories are often stored.
so close inside one's head.

Clean off the walls.
Sweep down the floor.
Take all with you.
Then close the door.

Walk down your road.
And I'll walk mine.
Unburdened now, with nothing-
But Time.

Flora D. Smith

Kaleidoscope

Listen, feel, experience
    His word; his Presence; his Love.

Speak, touch, share
    A prayer
        A soul
            A heart.

See, embrace, grow
    Beauty
        Life
            Faith.

Smell, enjoy, exchange
    Flowers
        Friends
            Concerns.

Swallow, soothe, give
    Pride
        Another
            Comfort

Seek, find, open
    His Kingdom; God; Yourself.

Mary Alice Austin

What Once Was

What once was real now seems
fake, what once was happy
now seems sad, what once
was good now seems bad,
what once was reality now
seems like a faint and distant
dream. What once was sacred
now seems like nothing,
what once was love now
seems like to hate, what once was
hope is now failure.

Billie Jo Burgess

Mom

Tomorrow is the day
that they lay you to rest,
I don't understand why
he took you, the best.

I have did much crying
shed so many tears,
my mind has wondered so far
so scared and full of fear.

I hope you're up there
happiness as you dreamed there to be,
I just hope and pray of one thing
that you will watch down over me.

Wanda L. Marquardt

Easter Joy

As the sun did begin to peek
two weeping women came to seek,
Christ the Lord, who was crucified
and at the tomb, they looked inside.
The earth had quaked at break of day
and caused the stone to roll away,
within the tomb, where He was laid
two angels sat, in white arrayed
and lying there, they also found,
the cloth with which He had been wound
the angel spake, "Do not have fear,
Christ is risen He is not here."

Nila Jo Silbaugh

Wild Red Rose

Velvet, scarlet, red
So beautiful and bright
In Mid-Summer's night,

Dew kissed bud
Has blossomed,
A wild Red Rose

Full bloom — to dance
In Autumn's cool breeze,
Sharing its beauty and fragrance,

To stay but for a moment,
God's precious gift
Red Rose of Love.

In Winter's cold wind
Petals fall free,
To emerge from darkness of night

Bringing beauty and fragrance
Into the Light of Spring,
To bud, blossom and bloom again,
The Wild Red Rose!

B. J. Crawford-Holcomb

Storms End

The angel's cried
one billion tears
and the earth
did drink them up;
in angered rage
the thunder roared
and lighting danced
throughout the sky;
eastern winds
predicting a change —
clouds in waiting
to transfer hue
from grey to ivory
nestled around
the idle sun
awaiting the storms end.

June Sullivan

Black Man's Freedom

Black man
wishin' to be free
Black man
hopin' to be

Black man
bendin' on his knee
Black man
prayin' to be

Black man
wantin' to be free
Black man
strugglin' to be

Black man
hangin' from a tree
Black man
FIN'LY FREE!

Antwanette N. Hill

"Picking Cotton"

Picking cotton
in the sun-drenched fields
her scarred, blackened hands
where a long time yields
her cotton bonnet
tied round in a little bow
a vision of the pain
as she crouches down low.
Her deep, brown eyes
and charcoal face
a painting of this picture
shows such beauty and grace.
Enslaved, held captive
in this cruel, evil world
picking tons of cotton
with her swollen eyes curled.

Christina L. Ruotolo

Child's Teddy Bear

Teddy Bear sits in his chair
He waits the child who put him there
The dearest one of all the toys
For he who cherished childest joys

Alas, how could that Teddy know
The little boy was bound to grow
So Teddy Bear waits all in vain
As always though he knows no pain

Though eyes are gone, one ear is torn
The fur all crumbly grayed and worn
For Teddy has no inner light
To guide him to a better sight

Our little boy is now a man
And answers to a better plan
He does not sit and wait decay
But readies for a brighter day

So Teddy still sits on his duff
Our man is made of greater stuff
How good the light that he can know
That he can grow and grow and Grow.

Virginia Davis Vaughan

"Immortality"

I will live
to see people die
What I would give
if this were a lie.

This world has
its evil ways,
time keeps going
never ending days.

I can't go back
to that year,
When I became immortal
death I had feared.

Alone and scared
still alive however,
It ain't so great
to live forever.

Won't fall in love,
it wouldn't last,
I'll keep going forward
and forget the past . . .

Danielle Gosselin

Sweet Sadness Of Today

Sweet sadness
of today
on thoughts
of yesterday
made sweeter
still
by memories
of thee.
O blessed bitter
pressing pills
these capsuled
memories
that give
to me
a clouded blinding
balm.

Peggy Stevens

Don't Weep, Rejoice

Don't weep for me dear loved one,
When it is my time to go.
Rejoice and be exceeding glad,
My sins are white as snow.

Don't weep for me dear loved one,
When God shall call me home.
Rejoice for I'll be singing,
Around the great white throne.

Don't weep for me dear loved one,
When Jesus calls for me.
Rejoice and praise His Holy Name,
For I have been set free.

Don't weep for me dear loved one,
If you are asked to wait.
Rejoice for I'll be waiting,
Inside the pearly gate.

Chrysteen Lilly

Sadness

A sadness can be anger
Or sympathy or pain
Or monotony of things we've seen
Until they're old and plain

Sniffling, sobbing misery
or just a lonely blue
Deep depression, or possibly
Just something else to do

Frustration, guilt, and mourning
Each of us felt them all
Or simple moods of brooding
Like a separating wall

The loss of something, great or small
Can cause our hearts to weep
Time will bring tomorrow
To put our pain to sleep.

Sonja Tonnesen

Postcard From Siberia

The children had a dog
But this year the dog died
They stared at the corpse in the snow
All they could think to do was cry
At least this year we eat!

Sebastian Ericsson

In The Beginning

In the beginning
there was me
a free spirit
open to receiving
the many experiences
of the seasons.
Alas, I have fallen
and known the brutality
of receiving winter's
freezing cold shoulder;
and yet,
I am always glad to openly see
the unexpected growths in me
because
there is nothing like
knowing with every spring
I have lived through another season
and tasted the assorted
bittersweet spices of life.

J. Davis

My Prayer

A precious one from us is gone.
A voice we loved is stilled.
A place is vacant in our house
That never can be filled.

Today I stopped dear Lord to think
Of all the things you've done.
Of all the tears you've dried for me
And all the battles won.

Of all the time my head hung low
Without a friend to care.
Now looking back I clearly see
That You were always there.

You heard my prayers when no one knew
The pain I felt inside.
So many times no words would come
And I just knelt and cried.

J. A. Blitch

The Thorn Tree

The Setting sun
Tinged the
Distant hills I knew,
red.

And here
Was swirled red with
Dust from cattle hooves,
and blue
From smoking fires,
The colors of
Our murrans' robes.

I'd been away
too long, and
longed for rest;
I nearly ran,
Without decorum
towards my home,
To take the
Thorn tree
to my Breast.

Peter Rigby

One Yellow Rose

Sprayed with golden sunshine
Whispered with a kiss of dew
A solemn yellow rose stands tall
For everyone to view.

Never has one shown such beauty
Nor has there ever been one so bright
But something different about this rose
Has come upon my sight.

Not only is this a flower
Given as a gift of love
But this is a great miracle
Made by two hands above.

Caressed by tender love and care
God placed each petal down
Upon a green foundation
So not to fall upon the ground.

The hidden message inside this rose
Before I could not see
To think He cared enough to share
Such magnificent beauty with me.

Amy M. McKinney

Rest Song

Good night.
Lay down close.
The dawn is soon to come,
And the night is not as long
As when we had begun.

In the morning light,
We'll both take heart
From fresh new insights:

Golden dream
Astride
Black knighted
Horse,
Light!

Lay down close,
Let's hug the night —
Let's sing a song
Before it turns to dawn.

Ligia Manjarres

I Lean Across the Miles

The life I live
    when we're apart,
The longings of
    this vibrant heart,
The journey near,
    the journey far,
The trip to my
    own wistful star,
The things I feel,
    the things I touch,
The things that mean
    so very much!
The truth and beauty
    that I see,
The dreams I dream
    so hopefully,
And all God's gifts that I explore,
All things that He has made me for,
All things I am, all things I do,
Have meaning when they nourish you.

Cy Anschutz

Outs And Ins

Out there is a world
Of wonder and joy
Of dreams coming true
And happy endings
All things fall in place
One way streets abide
There are no troubles
No worries, no problems . . .

In here is a life
Of wandering thoughts
Of visions of happiness
And patience for finality
Thoughts and ideas jumble
On six lane interstates
Sorrow and hope quarrel
As the toils of life
Weigh heavy the soul . . .

As all things happen so
My mind attempts perception.

John McGinnis

If You Go West

If you go west
you may learn to give up green.
So as you go
consider soft full branches.
Breathe in deeply
the fragrance of forests.
Remember berry bushes
and berries
bursting in the tasting.
But west may yet win you
with arid ways and windswept largeness
and tumbleweed sparseness.
You may see sky's starry cover
as brown earth's night-dressed lover.
And you may learn to love sky best.

Christina Watkins

Lying Together

As we lie together
Coupled by lust
Love is crippled
By lack of trust

We heap upon each other
Lustful taunts
For the purpose of gaining
Our selfish wants

For one another
We care little or nothing
And in the end
Regard each other with loathing

Together, living a life
Filled with the taint
Of the murder of love
By lack of restraint.

Zachary D. Stine

Pebble In My Shoe

This darn pebble in my shoe
I wish it would happen to you!

Oh no
Not now
It's my turn to bat
My turn to play
Well I struck out . . .

And all through the day I was thinking
If I just fixed that shoe right
I might be talking about a
Home-run tonight!

Jodi O'Brien

Untitled

Judge are we
by our manipulation
of 26 characters
and some extra
for supposedly further
clarification or is
it just senselessly following
convention?
Alas, the description
will never be the
described.
That which is, is.

Weiting Hsu

The Racoon

I walk alone on the sidewalk
Rejected by my own kind
I'm so hot yet so cold
Snow and ice cover the world
I walk with great difficulty
The humans follow me
One in uniform
Another with a box
Another with a stick
The ring wrapped around my neck
I was pulled up in the air
By the ring at the end of the stick
I was dropped into the square box
And taken to an unknown place
I am so sick
A man in white appeared
With a silver dart
And I was injected with it
And finally the end came to me
I went to sleep and met my fate

Norman Sadler

Untitled

Make still, the silence
of my soul.
Claim it as Your own.
Whisper sweet Wisdom
and Knowledge
to me this jewelless night.
In Darkness, I search
to find Your Heart.
O God, don't keep it hidden
form my sight —
To find this treasure I seek
though Hell and Light.

Caroline R. Bennette

Kill the Weed

Ignorance grows
like a weed
through the minds of those
supposedly intelligent beings
who preach hate
and are afraid to communicate
with a population of diversity.

Kill the weed
and cultivate the mind
then plant the seed
that will bloom in time
into an open-mind
fearless of what it will find
in a population of diversity.

Lynette Johnson

This Birthmother's Need

I have a need down deep inside
to find my son I was denied
and to hold for the very first time.

I have a need deep in my soul
to tell him why I had to let him go
to tell him how I love him so.

I have a need down in my heart
to tell him we were never far apart.

I have a need down deep inside
for him to look into my eyes
and know he is mine.

Denise Thorpe-Wamser

Accept The Challenge Of Life

Life is a precious commodity
not to be ignored or wasted.

Life is to be used to its fullest,
shared,
given,
lived.

Opportunity is present all around us.
Accept the challenges,
because it is the challenges of life
that make life so valuable.

Work to right a wrong,
strengthen a weakness,
develop a skill.
Maintain an optimistic outlook.

These are the things in life
that you will remember,
or more importantly,
these are the things in life
that you will remembered for.

G. W. Clarke

A Candid Approach To Life

I considered thoughtfulness
A way to deal with folks.
Then I added the kind of cheerfulness
One never hears in jokes.

Endowed with enthusiasm
Friends liked my amenity
Now friends are so numerous
Because of my sincerity.

bill wilder

Sweet Touch

The sweet touch of
your lips put stars in my eyes.
To see you smile is like a
light from the morning sunshine
shining down on my face. You
are like roses when you smile,
Blooming with laughter and joy
when night falls you're as bright
as the moon shining in the sky.
But like a rose you sleep
happy in the night.

Mitchell Parfait

Beautiful Land, America

Beautiful land
    With hope burning bright
Beautiful land
    For freedom's light

Beautiful country,
    Rich and so green
We're bordered by oceans
    With so much between

Beautiful valleys
    Beautiful streams
Beautiful thoughts
    And shining dreams

With people who love
    And people who care,
With great faith among us -
    Great things do we dare!

Connie Jones Prince

Untitled

My words are my weapons, my walls
Take them from me & you leave me
naked.
All of me a raw open wound —
Comfort me in your warmth.
Sheltering me in my pain
For this I cannot ask
I have no words
I am not afraid that you will hurt me
I am afraid you will not care.
— And that will hurt me until I
cannot move.

Cris Elaine Jung

Mild Moments Past

Brown Silk Skin
Unique beauty strikes again, Your
unexpected but still I would to invite
you in, your mysterious eyes, I wonder
what it is that you see, Pleasant hours
will remain, I want to feel you next to
me at 2:30 AM, I want to you before
the day begins, you are the smile that
I wear, you are the fear that I fear,
Lost in my own thunderstorm of mixed
emotions, that I surrender to you,
I'll take you on a far ride, From here
to crimson tide, time to rest your love
on me for awhile, to embellish in my
"Black Love Cave."

Pauline E. Chapman

Always Be There

It's good to know somebody loves you
it's good to know somebody cares
my mind is always on you
tell me you'll always be there

When I'm feeling dawn
you brighten up my day
your smile seems to glow
and show me the way

Because it's good to know
somebody loved me
it's good to know somebody cared
my soul will always be with you
tell me you'll always be there.

Always be there.

Paul R. Menard

Changing Times

Winter is evident
by the blustering cold
Summer smiles upon us
by a warmth so bold

Fall makes its mark
by rustling of leaves
Spring with smells of flowers
and buzzing of bees

Day shows itself
with warmth on my face
and slowly it fades
as night takes its place

To see these
all as I do
would mean giving up
something precious to you

I am forced to see this
all within my mind
My eyes see darkness
I am blind.

Christina Walker

I Am Schizophrenic

I am majestic,
With shameful rhetoric.
I am just like you,
You don't want to, or can't be;
Like me . . .
I am in my and your prison.
    You Are Free

I am free.
If I want to be.
But I can't be;
Yet I am, and I can;
And I am not,
Like you.
Yet you are like me,
    somehow.

One thing,
    at least,
    We Are.

Bill Fleming

Why God Made A Rainbow

God made the rainbow for people
to know that after a real big
thunderstorm everything is
going to be alright.
    He made the color blue from
the blueness in the seas.
    The pinkness from his blood
    The Yellowness from his
bright yellow sun.
    The green color from his
nature, pure grass.
    The colors are so light and
beautiful like a precious new
born baby.

Aimee Bosaw

Diary Of A Dreamer

In quiet moments
My mind sweeps me away.
My spirit carries me,
as time passes,
into the arms of Wisdom.
Here lies the fullness of joy.

Deep within my soul
lies an unknown reservoir.
It does not flow.
It waits.
In silence it cries out to be known,
to fulfill its intended purpose.

Who will discover it?

Suzette Marie Bowman

Arlington

Reflections of light
On lonely rows of white;
Lowly tombs each alike,
Each alone —
Silent Sentinels,
Reminders of the scars of war.

Joseph R. Foster

In Death

To oversee what will be done.
Let the children be kind;
My love's grief short;
And I, a sweet memory.

Marylou Dodd

The Space Man

There was a space man in the sky.
He's flying near, He's flying by.
He's afraid of people on the Earth.
For it is not the land of his birth.
So he will fly, to the sky,
and not return, so goodbye.

William E. Hargraves

My Dream

My heart it yearns a child to hold
My hopes, my dreams may soon unfold.
I want, but cannot have this dream
My tears are many, sometimes extreme
At night I know my dreams come true
Some child may someday need me too

Karen Loshe

The Rain

The rain —
How my heart has longed for it
and sighed for it
and prayed for it,

And it is here!!

Now my heart is glad for it
and beats with it
and sings with it.

And the thirsty earth is calling
As the silv'ry drops are falling
melting
swelting
pelting
Swiftly driven by the wind.

Quilvie G. Mills

The Irony Of Life

A different road,
I have chosen in this thing
called Life.

I know I am
here, yet I didn't choose to be.
Every day, I'm a step closer
to the End.

Ironically enough,
every day I learn more, live more,
love more,
yet every day, I have a little
less time in this thing called
Life.

Debby Mager

The Dandelion

Through the furry strands aglow
With friendly hints of sun below
The brightness of the daylight,

Blows a gentle, cool breeze
Past sentiments no soul sees
Dangling at a changing height.

Innocent love on the inside
Veiled beneath strands outside
Carried about in the wind . . .

Across the field it races
Until somebody chases
The thought of love again.

McLean T. Lutz

Darkness

How black is my heart,
As dark as my soul.
When death is on the horizon,
My heart's as black as coal.

No one, but me, understands,
And no one cares.
Except when the darkness comes,
Drifting on once-reluctant air.

Now the new light comes,
It is reflecting on the past.
From ashes to ashes and dust to dust,
Nothing seems to last.

Lauren King

Evil

Sun goes down
Full moon lights the sky
From the darkness
Open blood red eyes

Deep in the darkness
They sit and wait
Putting you
One step away from those pearly gates

Villainous and corrupt
Prowling the night
Swallow you whole
Feeding on fright

Scared to sleep
Cause they're watching you
Scared of the dark
Cause that's what it likes

Evil walks, in forms of the beast
Evil kills, without mercy
Evil deceives, with a smile
Evil, beware its kiss

Dorman L. Walters Jr.

The Ways Of My Life

The ways of my life.
Means the world to me.
Mostly out of life.
I just want to be free.

Free as a bird.
So anytime I could fly.
I just want the good times in life.
So my life won't just pass me by.

My problems concern people.
People that I care for and love
I want them to give me my freedom.
That's what I really think of.

To be free is like the silence.
Like a leaf going down stream.
To be cared for makes me happy.
Falling in love is my dream.

The ways of my life.
Means the world to me.
All I want is my happiness.
And the love that will set me free.

Lena C. Barraza

My Country's Flag

Pick up your flag
  and fly it high.
Be proud of it until
  the day you die.
Don't ever let it
  touch the ground.
Don't let anyone
  put you down.
Stand up for your
  country's rights.
It's what keeps the
  world going around.
Pick up your flag
  and hold it high.
Never be afraid
  to let it fly.

Agnes Bradley

Fear

As you come closer
I back away
Into a small corner
I want you to go away
I fear you, please leave
Don't touch me
I am scared
Who are you
I have no where else to go
Who will I turn to
It's taking over me
Help me, help me
Let go of me
I am weak, powerless
Don't do this — stop
Just get it over with
Please kill me

Jeanne Andrakowicz

Rules To Growing Up

Times are hard
and times are tough.
Things get bad
and things get rough.

You've got to learn
not to be so shy.
Not to do things bad
and not to cry.

Learn to stand up
learn to be wise.
Tell no jokes
and tell no lies.

Listen to everything
every word and every feature.
Mind your Mom and your manners
Pay attention to your teacher.

Follow the rules I tell
To grow up big and strong.
Stay cheerful and stay happy
and nothing can go wrong.

Amy Lunceford

Be True To Your Dream

Life is real and earnest
all things are what they seem.
But don't forget the magic
and the wonder of a dream.

With both feet on the ground
and your eyes upon a star,
with love to inspire you
you're destined to go far.

Be true to your dream
have faith in what you do,
believe love is for giving
and your dream will come true.

Be true to your dream
live in hope from day to day.
And the finest things you keep
will be what you have given away.

Be true to your dream
learn how to love and live,
for happiness is the return
you receive from what you give.

Marilyn Spears

Brother

Older, taller
working hard in college
confidently, constantly
Kyle

Jared Thompson

Perfect

I have no time to rest
I have to be the best
I have to try my hardest
Am I human or am I machine
I have to live up to her
no matter how it may be
I just cant be me
Must I keep on smiling
can I keep my head high
Would they still love her
if she were like I
they ask why I cry
then I wonder should I die
one day I bet
or someday I hope
they'll realize no one can be
  perfect

Malisa Dunn

The Mind Of Modern Men

Enter my mind
What do you see
Are you just dreaming
Escaping reality
Run from the truth
Hide in your lies
No one will find you
No one will try
Drowned in a pool
In this bottomless swamp
Nothing is true
And nothing is false.

Seth Westberry

The Beginning Of The End

How much time do we have
before the path
technology has set for us
ends?
When will society
do as it must
and pay the bill?
Change is needed
but the voice of change
goes unheeded.
The end is near
and I fear
that it will sear
the mind, body, soul.
We know of what to do
but society plays the fool.
It's now or never
and I prefer the former
over the latter.

Steve Alexander-Larkin

Memories

A house full of memories
A child full of pain
For a love that knows no boundaries
And a kindness to obtain
You look back so thoughtfully
At years thought wasted away
But with each new heartache
You pressed on for a better day
Now you hold the memories
That are dear to you like gold
You step back into the past
And watch your future re-unfold
So many things are treasures
Truths that lie deep within your soul
Secrets fester within that darkness
Mysteriously dwelling in that hole
But now you're a different person
An individual by far
Because experiences were the key
To what made you what you are

Jennifer Kyung

Angels

God sent his angels down
When life was hard to bear.
I did not know they were angels.
They did not make a sound
To tell me who they were.
They caught me unaware.
They were always around
When I needed them.
They were in form of family
And friends.
They showed me how very
Much they cared.
I knew on them I
Could depend.
A lot of their time they
Did spend with me.
Helping any way they could.
I thank God for them.
The angels God sent
In form of family and friends.

Cherrie T. Waters

Little Sunshine

Have you ever seen,
Such a precious sight
As a little child at play
Morning, noon and night.

A little one, so free from care
Trusting everyday,
The Lord above and us below
To help him in his way.

Little Sunshine on the earth,
You are so full of joy.
You run, you skip, you jump so high
And play with every toy.

Remind us, Lord, when we forget,
What you told us long ago.
We should forever radiate
The sunshine from our souls.

May we be like little children
In our attitudes toward life,
The rays of Little Sunshine
In a world so torn with strife.

Maridale K. Eidson

Love

Love is a very beautiful
thing, when treated with care it
can amount to anything. When you
believe in Love you can create
things beyond your wildest
dreams. Everything you've
hoped and dreamed of will come
true, life will be glorious, the
sun will shine with strong beauty
and grace, oceans will glisten,
skies will open up and seem to
hold you in their arms. All this shall
come true, but only if you believe
in love.

Elizabeth Emig

"My Tired Little Dove"

My tired little dove
who God sent from above.
You are such a good
little dove. You go up
and down the parkway, to
help those in need.
Indeed, you are a
special person, who is
full of love, "my tired
little dove."
I think about you and pray
that God watches over
you and keeps you safe
my tired little dove, who
I love.
I've been blessed to
have, come across your
path in life, my little dove.

Ru Caruso

I Pray

Each night I pray to God above
That I might dream of my lost love
If only I could just make sure
That she suffers in pain no more
If only just for a moment I could see
That she's as safe and happy as can be
If only I could see her face
And know she's happy in her new place
If only I could know this for sure
Dear God I would bother you no more
But see when you took my mother dear
You filled my heart with worry and fear
So please dear God a dream, just one
So that my heartache would ease up some

Patricia A. Masiello

Untitled

Gazing into the eyes of innocence,
lipid pools reflecting the past,
refracting the future,
into the contorted present;
eyes of pain from trust
thrashed down and hope
torn from the womb
of compassion
by dagger like claws of injustice;
bleeding and dying
in the gutters
as passersby walk blindly on
oblivious to all.

Johnedda Blessing Dolan

Peace Is The Answer

Someone dies in the night
Seems so wrong — just not right
Arresting one starts the fight.
Two sides against each other
Try to stop them — why bother?
Together — we go further.
Stand alone, sometimes you will,
But when it counts you will feel
Strength in numbers — there's a chill.
Together as one we're strong
Forming a bond lasting long
Peace forever — can't be wrong.

Melody Dudziak

For My Shogun

If I am the artist
Then you are my inspiration
If I am the obsessed
Then you are my infatuation
If I am the poet
Then you are my prose
If I am the fragrance
Then you are my rose
If I am the phantom
Then you are my delight
If I am the disillusioned
Then you are my sight
If I am the dreamer
Then you are my quixotic
If I am the dreary
Then you are my exotic
If I am the jester
Then you are my laughter
If I am the fairy tale
Then you are my "Happily Ever After"

Cynthia L. Roberts

Good-bye

The kiss of death has touched your lips
And taken you away.
So as you lie before me now,
Please hear these words I say.

My mind is full of unspoken words
That never will be said.
I know you understand this all,
Yet, these thoughts I still can't shed.

My soul and body throb so much
Because I miss you so.
And all I have for comfort now,
Is knowing you had to go.

Silvia B. Anderson

My Husband

The big tall guy
 in my life.
At times he thinks
and then we laugh.
 He can be kind
 with just a smile.
And when he holds me
 my sun just shines
But when he's gone
 my light goes blank!

Anna Macias Crowley

Correlation

The lessons learned, the message slow,
The things we think, we learn, we know,
Detain the mind, and make it slow
As if to say: I think I know.

David Moree

The Dream

A distant vision . . .
a proud and majestic tower of strength,
whose tattered remains
withstand the turbulent winds of time
that endlessly bear down upon man.

A light in the shadows for those
who have lost their way.

A reminder of the past for those
who would forget.

And a beacon of hope for those
who remember.

Charlotte Schneider

There Is No Turning Back

Am I in a dream or is this reality
It must be a dream there is no war,
There is no fatality
A peaceful place and a whole lot more.

A wild river waiting for me
Gliding along, riding the waves
As free as can be
I'm the only one who was brave.

Now I'm alone and I don't feel right
No one here to keep me company,
I see it, it's a bright light
Can I go near it, is it right for me?

It's him my savour
He's here to stay,
Between him and I he's braver
And he will never go away.

Here I can be me
Nothing here I lack,
I am what I want to be
There is no turning back . . .

Rebecca Jones

Untitled

Will they ever split the atom
They always used to say
No they will never split the atom
At least not in our day

Will they ever split the atom
They used to ask in fun
No they will never split the atom
You know it can't be done

Then one day the split the atom
With much unholy glee
And when they split the atom
A monster was set free

Now pandora's box is open
And genies at liberty
To wander throughout this sorry
World, to threaten you and me

Len Lagmay

Reflections

When you look at me what do
you see?

Not just a reflection, please
take a long hard look at me.

I know what I see, I see a kind,
caring person with a dream,
a dream that brings out the
very best in me.

I only wish my dad could see
what I see.

I wonder what he sees when he
looks at me.

Does he see a liar or a thief,
or maybe that isn't his image
of me, but his image of me,
as someone else sees me.

Emily Blake

Imagination

A basket of stars,
A rainbow of feelings,
A sky of seas,
Is imagination.

A cup of smiles,
A book of water,
A tree of sunshine,
Is imagination.

A wind of colors,
A road of eternity,
A hymn of peace,
Is imagination.

A soul of flames,
A stream of love,
A mountain of voices,
Is imagination.

Valerie Lau

Futuristic — Ponderings

The future sits before me
And I leave my past behind
I travel on unknowing
Of the way my path may wind.
It's one of life's great mysteries
To not know what lies ahead
I just keep stepping toward the place
I'll go when I am dead.

This world's in great confusion
of what it wants to be.
We work so hard creating
a future we can't see . . .

Angela M. Davis

I Share Your Sorrows

I share your sorrows,
I see your tears,
I cry your cries,
I feel your fears.
But yet I do not understand;
Why you have sorrows?
Why you shed tears?
Why you cry cries?
Why you feel fears?

Matt Forcum

Untitled

In mourning,
your veil is lifted,
and from behind the shadows
are the eyes,
the ice that melts,
and the love that's frozen
deep within you . . .

A kiss,
our kiss,
loving,
lasting,
lost within your pain . . .
The past resides within your heart,
and me,
laying there beside you,
waiting
for you to awaken.

David L. Cox

Love Is . . .

Love is harsh and is confusing
Though at times can be amusing
Taught to us by those who care
Love is something we should share
Though you may become depressed
Through love, problems can be guessed
Small things show your love for others
A hug is all you need for mothers
The thought is what should really count
Not what you give or the amount
Show your love everyday
A bright smile is one way
Love is often shown not said
Next time tell someone instead
Love is patient, love is kind
It's in the heart and in the mind
Show your love but not your hate
Before you opens a new gate

Jonathan Book

The Lover Of My Years

In the spring on mornings clear
On my window sill I sit
Waiting for the lover of my years
And quietly he comes unseen
Ah, the tender Zephyr
That refreshing morning air
That caress my face
And caress my hair
And caress my lips
With its tender tip of wings
While my eyes, my soul
On the quiet grandeur
Of God's creation feast
Then the radiant morning grace
On the horizon blue
Shows up his smiling face
And with his luscious hues
Brightens up the greens
The lover of my years fade away
I close my window and sit and dream

Santa Pi Rivera

My Little Sister

My little sister
Likes to play
With dolls; she
Also likes to
Play with balls.

My little sister
Likes to play
House; she also
Likes our mouse.

My little sister
Is sweet like
Candy; she is
Also very dandy.

Hey! What can
I say; well, just
Ask my sister;
She has a lot
To say!

Jessica Vilella

Untitled

Sometimes I feel alone
and there isn't any body at home
but one thing I can say that
I am wrong, because there
is some one at home.
Someone that cares and is dear
to my heart and that why
I knew it was right from the
start, because he takes
care of me.
He is there for me through
thick and thin, and that
is very kind of him.
But still sometimes I feel
alone, and that is very wrong.

Kristin Wilcox

A Flower Is Born

Our life is like a flower,
at first it's just a seed,
waiting for that special hour
to be more than just a weed.

While still beneath the earth it forms
its tiny little roots,
Protected from the storms of life
then through the soil it shoots.

Drawing toward the sun it grows,
searching for the light.
The Gardener is the one who knows
what it needs to make it right.

When weeds appear and they will,
the Gardener seems to say,
"Hold tight my little flower,
I'm here to guide the way."

Pam Pierrelee

Flow With Me

Flow with me
on the green grass
with castles of minds
and more . . .
Say those words
of the heavens,
speaking sceneries and
voicing the angels.

Do you have to go
far, far away?
Could you sit still
and limber and only
admire the operas of
silhouettes?

There are no more
words to try to understand.
What more is there?
Analyze, judge
release and forget.

Flow with me,
like ivory droplets
on my skin.
Call only upon
the distance that is
deep from within

Deborah Pospisal

My Kitty

Soft kitten, warm and cuddly
ever purring always snugly
rubbing noses, little grin
makes me feel warm within.

Sometimes playful with a string
always curious at everything
sharp claws and teeth and sense so keen
paws at you but seldom mean.

With a book or watching TV
kitty comes and sits by me
closes its eyes with a contented smile
dreams most pleasant all the while.

James Andersland

Officer Needs Assistance

Radio, Officer needs assistance,
and radio, tell them to signal 10.
Radio, I need another wrecker,
and radio, I'll tell you when.

Radio, I need a NCIC check,
and did I mention a local and S.O.?
Radio, give me a 10-28,
and please tell me where to go.

Radio, did you say a signal F?
And man, is that all you can do?
Radio, I really hope you don't mind,
If I take my frustrations out on you.

Did any one of us ever take the time?
And did anyone ever say?
That without any one of you,
It would damn sure ruin our day,

If not, let me be the first,
To say I really care,
I don't know about anyone else,
But I'm damn sure glad you're there!

Doug Esther

Times Change

Flowers bloom, then wither away
Mountains become shorter over time
Clouds get blown away
The seasons come and go
Trees bud, leaves fall
Tides roll in, then out again
The sands of time are always shifting
But one thing remains the same
   Mom and Dad

Mary Lee Dauksch

Music Of The Flowers

The fragrant odor of lilacs
   Herald a day in spring
Music of the flowers
   Cause loving memories to cling

On the fragrance of the lilacs
   These precious thoughts do come
Enhancing that noble flower
   On our coat of arms
   Pure, sweet, red, geranium

Our little house and garden
   Where flowers sing the year around
And for the birds of winter
   We spread bread crumbs
   On the ground

Looking toward our future years
   And the music of flowers perfume
Viewing our life together
   Where only harmony might bloom

Donald Rodger Long

Burglar

Muscular, thin
Robbing, threatening, Shooting
Always stealing from people
   Thief

   Dollar
Rectangular, green
Spending, receiving, giving
Going to spend money
   Bill

Dawna Walther

The Thumb

I saw you sitting there alone
Thinking no one cared but you
With just a thumb to pacify
While resting on cold steps
But I cared passing by
Others on the bus cared too
For we are not alone at all
We are all one together here
Each to his own purpose
Not independent of the others
All dependent on planet earth
Look around as you grow up
The connecting link is love
Not of self; but of others around
Put your tiny thumb to work, dear
Teach it more than self pleasure
The thumb is vital to idle fingers
Grasp this meaning to help others
You may be the thumb society needs.

Tigra Rivera

Forgotten Soul

An old man with silver hair
carries tales of yesterday.
And of untold wisdom;
that no one seems to hear.
    He wears a warn army coat
molded to his body, it has.
    It seems his only Friend
for it keeps him warm
in cold nights an hears his cries
    Where he sleeps?
A damp corner at a dead end street
he lays to sleep; with news of
yesterday.
    I read the paper this morning
found frozen, Hero; found frozen hero
forgotten soul;
His only Friend it seems
was his old coat
Oh! But a wooden cross
found tightly in his hand.

Vicky E. Young

My Special Friend

Pick up the broken pieces
Take them to your dearest friend
He'll piece them back together
For he's the only one who can
He'll listen to your sorrows
He'll nod a knowing smile
He'll stay right beside you
He'll go that extra mile
He'll lead you through the darkness
He'll chase away your fears
He'll take your hand in His hand
He'll dry your every tear
So when you need a friend
Who will always be there
Just look up to the heavens
For He's as close as a prayer

Marilyn E. Elmore

"A Butterfly"

A nice butterfly
Was fluttering high.

Stephanie Garbarini

To You With Love

Only the cool summer night
Compares to your beauty
So warm and pleasant
Full of mysterious surprise

The tone of your voice
Is soft and relaxing
Full of wisdom
And is overwhelmingly soothing

You innocence can be
Compared to a flower
Lovely and elegant
Still fragile and frail

You are truly the greatest of women
And as the sun does rise
So does my love for you
When I gaze into your eyes

Jason E. Mortimer

Do They Listen?

My daughter ate a mushroom.
She got a great big wart.

My son would pick at his zits.
Now he looks like s***.

What's wrong with these kids?
I've told them before . . .

If they do what I say,
then all would be well.

But since they don't see the wisdom
in just the smallest things

I keep these comments to myself
And things have gone to hell.

Don Bitle

Killing Time!

Time to kill
Is no thrill.

Time well-spent
Makes you bent.

Time it is;
Time it was.

Time in the Future
Is covered with fuzz.

Lee Christenson

The Walk

A walk in the clouds yes/no
Was it real or was it just a dream
For you see it was still all
a mystery
Was it true all those things
I saw
Those faces and the things
they said
Was it true about my ending
fate
Or was it just a dream
Those things they spoke about
seemed all to real
But I guess I shall never
truly know about my walk in
the clouds
Till that one day
For my true walk in the clouds
To put my mystery to an end

Arren R. Lilly

Unannounced

Frost arrived suddenly
Strangling, robbing the umbrage
Squelching fall's splendor
A boorish one-night act
Cheating Summer's finale
A succinct bleeding
Of dull reds and umbers
Sparks versus ardent flame
Had the trees upset Mother Nature?

Scott J. Palmer

"Wings"

If I could be a little bird
    I'd come see you every day.
    I'd flutter all around your room
    And talk with you and play.

I'd make you tea and cookies
    And plump your pillow up;
    I'd sing you such sweet melodies
    And cheer you right on up!

I'd bring you flowers every day
    I'd make you comfy too;
    I'd be the bestest friend ever
    If I could be with you.

If I could just be a little bird
    I'd spread my wings of blue,
    And bring all the prayers and wishes
    I've been wishing just for you!

Sharon E. Jackson

A Child Cries

The forces of despair within
Walls, created by fear screaming.
A struggle to claim the soul,
Driving sanity, to knot's ending.

Normal tolerance deemed forthright,
Thoughts, unable to be conveyed.
A testing to a smile's limit,
The senses hasten a woven braid.

The unexpected begins an ebb,
A deafening negative . . .
Starts the trial of tears.
Judge, jury, and you collective,
Caught - up in an angry web,
Hold dearly your temperance of years.

They are only children,
Incomprehensible, no motor skill.
Yet, when the bough breaks,
Loving eyes turn and kill.
Does reason run irrational,
think twice, lend compassion.

John Wall Duddy

Wind In Fall

Dreaming, I sat alone
in the forest's center,
watching, waiting for some
sign of changing seasons.

Then a silent release
marked a tree with absence,
the body drifted down
to rest with other leaves.

Southward pointing V's
soared across the darkened sky.
The zephyr whispered "death"
to the poor left behind.

Soon all will be vacant.
The monarch's wing will fly
when dry leaves are taken
for circus parasols.

White winter's peace will come
when night's gentle advent
dresses the freezing ground
in silver, sleeping robes.

David Moen

A Boy's Desire

The boy has his mind made
He wants to live where
they run for shade
Where the sun shines on
the rolling hills
The midnight air brings
soft chills
Mountains high as to scrape
the sky
The seagulls and pelicans fly by
The ocean warm and sand
all there
People surfing with golden hair
This is the place he dreams
of true
Yoh, this place is bitchin
Surfs up, dude.

Mike Midgette

Sourdough N' Cold

Pine trees silhouetted black
Against a sunset pale
Another night of frightful cold
A piercing coyotes wail

Ice crystals in the moonlight
Fall like gold dust in the night
My breath like steam drifts softly up
My ears sting from the bite

Gallant yellow flames of fire
That fight against the frost
Should its crackling battle fail
This warm life would be lost

And now the Eastern sky grows light
Another day I'll see
Traveling on thru mountains great
They seem to stare at me

And now below, a curl of smoke
It's there I'll cease to roam
My cabin rough, the smell of bread
How I thank God I'm home

Cary W. Phair

Wings

If I had wings
I'd fly so high,
Higher than the highest
bird; higher than the
Stratosphere.
I'd no longer be stuck
On the ground anymore.
I'd soar and soar
And when I landed
I'd rest 'till my wings
Hurt no more.
Then up again with one
Big jump, striving to be higher.
Then out of this world,
Lost in space with
No human race and never come
Back again. Then and only then
would I want to be on the
ground; for it's lonely
when you're the only human with wings.

Anthony Perkins

Memories

Your silhouette glides through my mind,
Stirring quietly in the darkness.
My soul envelopes the memory of you
as the light from your face casts a
glimmer of love into my heart.
My desire for you, my sweet love,
won't die.
But you've gone, and are nothing but an
apparition in my head,
Moving slowly through the myriad of
memories I have of you.

Angie Matroni

Just Open Up Your Eyes And See

Just open up your eyes and see
how pretty and precious the
world could be. Because of
most of the violence, we
really don't have a lot
of silence. If people and
gangs would not fight. Maybe
the world would have
more life. Share the world
with friends and others
be kind to people
like fathers and mothers.

Amanda Burns

Untitled

A soft intrusion steals its way
Into my thoughts of everyday.
A gentle echo summons me
From distant reaches of memory.

A faded smile
A warming tear
A familiar face
In time appear.

You reach for me
Than as before
A barren world
Bears life once more.

Bob Stanger Jr.

Tomorrow

To dream of beauty
And never to view its form

To wish for the sun
And feel the lash of the storm

To search for a smile
And find a tear in its place

To search for a star
And trip on a cloud of earth

To ache for life
And die at the moment of birth

To know of a better
And yet to accept a worse

Is to utter a blessing
When the lips would mutter a curse.

Bernice K. Gregg

Lonely Night

What a lonely night this is
Touching, pricking and searching
So many things I have to get done
Running around accumulating.
Drips, drops falling all around
now brothers and sisters
I want you to go with me and
say a prayer for all who needs.
I want you to go with me to say a
prayer, for all who needs.

Brothers and sisters come and go
with me, come and go with me.

Cheryl A. Pounds

Records

Everything that's ever happened
Over sea or on the land
Everything we ever say
All the performances of man

Each day that's passed before
All the days we've yet to see
Every moment, I am counting
Ends as part of history

Evidence we take a part
Facts we scrutinize
Failure to keep Good Records
May end in Hope's demise

In most everything my eyes have seen
In all the Stories, I have ever heard
In every thought, there seems a part
In what I've failed to learn

The duality of time
Divides my hands
From my mind
As my spirit wonders, free

Sharon Marie

Second Chance

Oh golden morning, you shined
upon my soul
gently healing, making me whole

Betrayed by love, my heart was left
in pain
But with your tender persuasion,
I will try again

To capture the elusive gossamer wing,
the silken thread of feeling, that will
make my heart sing

Jeanne Walker

A Snowy Eve

Snow was falling softly,
It was a lovely winter's eve;
The air was light and balmy,
All was quiet and serene.

Soon the earth lay covered
'Neath a blanket pure and white;
It sparkled with a lustre
That illumined the heavens bright.

The trees displayed their branches,
Frosted white, in lace so grand;
It was a scene so picturesque —
A winter wonderland!

Mary Jane Herbert

For The Love Of Filomena

As my world revolves around her
  My days are so complete.
As days keep passing us by,
  to know she is so sweet.
A man's love for a woman
  can always prevail,
like a puppy love letter
  lost forever in the mail.
When God had made man
  and man found a woman.
My love for Filomena
  is like being in heaven.
This poem is dedicated with
  love to my wife.
With her fulfilling everyday of my life.

James E. Lajeunesse

Life Colors On A Background

Infinity aids the
  brushes of the mind,
Each picture ain't done
  'til the end of time.
With increasing speed
  over canvas they flow,
Exactly their meaning
  we do not know.

The colors are added
  as free as you please,
Backgrounds as brilliant
  as new autumn leaves.
Just when it looks like
  a color is changing,
Her shades pull you in —

Beauty is caging.

Christian Heiss

Relationships

A seagull caught my eye
As it soared
Across the golden sun.
How freely it glided,
Carried by the wind
In the brilliance of the Sky.
Another gull ascended
and joined it in flight.
Together they danced,
almost touching wings,
Or crossing paths,
Or sometimes distancing.
As one they flew
In unpredictable harmony of flight:
Carried by the wind,
Free and unencumbered,
Sharing time and space,
Together yet apart.

Judith A. Principe

A Father Taken

I am but the wick of a candle
Surrounded by the wax of life.

Shining surprising brightly
In a sudden darkness
That refuses the sunlight.

Though gone from me
He is the fueling answer
To finding my way
In these darkest of nights.

Joan T. Petrosine

Do Ye Angels?

Tell me one in lofty flight,
Witness of His glorious might,
Do you remember your days
Of youthful glory?
Do you recall
How you grew into
Maturity?
Can you see the days
Of aged wisdom, when
You reflected upon the rich
Experience of life?
Do you remember anything
At all?
Do you remember anyone?
Tell me, one now absent to my eye,
Do ye angels every cry?

C. Shannon Roos

Remote Changer

Here I am — Lord,
  Wondering where it is;
Just thinking to myself,
  And watching my Coke Fizz.

My children had it last,
  Probably in the chair;
Lost for two months — now,
  And pulling at my hair.

I know you've been there,
  A story that's so real;
Children . . . losing the changer.
  Parents . . . depressed they feel.

I hear they have an answer,
  To the problem of the lost;
A beeping remote — at last,
  About thirty dollars in cost!

Robin Wood

Untitled

Just when you think
you have life figured out
it suddenly changes
and fills you with doubt

One day you seem
to find the meaning of life
and in the next split second
it's torn down by strife

The things you stood for
you realize were wrong
so you turn them around
like they were there all along

It's not one's color
height or weight
it's what's inside
that value one's fate

If we all come together
we find what's inside
what so many have feared
and tried to hide.

Bianca Conliff

Here's To My Boys

I don't brag I'm a seamstress
I don't crochet, tat or knit
Nary a quilt or even a dress
I can only sew a lit'l bit.

I've tried my very best
To make something diff and new
To please my boys, and
Hear it pleases you!

Take the throws to sit upon
Be it beach with sand 'n dust
Take down by the pond, but
Having fun is a must!

I'll never make a masterpiece
Or anything worth a dream
But when I'm finished
There's love sewed in every seam.

Clare Cunningham

"Love And An Elevator"

Love is like an elevator.
It goes up and down,
People walk in and out.
I only wish I'd get stuck
in it with you.

Jenny Bradenburg

Saint Elias, Saint Elias

Saint Elias, Saint Elias
why do you scare me so?
Ever since I was a
small child you saw
me come and go.
The church was always
filled with people, praying
to you for what was
once passed.
Your statue I shall never
forget, the way we
processioned on the streets.
The great devotion people had.
I wanted to put some
thing over your head Saint
Elias, because you're scary
face made me feel, you
should be somewhere else
instead.

Gloria Hagopian

The One

You Are My Love
My divine sweet Inspiration
The one I hold
To be as one
The love of my life
We are in euphoria
As only two could be
The warmth in your eyes
The taste of your smile
I hear it in your touch
I feel it on your breath
Our world of passion
Igniting like a burning flame
Flashes over the memories
Of yesterday and tomorrow . . .

Stephen Hegg

Wonders of the World

Oh what wonders of the world
Our tiny boys and tiny girls
With sparkling eyes and
tiny features
Oh what precious little creatures
They wobble and crawl
And teeter and fall
And their tiny first steps
Are the sweetest of all
Oh what wonders of the world
Our tiny boys and tiny girls
With tiny arms that hug
and hold
How lucky we are
With these treasures of gold
Oh what wonders of the world
Our tiny boys and tiny girls.

Wanda J. Turrill

Testament

I don't know about this Jesus
And these tales of God that tease us,
For He is I and I am Him,
The darkness joins us from within,
Kiss me, hold me, wait with me,
Who will rise to set us free?
Confusion, madness, the insane,
I open wide to taste the pain,
I stumble and falter,
This blood is my altar,
I cannot get up,
Please drink from my cup,
For now is the hour
To consume all my power,
To hear music in silence,
See compassion in violence,
To spread your wings and hope to fly,
So close your eyes and pray to die.

J. Felicien Brugger

I'm Losing Me

Who's that stranger sitting there
You caught me totally unaware.
You say you've known me most my life
They say you are my loving wife!

I look in the mirror, what do I see?
A stranger looking back at me!
They say I can't go to work or play,
A person my age don't act that way.

It really is a crying shame,
Some days I can't recall my name.
I can remember things from long ago,
Though yesterday, I don't always know.

They ask if I recall this or that,
Most times I don't know where I'm at.
Look at this, oh what a mess!
I'm having trouble getting dressed.

I have trouble when I talk.
Would you help me when I walk.
My biggest worry, can't you see,
I'm completely losing me!

Judith A. Cassidy

Looking Back

Looking back on yesterday.
Mistakes we've made along the way.
Second chances overlooked
as time slipped by within our youth.

Starting together on one road.
Turning sometimes out of control
We lost each other somewhere there
reaching out to no avail.

Drifting silently for years.
Shedding quiet lonely tears,
Waiting for the day to come
when you would leave and not return.

Looking back is always hard
Wondering if the day will come.
When I will find someone new
to fill the void left by you.

New horizons now appear
from far away as well as near.
Friendships grow from falling tears
as hugs replace the bitter years.

Cheri Knecht

Untitled

Through the looking glass
I go to a world of forgotten
memories and timeless smiles
it seems such long time ago
so far away so many miles

Through the looking glass
I go I see the road map
Of my life upon my face
the stitches of life upon
my belly

Through the looking glass
I go I can see in a distance
the lonesome happiness I
will have some day the
smell of playfully life
upon their faces

Clean the messes of mud pies
see the sleepiness in their eyes
tuck them under the covers and
wish them a future goodnight.

Sonia Deckert

True Love

Do you know how much I love you,
Do you know how much I care,
Your smile, your frown, your laughter,
I see it everywhere.

Do you know how much I love you,
Do you know how much I care,
No matter what goes on in your life,
You know I'll always be there.

Do you know how much I love you,
Do you know how much I care,
Each joy, each disappointment,
I'm glad that we can share.

Do you know how much I love you,
Do you know how much I care,
I love you more than words can say
And much more than you're aware.

Hannah Nugent

"It"

It brought out the colors,
sent darkness to the past.
It transformed the image
inside the looking glass.
It lifted the veil,
and brought forth the light.
It granted the passage
through endless insight.
It wore many faces
along the way,
and said every flower
has a place and a day.
And that each one of us
can rise above
and unite in its essence;
eternal love.

Ann Sullivan

My Garden

My garden is a place I go
just to be with me
to gaze upon the flowers
and converse with honey bees

Some may see
and some may know
the peace I find within
knowing that the flowers
don't care where I have been

It doesn't seem to matter
if it's morning or it's night

While sitting in my garden
all in the world
seem right.

Margi Kehres-Ulrich

The Stream

I sit above and watch you
As you ponder your way about.
You're clear and yet you're cloudy
You rush and yet you slow.

You catch the light without a thought
And let it go as quickly.
You're smooth and you are tossing
Never rough, but sometimes tickling.

You are old and yet renewing
Hidden places deep within
Beneath the swaying arms
You topple at your whim.

But peace exists within you
Under tumbling and turmoil.
Your face is like a mirror;
An armor to the sky.

Linda L. Awana

Nothing

The warm wind blows through the trees;
Laughter comes from the living leaves.
But I know that way deep down;
To them I'm just a clown.

The snow-covered wind bitterly blows;
The falling tears of a dying rose.
Stay? No matter how hard I try;
Deep down I know this is goodbye.

Margaret R. Gifford

The Bad Cat

At first she was very fun,
Now her bad side has begun,
Sometimes she scares the dogs,
And takes away your playing pogs.

In the night she is mean,
And cannot be seen,
Until the day has come again.

During the day a bird stalks her,
But that does not stop her,
She is on guard,
To protect our backyard,
And she chases the bird away,
She likes to lay in the sun,
To her the sun is very fun
She's the queen of the backyard,
She is the only guard,
She protects it very well,
And that is all I have to tell.

Ashley Neely

Dilemma

Oh! Grandpa, you're here!
I have waited so long
To ask you a question,
'Cuz I know something's wrong!

I really don't know how
It could possibly be.
I'll show you the problem,
If you'll just follow me.

Right here in Dad's dresser
Stuck back in this drawer,
Are what's got me bothered.
They were not here before!

See! How did they get there?
And now, what should we do?
We've got to return them.
How? I don't have a clue!

Here it is, Christmas Eve,
And everybody knows
Santa can't bring presents,
If we've got his clothes!

Geneva Reichert

Squandered

A tumbleweed stopped at my feet
I looked at it and then about me
There was not a single sight to see
As everything once had ceased to be.

I stepped around this tumbleweed
I turned in a great circle
And for three hundred sixty degrees
My eyes could only see
Nothing more than tumbleweeds.

It made me scared,
It made me sad,
I felt some guilt,
And too remorse,
But more so hopeless,
Foolish and lost.
For I had no idea that my neglect
Would have such a complete
And devastating cost.

Nancy Sullivan

The Vow

I placed a ring upon your hand,
It's made of precious gold.
It says that I do wed thee,
and take your love to hold.

Our love is much more precious
than this ring of gold,
for love is far more rich,
than all the shining gold.

The ring you have upon your hand
is a signature of our love,
that's recognized by God and man,
to signify our love.

I'll hold your love with dignity,
and cherish it for life,
for I am very honored,
to have you as my wife.

And as our days grow older,
and grayness does appear,
I'll hold you that much closer,
for I truly love you Dear.

Earl D. Higgins

Dust And Diamonds

Dust and diamonds
differ in dollar signs.

Youth and age
diverge in years.

Old and antique
contrast in demand.

Love and lust
discept in expression.

Want and desire
deviate with need.

Like and hate
clash in degrees of affection.

Envy and abhorrence
vary with confidence.

The strong and the weak
disagree in measured esteem.

Colors and skin
contrast in ignorant minds.

Black and white
are different only in the light.

Chevonne T. Siupa

My Best Friend

You ask me why I'm happy
When I'm alone, old and frail,
But an unseen friend is with me,
Guiding me along that lonesome trail.

He gives me faith, hope and courage,
Love for others that must be,
If only the whole world could see
What a difference He has made in me.

I thank God this friend stays with me,
Showers of blessings flow around,
Jesus Christ my dearest friendship,
Plants my feet on higher ground.

Lola Funk Anderson

Christmastime Birthday

It's your birthday and no present.
I know it's a dirty trick,
But this one year out of thirty
It will come with old St. Nick.

I know you won't be sorry
When you see what Santa brings,
'Cause I love you much too dearly
To give ordinary things.

So here's to a Happy Birthday
And to many many more
From your far away kid sister
To a brother I adore.

Lura Jean Hoffman

Hold My Hand

When the moon is full
And the sea is calm
My heart lifts up
And I feel the balm
Of the love that brought us here.

But now my love is gone
The days grow long
The winds howl
And the waves roar
As I wander alone along the shore.

But then my heart grows light . . .
I am not alone
"He" clasps my hand
And we walk on
As the waves rush upon the sand.

Please God, Continue to hold my hand!

Edna E. Henry

Over And Under

Over and under and away we go.
Up the mountain and through the snow.
Playing and laughing we spend the day.
How could we spend it any other way?
The air is so thin, crisp, and cold
internal exhilaration is taking hold.
Can you feel it growing inside?
Nowhere to run. Nowhere to hide.
Electrical excitement starts to climb.
I think that this might be the time.
We gather in anticipation
in our little winter nation.
Stop and listen to the sound
of snowflakes falling on the ground.
Sliding under the tree tunnel
hurling fast through the snow funnel.
A slide and a turn around this bend.
All of a sudden we're at the end.

Jay Whipple

Waves

As the rock on the beach must endure the waves
So must I endure life's trails
Constant and never ending waves
Yet must I hold steadfast

I yearn for the calm
But knowing this cannot be
I'll hold steadfast and endure
The wear of the never ending waves
And watch for the calm between each wave
Knowing at last there is rest

Linda Harman Bennett

My Guardian Angel

Staring innocently at me
Through the plates of glass
Lies a soft voice.
A voice so delicate, so fragile;
Not an angel could compare.
Though this voice has no hope,
No love; I feel her joy residing
Within my heart.
She watches over me day and night;
Her paws poised carefully
Among the boards of life.
She knows not who I am
Nor what I do,
Yet she continues to stare
As though she always knew.

Sydna Marshall

I Saw Him Truly Just One Time

I saw him, truly, just one time,
A breath, then he was gone.
Inside my chest, my heart took off
With wild, angelic song.
His smile, his walk, the way he smelled
All within me placed
A magic that would far exceed
The threshold that he graced.
The Gothic tower, a lovely church,
As old as my own love.
I stepped inside to stare in awe
At sculpted grace above.
A statue stood, its manner proud,
Loud praises to receive.
I could not shout, I could not speak,
My eyes . . . could not believe.
For there he was, carved into stone,
And I saw that he was mine.
But as I watched, they faded both.
So I saw him truly, just one time.

Anna M. Welch

Then 'N Now

1895

Little old ladies
   in crinoline and lace
Held dainty parasols
   to shade a fair face.

A gentleman spoke
   before trying to pass;
Stepped off the walk
   trod on the grass.

1995

Today, he first speaks
   to allay any fear
Before passing by as
   he comes from the rear.

Don't startle a lady
   as past her you race.
She may be well-armed
   with pepper spray and mace.

Helen Margaret Wilson

"The Rain"

I heard rain hit the ground
It was a pleasant sound.

Michael Rawlins

"Reflections Of My Son"

God shine down on Benji
today, as out the door he goes
to play. Keep him safe as
he reaches high, the tree he
loves way in the sky.
   As he reaches the top, my
heart skips a beat, I say
a player about those
little feet.
   God, where will they
take him in years to come,
when he's a grown man and
has a son. I hope a prayer
will stay in his heart and
he will remember the tree
as his start.
   Bless him and keep him
for I love him so much.
Please always bless him
with your gently touch.

Linda Caskey

On Relationships

We never talk.
We never listen.
And what we feel the most is pain.
The joys we feel in fleeting moments,
We cling to desperately in vain.

Whispers I love you
As loud as thunder
But lightening strikes
And senders burn.

We never talk.
We never listen.
But what is worse,
We never learn.

Donna P. Charles

"Eternal Whispers"

Out of the madness of the night
I try to rise above my despair.
Tears of rage burn my face
As I stand naked and alone
In the light of the moon.
The lies and darkness of the corrupt
Are the chains that bind me
To the pillars of truth
That are crumbling
Before my very eyes.

James E. Brown

The Lord Touches Me

Deep in my mind and I know
I cannot doubt the Master
Because my weaker soul was scarred
With time.
I bowed my head to pray
And he gently touched this life
of mine.
I'm so thankful, dear Lord,
And I do believe in thee.
Put your faith in God who loves you,
Because I knows he cares.

Sarah Collins Ward

In water
Have the form
Of a mackerel

In the sky
Assume the shape
Of a hawk

In love
Be
The flow,
Wind and water
Roving
Home

E. Johannes Soltermann

Spring

Spring is known for bright flowers,
it gives you the feeling of powers.

Your spirits rise so high,
they nearly touch the sky.

You turn around and see,
what beautiful things can be.

Your mind travels far and wide,
no limits will you bide.

What happened to you that day,
you will never say.

Someday you will understand,
what you held in your hand.

Now your thoughts are finished,
nothing is diminished.

Where will you go next time,
wait and see what you'll find.

Julie A. Korthase

Love

I saw me postulate from
whence you have come
entering slowly into my minds eye
melting, cascading down an
ebony curve, crashing into my center,
creating a forest of light.
You reach out toward my face
caressing each turn, each curve
until downward in my soul.

I see you; I see me
standing in a wide chasm
of destiny, of beginnings, of endings.
Finding ourselves floating
inside and out of
our own forgiveness.
To the heavens mouth
we gape letting our moist
parts entwine infusing
into a single organism,
a single life.

Eric Aguilar

A Family is a Treasure

A family is a treasure from way down
deep; our heart's are the key's to the
treasure's we each keep. Thru good
time's and bad we all must see, that
the key to the treasure is all we ever
need.

Lori Ann Smith

Untitled

There is a secret drawer . . . full of overflowing.
With treasures carefully kept (for may would have them)
They ask and reach and want . . . no demand!
It is a small quiet drawer,
Patiently guarding its holding.
I go there for a time . . .
Nothing is missing, nothing is changed,
It is not locked . . . only hidden.

Susan Baldwin

My Little Angel

My little angel appears to be,
There when I need him, it seems to me.
You see when in trouble, or maybe in doubt,
Something strange happens, and all works out.
A guardian sent from heaven, I do believe;
Always appears, whenever in need.
I look for my angel day in and day out,
And when he shows up, I know without doubt,
That God's watching over you and me!
Angels come in all sizes and shapes
So don't be surprised by the appearance he takes.
When you are troubled and feel depressed,
Have faith, your angel will help do the rest.
Now count your blessings each and every day, so your
Angel takes over to lead the way.
You'll get through your trials
How hard they may be, because
God's always watching over you and me!

Helen T. Freudig

The Ballerina

The poet is like a ballerina,
Her pen dances across the paper,
then finishes the performance gracefully.

Then the judges come in,
and take it all apart.
The dance is now finished,
and imprinted in your mind.

Heather McLean

"When I Think"

When I think of how your life could have been, it makes me sad.
When I think of how your life should have been, it makes me mad.

It makes me mad that you only had an hour to breathe,
It makes me sad that you had to leave.
I wonder what it is like to never see the light of another day.
To think it was just a matter of time before you faded away.

I do like to think that you are in a heaven of joy.
I like to think you are up there growing into a nice boy.
It makes me happy to think about you.
I hope you will always remember that I'll always love you.

Gabrielle Gonzalez

My Love For You

My love for you is
  a single rose
  Revealing its beauty in the sunshine.
   The velvet petals opening in the
  dawns early light
   I must borrow this love from
  Mother Earth
    and take it into my soul.

Allen Steinberg

"Bass Fishin'"

It's five in the morning, and I'm ready to go,
I need to hurry cause I've been to slow.

I grab my tackle box and my fishin' rods,
The bass waters make me feel closer to God.

I'm on the water now, can't waitin' to cast,
I pray I'll catch a trophy bass.

The bass is like no other fish you see,
Cause it could be anywhere, like under a fallen tree.

I'm sittin' in the boat thinkin' what to use,
Hmmm, it so hard to choose.

It's now six o' three and I made the first cast,
Please lake, give me a bass.

Chickity-chic, chickity-chic is the sound of the bait,
but be quiet, wait!

Bam, boom, there it is!
I knew this spot wouldn't miss!

It's hooked and I reeled it in,
The weight's ten pounds, let's do it again!

But will my luck for the rest of the day last?
I doubt it, but at least I have one bass!

Zac Scott

The Thing

Cloaked with darkness, in olive and green
pass the Men of Blackness, heard, not seen

Silent passing shadows, that follow the mist
came these Demons of Blackness, their weapon, the kiss
with exacting precision, they came on through the night
the command, spread out, cover the left, the right

They are coming, was the word spread through the men
what were they like, these Demons of Sin
on through the darkness, the Mighty Evil came
no one knows who, what's in a name

There they stood with deadly power and might
these Demons of Blackness, their weapon, the night
Lordly Conquerors, like Great Oaks, they stood
not one would leave, even if he could
with a mighty force, a shout, a scream
it fell deathly upon them, the horror, the Thing

Silently cloaked with darkness, in olive and green
pass the Men of Blackness, heard, not seen.

Ronn Durham Sr.

In Quest

Within the spaces of times past
The image of a vision lasts
And through the prisms of dark tears
Speak the knowing eyes of fear

Give man this vision, not just his sight
So he may breathe and see the light
And winds will wisp across the sea
To touch his soul, to fill the need

With sound of wave on moonlit shore
A quiet figure stands ignored
Hear footsteps walk a journey lost
And in the night two stars cross

Mark Culliton

Flyer

Kite flight
Aerial acrobat
Free wings afloat
In the light, bright aviary
  below heaven's way
Gliding upon spirit's breath
  whirling about
    flittering this way and that
      teetering on the brink
        of life's last gasp —

Reaches its tethered end
  spins out of control
    downward
      swaying alee

To find its resting place beneath the sun.
    Hollie G. Martin

Today's World

We were sent here for one purpose you see,
to hurt each other is what I perceive

We trust, we love, we really care
we bust our butt to do our share

But what do we get in return?
But belittled and criticized while we burn

Our trust doth fly with the birds,
When we spread the gossip with our words.

Our love cannot last for you see
that's not the kind of friend for me.

We walk this path, we'll always care,
But the questions is: Do we dare?
    Carol Meek

Loves Bouquet

Each precious flower in this bright bouquet
Reminds me of a sunny summers day long ago
When the sweet smell of young love filled the air
And you where there . . . with me

And if I close my eyes and take a deep breath
I can be there . . . And I feel young again
As you take my hand in yours and we walk down life's path
. . . Together

Every memory of you comes fluttering back like a butterfly
And lights upon my heart so gently
Young love . . .
True love . . .
Never to part love . . .

Like sweet honey to my senses I savor the moment
For I know that soon I will be back in my garden
Gazing at a bright bouquet of flowers
That will only last as long as the day

I breathe deeply and let the aroma fill the depths of my being
One last time before I go to return again another day . . .
Another time . . . When once again love is mine
    Brenda Nevels

Untitled

As memories pass and years go by,
Why must I keep crying this silent lullaby?
With the hurt and madness of the unforgotten tails;
Will it be gone by morn?
I am forever trying to put them behind, for my new life is born!
    Gail A. Gonzalez

"The Blessing"

My life has been ripped apart once again.
This time I've got the strength to go on,
No matter what the future holds.
I have changed through all these hard times.
I'm finely on the right path.
I cant help but wonder how long it will take
For the magic to come back into my life.
Now I have a magic that no man can ever touch.
It's the magic of a little hand, a little smile
The pitter patter of little feet.
It's the magic of a little girl who call's me
"Mommie"
My life is complete with the magic of this little girl.
I have always fantasize about it but I never
Imagined what beauty a child could bring to your life.
I finally have something that no one can ever take from
Me.
"The blessing of a child"
    Paula Hensley

Friendship

A single flower grows among a garden,
Surrounded by beauty stands the flower,
Blessed with the light of the everlasting sun.

Natural beauties are as one,
Each makes the other great,
The flower sustains the beauty of the ground as the sun provides
life to the earth.

A small seed, starting anew, slowly introduced to a guiding light,
As it grows, increasing in beauty with many virtues,
The sun's face beams bright, content with the friendship.

Each petal born, unfolds to show an encouraging pastime,
Savoring each moment while the hourglass filters through,
As the two are dependent on each other and flourish through this.

Suddenly a cold winter wind devours the blossom,
Stealing its breath, suffocating it with its frost,
The sun's glorious power melts the evil assassin,
Reviving her companion's life.

The flower may retire,
Only to return in new form,
Refreshed with the spirit of the ever glistening light.
    Angela Sultana

The Wind

I am the wind.
All day I leap and run;
Never tiring, never stopping.

Hopping over gorges,
Dancing through trees;
Never tiring, never stopping.

Whistling through canyons,
Gliding over ponds;
Never tiring, never stopping.

Although I must beware of the Jet Stream,
I continue my dancing;
Never tiring, never stopping.

At times I float over to distant China
And then hurl myself at Japan in the form of a cyclone;
Never tiring, never stopping.

Now I am waiting on Mt. Fuji; waiting for something to happen,
Suddenly another wind has taken my place,
And he is never tiring, never stopping.
    Jayson Leving

True Love

Is this what they mean when they say 'true love'?
Being apart for so few moments tears your heart in two.
His touch is soft as velvet,
His voice is sweeter than vanilla,
And his kisses seen heaven-sent.

Is this what they mean when they say 'true love'?
The time you spend together is as precious as silk
Your hearts are hard as steel, yet fragile as glass
when you're together.
You know you would give your heart just to keep his love.

Is this what they mean when they say 'true love'?
The relationship you thought would never end,
Ends in a shattering moment
Your heart is severed in to a thousand pieces.
The pain is immeasurable,
Balanced only by the deep love you still carry for him.
Is this what they mean when they say 'true love'?

Heidi Hansen

Planet Earth

When in the lofty scheme of things
Before Earth was infested with human beings
Mother Nature was in complete charge
All living things both small and large
Lived in harmony with one another
Until one decided to eat the other
Many years later with human arrival
One wonders how certain is life's survival
Can violence, greed and acts of passion
Be matched by love and human compassion
We pollute the streams and the air we breathe
Mine the Earth's surface and a mess we leave
Meadows, orchards, grain fields and all
Are replaced by another shopping mall
We admit this is irresponsible — and yet
It is nothing compared to the national debt
With all our intelligence it is hard to believe
We may make the Earth worse before we leave
There still may be time to restore Nature's worth
And become good tenants of our Mother Earth

Virgil Hunt

The Widow's Wish

Each day she visits his grave
    and places a rose on a cold tombstone.
She longs for the love and joy that he gave
    ...but now she must live her life alone.

With wrinkled brow and tear stained face,
    she gently bows as if to pray . . .
But from this sad and forlorn place,
    one hears only the wind whisper her wish for yesterday.

"If I could have but one yesterday,
    just one page from the past,
I'd wish for that warm Spring day,
    when in his arms he held me last."

"But the Spring of yesterday is never more to be,
    and time quickly steals away this mortal life's embrace.
But he and I through the endless ages of eternity,
    will share a special bond that transcends all time and place."

"So as in this life I breath my last December,
    my soul shall have no sadness of regret,
For caring for the one I'll always remember,
    Whose love my heart cannot forget."

Michael Beard

A Tribute To The Man I Love

My husband is my dearest friend, no better man my Lord could send.
Reflecting on the days of past, God whispers that our love will last.
Struggles in life have not been few, but faith in God has seen us through.
Drifting thoughts of now and then, God smiles and says "Don't follow men."

My husband makes my life complete, he holds me when I feel defeat.
Trusting God will meet each need, God reaches out and takes the lead.
Our love is strengthened day by day, as doubting thoughts are put away.
Serving God is our first choice, we pray in song and lift our voice.

I thank my Lord as night grows nigh, for sending me a man so dear.
He showers his love and serves the Lord, he keeps our home in one accord.
Lord, bless this man I love so much, he's filled with love and velvet touch.
But most of all, I thank You for his Christian wings that make him soar.

Candice M. Lance

"Another Way Home"

Now that the war is over, I've lost but I'm still living
I have almost nothing, and yet I still am giving

My mother cries all night and day. I don't know what to do
To stop the tears and ease the pain, I'll do what I have to

My brothers bleed incessantly; their wounds are open wide
All of which are mental scars of strife they keep inside

My children scream for fear of life since death is all they see
When they're frightened most at night, they still won't come to me

All we seek is another way home... a path to Paradise
to live in peace without heartache and sorrow in our lives

Ingar C. Moir

The Mortal Storm

Long may the flag of liberty
Of which we are so proud
Fly through the breeze o'er land and sea
And above that mighty cloud:
    The mortal storm.

Long may she keep the holy peace
For the country which she stands
And help the nations all to cease
The riddle of the sands:
    The mortal storm.

Robert Hudson Baker

"Need For Knowledge"

I look toward the light from within
to quietly ponder in solitude,
introspection.

From this point of reflection
upon my thoughts of life, and all the
various facets of it, what are
my views? Where do I stand? On politics,
religion, free speech ban?

Questions and answers galore
that I do not seem to have, much
less the intelligence to complete
this rhyme. What do they say about
the "stitch in time . . .?"

I have to find that road that will lead
me to where I want to go — I wish the
answers would hurry up
because they are coming awfully slow.

Michelle Fortin

Of

I dream:
Of candle light dinners — just the two
Of dancing, held close
Of kissing and snuggling on the couch
Of spiritual fulfillment
Of sitting together and watching the stars
Of financial freedom
Of an end to the days of loneliness
Of a mother far away I can't have
Of babies in heaven
Of a hug and a kiss when I've been gone
To know I've been missed
But mostly of understanding myself

Tammy L. Stout

"WHY — BECAUSE!"

Why is it when people die
Everyone thinks they have to cry.
And how come the first question is why?
We have to realize there is no why.
Because is really the word to select
For on to heaven ride the elect.

Because pain, sorrow and frustrations disappear
Contentment, peace, tranquility now are here.
Because one leaves crime, intolerance and hate
To become a resident where there is loving faith.
Because to depart this often wicked earth
To find his just and rightful heavens berth.
Because most of all the loving God above
Desires they be side by side in eternal love!

Henry G. Mueller

Winter (Visions Of Grandeur)

The mother gently tucks in her white blanket
    covering hills and valleys with a kiss of sleep
She sprinkles shining diamonds of tranquility
All around, the land sighs, satiated and the weak, yellow
    ghost of a sun peaks in timidly — hinting an
    inkling of warmth
    I step into this gift around me and my
    breath quickens, a feeling of excitement and
    contentment at the peace I feel — I am small,
    unguarded and my soul, it smiles.

Bridget M. Tracey

The Treasure

While on my usual course through the woods
An obscure object glistened from the path.
Almost elusive, covered by seasons of weather.
I whisked the sod away and pulled it from the earth.
A tiny locket, shaped liked a tear
Held it, turned it over.
Guess it must have been there years.
Anxious to see what story it told, I opened up the case;
One side held a broken heart, the other a child's face
What does it mean I pondered?
From my heart the answer came.
Offer your hand to the needy soul.
Who's lonely and broken inside.
Their tears they've buried
Broken hearts carried.
Feelings they have denied.
Open your hand and heart to love.
Your return will be with out measure
Freely give and you will see
That you have found the treasure.

Welda Brill

The Dancers

I went dancing the other night,
My pants were too short and my shoes too tight,
But I felt that I looked quite debonair,
Could I be a potential Fred Astaire?

I took to the floor with my partner in tow,
"Ginger" and "Fred" gyrating fast and then slow.
People were watching for we sure looked swell,
But suddenly I slipped, and both of us fell.

"Ginger" sprained her wrist and I tore my short pants,
After that exhibition, no one gave us a glance,
For people laughed at our funny, sad plight,
So we picked ourselves up and left for the night.

But I knew that we would return once more
And next time we'd be the "Stars" on the floor,
And we'd hear applause not laughter and jeers,
And we wouldn't depart with my partner in tears.

So this is the tale of my dancing one night,
When my pants were too short and my shoes too tight.
I still think I look quite debonaire,
But I'll never be a Fred Astaire.

Dolores J. MacDonald

Just We Two

Just we two stood on Rainbow Cliff
The rugged cliff between sky and sea.
Where one false step meant death below
But which failed to frighten you and me.
For in our hearts burned something bright.
Something until eternity we would share
It held us there between heaven and earth
Guarded by God's tender care.

A world was unfolding for just we two
A world of beauty, faith and new hope.
Not knowing the strength and faith it would take
For problems with which we'd have to cope.
But love burned bright the challenge;
A challenge making our dreams come true.
We left our cliff asking God's guidance
While chapel bells rang for just we two.

Georgiana Gross Kysar

Together Forever

Together forever, from this day forward
Until the end of time,
You know our love will grow ever stronger
The longer we're together
We'll share our days and nights
They'll be such great delights as long . . .
Yes as long
As we're together.

Together forever, from this day forward
Until the end of time.

Our love for one another can be taken
By no other . . . and together we'll discover
That our love for one another will stay true
Because you'll have me
Yes, and I'll have you
And together we'll see our lives through.

Together
Together forever, from this day forward
Until the end of time.

Kevin McNamara

Some Changes

Lord knows I've got to make some changes
  I've got some major re-arranging to do
  Time passes fast and I know it won't last
  I've got a lot to do and I'll help you too
  Can you help me . . . Together we will never be blue

I hope I've learned my lessons well
  I damn sure don't want to spend my time in hell
  Reach out and touch for those who can't feel
  Try to reveal for those who try so hard to conceal
  The truth that lies so deep inside
  Forever, forever no more lies

I've got to sing for those who can't speak
  Take a peek for those who don't, can't, or won't see
  Listen for those who cannot hear
  And live for those no longer here

Lord knows we all have to make some changes
  We have got a lot of major re-arranging to do
  Because we're living in a land that is mighty dangerous
  But, with all the love around
  No reason bringing armageddon down

    Sam Brooks

A Comet

A comet is just a rock in the sky.
With gases it flies. Who knows why?
It's a fuzzy cotton ball with a straight firm tail.
Not like sleet, rain, or hail.
Some can be big or some can be small.
But Hyetakute is not big at all.
In fact it's not big but it's bigger than big, it's bigger than tall.
It fits 1 full moon and the tail fits ten.
But look for it now, cause you might not see one like it again.

    Jennifer Miliaresis

The Falling Of Justice

The horse they ride,
One day they will fall from high.
There will be no ground from which they fall.
Falling into the echoes of their own plea,
All will be gone from them.
No second chances for they unfairly justified others.
The justified faces they see will remain imprinted,
In the eyes of the beholder forever from the
  stained tears.

    Rhonda Lee Winberry

Naked In The Rain

In midnight dreams, the rain's tender wet kiss falls on my naked face.
Winter's brisk breath takes heart and dries the eyes of sunken
  dreamers with morose tales forgotten in the sun's sweet embrace.
Running like a horde of grizzly eyed mad men to wade upon a
  temporary water slide of rancid rain and lonely leaves to
    come to the mouth of the death of it all and say
      goodbye to my forgotten companions.
Twisting and turning and leaping through each and every wet,
  wonderful kiss.
At this moment I am pure, happy, warm, innocent, guiltless,
  blameless, faultless, sinless, artless, stainless,
invincible and irreproachable.
At this moment I am what God intended children to remain.
At this moment I am naked in the rain!

    Matt Mohr

A Tribute To Old Blue

When Old Blue was new he learned a trick or two.
He would run, catch and fetch for a biscuit, it if was new.
He grew and grew. All the while to his master, he remained true.
He played hard. He had complete run of the entire yard, Old Blue.
Despite his size, he was nimble and, oh, so wise, Old Blue.
When company came, they soon learned he was quite tame, Old Blue.
He'd perk his ears and come running when called by name, Old Blue.
He'd sit on his haunches 'till all was quiet down country lane.
He repeated the routine as if it were a game until he became old and lame, Old Blue.

During his final days, mostly he sat with a far-a-way gaze, Old Blue.
His territory grew smaller. It was difficult for him to respond to his caller, Old Blue.

One night, the country air was very still and Old Blue settled down
one last time with a chill.
The end came peacefully much to everyone's surprise. For Old Blue,
there would not be another sunrise.

    Lou DeCrescentis

Pebbles In The Sand

Clear, ocean waves crash at my feet
  The heat from a bright sun roasting my body
Noisy seagulls step near for crumbs
  And always I see the pebbles in the sand.

Alone I sit on a beach; the beach; our beach
  We shared the best of times on this shore
That was before you stole all the shells
  Leaving me to see only pebbles in the sand.

No longer does the scene appeal to me
  The air is cold and chilling with you not here
The sand, the water, have lost their beauty
  Now there's nothing but pebbles in the sand.

Once you gave me the sun
  And chased all the rain away
    Yet now the rain falls so hard
      On the pebbles in the sand.

    Lori Prout

Babies Soon To Be Here

It hardly seems quite time.
I seems as tho just yesterday
When we saw the positive sign.
The smile upon your face, so true,
When I asked, "Well, pink or blue?"
The greatest gift, a girl or boy,
The happiness, the fear, the joy.
I'm getting scared, yet so excited.
Will I remember all I have recited?
Babies soon to be here.
I feel so unprepared.
Such a responsibility, I was very unaware.
The fairy tale has faded, reality sets in,
We are to be the ones on whom this
baby will depend.
So many unanswered questions.
So much we need to know.
Dear Lord please give us courage and
strength for where we are about to go.

    Marcella Moore

Forgive the Hopelessness

On the cluttered highway of life,
I left my car behind, as others drove by fast.
I drew from the trunk the parcels of my past.
My history was chained to the back of my leg
to follow wherever I led.
My heart still sat upon the shelf,
in the house where pride had fled.
I walked endlessly all the day,
neither blisters nor fatigue plagued me.
Though shoes wear out and linen shirts fray,
I'll walk until the sea.
I'll get there . . . someday.
No one offered me a ride,
so that I might decline.
Neither was I offered a meal,
that I could refuse to dine.
Pity . . . my only friend,
or at least someone to talk to.
When I discover I've been raised on lies,
nothing could ever again be true.

Lucas Steele

Dark Nights

I have been one with the night.
I have seen its velvety blackness
Envelope the paths of men.
The tears, the cries, the joys, the sighs,
All are known by night's moonlit eyes.

The darkest evils are hid so well
In darkness where Man fears to dwell
In the secret places the darkness swells
Only to be pushed back by first light's
Sunbeams we know so well.

Yet, heroic deeds shine in the
Dark with a radiance that causes
The stars to place second in glow.

So, I have been one the night,
Its blackness and its fears.
And yet the moments I remember best
Are those of mankind's gentleness.
I have been one with the night.

Stephen H. Gray

Forest Of Love

I was once in a forest
A forest of love
Everything was love, and making love
I felt like Satan because I had no love
Hating love, Scared of love, wanting love
But never getting love or feeling love
Wanting death for me and all
But all I wanted was love
In the forest, forest of love

Hal Parker

A Friend

Feeling alone and scared,
thinking that no one cares.
The road you travel ends,
and the pain will never mend.
You find a friend that you can trust
to share your feelings and your thoughts
One voice I long to hear
to know that you are near
Feeling alone and scared,
and knowing that some one cares.

Brenda Palinkas

Waiting For You . . . Which I Have Killed

Once again time passes through me;
waiting for your touch.
Rapid ticking of the clock triggers fundamental motivation --
you drift off,
Flying mystical innovations.

And still I'm waiting . . .

Hospital bed sheets are rough and cold you tell me.
Grasping my icy fingertips you whisper how my soul will keep you warm
quickly drift to sleep silently with out me.

How many times I've told you I'd see you through it all.
but tonight you leaped alone, closed your eyes to no one standing by your side.
Then there I was, held your icy hand.
Cried my single tears . . . with out you.

Standing in my single existence, invited darkness, enclosing all my
fears — and now you're trapped inside of me, crying yourself to sleep.
  Slip into a dream
as God makes a timeless angel.

And you sit up there and watch me, waiting . . .

Shay Carpenter

My Horoscope

I read my horoscope the other day, it was humorous but frightful in a unique way
The print was black, clear and clean, which made it easier for me to read
Not that I scan the daily for such news, but I need a little humor with my news
It says pay the pipers right away, if not my credit rating surely won't stay
Daily I'm at the end of the piper's tong, beat, beat, beat the tong plays on
I'm tired and weary from this musical fray, I cried, moaned, groaned and even prayed
But the piper's tong kept beat, beat, beating away
To make matters worse, the horoscope added "pay everybody else today"
To meet all those who demanded a tell, surely I don't have enough blood to sell
If I'd listen to all of them what would I be, for already I've become a twiggy
My bones have extended beyond my skin, I can't imagine how much I've thinned
And my baggy trousers keep falling down, alarmed I always look and turn around
To see if anyone is watching me, if so how embarrassed I would be
But alas, I'm a victim of the past
For each purchase I had made I'd swear "this is the last"
But the ad are so tempting as can be
Colorful, manicured, mannequin with designs of variety
However, this is the end of my woe
I promise not to read my horoscope any more

William Bryan

An Artist's Dream

Oh Yeah! I packed up my art supplies,
And raced out to meet the day.
I headed for the country
To paint it Autumn's way.

Sure! I found the perfect spot
Beside an old dirt road.
I set up my easel,
And the rest of the heavy load.

Good! I'd brought a chair,
Water, coffee and snacks,
Brushes, paint and wipe cloth
Everything an artist packs.

Ohhh! Autumn settles 'round me
In all the glorious hues . . .
Red and gold and russet,
And a sky of white and blue.

Oh! No! I searched and searched for a panel
On which to paint the scene.
And then my memory hit me . . .
I forgot to pack my Artist's Dream!

Jo King

His Legacy

Toby always seemed to be the one
Drawing the fire . . . drawing the beatings.
We saw the belt swing from fathers soft white hands,
slapping a rhythm, eyes bloating with anger, ego wide,
jaws set like frozen steel clamps, breaking.
His huge, pale body so agile with the target in view . . .
moving across the distance of the long house like superman
over tall
buildings, red cape billowing rage.
The house would be empty but for the silence of our brother's
unscreams, him taking the blows for us . . . saving us . . .
our shield.
We would do anything to keep him there.
And he took it, and took it, taking it into himself like food.
Filling his body with it . . . until consumed him like his father
and his father's father before him,
Carrying it on, passing the rage . . . like blood . . .
A legacy to be cherished . . .
Father to son.

Marcy B. Greene

"Goodbye" You Say, "Later" Too . . . Your Words Are Forever True.

Yes, Your eyes are brown, deep and true.
 Your voice is strong, no fear in you.
 Tall and tan, a real strong man . . . Yes.
You've comforted me. Can you possibly love me?
You've protected me. Can you possibly love me?
You've provided for me. Can you possibly love me?
You've sacrificed for me. Can you possibly love me?

Yes, My eyes are blue, I really miss you.
 My voice is meek, by far, I'm not weak.
 Thin and small, loving you here, with my all . . .
Yes, my love, with you . . . I've found strength from fear.
 I love you.
I've found laughter from tears. I love you.
I've found the beauty from within. I love you.

Yes, I give you a call; I say, "Is Gerardo there?"
 Mama says, "Si, momento . . . Gerardo, esta Faith."
 My heart skips a beat . . . you speak, "Eh, Faith how are you?"
 "Te quiero." . . . I love you, Yes . . .

Faith B. Martinez

Lonely Dreamer (A Tribute To Roy Orbison)

Oh, my lonely dreamer why must you be
so blue since you're not here we sure do
miss you, loneliness and pain never to be
explained, sorrow and grief comes like rain never
to go away; oh, my lonely dreamer.

Oh, my lonely dreamer don't be so blue, I
know you'll never be alone cause you're with
your blue angel my lonely dreamer, golden dreams
and memories often fade away, tears and heartaches always
stay; never to be together, my lonely dreamer.

Only the lonely knew how you felt cause you
was a legend of our time but nobody can take that
away cause you been through all the sorrow and
pain my lonely dreamer, golden dreams and memories
often fade away, tears and heartaches come and go as
misery comes to stay; my lonely dreamer.

Oh, my lonely dreamer don't go away, please come back to the ones
who loved you so; now that you're gone we are in a state of unreality,
only in dreams can we ever be together so please come back to me;
my lonely dreamer.

Jerel Fritts

A Mother's Prayer

O God, take care of my little boy in the jungle over there.
You'll know him with his deep blue eyes and kind of red-blonde hair.

You say he's not a little boy 'cause a change has taken place.
That's strange, 'cause I still see him with the ringlets 'round his face.

I can see his babyish smile — and hear his pitter-pattering feet.
When each day was an adventure that he so anxiously did meet!

The years passed all too quickly and he's far away tonight,
because someone decided — there's a war and he must fight.

He's tramping through the jungles and the mud and rain and heat.
Not knowing what's ahead for him or what he's apt to meet.

He's facing such grave danger all thru the night and day.
And he must have protection, thus to God, I pray.

Take care of my little boy in the jungles — dense and green.
May your love and your protection provide a protective screen.

May he in all his trials feel your loving care.
And know that you are with him in the jungle over there.

And let him have the courage as those dangerous paths he trod's,
to keep ever looking upward and to keep his faith in God.

F. B. Rinehart

Dream World

She said "It doesn't matter what you say anyway"
As I tried to impress her
It's all a dream you see, this world
And when I wake up, Ill be back to my throne . . .

Then the words ran slower for her
"And your looks are only a mirage"
There will be a crown waiting for me back in my world . . .

As she closed her eyes
"People are not obstacles, but goals"
And they will look up to me . . .

As she died
"It's all a dream you see, accept it as a game with your
 mind, but don't mind me"
I was only that sky and world away from going with her . . .

And I'll have my own water and my own trees
And even you will sing to me
And even she will sing to me

Ken Morris

Out Of Control

Let us forgive John Bailey
It occurred in the privacy of his home. He went upset.
He had lost his job at the office. He had to let his anger out.
The wife must have done something to increase his anger.
And so John threw a punches at her to let the anger out.

Let us understand John Bailey
The wife must have done something cruel to make him so cross.
And here was a young man with a chance,
To prove to the wife who was the boss.

Let us condone John Bailey
When the police broke up the beating that hour,
There was no way to fix the bruises.
For John's anger too quickly turned into boxing power
And all we can say for the wife is
She sure was lucky to have cowered.

Let us pity John Bailey
He has been through to much,
Standing there, his hands clenched with hate,
Out of work, upset,
Having to see that wife retreat to a corner, and listen to her fret.

Kurt Schultheis

Untitled

As the wind gently
blows into our face today,
I could not help but remember
the past that had changed us in every way.
The smiles on each of our faces
has always been shining since our young age,
but as we meet again in many years,
our smiles are the turning of a new page.
We search each other
for the young, helpless children we once new,
only to find that we have changed
into someone with feelings, someone knew,
and we understand and realize
that deep inside we're still the same,
and even though we've changed our appearances,
we still have the same identities, the same names.
The ground that we are standing on
is brown and filled with painful cries,
but the leaves upon our heads are green,
a symbol of love that never dies.

Taen Sayachak

A Dream

A dream is an idea that stands above the rest
it's a goal that sometimes seems unattainable
while at other times only inches from the grasp.
but the fingers will not close

A dream begins in the subconscious mind while
asleep or when sleep will not come. It then becomes
a thought that is focused on and which can cause
an obsession that can last a day, a year, or a lifetime

I like many others have seen dreams come with
the darkness of night only to vanish with the morning
sun. And awake thinking how foolish of me. But
dreams have inspired the world as we know it today

A dream is then only the imagination of an individual
and remains that unless acted upon. It sometimes
takes courage to take a dream of tomorrow and
with it step into the reality of today.

Tim Willis

Old Friends

Summer.
Long exhausting days of work and frolic.
A creature of energy.
A traveler with the sun.
Shaping memories is the true adventure.

Then arrives fall.
Short days which seem to be long.
A majestic soul.
A span of colors which always . . . listens.
The chores are passed by in awe of the beauty.

There awaits winter.
Dark frigid nights with days laced in magical icicles.
An animator of light.
A pause to be silent in a crystal sheet of white.
Reflection in the presence of a warm fire.

Here thrives spring.
Sweet smelling mornings growing into hope.
An artist of the new.
A stage from which to perform.
The reassurance that everything begins again.

Sara Kendall

Untitled

Two become one, joining, becoming complete
Separate too long, waiting passion released
Silent wanting and giving and feeling disbelief
As if it's a dream
Never so much intense yearning felt before
As if it was the first time,
Once again
Sensing every thought thru the beating heart
Unable to control composure
Totally free-holding nothing back
Speaking all emotions without saying a word
Making love to you.

Staci L. Row

Blue

Blue is a beautiful cloudless sky,
An amiable iris,
A soft touch of kindness,
A ripe blueberry.
Blue is a wise thought
A brave attempt
A brilliant fire work in the sky.
Blue is a comfortable pair of pajamas
and an interesting book.
A comfortable, cozy, and welcoming arm chair
And the richest crayon in the box.
A thoughtless attempt ended
with a gracious Thank You.
Blue is the most generous of all the colors.
The brightest color in the rainbow,
The color with a glossy shine,
And deepest of all sincerity.
Blue is a color like a dog
dependable and reliable.
Blue is the gentlest of all the colors.

Joanna Basile

God Cares

When at times you feel alone
And think nobody cares
God sends an angel to take your fears away.
He guides and directs you,
Through toils to hard to bear,
There's an angel beside you,
To assure you that God cares.
And when you wake up in the morning,
Feeling alone and that no one cares
God sends an angel to wash those fears away.
Always know in a life time,
That God really cares for you.

Rebecca D. Thomas

The Hunt

I love to go into old bookstore,
where the books are pilled high.
Row after row the shelves are stuffed,
some two books deep and as high as the ceiling.
The happiness I feel in the hunt,
when I spy a treasure high.
The feeling I get when I climb the little ladder to reach the
one old used book that is out of arms reach.
How high I am when I pull the old book from the wooden shelf,
protected by a layer of dust.
The tingling of a sneeze in my nose as the protected layer is
removed with a quick breath.
The sound of the crinkling yellowed leaves,
the musty odor that is allowed to escape on these cold winter days.

Darrell Roberts

Oh Daddy

Where is it that we stand?
  What happened to the day's we all walked hand in hand?

What happened to the peace, that held us all together?
  Where exactly is the love, that promised us forever?

What happened to the country, we all could stand up for?
  Every time I turn around, we're in another war.

What happened to the people, who always had a home?
  Now I see them on the street, so hungry and alone.

What happened to the vow's, you made your wedding day?
  I've watched so many couples, go their separate ways.

What happened to the Bible, that spoke the word of God?
  Now half of all his reader's, are out committing fraud.

What happened to the water's, that always stood so still?
  Now people's lives are gone, from over flowing spill's.

What happened to the friendship, that made us all as one?
  What has this world come to or has it just begun???

  Robin Decoito

It's Easier Than Not To Be . . .

The old tattered lanterns
that hung in his workshop
now collect dust in the basement.
And the footprints we left
when life was much simpler
still leave their mark in the pavement.

His jackets still hang in my closet
and his shoes that are so hard to fill.
After so many years and bitter tears, it's hard not to miss him still.

The one I once knew so long ago, still holds a place in my heart.
The memories of him right beside me
are inside me as clear as the day they were made.

And now my son who's just about ten
brings back the memories of way back when.
And I'll watch him grow from this boy into a man
to have what my father never had.

It's easier than not to be great,
even if great is in one person's eyes.
For what matters to one can still make the world go 'around.
It's easier than not to be . . .

  Drew Amendola

Silence Is Golden

You wish to be a teacher, or a preacher of the word.
Have you learned to listen or only to be heard.
To be continually speaking, how will you ever learn.
Sure you've gained some knowledge but where is your concern.
If you don't hold your tongue, your religion is in vain.
To talk about your brothers, is to show ones own shame.
So if you desire to help a brother through his trials,
Show him some compassion and listen for a while.
For truly these are his needs, to have someone hear.
To listen to his heartaches, to lend a listening ear.
For silence can be golden, in times such as these.
It shows you really care, about your brothers' needs.
A heart that's heavy laden, and weighted down in pain,
Surely should be heard, or the burdens will remain!
So if the opportunity arises take heed to what is said,
To listen with your heart, instead of listening with your head.
We sometimes lack wisdom, but this I can honestly say.
Our Lord gives understanding, as you come to know his ways.
The Lord reveals many things, this one thing I truly believe.
I may have written this poem, but from Him I did receive.

  Marvin Harris

"That Special Power"

Does life sometimes just let you down?
Does it seem to be so unfair?
Do you often feel so lost and alone?
Like there's simply no one to care?

For some, life seems to be such a struggle
And you may not feel very strong
You try to keep going, though it seems so hard
When the road is so lonely and long.

Sometimes the stress and pressures of life
Weigh so heavily on your mind
You search for the answer, but it just won't come
Why does life have to be so unkind?

There is a solution that will change your life
And in your pain, it is always there.
It takes no money or sacrifice
Its the life restoring power of prayer.

For one little prayer from deep in the heart
Can bring strength and peace from above
The darkness will flee, the joy will come
From the power of prayer and of love.

  Vicki Sias

Tracing The Family Tree

It's exciting to trace one's family tree,
Experienced is the romance of history,
News and affections are quote,
In a collection of letters and notes.

Genealogy is rewarding as it yields,
Information about folks, homes, cities and fields,
Folks as they get involved in a family pedigree chart,
Appreciation for the family history they will take to heart.

Every family has its keepsakes to treasure,
Sharing information with relatives is a pleasure,
Work backwards from the known to the unknown,
Air-crafts in wars some ancestors have flown.

Genealogy is never finished, per say,
New twigs are being added to the tree almost every day,
Through genealogy we are powerfully connected to the past,
Concerned persons will keep records that will last.

  Geneva Stockton Norrell

Ned's First Christmas Tree

I thought it was such an awful shame
That christmas day should be the same
As a common day for old dog Ned.
I found some greens to make a tree
It was pretty as it could be
With three red candles plus one red ball

The presents did look a wee bit queer
For I hadn't a thing but bones and bread
More appropriate than skates for a
  dog named Ned
I tied them on with string and knots
Then I waited as he bounded to the spot
He jumped and bounded to see what he got.

The tree and gifts were his, he guessed
He barked and barked, he felt so blessed.
One by one he accepted his prize,
The grateful glint shown in his eyes
Now each year at christmas time
Old Ned has a tree like the
  boys and mine

  Edna Schnell Case

Granddaughter's

A Granddaughter is a blessing to have
She will always be (my Little Girl) to her dad.
All frills and lace
In everyone's heart she makes her place.
Boys have their hunting, fishing and football
Little girls are always a doll.
She may play soccer basketball and such
But she always has a loving touch.
When she grows into her teens
We dream of her being the beauty Queen.
A granddaughter has a part
in keeping young a grandmother's heart.
It doesn't matter what she might do
Grandmother will always say (I Love you)

Verta E. Jackson

Night

I open my window
To let the summer breeze in
My bed seems so empty without you
It seems like yesterday I was in your arms
Together we were
"Forever" you said
Your love was a lie
Your kisses were not mine
Our love was like the summer
Hurried hot melting everything in sight
Our love was like the footsteps in the sand
Washed away by the crashing cool waves
And now I am alone and it is
Night

Shamila Malik

Nostalgia

What I dream, sleeps with me
until I wake and simultaneously
conceive a break in the doldrums,
rolling and resting for nothing and for no one.
The nostalgia of my moment fills me with a predilection
for the future, because all before me were sent
so that I would believe and be sure,
so that I would understand the signs constructed by my crimes.
And I would scatter my wishes out over the edges of the parishes.
And I would crumple beneath the weight of the world
calling to me from heaven, saying nothing
and no one will potentiate while the past and the future are even,
while the memory clings to solid things,
and life is loved through the joy it brings.
Nostalgic déjà vu in voodoo sense,
a claim on ignorance, a pretense.
And my dreams remind me of my life,
as I sit here and chew on a trifle.
Not a moment will be lost that wasn't won.
I almost see the future in the glare of the sun.

Chris Kiely

"Innocents?!"

Be still thoughts, Oh vindictive mind.
Vengeance not yours to seek and find.
Be still all those to right the wrong.
Forgive them now that weaken the strong.
For they know not the suffering they cause.
Thinking victory they've won, and blissful applause.
But burden they'll bare, they know not now,
They'll destroy themselves, no knowledge of how.
The price of deceit is the price they pay.
And the curtain comes down on the final play! . . .

Bob Britton

Morning

The glowing orb peaks up from the horizon and spills its light
acrossthe morning sky

It still persists in doing this daily — I know not why
What seemed the brave and fearless moon has hidden behind the earth
And shy little birds flock to the burning globe's fiery hearth
I lie awake trying to answer things meant to be left a mystery
Knowing that everything is what it's not when the blind me
learns how to see

I dare to ask the forbidden questions that when are unanswered
are to us so dear
Why do we seek what is already here?
And then in the morning everything is clear

E. J. MacLeod

Surrender

Deep in sorrow, lost in worry.
   The tasks of everyday weigh upon.
I hear you call, beckoning me, surrender.

Of where I'll live, of what I'll eat.
   Yet, the lilies are cared for.
I hear you call, summoning me, surrender.

Of life, of love.
   Too many to count.
I hear you call, begging me, surrender.

Surrender to you I do.
   I need not worry, I need not sorrow.
As the sparrow is cared for, I am also Lord.

Complete surrender you call me to do,
   my life, my love, my trials.
Let all be surrendered unto you my loving Lord.

For I am much more —
               than the lilies.

Prudence P. Parks

Dying Irises

I'm watching my Irises dying in the rain,
they were planted when my knees were in pain.
I hunger for the buds to bloom,
they were planted in area of lots of room.
I watch the leaves come up thru the soil,
fan out from my tail,
the stalks come up tall and long,
very green and strong.
The "falls" wasted away on the ground
loosing their colors as they were down.
Perhaps another day I can see them sway,
in a sunny time in May.

Richard W. Luedtke

Untitled

To see this world through the eyes of a child
You'll begin to laugh and even smile
The cares of this world will fade away
As you laugh with a child and see things his way

Take time to laugh and time to smile
As you plod through this world mile by mile
The troubles and trials that you face every day
Will lighten and not take your breath away

Take some time out just yourself and you'll see
That life isn't all just a grind and a spree
If you sit back and listen I know you can hear
The laughter of children light on your ear

Lynett E. Richart

To Roni

In the quiet of our dreams
slips the lives that aren't seen,
though we feel the fiber of what
we were, no better time then now
deserved.

Faith and love ours to keep as
our lives grow forever deep.
We are the guardians of our thoughts,
To keep us on the path lest we get lost.
Love is the truth that binds our souls,
from this day forward as our life
together unfolds.
Love,
  Ned
Edward A. Mandel

Forgotten Time

Anniversary clock enclosed in dusty glass
sits atop grandmother's laced oak chest.

Delicate ivory hands poised at a perfect midnight
wait patiently each moment in silent's rest.

Black figures flaked onto yesterday's dreams
still anticipate tomorrow's treasured hours.

Splintered wooden core grasps endless time
forever lost in a minute's countless powers.

Children's laughter touches ageless moments
winding rusty key to hear today's tick-tock.

Dust flies as time stretches its delicate hands
as life again returns to the anniversary clock.
C. Kay Bassett

Entwinings

Veils whispering in the night
to the sleeper — deep insight —
from Afar veils parted
waking the quiet one — now started —
seeing whence all spaces knotted
a single watcher now had spotted
sinuous strands of space — erased —
to behold entwined — lattice encased —
high above our sleeper noted
depth of space — fully coated —
each strand curved and twisted deep
fully spaced — with stars birthing —
light did curve on these strands all
and within each plate — a galaxy's stall —
to take our watcher — enjoined carted —
out in space-time — across veld started.
Thomas P. Lanagan

The Creator

God gave us this earth on which to live,
The woman the right of birth and their love to give,
The men to provide and hunger chase,
The golden rule to guide, and hate to erase.

The artist the right to see and paint the scenes,
Of all the things he has seen in dreams,
Of the tall pine trees with its boughs outstretched,
Reaching Heavenward to be blessed.

God gave us true love all to bestow,
On Him from above and the earth below,
Ten rules to guide us in sorrow and strife,
It is He we should love and to Him dedicate our life.
June Heitland

The "Re-Locating Blues"

The "Move"! It came upon us, without the slightest warning
The rug came out from under me! "I" went into Mourning!

The roots that I had planted for forty some-odd years
Were much too deep to ever cease the onslaught of my fears.

Confusion overwhelmed me while Denial reared its face.
Anger, it devoured me — Acceptance had No space.

To think a Corporation could simply "Slam-the-Door",
On my entire "Being", with No chance to implore!

Don't stay too long in comfort — You'll soon be on your way.
'Cause this "Global" Corporation will have the "Final Say".

We're living in the Nineties, unsure as they may be.
Change is always constant, so we are constantly to Flee!

But, oh the great excitement of the new folks we will meet!
It's just a different neighborhood; And state; And Home; And street.

We will still remain the same no matter where we plant.
It's just one small step forward, to Our retirement.
Michele M. Collishaw

Once

Once the words flowed without delay or obstruction.
So easily,
my pen filled paper with meaning.
So quickly,
my emotions escaped and gained definition.
The ink was dry,
and my mind was content.

Now the words are but a trickle,
seeping into dam after dam.
My pen chokes on its ink,
while the paper aches to be alone no more.
Emotions peer from a cell with no key,
as my mind floods with all that remains uncertain.

All that dictates my every thought and move,
rides a dark cloud destined for nowhere.
Searching for a window of escape,
I find my trains of thought possess no vacancy.
A ray of hope and understanding appears in the distance.
I open my eyes wide,
only to see the glass frosted with fear.
Colleen M. Morley

What You Mean

To me you are a springtime breeze
The way you refresh and make me feel
You're my favorite song that I can play when I need
You're the one that I needed when I thought that I didn't
The rainbow that brightens the life that I'm living
You're a day at the park and a twilight dance
You're the love I can see with just a fleeting glance
These aren't just words composed in my mind
For true love like mine is so hard to define
They're all sincere and straight from my heart
But I need to find out just who you are
This was written for someone unknown
But I know she is out there and
Wants to be shown
The love that I am so willing to give
To the one who can love without fear in her soul
Who I can squeeze and kiss and have and hold
David Carroll

The Stone

A cowboy was riding one spring day
when he found a grave along his way.
The stone was old, but he could see
the name of Anna — eighteen sixty-three.

Why is the grave so all alone?
Who is buried beneath the stone?
Was she short or was she tall?
Was she large or was she small?

What was the color of Anna's hair?
Was it dark or was if fair?
Was she young or was she old?
Was her life's story ever told?

Was she a mother or maiden fair?
Is there anyone left to care?
Does anyone know where Anna lies?
Does anyone visit with saddened eyes?

Nothing now is really known
about the soul beneath the stone.
He picked a flower that spring day.
Laid it on the grave and rode away.

John D. Loeb

Valentine's Day

Wanting and waiting for that moment all night
Each second lingered slowly
With every breath anticipation grew intense
Sweet reminders of perfect pink roses eluding to much more

When the bittersweet wine brushed the lips and warmed the heart,
relaxation sets in
The music heightens the moment
slowly swaying in each other's arms
Trying to fight the feeling once again
drifting off to dreams electrifying
hot breath, sinful on the bare neck

Awakening eyes are upon each other's
low whispers and silhouetted bodies
the slight brush of lips,
no was no longer an option.
As passion engulfs all surrounding space,
for a brief moment enraptured in each kiss
and away they flew.

Shelly Dawn Walters

Synergy

His eyes are laughing as he looks at me.
I melt, consumed by his passion and his lust.
He speaks my name in seductive splendor,
Giving a sweet but bitter yearning,
For something so beyond my learning.
He moves closer, and totally consumes me.
I'd give my all for just his touch.
He slithers snakelike towards me.
My knees are weak, my body limp.
As I remember no more
The wall I've built between us
No barriers are left,
My amour's down,
My senses flee me, and I give in,
Sinking—— Dying——
Afraid but elated.
To think I've overcome the other,
The essence of him that I received.
I realize at last, how much I like it,
I love him, and I care!

Genevieve E. Spence

Special Love

It's been so long since I saw you,
although time has no meaning to me.
The distance between us makes me blue,
but there's always hope, you see.

Maybe I don't know you at all . . .
or then, maybe you've found someone new.
But whatever, I will never fall for anyone
the way I fell for you.

You know when I'm happy or sad;
you know when something is bothering me.
You brought out feelings I didn't know I had.
You showed what love is meant to be.

I do wish always that you'll care,
If only a wee small bit.
Because the love we've shared is very rare;
so please, let's not forget about it.

I'll love you forever and always,
and you, I'll never forget.
I'll not pay any attention to the days,
if only the years would slow down a bit.

Helen Levatino

Pretty Girl On The Library Steps

Pretty girl on the library steps,
Paused mid flight,
Hair shining in the light, eyes perplexed,
Should I go up or down?

What lies behind those heavy open doors,
Dim corridors — musty odors of the past,
A trillion pages in old books,
The dates of long forgotten wars,
Dead heroes?

Shimmering sunlight calls
Excitement of a new day morn,
The traffic down below,
The shops beyond.

Oh, pretty girl, let me take your hand,
And lead you through the corridors of time,
The world of fascination and suspense, of what has been,
With wisdom of man's glorious hindsight, of what will be.
A world alive with quietness above the traffic's roar!

Oh, pretty girl.
Please take my hand.

Louise Bowman

The Dawn Of A New Day . . .

The dawn of a new day,
A select few minutes brightened by her presence.
Air alive with the subtle smell of her perfume.
The sweet sound of her voice as she says "good morning".
Like a perfect sunrise, the first sight of her beautiful smile
warms my heart and lights my day.
Her disposition always optimistic, her tone always pleasant,
she is a model of what defines a woman.
Though few come close in compare,
I hope to find one as fair and true.
Alas, an exchange of pleasantries and small talk
are all that can be afforded.
Knowing her comforting memory will remain fresh throughout the day,
I am forced to say goodbye to morning's first sweet breath.
With a smile and pleasant farewell, sealed by her soft embrace,
I reluctantly depart,
already anticipating the dawn of a new day.

Roger Lee Fronek

I Don't Know Who You Are

I'm saying hello to you though I don't know who you are,
I know you're out there waiting maybe sitting on a star.

I don't even know your name or the color of your hair,
I do know that you're special and you're waiting just out there.

I already love you and my heart fills up with pride,
I can hardly wait to see you — so we'll play seek and hide.

I wonder what you'll call me when you sit upon my knee,
And I wonder when you're all grown up what it is you'll want to be.

Even though I don't know you — I do know your Mom and Dad,
Two very special people — of that you can be glad.

They'll be there to lead the way and teach you all things right,
And they'll be there to tuck you in and hear your prayers at night.

When you fall and skin your knee or fall and skin your heart,
They'll be there to pick you up — it's written in their part.

They'll teach you about values, the meaning of trust and truth.
They'll even know where to find the fairy, when you've lost a baby tooth.

They'll teach you how to read a book and to wish upon a star,
And teach you to be happy and to be proud of who you are.

To help you learn the joys of life — I will do my part,
For I may not know your name — but I know you in my heart.

Sheila Brown — Grammy

A True Story

   Sitting around one day, feeling low and sad,
A man, a friend appeared to me, a friend, I never knew, I had.
   Sitting in my wheelchair one day,
A strange thing happened, a man stopped in to say,
why are you just sitting here in this door?
   I took my time, time to say, no one wants me anymore.
They told me, you will forever be in that chair,
   They told me so much, I was content to stay there.
After a long long talk, He listened and told me, you can walk.
   This stayed on my mind all that day,
   I could find no words, any word to say.
By him saying this, I knew not why.
He spoke again, asking me, will you try?
   I told him, they said, I wouldn't walk no more,
   He said to me, If you try then you'll know.
As I sat there, not knowing what to do,
He spoke and said, for now, I must leave you.
   Still shocked by what he had to say,
   If I had not had the courage to try,
I wouldn't be walking today.

Larry Landrum

"Michael"

If only to touch you one more time
To feel you inside of me would be divine
To have your arms around me as never before
I would fall asleep to awake no more
The peacefulness of your body against mine
The beat of one heart as two entwine
The feeling of togetherness
and yet the distance of apart
Is this an end to a beginning
or possibly a new start?
Time will tell what our future holds
To be loved by you or one I am told
No matter when the resolution of our souls will meet
I can promise one thing
I will not settle for defeat

Heather McKee

She Who Flies

My valkyrie wields high her arm;
Hordes attend her word, and they are moved.
My amazon rides headlong to the battle;
Gladiators fall before her deft design.
My warrior's besieged by the throng,
And all who feel her hand respect her call.
She sought not discord's sting, nor weary heart,
But, set against, relinquished not her will.

Her wounds have sterned her soul against the dark.
How I ache to save her, would my reach not fail!
I may know of her travails yet not impede them,
Nor shield her path from fools' and madmen's rail.

Haven will I be to she who flies,
Refuge from the lightning and its thrall.
Until the sun forever close my eyes
I will remain her home. I will not fall.

Patrick Breslin

Roses In The Sky

To Bruce Benham, From Keith, 3-9-95
There lives one red rose.
In a field of viny forests of petrified trees.
Vanilla gardens bloom unforgotten love.
Red petals drop day by day in a sea of tranquillity.
Desert skies burn as colors of our lives turn into sweet sunsets.
Roses lay across the sky.
Smell each color everyday.
Every Arizona sunset reminds us of you.
In the sky forever.
There is only one red rose.

Keith Benham

My Light

It's very dark when the power is gone.
I looked at my watch, it was a long time
till dawn.
A battery radio we had, but not a T.V.
My boy had his flashlight cause he
wanted to see.
I found mine, but the batteries
were dead.
I forgot to buy new ones, something's
wrong with my head.
I said to my won, "love ya man"
Though I felt like a dud.
He held on to his prize and then
said,
"You're not getting my light bud".

Gary C. Rasmussen

The Renewal Of My Soul

When all seems lost and I've lost my way
   and friends are lying low,
I wrap myself in a blanket of faith
   and will sleep on a cushion of hope

My guardian angel sings hushed lullabies
   that melt away my fears;
Prayers are a comfort and help close my eyes,
   and I know that God hears.

I sleep peacefully and awaken refreshed;
   alert, now, and ready to go.
I give thanks to God and my guardian angel
   for the renewal of my soul.

Margie Parks

The Whirlwind

A Whirlwind is a Powerful force,
Swallowing anything in its path.
So powerful that resistance is denying the inevitable.
Taken from reality is the only outcome.

A Whirlwind is a Sturdy animation,
Selling itself to only the strong.
Stopping at nothing to consume all energy that exist.
Tallying victories against its victim.

A Whirlwind is a Persistent intensity,
Spiraling into innocence.
Surfacing only to declare victory against its prey.
Tying together Nature and Man.

A Whirlwind is a Woman untamed,
Spelling Love with every action.
Solely as an act of Nature, risking everything.
Teaching Man all its potential.

Mark N. Webber

Light To Dark To Light

As we wake up from an endless dream,
the world has changed to such an extreme.
The grass is wet from the morning dew,
and the day is starting just anew.
The flowers stand high for the rays of the sun,
they stand so proud for they know not what is wrong.

Everything has died.
The lights are gone.
The world is filled with darkness because the sun has gone.
The wind is scattered around the sky,
and the cold air is only now passing by.
Death arises upon the ground.
Yet no one knows when the new world will be found.

Ninaki Priddy

Wedding Prayer

I prayed Lord for someone to share my life
To do your work side by side
For a born again Christian Wife
Thank You, Lord, for my beautiful bride.

I asked you, Lord for a holy man
One I could cherish and love
As down life's road we walk hand in hand
As you look upon us from Heaven above.

Now we are one
Our love's happy and strong
We're serving faithfully Jesus, the Son
To Him our hearts will always belong.

Patricia Isenman

The Death Angel

He comes like a thief in the night,
  Slowly, like a fox, he comes for his prey.
When he comes there will be no fight.
  Those that go get no chance to pray.
You can be a child of eleven,
  Or an adult of eighty-three
He will come to take some to heaven
  Or hell is what some will see.
Those left behind shall mourn
  And there pain will live on.
Children, Still will be born
  And there lives must go on
When he will come no one knows,
  Are you ready for where he will go?

Rachel Thomas

Black Boy

Little black boy, who are you?
Smile, boy, I can't see you
Speak boy, I can't hear you
Little black boy, I see you, in the field, in the street
working, struggling, on strong feet
dirt, sweat, hate from the soul streams
searching, touching, holding your dreams
pain, anger, rage, color your face
to hide, to run, there is no place
to escape the torture of the past
sleepless nights, full of fear, last
while the world slumbers without care
kneeling, praying, shedding a tear
Little black boy, I watch you
Come, child, rest your head
Share my roof, share my bread
Cry, child, cry, let it out
Pain, hate, loss, of this I shout
Listen, world, His future you hold
In your soul, love grown cold

Christopher Graf

Love Of Life

When I took at you
I see a heavenly light
Oh what a beautiful sight
A walk in the forest
A choir or a chorus
It has found me tonight
I have longed for love in this world
When I saw you, instantly I knew it was you Girl
With your hair at shoulders length
I knew I had found all my strength
You are a beautiful sight
without you I have no life
See in me all that I see in you tonight
I look into your eyes and see the love of life
I know now that I have to have you as my Wife
That me might share all we have in life
To know we share a love for life!

Brett Sonia

Is It Time To Go Home?

Softly now the light of day
Fades upon my sight away . . .
Quiet and peaceful in sunbeams
Hidden like tomorrow's dreams . . .
Engulfing warmth, love's light streams

We all do fade as a leaf
In Autumn's spirit of belief
With promised whispers of the Spring
New buds on branches make birds sing . . .
So "Death where is thy sting?"

And tho I'll fight with all my might
For strength to enter this new plight
I'll listen to the voice within
Who'll tell me if it's time to win
Or let go, let God, and go with Him . . .

Where there's no more suffering or tears
We all make this journey through the years
While loved ones, family, friends await
With open arms, joyful spirits, love so great
Shining peace welcomes me on my way back home.

Lorna Punches Heiser

Whimsical Lover

Lover say. Lover do.
I'm confused but you say never mind
Instead you playfully reassure me with a cool embrace in the
afternoon sun.
And I love you my whimsical lover.
In the morning, distant and unreachable, you stare out in stony silence
And I, too meek to intrude, carefully read the messages on the cereal box
And find hidden words that describe you.
You're something on the outside and different on the inside.
You're wholesome, nutritious and good for me.
You're my recipe for a party and my favorite dish.
In my mind you are the ultimate lover
And there is no reason for me to ask why.
I am your lover too,
You're rich, tasty and wonderfully nutty blended lover.
And for this I know you really love me
And in return I will always love you.

Edmund Siejka

Untitled

Send me a post card of thoughts — letters of hate
Paint a picture of lust — pornographic literature
Telegraph me your thoughts — the room in your brain
Rain drizzles down the fountain of future sanity we now see it
Tonight is the last night of peace-justice-the american way
closed captioned T.V.
For tomorrow will open our eyes — and see
The deaf will hear and converse with the mute
All war now ends — it's time for world peace
With all now quiet the restless now sleep to awaken the dead
We can take wisdom from the temple
Passion everlasting
Faith is what keeps me going
The resurrection is an on going experience
Listen to my tales — for I speak of the knowledge
The door still remains open for you to pass through
Test you nerve and morals-bring open your heart
Morning has come to flourish our thoughts-heaven-love
Come on with me through the garden for the green fields and
pastures lie ahead — do you have any thoughts — speak

Mike Tyler

Thank You

I love to sit in the garden and watch
Our sons and the flowers grow
All that color and activity makes for quite a show
The grand long rope swing, hanging from the lovely old tree
What a delight as they alight, and fill the air with glee
Scattered among the ferns and flowers growing without a care
Miniature versions of cars and trucks and tractors here and there
They make the plants seem larger, the lawn a great expanse
For treasure hunts and picnicking, and grass stains on little pants
I love to sit in the garden and watch
Our sons and flowers grow, and it makes me smile to know
That the one who planted all this beauty is the one that I love so.

Tami S. Campbell

The Angel, The Prophet And Me

I was walking along one stormy night
I was feeling sad and not all right
The skies opened the sun's rays shined down and I
   Looked up and before my eyes there were
   Angels dancing, it was like a ballet
There was a figure out in the distance that spoke in
   A kind voice and said "let the bad things pass and
   Think of the wonderful things you have done"

Harvey Karon

Living The Lie

Where is the line between the realities of today
and the dreams of tomorrow?
It all seems to muddle together
as if to say — try and find me, if you dare.
But then one day, reality sets in
and the dreams are gone.
The time has far past
and tomorrow is gone.

Is there a place where our dreams lie dead?
With only a glimmer of hope to resurrect them.
Let me believe in that.
Please let me believe in something.
So dream your dreams,
look to the future —
but don't make the mistakes of many
and find yourself living the lie.

Diana M. Tosado

Best Friend

Gaunt as ages long dead,
the old dog scoured the roadside
in search of survival itself.

But time kept roaring by,
indifferent as water over stones
or wind through trees bare as bones.

In the wintry headlight of night,
a thousand faces streamed along
cold, dull and mute, eyes far away,
minds, too.

Black as the night and weak with dread,
the old dog rolled back its head
and howled at what it could not see then,
or now.

Back there beside the road it remains,
black as always, black as the night
in which it stays.

Leslie Brumfield

The Goddess Of Nature

To see her glorious beauty is an everlasting treat.
To hear her heart roar like pounding thunder.
To feel her sensational vibrations sending shivers up he feet.
To taste her sweet nectar like a moist zephyr.

The life and light of many cities, oh what a feat.
Her grandeur to find is for that of the explorer.
Yes, Utopia needn't exist without her or I'll weep.
Over mountains — down the valley, to paradise for the adventurer.

To know and behold her beauty is a joy to seek.
To view the rainbows above her is a blind man's hanker.
To fall in love at first glance after we meet.
To be full of love and yet still hunger.

Her elegant cascade is the quest of the meek.
For most men, her beauty is like a stranger.
She's a cataract to lust for which makes the knees weak.
One taste of her moist atmosphere will cause the mind to wander.

She's like no dream to ponder when you're sleepy.
She comes in many sizes, shapes and ventures.
She goes by such names as Angel, Victoria and Fairy.
She's "The Goddess Of Nature," a waterfall — a true wonder.

Thomas Edward Champ

My Prayer

Give me time and patience, Lord
and understanding to accomplish
my goal, Give me the wisdom
to accept and resolve the little things.
Help me to see the good in others,
And to do what I can for the needing.
Keep me from selfishness that
can hurt the ones I love. And
give me courage to face each new
day. Teach me to be tolerant of
others short comings and do my
part to help them overcome them.
May I always have the foresight
to aid the oppressed, listen to those
who want to be heard, praise
when deserved and to give advice
when wanted and to be constantly
able to help my fellow man. Amen

Garnet Winchel

Time In Time Out

White clouds are banks of snow,
In a sunny blue sky and idle time
Goes drifting by without purpose and
Without aim, it's all a careless little game.
Idle time passes and drifts along hardly
Noticed when suddenly the mind quickens,
Like the beat of a drum or the shrill
Of high pitched trumpets. A shiver of fear,
Tragic sense of loss and stark wonder, how much?

Like a shadow alongside the highway,
Appears a thorny bush — dried up are the stems
Blood red are the petals of a rose once luscious
And bursting with nectar and sweet smells.
Black speckled and yellow bees flew in and out
Briefly settled for a feast — time in and time out,
They scattered round about, finally they too
Became like dried up roses with blackened petals,
Falling on pure white sand, or like a dead star in
The universe looking over no man's permanent land.

Lee M. Wheeler

On Loan

The child is not mine, but was placed in my care
for such a short time for me to be the caretaker.
To carefully weed out that which would choke out
his strength to grow and cultivate him to bring out his beauty.
To love him as God loves me.
To be ever so careful to guide him upward, so his
face looks up to the heavens toward his true Parent
and listens to Him with all of his heart.
For he is not mine; he is the Lord's. He has
placed him in my hands, entrusting me with his most
precious possession.
His talents I did not give him, but God gave me
a way to help them grow.
He made him the way he is; I cannot take credit
for them for I am just his helper, doing the best I
can in the short time I have to get him ready for this
world of our's. To shield him as much as possible.
To give him strength where possible. It is not an
easy job, but I thank God that He has given him to me.
He is not mine; he is the Lord's

Deneene Oleneack

The Soul Maker

The biggest job that can be had
Is the one that has no rules.
It doesn't come with instructions
It is not an occupation for fools.

What is best for me, may not be for you
My instinct must decide.
I may have pleasure just for a moment
But the scars will be left inside.

A flash of time is all we have
One's life is not so long.
Can I not see in the future?
The eyes that hold a song.

God, give me divine wisdom while I shape this soul,
There are treasures still yet to be found.
The gift is to watch this life unfold
For this I hang around.

Mary Taylor Minnix

The Day Of The Fire

Look at the fire reflected in her eyes,
She can't bring herself to say the word good-bye.
Everything she once had is consumed by the flame,
She sits and watches her things be put to shame.
She feels undescribable pain,
Why did this happen to her she asks in vain.
What will she wear?
What will she eat?
Where will she lay her head down to sleep?
Where will she go?
Where could she stay?
A lot of hard decisions will have to be made today.
She doesn't know what to do right away.
The fire is out and she finds a place to stay.
She decides that she really will be ok.
She didn't burn, she is still alive.
You can tell by the gleam in her sparkling eyes.
She will live through this tragedy and take it day by day,
Because she figured out there really is no other way.

Angela Johnson

You Touched Me

I search other faces
Looking for your look
Trying to find traces
Of you in them.

He has to have your happy smile
And your caring eyes
But as I look I know all the while
There will never be another like you.

I thought that it was love
So I gave you all I had
And I didn't know when to leave
Never knew I could hurt so bad.

Your love for me was never there
Though I wanted it to be
You came and left without a care
But for me there was no way out.

A heart only knows what it feels
My heart won't let go
You're not coming back and I'm moving on
But you still own my soul.

Lois Savoca

Love Life

As I rise in the morning, I say a quick prayer of hello
And dash out the door to the routine life that lies ahead.
Missed an accident on the corner and almost hit a cat,
Yelled at a man for stopping at the yellow light,
Switch the station on the radio and pop in a tape.
Wonder how much money I have maybe I'll stop for a coke
Or maybe I'll swing by the mall and see what's up for sale
Got to start work in an hour I'm now on the clock
Cruisin' down the road I see a family and smile.

Now my day is ending, I can slow down and relax.
As I drive down the road I look back at the whole day
And imagine the sleep that lies ahead—how wonderful.
I stop at a light and I look up at the shaded sky
A gentle blue, pale, pale pink and a light purple.
The sun, slowly sliding out of sight and below the earth
Makes the sky glisten and I think of the master painter.
The man behind me honks his horn, the light is now green.
Oh, I'm sorry, I was just remembering how much I love life

Sarah J.

Life

Life is ticking away.
We can't wait to pray.
Our Lord Jesus Christ wants to hear it.
To Him, we are mice living under His arm,
Doing each other no harm.

Oh! Then I awake and it's just a dream.
The world is horrid still. You know what I mean?

Life is ticking away.
We can't wait to play
Little, dirty tricks on each other.
But while everyone is bad,
Our good brother, Jesus
Looks down on us crying.
We're disobeying Him once again,
Thinking it's O.K.,
But we're lying.

Please listen and learn.
Let Jesus give you a turn.
Live together in peace.
Please do it for God, at least.

Isaac Harrison

For Good

A light durable but soft
is kept in the attic of your house.
It stays among the goods you store,
those you dare not remove for good,
your mother's soft blouses and skirts
the ones you saw her wear the year
before she was gone for good.

Hurriedly packed packages and strings
familiar combs, notes she wrote and
half solved puzzles in fading magazines,
lottery tickets never checked to see,
shoes kept for decades — the ones
she had you buy her from Rome —
stay lifeless unattended and remote
in bags and boxes on the floor,
kept lighted and half dusted in
what is now her chronological home.

Bruce Nassiri Kermane

Aeschylus

Release yourself to that one encompassing abandon that claims
my very soul
if not
Release me from the wounds that break my spirit
Let me show you life at its fullest
Embark with me on a fantasy fit for a princess
Angel that you are,
sweet innocence radiates from your eyes
basking my soul in such rays that make me wince upon glancing deep
into their mystery
Men have loved before and will love again
but none could eclipse this slow burning flame within my heart
Caress me and I'm lost as a babe newly born
groping, waiting once again for your gentle touch
Kiss me and I'm transported to a place of wondrous beauty
far exceeding that of the Elyssian fields
yet shamed by your unadorned loveliness
Close your eyes
Close mine
The dream has already begun.

F. Ian Fitzgerald Farrell

As The Sky Goes By

The boundaries of
where our eyes can see
Words of a dream felt, touched upon,
tasted, seen, heard
a dream.

Life twisting,
turning reaching into moods.
Can you see yourself in you?
Blackness surrounded by character.
Blackness surrounded by mood. Blackness
to be played upon.

In the boundaries of
where our eyes can see.
Darkness, soft light shading
into the night.

Blackness
a reflection of life
to be played
upon.

Raymond Cheshirer

Seeking Out A Dream

The years have past,
the years have gone.
Now it's time for something new to spawn.
The unknown triggers your eyes at dawn,
flying off a mountain into the sea,
chasing away all fears and misery.
A bird is happily sitting on my shoulder,
In the morning,
He says you've learned how to fly.
What could that be?
Have I reached nirvana?!
If I can fly I'll be free in my heart and soul.
No more strife no more apathy,
the blissful kiss on my head.
Is this really happening to me?
Have I reached total peace of mind?
What have I found?
What can I find?
of all things of all mankind.

Ian Wolf

Emptiness

I am like a lonely star in the sky
Like an empty shell in the sea
Like the silence of a graveyard
Like a flower without leaves

I am like the rain that kisses the earth
Like a whisper thru the wind
Like the sound of an old bell
Like a night without a dream

I am like a stone next to the road
Like the joy after the fear
Like a child who lost his toy
Like a mother without tears

I am like a musical note
Like the end and the beginning
Like a castle and a ghost
Like a life without a meaning

Norma Vega

Our Beautiful Rose

Mother Earth is like a beautiful rose,
its stem with many leaves are like the cosmos are to Mother Earth.
For as long as the stem with its leaves continue to grow . . .
our beautiful rose will always be . . .
existing till eternity.
But, If one of these days the stem and leaves dry out,
so will the beautiful rose.
Yet, if only the beautiful rose dries out,
the stem and leaves will continue to grow and exist,
but, without a beautiful rose.
This is then how mankind must learn to love and respect Mother
Earth as if it was a very beautiful rose indeed.
For if mankind continue to destroy Mother Earth the cosmos will
not have a beautiful rose anymore.
Mankind then cannot exist at all with only a stem and leaves.
It needs its beautiful rose in order for mankind to exist.
So take very good care of our beautiful rose,
Mother Earth,
It belongs to all mankind.
It must be shared with all mankind.

Carlos T. Ramirez Jr.

Separated

Two worlds that collide
Two kinds of people black and white both
alike, both have feelings, both have fears, both
have dreams, both smile when they're happy
and cry when they're sad. Separated because
of hate. Blacks hated whites for making
them slaves in the 19th century. The
hatred spread into the 20th with
blacks being called niggers and not being
given equal rights. Black children went to
Black Schools white children went to
White Schools. One nation separated by
color of skin. One man had a dream his
name was Martin Luther King he stood
up for what he believed. The boycott
began to unite black and white. People
said "Never will come the day when hate will
disappear." It never did. There's still the KKK and
hate in the world today. One world, one man, one dream.
Two things that collide Hate and Respect.

Faith Posten

Sympathy

The tears of grief welled up inside
Please let them flow like rain
To comfort, cleanse, and nurture you
And help dilute the pain
Like a cold and bitter winter
Trees bowed from ice and snow
And bone chilling winds raging round outside
Threaten to dampen the fireside glow
But then spring comes with sunny days
Bringing warm and melting rains
Your grief subsides; your soul revives
Allowing you to smile again

Gerdine Newsome

Tapping The Tables Of Time

Tapping the tables of time
Sipping soups sorrowfully solemn
Keeping my capers carefully quiet
Dying while dining doubtfully done
Lying while living, leaving, left
Pondering poems, picking up pieces
Changing my chances of choices
Saying I'm sorry silently so
Thinking my thoughts thankfully not
Wondering my wanderings, wanting, and wishes
Fighting the foe from my feelings
Hating my happiness haunting my head
Ending the ebb of emanating emotions
Dizzying the drifting, dead and doomed
Missing the moral memories once molded
Tapping the tables of time

Shannon Phy

Surrealistic Dreams

Your dreams will bring you wisdom
As time slips away
Never ending, no beginning
Stories that unravel before you close your eyes
Dreams fall like rain as the night passes by
There's a place in your dreams where the imagination runs free
And the night holds no uncertainly
Dreams are filled with memories
With promises of laughter
And whispers in the dark
As darkness fades
Dreams come to an end
Unaware of all the lost dreams that dance in her head

Amy Sasali

Things Are Changing

Things are changing as they should,
Things are changing as I know they would,

Things are changing everyday as I know
it is God's way.

Keep the faith and chin up high because
we know Gods on our side.

Let temptation come and go, we don't
need it, it's Gods show.

Work hard and honest everyday and you
will find the one true way.

Things are changing everyday as we
know it is Gods way.

Tom Ganley

"My Sister"

My sister means so much to me,
Always my friend, Always will be.
She's always there when I need to be heard,
Usually listens and never says a word.

She'll give me advice, her point of views,
But never puts me down when I don't follow through.

I love you sis as you should know,
My thoughts are with you where ever you go,
Remember the good times, keep them in mind,
I love you so much sis, you're one of a kind.

So when you travel day after day,
Remember I'm with you every mile of the way.
I love you sis, this is written from my heart,
As long as we live we will never part.

Brenda H. Ball

Smoke

I never saw the smoke again
that fled the towering chimney;
it unfurled around an evergreen tree,
crouching in the greenery;
I mistook a cloud of mist for it,
I wasn't dismayed one bit;
I asked a meandering fox
for word of its whereabouts,
it eluded my continuing shouts,
a robin perched atop her nest
pointed to a distant cloud
and said: "It joined that cloud in the West".

Frederic R. Martin

The Prize

Only the foolish fail to realize
the simple truth of the prize.
Joyfully given, innocently received.

So many rush blindly
down the mirrored paths.
Thinking only of gain,
never noticing the loss.

Few take time to stroll
through the gentleness of the garden.
Not many savor the morning dew
pooled gently on the delicate rose petals.

As bewildering as this may sound,
A great twist of irony is easily found.
The blissful moment of birth...
Begins the journey toward death.

The roads of life may seem long and never-ending,
But if you will take your time
You may just one day find
The simple and evading truth...
Life is a prize.

Donna K. Thrash

Quests

Here's the part that would not write
Though scribbled at it day and night
Then flashed to mind a reason of why
So sat me down for planned last try.

Tis said that you can invent your self
Let's add a Do to get off of the shelf:
All a flutter as with butterfly wings
While heart within it sings and sings . . .

Ruby B. Snow

Trout Are Wonderful!

Some people think of a trout as a fish in a creel
Not the glorious singing of a reel,
Nor the arch'ed flash of silver, gold, or crimson
As a gorgeous fish leaps high above crystal waters
To dive with warlike fury upon its prey.

They don't know the thrill and tension of a quivering rod and line,
Nor have they caught the gleam of reflected sunlight in the foam,
As the feisty trout sweeps downstream
Finally free — away
With but a feathered hook, reminder of the fray.

John R. Snow

Dreams Confiscated

Step right into my lair
enjoy the fruits of your electric chair
and all the thought crystals of desire
you have an appointment
with the butcher of telepathic defense
his name happens to be Charles
but could also be Ben or Betty Sue
who ages back at you from the mirror
off course it's not you, but it could be
if you sell me your soul
you don't believe in souls anyway
Do You?
Excuse me, what are these electrodes for?
Faulty neurons for this efficient machine.

Kurt Gonnerman

"God Spell . . . God Spell"

Come my love, help lift this burden off my
weary back

Sit, dine with me my love, let me rejoice in
the pleasantness of your company

Savor my mind, drink my needy soul — consume
my lonely heart with gentleness

Come my love, secure this axis' spirit . . .

Does thou tease in anxious whispers, shouts
and screams?

Dare I admit!!!

"GOD SPELL"

Indeed the spirit moves over still waters . . .

Mia Alicea

While I Am Young

I want to enjoy life and have fun,
I like to joke and laugh with everyone.

I want to be happy my whole life through,
Because there are too many sad people I once knew.

I like to smell the fresh air and flowers so sweet,
To feel the gentle rain and the mud squish beneath my feet.

To see a beautiful rainbow up in the sky,
To hear roaring thunder almost makes me cry.

To gaze upon the stars on a dark, dark night,
And to see the universe from a different light.

I want to enjoy life and have fun,
These things I will do while I am young.

William Ferguson

The Beauty Of The Sun

The sun's rays poured through the mountains and the trees
The power of its beauty seemed to echo through the breeze

The birds seemed to soar to the highest peak
Without even the thought of becoming the least bit weak

All the land animals gathered with a certain feeling of pride
In their lonely caves, they no longer felt the need to hide

The leaves turned bright as the branches grew strong
The roots regained their vibrancy after being dead for so long

As the sun's warmth continued to rise, the flowers followed its lead
Each of them had been blessed with a strong eternal seed

Such a beautiful sight is hard to come by
Its beauty is far more precious than even you or I

Sooner or later the sun will no longer be in sight
For all the animals and trees have been laid to rest for the night

The beauty of this picture will forever stick in your head
The happiness it brought you shall never be dead

Until God's work is again in plain view
You will realize how its beauty inside you grew

All the struggles of pain that seemed to weigh a ton
Were simply lifted when you noticed the beauty of the sun

Crystal Worrell

Tears

Beads of salty water, rolling
softly down my cheek —
flooded over from a heart
that is too full.

Are they a cause for shame,
a sign of weakness in myself,
that I can't control them
when they start to flow?

. . . Or rather — do they give release
from frustration, worries, fears
that otherwise might
tear my heart in two?

. . . And . . . when these tears are
caused by joy,
when my cup overflows,
do not these tears become
the wine — to celebrate with you?

Mary A. Ryk

My Dad

My Dad was a great man in every way,
He was a jack of all trades, so they say,
Polio attacked him at 17 months,
He didn't let it get him down
Or stop him at all,
If he fell, he picked himself up and stood tall,
There was never a day that he gave up.
He did everything he wanted to do,
Great aspirations he had and inspired me so,
He left a great legacy to his grandchildren,
They all looked up to him.
Life with Dad was never grim,
Even with his affliction, he was a sportsman,
Teacher and craftsman,
There aren't enough words to describe Dad,
He will be remembered forever and ever.

Marilyn S. Mossy

Best Friends Are Friends Forever

My friend I will see you someday,
you are in a better place and there is no suffering there;
remember all the good times, so many times we laughed,
but then there are those troubled times I'd soon put in the past;
I wish we could of kept in touch more often, so much time had passed,
you must know I thought of you even when I wasn't there,
I wondered how you were doing, I hope you know I cared!

I know you went thru a lot in your life,
I wish I could of been with you,
but I know this place is where you should be,
there's nothing there to harm you.
Someday we will be together and when we are
you can show me this place that I'm sure is really beautiful, so
please be looking for me, for when I see you I'll greet you with open
arms and still call you my best friend!

Nancy Ramey

Before The Buzzer

As I stepped onto the rink, I felt the chill of the
ice. As I skated through warm-up listing to the
blades of my skates slashing through the smooth
cold ice, the sound of the frozen puck gliding across
the ice fills my head. As the goalie stands between the
pipes like a knight in armor, I charge the puck with the
blood flowing through my arms. I shoot the puck and I
watch it fly through the air and past the goalies glove
and hit in the back of the net. That is when your nerves
go away and then the adrenalin starts to pump. When the
buzzer sounds I am ready for the opening face-off.

Rusty Johnson

The Humor In Emotions

Have you ever bothered to look at the sky,
Watch the clouds, maybe the stars.
Have you ever walked for hours alone,
perhaps collecting your thoughts.
Have you ever driven hundreds of miles without a radio,
Looking at the scenery.
Have you ever laid in bed at night crying,
Just to relieve stress.
Me neither just checking.

Nathan M. Walenta

"My Angel"

Is there someone watching over me,
To guide me through this life,
Someone to care and comfort me,
My remaining days of life?

At times I used to think there was,
But then I am not sure.
Sometimes I feel that an angel does,
Or is that just my cure?

Whenever I fall deep in sleep,
These certain dreams occur,
That when I wake my eyes both weep,
To some that sounds obscure.

One day I will see in the heavens above
The people I have met in life,
But for now I will keep on dreaming of Mom,
My Guardian Angel of life.

M. Donant

What Do They Expect —

Airing their laundry out . . . 'n Public??
Dirty panties/dirty bras? But to become?
Human sacrifices perforated 'n psychological —
Dilemmas!?? 'N she should do so well??? Assuming —
Position . . . like neo Nazi?? What happened?
To respect? Self . . . or property she yelled!!??

Raved n' ranted!! While driving . . . almost had . . .??
5 Wrecks? Within . . . quarter uv'mile!!? That Tuesday —
Morning blaming me for her? . . . Not skiing for 5 yrs.?
Her left leg . . . not touchable?? Smashed Tibia or —
Shin splint!! While explaining? To Novices Teacher . . .
of Treacherous slopes uv'extreme skiing out of . . .
Her league by gravity's concern that snow shoe rabbit —
Is now deceased by hook or crook uv . . . old man Winter!?

Doesn't explain that after breakin' up!? She wanted —
To keep poems dedicated to her? And the necklace uv' . . .
Our engagement!? Afro beads 'n beautiful color ceramic . . .
Earth clouds of clay!? For her desire to serve . . . coffee?
While wearing French maid's.. dustin' outfit! 'N talkin' . . .
Polishing my head off . . . like secretary takin' stenography!??

Philip Sherrod

Untitled

Drifting in this corridor,
Making my journey from season to season.
Must everything digress
into the silent droning
That paws my ear to agony?
This propagating ailment
Where only the simple is amiss.
And still the quizzical condition remains unparalleled.
Yet everything is not lost
And simplicity is still a virtue
with a peerless and quaint quality
And being lost is far from amiss
If you know where you're headed.

Jarod Thomas

Missing You

I feel a yearning, for my son,
As all the seasons come and go,
And yet my son forever lost;
but not really lost at all,
For my son is with, 'Our Saving Saviour,'
Our saviour, Jesus Christ.

This yearning, that I have,
Comes now and then throughout my life.
I feel it deeply in myself,
It tends to make me cry.
But my prayers that I send above
bring me joy and peace,
For my son I know is with Our Saviour,
Our Saviour, Jesus Christ.

A. Lillian G. Baros

Untitled

I see a woman who sits across the way; a lady
Her sleep so peaceful
Her skin so smooth
I watch her breath
And I wonder,
As I see a subtle grin,
If her dreams are as beautiful.
Or if I shall ever feel this way again.

Ben Noakes

Morning

The cool crisp air awakens my senses
    as I walk in darkness toward the lake.
The silence is broken first be a Loon
    and an unseen ballet by fish adds an
        arrhythmic beat.
The secret ingredient of lake mist
    blends the night into day,
As blurs of gray
    start to take on color and shape.
The sun's warmth is now felt,
    a pause of all noise echoes.
Suddenly all the birds are saying hello,
    the last of the deer return to the woods.

I stand alone.

Many would consider this a work of art,
    but it is nothing more than a crayon picture
        with stick figures.
Without you there is no depth,
    no soul of a true masterpiece.
I see just another cold, lonely day break.

Eric Benjamin

Eyes Of A Storyteller

One raise of an eyebrow
Then two and in the glow of a mind at work
You begin to see things in your own light

You cruise through your vivid tunnels of illusions
Some bordering on happiness, sorrow, or fright

Moving past those visions both big and small
A picture show runs through your imagining hall
Seeking a sort of entertainment bliss
Nothing in the moment is there you miss

Creating characters along the way in your own form of magic
You paint them either villainous, heroic, or even tragic

For whatever fiction your mind plots,
it must be said, you have the eyes of a storyteller

And blue in color, these eyes are inspired, whether on a day
which is bright, or in ominous shades of gray

William A. Berg

Endless Dreams

I'm dreaming of an endless day;
a time when children laugh and play.
A day when there is no more pain;
and people will succeed and gain.

I'm dreaming of an endless time;
when some will sit drinking wine.
A time when men no longer fight;
and children's eyes will shine with light.

I'm dreaming of an endless life;
a time when I may be your wife.
A life that will continue on;
even though you've long been gone.

I'm dreaming of an endless place;
somewhere I can see your face.
With memories that we've been through;
and I'll tell you how I love you.

I'm dreaming of an endless sky;
a place to go when we die.
A sky that we will see together;
and be together always and forever

Anna Heimark

The Nightingale

What makes you sing when it is night,
While others sing when it is bright?

Perhaps the darkness begs a song,
To make the nighttime seem less long.

The eerie, dark, and lonely hours,
Can veil nature's brightest flowers.

But night seems brighter when you sing,
With gentleness upon your wing.

Your playful notes can warm the frost,
And give us peace when all seems lost.

Why do you sing when it is night?
To give us hope till there is light!

Meldin R. Merill

Treasure The Mother Earth

Feelings of laughter float to the sky
The mother earth, the feelings must glide.
Through the earth soaring so far.
Think of the shadows reach for the star.

Leave all lost love being here with me,
Wondering illusions the depths that I see.

Feel the burn the hunger intense,
Listen to the baby and all that they sense.

Feel all the love and emotion around.
Think of the love that once filled the ground.
Listen to the words and feel its soul.
Listen to the love and all that's untold.

Kadie Watts

Untitled

Walking through the world of green.
Where the giants dance and the little birds sing.

The earth crunches below your feet, tip-toe, make yourself discreet.

Your life starts here on this dirt trail.
Go left or right just don't fail.

People's prints from times before show the way they choose more.

You decide to go straight instead.
Make your own destiny of what lies ahead.

There's a pond where people have stopped to rest.
Which way did you go to pass this test?

We took the road that was most used.
But this isn't the destiny we choose.

The footprints we followed show there is more.
They will lead us to what we are looking for.

I went off the trail to the land of the green.
Where I danced with the trees and the little birds sing.

The wind carried me to this pond where I rest.
Neither left nor right helped me pass this test.

I followed my heart and held the hand of my fate.
All this I've learned by just going straight.

Liz Velazquez

Snow Walking

Pound, pound, pound, pound,
Go my feat upon the ground.
Thump, thump, thump, thump,
Goes my beating heart.

The wind flows across my face,
My breath swirls forward in white clouds.
My sight sees nothing stir,
For there is nothing about.

I travel across the barren wasteland of snow,
My feet leaving a trail behind me.
Everywhere I look I am alone,
Yet some how I know someone looks over me.

I look behind me to see my trail,
And I see a trail of two.
I raise my head and howl to the moon,
And somewhere close by comes answering call.

I am never truly alone in this world,
Even though the road I travel down is barren.
And he carried me across the snow,
When it became too deep for me to travel.

David A. Wardrup Jr.

No Wanning Years

For over half a century
    We worked, we planned, we loved
Our future was never a mystery,
    We planned to meet our God above.

Our farm is a haven far all.
    He loved nature, and his work
He knew ass the cows by their bawl
    Caring for them he'd never shirk.

As life, and years moved ahead
    His footsteps were slowing
But he lived, and planned, the cattle he fed
    In the evenings we'd hear their lowing.

God gave me a great man
    To have for all these years,
We didn't know God's plan
    But early one morning, he answered my fears.

God took my life, my love,
    There'll be no wanning life,
Now he's with our maker up above
    And I'm trying to deal with my strife.

Josephine A. Kissack

"Michelle"

I've never seen anyone looking so right
never seen a star shine so bright — you are
a lady — and I have never seen an image
light up the magic sky you shine so bright
I want to hold you tight and never let
you go.

Always wanted to asks you out, always
wanted to let you know that I cared.
I will never let you go you'll always be in
my soul. My darlin' Michelle the love of my life
always looking so nice. Did you that I
cared. I just want to be with you
My darlin' Michelle.

I just can't keep away from your eyes
can't keep away from my love. Ill never
be to far away. My darlin' Michelle.

Thomas Jackson

Just Another Day

As the sun sets and nightfall begins,
A day is done and a chapter ends.
"What have I done?"
"Where is the mark I have made?"
"Did I make it the best or make it the worst?"
"Did I finish last or did I finish first?"
Even if I fail or if I succeed
I still am planting tomorrow's seed.
What will happen in the future? I do not know,
but from the seeds I plant today and tomorrow,
The future will grow.

Geoffrey Marberry

Untitled

A long and dreamy night filled with bewitching beauty.
When I am around you, I feel every breath inside me being
sweetly devoured. Your kiss leaves me in a weakened state,
craving life. You look at me with your darkened eyes. I am
drawn into your soul. I can still feel your flesh pressed
against my mouth. You are like the rainbow that appears
after the storm. A warmth that melts the chill of winter.
I am in love, crazy glorious love. My love was sent to the
angels. A misty silence was awaken. They saw my dreams
and heard my thoughts. They wiped the tears from my
pillow and brought them to heaven. A remarkable gift
was then handed down. They sent you to me. A strong and
gifted man. With a heart full of passion, a mind filled with
strength, and a soul that is forever. Joined with the one
woman who knows how beautiful and true you really are.
Now and forever.

Lynda D. Rowse

Seven Times A Day

There it is, that loud ringing.
Ringing right in my ear.
There it is, that enormous blunder of chairs
screeching and scraping across the floor.
The feet shuffling, the pushing and pulling
has started once more.

It hurts my head so — everyone screaming.
It hurts my body so — everyone shoving.
I need more time to get to class.
And then, just as abruptly as it started,
it ends.

There is silence echoing in the halls
No pushing, pulling, or shoving
No screaming, no feet . . .
until next time that is . . .

There it is, that loud ringing.
Ringing right in my ear.
There it is, that enormous blunder of chairs
screeching and scraping across the floor.

Amanda Carrico

Nature Of Peace

As I walk along a wooded road, the beauty of Nature
surrounds me and my inner peace strengthens.
Throughout, my spirit rings with joy. Before me lies an
open field in which a herd of cattle grazes and I stop
along the road to watch them feed. The wind blows
gently to rustle some leaves and the sun is shining on
my face. In the distance glides a hawk through the sky
and I stand in awe of the majesty of Nature. She is a
most beautiful apparition.

Craig A. Metcalf

Have You Ever Dreamed?

Have you ever dreamed to be what you are,
But afraid to reach for your own special star?

Have you ever wished to sing like a lark,
But sit all alone, afraid in the dark?

Have you ever wanted to play like a child,
But afraid that others might think you too wild?

Have you ever noticed how quickly time flies;
As one child is born, another one dies.

Look deep in your soul and let yourself dream,
For things are not always just as they seem.

The fear that we have is always our own,
While the time that we're given is only a loan.

Go back to the time when you were quiet young.
Let the music play loud and your songs to be sung.

Look up to the heavens and shine like that star.
Your dream is quite close, it's not really so far.

Just let go of your fear and be what you are!

Jeanne Jack

Today

Today I want to run you, be next to you
    Let your eyes and mine embrace
Loving you from affair is interesting
    I feel the need to hold you, not mold you

Today your image is in my heart and mind
    Now divine so fine I am not blind
Just to often love is hard to find
    Thus come into my arms hold my charms

Let me remember man can be warm
    And oh, so tender remind me please
In a friendship gentleness can prevail
    Any affection between us does sail . . .

S. H. Clarke

Fog

Fog . . .
    is mystical and musical
        like butterfly wings touching the softest of mosses.
Fog . . .
    peeks around trees
        playing hide and seek with the deer.
It joyfully rolls along oceans
    gently caressing and soothing the mighty whale.
And when it has permeated all that it may with Love . . .
    Fog gently lifts its velvety body
        back to the heavens
    To lie like a blanket
        tucking in the stars
            until night comes again.

Anne Carpita

Precious

Feeling of emptiness when you are away,
Under your spell is where I wish to be,
I dream of your beauty from day to day,
As I yearn to embrace you close to me,
Your hypnotic eyes which would make me stay,
To cherish you heart, your love endlessly,
Precious is the view from a man in love.

James Marquez

On Becoming Eighteen

Now that you are eighteen years old
(although you have been this age a number of years),
Here's hoping that you realize that you
are not quite dry behind the ears.

A whole new world is before you.
Take your time — Think — Talk — Think again.
No need to hurry.
Now is the time to go slow — enjoy.
But don't change your friendly, smiling ways.

Life ahead is a long, long time.
Even though it's hard to realize now,
Your decisions should include visions of tomorrow.

Marjorie H. Baker

The Course

I once had a horse, that had a course,
The he always took.
One day the horse, was on his course and
I saw him fall in the brook.
He came out soakin' wet,
so I took him to see the vet.
But, the horse
Died of course.

Alan L. Ganshert

Aspirations

Someday I guess I will learn how to fly.
I used to take lessons,
but the teacher didn't like me —
so I quit.

I used to take lessons,
but they were too hard —
so I quit.
Everyone said I should have kept going;

But they were too hard.
I tried, really I did, because —
everyone said I should have kept going,
but flying is not very easy.

I tried, really I did, because —
I wanted to be better than everyone else,
but flying is not very easy.
Someday, I guess, if it isn't too hard,
   I will learn how to fly.

Elia J. Nelson

Our Crazy World

This whole world is going crazy,
with people in general getting so lazy.

Some one in need, of a hand to get by.
A cripple who needs help gets a little
white lie.

A child with hunger in a desperate time
of need, with children at home the first
that you feed.

When a cry for help just goes unheard,
A scream and a yell no reply, not a word.

So why can't we be friends with out
questioning "Why"?
When some live all alone and that's the way
they die.

Jerry Rathe

Black Dog, White Dog, Brown Dog, Big Hog

I have a Black Dog he used to be brown
I don't know why but he likes to go to town riding around with
   the window down.
I have a White Dog he has a puppy face, I don't know why but
   he's a disgrace.
He scratches the walls, he scratched the halls, he even scratched
   my rubber ball.
I have a Brown Dog he is a big hog, he eats everything he sees.
Once he drank orange juice and ate pickles and peas, but that
   was only what he had for lunch . . .
For dinner he drank purple punch and pig meat from the market.
I actually have one dog with all those colors . . . and red.
He does all those things and his name is Fred.
He needs to be fed then he'll go to bed he's a sleepy head.
G'night Fred!

Alexis Boatman

This Deadly Game

I am fat and ugly I say
when I look in the mirror each and every day

If I could only lose a few more pounds
maybe I'd sleep a night that's sound

I wish I could change this focus
go one day and just not notice

I fight and battle everyday
Lord, please just take it away

I wish I could see myself as You do
I'm sick, it's like a constant flu

Depression fills my mind
I swear, this will be the last time

I'm scared and sad all my days
if You could only let me be happy, I pray

I won't ask You for too much
but will I ever live without this crutch?

I want to look in the mirror one morn
and know my life has been reborn

Bulimarexia is my name
I want to end this deadly game

Theresa Rohde-Walls

Yes, I Know It

You keep telling me I'm old and gray
But don't forget you have to pass this way
Don't remind me I'm old
I lived this life and know it's so

Take time to see me, don't leave me alone
I still need people, not to sit and moan
My body has changed, but my mind is clear
I still care for you, all the moments I'm here

I cannot do as before
But can still help you open life's door
I need your compassion as well as your love
Before I meet my maker — above

I still have many things to say to you
If you'll just listen than I'll be through
So don't leave me sad and blue
Come and say **I love you**

Louis F. Green

The Human Race

We are all a part of the Human Race,
We join in at birth at a steady pace.
Don't stray ahead,
Don't lag behind,
Just keep up with your fellow kind.
Different culture,
Different creed,
We all must race at the same speed.
We take in life's wonders with every stride,
Man and Woman side by side.
We join in when we first are born,
Into a world where Hate does scorn.
We keep our pace when we're adults,
Not always avoiding life's cruel jolts.
And when we become Old and Wise,
We finally begin to realize...
We are all a part of the Human Race,
We all must run at an Equal pace.

Lesley Marsh

The Sea

All my life I have loved the sea, the potent feelings it stirs in me
The way it moves, it takes my blues
And puts my heart where it wants to be

I sail forth at the break of day, set my course an make my way
I speculate, and navigate
The game is set, now I must play

My ship and I, a team, as one, from dusk at night till morning sun
We conquer the ocean, we feel emotion
A battle lost, a battle won

The sea's my foe and yet my friend, each journey's start a journey's end.
To sail the world, my plans unfurled
My hopes and dreams together blend

On deck I stand, at one with time, distance all around, sublime
This mast so tall, I feel so small
I'm master, yet it is not mine

I fell it live and die through me, that wondrous entity, the sea
It takes my soul, and makes me whole
Its power sets my spirit free.

Jane Turner

They Are With You To Raise

A small hand
grasping yours
as you guide their way
through this big world.

They look to you —
for answers,
They look to you —
for security,
The come to you —
for affection,
They are with you —
to raise.

Be patient, be kind
help this little one grow —
broaden his mind.

Do not pervert it or tear it down
make the child feel important smile — no frowns.

Children are blessings
an investment in our future teach one to love
and the world becomes a better place.

Allyson Hester

O Hellish Fate

When will I see the dawning of eternity?
When will I leave this grade to view the universe entire?
When will all colors fade, to blend with nature's perfect jade?
When from this masked parade retire,
When in the grave my body's laid,
Then will I say the price is paid.
When I have wallowed in the mire,
And struggled through the fire,
And the lyre of my desire has lifted, lifted higher.
All my joys from Hades bought
Have cost me endless, wasted thought.
And all my grief has come to nought.
My dreams from Heaven snatched are gifted in array,
But they have smashed and drifted all away.
Jailed are my senses, bound with thongs of steel —
Caged in an unseen world, where only death is real
   Marooned and desolate,
   O hellish fate,
   Eternally damned fate.

Lydia R. Kraemer

Unfold Your Word

When I unfold Your Word I see Light
Let it strengthen me with power and Might
Your Love is seen through all the Pages
Through all History, down through the Ages

Your Word is a light unto my Path
It's your Greatest gift that I Have
To see how Jesus came and died for Me
To open my eyes so I can truly see

You've allowed me to know and love you
Your word teaches me what I can do
It teaches me I'll live in Heaven Alone
If I believe and trust in that love

Your Word is worth more than pure gold
I will trust it more as I grow old.
It teaches me of the maker of Heaven and Earth
Your Holy Spirit and the one new Birth

Your Word Teaches me if I have Faith
You will deliver me and see me through
It gives me power and strength
to do all I can do for you

Linda M. Dawson

My Australia

It could have been the Serengetti
It wasn't.
O vast land, endless in your grandeur,
A stale piece of crusty toast
Showing off.
Young girl dressed as a fairy
incandescent light frolics upon
your leaves, the gods down for a tune.
On and on and on they whirl . . .
Oh please end, I beg them to stop.
Milky Way vomiting star matter,
Swallowed by a ravenous horizon.
Up comes the sun a bully in the sky,
blazing fist swinging madly into the mud.
I feel so small in Australia.

Kristina Faragher

Art Always Has The Answer

You might not have all the answers,
but to use your mind and imagine
can bring forth a wonderful creation
if, you know how to make it happen.

Art is a piece of the artist's soul,
to express feelings or emotion.
But to understand what the art is saying
again, you need your mind and imagination.

It is art that helps us understand,
in ways other things cannot,
It is up to you to use your mind,
and pursue the answer in which You can only find.

Jonathan Paek

The Masquerade

He came into my life
bearing gifts;
love, hope, passion.

Winning my trust, he swept
me off my pinnacle of faithfulness,
and introduced me
to a dance of deceitfulness.

He rewarded me with ecstasies
beyond the imagination!
He laughed at
my fears and questioning.

He broke my spirit and
pierced my soul.
He robbed me of my knowledge and
understanding of the word.

At last, his identity revealed, he
left me, naked and lost;
seeking another victim of his Masquerade.

Barbara Valerio

The Highway

On the highway of life I began to cruise
which roads to follow, I started to choose
Behind the wheel lost in thought
memories of a dear old friend I sought
and for each turn around the bend
I prayed our paths would cross again
but the more I drove, the more I learned
there are just too many roads
and too many turns . . .

Dara Podber

What Will It Be Like?

What will it be like to see God on His throne?
What will it be like to know what is unknown?

What will it be like to walk on streets of gold?
What will it be like to never grow old?

What will it be like to have a mansion there?
What will it be like to never lose your hair?

What will it be like to see the angels in His glory?
What will it be like to hear of our life story?

What will it be like to live in the sky above?
What will it be like to always and forever love?

No one knows what these times will bring,
Only God the Father our Almighty, Heavenly King.

Laura Schmidt

To My Beloved Holly

It's not about things — it's all about feelings
Intangible emotions that lift our souls above that which we are.
Intangible, but yet as real and powerful as life itself.

Oh what could I give to represent my love?
I realize that nothing is sufficient to represent this.

Oh that I were a poet.
I could move your heart with words.

Oh that I were a sculptor,
I could fashion my feelings, then you could hold my love.

Oh that I were a carpenter,
I could build a life without pain for you.

Oh that I were a romantic,
I could swoon you away with me forever.

But alas, all I have to offer is a smile,
a kind word, a soft kiss and my love.

I cannot explain emotions
I can only give images and invoke emotions with tongue and pen.

Let actions show you my love,
Nothing less will do.

Scott Sudweeks

Space Of Freedom

Sunshine flows over the sparkling Lake Superior waters.
Big sphere of red-orange fire.
The warm white sands of the shore.
Skies of blue, with icy white pillow clouds.
Brings about a feeling of peace, serenity.
As I sit to watch the cool water wash up to its shores,
hits the rocks flies up high, higher and back out again.
I clear my head with the brisk, crisp air.
Fresh!
Warmth comes over me.
This is my space of freedom from all the worlds heart aches and pains.
Here I can breath breaths of life.
Here I am alive.

Susan A. Johnson

BATF

All power to the people? Flush the John!
Bite your tongue Jefferson, if you could see
Us now I wonder if you would agree
No Bill of Rights should have been placed upon
That document you dreamed in days long gone
When some men held that all men be free
And with those ten amendments they would be;
Power corrupts and now comes a new dawn.
That an informed electorate could rule
Themselves and curb the innate greed of man
For power over all of his own kind
But greed makes reason seem an arrant fool
No gospel, law, amendment you wrote can
Reform our delegates or change one mind.

Joseph E. Barrett

A Valentine's Lament

Our relationship is hard to define
I know only my emotions
and wonder of yours.
On this day hope and love spring eternal
but whatever will be, will be.
Fear not of being whisked away by cupid
for he is me.

C. Paul Weber

Made For Me

The years of depression, the
hardship we never forgot.
For a large family we always had
beans in the pot.
Dad accepted any work for pay
mother washed clothes on the board
and so tired at end of the day

My birthday was celebrated, when
I was the age of three.
Mother made a rag doll Annie for me.
She slept with me every night,
I held her close and oh so tight.

The only doll I ever had,
The puppy pulled her leg off and I was so sad.
Mother wiped tears from my eyes and
repaired it which made me glad.

Lucille Tripp

Imagine

Imagine what you would do
if all of a sudden, out of the blue,
someone came up and said to you,
"You can't do that, you're a Jew"

Imagine how you'd live you life
when if you were a Jew
then so must be your wife.

Imagine having a curfew each night,
imagine seeing the most terrible sights,
imagine living with the most awful, terrible, very bad,
no good Nazi fright.

Imagine having friends murdered,
or being taken away from your mom and dad.
And now you come and tell me that you have it bad.

Kate Bastida

The Ultimate Challenge

It is in times of uncertainty
When the strifes and troubles in life appear to be
unsurmountable!
It is then, at this crossroad,
That one will find what he is made of.
Many a man have tried hard, yet failed!
Many have lost their lives along the way!
Far too many concede to defeat,
Only to accept failure at face value.
Never to challenge the struggle.
There is nothing wrong with failing!
For to fail, helps keep sight with success.
One cannot succeed in all life's endeavors!
So to understand ones triumphs is great!
Yet, we must also live with our own shortcomings.
Let us look beyond these obstacles!
For to conquer these distractions,
Is to have accepted, learned from, and found . . .
That you have kept a perspective with failure.
Then, and only then, can we truly understand and appreciate
The conquest . . . Of having arisen to one of life's many challenges.

David Alan Doeing

Yesterday, Today, Forever

Matthew, 7:14
Are the three, times in life,
    That we all, must pass through,
The Maker, of Heaven, and Earth,
    Loves us, that means, Me and You,

He sent His only Son, Jesus the Christ,
    To be our Lord, and Saviour,
Jesus, took our sin's upon Him-self,
    Shed His, Blood that sin be covered over,

He gave us the Bible, to tell of things past,
    And times to come, while the world last,
So we have no reason, to doubt, but fear,
    Come, ask forgiveness, while still here,

Let's get our mind, and feet,
    Set on the strait and narrow way,
For on that path, we will meet,
    Jesus Christ, Lord, of all some day.

Orin P. Lewis

Windsong

Winds of the ocean, blow from me,
And blow to the one I love
Who lives on a green hill over the sea
In the land of the cooing dove.
Blow gently over the vine-clad house
That stands upon the hill
To ruffle the feathers of the vanishing grouse
And answer the whippoorwill.

Weep softly through the willow trees
To ripple the murmuring brook,
And tell the busy bumblebees
Of the love that she forsook.
Blow back the formless breath of life,
You salt winds of the sea,
For I come soon to take a wife
In the hills of Tennessee.

Sigh softly as the doves that sigh
In the humid afternoon
And sing of love that will never die
On our wedding day in June.

Cecil Haywood

Who's Complaining?

Who is the one who says it will be good
When the kids are grown and on their own,
That time doesn't count; we could
Pretend we're young and dance and play;
Ignore the creaks, the pain; don't groan
Because it sounds like we are weak, not gay
And uncomplaining?

Ah, ha! I checked it out today, to see who
Says all this to us who are old and gray.
As I thought, the speaker had hair so bright,
Skin soft, smooth. She may be, too,
Forty years but looked as though each day
Has been free of strife and struggle,
So, she is gay and uncomplaining!

Now I think it is time to pull up chairs,
Tell this cute and young and bright-eyed
Miss that time takes its toll on all of us.
It creeps up quick, sags our skin, greys our hairs.
So, young Miss, we'll see you there.
Who's complaining!

Doris W. Wagner

Life-Shoes

Life is like our shoes;
The old and the new.
The tired out and the kicked around —
Some are polished, some are not.

We have many pairs —
We have many colors —
We either fit well or we do not.
We get worn down and are thrown away.

Doctors, lawyers, teachers, psychologists
Mend us like a good cobbler.
They give us new life and resole us
So we are kept around a bit longer.

Chris Westbrook

Trail Of Tears

Minds are confused.
Eyes are burning as brown dust and sand swirls with harsh wind.
Many have fallen asleep on our trail, but unfortunately never wake up.
My legs are sand stained and scraped.
My moccasins are worn and full of holes, but yet we keep walking.
All the horses are restless and refuse to go to an unknown area,
but yet we force them.
Many of them have been left behind
so that there would be more food to go around.
Even though everyone is tired, we don't stop.
Even though everyone is hungry, we don't eat our fill.
We just keep on moving. I miss our old land.
I hate this Trail of Tears we are riding on.
I fear if I sleep, I will not be able to wake. So I don't rest.
Many of my family and friends couldn't wake.
All I have left is my father. He is getting ill though.
He is always tired, but I understand that well.
I have many cuts and sores that will never heal.
I can look down and see my ribs. I don't have very warm clothes.
I feel so bad about leaving my beloved land.

Jessica Scruggs

A Burning Hope

Days have passed to months and years,
I'm still hunting in the shadow of dark fears,
The glowing light, where are you?
I will chase and chase till I am blessed by you.
The heaven the earth, the mountain the sea,
Who stealthily cry in agony are waiting thee.
Oh blessed! Oh sacred! Oh glorious light!
To fight the evil darkness you are the only might.
The lashing waves of the angry sea,
The gushing blows of the crazy wind,
The howling of the neglected beast,
Are madly echoing in me in search of thee.

Amina Muniza Karim

Fairyland

Fairyland, where the fairies play,
  In the dusk of the night and the fire of the day.
Deep in the wood, lies the forgotten place
  Where the fairy hides her gnome-like face.
Look! Can you see it, just 'round the bend?
  Then the vision had faded, has come to an end.
Vanished from sight-wasn't it just there?
  Lost and forgotten, to no one knows where.
Perhaps on some golden September morn,
  The elves will come forth, with flowers to adorn;
And then just as quick as those sprites do appear,
  Away they will scatter if you venture too near.
Away to the land where the fairies play,
  In the dusk of the night and the fire of the day.

Tarelle K. Simmons

The Arena

My first real spectatin' at these games
The crowd's in an uproar, glad I came
And here they all stand up to pray
Looks like a sell-out, all the way
Must be some action, sure moves fast
Right from the front row to the last
Some thumbs is up, some thumbs is down
Some folks just turn their heads around
And I don't understand, but I'm sure tryin'
Which is Christians and which is lions

David W. Sjoberg

Those Wise, Wise Eyes

We're all familiar with the expression concerning the eyes —
  That the "eyes are the windows of the soul" and even if we tried
We could not disprove this observation that seems to perpetuate
  Itself as time goes by. There's not only a feeling that seem to emanate

From other's eyes but a whole personality may even express
  As in love, hate, anger and many emotions we may not even confess.
You've seen those who seem to radiate life and love and peace.
  They set your mind at ease and their company expresses like a feast.

And we all have experienced the darker side of negative expression
  Which radiates the opposite and leaves all involved, feeling somewhat less.
Wouldn't life be great if we could just try to keep a light burning
  In the windows of our soul — a light to guide a peace returning.

Lucile I. Burke

Family

Everyone always seems to be in such a hurry —
We have enough to think about, but shouldn't worry.
We spend our weekdays running to and from work
If we don't slow down, we will all go berserk.

These days, a one-income family may be a thing of the past;
With the cost of living, paychecks just don't seem to last.
But if we put our minds to it, and keep juggling our time
Keeping family and God first, with work one step behind.

Everyone should just relax and think about family;
Their love and support is the answer — you'll see!
Sharing quality time will mutually pay off,
Whether it's at the park, softball, or just playing golf.

The hard work is all worth it for just one hug,
It is better than lots of money in one big jug.
I am happiest when I know my children are having fun,
Whether they are at church or just hit a big home-run.

A child's smile is priceless and wonderful to see;
My day is made when they say they love me.
They are a gift from God and I hope and pray
We will always be together each and every day.

Sharon Waldrop

Untitled

I've let a rose
take the place of self-esteem
I've let your tears of contrition
fill the hole in my heart made by your fists
I've let your repeated promises
replace the words that have stripped me of my confidence
I've made your sudden anger
a substitute for feeling
I've become nothing.
I am — nothing.
I let you teach me that
because you love me.

K. Allyn

In My Dreams

It happened in my dreams last night, many years ago.
We met beside a babbling brook, playing in the snow.
I was about the age of twelve, she was only ten,
Still I ask, if that afternoon, I couldn't take her for a swim.

It happened in my dreams last night, many years ago.
We use to go to parks and beaches, when it wasn't cold.
Where we would romp and play a bit, like when we were kids.
Till now and then when it got dark, we got a little bold.

It happened in my dreams last night, just a few days ago.
She came to me and ask me if, she could have a key.
I took her in my loving arms, and held her close to me.
Then told her that she could have, anything that belonged to me.

Now we were wed for many years, our children are all gone.
But I still love her as I did then, back there on the farm.
It happened in my dreams last night, when she came back to me.
But I awoke to find that she, was not in my arms.

It happened in my dreams last night, many years ago.
We met beside a babbling brook, playing in the snow.
Now I'm in my seventies, just sitting home alone.
For my love of fifty years, to heaven had to go.

William A. McDaniel

Snow White

Oh, beautiful girl, America!
You are lovely, pretty, and bright.
I know you girl, Snow White,
In legend and in dreams of mine.

I am Oriental in origin,
A prince from the East.
I journeyed West to America, a far land
Because I love your beauty:

White as snow, sparkle as stars.
Wraps in blue robe of the oceans.
I long for your lips, red as blood,
Flowing in my body and yours.

Come here, Snow White! My princess.
Stretch arms in arms, lips on lips.
Let us offer the kiss of loving, passion.
Oh, my darling, Snow White, American.

Tien Van Pham

Dear Sister Ruth

Here's to my dear sister Ruth
Who n'er saw me when I had one tooth.
But now that we're older
We talk shoulder to shoulder.
She's learning that I have some couth.

Her kids now have found a new Aunt,
One who never said, "No, that I can't."
Although I'm afar,
They'll find out who I are,
Just a loner who'd write rather than rant.

So, just write my address in this book.
If I move, I won't make you all look
Far and wide, I may go
But just want you to know
In my heart you all have your own nook.

Carol L. Thompson

"Gems" Our Children

Their lives are undaunted, their world always
    haunted as they grow from day to day.
Their minds are like sponges as time and life
    plunges, its raw and unkind ways.
But you see it in their eyes, and it's etched
    in their faces. There is no trace of prejudice
and there are no races.
So let them grow and help them be strong, because
    the world to us does not belong.
For they are the "Gems" whose lives are uncut.
    Let them grown, let them prosper, And lets
not betray their trust.

Michael Pearson

Resting Place

The sky so blue above my head,
The grass so green below.
The sun is like a large red ball
Warming the place in which I lay.
The flowers with their fresh, sweet
Smell, the birds sing their lovely song.
The deer peeking from behind a
Bush, the creek soothing with its gentle sound.
Peace is all around, happiness
never far away, here in the gentle earth.
The softness in which I lay

Joyce Kempf

Doubts

How can I know of thee and thine
When I don't understand what's even mine

How can I know of he and she
When I can't fathom even me

What do I know of others — friends and lovers
When I do not know of me — of what I am to be

Is there a light in all the dark
That someday gives a tiny spark

A signal that I have truly found
My own true soul on hallowed ground

A soul that shares my doubts — my fears
A soul that's mine — all mine — for all the years

Jeanne E. Crittenden

Little Boy, Strong Youth, Grown Man

    I tell you, Old Woman: I am that little boy
Who heard Sojourner Truth ask in Delaware:
"Whom shall I send?"
And my young heart said — "Send Me!"
I am the strong, young athlete with set face,
Moving with cool aplomb and firm stride
Who walked through the jeering crowds that called me names
— I who heard Old Booker T say
"Cast down your bucket where you are — "And I said I would
And now you see the fully grown, young man
Standing tall in my three piece suit
With the knowledge that greater is He that is in me
Than he who is in the world
— I heard the voice of Frederick Douglass
Urging me to move steadfast, Oh Freedom.
And I said, I would.
    Old woman, I must go
And walk the road of Moses across America;
For I have three promises to keep.

Timotheus H. Carson

Untitled

The leaves are blowing softly
Whispering in my ear as I walk by
The colours are intensified by the grey sky
As if they were trying to brighten the world on their own
A cold breeze blows
Yellow and red fall around me
I reach to pull one out of my hair
It is brown along the edges
Winter will be here soon, I think
Pulling my sweater around me
Watching the leaf fall from my hands
Denise Kahle

Rain

As the raindrops do their dance across the sky
A tear shines
Freely dropping upon the earth
The tear falls from my eye

Quenching the land beneath us of the thirst within
My soul in turmoil
Feeling its powerful then easing plummet
My soul gives in

Their emotionless music playing softly in the distance
Yet my emotions waking
The wind joins in their song
My emotions freed of resistance

The cleansing of both sky and earth
A lightness fills my heart
The sun in all its glory awakens the earth beneath it
And I join in its rebirth

The sad raindrops upon the leaves now glisten
My eyes brighten at the beauty
Its warming stirs all that was hiding from the rain
Now I am free to listen
Lori A. Lawton

Where Does A Child's Life Begin

Where does a child's life begin,
At the age of one, five, ten, fifteen years of age.
Where does a child's life begin,
When she or he can say Mommy or Daddy,
or when does a child's life begin,
At the age of five, when Mommy says you know right from wrong,
or when she or he sees Mommy and Daddy fighting and asks them to stop.
Where does a child's life begin,
At the age of ten, when a child is caught kissing another child.
or when a child is caught stealing from another child.
Where does a child life begin,
At the age of fifteen when Mommy and Daddy say congratulation to
   your graduation,
or when the police says congratulation the other child you shot had died.
Where does a child's life begin?
John Pecoraro

The End Of A Long Journey

I think I'll start for home now. You come, too.
We've planted the seeds in the fertile land. The
warm nurturing sunshine and gentle sweet
smelling rain have freed the buds from their bonds.
The poppies and lilacs have weathered the storm
and bloomed beautifully. We've picked the
wretched dandelions and all the nasty
weeds. It's time to leave the flowers in their
garden. They know we won't be far off when
the fall arrives, that is, it if ever comes.
Dawn Leas

Ode To Caregivers

Somebody's grandmother, mother and wife —
What a full and interesting life!
What's behind those far-away eyes?
More than any of us realize!
Now she is old and tired and worn,
Looking lost and oh, so forlorn!
Help her become a part of this place,
Enter her world, find her a space.
Protect her from unfamiliar ground,
Let her babble and meander around.
Tell her you love her ever so much,
And she will respond to the feel of your touch!
Never forget to be gentle and kind,
Be cheerful, no matter what's on your mind.
God, in his wisdom, remembers your deeds,
And He will repay you as your life recedes!
Dorothy G. Wright

Confused

So intense are my feelings,
There is no escape
I'm running in circles
But my life stands still.
They all say they know,
but none ever feel
all of the lies, all of the tears
I put up a show, just to prove a point
actions are nothing, thoughts are kept.
Don't push away
Don't come too close
They all go, those who were never there
You think you are, but I know you aren't
You can't see, the light is blinding
Please just let go, I don't feel
myself hanging on. I don't know
who everyone is, but I know everyone's
name. I am lost, yet I know
exactly where I am.
Kimberly Van Heel

"Being With You"

In my dreams I see a place to play,
somewhere that I can stay all day.

I can not be harmed in any way,
all my fears are swept away.

All my fantasies can come true,
but the only one I really want is to be with you.
Amy Throndsen

Rose And The Honey Moon

My name is Rose Ann Larue.
Every night I go to the Honey Moon.
It's very beautiful and sweet
I don't know when we will meet
I would only wish for one wish a day
and this is what I would say.
"Honey Moon, Honey Moon big and round
I know that you are in the sky, and I am on the ground.
Now I will wish thankfully all a round
up and down from the sky and here on the ground."
But one night I cried, because there was no Honey Moon in the sky
So I sat on a rock for a long long time
and said "Honey Moon, Honey Moon come back to me"
then I looked in the sky, and there was thee.
Stefani Diane Peoples

Forest Retirement Community

The residents are putting on their finery
For Fall;
Brilliant crimson sweaters, gold sweat suits, and maroon
Mufflers
To cover the drying
And the dying.

But wrinkled brown spots
And gangly bare limbs
Are already showing;
And crisp, crackly, leafy discards
Are piling up for children to walk through.

A quiet visitor can hear
Sighing and moaning
And crying in the wind,
A perennial forgetting that dying
Is the way to
New Life.

Sallie Dewberry

Chile And Me

My passion revives beneath Chilean skies,
So far away from where I live,
Its people gladly welcome me,
And of themselves they freely give.

The Andes beckon from smoke-filled streets,
Oh, take me there señor,
I want to dance to songs of clouds,
Oh, take me por favor.

The great Pacific Ocean surf,
That splashes on the Chilean shore,
It sparkles through the bus's glass,
Have you heard the sea lions roar?

I toured the valley vineyards,
I tasted many wines,
I savored native Pisco Sours,
And pleasant Chilean times.

My passion cries for sunset skies,
And violins so sweetly play,
The memories of flirting smiles,
In Chile my heart remains this day.

Brenda G. Munford

Untitled

Were travelling on the cosmic wind, don't forget to bring your heart,
Tuck it safely by your side, cover it with care
Watch out for thorns on rosebud stems, they may create a tear.
Now travelling in this space and time our company is near.
So lovely is the touch of life, we feel no breeze of fear.
This Angel Guards us with her life, she spreads her wings with care
To shield us as we fall in love, were truly going there.
Her shadow cast a shielding shade to cover where we dwell
For in this place called love we live, she's living just to tell
The brightness of the sudden flash that signaled our embrace
When we decided holding hands to enter into this place
Dark corners were revealed with light, disappearing in a flash
Leaving just a small white dust that we call soot and ash
No past or future could we see except the living now.
To cast its image in our minds and spurn us on somehow
We begin by seeking outside ourselves that place where we should be
Our vision pierced the dark abyss and reflected back to us
Creating light beyond our eyes enfolding both of us
We fell into this place called love and dwelled and lingered there
Unfold it now and spread it out for all our friends to share

Daniel Swift Tyler

"... For Reasons ..."

Sometimes, in habit ...
Occasionally, in the heat of the moment ...
Often, in a session of passion ...
The times, my mind believed it was possible ...
And my heart desired it to be ...
... But it wasn't until today, it came true ...
I fell "in-love" with you!

Michelle L. Montague

Middle Of The Night

When I called to him that night, I didn't get a response
But I waited so patiently to find some answers
For I believe this was just a nightmare
Of which I would soon wake up from

But my eyes were wide open
For he had gone far away
On this dark and lonesome journey
Of which he would not return

But my questions that I had, could not be answered
For I was, somewhat confused
Of the thought of him leaving
Without even a word of goodbye

But the choice of him leaving was not his
It came as a surprise, in the middle of the night
But when I heard of the circumstances
I knew my heart had been torn apart

But his gentle eyes, I cannot forget
Nor will I ever forget his smile
Because he was so very special to me
In a way that no one else, could understand

Easter Johnson

The Sun

In the morning the sun hits us like
a tidal wave. The sun is like love.

It has its ups and its downs. Sometimes
it fills you with happiness and
sometimes with dreariness. Like
I said it's like love, very distant.

If you look at it, it might even blind you.
I guess you just have to take it slow.
If you take it too fast it might
burn and scar you. If you take it too
slow it may never come out. The sun
I guess is Love.

Nina Marie Petrelli

A Wheel

A wheel, within a wheel, circled by a wheel.
Which am I, is Us and which is them?
We alone, are separate, together all are one?
We depend, support, then reject again.
Join together, split apart,
Fear alone, afraid to need.
Drawn together, flee apart.
Must create, sustain and recreate,
Fear drives Up, love guides us,
We search to know, and hide from truth.
He calls us, not me — but us.
To join; as me, within us, circled by Him.
A wheel, within a wheel, circled by a wheel.

William B. Strange Jr.

"The Magic Of Love"

We have never seen a sunrise together,
nor have we ever seen it set.
But the love that we share
could never be put to rest.
The days come and they go,
and never once seem to last.
The whisper of your voice to me,
proves our love is for eternity.
In good and bad, you are here with me,
to kiss away the hurt and tears,
never leaving me alone.
With beautiful memories, our hearts will grow.
So have me in your memories tonight,
hold me near and very tight,
and I know you'll feel my love
each and every night.
So close your weary eyes my dear.
Sweet dreams instead of tears,
for I will always be around,and my love will always be there.

Joseph J. Shahayda

Checkmate Fate

This is a tale, a horrible tale,
About a friend of mine.
This friend of mine, this dear friend of mine,
Suffered a horrible fate.
This fate, this horrible fate,
Made him shrill and scream.
His fate, his horrible fate,
That made him shrill and scream,
Death was his fate, his horrible fate,
A taunting checkmate, was his fate.
His fate, his checkmate fate,
His taunting checkmate fate,
Pierced his heart with knife,
A cold and chilling knife.
This knife, this cold and chilling knife,
Made him bleed and bleed.
This was his fate, his horrible fate,
His taunting checkmate fate.

Dave Petty

A Poem Of Marriage

Ten years ago . . .
A lifetime. A mere drop in the Ocean of Existence.
I met you . . .
Friends. So Special, yet so Uncomplicated.
We took a Chance . . .
Our lives were filled with Questions. Our Hearts seemed so sure.

You made me Laugh.

We have Changed . . .
I know. We are Closer than ever before.
Sometimes we cling to each other . . .
Like Forlorn children. On a turbulent homemade raft.
Then we remember . . .

And we Laugh, together.

Sometimes I feel Sad . . .
A longing for the past. Family and Old Friends.
But, no Regrets . . .
Only Gratitude. Accepting me for the way that I am.
Encouraging me to take My Own Direction.
Loving me Unconditionally with Intelligence, Tolerance and
Admiration.
And for still making me Laugh.

Wendy Wrzos

A Strive For Clarity

I start with a thought and develop it into an idea.
One that I must share . . . with you.
With the world.
Only I can't tell you, I can't.
I am in a room with windows.
Everyone looks in at me, they see my mouth move.
They can't hear the words.
They see my eyes widened.
They can't hear the words.
They see the expressions on my face . . . the feelings in my heart,
they think they understand.
They can't hear the words.
I live in a soundproof room.
I strive for clarity, I strive to be understood.
I strive to break the glass . . .

John R. Scott Jr.

My World

High toward the sky we did climb,
to get a glimpse of His written rhyme.

Upward and skyward unto the peak,
did we pursue just to seek.

Once at the top did we discover,
a calmness that caused us to shudder.

Could we but see an endless sea,
a domain bequeathed for you and me.

From that perch did we come down,
to realize what we have found.

Roland B. Davis

Tree

Tree,
Giving its life,
feeling hate and strife,
This tree cannot flee,
but face its penalty.
How can this person cut this tree,
and be so mean and greedy?
Does he have a family whom is needy?
The man raises the axe,
Chop!!! Chop!!!!
Splinters of wood go flying.
A deafening sound fills the air.
I look.
The space where the tree was is now empty,
except for a stump.
All I can feel now is pain and sorrow.
But wait!
I see a girl planting a fresh new tree!
A hero she should be,
I hope they don't cut down that tree.

Jake Pinon

Voyage

I'm trying to name myself again
Seeking refuge in another strange bathroom
Mirror says foundling orphan huge-eyed and clumsy
Fill out the trembling outlines of my face
Too young today, and teen aged lost
Hoping discussion, dissection, and transcription
Will crystallize the liquid present of Thursday chatter
More lucid now, now than usual
Bathed in spurts of my own internal babble
Reflected girl with the black bag of everything
Drawing distracted swirl pictures and silently
Aspiring to divinity.

Amy Traub

What's Crashin' In?

The world is crashing in on me
The world is crashing in on me
For reasons I can not see
    The world is crashing in on me
    The world is crashing in
Oh why can I never win, for me?
    It seems everyone's yelling in poetry
    and
    Everyone's yelling at me.

Kathleen Setzer

Web And Life

The hours it takes to spin a spider web is a life time of you and me.
The web starts out small, like we do in life.
The web grows slowly around and around as we grow experiencing new things: Love, hate, friendship, heartache, freedom, loneliness, happiness, sadness, birth, and death.
The web is broken by some unexpected monster, as our life is broken by some unexpected monster. But time cures everything. The web is rebuilt just like our life is rebuilt back to our utopia.
The web and our life are never expecting a monster, but if he comes again we can always rebuild.
If the spider can't catch his life in his web he moves. Just as we move on to new land to catch our life, whatever it may be. Then we both rebuild in hopes of a better life in our new utopia.
Maybe living and dying as neighbors.

Michael David Somich

Chocolate, Chocolate (For Kids Like You And Me)

Chocolate, Chocolate, I love my chocolate bar,
I like it better than vegetables by far.
If everything was chocolate I'd not refuse to eat,
With chocolate syrup in my milk and chocolate eggs so sweet.

Chocolate, Chocolate, when I grow up there'll be
A kingdom of chocolate for kids like you and me.
I'll have a swimming pool with melted chocolate
You can jump right in and sip and sip and sip.

I'll build around my house a fence of chocolate bars,
Chocolate trees with mint leaves that reach chocolate stars.
When I become sleepy my moon with chocolate beams
Will beam me up to ride the milky way of dreams.

Chocolate, Chocolate, if ever it should rain,
It'd rain chocolate sprinkles on chocolate cookie lane.
How can one be angry, have a sour face or fret
Living on Sweet street in a world of chocolate.

Eleanor F. Basinger

A Sonnet

On some mornings the sun shines through my windows
Casting shadows on the wall
Of the bars across my cell
Then on my bed they fall.

Doubly trapped within my cell, I lay upon my head
Another day of squandered life, another day of dread
Beneath these shadow bars where hope is lost to all.
Another challenge for my soul to answer this day's call.

But in between these shadow bars are wider bands of light.
It is here I lose my fear, finding answers to my plight.
I find within these lighter bands all darkness is dispelled
fear and apprehension, doubt and worry quelled.

No longer trapped beneath the bars, now my soul sees clear
I can survive another day! Perhaps a week. A year?

Robert Roston

Night's Dark Tail

Swiftly, night approaches on padded, furry paws,
stalking his enemy, light
The tread of night is sure and stealthy and,
with teeth bared and claws sharpened, he surprises his victim.

Woodland wails erupt as night switches his dark tail,
shadowing what should have been a vigilant hawk's meal.
Night assails the grumpy owl
who hoots his defiance as he flies in search of food.

Night curls around the tiny cub,
and purrs his lullaby to forest babes.

As the moon glides into satin black,
night rises from velvet haunches, growling to no avail.
He climbs an Oak, rustling leaves as he ascends.
Attaining the highest bough, night waits disdainfully,
hissing dire threats at the misty moon.
The moon dims, leaving night the victor.

Night dozes, unaware that his enemy has planned a fresh attack.
Dawn approaches and the fight is quick and merciful.
Night hides within the deepest cave
to lick his wounds and wait his turn.

Linda Darlene Evans

God's Painting

Lord, as I traveled the highway early one morning,
just as the break of day came dawning.

I was captured by your work of hand,
as you spread light upon the land.

The beauty that morning that filled the sky,
was breathtaking and a wonder to my eyes.

The blue turned to pink with a touch of gold,
then came yellow, purple with red, my precious Lord,
it was beauty to my soul.

At a distance I could see the sun's streaking rays,
through the clouds, leaving me in a daze.

Oh Jesus, if I could have stopped the world, and time could have stood still, but the traffic on the road wished I would speed up for it was not your beauty that gave them their thrill.

Someday Lord, I know those skies will open up and you will come for me.
On that day Lord all the speeding world will stop to see.

Sue Poole

Winter Day

One mild winter day
you came my way.
We knew from the start
that this love was straight from the heart.
We figured that this love would last
because we had learned from our past.
The years have gone by and now we are on number Seven.
Through all of the ups and downs, it still feels like Heaven.
We have joined our families together as one,
and each day we learned to have more fun.
You made me very proud when you became my wife,
it is something I will cherish for the rest of my life.
I love you all more in every way.
I thank God for that special winter day.

Brian L. Poppe

Why Them?

Why them? Babies born before their time.
Prematurity their only crime.
The pain, the sorrow,
The waiting, the guilt.
The wishing, that I could take their pain away.
The prayer that it will be O.K.
The hoping to take them home at the end of the day.
We can't give up hope,
But pray for strength to help us cope.
To listen, to understand,
To give a helping hand.
It's no one's fault, no one's to blame,
But still there's the pain of knowing what you could lose.
Better doctor's and nurses we could not choose.
To bring home a healthy child is well worthwhile.
You may think the circumstances are greater than mild.
Nothing is more precious than a child.

Ashley Savage

Our Deep Song

Don't become disheartened my love, the tears
I shed while in your arms were tears of joy.

What ecstasy
What fulfillment
What total love

Looking into your eyes becoming lost in our love.
Your gentle caress
Your soft lips
Upon mine

Our bodies engulfed in one another, coming with the
rhythm of our breathing into each other being.

Rhythm
Rhapsody
Song

Carol Manzano

"Perpetual Productions"

I went to the river to look and to see.
I heard from the Lord of the gods over there.
I've heard of a Sword that turns in every direction.
They shine in the Glory of the Fruit of Perfection.
Jesus took me down into the river, the great river Euphrates.
I descended down into the River to see.
The depths of the Creatures, iniquity, He has them imprisoned there.
There is nothing but deception, in destruction.
Before the Flood of Noah, they were cast down by the Sword of the Lord
The Queen of Babel, seeks her frog to kiss,
He can draw fiery missiles from the Rock.
The Lord can open the Rocks of Life giving streams of Water.
And the Lord can turn the Table on You.
You were a Name and Are a name, But your Name shall be erased.
Christ is a Rock on the Path in the way.
A Resting place for those whom are willing to Live.
I Looked at the River from its four sides that I see.
There's nothing over there greater than HE that in ME.
In the Dark Room, there is No darkness to God.
In the New Room, Holy Works To His Majesty!

Brian F. Houle

To Kathryn

She said, "It's naught to write a poem."
I try and try and still can't do 'em.
The rhyme and meter, the tone and feet,
I'm up all night until I'm beat.

Is anapest the thing to do?
Is dimeter one foot or two?
Is verse that's free the modern thing?
And how will dactyl, trochee swing?

And how does one select a rhyme?
A a, b b. is that the line?
Or is a b. a b the best
Technique and style and all the rest?

I sit and think, my head's aspin,
Is psalm a her, an it, or hymn?
"Try parody," they all advise.
Can't find a thing to paradise,

I can see that poetry
Is not to be my cup of tea.
I'll have to stop and then admit it
But, by gosh, I went and did it.

Max Hammerman

Slept

As you slept,
I sat and watched.
Watched you dream,
Thinking what you could be dreaming about.
I sit and watch,
I stare at your beauty,
Stare as you dream.
I could sit here all night,
Just watching you dream.
A halo of beauty surrounds your sleep,
So peaceful and serene,
I have to sit and stare,
I could stare all night.
I wish I could tell you my dreams,
But I can not,
So I sit and stare into your dreams.
You dream asleep,
I dream awake,
One day we will dream together.

Douglas Pregman

Project

It took place on a feria
It was a holometabolism
It took hyperalimentation
Indemnization was not required
Death almost came from hyperemia
Magnificent metabolism resulted

Its shape was cabalistical
Its body was bulbul
Its color was burnt sienna
Reminding us of bronchia
Its meal was of butyraceous

Our attitudes were not bumptious
We were betulaceous
We were on beta-adrenergic blocking agent
It was like a pageant
We're of berkelium
Our place was of beryllium
We were at a place of berth
On the planet earth

Randall Winston Pretzer

The Tapestry Of America

The United States of America
Is a rich melting pot,
Brimming with ingredients
And overflowing with thought.

It is an ornate tapestry of interwoven threads
That depict culture, career, tradition and life.
Each thread is a symbol of a person or deed
And the stirring events of triumph and strife.

This carpet has imperfections.
A single loop may go wrong.
But the entire piece all woven
Is extraordinarily strong.

Unravelling and fraying
Are forces to combat.
We are mighty and powerful,
Not a weak doormat!

All that has passed
And the web of eternity
Will be recorded
On this living tapestry.

Wendy L. Schmid Tetrault

To Be Or Not

Here I ponder life
As countless numbers ponder life's maze.
Filled with strife
Constantly living what seems a haze,
Looking for that silver lining
Everyday the sun shining.

Will I find peace of mind
As I wonder from day to day
That pot of gold will I find
To have life go my way
To grasp the golden ring it seem
Is only just a dream.

Maybe I shouldn't dwell on the negative
Maybe I should be glad to be alive
I have but one life to live
Happiness is all I should strive
Or maybe it's true what most say
You can buy with wealth
HAPPINESS EVERYDAY!

Jeremiah Blackwell Jr.

Image Of A Mystery

Our God a Holy Mystery,
Never changing and capable of all.
We sense the complete essence of his being,
Happily awaiting his beckoning call.

Not ever alone His presence always near.
Forging on with assurance as we live our lives here.
For with our God there will be no fear,
If we live in his word all our journeys will be clear.

He is the flowers in the mountains,
In the eyes of a loving friend.
We hear Him in the music,
And on the gentle winds.

If you have felt his power of healing,
And seen the wonders His love can mend.
Then you must share with all man kind,
That our Lord shall come again.

Connie Lind

Dreams

A third of my life is escaping reality
Off in some dream world you see
Visions and thoughts of a uncontrolled mind
Reality in them I cant find
Without them they say we go insane
But I don't remember them so whats to gain
So maybe there are two worlds only are mind knows
And while one sleeps the other one grows
Or maybe the insanity of the world causes sleeping minds
To unfold as are body curls
Or are there to persons in this flesh
One walks the day and one walks the rest
So what is the purpose of fading into some dreamland
Into a world we don't understand
Or is it the other way around
That in this dream world were boss and can be found
And in the awaken world were lost and bound

Two thirds of my life I will see
And one third of it will be a dream to me

Debbie Ewing

The Saddened Face

The saddest face I have ever seen was on a child, aged eight or nine.
Time has passed, but for reasons unknown I couldn't get her out of my mind.
We had gone with some friends to the city, for lunch and to see a show
Amid traffic, horns and wailing sirens, and bright neon lights aglow;
in the crowds of people my eyes focused on a woman who guided a child.
I seemed to be drawn like a magnet, for the little girl had no smile.
I looked at many faces of the strangers who passed us by,
but no one cared to notice the small child that caught my eye.
Her lifeless sleeves hung limp and empty, waving with each puff of air
though her steps were quick to follow the older woman in her care.
For just fleeting moment I tried to vision her at play;
She couldn't ride a bike, swing or see-saw, or hold a book in any way.
Never could she hug or play with baby dolls, or jump rope with a friend,
to even dress or feed her-self, on others she must depend.
Had drugs or medication caused this child to live a life of gloom?
What had prompted the growth of malformation, or disfigurement in the womb!
On each shoulder grew a baby hand that looked like tiny angel wings;
and yet we worry needlessly each day about silly trivial things.
When-ever I feel disgruntled, my disappointments I quickly erase,
for there comes to mind the armless figure, the little girl with the saddened face.

Ruth V. Shillito

Letting Go

Too many fights, too many tears
too much hurt over the years
too much pain, kept inside
has built a wall, to protect my pride
too much anger, fills my soul
too much sorrow, took its toll
this is reality
and I can't go
with one true remedy
to learn to let go
Letting go
is easier said than done
Forgiving and forgetting
is a battle rarely won
so let my tears
carry the pain
away with the river
away with the rain
I tell myself to start anew
I'll find the strength to see it through

Maggie Valladao

. . . Tomorrow?

It is daybreak. Another day — I try to reach her.
The task for me is impossible, yet I still must try.
I should not pity her; for my pity she does not want.
I cannot get too close for fear that I will break.
We live in the same house, yet in different worlds.
How can I make her see? I know not with her eyes.
How can I make her hear? I know not with her ears.
My heart is breaking, but I know I must be strong.
She stumbles through the day as I do through the midnight.
To light her way — Oh! I wish that I could.
But her darkness is too thick to penetrate.
To put the world at her feet would be so simple.
But is the world what she wants? How can I know?
Not through her eyes and not through her words.
If my eyes I could give; the world she could see.
My ears I would give; the birds she could then hear.
But does she want them? Or is her world enough for her?
Her mind a open field where the flowers have not yet bloomed.
Is her heart scarred with pain she has to bear? Will I ever know?
It is now dusk. Another day I have not reached her.

Jenger Laine Hutto

My Grandfather

I remember seeing my grandfather unlike himself,
Lying there so cold and lifeless.
I also remember hoping he would
open his baby-blue eyes once more.

I remember hearing crying and grieving people;
hearing his rolling laughter, while playing with his
grandkids, and the slamming of the hearse door.

I remember smelling the unforgettable odor of a
funeral-home, the various kinds of women's perfume,
and all the elegant flowers in the room.

I remember tasting a lump in my throat as big as
a fist, the taste of love when upon my cheek he'd kissed.

I remember touching his unlively body, and wondering
why he wasn't touching me, why he had to go, and why
it had to be.

Kerry Rodgers

Grandma

At home I feel safe from all worldly fears
Your gifts were generous my first 12 years . . .
My stuffed bunny, a comfort. My soft doll, a friend.
A story worth telling of love He did send.

The big old house and the garden of flowers
Opened my eyes and filled my heart for hours.
The fun we had and the stories we read
Helped me weather the storms I had ahead.

Thoughts of you linger, they're greatly preserved.
Your sunshine and warmth was never deserved.
Your soft voice and your singing I always will miss.
Yes, snuggling and cuddling and your sweet kiss.

You've been gone a long time — I'm almost grown.
You gave me more happiness than anyone I've known.
I've loved you, dear Grandma, you've been my best friend
Only God in Heaven knew why it should end.

Someday in the future when the world gets too old
We'll walk again together — but on streets of gold
I'll pray and have faith and serve God on high
And before I know it, the time will draw nigh.

J. L. Lange

The Man Of God

Man is kind
Man is good
Man is wonderful
but Man can't compare to God
God is something out of this world
He's not replaceable
but reuseable over and over again
No matter what's the problem
God will solve them
Man may get tired of you
God will not
for he wants you to come to him
do as you're told
Your prayers will be answer don't look to man
look to the one who created you
Who made you to who you are today hold on
Your dreams will be coming Just keep praying
and look to the Man
the Man of all Men
the Man of God

Verda Essex

On A Friend Dying "Acceptance"

I have a friend who's very ill . . . she may surely die
Her cancer's back and in control . . . there's not much left to try.

The chemo may or may not work . . . and if it does how long
will it be this time before something else goes wrong?

Her friends and family will pray for her . . . and try to
understand whatever answer comes to them is strictly in His hand.

One day at a time is what we're told is the only way
to live . . . I pray dear God you'll give to her all the
days you have to give.

Kathleen McCrary

Searching

Have you searched for God in the meadow
or out on the stormy sea?
Have you seen His face in the clouds above
or heard His voice in the trees?

Or have you lived in selfish pleasure
and idled the moments away
Then suddenly come to realize
You've never learned how to pray?

It's sad to see people searching for self
in this dying world of sin
When the only real way to know who you are
Is to lose yourself in Him.

Betty L. Raines

Dark Before Dawn

I am acquainted with the darkest nights
Which know no bounds and will not let me be.
The nights spent in sorrow, anger or fright,
Or in darkness unending as the sea.
The hours melt forever into each other
And time stands still for lack of will to move.
Thoughts are often projected by the weather
And music whispers soft but does not soothe.
The night he died he left and left forever
It was by far the darkest night of all.
The heart was bruised and cut and severed,
And angels wept for his eternal fall.
But now the sun creeps shining, bright and soft
And thoughts of him are banished, for now, and lost.

Joy Bellmay

Labyrinth Construction

Funny fellow, sometimes twelve, sometimes eighty
Sculpt your orbit in a languid, accessible way
Your goals are crystalline, and stowed in the gray
In whole shared with none but, in piece shared with some

Honesty, your ultimate bequest, may never be delivered
Too risky, to treacherous to remember

Realist you bellow to the golden pink skies
Unlikely, with a core so mellow and frightened

Gray skies leave you twisted on the cold straw dreams of what is to come
You have waited for the equidistant which was and now moved to recollection
Still, you linger on
Each message learned has cost you much
And still you move in easy orbit, never learning what this learning cost

No change in sight as the day star sets amidst the gray
Funny fellow driving around on the labyrinth you construct

Adele A. Etcheverry

Merry Christmas — 1995

Nowadays it's like in Hickory, Dickory Dock,
As at home we sit all around the clock.
This is due that after a lifetime of travel
And adventure we now have seen it all unravel
It's hard to explain to our friends around the globe
With only this — another Christmas letter to probe —
Why this should be at our early age
As we are still in our eighties on this page.
We can't really lay claim to having seen it all
Because Eleanore is still able but not old Paul.
Our winters in Florida are also on hold
Our time with Medics is too much to be told.
The calendar is full with appointments to keep —
A tiresome nuisance but does fill the week.
Lest you think this all is but a tale of woe
Life still looks good we want you to know.
Now we must mention our few days at Bucks Lake
For the first time our stay was shorted for Paul's sake.
To our friends up there and over the world so wide
We send you our Season's Greetings this Yule Tide.

Paul Ziegelmaier

Ode To Alvin York

Over the top the many young blokes went
To go forth to where they were sent
To seek the glorious success of a victory
Upon a ground that is not the playing ground of a gent

Upon this ground those before them did impede
The abounding efforts made by others in deed
By those who had occasioned to proceed
Those who now hurled themselves forth in the moment of need

Those before them did in their moment of surprise
Bring themselves in their might to arise
And began upon their heights to surmise
That they were host to a party of size

Though challenged by this unanticipated sight
To array and flex the cumulation of their might
To bandy now where from here would go this night
That had for so long for so many been such a fright

Upon this play ground of debate stood a fork
Where men from Sacramento to New York
Would face the stifling specter of the Stygian Stork
Including one whose name was Alvin York

David LaValley

Her Black Feather Boa And Baby Doll Eyes

It was the time of the black feather boa and
all those leopard printed things,
sometimes garish high platform shoes that did not match and
she walked like she was trying not to fall down in them.
She had those big big Japanimation eyes, huge like baby dolls and
Disney fish and she felt like an actress in a bad movie,
standing on the street corner in a far away city
where she had never been.
The backalleys and the beer/sweat/cigarette smells
stuck to her clothes - even when she got home
and took them off she could not forget.
She danced out too close to the edge of the pier
one day in the wintertime when there were no tourists fishing
and holding hands looking at the ocean.
She spun around to the music inside her head and
briefly felt no more pain.
One bare foot came down from a twirl on her toes
but she lost her balance. She did not feel the wood beneath her,
only the push of the wind and falling. Her eyes snapped open
from behind shades that had not fallen off to see the ocean
rushing up to meet her. Her breath caught in her chest
and she realized in the seconds before she hit that she would
never again dance too close to the edge.

Tiffany Bolz

The Eastern Star

There was a feeling of magic in the air,
That filled the heart with unsaid prayer.
A very bright star shown high above,
To light a manger with divine love.
For, this is the night when love came down,
From heavens most glorious king.

The sky had changed from night to day,
Their halos were so bright.
Shepherds in the fields below
Fell to their knees in fright.

"Fear not", sang the Angels in voices soft and clear,
"Born with grace, the Prince of Peace",
Is found this very eve.
Laying in a manger adorned in swaddling clothes,
His mother Virgin Mary is singing lul-la-bies of joy.

The shepherds did not answer,
They all stared at the sky.
Glowing with hundreds of angels, singing praises
to The Lord on high.

Cynthia Delligatti

"Ardor Afar"

Like a ship sailing in the distance, I see you.
Like a muffled whisper, I hear you.
I see the wind blow the leaf away rapidly,
Like the leaf, I feel you.
The more I see you, the
More I realize you're not here.
The pain is fatal and the wound deepens.
Breath on my hair,
Arms around me,
Heartbeat on my lips,
Never to feel.
If only you could see.
But what would you do?
The answer still rings harsh in my head,
Nothing.
Although I could never reach.
I wonder,
If you knew,
Would it change?

Jackie Raimondo

Missing You

My love it was twenty years ago today
Yet it seems as if it were yesterday
Suddenly you were taken from me
But again some day your face I'll see.

I still love you so much my dear
Almost as much as if you were here
I miss your warmth and tenderness
The special feel of your caress.

Your once warm body has grown cold
Unlike me, you will never grow old
You will never know the sorrows
That I will feel with my tomorrows.

Your handsome sweet face others can't see
Is always here in front of me
Sometimes in my mind, I still feel your touch
That wonderful feeling I loved so much.

Sleep well for now my love
Dream of me from your home above
Someday God will come for me
Together forever we will be.

Chloe Ann Capps

"Hear My Voice"

Writing my thought and experience, as they unfold.
Knowing that I've touch someday heart and soul.
There must be someone, who would hear my voice speaking such
familiar words, and feel what's to-be felt for we stand alone;
Hear my voice, share the Joy of my laughter, and feel my pain!
Understand that we're one in the same.
Friends, my words will speak for me.
Respect if you will the simplicity and style: presented to
you worthy, and worthwhile.
We've felt the winds that we can't see,
We've drunk the waters, which have no taste, yet our thirst is
quenched. Though our hearts beat rhythmically, we can't tell,
yet blood flows from cell to cell.
We've lived to see and often try to explain the mystery that
heaven must proclaim
So sense you're out there some distant near,
Hear my voice:
As the curtain of darkness rises knowing that the sun doesn't lie;
come let us gather to reread the words of the poet if to find
and believe what has yet to be Discovered.

William E. Alexander

Flowers

Flowers fall to the ground,
Sadly weeping all around,

Petals crush beneath thy feet,
Quietly whispering soft and sweet,

Precious lives not yet full,
Are silently ending with a pull,

Children tug not knowing why,
These beautiful flowers shrivel and die,

Their right to live has been swept away,
When the children want to play,

How unfair it is for they will never see,
Another ray of sunlight or a busy bee,

The morning dew won't settle there,
Upon the stems that now are bare,

All because a child's hand,
Has taken the flowers from the land.

Rebekah Buzolich

Mother Oh Mother

I feel the coolness of the rain,
And it brings back memories of you again,

The love and tenderness you showed to me,
Now long passed I finally see,

You gave me life and showed me the way,
Telling me of what was to be if I
   should sway,

And as I grew I thought you'd always
   be there,
I was living never having a care,

Then in a fleeing moment day became night,
Darkness fell upon me as though I
   had no sight,

What once was will never be again,
For your life had finally come to its end,
Mother Oh Mother who's love gave me
   the will to fight,
I will see you again when I'm
   called into the light.

April F. Mora

For Mom

The last four years have been so hard watching your mind fade away
Now we have to say "good-bye" as in front of us you lay.
As we think back over all the years both you and Dad were there,
We cannot remember ever when you didn't have time to share.

You nursed us through our illness and chaffered us about
And in all the years we remember, we never did without.
You showed us so much love in everything you did
And both had so much pride in us and all our kids.

So thank you for the laughter and the good times that we shared
Thank you for the things you taught us all with love and care.
Thank you for your helpful ways, the comments, hints and such
And even when you're criticized, it really wasn't much.

We only hope as you looked at us with eyes that just seemed to stare
That somewhere in your fading mind you remembered how much we care.
So Mom we say "So long" for now as we all feel ever so sad
But happy knowing that in Heaven you are again healthy and with Dad.

Nancy DiMaio Giangiulio

The Crags Of Thought

All through the ages Man has climbed
As the secrets of God he's sought
Scaling the heights though dim and obscure,
Climbing the crags of thought.

When he reaches an apparent summit
Broad vistas turn and twist
And endless beyond, rise crag upon crag
Shrouded in fog and mist.

Endless, forever the search progresses
The boundaries of Truth diverge.
Crag upon crag, they urge man onward,
But the boundaries of mind converge.

Though dimly and darkly the mind perceives
The wonders God has wrought
Still must we climb, step by step
The endless crags of thought.

Edwin M. Johnson

Truth, in the end.

And a dark black past erupts from somewhere deep inside.
As some mucky thing eats away the last of my humanity.
The heavens fall to sunder from a prick of pain that once was my sanity.
A longing dream I once had, now just loose words on a liar's tongue.
Dark fall, where upon I enter the hellish twist of fate that sups on my desires.
Wisps of thought elude my gentle caress of hate.
The well's dry and the dream has died.
In hope there is death and wishes turn fatal just as lies desire to be the truth.
Pain
Hatred
Joy
love is divine but death is eternal

Glenn Waterman

Passing Reflection

Hope is fading from my soul
I ceased listening to your music
a long time ago
pain reacts when the melodies flow
it is easier to listen to the silence
hear the collapsing of my heart
ice breaking on the lake of insincerity
to be so grand posing high upon your stage
your lights gleam so brilliant
The light is dim in my eyes

Lisa Marie Griffiths

Your Shadow

In your sleep I watch over you.
In the darkest hour I am know to you.
You do not realized the power for which I have over you,
    but you can feel it.
I am, like a phantom, a soul without a face.
My heart is still until you enter my mind.
Then the racing of my heart nearly kills me.
The love for which I am with you.
You love me too but you are not aware of it.
When midnight comes I cover your face with my hands and it
    strengthens me.
I am part of you that is taken for granted.
You think that I am item for which you can just ignore,
    but I am not.
I follow you where ever you go.
In the dark I am invisible but you can see me.
I do not hide only because you do not care.
When I look at you, you look away.
Please dear love, do not fear me for I know all you secrets.
You hide them in me. I am you shadow.

Wendy Wise

Be Your Best

Try your best in all that you do
but make sure it's not to impress others — just be you.

Keep in mind how truly special you are,
there's no one like you near or far.
Dream your dreams and watch each one come true;
always remembering, just be you.

Never be afraid to fall and stumble
but keep your faith nearby always be humble
The progress you make is never a mistake
it comes from a little hard work and God's grace.

Some lessons can only be learned by heartaches and sorrow
the person you are today isn't the person you'll be tomorrow;
but if you're strong in character, inspired by truth
and grounded by faith the person that you'll become will be
the best of you

Tamara A. Gates

Against All Odds

My knees are knocking
    but I'm standing at the plate
This road has been long and rocking
    But finally a big league date.

I'm up from the minors
    from Hardknocks U.
My hands are tense and my heart's beating too.
    A fast ball and it's over the fence!

But it's a swing and a miss
    Hey I've been there!
Back on the bench
    But I'll get back in that box with a double dare.

Ball one, outside what a call.
    The next one, a curve low and inside, Strike!
Could it be true? I don't care.
    I'm swinging till I'm blue,
because I've watched enough balls go by
    because I've graduated from Hardknocks U.

Steven J. Lytal

Etchings Of Love

For every little hand clutching Mother's knee
For every pair of little feet walking piggyback on Daddy's
Or for every pair of little eyes staring in wide open wonder
There is a sketching of trust
Etched in all humankind.

For every pair of little arms reaching out for a hug;
For every little heart going thump, thump, at a rapid beat,
And for every little body wrapping around Mother's skirt
Speak of a sketching of love
Etched in all humankind.

For every little grandchild seesawing on Grandpa's leg
We are reminded of the need for bonding,
That for love no child should have to beg,
And that any sketching of love should grow big,
Rippling through the rivers of life in all humankind.

Every little hooded head, every little smile,
And every little chuckle
Speak of a sketching of unadulterated sweetness, sweetness,
And that there is an etching, sketched in the beginning,
Of love, trust, and sweetness in all humankind.

Ann Hobgood Wrenn

Children

What have we done to our children,
By letting them grow up too fast?
They can't read, write, add, or subtract,
And history's just in the past.
They go on-line with computers,
They're making babies and killing
In their gangs or by themselves,
Just seeing which is more thrilling.
When they're caught and alone they cry,
"Accept responsibility?!"
What do you mean, it's all my fault?
It can't be me, it's the tv!"
Can we undo what has been done?
Or is it too late for us all?
Let's teach them in school and at home,
There's more to this world than the mall.
What have we done to our children,
By letting them grow up alone?
Fix what we've done to our children.
Don't make them adults 'til they're grown.

Kathryn Bates

The Men In Blue

They stand in line, on graduation day
chest pushed out, with heads up high
proud of the star, that is being worn
serving the city, where they were born
they are cursed and spat at, called dirty pigs
"hold thy temper, "you dare not explore,"
police brutality, is what they'll shout
all over the headlines, what it's all about
now you do a good deed, go about your job
no one to see, the good you have done
one gloomy day your duty calls
slain by the hand of assailant unknown,
be it knife or a bullet, that scars the spot
instead of the star, proudly worn on your heart
how brave he was, all voices will say,
but it's to late, praise he cannot hear,
lets get together, and praise them now
for the symbol they stand for
and the good they have done.

Rose M. Gasca

Untitled

As an immortal child, I watched the sea,
    I moved along impoverished cobblestone streets.
As a youth looking fearfully at life, I flee,
    Yet, from night to dawn of daylight, we shall meet.

In a flood of progress,
My beliefs are shattered,
Revealing an untamed, uncreated heart,
    Neither hot or cold,
    Nor bought or sold.

Bereft of the fascinations of fairies,
Under staves of barbarians,
We only know we.
    Matter it not how we leave youth,
    Whether it reveal secrets of truth.

Like the placid streams of night,
I reveal the pale moon light.
    From the ridge to the valley,
I step from shadow to shadow.
    Upon the hill of kings, I see a sepulcher,
    And I am home.

Joseph L. Huelsebusch

Stephina

At Christmas time you are a special Christmas gift to me.
Throughout the year you have endured my failings and faults
    that sometime cause you pain, sadness and anger too.
My dear I know you are not an easy forgiving soul but listen
    to my plea of sorrow and anxiety too.
For I am a weakling too and I suffer painfully when I see you
    sad and angry too.
But I love you so and I look to you for compassion, comfort and
    love to survive the loneliness I feel when you are apart from me.
My dear, you are stronger than I for I am a weakling without you.
Your support and love for me is my fortitude for all my fallings.
As you know I have so many.
Yes my dear when you take me in your arms and tell me
    how much you love me.
You give me strength, hope, joy and happiness which are
    the breathof life for me.
The spirit of your love gives me the courage to keep on living
    from day to day.
Yes my Stephina, you are my special Christmas gift that Jesus
    gave to me to help me live from year to year.

Pedro Gutierrez

Once Bound, Now Free

Hopelessness and despair is the world in
which I dwell, a weakened heart crying out
to be rescued from this hell
    As one with darkness, he once again came
whispering his promises then leaving his stain
    Empty are the days that come, empty are
the days which go, bound am I in his lifeless soul
    As though a star fell from the heavens
my eyes looked upon this great light, as
if wings of an angel in my heart He took flight.
    My soul, awakened and I heard His tender
voice say, 'I died for you and all my promises
are forever true' To the floor my knees
went, my soul filling with the spirit He
sent look at me, can you see
once bound, now free praise God
    I'm free

Caroline Cress Dixon

Untitled

The young and the old
Share a wisdom.
Their eyes wide with wonder
Behold magic
Where others see none.
But as the children grow — they forget.
Living by the ticking of clocks
In constant motion.
Driven. No time for foolish whimsy.

Only when their bones creak
And hair turns gray do they become
Again as little children.
Wisdom returns
Secrets long forgotten — remembered
And they laugh and play,
And sing and pray
Like those children
So long ago
At their mothers' side.

Lynette Brewer

Predication

I have been reflecting on the things gone by,
on the things undone.
Wondering what time has in store for those who are not here.

Who will be inspecting the things I will try,
the things left upon
timeless wandering and more, by those who do not fear?

Will they be rejecting the things they spy,
the things left unsung?
Perhaps starting anew, preferring new creation, the proclaiming of jeer?

Will they be accepting of the things they descry,
of the things they can spawn
and enhancing, modifying: A new situation of change now in gear?

So, while I am reflecting on the things gone by,
on the things undone,
wondering what time will have in store for those who are not here,

I will consider it respecting to the things I did try,
to the things I dreamed, not yet done.
I will dream of a door through which is the expectation
of the things I hold dear.

Mark W. Emerson

70

I Can't Escape You

I can't escape you. Though I've attempted laving guilty fingertips of
The natural redolence you've left behind, your flavored scent subsists
Among edges of nails that have scratched and searched an anatomical
Wilderness that remains esoteric to unfeeling hands. Swaddled in a
midnight grapple, I taste ticklish lips and hush whisper stained
Orisons against saturated bliss and while relearning to breathe, I
Guilelessly swim downstream as we church barbarous hips into silkened
Puddles of cream. Lover's legs lengthen a lick-starving body quake
Seismographed and grazed upon by mouth, cheek, and nose voraciously
Tongue-teasing two strong ankles and ten lonely toes. Cardiac
Palpitations pump a detonating funk that penetrates three humps and
One bump in double trouble time count as if our musical souls sang
Without making a sound. Within your wings, Land Of Nod dreams weave
Easily like two Angel's fleeting flight from a private Gethsemane.
And although I've dammed your rivers from my sea, and a dew trickled
Dawn sunbathes separated mornings, I can't escape you:
Not even if the alluring path to your door burned the bottoms of my
Purposive feet, or if your Adam's apple kisses ceased to be sweet.
Not even if I drown in what I've been blessed or chased by Essenic
Winds of Jehova's inquest, I can't escape you.
Not even when I'm dressed.

David Aikman

Looking For Miss Right

You go out there every night
So sure you're gonna find Miss Right
Your eyes meet and you walk over her way
She asks you to sit down and stay
She wants to buy you a drink
The whole time she's talking you're trying to think
She looks at another guy
You try to look interested but start rubbing your eye
You just want to turn out the light
She wants to hold you too tight
She rolls over and calls you "Hon"
If she'd just shut up this could be fun
She's cute but she laughs kind of loud
You didn't notice that so much in the crowd
It's time to ask her to go
That empty feelings back and you feel kind of low
It's happening again You just want to be friends
You keep saying you don't want to fight
At this rate how can you win
Never mind, a new girl walked in

Susan Fowlkes

A Feeling I Have

I love you more than words can say
More than symbols can be seen
From the depths of my heart
I love you more than anything
Anything in this world
Anything this world could ever possess
This feeling of love I feel is like nothing
I have ever felt
I don't think I could feel this way again.

Violette Ezra Williams

Final Wish

Let a cardinal sing me to my grave
And finches, chirping, fly a summer sky
These are my friends
Treasures in my life
Their scarlet, golden, many colored wings
Have brightened days weighed down
Their generous songs have helped my spirit soar
So, too, escort my final journey
Bright color and song to the very end

Carol W. Seefeld

Room To Bloom

Make room for you to bloom?
Why not?
Here we are — so near each other — yet —
    each of us in our very own spot

We grow — we blossom — each at our own pace

Your blossoming out gently touches and steadily moves
    me aside

When I blossom — I will touch you gently and
    steadily move you aside —

It was your permitting me to lean on you that was the
    strength beneath my last blossom.

Not you? Does it really matter my friend? I am here —
    Strong at the moment

Lean on me! Grow and blossom!

Your beauty enhances me — until I can bloom again.

Marionette Sanders Daniels

Grandpa

Whenever Grandpa comes to mind,
I smile a happy smile.
And think of all the summer days
We'd sit and talk awhile.

This little man with eyes of blue,
And hair of silver gray,
Would smile his magic, childlike smile
And chase all blues away.

He was a very patient man
Who gave his heart and soul.
He showed me caring through his love.
This was his lifelong goal..

He made my life so very rich.
He taught me how to care,
And see the beauty in all of life.
This lesson he did share.

And now my Grandpa's gone away
To a land of peace and love.
To a land where angels sing their songs.
To a land of God above.

Sheila B. Roark

Life Is Principle's Harmony

What is there about this life that makes it seem to rhyme,
Like the principle of music with its harmony in time.

Not the time that passes by and seems to change our face,
But the time that keeps the music within an ordered pace.

A rhythm that's so steady that no note is out of order,
While within this count of time, is freedom without border.

If we could see that life is like the music that we hear,
Ever so beautiful, so glorious, so dear.

Always harmonious while Principle is unfolding,
Orderly and graceful in the voice which is beholding,

Aware of its own harmony where love and joy belong,
Where peace, freedom and wholeness sing one blissful song.

Patty Hanson

The Stars In The Sky

The stars in the sky glittered like gold
I wish one of them I could hold
The stars are so bright
On this full star night
Kelli Baker

Heart Of Stone

I thought you were my own,
but now you're gone, and my heart
has turned to stone.

I sit alone by the phone, wondering
where your love has gone, feeling
nothing but a heart of stone.

I think with my head, because without
your love, I feel that I'm already dead,
since my heart has turned to stone.
Clara E. Schuster

She Is My Mom

See the lady over there, the one with
the beautiful silver hair
The one with a smile upon her face
She loves the whole human race
She gives of her self to help a friend or
anyone in trouble
No matter where or when
She loves everything God put on earth
Animal or people whatever their worth
As for a wife you could not find one better
She would be there through all kinds of weather.
A mother and wife the greatest yet
Loved by all this you can bet
Everyone first and her self last
This is how she has lived in the future and the past
You ask how I know one with so much love
And one who was blessed from heaven above
I will answer in just three words
Three words that mean a lot to me
She's my mom.
Robert Wilson

Winter Mood

The mornings are cold and quiet
The streets seem empty and foggy
The trees stand still
with their branches empty
and the wind kisses my face
with its icy touch.

The ground seems hard and lifeless
The grass has lost its color
The smell of burning wood
fills the air with its aroma
and a sense of loneliness
is rooted inside my heart.

Spring will bring new life,
new buds, new grass and flowers
The trees will grow new leaves and
birds will come again and sing.

The sun will bring us warmth and light;
children and their laughter
will find the streets and new hopes,
new dreams will fill my heart.
Martha Schneegans-Avilés

"Mama's Black Son"

You know who you are,
you Beautiful Strong Black One.
You know who you are, Mama's Black Son.
Why must you pull and tug at my heart?
Why must you destroy what I've begun to start?
Why must you lie, cheat and steal?
Be honest my son, God fearing and for real.
I know what you're doing out late at night.
I'm your Mama, son, you're my star shining bright.
I had such high hopes for you, my son
It's not too late you can get a new life if you really want one.
I didn't bear you to loose you dead on some street.
This drugging is nonsense, it's got me dead on my feet.
Start anew and let your soul be free
come back my son, come back to me.
You know who you are,
You Beautiful Strong Black One.
You're Mama's baby, Mama's black Son.
Marcy R. Dorsey

Goodbye My Friend

Goodbye my friend and may God bless
And keep your soul close by
We wonder "Why God's plan is this?"
We mortals should not try.

Goodbye my friend — your death so unexpected
We never know whose turn comes next,
Prepare to be respected;
We learn this in the Bible's text.

Goodbye my friend, whose luck at chance was ample,
Card games were fun, you had great skill,
But then your heart — it took the final gamble
And lost to God's own will.

Goodbye my friend, we'll meet you there
When God decides it's time;
We treasure now your memory
And see you down the line.

Goodbye my friend of many years
Our friendship did not end
For us here fighting back the tears,
I pray God's Grace He'll send.
Helena Collins

How Soon They Forget

How soon they forget all those promises made,
As they waste our tax money we so faithfully paid.
How soon they forget the poor, elderly and ill,
As they feather their nest on Capitol Hill.
How soon they forget they're working for us,
As they bicker and disagree on what each party does.
How soon they forget how much everyone pays,
As they scheme to give themselves another big raise.
How soon they forget we can't hardly get by,
For there's too many greedy fingers in the "political pie."
How soon they forget we've had all we can take,
Of eating beans everyday, while they're having steak.
How soon they forget we're tired of their campaign games,
As they sling mud and call each other dirty names.
How soon they forget we deserve something more,
Than the elephants and donkeys always in an uproar.
How soon they forget it's disgusting to put someone down,
I wish I could vote for a nice character, like "Bozo the Clown".
Violet J. Samson

Visions Unaware

Open your eyes man!
Can't you see the waves
crashing against the rocks?
Can't you see the salty sea air?

Open your eyes man!
Can't you see the gulls,
flying, there along the shore?
The couple standing atop the cliff
embraced in passion's mastery.

Close your eyes man,
tell me what you see.
The crimson tide driving toward shore,
the horizon dipping deep, into the pool.

Close your eyes man, tell me what you see.
Is it hope,
endlessly lost in the light?

Alfred James Cole

"To Beard Or Not To Beard?"

Oh bristly appendage
both comforting and opposing
My inseparable companion, phantom image
Constant reminder of necessity

To be or not to be is not the question
To beard or not to beard begs intention

If I beard
You will intrude upon my profile
If I beard, you do same

I look upon my image without destination
and contemplate the either, or
tempted to obliviate but stop
at total destruction

For what is mine will always be
Regardless of resolution
So, I beard
Only to confront
once again, thy bristly appendage
I call mine

Phyllis L. Hunt

"Heaven's Tiny Angel"

Written and Dedicated to My Sister Eileen,
Upon the Day of Her Birth 6-15-71
In this world of hate and crime,
a little light shines through,
this part of you which Heaven sends,
to love a life that's new.

A baby wins the hearts of all,
a life so small and warm,
their tenderness sent from above,
a gift the day they're born.

Their skin so pink, their hands so small,
their eyes like gleaming pearls,
within your arms is held with care,
a precious, gentle world.

Heaven's tiny angel,
that's what babies are,
so, may all babies everywhere,
shine bright, like Heaven's star.

Susan Ongirski

Frilley Milley

Frilley Milley is a girl age eight.
Has a friend her name is Kate.
They go to school they're never late.
They listen to teacher what she states.
They write with chalk upon the slates.
They know to learn helps their fate.
They leave for home their mothers don't wait.
They laugh and play, run and skate.
They tell their secrets by the garden gate.
They promise friendship in a future date.
Frilley Milley and her friend Kate.
Here comes Willey with fishing pole and bait.
He likes to tease Frilley Milley and Kate.
He thinks he's smart and oh so great.
He calls them dumb and says they're quaint.
My, mother says one day if we wait.
It's like a balloon that will deflate.
Willey will stop teasing by the garden gate.
They'll all be friends in a future date.
Willey, Frilley Milley and her friend Kate.

Margie Knight

Shiver With Me . . .

Left my mind somewhere back there,
Blow-dry the shakes out of me.
Stomach cramps the daylight,
Sacrificing scars.
The tracks will eat me alive forever,
The skin left under my nails.
The nervendings under my skin,
Satan's spawn, my closest enemy,
Bad habits are easy to make.
Too personal, too, too personal,
Alive in a sense, never the same.
Conformity lost, even after I found it,
Who is the woman who writes the verses?
Surely not I, not any more,
They all know, dead or alive, they know.
They sing the same song,
Scratch the same flesh.
The cross of nails forever on our backs,
Hot flashes, cold, seems forever.
When did reality stop?

Sara Stroosnyder

In Loving Memory

There was always help and comfort when
You were around. A scraped knee along with a
Long frown, but with your tranquil touch it was turned
Upside down. Mother, oh mother you were
Life to me, now who's gonna be there to bandage
My knee.

Rolling through life, lonely I am. Needing to
Hear your voice say, "I know you can." Longing
For the safety in your kiss, clouding my guilt in
A state of bliss. If only I knew what I know
Now, my face would be banished of this sad
Brow.

Once in a while a good day will stroll by,
Only to be taken over the question "why",
Praying to a God who will not answer me; when
Will I open my eyes and use them to see. That
These somber questions which linger so, can only
Resolved by........me

Peter Labore

Given To You

Time is so special now that I have you.
The words spoken and the things we do.

The time in the night as we lay entwined
Touching each other leaving the world behind.

When all stops that surrounds but you and I
The lust I see within your eyes, you read me too.
That is why time is so special now that I have you.

Susanne A. Jajkowski

Winter Past

Search me now and see me gently
  Idle into that soft green meadow
Where the spring breeze is whispering softly
  To the lazy rows of lush grass weaving
  Of an elusive past; but now the meaning
This wake-up call is singing is of a time to grow.

Look inside at the water barely ripple
  Moving slowly towards the outlying earth
To encompass the pond, while the minute movements trickle
  In remembrance; but at the moment
  It is enough to have your energy spent
  In circling the eater and measuring its girth.

Be still, my heart, in peace and tranquil ease;
But stir not that dark memory.

John Vaught

Family

A family sticks together,
Through hardships and pain.
They love one another with all their heart.
They laugh together
And talk together.
They enjoy the little time in which they share together.
During hard times
They don't fall apart and each go their separate ways.
Instead, they hold hands, combine their strength
and become stronger than before.
When one slips and falls,
The rest will reach down and pull that one back up.
They take care of one another,
Help one another,
Love one another.
Together they can make it through thick and thin.
They are something special, you see
For they are a family.

Sabrina Royer

Women Of The Past

Women of the past
Weaving their way to freedom
Paving the way
For people everywhere today
Linking arms through history
They have fought and cried and sacrificed
Some have even died to change our lives
We must keep what they have done in sight
Never forgetting that freedom is a hard won fight
Never forgetting that freedom is our precious right
Women of the past
Reaching out into the future
We are all a link
In the chain of freedom
Linking arms through history
Holding hands for equality
Becoming one
Through you and me.

Linda Tringali

"School Daze-Grade 3"

Get your face outta my face,
You're not respectin' my space!

Last one to seat is rotten egg!
He tried to trip me, he put out his leg!

    Please be quiet, sit down.
    You don't want me to frown.

I don't feel good, would you feel my head?
I probably should be home in bed.

He called me a name.
No, I'm not to blame.

    I'm going to count to 2.
    I want absolute quiet, too!

He started it is my claim,
He's the one who should feel the shame.

He butted in line.
He took what's mine.

    Please stop! I can't take all this stress!
    I want to go home, I must confess!

Sharon K. Preston

A House Wife's Soliloquy

Oh, this April day's so sunny,
I just can't be content
  To be scrubbin' and be bakin'.
I think the Good Lord meant,
  For His children to appreciate
His wonders as they're sent.
  So, I'll discard all my dust cloths,
plan dinner out of cans,
  And go walking', just a walkin'
for to see the new born Spring.
  Oh, I tell you folks, it's worthwhile,
just to give yourselves a fling.
  It will lessen every sorrow, every duty,
every care,
just to spend some time with Nature
  You will surely find God there!

Helen Wilson

My Lovable Man

He came into this world not so long ago
It was November 19, 1982, in fact
I am unaware of his looks at birth
But just look at him now!

He has blue eyes that shame the sky
And a smile to light a heart aflame
His hair is undefinable
But it frames his beautiful face

I love him for his humor
Others love him for his looks
But he is my sunshine
My world is dark without him
Like an ending world facing cold doom

It is this way to others
Because they do not know
They linger in his shadow
These ones are not for me
Adoring are the girls beside me

They ask about him
And I tell them he is my lovable man . . .

Kimberly A. Jaus

"Happy Memories"

We live way out in the country
It's called, 40 up and plumb -
Our kids grew up here and loved it,
Oh, how this place did hum —

They had calves to feed and cows to milk
Some chickens to care for too —
A few goats to play with —
- you name it, they had that too!

They rode horses - made carts -
We had a few ponies too —
They sure are cute when they are born
We'd laugh, what ever they'd do.

Now, all our birds have grown up
And come home with children of their own
- This old house rocks with love -
And memories return, to our throne.

Connie Stratton

There Is A Soul I Know

There is a soul I know that lives in the
world to come. He sits in silencing thought
throughout the days.

There are few that can follow him when he
speaks his words of wisdom.

His faith remains in God, and all of the
revelations to come; he knows there is a peace in
such a faith.

The motionless expression upon his face
isn't one of ignorance, but one of the wise.
His grey eye reflect the feelings of our world today.

He speaks of the events to come, and their destruction.
"The knowledge of the future comes from the
Holy Nation from above; he proclaims.

There is a soul I know that lives in the
world to come; a wise man that could tell your fate,
but how shameful that such a wise man can be
so foolish as to dwell on tomorrow while wasting today..

Bonni Gerber

At The Concert Hall

Now, I must be really awake
since I sense music all over.

From wind and trees, cellos, oboes,
soft sands and moons, swift dreams and rocks,
light blocks of light and shadows again.

What is this? I might never know
but amazed so far by the many crisp sounds.

Am I the only one in this silent dark
track of events — stepping out, rather than in?

But no. Wait a sec . . . What do I have?
See here: A silvery touch, a quiet triangle.

Cellos are older, harps may be wiser. Perhaps . . .

But I got this trinity without really knowing
what I should do. From no one to inquire.

Script is blurred and a frantic man only,
con brio his arms, giving us orders.

So far I am out, but why don't I wait?

It has been dead long, and not quite too easy
to keep in the silence (my out-of-ways way).
For good now, hand-soul: Let's hit the iron!

Carlos Cortinez

Life

Life is like a rose, so slowly it unfolds —
You scarce can see it bloom
Before it's reached its doom.
It may be full of sweetness
And its fragrance that of bliss,
But when it fades in beauty,
Stop and think of this:

A rose is just a flower; life is only dew
One moment you are here, the next we may miss you.
Others come to take your place among the snares of earth
But not a one can mimic you in charity or mirth.
No one else can really see the things you used to do
In the actions of some other flower that wakes in coming dew.

Sally A. Mathis

Ode To Death

As death raps gently at my door, somehow its sound is so loudly heard.
Its rapturous tune never ending, Oh God! How it hurts, my mind
darts here and yon. My pulse, how it quickens, am I troubled, yes, yes
deeply so troubled. Oh! But the fear is so new. I feel so helpless, so
empty Of you whose blood flows through my veins and of my kin, and
their kin and their kin. I see shadows growing near, the darkness, oh so
near; they softly edge o'er the hills, coming ever so close.

Grandfather of mine, I cannot forget you, the heritage you bestowed
upon me. I am in pain, and misery, as though my world is beginning
to crumble. When last I saw you, I knew that you were weak,
but I couldn't dream that it would be so soon.

Alas! What more can I say, nothing, will remove the pain, the hurt.
Sleep on my grandfather, suffer no more, yes sleep, lay your soul to rest.

Evelyn Gibbs Scovel

Pines

There is a quiet coolness here between
The trunks of pines, tall standing in a glade.
They do not bend their boughs to offer shade,
But on each outstretched arm there is the sheen
Of sunlight, dimly mirrored in a pool
Of shadowed gray: A carpeting beneath,
Where tiny pine swords gather, sheath on sheath,
To form a many-pillared vestibule.

Beneath these colonnades there is no breeze.
The air is hung with pungent, spicy scent
And one can hear, with ear to brown earth bent,
The gentle, muted language of the trees.

Reba H. Herman

Untitled

We start out as children;
From the gift of God.
I've look upon the adults as monsters.
They look so tall and so high,
We watch their every movement,
And look upon their face.
Sometimes they are smiling
Sometimes something is in their distaste.
Let us not forget the wrong things
And the things that are right
We learn from experience some things may cause fright.
Soon it will be our turn to be a mom or pop
We look back and say "Thanks a lot"
That's when new things arrive
We try to find a way out.
We watch our children grow up
We know we were there
Thank you God for a life.
That I could bear.

Joseph E. Breyan

A Dream

In a dream I lay there
With my fingers entwined in my hair
Dreaming of the girl
I thought so cool

With her skin so soft and eyes so enchanting
Her thoughts were beauty, her time was short
We filled the day with fun and laughter
And then she was gone, with others she rode

But to me she was alone except for our dreams
Her hair blew with Chestnut brown
As we sway down the track
The water did splash and dazed she was

As we stepped to get off, her body did sway
As she walked down the path, I could plainly see
She was the girl to be
In my dreams of memories
Roberta O. Malcolm

Hello-Goodbye

From a child's laugh to a lover's sigh
With today's hello begins goodbye.

We deny death's shadow maybe cast.
We deny the chance this day's our last.

Banishing the night with the soul's glow,
In the dawn's first light we say hello.

We grasp life's lies and tales to tell
Deep within our hallow shells.

Denying man's limited powers
To live a life of farce for hours.

Afraid to feel love's piercing dart,
We say hello with timid hearts.

To say hello without the fear
To anyone who will come so near.

We say hello with courage untold
And say goodbye as life unfolds.

For tomorrow's dawn may bring goodbye
Known or unknown, death's final sigh.

We are mere pawns playing the game,
Where life and death become the same.
Colleen Hillseth

Our Class

Comes, join us in class sixty-O
Led by Mr. Komito!
You'll learn to capitalize proper nouns,
State capitols, and other towns.
You'll discover how Lincoln freed the slaves,
And prehistorics lived in caves
You'll learn about snakes, and graphs and snails
And high adventure ships with sails.
And if you're mathematically inclined,
There's nothing like equations to clutter your mind.
One of the first to come to the door,
Is a handsome young student named Gabor.
You'll get to know petite Marie, and our class comedian Mr. G.
You'll meet sweet Nancy with brown flowing tresses
And her gentle mother who sews her own dresses
And Mrs. Gellers' subtle smile, makes a trip to school worthwhile.
There are some whose names I don't recall
But we're like a family, one and all.
For a friendlier group, you've far to go.
Like the group in class sixty point zero.
Barry Golub

Battered Woman

Oh, how I love my man
I gave him the best, and all that I can
You rape and slap me with physical might
You insist, this is your God given right

Your language is nasty, and call me a whore
Before we were married, you never had this side before
You get so angry, jealous and knock me down
Even with the children around

We have problems, and a need to talk
When I do, you simply balk
You frighten and threaten me with harm
Our marriage is a shamble, you don't give a darn

Our family is broken, all because of you
The children confused and frighten too
What happened to our sacred vow
To love, and honor each other, no matter how

A counsellor, a preacher, or help we do need
To stop your violence, indeed
I will no longer take it, I will take command
To leave you, this is out of hand
Louis Freeland Green

"Oceans Of Love"

I found reprieve and a berth, aboard a vessel
She showed me there was laughter, in the sea
Away from the shore was a world apart
The ship, the ocean and me.

Awake to a morning with a turquoise sky
Then in a corner, it's set aflame
Autumnal colors, crystalline and clean
An explosion of roses, it's daylight again

The sun that has labored hardest of all
Released the stokers, its light no longer carrying heat
Stretched to all its grandeur, for just a moment
Then slipped away, to sleep

You lit with stars, this velvet of black
Giving comfort with a love light, found only in eyes
A cool breeze and ocean spray, then was your gift
As fresh as the kiss of new snow

"Ocean" how could I not
In some secret cove of my heart
Have found in you a harbor
A place to anchor my soul.
Roderick Caldwell

Ballerinas Of The Water

Flute echoes across the water,
reflections light the stage,
a sea lion comes from beneath the wharf
he twists and turns, slowly in the water,
he floats, turns and dives, beneath the surface
them nose first, comes up,
he twirls about gracefully, he dances,
like a ballerina of the water

Meeting his mate, they dance,
close together, slowly, gracefully, they entwine,
swirl and twirl together,
dancing the dance of love,
like ballerinas of the water.
When the dance is done,
they part, and go their own way
and they swirl and they twirl
and dive beneath the surface,
like ballerinas of the water.
Merletta Ann Tindle

Look Up

While rushing through my busy morning
just the other day
I knelt to watch a tiny ant
struggling on its way

It wrestled with an object
at least ten times its size
then picked it up and continued on
much to my surprise

As I rose to walk away
something caught my eye
a busy spider spinning a web
in which he'd caught a fly

Time to go I said to myself
as I sprang to my feet
I too have chores that must be done
to make my day complete

Just then my eyes turned toward the sky
and I pondered carefully
perhaps I'm not so big after all
could something bigger be watching me?

Dennis L. Rodenhofer

"Little Things Mean The Most"

Please God help me to see
the beauty that lies right in front of me.
Nature itself exhumes a lot of love
from billowing clouds to a soaring Dove.
From all the sunrises to all the sunsets,
the horizon can be the "beautiful-est".
The birds, the flowers, the stars up in the sky,
just being outside gives me a natural "high."
But from within the heart comes even more beauty,
Like the love of a child (who's a little "cutie").
He trusts and cuddles and loves so freely;
the apple of my eye and I love him completely!
A warm smile, a gentle touch;
A simple deed yet it means so much.
To be there for a friend, and show you care;
to listen, to hug, and to be able to share.
To send a note and spread some cheer;
it'll make them smile from ear to ear.
To spread your wings for over a mile;
to live your life, and be free for a while . . .
From inside or outside and coast to coast,
it's still the little things that means the most!

Linda Hirschmann

Humanity

I have more love and passion for life than no other,
I can call every man my brother.

One big family is all we are,
it doesn't matter if you walk, ride a bike or drive a car.

If we could see past the clocks, smog and debris,
we would see a world custom made for you and for me.

Why we continue to destroy I can honestly confess,
I don't have the answer, but let's try our best.

Babies are born with such innocence and purity.
Let's not make drugs and gangs their destiny.

I put this in words to remind the world of what it
already knows, there is more to this wonderful life than
just the status quo.

Timothy T. Thompson

The Island

The clearest water you've ever seen
Its reach is endless, or so it seems
Looking out from a mountain top
On the island all alone . . .
A dot on the map surrounded in blue
The wolfs howl chases after the moon
And I feel freedom like I've never known
The Isle Royale stands alone . . .
So much like me, waves crash ashore
And wash away what was before
Ever changing, never still
I wonder if I ever will
Find a way to make myself evolve
Into such a perfect love
The greenery wild, all overgrown
The Isle Royale stands alone

De Hunter

An Unfinished Beginning

When I think of you . . .
It keeps me from being blue.
But when we argue and fight,
I can't fall asleep at night.
I think about how happy we've been
especially when we are together.
The places we have seen,
and the memories that are forever.
Sitting in your arms is enough for me
on a normal day, in front of the T.V.

When I think of you . . .
there's something that I feel is definitely true,
and that's the love I feel for you.

I have forgotten through the years,
through the many hardships and tears
that love can exist in my heart.
But now, through your bright ambitions
I can find and give definition
to this feeling I have inside . . .

Christine Tran

Gran's and Grampa's Christmas In Their Golden Years

*(Dedicated to our children, grandchildren and great-grands
Who make our years golden!)*

Gram and Gramp are havin' Christmas, all the kids are comin' home.
They will all arrive tomorrow, but tonight we're all alone.
So, we're dancin' on the carpet (neat!)
A-doin' it in our bare feet!
And, wow, it feels so funny
O-o-o-o . . . it tickles, Honey!

Jingle bells and laughter pealing — Christmas tree up to the ceiling!
Kids a-throngin' in the driveway —
        bringin' presents through the doorway!
Birthday cake for Him Who sees us
Children in exuberant choir!
Singin' "Happy birthday, Jesus!"
(S'mores now roastin' in the fire.)

Turkey splutterin' in the oven —
        great-grandchildren full of lovin',
Gram's and Grampa's pride's a-showin'
        by the special way they're glowin'!
But Gram's and Grampa's biggest treasure,
        celebratin' Christmas cheer,
Is the deep love without measure,
        that our family shares all year!

Faythimes

A Wish in a Dream

I'm sitting here all alone again tonight to
wish upon a star so bright and if I may
wish on you I may wish a dream come true
To those who hear to those who prey I may
say that it's okay.
    Cause I'm here just waiting for you and you're out
there out there somewhere and who knows
where our love goes and who cares that
our love is there.
    So I'm wishing upon a star tonight to hope
that things will go right I prey the Lord
above you that you will be so darn true.
Will you kiss my lips and never let me go
Will you hold me tight and say you love me so.

Tracy Vicaro

Fear

I'll hold you down, hold you back.
I just can't let you go, you can't push me away.
I'll always be with, you walk at your side.
I'll hold your hand, if I can.
I can cut you down, you'll feel so low.
High for a moment, maybe two, but I'll come to meet you.
I'll take you home, but won't let you go.
You can sign me off any time you please, but I'll never leave.
Don't turn around, don't you dare.
I'm always here. Don't turn around, look away.
You can't look me in the eye.
   Are you afraid to die?
   afraid to leap?
   afraid to lie?
   afraid to love?
   afraid to look too deep?
   afraid to cross the line?
   afraid to look too far?
   Are you afraid you'll find yourself mine?
Too late.

Cara Lynch-Passarelli

Southern Sunsets

The fields of wheat flow with the wind,
And I look forward to plowing them again.
The sky of the South makes everything right
When one watches the sun yield its post to night.
O, dear Lord, don't let this moment pass,
That I might see this spectacle times to come, alas!
As Apollo's chariot approaches its heavenly stable,
And the Southern landscape begins to fade,
I stop my work and store my spade
Where to find it and play with it, my children are unable.
The Lord has blessed us with this and His Son,
I thank Him for them as the land sinks into oblivion.

Mitchell Albritton

To Akita

"I am indeed quite fortunate,
that I cannot heave my heart into my throat
to speak to you the words
you so deserve to hear.
Instead I beg you,
let me turn my heart into a dagger
that may be thrust through my soul,
so that I might press against your lips
and show you with a kiss
the feelings I have for you.
The feelings that my throat
can only say with words . . .
I love you."

Kevin W. Good

Shoe

I allow television to mold me into what I am today.
T.V. is my morning call, my good night kiss.

Teaching me to live, eat, dress
To love, hate, kill and die.

The deficit, the ozone layer, wars,
Terrorists, drugs, muggings, gang violence
And nature's phenomena.

I have become completely dependent upon my friend,
My informer, my educator and my companion.

I am lost without TV's influence and guidance.
No wonder I don't know how to read or write.

But I am well informed.

Today I went out. I wore one brown shoe with a tassel
And one black shoe with laces.

Everyone stared, some with pity, others with perplexity.
All I could do was run home to my understanding buddy.
Slamming the door shut to escape the realities
of the outside world.

Who needs it anyway!

Olivia A. Hoffman

These Three Mice

As the years go by and by, you've seen three children grow
From little ones that used to cry to adults more mature,
And as you sat, day after day, thinking life was slow,
It seems now years have passed away, invariably, gone for sure.

You labored hard to mold each child to perfection, through and through,
And even though you always smiled, the work you did was rough.
Many hours, end on end, with countless things to do,
Making sure to always spend time with each of us.

But these three mice are not so blind; we see what you have done.
We know that we could never find a better life than this.
We each thank you as much as one can for what we have become;
Each girl a woman, the boy a man, but childhoods we'll miss.

John White

Marshmallow

I am a symbol of sugar, now enjoy me
I help make foods like rice krispies treats, marshmallow cake, and
smores oh smores
I look like a pillow, a cloud, and I am a white cylinder
You can not stop eating me
You just want more
I am chewy, sticky, and yummy
I am sugar, pure sugar, white crystals of sweetness
Eat me, eat me, just eat me you know you want to
Oh stop torturing yourself just do it eat me
Put yourself out of misery just Eat Me!!!!!

Gus Rhodes

Log Cabin

My log cabin is home to me
It rests among the tall pine trees
The train whistle echo's through the hills
Leaving me with a wonderful thrill
The young deer graze nearby
Looking at me to say "hi"
When the sun rises over the mountains
Is reflects a beautiful light upon my window
In winter when the snow is heavy
The crackling fire keeps me warm
I hear a sound outside my door
My animal friends are hear once more

Charlotte Burke

Ecstasy's Blindness

Ecstasy's blindness through stumbling time
Is falling, is bawling, and calling a rhyme.
Clawing a way across endless conclusions
Tripping and slipping on blank dissolutions.
What's there to say among crumbled and cracked?
To miss but a kiss has more strength to attack.
Is nothing a something that has not a name?
Do you think, talk or feel when it stakes its feared claim?
Craving one's saving the hopeless but pure
Forsaking the rest that will have to endure
What has not been passed upon lips that once told
Of things unimagined by young and by old.
Wanting so badly, you almost can taste
The sweetness surpassing that which life is based.
I only can hope that it's not too far-fetched:
This painting of hope and desire I've sketched.
It's a sad thought to think that we all can't be free
Until ecstasy's blindness finally can see.

Stacy Taladay

Speculation

Do you really understand that we live an illusion,
or have you a different thought and conclusion.
Merely conceived ideas from mind and soul,
are not enough to grasp firm and forever hold.
For to understand how this world works and turns,
you must first judge, from mistakes everyone learns.
So, do not draw conclusions of a nature unknown,
for on this dreary path the direction may never be shown.

Christopher A. W. Webb

"Fear"

So many times I am afraid
Afraid to dream
Afraid to hope
Afraid of what might happen
If I get my hopes too high
There is always a fear
Of disappointment lurking
In the shadows of my mind
A part of me yearning to be loved
While the other withdraws from all emotions
The fear of losing
The hope of holding on
Oh how do I fear, fear
Oh how I do dream
Oh how I do hope

Rose E. Gerard

Seasons Past

I wished Winter into Summer, the night into the day
Then before I knew it I had wished it all away

Alone by the window, in the kitchen, at the table
With my coffee in a milkglass cup I feel like some old fable
A bird now perched upon my sill peers at me through dirty pane
The window I once buffed with hand is only rinsed by rain

I stare too long at photographs, reread letter's I've reread
Carry on a tête-à-tête with the cat . . . the dog . . . the bread
The phone I used to damn for ringing lies too quiet in the cradle
The soup that used to fill the pot now scarcely fills the ladle

I wished Winter into Summer, the night into the day
Then before I knew it I had wished it all away

Cheryl Allbaugh

Remember You

Will I remember you
after this relationship is over,
when love is old no longer new?
Will I remember that sun comes up and down
and the moon remains spell bound,
in space, to adorn my face
at night as I try to sleep?
And a cock does crow abruptly at dawn
and I must go again,
cause I remember it's on my agenda to be gone.
Do babies recognize
the smell of mother's sweet milk
and that when it drips
it's time to sip and give nutrition
to life newborn, I'll remember you
as long as I remember my name.
When cars go by I'll think of you
and cars go by a lot.

Candy Cole

Untitled

i remember dreaming once
    that snakes could talk
    and they would fall out of trees and ask you about your day
i remember dreaming once
    that lips touched mine
    and that was unconditional
i remember dreaming once
    about a planet with four moons lighting up the night sky
    and colorful rains of green and orange
i remember dreaming once
    about red hair, brown eyes
    long legs, and rather large breasts
i remember dreaming once
    about a god
    who sits on a stiff throne all day trying to decide who's going

    to win the next war, and the next election
i remember dreaming once
    about walking through a paradise
    cradling my newborn son in my arms
god save me if the day even comes when I can't dream

Brant Gonzalez

"The Unforgotten"

The famous, Will and Wiley, no longer pals can be
As life from them was taken, in an airship o'er the sea.
It happened on a pleasure trip, while traveling in their plane,
From Washington to Siberia, 'twas then their trouble came.

On way they'd stopped at Juneau, to await the terrible fog.
They feasted with the natives, then while sitting on a log..
They gazed up at skies above, to decide what they should do
After thinking quite a while, bid the natives sad adieu.

They left in spite of it, as they had done before,
But they've done it once too many times and they'll never do it more.
They were widely known upon this earth and were friends of everyone
Wiley, as a pilot, great, while Will was full of fun.

He was a humorist in our shows, where peopled always go
When they'd hear the great news coming of Will Rogers in a show.
Now we'll no longer see him, or see Wiley in his plane
These men, so great, lost their lives, they'll never lose their names.

They will always be remembered, by the good things they have done
Not by harm they've done the world, but they the name they have won.

Ruth M. Peterman

On Death's Door

In the face of death I see
The full extent of life's mystery.

Material things we think we need
Are unimportant to us, indeed.

Faded memories become much clearer —
Family and friend becomes much dearer.

Seasons may still come and go —
But they now contain a special glow.

Things which once were critical matters —
Now become just idle chatter.

My heart is now full, yet lighter.
Days once dull, now seem brighter.

Death is no longer a dreaded foe —
But something to embrace and hold.

For now in death I can clearly see
What the afterlife holds for me.

No more pain, grief or sorrow —
No more worries of tomorrow.

Just a life spent with God above —
Basking in His infinite, undying love.

Carol Spitzer

Of Time And Shadows

Your shadows gone in the hours that were lost
   Strike light incandescence when mind's illusions dissolve
     in your reality's presence; and it glows; and the joys,
      oh, so much more than a thousand fold.

Hurt pride! Heart lost!
   Treasured moments that were lost
Now in timeless space a void;
   Memories gone to naught.

Come shadows, come spring
   Come drifting leaves; snow blossoms on the hill,
one after the other come and go
   but leave wound's gaping and unhealed,
Pain after pain and yet more sting
When do summer you gaze and lull these nightmares
   Into A Dream?

P. E. Bryon

"God's Love Is Great"

God's love is great!
How good that is to hear.
When you're confused, he leads you straight
without having doubt or fear.

So many times we stray from his love.
Without thinking of what we do.
We put other things above.
When he should come first instead of soon.

But he is forgiving.
He will never let you down.
Without his love it's impossible to go on living.
Just listen to his word, listen to the sound.

Whenever you think you don't have a friend.
You should think twice, because God's there.
He listens to you without end.
And if no one else listens remember that he does care.

He comes first in my life.
That I'm happy to say.
I know that for me, he was sacrificed.
So for all people without God, I pray.

Jessica Harper

I Like

Gentle april showers, on warm spring days
That soothe my body till I feel crazed.

Snowy, icy capped, mountain peaks and plains
Viewed from afar, as I lay and listen to the rains.

Warm, june summer sun, fluffy clouds in the sky
Gazing hypnotically, as each cloud sail by.

Lying lazily on the beach, waves beckoning me near
Drifting thoughts, gentle breezes, caressing my ear.

Moonlight walks in the park, on starry autumn nights
Lovers embracing, whispering, as they wander out of sight.

Birds chirping happily, as they gather twigs for a nest
Knowing soon they can settle down to lay eggs and rest.

Blue skies, bright sun, shining serenely down on me
Fisher boats drifting slowly, seagulls circling the sea.

Girls and boys laughing gaily, as the wind blows their kites
Listening to schubert's trout quintet, are the things I like.

Dealia Gwaltney

Untitled

Hunter's rifle rests beside
Gold and emerald arches
Riding in tribulation
Of what must stand.

And the curtain falls
Beside her olive knees,
Khaki shorts and belittled
Entering her awesome expression
Like she's wanting, wanting what makes her human.

I understand ideas,
Transforming from latent scribbles
On wrinkled skin of pubescent angels
Mocking, but laughing at the taste
Of humorous endowments.

I understand her need, for I've seen her fancy
Innocent little birds,
That whisper ominously into crumbs of crackers.

And the curtain opens upon her show light glitter
making everyone famous in historic fantasy,
And in the tender hearts — Of the wicked tamed.

Erik Christian

Why?

Why us it only I
Feel left out, the odd
One, scrabbled out like
A foreign race from everyone's mind?
   Why us it I only
Wish to take a step
Towards the lucky ones
Without them taking
Two steps back?
   Why is it you want
What you can't you want,
What you can't have? Is
It because you want to
Be cared for the slightest
Bit, to be accepted for
Who you are or not to have snickering behind
Your back as you walk by?
   Yet I only walk on,
Head high, heart crushed,
Thinking to myself . . . Why?

Jennifer Doerr

Lowdown

I feel so low down.
I slept well last night
I ate good this morning too,
But still I feel down

I do miss you my Angel
Your blue eyes, pretty smile
And hair of gold.
You are the one I adore.
I hear the phone.
Is it her I wonder?
Hello!
I was just thinking of you!
I felt lowdown, until I heard you voice!
You are my life my love
Let's go to the shore
Lowdown no more.

Robert J. DiGennaro

A Lover's World

A ruby in garnet splendor glows,
And a soul shines its diamond-strength..

Come, sweet to where the new world lies,
Out where the stellar-vast lights beam,
Where soft clouds are beds of calm.
There skies in silent orbits move,
Where passions, red as roses bloom,
And lips in their ruby press tantalize.

O come where music is a joyous dream, a lark,
Where notes are a gloss of sapphire blues,
Jewels, my dearest of our dream netherland,
Where only we lovers can ever trod.
Where a mind truly moves and flows,
In our sweetly fragranced land of dream,
Where our souls by silvered glasses gleam,
And our love remains a constant happy glow
Our joys a smile as wind-kissed roses blow.

O blessed be the soul that reaches so high!
May such peace of mind be ever, ever nigh!

Anthony Trent

The Love Of My Life . . .

He's the love of my life and the life of my love,
He's the Son of my Heavenly Father above.

He was born of the Virgin hand-chosen by God,
Who watched o'er from the crib 'til on Calvary He died.

He's the one my heart clings to when it feels deep pain —
This Physician Divine heals my soul, grace to gain.

He's aware of my troubles, my sorrows, my fears,
In Him I find comfort when I'm drowning in tears.

Now without Him my life would be counted a loss,
But He changed all of that when He died on the cross.

He's the first one I greet when I wake up each day,
And the last one to whom every "Goodnight" I say.

He's with me every moment, each heartbeat we share;
Though I sometimes forget Him, He'll always be there.

He knows my every thought, word and deed, each desire,
All my faults that must die in the crucible's fire.

He'll lead me and guide me, 'til my life here does end,
He's my Savior, Protector, Good Shepherd and Friend.

He's the Son of my Heavenly Father above,
He's the love of my life and the life of my love!

Patricia A. Sibley

Melinda McKay

Have you ever heard of Melinda McKay?
She said "there's no God. He's not in my yard."
Melinda McKay had to have her own way.
She was selfish and mean, She thought she was queen.

She hated her sister, her dad and
her brother. She secretly hated
her own dear mother. She often felt
sick. She didn't feel. She was
lonely and frightened, but she wouldn't tell.

She cheated at games, her friends
wouldn't play. She lied, she stole,
she scratched and she bit. If she
didn't win, she threw a fit.

One day in her yard, some birds came to
sing, She sat all alone not hearing
a thing. The tall trees were budding,
their leaves set to unfurl. She never
looked up. What an unhappy girl.

Melinda sat pouting, not daring to cry.
Blue skies overhead, white cloud drifting by.

Jane Murphy-Duff

American Impasse

God blessed this country that gives pride to all
It has come to rescue the weak and the small
Our soldiers have ventured to help lands of the poor
And fought many battles to bring peace to their door

People have come here who have braved the sea
In search of a land where they might be free
They came from far places all thinking the same
And many went on to reach high levels of fame

There were dangers at first making life hard
And some were assigned to watch and stand guard
For good reasons they came and never lost sight
That our beautiful land was well worth the fight

Problems have touched us and oft been solved
By people of greatness who became much involved
But America has one now that could be the ending
It is known to us all and called deficit spending

To those in high places who promised to lead
Sit down to the table and lets start to proceed
You must balance the budget and let us stand tall
As the world prays on that our nation not fall

Martin Fleming

Matriarch

A special Lady of beauty and grace,
Always a lovely smile on your face,
Bluest of eyes shine with a gentle glow,
Love for your family just seems to grow.

We know you always will be there,
Our joys or sorrows you gladly share.
You walk beside us hand in hand,
Tall and strong with us you stand.

Birthdays may come and go each year,
With each passing one you grow more dear.
You tender heart you share each day,
With all who need you along life's way.

You're so soft with the sweetest scent,
Thank you God for this prize you sent.
Of all the Mothers from Heaven above,
God gave us you Mom blessed with his love.

Joan Daly

Soft Secrets

I ran up to the stars last night
Thought maybe they could shed some light
They glistened as they listened and then turned blue
They listened of the love I couldn't tell you

You see I dream of you before and sweetly into sleep
Then first thing in the morning treasured moments I will keep
I tuck safely in my memory as if they really happened
Before reality sets in and flaming ecstasies are dampened

Patricia A. Lewis

Keep The Hope (O.K.C. Bombing)

The bomb went off, the building went down
Killed innocent loved ones five blocks around
Babies so young with no chance to see
The world so beautiful as it can be.
Mothers & fathers, other relatives too,
Trying to live to be rescued!
There is a chance more is alive
Keep the hope they may survive!!
The person who did this is so unreal
He has no heart he cannot feel.
Say a prayer for the victims right now.
Pray they make it through this somehow!

Amanda DuBuc

You, Me And The Rain

As I wake to hear your cries,
I rub my tired eyes

It doesn't matter that the time is unclear,
while the morning light draws near;

As I feed you in my arms,
the night rain has many charms;

Everyone else is asleep,
this moment is ours to keep;

With its pitter patter pace,
I wouldn't dream of another place;

With each tiny drop,
I whisper "Don't you ever grow up";

Now that you are fed,
and I lay you back in bed;

When in years to come and I hear the night rain's song,
it will be nights like these that I will long;

When you hear the rain - don't be blue,
think of how much I love you.

Kathyrn A. Adams

Forgive Me

   Begging and pleading for your entrance, wild with passion
neglected by desire. We . . . body . . . cries for thee please . . .
Forgive me God, for I lust for thee. I need thee to break my
strength. Oh! God of formality of so many profound words whisk
these naked, provers fantasies from my thoughts. Come closer to me,
wet my lips with yours, cream my fantasies, dance with my dreams make
love to my soul and when you are done leave only a shell.
Forgive me
Oh! Lord for I have placed a mortal body ahead of my prayer, ahead of
my daily verse. I have let this mortal comatose my soul, I have let
this mortal walk around inside my innocence. And now I want more
I want to lose myself inside his presence, I want to spread my wings
and let his body like the mind flow through me, and when he is done I
want to say "Forgive me" . . .

Florence M. Mills

Immortal

Twisting, turning, creeping, crawling.
Waiting, burning, jumping, falling.
When does it end? Who can I tell?
Will it be heaven? Will it be hell?
My mind is made up, I'm not one of you.
You're not yourself, What do you do?
It's crashing, Can you feel it?
Life, as you know it, coming down.
The weight is too much, I can't go on.
You say you know, but I see right through.
Your mind is weak, your thoughts mean nothing.
You call yourself free, you say you can fly.
I know better, I see you in your cage.
I see your death, I've watched you die.
I see them coming, just like before.
Can you hear them?
Have you done what you were here to do?
Is there more?
Make your choice, I hear the bell.
Will it be heaven? Will it be hell?

Michael Johnson II

The Green Eyed Angel

This is a thought to behold,
When we are in Heaven with streets of gold.

Will this that I am asking be true,
If your eyes will have color of brown, green, or blue.

Well, if these colored eyes in Heaven can be found,
There will be beautiful angels all around.

But I want you to look for the angel with the eyes of green,
For I am one angel I hope you have seen.

With my green eyes, all dressed in white,
You will never more have me out of your sight.

My eyes of green and yours of brown,
We can hold hands and fly with our golden crowns.

We will be as happy as two angels can be,
In Heaven with Jesus for all to see.

Maybe the Lord gave me my green eyes at birth,
Because He knew in Heaven what a green eyed angel was worth.

And He let you have me for yours for a while on earth below,
So the brown eyes and the green eyed pair could get ready to go.

Just to be in Heaven where there is no night,
You with your green eyed angel all dressed in white.

Clara Baugus

Where Are You?

   Please tell me why you left
You know I'm a part of you
   Sometimes I cry wishing you were here
You miss the opportunity to watch me grow
   I resent you in some ways but I love you in other ways
The pain is never going away
   There's so much you missed in my life
After 12 long years you walk back into my life
   Now that you're older and older and growin' sicker
I look into your eyes and see the pain that you suffer
   You don't show me love and I can't show it to others
Maybe cause you were hurt by your father
   I still give praise to my mom the one who raise me
After you left the burden in my life
   Like you I won't run away from my problems
But deep in my heart "I Love You?"
   In the back of my mind I still ask always
   "Where Are You...Daddy?"

Tamara Wright

The Prodigal Son

She stared at the picture of her little boy,
While in the other hand she held a letter,
And his once favorite toy.
She stare — dry-eyed — no tears upon her face,
Then set the little photograph back down in its place.
She remembered everything about him, her little son,
But she never tried to remember the older one.
She'd realized it way too late,
And the hands of time she could not rotate.
He'd become her prodigal son,
And she just couldn't forgive the things he'd done.
Perhaps, if she'd been able to forgive, her son would still live.
But like a sea star she wouldn't let go,
And now he lay six feet below.
She'd relived the nightmare a thousand times:
The telephone, his voice, ringing in her mind.
She remembered the church bell's toll,
And how sweet it felt to finally let go.
She knew her prodigal son felt it too,
But it was far too late to start anew.

Oranda Davis

The Hour . . .

The hour of awakening
is now upon my soul;
As I sit by patiently,
and wait for the truth to be told.

This evil act, this senseless death,
has torn my world apart.
Time will never heal
the emptiness in my heart.

In the quiet of the night,
in the quiet of the dawn,
I think of him and wonder,
how am I supposed to go on?

Then I remember . . .
I remember what I already know.
I see his face, I hear his laugh,
I remember a man named Joe.

From this pain, I will draw my strength,
and find my will to live.
From this pain, I will be reborn,
and find the strength to give.

Katrina M. Slavey

The Mysteries Of Life

The things we don't understand
Are sometimes the most beautiful to look at . . .
The mysteries of a spider's web,
The beauty of a bud blooming —
The look of wonder in a child's eye
Wondering why things are just that way —
The wonderment of love,
As I look through a window pane
Watching a child run to and fro,
The prayers of a child who talks to God like the Father He is
Instead of the ruler with a list of all of our good and bad deeds,
The hope we have in our eyes . . .
When there seems like none is in sight —
Then, there is the look of love,
Which is unmistakable —
Yet never looks the same in another's eyes
These are the things that cannot be explained . . .
Or understood
Yet are the most beautiful to look at

Angelica Z. Yguado

I Promise

I Promise to hold and cherish you
for there is nothing else that
will bring happiness.

I Promise to take care of you
for that is what a man
does with a woman.

I Promise to not let go of you
for that is what both
you and I want.

I Promise to be there for you
for that is how available
I will be to you.

I Promise to make you happy
for unhappiness is not foreseen in our future.

I Promise to make love to you for that is our intimacy and
when our souls become one.

I Promise to love you for that is what joy, truth, and
happiness will be for each of us.
I Promise . . .

Juan M. Morin

Veteran

When Nimitz, Halzey and me were out on the open sea,
We sailed on our ships into the face of our enemy.
We endured the dangers that came our way so we could
make history, then came home to our families.
We veterans of today can look back in pride, and say even
with God on our side a lot of men died.
We veterans must take our stand to make these younger
generations understand that our flag is not just a rag.
There are veterans still in pain. So don't let what we fought
for die in vain.

Leonard A. Bell

God In His Wisdom

God in His wisdom changes our lives
We grow and move forward
And learn from our strives
The pain we endure makes us braver and strong
That our days on this earth may be happy and long
Stay close to us Lord and center our thoughts
On goodness and patience
And all that you've taught
Humility and caring for our fellow man
So when problems arise, we understand
That man and woman can walk hand in hand
Equals to be in this great land
Not jealous nor envious of one another
But able to share as a sister and brother

Elizabeth Krause

A Dream Come True

Lying beneath the stars, above the sand
the ocean waves whisper in the darkness
like a falling star a tear streaks across my cheek
disappearing in the smile on my lips
my thoughts wander dreaming about you and me . . .
Years from now . . . lying beneath these same stars,
above the same sand, and feeling that same love.

Fate has brought us together . . . now it is up to us
to make this . . . dream come true

Jennifer S. Mingo

Misplaced Foot

Before, I gazed into her eyes,
  But now I gaze through them; for this flower has been stepped on.
The gardener, having planted her roots on his walking path, left her
  only to be crushed by the misstep of his foot.
But this foot goes unhated,
  For it is also the foot which cools her thirsty throat with water
  and by which she calls Daddy.

Why Daddy, why?

I want nothing more than to build the fence which would protect her,
  To paint the sign saying "Wrong Way".
But then, after the misplaced foot,
  My feelings turn to rage.
All I want is to take this flower from him.
  To carry her pedals to a safe place and protect her.
The walks continue . . .
  Bringing the foot with them.
With each misplaced step,
  She's pushed farther and farther down, until finally the
  soil becomes her protection.

Why Daddy, why?

One day the flower was pushed too far into the dark soil and suffocated.

Mark A. Pack

The Day I Killed A Man

It was hazy, but when I look back, I can clearly remember the day
I killed a man. And I see the reflection of Fred something at the
Vietnam memorial. And all he is stone. And I have left him down.
How I thought about him as I reached down and pulled out cold steel.
From behind, a bang and a glorious red fountain covered me in warmth.
I laughed about my accomplishment, but Fred went the same way —
and then I laughed at my youth. I'm all covered in it and you're
all covered in it and one of us lies dead.
  Now, as I reach down in my soul and pull up what's hiding,
I sob because I did it to be accepted. I cry as I remember the
day I killed my brother.

Brendan Jennings

Wet Music

Wet music plays down my window.
I can hear the thunder sing.
The lightening flashes, crashes cymbals in the air.
The trees dance with the wind in crazy moves.
I yearn to join the party outside,
but I cannot.
I can't sing that music or dance those moves,
and no one can tell me why.

Amy J. Fischer

Untitled

Knock! Knock!
Hello! Welcome to my mind. Please, come on in.
Excuse the pain; let me remove some fear.
Have a seat in my loneliness.
Can I get you a cup of depression?
No! Thank-You! I can not stay long.
I brought you your products, you ordered
  in prayer
Here is your peace, and this is your joy;
  Both carefully wrapped with love.
Here is another box — a gift — from ordering
  from me.
When my visitor left — I opened my gift.
My lamps started to glow, as I held in
  my hand, a cup of grace, Was given to me.
In a humble box — wrapped with love;
  Especially For Me.

Jo Anne Adams

Seasons And Reasons

The fields, the streams, they're not the same.
I hate the snow, I hate the rain.
But you loved each in its season.
And, son, you had good reason.
You enjoyed God at His best.

I take your rod and gun in hand,
And I still can't fully understand
Why God cut short your "season",
But I'm sure He had a reason.
Now-enjoy God at his best.

I pray each night I did not fail,
And I hope my guidance did prevail.
I pray that God will understand,
And grasp you with His powerful hand.
Until I have a reason,
Enjoy you new-born "season."
And - enjoy God at His best.

  'Till we meet again in God's
    Reasonless, seasonless Kingdom,
    "Dad"
Bennett P. Davis

Relife

No one can love me, that's why they hurt me,
I'm nobody's baby, that's why they hit me,
I'm just a girl, that's how I was born,
It's not my fault, I'm made deformed,
So let me hide away from them,
  Will someone be my mommy?

Frightened tears are running down,
Can't catch my breath to make a sound,
Please take my heart away from good,
They think that I fell down.

My husband doesn't love me, that's why he hurts me
I was pregnant when we married, that's why he hits me,
I try to do the best I can,
I'm less than dirt without a man,
So let me hide away from him,
  Will someone be my daddy?

Frightened tears are running down,
Can't catch my breath to make a sound,
Please take my heart away for good
I told them I fell down .... again.

Judy R. Jones

Lab Results

Late afternoon sunshine pressing through dusty venetians
lighting up
beautiful young faces beneath shiny, bald haloes
I looked up, sensing your presence standing there;
knowing you
Child of the Crab; soft, gentle, trusting violet eyes
sun touched, smoky light brown hair, soon to be torn away
wanting you
to be the one to survive; feeling already your
departing soul.

Oh the anguish in your mother's eyes, begging us to say it is
not you
All the tests are clear, the claw of the crab has dropped
  its vice like grip;
the monster has shambled away.
not so
It can not be for you, a child's carefree, eternal existence here on
earth, not adulthood; not aging
not life
Only for you, there will be the merciful clasp of eternal peace.

Jane Mason

Untitled

In between the light
I feel my way through walls of music
Whose rhythm guides me forward
Spinning my thoughts into blankets of
Warm nothingness

Biting my skin, tenderly, the teeth of life
Leave their marks
Impressions that make me question all

But who is beside me?

No one.
I can put my feet up on all coffee tables
The possibilities are as endless as I am

I twist and push

Getting nowhere, but not remaining where I am
Currently

Beyond all boundaries I find my song
The music has left the pages of my world
But lingers like a soft ringing in my ears

It sounds on and on . . .
   Incessant like the moon
     Meredith R. Tolan

Together

Together on a rainy day
The sun still shines in your smile
Together on a cold and wintery eve
It is filled with a warmth form deep within
Together on a dark and gloomy night
The night is filled with light from the twinkle in your eyes
Together all the sunshine, warmth and light
Are missed when there is no together
Together is one of the must enjoyable things in life
When there is someone you want to be with together
Together everything becomes one
Living, warmth, light and happiness
The only thing missing is loneliness
But that is okay
That is something we will ever know
As long as we are together
    Robert Funk

The Caterpillar's Dream

Emerging freely into the air
  from a confining life of solitaire
And now you see the world
  From a different view
Facing new challenges
  Starting anew
Forgetting your past
  Constantly moving on
What once was looked up to
  Is now looked down upon
Setting yet another site
  And leaving a mark
On each goal you alight
  Aware of the danger
In each path that you choose
Not gambling on odds, in which you often lose
Proud of yourself, not flaunting but bold
Graceful, flamboyant, truly a sight to behold
And someday I'll be like you, because I set my goals high
To spread forth my wings, to become a butterfly
    Anthony Kelley

Rugburn

The bomb went off Saturday.
Pieces of my mind and soul
Flew everywhere.
I scrambled around trying to pick up
Each and every last piece.

But I couldn't,
They went too far.
I scrounged for another hour or so,
But I couldn't complete the puzzle.

What was left of my mind began to rationalize,
What was missing?
All of the mechanical parts are here.

What was left of my soul began to think
Of what I needed most right now,
And of what piece I needed to find
To survive.

That missing piece was you.

And then I began to cry.
    Liz Coffin

A Utopian Dream

The Olympics — what do they mean?
They stand for peace
And a Utopian dream.

The five rings bind and tie
All nations together,
Attempting to create unity forever.

Hundreds of countries participate every four years,
In hopes they can create harmony
And dissipate all fears.

When our country takes part in the Olympic Games,
No one should focus
On the famous athlete's names.

Instead everyone should think
Of this great opportunity,
Which is to create peace, harmony, and unity.

The Olympics — what do they mean?
They stand for peace
And a Utopian dream.

Let's try to make the dream come true.
    Deanna Griffin

Peaceful Man

Yihtzak Rabin now is dead.
But it is not the same for the fight he led.
Standing there, sharing his vision,
Shot by a man of his own religion.
Shot three times in the heart and chest,
Two days later his soul laid to rest.
The nation he led now in sorrow,
What will happen-come tomorrow?
Leader, father, grandfather, to many a friend,
His long life met a premature end.
Across his coffin laid his flag,
Morale is low, and spirits sag.
Many people are now in grief,
But also shock- and disbelief.
The man who led a country so great,
But now who knows his nation's fate?
The newspapers all reported his death,
Not a warrior, but a peaceful man- to his last breath.
    Paul Wright

The Longer I Live

The longer I live the more I realize
We are all different
  but yet, very much the same in likeness . . .

The longer I live the more I realize
We should each moment
  Look at who we are and celebrate, celebrate, celebrate . . .

The longer I live the more I realize
We have a choice and
  with kindness we should embrace it . . .

The longer I live the more I realize
We cannot change
  who we are nor can we change the past . . .

The longer I live the more I realize
We have to make a decision
  to change our way of thinking . . .
and so, the longer I live
  I realize we all have our own uniqueness
and with respect for ourselves and others,
  accepting our differences, and working
together, we can be a powerful team

Mary Brett

Women's Talk

Two women meet for lunch one day,
To catch up on the news.
The subject swiftly turns to Love,
And both have long reviews.
One speaks of love with dancing eyes,
The other looks forlorn.
For she can only glare at love.
Her heart so badly torn.
"But why," one asks, "Should you be sad?"
"We've had our loving days."
The sad reply is spoken low,
"Love always drifts away."
"Then maybe, friend," says loving eyes,
"It was not love at all."
"Love does not die, just change its course."
"Love weathers every storm."
"What must I do," the sad mouth asks, "Try all that love directs?"
"Should I just keep on searching, make true love's gain my quest?"
Then loving eyes just folds her hands,
And utters softly, "Yes!!"

Bunny Wylie

Atlanta

Atlanta, a city that's great;
Atlanta, too busy to hate;
In Atlanta, queen of our state;
We like to affiliate!

In the corporate world, we rate high;
Architecture reaching the sky;
Home of Cocoa Cola and Delta too;
The King and Carter Centers serving you.

Education, a priority,
Our many colleges offer the key;
Successful careers and honors we stand;
In celebration — Strike up the band!

Atlanta, we truly love you;
The Creative Arts we pursue;
Housing and Health Care you provide;
Sports and Recreation in which we take pride.

Atlanta, in God we abide,
He, the Power, forever guides
Our thoughts, our plans, our destiny;
Bring peace to us, eternally!

Helen B. Norton

Persimmons

Crows like black specters,
nondescript brownish grasses
frame the picture made by turning leaves,
golden harvested vineyards
soon to be bare and dormant.

Orange balls hang
like left-over Christmas decorations
from persimmon trees
stark against the dark winter sky.

A few early narcissus signal
that this will pass and come again.
Each year
another winter of remembering.
Each year
another dark winter of longing.
Until spring
brings sunlight and wildflowers
and the green grass of hope.

Shirley Spina

Only A Kiss

You say a kiss is only the imagination,
But I think that you are very mistaken.
How can you think of it so cold and heartless,
When it can mean so much to even the thoughtless.
It's only the imagination so you say,

Well I think not in any such way.
Why a kiss is love and passion combined,
A warm caress from me to thine.
A pressing of lips from one to the other,
That makes it more than a kiss from a brother.
It is a beautiful thing that only two can know,
That often inspires a love to grow.
It's the sun that shines into my life,
It's the thing that helped make me your wife.
A kiss is a song that lifts the heart,
And makes two sad when time to part.
Oh I wish to God I could make you see,
Just what a kiss can mean to me.

Ollie M. Bohlen

Six Ways Of Looking At A Cat

I. In the slums of some obscure back alley,
  The only ray of hope
  Is the gleam of a blind cat's eye.

II. Cars honking, people shouting,
  Feet stomping, glass shattering —
  The chaotic din of the city
  Is just the lazy cat's purr.

III. Amid the lustful harmony
  Of the two naked lovers,
  The wise cat sits,
  Quietly licking its paws.

IV. On the first day, God created light.
  Then He divided the light from the darkness
  And saw that this was good.
  Later, God combined light and darkness
  Into the image of the cat and saw that this was also good.

V. All the rivers, lakes, and oceans of the world
  Find their source in the movements of the cat.

VI. A desperate girl turns to prostitution for money.
  The cat has just lost one of its lives.

Nancy Koven

Little Big Girl

Little big girl lying there with a smile on your face.
You're so fragile and beautiful, modeling your veil of lace,
Some day Jesus is going to come and make you whole and free,
Then you can come and go as you please, just like mother and me.
So as you lay day after day, remember Jesus is going to
make your dreams come true.
So little big girl, on days you are down and out
Try to smile and not be blue.
Though your body is twisted and small.
Your heart is bigger than mine.
So as life goes on, keep believing is Jesus.
For we all know that He is gentle and kind.
Remember this, God loves all and for those to Him is true
His reward is to take them to his home above the clouds of blue.
For your love of Him, His return is to take you
to heaven above.
There you will walk the streets of gold
As your reward for your love.

J. Russell Brooks

Untitled

Blessed be the name of God
The Divine gift is wisdom
And knowledge of the Creator shall be pure
Come and join the gifts
For the Creator has many
The King (of Heaven) has his treasury full
And the Queen's wisdom has endless riches
Therefore be wise and pray for the greatest gifts
For many poor persons seek the riches of God

Daniel P. Winn

A Wider Sky

I want a wider sky, I desire a deeper space,
I need to hear my sight and feel the texture of sound.
When young time inches slowly past our sight,
We do not understand how to hold on and allow the time to flow.
With adult eyes this time can be seen racing by,
while the lone days hold us hostage with their weight.
The years change clouding or clearing our vision,
Like an hour glass that's nearly run its course,
the sand seems to flow faster, and faster, faster, and . . .

So I see my time running short, the joy and happiness covered.
Buried under six feet of seconds, minutes, hours, days, months,
and those impossibly short years.
Like a child hurling pebbles into the surf, I try to hold back time's tide.
My life has learned what rules reality and it is not love.
Rather minutes, miles, and money are the everyday Lords,
All measurements of how humans are parceling out ourselves.
Adult years do not make me a man, but the measure of a man.

I need to hear my sight and feel the texture of sound;
A world where reality does not abound, then Love might survive.
I desire a deeper space, I want a wider sky . . .

Frank Bedros Bozyan

The Sun

As I lay in a patch of clovers, I can see and smell the
Honeysuckles growing on thin, rope like vines.

As the wind blows the branches on the trees sway.

Birds are chirping
Grasshoppers play in the tall grass.

Looking at the sun,
I know it is going down.

Everything is silent
The color of the sky runs black.

Melissa Hamrick

God's Call

It was the day of communion when we would renew our vow
But little did that little church know that God would work now.

He spoke to a young girl's heart and told her of his love,
He showed the plan he had for her life and the wonderful gift from above.

So she decided to do what he'd said to go out and spread his love,
To show all the world the love of Jesus and her heart soared like a dove.

But she made a sacrifice, when she left the comforts of home.
But, oh, the love of Jesus could be seen wherever she'd roam.

And maybe someday she'll go back to that little church she called home.
And maybe somehow the people will know from them she never did roam.

And maybe they will understand that she carried them deep in her heart.
So from their presence she may have left but her heart did not depart.

Angela Detter

Who Comes This Way?

Who is this that comes my way?
Just another person who I have not seen ever.
Is he someone with a great purpose in life or
is he just another person who is minuscule to my purpose to him?
Why shall I question myself with his purpose when the direct
effect shall be on me.
Who is it that comes my way now?
It is only me, maybe I should look again to think about what
I just said.
I looked once again I see what I see what I saw before, me.
What am I doing facing myself? Are you my greatest challenge?
To my surprise he answered "I am you and much more than you,
the reason why you are not what I am is because you will not
let yourself be that person that is best for you, so your answer
to the extreme question you have asked is yes, no and maybe."

Makalani Bomani Aswad

"Look Up From Down There"

Glancing upward where winged creatures take flight;
where the dusk and the dawn share the same light;

Often, as always, once seen, a picture captures most,
barely creating for the canvas, a silent spirited ghost.

Where is the memory of past or distant dreams?
Or present images of what could be; it seems

To gaze up recalling a thought of what could have been;
staring at the last moment and starting over again.

Upward into a foundation untouched with once being there,
or simply holding onto a wish or secret not made to share.

Each discovers a new path — the way is long and bold,
sweeping under the feet; the touch is crisp and cold.

Where ever it leads, the soul of all is pure and good,
however hard to capture the sights, once it's understood.

Look at what is only above the level of your path;
lift, movements taken forward, must hide the fallen past.

How easy to stop short and give into painful fear,
throwing "almost" away, because the present is right here.

Easier it seems — the light glows and notes the way,
interrupting the darkness of thoughts — hear the music play?

Where there is power to remain — resist the urge to hold your stance;
shift the gaze of the windows — lift them — focus on the chance.

Escape the trap dealt to yourself — loop up from down there!!!!
Because only from down there — can you see to Anywhere!!!

Darlene C. Callahan

No Painting

What man can paint,
The forest true,
Can he paint the tree to move
as gentle breeze goes wandering by?
Can he paint the smell of new spring
flowers, on canvas tight?
Can he paint the water
as it flows over the rocks
and washes onto my feet?
What sound can his brush make
That I would know an eagle has flown by,
Yes he may paint a spot from here
and there, but can he paint the smell
of a new spring rain,
What paint can raise on morning bright
when the mist rises up to my head.
That I may see a thousand colors in a
hundred places that no man has ever
painted.

Donald Carroll

Silent Strength

I always thought a push and shove
Was just the way you love
So I left and cried
And went out and tried
Your cruel way of wording things . . .
Spoke the truth and "flew with wings"
With your evil eyes you stare!
And not one tear you share
But your laughter shines through
In everything you do!
Each and everyday I took a step
It was you who never slept
"Others" comfort me with riddles and rhymes
But, it is "you" who stood the "test of times"
People say that I'm the strong one
But you were the one who never had fun
Because you always had to yell and scream!
To make me fight for the dream!
So, for every step that I take tomorrow
I know you will push me and take the sorrow . . .

Janet L. Bennington

The Silent Plea

I was conceived before the foundations of the world existed
And you want to kill me
My father was the one who put you in existence
Yet, you still want to kill me
I did you no harm, never laid eyes on you, and never trespassed in
  your world
Why do you wish death upon me?
Is your world so bad that you want me killed?
It can't be so bad if you're alive, if it is, would you wish
  destruction upon yourself?
I don't want to be destroyed, nor do I want you to be destroyed
I just want a chance to live, to see your world
I just want to be held, to be cared for, to be loved
You did not make me, so don't destroy me
I am a gift to you, do not refuse me
I can offer great things to you, to your world
All I want is a chance to live, a chance at life
So please, choose me, choose life
For I am life, I am the unborn.

Richard N. Keyser

My Baby

How much do you love me mommy, asked my child today.
More than life itself I answered, hoping that would assuage.
She's only three, you see, My Baby really needs me.

"How much do you love me?" "Can I get the shoes I want?"
Love is not measured by things I quickly replied.
She's only eight you see, My Baby really needs me.

How much do you love me Mom? This question just goes on and on.
I cook and clean and sew for you, run errands all over town for you.
She's only fifteen, you see, My Baby really needs me.

My Baby called the other day, "How are you doing?", I asked.
"Just fine.", she said. Just called to say, I love you mom.
She's only twenty-three you see, My Baby really needs me.

My Baby came by the other day. I love it when she visits.
She asks for my advice, though my grandchildren are perfect.
But she's only thirty-two you see, and my Baby really needs me.

Many trials and jubilations together we've come through,
I love you mom she says to me, You know I love you too.
She's only sixty-three you see, my Baby still needs me.

Kimberly R. Humburg

A Summer Storm

Sitting on my patio one scorching summer eve,
Gently rocking, in my hand a cool glass of ice tea.

Suddenly, loud drum rolls of thunder go rumbling thru the sky,
How sensitive to dog's ears, these sounds so near, yet so high.

Wondering what these shocking roars mean and to us are saying,
Trees and bushes to a definite beat in the heavy rain, are swaying.

The lights quickly flicker and move me into a cool evening dusk,
With sounds of sirens and fire trucks, off to far away places rush.

The birds harboring in the trees, worms below for their meals,
Sweet sounds of cars splashing the wetness of rain from their wheels.

The storm is over, drops gently falling a soft pitter pat on the grass,
With flowers in bloom and their heads hanging, as if embarrassed.

The rain stopped, lights come back on, this has cleared my mind,
My quiet wonderful moments in the darkness are over with time.

Sandi L. Bernauer

Beauty In A Beast

Alone in the night, darkness all around.
Distant thunder, tonight's only sound.
Flash of lightning, dancing in the sky.
There in a moment, just as quick, good-bye.

Silence again, a quick show of might.
A warm breeze blows, ever so slight.
Leaves start to move, silence they break.
Dance in the wind, a rustle they make.

First drop of rain, drops to the ground.
Increasing in number, dropping all around.
Sweet summer rain, warm in its touch.
Life to all, appreciated very much.

Pools of water, collecting everywhere.
Where they lie, they don't care.
Lightning gets closer, flashing quick and bright.
Breaking the darkness, darkness of the night.

Thunder roars, following the flash.
Across the sky, another bolt does dash.
Slowing rains, the storm starts to cease.
Final farewell, for a passing beast.

Patrick H. Boyle

I'd Really Like To Be A Star

I'd really like to be a star,
I could have any life, any car.
I would go on all kinds of dates,
with directors and stars from all countries, all states.
I'd do commercials and movies,
and a duet with the Newsies.
I'd work with Tom Hanks,
and get makeup tips from Tyra Banks.

The only thing I worry about day after day,
is not making it to even broadway.
Sometimes I get scared,
kind of like when you get dared.
I usually think, "what if I don't make it?"
Will I just have to quit?
Then what'll I do?
I will have to get a career that's brand new.
All I want is to be an actress,
nothing more, nothing less.

This is my life long dream,
all I need is a little self esteem.

Jodi Wittig

Precious Young People Of Color

My black sister, he says he wants to get with you.
With what does he want to get
the body or the mind or the spirit?

My black sister, maintain you dignity,
maintain your self respect.
Be willing to extend, but don't always give in.

My black brother, do you know where
you've been and where you are going?
Set your priorities; know you history
and positively influence your future.
Be strong, never knowingly go wrong.

Love and respect your black women.
Someday she might be all you have.
Don't be against her, always be with her.

Precious young people of color,
we will soon be the foundation of the black family.
We must uphold our roots,
for if we don't, someone, somewhere will snap them.

If we all stand together and become one,
we are sure to find love, respect, and pride.

Carmen Kennedy

As I Watch . . . I Wonder

I sat at my window watching the sun come
through the trees.
Wishing you were here with me.
I see all the blue birds flying so wild
and free.
Thinking what freedom means to both you
and me.
I watch leaves fall from the trees.
Thinking how I wish you could have fell
in love with me.
Watching the rain hit my window pane.
As I wipe these tears I've cried away.
As I watch the sun go down.
I wonder where you might be.
As I watch the moon above so bright.
I wonder if you're safe tonight.
As the stars seem so beautiful and carefree.
I sat here thinking how lucky she must be.
Wishing and wondering why wasn't it me.

Suzanne Craig

We Must Not Give Up! Never give up

We see around us the hatred and suffering
As sisters and brothers, together we fight,
We must continue to help our own brethren
Despite all the evil and pain in our lives,
We must continue to live in the light
We must not give up!

We see our families falling apart
Behind every mask there is love in our hearts,
Communication is a part of our living
Something we must for all times repair,
Sacrifice is a part of our giving
We must have hope instead of despair,
And never give up!

Shootings, death, drugs and disease are among us
Oh, how we must feel about this world,
We must grow to love one another
And stop this hatred we have for each other,
We must build and bond together
Live in the light, touch one another, and never give up!

Cynthia Anne Renée Armstrong

Stop

Stop the pain that feeds upon my heart
As though a ravenous hound has gone without
On a cold winters night.

Stop the untruths that burn my ears
As though my wounds where filled with salt
And my soul filled with fire.

Stop the mistrust, as the ugliness of it
Forms bitterly on my tongue
And breeds ill words upon my lips.

Stop the dreams that haunt my nights,
So that I might have one safe haven from the pain
That finds me and shall always find me . . . unbroken.

Stop the secrets that hide me from the life I cannot find.
For every unhappy moment brings me closer to death,
And further away from the feelings I need to share.

David DuChemin

Till We Meet Again, Grandpa

God saw you were getting tired
And a curve was not to be
So he put his arms around you
And whispered "come with me".

With tearful eyes we watched
As you slowly faded away
Although we loved you dearly,
We could not make you stay.

A golden heart stopped beating
Hard working hands to rest
God broke our hearts to prove to us
That he only takes the best.

It's lonesome here without you
We miss you more each day
Life doesn't seem the same
Since you went away.

When days are sad and lonely, and everything goes wrong
We seem to hear you whisper, "Cheer up and carry on."

Each time we see your picture you seem to smile and say,
"Don't cry, I'm in God's hands we'll meet again someday."

Dave J. Gallegos

89

Kafka

The world is not a good place for sensitive men,
At least not for men like Kafka
Who wrote about the unpleasantries of the unconscious,
But didn't materialize collected nightmares.
Yes . . . People write about bad dreams
Others manifest them, both co-create them.
It goes without saying that if a person thinks,
upon something, he or she becomes
The conception of his thoughts, or his thoughts
A conception of the man?
Who's to say.

There's a thin line between
That which we believe to be reality,
And that which is reality.
We can only speculate the notion.

And there exists a thin space between nightmares and hope
Both dwell in the same realm.
We can only live the possibilities.

Vernon Demetrius Odom

Your Body

Your body begins with a roar and a screech,
soon it will quiet and find some relief.
Your body's career lifelong is to fight,
it's designed for plenty of sleep thru the night.

Your body was built with this in mind,
looking up Genesis 1; verse twenty nine.
The God said, I will give to you,
every seed bearing plant and tree that has fruit.

Your body requires a little spring cleaning,
like a house whose cobwebs extend from the ceiling.
Remove all the cholesterol, bad minerals, and plaque,
and make sure that garbage will never come back.

Your body stands guard against the pollution,
it wants you to know there is a solution.
The body instinctively battles with cells,
Immune system dictates, it hollers and yells.

Preservative, additives, to name just a few,
create a disturbance, a breakdown, a feud.
Given the right ammo your body can win,
you could be retiring, good health to the end.

Bonnie Luksis

When The Earth Is Flung From It's Orbit

The day politicians tell only the truth,
When teenagers stop shouting things uncouth;
When taxes are a thing of the past,
And appliances are built to last,
When all hate is replaced by love,
And people in crowds no longer shove;
When our bodies no longer deteriorate,
Each one has found the perfect mate;
When people stop destroying each other
And truly start treating each one as a brother;
When there's no more murder and no more crime
And a dollar's worth a dollar instead of a dime;
When youth is respected, and age is revered,
And war a solution no longer feared;
When ugly turns pretty and pretty turns real,
No one's afraid to say what they feel.
When the air that you breathe has no pollution,
Every problem has a solution.
The earth will be renewed and totally fit
The day the earth is flung from its orbit.

Donna McCourt White

Life's Advantages

Arise! Electric cockrows hearken slumber's fate;
No matter that the time is chasing time.
Red robins warble gracious hymns of Spring;
Smell, taste, drink in white resplendent prime.

Look! Towering arbors frame azure skies;
Wild wind — God's breath; limbs sway — a heaven-kiss.
Bathe quiet pleasure in the rushlight of day;
How blissful an existence such as this!

Alas! Old sun grows dim, gray shadows fade
Yet mindful souls vow still to elevate.
An opaque curtain calls to life the dusk
Who promises exotic gifts await.

Teri Ann LaBuwi

The Glistening Stone

Warm, the dampness that surrounds the trees,
Pale and bothersome- like water that dares not seep,
Outstretched, the milked honey likes the bees,
To see the sap — tickling irises that she cannot keep.

Wrath spills into a violet-filled scream,
A meaningless thought leading to a meaningless deed.
Hoping the belayèd root can save the last fulfilled dream,
Only to babble and look away — drowning the seed.

Going only to shadow the feel less seclusion,
A spoiled laugh echoing the mind asleep,
Desires crumble the prophesied cliff.

To nibble on the moss she left for the stiff,
Leaving a weeping tear; to dry in the whiff . . .

Charlie Weisent

The Reflection In A Cracked Mirror

I squander in trivialities that pull me down
    with a force beyond hope, beyond will.
I fly as if weightless in a sea of laughter
    constantly floating above the hatred.
I tread with fragile limbs of steel
    view the pull as a force towards revelation
        experience the flight as a progression towards reality.
It is I who suffers,
    who overcomes, who learns, who grows
It is I who possess the sight
It is I who performs the deed
I live in a cracked mirror
I house a kaleidoscope of distorted beauty
I am a reflection of you.

Jill Wilson

Wait For Salvation

Someone visited me yesterday and I know him well,
he came before, yet then too he fell.
His face is featureless with hair of flame
evil whispers, to call my name.
Here you see him, black robes of fear.
But there you pass, your screams so near.

This is not his world, and we aren't his to keep,
until we do die, and then they will weep.
The spirits above, they sense the pain,
below on Earth begins the rain.
While those below, they gain another
to initiate as their newest brother.

I will never go with this death, luckily saved,
the torture of it I have steadily braved.
He will come again, but I can live,
until I rise to life that only God can give.

Sarah Basiletti

Untitled

As I was walking down the street one day,
a billboard caught my eye;
The rain came pouring that day,
and tore it half away;
The other half remaining there,
made that billboard say;
Go smoke a coca-cola, tomato catsup cigarettes,
watch a box of cough drops, dane with a bag of cigarettes;
Get pruna for your horses, which is the best in town,
And overcoats are selling out, each at five cents down.

Albert E. Strasbourg Jr.

Today Brings Tomorrow

Like the wind blowing through the leaves of the trees,
Like a man proposing marriage on bended knees,
The sun sets night after night.
Yet rises like an eagle in flight.

Yesterday was sorrow,
And today brings tomorrow.

The haze in the sky,
The clouds passing by,
The rain falling on the earth,
Watching a child at birth.

Yesterday was sorrow,
And today brings tomorrow.

Crawling and walking,
Running and talking,
Yelling and screaming, singing then dreaming.

The world can be in the palm of your hand.
Because in Gods eyes this was all planned.
Yesterday was sorrow,
And today brings tomorrow.

A brand new dawn, and yesterday is now gone.

Christine Ryell

Spring Morning

Oh what a Spring morning, when the sun is shining,
   the winter snow is thawing, the animals are
barking, the birds are scratching and searching for worms beneath
   the snow or under bushes close
to the house. Winds are howling,
   temperature is rising to around 60 degrees. Water is dripping
from the roof top from past weeks snow.
   Such beauty, when one season is pushing its way to
freedom. Winter is saying last good-byes.
   Snow is saying I protected you. Spring is saying my
turn to warm you with sunshine. Rain is saying I come to make
   things grow again. Giving thanks
because only God can make a morning.

Charlotte A. Trapp

Poetry

Poetry is not words . . .
but your heart granting a wish.
Another soul set free.
For poetry can be anything your mind is.

The one true thing that makes poetry come alive is to give your
mind another adventure.

The heart and soul wanders in and out,
but poetry stays in the hand and heart,
so, when the heart makes a wish,
be sure to have paper and a pencil.

Shelton Simmons

Tales Of The Orient

— Calendula
   its smile of poison,
Calao,
   Covered with marble
   In typical tropics
   Ready for a fire celebration.

— Sentimentality no longer exists
   engulfed since the beginning of time
   by pink swamps.

— So many smiles
   lacquered
   at mezzanines
   from the towers of Babel.
   Under the calming lash of the great Vizir
   Two rubies are fading.
The prayer has begun . . .

Georges Pinel

Blue Diamond

   An ugly rocks was found one day.
It was just laying there. He picked it
up and thought for a moment. Then He
decided to use it for a purpose. He took
the rock to His workshop and began chipping
away at it. He chipped and chipped until
He saw it was a fine blue diamond. He then
polished it until it was perfect.
   Who is that precious gem? I sit you? Is
it me? Only HE has the answer.

Janis Cox Chaney

Grandma's Tears

Twelve years have gone since Grandma left our world and entered His.
It's been that long since I have been in the church that Grandma lived.
As a child I remember sweet Grandma praising to the Lord.
And as her eyes would fill with tears she would tenderly hold me close.
I often wondered why she cried and never asked her why?

As the song and prayer filled the church today, my eyes began to cry.
And as my daughter looked at me, she wondered why I cried?
Through my tears I smiled at her and, in return, a glowing smile.
I realized that Grandma's tears were not of sadness or of hurt.
They were tears of joy and gladness that Jesus filled her heart.
And now her joyous tears hold meaning that never will it part.

In the church that Grandma loved so much,
His warmth and love had filled my heart.
So, thank you Grandma, thank you God,
For bringing me home to your kindness and love.

Shari J. Valdon

Sanctuary In Prisms

The weeping of brightness is not easy to see
for in light there tends to lie joy.
If only to hear what a shadow could feel
it is certain that joy would transfer.

Conformity is forced in a spectrum of choices
forced and compacted into visible tears.
The light we envision is often formed of unwillingness
which in our arrogance we choose not to see.

There is sanctuary in prisms, and no relief at night,
safety in colors, not whiteness.
And the pleadings of light bulbs are invisible to us
that we might be comfortable in sight.

Stephen James Toulouse

You Took Me By Surprise

Unknowingly and much to my surprise, several months ago when the cold winds ran through me and chilled me to the bones, when the skies were gloomy and so very gray, a seed was planted deep inside my soul. It was a very special seed, One that didn't need the warmth of the sun or the water from the rain for it to begin to grow. It was a seed that began to sprout its roots from the mere sound of your voice and the kindness in your tone. Although we had not psychically met, and you were so far away from me, I could still feel the tenderness of your heart, and could see the beauty in your soul. Suddenly the cold winds would subside and the sun would shine in my heart warming the coldest of days. I knew you then only by the sound of your voice. It was a voice that stayed clear in my head when I would go home, and echo in my mind with thoughts of you all night long. I would think of the things we had said to one another and look forward with great anticipation to the following day to once again here your soft words. When we finally met, all the qualities I had invisioned you held, I could now see in the softness of your eyes, in the charm and warmth of your smile, and felt it in the gentleness of your touch. Since then and still to this very day, my love for you continues to grow. It has blossomed into a beautiful bouquet of the flowers of love, and has taken root deep inside my soul. And now, with each and every waking moment of every new day, and with every breath I take, my senses are filled with the sweet fragrances of you.

Richard Jouney

Her

Staring into the mirror,
Who is that she sees?
A reflection of her sanity.

Her skin as delicate as lace,
A single tear falls down her face,
Blue eyes crying,
Her soul dying.

Her heart so empty,
Too much room inside,
All she wants to do is curl up and hide.

Her mind cluttered,
Everything is just muttered,
Never heard,
She is quiet as a bird.

Now she lay down to rest,
Place your head upon her breast,
Listen to her heart go beat,
She's just lying there on the sheet.

Elinor Reneau

Hindsight

In the morbid grip of vice lies not the greatest danger.
In pristine love our naked soul becomes the vicious stranger.
For what we know to be a snare we shun without a qualm.
But what is pure and innocent we flee to seeking calm.
The seed of our humanity shall come to it's fruition
Betraying us with naught but our own faith and intuition.
The place we ever hailed our hearts' own haven safe and warm
Becomes our very prison in the tumult of the storm.
For none is sacred but the Lord. To love each other strongly
And not to, hand in hand, love Him, we love each other wrongly.
For we may come, but might must go, our love thus interrupted.
Or granted stay, we run the risk our love will be corrupted.
To give ourselves we lose ourselves in parting, and we weep.
To give His strength, we see through tears,
we give what we can keep.
We are the Potter's fingers in each other's sculptures molding.
We must not cling, but glide and learn that loving isn't holding.
For clay stuck to God's fingers is a selfish broken heart.
To shape in motion makes both loved and lover works of art.

Tricia Stevens

The River

On the bridge I stood and stared
into the somber water. Wild thoughts
raged in my head, and the river whispered:
"Come along, come along!"

Out of my loneliness comes moaning the
Question: "Why, what for?"
And the river responded:
"Come along, come along!"

The question "Why, what for?"
Stays without answer,
yet out of the depth entices:
"Come along, come along!"

Fascinated I stood listening to the river.
Out of the darkness ancestors spoke to me:
"Come along, come along!"

I sighed in chorus with the waves.
Redemption was my hope and the river
murmured: "Come along, come along. On my
waves I will carry you until eternity."
"Come along, come along!" roared the river.

Myriam Nolcken Nau

Eternal Life

It's time to say goodbye my dear, but do not think you've lost me.
Just lay me down in some plot with living things around me.
And in the Spring a part of me will join the grass there growing
To feed the hare and then we'll both go romping through the meadow.
A part of me will vaporize and heavenward go floating
To join the clouds and travel back as rain or weather snowing.
A part of me will join the rock, for centuries thereafter
I'll feel the sun and snow and rain and seem to be immortal
Or blow as dust to some far place and new adventures find there.
So do not weep and think I'm gone, just very busy living.

Charlene Bresnahan

Snowflake Lives

Every snowflake is different; no two alike
Just like the snowflake, we co-exist with
no one else quite like us.
No one of us the same. Yet we each have our own beauty.
When a storm comes, a snowflake will be thrown
in many different directions
It will be bought up or down; blown to the left or right;
often blowing in circles.
But no matter where it is taken
It always lands right where it should,
Exactly where God knew that it would.
Our lives are like the snowflakes;
when the storms of life come we can be brought up or down
in circles — all around.
But with God's guidance we land so perfectly,
Exactly where He wants us to be.

Lisa Carrube

Meditation

I am not my body, not even my mind,
I am the Spirit we all want to find.
I am not my emotions either,
I am the Spirit who lives for ever.

The Spirit this radiant spark of God
Lives in me and in everybody's heart.
That's why we are all brothers in God's garden,
If we would love each other
We would find on earth — Heaven!

Eva Martin

A Reason To Share

Scenes in my mind's eye, tells me that it's no lie.
I often see visions of a lonely past.
A time that someone special would die;
Even at this painful time, I will hold in my muffled cry.

My mother, father, grand parents and even a little son, too;
Have left this world, and my world, and at times, I am quite blue.
So I will use my talents, singing my songs;
Which I know will come off as true,
That I gave of myself, relieving my grief, as I sing my songs for you.

Singing for those that are left, getting relief from the lost I can't regain,
As time will past, I must go on; no more to endure the pain,
Of never hearing their voices again.
Not a song or words given, even as a slight demand; And even though,
I have searched my mind and my soul, I conclude with this plan.

I plan to sing and sing I will, until the day I die.
I will leave my heart in the songs I sing and that will be no lie;
To explain to my child or a very special love, that life has been
    great to me;
Yet, Family and friends have come and gone as I was forced to say
    good-bye.
Now when I die, no more to sing and no longer to hold in my muffled cry.

Tony M. C. De Carlo

Dragon Speaketh

The Dragon Speaks.
I heard that somewhere.
I wished I could have been part of its breath.
I yearned to become one with its thoughts.
But I was just to far removed.
My aspirations are not what is mirrored in its philosophies.
It pained me.
Yet only for an instant.
Intellectually I did not understand what my heart was shouting out.
So the shouts fell on a deaf mind and withered away.
So the pain was unfelt and withered away.
Intellectually I am so extremely sane.
But Ho!
The Dragon has spoken and sides with my heart.
A Dragon refuses to be overpowered.
It speaketh for my heart.
Already it takes over.
The Dragon speaketh for my heart.

Sarah Crouch

Will

I wrap my self with
The most austere eloquence
I sing unspoken phrases
    Lightly
Still grasping those fragrances
Unwilling to erase them
    Ever

I look up
And turn around the vortex
of my pilgrimage
I cancel my distractions
And I stop pushing the gates of heaven
    As well

Not time
Not they
Not anything will sweep away
Those words that can't either be bottled

I won't stop my ride
Half way before grace

Daniel E. Navarro

She's gone, that's all I know . . .

She is gone, that's all I know
As I sit in the dark of my soul.
My dry cup runs over still —
The why not mine to know.
At the Station today, gunned down,
(The whistles covered the sound)
As Bullets entered her body; My Love,
lonely, entered the Train Hellbound.
So now this ride. I ride the way
Along these dark tracks others trod.
The Blackness, my friend, covers my face
As I sit here questioning God.

Ashton Shane Jolley

Understanding

Sometime's understanding is hard to get,
and people say thing's that at the end they regret,
The problem is pride won't let you think,
So deeper into misunderstanding you begin to sink.
The only point you want to hear is coming from your pointed head,
You won't consider taking time to hear what someone else has said.
Understanding is so hard for you because you're always right,
And trying to get you to see another view,
would take most of a day and night.
So if by now you haven't come to an understanding of what I've said,
Then just forget the whole darn thing and rest your pointed head.

Lloyd R. Williams Jr.

Untitled

Do unto others, the Golden Rule says,
as I'd have done to me.

It all seems so simple and clear,
we could live in harmony.

But instead it seems, the world's gone mad,
hatred and contempt seem to thrive.

In a world that's so crazy and full of distrust,
it's faith that keeps it alive.

A faith that's not seen, but provides hope,
a faith beyond our understanding,

A faith that is true and ever so real,
it shines bright in a world so demanding.

So do not lose faith, put others first,
remember we're in God's hands.

There is peace in this age, if we look to Him,
Have faith in His commands.

Connie M. Ambrecht

"You Told Me"

You told me I was a mistake, that all I did was take.
You told me time and time again, that I would end up like him.

You told me you had no life, that all we did was fight.

You told me that he left because of me, but all it was, was greed.

You told me you didn't love me, that you didn't need me,
that you hated to see me.

You told me you didn't want me, you'll be happier without me.
You told me I was wrong, I knew I had to be strong.

You told me to leave, that you had enough of me.

So when you kicked me out, I didn't shout.

I just walked out the door and ignored what you told me.

Heidi Watson

Proud

You don't know just how I feel
Because I'm too proud to cry.
My feelings won't be shown until
It is my time to die.

On that day I will be brave
And let my feelings show;
But until then you won't understand
Just how much I know.

I know that you are always there,
Until death do us part.
You realize I'm not one to talk,
You know that in your heart.

My ambitions may have fooled you,
My work it sure was grand;
But to share with you the things I know,
This day I've carefully planned.

You've tried to get inside me,
You've tried to be a spy.
But you don't know just how I feel
Because I'm to proud to cry.

Kristen Fidh

Love In My Heart

There is so much love in my heart at times
That I must give it away or my emotions climb
To a point where I can no longer anticipate
Just what I will do when I cannot hesitate
It flows so freely that I cannot control it
It's like a heavenly high and I must behold it
I will spread it around like a good chocolate frosting
I will lend it to my friends who may not even be requesting
It will run like the wind to each soul I may meet
It will trample hate and greed and make their life sweet
I wish I had the powerful love of God
To have that much love would surely make a human feel odd
But, maybe it would be a good thing to know
Just how much love the Divine truly shows
Then we would realize what it is that we are
Where we are to go and just how far
The love in my heart goes up and down
From spilling over the top to nothing but grounds
A steady stream would be just fine with me
A steady stream of love would surely set me free

Cindy L. Salow

A Poem To Selena

Music lived within you
you said it
A part of you is not here
. . . It has gone away
Your other part is music and it exists.

You will live in the muse of the poet,
You will live in the singing of the artist
In the vain dreams of the beggars
In the virginal conscience of children
Even in the apparent calm of silence.

Your figure will cross the stage again
Pleasant beautiful star
You are not here, thousands will emerge
as an answer.
Other faces, other bodies
Other appearance,
and at the end Selena's like your essence.

Manuel Cortez

Thalassic Gestures

Among the magical hymns in my brave mexican tongue,
I stand erect in gold.
At last the liquid psalms shall scream through the tired masses,
and I shall lead the celebration with large victorious strides.
We shall dance atop the oceans and equal the passion of
every wave.
With thalassic gestures we'll march wildly in geometric strides;
and sail like young sailors who laugh in robust fashion.
With our brown finger-like projections we shall scribble
our cultured anthems in the sun's sky;
and warble a holy, damp chant to request
the new season of sun games.
For the penetrating ceremony is herald as it is ancient
and we shall plant our civil solace in this garden.
The mild kindness is over,
The collaborate bliss of the wilderness is 10 billion strong.
The brine will not be forgotten for
the forest is brown and green.

Gilbert V. Estrada

Go On And Be Strong

I thought my heart could never love again,
Until I found You.
You were always there by my side,
But you were so quiet, I could not hear you.
While others tore at my soul,
You were there to give me the strength to carry on.

I've turned my back on You in the past, and did
Not believe in what You were trying to tell me.
You told me I was good and strong, and could face
My life's burdens.

You were the old friend I'd forgotten, but
Needed the most.
You restored my faith in myself and let me be me.
You said that You would always love me unconditionally.

I treasure what we share with each given day.
The sunrises, sunsets, and even the rain.
I thought that I was unloved and alone, because
I did not remember You.
But now I do. I hear You say to me,
"Go on and be strong."

Linda S. Rickards

Your Eyes Against Mine

Standing twenty feet from me, your eyes focused on mine.
Curiosity and flirtation came from my eyes,
coyness, and boldness came from yours.

Your eyes began measuring, began tracing
my clothes, my shoes, my arms.
My eyes started to hold, to touch
your shirt, your skirt.
And as our eyes pulled at each other,
stroking lips and cheeks, tugging flesh and hair,
others stood unmoving.

You, bold as an eagle, flew into my eyes,
and showered me with a flurry of blows
which turned my skin blue.
I, dark, grim, went into your soul
and threw innocence into a chaos of lust.

Upon separation, your eyes, my eyes,
died from the sudden loss of passion
died from the sudden loss of a war fought with tongues.

Rhett Valino Pascual

Need Forsaken, Created

As I lose myself deliberately
In the moist web of dazzling light
Bedecked with the intricate pattern
Of multi-faceted raindrops
That shine like crystallized diamonds
Butterfly whispers
Float my careening mind
Over tumultuous waters
They engulf my carefree worries hungrily
My heart leaps from somewhere inside depths of myself
And rips through my skin
While tears of joy
Drip continuously and methodically
From the tips of my eyelashes
I am trapped in a perfect prism of ecstasy
Warmth rages around my body yet
Entwines all through me
Wishing to idealize this tired old world
I isolate myself from any part of me that feels forsaken

Lisa M. Tobelmann

Devil's Dance

Hark! The evil bells do chime,
As the sun sinks low, and the moon does climb.
The sky runs red with an eerie glow
The darkness that's coming, runs black and slow.

The drugs come out, the young folks grin,
Now, the devil's dancing his evil dance again.
The boys and girls think they are having fun,
But the devil knows they're on the run.

They are running from life,
As fast as they can.
The devil knows,
They're running into his hands.

Listen to me, do take heed,
Those terrible drugs, you do not need,
Respect yourselves, look for the truth,
Life is worth living, both for your loved ones and you!

Phil Castle

My Secret Place

When day is done and it's time to rest
It's the time of day that I love the best
I wander up the country path to a place upon the hill
I cross the green meadow, so quiet and so still
In spite of my worries and all my cares, I pick up my pace
For I'm headed to the spot I love, to my secret place
Soon I reach the flowing brook and at the edge I sit
Thinking of the day just past and contemplating it
Am I that important? Does it matter anyway?
Things that are upsetting, are always in the way
I gaze at God's given beauty, the nature of the trees
And all the flowers, gently blowing in the breeze
What insignificant part do I really play?
In this selfish world that I face each day
This is my sanctuary, a place of quiet peace
A place that I can talk with God and all my troubles cease
The beauty before me, confirms that I am blessed
And each days problems seem to be only a calculated test
For traveling to my secret place is only a small part
The important thing is my walk with God and what is in my heart.

Nora Catherine Waters

Reunion

I opened the door with a habitual twist,
a familiar motion, a flick of the wrist
his eyes pierced my tender skin
I motioned for him to come in
he opened his arms for an embrace
into his neck I buried my face
the small of my back he rubbed slow,
what was I thinking when I told him no?

She opened the door, with adoration on her face
her eyes were pleading it was a disgrace
I opened my arms and took her in
she is really quite fragile, I know where she's been
it was familiar to comfort her, just like so long ago
but when if ever will she let me go?

Elizabeth Martini

To My Papa

It has been so long since God took you away,
Destroying all who love you on that dark fateful day.
"Why did you have to go," I ask each night in prayer?
Hoping that when I wake up you will be standing right there.
My life has been so rough without you by my side,
Here to help me through everything, going together for the ride.
I was still so young when you were buried that day,
I cried through it all, praying that you could stay.
So much has happened while you have been away from me,
I have grown into the young man you always wanted me to be.
You taught me the way how to be a good man,
I was too young to see then, but now I understand.
When I have my children to carry on your name,
I'll teach them the right way so that they will be the same.
Even then as a grown man many years from when you died,
I'll still be your "little hamburger" that was always found
    at your side.
The next time I see you as my life comes to an end,
We'll be together once more, this time as two men.

Matthew Huff

From A Raindrop's Eyeview

The rain keep's falling
I can hear it calling
It wants me to follow
It up to it's home
Up in the clouds I fear
To look down from up here
But when I do
My home I see through
A raindrops eyeview
To a raindrop all is huge
Natural resources were not given as a gift
But to be used wisely
I now know what the raindrops are saying
So whenever I see rain I think about my experience

Deanna Gray

Mother's Love

A bushel of giggles stuffed inside chubby cheeks,
A whirlwind of mischief traveling on tiny feet.

A master of exploration with eyes wide with wonder,
His love is so sweet but his anger like thunder.

I love his peanut buttered hair and chocolate smudged face,
My gift from heaven, so bright and full of grace.

My innocent inspiration, my treasure, my son.

Cindy Rawdon

Song Of The Hives

Listen! Below the silence — a cacophonous roar, a billowing hum —
too loud to hear —
What is it? History, my dear! And from where? So clear now to my ear?
From us! Each tells of his life and his words come clear!

So — raise your voice. Join the chorus.
Though none can tell All — all must speak for us!
Add your tales of a life lived —
Yours and mine, hers and his and all of ours!
Deaths and births, meetings and partings, sieved —
Murders, mayhem and mirth, showers and flowers,
Or "two of each into Noah's Ark, squeezed".

Our Eras set the patterns, we all set the beat.
And we all form the measures, slow and sweet,
Or — quick-step marching toward a greater Worth!
Yes — we all perform in the Symphony of Earth.

LeAnna W. Groh

Turn From The Drink

5c, 10c Always asking for spare change
When you knock on my door,
You look mighty deranged
Please can you help me
This is always your line
When all you are thinking is
I need a bottle of wine
No shame, no feeling,
You're bold in the mind
I pray for your soul
That this prayer reach you in time
Please listen, stop drinking
Don't do this to yourself
You were once a good person
With plenty food on your shelf
Now you're hungry
And bummy, without self respect
Put the drink down and have no regrets
You still have time to clean up your act
So take this chance and don't turn back

Rose D. Lewis

On The Wing Of An Angel

When two people are meant to be together,
When destiny has feather kissed their souls,
They will be together for eternity.
Over the years their love can only grow stronger.
Through the decades their love will continue to bloom,
And even in death their hearts will remain adjoined.
Something so strong and pure, only happens once,
It is a gift given to you on the wings of an Angel,
And it is blessed by God.
Some have passed it up and lost it forever.
The lucky ones, the ones who realized it for love,
They are together to this day.
They will be together forever, and will love, cherish, respect,
And honor each other for eternity.
They will also teach, not only each other,
But every one they encounter, of the precious gift of love.
Always hold love in the highest respect, never take love for granted,
Always know that with love comes faith, and never despair,
Because when you least expect it, you will feel the slight brush of an
Angel's wing, as she bestows the precious gift of love unto you.

Kyra L. Beaupre

Through A Mother's Eyes

Happy Birthday dear, my angel sent from heaven above. Such a
special gift from God, made by the Potter's hand in His own image.

Your raven dark hair, your soft brown eyes that sparkle like a rare
diamond that radiates your zest for life,

Your lips God formed like tulips that speak only that gentleness
of your heart.

Some would say this could only be seen through a mother's eyes.

I know God sees her as a precious jewel being polished to shine for
His glory.

Thank you God, for trusting such a rare and unique gift to my care.

God bless you, I love you,

Mother

Happy Birthday, Nishma
31 years 3/24/96

Sonya Kerstien

Rain Of Tears

The day it was Good Friday, and the skies were dark and grey.
I woke this April morning to a hazy sunless day.

My friend that day had told me of the memories of her youth,
That every year, Good Friday, it would rain third hour past noon.

For that's the day God's only Son had died upon the cross,
And He would weep his tears of rain in memory of His loss.

And so the day went on and I thought of it no more,
Until it came third hour past noon, the skies began to pour.

The wind it howled, a lonely sob of thunder filled the air,
And birds fell silent as if all God's creatures were in prayer.

Trees in solemn dance swaying branches towards the sky,
As if to say they love Him, as if to say 'Goodbye'.

And so I walked in rain that day, the first I had in years,
And mourned with my sweet Father in His loving rain of tears.

Amy M. Bange

Blink And You'll Miss It

Open your eyes, blink and you'll miss it.

The road doesn't curve, split, or divide. It goes on, silent and
weary, miles from nowhere. No reduced speed sign to provide a sign
that you're already there. Just a pile of wood, a few nails, and a
painted skate board incline. Blink and you'll miss it, it's so benign.

Open your eyes, blink and you'll miss it.

The Baptist Church towers behind the cottonwood trees.
No Smokey Joe's Saloon in which to dine and the school
doors are always open. The children run free
flying kites, playing basket ball games with no broken rules.
Blink and you'll miss it. A town in glee.

Open your eyes, blink and you'll miss it.

The little brick roads will lure you their way.
No bars on the windows, a cottage, so quiet and quaint.
Time will pass by, hair will turn gray.
Children will grow and go into the world where they be will tainted
by the sins of the signs of the day.

A town without signs without the sign of the times. Open your eyes,
blink and it'll all go away.

Toma Clark

'Tis Eastertime

God is not dead, like people say,
For I just talked to him today,
And he assured me with his love
He's watching o'er us from above.
Just look around and you will see
How much He, cares for You and Me!

We watch the seasons come and go,
Spring, Summer, Fall, and Winter's snow.
The Winter's past, and now it's Spring
When God brings new life to everything.
The trees they bud, and the daffodils bloom,
And the whole earth looks like God's living room.

'Tis Eastertime the world around,
In each Christian's heart, new joy is found
When we think how Christ from the grave arose
A mighty conqueror o'er his foes.
He had died on the cross, and bore our shame,
May we now bring honor to his name.

Charlotte E. Armstrong

Proudly Myself

I am a simple housewife,
A housewife, I have come to be . . .
   Proud of my life, my love,
my children, have become
so important to me . . .
   I am a simple housewife,
brave, true an strong . . .
   Never have I wavered
my life to be something that is wrong . . .
   I am a simple housewife,
my children I hope will be,
caring, aggressive and strong
with whom they choose to be . . .
   Loving them forever
comes so easy to me. Happy
is all in life I hope they will ever see.
   I am a simple housewife,
a lifetime it will be, to raise
my children with pride and dignity . . .
   Simply true and honest is what I dream my children to be . . .

Pam Albrecht

A Strand Of Hair

Noted authorities in the field have proclaimed it to
be, just remnants of a once living cell;

But for me it serves as a telescope into my past,

A pathway leading from the corridors of splendor —
To the threshold of my present despair,

Corridors filled with the candor of expression during
afternoon summer strolls through Central Park;

To the blistery winter Christmas Eves where comfort
was encountered in a cup of hot chocolate,
and your warm embrace;

Oh my love, why is it that you've ceased to exist
within my life?
Is it that I've smothered you with an over-abundance
of affection?
Or is it that I have fallen short on a duty owed?

Is it as they say — just a part of life's evolutionary cycle?
or is it just; A Strand Of Hair?

James T. Minor

Deception

Tell me a tale that will never come true.
Make sure you color it with your own special hue.
After all, my love, you need to know I love you.
Now, cross your heart and hope to die,
Knowing you'll deceive with a despicable lie.
Why can't you tell the truth, that you will not try!
That package of misery you wrapped up so neat,
Just crumbled in shambles on the toes of your feet.
It's truly a pity, you aren't more discreet.
Now, don't be alarmed, dear, that's not your style.
Smooth it all over with your delicate smile.
I'm sure you will create something in just a while.
Now, remember this day, honey, you're in for a treat.
I hear pay back is hell, and revenge is so sweet!

Cyd Charessia Behrensen

Untitled

They followed all the rules, you followed none.
Still I loved you most.
Entranced by your spirit, you've stolen soul.
I revel in my captivity.
What once was mine, is now lost to me forever.
Locked behind your dark eyes.
A perfect dream, it smashed through into reality.
Only to be reabsorbed once again in illusion
The feel of your touch, the sound of your
breath, the taste of your lips never to be
tasted again. All etched in my mind
as though carved in diamond. Nothing
can cut me like you did, your hard
sharp edge as light as a feather,
leaving scares never to fade.

Jennifer Kearney

A Grandmother's Final Prayer

Dear Father in Heaven I pray,
that you will look after my children here today.
It was not my choice to now join thee above.
Help them to understand that they still have my love.
I won't be here today father, to wipe away their tears.
I can't encour age their dreams or help them to overcome their fears.
But in my heart I know they will be fine.
For each possesses a unique strength as they are mine,
All that I have for them are memories.
If sharing warm summer day, of apple pies, love and laughter.
So I'm leaving them in your care Heavenly father, watch over
them for me I pray both today and ever after.
   Amen.

Jeanette Putnam

Directions

I explore life's many paths in my dreams,
Braving virgin avenues, losing myself in intricate labyrinths,
Deep in the recess of my mind.
Tossing caution to the wind,
Roaming the winding paths, smug and unafraid;
A luxury only allowed in dreams.
I seek the paths of reason, roads I'd dare not travel in the wake of
consciousness.
In my minds eye, I see paths, that beckon me enter,
To cross the threshold into the nether regions;
Where dreams become reality, and
Fiction becomes fact;
There's fear;
Here.
I want to turn back;
Back to the safety of my dreams.

Amelia Roland Washington

Dying Room

A little girl with stiff black hair.
Stranger will strap you to your potty chair.
Don't bother with tears any more
or you'll be locked behind the door.
The dark dungeon with the smell,
where your body becomes a shell.
In your crib you sleep with five.
All live but none are alive.
Birthday, Doomsday it's all the same to you.
Your face and eyes have no hue.
It's easy to close you out because ignorance is bliss
and you are someone that no one will miss.
Born a girl, for that you are shamed.
And only God knows your name.
Precious flower without a bloom,
today you're going to the dying room.

Amy Timberlake

"Yore" Genes

It may be, you'll hear tales of yore,
From one, who thinks, he'd lived before.
But don't you be too quick to find,
That he is quite out of his mind.
It may be, there's some obscure link,
That causes some to really think,
That they had lived another day.
It may be, that it works, this way:
It may be, all those chromosomes, and genes.
Are like the chips, in our machines.
It may be, that they stay alive,
Where other things do not survive.
It may be, in our ashes, and our dust,
These genes are saved, from rot, or rust,
And, helped by earth, and air, and rain,
We eat them, back, into the brain.
It may be, this will serve to show,
That all those folks, who think they know,
That they have, surely, lived before,
May, in their brains, have genes of yore.

Frank Greenberg

I The Spider

I, the Spider, hear time whistle through my silk web.
For the wind has taken half and I must build a
new one to hear a higher pitched whistle.
And I wonder if I will ever come back to this golf
course to hear a golf club slam against the ball.
Time sounds like a golf club slamming against the ball.

Dan Shier

Untitled

The angels sang a song today as they danced among the clouds
With hands clasped tight. They circled and their voices heard aloud
They took her soul and rocked her, they held her with such care
We could not cry no longer, for we knew that she was there
We did not want her to go away, we did not want her alone
We tried so hard to keep her here, but we knew she had to go
She went to be with family, and loved ones long since past
We knew the pain inside her was finally gone at last
She looked so pretty in her gown of pink, each hair was just in place
The slippers made with hands of love brought a smile upon our face
She's looking down, I see her, she's kneeling now in prayer
Please do not cry my children . . . in your hearts I'm always near
The angels sang a song today, they took our mother home
No one so loved is ever gone. And we will never be alone

Cathy D. Albert

The Gift

Guess what I saw today? You face,
in the clouds. Soaring ever higher
into the universe, to join me there.
In my heart I felt our love, so true,
so real and so complete. From my
eye, a tear fell, resonating joy for
all those aware to feel. My frown
turned into a smile, when I felt
the love of our beings join out
there in the universe, for all to
benefit from. All goodness stems
from this unconditional love.
Trust in this and we will soar forever more!

Sheila K. May

My Life Will Bud Again

One strong tree stands silent on a hill
The breeze has died down to an uneasy calmness
Large clouds form overhead, filtering the moonlight
In the shadows, there is but one leaf left behind
It hangs on to a weary branch, not daring to let go.

As I watch this leaf clutching to its base
I realize, it is I hanging on, although tired
Hanging on to my fears of falling and failing
Yet strong and determined to remain grounded
Feeling the aloneness in the world around me.

The leaf tires and falls, floating quietly to the ground.
It is lost, among the vast majority of the others
A warm breeze blows gently past my face, reminding me . . .
Like the tree, as I shed my burdens, my life will bud again
Only then, can my new journey once begin.

Jerrilyn A. Murray

The Real Blasphemy

Holy Cathedral Eyes
worship chanting scenes
of Gothic sculptured thoughts.
Sound echoing off marble minds.
Penitent acolytes soundlessly sweep past
with bowed brains.
Reverently pause in the silence
of this holy place.
Scenes of suffering, a monument to peaceful slaughter.
Lips move remotely,
aspirating prayers that passed through them as children.
Young questions starved from memory by dark robes.

Holy, holy, holy horde
give up your power and might.
Divest your minds of the right of reason,
lest the truth should come to light.
All power and money are ours forever and ever.
Or until you awaken. Amen.

John Cashman

The Angels Are Crying

The angels are crying because lives are in turmoil.
The angels are crying because children are hurting.
The angels are crying because death cradles us in its arms.
The angels are crying because disease, hunger and poverty
are too overwhelming.
The angels are crying because hatred is dominant over love.
The angels are crying because violence controls our country.
The angels are crying because the innocent are suffering and
nobody is responding.
The angels are crying because we, as a whole, fail to see.

Jonelle Newman

If Only I Knew

When I thought to never find love again, we met in a foreign land.
When I wondered why me, he said that from across the crowded room
  I looked so strong, just like the leader.
When we talked, it was as if from a lifetime of knowing each other.
When we touched, it was electrifying, as if we lit up the city.
When he held my hand in his, it was instinctive this trust I felt.
When he looked into my eyes, it was as if he could see into my soul.
When we last talked, through tears I tried to hide, he heard them in my voice.
When we said goodbye, I thought we would last forever.
How was I to know that the telephone would not be enough?
How was I to know how much I would miss his arms around me?
How was I to know that my true soulmate would be lost to me?
How was I to know he would not wait for me forever?
How was I to know that what we once had would never be again?
How was I to know how lost I would feel without his love?
How was I to know that once where I was strong,
  I am now weak, no longer a leader?
If only I knew . . .

Jacqueline M. Caldwell

A Love That Lasts

There comes a time in your life
When everything is going wrong
Nothing seems to be just right
And the road seems just too long

You'll look back and remember certain times
You'll see a familiar face
You will face the facts and learn to walk that line
You're sent to a special place

Thoughts of someone who really cares
You know she will stand by you
She knows that you may be scared
Chances are, she's scared too

Just remember you have a guide
A person to help you through it all
Tell her feelings left inside
So she can catch you when you fall

Anyone can walk in and out
They can show how life can be fun
But one woman can show you what it's all about
That's the love between a mother and her son.

Enrika Norman

Hello: Good-bye

I said hello to the cutest little one, arms so slight,
Just a few days ago,
And held her tight, and wouldn't let go.

I said good morning to a radiant little sunbeam
Just hours ago.
She was going roller skating and, "Mom please come,
And don't let go."

I said how are you to my radiant sunshine,
Her eyes across from mine.
"Oh don't wait up, I'll be home sometime."

Someone said hello remember me?
She sure looked familiar,
But no, couldn't be.
My little girl was a sunbeam, holding onto me.

Lisa Hannahan

I Do Not Crack

On the seventh day I come back to the people of Eden,
models with God's hung over their shoulders.
The heads are bowed and the sea is red watercolor.

It is not finished.
There is one hill left to climb.
Afterwards — criminal gone, villain bused, the middle down.
The depressed cry on the hill.

I do not crack
but swing from the tree while spirits encircle me.
Until, at last, there is only eternal life.

Family disassociation in it and the young man who never wrote about
the white bed curtain close to the moral bed.
The bridges fallen on the old road — still waiting, speechless.

The fear of the deed devours me.
Darkness falls,
gloom encompasses a black sky with no more dreams.

A white coat no one can button or see really there?
We wear them
and suffocate on Sunday morning.

Amy M. Eldridge

What Is War?

War
What is war?
Is it evidence of hate
Or is it god's simple twist of fate
Is war something we love
Or is it something we have had enough of
Does war bring an end
Or with war does a new world begin
Is war our society's uncontrollable death
Or is it a brand new breath
Where is a war
Gettysburg, Korea, England or the Pacific shore
When it is over said and done
How often has anybody actually won
Why does a war start and why does a war end
Why do people lose and why do people win
Is war a problem or is it a solution
Are we destroying earth or are we making a contribution
This question when will we ever get to the core
What is war

Erik Potter

When The Hills Rejoice

Behold! Behold! Behold! The sky, the sky so mysterious in hue
Awesome, so awesome, frightening, fearsome in azure,
azure
Blue
So sombre, so sobering, all heav'n, all heav'n
A' ring
Earth's music, frivolity, those hot mouth women of Babylon
those
raucous
din
A' stop
what
A
thing
Those voices, those voices, methinks, methinks a million
thunderings
The King of Glory! Oh blest story, He comes to reign
When the hills rejoice

R. Green

For Sam

Countryside goes rolling by
Raindrops fall from a dark gray sky
Thoughts of him fill my head
"I need you Dad", was all he said

Held him close and cried today
Then packed a bag, on my way
Take care of you Mom, I'll be home soon
Just four more days till Friday, noon

Precious moments I'll miss today
Sometimes just don't know what to say
Business trips are hard to do
When you've got a son who needs you, too

Yes, I love that little boy
He's Daddy's special pride and joy
Tears run down those cheeks so red
"I need you Dad", was all he said

Someday he'll understand, I pray
Why Daddy had to go away
Sleep well my son, I'll be home soon
Just four more days till Friday, noon

John Troy Calaway

A Moment of the Woman

Flame brothed and back hit,
    something cold transcends my spine.
Beginning in the outskirts of sight,
    and drifting 'cross my mind.

From the wisdom on her face,
    like a mountain stands unspoken.
To her fluid style of grace,
    that keeps my conscience broken.
She always feeds me smiles
    which rule me with their might,
And creates forever whiles
    that forever bloom delight.

You might even catch me caught,
    yeh, strolling really high.
'Cause she can freeze me in my thoughts,
    and stop me in a sigh.

Wes Martin

Passion For One

The passion is my heart,
Is like love between two people,
You're like a bull's eye on a dart board, me being the dart,
I just can't seem to hit the right spot,
The more I try, the more I lose,
In my eyes I see one lingering picture,
Two birds, flying high above the world,
Through the misty rain
One is shot down, like a dead rose,
The other flies off like a careless butterfly,
He pays no attention to the others,
The passion in my heart, is like an eternal flame,
It burns higher and brighter every hour,
Never burning out,
Growing greatly upon the world,
Like an endless forest fire,
Everything in its path, is being destroyed,
There is no life left,
Unless we take it into our own hands,
listening to the passion in our own hearts.

Amy Cano

My Morning Son (Eli's Poem)

My Morning son shines so bright
He awakens me, moves me, even in the night
The twinkle and sparkle that shines in his eyes
Keeps my life turning, and turning clockwise

So much joy, love and innocence
So many questions and growing sentences
His curiosity leads to discovery
And I love how he's made me a girl so motherly

I know he's the reason I was put on this earth
And any pain and suffering now seem of worth
But when my time comes and I'm not there
Will he ever know how much I care?

I want him to know he's my Morning son
The one who brings to me so much love and fun
Teaching him life is my duty
But he teaches me to see all the beauty

My Morning son shines so bright
He awakens me, moves me, even in the night
The twinkle and sparkle that shines in his eyes
He is my life, my world turning clockwise

Diana Best (Di Rice)

Empathy

Alone
and under the stars.
Strolling through the kingdom of cages I feel
frightened and defenseless.
And for no reason,
the beasts are jailed.

My gait, interrupted by an inviting gesture.
The wisest elder comes to greet me.
He grabs the bars and silently
looks me in the eye. The sounds of
a hundred screaming creatures fill the hot air.
Under the long branches of an old tree.

Our bond is obvious. Minds
connected by an age old cord, the anger is mutual.
I'll have him know that
I too think of my children and
weep for them.

Jordan Bria

Truth Or Dare

The Truth crime would be easier.
The Dare hard work.
The Truth living single would be easier.
The Dare till death do us part.
The Truth birth control would be easier.
The Dare raising children in all this crime.
The Truth bottom of the bottle would be easy.
The Dare never breaking the seal on the bottle.
The Truth renting my home is easier.
The Dare thirty more years and it is mine.
The Truth hiding your true feelings is easy.
The Dare letting someone in to love you.
The Truth thinking that no one can do your job.
The Dare knowing everyone is replaceable.
The Truth always taking the easy way out.
The Dare living with what you see in the mirror.
The Truth Or The Dare: Which is really easier?

Jeffery Grigsby

The Dog-Matic $

A fighting-daily is to have a dollar.
Dough comes and goes like the snow and the rain.
A paycheck may disappear as if it were a falling star.
Spending to some has become just routine.
All the rolls represent a mirage.
A miser hoards cash as if it was the bottom-line.
We work for a necessary wage.
Jack determines the social playground.
Cash in the economy can go on a rampage.
Buck has its own sound.
Dollars, dollars, we don't get enough to meet our expectation.
Greenbacks will always stretch to the limitation.
This adds up to just plain civilization.

John A. Conner

The Pass

Driven out pushed hard to move
the big greys pounding fast across the flats
claps of flash shredding the wind in secret colors
old tall's misting out their pine scents
stand sentry as the great pass flattens
here clouds of snow geese collide the silence
with unforgiving ascent the flawed are left to nourish the marsh
as the moon preys the sun
the coon ply's its hands
night sneaks to life as
the fall grasses on kenosha
lies in dew

Pete Bowden

The Marriage Mast

As nature's winds fill the sails on a mast,
So we gave a billowing surge of love and
Understanding to our marriage.

Our sails were filled with hope and faith
as we navigated a life
of give and take.

At times the waves broke over our bow.
We sailed through the most brazen of storms
and eventually reached, without great harm,
the calm of an open sea.

During the stormiest of our voyages,
we never left the helm, but
our sails are now permanently lowered.
Our tides will ebb and flow no more and
I, alone, now stand at harbors watch
I miss you. Oh Captain, My Captain!

Maxie Taylor Weaver

Every Rose Says I Love You

I was thinking how much I love you.
What is the best way to let it show?
So I went to buy you a dozen roses . . .
Just to let you know.
While I was there waiting,
A troubled looking old man came in.
He wanted to buy some roses for his ex-wife
For all those years of making her life such a mess.
There was also a young man who came in to buy some roses
For a girl that he really wanted to impress.
So when the florist came out with your roses,
She told them that there were no more roses left.
They both looked so very depressed.
So when you only count ten roses,
Remember every rose says "I love you".

Roger A. McGinnis

Caring

Is anyone happier because you passed this way?
Does anymore remember that you spoke to them today?
The day is almost over, and its toiling time is through,
Is there anyone to utter now a kind word of you?
Can you say in parting with the day that's slipping fast,
That you helped a single person of the many you have passed?
Is a single heart rejoicing over what you did or said?
Does the one whose hopes were fading now with courage look ahead?
Did you waste the day or use it?
Was it well or sorely spent?
Did you leave a trail of kindness or a scar of discontent?
As you close your eyes in slumber, do you think that God will say:
"You have earned one more tomorrow by what you did today."?

Olivia Spagnola

"It"

It has been gone for quite a while, but I'm afraid that it's back.
It and I are old friends, but at times I'm not very fond of it.
It can be your best friend or it can be your worst nightmare.
You can't see it, unless you feel it. You can't touch it
    but you know it's there.
Be careful, it can make you crazy, but it can also make you whole.
You can tell who has it, who lost it, and who will never get it.
What am I to do with it? I want it, but sometimes I'm not sure.
Maybe it has a new side I've not known.
If you feel it and need it, that's fine, just be cautious of saying it.
Once you say it, or if you even write it down, it changes.
It will change you, it will change the person close to you.
Most importantly, once you say it, you can't take it back.
Now, maybe I don't want it to go.
You can fall into it, in a matter of days or it can take years.
But if you have it, it can last forever.
It wants you to call its name and it wants to be heard.
It came to me, and told me, it was here if it was needed.
If you are blessed enough to have it said it back to you then it's ok.
If not, it stinks. Well, do you finally get it?

Bruce Thayer

"Stifled"

The ropes they're being cinched
makes a future crawl inch by inch.
Who is this daring one?
Thee who stifles my tongue,
All the joys I've grown to adore,
One tries to absorb me all the more,
No one soul can ever control me,
However to some, seems a possibility,
If they ever fool themselves to that degree,
I'm destined for the battle to be free!
Once that magic force is lost,
Change is on the horizon at any cost
That bright star shines somewhere in my reach,
To obtain it is something one cannot teach.

Carol Fee

"Silent Music"

I sat on the porch —
The wind slapped my face —
Inspiration struck me —
And I started to dance —
Birds chirped happily —
And I started to sing —
I was happier then I've ever been.

Then I got slapped again —
Falling to the ground —
I realized it was probably a dream —
But, who cares as long as I can be happy again.

Kelly Kurczab

Two Points Of View

Life is a two-bit carnival that sneaks into town on flat-bed
trucks with creaking axles in the early morning fog and rain
Its rickety roller coaster runs on rusty tracks that only go down
and the Ferris wheel conks out when your car is over the motor
The carousel music is tinny and too loud
The pizza is cold
And the popcorn is stale
And the fat lady ain't so fat
And the fire-eater is a fake
Life is all messed up

Life is a walk on the beach on a Sunday morning
It's the high school band in full dress turning into
Central from Main and never missing a note or a step
   It's the home team's halfback busting through tackle
and going twenty-five on third and eleven
It's a baby crying in the back of church
It's lunch at the Ritz or Burger King or a family picnic anywhere
It's the smiles of those 'very special' Special Olympic winners
Life is beautiful!

Frank Barnicle

The Nine Planets

Mercury is the first one.
   It is the closest to the sun.

Venus is number two.
   It is one of the closest to you.

Earth is the "third rock from the sun."
   It is my favorite one.

Mars is number four.
   It is like a red hot core.

Jupiter is the daddy rock.
   Way, way around the block.

Saturn has 1,000 rings.
   A lot of beauty is what it brings.

Uranus is number seven.
   But it is not as far away as Heaven.

Neptune is the eight.
   You may not get there, but have faith.

Pluto is a freezing place.
   To keep warm, you would have to run at
   a blinding pace.

Cody Likiki Kanekoa Selman

Burn Bright

I think of things a lot of the time
But I never know when it will rhyme
I think sometimes life's too hard
But then again, I've come so far.

Life has hardships everyone knows
But sometimes a little light does glow
Like a candle glimmers, you are there
But sometimes I'm afraid the spark will wear.

Down to the wick it may go
But I'm ready to see it dwindle
Long and steady like a coal.

The coal burns long like you and I
Life has its hardships everyone knows
But sometimes a little coal burns bright in our soul.

Linda Sue Kennedy

My Dream

The night is still, a gentle calm, warm
And comforting as you come to me

You hold me ever so tight and I can only hope
That these moments I will not forget

Your gentleness surrounds and envelopes me
In a mist and you will not let me be

Splendid colors and waves of emotion shoot
Through me like a celestial comet

What delightful thoughts and images you
Bring, yet I struggle to be free

A new day is dawning, and you "My dream"
Must relinquish to the awaking conscious of
that which is me

Judith S. Howard

I See America Sitting

I see America sitting, the various sitting I see

I see the children sitting in front of the tv,
   their rear ends getting cushioned already

I see the youth of today sitting in front of a tv, with
   cords of evil, and control pads, that really control them

I see the drivers of this age sitting in their cars,
   just driving

I see the workers sitting around eating and smoking
   their lungs away

I see the government lounging in their rich homes, and on
   planes as they sit letting us other sitters rot

We all sit around, that we should not, because we are
   losing ground in this world of ours.

Michael S. Girvin

Untitled

Let me in, to hold you in your
moments of rushing pain.
Let me brush you into safe sleep.
Let me take you to my love, my softness.
Let me show you heaven.
Let me be with you. Let me in.
   And when it's all over and passed,
   let me stay.

Carolyn Elizabeth Seib

The Nighttime Sky

When I look up at the midnight sky,
I see the moon glistening in the shadow of darkness,
As I look up at the sight,
I see a golden cross sparkling around the great moon,
I feel the Lord is letting me know he is watching over us,
As I lay in bed staring up at the peaceful, nighttime sky,
I feel nothing could go wrong,
While I still gaze at the blue 'yonder sky,
I see a grand white passageway, opening up around it,
I feel someone has just left this beautiful earth,
And as I look up, I think of my grandparents,
And each night when it opens,
I feel my grandparents are sending down their love for me,
And when God opens up that glistening passage for me,
I won't be scared,
But for now,
I will live life to the largest extent I can.

Tina M. Adamo

Do We Realize

Do we realize how happy we are, until something makes us sad,
do we realize how good something is, until it goes bad.
Do we count our blessings, until they've come and gone away,
do we realize how fortunate we are, to wake up every day?
We take so much for granted, we never stop to think,
are we one that needs that pill, or can't get by without that drink??
Life is kind of funny, as it continues day to day,
and if you've not very careful, it could be you that lives that way!
so you have to make sure to thank him, the Lord from up above,
because without him watching over you, and giving you his love;
You might fail in achieving your goals, your plans may go astray,
so make sure that you thank Him, each and every day!!

Jeanette K. Clark

Untitled

I am a clown who welcomes all art . . . Music night and day
Simplicity of musical notes brings scattered parts together.
Skip a note, skip a beat music moves in time
Till we become something else, changed,
Transformed beyond our will with a sense of tranquility.
Pores are opened, minds are cleansed, breathing deeply, ahhh
Preparing our soul for communion with the Divine
In the Eucharist, in praise, adoration, mystery . . . Ahh!
Music bringing one to prayer, to contemplation
Entering into a world of life, death, rebirth.
Soaring stirring hope, idealism and passion
For the journey of life that has been mirrored
In the music itself, over and over we may play
The sound like faithful friends that never leave us
Putting us in harmony of a higher perfection.
I feel the tingle within my soul and I heat the sound of music
When I see you have found within yourself to laugh,
And have taught yourself to believe.
Helping you reach the child like nature within you
With liberated chuckled and belly-laughs, for I am God's clown.

Ida Reifsnyder

The Blue Below Heaven

Why is the sky as blue as can be?
Does it symbolize peace or a chance to be free?
Let the beams shine on you for as long as they can.
Because your destiny is not in your hand.
Don't ever turn back, it's never the end.
Others will criticize you because they are your friends.
The fluffy white clouds that floats in the sky
For everyone to see as they pass by.
The birds are a token from high above,
That God has created for everyone to love.
The night will depart sleek but fast
Leaving the sky left in the past.
The stars will come out with their vivid white glares.
Waiting in the sky to show off in pairs.

Mike Hum

Battle Cries

Above, the moonlight shimmered bright,
Below, the seagulls in their flight
Did catch the sky upon their wings
What wondrous songs the birds do sing.

The fishermen, both night and day,
Cast our their nets into the bay
To swallow hole the unarmed fish
With eyes of fright and death a wish.

The birds do sing tearful songs,
The churchbell rings with violent throngs.
Another day of death is done
The fishermen again have won.

Ingrid S. Donaldson

"My Angel Of Hope"

Bright angelic vision
in the middle of the night
Shocked! I was awakened
at your touch, oh so light

There wasn't any warning
no time to respond
Through my ceiling you vanished
Like a song bird, you were gone

Why I was chosen?
To glimpse your pure light
I'll always wonder
Late! In the night

That your spirit is holy
I know now the truth
One touch, from your wing
brought back a lost hope of my youth

Now when I die
I'll be happy to see
Your silky white wings wrapped around me
As I'm judged by God, our King.

Robert L. Perkins

The Gambler's Prayer

God just don't play Bingo, Lotto, or Black-Jack.
Nor have I found his blessings much, sitting at the track.

He doesn't help much at Craps, Or turn the Roulette wheel.
But it's him I find I cuss the most, When there's no money for a bill.

He wasn't with me at the Drawing, for that brand new red Corvette.
I've just about determined, that God just doesn't bet.

I lost him at the slot machine, along with many bucks.
But I ranted and raved, and told him how it sucks.

Twas not his hand, that touched my shoulder, as I dealt another hand.
But, I certainly told him what I thought, as I lost another grand.

The phone is shut off and the rent is past due and the cupboards
     are mighty bare.
And it's all his fault, not mine, that life is so very unfair.

And as I wander through the park, a broken, lonely man.
It's not till then that God reached out, and took me by the hand.

Larry Boatman

The Rooster And The Hen

Feathered and friendly are the Rooster and the Hen,
Well liked worldwide and their uncounted kin.
He's a macho mannered male, there is no doubt about it:
Whenever he sounds off, he will loudly shout it.
He's plume-tailed and handsome, red comb to yellow feet.
She lays eggs, then cackles, in a tone that's quite upbeat.
She hatches her chicks, watches over her brood,
Keeps them close with her wings in a motherly mood.
As they scratch and peck food found on the ground,
Squawks and clucks, chicken sounds, abound.
They eat all day roaming 'round the yard or pen;
And this they've been doing since Who knows When.
In the henhouse they huddle and roost at night;
Within is dark and quiet, unless something causes fright.
Early morn he wakes all with his Cock-A-Doodle-Do,
Loud blasts rousing early and late risers too.
Content with fowl life, they require not a lot,
From fluffy, yellow biddies to simmering in a pot.
A familiar, farmyard family, who serve beyond the end,
The funny, feisty Rooster and his mate, the fetching Hen.

Louise Foster

The Pine

The sun rose slowly o'er the hill.
Cold, dark night with light did fill.
Alone did stand a wilting pine.
And I remembered songs of thine.

They took me through the lengthening day.
And in my heart at night did stay.
Gone away was grief and strife,
I found I'd lived a happy life.

The winter nights beside the fire,
No children left for us to sire.
My spirits down, consumed by age,
Withered hands were clenched in rage.
Each day of work on face now told.
The youngest dreamer now grown old.
You always came and took my hand
And forced my bony legs to stand.

And until the last cold winter day,
When I finally passed away.
I stood with you, my hand in thine,
Upon the hill which stood the pine.

Randy Burd

Seasons

Leaves of red, yellow, gold and brown
Slowly drift to the ground.
They float and glide through the air
Touched by the unseen hands that put them there.
Snowflakes of billowy white
Slowly drift to the ground in flight.
Snow on the ground slowly starts to melt
No more beautiful sensations would ever be felt.
Flowers start to form buds soon
They begin to grow and start to bloom.
That means spring is almost here
When cool breezes whisper in your ear.
Spring means summer is now so near
When grass is green and skies are clear.
Just as the water in rivers flow
Seasons come and seasons go.

Crystal Powell

Going To School In Colonial Texas

Going to school was never easy,
All the chores, they kept you busy.
Yield the ax, kill the deer,
Mend the shirt, another year.

Never a minute, was there to spare,
And lack of money, caused despair.

The government tried to support the schools,
But there were no teachers to make the rules.

Formal schooling was only for boys,
The gals, they said, should learn only poise.

Reading, writing and 'rithmetic,
Learn the basics and make it quick.

Cooking, cleaning and sewing too,
These are the things the girls must do.

And so the boys, they learned to cipher,
While the girls were taught to diaper.

As Texas grew in sense and size,
People began to realize,

No matter what, girl or boy,
An education we must all employ.

Tricia B. Rosier

Letters Of War

To the end as I fight, finishing
Off my soul; writing, writing
   Letters of war

They tell a tale to me and
To others; discovering, finding
   Letters of war

Just and unjust, peace and illusion
Looking, listening, making, searching
   Letters of war

Crescent moons are being read,
Helping you to think and teaching you to fight
   Letters of war

Caress your thoughts, release them, tell
Your bloody tales and let them loose
   Letters of war

To the end as I fight, finishing
Off my soul; writing, writing
   Letters of war

Felicity Gaudet

My Soldier

This message came to me to show you the light.
I won't tell anyone it is just for you.
My hand was guided to deliver this message for you and
Only you. When you read this poem, you'll know that this
Hidden message is just for you. And only you will know what
to do my Injured little soldier.

My Injured little soldier, let your heart heal and mend.
My Injured little soldier, let your mind rest and be at peace.
My Injured little soldier, let your soul and spirit become one.
My Injured little soldier, let me comfort you.
My Injured little soldier, let the light within you come out.
My Injured little soldier, I will always love you.
My Injured little soldier, I have gone on to watch over you.
My Injured little soldier, just listen, listen with your heart.
My Injured little soldier, open up your mind and you will begin
To heal with time. Now go on and be at peace for I shall never
Leave my Injured little soldier.

Sheila Wright

A Place Like This

The sea . . .
Salty air clinging to my cheeks.
Sunrise . . . softly gripping my feelings.
Stretching dunes . . .
Where I want to run, wild and free.
Myriad abundance of tiny shells by the waters edge.
And down in the deep,
The seldom seen, and extraordinary
Citizens of earth who live below there.
What kind of a mind
Designed a place like this?
Wind swept and beaten by storm and tide . . .
While walking here,
I have learned many things,
About myself.
Revealed, in quiet,
In sun, and wind . . .
In surf and the ebb and swell
Thereof,
A vast and ancient ocean.

Sherry Dixon

Spring

Spring is in the coming,
and my yearning soul doth seek
an outlet for its restlessness
Brought on by winter's keep.

Be still, for March winds still blow cold,
and April showers will seek snow
to melt in hidden woodlands deep.
Heralding the seeded plants to grow.

Then shall my feet seek nature trails,
And woodlands beauty free and pure
Shall calm my heart with God's great glory
For which man's praise is but a prayer.

Lila Rose

Ode To A Dear Departed

Your spirit has flown to a land far away,
Higher than any eagle has dared to soar.
It has traversed over hills and mountains high
To that place where pain and tears will be no more.

Up there is a mansion just waiting for you,
Where you will discover a beautiful place.
Where all of your fondest dreams will come true,
As you bask in the Savior's eternal grace.

You will find more peace than you have ever known,
As Jesus sheds forth both His light and His love.
You will experience harmony and rest —
Oh, the bliss you'll feel in that heaven above.

Throngs will be waiting to joyfully greet you,
To a land where night and sorrow are no more.
Eternal bliss will be your reward and joy —
A crown of glory awaits you on that shore.

Edward S. La Pointe

Spring

The bursting forth of spring's warm song;
Heralds spring's arrival after winter long.

The snows once held in winter's arms:
Now runs, and dance to natures charms.

In headlong rush across the land;
To feed, to nourish, then vanish in the sand.

To continue to its mother's breast;
To flow with her to their ocean nest.

For spring is here, she has arrived:
More wondrous than man could contrive.

Her gentle rain has cleansed the air:
She purged the soil with gentle care.

Seeds spring forth in her warm embrace;
to fulfill their promise in majestic grace.

Godrich Hall

The Close of Winter

Spring has sprung.
As if a life giving bell has rung!
The birds all know the songs they've sung,
the grazing animals wait for new grass on their tongue.
Everything is beginning to green.
It's not as if this has never been seen.
What does this mean?
The beginning of a beautiful scene.
Although the rains can be a bummer,
spring has sprung and brings with it,
summer!

John E. VanTine

Can You Make

Can you make a tree grow, can you paint a rainbow;
Can you put the sun into the sky.
Can you make a river blue, and make the moonshine too,
Can you teach the birds how to fly.

Can you make the grass grow, can you bring the winter snow;
Can you paint all the leaves in the fall.
Well, you can't you know and you'd better say so;
And know there's a God that does it all.

Can you make the birds sing, can you grow a lovely spring;
And put the fruit on all the trees.
Can you make the oceans deep, and make a mountain peak;
Or make all of the little honey bees.

Can you make the star light, can you change day from night;
Can you make a butterfly so small.
Well, you can't you know and you'd better say so;
And know there's a God that does it all.

Susann R. Grimme Bunner

Death Of An Angel

Some time last night my angel died
Those who she loved fell down and cried
All but the one to whom she lied
Last night when my angel died

The Heaven's skies have lost their light
Why didn't life treat my angel right
All my dreams were gone from sight
When my lovely angel died last night

I saw her body laid to rest
My sanity put to the test
Her cold, white body sadly pressed
Inside a chilling, metal nest

When I slept, her soul was in my bed
When I woke, her vision, in my head
When I spoke, her love with all I said
But alas, my poor angel, forever dead

James Moore

"Six Strings"

It sits there in its loud silence, waiting for me to play her.
My figures don't hurt and my technique is fair.
When I get bored I touch the thing deep within.
After I'm done,
I sit and sulk all the music, silence and the way of the world.
Loneliness, boredom, and sterile repentance are my life.
But when it's over she still sleeps in her darkroom
waiting for me to play her.
Play her hand and nice.

Carlos Aterrado

Love To Sing

There's nothing quiet as wonderful in all the world as song.
Especially when I can get my friends to sing along.
But even when I'm alone a song is company.
I sing of places faraway that I can't wait to see.

I sing about my dreams and know that they'll come true someday.
And when the doubts and fears creep in, a song shoos them away.
Sometimes I find it hard to say the thoughts inside my head,
But then I think of music and I sing my thoughts instead.

Sometimes I feel like I'll just burst, and run off to hide,
'Cause no one seems to understand the way I feel inside.
But when I sing, my spirit lift. It never takes that long
Because there's something magical inside of every song!

Misty Wheeler

Who Is She

Her hair is brown her eyes are blue
Who can she be
If I only knew
I vision her in the day
I see her in the night
But something is still not right
Each time I face her I become more attracted
Maybe from the way she has acted
Her inner beauty mostly still unseen
Keeps me wanting to know more
Of what seems to be an on going dream
It might be in her smile
It might be in her face
It could be in her voice
or maybe her grace
But for now I sit and think
Who can she be
Her name may be my link

Jacob J. Brown

Personal Peace

Peace comes softly: A gentle touch,
Pink-trimmed clouds guarding the lane,
A returning smile for one just given,
Or the steady murmur of drops of rain.

Peace comes gladly. It opens its arms
To the grace of a cat, the lick of a dog.
It points toward sunsets and greening farms,
The song of a bird, the swirl of fog.

Contentment lies in quiet nearness,
Understandings that need not be said,
Rhythms felt in muted music,
And gentleness in nuptial bed.

Dorothy I. Sweitzer

Castle

In this castle, I'm kept a prisoner,
A prisoner to my very flesh,
Oh, the hours to endure,
Of the cruel "every day" mesh,
Washed away; My idle identity,
I am just a slave to endless dust,
Gazing at the colorless picture of "used to be,"
A feeling of loneliness, that devours my trust,
Left with only four walls and its stony stare,
Insanely held for evermore,
Buried in this atmosphere,
Leaving me with only fantasy to explore,
Strict my dwelling, surrounded by pain,
As my fire for life, struggles to remain.

Barbara A. McCornick

Forever

   Life has challenges that sometimes seem overwhelming
Our strength in mankind is measured through illness and
transience, sometimes making our inner being almost unbearable.
As time goes on, we become stronger, while life's questions continue.

   Some challenges are difficult to understand, but be assured,
things don't happen without reason, we just don't always know
why . . . Until later, perhaps years later.

   As we grow, we learn, and as we learn, we accept. As you
grow older, the pain will disappear, but you will continue holding
onto the fond memories which will once-again make you smile.

   Eternity is forever, and when one reaches that cycle in
life, loved ones shall remain together . . . Forever.

Sandra Webber

His Unknown Reality

Harsh winds in your head
Dark dreams flood your bed
Stormy days go by
You think you can fly

Waking up in strange places
Spending your life in dazes
The demons have control
They take over your soul

Hurting the ones you love
With the power of the drug
Not coming back to reality
Not even for me

Now the days turn into years
When you've been living your life in fear
Never knowing who you are
Never seeming like you care

Will you ever come back to me
Back from your unknown reality

Michelle DuJardin

"One Breath"

The night sky fills him with wonder and longing.
The stars contain too many secrets.
Always present are the questions,
Never are the answers revealed.
Enemies around every corner,
Denying everything that he knows to be true.
There is no one to talk to.
No one to trust.
Loneliness and hopelessness cloud his mind until
The fog is all-consuming.
Standing on the edge of the abyss,
A voice calls to him.
It is the voice of someone long lost,
Calling from the far reaches of space and time.
He steps away from the blackness momentarily,
For he knows that he can never stop searching.
Someday the stars will reveal their secrets to him.
The truth is out there.

Heidi Haserodt

Unrequited Love

I searched for you, for oh so long —
discouraged, then, . . . all hope had gone.

Then there you were, my love, disguised —
at first stranger in my eyes.

I felt your heart reach out to mine,
felt hearts, spirits, souls entwine.

The feelings you evoked in just an hour,
have left me wrenched, confused, unpowered.

Too late to turn back now, the coals are stirred,
the embers flames are burning now,

I was careless, thought I was so strong,
How easily, you stole my calm.

Would that I could, just walk away,
and return to calm of yesterday,

I cannot, you are here with me,
As the salt is with the sea,
Although, our love was not meant to be,

Pray soon the calm will be restored . . .
Though broken, as the mighty wave beached upon the shore,
Some day, will renew its strength to love once more.

Josephine C. Gilbert

This Loathsome Reaping

Teardrops falling from an open stain,
Collectively cluttering the calming rain,
Soundly sleeping are the sorrow's seers
That cause fear, by the numerous ears.

Tensely tormented without bounds,
A young yearling learns the sounds.
Beating bold, and boastful in her mind
Is this haunting havoc controlled by time.

Talons producing many piercing pressures
Create relief by such desperate measures;
Within our sovereign social souls,
Can one fathom but all of the tolls?

Or might one pay to please his maker?
Or bid his time a lethal taker?
But, the clock will tick its tock past
Her scornful soul that danced its last.

Then, the stains will all but shine,
Beneath their memories for all time.
So for now, the sinfuls' sorrow is sleeping.
But how long, must we hear this reaping?

Gregory Owen Thomas

Dust

I started my life, when I was eighteen
    I had everything, I needed it seemed.
I thought I had love, oh and I had a dream
    It was just he and I, and we could do anything.
What I didn't know, and what you should consider
    Is the way things change, when you're beaten and battered.
Your heart learns fear and then it learns anger
    And you find that it's more than your heart can handle.
The love is gone, and there is no trust
    All he's left behind is just some dust.
So, teach me to care
    Teach me to trust
Teach me to love
    Before my heart, turns to dust.
You haven't much time
    It's beginning to fade
Oh, teach me to love
    Before my heart turns to dust.

Denise McKeehan Riggleman

Memory Lane

My darling, let us roll our wheelchairs
To the end of Memory Lane.
We'll hold hands and talk about
Those good old times back then.

Yes, we'll laugh and joke and reminisce
The fun we used to have,
And we'll sing our favorite songs
At the end of memory Lane.

For we have reached a turning point
In our journey through this life.
We've run out of streets to cross
But we still have Memory Lane.

And now, by starlight, I can see
The sparkle in your eyes
As we pause to say "I love you!"
At the end of memory Lane.

John M. Denney

If Only I Were a Bird . . .

I wish I were a bird so I could soar thru the sky,
I would fly through the clouds and look God in the eye,
I would constantly be looking at all the beauty there is to see,
I would go wherever I wanted and be all I wanted to be,
I would use every minute and waste no time,
I wouldn't listen to gossip and would see no crime,
I would spread my wings as far as they would go,
I would never be in a hurry, I'd go real slow,
I would sing as loud as my lungs would allow,
And I wouldn't wait until tomorrow, I'd do it now,
I would breathe fresh air every single day of the year,
I would always be brave and never fear,
I would share with everyone all the love in my heart,
For hatred and vengeance just tears us apart,
Loving and caring is what it's all about,
In my little heart there is no doubt,
If only I were a bird I'd soar through the sky,
I would always be happy and I would never cry.

Janice S. Craig

Ignorance

Scratching at the wall of sanity,
stretching out our hands and probing
the depths of mortality.
Boredom preys upon me like a vulture
on a dead carcass.
Sucking and draining the mere life out of me.
Slowly my eyes fall shut leading me to
a new dimension under bright lights and loud noise.
But just a quickly as I reached this netherlands, I
am pulled back to reality.
Silently the ignorance falls around me raining
down upon my head resting upon my shoulders
to exhaust me and take over my mind.
I fight to hold on to the ever fading visions
that so long ago entertained me.
It's too late.
I've lost.
I walk in the midst of the ignorant,
and march to the beat of the dead.

Jennifer Kay Holbrook

Amy

It's OK to doubt,
    Long as it doesn't consume.
It's OK to have undying love,
    Long as it gives you room.
It's OK to seek happiness,
    Long as you know what's true,
It's not always someplace else,
    Look inside of you.
It's OK to take the blame
    But not always - not forever,
Once in a while share it with,
    those who shared the endeavor.
It's great to think you're always right,
    but don't stand too long alone.
It's great to ask for opinions,
    but don't give up your own.
It's OK to say you're wrong,
    if it causes you much sorrow,
take heed to know what's wrong today.
    Changes your tomorrow.

Jeanne Roberts

Untitled

Never forget where we came from,
Never forget why we are here,
Never forget the reasons of oppression,
Never forget the unfounded fear.

Always remember to keep on trying,
Always remember the goals we share,
Always remember the importance of family,
Always remember the debt they payed.

When we hold our dreams and believe
they will gain substance and appear,
but if we don't go forward and continue
to go back, The world won't care nor
remember those people called black.

Donald Williams

Tough Times

When time are tough and things just don't seem right, lift your head
up to the light. Up there you will find all the strength that you
need for God is there to listen and lead. So tell Him your
worries or your doubts and listen to Him and take that route.
Sometimes the route may seem so long, but God is with you so you
will be strong. Don't be afraid if your knees grow weak He will
make them strong for he knows we are meek. So take His hand and
whistle on, and He will carry you safely from dusk to dawn.
His arms are warm and never tire, so lean on him
through wind and fire. Don't look back to say 'why' just look
forward and up to the sky. The sun will shine, the clouds will part
for you have God in your sight and your heart.

Shirley J. Rosko

The Gray Dawn In 1942

On May The 12th in 42
Morgantown's clock struck half-past two.
Out of the clear came a rumble and a roar.
People on the street were silent.
They'd heard that sound before.
After the silence of ages it seemed.
Every ambulance in the town screamed.
Then went Firemen, Red Cross and Safety Crew.
Where they were going no one knew.
Everyone followed the crowd to the mine.
Only families of workers could get past the line.
No one was sure just who was inside.
We just waited patiently and silently cried.
The Safety Crew labored all night with out rest.
The families waited and hoped for the best.
I'll never forget the grey damp dawn,
we suddenly realized the hope was all gone.

Gertrude McClain Allen

Williwaw

In your dreams
You ride a dog sled across snowy fields
Your eyes blue as the sky above Anchorage
You drift in a kayak
Past pink Mt. Roberts, Thengit totem poles
You squat, savor silvery salmon
Hold Eskimo babies
They look like Japanese dolls
Your calendar of Alaska
Still hangs on your wall
I sit at your bedside
Wipe frost from your cheeks
Brush snowflakes from your hair
Icy williwaw blows a blizzard that buries.

Jean Pollitt

Special Love

Over the years I never knew
That I could find someone like you.

To know that living is also sharing
To find such strength, love and caring.

We share the joys and the sorrow
I love you more with each tomorrow

During those years way back then
Who would have known we'd be more than friends

We've been through some rough times that weren't so bad
We're still together, and for that I sure am glad

In our hearts we are as one
And for us love's just begun

Because of you, I have a life
And now, my Love, I am your wife.

To share my Love and life with you
Now I know dreams do come true.

Ruth Ann Johnson

The Nature Of Love

Love?
What can I say about love except that it's a part of nature
And a part of life.
Like the waterfalls that pour freely in the mountains
Or like an eagle that soars gracefully in an endless sky,
Love roams throughout the universe in search of
Something . . . or someone . . . to hold on to.
But like nature, love is subject to its ups and downs.
Just like hurricanes tear apart innocent cities
And just like floods rob people of their homes,
Love can diminish a virtuous soul that is desiring to
Experience this miraculous sensation.
On the other hand, love can be like a blooming flower:
It grows and blossoms until its beauty causes your heart
To melt in utter amazement;
Or even like the calm, cool waters of the sea, love can
Surround your heart with tranquility.
And if you ask me what love is,
All I can tell you is that it's a natural "high" that
You don't want to miss.

Edwin Rivera II

From Darkness To Light

Many a times, I wanted to stop,
the darkness around me for once.
To struggle no more, to suffer no more,
just to become part of the dust.

Many a times, I wanted to yell,
at the One who lives up above.
For bringing me here, for cursing me here,
because of my parents' own lust.

Many a times, I just sat and cried,
wondering why life has to be.
So cruel and hard, so tough at times,
for people like you and me.

But most of the time, I got down on my knees,
asking Him to show me the light.
To help me cope and fear no more,
to help me put up a fight.

So if you are down and gonna give up,
do not cut your wrist with a knife.
Just ask the Father for strength and courage,
and He'll give you eternal life.

Lysette Fontan

Economy Delicious

"Waste not — Want not"
  Is an adage old but true.
I find that in my daily life
  It's just the thing to do.

If an egg I do not have,
  And need to bake a cake,
I find that recipe I've saved
  That not an egg does take.

Or, if I have some bananas
  That are just too ripe to eat,
I make some loaves of banana bread
  And we really have a "Treat."

So, if I waste not anything
  Including old recipes,
I find my self not yearning
  For foods my palate to please.

In case I get more baking done
  Than we are able to eat,
Do I ever need to let it get stale?
  "Not with neighbors across the street!"

Verda B. Lester

Untitled

Lightning sounds the drummer's retreat
All about the floor lay the party remnants:
  clean glasses, empty ash trays
Keep me from tomorrow as today goes crawling by
In the hall, a sound
  no, not a sound, a whisper
The rain beats gently on the roof
  a car door slams and then another
They drive away into the dank
  doors slam, floors creak
Tears for a fictional friend
  the rain, it is so soft
The light, it is so bright it hurts my eyes
Tired, too tired to sleep
To hear his voice, enough for me
  go to sleep, but don't dare dream
Reality, an unfair illusion
  sleep, my only escape
Hold onto the night for the day is fleeting
He calls to me and I succumb

David D. Denton

"Creativity"

God is here God is there God is every
where in the atmosphere, God is a king
and I follow his law, he gave me the
talent for me to draw, while I was
young I went through the wrong, but
the more I believed my mind just got
strong, I created drawings, that I
thought I could never do, made letters,
characters, and mixed colors too, I did
all of this striven and thinking, a good
steady hand is what I'm fixing! Now I
know what Graffiti mean, it's the best
type of art that I ever seen, Graffiti is
good and some is bad but the one
that I draw will make you glad! I got
better and better day by day and now I
have new toys to play, markers, sprays, papers,
and walls, now I'm the one who is having a
ball! I write this poem so you won't be
late to draw and paint the way I create!

Jose Caraballo

Liberal Or Illiberal???

In a world of redemption and fantasy
We try to make it look easy
Were we try to kill a silent death
In the eyes of evil shall we live
The sense of reality is much fake
For those misunderstood mistakes
In a world of idols and fools
Which formally people make worse
We're so fragile we still break
And we seem to be a freak
In a forsaking world of problems seeming to be unsolved
Delightfulness seems to dissolve into hate
Seeming to expose ourselves and our world
Our powers of imagination seem to hurt more than the fantasies
In a world were I think people hope
A many of humanitarian and devil
Very much we seem to look evil
We seem to be very ill disposed with each other
But do we care for one another
Most ill humored people get what they want why are we so
scared?

Ashley Earle

Darkness

Darkness comes in the still of the night
  an stays 'til the dewy morning light.
It plays with your unfettered emotions
  and holds for you all kinds of devotions.
In the darkness, visions preconceived
  heighten the heart with visions believed.
Imaginative minds create images in darkness
  and change them quickly to stone cold hardness.
Darkness veils many hellish and vile things
  and brings back memories on raven's wings.
It brings out the worst of sinister lies
  filled in dark, cynical and brooding eyes.
Darkness can suffocate any rayless room
  with abysmal penetrating gloom.
Darkness can pervade all that it touches,
  unless we release ourselves from its clutches.
As soon as darkness looms upon a heavy heart
  the morning comes to illuminate the dark.
With darkness gone and light enveloping us,
  our minds are free of the fear of darkness.

Joi Sheldon

"Rebirth"

I sit and stare out the window
Searching for words to describe my feelings.
Few are found in what I see
Through the panes of separation.

Leaving my months long prison I realize
The winter winds no longer howl in anger,
Replaced by the gentle whisper of spring.
The dark clouds that filled the sky
Have given way to birds on wing
Carried along on the gentle breeze
That caresses my soul.

No longer does death lay at my feet.
Instead, sounds of life surround me.
Stretching out my lonesome arms
My lungs fill with a fragrance so sweet
And the warmth of the sun thaws my frozen heart.

Once again . . .
I am overcome with the wonders of youth
And a strong desire to live,
Not simply exist.

Steve Thrash

"Why I Teach"

They come to me with many faces
From distant lands and faraway places.
They come from every walk of life
They come with awe, they come with strife.

They come to me with different views
of life and learning and following rules.
They come to me with knowledge and skills
That need developing for the fruits they'll yield.

Many bear problems that life has dealt
Many have scars within that's kept.
Some have talents they share with pride,
Some have them buried deep down inside.

I teach for many special reasons . . .
to guide, to love, to help all people.
I teach them how to learn and discover
To live a life of lifelong wonder.

But, most of all I teach to survive.
It's in my heart and in my eyes.
I teach because I'm a teacher you see
and all God's children belong to me.

Betty J. C. Wright

Eight Souls

Fifty years raising children, always hoping to win
A godly record, eight souls free from sin
She made us learn, she made our beds
She made our clothes and made our breads

Up before dawn, last to say it's done
Her hands were busy past set of sun
Worried as her hand touched a fevered brow
All eight survived and only God knows how

Tools in hand, at her side a baby
Working like a man, yet, definitely a lady
No time to cultivate friendships of her own
With positive will she had to push on

When the gates open her prayer is mine
All eight souls in heaven will someday shine
Please Lord, not only eight souls for thee
We're gathering in more for heaven to see

Dear Lord as children bowed on our knees
Look favorably on us and answer our pleas
Stretch out your mercy, forgiveness, love, and grace
And prepare in heaven each grandchild a place.

Nancy (Glenn) Powell

God's Masterpiece

Sincere congratulations to Mother and Dad on that brand new baby,
who's come to live with you.
A pretty little girl from above, that God made to be perfect,
His little angel from above.
He gave her little curls and big brown eyes.
He gave her strong arms and legs too,
For she's just the perfect baby for me and you.
He also gave her a beautiful smile,
That would win any heart,
Specially your Mom's and Dad's.
But we can't forget Grandma and Grandpa, too,
For she will be their little angel, too.
God made each precious baby from above and sent them down
   for us to love.
God's masterpiece from above,
This little girl for us to love.
We thank you Lord for her,
We will always love her.

Arlene Schmidt

"Shooting Star"

Certain thought, that I read, remind me much of you
Stirring all of my emotions, while they often make me blue
One thought that stirred me up, from my head down to my toes,
brought back childhood memories. — Well this is how it goes . . . —
"Beauty is never very far, a simple rose, or a distant star"
The stars were our own secret — they could talk — (and this we knew!)
Now, alone, I talk from a distance, to the stars as tho they're you!
And beauty wasn't in the rose, you'd hide behind your back . . .
But in the joy you got from all giving, because you were Jordy Mac
You were so much more beautiful, than you were actually tall,
And the hole that's in my heart, is anything but small!
Reliving childhood days gone by, desperately wishing you were here,
I look up to the star filled sky, from my eyes are falling tears.
I know you hear my pleading heart; but show me,
Jordy, fly!"
Well, he made it clear — he is the stars, because
He shot a few across the sky!

Lori MacWilliams

Fatal Pain

I hear his heart crying with fatal pain;
His dear voice, screaming out.

I sense his fear of death being near,
Yet still I see the good Lord is here.

"Be not afraid," I say,
It is time to appreciate this day.
The hands of the Lord are upon you;
In a better place you will stay.

One day we will meet again
And more good times we shall share.

The fact that you are gone away from us,
Your loved ones, isn't fair;

But I know, in my heart,
That some blessed day,
I, too, will be there . . .

Jodi R. Nedwick

Who Am I?

Who am I that I should survive. Survive what you say?

Survive the torrent rain of tears, survive the sharp lightning bolts
of pain, to mount upon and learn to ride the winds of despair.

Who am I?

I am one that they thought should have been aborted. I am one that
they told I had no imagination.
I am one that had no physical beauty to man, I am one that they gave
no foundation, I am one who
ran wild in the streets; I ran for the fun and I also ran for my life.

So who am I.

I could be any fathers daughter, any mothers little girl, any
husbands wife or any child's teacher, I
Am A Woman.

Lisa Marable

Beautiful Things

There are many beautiful things to see if we just look around,
From the magnificent eagle on his perch to the tiny ant upon the ground.
From the flowers swaying in the breeze beneath the willow tree,
To sand dunes tall against blue skies reaching to the sea.
And watch the water as it flows and rushes against the rocks
And travels on for miles and miles and never wants to stop,
From flowered kissed hills to meadows green to snow peaked mountain tops.
All these are beautiful to see if we just make a start,
To see them not only with our eyes, but also with our heart.

Selena LaMar

The Ninth Sound

She lies in the withering grass gazing up into space not knowing
what she sees or what place waiting for the cow, a bovine, lean,
not mean to tell her why the grass is no longer green.
A moisture fills the air as a dark curtain blankets the night, the
arrogant osmotic of jasmine has deepened her sense of befuddlement,
the stars hasten the night with their near yet so far away light.
She hears four steps forward and then four steps backward followed
by a thud. She rises from the grass in a hesitant manner then
seeks out the ninth sound. As she gazes around she soon sights
the reason for the sound, the cow, a bovine, lean, not mean stuck
in the mud. She hastens to the scene and comes upon the cow
already in recitation, "When the nourishment of love was spread
around a bull, a cow, the grass on the ground, there was a
direction that all should take for not only was the green grass
at stake but all animals were bound to keep love around and now
that it is no longer so where is that love nourishment to go
but to the ninth sound". Hearing this the girl went home and
took to her bed and that night she prayed to God that the grass
would turn green, that love was not dead, that the cow be found
and that she be spared from ever again hearing the ninth sound.

Ron Jones

The Inner Peace

The inner peace
Soft and flowing
Perfect balance
Perfect form
Then suddenly I am jarred away.
Disgruntled, falling into a new, uncomfortable life.

Never before had I lived in that life,
As when I lived inside of that life.
It calls to me
I hear it speak,
"Come back to me"

Heather Barnhart

Dreams Turned To Dust

Last night I had a very unusual dream,
Full of sunlight and moonbeams;
In this dream I met a man,
He had nothing to offer but his hand;
In this dream I fell in love,
What's this love and life stuff of;
In this dream it was black night,
And this man he touched me light;
In this dream I prayed he'd care,
And my feelings the man did share;
But in the morning hours I awoke,
To find my dream was just a joke;
So now I sit in the dark and stare,
For in the morning hour began a nightmare;

Kathleen Bahr

Black Women

B is for the blackness in our skin that holds the key to our beauty.
L is for the love we share with ourselves and others.
A is for the anger we have towards stupidity.
C id for the care we show towards others.
K is for the kindness in our heart.
W is for the will we have to try to keep our black nation together.
O is for the other nationalities we show concern too.
M is for the motherly love we give our children.
E is for the extra work we do to fix what our men has destroyed.
N is for our name. Strong Black Women.

Virginia Haymore

Divine Intervention

To all the people I have fooled in this world,
there is none that I have fooled more than I.
Absent from confidence and the passion to know,
I see, but my senses lie.

Be patient, my friend, and your day will come.
Friends are fortunes even if there is only one.

The sun will shine in your darkest night.
Within every cave, hides a little light.

Success, fame, and to immortalize your father's name
completes a mortal goal.
To pass it on and become one
builds the strength of the mighty oak.

Believe in these and let whatever may come be.
Repel all fallacies.
Believe in these and let whatever may come be.
Heed their truth.
Beware of its insanity.

'Lil' David Remillard

Everyone Says

If everyone says something different what are we
  Really saying
Does the message get across or is it bleeding in the
  Moor
Hearts will beat and winds will blow
I know that love will come and go
I thought with you my place was safe
Now I pace this earth
A lonely place
To smell the rain of storms gone by
To float the streams of tears I've cried
Still I think we had a chance
But that's the last of our romance

Leslie Pears

Someone To Be There

So much has happened, I can't slow down.
I'm running in circles, painted like a clown.
My nose is red, my face is white.
But with shadows in hand,
my heart is the night.
Someone to hold me, I need a friend.
Someone to tell me it's not the end.
Never have I felt this much alone.
Like a tiny puppy without a home.
I only wish for someone to be there.
Someone who'll never leave,
  who'll always care.

Jennifer Spink

Reflections On Music

Music is a way to escape, to let out our feelings. Like
clay, it can be shaped to please and to entertain. Like a bowl,
music an be empty or it can be full. Music can tell a story or
sing a song. Music is the voice of the soul. Rhythm is the
thought and harmony is cooperation. Something as pure as music
is heat to melt ice, paradise for the mind, notes as natural as
heartbeats, colors flowing with warmth . . . or it can be cold.
Music adds flavor and acts to clear the mind. You can use music
as a sword to excite and a shield to relax. A bridge to an
unknown land, music can be shared as a gift for many people.
Gold can be purchased, even though expensive, but music is
priceless, like disposable art or timeless artifacts. As
Aristotle said, "All that glitters is not gold."

Steven Johnson

Eternal Spring

We run, we skip, we laugh and sing
For well we should! The time — is Spring!
  The nights are short, the days are long,
When Springtime — calls to Summer's throng.
We run, we skip, we laugh and sing
But then — a bruise; a bump on the knee,
  God reminds us, of our mortality!
  Sometimes when life, is at its best —
When all seems calm, at peace, at rest,
  The reality that we are dust —
For God reminds us, as He must!
  This life was given here — on Earth,
Some years back, upon our birth,
  For all to Him, we shall return.
For deep inside — our souls, we yearn,
  To go to Him, for in His rest —
It's Spring and Summer at its best!
  To run, to skip, to laugh and sing,
To Him eternal praises bring. We run, we skip, we laugh and sing.
Thanks be to God — For Eternal Spring.

    Neil John Zeilenga

"I Wish, I Hope, I Love, I Dream"

I am a rose in a garden of thorns.
I am a dreamer in a land of sleepers.
And I am a warm heart in a quarry of cold stones.
I will bring people to their feet in a place where they have no legs.
I will grow wings to fly from a land of shattered dreams.
And I will sing a song of love in a place where the devil screams hate.
I think beauty can only be found in the eye of the beholder.
I think wisdom is experience.
And I think a heart can sing a chorus of different songs.
I can be your friend in a world of enemies.
I can listen when your neighbors have all gone deaf.
And I can feel the pain of your hurt.
I cannot imagine a world without laughter.
I cannot stand for the ignorance of the intolerant.
And I cannot shed a crocodile's tear.
I wish for fate to twist me gently.
I wish people would admire beauty, not worship it.
And I wish being in pain didn't hurt so bad.
I wish, I hope, I love and I dream.

    Debbie Peterson

The Mind Master

Blood stained concrete and a life filled with hate.
The same cycle of uncertainty seems to be their fate.
Emancipation only served to open the gate;
to another mater with a plan to annihilate.

Feeling good, yes, feeling fine.
Selling their souls for a nickel or a dime.
Not realizing that it's a battle for the mind.
What's it gonna be? We're running out of time.

Tougher legislation, yes; government regulation,
Voter registration, Better race relations,
build more prisons for longer incarceration. Lets arm the population!
We've got to save the nation form this evil infestation.

Blood stained concrete pictures plan to see.
Children killing children and they're dying in the streets.
The Mind Master's got them his music to repeat.
Another child dies and a family sits and weeps.

Stop lights in the grave yard; the policeman's on his beat,
directing all the traffic, seems the hearses never cease.
Of a certainty there's no tomorrow just bitter pain and grief.
Can we break this cycle, is there any peace.

    Glenn Johnson

We Love Our Flag

We love our flag, and hold it high
For those who live, and those who die,
For country and for liberty,
That all imprisoned souls may see
The stars and stripes against the sky.

And when there comes a battle cry,
We cheer it as it passes by,
And sing in grateful harmony,
We love our flag!

Tho' many years ahead may lie,
Over our nation still she will fly,
Swelling our hearts with joy that we
Live in the land of the brave and the free.
Filled with pride we can't deny,
We love our flag!

    Ruth Ward McClement

Fallen Asleep

Sailing to the land of sleep and slumber.
Soon the waves will drag me under.
A short struggle and then I'm free.
Sinking deeper, deeper into the sea.
Waves of covers wrap me snug and warm.
Angel fish surround me, I keep from harm.
Suddenly I feel a brilliant light.
Spewing like a fountain, I realize it's night.
Flashes and claps and drops of dew.
"Steady as she goes," yells the Captain to the crew.
She creaks and cracks,
As upon the rocks we dash.
Soon the waves will drag me under.
Sailing to the land of sleep and slumber.

    Nathan Gould

What Are Friends?

Friends are people you can depend on.
Will be there when you need them
They won't lie to you
When people talk behind you back
They tell you
And they don't tell the guys you like
You like them
They give you shoulder to cry on
They get excited when you've excited
If you are upset they cheer you up
I wonder what it would be like with out friends
It would probably be horribly not to have friends
You wouldn't have anyone to tell your deepest darkest, secrets

    Mary Ann Johnson

Bread For The Birds

In the early morning. Maybe snow on the ground
Most everyone is asleep, don't hardly hear a sound
I gently open the door with bread in hand
To feed the little birds, creatures of the land

To see them in hunger, pick up every crumb
Raising their heads, keeping an eye, if anyone comes
I ask myself, on earth He lets us live
It is our joy, love and compassion to give

Divine creator of the world, he spoke the words
He provides for all, even bread for the birds
No blessing is greater or brings mere joy to man
Than one that's given, touched by God's loving hand.

    Ozo A. Sutton

You Decide

When we awake we face each day with a clear choice.
To be in a bad frame of mind or to openly rejoice.
We can say thank you Lord for another day to live.
Or we can expect the worst that the day can give.

These decisions usually impact the rest of the day.
Making us happy or sad when at school, work or play.
The choices we have are much too numerous to count.
Basically we can do good or just let our troubles mount.

Being light hearted and happy are guides to the good life.
But heavy the load when a day is filled with anger and strife.
You will always be an example by the decisions you make.
Whether good or bad may alter the direction a life may take.

At the start of each day we each need to do a mind check.
Will I be a good influence or just another pain in the neck.
You can bring happiness to someone with just a kind word.
Or destroy a life with barbed words as sharp as a sword.

Doubting usually brings nothing but worry and fear.
So try to set your direction positive and very clear.
Decide each day to be the best influence you can be.
It will make your life far better, try it you'll see.

Donald L. Parmer Jr.

Morning

Dark and bleak it showed itself
And snow was in the air.
The wind was whistling through the woods
The trees of leaves were bare

The sky was filled with ominous grey
And clouds were heavy laden

The waves beat down upon the shore
To wash away the sand
And I upon a high far knoll
Did watch and take my stand

As I looked upon this wondrous scene
A thought passed through my mind
What beauty hath our God wrought
And to it, I so blind

Now as each morn comes slowly through
That black and dreadful night
I wonder if, like the last, it will be
Such a great and glorious sight

Gerard P. Boe

Missing You

I see you,
You see me.
But you don't care about me anymore.
I'm just a memory from the past.
Just a face in the crowd.
You don't care about me.
But I still care about you.
You said you just wanted to be friends.
But now, we aren't even that.
Why did you take your love away from me?
Did you think we weren't meant to be?
Why can't you see,
I love what we used to be.
I want the old us back.
Your love is what I lack.
I miss you,
But you don't miss me...
Do you?

Angela May

My Sister And I

I have a little sister, her name's Amanda Sue
She likes to go where I go and do the things I do

But that's not always possible, because I'm telling you
That I have just turned six years old and she is only two

You may not know we're sisters, we don't look alike you see
'Cause she has short blond curls, not long brown hair like me

She's really very smart you know, for being only two
She knows most of her ABCs and can even count four you

I love my little sister, we are the best of friends
We don't always get along though, because it just depends

On if she's tired and fussy and hasn't had a nap
Or if I'm feeling out of sorts, cranky — stuff like that

We're just like other sisters and sometimes fuss and fight
But then we make up, hug and kiss and everything's all right

We have such fun together when we laugh and run and play
But I must be very careful, 'cause she says exactly what I say

And I wouldn't want to teach her bad things to say you see
I want her to grow up and be the best that she can be

Soon another year will pass and I can't wait to see
What we'll be doing when I am seven and she has just turned three

Donna S. Perry

Untitled

One day two worlds collided, facing similar strife
The paths they travelled were so alike
They gave each other new life.
They came full circle face to face
Different roads along the same course
As time passed they both found the need to fill a loss.

Suddenly two minds collided
Their thoughts and dreams they'd share,
One could not reject the idea
More than just friendship was there.
Believing the other's words, strangers in the least,
As it turns both minds found a state of calm and peace.

Without warning two hearts collided
Unprepared and not ready to feel,
And from this union they created the strength
That would help the other one heal.

These hearts had loved different loves,
In their own realms they dwelled.
But one day the hearts and minds united,
Making their very own world.

Kimberlee Posner

"A Trip"

A trip
What fun
We're off to view some sights across the sea
Paris
London
Venice too! (that's in Italy)
The things we saw
I can't believe
That I was really there
Of course I know
I wasn't
But rather in my rocking chair
The trip I took was on a screen
In the corner of my room
But what a way for a lonely old lady to escape her day long gloom

Karen Samaritoni

Who Me?

A mirror reflects the truth
The self righteous stand before an image of superiority
Their eyes manipulate their own self worth
Indulging on a mission of insecurity
Pressing deeply into the shoulders of others
Authority obtained by means of intimidation
The intimidators claim victory
Calculating minds hunger for power
Mindless calculators distort the truth.
Confusing intelligence with inferior greed paves a path
   of desperation
Defending what is wrong by offending what is right
Ignorance remains stabile for as long as it's supported
Intimidation's climb to the top was swift
Instability's descent is swifter
Exposing deceptive builders who saw master carpenters
   before the looking glass
Eventually shattering a fraudulent foundation every
   step of the way.

   Camille Ciampa Passanisi

Red

Red can be happy,
Red can be sad.
Red can be good,
Red can be bad.
Red is the color of my father's car,
Red is the color the sun looks from afar.
Red is the color I love you can see,
Red is heart to you from me.
Red is ladybug kind and sweet,
Red is the color of a peppermint treat.
Red is the color that says danger is near,
Red is the color that says, "Stop right here."
Red is the blood that Jesus shed,
Red is the hat firemen wear on their head.
Red is Santa's suit at Christmas time,
Red is the lollipop I bought with a dime.
Red is the lipstick Grandma used to wear,
Red is the color of a Valentine bear.
Red is my favorite color you see,
Another color just isn't for me.

   Amanda Caler

What God Could Not Give Me For You

The simple things in life and nature if
you're the right one, this is what you'd mean to me.
If god gave me all the stars in heaven,
as a trade for you. If he gave me the sun,
the moon and the earth it still would not do.
If he gave me all the silver and gold
that has ever been found. Or the songs of
all the birds your voice would have a
sweeter sound. And if I could number
every grain of sand that is in the sea.
Then maybe I could begin to count all
you'd mean to me. For if, I knew every
star by name that god has hung in
the sky. Then just maybe I could begin
To tell you why. Why I'd love you the
way I'd do and what you'd be worth.
For I could not count the price of you.

   Melody Cain

The Recovered Addict

Destitute, confused minds
Looking for their kinds
Lurking around dark streets at night
Hoping to keep out of mom's sight
Unrealizing the all seeing eye of God
Keeps track of everywhere we trod
Sniffing, smoking, snorting, drinking ourselves a mist
Forgetting that we are God's-tis, tis
Falling! Falling! Into the deep dark hole
Desperately we cry, Lord save me from the gates of Sheol!
Suddenly we are awaken to the beautiful sun
Given a second chance to prove ourselves to The Son
Thank You! Thank you my God! For saving me from that awful strife
I greatly appreciate this gift of new life.

   Corinna Miller

A Ray Of Hope

Accidental grief bestowed upon my family
For living a life of depravity
Making God cast aspersions upon my soul

Now I wait in darken room
Living life unfulfilled within the doom
Waiting and wondering which path to follow

My identity has vanquished, disappeared
For I live my life in sorrow and fear
Knowing that the Reaper and I must elope

Now I search for God to take my final breath
As I pray for my tranquility which is death
I no longer search for a ray of hope

   Raymond Matteson

Secret For A Good Life

Enjoy each day as it comes,
   be creative, be happy, be honest.
Live your life to the fullest,
   leaving today's and tomorrow's turmoil
   in God's hands.

Learn what you can . . . enjoy it, share it with someone.
   Love and be loved.
Touch someone. It will brighten your day.

Don't put off for tomorrow what you can do today.
   Do not worry about getting old.
Take good care of yourself.

Life is an adventure. Be excited about it.
   Wake up each morning with a smile.
Do not miss the joy of a new day.

   Jeanne Skeen

A Spirit Lost

Who am I, he cried, to the masses' delight,
A reflection of the bitter dismay
Over their own life's inequitable plight
Still, others would arrogantly say
I know who I am, so tell my why
should I care about your sad state,
Physician, heal thyself the Scriptures cry,
So now, no more foolish debate
Mind and heart are closed, my eyes are dry
The dream is dead, as is the King
No stirring compassion occupies my soul
as I await Death's final sting,
For in my world, the King is I, Sheol

   Fred Greene

Vision Of You

I look out my window and up to the sky.
Watching the stars shimmer like diamonds above.
With a smile on my face and stars in my eyes, I closed
My eyes and had a vision of you!
You were my knight in shinning armor upon a strong white horse
Then you were my lover and lifted me up into the air and
Swung me around.
It felt just like I was flying.
Then you set me down and we looked into each
Other's eyes. We leaned forward . . .
I woke up from a pitter patter on my window.
I will remember that night, cause that's when I had a
Vision of you!

Cassandra Beach

One Loving Word

Don't wait to write a novel to send
To gladden a heart of an absent friend;
Go on, send now just one loving word
So a lost heart may be gently stirred.

Lots of good friends are lost in the sea
Of life that clutter you and me;
They might have been our friend for all time
If only we'd sent that loving line.

It's never a long speech that saves
A friend from life's angry waves;
It's just our simple, sincere word
That makes our friends heart feel stirred.

We wish to speak like angels would,
Forgetting, that each of us truly could —
A message to an absent friend will be heard
Tho' it is just one loving word —

Friend.

Kay Jones

"Windows"

We are all considered Windows
  with many divided panes
  through each one
  a bright light
  sometimes fading to a calm darkness
  only to become awakened
  when washed clean of the shadows that hide behind the light . . .

We all fear of lifting our shades
  opening our blinds
  hoping to never see what we may find . . .

We fear the rocks tossed our way
  for fear they'll shatter us . . .

Yet everyone, at one point in time
  must open their windows
  and follow the bright light that lies ahead of us all . . .

Laura J. Moore

Columbia River Fog

I've seen it come as a rolling sea
As vague and as true as eternity,
As white and soft as a woman's hand
Above and within the solid land;
As sad as a weary soul's lament;
As weak as a salmon spawned and spent;
As pure as a new-born baby's breath;
As calm and sure as life or death.
Of beauty and youth — of prayer and vow,
Akin to the sun and the set of the plow;
To the rain — as vague as men.

Helen LaRoy Fallert

The Little Birdhouse

I have a little birdhouse that sits upon my back fence,
To build it was not much expense.
And the joy it gives my little feathered friends;
Far exceeds the trouble it took I contend.
I watched one day as two little birds inspected it together,
For they knew that in it they would be safe from hawk and weather.
They jumped up and down and flitted all around
That little house I had made from a few scraps of wood that I had
found. Each morning they sat on the TV antenna so high,
And sang until noon came nigh,
Just to say thank you friend for thinking of me and mine,
The little house you built will do just fine.
Now when I go outside to work in the yard,
The little birds are there to chase the mosquitos and be my guard.
The family now includes seven,
And they're all as blue as heaven.
I sit on the porch and watch them play,
And just wish I had built that little birdhouse a sooner day..

Zola Annella King

Dead of Winter

Close by the doorway, he paused to stand.
There he wistfully took her hand.
All were watching, did not speak,
as a silent tear rolled down his cheek.
And through his mind the memories ran,
of when they met in that warm summer sand.
Her eyes were still, drawing very cold,
telling him he'd never again have her hand to hold.
Treasuring their last kiss, he unwillfully lingered,
drawing away, he slipped his class ring from her finger.
With a quiet sigh, he bent very near,
whispering a final "I love you" in her ear.
With the ring on his finger, he kissed her goodbye,
knowing she loved him, he began to cry.
The door opened slowly and the harsh winds started to blow,
as they carried her casket through the deep winter snow.

Melissa Letsch

My Only Son

You are my first born, my only son.
And from the time you opened the womb,
I realized the miracle God had done.
For you, I knew, we could make room.

You brought us joy and so much fun,
Eager questions, wanting to learn.
Happiness, tense times, all, my son.
You brought us each of these in turn.

You are a man now and on your own,
Blessed with a wonderful wife.
She'll stand by you, you aren't alone,
She'll help you establish your life.

God's blessed you, not only once, but thrice,
With fatherhood, He's lent you life,
To enjoy, so son, try to be nice,
Please son, they're only two and wife.

Son, I've turned you completely over now,
To Jesus, my precious Lord,
I know He'll take care of how,
You live your life, and He'll be your guard.

Pansy Wright

"Are You My Friend?"

Are you my friend?
A true, blue friend?
Or are you my enemy in disguise?
Someone out to destroy me?

I thought you were my friend
I find that I was wrong
You stabbed me in the back
When I wasn't strong.

This makes me sad
This makes me blue
To find I've lost
A friend like you.

But who needs a friend
Who stabs you in the back?
Life is too short for
such as that.

I've learned a lesson the hard way
seems like I always do.
But I lost the one I love
because of a so-called "friend" like you.

Joni Smith

"Grandma"

I stopped in for a visit, to talk with you awhile.
I've always enjoyed time with you, you've always made me smile.

And when I went to leave that night, I said that, "I love you."
You looked straight into my eyes and said,
  "I love you, too!"

Less than two days later, I learned you passed away.
Those last four words you said to me, still echo yet today.

It's been awhile now Grandma, that we have been apart.
There's not a day that passes by, that you're not
  in my heart.

Sometimes it gets to me, you know, a sadness deep within.
I feel that you're still here with me,
  but you're up there, with Him!

Grandma, you're in heaven, I know that in my heart.
God took you there, I've known it,
  since we have been apart.

And grandma, I would like for you to talk to God for me.
I'm glad that you were in my life,
  could you thank God, personally?

Carmen M. Coppler

"Rebellious Heart"

I had hate, he gave me love
I gave back anger, he loved me more
I held fast and would not move
With patience he stood at the door;
I ran on, he let me go
I stopped to rest and he was there
One step ahead, now face to face
I shook my fist, why do you care?
In answer to my foolish question he asked child
Why do you cry?
I am the way, I love you so
Upon the cross I gave my life!
He gave me love, I loved him back
Rebellious heart to run no more
On bended knee I knocked and waited
Forgiveness opened heaven's door!

Deanna David

Windblown: The Old Romany Way

Sooty black ringlets whip against sootier cheeks.
Earthwater pools reflect in liquid gray eyes.
Smudged palms leave streaks across starched white linen
as she binds up her tresses to collect firewood for tea.
Her printed skirt swirls around her slender frame;
tanned as an olive branch, she'd grow pale within the confines of
a Black Forest cabin.
Patches of rust on golden hoops scarcely compete with the patches
of decay on the rim of her grandfather's wagon.
A copper bracelet falls from her wrist as she dodges the wiles
of a scampering camp dog with the nimble grace
of her father's fiddle-playing fingers.
She pays no attention to its fall, nor to the wayward glances of
mustached Gringo traders, for she is a Gypsy girl.
Windblown.
Carefree.

Kara N. Vozel

The Volunteer

Venturing whenever your heart might guide,
  you quietly sit by a lonely one's side,

Offering your hand to softly hold the hand
  of someone fragile and old,

Leaving your personal needs behind,
  you set your sights on just being kind,

Unselfish in your giving,
  you make lives worth living,

Never a thought of the times you have spent
  or how much of yourself you have given or lent,

Thinking only of those you might serve,
  giving the tender care they deserve,

Ever mindful of the world and its needs,
  your heart full of love is the one that succeeds,

Enthusiasm, excitement and tenderness are there,
  proving to all you're that someone who'll care,

Remembering the gift without the giver is bare,
  your heart will be open and ready to share.

James E. Moore

Bad Mood

I'm here in my head, she says
"no entry" by her beclouded eyes;
reluctant doorbells to the shelter of her skull

Hold it all in, she believes
fearful thoughts can't come out;
emotions are washing their hair tonight

I'm grounded, she wants
no TV or telephone to ease the silence;
just discomfort from her own company

I'm sick, she calls in
from two-faced smiles and cubbyholes;
reality is not a choice today

Her friends, she takes a bottle, a cookie, a smoke;
sleeping too much, groggy awakenings

You're out of your mind, she hears
voices around her calmly interrupt;
her eyelids lifting to see only a mirror

Let me in, she remembers
familiar eyes bearing into hers;
light, love and humanity embracing wholly.

Laura Fern

The Quickening Breath Of Middle Age

I saw myself in the mirror today . . .
changes came silently while I was busy . . .
lines wink back and my eyebrows are falling . . .
who is this woman? Much heavier than I . . .
looking tired and sad . . . but . . .

I noticed my co-workers today . . .
young women, busily being 29 or 32 . . .
slim and trim, in the corporate mold . . .
I am alien, clumsy, much different from them . . .
looking tired and sad . . . but . . .

I saw a picture of me today . . .
many years ago, many lives ago . . .
funny, I don't remember ceasing to be her . . .
but the mirror says I'm someone else now . . .
looking tired and sad . . . but . . .

When I was young, my soul was silent . . .
Now my soul is becoming vocal and free . . .
If that is the price for youth lost . . .
then I'll take this woman, looking tired and sad . . .
and learn to love her.

Marilyn J. Montgomery

Heaven On Earth

There is a place in the sky where everyone goes
No one knows how to get there cause it never shows
When you're gone, and are all alone
Your soul floats away for in the sky it will stay
Your soul starts flowing you don't know where you're going
It could be carried away in the dark or in the day
And when you get to a gate, it's up to God to decide your fate
No turning back, no holds barred
you've waited too long and come so far
For there is some difference between heaven and earth
It ends with death and begins with birth

Veronica Baer

Quilted

the yellow sun in her blinding splendor
wakes us in the morning
she quilts her many children
yet here I sit on the edge again
in another game of blanket
tug of war.
I feel my warmth escaping

puffy eyes glazed and glowing
watch the evening fade
into a sea of peaches
Night's darkness opens himself with a sob
letting the rain slide through the trees
leaving me dry
yet tasting his many tears

Blanketing the plush lands
alive with vibrant colors
greens
violets
reds
blues
I sit and take in these precious sights
from under the warmth of my quilt

Leslie R. Artz

Excerpt From . . . "The Guys We Left Behind"

And that's the way it was, that's the way . . . 'cause,
into that valley of death walked those five-hundred,
into the valley . . . stalked and blundered.
And later . . . shocked . . . they wondered exactly why
They'd been mocked and had to die.
To die in 'nam, to know you're through.
To defy, as a man, and know you've been true.
Well . . . it's past all fool's humiliation,
That last call . . . a cruel invitation
Just realize there's no compromise,
To recognize . . . as you cower, demoralized . . . your last hour.
But then, lest we forget, there also were the men we'd never met,
Who chose, of their own accord, who chose, who could afford
"Courageously" . . . to remain behind.

Twelve of our units . . . by dawn they were gone.
Gone from the earth which gave them birth,
Their bodies rotting and bloated, and nature plotting as she gloated.
Because . . . into that valley of death went those five-hundred,
And . . . t'was their last breath because they blundered.

Celia Huntingdon

Temporary Loss Of Consciousness

The rain falls to the earth, pounding like the feet of men
as the throbbing in my head at the memory of her
a cloud of dust the burnt cinder I was becomes
with every drop of water, with every beat of my heart
when the tears fall like rain and make pools of blood at my feet
while inside the blood boils to the top and spills out of every pore
I kneel there, soaked, in blood, in tears, or merely in water
in matters not — they're all the same
each tear falls as if it were the first
as I mourn the dead and dying . . .
I lie there at her grave, broken
shards of my soul lying about
a broken mirror with fading reflection
and each fragment is crying her name
no matter the shape each one shows her face
and so I lie there, we, the forgotten of the world
apart of life — together in earth
and who will follow? None to cry for her, none to pick up the pieces
the clockwork hearts beat on, the feet trample onward
and cold wind whispers her name

Brian Cochran

Violence In The Media

It's hard to deny what clearly we see
    But yet there are those who just won't admit
That the violence displayed on T.V.
    Motivates notions for crimes to commit

Granted . . . violence has always been here
    Way before we had so much to review
But why encourage what year after year
    Has been a national tragic issue?

With more and more youth clashing with the law,
    I have to wonder about role models
Was it their parents, or T.V. they saw
    . . . Who was home developing their idols?

Children are seeds our future grows from . . .
    When under our care . . . their conduct, we own
In place of rage, let's cultivate wisdom
    They don't know the way . . . don't leave them alone

If you don't raise them, the medial will,
    And their eyes and ears are willing to learn
As parents, this is our task to fulfill
    . . . Don't throw it away . . . it's your divine turn

Bob G. Martinez

Untitled

With quiet resolution,
    stepping into and out of myself.
Seeing in your face,
    what is the wonder of me.
Softly embracing my body,
    touching my heart.
Opening and closing
    the very secrets of my soul.
Knowing your gentle, sweet laughter,
    I have come to know my own.
Flashing in your eyes,
    forbidden passion, unmasked innocence.
Fingertips caress my face,
    they calm me, excite me.
What is the wonder of you?
    Where is your secret hiding place?
Come to me for just a while,
    where minutes turn into hours.

Denise L. Tonkovic

The Savior's Love

How will He love you? My dear child
    just count the ways;
He'll love you through the long, dark nights
    and through the sun-filled days.
He'll love you when you go to Him,
    head bowed, on bended knees;
He'll love you when you go your own way —
    turn your back — not seek to please.
He'll love you when you make mistakes,
    and long to run and hide;
His back will never be toward you,
    he'll be there — by your side.
He'll love you when you're thankful
    and sing praises to His Name,
And even when you've sinned
    and hang your head in guilt and shame.
My beloved, this He promises,
    that whatever you may do —
His love is forever,
    unconditional and true.

F. Katherine Ullrich

My Heavenly Angel

I don't know the name of my angel there the guardian's of life and I
dream they that help me reach goals destinations, with that I'm on
their heavenly team I have traveled many a journey with-out them
I'd be in despair that's why my Lord sent me an angel,
my Lord sent me a wonder to share

If I'm lost or can't make a decision my mind will unravel like rope
Cause my angel has guided and nudged me they're the keepers of
magic and hope my angel knows my every movement leading my path
thru the night like a scout my angel is watching till my angel knows that
I've seen the light

When I feel I've carried the whole world on a mission that I had to
tow then my angel who and then will show me the light colored prism
rainbow the motto of any sweet angel is for us to lead a good life
Were promised a bright new tomorrow when we've loved then will end
our strife their voices are whispering secrets, yes they watch me
where-ever I go if I stop and I have to wonder they'll send me to a
place that I'll know

My angel loves whistling a rhythm a tune of a one for my ear
In a soothing and in a sweet melody it's one that I love to hear
When I hear rhythm or singing it's music of a mystical chord
I know that my angel is saying, yes it is...it's a call from my "Lord".

Ronald Celis

"Epitaph"

The man whispered in horror as he sat and he shook
Only did he scream in torture when his soul was took.
Then it all ended at the blink of lonely eyes
It was all a dream of my awaited demise
But was it over when my sleepless dream had ended
Or was it just Hell's prologue as I had descended
And could it be mended; the pit in my heart in which I fell
Whether it can be amended or not I shall die as well
So don't ask me and I shan't tell lies of truth that poison our land
And don't bring me water of well of feed me by a caring hand
Let me be damned; this is my home and exiled domain
Bask on the sun's land and I shall bask in my own pain
Let fire fall like rain from the black clouds that serve to deliver
Heaven's wrath
And call me insane but "I love you" shall be written on my epitaph

Daniel J. Quigley

Mothers

Mothers are there to help you out,
When you think you're going to pout.

They're always there to lend a hand,
When you're off in la-la land.

You may have hardships and have strife,
But I have found through the course of my life,

That my mother's helped me through thick and thin,
And has been at my every whim.

She's always been there for me through and through,
I hope you have someone that dear to you.

I owe my undying gratitude to my mother,
Because she's so special to me:
And she's unlike any other!!

James Nelson

My Katelyn

Descriptions, there are many
But, you need to truly see
The beauty of my baby
That has all-encompassed me.
Her eyes, her smile, her laughter —
They'll speak deeply to your soul,
Asking you to look within and see how far she'll go.
She's more than just a child to me;
My life on her depends.
The days and nights are sweeter now
Due to the love she lends.
She's the beauty from the Lord above,
As He would only show.
I only hope your heart will meet
The Katelyn that I know.

Kristin K. Malley

Shoreline

There were clouds on the shoreline of his mind
Behind, behind, it came to mind

Where will I go? Where will I be?
What will happen soon to me?

The waves are breaking
Making, making
Timeless moments
Shifting sand

Upon the shoreline never trodden
Lies the future of the one
Who will walk with head uplifted
Born again to weep more

Gary Scarbeary

Gunman

```
                 I
HAVE    HAD                              A
PIECE SINCE BEFORE MY MIND CAN RECALL. LOCKED
AND LOADED IS HOW I LIVE. VENGEANCE IS MY ART.
TO WOUND WITH CRUELTY THOSE WHO WOULD ME IS MY
POETRY. I LIVE AS DID THE WARRIORS OF OLD. BLOOD
CALLS  OUT FOR BLOOD. IN MY
LIFE NO      ONE  IS  MAN
ENOUGH TO  FACE  ME  FOR
FEAR AND I      ARE      ONE
IN THE SAME.     I SIT ALONE
AT THIS APEX.
A HEAVY PRICE
FOR RESPECT.
```

Michael B. Miller

Courtney

When she is fast asleep under an
iridescent moon,
When all is quiet, I sneak into her room,
checking for her breath, through
a shaft of light, I think of this
day, turned swiftly into night.
Silently I watch her dreaming
there, blissful, peaceful, asleep.
Quickly time is stolen away,
leaving memories to keep.

Teresa Jager

A Poem For Norma

We walk together hand in hand
At times it seems like a foreign land.
We reach the sky to see the first star
I hold you close, but yet you're far
You shiver against the cool night air
I lightly kiss your cheek and brush your hair.
I take your hands and pull you near
You tremble in my arms, full of fear.
I search your eyes and see the love
You came to me from heaven above
I'll love you always and always care
Together our love we'll always share
We'll love each other for ever and ever
We'll never be apart, never, never.

Steve Elliott

God Is Love

Demons entwined along the vapor of
my soul, realizing the folly of all my
goals. Efforting, straining, groaning inside,
worrying and wondering, overwhelmed without
trust, hiding the truth —
    God is just,
Whining, crying — squirming worms
engulfed in liquid flames that burn.
Confused by the signs — drunk on our ego —
refusing to accept that we don't know.
Stumbling and falling on our desires —
speaking all truths from the mouths
of liars. Our eyes wide open, but not
to see — sounds muffed by our
crippling disease. The simple truth we
can't be worthy of and makes us look
for something greater
    Than Love —

Burke Foster

Anniversaries (Intimate Moments In Our Lives)

This is the time to reflect on the days gone by.
To remember the special time that we have shared.
The togetherness, friendship, joy and laughter.

Certain events arise as virtual photographs in our minds.
Like sharing special foods, and drinks.
Lying by a dancing fire, our passions at peak.
Enjoying soft spring breezes, under clear blue suntan skies.

Walking hand in hand and dreaming of tomorrow.
We comfort each other through our times of sorrow.
A listening ear, a gentle hug, and warm soft kisses.
Can return our wonderful bliss.

On this special day of happiness and caring.
When we are remembering those first days of passion and
wonder.
Our hearts pounding like rolling thunder.
Lovingly embrace one another, and never let go.
As we experience this Anniversary's intimate moments . . .

James S. Wilson

If Ever

If ever I see,
The way the old place use to be.
If ever I wonder,
The rolling hills and the sound of thunder.
If ever I do,
The way my grandfather had to.
If ever I believe,
In the good Lord's love for him and his memories.
If ever I make a fuss,
I remember I put him in God's loving trust.
If ever there should come a time,
I will have him in my heart and call him mine.
If ever I should shed a tear,
I will remember he had no fear.
If ever he should pass away,
I'll remember the way things use to be and the way things
    are today.
If ever I forget,
But then again . . . not yet.

Mary Holzinger

Crushed Velvet

Condemned to lounge on mattresses
First fashioned for a privileged few
Alas, today their worn and willing seams,
For her shall have to do
They're old, (no, not antique), just second-hand
Yet she pretends
The noble and the affluent
Are still her closest friends
She carries straight and tall her shaky skeleton, with pride
A habit, dragged in plastic sacks
She'll look into your eyes
Then shut her own to view the past
The girl
The starched, white dress
Now nourishment and shelter
Will define today's success
Tonight, she'll dine with princes
As the city's sidewalk guest

Gina Kent Silvers

Dreams

Dreams are just images, kept locked in our mind
A place you can find happiness, time after time
A place you can be whatever you want to be
Allow our imagination to run free
Where clouds are always fluffy, skies never gray
And where the people you love,
Never go away.

Stormie M. Polhemus

Upon Graduation

You came to us so small, so sweet
tiny hands, tiny feet.
You've grown so much, a woman become,
to us a joy, a rebel to some.

To watch you grow has been pure joy
from dolls, to dogs, to horses, to boys.
Face always hidden within a book
always moving without a look.

Another threshold all but done
it has not always been much fun.
But we made it through, we lived, we did
and from it all we got one great kid.

So from the hollowed halls you go
the knowledge you've taken, how you'll sow
I told you to listen, do well, just pass
Come June'95 you're out on your a**.

Jerri Bailey

"Unforgotten Memories"

An old man sits in a rocking chair,
Gallant, grinning always there.
Shakes his head at the world he knows,
Remembering the past as the present flows,
Asking himself what happened to his life,
Trying to laugh at all his strife.
Seeming lively and feeling fine,
Covering up the pain and lines.
No one knows what lies ahead,
But soon this loving man maybe dead.
As the old man waits for death to near,
Relatives gather and all have fear.
Soon this man they loved so much,
Will meet his end and death shall clutch.
Rocking on through the ages,
Love and fear in all the pages,
His life is now gone,
But his memories live on . . .

Kim Delloma

Untitled

The day we met who knew we'd meet again
To find us in love after being friends
We never knew our feelings could be strong
Then you walked away with no worries at all
You stayed gone thinking of me for so long
One day you came back wanting me to fall
Looking in your eyes is all I needed
And I too had those same feelings all over
Now as the days past slowly as I plead
To have you back in my arms forever
Your life is just a memory to me
Now our love has come to an early end
Yet I know in heaven you're with me
If only this time you could hold me again.

Nikki Howard

A Gem He Almost Missed

He stands alone, pondering existence,
  Eyes locked on the horizon.
If left alone, he stands no chance,
  His sun will set . . . Or is it rising?

She came to him, a gem he almost missed.
  A friendship grew pure and stable.
He knew his search was over when they finally kissed.
  She gave him strength that made him able.

He pours his soul into his lance,
  She adds her grip for confidence.
Together they will slash on through
  The web of life that holds them true.

Now they stand together, destined to be one,
  Fate is theirs without surmising.
They turn to the horizon, and gaze upon their sun,
  And sure enough it is rising.

John Zengel

Twenty-One Years

Sweet lady, I know —

  (all passes)

    Mud to flowers — (flowers to wilts)
    Sticks to leaves — (leaves to fallings)
    Worms to butterflies (!) (and even butterflies to snow)

  (all) I know (passes)

    Mothers (to age) and fathers (to graves)
    Children leaping to life (yeah, toward death)
    Between the blinking of my years — Oh light!
    (all to darkness) and even I and you (we two shall pass)

  (and) I know —

    All the raw ragged edges of this being human
    So softened by your lovely ways
    That miracles of light and sound overwhelm this one
    (blind and dumb, stumbling, smashing in singular pursuit)
    But in times with you — no care (of timelessness)

  One is two —

Sweet lady . . .

                    ah . . . sweet lady.

Richard Travisano

Wind Song

The wind blows music plaintively singing
  through my hair. It rushes up along my
cheek placing kisses on my mouth and,
  talks into my ear.

I watch it come — rustling up from the
  hollow there, skipping, flirting around
every fickled hill, blowing gaily across
  wood and glade, on its way to me.

I reach out to catch its joy, to hold its
  secret in my fragile hands and, look
eye to eye into your cherished face —
  hearing songs of a hallowed time.

I run and fall and, stumble too, looking,
  looking for you — I cannot feel, I'm
deaf, I'm blind, my mouth will not speak
  — help me please.

Norma S. Taylor

One Last Tear

And when he opened that final door,
he was swallowed by a lifetime of shadows.
There, immersed in darkness, were his fondest dreams —
unrealized and bitter —
now skeletons to haunt and torture him.
At their feet he wept, for the hell he found
was of his own making.

Karl E. Glasgow IV

Why Does It Hurt So Bad?

Why does it hurt so
bad when your heart
is crying? Why do
you feel the pain?
Why does your
heart break even
more when you see
him with another girl?
Why does it hurt to know you're
dying inside for him and he does not even care?
Why does it hurt to know
he probably doesn't even miss you?
Why does it hurt so bad when you see
him and her out in public and he's holding
her close and kissing her?
Why does it hurt when you look back on
all your memories with him and cry?
Why do you wish you had him back
after he hurt you so bad?

Ashley Foster

Why Try?

Try?
What is try?
Try is what you do when you really don't want
    to succeed
Why try?
Why play the game?
Why not succeed?
Either you want to succeed or you don't
Why go through life trying to accomplish goals
    that don't fit you?
Why not re-evaluate yourself and set goals
    that do fit you?
Then, you will succeed.

Cindy Torres

Zoom Lens

in a fish eyed frenzy I step aside and try to hide
as the hordes of flesh mongers slide past me
on the way to a feast, a feast of sin,
of eating and drinking the blood of those
more fortunate than ourselves,
those allowed to pass on into the arms of God
instead of having to watch as the demons devour what is left.
My chest heaves and I cannot breathe from
the pain of trying to tell them what they do not want to hear,
they want only to become like the animals
to forage through the wilderness and carouse with darkness.
I walk with them, crawl with them, cry with them
as we remember what it was like before hope was a memory.
But while I want to rebuild, rework,
give birth to all the dreams
that were trampled on by people who called themselves Gods,
they just want to forget and live like . . . demons,
lost in a world that can never warm them
like the baths of hell.

Bo Buchanan

The Water Room

sun rays
flood cold currents
    streak seaweed beds
    wind down coppery vines
    into sea grass

up near the surface
phantoms glide like shadows . . .
    a grouper cuts away
    cruising slow
    she comes in close
    suspends —
      her stare
      x-rays the wall of glass

she tugs me like a magnet
and the wall melts down . . .
    a fetus
    almost transparent
    mouth slack —
    I gulp for air

"breathe water . . . like a fish . . .", she whispers

Janice Burchard

The Egalitarian Tradition

In the days of yesterday, I was me and you were you,
Male and female, we crossed no lines.
The woman's place was in the home,
The man's was in the world.

Through strife, economic change, and finally recognition,
The woman's role has digressed with time.
Now she can taste the world,
While the man picks up her stride.

Who was it who said, "a man cannot nurture
And a woman has no muscle or brain?"
Let the truth be known, both possess the same.
One may be left brain, and one may be right,
But what difference does it make, if together they thrive?

You are male and I am female;
The main difference is our sex.
We share the responsibilities of the world together,
And with flexibility nothing is too complex.

You are man and I am woman,
But in the Egalitarian tradition we are equal; we are one.

Michele Morris-Jones

The Old Man Suitcase

The old man stepped upon the porch of the county's Old Folks Home
He'd come to spend the rest of his days, never again to roam

He'd traded in his dreams for three meals and a bed and he knew
this was what he would call his home till the day that he was dead

And his lifetimes accumulation he held in just one once proud hand
It was all he'd ever have to show for his many years in this great land

It was an old tattered suitcase, all worn now to a shred
but it told the whole life story of the life that he had led

It held pictures and ribbons and a small pair of shoes,
they sometimes brought him laughter and other times the blues

Yes its contents told of many of his life's most foolish schemes
but it was his record of living, his diary of dreams

Joe B. Karnes

My Father's Glass

My father had a special glass,
forever at his side.
He thought his children could be fooled,
so the glass he tried to hide.

The golden spirits quickly drained away,
his health and life did follow.
Every dream . . . every love . . .
Disappeared with an endless swallow.

The day my father passed away,
I searched to find that glass.
Thoughts of it shattered, useless and broken,
gripped my soul and would not pass.

But, as I held it in my hand,
with such sadness, poised to throw,
I found it would not leave my grasp,
my tears would not let it go.

For this was all that I had left,
my father's most prized possession.
I'll keep it forever at my side,
To remind me of his obsession.

Sharon Galiatsatos

Patience

I stroll about the carpeted halls,
Wandering, searching,
For the one person that's always on the top of my mind.

I round a corner, and alas!
The tall, lanky figure looms from the crowd.

As he looks my way,
My face begins to glow and breaks into smiles.

He approaches and my heart bursts
over his simple acts of friendliness.

I ponder and hope over him.
Wishing I knew his thoughts,
But I have to wait with that one, horrible word
Patience.

Jillian Loveland

Best Wishes To The Miser

There will be no pockets in your shroud, my brother.
There will be no pockets in your shroud.
For you cannot take it with you, my brother,
So you'd better spend some now.

Give it to your father, give it to your sister,
Put a smile on the face of a child.
There will be no pockets in your shroud, my brother.
So you'd better spend it now.

Endow a library, or a hospital,
Fix an old widowed lady's roof.
Spread your money around; don't bury it in the ground.
Enjoy spending it on others now.

There will be no pockets in your shroud, my brother.
There will be no tears at your demise.
A miser's not missed, who'd no smile, who'd no kiss.
Find joy in sharing now.

There will no pockets in your shroud, my brother.
There will be no pockets in your shroud.
For you cannot take it with you, my brother.
So spread some around right now.

E. M. L.

I See God

I see God in every flower,
In every blossom, in every bud,
In every color, pale and bright,
In every sweet and perfect sight,
I see God.

I see God in every hill,
In every peak and every valley,
In every stream, in every sea,
In every rock and cliff, I see God.

I see God in every sky,
In every planet and far off star,
In noonday sun and winter moon,
In clouds that go a floating by, I see God.

I see God in every storm,
In every mist and every gale,
In every warm and gentle rain,
In every thunderous icy hail, I see God.

I see God within myself, in every living creature,
In every spark of kindness shown, and everyone I know,
I see God.

Carol I. Ferguson

Reticence

In your eyes,
I can see forever.
In that black void,
I can loose myself.
There is no time,
    No feeling,
       No sound.

Only space.
You speak,
And the silence shatters.
The pieces fall to the floor.
A million shining silver splinters scatter.
I try to pick them up, while dropping tears.
Mournful at its loss,
I try to fit them back together,
But it will never be the same.
I look to you for help,
But all I see is the black void of your eyes,
as you turn to walk away.

Justine Simonson

"My Uninvited Guest"

Death came knocking at my door.
I said, "Death who are you looking for"?
Death said, "I came to take you away
To a place where you'll forever stay".

I told Death, "Please leave me alone.
I'm not looking for a brand new home".
Death said, "I came because it's my job".
I told Death, "Hey, look down the street at the mob".

I said "Death, I can't go with you.
I have entirely too much to do".
Death said, "Hey it's your time to go!
Please, don't make me take you so".

I decided to make death's job hard.
I tried to convince him of others to part.
Death reminded me that it was my time to go.
God gave me peace of mind and I surrendered so.

Death came knocking at my door.
I said, "Death who are you looking for"?
Death said, "I came to take you away
To a place where you'll forever stay".

Darlene L. Henderson

Chrysalis

Glass frosted prisms
wedged in barbed fences,
shelter the butterfly . . . slumbering still
in its cocoon of life.
Sentient caution, tender as such, patient yet wary as
light years do rush
brazenly, brashly, foolishly sought
until in a crackle, the butterfly emerges —
in the flutter of early light.
The Chrysalis — Shatters
millions of pupa
dried and scattered,
empty, forgotten,
no longer needed.
The Butterfly evolves a passionate flower —
slaying the world, with grace.

Donna Rorex-Griffin

Ash

The sad joy of autumn lies
in her golden October
a bitter-sweet, pungent smell
of smoke on drying leaves
slanting beams calling out an end
to the one who disbelieves fate
yellow warmth who's ending is a birth
to her ancient child's wonder
for things earthy and kind
the reddened sun, so tired and
soon to sleep, whispers direct
to her heart of a Californian dream
and lulling movement among the trees hides
the short diversity of loveliness
from her late afternoon
sunlight through the spotted
canopy to the soil dark and quiet
with its familiarity of solitude
in the sad joy of her golden October.

Aislinn Race

A Tribute For Oneta

O-ne day, I met you in a pace of life
  When I thought, time was in jive
  Because, you were there smiling
  With an open arms that were willing

N-ot a thing that you have criticized me
  Nor rejected, pushed and misjudged me
  All you did was show your love and respect
  With my aspiration, it is what any human would expect

E-ven though, your health was a big battle for you
  You were performing life's duties just like we do
  How precious were your hands to cooked in every gathering
  And so sweet of you for all the gestures and caring

T-ruly, you were a very beautiful person
  Who disappeared from your family too soon
  Today, we are missing you terribly
  For we treasure your memories tremendously

A-fterall this hour, I wish you are still alive and with us
  So I can show you more my gratitude and fuss
  For the reality that you gave birth and brought up Ron
  Whom I am spending my whole life through — your son.

Maria Grace Burris

Dying Abused

She lies awake in her bed,
But all she remembers is the color red.

It comes through her mind, the horrors from the past,
The beatings from her mother and the big huge outcast.

In her body she feels the pain,
Then pictures the future with a cane.

She's got to leave before it happens again,
But falls asleep before the end.

Andrea Masemer

With Death At Our Side

With my sword held high
Blood drips on my face
I see you lying there,
But couldn't see your face
I stood there in thought for a minute
What I decided was I could but I didn't
Then I walked away,
Knowing the battle has been won
Looking down, I saw dead bodies,
None killed by a gun
All this death and all this mayhem.
Am I the last alive? Or will I be the last to die?
Then I draw my sword and throw it across the land,
Because now I'm still alive and fought with my free hands.

Brad Butin

Mythic Man

You are Pygmalian, I Galatea,
Matter and essence awaiting the artist's touch.
Exquisite hands melt my skin, electrify my veins.
Vital eyes ignite my mind,
Infuse my consciousness —
I come alive for you!

Love of mythic proportions,
Feast for the senses,
You are the food that fills me up,
Fuels my appetite for more.
Soul unbound, flesh of my soul-satisfied,
We are kissed by the Gods!

Holiest of passions, most carnal sacrament,
It could not be a sin to taste
What heart and soul foreknow.
A fusion lodged in destiny —
More so would be sin to deny
This sweet, sweet alchemy!

Stacy J. Basham

Alone Life's Way

As alone life's way we go,
What kind of a light does our life show,
Does the world see Jesus as we go alone?
Are we serving him daily with a smile and a song.

Someone is watching us each day.
So let us be careful of the words we say.
Be kind to your neighbor, help someone in need.
Be sure to serve Jesus in both words and deeds.

We can be in church every sunday,
Read our bible every day,
But what really counts for Jesus is
How we live our life each day.
So be careful fellow christian as you go alone life's way.
Be sure to live for Jesus each and every day.

Sylvia Garner

The Empire Is Silent

The Audience reveled
And Caesar hiccuped,
the Empire fat on wine and debauchery
Whorls of silk and naked flesh to satiate the hunger,
feasting the fat with ulcers of pride

The reveling went into the night
And Caesar sniffled,
a whisper of worry, the untouchable god
With wraith fingers of mortal ailment,
dismissed, laughed at, nervous tongues say there is no fear

The purple of dawn, revelers sigh
And Caesar died,
As all Gods faded into blurred stupor memory,
their pious fans look elsewhere
The sound of howling ivy on broken cobble,
the Empire is silent.

Lériget de La Plante

Love And Hate

Love is like a filled glove,
because there is always someone to love and care for.
So, let your glove be filled with someone to love and care for.
But, hate is like an empty glove,
no one to love and no one to care for.
So, don't let your glove be empty,
let it be full with love not hate.

Marie Wessinger

Lines Only Tied To Earth By Paper

I rejoice at the color and vibrations of springtime —
At Hyakutake comet strobed with dazzling sunlight,
At eloquent music keeping breath by me,
At the caressing of a soul with a touch,
At night's beginning for having lived today.

I treasure life with these words
exploded on this quiet page.
It's not a ramble through my emotions
that takes me through this life.

I found a rhythm, a path, a web, a weave, a movement.
And from my vantage point in this sprawling universe,
these lines are only tied to paper on one end.
The effort and desire to know life
hurtles at a shocking speed out beyond the comet,
out beyond anything I can see, feel and imagine.

Frank Van Creef

I Am Dream

As the dim moon light shades off a darkish glow to guide my sleep,
I am mesmerized by the sweet melody of the midnight whispers.
Beloved sounds of mystery lurk in the dancing night. How I caress the
passion of the night's shining armors. Persuaded by a kiss of purity
flown to me by the midnight breeze, I can tip toe through enchanted
gardens of dew glistening roses to come upon romantic forests, ever
aching to be my shelter. Twisting turning vines are plunged up through
ponds of wine to guide my destined travel. Ensorcelled by a passion so
rare to the human eye, I am withdrawn by a source unknown to me. A
whisper that time will pass, and time is still, and ever will. Not afraid.
I follow speaking Wiser that tells me all of what I shall. His love
turns to echoing songs that would enhance my mind, my soul. I am
one. I am night. I am rose. I am sleep. I am the melody that plays
within. I am dream, now let me sleep.

Erin Espy

Looking Forward

Adults killing kids, kids killing kids. Where does it all end?
What do they have to look forward to?
Gangbangers killing your kid for their shoes.
No parents to show, how we all should grow.
Kids are living for the day because they feel they have no future,
No hope. It's a never ending cycle of pity and dope.
So much food in the world why are so many kids starving to death?
Society doesn't care about the no name rest.
Pollution and the killing off of the rain forest.
Solution or have we of the human race destroyed the Earth and our
fate? The rich don't care about the poor,
It's as if they were dead. Political corruption so bad,
The little man can't get ahead. As you see.
Money and greed is the root of the disease.
Religions arguing with religions to the point of war.
Fighting over land that was never really theirs.
The ignorance of people, if they would just look back and see,
Why God gave us this planet to live on it peacefully.
It's a shame we have to live this way.
That's what we've got to look forward to today.

Michael L. Chamberlain

Childhood

I miss my childhood
the innocence
not knowing what happens
not knowing the truth
no worries at all
just about making friends
no cares in the world
just playing, having fun all day
not knowing what's in store
not knowing the future
not needing to know
just asking simple questions
what, how, and the famous why
life used to be so easy
so simple
when you're little you don't even care
if your hair is out of place
or if you forgot something
because everything will be alright
childhood, the innocence, no worries at all

Sarah Gelletly

Frederick Douglas

Frederick Douglas was a tree
Bound by his roots,
Not able to leave,

He wished and dreamed
About being a bird
So he could fly free and even be heard.

Then the snow and ice came
And beat down on his limbs
And when it was over
He was twisted and broken

Now he was stronger
And summoning all his will
He changed into a shadow.

Skipping along
Past the night
Trying to flee from the evil in sight

As the warmth hit his face
The shadow fell away
To reveal not a bird or a tree
But a beautiful man who became great as a king

Terra Gray

The Charge Of The Light Brigade

I received a shock that's with me still
　from the electric charge on my utility bill.
I went to complain and the saints preserve us
　was referred to a dolt in "Customer Service".

One would think by complaining I'd broken Ohms Law;
　this from the most ignorant specimen I ever saw.
To put it bluntly, not being subtle or profound,
　he didn't know his amps from a hole in the ground.

It seems billing is based on an average use
　of kilowatt hours.
(Probably read by the meter person who trampled
　my flowers.)

I'd been gone a month so asked what they could average;
　he got red in the face and almost turned savage.
Said he, "I'm tired of explaining to every ignorant jerk
　the way that our electrical charges work."

There was no use to argue; they have all the clout —
　either pay what they say or your lights go out.
If into a light socket I could manage to screw 'em,
　I'd give them more power and yell, "Sock It To 'Em".

Jack R. Jones

Stormy Sea

On a stormy sea of moving emotions
Tossed about I'm like a ship on the ocean
The face in the mirror that's looking at me
Can't be what everyone else can see
Hearing the sound of my own voice
Speaking to me saying I have no choice
My heart is filled with uncontrollable desire
Panic rules the moments with no mercy nor desire
My emotions fooled me into going back
Spoiled the memories that I left on the track
But I'm woven in a fantasy can't believe the things I see
This is all that I am and all that I will ever be

Allison Gregory

Ponds And Lakes

Whenever I go to make a pond,
of it I'm always very fond.
And once I went to make a lake:
Of course it was a fake.
It wasn't big, just the size of a quite enormous fig.

Then I made a boat and set it in to float.

Then suddenly the sun shone brightly!
The sun said: "I have no fear to shine so you can cheer."

Daniel C. Mayer II

Untitled

I can't face the night alone
Darkness has taken away my light
In my soul . . . in my bones
Baby I need you here tonight
Deprived of comfort . . . deprived of sleep
The tears I cry, I cry for you
Is it right to know I weep
When events are misconstrued
Surrounded by a wall of bars
What's a boy supposed to do
Musical mobile of trains and cars
Doesn't help me forget about you
In my mouth I put my thumb
That helps me crack a little smile
That gets old and I feel dumb
Because I'm missing my blankey all the while

Thom C. McQuestion Jr.

Wings Of Harmony

With thorns of iniquities streets of confusions,
We look through eyes of illusions.
In conflicts with spirits,
Wings of harmony will not be found,
Empty souls lie to the ground.
To void to think,
No fullness in a drink.
To cry in questioning loneliness,
Can a sparrow nest in a tree of barrenness?
The word of heaven you can feel,
God will send his peace to heal.
Heave the seeks of evil and wrongs,
The spirit will stand again, and strong.
Blossom clean and clear,
Love will come the more near.
Bold and positive look through the wall,
Rejoice and hear the eagles call.
Never hold to the earth to keep a
Spirit that must be free.
Let us soar on wings of harmony.

William Runnels

Untitled

The rain is a baptism on my skin
It chills to the bone and invites me in
First a slow muffled patter
Then the sky erupts and nothing matters
Streaks of light in the sky
Heavens demon is alive cleansing the world of its sins
The growl of the demon begins
Awake is natures rampant child
He starts the storm and sits back with a smile
The tapping can drive a man insane
But it's rhythmic to a lonely man's brain
The hush is calm
As I notice the wind has gone

Jeff Mansch

Summer Storm

The rain is teaming outside the log cabin.
The air, fresh.
The breeze a welcomed relief from the non-stop humidity.

Pelting teardrops from the sky hiss and spit against the wooden porch.
Thunder crashes in the distance.
A child's voice exclaims in alarm and fascination.

Crash!
A flash of lightning.
The thundering roar rages across the blackened sky startling a few
that "whoa" in awe.

The pattering: continuous, insistent, relentless, hard hearted!
Thunder screams across the wind.

Silence.
Drip, drop.
The aroma of charcoal burning in the air.
An evening sun streaks across the sky; rumbles of thunder roiling in
the distance.

Maureen McKeown

Eagles

The wind of God
The burst of wind
We all sing together in the heart of blind
Soaring through the clouds
Flying through the sky
Now they'll say goodbye

Jenny Schmidt

Ode To Adeline

The first time we met, do you recall?
It's hard to forget, that trip in the fall.

To the city bound, not just to look around
Husbands were drifted — had to pass a test
At the governments request.

A baby on the way, three for me, four for you
The layette I bought gave you the clue.

Little yellow house, with a porch rail
Crowded post-office lobby, — waiting for mail

Silk stockings worn, though they were torn
Nylons came later, a gift of the war.

Regularly walking our kids around the blocks.
I'm sure by us the natives could set their clocks.

So here to 50 years of memories, some joyful and some sad,
But one thing for sure not all of them bad.

Margaret Twitchell

Final Moments

The time now has come, to leave this world behind,
    I must move on, to join those for whom I have pined.
Loved ones gone before are standing by — they're near,
    They're telling me — that the final moments are here.

It seems rather strange, to find there's no more time,
    But don't fret for me — they tell me, I'll be just fine.
So much in this world I've not yet seen, nor done,
    But there's no time left, to accomplish even one.

I do have to wonder, where the time did go,
    If it could last forever, this I would so vow;
I would do much more, every second, I'd fill —
    And treasure each moment, as I climbed the next hill.

Though I thought life long — it really was so short,
    Although overall, it was certainly a lark.
No matter the trials, no mater the strife,
    Through joy and sorrow — it's been a wonderful life!

Opal Gibson

"Love In The Night"

The sun sets softly over the hills,
the skies colors are so soft and beautiful.
But the beauty is no match,
for the one in my arms.
We lay quietly waiting,
waiting on the moon and the stars.
The first star appears,
twinkling like her eyes in the moon light.
The gentle kiss of her lips,
makes me wish time,
would stop for eternity.
I whisper softly in her ear
I love you forever,
and forever I will be here.

Brett Popov

Forgotten Realms

Epic battles fought at noon
Heroic struggles across sandy dunes
Cross country flights on my condor's back
Escaping death on a pirate's rack
Launching myself on a trampoline
In search of galaxies yet unseen
Half remembered dreams of childhood days
Forgotten realms of days at play

Joshua Hall

Growing Up

Restless in the wind
leaves blow with a trace of regret.
Sighing, softly singing
a sweet sound like mother's lullaby.

In strong arms she holds me
rocking like a tree in the wind.
Safe and joyous, her smile is sunshine
driving off the shadow night.

Strong hands smoothing my worried brow,
rustled by a wind of change.
Pulling me to my destiny
she the branch, I the leave.

Jennifer L. Tafe

Forgetfulness

Forgetting is a great aspect,
if it's the right thing you're forgetting.
When you forget to brush your teeth,
your breath will send out a warning.
When you forget to call someone,
that person will be sure to inform you.

But the aspect that I think is great in all men, is the ability
to forget the color of one's skin. Once we overcome this
remembrance of the color of one's skin; We will all be better
off, and maybe, just maybe the world would be able to forget
to be prejudice.

Credella Parker

God's Road Map

Believe that Christ is the son of God
That's the very first thing you do
Because if you do not believe in Him
You will never be able to carry through

The righteous path is lighted by God's word
Who in this sinful world has not heard
It seems strange and false to me
To think there is anyone in this world that is not free

Free to choose their way in life
What path to follow, what kind of strife
The path of darkness leads to sin
There is no guiding light therein

So choose to follow the path of light
You can be sure you are doing right
God will guide you all the way
His word and prayer lights the way

Olivia Hodge

Girls

    They fall in love with you,
They are beautiful, some are tall,
    Others are fat some are skinny, others
are pains, most of them are good-looking, most
of them are divorced, married, or single, some
of them are good. Others are bad, other you have to
leave them, some of them you have to break up with,
some of them are so stubborn, pigheaded, rude
some are Lawyers, Doctors, Bus Drivers, Teachers,
others are good to have around, some are small,
some are smart other are dumb, others stay
home to do housework, some of them ask you
go to the store, others mouth off of you. Most of
them likes guys with after-shave lotion on.

Joseph Edward Grover Jr.

No Way Out

He once was a man, so tall and strong,
His good looks promised nothing could go wrong.
He was virtuous, ambitious, pious, and devout.
Health was a subject he never thought about.

He was a fireman who treasured each day on the scene,
He advanced through the ranks, for he was calm and serene.
Off duty he was at home with his children and wife,
Or in his garden nurturing his plants to life.

He talked of the past and his family tree
But never realized he would never be free
Of the disease handed down to him through the years
That had blinded his friends and crippled his peers.

Now he sits in a wheelchair with one of his legs gone.
His body is boney, his face wrinkled and drawn.
He is still a young man of forty seven years
So why is he old . . . why all the tears?

To this young man, Diabetes is no joke,
He knows it's a killer and no respecter of folk.
It has cost him his job and his bank account
But his main fear is there is no way out.

Linda Peeples

Fall's Violet

In fall, when maple trees indulge
In phantasmagoric self-display
In one last bacchanal before their naked sleep,
The wild asters, with genes perversely programmed,
Resist the lemming march
But can not stop its toll.

In fall life's progression juggernaut
Can not be stayed;
Nor, on reflection, would we wish it so.
Nor would wishing will it so.
Still, the shiver in fall's darkening sky
Bespeaks anxiety as well as evening's raw.

In fall what joy is in discovery
Of the stunted violet that resists the downward flow,
And blooms again for us in some unlikely place;
The path between the corn fields, the pebbled driveway's edge,
Or by the old stone wall. The violet
That shows for us again this unexpected time
Speaks to our hope, as day gives into night,
And evening cold sets in, of resurrection.

J. C. Wood

Shadows After Dark

Some love the sunshine, fresh air, the park
I love the shadows that appear after dark
The young and innocent feel safe in daylight
I need the darkness, the blackness of night
This world is my kingdom, it's here I rule
My victims the tainted, the useless, the fool
They don't care what I do, the people of day
Their world is color, mine shades of gray
They want only nice things around them to see
So they ignore human refuse, they leave it to me
But they're only human, I am not of their kind
They are happy to stumble, emotionally blind
I'm sorry I sometimes get into this mood
I hate being near them but I need them for food
Here comes one now, in this doorway I'll wait
They never see me, until it's too late
Now into my body, his lifeblood will flow
I have just cancelled his small part in life's show
How utterly foolish that look on their face
When they see me and know I am part of this place

Kenny Hayes

The Gift Of Love

Love is what is never seen; by heart alone it's felt.
It heralds dreams, enlivens thee; for pain and grief do melt.
In every way it stands for what is known, so good and right;
For every creature here below, it is the source of light.

It brings, to faith, a balance in our burdened earthly beings;
While faith lives for the future, and for things we aren't yet seeing,
Love abounds, is ever-present, both tomorrow and today.
And while we cannot hope to see or touch it, in our way,

It gives to us a wondrous joy, such warmth so undefied;
That witness to such acts of love, these cannot be denied.
In special ways, it feels within, as though thy heart be lifted;
Though many who may choose to flee, will never be so gifted.

Some run from it, they hide away, inside their angry hearts;
Their twisted "truth" and bitter scorn ensure their fiery darts.
When given but a simple choice for love and truth and life,
They cast their stones and curse aloud;
the course they choose is strife.

And in the end they had a gift, asked only but to take it;
Instead they ran a tragic race; alone they could not make it.

Roland E. Blankenship

I Am

I am alive
I wonder about people
I hear about wars
I see death and life happening
I am afraid

I pretend war isn't there
I feel the feelings of others
I touch each life I can
I worry about others
I am sentimental

I cry about death; I understand not why it happens
I say that they are in heaven
I dream that they are too
I am worried also when I know that they're not there

I try to understand this world we're living in
I hope and pray it will change someday
I wait to see it through
I strive to be helpful in His plan
I am sure of some things too, that will help to change this world
of death into something that is new!

Matthew John Sprink

Time Will Tell

Time will tell
What time need to tell
When you do what you need to do
For time to tell
What time need to tell.

What you do today,
Time will tell,
For it will be history for you.
What you will do tomorrow,
Time may not be able to tell,
For nobody knows tomorrow.
But you're alive today,
So leave tomorrow alone,
Live for today alone.

Make your life history today,
For you might be in the grave tomorrow;
And this — time cannot tell, but time can tell
And tell what you do today.
So Gentlemen And Ladies ! Live one day at a time.
Do some good things today for generation of tomorrow.

Arthur O. A. Nakpodia

Spring

Tis a touch of springs that I sense as winds swirl the blossoms about,
Tis spring again, ahhh yes, tis spring indeed!, I loudly shout.
The changing of life with the arrival of gentle falling rains.
Vine covered picket fences, and honeysuckles draping the lanes.

Nay I say, mere men will never grasp the secrets nor the reason,
And most will remain so, mystic creations season after season.
The many fragrances of perfect blooms from the plants and trees,
As I eye the work of scouring ants and tiny, buzzing, honey bees.

The singing of birds in the nearby forest with their many melodies,
Their colors, bright and in so many hues to the eye they please.
Our creator in his infinite wisdom knew we required such splendor.
Such glorious and endless wonders, we must say thanks to the Sender.

Of all the wonderful seasons, Winter, Summer, and colorful Fall,
Spring is so fulfilling to my hungry soul, it is the favorite of all.
If I were only a painter and could all this wonder capture,
The miracles of Spring would keep me in an endless state of rapture.

There cannot be any other season that matches this annual scene,
Of life renewed, across the meadows, and streams, so serene.
Aye, is it any wonder young and old alike have cause to sing,
There's much to be joyful about, this new, and beautiful Spring.

Joseph A. Johnston

The Perfect Creation

God stayed busy for a span of time,
creating things that was on His mind.
Making things for you and I,
that would be pleasant to the ear and eye.

He made the birds to fly and sing,
He knew the pleasure that they would bring.
The bunny hops and the butterfly flies,
big round circles for the hoot owls eyes.

Flowers that peep through the ground in spring,
everyone knows that is a pretty thing.
Clouds that are white and fluffy up there,
tossed in a blue sky with loving care.

Trees that bloom with pretty flowers,
that send out fragrance for hours and hours.
Steams and rivers seem never to end,
roads that twist and climb and bend.

Wild animals that roam in a jungle deep,
with spots and stripes and some that creep.
When He finished His task to create the world,
He created His masterpiece — A boy and a girl.

Della L. Stutler

Untitled

With a face set like flint
And not a care in the world,
She continues her never-changing routine.
She has the power to control all,
But is controlled by a separate power.
People can't find enough of her.
They fall victim to her heartbeat.
Always wanting, needing more,
But on her wings she does fly.
They try to trap her, hold her,
But she will always slip away.
Forever young she will be,
With her shining crystal and swirling dance.
Moving forward, never looking back.
The past is gone, the future becomes the now,
And the now, it becomes the past.
In each hour, each minute, each second, each TICK.

Mary K. Zmuda

"Dark Of The Night"

The night has come and it's taking its toll,
on the lives of the young and the old.
It's all around you and there is no place to run,
and there's too many hours before the rising sun.

The curtain has come down on all of the land,
and darkness is coming to play its hand.
No one knows whose life it will touch,
or who it will deliver, or who it will judge.

In every corner and around every turn,
the sea of blackness is beginning to churn.
Swiftly it seeks out all light to devour,
blacker each minute, hungrier each hour.

It's coming for you and everyone you know,
and you can't escape when there's nowhere to go.
It will search you out wherever there's light,
and drag you, screaming, into the night.

If you have faith, it might get you through,
if it is strong, and as long as it's true.
Then pure is the light that comes from your heart,
that casts out the shadows and conquers the dark.

Stephen D. Strzelinski

For Sale, By Owner

Uplifted and surrounded,
A pale, halo of light.
To prey upon a weakness.
Deliverance, this endless night.
Endearing are the promises,
That never will grow old.
I'll see the world through youthful eyes.
Live on
While those around me die.
But what then of the ever aging
Poison in my soul?

Sarah Johnston

A Loss

At eighteen, I lost a man dear to me
It was my father, as you see.
He left for work, and took out his gun
We were all completely stunned.

After the shock and mourning ends
My family was in terrible shape.
Alcohol, pills, food, whatever it would take
To dull the pain of our heartbroken state.

I was to be married in a very short time
And everyone who came said, "what a beautiful bride"
Oh! If they only knew how I cried and cried inside.

Diane Patrone

He Hears

If I think, that know one cares,
Forgive me Lord, for you are there.

When wondering, how, when and where,
It's only you, that can answer my prayers.

At night, at dark, it's silent with stars.
I look above for comforting love.

So as these eyes close tonight.
Watch over me, til morning light.

If you call, before I awake,
Take my hand, lead me to the gate.

Molly Trogdon

Love: Pain

When I was in love with you
I could handle the pain
When I wasn't in love with you
I handled the pain.
Now I don't even like you
Now I can't handle — the pain.

After all these years
The pain and tears
The hurt; still with hope
You'll grow to know
Kindness, niceness, patience too
What a wonderful new world, it would be for you.

If you could hear, the things you say
The way you say it, you would change your ways
You can't stop my love for you
I just hoped my love, would help you love you
But as the saying goes
"You can't teach an old dog new tricks"
So why keep on keeping on; throwing the stick.

Gail Fisher

Untitled

Tonight I said a prayer for my children
Talked to God like I've never done before
And asked him for the wisdom to make them understand
Why the world doesn't seem safe anymore.

For the Why lives in blown up buildings
Amidst the concrete and the steel so many died
How do I find the answers to their questions
Without showing the rage and anger I have inside.

How do I answer why mommies kill their babies
Or why daddy hits mommy and she bleeds
How sons can coldly kill their parents
And excuse it all as if it were a good deed.

Can I find the words to speak about prejudice
To explain the hate and treatment that's so cruel
Why a cross or swastika can be displayed as public symbol
But not one prayer can ours kids say in school.

Tonight, I said a prayer for my children
I spoke to God to help me formulate a plan
But before I can start to answer their questions
God has to make this father understand.

Steven R. Fritz

The First Vespers Of Spring

And snowflakes fall and rise to the rushing wind,
And the ice forms on the rained-frozen trees,
And the summer grass is no longer to be seen,
And the secrets of the winter snow beset themselves.
The crocuses resurrect above the snow,
to triumphantly greet the coming Spring.

Helene J. M. Kozma

Love

Healing, and serving.
Then betrayal?
Whippings, and thirty-three thorns.

Humiliation, and condemnation.
Then denial?
Fallings, and three nails.

And one stab,
Then death . . .

. . . at this point the gates of heaven opened, lovingly.
You may now enter, but slowly!

Euie A. McKee

Untitled

Many roads to cross
    So you pass them
Many words to say
    So you speak them
Many feelings to express
    So you tell them
Many smiles to share
    So you experience them
Many tears to shed
    So you discard them
Many bewildered moments
    So you wonder
Many happy moments
    So you sparkle
Many confused times
    So you're troubled
Through all this power of awareness, power of perceiving,
power of sense, touch, reaction, you also have the power
of the mind to move ahead.

AnnLouise F. Juliano

Moon Dust of Night

Moon dust of night's passion gently touches the wounds
crushed petals of tomorrow spill down to the rigid truth
shadows marked by angels fill the air
somehow in the madness, I wish I wouldn't care

Time's power swallows me in
distorted reflections taste where we've been
satin tears await the rain
sudden swirled emotions seem impossible to tame

Bitter-sweet feelings lose their painted tone
water-colored raindrops silently perceive the unknown

Innocence destroyed in countless ways
dreams silver-line the remainder of my days
thoughts captured in pollution of you
anger stales as I ponder the wonder of what to do

Flames of deceit freeze in your eyes
falling fast, I feel myself fading away to distant skies

Nita Guidoux

The Letter

The brittle, yellowed paper
Tells a tale of long ago
When a country torn by battle
Saw a time of grief and woe.

It's a story of a soldier
Who defended home and hearth,
Of the journey he had been on
And the sorrow in his heart.

It tells of friends who fought beside him
And the horror he had seen
Of the prison he was held in,
Of the fate of many men.

How they all would be held captive
Till somehow this strife would pass,
But to wife and friends and family
It was word from him at last.

At the end there was a prayer
For his loved ones far away
That the Lord would watch and guard them
Until he'd be back some day.

Sharon Carter

Queen

She's a mother, need I say more
She's the maid the shirts adore
She's the cook, makes tummies glad
She's the wife, Oh happy Dad

She's a nurse, the one you trust
She's the shrink for the best of us
She's the man when dads at work
She's the Judge when there's a quirk

She's a lady, when day is done
She's the friend just one with one
She's the person when a person is needed
She's the mom with whom we pleaded

She's a teacher when we are wrong
She's the wreck when we are gone
She's the grandmother who stands so tall
She's the Queen, the one and all

RenaMarie Lavery

Chaos

Four score for seven years in prison? Good deal if you don't
fumble the football your fist and beat the floor the geek, he
needs it as much as the Gerber Baby wants a spanking. So turn
your head and coughing on the smoke your hash before it's
made legal because then it won't be so fund the war all you want
but you can't stop the military from mailing you that yellow
piece of paper-punching pencil-heads should volunteer them-
selves to fight to save face. Wait, what's that the sound of the
charge! I can see the whites of the eggs are supposed to be
better for you but the guy at the gas station says you need gas
to live. Keep your hands and feet off the grass stains don't
kill babies either so why not try bud dry? You don't believe me?
That's what the doctor said no more jumping on the bandwagon
because we all know it's just how drunks get from place to place
and playing, volleyball in the rockies looks more fun when
drunk. I am freethinking, free-speaking on a point of personal
privileges for all that's my motto includes association, conglom-
eration, constipation, nighttime sniffling, sneezing, coughing,
aching, fever, stuffy head so you're drunk again medicine!
Spank you very much!

Ben Jackson

Ode To My Son

"My son is dead," cries out my anguished heart, "My son is dead."
No more will this gentle giant stride across the land in his slow
    deliberate manner.
No more will I hear his quiet voice speak of things he loved.
No more will I feel his comforting arm about my shoulders and hear
    his voice reassuredly saying "It's okay Mom."
What then is left? Ah, the comfort lies in what is left
For he shared his soul as he lived, touching so many lives both old and young.
He left much love which will live on long after his passing.
He left memories of a tender man with a heart filled with compassion
    for his fellow man.
He left with those around him his love for the beauty and joy found
    in the great outdoors.
He loved the desert and all the beauty God had hidden away in its many
    nooks and crannies.
He loved life, but even more important, he loved the people
    surrounding him in that life.
He was a free spirit that could not be pressed into any conventional mold.
He was not a saint, but he knew the Lord and . . .
He was my son, my joy, and my heartache.
He was a special gift from God to be enjoyed for only a short while.
He is with God now while his memories continue to sing in my heart.

Joyce May

A Winter Visitor

More appealing than the sublime cardinal or the dashing jay,
your cheering presence brings life to the dreariest winter day.
Out from sheltering holly you loop to alight on the dogwood tree,
and announce your arrival with a buzzing "chick-a-dee-dee-dee."

Nervously you accept my invitation to dine on a winter offering
of black sunflower seeds, which you deftly seize and take to wing.
You flit to above oak to hammer at the seeds with your tiny beak,
pulverizing them to the required digestible morsels on which you feed.

The unmerciful wind raises a tuft of feathers while you pause to rest,
only momentarily however, for nature drives you to an endless quest,
to confront the daily problem of maintaining a minimum body heat.
To and fro you dart, forward to feeder, and again to the oak you retreat.

My human subjectivity is of no concern to you, my tiny winter visitor.
The joy you bring to me passes unnoted by you as you work at the chore
of keeping your inner warmth and enduring another day of numbing cold.
Heat to survive the frosty night and again the morning sun to behold.

Yet, oh chickadee, recognize that my odd nature often depends upon
an inwardly created world which beyond objective fact transcends.
Though you are not aware of how very much you give back to me,
kindly act as though we are friends as you feast upon my seeds.

Ronald W. Brown

Self Made

When viewing a painter his picture starts off
looking like nothing, but a child's paintings,
but with each stoke of the brush, the shaping
and shadows to the highlights, you're starting to
develop your scene. Then you step back for
the whole view and it's turned into something
very beautiful.
    Like life you're so natural and innocent you
don't have a clue. When you get older you're
in touch, but still it's trail and error, but
with patience, and compassion for yourself,
what you do and who you love, when you step
back for the whole view, look at the good,
don't take what you have and who you have for
granted.
    Look underneath the layers of paint, and
remember the work. That all things that make
things are beautiful.

Victoria Costanzo

No Path Needed

She walks slowly through the woods because there is no trail.
Will she make her destination, find a new way, or fail?

At first her way was fresh and bright!
There was a path to follow, wide with light.
Many travelled with her, some slower, some fast
One running to the future, another walking from the past.

Then came a storm and the bright was gone
Only angry flashes to keep moving on.
Things flew at her from nowhere cutting her hands, a knee
She said to herself, "This way is not for me."

She ran to the woods, found a place to hide.
Shelter — warm and dark where only she could reside.

The storm finally lost its rage
Then the cave began to feel like a cage.
The rain was still falling when she stepped out
Her path was lost, she began to feel doubt.

Creeping along — one step, now two
She looked through the rain then knew what to do.
She could walk through the woods no matter what would occur
The way to find shelter would always be with her.

Ronald J. Brick

Rainbow Memories

After the shower, the rainbow,
  arching across the sky.
The colors bringing memories
  of days that are long gone by.
Falling like teardrops, they bring
  scenes of blessings and happiness,
  recollections that make my heart sing.
Purple pain, blue hues, rosy glows
  and golden memories passing by.
Flashes of joy and sadness,
  bits of love and gladness.
A visit through memory as I gaze at the sky.

Cleta E. Colbert

Hiram Ulysses Grant

He had an
Irresistible urge for and
Reveled in the consumption of
Alcoholic beverages. He
May have been the only
Undeniably
Legitimate chance for the
Yankee's success.
Somehow he
Skillfully yet successfully
Emerged to defeat Confederate forces at
Shiloh, Five Forks, and Appomattox Courthouse.

Good thing for us that this
Relentlessly stubborn
American fought for the
North instead of
The South.

Jeff Kidd

The Weather

The weather, was lead by the feather.
To fallow the swallow that was not hallow.
He eats the seeds that came from the weeds.
When it's hot, he drinks water, from a shallow pot.
On the spot. When he rang the bell.
A feather feel in the air.
It was a feather in the weather.
From the swallow that was not hollow.
Who ate the seeds, from the weeds.
Drank water from the shallow pot.
When he gets hot, on the spot.

Sandra L. Duncan Quinn

The One Soul

I am always with you
In the one soul
Where there is no separation.

I walk with you.
I talk with you.
I dream my dreams with you.

And sometimes, my love, I even dance,
Sculpting space in a million myriad shapes
With my body.

You are always with me.
You breathe with me.
I feel the beating of your heart
As I feel the beating of my own.

Patricia Brainin

We Are The World

For hereby today
I shall announce by grace
This planet stick together
With drugs in our face
Killing America
All the way around
Dying by drugs
Shipped and found
Murdering youths
Guns on the streets
We must try to stop
At our generations defeat
What kind of better,
We are the word,
A better nation
This would be
If we all got along
Save this generation youths
From going bong
We are the world and the children rest in peace

Dana Nicole Bell

Search

Always looking . . . searching for something.
What?
It escapes me.
The ache, the yearning burns inside.
Something must quench the fire!
What?
What?
An age of questioning.
We are not what are parents were.
The world changes . . . faster,
Faster than the mind can comprehend!
Always looking,
It escapes me.
Were they happy?
Those before us
Adapt . . . or die.
The only constant is
Searching for something
To quench the fire.

Melissa A. Stewart

A Touch Of Mary Ann Hatfield

Mary Ann always had a plan —
To be a helping hand;
To send peace through the land.
She'll always be my fan!

Because she is of kin —
She'll always be a friend.
We'll heal and mend;
We'll carry time to the end!

We'll always use her approach —
We'll consider her a coach.
Do not let others poach,
Nor smoke a roach!

To tithe the kins —
To always favor our friends.
To heal and mend;
To love till the end!

Let others hear the plan —
Always be a helping hand;
To always bless the land.
Because our land, will always be Mary Ann's!

Ray Allan James

Keep On Keeping On

I never said that life would be easy for you.
I never said that life would be fair for you.
Cause it ain't easy to ride the mighty clouds of life
when you been knocked around, but when life knocks you down,
You gotta get up and ride again.
You gotta keep on keeping on, keep on keeping on.

My brothers, my sisters, lost in despair.
So many have trod this path before, and you are not alone,
for my God walks with you. So, when you're at you're lowest point,
late in the midnight hour, just look inside yourself for
strength, and remember who you are. For you are a proud people,
You are a mighty people. You are not a lost people.
You gotta keep on keeping on, keep on keeping on.

Don't let nobody steal your joy, for it belongs to you. They
can't take it away, unless you give it away. So hold on to it,
and wear it in your heart.
You gotta keep on keeping on, keep on keeping on.

Lillia H. Sessoms

City Streets Don't Lie

The brightness of the midmorning sun
Lights up rows of boarded-up buildings
But offers one little consolation
Along these lonely city streets
That lead to a dismal desolation.
There are people here they say who care
But many for the wrong reasons.
And absent are the kids playing;
For them there's always the fear
That death lurks somewhere near.

From out of nowhere there's commotion;
A speeding car, the screeching of tires,
Piercing screams, the clatter of gunfire
Proclaim it's still the killing season,
The peace broken by another drive-by.
The ensuing stillness, a bellowing cry
Of grief and disbelief, the pools of red
Leave no doubt. Another person is dead.
The sights and sounds of city streets don't lie;
Crimes run rampant and the murder rate so high.

Michael M. Doyen

Prayer Of A Blue-Collar Working Man

Lord, please have mercy on a working man,
Who's only trying to make a living as best as he can

Protect his family, his kids and his wife,
While big business destroys his standard of life

Ease his insomnia, his fears, his pain, and his tension
Since he's found out the union has spent his pension

Father, calm his heart concerning NAFTA and GATT
His job will go to Mexico, and that is that

Lord, his heart is filled with bitterness and rage
He knows that soon he'll be making a minimum wage

His hopes and dreams have been all but shattered
While the corporate giants scoff as if it mattered

Now the strike is on, how will he eat?
Lord, who'll feed his family, or put shoes on their feet?

Lord, you know his heart, his motives tell no lies
as more of his world crumbles, a little more of him dies

Lord, give him courage as only you can,
Sweet Jesus, have mercy on the blue-collar man.

Michael Gammill

Ragtime

The songs played on piano tiptoed around the room
Were cups on a table casting shadows
Late evening breeze through open windows blowing
Crickets after dark mustering the night
Car tires rolling on gravel
The dust rising up behind them
a haze between then and now
Reading the old thermometer
That used to be out on the porch
And cheerful voices in ones and twos
Quiet gentle laughter off in some shaded nook
And conversation not discernible
But music to the ear
Just as those old rags dress out the piano
in shades of melancholy recall
Never far

Mark W. Bailey

The Dancer

She stretches each muscle precisely
Like the machinery in a Swiss watch
Each string of flesh rolls up or down, finding
Its place in the bouquet of her physique;
Her face deep, motionless and self-sufficient,
The calm surface of a lake at noon.
Regally ignoring her audience, she does what she has to do,
Celebrates her self,
Her shape a dance in itself wraps arms like wings,
Spiraling towards heaven
When she reaches for the ceiling,
Her fingers late March buds
Waiting to unfold.
She is not rooted, defies gravity's laws,
Curling, bending, prolonging
A body built to excel.
Her performance is praise to art in its purest form:
A woman at ease, in love with herself.

Miki Tallman

I Am Happy

I am happy, I am I say; just because I was born today.
I am happy, I am I swear; lost my first tooth in a pear.
I am happy, I am I say; for this was my first school day.
I am happy, I am I insist; I just had my very first kiss.
I am happy, I am I state; turned sixteen and had my first date.
I am happy, I am I relate; all grown up I did graduate.
I am happy, I am I allege; just now completed college.
I am happy, I am I propound; that special someone I just found.
I am happy, I am I carry; at the chapel I will marry.
I am happy, I am I admit; for now I have a new born to baby sit.
I am happy, I am I say; giving my youngest daughter away.
I am happy, I am I say; I'm still alive, here for another day.
I am happy, and will be for a while; for I have all these things to
keep my smile.

Chad J. Allan

His-Panic/Her-Panic

padded walls provide no comfort against my bleeding head,
i look up at you but only bruise my eyes,
you embrace me with tangled arms but scar my back,
to walk upon your river of fire — i writhe between memories,
pounding on your shield of passion only blisters my fingers,
speak to the serpent that i can feel, smell, and taste, but can not
see — he shall tell of the time i looked under "lover" in the
dictionary, yet despite your tempting scorn, could not find you . . .

Maria Ines Ocampo-Diaz

Of Earthly Desire

I am flesh, gone is my spirit.
You are my salvation
I am your soul.
Take this flesh that lusts for you,
make love to me that I may taste the sweets of thy fruit.
Am I the very bounty for which you ride?
Mount me.
Eat me.
Consume my everlasting passion, for as I am, I am void
and when you eat all of me
I shall be whole again.
Lick me dry, devour me with thy fire;
Leave that of which
when blown by the blue breeze of autumn's day
becomes more of what shall never be.
Cradle me in thy strength,
I am yours
Behold!

Tara Janosh

Protoceratops

A big fat pudgy dinosaur
Roaming down a lane —
Running, romping, stomping
This creature is insane.
Born in an egg so hard to crack
The dinosaur almost broke his back.
Falling down on his behind
Needing aspirin for to find.
With a beak-like mouth
Whose name means first horned face
He is always moving
In a dizzy pace.
Living in a fossilized cave
His face is hairy from forgetting to shave.
Other dinosaurs try to steal his eggs.
When they come out they have no legs.
This dinosaur wears some stinky socks.
He sure is a fool but he really rocks!!!!!!!!

Christopher Ghattas

Planet A-Z For All

From Afghanistan to Zimbabwe, a Family Planet
That straddles Humanity in a terrestrial ball
With single umbilical cord, webs races of one Creation
Language and habits may local be; Trade excites exchange
Travel transports diversity around imaginary boundaries
Distance, only physical, as everlasting water'n air wing on

Folly draws line; no hold to crossing Air and rushing Water
For breath to creature that must respire
From earth comes hum(an) us; to earth-the way we were
Life overs man-knowledge; no manufacture, no design
Over mere temporary dominion, that doodles futility
As Mother Nature goes about business, nevertheless
Materiality perishes, never to cross borders to eternity

Love is shinning amour, more precious than ornament
Whose sister-in-nature is Peace
With them continuity protects
If eyes could see . . . through the maze and fog which dense to hinder
Wonderment . . . of great Light from beyond that pans on the beauty
Of all things, with Splendor and Power in majestic creation-state
Form His Alpha and Omega into Planet A-Z for all.
Ukagwu.

Uju N. Afulezi

Passage

I looked across the mountains and into my soul
    and found a yearning to be free.
I looked at the snow-capped peaks
    and found a need for purity and truth.
I looked at the ever-green slopes in the distance
    and remembered the vigor of youth.
And I cried inside my being for the beauty
    of that which I had long ago squandered.

Suddenly I wanted to run after those who still
    possessed all that I had lost.
My throat ached to cry out to them
    to warn — advise — exhort — plead.

But no. Their ears would be as deaf as mine had been
    because — for a time — they are still immortal.

Dorothy Anthony

The Joy Of Pianist

Out of the great and small silences
Into the wonderful singing kaleidoscope of sound
From the loving caress of the keys
Across the rippling waves of music
Between the dancing, drifting notes
Among the lovely mellow tones
During the simply beautiful melodies
Through the rich and complex harmonies
Along the smooth and flowing lines
Inside the comfortable warmth and depth of feeling
Past the tremendous colors of expression
Around the intensely delicate shadings of mood
Onto the careful shaping and finishing
Toward the final exhilarating echoes
Through the joy of performance
Into the enchanting world of musical magic
Beyond

Kathryn Johnson

The Wind And The Wolf

The wind and the wolf
together always like lovers.
Singing their lonely song
under the dark cloak of night.
Hearing nothing but one another
content in each others company.

The wind gives the wolf
the smell of his next meal
while the wolf gives the wind
someone to sing and dance
with in the night.

Each complementing the other
in the loneliness of night
they are always together but never alone.

Joyce Logan

Untitled

A blooming rose, a bed of sand,
a grandfather clock without any hands.
A second to spare, a minute to lose,
only a drunk now drinks the booze.
A case of coke, no not the drink,
a dead person lying over the mirror by the sink.
A nose of steel, a package of white,
another death on this lonely night.
Is this the way we imagined it?
A world where nothing ever can fit?
Is this how it all shall be?
Do we forever close our eyes to a truth we don't care to see?

Rebecca Reisch

133

A Departed Love

Sandy sidewalks stretch on forever,
trimmed towering trees stand over my head.
The fall of the sun brings yet another night
as my dreams of fear come into sight.
Shattering of glass onto the floor
bringing new meaning to sound, he is with us no more.

The laughing of children, they do not know
that this death has entered my soul.
Fluffy gray cat glares at me bringing new hope,
that was meant to be.
He looks at me as if he knows promises
I have yet to hold.

My future looked bleak, but now I know that
I will live to be 100 years old.
I am not alone as they may hold, tomorrow is
another day about to unfold.

Lauren Queen

Untitled

Life has been nothing short of blessed since you entered mine.
A day with you is a lifetime of pure joy.
A second without you seems like a lifetime alone.
But when we're together it's as if time can't touch us.
We need not wish of forever.
Our hearts were combined long before we even know.
Thanks to you I've never been this happy.
Many a time we shared one another.
Memories beyond numbers we carry.
Throughout infinity we will always be.
Because we've made a bond that no one could ever break
You and only you will my heart belong.
As no one could ever take your place in my heart or my life.
Through a lot we have been.
But because out love is so strong it will never fade.
With each other our lives we will spend.
As the love of my life.
I love you
And always will.

Amanda Schwegel

Flowering

The fruitless fruit trees are flowering
and people plant pansies and petunias
While wisteria winds around and up to hang
and droop and tulips stand as straight as sticks

Some women simply have power over men
while others cosmetically incline their lines
Some men make money to flaunt their pastimes
while others live only pre-learned disciplines

Cultivated gardens
carefully cut, teased and combed
Vie with hordes of windblown and bird-dropped seed
to feed the sun and quench the rain

Which falls on sun-bleached bones and dry sand
where gray jays and nutcrackers shout,
Which falls on bogs and muddy meadows
where mushrooms and field-mice cower

Each being awaits its moment of display
to laugh and cry its cuteness and fire
To be seen, desired
and with relish and relief devoured

Keith Kilburn

Our Choir

Oh what a beautiful, wonderful day
One in which our dear Lord enables us again to kneel and pray.

Of our choir we are very proud.
Every day, whether it's sunny or a day with a cloud.

Tho some of us are in our golden years
Our choir has taught us to face anything without any fears.

We thank God for our wonderful directress, who has brought us so very far,
To us she is the same as a tank full of gas is too a car.

Our directress possess a vast amount of dedication and love
Virtues that were bestowed upon her from our Heavenly Father above.

Through the years God has called some of our fellow choir
Members to His Heavenly home above
Tho they're gone from us, for them we will always, in
our hearts have a super abundance of prayers and love.

We don't sing or perform for recognition or fame.
Everything we do, we do it in our Heavenly Father's name.

Anna P. Swanier

The Golden Gate

Behold the earth where man does dwell.
 Beware, for even his soul he does sell!

Here on his world the gift of life is cheap.
 He knows nothing of love; nothing of the spirit deep!

Son battles against father, and father against son.
 Neither ever realizing what has already been done!

Even the earth cries out to them, yet they do not hear.
 For they are too blind with avarice to even fear!

They lie, they cheat, they steal and even kill.
 They have already broken the most sacred seal!

He has turned his world into a pool of vice.
 Along the way, he has never thought twice!

He thinks his world will last forever.
 If only he knew what he is about to endeavor!

Consumed with hatred and self-pride,
 None will mourn him when he has died!

Let us abandon this world where there is no care.
 This place among the stars filled with despair!

Alas, is man's world consumed in hate.
 None of its beings shall ever pass through the Golden Gate!

Robert Loring

Different

The one and only orange banana,
The lacy, feminine bandanna.
The only stoplight with lavender spots,
The only cook with hot pink pots.
The only dog that dares to meow,
The one and only three horned cow
The princess who's quite fond of the dragon,
The pioneer with a gasoline powered wagon.
The sheep who took karate classes,
The fashion model with horn rimmed glasses.
The old gray mare that ain't what she's sposed to be,
A little off the wall, that's me.
Once I heard a story from a wise old owl,
About a hungry wolf upon the prowl.
The wolf attacked some sheep one day,
And only the one that didn't run with the flock got away.

Samantha Davila

Untitled

No matter how I treat, you're always there for me.
And forever in my heart, I know you'll always be.
You've been there though the good and bad, each and every day.
But I know one day you'll leave me and we'll go our separate ways.

You see, you'll be gone to heaven and I'll be here alone.
Wondering why life's so unfair and wishing you'd come home.
Reminiscing on the good ole days and how you made me smile,
Remembering how we played around to spend quality time for awhile.

I'm grateful that you're in my life and so close to my heart.
But I'm well aware that when you go, my world will fall apart.
Since I can't imagine being here without you by my side,
I'll have to guess that I will feel like a part of me has died.

But while you're still here with me, I'll treasure what we've got
And no matter how you look at it, that's an awful lot.
I love you more every day, tomorrow more than now.
And I hear you say love me too, with every little meow.

Dawn McIntosh

Purgatory

So here I sit pondering life
Just to meet my friends, unhappiness and strife

Most think my body an empty shell
Contained inside my private hell

Condemned to spend the rest of my years
Drowning in invisible tears

Learned people poke and prod and feed me full of pills.
Unfortunately they cannot help my ills

I don't want to go on but am told I must
Though years ago my broken heart began to rust

With intellect and mind in check I could climb that corporate ladder
Firmly seated on the ground I look up, just to find it doesn't matter

Because my will to go upward has soured
People see me as a coward

I know I will find happiness before my death
Although I fear it won't be until my final breath.

Christopher D. Beverly

The Book Of Souls

Why do I turn these pages?
There is nothing written here.
The book is empty.

Am I searching for my dream?
The world I've searched for hope
The world is empty.

Destiny evades the lowest soul.
Where do they go when their time is done?
Between the pages of dust-covered books.

I turn then, lost souls,
Who wait for their lives to be written.
I have no pen — will they forgive me?

Night cold threatens to close the book.

Upon these pages, upon these lost souls
There should be words written.
But it is better to have empty pages,
Than empty words . . .

Linda DeRoch

Rain

I think if it made my house an ark,
I would still love the sound of the rain.
The world comes alive when it taps on the roof,
Or beats on the window pane.

And I love it when wind comes along for the fun,
To slam it against the door.
My spirits rise and I laugh and sing.
I'm thrilled to the very core.

Since each has its task, the wind and the rain,
They may as well do it with flair.
The rain has to wash the face of the world,
And the wind has to comb its hair.

So I leave my body of flesh and bones,
And soar with the wind and the rain.
I cleanse my soul in the soft sweet drops,
While the wind combs the webs from my brain.

Sue Cole

I Am

I am . . .

  on a hill top gazing at the stars,
  and the darkness that leaves scars,
  scars so deep, stars so bright,
  night so dark . . .
  dark like me.

Thoughts . . .

  roam to and fro through my mind,
  right and left and far behind,
  behind me, minds that see, far from me,
  to be . . . so black like me.

I've noticed . . .

  the difference between the two,
  the stars and the night's blackish blue,
  bluish-black, two stars hidden back,
  night so sweet, too sweet to be . . . black like me.

I've realize . . .

  somehow the two are always together
  so, we down below can see the unity.
  the unity of bright and dark . . . which is dark like me.

Naomie St. Louis

Rebeca

It was a cold winter morning when I gave birth to Rebeca.
The snow storm had made it nearly impossible for Dr. Kahn
to arrive on time.

It was painful.
The contractions.
The pushing.
The exaltation.

Seven hours of labor. The family awaited.
Richard was so impatient.
He fainted as he watched her little head come out.

Mama Joan assisted Dr. Kahn. She knew all about labor pains.
She brought me into life. She brought my brother Joey.

I felt the pain. I pushed with all my might.

Finally, Rebeca came out.
Dr. Kahn slapped her buttocks. But my child did not cry.
My Rebeca had died.

Naite Mascaro

You

You were with me in the time that was. I loved you.
With a passion beyond time, I could not forget you.
The years we had together, happiness building on sorrow
our love reached a crescendo. Then, it was over.

God called us Home to a place where beauty reigns
where light, love and joy replace earthly pains.
There, we learned another love, for everything and everyone,
everlasting and unconditional. In heaven, all are one.

Yet, in that place of beauty, I needed more
. . . Of less, to make my Spirit soar.
In a heaven, where happiness has no limit,
I yearned to leave, to imprison my Spirit.

Within flesh and blood, I would endure.
In a world of trials and pain, I would remember . . .
You! Your Spirit, the one that I love
was destined to follow me from above.

So that here among the squaller of this incarnation,
our Angels can guide us through time and nation,
past heartache and suffering that weighs so much
to the day we rise above Them . . . And touch.

Alfred R. Hughes Jr.

"Sad Reality"

In the darkness of my soul, you emerge without dimensions,
your presence is atypical and to my dismay predictable,
and when I perceive the cruelty of your sad reality, yet intangible,
painfully, I surrender crying and swathe under your unjust wings.

But I don't want you. Not your misery in my existential ambit; and
far less, your unasked ignominy that lavishly is extended to me, to
carve my own entrails with torture, reducing disparagingly my matter
into particles before the world's eyes, leaving me nothing but a
perpetual wish to abort you and return your hate.

To avoid your oppression, and in vain, I seek console in the glorious
things of my life. But, behind the glow, the blessing and sweetness
of my descendants, behind the purity of their tender beings and warm
spirits, behind the man's love that fulfill my days with care and
respect very precise,

behind fresh memories of tropical mountains, they my eyes have not
seen in a decade, behind its green of jungle, crystal curtains of
water that fall in countless cascades, and even behind the legends,
art, folklore and magic of its wise indian natives, sadistically, you
emerge to anguish me with your grotesque liveliness day after day.

Just because, I carry the social guilt of having my roots in a
faraway land and an unique epidermic tinge. Don't prejudice me
anymore! You are morally incorrect! The language I try to speak,
it's not different than yours! It's all about love and respect! The
universal language, that dreams to master the complex and
insensible mankind.

Maria G. Austin

My Secret Fire

You have sparked a flame deep in my heart,
I hope it will pull us together and not apart.
This flame burns for you day after day,
I wish I could tell you, but what would I say?
My heart is full of love and fear,
As I sit here and cry my last tear.
I must be brave and wipe my face clean,
I must be straight forward and never mean.
You must know you have filled me with lust and desire,
You must know that you are my secret fire.

Candy Alaniz

I Know How It Feels

I Know how it Feels to be — Abused
I Know how it Feels to be — Confused
I Know how it Feels to be — Defamed
I Know how it Feels to be — Devastated
I Know how it Feels to be — Disappointed
I Know how it Feels to be — Disrespected
I Know how it Feels to be — In Distress
I Know how it Feels to be — In Disrepute
I Know how it Feels to be — Dissolute

I know how it feels to be — Ab-so-lute
I know how it feels to be — Ac-claimed
I know how it feels to be — Ac-ceptable
I know how it feels to be — Ac-countable
I know how it feels to be — Ac-knowledgeable
I know how it feels to — Administrate
I know how it feels to — Affiliate
I know how it feels to — Affirmate
I know how it feels to — Be-trothed
I know how it feels to — De-vorced.

Norma A. S. Robinson

Grandmother's Wisdom

Oh! How I remember the times long ago,
When my granny sang to me the songs I
     loved so.
Her little hands were wrinkled from the
     times she spent,
Washing and cleaning the things we took
     for granted.
She had a way of telling us the things we
     need to know,
And if she ever got mad, she wouldn't let
     it show.
She isn't with us anymore she's with the
     angels you see,
If I had one wish today that one wish
     would be.
That I would have the Wisdom that my granny
     showed to me.
I didn't understand it then, but now it is
     so clear,
When I think of lovely things I feel her very near.

Joan Hilton

Beyond The Sun

The lovely lady drifted out of the mist,
Along the seashore; she was smooth and sun-kissed.
When he spoke to her, he was charmed by her class.
She spoke softly with a delightful tinge of sass.

He was intrigued with her honey locks,
Her shapely feet, no shoes nor socks.
Her frothy white dress, wet at the hem,
As spindrift swirled and she lifted her chin.

She savored salty breezes and golden sunshine,
And he knew he was smitten; she was sublime.
His happiness soon shadowed with fear.
He couldn't touch her though she was near.

Then her laughter rang, sweet and low,
And she ran through sugar sand, white as snow.
He chased after her; he had to know her name.
All he got was a teasing smile, and a funny game.

At last she stopped and gave him a wistful smile.
Sadly he watched as she drifted skyward awhile,
Then faded into the mist from where she'd come.
She had to return; she was an angel from beyond the sun.

Barbara F. Lamb

By The Ocean

By the ocean,
The sea gulls sit on rocks,
The tide is going out.
The shells washed up on shore,
Lay untouched by the harbor.

The fishes are near the surface playing,
Playing till the fishermen come.

The dolphins and whales are exquisite,
Their skin glistening in the early sunlight.
The sea otters are swimming their morning swim,
Getting ready to rest their day off.

The waves are rolling in with the wind,
The ships are sailing over the smooth, clear surface of the ocean,
The breeze is carrying a light, sweet smell of saltwater,
Promising a day full of fun.

The wonderful sounds of the ocean are singing to you,
Welcoming you with a promise never to be broken,
A promise of a wonderful day,
Down by the ocean.

Elma Sun

"Feelings"

This rage that seems to be growing
inside of me,
Visions of you are all I see.
Will this pain ever part,
Will I ever be able to rebuild this
broken heart.
Is it something I've said or done,
The love and warmth we could of shared
was hotter than any sun.
Things always seem to be the opposite
of how they really are,
I guess I didn't realize the distance
between us was so far.
The tears that stain my bedroom pillow,
Remind me so much of the trunk
Of a weeping willow.
The sun will rise and the sun will set,
The special feelings for you I will
never forget.

Michelle M. White

"Briana" Or "A Magical Place"

Sitting and singing
in the sand for a while
gathering rocks into a pile
pondering, wandering
shuffling in leaves
quietly delighted by all that she sees
grasping flowers
by petals or stems
unknowingly crushing while carrying them
toddling, tumbling
twirling around
excitedly giggling as she falls to the ground
Splashing in puddles
with hands and with feet
chasing small critters
always just out of reach
Swinging in sunshine
a smile on her face
She's in her own world
what a magical place.

Wendy L. Garrity

I Was Born

I was born bond nor free,
Black nor white, good nor bad,
Right nor wrong. For I am of God's
earth, and who is to say whether it
be bound to any man or free to the winds
or whether it be bright as the flower gardens
or solemn as the graves of evils or whether
it is good soil for the harvest or soil
where only death may reap. Whether it
should prosper or stand motionless.
No, I know not why that I am or
what I must do. Yet, by God's wisdom
I will succeed for I "WAS" born.

Janet L. Bell

Who Is The Man In The Mirror?

Where does life sneak off in its silent tread?
Where has a year and then a decade fled?
When do the minutes find the time to flee?
Who's standing and reflecting, who is that that I see?

Wasn't it just yesterday or was it the day before?
I climbed the steps of life and opened up its door.
I sipped its nectars sweet and heard its melodious notes.
I dreamt its wondrous dreams and crossed its hidden moats.

Through it all I never dreamt would come a certain day.
In my mind and in my soul I hid it fast away.
Now as I stand and reflect alone, I swear it can not be.
But staring back with God as my judge the old man in the mirror is me.

M. M. Stiff

"Angel's Blush"

As day breaks and the sun starts its rise,
there's an "Angel's blush" on the eastern skies.
The cotton ball clouds turn to blaze orange and bright red.
Creating a welcome from the angels to the dying and the dead.

It's a sight so beautiful and tranquil you hold your breath.
A glimpse of what awaits beyond this life of the flesh.
From a God all knowing, so gentle, so kind.
Who takes us all home only he knows our time.

For some it seems too early for others too late.
But God knows our time, in his hands is our fate.
So if life weighs you down and you feel caught in the rush,
get some rest, get up early, and go. Breathe in the "Angel's Blush."

Mark R. Hansen

Untitled

I don't have floral manias,
but I seem to like Gazanias,
and what one may suppose is,
that I'm really fond of roses:
Troubles come with many plants,
mildew, snails, aphids, ants,
plus, what no one ever needs,
a raging plethora of weeds.

Here's a garden poem, and,
I hope that you will understand:
When I received your mail today,
I was set to cast the thing away . . .
Not your letter, it was fine,
but the poem that was mine.
And now it may be destiny,
my printed poem I may see.

Richard S. Melville

Feelings

That single tear dropped from my eye
probably the saddest tear I've ever cried.
Warm and moist before touching my flesh
When touching my skin it becomes bitter and no longer fresh.
The millions of thoughts that helped make that tear
are the thoughts that I mostly fear.
Others see just water running down my skin
to me it's where the pain begins.
Is there any cure for this horrible disease
much worse then just a cough or a sneeze.
It seems like a lifetime of pain.
I wonder if I can ever stay sane

Amanda McCart

Untitled

Dark is beautiful
and I've found no one as beautiful as you,
and this is why I write this poem to you.
From the pitter patter of my heart, to the
sounds of this pen gliding across this paper from you all I
ask is one small favor.
For you to remain kind, nice, tender, and true, and forever
will I write sweet poems to you.
Dark is beautiful
For you're remaining to be the same, let it be faith and
understanding of the reason for which I've come.
Hidden away from light in a small gloomy place, your beauty
is radiant through the darkness beams upon my face.
Comparable to none for you are quite unique, I've come to
the end, for this poem has reached it's peak.
No matter where you go think or say
Dark is beautiful
and I love you in a special way.

Troy Wayne Murphy

The Father Down The Road I Go

As I've traveled down the road — I have seen and done some things
I've learned about hard luck — and the suffering it brings
I have heard a lot of stories — some are true and some are lies
I've seen people having fun — more with misery in their eyes.

The farther down the road I go — and the more of life I see
I wonder who it is in charge — who controls our destiny.

I see those who travel light — with a black cloud overhead
Always reaching for the sun — but they get the rain instead
Some people have a good life — some more than their share
And long ago I learned the truth — that life just is not fair.

So the farther down the road I go — and the more of life I see
I don't know who it is in charge — I just know it is not me.

Willie O. Moore

Nature's Beauty

Quiet you sneak, to take a peak.
At a beautiful deer, that's out in a clear.
Pulling your bow, so you will have a beauty to show.
Trying your best, to hit him square in the chest.
Nervous you are, he's not that far.
Holding on tight, hoping he won't fight.
Letting go of the string, watching the colorful arrow fling.
Watching the arrow enter his chest,
You hope this is the place he will rest.
Everything stops, and nature's beauty drops.
People say it is bad, but it really is sad.
To see the deer die, you want, but can't cry.
Rest in Peace my beauty.
Everyone knows this is not fun, but it is our duty.

Delaina Bonwell

The Little Ditty

I came without invitation, little ugly and loud
They wagged their tongues, and shook their heads
No pillow for my head
I went to the county, much as a stray cur
Loved by none!
But wanted by one
He got in this buggy, train and jitney
Just to see little, ugly and loud little ditty
He bought little clothes so fine, red cap, red shoes and socks
They, ditty's mother and he placed in a box
They came to the home to get ditty
He'd soon be leaving the great big city
The clothes from the home quickly shed
Now he was bernard, dressed in red
By jitney, by train, by buggy he came
The little red suit and his own little name
Ashleigh turned out to see
This little lad
You could tell by their faces they were very glad
No longer will little ditty be sad

Geo Bernard Creech

Baby

Velutinous skin,
eyes of the sun,
smells of springtime,
giggles like the sounds of bells,
facial expressions like the sky,
as curious as pandora, and
nails as small as raindrops.

Unable to communicate
unable to support themselves,
little control over their muscles,
little knowledge,
drools like a water faucet, and
completely helpless.

Carefree, untainted,
not corrupted yet by the crime of society,
tender and loving,
harmless and cuddly.

Brought into existence,
inexperienced in the ways of the world.
Innocence!

Katherine Noel

I Thank You

If only I could tell you how I feel,
How you made me see you were someone who cared,
You showed me I could trust you,
When you sheltered me with the hugs you had shared.

You made me believe,
That someone on this land wanted me to smile,
You showed me the path,
When you came for a short while.

Every waken moment,
That I had sorrow in my eyes,
You gave me a sign,
And made my spirits rise.

You were the first person,
Who showed me I am who I must be,
And therefore with your memories in my heart,
I am the person everyone will see.

And so I thank you,
With all of my heart,
It is you I shall LOVE,
Even though we will forever be apart.

Julie Lawson

Awakened To The Love

All I remember was the fear,
the hopelessness, the quietness of strength.
I forgot the reason why.
The reason for the pain.
All I remember was the guilt,
the sorrow of your disappointment.
Years have passed.
Everyday I prayed for your love, your understanding.
I never saw it, I never felt it.

Yesterday,
my eyes opened for the very first time.
All around me was love, the solution.
The pressure was released,
the penance was given,
the forgiveness was received.

You helped me these years
and I was consumed, never saw the quest.
You gave me what I needed — to be me —
and yesterday,
my eyes opened for the very first time.

Beverlee A. Kaster

Dear Lord In Heaven

Can you hear me when I pray?
Am I forgiven for things I say?
Lord I've done many wrong things,
forgive me please and let my heart sing.
Why do we lose sight of what's right?
Does this happen just over night?
Guide me my Lord, take my hand,
I need your help to even stand.
Do I come to you only when things go wrong
or do I come to you all the year long.
Lord, I can't forget you-never could it happen
you light up my days and stop all that saddened
I must stand before you sometime someday
will I hold my head up, yes Lord I pray
I only want to please you and hear your voice say
you walked with me thru life
You live with me today
If I deserve this great reward
I'll need all of your help my dear Lord.

Nita K. Malone

Summertime

Summertime — is here again in all the
　Beauty nice warm fresh air — and
With beautiful flowers are blooming all over
　And the vegetable gardens are great
The bird's are happy singing their sweet songs all over — and all
The animals are doing fine in the nice
　Sunny warm weather — as
The green grass is growing and doing fine
　Waving in the wind — and
The crops in the fields are growing great
　After all the great moisture
So the people are enjoying the great
　Summer weather — in vacationing
Camping — fishing — picnics — ball games
　Radios and walking in the fresh air
Also visiting friends's and family weather
　Out in the nice sunny warm weather
As summer time — is the time to enjoy
　Nice fresh warm sunny weather
After the long cold winter weather is over again — it's summertime.

Irene Mary Jarson

A Part

The wars that frighten children,
drugs that kill us all.
The sound of guns when they are fired,
and all the victims that fall.
The laughter that hurts when someone stares,
The finger that points when no one cares.
This world is dying,
the children are crying.
We need someone to love us,
Someone to get rid of all the hate.
As we all live and lie,
We need someone to catch us when we start to fall.
So when someone offers to love you,
reach out and take their hands and together
We can make a brand new start,
In this world that has suddenly fallen apart!

Emmie Twigg

Untitled

As the waves crash onto the sandy beach of time
And the wind whispers through the palms of change
Like a feather across my deepest emotions
　I thank the spirit
　That has brought this to me.

As I climb the House of the Sun
To the temple of my mind
My arms outstretched to the sky
　I remember what joy has
　Brought me.
Even when the Great Star disappears from the horizon
　I will always be.

Paul Vivian

Month By Month

January — beginning of a new year
February — "Be my valentine" are the words I hear
March — An Irishman's knocking at my door
April — The easter bunny brings me candy galore
May — A beautiful basket I received from I wonder who
June — I made a lovely bride on the day I said "I do"
July — Let freedom ring for the rest of my days
August — I hurry to catch a few summer rays
September — Labor day — I work so hard to
　bring home the dough
October — Little trick or treaters to my house come and go
November — How very thankful I am
December — Jesus was born in Bethlehem

Janice Schultz

Sondra

Maybe it was your eyes, friendly and alert.
Maybe it was your lips, tender, never giving hurt.
Maybe it was your hair, dark, soft, flowing.
Maybe it was your smile, lively, glowing.
Maybe it was your mind, inquisitive, creative, knowing.
Maybe it was your heart, loving, compassionate, growing.
Maybe it was your walk, your talk, your actions untold.
Maybe it was fate, luck or unseen designs that unfold.
It is one, it is all, it is more — that are the sum of my life.
It is you, my friend, my love, my wife.
It is all these things and more, true, through and through.
Whatever it is, I thank God I love you.

Okey Nestor

The Greatest Thrill Of All . . .

Little League was my dream when I was small.
    I used to sit and imagine — smacking the ball
        . . . over the heads of the basemen
            . . . past center field.
    And listening to the roar of the crowd as the ball reeled
        clearing the fence and into the stands.
        The bases were loaded! Just listen to those fans!
            I was a hero! Wasn't it grand?

And then I grew older and fulfilled my dreams.
I played first base, struck out batters amongst the screams
    of fans attending every game.
I wallowed in glory, pride and NO SHAME!

But the greatest thrill of all I can say
    Wasn't the home runs — the outs —
        or the fantastic plays.

It was knowing that sitting in those bleachers each day
    Sat my Daddy . . .
        Proud of me in every way!

Rita Peters

Hasta Velveeta, Big Guy

Gouda by my love, and farewell to thee
My paramoursean that could never brie
I swiss you much luck as you romano 'round
From cottage to port, new loves to be found

Go have Lynn Berger and Cammie Bert, too
Crackers standing by for a chance with you
They're not good enough, the blood must be bleu
It's all in a name, new money won't do

Keep searching, I'm sure true love you'll find
At the grand Cheese Ball—meet one of your kind
You'll choose her so fast, her mold you won't see
This woman with a shredded history

By day she'll play your little game for fun
Melting your heart, telling you you're the one
But into the night, she'll find cheddar men
And fondue them all, again and again

A master at it, she, too, has your knack
Just ask in Philly and in Mont'rey Jack
So you've made this choice—go live life your way
You're cheesy, my love; not choosy, dare say

Sabrina Valentini

The Cliffs Of Moher

How majestic your walls as they
Fade away in the mystical mist.
Jagged rocks and lapping waves
Celebrate their union with white foam and a
Melodic crash that stirs
My emotions with a calming charm.

No one of this earth could have bore thee, but
Only be humbled before thee,
For your wondrous sight arose a calm like the
Night and silently engulfed me.
All my fears, joys, and pains were washed away
As the waves rolled out to sea,
For my heart could only hold the beauty
And awe that lie outstretched before me.

Monique A. Cureau

"A Friend Called Jesus"

I love a friend called Jesus
He's more than life to me
I met this friend called Jesus
As I sat on Mothers Knee, He has
always loved me, He died to save
my soul, I know that He still loves
me, as I am growing old. I invite
you to love Him the way that I do
you will not feel sorry, He has good
news for you. He is building mansions
for His holy kin and we will soon
be leaving for a world that has no end.
There will be no night there for good is the light.
I'll be praying for your lucky day and night
Oh! Don't live without Jesus,
you will surely die if you live with out Jesus,
you'll miss your home up in the skies.

Kathleen Buchanan

Ending Of The Storm

Majestic in its stance and stories to be told
This barn is more than lumber, this barn is more than old;

The Earth beneath is solid, for miles does it span
Within it grows a future, upon it stands a man;

His heart is filled with glory, but glory endures pain
He's built four walls without a roof to shelter him from rain;

The worst is almost over, the clouds are passing by
Now put the storm behind you, let sunshine fill your sky;

You're merely seeing black and white, you're only feeling blue
Your rainbow is inside you trying to break through;

For every lot of lightning, the trees draw back in fear
Although they seem untouchable, they're not what they appear;

Fright is not our secret, it's weakness that we hide
Weary and defenseless, it tears us up inside;

Now look across the acres, now focus on the view...
This land is full of wonders, this land's a part of you!

Amy Landcastle

Night Birds

At night the road stretches on in endless silence. The land seems
dark and still. Yet, if the eye is skillful one can capture glimmers
of life everywhere. The nightbirds flee from the warmth of the road.
At a glance, there is a fear that I might damage a fragile wing, and
these gentle creatures would with broken wing fall back to earth,
    with loss of grace.

What sadness this would bring to my heart.
For each one is counted as a priceless work of art to my soul.

The nightbirds flee from the warmth of the road. The road stretches
on in endless silence, and my mind ponders The simple beauty
around me. My being longs to rest in this peaceful silence.

The nightbirds flee from the warmth of the road. With gentle grace
and fragile wing, tangible for only a fleeting moment. Then, they are
gone as if only to have never really existed. My mind holds their
image in a place saved for priceless things that upon recall, give me
peaceful pleasure.
The nightbirds flee from the warmth of the road. With gentle grace
and fragile wing, they soar into the dark sky With their own song to
sing. They seem as we, fragile, tangible, but intangible. Here for
a fleeting moment, then gone in a flight of endless freedom.

Linda Tickle-Golden

Spring

March is ending April is near, I'll
be glad for the buds to appear.
Yellows, reds, blues, and greens,
all come out at the beginning of Spring.

The sun is warm on your face so sweet,
making you feel wonderful, joyful and complete.
Winter is over, snow has passed, there will be
fishing, swimming, and laughter at last.

Birds will start to build their nest,
singing as they fly about their task.
Babies will squawk for big fat worms,
with mouths open wide waiting their turn.
Oh! Beautiful spring.
Mary L. Cable

Was Her . . .

She knew what she wanted, she seemed open and happy
She is beautiful and intelligent, she has her faults
She wanted love and compassion, with keeping her laughs and freedom
She needed a friend and a lover, to caress with a shoulder to cry on
She longed to be swept off her feet, by a real man, someone with class
Someone with money, and someone with charm, someone protective to
    keep her from harm
Someone with a sense of humor, to keep her laughing, even through
    the hard times
Someone who is romantic and kind, someone steady with a creative mind
She still wants to party and have her fun, although she love to
    settle down, but no with just anyone
She needs someone unselfish, respectful, and mature, someone
    healthy with good posture
He must have respect for the way she lives, he must be willing to
    take the love she gives
He must be devoted to what she was wished
He must be willing to keep the relationship at a moderate pace
She knew what she wanted
She just couldn't see it staring her right in the face
She knew what she wanted
. . . But all he wanted
    . . . Was her . . .
Steven T. Smith

Invisible Shadows

A swing in the breeze . . . platform in space.
A branch overhead . . . daydreams in place.
Green vaulted ceilings . . . limbs in array.
A place for thinking . . . with rhythm's sway.
That house of my youth . . . dropped from decay.
The tree has fallen . . . but memories stay.
Unseen shadows . . . shading my days.
Lee E. Welch

Recollections Of Fall

If autumn leaves of gold should fall
Through azure skies that I recall,
And blanket all of lovely spring,
They could not hide a single thing
Of you that I recall.

I recall moonbeams dancing in your hair,
And your perfume lingers in the air
I recall the moment that your lips met mine,
And the love light in your eyes divine.

Dreams of you spinning in starlight
Soft breeze filling the autumn night,
Oh, I recall, yes, I recall you still,
And I always will.
John Hill

"I'll Think Of You"

*To My Beloved Brother David Lynn Wilson, Cushing OK,
Gone But Not Forgotten*
    I remember when we both were young —
we always had so much fun;
    Hand to hand, just you and I —
there wasn't a dare we did not try;
    Even though we weren't always together —
I hope we can stay Best Friends forever;
    The day I had started to wonder —
was the day they put you six feet under;
    But even though life has its Tolls —
it can't take away, what's in our Souls;

    I'll think of you —
    When the sun comes up;
    I'll think of you —
    When the sun goes down;
    I'll think of you —
    both day and night;
    Where ever I go —
    or whatever I do —
    "I'll Think Of You"
Michele R. Wilson

"Summer Evening"

The Sun hangs briefly like a red ball of flame,
Then plummets quickly beyond the Western horizon.
The darkness of early evening surrounds me,
Then the stars brighten and the moon rises, playing
    hide and seek among the clouds.

The trees sway in grotesque dancing patterns,
As the wind moans its way through the branches.
The billowing clouds move across the night sky,
Finally disappearing from view across the distance.

In the solitude, the fireflies mingle with heat lightning
    And the sounds of Summer,
As fresh breezes give promise of a cooler Tomorrow.
The oppressive heat of the day has lifted,
But the closeness lingers, clinging, with the tenacity
    Of a Summer evening. The night is here.
Lowell Moore

My Death And Funeral

Today was the day I died, leaving my spouse without saying good-bye
She may question whether she's to blame, now that her life is
    not the same
She will not quite understand, why death dealt life such a hand.

For death is nothing to worry about, I did not ask for it nor can I change it
But I changed the way you live, my life was in you
It will always be there, you will see me in others
For there is a part of me in you that will never die.

You may walk along an empty shore
searching for an answer, looking for the truth
But all you find is a cold brisk breeze
and the autumn leaves that float as they fall
for each leaf tells the story of us all.

Your memories are the flowers places over my tomb
Just as the unborn child cuddles in the mothers' womb
Forever . . . This is my place of rest
Now the born child suckles at mothers' breast
For we celebrate the miracle of birth and the mystery of death
With all those gathered here in memory of me.
Daniel J. Hart

The World

As the wind blows away I hear the trees gently sway and the waters ripple away and I still stay. Then it starts to rain, the rain travels near and far some times all the way to Zanzibar. As it grows colder the rain turns to snow, it turns the mountain white what a magnificent site. Then feeling tired I rest my head on the nice soft dirt and look up at the breathtaking blue sky and wish I could fly. Then I doze off into a long nap. When I awaken it is already the next day and just the same the wind blows away and the trees gently sway. I don't want to miss all of these things so take care of our world and keep it clean for generations after.

Meredith Epstein

Cold

Cold,
 as a body without love.
Cold,
 as a leafless tree on a winter's night.
Cold,
 as the hard, frozen earth.
Cold,
 as a new born baby upon its birth.
Cold,
 as the north wind's breath.
Cold,
 is the body without love.

Ginger Crawford

Wolves

Wolves are wild,
Wolves are free,
Wolves are in you and me.

Wolves have spirits that cut like an
arrow just like an Indian farrow.

Wolves are spiritual,
Wolves are guards,
Wolves are in our hearts.

Wolves have the right to be here just like
you and me, but if we keep killing them
no more will they be!!!

Laura L. King

A Special Moment Of Love

Love can be good, love can be sad
Love is sharing the good times along with the bad

I've waited a life time for someone like you
Someone who loves me and will always be true

No more days filed with gloom and grey
Only happiness will fill each of my days

A love like ours is one of a kind
Rare and unique, and very hard to find

Some people search their whole life thru
Just to find someone, someone like you

I found love when God sent you to me
I know in my heart it was meant to be

A long time I've waited for our special day
A day when all my heartaches would be taken away

United as one, a family we'll be
I love you dearly, I'm asking you, "Will You Marry Me"

Connie Adams

"The Girl Next Door"

She was a cutie, always under foot and in the way,
I'd tell her, "Go find your doll and go play."
She'd cry, "You're a meanie. I'll grow up it won't be long,
When she didn't come around, I thought something wrong.
One day I asked Mom, "Is she sick?"
Mom answered, "No just growing up and dating Nick."
"Dating? Has that much time gone by?
She can't be, she's just a kid," I said with a sigh.
She used to say, "Wait for me, I'll grow up someday, you'll see."
I'd say, "You do that, but there are places I'd like to be."
She cried that day as I left her standing there,
Gone a short time, I realized there were things with her I would share.
I rushed back home to see her, but Mom said, "You can't, it's time you knew."
I just want to see her, that was all I wanted to do.
She was getting married, when she told me I cried,
I said, "It can't be." Yet here stood a blushing bride.
Putting her arms around me she said, "I told you I'd grow up someday."
I wished her well, turned to go before she saw the tears as I walked away.
Time has erased the pain, I don't hurt anymore,
But I'll always be in love, just a little bit, with "The Girl Next Door."

Kenneth Edwards

The Painful Journey

When we are born, if we'd only know
The burden we must carry and the long way to go,
We probably go back into the mother's womb
And refuse to come out, but prefer to go to the tomb.

However, we are born, we grow, reproduce and die
We must face the misfortunes from which we cannot hide
This is a long journey and we must learn to face
The prejudice of people, the injustice and disgrace.

The world will never change. It is an endless cycle
The kings were ruthless and idle, it is written in the Bible,
What is now, already was, nothing is new under the sun
It's so scary, we want to escape. But there is no place to run.

With outrageous misfortunes, with many ups and downs
We finally are older. Now! It is time to leave the towns
But when we realize that death has come for us,
Now we don't care the suffering. But we must die without a fuss.

Tavita Martins

Winning

In this world of toil and struggle
in order to survive,
sometimes we have to push and shove
just to stay alive.

When friend against friend becomes necessary
in order to perform our jobs;
then in our necessity to compete, down the hall we trod.
We think that if we hurry and claim that special place,
that every thing will be o.k.
Let another be misplaced.

But as you sit there on the spot
you so hurriedly gained, you see
The face of a precious friend who wishes there to be.
Your conscience starts to bother you
a lump comes in your throat.

You realize you didn't win. You have no desire to gloat.
Sometimes when we step back and let another win,
we really are the winner, because we kept a friend.

Thelma P. Williams

Teddy Bear

Darling tattered teddy bear,
With flattened nose and tattered ear.
The favored friend of one so dear.
He talks to you, he likes you near.
The two of you go out to play.
Many are enchanted nights,
He on the left, you on the right.

Remember the swim in the wading pool?
There were trucks, "Baby Moses," and you.
A little tow head with tear filled eyes,
Brought "Teddy Bear" for Mom to dry.

Darling tattered teddy bear,
With needle and thread,
I'll sew your ear.
The favored friend of one so dear.
I'm very glad that you are near

Diane Douglas

"Harmonious Sight"

Just open your eyes and see,
see the many great things left in the world to be seen.
Through the turbulent tides of hatred
and the aura of animosity,
Sight will rise.
Just open your eyes.
"We the people . . ." will open our eyes and see,
see the truth and will disclaim any parody.
We will look and see what we have done,
Learn the truth that people of every nation are one,
same alike with no difference between each other.
Then at that moment our goals and accomplishments
will have a significance with one another.
Education, indifference, and toleration are the key.
Just open your eyes and see.
One day if we learn, we can live in peace and harmony.

Adnan Hafeez Syed

Nature

I walked to the pastures to see the flowers grow.
There I saw the beauty of fence posts standing in a row.
How could I ever live without these beautiful sights
Watching the beauty of animals and birds in flight.
That is why nature and I will always be friends.
For me, being in the fresh air and among the trees,
is a beginning, not the end.

Jay C. Beck

Survival

A creature, whirring through
the corridor of rocks.
Moving swiftly, knowing that its life
will soon be ceased.
Ghastly enough,
he keeps on going knowing that if he stops
his predator will become content.
It passes by the stork-like bird,
dabbling in the eerie pond.
It wonders, why me?
The primitive creature darts through the moist moss.
The huge world seems like a maze to him.
It comes up to a rock, pawing to climb up
he sees a pleat in a nearby maple tree.
His slender body squeeze through the rugged bark.
Knowing that it is unscathed
it thinks about how engaging nature is.
It lays down to rest, knowing that
tomorrow it will happen again.

Danny Jimmerson

Why?

People much more learned than I
Have asked the age old question, "Why?"
Why we're born and live and die
And what it is that makes us ply
And plod and trudge this whole life through
Even though the days we rue.
Most, ever onward dreams pursue
Even though rewards are few.
Some people live a lifelong sigh
And struggle on without a cry.
Others that we think thrice blest
Willingly go to an early rest.
What gives the soul that inward spark
And makes us struggle through the dark?
Toward some unknown distant goal
Our ships sail for that mysterious shoal
Not knowing what awaits us at the end
Through deep chasms we descend
To some unknown eternal fate
When death flings wide that one way gate.

Mary Albracht

Playing House

Loneliness, guilt,
the emotions of love,
are mixed with sadness and longing.

You reach for me, I pull away.
My feelings confused,
doubts flood my mind.

I ache to return to happier times.
Times of fun, flirting,
and childhood innocence.

We are now older,
serious emotions come into play.
Along with reservations about commitment.

We compromise on a relationship.
That begins with insecurities,
disappointments and doubts.

We are two children
playing at house.
Unsure of the outcome,
continuing the game,
regardless.

Kathleen Nevins

Grandpa

I watched as he wandered the wooded trails
And took in all of nature's wondrous beauty.

I watched as he cared for his horses and dog,
For they were part of the beauty of nature.

I watched
As he talked and listened to;
As he laughed and cried with;
As he praised and prayed for
His family.

I watched
As he read God's word;
As he sang praises to God;
As he prayed . . . full of faith.

I watched.
He unknowingly taught.
I learned.

Thank you, Grandpa, for being you.

Jamie L. Walton

Turbulence

The world, our world, composed of land and sea
Where all things live and die, 'til souls are set free.

How long will it last?
Will it always be?

Generations, future and past
Life and death surrounding me.

Beauty, majestic splendor, fields of gold and greens
Ugly, barren wastelands, dead waters, empty dreams.

Peace, love, clean fresh air
Spring flowers, sweet mourning doves.

War, hate, famine, despair
Quakes, floods, people mourning loves.

Good here, Bad there, Turbulence is everywhere.

Like oil and water, hot and cold
A son and daughter, young and old.

When the two meet, will they mix together? Even out?
Will they explode in angry thunder, scattering everything all about?

Who can answer this? Who stays? Who goes?
What can we do? Who wins? God knows!

Joan C. Shears

Untitled

I want to be a princess
I want to be beautiful
  but the fact remains
I want to be special
I want to be an individual
  but the fact remains
I want to be someone
I want to be anyone
  but the fact remains
  the fact remains
I saw you standing there
  a little frightened
I watched you silently
I began to study you
  began to know you
  began to want and need and love you
And then it happened
  you turned and caught my stare
I was embarrassed, but before I shyly walked away
I memorized you

Andrea Osborn

Trip To The Moon

Life's just one long trip
A cruise on life's ship and oh
We had so much fun following the sun.
We climbed the steep heights
To fly colored kites and
We danced through the nights
Till they put out the lights.
We've done it all and had quite a fling
I'd do it again if there was enough string.
But now it's a game gone silly and tame
Because past, present and future are all the same
Since you, my love, can't hear my plea
And there's no one around to set me free.
So come back to me soon
We'll climb the string and fly to the moon
We'll be way up high where stars never cry
And the sky is so blue, so peaceful my love
So new . . . so true.

Sylvia Kogel

Memories From A House

As I stand by the road
My stories have long been untold.
My floors have fallin':
The neighbors stopped callin':

The sounds of children long have past.
I know not how long I will last.
Now an empty house, when once a home.
Time has come and left me quite alone.

No more gardens, No more tears,
The folks have left with all their fears.
The cows don't moo, the hens stopped clucking.
No woman on the porch, no corn she is shucking.

Visitors came the other day!
They explored the grounds, were then on their way.
To hear their voices, to feel their heat.
To have their presence was oh, so sweet.

Maybe they will come again.
To have a guest is to have a friend.
One just may live forever,
When there are memories for generations to treasure.

Keri Linton

Construction Fantasy

Come walk with me where the yellow giants play
And let us see if we can perceive the plan
Of their constant growling, ever-creaking way
That moves earth from here to there in caravan.

Their heavy clanking treads drown out what you say
And tremble the limbs of each observing man.
They fill the air with a breath that's dark and gray
Spouting upward in a murky heavy fan.

The crescendo tones of their voices convey
The strain encountered as teeth meet the hardpan.
How quickly do they change the scene from hill way
To vague flatness like some modern artisan.

Come, walk away with me and let the giants play
For too soon we'll know what is their precise plan.

Donald W. Young

You Took My Life From Me

I was brought up in a normal way, taught between right and wrong I never went out of my way to hurt any one in any way, I had my dreams and hopes of what I wanted to be, and had dreams how love would some day come my way, but none of this will ever be. You took my life from me. You took my life away, and I never did any thing to you. I was just walking down the street, and you came riding by in your car and shot me, I did not know you, and you did not know me, why did you take my life from me? I went to church every Sunday, and prayed for a good life with a family, I would have gone out of my way to help you, just like the Bible taught me to. You took my life from me. You have made my family unhappy, and I am sure they dislike you too, they always wanted the best for me, and if they knew you they would wish the same for you, I don't understand why this happened or why you chose me, I hope you are not amused for what you did to me, but I would not be surprised if you are somewhere bragging for what you did, you must be full of hate and anger too, it takes all my strength to ask God to forgive you. You took my life from me. This crime in the street must end, or the freedom we know will cease to be, too many innocent people have died like me, we have to sweep this dirt away, we can't let bad people like you continue to take our life away. You took my life from me. You must be made to pay, by someone, someday.

Leonard Tabb

144

Tawkin' Texun And Yankee Translation

It ain't 'nuff we say yaawwll with uh draaawwwll
'Nstrech ever syll'ble tuh tywo'r thruhee.
We jess' don't hurry ar tawk thats aaawwwll
'Cuztawkin'z like craws'nuh cruheeck.
Yuh wuhait'll yuh find uh shayuhluh spawuht
Witha rawk tuh suhppowert ever steuhp.
An'yuh thaink fuhruhminit'n startoff slow
Caawwz ifyuh huhrry y'endup all weyut.

It's not enough that we say you guys really slowly
Making two or three syllables from each.
We're only taking our time expressing ourselves verbally
Because talking is like crossing a creek.
You thoroughly search for a shallow spot
With a rock for each careful step.
And pensively step slowly from rock to rock
For a hasty move will surely get you wet.

Allen Briggs

The Deep And The Dark

In the deep, dark woods
Trees pull down their hoods
Making long black shadows
Casting deadly quiet over the night
Shapes seem to move
As you look at them
Knowing you are lost
Lost in the deep, dark wonderful woods
You shiver and freeze
All because of the icy cold breeze
The moon guides you
But you still feel lost, really lost
Just before you're about to cry
You search the woods with your eyes
Looking for help or
Looking for trouble?
You think twice
You turn around with a frown
You're sure now you are lost
Yes, lost forever in the deep, dark wonderful woods.

Michelle Walters

My Loved Ones, My Friends

To my loved ones, my friends
How my heart aches for you;
How I want and need you by my side.
You are my love and joy, I cry . . .

When all around me are Praising God.
How I long for you.
Even though God's precious ones are there,
If it were not for Jesus, I would be standing alone . . .

With up raised hands and singing voice,
I picture you there.
For if I lift you up before the Lord,
He has to hear my prayer.
"Come Lord Jesus, live in me,"
"Forgive me for being blind."
This is all you have to say, with true heart.

Leave the rest to Jesus, for He's standing there.
With open arms and tears of joy He welcomes you home.

Then we too, side by side this time tears of Praise.
With hands upheld, we glorify His name, for what?

He's changed our lives, we're His, We're Together, forever!

Donna Durante

Soft Round Tummy

Soft round tummy how I wish you could talk —
I so wish to hold you — to teach you to walk.

I want to love you and hug you and rock
In the old rocker that your grandma so rocked.

So many people already love you —
And we haven't yet seen your little life new.

I think you know how special you are —
And I'm awaiting your birth — though the date seems so far.

Late at night as I lay all snug in my bed —
I stroke the lump in my belly I believe is your head.

I stare at my tummy and know you're inside —
I know the fear and excitement from you I can't hide.

Although raising you will be quite a chore —
Somehow I know you'll make it a time to adore.

Hard to explain- the feelings felt for you my child —
Then softly inside me you kick and as suddenly I smiled.

Silently I love the child that waits inside of me —
Anxiously I await the child I want the whole world to see.

Monica E. Coutee

The Lord's Welcome To A Lovely Woman

Lovely woman, come on home.
There's a beautiful mansion
Where you'll never more roam.
He's made a place in Heaven above,
Where you can be with the one you love.

You'll walk the land of milk and honey,
The light will be as bright as the sun,
And you'll have the love of everyone.
Jesus will be there to let you in,
He'll be happy he forgave you of
All your sin.

He'll say, "Woman, I have a surprise for you."
Then up will walk the one to whom you were true.

The boys and girls; she had quite a few:
And some went on to meet their dad, too.
Oh! What a blessing these children have had.
To have had such believers as their mom and dad.

Marion J. Lewellyn

My Life Is Shattered

You told me life would be fine
    You lied it hurts all the time
You told me the pain of her loss would go away
    You lied it's here to stay
You told me to say goodbye
    but all I can do is cry
You told me grandpa was remarrying
    so you went to the wedding
My birthday is here
    I feel cold this year
You told me grandpa wasn't coming home
    he's helping her for close the sale on her home
My life is shattered
    now I feel so shallow
I can't forget the pain that it's caused me
    I can only remember how you looked or felt
My life is shattered
    in the pain inside me

Pam Stiles

A Morning Prayer

Bless me Father, on this day of days
Give me the strength, to live in thy way.
Allow me not a hand to lift to cause Thee hurt.

This day is before me, with its trials and strife
Bless me Father, and guide me right.
That I may be gentle, and honest and true and useful to you.

Restrain my life from cross words today
And guide my thoughts, should they happen to stray
Each deed I do, may it merit its reward
In thy greater Honor and Glory, my God.

Life is so short and soon I'll be gone
Let me remember this, as life goes on.
So Bless me, Father, and keep me close to Thee
Now and throughout eternity.

Stella Lemanska Olbris

Staring

Sitting up here on my wall
Staring from nothingness to nothing at all.
And now here I go again, thinking,
Thinking of you, the thoughts are sinking.
The clouds start gathering above my head.
Everything goes still, almost dead.
My mind starts wandering to distant memories
I look up at the dark sky and fall to my knees.
Mumbling chants, pretending to posses knowledge.
With all my thoughts, I've been pushed to the edge.
Here I am kneeling on this wall
Afraid of loosing it, afraid to fall.
The world starts to circle around my head.
The dream keeps appearing that I'll soon be dead.
And here I am sitting up on my wall,
Staring from madness to nothing at all.

Shannon N. Butts

Mother

Gentle hands, loving ways, kind spirt, non-trying days.
She gives her life, to keep us safe, and helps us out,
everyday, She's better than gold, and kinder too
without her love, we would forever be blue. All Mothers
are special, but for me I think, mine is the best God ever gave.

Jo Ellen Brake

"Kitty"

My father's voice sings out
no hint of shadows yet to come
bright light of our young lives
Kitty! Kitty! Wake up buttercup
get up buttercup. Here comes the sun!
But dark clouds went over. She was gone
rain, rain, rain. We all cried
she is gone!
Like clouds going by in a summer's sky
she can't, she won't come back, but
I found another love to match
venus in the evening sky
daughters born that mirror Kitty
thank God for such reflections
two girls. Gifts from heaven
Kitty would love you all
only she could be here
never ceasing, never ending
love is eternal!

Jeff Cunningham

Listen

Listen! Can you hear the angels?
Their wings are all a flutter.
For me it is a day of sadness.
They have come to take my mother.

Listen! Can you hear my tears?
They cascade from my eyes
Like dew from an early morning rose,
Each drop whispering my goodbyes.

Listen! Can you hear my heartbeat?
It's like thunder from the sky.
The clouds are gray and lightning streaks the heavens.
Why do you have to go mother? Why?

Listen! Can you hear the angels?
Their wings are all a flutter.
For them it is a day of celebration!
They have come to take my mother.

Rita Bryant

"A Tribute To Mike"

I know you are gay and that's OK
But be careful you don't get AIDS.

It's your lifestyle and your choice
but I don't want you to die from a
    deadly disease.

Please be careful and take precautions
You're my friend and I want you around
    for along time.

We are the same age and let's be
    here in this life for little while
    longer.

You have your life and I have mine
But that doesn't change our friendship.

I tell you this out of friendship and caring,
Please live your life carefree but be careful.

If for some reason you should get AIDS.
I'll stick by your side as much as I can
But it will be hard to watch a good
friend die of such an awful disease.

I will never forget you, Mike. God bless.

Rebecca S. Cook

Sudden Death

Where is your spirit, Where is our soul, Why did you have to go?
Did you see the tunnel, then the light? I hear it is very bright.
You were gone before I knew. I wanted to say goodbye to you.
I love you so, I wish I could go. But it's not my time, my journey's
    not through.
The sun won't shine, the snows not white, my souls in shock, I
    hate the night.
When morning comes it scares me so I want to keep hold and not let go.
I do have faith in the big plan. I know we will meet again.
We've been through all the trials of the heart, they could not pull us apart.
Our Bond was strong we would not let go. That's why it so
    hard for me to close.
You were my heart, you were my soul I need you to help me grow.
I miss your love, your funny ways, I must keep you in all my days.
I see you in us as we get through. I only wish that I could see you.
You were my morning, my noon, my night, my mate, my friend,
    also my light.
If you could send the tunnel for me so once again we will be.

I love you, Chris
Julie Ann Stuart

Old Mother

Deep in her own years
She sat like royalty in her chair with wheels
Deep in her own memories
She picked flowers with her sister
Deeper still — the young ones
As they frolicked about her

Brought back with a jolt
As the nurse gives her pills
And says supper is ready
She eats with strangers who have nothing to say
Or babble incessantly about things of which she knows nothing
She longs for things past
And closes herself from the present we have
Leaving us fearing old age
As she lived it
Deep in herself and her memories.

Bobbie Fishburn

April 19th, 1995

Life is so precious and dear,
that when taken away we all have fear.

Cherished memories becomes our comfort
when our minds are complete disarray and out of sort.

Through crisis we reflect back and think
we were just there, all in disbelief.

It has been but just one week
all of us feel empty and bleak.

With faith and God the voids will soon fill.
There is hope, there is light, just like
sunshine coming through a window sill.

Oklahoma has been hurt, Oklahoma is strong,
in years to come we will go along this path,
reminiscing with a tear and with saddened face,
Oklahoma has survived with a lot of faith.

Debra Strong

"Daddy Still Loves His Daughter"

It seems with my unexpected disappearance, I have left a
tremendous void in your life. I also had the miserable
task of leaving my other daughters, my sons, and my wife.

If you'll give me a moment to explain, I'll try to let you
know where my feelings lie, by telling my heartfelt story
in truth, through this capable writer's eye.

I can't tell you how sorry I am to leave you all with so many
questions, but, please feel assured my sweet daughter,
my love and emotions are too abounding to mention.

I've seen you with life and its hard times, only to see
your strength shine through. Oh, I miss you so very much
my dear, all the time I could have spent with you.

So, please don't feel you've missed getting to know me,
because with me looking down from above, I can see what
I've missed by not being there for your love.

So, keep thinking of me as being in a better place, and
I know you care because of the smile on your face.

Make sure you keep your head up high, and don't let
the hard world lead you to the slaughter. And, please,
please, always remember me dear, that your
"Daddy still loves his daughter."

William T. Travers Jr.

Rainbow Colors

A rainbow is a reminder
of God's beautiful colors,
displayed on a circular arc.
Colors which are not understood
or noticeable in the dark.
The colors are bright
and beautiful for a while,
and they soon fade
before your eyes in no style.
A rainbow is a beautiful sight in the sky.
To catch the eye of a passerby.
A rainbow almost makes you feel
the presence of God.
Only God can
make a rainbow.

Patricia C. Jackson

At The Cabin

Just a few more minutes Lord
    Before I tackle dirty dishes and unmade beds,
Jut to look out on your world
    Clean, white and quiet this morning.

Came up for opening of trout season
    The morn showed soft new snow,
Fell so gently and carefully in just the right place.
    So like your doing, Lord.

The morning sun is bright
    The world is clean and right
All the struggles of war, crime and bustle
    Seem so far away.

I sit, gazing out in silent communion,
    Renewed with content and love,
A great day ahead - life is lovely,
    People are beautiful and your world is good.

Lahoma M. Cook

Holding It Together — Together

Just the two of us isn't enough, there's need of a third to bind us.
When problems and troubles and heartaches come we need a
    third to remind us.
We are not meant to do it alone, not even the two is enough.
The third is the cement to hold it together when things get really tough.

With God there's the strength and wisdom and love, enough to
    keep us alive.
With God, there's a reason and will and more than enough love
    to survive.
Through darkness and drear and black nights of stormy clashing
    weather
Holding on, cleaving to God, we can hold it together —
    together.

Roseanne Casamassima

Ode To My Sister

If you should go before I do — in all things on earth I'll remember
you — I'll see your face in twilight dim — and hear your voice
In each church hymn — when I walk in a garden you'll walk
with me — along the beach and by the sea — In the woods
when autumn comes — together we'll walk arm in arm — in the
rain you'll call to me — in the show you footprints I'll see —
and when the sun is shining bright — and when the sky
are clear at night — I'll be content because I'll know —
you go with me wherever I go — But if I should go
and leave you here — Remember me and keep me near —

Lela Gayles-White

Time Eternal

One moment, one moment, one moment please clear.
Without the noise, the hustle, the bustle drear.
Without the grown folks' playthings, that cause pain.
Without the confusion that we all know, that leaves no gain.
With precious life, silent, golden, yes precious it be.
With precious life, that came about, from a struggle to be free.
With precious life, a gift, the master gave to all.
To have, to hold, to walk not crawl, stand tall.
To live to the utmost, all needs met, no fear.
To have a happy life, a peaceful life, no tear.
One moment, one moment indeed, one moment dear.

Al G. Rowls

Harry

The old man sat with silly smile
some say feeble minded he was
His family deserted him to a life with new friends
The old man longed for earlier times — working for
the same company for 14 — 22 or was it 27 years
The old man did not really know
His mind had grown old
and his body weak
He was the definition of aggravation to some
and the definition of joy to others
None of this matters anymore
For the old man is no longer old
He is gone

Michael D. Allen

God's Servants

Are you in loneliness,
Let me befriend you,
Are you without love,
Let me love you like a brother or sister,
Are you lost,
Let me help you find your way, again,
Are you cold,
Let me warm you,
Are you hungry,
Let me fill your stomach,
Are you sick,
Let me make you well,
Are you hurt, sad, angered,
Let me help, you to heal your soul,
Are you poor,
Let me make you richer than the rich,
I am not contented to walk by,
without compassion and helpfulness,
for you, because I am living in the blood of Jesus.

Rosemary Perronteau

Untitled

My tongue is dry and cracked — a sponge in my mouth,
Dirty, rotten, carnivorous pigs have stolen all of my water,
"You know, a person needs water to live"
"No crap!" I scream back to a crowd which moves
to a monotone beat; tilting their heads to see me.
But, for a moment, the sandstorm ceases scraping the flesh from my eyes,
Raindrops the size of cockroaches fall into my tongue.
It unshriveled — I could dance and sing and roll
in the dirt which crawled into my pores and whispered
"It is good"
Then it stopped; ripped away, like a gift I didn't deserve.
Now I throw sand at myself and scrape my own eyes
praying it returns.
Finally, I crawl back into my burrow to live
like the pigs who ruined me
I crawl back, without water.

Hope Bursenos

The Man Who Could Not Give

Alone, I try to mend after you decided to depart.
In order to begin my healing, I think back to our start.
You needed someone to love you, someone you knew would care.
You talked of life and love; the future we could share.
I tended you in illness, my heart was slowly one.
There were some times of happiness, we even shared a son.

Then you began to turn from me, even words faded away.
The loneliness became too great, I was hurt in so many ways.
Your friends were more important. So often you'd be cruel.
You kept right on taking, you played me for a fool.
I have nothing left to give you. You took all I ever had.
I'm just a little older; more wiser, yet so sad.
I know time will heal my wounds, once more I'll love and live.
But, I'll always feel some sorrow for the man who could not give

Jenny Christofic

"When I Kneel To Pray"

Dressed in whisper pink soft voile
With scalloped lace and satin bows
She kneels to say her bedtime prayer
What's in her heart . . . only God knows

After she prays, now I lay Me Down To Sleep
She asks God for a special gift of love
She ways, Dear Lord please send me a Mother
I know you have one up above

She says I need a Mother
To help me through the days and night
God I know you hear little children
So please . . . for me make things right

I will always try to show my thanks
As I grow from day to day
I'll always remember to say Thank You
Each day When I kneel to Pray

Viola M. Kiliman

Grandparents

When she was born; we jumped for joy.
A girl she was; and not a boy.
We anxiously waited; for this event.
The months and days; each came and went.
We waited all night; into early morn.
Arrival proved; an angel was born.
Her hair was long; and dark as night.
Her body perfect; a beautiful sight.
She's growing daily; our pride and joy.
And now her mother; just had a boy.
What more perfect combination?
Than two loving grandchildren; a new generation.

Charmaine Ratcliffe

True Love

The kind of love considered to be true,
takes the willing and wanting of two.

Sharing moments of laughter and sadness,
considering not the difference as madness.

Loving one another with no limitations,
accepting each fault with no reservations.

Feeling together as one true pair,
remembering to tell one another you care.

Be willing to give as well as receive,
having no will to ever deceive.

This is considered love of true kind,
but it doesn't happen often or is it easy to find.

Ivano Vit

Great Despair

There was a time in my life
When I lingered in Great despair
My heart was crying constantly,
but you could find a smile there.

The pain that held me hostage.
Was awful and cruel indeed
But no one heard my silent cries,
Nor all the tears that swell in me . . .
My pillow wet, no dignity.

I've know of hurt, but never where
I lost my heart and mind . . .
and now I feel the aching of that
awful, awful crime . . . Your suicide
heavy on my mind.

I wonder through a hazy world
of rain clouds, and covered dew
And it takes me back . . . to a time
of life, that I often knew . . . And in
My great despair, I often let it, linger there.

Angelina McLaughlin

My Yellow Rose

I was blessed above them all
A gift from God I said,
A yellow rose within my garden
A princes in her bed.

Although it rained and clouded over
December 3rd, a day so dear.
I prayed, I said, so many times,
And God, at last, did hear.

She dressed in yellow, like the rose
The petals, bright like the sun.
I'll never forget how cute she was that year in '71.

This yellow rose that grows with me
Is special in every way.
My love for her does strengthen with each and every day.

Although the petals sometimes fall and sadness often appears
My life is still complete through all the sadden tears.

My world would have no time my garden would have no growth
Since I have prayed to God he has granted me both.

I wish this rose could see herself the way I see her best
Just as she is without a doubt Amee, you're far above the rest.

Tommie Keel

God's Tinted Flowers

When God planned His various gardens,
His beautiful flowers were not all painted white;
For with hues and precious colors He saw,
His garden would be more lovelier bright!

Each lovely flower was tinted with tenderous care,
To reflect a bit of Heaven's glorious light;
Placed in His garden to revel, in Infinite wisdom,
All colors were much beloved in His sight.

There be so many precious tinted flowers,
Striving to but bloom in their garden land;
And be it known, no matter what the tint,
'Twas conceived and tinged by the Master's hand!

I care not what may be the tint nor shade,
'Tis but another of God's precious flowers I see;
My hand I stretch forth in respect and love,
To my brother's hand outstretched to me!

Lloyd N. Cooper

Suicide

Forever darkness surrounding thee
gone is the light taunting me

Blackness also is quite common
more often referred, as a pit with no bottom

Falling it seems with no known escape
death is upon you, make no mistake

Saying goodbye is not so bad
leaving behind all that you had

Try and try to squeeze thru its grip
you lose your balance, then you trip

Think you may, think you might,
banished are you from true sight

All these emotions stirring inside
stay in control or say good-bye

Disillusioned or so it seems
completely shattered are all thy dreams

Don't give up, don't quit fighting
talk about it, come out of hiding

These are my words from me to thee,
suicide won't set you free.

Thomas M. Phillips

We Live In Different Worlds

Social life is funny
We all lead a different life
But we all cope with everyone
We deal with habits of every way
And some stir our nerve!

Annoyance and criticism is a part of life
Friendship and happiness help heal the hurt
Sometimes we wonder why people are
The way they are
We regret what we say sometimes, why don't they regret?

We all are so different, yet so the same
For some reason I don't like this social crud
Why we must play this game
The reason I just don't see
There was a guy that played too much and is dead!

This world is very cruel
Only the kind are survivors
This is silly, I want to yell
This game I'll probably fail

Thomas Lee Turner

No Man's Land

There lies a field between the foe
Covered by rock and barren earth
Which can tell a story only of woe
And fascinate the mind beyond that of mirth.

Here men fight and heroes become
Here men die by bayonet, by gun.
This land has no virtues, neither law or code.
This land fells the strongest and those who are bold.
This land has no value and yet a price on its head
A debt paid in full by those who are dead.

To whom does it belong? The soldiers who fight?
The great Lord above who looks for the right?
No, not this land can any man claim
A land soaked in blood and fought for in vain.

Harold S. Davis

Laundry

Rhythmic running on the pavement
Footfalls slapping in the dark

It's the agitation of the wash cycle.

My initial labored breathing
signals my machine is out of round.

I adjust

One washes my clothes,
   the other cleans my mind.
Both rinse away the grime.

The quiet soak process finished
I emerge from the shower replenished.

Armored in fresh apparel
Shielded from the elements of daily life

Briefly

For the spin cycle begins.

Angie Goodman

The Unsigned Card

Every year on Mother's Day five new cards came in the mail, to
let Mom know how much we loved her, and that we all wished her well.

This year Mom placed four new cards upon the mantle shelf, and
one beautiful old unsigned card that stood proudly by itself.

One child passed into the arms of God and left his family behind,
but before he went he bought his Mother a card, he just never
got it signed.

Now even if the unsigned card becomes aged and tattered with
wear, she will place it beside the new ones with tender loving care.

The memories of her son shine on, even though losing him was
hard, so every year on Mother's Day she will share her unsigned card.

Lavina M. Greenough

The Picture

I started into the face of a little girl today.
She was only in a picture I had carefully packed away.

I wondered all about her as I looked into her eyes.
Then something deep inside my soul told me she'd often cried.

I felt a strange connection as her eyes pierced through my heart.
It didn't take long to realize I'd known her from the start.

She was a special part of me I had somehow tucked aside.
And as I stood and stared at her my eyes began to cry.

I wanted to embrace her and tell her she was good.
But the words didn't come so easy and I wasn't sure I could.

Her little face stared back at me as if to almost speak.
And as my heart reached out to her I knew what I must seek.

The sadness and the loneliness could somehow now be stilled.
For as she entered in to stay my emptiness was filled.

Marie T. Vande Zande

Untitled

I am a traveler,
A traveler through the corridors;
Some reveal themselves to me easily;
Some are elusive and impalpable;
There is a path for me in between these corridors
But right now, I am just a traveler going through the corridors.

Sarita Battish

Untitled

I have to say dear Mom and Dad
You mean the world to me.
In spite of my behavior
In my heart you'll always be.

You're more than just my parents
You also are my friends.
For it never fails through thick and thin
You're there until the end.

I have many fond reflections
Of Christmas in the past.
You two were there for most of them
Thank God those memories last.

If I had a lot of money
There's so much I'd give to you.
But considering I don't
These words will have to do.

First you'd get an angel
To keep you safe from harm
And blanket you with love
To make sure you both stay warm.

Steven Speranza

The Eye Of The Storm

In a couple of hours
   My life was turned upside down, inside out,
Shattered, like the windshield of his car.
   Suddenly, I'm alone.

Everyone thinks I'm so brave, so strong.
   They cannot see the storm of grief
   That surrounds me and fills me.

I do not try to avoid the storm. Rather
   I want it to overcome me and
   Destroy me and wash me into oblivion.
So I embrace it, hunger for it, reach
Out and let it sweep over me and through me.
I let go and fall into the maelstrom.

But in the center of the storm is
   A place of calm — the eye of grief.
All around me, the storm of emotions is still
   Swirling and raging.
And I know I soon will feel it all again.
But this calm I feel, this so-called strength,
Is merely the unnatural quiet
Of the eye of the storm of grief.

Paula B. Gray

Our Space Pioneers

Flying soldiers into space, pioneers of the human race
Knowing not what lies ahead: More knowledge for man or sudden death.
Yet on they go up in the sky, going where birds will never fly,
so close to God where all is calm.
And though some perish as they climb and others died upon the
   ground, yet new resolve again is found.
To keep on trying is our way, not on the ground will man e'er stay.
We all keep trying all our days, to return from whence we came.
Some make it back so very fast, or so it seems to us,
but we who are left behind feel such a loss.
Our only consolation is that our time draws ever nearer, and
soon we'll go home again.
We each have something on earth to do and when it is done
   our day is through.
So live your life from day to day for soon, so soon,
your day will come.

J. Everett Villines

Dust

This prairie dust is the kind
that settles on a man
I doubt that you could ever find
dust that clings like this dust can.

But, you know, it ain't so bad
takes gettin' used to though
'Bout 20 years of dust I've had
and 20 more to go.

That prairie dust means movin' cattle
Means drovers and a herd
Means lots of work, life in the saddle
That's this man's life by third.

The other thirds are homes and wives
and maybe children too
but somehow in these cowboy's lives
these things he doesn't do.

Well you can't blame him much, of course,
his way of life is such
that he just needs his dog and horse
so who would want him much?

Gwenn Ward

Intrinsic Sleep

Now you're sunken into your sleep.
Now you're drunken with the dreams you dream.
Now night passively arrives with its swift escape from reality.
Consciousness surrenders to unconsciousness, surpassing in surrealism.
A gentle caress of peace, ease, and blissfulness, or . . .
Drowning in a sea constructed of anguish,
No one can hear your desperate, but silent cries.
Your greatest fears, flashed before your minds eyes,
In a timeless region where the uncanny lies.

But now the dreams, majestic or calamitous, must all subside my friend.
For night now rapidly approaches its predestined end.
Consciousness invades unconsciousness.
Lying in a deep bed of incense.
Awaking to the grand aurora.
The sun reveals itself over the distant horizon.
Stars vanish into the vast dawn skies.
An this essential process takes place while last night dies.
Now you awake with the vague memories you keep —
    from your intrinsic sleep.

Simeon Gonzalez

Untitled

It was the night before Christmas, the snow was deep,
I looked out the window to take a peep;
I saw the tracks of Santa's sled,
And heard his reindeer over-head.

As fast as I could I jumped into bed,
Quietly pulled the covers over my head.
I lay very still and pretended to sleep,
As down the chimney old Santa did creep.

I jumped up early long before dawn
Because I knew old Santa had come and gone.
Dad said, "No, Santa had not gotten there,"
But I said, "Dad, I can smell chocolate candy in the air."

So we kids ran to the Christmas tree,
There were dolls for Polly and Me;
With long curly hair and eyes of blue,
They were so pretty we didn't believe it was true.

Brother had some trucks and a ball,
To us kids it seemed to be the best Christmas of all.
Mom and Dad had a big smile on their face,
As we kids scattered toys all over the place.

Mary Warren

The Reader

A union of the spirits,
Of wind and sail and time,
Gossamer wings and other strange things.
Were his to seek and find.

Across a hundred centuries
To distance stars and beyond,
He travelled onward with memories,
Of golden days now gone.

For he was a questing seaman
Whose ship, his searching mind,
Feared not the wind, nor mankind's sin,
Or the binding chains of time.

And he sailed across the landscape,
On the sweet prairie breeze,
Where the grass is the sea and the waves are the trees.
Over towering mountains and stormy oceans green,
Caverns deep, where dragons sleep, that only the brave have seen.

And I have known this sailor of time, have sailed his endless seas,
Have felt his pain as though it were mine,
For could not this man be me?

Jim Pugh

We Died Before We Died

Today, to be faced with the grim reality
    A dead mind may proceed the body in actuality
If so then perception is naught
    As everything viable begins with thought

The mind is our cerebral soul
    That steers us along Life's rocky shoal
Our psyche is our very essence
    Breathing individuality into beneficence

We have lived that we might ponder
    Conjecturally with hope and wonder
Having traveled the world so far to date
    To share creativity thats' hopefully innate

And now to be dealt the brutal blow
    That our mind may be the first to go
Oh! Fate thy wicked sting
    Take our body - before our mind - and ring

The Bereaved Bells of Life to deplore
    The theft of an active mind before
A bereft body that's unwilling to surrender
    "We died before we died" - despite loving life so tender!

Wayne Field

Untitled

I look for you
I cry for you
And yet I can't find you.
I protect you
I care for you
And still I can't touch you
I caress you
I hold you
Even though I can't feel you.
My heart loves you
My mind wants you
But my eyes are too blind to see you.
I live in the past
And there's always something in me
That doesn't want to find someone new.
Still I keep up the search
To get that other someone.
Funny for me, everything leads back to you.

Tricia Winden

Mr. Morning Star

Standing at the courtyard door,
Slowly sipping a special cup of tea,
Picking up the message telepathically,
He wants to be with me.

A small man with a child-like head,
Bobbing full of gray-white hair,
A spark of Divine Intelligence,
Stepping up to greet me, so gently,

Lighting my way, says, "Will you give me a lift?"
"Meet me where Hope stands with the Morning Star,
At the intersection of the Early Nineteenth Century,
And Twenty-First."

I hear only children at play,
In a small quaint town centre,
Where big hearts sometimes hold small minds,
I hear him say, "Will you give me a lift?
Earth time; now, four o'clock, today?"

His arms gently grip me up, I ascend (as he ascends),
From my small mind into the Unlimited Big Bang Mind,
Beyond all space and time.

Zania Reigh Creigh

Wings

Fly to me, butterfly, have no fear
Fly to me, bright butterfly so small
I'll watch you soar through the air
I'll catch you if you start to fall
Fly to me, little butterfly
For I have watched you grow
From a brown caterpillar bound
So closely tied to the ground
I watched you in your cocoon
Many dark nights under the moon
I watched and waited for a time
Knowing you were becoming strong
And what joy I felt when I watched
You struggle hard and long
To free yourself from the bonds
Fly to me, butterfly, for don't you see
The wings were what were meant to be
Fly to me, butterfly, for now you are free.

Debbie Holmes

Break Up

They sat in Shoney's across from me
He is stony silence, she in spurts of
quiet talk and tears.
Her heart was bare for all the world to see.
His eyes were cold, while her's reflected all her fears,

The tears that told a story, familiar and sad,
Why did it hurt to watch her pain and see
An end to all the dreams she had
As they sat in Shoney's across from me?

LeNore Kosovec

Feeling Icky

Feeling icky, finger's sticky, stomach's full of goo
Ate a doughnut and some chocolates, had some ice cream too.

Feeling icky, wasn't picky, when I ate that junk
Munched a pickle, finished the chips, took a bath and sunk.

Feeling icky, kinda sicky, "Gee, I'm really full".
Woofed down candy, licked a lolly, better stay home from school.

Feeling icky, not too chicky, dunked my cookies just right
Have one left, "What shall I do?" Aw, heck. What's one more bite?

Becky Lofstrom

Death, The Angel Of Mercy

When it is time he does not knock on the door — he merely walks in.
Whether there is suffering of men, women, or children he sees all,
Death would rather not come forcefully as when we take a life or
 our own, nevertheless — he comes whether we are ready or not.
In times of trials and tribulations he comes.
Whether in times of peace and sunshine he comes.
We do not have to call on him as in prayers or in killings because
 eventually he will come to someone this day.
He is an angel of mercy because he comes as he alone can let it alone . . .
 Restful asleep . . . Or in pain somehow he comes.
No doctor can call him and tell him for he has his own time and schedule.
He sits back watching and judging the time, he then goes to God
 to tell that the time has arrived.
He more than the doctor knows the factors beyond medicine's door.
He wants us to live as long as possible but when the body cannot
 its strength fades and calls on him.
Angel of death cares and when he cannot see and stand any more, or
 he hears the call however it comes-he comes in his own time, and
 when he is forced to come he is sorry for those left behind of the
 family but when that body calls he cannot hold back — he is the
 angel of mercy.

Steven W. Lee

Branches Soaked In Anguish

Imagine a poplar full of
Mellifluous skittishness
And its dreams scattered over
Eyelids closed, and furthermore
Postulate a day drowsy
With sorrow for poplars
Fearful and morose.

Then by a route remembered
From somewhere (The Book of Living;
The Book of Existential Prose!)
Theorize upon fading footsteps
Of all those oblivious
Images of yours.

And then enchanted
(And let us say, calm)
While the earth is laving
In the roots of trees
Recall the loneliness of all barren graves
Recall the barrenness of your sullen knees.

Djordje Minic

Last Time

Touching you for the last time felt so good.
Making love to you is a feeling I'll never forget.
The moments we've shared have reached out before me.
Strangers in the shadows watching it rain.
While the lonely one feels so empty, lost, and deranged.
Your feeling I'll never outgrow.
The love that used to be, I no longer know.
Discovering your soft whisper won't be there.
Only time can take us anywhere.
Tormented and torn apart.
For the last time I lay my hands on your sacred heart.
Truth can't speak alone.
Colliding souls now drift gently to shore.
When all our faith is nothing more.
Sensations controlled by the mind.
Broken promises have been left behind.
The burning I feel it's never seemed so real.
Breathing on your skin for the last time.
For the last time I lye holding my restless heart.
When from this day forward one world breaks apart.

Denise McAllister

God Be The Glory

When you see me singing and praying,
Also, shouting and dancing
God Be the Glory

There are times you will see me teaching and preaching
God Be The Glory

Sometimes you may see me walking and talking,
Sleeping and resting, the sun began to rise
Then, I began to praise God to the highest
God Be The Glory

Late at night when it is quiet, I decide to read and do a little meditation
While I wait on God to give me some inspiration and
Jesus to come with some relaxation and
The Holy Ghost moves with motivation
Then I began to glorify God in my spirit and body
God Be The Glory

Through my good times, bad times, and hard times, thank God
I gain Christ mind without a dime.

If we glorify, we ought to glorify in the Lord
For ye are bought with a price, therefore,
Glorify God in body and spirit which is God's
God Be The Glory

Eunice Condry-Morgan

A Bird

He holds his head high, always searching for the wind
The wind that will lead him to forever
The wind that will take him soaring
The wind that will take him to freedom

He sings his mournful song, always searching for the notes
The notes that will call his eternal love to him
The notes that will warn the world of the unfearing
The notes that will be etched in stone in their minds

He spreads his wings each time the breeze flutters them,
waiting for that wind
And until the day it takes him to the skies, he will wait patiently
Holding his head high, singing the same mournful tune
The same mournful tune I sing to me

His eyes rest upon me, a strange creature that somehow belongs there
In his world
He does not fly away, for he knows all too well that I am him
Waiting for the wind that will set me free
Searching for the notes that he will remember me

Anna Lisa Bitgood

You Can Be My Parents

You can read me a poem about love or of life.
You can sing me as song, weeping sorrow and strife.
You can spin me a story of your yester years.
You can tell tall tales, igniting my fears.
You can admit to the truth, say how you feel.
You can lie if you wish, some things you conceal.
You can love me, but don't ever stop.
You can be my parents, the only ones I've got.

Becky Schultz

Autumn's Seasoning

Tell me of your Autumn
Is it shades of color
    or branches of gray?
Do leaves dance in the wind
    or fall to the barren earth?
A part of the cycle of being
    or a death of all that was once beautiful?
Please tell me of your Autumn
    for then I will know of your soul's seasoning.

Amy Lynn Rettammel

Afraid

Afraid of the hurt I feel inside,
Afraid of the smile I hide behind.
Afraid of pretending to be someone I'm not.
Afraid of standing in a thousand and being a dot.
Afraid to be alone by myself and free.
Afraid to feel too much happiness and glee.
Afraid to care and love and to
    be free like a white innocent dove.
Afraid of being alone in life
Afraid to care and to be someone's wife.
Afraid to open my heart and to be
    careful so it won't be torn apart.
Afraid to be special to someone,
    'cause I've felt my heart has been shot by a gun.
Afraid of the holes that have been left behind.
As if they were meant as
    a reminder, a sign.
Afraid of the signs that were left to me, because
    they remind me of what never can be.

Melanie D. White

To A Boy

Tell me little boy what is your name
Where do you come from and what is your game
Have you seen the sun dance on the water so blue
Or watched a snail crawl up and over your shoe
I talked to a mocking bird once upon a time
And to a spider named Charlie I took quite a shine
There was an ant named Mabel who played on the table
I sang to my horse in a voice full of glee
A tune called guess what — love lifted me
I called out one night to a cricket in a storm
Come inside and I'll keep you warm
There are games with rabbits and dogs and cats
That will send your mind whirling right through your hat
I know I have been there and I'll take you along
Just give me your hand and fill your heart with a song
The games are useless if you don't find a way
To let your spirit wonder in whatever you say
The time can be ten minutes past yesterday
Or twenty minutes before tomorrow
The gist of the game is to chase away sorrow

Jean Sublett

Twilight Loneliness

He stood quietly and motionless at the over pass
Looking down at the criss-crossed empty tracks below
A heavy duty metal fence shielded him
Just in case a dizzy spell would hurl him below

His stetson hat was cocked just right and with class
His eyes shaded to shield off any afternoon glare
His clothes were neat and clean and fitting well
And if one cared to look, his shoes were ashine too

A wrinkled face and stooped back spoke of a life's end
His tired form said the years might have been hard
Where were all his friends and children
For he now stood alone on Main Street U.S.A.

And I wondered if someone awaited him at home at all
Maybe a wife who could have shared his quiet afternoon
Or walked to the Square with him to watch the trains
For only his fading shadow was here with him today

Did he now think of yester years or of future repose
Did his soul feel a pain or his mind hug a futile chuckle
I would pay to intrude into your wise thoughts Old Timer
Or have we all erected you as a Monument to Loneliness?

Syokwaa Mulumba

The Gypsy

Who can ever forget
That romantic moment when we met
Those great love songs
Songs that keep my love and heart strong

I think of you
Beautiful, embraceable you
Like a bison you roam
Linda, my buddy, along way from home

I'll be seeing you
My sleepy time gal
Where or when I can't begin to tell

I can't forget and still remember you
Dancing in the dark by the light of the moon
That old feeling, like old times it haunts me too
The port, the harbor, and its erie tunes
Yes, I remember you

We'll meet again, I hope we do
If not, I have my devotion, memories and melodies of you
It's ironic, when I play deep purple or serenade in blue
I miss you . . . always Ronnie

Theard Ronnie Lowell

Lament

I hope for joy, but soon I'll wear
   the somber robe of sorrow
Today... I smile but tears and heartaches
   will I have tomorrow,
I hope for all that's sweet.
For life like purest gold to glitter,
But I am disappointed
For the fruits I reap are bitter.
When I wish for lilies white
Then only roses bloom,
And when I wish for peace
I hear the troubled trump of doom.
When I wish for starry nights
No star shines in the sky,
I see dark clouds only and hear
   the night winds sigh,
Sometimes I wish for fragrant flowers,
But stagnant rills abound,
And now I need you more than all,
You cannot, dear, be found.

Dorothy E. Mittoo Walker

Grandma And Me

My name is Angela and I'm not one two or three
for I go to school now, yes indeed. My Grandma is special
she dances, plays, and sings songs with me. We make up
our own toons and animal sounds to. So you see I'm
no longer one, two, or three. Sometimes she acts foolish
but I know it's just for me, that's my Grandma yes
indeed. We live so so far apart and sometimes
it really breaks my heart.
We talk on the phone when afar, she calls me Honey
and I say, Hello Grandma, she visits in summer
and what a treat, she really is so neat I think!
The two of us read books, and walk, and talk I'm
no longer one, two, or three, almost grown yes indeed
I know my prayers now, and she thinks that's
Just great, I'm almost grown for goodness sake.
If I had one wish it would be that my
Grandma could come to live with me. So you
see I'm no longer one, two, or three and Grandma
and I are best friends yes indeed.

Judith J. Arruda

My Red Bike

My red bike is the best bike around
it maybe old but it gets me around.
   Even though I found it in a junk
yard broken and bent and the paint has
rubbed off and the rust has set in.
   I got parts from other bikes in that
junk pile that I have found. I put
them in my bike like putting a jigsaw
puzzle together one piece at a time.
   Then I painted it with care a red
color it was rare. As the paint dry over
night my expectation was that of a child
on Christmas day. It looked like a new
bike when I open the garage door on this
beautiful day in Spring just right for
riding a bike down the street I mounted
my old red bike and pointed out to the
street. I started to peddle it down the
road the wind rush by my face that made
me free that old red bike and me.

F. W. Rook

Let The Games Begin

They come from around the world
to a place where only champions will meet
for it talent was measured like mountain
they would all be known as peaks

Like those that came before them
whose legends haunt these fields
they've given their minds, souls, and bodies
in an effort to perfect their skills.

Like Owens, Spitz, Rudolph, and Kersey
it's not about being a household name
for my friends, the truth is simple,
they've trained for years to play in these games

And oh, how we sit in anticipation
with rewards of bronze, silver, and gold
but there will be no losers here today
if the truth would dare to be told

So when the crowds have gathered
and their flags stand proudly and blowing in the wind
it is indeed an honor and privilege
to say "let the game begin!"

Arzo Grayson Jr.

My Thanks To Each Of You

You make my life worthwhile,
And when I see you all with a smile
It makes me want to stop and pray,
And thank God for sending each of you my way.

Thank you all for the patience and understanding
I require a lot of, now and then,
It's not easy trying to finish each task I begin,
But I'll keep on trying to do all that I can do
To make life real happy for each of you.

I want you all to know
How very proud I am,
That you count on me
In so many different ways,
And welcome my encouragement
Along with a lot of praise.
I feel so very blessed,
To have the three of you
You've made all my dreams come true
And I'll give all my love to each of you.

Joyce Oliver

I Thought Of You Today

I thought of you today and a tear of joy came my way but don't dismay
it was a tear of joy that came today.

The way you tell me you love me or tell me you need me brings joy and
I know I'm not just a toy.

Trust in me and you will see just how I need you as much you need me.
Together we will always be.

I thought of you today and a tear of joy came my way, for by my side
you will always stay.

William B. Nesbitt

To Be Set Free

To run like an Elk, thru the tall green grass.
Away from the danger of a wild sleek cat.
To leap and scramble up a big oak tree.
Like a leopard to rest, in its branches, as they held me.
To set at the tiptop of this great tree.
As a beautiful butterfly on its green leaves.
And fly away in the evening breeze.
Above the stars, the moon, the galaxies.
To sore high as an eagle, to heavens shore.
And there to live, for evermore

Margaret Myers

First Flowers Of Spring

Bitter does the north wind blow,
as it wilts the garden row.
It won't be long before you know,
that spring's life blood again will flow.

For though that wind may seem bitter cold,
it drains your life. It makes you old.
Forget you not where you come from.
Always remember the begotten son.

Rejoice when this wind does hit your face!
For this winter landscape is not your place.
It is but one path in which you have chose.
One that's been traveled by many a soul.

So chin up! Praise God! And all living things.
Always have faith in the first flowers of spring!

Susan Epps Ward

Why Can Not I Get Another Voice?

How can I tantalize a traveling soul
Swimming under an unknown skin?
My snake-shaped hands dream about exploring ancient and missing
secrets. A broken bowl
　[a heart in its womb]
An useless mirror
　[a skeleton on its face]
A timeless sign
　[a ghost screaming alone]
Where are the forbidden answers?
Where was the first worthless question?
My brain
A hopeless drop falling down
Deeply in the darkness, on the ground of the abyss.
I [desperately shouting among lonely street-walkers],
Just a bleeding body with its history forgotten
With its hidden desires
Endlessly lying
Kissing the last dust.

Raul Vallejo

Needy Not Greedy

Which one are you: Do you want more than your share?
Or do you have plenty and able to spare.
How do you view it: You don't need to stow it.
Money won't rust, your bank account won't bust.
We can't feed the whole world: And forget the needy here.

Some children go hungry to school:
Some days they have only one meal.
So stop being greedy, and give to the needy.
You'll have your reward just trust in the Lord.

Carolyn M. Warner

Treasured Memories That I'll Never Let Go!

　　Running through the rain, so cold to the touch. Telling my Mom
"I Love You thissss much!" Sharing a chocolate shake and having a
fish filet, just because I was a good girl today. Stealing flowers for Mom
on the first day of May, we wondered if she knew, what would she say.
Picking blueberries in the summer was fun, for all of us, not just one.
　　The way my Grandfather used to make us smile, for us grandkids
he'd go that extra mile. Fresh fallen snow as it hits the ground,
it's as if you can hear a pin drop, not a word, not a sound. One day
it's "Let's make a snowman!" And the next day "How about a snow
angel!" And the next day it all melts away, "Oh well, there's always
tomorrow!" My Mom and Aunt Jen walking along the beach shore
searching for shells, ones like they've never seen before. My cousin
Ray and I snorkling in the ocean shallows looking for treasures, some of
the things we found made us laugh, some we kept, some we threw back.
　　Sliding down Mr. Holly's hill in the snow, my brother made
bumps in the middle and when you hit them, boy, would you know!
All of us sitting down for a well rounded dinner, Me, Mom and Dad,
my brother and my sisters, looking at each other, who would think,
we would all be apart faster than you could blink. These are some
things that I'll never let go, but with every year, every day, every
hour, they just grow and grow and grow.

Margaret C. Arruda

Life's Secret

Confused of life you seem to be.
Although they claim it's destiny.
To be just who are this day,
although your thoughts are miles away.
Life is not fair,
and you should know that each and every person shows,
quite a different point of view on things they know and things they do.
Yet, life's secret proud but true,
will not just once show its face to you.
So if not found upon first try,
don't feel life's best has passed you by.

Janet M. Kish

Billy's Wish

Little Billy likes to hunt and fish
and his dad sure does too
He has seen the chance to make a wish
so maybe now it will come true

He was outside late last night
when he saw a falling star
He knew to wish with all his might
but it hasn't come true so far

He just wants to have a friend
who would understand everything
Someone to be there to the end
and for him would do almost anything

Oh, lonely day which makes him sad
but who should ask him to play some ball
Well, who else but his dad
Little Billy's wish had come true after all

Karyn Ross

It Is Sad

Arthritis, though an aging woe,
need not hurt 'til tears do flow.
Two centuries ago in the Southwest,
the natives knew how to put it to rest.

Modern science passes this by.
It's too simple for them to try.
Just crush a chile and put it on.
Your arthritic pain is quickly gone.

You can't take any old chile pod.
There's only one that will do the job.
It must be picked at a perfect time
full sized with a bright green shine.

We wanted to share this pepper's magic.
Washington though says it would be tragic
to sell pepper juice for arthritis to ease
without years of tests the officials to please.

Centuries ago the Indians shared
benefits openly because they cared.
Today the benefits go to only the few
who secretly bootleg this natural brew.

Cleve Anderson

What Life is About

You will find when you walk through our door, an old farm
house with unscrubbed floors, cluttered up cupboards, worn out rugs
toys everywhere and stains on the couch.
You will find when you walk through our door, a bright burning
candle with treats on the bar, spills in the refrigerator, garbage
not taken out, a VCR playing and children walking about.
You will find when you go upstairs, six unmade beds and
stuffed animals everywhere. Dressers so packed that the drawers
don't close, night-lights still shining and pajamas on the floor.
You will find when you walk through our door, a mom and dad who
live for this all. A loving little Louie, a cheery Charlie Brown,
a happy Miss Hillary and Marylou last to come.
And we all know when we walk in our old house,
our love and our happiness is what life is about.
For our greatest asset is our family and our love,
and we thank our Dear Jesus in the Heavens above.

Mary Jane Hengesbach

Remains

Remains of an old farmhouse . . .
Foundation made of large stones
Not one possessing the same shape or form.
For the home they were the backbone.

A lilac blooms so fragrantly sweet
being now in God's care.
For no human hand takes time
to see that it has flowers to spare.

An orange blossom will bloom soon
Which stands in a corner so forlorn,
No one will stop to smell its perfume,
Because the building from its foundation has been torn.

A wake made of bricks still remains.
Because of the growth of weeds it can't be seen.
And all that is left of the water supply,
Is an old rusty pump beginning to lean.

Time can destroy a house that was once a home,
To many people, only our dear Lord knows,
But memories will always remain
Of the old farm-house whose foundation only shows.

Betty Chupka

Back To The Days

The divine spirit goes back in part
To rekindle hushed secrets gone by,
Fondly remembering the perfume of the heart
As watching the sudden triumph rainbow in the sky.

The thrill of tender feet touching the russet earth
Lingering in mind like springtime so royal,
Running freely in the swift breeze brings rebirth
For the zest of the pure mind is so loyal.

Recalling the touch of the dewy sweet wild flower
Held in the tiny pearl soft hand,
Sends waves of contentment to a soothing tower
Of the child like thrill fading in nature's land.

Seeing the first tide of skylight charm
Waiting in the silence of the shadows,
The humming young soul feels no harm
As it gazes at the stars so fair in the meadows.

Back to the time of a drowsy fun day
Does the fiber of the youth recall,
Forever spinning on a glorious pathway,
The timid mind stands forever splendid and tall.

Charlotte Campbell

Summertime Fun

Partying Day and Night
Sometimes out looking for a Fight
Cruising Late Chasing Chicks
Vodka and Lemonade, a good mix
Working little, more room for fun
And still having time to lay out in the sun
Making sure I still workout
Still in shape, Without a Doubt
Spend sometime on the golf Course
Even rode a Horse
Once in a while We TP
Only buy the Cheepie
— Spending time with Friends
I'll remember this forever
because it was like never
Pictures and stories we will share
Had the time of my Life
We were THERE
For the Summertime Fun.

Ed Leadingham

Mama Was Right

Holy union committed her to foreign lipstick shades
on his shirts, and nights spent in alcoholic solitude;
Sunrise brought to her the cleanness of a new day
and the dread of another filthy evening
Her entertainment was the snap! of kitchen cheese-traps,
the slow red change of clock numbers in the dark;
His entertainment was the ever-flowing anesthetic of draft
as he pocketed colored balls — stacking more of her quarters
on the altar of a green table.
Giving birth brought only warnings of eviction.

The last night he hung her heart on a barroom coatrack,
she quit lying to the phone.
She took her bundled doll and trudged
twenty-six miles of swallowed pride,
and snuggled into an almost forgotten faded photograph
that was mama's house.
In her old frilly room (wasn't she once a child?)
they slept from hell to heaven, sharing her teddy.
(he'd pocketed the eight ball too early in the game)

Kimberly Lewis

Untitled

In the front of His house you will see
An alter to pray for you and me.

As you kneel there, while to the Lord you pray,
He makes your heart feel different in a very special way.

Because this is a place set aside for prayer
Where only you and Jesus spend time together there.

You can thank Him or praise Him, or He can cleanse your heart,
Or into your life He can become a part.

This place in His house is always open to you
So come to Him and He will surely bless you too.

Because spending time with Jesus is a precious thing,
Into your heart a gift of love He will bring.
Gina S. Shiraga

Sharon's Psalms

It's dark and it's cold, the windows quiver in the wind
Lord, I'm afraid of tomorrow!
"Don't be — I know where you are"

"I'm sick and I hurt, this pain takes my breath away
Lord, I'm afraid of dying!
"Don't be — I know where you are"

This place is cruel and heartless,
Lord, I'm afraid of being lost!
"Don't be — I know where you are"

My protector knows all my hurts and fears
He knows where I am and He knows all these things
Even before I cry out to Him!

He comes to me, when I cannot come to Him
He wipes away my tears before I tell Him where I hurt
He gives me strength to face what I cannot see

Praise God! He's prepared a mansion for my comfort
Praise God! He's loved me for all my yesterdays . . .
Praise God! He loves me where I am right now . . .
Praise God! He will love me for all my tomorrows!

Praise God!!
Sharon L. Overholser

Vietnam Dateline 6/2/69

Perhaps, he fell on Hamburger Hill
or during the bloodily seige of Hue.
Wounded, as he bled
his mind confused, bewildered and afraid.
Out where the missiles soar and the cannons roar
thousands of miles away.
Oh, somewhere in Vietnam
a soldier died today.

Not a soul was near to lend a helping hand;
not a soul to hear his final anguished cry.
And even the sun
so commonly true, deserted the dark blue sky.
Two frightened lips moved quietly
in a solemn effort too pray.
Oh, somewhere in Vietnam
a soldier died today.

As his vital life's light grows ever so black,
in so dismal a plight his mind wanders back
to a dearly cherished home.
What a price he would give to again relive
all the tender joys once known.
Now even the memories fade.
Oh, somewhere in Vietnam
a soldier died today.
Jeffrey Prince

Feelings

Feelings of the body, of the mind, and of the soul
emotions we all experience, both the young and old.
Feelings of the body, the sensation of touch
To hold another person that you care for very much
Feelings of the mind, the psychological sense
To understand another person and to know how love is meant.
Feelings of the soul the one we just can't hide
'Cause feeling of the soul is one we all live by
All of these emotions are different, but the same
All of these emotions in us they will remain.
For these are not just feelings that we take in stride,
This is our way of living
For this is our way of life!
Kathalene E. Jones

As He Dreams

As he watches other couples on the pond
Their laughter rings through is ears.
He smiles —
Out of the blue he thinks of her.
He drifts into a dream world of all the good and fun times they shared.
He still hurts from losing her, he doesn't know what he did to lose her.
Listening to the wind across the pond he can still see her sitting
    by that big oak tree smiling at him.
But now all that he has left is a picture and the memories of her.
He rises and wiping the tears away he knows someone is out there
    waiting for him to find them.
But he's afraid to fall in love again, by chance he gets hurt again.
He is healing but it takes time.
Lynnette K. Lamb

Cherish

Her Genuineness Is Faithful . . . Indistinct
    For she requires no indorsement
Beauty opposed
This she can't conceal
Witty . . . never indelicate
Her virtue never diminished
To her I'm captivated
No singular character is unique
United they make her precious
Brian W. Lockrey

"A Jazz Age"

I was a nifty dresser, not too long ago in time,
But now my threads are corduroy with creases not too fine,
The gals that once looked twice my way now never turn their head,
Except to look at other guys, my book has all been read.

The pride I took to wear my clothes of finest gabardine,
Was as a peacock struttin' front of hens that were a dream!
My throne was on the bandstand and the music played was "Jazz",
I worked the finest ballrooms and my life had such pizzazz!

As years go by we wonder why the songs we knew have changed,
The fox trot time is now a rock — the music's re-arranged,
No, things aren't like they used to be and ballads disappear,
The Rock-beat drum's monotony disintegrates my ear.

I miss so much the big bands sounds with brass and saxophones,
They've been replaced by "Amp" guitars with deafening grating tones,
Each generations style thinks that their sounds are "just the best,"
Just like the three piece suit was never worn without a vest!

It's hard to let the old styles go and hope they might come back,
But if they should I won't be here, not me or Freddie slack!
I'll find my friends like Miller, Duke and Perry Como too,
I've transferred to some higher gigs — my dues paid up — I'm through!
Herb Walsh

Kismet

Have you seen the sparkle of a summer sea
Splashing on a sun-drenched beach?
White fingers of foam that reach for land
Then disappear beneath the thirsty sand.

Look at that leap of spume as it shoots high
Above the jetty's mossy rocks!
While underneath the steady beat
Of rhythmic tides repeat — repeat!

What constant surge of nature's call
Sends seas upon their constant course?
What secret message does it hear
To follow paths, to me, unclear?

I listen for some guiding force
To drive me as the sea is driven,
To bond with elemental time
And fulfill the destiny that is mine.

Marlyn Honey Perkins

Untitled

My one true love
Though we are two
We make up one heart, one soul, one mind.
Forever we are as one
A bond so strong that death could not
Tear us apart
Forever my love we will be
It is our destiny to live, to love, to be
Free together
To know joy and sorrow. Passion and ecstasy
We are forever entwined my love.

Rosiland Leaphaft

My Grandpa

I have no money nor a car,
I need to go home, and it's quite far.

I've gotta go see my grandpa — before he dies,
I must see him and tell him goodbye.

I love my grandpa — I need to see him again,
Before he leaves to the promise land.

I'll miss my grandpa when he's gone,
But I know my life must go on.

Yes a lot of tears I shall shed,
but I still have the future ahead.

I cannot let my life go down hill,
for I know that is not my grandpa's will.

Cheryl Churchill

Indelible Ink

To lift the child up with a pat on the head
and give kisses and hugs when you tuck them in bed.
You affect their perception, in fact, how they think
and put a mark on their soul like Indelible Ink.

To harm them, neglect them and treat them with spite
and leave to discern for themselves what is right.
You too are affecting that child on the brink,
and will leave their soul scarred with Indelible Ink.

For who do we see for lost souls of this land?
Who is responsible when terror's at hand?
The first one to look to's in the mirror, I think,
for Our writing's on the wall with Indelible Ink.

Kim Lewis

Untitled

I remember as a child, wondering what I would be like all grown up.
The imagination of one so young can not comprehend the roads
that life takes us through to become adults.
How could I have known that my heart would have to endure so
much pain and still keep beating.
That happiness would come only after the price was extracted
from all that I am.
How could I have known that becoming an adult meant surviving
all the predicaments I allowed myself to be in.
Becoming an adult meant dealing with reality and not what I
wished everything to be.
How could I have known that there was so much to learn, that
I didn't have the answers just because I came of age.
I remember as a child, I wondered what I would be like all grown up.
I'm all grown up now and I am me.
I have strength, compassion, patience, and happiness in littlest treasures.
I don't wonder anymore, I just take it from day to day.

Kathleen H. Smith

God's Gifts

God gave his gifts to us to use, a rose, the stars, the moon.
Why must we search for other things?
Things that fade so soon.

He gave the dew in the early morn, the sun at noon-day bright,
A rainbow when the clouds pass by
There is no more beautiful sight.

The hills crowned with their cap of green,
The valleys of purple hue.
The lakes and rivers to reflect the sky of glorious blue.

The clear cool streams, babbling down
Over pebbles, shiny and bright.
The ocean bringing waves to every shore,
Just for a child's delight.

The wind to cool a fevered brow, the desert for the artist's brush.
The beautiful black of a raven's wing,
The song of the lowly wood-thrush.

Why do we seek to destroy God's work,
and replace it with work of our own?
His hand designed a more perfect world
Than man can build alone.

Marie S. Austin-Tyrone

Peace Of Total-Self

One frequently hears the phrase "peace of mind"
Yet it is a mistake to stop at one's wanting it
Because one is composed of more than mind,
Splendid energy it is, however, all one's energies are important,
It is vital to want, cause and have peace of total-self
And this includes one's physical body
An energy that is often dismissed as being unimportant,
To have peace of spirit, of soul,
Of all other energies of which one is composed
Is complete peace — an active and vibrant
State of being, living and functioning
That keeps one's energies free, flowing, lucid,
Peace of total-self is attainable here, now, continuously
And it is the complete right of each individual to have it,
In deed, there are a number of people
Who live peace of total-self,
It is essential and one aids oneself enormously
When one lives thusly in limitless ways.

Guen Chappelle

Christina

In the music room sat a piano grand.
The sweet and haunting music came from the hand
Of the beautiful girl sitting there with skin so tan.
Our "Granddaughter Christina."

Brown hair down on her shoulders,
Soft eyes big and brown
It all mingled together with the unforgettable sound
The music from the hand of our Christina.

The seeds of music had been planted in her life to enjoy
so artistic, she is our pride and joy.
She is so sweet and yet at times a tomboy,
Our dear Christina.

She is fourteen, a teenager not sassy.
But helpful to me she gives me hugs and laughter.
She always takes time to be.
Kind, sympathetic. She is a jewel to me, my Christina.

As she grows up and starts a family of her own
I hope she'll remember the seeds that have been sewn
And teach them to her very own,
Our granddaughter "Christina."

Eloise Callin

Not Much Time

The things we've been through
The things we've tried
I thought that we would always have time
For each other and others
To spend time with love
And honor
Not trying to ignore each other
Not lying on our death beds
Alone crying for our lives
And each other
We've wanted to do so many things
Now we don't have much time
Not much time to do anything
For anyone or ourselves
Now because of you I am dying
You lied to me and everyone
Now look at what you're faced with
Not much time

Lindsey Clark

Father

A silent whisper
A lonely dream
A world sliding by without you.
A cold grave is where you lay.
Why does it have to hurt?
No memories to share.
Dreams I can't bare.
You're a part of my world.
I can feel you in the wind.
I can see you in the sky.
I can smell you in the air.
It took me so long.
To accept you.
I wanted something that was too far for me to reach.
It still hurts me..
But I can now sleep.
I can dream
I know you're there
along with me.

Tanya M. Coburn

"Seeing Outside Ourselves"

Don't let the brilliance of your own light
Blind you to another's softer hue

For greater things might quietly come
From one deemed less by you

Revel not in personal glory and fame
For the time will come when you're not
remembered by name

To be remembered for acts and deeds
Meeting the challenge of another's needs
Is a greater reward for our time here
And our purpose for being, becomes quite clear

To help, to serve, and to be a friend
Our reward is love at our journey's end.

Beverly D. Collier

Kaleidoscope

If we are not on this world for love,
   then what else?
A life without love
   is like a kaleidoscope of blacks, and whites and grays.
There is beauty to its shape and form,
   but it is dead . . . it has no warmth.
Such has been my life
   love has touched me, then escaped me.
I, too, have been left cold.
   Until you.

Ronald J. Light

Love Me No More

I don't know where I'm coming from
and I don't know where I've been.
But I do know the future is dim
and soon it will end.

So for you, go on, forget what was said,
for the memories I have
will last to the end.

So for me, my mind, wonders what if,
and if is no more.
So fly and be free,
because I know you love me no more.

Kimberly D. Lawrence

Next Time I'll Call The Plumber

I knew when I tried to fix it,
That I would have to use my brains,
But now that is all over,
I can shoot my worries down the drain.
I hope Mom and Dad don't see it yet,
Because I might have made a mistake.
I took off the lid, placed it on the ground,
And got out daddy's wrench,
I twisted the plastic tube inside,
And dropped some perfume in it.
But when I tried to make it work,
It spouted two feet off the ground,
So then I put some heavy rocks in it,
To really make sure it stayed down.
But I still thing there's something wrong with it,
I think it used to be round.
So I put all my tools away,
And turned off the light.
I shut the door and locked it,
Well, I just don't think I fixed the toilet quite right.

Risa Lin

The Rape Of Persephone

Child of the Fair Earth born,
a flowery infant of tenderness grown,
Demeter smiled fair on Her own that morn,
and two stalks grew for each seed sown;

The soft winds blew, and all was calm,
for the half-score years Demeter's child grew,
Creation was graced with the tender maid's psalm,
and Demeter's tears were fair, and few;

Then the Child of Earth drew another fate,
Stolen away by the great God of Hate,
There, away from the sun's light, was she kept,
She cried as innocence, from her, was swept;

Hades had stolen Demeter's fair child,
and, without her, Earth's grief turned wild,
Her bitter tears stung cold, bare ground,
withering any and all life they found;

Captive within the fires of Hades' lair,
dwelt Earth's child, no longer a maid,
The fate of Demeter's child, never to be free,
The mournful lament of Persephone.

Esther Mitchell

The Difference

There's a difference between you and me
There always has been
Somehow you could fly
To me that was a sin

There's a difference between you and me
Although no one else can tell
I always dragged you down
I was better off in hell

There's a difference between you and me
But the world is blind to it
I always struck out
You just took another hit

There's a difference between you and me
But it was meant to be
We're locked up in each other
And someone just lost the key

Rachel Comerford

Someone Cared

It is good to know that all my pain,
has not truly been in vain.
Even though I could not see,
He has cared for me.
When I was enveloped in my sorrow,
I never wanted to think of tomorrow.
When I was lost in my despair,
He would show me that He cared.
Even when I was alone and in tears,
He was there to lend me an ear.
He's carried me through my desperation,
And has seen me through my elation.
When my world was so shook,
it was in His book that I would look.
Sometimes I feel I'm going crazy,
but He is my rock of sanity.
It is good to know that all my pain
has not truly been in vain.

Kathryn Conaghan

God Is A Lamp

The love of God is a lamp unto my feet,
his mercy a light unto my path.
Sometimes my flesh trembles for fear of defeat.
I'm afraid of thy judgments and wrath.

His righteousness is bright as ten thousand mornings.
His commandments to me he does teach.
I shall live by His Testimony and understanding.
His words are pure. Holy. His promise he'll keep.

He is a God of hope, not darkness and gloom.
God is the Lord, the Master of Light.
Christ the Saviour, a King that's coming soon.
Rest in His shadow. There is peace sweet delight.

Franklin Speck

On Your Birthday

When you were born in Centralia,
Did you hear the geese fly
With all those quacks and calls,
Interrupting the sky and
Introducing you to wildness
And nature? That must be why
You are so special.

Or perhaps you listened to the corn stalks,
Quivering in the wind's air.
On the Illinoisian landscape
You made your first lair
Of Wildness and Wilderness
Woven with love. That must be why
You are so special.

On your birthday
Can you ever think when
Nature was out of your lifestyle?
No! Not now or then?
Forest, brook, dogs and again,
We love you because you're so special!

Aurelle Sprout

He Lives

I love the gently falling summer rain.
    The thunder storm is gone.
The lightning flashes no more across the sky.
    Only the steadily falling rain.
Drink thirsty earth, long parched by burning sun.
    The browning grass will turn to green again,
The wilting flowers lift up each drooping head.
    All earth refreshed by God's own miracle,
Radiantly proclaims "He is not dead."

Gladys Loveland

"Love"

Love is like a breath of Spring
You sit and dream of the joy it brings
The world is all at your command
Until you find what love can stand
Of all the things you share the most
Is what your love can give to both
For years you struggle for what you want
But love alone is not that strong
So life goes on as you can see
The things you dreamed of could not be
So please don't throw your love away
Because things did not go your way.
There is one thing you need to know
The love you cherished will never go.
For in your heart you still can say,
"In spite of all the things unseen, my love is here to stay."

Marie Cigna

I Can Swim In Your Eyes

I can swim in your eyes so deep and dark,
Like twin pools they are, so clear and calm.
Eyes that will never harm or show ill will.
Eyes that are always looking for a thrill.
Eyes that are portals to the soul,
Keys to the universe within, and reflecting the macrocosm without.
I can swim in your eyes so cool and deep,
Sweet memories, are mine to keep.
What is it that attracts me so?
Is it the depth of passion they show,
Or is it their warm inner glow, that beckons me so?
I can swim in your eyes as you can plainly see.
Eyes that have depths as deep as the sea.
Eyes that are always watching me.
Those eyes so penetrating, fanciful and free.
I can swim in your eyes and dwell there for a time.
The calmness I find there makes my life so sublime.
For, I can swim in your eyes for the rest of time.

Vasco R. A. Pires

God's Love

High above the Sistine's walls, a painting may be seen,
Of God's great love for all Mankind,
And what is needed to receive.

God moves swiftly, on Angels wings, to Adam who lies below,
Too weak to stand, he lifts his hand,
Allowing Divine Grace to flow.

Empowered now, Adam takes Command,
Of all the creatures in the Land.
We know the rest . . . the Garden test . . . where
  "Adam's Fall condemned us all."

But God's love would not let us, in exile stay,
He sent His own Son to show us "The Way".
Another Garden, another test,
The "New Adam's" hand was laid to rest.

Grace twice rejected, Man continues to fall,
But there is a saying that "Love Conquers All".
The Lord left His Peace and Forgiveness too,
And from Heaven sent His Spirit to make us "new."

The Journey's not over, but one thing is sure,
God's love for us, will Always endure.

Jeanne M. Smith

The Seashore

I walked along the beach today, alone.
Oblivious to little children about me,
Oblivious to the hour, the day, the month
Lost in a world of timelessness and turmoil!
Lost in feelings of depth and despair,
Empty of soul and substance as the seashell.
Uncontrollable emotions were drowning along the way.
Life was a struggle past reef and rock
A meaningless glob on the face of the Earth.

Then suddenly, like a baptism
Love gently lapped at my toes;
Sunshine gave warmth to the body
Sandpipers and gulls gave flight to my presence.
Conversations of sea-wonder evolved, discoveries along the shore.
Azure-blue skies, sails in the distance,
I became filled with newness and vitality,
Bathed in God's love, immersed in His presence.
I was not alone, I was alive!

Marjorie Meek Craig

The Artist

Three Graces, three Muses
One a Painter, One a Potter, One a Dancer
All come to say au revoir
To the artist supreme
Who wanted to be immortal

And he said "My paintings, my paintings"
"Why don't they see me in my paintings?"

They who inspired his vision
Three graces, three muses
Celebrated his art and amour
Fondly shared by committee

Two doors beckon for admission
"Artist Poet" Artist manque

The Eternal Arbiter
Is a fair judge
For the way we live
For the way we die

Sired by the three Graces, three Muses
In a concert of love
Redeemed in Purgatory

Ida Segal

Alone

Alone . . . I like being there . . . it gives me my space,
  it gives me my time . . . it is my own.
    Being alone!

Lonely . . . is having no one who cares . . . no future,
  just existence . . . day after day
    Year after year!

Alone . . . I crave it sometimes . . . my time to think
  my time to remember . . . my time to grow
    It is my own . . . being alone!

Lonely . . . is a depressing state . . . I try not to go there
  It makes me feel sad . . . it makes me feel helpless
    Year after year!

Alone . . . for me is a positive time . . . pleasing only myself
  I've had many years of going there
  I like to go there . . . being alone.

Lonely . . . is getting old to me . . . no one to share what I think about
  When I am alone . . . life shouldn't be like this
  So empty
  being on my own
  Alone!

Susan Winters

I Finally Realized

After all this time I've finally realized that I loved you.
I know it took so long and I'm sorry,
But this time I mean it so don't worry.
We can finally be together,
For now and forever.
All our problems are solved,
We can be together for one and all.
You and I are meant to be one,
My love for you weighs more than a ton.
Please don't be frightened from my love for you,
For I am still hoping that you love me too.
I have been depressed and weary,
Without you my life is dead and dreary.
I have cried and mourned so that someday we could be together.
Now here is my chance.
Finally we can be one forever.

Victoria C. Smith

Sullen Flag

We see the flag across the sky
Proudly speaking to us
And many are the ones who die,
While many act fallacious

Beyond reproach is our banner
And men and women who fight for her
Suffering in their muted tones
As the sun forever bleaches bones

Distant shores have seldom seen her
And when they do, freedom is often sure
I guess the real sadness resides
With our loved ones who've lost their lives

Oh, tri-colored cloth so softly weeping
Gather your chicks for their safe keeping
Warm our hearts, stay the freezing
For those who scoff are not through teething

Flying at half mast as they die
Moving solid men to ask why
So when questions of security arise
The protected suggest, "drink's at five?"

Michael Robert McCarthy

Felt Like A Woman

She had not, felt like a woman for so long.
She wanted to slip into a Frederick Bra.
A black lacy shelf, lifting up and parting her soft breasts,
Dressed like a lady on the outside,
Yet underneath lacy black on soft white skin,
Making her feel like a whore.
Her added weight bothered her some,
Yet! She felt she could make a man explode,
She like a lady of the night,
Black silky lace over her white skin,
Soft warm sweater rubbing exposed nipples,
Cold making them hard and protruding,
Tingling for a man's caress.
So long since she felt passion in the night.
Longing for warm hands stroking, clasping her,
Making her feel like a woman again.
Taken as a woman of the night,
Daytime treated like a lady.
Oh! Where would she find such a man.
That could make her explode with passion once again.

Madeline M. Queen

Will

In the cheat and heat he will think of a better field,
    And imagine a better yield.
A field where the crop is good and makes what it should.
    One thought will take him there like any working vision would.
The thought will come easy despite the dust of the field he's in,
    And he will grin as his sweat rains down without end.
He has seen life, and a hard life can be rich or poor.
    He will continue to try hard to make all the hard work mean more.

In the cheat and heat he will think of life.
    He will think of the kids, his dog, and his wife.
He will think of his mom and all she did for him all the years,
    And he will say thanks as the final terrace nears.
He will think of his dad and all the things he had to say,
    And he won't be able to think about a happier day.
In the cheat and heat this aging man will think hard it will seem,
    Only to find his life, a dream.

Vincent Shane Hesting

A Cry For Help

Did you ever really love someone
And know they didn't love you
Did you ever feel like crying
And think what good would it do
Did you ever see them walking with their head down low
Did you ever whisper I love you
But I'll never let you know
Did you ever look into their eyes
And say a little prayer
Did you ever look into their heart
And wish that you were there
Love is fine but hurts so much
The price you pay is so high
If I could choose between love and death
I think I'd rather die so when I say
Don't fall in love or you'll be hurt before you're through
You see my friend
I thought you knew that I fell in love
With you

Barbara Stowers

Continental Drift

That space in my life that I long for
Grows wider with each passing day.
Once would not fit a flea
'twixt a fault that now seems
A wide, percale, billowing sea.

That love of my life whom I live for,
Now rests on yon eiderdown shore,
And the cold coast that's me
Lines a smooth, icy, sheet
Where once was a tropic 'paree'.

That printed, patterned, 200 count water
Yawns treacherous; and should I dare cross?
Or avoid sirens' song,
Lest I sink 'neath it all
Should refusal be my new port of call?

That land called our earth is moving,
Growing closer, then farther apart.
And it's easy to see
Mother nature's Decree
Might apply to the bond known as "We."

Kim Shelton

Sky Bear and the Comet

It was during the time when the comet came
to visit Sky Bear that you went.

I was watching a not-so-bad
indian movie on T.V. and
beading a rosette,
blue like the sky,
red like the dawn,
black like the night,
round and round,
circling like the roundness of life.

The roundness of the bracelet you gave me came undone.
When it broke I knew you were going.
I tried to prepare myself.

This morning there is
frost on the grass and
I sing the morning song
in my car on the way to work and

I know that, like Sky Bear,
you have circled away from me and away from our light
that was bright and brief as the comet.

Elizabeth Blue Turtle

Free

Black black is all I see
   Yet I know the sun shines
    and the grass is green
I run until there is no longer a path
   and on this unpaved road I move
   Till I leap off reality and spread wings
Here I soar higher than consciousness itself
   gliding through space that has no time
Looking down on Sister Earth
   blue and brown so pale and bare
   To many humans a poor sad lair
It was among the cooling stars somewhere
   that I forgot my skin my outer layer
The sun bleeds and in Her blood my soul danced
   Round and around on this galaxy I pranced
Breaking free of my old delusions
   crash and collide into that cosmic revolution
Freed from tribulations of existence society and self free
   Breath deep Mother Universe breath deep I'm free
     Prescilla Acuna

A Thought

Where I was wrong?
Where did I not stop?
Or is it just a thought telling me . . .
   just go on.

My life will be complete
when I go on too deep
to dig the best out of me.
For the best in me
is the reflection of the best in you
The love and
happiness given to me.

It is sad for those
who can not love
for they never experience
anything out side their being.
     Wasima E. Alvi

The "I AM"

Precious JESUS! Love Divine!
Redeemer of this soul of mine.
Almighty in power — the great "I AM" is He.
I am the Way, the Truth, the Life. No one comes unto the Father,
but by Me.
Sing unto the Lord — rejoice in Him, always.
Everlasting life with Christ Jesus, is our hope and stay.

HE IS ALIVE! Alleluia to our risen Lord.
In thankfulness and gratitude, let us rejoice with one accord —
Majesty, honor, glory, and praise, be unto our Savior and King
   adored.
     Ethel L. Voelker

Father's Day

I can remember when I was a girl,
I made my Dad cards with flowers and swirls.
He'd open and read them, hug me and say;
"They're wonderful Dear, surely none can compare."

But now I am older and much wiser too,
I no longer make cards out of paper and glue.
I show him my love through obedience and trust
and I know if I need him he'll always be there.

My Dad is a strong man so loving and kind,
If I searched the whole world not another could I find;
So Dad on this Father's Day it's my turn to say;
"You're Wonderful Dad, surely none can compare."
     Liane Spain Nicol

Salutations Of War

The prickly paired fangs of damnation's fate has spirited its
   venomous treachery at the flesh of those that do.

The influenced tumble down the cobble-stoned causeway of moral
   defecation, bleeding to the pit of the master of disaster.

Soldiers of sense clang away at the silkened threads of deceit
   sweating tears at
the thought of so few who lack the heavy metal needed to crack
   the skull of sordid serpentry.

Hazed muses blue the skyline as the souls of the silent servants of sin prism,
   crackle and explode in bell tolled concert to the symphony of death.

Dreams of wild horses roam desert's cavalcade of destruction so, monk's of
   ministry mirage the oasis of the meek in a stampede of heralded mortality.

Crucified victory and rituraled defeat hang in the balance of infinity's vortexed
   battlefield — greetings and salutation to all men!
     Orrin Keith Loftin

Love Is

Love is not a place or time or thing
Love is the joy a smile can bring
Love is God's peace though your heart cries
Love is the starlight in your eyes
Love finds a way through joys and sorrows
Love fills all yesterdays, now and tomorrows
Love lives in hearts, in souls and emotions
Memories, plans and deep devotions
Love is strong, gentle and kind
Love is a stabilizer that does not bind
Love never pretends wears no disguise
Love is deeper than oceans higher than skies
Love is the Christ in you and me
Love is the truth that sets us free
Love breaks the barriers of fear and distrust
Love gives us courage to do what we must
Love it the balm that paves the way
Love is the faith you find when you pray
Love is all this and even more
Love is the key that unlocks any door.
     Pearl N. Sorrels

'Tis Spring

'Tis Spring and flowers are blooming everywhere.
Tulips, Iris, Daffodils, and many more here and there.
It looks like a huge rainbow of color and hue.
Every color in sight — red, yellow , purple, and blue.

God made these little breaths of spring to enjoy.
Most of them are plucked by a small girl or boy.
Taking them to their mommies with pride.
With a smile on their faces; poseys behind their backs they hide.

They hand them to Mommy and say —
"A flower for you, Mommy, what a beautiful day?"
How can they resist a hug and a kiss,
When they say something as precious as this?

Did you ever wonder what the little flowers would say?
If you asked them,"How is your day?"
Why they'd answer you and say, "My day is just fine;
God made me, and I'm one of a kind."

No two are alike, each different in some way —
Many may look alike, but God would say,
"I made each of you different and not alike;
You're just like people; different, even their psyche."
     Carolyn M. Wilson

The Pleasure Of Your Smile

I waft deeply in the pleasure of your smile
It treats me like a gentle breeze
On a hot and sultry summer day
As a rainbow peers aft' endless rain
And clouds fast fade away

I'll store it in that special place
Down deep within my brain
When things go wrong, I can't erase,
To recall it once again

Memories are made, you see,
From moments such as this
A smile can be as gentle
As a lovers well — placed kiss.

Blondine Louise Reddick

Dusk Of Selfishness

By this early spring morning
Where the sun is still in shadow,
The silence makes me feel the immensity.
The singing birds light up this consciousness:
I am fully a part of this nature.
The desire to escape
creates all the misery of our life.

Gapless is the space
Between life and death.
There's just life
Which each moment
Falls into oblivion
For an eternal life of renewal.

Only harmless action
Brings fulfillment in our daily life.
Without overture
Just an ego movement
To preserve the little we have seized.

Spaceless open-mindness
Is where love bursts forth.

Alain Bechard

Time

The amount of time we all have got
May seem to many as not a lot.
Some have more and some have less
And we all want more than we have, I guess.
Now the fundamental issue is how to spend it
And we can do a lot to really amend it.
When you hear people say they're just "killing time"
Tell them smelling the roses and admiring the sky
Will help them find out that time does not die.

Jeannette Frantz

White

White are the angels high in the sky,
White is a harsh cold wintery sigh.
White can be the clouds passing by,
White is a person saying my my.

White is the sound of paper ripping,
White is the sound of water dripping.
White is the sound of something growing,
White is the sound of some thing flowing.

White is the color of heaven,
White is the special color to mention.
White is a spring moth,
White is the feeling of a silky, soft cloth.

Justin Emery

Serenade's End

There was once a time not long ago I met a young woman,
Together we played a song that was as sweet as honey and smooth as glass.
The notes were always on key and never sour.
We played together for many years,
The sounds we made I never was quite able to remember them alone,
However when we were together it all seemed to come naturally.
Once when I was a young woman I met a man that forever changed my life.
Never before was I able to play songs and melodies of these sorts,
for the reason that
when I was with him my heart was alive and filled with love.
I closed my eyes one day and he was gone,
The music stopped and the sweet sounds died around me,
Yet I never forgot just how we were together.
When we were young we each met a person that made our lives whole.
Sounds that we ne'er heard before were played.
His love for me, my love for him has in no way died.
But the sounds that we made together have.
The sweet sound of honey has gone sour,
The smoothness of glass is shattered,
and we are both alone in a deathly quiet world.

Ismeil Abu-khdeir

Snow

Snow . . . snow . . . snow,
Fall gently, forcefully, whirling and swirling,
From the skies the unrelenting wind will blow
Your delicate patterns all around us
In this season called winter.

We are awed by your beauty at season's first
When we awake and find a burst
Of the most beautiful crystals dressed in white
You bring out the youth in all who delight
In this season called winter!

Oh quickly, come, build Mr. Snowman with his magical gait
Why, indeed, we could build him a mate
And when the chill in the air does our rosy cheeks make
Indoors we will scamper hot chocolate awaits
In this season called winter!

Isn't it grand, this time of year
When the fresh snows fly in the wind chilled air?
Soon, we know, the winter will end
But not before many happy days do descend
On the Families and friends who cherish and love . . . winter!

Patricia Akey

Lost Summer

From my hospital window
Through misty, feverish eyes I see,
Green shaded patches and far-away hills.

Though my brow and body are beaded with sweat
My mind wanders about in half delirium wondering
if this wounded soul will ever again have the
strength of the eagle soaring and undulating in
that cloud visited sky.

Doctors and nurses hovering about in a haze
Faint murmurings I can't quite piece together
It would be so easy to just close my eyes and be gone

But I mustn't, I have to hang on,
What an injustice for those who shed tears for me.

I have to grab the strings of life,
I have to hold on
I cannot let go
I have to be strong.

Yolanda Porras Lopez

"Celebrate Life"

I celebrate Tommy, I sing myself.
I ponder my life and what makes it worth living.
My friends and family are all a part of me.

I sit, and remember the past.
Memories and times almost forgotten,
Tucked carefully away in the back of my mind.

I sit, and think of the present.
Of what my life has become,
Of the joy and sorrow of everyday life.

I sit, and imagine the future.
Myself five, twenty, fifty years ahead.
Will be I alive, dead, happy, or sad,
Or will it even matter to me.

I sit, and as the future becomes the present and the present the past,
I think of my life and what it is worth to me.
I celebrate my life, I sing myself.

Tommy Adams

Mirror In A Box

A signal of light has appeared in my sky
As I leaf through old poems that no one would buy
I must have some jewel — some thought for the age
A capsule of wisdom in a twenty-line cage
"One" only one boldly written in caps
Instruction for entry and time to elapse
I sort through my pages and see my obsessions
Dramatically long-winded, purging confessions
My heart broken sonnets all drunken and cursed
New love and rosebuds resound the reverse

This one is manic — called "suicide line"
One that the words never bothered to rhyme
Birthdays and get wells for friends of the day
All put to verse in my vintage old way
Now at my "Robert Frost" fork in the road
My own Gitcheegoomee shore to unfold
Listen my children and you will see me
Relentlessly seeking my Annabellee
Thanks for the wake-up call so high tech
This contest provided my thousand mile check

Dolores Cortese Molaf Adamsky

My Reason For Writing Poems

If I may brighten up someone's life,
by some of the things I say.

If I could just help make someone
smile, even make someone's day.

I use humor, people, some animals, and
even things, and places far and near.

In doing this I may touch someone, make someone
happy and some may even shed a joyful tear.

I will not write of race, color, and
I do not believe in discrimination.

I believe in God, all people equal, we should love
one another, help each other, in this great nation.

I write religious poems. I really believe
this helps their heart, their soul and their mind.

This I do in appreciation, for knowing
it will last us for all time.

When reading these poems, don't think of me,
think of happiness, and love, this will be a lift.

Go through each day, helping people, making
people happy, and this will be our gift.

Ronald L. Cloud

As One

The sun will always shine,
  even when I frown.
The rain will always stop,
  even when my tears continue flowing.
The night will always come to an end,
  even when my sadness stays.
The flowers will always bloom,
  even when I wish myself a child.
Spring will always follow winter,
  even when love doesn't follow loneliness.
The world and I are similar,
  changing minute by minute.
In our hearts we are one,
  though different we may be.
Hold Hands as you walk through life,
  use your heart to see;
See the beauty in everything,
  see me in you as I see you in me.

Andrea Robidoux

"Amandinus"

Let me sleep inside your mind,
I'll interpret your dreams.
I'll whisper to you if you're still alive,
And solve your internal mysteries.

Let me be your Amandinus,
The author to your life.
The answers to your questions.
The truth behind your lies.

Mysticism plays its role,
And the stones all look the same,
Except I, who wears the Amandinus stone,
And knows the significance of your name.

Do not crucify my existence,
For I know what you read on the inside.
Yes, I, who wears the Amandinus,
Can tell the stories you hide.

Jill A. Hoff

Loneliness Turned For The Better

Now I am lonelier than ever. I see nothing
coming my way. My life begins to show no meaning,
because of loneliness I feel inside. I hide from my
friends in fear that they would find that I have
the loneliness for a companion in my life. But as I
come from my hiding place to be with my friends.
They I find have a companion, and they pity me for
not having a companion, so I laugh in their face and
quickly run to my hiding place. Were a young man
comes to my rescue. For he has seen me running to this
so called hiding place of mine, and in fearing for my danger
swept me away in his arms and kissed me. But it
did not stop there for I had found a companion
right for life and loneliness had been swept away and
in its place stood love.

Brandi Dougherty

Beauty Beyond

Pink sky laced with ribbons of white,
Songs of dawn echoing through the trees,
Warm breezes that bring forth the smells of yesteryear,
Darkness fading into the birth of all that is new,
Nature embracing its purest moment,
Mists of dew gently showering earth's beauty,
Blankets of delicate freshness lightly draping the flowers' rainbow,
Inner peace lies within the serenity of creation in its waking emotion.

Wendy A. Jones

"Another Soldier! . . . Coming Home!"

There will be angel's of the Almighty — whom shall gather around
his soldiers! And present them before the King! When these soldier's
leave this world and make that journey home to heaven! And these
same shall hear! "Another Soldier! . . . Coming Home!" . . .
"Everyone! . . . Get ready!" . . . "Here he (she) comes! . . .
"Welcome!" "We are glad that you are here! . . . We are glad
that you are home! And those angel's gathered about! Shall
assist him (her) around! And bring that soldier as well before!
To see and to meet the King! And all of the
pain and all of the tears! Be there any found! Shall as well be
healed! And wiped away for good! And for these soldier's there shall
be! Found no more sorrow any longer! And he (she) shall be given —
either new orders! Or another way of life! Given riche's and a mansion!
On behalf of his pain and suffering! And for standing; . . .
"First! and foremost! "Beside and for 'the Almighty God' of heaven!
And before the King every soldier's knee shall bow! And give praise!
. . . Glory! And thanks! — To the King for receiving him (her)!
And for the forgiveness of his (her) sins! And to the "Almighty"
For eternal life! — "These are the orders! And these shall stand!" . . .
"In God's name and his majesty! . . . The King!"

Paula S. Ridolfo/USNR-IRR

Salute To Spring

Now, Spring is just around the corner from us,
Sometimes we even feel its warming breath,
In the still of the night if we would listen
We'd sense the sap moving up in the trees;
There is a mystic ocean 'neath our feet, on which the flow'rs are now sailing,
The crocus and other sweet-looking blooms will soon reach port
— our very eyes! We'll see the flow'rs, and hear a myriad of birds
Singing their songs of gratefulness to God,
And if we went to the hills or the mountains,
We'd hear the streams sing out their Spring fresh songs!
Our world puts on a grand celebration — A feast on sights that
dance on sounds; it's time to dress the heart in gratefulness
To thank our God whose world this is!

Thank Him for all the people whom we have known —
They've been the soil of our cultivation
Thank Him deeply for having called us His own —
We couldn't have made it alone on our own!
Thank Him deeply for the renewal of our world —
The celebration he provides, the resurrection that he is to us,
Though we would die, yet we shall live!

Joy P. Anciano

The Wall

It was in the Spring of 89,
When I first saw the Vietnam Wall.
I lingered, looking at the names
for those I served with, whose
names are framed for the eternal roll call.

As I gaze upon the wall,
I see my buddies name,
and memories, now do linger on,
of that day, he gave his all.

I shouted, screamed and cursed myself,
Why, Lord, did Robert die,
When I did promise, his Mom and Pop,
He'd always be with me, at my side.

Now I kneeled, down in prayer,
thoughts of times gone by,
When I felt someone squeeze my shoulder,
as I look and see, a Motorcycle Policeman,
looking down at me. I understand he said
to me, for I was there and do believe.

Stephen D. Pommer

Friendship

I thank you my friend for being there for me
at times when I needed the company

You came into my life when I was down
and I am happy you're still around

In times of anger you choose to see
only the good that is in me

You overlook many things that I do
and make me realize our friendship is true

All you want is a hug now and then
I thank you for this my Feline friend

Kathy Herne

"Thirty Plus One"

The sky did shimmer with moon full and bright
The stars diamond lights lit up the night.
But, wee hearts were heavy with a great sadness
Absent of smiles and anything of gladness.

The lady they referred to as their mother
Closed the door — walking out on sis and brother.
The tiny souls were overflowing with fear
That far away night of thirty plus one year.

Up the long and winding, landscaped drive
Drove in a truck complete with bees and a hive.
Peering eyes searching through mucky glass
Was a gray-haired, wrinkled-faced elderly lass

Showing missing teeth with grin from ear to ear
Said, "Come here hon — it's been thirty plus one year."
"Is it her, could it be true?" Says brother
"Open your heart for the return of mother."

Patricia A. King

"Without God"

I hope I never get to the place
In life when I am to myself
I want to be humble always
For if I am to myself there's no place for God,
I shall always need Jesus to
work himself in me!

All else is self destruction,
To be without God is truly lost;
A life without is hurt, pain
I've chosen to like, never to part again;
I'm not ashamed to acknowledge
my trust friend!
I now know true love;
He has accepted me once again...

Bernetta Green

Faith

Faith gives hope in troubled times
    to bring to order what went out of line
Faith gives love that comes from the heart
    to lift you up when life falls apart
Faith gives confidence to get you through the night
    to wake up restored facing the new light
it strives to keep our heads held high
    knowing when to laugh and when it's okay to cry
Faith comforts you in your time of need
    when we are lost it's there to lead
Faith means holding firm in your ideas
    and fighting for what's right through smiles and tears
Faith means trusting something seeming so unreal
    that your true self one day may reveal

Barbara Webb

A Memory Lives Inside Our Soul

A memory live's inside our soul
It's printed there for the heart to see
Ever lasting ever present the memory will always be.

When love is lost or goes away
The memory of it is here to stay
I shut my eyes and see your face
I feel you holding me in a warm embrace

Every where I look every thing I see
Reminds me of what use to be
I really thought we had it all
I wasn't prepared for the fall

So you go your way and I will go mine
We will travel different paths
Other arms will hold us close
Other loves will come in time
One thing I am certain of your memory is mine

A memory lives inside our soul
It's printed there for the heart to see
Ever lasting ever present the memory will always be

Naoma J. DeWitt

"Thoughts"

I sit upon a pile of trash and watch as robberies, murders and rapes go on around me.

I take a walk in the park, but the hard broken concrete path hurts my feet.

I take a deep breath of fresh air, only to feel my lungs burn. I begin to cough due to the toxic fumes from near by factories and over crowed freeways.

I go down to the lake to relax from a hard day at work, reproducing generic copies of stolen thoughts. Yet even here I receive no solitude, as bloated dead fish float past my feet, surrounded by a green foam, atop a black sludge film on undrinkable water.

Our justice system failed, our values warped and morals diminished. I think to myself . . .

Thank God I'm In America.

Lary R. Blodgett

On Eagles Wings

You walked through the water and through the flames,
I bare you child upon eagles wings.

I am your stay and supplier today,
I'll walk right beside you each and every day.

Some days you'll trod where you've never been

But
I will uphold you through thick and through thin.
My Holy Spirit is with you to teach and to guide,
You are always in the center of my eye.

I will keep thee as the apple of mine eye.

Do not be afraid of their terror you see,
I shall deliver thee quick with no sorrows to be.

I am your Almighty God,
forever to be.

I am thy shield and exceeding great reward,
Love and Adore me,

I am thy Reward

Linda Ramey

Fighting Spirit

Every step I take is with my head held high,
And my sword upright,
Always moving ahead without fear,
Doing everything I think is right.

There is no one to stop me,
And nothing that can come in my way,
I'm inching towards my goal,
Regardless of any obstacles that in my path lay.

In one of arms, I hold a weapon that can destroy my enemy,
And my other arm is always ready to hold,
And embrace those who are friendly.
I do no wrong, so I expect no wrong unto me.

I'll be always fighting against the evil
That I may or may not see
Even if someone kills me, my sword will be still held high,
'Cause it won't be me but my body that will die.

Gulrukh Irani

The Beauty Of A Rose

Rose petals soft as kitten's fur
In silence almost seem to purr
An invitation: Stop, behold
This beauty fine as precious gold.

So delicate a rose in bud,
How could it grow in thick black mud?
Exquisite daintiness from dirt
One Power alone could thus convert!

But lovelier still a rose in bloom,
A single flower transforms a room,
Extending from a slender vase,
Epitome of fragile grace.

A dozen roses in bouquet,
Like glowing coals, merge, one sachet
Whose fragrance sweet, distinct and clear
Pervades surrounding atmosphere.

Wherever found in Nature's scheme,
A rose remains a joy supreme,
Reflecting, as a jewel rare,
Its Maker's beauty beyond compare.

Mildred Becker

Searching

Searching, the flow of life,
Without which and its goals,
Aimlessly, we would wander.
A life without meaning.

We search for belonging.
We search for riches and pleasure.
We search for peace and freedom.
We search for justice and fairness.

Above all, we need love.
Let us not search elsewhere,
For all other search is centered in self.

Without Love, self is incomplete,
For the goal of Love is, completion of self.
Joined in Love, all else is found.

Thus, search for Love.
And when found,
Love!

John Nevshemal

"Thoughts"

A face so ashamed —
whose analytical criticism
shakes the world.

With each mighty blow
the mementos of familiarity are crushed,
overthrown by a new sinister anarchy.

Shall it rise above the depths of evil?

Will it take off its unthinkable mask
and become again the passionate flower it once was?

I see the face of familiarity —
I see the desperate smile ready for a return.

I feel the embrace —
a resemblance of some kind memory has just blown through me.

Lauri McElveen

The Lion, The Leopard, The Cheetah

Lion is a big, powerful cat.
Wouldn't if be interesting if he had a hat.
But someone might knock it off with a bat.
But he might be too fat because he eats all that meat.

There's a leopard cat, a leopard frog, a leopard seal.
To reveal a leopard cat, you would die
Cause it might attack.

Cheetah has slender legs.
But he might step on a blender and go around
And end up in a playground.
He might try to eat a child, but he could go mild.
He really needs to go back to the wild.

Jessica Muñoz

Not As Helpful As A Hug

The grass was green upon the hill,
Where the lady went to get away from her bills.
She couldn't stand it anymore,
That's it! She yelled as she kicked down the door.
Everybody looked and stared,
But nobody really cared.
She headed for the hill where the grass was green.
She couldn't understand why the people were so mean.
Upon the hill as she knelt,
She prayed to the almighty one for just a little help.
Near dark, she made her way back to her house,
Which lived with her thousands of roaches and a mouse.
She walked in and what did she see on the floor.
A pile of money and her broken door.
She looked up to her ceiling and said, "Thank you very much."
There came a whispered reply, "You're welcome, but it's not as helpful as a hug"

Athena Hamilton

In Your Presence

When I stand In Your Presence there are no words in any language in the world that can express the feelings and emotions that I feel toward you, In Your Presence.

There are more feelings of frustration, distraughtness, and anxiety that grip me because I can not adequately express my feeling due you while I am In Your Presence.

But to stand in awe In Your Presence and give you honor for who you are, is the only expression without words that I can express a beauty to behold In Your Presence.

You are a beauty to behold in your presence.

Paul Lucia

Dance Therapy

Crazy girl, pretending rhyme,
dancing on the winds of another time;
searching she knows not where,
then hiding amid the clouds.
Magically born in a dream,
tragically lost in a dream.
No matter where she roams
she stands in desperate music bound;
spinning round, wildly dancing down.
Waking, slowly waking...
wholly breathing in the morning.
Sweet distant music entwines enchanted visions
and softly veils the afterglow of inspiration.
Crazy girl, pretending time,
dancing on the wings of another rhyme.
No matter where she roams,
she stands in desperate music bound
to dance alone;
just to dance alone.

Amy Metal

"There's A Grave"

There's a grave, I go see and in that grave you're sleeping you're still part of me.
I place flowers there with love from my heart.
And sometimes. I ask myself why we had to part only God knows the answer and someday he'll tell me for I belong to you and you belong to me.
They say once in a life time a true love is borned and I know you are mine and I know I was yours and I can hear the preacher say till death do you part as we said I do it came straight from the heart and some look at a grave with death on their mind and in that grave I see you resting for only a time and some day I will join you for it's God's will to be then will be together forever to be.

Helen Gray

Untitled

Your earth-toned arms,
with such power and grace
will get no chance
to hold one in a strong embrace.

My runny nose will never be wiped
nor my excuse for absence ever be typed.

You conceived me dear mother
before you were wed
you made your decision
now your only child is dead.

Linda Lewis-Everett

The Gunfight

The warm breeze blew the dust into the air
But still could not effect the cold harsh stare
Clicks of the spurs could slowly be heard
But other than that there wasn't a word
One could see the fear in the two men's eyes
And feel the pain of the women's mournful cries
they stood there staring at each other's face
neither wanting to die in mortal disgrace
and as the guns are drawn and the hammers cocked back
from the barrel comes the thunderous clap
and when he is struck by the fiery hot lead
in one last breath he is dead
and the victor rides away feeling proud and strong
until a faster challenge comes along

Matthew P. Owens

Faces Of Death

Death looks us in the eye
    different for many.

A face of kindness if met timely?
A face of peace if met after affliction?
A face of shock if met accidentally?
A face of regret if met intentionally?
A face of alarm if met prematurely?
A face of horror if met brutally?

A combination of
    kindness and horror
    peace and regret
    shock and alarm   or
a mirror image?

It appalls yet entices.
What face will be met?

Whom to tell if I'm right.
Diane F. Dobrolski

A Mother

Wherever you go and whatever you do she'll always
    cherish her love for you,
It's in a smile, a nod of the head, a gentle touch
    or a tear she's shed;
It's in her forgiving, her anger too and everything
    she's done for you.
The good times and bad times, the sickness and hurt;
    the heartaches and failures we all can relate.
Sweet tender moments when she hugged you so tight,
    covered you up and kissed you good night.
She sacrificed much and made choices too, so our
    dreams and wishes could all come true.
As time went by she watched you grow, always at your side,
Never complaining but always yearning for the child
    she loved with pride.
It doesn't matter who she is or whatever it is she does,
    she's just a mother like any other who is blessed by
God above.
David M. Oster

"Memorial Day"

I am trapped in a refrigerator box
Frozen in space
Stifled in 1:4 time
My life made invalid by your absence

There is a peephole in the box
And every time I look out I see you
Every time every time
And I see your life going on going on

I see an outside world
Where children grow
And adults forget, and I watch
I watch through a fog of sadness

And granite heavy regrets
Through I strain my vision and I strain my muscles
To glimpse you as you drift away from me
I watch through the peephole

As you finally disappear in the distance and time goes on no more
Everything, every thing becomes just waiting
Waiting for you to come back
are you coming back.
Gerald Matteson

Ashborn

The first four hundred years,
nested in scented leaves,
crested in gold, reddened, redolent,
she roosted in her piney tower crowing
crow-crow-crow-crowing
or woohing like the mourning dove
wooh   wooh   woohhh.
She crowed and woohed and fluttered;
got, even, sometimes unboughed.
The first four hundred years.

Then ashes started burning down
down in the deepy down
and the nest slowly — oh! so slowly —
the roosted Phoenix nest took fire
(a yellow burning under the dark)
and up she went: all four hundred years of her up.

Now five hundred years old she finds the ozone pure
in the high altar of sun rises and sun spices
and her feathers never have ever looked better,
singed only slightly from her flight with fire.
Mary Aswell Doll

Our Wedding Toast

Now that, our bright future, we're planning,
    with hope and anticipation,
May we give thanks for what we have in each other,
    with much appreciation.
May we always be compassionate,
    and sensitive to each other's needs.
May we always treat each other with respect,
    with love, and trust, and by deeds.
May we feel, long after we're married,
    as happy and in love as when
We first set eyes on each other,
    that day — remember back then?
May we always be supportive of each other,
    and when we live our married life,
May we stay together until we're old,
    and never experience strife.
May we pray to receive special blessings
    from the Good Lord up above.
May we live our lives in harmony,
    in happiness, and in love.
Irene Andrighetti Dietz

Time

When I was young and small
Time hardly moved at all
Will Xmas ever get here?
It seems almost like a year.
Where is the snow? Summer was so long ago
    Time goes so slow
The years pass by, I meet this guy
He's young and fun-calls me "Babe"
I don't want to be an old maid.
If I wait till 28 I'm sure it will be too late.
    Time goes so slow.
The babies come one, two, three
Joyous and painful-the moments be
Four, five, six come along too
No time to think or even be blue
And now I'm sixty-five
Where did all the time fly?
Precious time slow down a bit
I have much to do before I quit
    Time goes so fast
Marjorie L. Heinrichs

Coming Back

Being young isn't always the easiest thing to do.
It's a time of trials and learning all about you.
But for some reason maybe you just don't care.
You beat yourself up because life just isn't fair.
So you do what everyone else in your position does.
You go out alone trying your hardest to catch a little buzz.
It takes you where you want to go, but only for a little while
You come back exhausted because you feel like you've traveled
thousands of miles.
Where did you go? What did you see?
Was that you I heard trying to call out to me?
What did you do while you were up there all alone?
Why didn't you speak out and make yourself known?
You missed a lot while you were gone all those years.
It's time to be brave now and face all your fears.
It won't be that bad if you avoid your old ways.
Don't fall into that trap that will lead you back into a daze.
Being alone is something that shouldn't bother you anymore.
Now that I'm here let's show everyone the surprises you have
kept in store.

Alex Gonzalez

Nature

I was on the river of rocks and sand,
of mountains and trees,
the minnows and tadpoles and fishes,
you'll see, going down their river stream.

The sun will touch, the mountain tops.
The birds will sing, upon the tree tops
the frogs will sit upon lily pads.
And snakes will crawl upon the ground,
rabbits and squirrels roam the land,
from earth and sky, nature begins.

Richard Clubb

Untitled

Many years have past and we still bear the emptiness of a life lost
   from our grasp
Beauty turns to sorrow, the futures race past
A bitter desire, a dream, reality; shall we dare ask?
A misplaced image of you gazing through frosted glass
We've grown old, our youth lying in the shadows cast
We walk this road only to part like the fork in a path
And off in the distance muffled a familiar old laugh

Kevin Wayne Cookemboo

Oh My Beloved

The way you make me feel is unlike that I have ever known.
The touch of your hand and the softness of your kiss
Makes my heart overflow with passions that make me glow.

You put a spring in my step and make everything look anew.
Before you came into my life, I never knew dreams could come true.
When love has finally found you, there is nothing you can do.
Oh my love . . .
How lucky I am to have found you.

Nevertheless, I do wish for you to know that I truly care
And that you are my only one.
The kindness of your heart and the sweetness of your smile,
Makes me feel like a bird
Whose flight has just begun.

Oh my love,
Words could not fully express the way I truly feel.
But always know that I will forever love you
Through the thick and the thin.

Sharah T. Horton

Our Home

Our Home
   is a peaceful corner in life's tumult
   where we can rest at the close of day.

Our Home
   is our fortress from all the cares of the world
   and our shelter when plans go astray.

Our Home
   is a place of love and special comfort
   when we have days of grief and stress.

Our Home
   is filled with love, hope, laughter and security
   where our friends and family find sweet happiness.

Our Home
   is contentment and warm peace of mind
   with two hearts and minds entwining as one.

Our Home
   is where kind thoughts and prayers guide us
   from early morning until God's day is done.

Jane Johnson

The Music Man

Dedicated to Ben Pitt, 8/20/95
His music may be gone;
but his lovely tunes, still lingers on.
Oh, that man could play.
Sometimes, he would blow that horn, all night and day.

He could hit the low notes;
and, he could hit the high notes;
and all the notes in between.
He was like a good tailor, stitching a perfect seam.

When he picked up that horn;
he couldn't put it down, until the crowd was on its feet.
He would play, and play, and play;
without rest, or missing a beat.

When, the music man's, final note was played;
it was a very, very sad day.
But, we need not worry, or to ask why.
Because, he is up there, with the great one;
who rules the deep blue sky.

David J. Smalls

Screen Door

Just remembering that rickety old wooden
   screen door, and the shape it had been.

Sagging and paintless, with screen full
   of holes, to let the flies out and in.

We would slam it shut, in from our
   day of school.

Mom asked if we were born in a barn;
   for slamming doors, she had a rule.

Twenty times in and out, counted a loud;
   perhaps you'd remember next time.

To come and go quietly, and dare
   not repeat, this mortal crime.

Years have passed, the house torn down;
   mother left us long ago.

What brought back these memories
   of days gone by, I just don't know.

Carol M. Powell

"March 2nd"

My dear Son, I'm so proud
  of the man you've become,
It doesn't seem that long
  since you were so small and young.

I worried so much before
  you came into this life,
If it was right to bring you
  into a world so full of strife.

I was so afraid and uncertain
  of our life ahead,
But decided not to worry and
  just prayed to God instead.

Then on a beautiful Sunday morn,
  You decided it was time to be born.
And when I held you in my arms that night,
  I knew then that nothing could be more right!

I thank God always,
  when I pray,
I thank him for the great son,
  he gave me that day.
    Sandi Lima

If

If you could have stayed here with me,
My life could have been so much simpler.
If you could have won the battle,
so many hearts wouldn't have been broken.
If you could have shared with us,
there wouldn't have been so many unanswered questions.
If you could have only said goodbye,
there wouldn't be so many quiet moments and sad eyes.
If God didn't love you so much,
He would have shared you with me so much longer.
If and if and if
If I could have been more understanding and more patient,
I could have been stronger for you.
If I ever fall in love again,
will I ever be able to love like I loved you?
If someone falls in love with me,
will they make me as happy as you did?
If I give my heart away,
I know you'll always be in it —
for you were my best friend — you were "My Hero."
    Kate Barreca

Little Boys

Burdock, mud and grass stains,
an unidentifiable room when it rains,
wall to wall, games and toys,
there is no doubt that they are little boys.

Snowball fights and building snow forts
sliding, building "Frosty" and sorts,
little boys climbing tree's,
wiping the tears because of skinned knee's.

Soap in the eyes from shampoo
get a wash clothe quick, to make it like new.
In come snakes, worms and ugly bugs,
but don't forget "I love you mommy" and group hugs.

Torn shirts, patched up jeans,
"Awe, mom. Do I have to eat the beans?"
"Don't forget to brush your teeth."
"Wash your hands before you eat."

They say their prayers, you tuck them in,
it is bedtime, you think with a grin!
"Aren't they cute, my sleepyheads?"
They look like angels tucked in their beds.
    Tina Spaulding

"Love Hurts"

The love I have for you is strong; Yet I feel so weak
How the earth revolves around me
Though it seems it's staying still
I say these words; For I only care
You have to understand
Listen very carefully
And to use all your strength so you will be strong
Though you can use your strength to tell me so
But if you're too weak and will not try
Then I will keep on speaking till death do us come
And when it happens
I hope you will listen and be strong
And for me to tell my love that is so strong
    Melissa Maloney

Ohio Landscape, Winter

Snow whirls like tufts of the Pharaoh's hair
before his sarcophagus was sealed.

The Waffle House outside Columbus
is open 24 hours.

Farmhouses are bruised and naked
behind their gray shingles.

Trucks stop at liquor stores
their drivers frail and poker-faced.

They have voices, too.
They are trying to explain everything.
    Ira Shull

The Lonely Heart

I come to you each morning with hopes and dreams
I hope you will care and understand me
For my nights were short and filled with tears
Everyone was busy doing their thing
For tomorrow will be better
You will lift my spirits
You will build me up, cause I'm down
I was just lonely and had many fears
Fear that I was not loved, loved by no one
No one at all
"Just eat your dinner, watch T.V. and get out of my way"
For no one knows what I have to do for you tonight (teacher)
For I did net tell, I told no one at all.
    Paula Costen

Love Is Like The Ocean

How can you explain a hurt,
that runs so far and deep inside?
You can laugh and smile,
but the crying doesn't subside.
To me, it's like the ocean,
which seems so blue and clear.
But when you go down deep,
it's full of darkness and fear.
It seems like it goes on forever,
that the happiness would never end.
But then you reach the shore of reality,
that sometimes isn't a friend.
But after every ocean, there's a lake,
which eventually runs into a stream.
So, I pray for you the pain will lessen,
and maybe soon it won't be so extreme.
    Michelle Ann Rogers

Gone Away

Once you called my name, I always answered the same way
As I did before, but now you've gone away

I always see your face, it's always in the same place
But now you're gone, and its been oh so long

When you came to me and said you were leaving me
I really could not see what was supposed to be

Now you are gone, oh so far away
And you are gone, never to come home again

And when you said to me that you wanted to be free
That having a family was not for you anymore

You were gone, oh so far away
And you were gone, never to come home again

Then when you came to me and said you'd been wrong
That life had shown you what I knew all along

The children have all grown, gone their separate ways
Father time has strayed, no more years to save

I said you're gone, and its been oh so long
And you are gone, never to come home again
Now you're gone

Mark E. Andrews

Lines On Paper

Burning tears from my heart leave
me restless within the darkness of
the night. They soak the pillow.
My mind tumbles "regain control,
regain control" I am unable.

The clock ticks upon the far wall
exhaustion seeps into my mind into
my soul, slip deeper, deeper into
sleep the tears eventually stop
they wait for another day.

Lightning flashes, thunder rumbles
within my dreams, tossing and turning
nightmares that became reality cause
me to cry out, no one hears, no one
ever heard that little girl I once was.

Pen to paper became my salvation, my
sanity. Poetry, Gods gift to me. The
years have been long although I am young
I pray, someday I'll get an answer,
Lines on paper, scars from the heart.

Jennifer Baughman

"Of Times Gone By"

Passionate, elusive thoughts pervade my being.
They creep slowly, very slowly, as the night air beckons for the
peaceful serenity that befits the twilight hours.
I yearn for the comfort that it brings; for I am troubled,
yes, deeply troubled, and my soul seeks for tenderness that
only he could bring (me). As I gaze aimlessly at the
quiet still of yet another restless day that has climaxed
into night, the hint of his passionate kiss bespeaks it all.
My mind now drifts, to the times that we shared together.
Those intimate, undisturbed moments that left me breathless,
in awe of his being, (yes), of his very existence. What he
meant to me, and what he is now, is but a distant memory.
Silence now kisses the baby fresh dawn of a new day's
presence. All traces of the preceding night are but a
charming, yet ever-present testimonial that knows
NO BOUNDS!

Denise Dudley-Ruffin

I Cry For You

I set here wondering — what should I do
As I hear johnny — beating up on you

You scream and cry out — cause you are scared
Johnny — yells — to shut-up
Before he put — a — gun — to your head

I want to help — so I run to a neighbor's door
To use the phone — cause I have none — no more

My loud banging echoed — as I knocked on her door
She speaks to me softly — so she couldn't be heard

The heck with this mess — the neighbor — said — to me
I just — don't — want — to get involved — you see

She heard you cry out — please — please — no more
Then she swiftly — closed — her — apartment door

So — I go back home — with tears in my eyes — "crying"
Lord — please let — my friend stay alive

As I get to my door — I sank to the floor
My heart is heavy — for my friend of course

The police are there — and break down the door — to stop
Johnny — from hurting — my friend — again — once more

Dorease S. Russell

A Sheep Herder's Day

He opens the gate at sun rise each day.
And watches the lambs gamble and play.
Then drive them out to graze or to drink.
Of his own poor self he does not think.

Down through the coulee they went.
Spreading all over till the dog was sent
Away out around to gather them up.
The Old Sheep herder loved that pup.

Then on a flat where ran a stream
There in the shade he could rest and dream.
While they drank and rested awhile
Then they grazed on for another mile.

Now he turned them around and started them back
Slowly he walked till insight of his shack
Now the woolies are safe with only Bow-wow.
So he goes on home to milk the old cow.

And this is a day in the life of a man
Who has no worries and eats from a can.
Each day is a pattern for the one coming up
So he sleeps and he eats and he feeds Old Pup.

Vera Easton

"The Rainbow"

God put a rainbow in the sky,
I'm sure as a child, I wondered why.
Why was it there; all pinks and blues,
My Dad answered, "for me and you."

As I grew older; it was still around.
These beautiful colors that I had found.
I still was curious; so I asked once more
Dad couldn't answer as he did before.

He was up there somewhere with pinks and blues
Looking down here on me and you.
As I tried to explain to my Grandson
Why he couldn't see him, as I had done.

The clouds went away and the sun began to shine
A rainbow appeared for that grandson of mine.
He looked at me with a question in his eye.
I said, "God put the rainbow in the sky."

Holly B. Terrebonne

Alone

As I sit looking out the window, I wonder was this meant
to be? As I gaze across the meadow looking at the bright
green grass and tall growing trees.
As I lay awake at night lying in my bed I tell myself
not to worry. I won't be alone forever. As I stand under
the sun so bright and the sky so blue, I wonder if that
special someone's out there waiting for me.
As I sit by the telephone waiting to hear it ring, I wonder
does anyone really care? As I walk through a field
of flowers so tall and still, I wonder did I do
something wrong? This really isn't fair.
As I lay asleep I'm dancing with you in a ballroom
so luxurious, but still I wonder who? Where? When?
How? And Why? As I stare into a crackling
fire, I ask myself will I find someone before I
die? As I walk through my life I look up at the sky
and ask God why? Why try?
As I stand in line at the store, I wonder, am
I paying some fee? As I sit looking out the
window I say maybe . . . maybe it was meant to be.

Nicole Ruano

Tea at Three

Not every day, but most days
When the clock strikes three
Laundering, ironing, cooking, and cleaning stop,
The old water kettle is filled to the top;
Stove burner set for near full heat.

Anticipation sets in of what the day offers in treats,
Cheese and cracker were perfect for yesterday,
Baked apple with cinnamon for today.
Sunday we'll have the last two slices of cake . . .
A special gift from a dear old saint.

This is our time to share our minds wonderings.
We exchange philosophies of life, religion, weather,
Growing plants, old dogs, and other things.
There is joy in our hearts to have lived so long,
What determines such things we wonder aloud.

The conclusion is so clear, what took so long to see,
It's the tea of course, it's the tea.
The clock strikes four, tea time is over,
We agree to arrange our tomorrow
To be together again for our tea.

Dorothy McClelland

An Emotional Mom

To smile, 'tis too much of a chore,
Now, that you have gone away;
   But, by your decision, I must abide.
You know, I'll miss you so much more,
With each and every passing day;
   Emotions engulf me from deep inside.

When I read your despairing letters,
My eyes begin to fill, then blur;
   Those thoughts echo want might have been.
As I stare at your graduation picture,
I mourn the wonderful child you were;
   You will Never be so innocent again.

When I try to talk about you,
My voice is silenced by the tears;
   That insist on trickling down my face.
As a Marine, you'll do what you must do,
But that does nothing to calm my fears;
   So I'll put my faith in God's saving grace.

Remember, as a Christian, to always trust in Him,
For God will always help you each victory to win.

Carolyn Rebecca Cauthen

My Special Hoe

I entered on life's center stage, with my special hoe in hand
Life's row already planted, stretched before me, out across the land

With my partner by my side, we toiled along life's row . . .
The rain, the wind, the floods, so difficult to hoe.
The rocks and weeds abundant, appeared anew each day.
Why is this row always up the hill? No one around could say.
I chopped my toe a time of two, and suffered through the pain.
Just start anew, there is sure to come, cool gentle falling rain.
The row is level now, the rocks are but a few.
The hoe no longer heavy, rows end still not in view.
My partners voice beside me, as we toil along the row.
Be careful dear, do not chop your toe again with your special hoe.

Victoria McGhee

Untitled

I dream at night I'm walking
down a long and dusty road,
back to the age of innocence
when life was not such a heavy load,
where lovely rainbows shimmer after a
   soft summer rain,
and childish laughter echoes in my memory again.

The mountains so ageless in their beauty set in time
and stars and moon at night in virgin beauty shine.
The wildflowers kissed by springtime
as winter's frost is all melted away,
and then, alas, I awaken from my dream
and have to face another day.

Violet Austin

Hunger

I am wrapped around a hollow ache
An emptiness that reaches so deep
A thirst so enormous it cannot be slaked
A need for which I can only weep
I remember your warmth, your smile, your soul
Sustaining my heart before you were gone
Then I was complete and whole
With your arms around me making me strong
I hunger now for that strength you shared
For the part of me that was stolen away
When the doctor came and shook his head
"I'm sorry" was all he could say
Alone now I must face the pain
Of knowing my hunger will never cease
Yearning to feel you beside me again
And waiting until I too am released

Lydia C. Nussbaum

Motherly Love

Mother loves you before you are even born;
She loves you all the way up to the day she is gone.

She's there when you're a toddler and need her the most;
She's there when you're older and on the other coast.

Always by your side, especially when you're down;
Seems to know how to wipe away your frown.

Teaches you everything from right to wrong;
So the world we live in, you can get along.

When you leave the nest no matter how far apart;
Mother always loves you deep from her heart.

Thomas E. Kelley

"Wind Lilts"

You heard my song . . . your life began . . . I am your breath . . .
life is your plan . . . you use me each moment . . . and think of me
few . . . you only see me . . . move things as I do . . . sails would
not sail . . . lest my lilted tune . . . I move the clouds . . . to
shade you at noon . . . at times I'm scary . . . when so hard I blow
. . . I cause such terror . . . I'm called tornado . . . but I only
meant . . . to give you a stir . . . never to cause . . . such fear
to occur . . . when you really listen . . . as I sing with ease . . .
you dance around . . . and call me a breeze . . . I am in every . . .
living-breathing thing . . . I'm even in bells . . . each time they
ring . . . I move the mountains . . . I move the scents . . . yet I'm
but one . . . of your elements . . . so look for me . . . in all
that you see . . . I'm an invisible-immeasurable key . . . now you
must use me . . . in journey and search . . . as it's me you breathe
. . . in each given lurch . . . so let me swing . . . and lift you up
. . . you're never empty . . . I fill life's cup . . . I'm a part of
. . . fire-wind-and song . . . I love this earth . . . where I move
along . . . I'm here behind you . . . to be your shove . . . to watch
you grow . . . to heights far above . . . I'll lift you high . . . in
space without end . . . you can't leave alone . . . 'cause I'm your
"Wind" . . .

Shirl Willingham

All The Noise

It's alien to me now, living in a small backwoods town,
all the noise I used to know . . . I think back on the sweet home,
every once in a while, and hear the sounds that never seemed to quit.

I remember staring at that infamous skyline, aglow with living
light, across that deep black murky lake . . .
You could hear the fluorescents buzzing like a thousand million
flies above your head — and in the distance
may be the North West Side where I once lived — you could
hear the trains running on their dilapidated tracks . . .

It was a 24 hour panic in the sweet home, but it was what I
knew to be true back then . . . all the noise.
And underneath all that, straining hard to hear below the
industry, Tony yelling for Carmen to ". . . open the God damned
door!" She would call the cops — she always did.

Now I lay me down to sleep to wait for the siren's shrill scream.
All I can hear are the crickets and a low but steady electric hum . . .
my ears how they've rested here in the new home, and I love it, but
I will always remember the noise of the sweet home by the lake.

Sonia Smith

When You Smile The Angels Will Sing

To follow the sun will bring a shine to your smile,
  For at sunset you will find the shine of the moon on your smile,
At sunrise you will find a whole new day bringing a new smile,
  For this day the smile of happiness and love will be yours,
    And you will hear the angels sing.

Tom Davis

Come Back

Every time I look into your eyes,
I remember telling you all those lies.
And now I wish I'd never done so,
Because now you're leaving, and I don't want you to go.
I would do anything to keep you here,
To feel your skin and heartbeat so near.
To touch your hands, to kiss your lips,
To stroke your neck to your finger tips.
I would never hurt you or lie to you again,
Give me just one more chance, and a new place to begin.
And I know it's hard to forgive and forget,
But just remember the first time we met.

Margaret Olvera

The Light Of My Life

Sitting upon the earth, I wonder what it's worth,
the gold nugget that radiates heat to my skin.
And I think to myself, oh God, there's not much left.
For the day that was once here is about to end.
Now the darkness creeps in,
and a chill hits my skin.
The heat I once felt is now gone.
The night draws nigh, and a tear falls from my eye,
as I realized that my love is now gone.
The blackness, the emptiness, the coldness is here.
There is nothing to look at, but much to fear.
But, if I sit here a while I will soon smile, for the darkness will
soon be done.
I'll hold on tight through this gloomy night,
for, in the morning there will be a rising sun.

Brandon D. Beasley

No Cure

Where do we turn?
They call it AIDS
It attacks the body, the mind, and the spirit
Leaving its victim vulnerable to all
But there is no cure

Where do we go?
They call it Cancer
It wages war on specific parts of the body
Breaking its victim down
Yet there is no cure

Who do we ask?
They call it racism
We battle each other, without knowing one another
Battering the strongest soul into submission
No one will use the cure

When will it end?
They call it Bigotry
They call it Ignorance
They call it Hate
Whatever they want to call it
There will be no cure, until we stop it from spreading

Leah Z. Carmel

The Bliss Of Blue

While I stood on the Pacific Beach
And gazed with awe at the cosmic blue,
Kissing the Ocean within its reach,
The color that filled is the noble blue,
The color I love is Royal Blue!

The blue Sapphires from Kashmir all,
Were Marco Polo's visiting call!
At the Great Khan's court, the warmth that grew
Was all due to the precious blue!
The color I love is Royal blue!

Bleeding blend of blue and red
Love of labor the World they spread,
The Seven Red Stripes and Six more White,
With Stars on silk, Blue and bright
The flag of the U.S. stands for the Right!
In the maiden's deep blue eyes,
Passionate, lovely, bold and wise!
The blue blood flows in Royal veins
And in Oxford, Cambridge, Navy too,
Blue is there! Everywhere — with all its bliss in guise!

Arun Narasimham

Caring

Life is sweet if you care.
Doing for others is a way to share.
Give of your time, your heart, your mind;
Say something thoughtful, good and kind.

Take a moment to look around;
A friend in need can be found.
Lighten the burden of someone near.
Think of a way to bring good cheer.

When life is hard and days are long,
That is the time to sing a song.
Just help someone along life's way
And it will be a better day.

Do this always and you'll soon find
Life for you will be good and kind.
In caring for others you have won
A place beside God's own Son.

Jan Sneed

A Thousand Winters

A thousand winters have met the skies . . .
Spring has come to greet these eyes.

Winter's earth had turned cracked and cold . . .
Spring's warmth has returned to hold.

Winter's leaves had strayed away . . .
Spring's imparted them to stay.

Winter's breath had left all serenity . . .
Spring's embrace is for all eternity.

Winter's snow had showed its promise . . .
Spring's flowers will plant true bliss.

A thousand winters have met the skies . . .
But spring has come to greet these eyes.

Deb B. Stultz

Uncentered

Lunar Light through window creeps
I lie alone, unable to sleep
At one time I was happy, but now I weep
You used to call me your "Golden Goddess",
Back when your feelings ran deep.

But soon I bored you, and no longer
amongst the stars do you wish to make me dance,
no longer on the moon do I sit.
Right now things are black and desolate.

I am empty, my soul hollow, no longer
is my laugh gay, my eyes no longer twinkle,
part of me died, my spirit crippled

Angela Oakgrove

"Elegance Joy"

In this world of uncertain things about!
Life goes on without a doubt.
But children add that special touch of
Love and Joy that means so much!
As toddlers they cuddle, kiss you and cling;
They look for your guidance in everything!
But as they grow — you see them form.
From little people, to a mind of their own.
The love that you gave!
The rules that you had set!
Comes back to your heart, repeating no threat.
The greatest joy, that could never be bought
Is to have your children repeat what you taught!

Betty Nadile

For The Love Of Night

Right now, the moon is sinking its incandescent light
back through the sky
Frightened, the stars lay behind like children who have lost their mothers

An innocent bystander I am —
as the sky soaks up this wondrous vision
What if, in all its glory, I murdered the sky's evil thoughts
and my chivalry saved that giant fluorescent angel
from dying away?

The stars would regard me as a hero
The knight of nights
The horrid sky, drawing its sword
would pierce my senses
with the on — coming dawn
but would surrender to my love of darkness —
being shattered to pieces of bygone days

And the moon would eternally beam
upon my victorious face

Marta Coppola

The Birthday Candle

She kicked a can into a gutter,
It echoed down the alley.
Someone turned their porch light on,
Expecting some new tragedy — but let down.
She wanted to be rocked again in the cradle
It was so much easier back when . . .
She needed some understanding
A shoulder to lean on then . . .

And the rain seemed to keep on falling
It seemed to burn much more tonight.
More than her heart can handle
More than a candle's light.

Little girl, you weren't taught of life
Not when you're five years old.
Time threw you into old age
Made you walk, when you should have strolled . . .

Andrew G. Ebel

Circadian II The Soliloquy Of An Assassin

My Brother, the choice is not mine,
But this is the way; At least for a time.
One day it will change, and glad we'll all be.
But that is not now, Today — Destiny.

There are Laws of the Universe. Of this, no doubt.
Your body is trapped, but your spirit is out.
In a short while, you will be free.
To roam through that universe, eternally.

Your mass will change forms into another.
Your spirit ascends the scale of some other.
The last of life will be harmony.
'Til the moment death does claim thee.

My heart is bereft;
at the thought of your death.
I assume responsibility.

Make peace with it all, for your maker calls.
It is time to set your soul free.

Fight if you must.
But, in God trust. He is divinity.

For you now, I pray. No words left to say.

Mykel A. N. Hawkeye

175

Helen

Her apartment's walls are yellowed, cracked with age;
  reek of liniment, spent cigarettes, something sickly sweet.

She sits before a thick window;
  stares out over the city's lonely roofs
  into winter's hanging gray afternoon sky.

Forgiveness is her dream.

Her heart longs to purge the years of shame
  she has so carefully acquired.

In exile from those she loved, she hopes to find their mercy —
  a pardon for their Magdalen.

Over the building tops,
featherlight shavings of snow swirl noiselessly through the air:
Turning, twisting on the wind,
a frenzied swarm of silent,
icy white bees.

  Brian Field

Cosmic Starcase

Lightning bolt pierces the midsummer aura
Electric color, bursting auroras!
Red-orange-yellow sheets of blazing, hot fire
Alive with passion's burning desire.

Mountain peaks over feather canopies stand
Silently powerful, calming the storm.
Green-velvet emeralds dot the moist, rich earth, a
Soft, jeweled comforter warming nature's heart.

Midnight twinkles over earthly realms in a
Heavenly circle of galactic gems.
Indigo breezes waft magical moonbeams to a
Mystical castle of prophetic dreams.

Rainbow spectrum forms a crown of flames, a
Breathtaking, celestial windowpane.
Violet hues transformed in the night
Unique, eternal, expectant

Sunlight!

  Darla Billington

Where Have You Been

I have been high with excitement and low with pain.
Walked on a cloud and loved in vain.

I have captured the brass ring and touched the sky.
Lived hard, played hard, and at times, wanted to die.

But none of this prepared me for what was to be.
That I would love you and you would love me.

Where were you? Why weren't you here?
The answer, of course, is all too clear.
I simply wasn't ready or over my fear.

Now, I can settle down.
Head on straight and feet on the ground.
Happy and thankful for the one I've found.

Let's take a long time to cement our love.
With fidelity, devotion and, help from above.

So, happy birthday "Kitten".
Seems like the love bug has bitten.
You mean a lot to me.
And, I've been set free.

To love, nurture and care.
All I need is for you to be there.

  Howard Reeves

The Little Church On The Hill

There once was a little church that stood on a hill,
and if you look closely you'll see it there still.
Though the name has been changed, and the outside too,
the people within are the same friendly people they always have been.
Over the years our loved ones have gone, the ministers
too, and many we've had, most have been good,
but some have been bad.
Many a time we thought we couldn't go on,
but with God's help, we've struggled along.
Then we were blessed with help from above, and
though we have a different look, we're the same
little church that still stands on that hill,
You may have to look closely but you'll find us there still.
We're Methodists by name, and proud of it too,
because that church on the hill, will always be
home for me and for you.

  Jeanette Allan

"A Secret Recipe"

What a wonderful way to fulfill your dreams
a day where only the sunlight streams
uniting two people, becoming one
the love you share never undone
the union of marriage, a special bond
with God's blessing to look upon
as you journey begins you're sure to find,
commitment and endurance you won't mind
the path of travel will soon unfold
plenty of discoveries and memories to hold
like a favorite recipe that is always tasty
the ingredients to marriage is never hasty
start with warmth and understanding
add devotion and an abundance of caring
mix with tenderness and compassion
combine with love so everlasting
remember amounts can't be measured
so use your judgement and don't forget pleasure
most of all be true and kind
honor each other until the end of time.

  Deborah Cotov

If Only . . .

If only . . .
The harmonized song society's dreams.
If only the human race would look past color,
  Justice could smile knowing she upholds the will of her people.
If only anger could be handled maturely,
  it would be safe for neighborhood street games to linger
  into a blanket of darkness.
If only people turned to a healthy means to cope with reality,
  Drugs would no longer mediate joy.
If only abstinence was routine for every female not responsible enough,
  abortions would be illogical;
  children could dance in the light.
If only knowledge was power,
  the individual would be praised.
If only . . .
As long as the world sings this reprise,
when all is said and done humanity will be exactly where it started.
The beginning . . .
Doomed to repeat the mistakes made because of
selfish ignorance.

  Yvonne Latour

One With The Earth

I walk through the woods, down the draws and up the hills, my heart is full of joy, my mind at peace, and my spirit soars as if on the wind itself. I feel the cool fall breeze as it passes my hair and I feel the earth firmly beneath my feet. The Great Spirit envelopes me and although I am alone I am not lonely. Even the wind seems to have an almost human voices it makes the oaks and cedars sing. I am one with the earth and she with me.

I walk amidst woods so the woods live within me, within my heart, within my soul. Every bird that sings, every flower that blooms, every tree that grows becomes a cherished memory. A memory I will take with me unto my grave. In my grave I will become dust and join with mother earth from which I have come. For from dust was I formed by God and to dust I shall return.

it has been ordained by the master of the universe. He is the Author of all things. He formed even the leaves upon the trees, built the hills, and sent the rain. How great, wonderful and mysterious are His ways. I will praise and worship my Creator who has made all things so that in their beauty and complexity they might proclaim His holy name.

Matt Atchison

Someone To Love You

Someone to care, put your
arms around yourself, for there you'll
always find a gentle loving teacher
with your tender heart in mind.
Sweetest ways about her, the
spirit like a breeze will flow
around you like a leaf upon the
trees.
The light is shining softly, as a
glimmer in the dark, a peek of something
greater as the distant memory fades
the love of someone closer, is the you
within yourself.
I too have walked your lonely path
looking to the sky, not quite alone you
see, the Great one by my side. But
thru the distant misty past the one
I should have Loved was me.

Audrey Cook

Oceans That Never Die

A joyful star peaks trough a far off storm,
Slowly bringing light to an ocean it loves to warm.
Then sounds of the surf, woke him very early,
As living mountains of liquid, burst forth in a flurry.
It's time for a stroll under a colorful sky,
This he loves, the compelling waters know why.

Maybe majestic forests that end at the seas,
Or hiding creatures that plays in its trees.

The pounding surf then hums through the ground,
Stirring up a doe, as it turns toward the sound.

A sea lion bobbing in the splendor of the waves,
Catches the wondering eyes of the deer as it plays.

Proud waves roll at the shore to be spent,
As a great mind purposes why they are sent.

Lone man looked on, then wept,
Precious magical memories kept.

The landscape grows, the years pass by,
Guarding oceans that never die.

Lexie Davis

"Old Cedar Stump"

Alone she sat, on an old cedar stump, and thought of her accident dreams. They drifted in and out, and wove to and fro, and bore a likeness to vague, it seems. Absently she watched, spring bugs fly about, as her moments of life came to mind. She couldn't refrain, her heart was in pain, and her gut tightened up in a bind.

She wondered where it went, was her time wisely spent, did she really do some of it right? Guilt crept into her soul, she felt such a fool as she sat there long in the night. She didn't get cold, but abruptly felt old, and she suddenly felt her years. She found some relief, in feeling her grief, and welcomed the sting of her tears.

Too tired to try, she just sat there and cried, her emotions flew out in a burst. At one point she smiled, as her life she filed, and realized she wasn't the first. Her face feeling puffed, she'd had quite enough in dwelling on what was her past. To her it occurred, she should not be deterred, for she was certainly not the last.

And now she laughed, and silently sassed herself for feeling so down. Her worth she saw, her goodness she felt, and decided to forgo the frown. Then she watched the stars, they are what they are, her bad feelings she opted to dump. Sadness was cured, in a sense of the word, just by sittin' on that old cedar stump.

Tracy Lynn Davis

Poetry To Me

I dream of being a well known poet
For miles around people will know it
Words, experiences, knowledge, and grace
Memories and moments, a girls beautiful face
My pen, my thoughts explode from my mind
Confusion and mysteries, changes past time's
Heart aches, rainy days, inspirations running free
Extracted thoughts in ink for the world to see
Beautiful sunsets, an eagle flying, captured when I write
The beauty from me to you, use your sight
This poem comes from miles away, with a poetic passion
Can you feel my tremendous attraction
For the love of words I use to depict
Here's my personal feeling, Michael Nash's script
Hopefully the message is clear and concise, I'm trying to imply
My love for poetry is the reason why
Here's the paper that holds my dreams
For the world to see and feel what I mean.

Michael Nash

Faces In The Sun

The madrigal in the fields of a Texas spring all too soon
succumbs to the invasion of sunflowers
reminiscent of an Alamo's stand long long ago.

Bold, unaffected by the searing heat
the sunflower arrays her blossoms to the four winds.

Encircling her territory with her woody prickly stems
      and sticky leaves,
she embraces the bumblebee and teases the children of the wren.
Her root system is shallow, yet defies the strongest intent.

Her season of choice (its lease too long for the faint of heart)
eventually surrenders to the cooling influence of fall
and then to a cowardly winter.

But, she'll return,
as sure as the oppressive passion of summer
withers the grasses of the field and the humid night air
      opposes sleep.

Kay Kocour

I Never Had A Mother

Mother? Mother? Where are you, Mother?
I know you were too busy for twelve.
Too busy for cuddling.
But you took time to be cruel.
Children divided into loved and unloved:
Some could do no wrong; some could do no right.
I wanted to read books, escape into another
  world and be ignored.
I even tried hiding behind others.
Thought if you didn't see me, you'd forget about me.
You demanded my presence, to be pointed out, to be
  laughed at, to be called ugly.
You said I couldn't sing, not even hum a tune.
So I tuned you out. You got a switch.
I tuned you out some more. You got more switches.
When people said I had grown into an attractive
  young woman — you tuned them out.
I forgave you because I was your child.
But I never had a mother.

J. J. Jackson

Old Photographs And Memories

I found some old photographs today, all yellow from time and age.
Dressed in faded color, some black and white, and a few on a page.

I saw Dad in his black leather jacket, so handsome and tall,
I held some of Mom with her eldest to youngest, proud of us all.

Isn't it funny, how we remember so many places? We can recall
tiny details and funny faces — yet we forget things that happen,
important events, then we stop and wonder where it all went?

As I viewed many pictures over again, I found I was hungry for more.
I wanted to go back in time to then,
and put things back like they were before.

'Twas not events the pictures made me remember, but rather
the feelings I felt and expressions found in our eyes.
We will never be the same, so young and free,
and I cannot make things the way they used to be.

Now as I look on the past, I wouldn't want to change a thing,
'cause I love you for who you are today, but to yesterday I cling.

I consider myself fortunate that all of you were loaned to me,
I'll always hold you dear to my heart, locked inside my memory.

I was looking through some old photographs today - - -
I just wanted to say — I love you all — ALWAYS.

Lisa Lennon

The Eternal Bond

To witness a sister as delightful as mine,
Paints my heart with bliss-there's no denyin'.
For we carry between us a special bond,
And like a river it flows on and on.

Those precious memories that we often share,
Moments like when I'm fixing her hair,
Or reading a bedtime story that she loves.
These times are what our bond is made of.

Our unity is immensely pure and sincere.
It is a chain-unbreakable and secure.
Each link is intricate and firmly unseparate.
Not even fire nor a chainsaw could make it
  disintegrate.

This cherished bond will expand and grow,
As does of a baker's kneading dough.
Elastic and limitless this bond shall be,
'Til it reaches far beyond the vast sea.

Lily Truong

Black Love

What is that I smell
It is black
What is that I hear
It is love
What is that I see
A kiss
What is that I feel
A rose
What is it like
A kiss of rose
Why
It is unconditional
Why
Neglect does not phase it
Why
Its beauty is relentless, yet forgiving But . . . Why
Yet one touch draws blood, causes pain.

Patricia A. Raymond

"Peace Of Mind"

Sun rises,
today is a new day...
The sky is so blue,
the atmosphere is so clear
new things have come to life...

Trees blow so widely leaves fall so peacefully...
A bunch lands on the ground,
many different colors and sizes
reflecting so many things...

Birds fly so high,
so high into the sky where no one knows...
Ten birds fly in one path,
others fly another, and some birds get stuck in the middle...

Lights light up the sky so bright, so beautiful..
Water starts to flow waves come together,
ocean meets the shore...

Sun sets, the day has come to an end...
Blackness enters the sky
stars enter the atmosphere
all things come to a rest...

Michelle Koza

The Loves Of My Own

I love to watch whispering snowflakes floating down
Dressing God's forest with a glorious white gown;
  My children's arms embracing me tight
  Which feed my love's greatest appetite;
  And the taste of air after the first rain.

I love to stroll beside the perfumed sea
Searching at length through old debris
  Found in the ocean's ancient caves,
  And to watch the rhythmic roll of waves;
  To taste the misty froth again and again.

I love to sit by a lazy evening fire
Puzzling my mind with odd satire
  Of visual fantasies only I can see;
  To believe it's God's will what happens to me;
  And to listen to the roar in an ocean shell.

I love to see those laws of nature since the birth of time
As night draws its curtain and the stars brightly shine;
  The silent beauties of dead years; the first sleep of night;
  To know without doubt, what is wrong, what is right;
  And the possible loves tomorrow might bring.

Paul L. Adkisson

Is It Time?

As the church bells rang in the town square,
I wondered if it was time for sunset or sunrise.
Is it time to stop bargaining away our national forest?
Or is it time to plant trees and provide homes for creatures of nature?
Is it time for the wholehearted religious person to come out of hiding?
Or is it time not to have something to believe in?
Is it time for politicians to address moral issues?
Or is it time to hide them like a bad memory?
Is it time for world peace?
Or is it time for third world countries to rule through terrorism?
Is it time for racial warfare?
Or is it time to love one another?
Is it time to abuse loved ones?
Or is it time to hug and kiss them goodnight?
Is it time to sleep or wake up?
Is this just a dream? or is it.

    Erich L. Kaney

Perspective

Mountains, ageless in beauty, span the earth
From north to south and east to west they stand
Above and beneath the ocean's cool surf,
Worrying not with the passage of man.
Man is as the snow on the mountain's peak,
And in the glistening trees that do sway
Backward and forward till winter's last week
When the shining snow slowly melts away.
The life of man born of woman is short
And full of trouble says the Lord our God;
The ship sets sail from a calm, serene port
Only to sail a stormy sea of blood.
  The sun also rises and sets, but know,
  The earth is brightened by its glow.

    Joe McNees

Your Hands

Your hands they tell the story
  Of fifty years of love and strife,
They tell of sorrow borne and victories won,
  Together in your life.
Fifty years ago today, when you
  Clasped your hands in love,
God smiled on both of you,
  His approval from above.
So he sent you precious spirits, because He alone did know
The love, the care, the attention
  Your precious hands would show.
Those hands have served your God, and fellow men as well.
The lines, the wrinkles, and the roughness,
  Alone a story tell.
Your hands will go on serving
  "Till death they are folded there.
"Well done, thou good and faithful servant,
  Be free from earthly care",
For in my celestial kingdom, your hands have work to do,
As you travel heaven's highways, hand in hand — the two of you.

    Lavelle W. Despain

To Debbie

My bathroom counter was so clean and clear;
But now what a mess, what a smear;
I know my daughter is home,
It's so crystal clear;
I wouldn't trade her for the world,
she'll always be my baby,
so precious, so dear.

    Timothy W. Nehls

Friendship

I have a special friend,
  we share a special friendship.
My troubles she can mend,
  with just a friendly tip.

We share our deepest thoughts,
  about everything from "A to Z".
Our friendship can not be bought.
  She means everything to me.

Sometimes we don't get along —
  and it seems it wasn't meant to be.
But strike up the band and sing a song . . .
  for now, we are friends for eternity!

    Ashley L. Dettmann

One Starry Night (Dedicated To Warren)

Their faces so soft and glowing
The language of love is knowing

Surrounding us the moonbeams pranced
Twinkling brown eyes met and danced

Those sparkling eyes that reveal a truth told
Communicating the poetry of love to behold

The night air still and cold as they walked
Consumed with happiness as they talked

Of hopes and dreams for a future yet unplanned
The energizing forces of love's emotion unbanned

A black velvet blanket above held a starry night
And he softly whispered, "you're a beautiful sight"

Capture each cherished moment and seal it with a kiss
His masculine arms and mellow voice are musical bliss

My darling imparts secrets that warm the heart
Clingingly embracing ever so reluctant to part

Give completely without restraint my Italian troubadour
Obligate yourself to love and be loved with all its splendor

Oh if only time itself could stand still, they would pray
But those incredible hours must pass on . . . Night into day

    Martha L. Chainey

War

Your gaze shot through me,
Sparking a fire.
Your stare rooted me where I stood,
Your eyes stole my heart away.

Your look told me I had captured your heart.
Your mouth, however, mumbled,
"Our friendship would be destroyed."

My mind knew this was true.
My mouth told this to you.
My heart swore never to love you again.

My mind, my heart, are at war.
Neither side is winning.
My mind uses logic as its weapon,
My heart uses my emotions.

Which will win?
Will I profess my love?
Or deny my feelings, to myself and to you?

Which should control me?
My head's logic?
Or my heart's emotion?

    Elizabeth Gendreau

Voices Of Incest

The grey-bearded, heavy-set elders,
like tanks from Tienamen square,
rumbled their word in a cadence,
"Your memories we will not hear."

The therapists, brave and a few,
stood vulnerably facing the tanks.
"Your daughters are speaking the truth.
We're joining them here in these ranks."

The guns from the tanks just exploded
and burst forth with fierce legal fire.
The therapists fell where they stood
and burned on the paperwork pyre.

The silence. It deafened us all,
until, oh sweet sound, it arose.
The sound of the voices long-silenced,
the song of the daughters in prose.

"We remember," they quietly whispered.
The new voices said, "We recall."
"Now both of us know just what happened.
And you cannot silence us all."

Anne Hart

A Mother's Love

When I was wrong you let me know
when I did right, I could see the glow

Stern and strict, a Mother's right
still you protected through the night

Always seeing, that there was good
always knowing, you understood

You taught and molded, hoped and prayed
always knowing I would leave someday

These things and more, I owe to you
for teaching me just what to do

A Mother's love, I can't repay
only cherish it every day

Over the years you won the fight
thank you Mom, I turned out alright

Ron Mobley

A Profile Of A Man

I would like to share with you — A Profile of a Man.
You search for truth and love — but to find it? Rarely, anyone can.
Yet I found these life's treasures, beholden in the "Dancing Man".

He takes those filled with trouble or pain to search within themselves
    To find the joy they can gain.
When desolate shadows and clouds overcome my mind,
    A power of kindness, gentleness and strength in him, I find.

His love is bountiful, his soul is beautiful,
    And overflowing charm he does possess.
Turning moments into magic and hours into happiness,
    For all to assess.

His sparkling wisdom changes sadness to laughter, and fears to expectations,
    In the many lives he may touch.
This Dancin' Man, while turning sweat to diamonds, and tears to love,
    Never really asks for much.

Not, much. For pleasure — golf is his game.
By reputation — Kellum is his name.

And each enfolding year that we share pleasurable moments of time,
    I feel privileged that he's friend of yours and mine.

Patricia L. Simeone

The Lost Boy

Love and death began with,
pounding on the wooden planks
ending with a swish.
She glanced my way and then I knew,
she felt the same as I.
We were meant for destiny,
but destiny was not I.
She left me standing in my shoes a broken man.
Me, my shoes, and my bottle
they resolved my differences,
they became part of the man.
They got me further down the road.
Until the night of danger came upon,
and the bottle became my closest friend
as death took me by the hand.

Jennifer Errett

Precious Memories

Etched in my mind is a vivid recollection of childhood memories
augmented by the yeasty smells emanating from the old wood
burning stove.

Suffused light elicited from a solitary brass oil lamp bathes the
knotty pine panelled bedrooms while casting quiet shadows on
hand-sewn eiderdown quilts which adorn feather beds fit for a king.

This eternal beauty, a sprawling farm, perched at the doorway of a
cascading landscape, is resplendent with a tapestry of sweet,
succulent strawberries, daisies, and clover.

Massive white birch trees and like spires, erect and proud,
bordering this bucolic countryside, creating an aura of peacefulness
and serenity. What precious memories!

Holly Draudt

Funeral Arrangements

After her stroke
grandma lost words, even names.
At the nursing home
Grandpa fed her twice daily
for eight years
as if the food would heal the irreparable.

When finally she left us
for someplace where words are unnecessary,
two days before their sixtieth wedding anniversary,
the minister praised my grandfather's efforts.
"She served me well for fifty-two years"
was all Grandpa replied.
As if she were a maid, a pet, a thing.
And so I relish the memory
of her finally resisting him,
refusing to get in the car
or sit where she was told.

Susan Notar

Wonderings

I do not understand love.
    Why people feel it
    Why others don't
    Why 'Love' hurts sometimes
But, most of all I do not understand
    Why love is so hard to understand.
What I understand most is pain,
    And how it happens.
Without 'Love' there would be nothing to;
Separate man from machine.

Joel B. Dunafon

Dreams, Nightmares And Prayers

From the shattered dreams of a distant past
To the future of a man always ranked last
From the emotions of a man Possessed by rage
To channeling that rage on to a blank page
From society shunning him and putting him down
To that man left standing on deadly ground

A mothers scream of parental rage
Trying to force a child to come of age

From all the things you wanted to be
To failing and ending up in misery

For all these things written surely indeed
Time waits for no man a tireless steed
Stalking the grim fate of us all
for no man walks eternal, sure to fall
all these things are not cast in stone
The future is for you to write, you alone.

Daniel Bligen

Untitled

Comforting moist blackness,
Clean fresh earth,
Slowly moving from your place to mine.
Decomposing is our life.

Tremors above, scratching sounds, light is visible.
Large alien eyes look upon us,
Dry rough tentacles pluck us from our damp dark world . . .

TRANSPORTED

Impaled, not once, not twice, more.
Sharp cool metal through our flesh,
Jerked and squirming,
Unheard screams.

Plunged into liquid cold and dark,
Alien creatures swim and bite.
Pulled from their grasp . . .

DISCARDED

They dig for another,
And again it begins.
Oh the life, the insignificant life
Of a worm.

Anastasia M. Smith

The Dreamer

There once lived a man who had a dream,
That a race of people would
one day be redeemed.
His dream of love and peace would touch the world,
In the Heart of every man, woman, boy and girl.
His march for freedom and equal rights,
Was the dream he had that night.
He was stoned and taunted
with racial slurs,
But in his dream he would
not be deterred.
Brotherhood for all is
what he preached,
In his dream he hoped
was within reach.
Until one day when he was all alone,
His life suddenly ended but his dream lives on.

Darrell Castle

Rite Of Life

This is the day of the dead. Kick up your heels.
Dance! You have all the time in the world and no time at all.
 It is the creative process that man thinks will make
him immortal.
 But what is death? Why do we fear it?
 Death is merely boney, cold, seductive fingers, a stepping
stone to another signpost. This signpost bears the words,
"Journey Down the Road."
 This road is a road less travelled. Down this road is a
ride. This amazing ride is called "Life."
 Our ride will end, too quickly. Nothing can we do to
make it last longer than intended. Drink full from the cup,
order good wine, or don't drink wine at all.
 The children are all gone, we hear no laughter, we see
no tears. We're all going to the same place, which is no place.
 So, add spice to a short recipe called a lifetime.

Natasha E. Gates

Why Did It Have To Be Him . . .

He was: A very sensitive and caring young man.
He was: Someone who made you feel
good about yourself, someone that made life worth living.
He was: Someone that brought out
the real you, someone who was joyful true
He was: Someone that gave you courage to be strong, someone you
could trust to help you along
He was: Someone that you felt
like being around a lifetime . . .
At times we both grow, and
learned things together, cause he was my dear friend . . .

Your warm gentle smile, will be sadly
missed by a dear friend . . . Who cares . . .

He departed this life on Friday
March 22, 1996 . . . In Columbus, Ohio

He leaves us to cherish his memories:
To his dearly beloved toddler daughter, that was in the
apartment with him, during the time of the shooting . . .

Why did it have to be him . . .

Connie R. Norris

Altered Reality

Help, I'm falling thru the world of Vorr. Fleeting glimpses of men of
Ore, and kings and things of nevermore, existing in the world of Vorr.
Powers that be beyond compare, just waiting for myself to snare.
Where space and time and things of kind, existing only
In your mind.
A world of beauty, bleak and dark
A world of passion, and lonely hearts
A world of horror, love and peace
Of ugly things, and golden fleece.
If traveling thru the world of Vorr,
You wish to come back never more.
Take hold your life and be concise
Don't force yourself into a vice.
Bit if the world of vivid time, and
Space and things of equal kind.
can't hold your young old feeble mind.
Then doomed you are forever more
To travel thru the world of Vorr!

Dennis W. Brooks

Autumn Leaves

Leaves of our lives —
How verdant in the springtime,
How sharply etched against the
morning glow.

How large they grew in summer,
As swollen as our dreams,
But tight they held onto the bough.

Now autumn comes;
Like ripened fruit unplucked
They soon begin to fall.
Their golden span is short.

Soon wintry winds will start to blow,
Casting them downward
Into the dust, where all must go —
Our dreams, our garments, all must go —

Until another springtime!
When will it be?
A. Louise Eckburg

Time To Sleep

Hush now, daddy, and go to sleep,
and pray the Lord your soul to keep,
and if you cry out in the night,
I'll be there to calm your fight,

I rest my head and listen, as you tell,
your stories of the war, I know so well,
such a hero you are, so tough, so strong,
dying this way seems so wrong,

It gives me peace that you understand,
when you pass you will go to a better land,
where Jesus, Grandmother, and Grandaddy will be,
and please, don't forget to wait for me,

And when it's time for me to go,
there you will be, this I know,
with a hug, and a kiss, and a big smile,
we'll be together again for a long, long while,

Hush now, daddy, you must go to sleep,
for now it's time for me to weep,
Can you hear the angels tender sweet song?
Fly with them to heaven, where you belong.
Jacquelynne Janssens

Insomnia

Turning tossing, stopping, stuttering
gnashing, biting, maddening, maddening,
this strange thing I hate the most, take in, take one.
Take Spirit,
On Ghost.

Why must it happen, when will it end,
Oh, just to sleep at one within!

Look through the light see what you see
Shadows, Darkness, through one
who is me.

Why do I sleep if sleep has no end?
Can I succumb to the shadow within?
Dreamscape and nightmare have their domain
Darkness and Light fight to remain

So I close my eyes and open my mind
To see what lies in the shadow behind.
John Edvalson

To The Lady I Love

I can not offer you a mansion,
only a castle where you would be queen.

I can not offer you the world,
but I'll share with you all my worldly things.

I can not offer you half a century,
but I'll share with you all that life has left for me.

And I would never ever share,
the love I have for thee.
Neal M. Edwards

Friends Are Forever

Everyone needs a friend to talk to,
Even when they're down.
A friend will always listen,
And always be around.
Friends could never hurt you,
Or leave you in despair.
Just when you think you're alone,
You turn and they are there.
Friends are people who love you,
And who will always care.
So, if you want a friend,
Then be a friend, and show that you care.
JoAnna O'Day

Poetry Of A Troubled Soul

Hopefully happy,
I sit and think
I wander through an oasis of thought,
Yet, for some reason have nothing to drink

Deep and true runs my mind,
Though shallow and false
My thought is now lost
In its long endless halls

This is when I feel best
This is when I get my rest
The thought that I had is now long departed
Gone to the regions forever uncharted

I am chilled by my own breath
Is this like a brush with death?
I begin to question my own sanity
or is it my insanity?
Adam Oaks

Boy

Distant,
Reluctant,
And
Scared,
The young boy sits upon
His rock
Under
His tree
And looks up into the sky.
The evil sun peers down at him with his
Wicked smile
Of
Heat
And
Endless fire.
He knows what they boy wants.
And that, of course, is why the rain did not
Fall
That day.
Or the next...
David Orvis

Election Year

Form — from stillness it graduates
And doesn't end until it fades to all.
That's what wins elections — form.

His figure stepping from a foul fog,
A leader fading into view
To mount Washington's steps
Amid cheering crowds
With laurel crown and a procession
Of victor's spoils from democratic conquest.

Stretched hands grasp for images,
Holographic — fingers go through
Holographic — they pass right through.

There once was an ancient city in Mexico
Bigger than Rome.
I forget the name. Can you believe it?
Bigger than Rome
But I forget its name.
Forgotten . . . Forgot . . . For . . . . . .

Keith Boggess

"Winter At Eight"

I ride a banana seat bike at break neck speed
White wicker basket attached to the handlebars
in the dead of Southern winter
hoping for light a little longer
Next time past the house, Mother will call
"Too dark," "Too cold," "Dinner's ready"
The big yellow-orange tabby sits on the
back step, patiently awaiting his evening meal
Later he will purr full of unforgiving, inconstant affection
Times tables are too hard
There are good books to read
A funny T.V. show is on
The baby wants to play.
Gibbles, gurgles, and cries dimpled and chubby and red.
Mother fusses
Times tables must be learned.
Put the books away
Bring the bike in
Put the tomcat out

Crystal Richardson

Eagle Vision

Having faith and courage — to soar as high
As the mountain range
Wisdom reaching new heights

Sight as sharp and clear as a crystal point
Depends against all fear
Talons lift when spirit is low

Insight to past, present, and future
Let eagle guide you
To believe in your dreams — you may not have known

Eagle — strong as a rock, peaceful as a dove
Feathers as gentle as the summer breeze

Let your soul fly on the wings of the eagle guiding you to open
Your heart and soul — to healing

Safe and secure wrapped in eagle's wings
Wind whispers messages to all who would listen
The moon and stars in the night glisten

Supported by the sky — we can try to fly
With eagle vision — we too can see

Believe in your dreams — know the universe holds you
You can fly to the heights of eagle in heaven on earth

Kindra Erica Oshrin-Mohr

A Child

A child was buried today,
He died from a serious disease.
This child was beaten to death,
Perhaps because he didn't say please.

Adults around couldn't hear his cries,
Beaten into a world of silence.
Adults around just closed their eyes,
While the child lived on through the violence.

As life slipped away from the child,
His soul moving away from his little body.
The last thing his human form heard,
Was his parents fists telling him he was naughty.

His soul in its way to heaven.
The angels will let him laugh, be a child, climb some trees,
Some where inside my heart,
I can hear this child saying please.
    Please adults won't you listen,
Try hard to open your eyes.
    Please find a cure for this disease
Before another child dies.

Teresa Lorraine

A Letter From Molly

Just the other day I got a letter from Molly after I asked her to play
she wrote,
I don't think so Tommy, my dad says he wants to play.
He tells me he loves me, but when our playing time's done
He swears bad things will happen if I ever tell anyone.
I cry in my room wondering what I did that was so bad.
I wonder if I'm the only girl who despises her dad.

I tried to tell mom but then daddy walked in
and before I could say a word, I had paid for my sin.
He slapped me and he hit me and then I started to cry.
Daddy said I was evil and that I deserved to die.

I'm sorry Tommy, I liked playing with you instead.
You never have touched me the way that he did.
I'm only saying bye to you, you're the only friend I ever had.
I can't live in this world anymore —
not when daddy says I'm bad.

Hugo Barraza

Wounded Hearts

The present and the future
look so empty and so dark.
With bitterness and anger
filling up a wounded heart.

Memories seem to haunt us
with the lessons we have learned.
Afraid to take chances . . .
afraid we'll get burned.

For love is like a knife
so painful on both sides.
And never seems unshakable,
but changes with the tides.

To love or not to love?
Is the question always asked.
The answer would be easier
if we knew the love would last.

But no one can see the future
because they're always looking in the past.
And can't see that the love in front of them
might be the love that lasts.

Vickie J. Harris

Who?

Who helps you conquer all your fears or dries your everlasting tears
and helps you beat pressure you get from your peers
Your one and only best friend

Who tells you secrets they tell no one else
or helps you get through the deepest, darkest trails
and brings you back up when you think you have failed
Your one and only best friend

Who helps get you out when you think you're in trouble
or picks you back up when you've fallen or stumbled
and makes your life float like a colorful bubble
Your one and only best friend

Who is always with you when nobody ares
or helps you get by when life's just not fair
and will stand by your side and your burdens they'll bear
Your one and only best friend

Jennifer Erin Enoex

Mammon (Money)

They say,
  Mammon can buy anything,
  I say to them, But not love
They say,
  Mammon is everything,
  And I say, but neither you nor me
They say,
  Mammon makes you happy,
  But I say, not true, you would realize soon.
They say,
  Mammon is the root of power, (yeah right)
  I tell you, this is but lies, all lies.
I say to them, Mammon is the root of all evil
  If asked why, I would give these reasons:
    Because of mammon you steal
    Because of it you fight because of mammon you go to jail
    Because of mammon you kill
    Because of mammon, There is "Hate"
    Everybody can see now that, truly truly, Mammon is and
    would always be the root of all "Evil"

Anne Otum

Tears

I had to hold your hand and watch you die,
You, who had nursed me through so many
Illnesses! I could not keep you here.
The doctor was the first to give up hope;
He merely promised you would have no pain!

You gave me life, then gave yourself to me —
Both you and Dad — freely gave all your love.
The three of us faced everything together.
Our love grew ever stronger with the years!

When we lost Dad, I almost lost you too
But, for my sake, you built a life with me.
My dearest friend, you always gave me strength;
You were my anchor and my haven. We
Had many years — to few — together! How much
We missed our Dad? Dear love, how could we live
Without the best of husbands and of fathers?
But you creatively succeeded in giving
Me a home, a base for work and life.

And then, alone, I had to watch you die.
All I could do was hold your hand and weep.

Marion Sonnenfeld

"I Love You"

Kissing you was not what I had planned,
Now I'm not so sure just where I stand.
It was only good clean fun,
There's nothing like a little tongue.
I'm too young for sex,
I'm not ready for anymore kids yet.
But my only crime is caring about you and the kids.
I won't leave you, so please believe it.
We've been together for five months,
And it's been great.
We both wanted kids and we wouldn't wait.
What I'm trying to say is you and
Our kids are a part of me and that will never change.

  I Love You

Briana Michelle Warren

True Love

It's hard to express the way I feel,
But when I got to know you
I felt a love so true.
Now, all I am, all I want, is you.
Ever since that day,
I can't help feeling this way.
I found a feeling deep inside,
That I knew I couldn't hide.
These feelings kept on growing
Into the way I feel today.
I thought I had felt true love before,
But this is a feeling I just can't ignore.
And if what you say is true,
I know you feel the same way I do.
There is a place in my heart only you can fill,
And when I think of what might have been,
My feelings grow stronger still.
I'll do anything to be back with you,
Because these feelings are like a burning fire,
For you have become my heart's desire.

Jamie Ellis

Dream

What if it's all a dream,
a dream that will never end.

If we are all just roaming the earth,
without knowing why we're here.

Or if someone's just thinking of how life could be,
and we are all in their mind.

What if this is our heaven of hell,
or somewhere in between.

If all of our actions are controlled by destiny,
and we are the puppets of fate.

No one has any proof that this is real,
for all we know it could be a dream.

Peggy Wilcox

Peace

Peace is the moonlight glistening on the rippling waves of water
The gentle slapping sound gracing the shore
There are no intruding sounds but the infrequent hoot of an owl
The stars watching over one and all during their night-time vigil

I listen and marvel at the serenity within my heart
Then hear the croak of a bullfrog calling to its mate
And smile at nature, this beautiful sight and its sounds.
And peace. And peace.

Sue A. Strobel

Daddy's Girl

Daddy's girl . . . what a joy was to see her arrive to the light,
with her innocent looks and cry of fright.
I searched to the heavens with a sight of thanks,
for such a beautiful angel that I hold in my hands.

Daddy's girl . . . watching her grow with such independent way,
that she can conquer all that stands in her path.
With daddy by her side almighty Knight,
cautiously attending to her first steps in life.

Daddy's girl . . . fake lip-stick and make-up she tries to put on her
face, working hard as she could to fit in high heels and a big dress.
The time will come when she will soar through the skies,
in search for that love that will fulfill her life.

She will always be . . . daddy's girl.

Dick G. Elias

"Star Soul Searching"

Here I lay on my bed
Staring out my window
My eyes are tired and turning red
From searching through the stars for my soul

Stars, stars, what do you think
As you twinkle and shoot through the sky
Stars, stars, maybe if I don't blink
I can catch my soul as it shoots by

As I lay and stare at the sky
My heart wishes and ponders
Upon every star that twinkles by
While my poor soul just wanders

I have laid here and looked at the sky
The whole night has gone by
As each star twinkled and shined
I never found this lost soul of mine.

Judith Greer Edwards

What Matters

What will the world be like when I'm gone?
Will Brokaw and Rather still battle it out at 6:30?
Will Dave and Jay still battle it out at 11:30?
Will John Madden still over-analyze every play?
Will kids still call each other names?
Will people still get stung by bees and jellyfish?
Will my car still smell the same with someone else in it?
Will people still laugh and have fun?
Will my family still talk about me (and to me)? . . .
Sure all these things will still happen,
But they won't be the same.
I won't be here to let them mean what they do now.
The world as you know it will cease when I'm gone —
Just as it will when you are.

Jude Thaddeus Silverman

Why?

I never understood why politicians never do what they say they will do.
I remember a day when it rained so hard the flowers died
Now I know the truth
I never heard the truth before I questioned it.
If only it would have happened sooner.
I have imagined the future, it excites me.
Nobody told me, I had to find out myself.
I have searched for the answer to many things.
Like a diver I accomplish things without a splash.
I am only now a beginning the great adventure of my life.
I am still surprised at the endless groves in my life.

Patrick Hardy

Mother Nature

Mother Nature, we have robbed her so,
I hear her cry in the wild wind blow.

We have tasted all her sweetest fruit,
Yet, never a praise of gratitude.

We have ripped into her breasts to steal her gold,
Yet, it was sacred, we were told.

We have drained her of significant power,
Yet, we won't hesitate to pick her flower.

By given us beauty she has shown her love,
Yet, soon she will not be here for the sun to rise above.

For, just like a mother she would give up her life.
To the very same children who hold the knife.

Mother Nature, we have robbed her so,
I hear her cry in the wild wind blow.

Lara Rose Alorro

Ode To An Ultrasound

My mommy said they shouldn't know if I'm a he or she,
she said, "well, gee, that's half the fun" — not knowing what I'll be.

But daddy said, "we should find out if we're to make a plan,"
still, he agreed to mommy's way . . . he's such an agreeable man.

So who'd a thought if the other day when mom was such a sneak,
when daddy wasn't looking, she and the doctor took a peek.

When she found out which kind I am, why she was tickled pink,
but she couldn't help but wonder if my dad might make a stink.

So she waited till real late that night to whisper in his ear,
"I have some news to share with you, my precious darling, dear.

I know I said, 'I want a surprise,' I said it every day,
but I got so excited and I just got carried away."

He said, "you indecisive girl, would you make up your mind?
I can't keep up with what you want, it changes all the time.

But since you have a secret that is known to only you,
perhaps you'd like to share it so that I may know it too."

So mom revealed to dad that night, with much delight and joy,
"My darling, we are going to have a bouncing baby . . ."

R. Panel

Dear Steve

Once we shared a body . . .
  Genes, origins, oxygen, nourishment . . .
We felt fulfilled . . .

Then you became separate . . .
  Learning, growing, searching, wanting . . .
We felt unnecessary . . .

Soon you will stand alone . . .
  Educated, confident, self-sufficient,
  handsome and clean and eager . . .
We feel proud . . .

and all that you are
  is more than we hoped for
    more than we gave you
    more than we ever dreamed could be . . .
We feel fulfilled . . . unnecessary . . . proud . . .

Awed.

Connie Blackmer

The Philosophy Of Camaraderie

Enveloped in the coliseum din of other customers,
I observed the movements of Aristotle as he
attacked his cheese omelet with a spoon across
from me.

His fork was dirty, you see, so it seemed
only logical to the hungry philosopher.

Discussions circled the greatness of platonic
encounters like this one and our personal Greek
tragedies; his thoughts and opinions cradled by
the dance of auburn nymphs in the sunlight behind
him. What an elegant case for such an aloof mind.

He finished his eggs and said with a contemplative
gaze, "You have a pretty face."

My cup of hemlock seemed to grow cold just then,
so I pushed it aside and he strolled away,
with his confident toga wrapped around him
more tightly than any unshakable theories
I albatrossed around myself.

Ah! What good medicine friendship does make.

Monica Lynn Jackson

Glass Baby

Hearts at war
Don't know what to do with crystal.
A glass baby without flaws —
Not even a scratch — when the sun is right,
Reflects space fighting for air.

Imagine: No powdery infant smells,
No coos, just the clinking of limbs
Keeping them awake at night; the cold
Shock of the bauble against their pink hands;
Never a cry nor a demand for the breast.
Something to be thrown in the road!

Squeals of brakes,
Cars locked in fetal positions,
Passengers staring through cylinders of void . . .
By summer, weeds had diapered the asphalt,
Green spears had grown around clarity, and when the wind blew,
Something gossamer with no place to hide
Rocked in a cradle of grass.

Phyllis White

Who Are You?

A mirrored face hangs upon my wall
And all day long I stare into its eyes,
Wondering what I see,
Wondering what they see in me;
Framed by the scars from
Youthful crimes, they have thoughts
I cannot quiet and questions I cannot avoid —
Like how and when,
And when and when and when,
And if . . .
There are times when the world is so
Close I can hold it in my arms and feel
Complete, I can go to sleep and know
Nothing will be gone when I awaken;
Then there are times
(Such as now)
When the world is a mirror
And all I see is myself,
Looking at me and asking me
Why I don't look the other way.

Harlow Blackmon

Jesse And Jake

The things that separations can cause
Kids torn between two parents
Who feel so lost
Dad says we can come for four days
So you take off to get them
You're in a daze

It's been so long since you've seen them
My how they've grown

The time flies by and it's time to go
God, how you hate to tell the boys so
They try to act big and take it in stride
As they hug you and kiss you goodbye

Connie Rose

Young Love

Oh how I love the young beautiful one.
Thou are radiant as the glowing moon.
The long hair that flows looks touched by the sun.
When you slip from my view I'm lost in gloom.

Your young beauty grew my great attraction.
For no one else such feelings did flow.
Which I never could find a distraction.
Your beauty caused an eternal glow.

By chance in future years you may not fade.
Or thine young body wither with old age.
But the eternal glow may come to shade.
Causing my heart to release from your cage.

If nature takes course my love fade none.
No matter what you'll always be the one.

Justin Younie

The Song

A gust of wind to let me know my heart is still a flow.
The meadows full of rain dew on my face, drips fall to my lips.
Hungry for a mist of that fresh breeze to blow through my hair.
The humidity how it sets my heart on fire too long to see the flames burn.
Nothing more than a strike of lightening to gleam in my eyes.
For never more will I cry again, but only to glee in my victory.
Holding on to the past will no longer last for I walk, as I walk along
I can still hear my favorite song.

Thirisia Broadway

April Rain

I sit by the window watching the April rain. Watching the wet drops
of summer fall on the window pane. I look out on the dampening
earth, the grass becoming greener and the air becoming moist. I
remember the summers past, looking out the window into the rains
of time. Remembering when I played in the yard and danced in
thunderstorms. When the kids jumped in the yard, splashing and
having water fights. Their bare feet were protected by the wet bed
of grass with no fear of branches or sticking roots.
Those were the days, when you could go out in heaviest rain and have
fun, not have to worry about catching a cold or getting the sniffles.
The April rains were there for the children. The grownups could enjoy
them but not the same way. They could enjoy it watching their
children play and remembering their own times. Every year they came,
all the kids waited for them and when they came, the kids put on
their shorts or swimming trunks and slid and sloshed around,
filling buckets and cups with water chasing each other around.
The world of youth being relived through others beyond the
glass pane. We always watched them play, that's the magic of
the April rains for us. Watching our kids enjoy the magic. And
some day they will be where we are watching their young play.
The rains of April, the innocence, the magic, the warmth, the
frolic. When the rains come, everyone is a kid.

Michael A. Ritchie

My Shepherd

My shepherd watches with an angel's eye,
From gallies and ravines, he shields me,
From thickets and marshes, he protects me,
Poisonous weeds and grass, he uproots
To clear my path.
My shepherd keeps me away from harm.

When I fall he picks me up,
Cradles me in his strong arms,
Wipes my tears and heals my wounds.
His loving words and tender touch.
Soothes and mitigates my bruises.
My shepherd keeps me away from harm.

When I am lost and can't be found,
He rummages through the bushes,
Turns every rock, looking for my tracks,
How can I not love my shepherd?
My shepherd keeps me away from harm.
He is my shepherd, who died for me!

Amelia S. Hernandez

The Verdict

Thank you for the happiest day of many years. Just to see the smile on your face, eyes shining so bright, the touch so soft and gentle, what a beautiful day.

The sky is so dark, the thunder rolls, the wind very strong, I can hear that soft voice saying where did we go wrong.

"The verdict" was read, as we clutched each hand, there was peace, joy, and happiness, we just whispered thank you for this day.

I don't know what tomorrow will bring. It may be gladness, tears, and sorrow, this day, this time, this year, the love of my life will forever be.

Thank you for this day.

Sarah R. Fornis

The Red Leaf

Swinging on the hammock, caught a glimpse of something bright
in the corner of my eye. Got up to see what it was, what it
was doing, where it was and why.
It was a red leaf. I stood up under it. The sunlight made it
shine different from the rest. Even though there were some other
red leaves, I had to have this one because it was the best.
I climbed up on a chair but it was way too high. I could reach
all the other red leaves but this one stayed in the sky.
I got a taller person's help but even he couldn't reach this
great thing. We tried and we tried and then I learned something.
Some things no matter how beautiful need to live in the mist.
I looked at the red leaf and I planted a wish.
I wished that this leaf lived from infinity till. If I picked
it, it would die, so God made it unreachable in his will.
So I hope this leaf clings tight for his life, when the leaves
are taken when the wind cuts like a knife.
Cling little red leaf, never fall down. Forget about your friends
who are on the ground.
Always be strong, never be weak, and I'll see you next fall
pretty, little red leaf.

Shanee Howell

Tapestry

Dream on oh stupid fool . . . your destiny is woven.
At the very start of life, your date of death is chosen.
Like little threads of color in the tapestry of time . . .
The only thing that really counts is your ultimate design.

Kelly Marie Bunetta

Time

Once, great voyagers   daring wind
                    and
                    sail,
          sliced open the seas
          with "faith" to prevail.

          Thrusted abreast on
          a sand salted shore,
       they found themselves a
       "world" unseen before.

Now, great voyagers   daring faith
                    and
                    souls,
          slice open heavens
          to define "black-holes."

          Thrusted abreast the
          universal shore,
       they found themselves with
       "worlds" yet to explore.

Will great voyagers   dare to find
          God's
          "Time"
       preserved in dimensions
    reserved — just — for mankind?

Kathy A. Hamlet

My Best Friend!

You are my strength and my shield, my solid rock and my foundation.
You give me strength to handle life's daily battles.
You shield me from those battles that I cannot win, and give me the
strength to try again.
You are my shelter when life becomes too rough for me to handle
alone, You are my shelter when I feel all hope is gone.
You are my lifeboat when I am drowning in the sea of despair,
You are my courage when I have been beaten down by life's
hard knocks. When I feel that I am all alone in my misery
and despair, you take my hand and tell me that I am not alone,
because, my best friend is there.
You are my partner in all things. I can always count on you
to be there. You stand by my side in the good times, and
you do not forsake me in my time of need.
You are my best friend and Jesus Christ my King.

Janis Dawson

Observation

Winter blasted cold in the face of my fury
    Beneath the beams of rotted oak and mahogany.
How those years tumbled on —
    Many forgotten and housed with the termites
    In this quiet domicile.

At last life leads to this proposition of gangly measures
    Filled with all the uncertainty of youth
    And with all the solitude of death.
Simplicity gives way horrid reality
    As that reaper waits outside in the snow with his sharpened
    profile.

Ages past and all lost worlds converge in my burning brains
    Allowing me to forget my bloody, frozen body —
    Alive by measure of anger and abundance of fear.
That carnivore loves me, you see,
    Just as the honeybee loves the flower's style.

In this old sanctuary, broken and abandoned but by me,
    Worshippers gather no more inside its simple boards —
Only a young body with a tired, old soul stopping to rest.
    Sitting in remembrance of all that has gone before,
    Staring into its dim halo, and contemplating my next mile.

Sarah E. Land

A Sonnet Of Hope

Hope is the future of better things:
The bloom of a flower, the green grass and its dew!

Hope is the morning of a new day with a frontal bay-window view
    upon a peaceful sea.

Hope is caring and continuing to care and not knowing why?

Hope is asking a question; Knowing you won't get an answer
    there is none!

Hope is a distinguished treat; a gift to a human being
It is a tender caress of a human being to another.

Hope is faith; Faith for tomorrow. It is a sonnet that cries
    within the inner being!

Hope brings a squire to its knees in the hope of not having
    a solitude tomorrow.

Hope can give backbone to the smallest player and make him great!

Hope is the aureole of a rainbow; Peace, tranquillity for some;
A clear bright view for another.

Hope is an awning for the majestic dignified heart.
The heart the pump of Life!

Hope is energy; The energy of life.

    Ramona Reyna

Untitled

Loneliness is like the vast desert.
Empty, except for a few tumbleweeds of
memory floating across the desert floor —
reminding me of past love.

The sun beats down and nothing grows.
All inside me burns like an angry fire
That cannot be quenched.
My feet from this endless walking alone
have begun to ache.
To say nothing of my heart.

Off in the distance, I hear people laughing
and gathering around a dinner table.
The wind of silence blows continually —
Wiping out all happy sounds that
my weary mind attempts to imagine.

    Linda S. Chakoian

To My One and Only

I love you more than words can say
I love you more and more everyday
You are always in my thoughts and dreams
If I knew I would have to do without you
I would scream
Your love surrounds me
And I'm as happy as I will ever be
You are always in my heart
So I know we will never part
You give me courage to get through my greatest fears
And I could never do without you dear
Anytime I get lonely
I know that you are my one and only
And I know the sun will shine
because you are my valentine
And that is my rhyme for you
because no other one could ever do.

    Julia Beth Hall

Open Mind

What can I say to make your day
Something to look foreword to?
The memories of fun in days past
The warmest of feelings that really last

A sight or sound that takes you back
& brings into today the things it lacks
shut your eyes and let your mind
Be open to memories of a festive kind

Don't worry what today may lack
You've got your memories that stay intact
Today's events will be tomorrow's past
So live it up, the blues can't last

    Eileen G. Arends

Sorrow Rain

When you're down and feeling pain, you're standing in the
Sorrow Rain.
When you have tears running down your face,
or you feel small in a big place
when you feel like a tattered mane you're standing in the sorrow rain.
When someone dies and leaves forever, or a friend moves away
and you think you'll never again be together,
and everyday your sadness is the same
you're standing in the sorrow rain.

    Matthew P. Zimmerman

The Endless Pains Of Hell

A dream conveys me to a crowded room.
The room is filled with angry men:
A battlefield of shouting, fighting men —
I try to find a door: There is no door.

The men in blue are shouting: "God is blue!
God's holy skin is colored blue!"
The men in green are shouting: "God is green!
God's holy skin is colored green!"
The men have all been slashed and stabbed —
Their swords inflict the endless pains of hell.

    Moses Grady Farmer

The Edge

I stand on the edge
Teetering above the dark sea of madness
It is as black as my soul
Is there peace in the depths?
Or only turmoil beneath the surface?
Is it worth hanging to a hope of sanity?
O for a quiet bed for a weary
traveler who cannot go on, and cannot turn back.
Is this purgatory?
It isn't living
It is death of the soul
Is the emptiness a lack of pain?
If I fall will the warm water
baptize me with peace?
Or will it take me to some
new level of agony everlasting?
I can only wait
To find myself falling
Or hold on to the memory of hope
That there is such a thing as mercy
And a new path will lead to life.

    Kim Faulkner

Colors

Blue is for the northern star, with its big blue points,
so near, so far.
Black is for the sky at night, when I'm there it gives
me such a fright.
White is for the stars so bright, so bright, and down
on earth they are such a sight.
Pink is for the lemonade you drink, there's lots of
ways to pass the dry and hot summer days.
Red id for the beautiful apples you eat in the spring,
also the roses that bloom in the spring.
Purple is for the plums, so ripe so good.
Yellow is for the bright sunshine that helps to grow our food.
Green is for the christmas tree, its big green needles
so pretty is thee.
Orange is for the orange you eat.
Brown is for the oak furniture you but at the store,
is it not neat?
Grey is for the little mouse who is scampering
around my house.

Eric Lee Peeples

Lines

They begin._____
When one ends, another begins.
Like the days of your life, they start again and again.
Like the lines of the page, the continuation is essential.
_____To cause their abrupt end is an abomination
Live their example.
Continue till the end.

Jarvis L. Reed

Loco Weed

Egad! The lass has swept me off my feet;
For I looked deep into her baby blues.
I fear my racing heart just skipped a beat;
My socks are damp from sweat inside my shoes.
A giddiness has caused my head to swim;
For shame to let such beauty run amuck.
I'm trying hard to look so neat and prim;
My lips can move, but Lord! My tongue is stuck.
Moon madness grips my soul from head to toe;
The coyote in me wails its wistful howl.
My dignity has fled from me I know;
This bonnie lass must really be some gal.

For someone who has learned so much in school,
I must confess I'm acting like a fool!

Jerry P. Morgan

Untitled

If when I talk I seem to be shy
I'll tell you the reason why
It happened so fast and without warning
I met a person so nice and charming
We could never become sweetheart
As to God she pledged her heart
She never dreams of becoming a wife
As God's love and words guide her life
As we talk it seem her only love
Is her church and her God above
With all of this love for God in her heart
I hope a friendship it will let us start
A friendship with her would be very dear
As God and his love would always be near

Fred Griggs

The Song Singer

Oh dreary day, oh dreary night,
On metal chariot I ride,
Of soundless strife I fill my life,
To fill my dreams I must abide,
And seek to void the endless quest,
And sate my thirst, and still my breast.

In brief repose I surf, I seek,
Of magic pictures, sound and screen,
To brief a time to fill my rest,
My senses pause, on bated breath,
A prince, a sound appears of song,
And fills my world with what I long.

His black eyes flash with spirit strong,
His lips are sweet, his brow divine,
To kiss, to hold, a dream to belong,
He stares at me through plastic time.
I gaze, and long for dreams to be,
And curse the end of my reverie.

Joan M. Fernholz

What Is A Rock

A rock is millions of tiny particles sometimes naked to
the seeing eye woven tightly together by the pounding and
weathering of the waves. With each wave a new particle is attached.
Many people look at rocks and kick them aside — yet look deeper
— break it apart, chip by chip and its beauty begins to unfold.
A thousand years of the pounding and weathering and natural
forces of nature have created this hardened mass — such a
beautiful piece of art, yet so seldom seen as such and tossed
aside. Even the ugliest of rocks have their own beauty.

　　Look at the colors — see the sparkling
　　of each minute particle when held to the sun.
　　Look closely, for it is unique unto itself. Just
　　as no person is the same, no rock is the same.

We've all been weathered and shaped by the forces of nature
and life itself. With each new generation a new life begins and
new particles are passed on. Sometimes good and sometimes
bad, but where is the uniqueness after all is passed on and
attached. It needs to be rediscovered and remembered.
One needs to find their own center and core.
　　It is there — somewhere — I know

Kimberlee R. Y. Sanborn

Nature

Summer; it comes on the wings of a rapture and with its feathers of gold,
Shine in the light — what a heavenly sight — and now only memories
　　of wintery cold,
Grass green and the air is clean and bees for the purest flowers, seek,
And all the things the good earth brings just like a huge bell
　　and how it rings, if nature could only speak . . .
Fall; blistering winds refreshing rains and all its color vividly bright,
A rainbow planned by natures hands and all prepared to sooth your sight,
Leaves will fall high and small winds and rains the country will sweep,
And a little snow, well not yet although, well to tell the truth I
　　really don't know, if nature could only speak . . .
Winter; it creeps on like a lion and then with a sudden spring,
Freezes your toes and frosts your nose but puts some love
　　into everything, everything is white and Oh!
So bright with mother nature's beauty unique,
It's plenty cold, yet for all the gold, if this was all yours
　　not one ounce would be sold, If nature could only speak . . .
Spring; flies in on a cloud, fresh and clean, wintery cold is gone,
The birds sing, of everything, oh what a ballad what a beautiful
　　song, there's a little bit of heaven everywhere
　　things are clean and neat, Like a child at it's birth,
　　like the Heavenly mirth, If nature could only speak . . .

Catherine Dumar

Bon Appetit

Farewell my love — my love for Apple Trees
For I am sailing to a land but not across the seas
Which have no apples such as these —
But Hello Avocados! My new professed acclaim —
I must devour some more, before I go insane.
Peel the skin and show me the stone.
Not gold ! Behold ! It's only brown I'm shown.
"Give me something new" I yell.
What do I see? No not a gazelle
But a Radish.
Delish, Delish, you little Radish on a dish
But your bite has caught my tongue
And it is now time for a new song to be sung.
"No more fruits — bring me wine
Accompanied by a roasted swine.
Give me substance, give me flavor —
Something which my knowledgeable mouth can savor".

Andrea Heydlauff

The Widow

Her voice would falter and her eyes would fill
As she spoke of her man, recalling him still;
And their life together — a long span of time.
It was his death evoking those memories sublime.

A young woman, she was when first they had met.
It was something in his aura that made her forget
Those ills of a difficult and impoverished life,
Replete with all of its painful and consequent strife.

Commencing marriage with hearts full of hope,
It was love that made life easier to cope.
And then came the children, one by one;
After the fourth, this part finally done.

A struggle it was, with good times and bad,
As children left home, their lives would be sad.
Alone again, but with dreams now fulfilled:
With the power of love adversity was killed.

Then, although happy yet said, he welcomed his God,
No more burdensome paths would have to be plod.
But she, without him, somehow was incomplete;
Only their reunion this impeding plight could defeat.

George H. Harhigh

Reality, Fear, And Truth

Reality came over for dinner one day,
and asked me to look in his eye.
What he needed to know was I going his way,
or simply saying good-bye.

Fear came along next and she told me to say,
that Reality should go take a hike.
But I needed to go and to find my own way,
since my own life I just could not like.

Truth appeared last always willing to shine,
though a little bit painful to see.
She gave me a map and a hug which was fine,
and I knew what I wanted to be.

So here I now walk down the path of my life,
skipping steps as I go in my stride.
Whether it's glory I seek or unending strife,
I know Reality walks close by my side.

So-Woo Lee

Untitled

A stranger ate my bread
And in the meantime as I lie, I disguise
As her eyes roll to the back of her head
I cover up
I play the game
I caress her body
I underestimate the strength
And in the meantime, I nod
And the stranger moves towards my wine
I wake to the senseless bottle
Barren as the bottle is
Barren are thoughts
I'm empty on my berth
So content
I lay with insensible eye, motionless and consumed
Silent and deserted
And in the meantime she returns
In her arms she holds a loaf of bread and a bottle of wine
I'm dependent
I smile a child smile

Jennifer Miller

Fruits Of The Spirit

There is a garden for a Christian to grow
The fruit is as sweet as you'll ever know.

The seeds are watered by the dew.
When they mature there is a clue.

Love, joy, and peace abound
Patience, kindness and goodness are found
Faithfulness, gentleness and self control
Blessed until the harvest, saved be their soul.

Donna McDermed

Mistress

Day by day my patience grows dim. Like the wick on a stick of dynamite. As the wick of the stick burns, tension builds. What I thought to be lost forever, I found it not to be. Like a mistress in the night you swept it from me. I thought and thought of what it could be that you would want from me. I came to my senses and found it to be, that it was my heart you had taken from me. I find myself wandering just to find you, so I could kiss you and say, "I Love You." I come to your house and gaze through the window. I see a silhouette figure against the couch. Why of course, it's you, ever so true in thy beauty. I walk to your door and tap on it as though I did not want to. You hear the gentle rap at your door. I see you there before me, so I place my hands on your cheeks and gently pull you towards me to kiss you ever so sweetly upon thy lips. I whisper to you that I love You and this I hold to be true. As I walk down the stairs, I find it to be that I have taken your heart, just as you have done to me. So I promise to thee that I will Love You for all eternity.

Joel Wozny

Untitled

I take your hand and hold It in mine,
I promise to love you till the end of time,
I'll always be there if you should fall,
I'll always be there through it all.

I promise my patience, understanding and friendship too,
I promise my heart filled with love for you,
So in sickness or health,
Whether poor or all the wealth.

I give you these rings to wear for life,
and a bond & love that will last forever,
    as husband and wife.

Peter Di Rienzo

Sitting By A Grave

I set here by this grave so deep
Wondering if tonight I could sleep
My baby so little my child so sweet
How she kept her room so perfect and neat
Her hair so silky, her cheeks so soft
I would rush to her side whenever she coughed
I'll never forget that day or that call
They said she had a terrible fall
I rushed to see her, by her side
But when I got there they told me she had died
I try to go on everyday
I try and try in everyday
I sit here by this grave so deep
And wonder if tonight I could sleep

Jaime Miller

Overlooking The Holler

As I sit on the mountain top overlooking the Holler,
I silently observe the chirping birds, the rustle of the leaves
    the unique rock formations.
There is peacefulness in the gentle breeze against my face,
    the warmth of the sun, the aroma of creation.
Time does not exist at this moment because my soul
Is free of the constraints of this life.
A small leap and I shall fly away to a place of divine eternity.
For a second I am faced with turmoil, then
An awakening, for my life is not yet fulfilled.
There are so many things to experience and people to love.
A calming determination fills me with a sense to accomplish,
    a life to complete.
I know that all things come to pass,
But through their passing, they leave a mark of wisdom on the soul.

Elizabeth Loebach

Eyes Of A Cat

What does a cat see with her eyes?
She see's a mouse, and that's no lie.
She see's a boy cat, and is shy.
My cat got my dad's tie.
And she always eats my pie.
The cat see's bird in the sky,
And the cat wants the bird, "Oh My!
Only if she could fly!
She will live along time, until she dies.

Deborah Healey

The Sleeper

The sleeper dreams as shades of day, enfold and take him far away . . .

Behind the dumpster in the dirt, the child of innocence is hurt
The sad remains are all that's left from obscene blows
And no one sees, and no one helps and no one knows.

The sleeper twisting, shifting slight, embraces full the deep'ning night.

A woman screaming in the hall, beseeching for the life of all
Her children hungry, dazed and harmed
Yet no one cares to sound alarms.

The scent of Jasmine sweets the air, and weaves the sleepers dreams in there.

A frightened beagle vainly cries and longs to see his masters eyes
But he has gone, abandoned, fled, The needle comes, the Beagle's dead.

The moonlight slowly fills the skies, and bathes the sleeping sleepers eyes.

Through every beauty man can know, or see, or hear or touch or grow,
Such travesties obscure the man,
Infect the world and change the plan . . .

As daylight comes, then swift is gone, the sleeper shrugs and
    just sleeps on.

Robie Lester

Pandora's Box

Tucked away, behind your porcelain doll, a box of silver and
gold lays. Mystic this box. Sealed shut by black velvet ties.
What secrets could you hold? A small note beckons you;
"Open not this box. True feelings lay within."
    Untie the knots. Just a peek will do. The curiosity grows
strong. I must see what's inside. What will I find? I've
come this far. Slowly, the lid is lifted. A hush fills the room.
A feeling unknown creeps over you. Could this be wrong?
    A touch caresses your face. A heart warming hug encircles
you. A gentle, caring kiss felt on your head. The meaning of
my life is now known. Kept in my box for many of years. All my
laughter, all my kindness, you have felt.
    Now you know what lays inside. Tell me, will you close
this lid once more?

Paul T. Davis

A Rose For Sharon

I met her on a midnight still
As I sat beside the window sill
She spoke with ease as she said what she pleased
And I quietly thought "Oh God what a tease"
But then one time, once when she spoke
Of her my judgement in pieces it broke
The smiles they hide the tears inside,
And her heart with pain, it soaked.
Confusion is the devil's friend . . .
mine enemy always be
Is what the sorrowed Rose of Sharon
had all appear to me.
What had she done besides love the one
who left her in a heft.
The one she took and stood beside
and said "I do" till death
This is a rose for Sharon
for I do love her still
And as the nights roll by..on look I
sitting quietly by the window sill.

Phylicia Anderson

Untitled

Flowers crammed in a vase without boundaries
People in the world
Confusion and chaos
A book full of words
Things defined and not
Questions around each corner
Lost in a world full of leaders
People are like
Flowers crammed in a vase without boundaries

Nona Michael

Interment (An Italian Sonnet)

I felt the embalming fluid flowing
beneath my skin, which was covered with thick
blots of powder makeup. My numb arms stuck
to my side, bent at the elbows forming
a tangled loop of fingers pressed beneath
my petrified breasts. Dried, puckered lips cracked
at the corners of my mouth. And I'm packed
within a box cushioned from head to feet.
Yet, my crusty eyelashes held the key
that unsealed the passage of my new world
inside a realm of heaven or of hell.
Yes, I have to open my eyes to lead
my spirit out of this corpse from peril
overcome my fear of death and prevail.

Deaette Smith

191

"I Am"

I am complex of the human race,
I am respecting of nature and an ally to her mother,
I am truthful and up-front,
I am honest and blunt,
I am a man for women,
I am sensitive and caring,
I am loving and sharing,
I am asymmetrical,
I am accepting and pure,
I am sex and sexual,
I am a lot of things,
I am only a few,
I am but one man,
I am but one man for all women and men,
I am Asian Black Latino Straight Indian White Colored Gay . . .
I am all but all in one,
I am a aunty uncle brother mother sister father lover . . .
I am an open and blank journal to be written in,
I am open,
I am.

Brant Rawls

A Penny For Your Thoughts

It's been a long hard road this life of mine,
My surface is dull and I've lost my shine.
For forty-four years I've been around,
I've seen people up and I've seen people down.
I've been to the east and I've been to the west,
From a young girl's breast to a business man's vest.
I've been to the north and I've been to the south,
From an old man's fist to a young child's mouth.
I was lost in the dust at a Texas rodeo,
And lay there hidden for a year or so.
I was buried in a shell in the sand on the shore,
Until the tide washed me out in the dawn of the morn'.
I rode the Mississippi on an old steamboat,
And climbed a mountain in a old timers' coat.
I was thrown in a fountain to make a wish come true,
And given to a blind man to help buy food.
People and places, I've seen so many,
And I'm nothing more than a little copper penny.

Dwan Raper

That's My Job, O.K.?

I left you with a job to do . . .
Spread love an joy each day . . .
If judging has consumed you . . .
That's my job, O.K.?

You're not in charge of everything,
Nor accountable for all deeds . . .
My job's to rule the universe . . .
You're to help with people's needs.

If you're watching someone's walk . . .
Judging what's in their heart . . .
You risk from me displeasure . . .
And it could keep us apart.

So do the things I told you to . . .
Fill your heart with love . . .
Minding your own business . . .
Is an order form above.
  Love,
   God

Jill Loustalot Martin

Lord, Help Me!

Lord, help me to be the best that I can be
Counting on your power to sustain and to charge me
Each needs improvement, not a one being perfect
Lead me on the route that you desire me to grow

Lord, help me to be a good person to all
Not believing anyone on this earth above or below me
Show me your plan to make relationships healthy
To be one who loves, and can give of my talents

Lord, help me not to fall into dwelling in self pity
No matter how bad, there's always someone suffering more
Aid me in putting that negative energy to positive use
Allowing time for my needs, but not to be consumed by them

Lord, help me to put my best effort into all that I do
Excellence not the good, but my aim self-improvement
This will take work on my past that I need to expend
In spite of your miracles, we can't just sit and wait

Lord, help me to strive to live up to your word
Trying with all effort to be exactly like you
An impossible task, to achieve such a glory
But always working to improve; to please you, god almighty

Sue Regina

If We Would

If we would truly let Love abide:
We would know that there is a presence, that permeates the universe,
We would see that every soul is connected, it all begins at birth.
We would understand why we were created, all as a part of one,
We would understand where we are going, and where we have come from.
We would enjoy the beauty of sunshine, and dance in the rain,
We would feel one another's hurts, and share in one another's pain.
We would cry along with the hurting,
We would bear one another's burdens.
We would greet one another with a smile, and be careful when we frown,
We would lift each other up, and not tear one another down.
We would pray for one another always, because that's the only way,
We would help one another through pain and sorrow, as we live from day to day.
We would understand that riches and wealth, is only a passing phase,
We would realize that the awesome presence, can never be replaced.
We would understand our purpose, the mighty plan unfold.
We would all join hands and run this race, the young and the old.
We would understand that when this life is over, nothing will really end,
We would only be transformed, to return to where it all began.

Renata Bigham-Derry

Happy Birthday Mom

Light that beams and glimpses your face by the morning star.
It's off to work each morning you go, that seems to be so far.

But not today, for it is new emotions and a new high.
The light which touches you now, does not come from the sky.

Enriches the lives of all you come to meet
Better off from there on out because of your awesome heat.

From now, today the future is becoming better and new feelings
and excitement will be there too.
It is not because this is your day but because of that which
comes from deep within you.

The impact that you have given freely to share.
It is a life unlike my own that I cannot come to compare.

I love you mom and that is all there is to that.
The magic that you have created for me could have never come from a hat.

I wish words could be more powerful in which the way I feel;
but it will always be my heart that you will have forever to steal.

Happy Birthday Mom, and those words come from no fool.
Your day from here on out is now brighter and yours freely to rule!

Jason O'Rullian

"Ode To A Lover"

When I'm alone,
All I think about is you
You calm my fears and soothe my pains
My love, I must praise thee on a job well-done

I look into your eyes and swoon,
For they're almost as handsome as you
A bluer blue could not be imagined;
Your eyes hold your soul

Your voice is like Nature herself speaking,
So soft and gentle
It flows away from your sculpted lips,
And carries me away

When you kiss me, I feel faint
Magic runs through my veins,
As does temptation oh-so-sweet
My mind reels just thinking about it

You're the yang to my yin,
The darkness to my light
Or is it the other way around?
Sometimes it's hard to tell

Brandy Woods

Artistry

An artist with only color and a tiny brush
May produce a painting that will inspire us.
A soft still morning of a gentle spring,
"A few strokes here and I'll have the thing".

A poet weaves a tapestry word by word
Of the things he has seen, felt and heard.
A soft still morning of a gentle spring
"What could be more lovely? Inspiring!"

The musician takes the words the poet has written
And he makes them purr like the proverbial kitten.
A soft still morning of a gentle spring
"Of such things are the songs I sing."

For a pilot, the essence of art, song and word
Is just to go soaring in his beautiful bird.
A soft still morning of a gentle spring
"What a day for a ride in my flying machine."

While flying, you get back more than you give
For not to have flown is not to have lived.
A soft still morning of a gentle spring
Carries the memory of a pilot still doing his thing.

Vincent Young

Good Bye Old Dog

There you are boy
My buddy, my friend.
It's okay buddy,
You are nearing the end.
I'll stay beside you.
I won't leave you here.
I'll cradle your head.
You'll have nothing to fear.
You will just fall asleep
and your heart will be free.
Then we will drive home to your favorite tree.
I'll wrap you in your blanket,
One last time kiss your head.
As I lay you down, in the earth by the shed.
Then I'll say goodbye and my heart will break
and all of my love up to heaven you'll take.
I'll miss you boy.

Linda Holmes

I Have My Own Beauty

I am a supernaut of the new frontier
I groove in my own dimension
I exist in a time warp all my own
I have my own beauty

I'm pro-choice, no choice
Any choice I like
If you don't agree with me, that's okay
I'm used to it

But I'm through with being trampled on
For seeing things my own way
My friendships are blind to color and sex
And I've learned to forget the boundaries I've been taught

I'm electric, electric
I have my own beauty

Randi Padgett

Return To Senses

My pain is shared — yet I feel it is not felt.

Things said in anger to a listening God — or is He?
    For I feel it is not heard.

My tears, burning my cheeks and eyes, turning into sobs,
letting it all go — still I feel no relief.

Missing the scent of another —
    on the pillow next to mine;
    in the air of my home.

Missing the evidence, the sight —
    of rumpled clothes on the floor;
    of another in my bed.

The emptiness of my heart is all I taste — the others are empty,
    except the bitter taste of alone-ness.

I desire, I long, for return of senses.

Kathryn Nader

Season Of Love

Fall is gone and winter has moved on
Summer is yet to come.
For in our hearts, spring has sprung
In my love you shall forever stay.
You calm, your beauty, your graceful way.
As we walk along, hand in hand,
Our hearts leap, are light and gay,
While forever the bands shall play.
If there was but one way I knew,
I'd tell you how much I love you.
Your calm, your beauty, our love a new.

Mandy Fitzmayer

Picking Up The Pieces

Relationship is over
Broken hearted
Hurt and anger
Dealt with in time
Pickup the pieces
Start once again
Be thankful for your family and friends
A lesson I've learned throughout all of this
Men come and go
Family and friends never left
I thank them all for standing by me
And I honor them as they honor me

Linda Marie Neese

"Ode To Life"

Sometimes it's hard to comprehend
Why there has to be an end. Why must we die?
We wonder why, we even bother to be alive.
The clue to live in happiness, is to take each day with gentleness.
For life can be magnificent,
When every day is fully spent.
Life is not just what comes and goes,
But those friends who share and feel our woes.
And if each day does come in vain.
Then what cure shall relieve our pain?
For it's sad to say but some day soon
We shall have to face our awful doom.
However, we must learn to be strong,
To distinguish the good from the wrong,
To look at life as a bridal gown,
And to realize our God shall never let us down.
So let out those tears that hide from within.
Revealing your inner hurt is never a sin.
And always hope, hope for the best.
This way you'll always ace the test!

Linda F. Diaz

Visualize

Education will open their ears and eyes . . .
Revealing enormous surprise,
That would have, otherwise,
Been disguised as drugs, crime
And parents ties
To a child and welfare.

What we have realized,
Is that welfare buys
Illegitimacy on the rise
And hopes turned to lies.
All that remains are the fictitious highs,
Of youth — between there and nowhere.

So the teen is reduced to sighs,
Having missed a slice of the social pie,
Having been povertized
By a system that vies for the fittest —
The educated who can visualize
Their future . . . and care.

Robert D. Reed

Saratoga

Oh Hale Ye Oh Hale Ye Men and forces for Gentlemen Johnny
comes with his British Army, on horses. They are armed with
guns, rifles and knives.

We will prepare and out number them. When thou gentlemen
Johnny may come
with his British Army, we will fight for our rights of
Independents to be free.

When thus must occur, blood will be shed, lives will be
taken, tears will be shed,
and hearts will be broken. Families will be shattered,
injuries will occur.

We will remember thus who fight heroic, for the ones who
cease in war, we will pray that your families broken hearts
will mend. Injured or wounded we will show respect and
fight on for you.

The Independence we want and need will only come if we
proceed. Then we will be free, of King George the III, not
the great. Whom he serves for the King will fail, we have
our determination and our Lord whom we can do anything in.

Carolyn Ann Royer

Free Falling

Feelings burn through me as His crystals tingle my soul;
I am a pot of melting gold on a heated stove.

Water and sand together create a beach, He is the moon;
Controlling the tide and its motion, beauty is before me.

I reach out to capture and share His hushed breath;
Two shadows mingle on a lonely slate wall.

Allowing the sunshine of His smile to heal my unkempt wounds;
Ties of passion bind these hearts together.

Soft smiles and small caresses equal an entire chapter;
This novel is not yet completely written.

Lighting the way is my angel, who believes in my every step;
Sheltering the storm, but allowing the rain.

If this be my only chance, let the fire within me release itself;
For He is the love I have held dear from the first day of my life.

Janet L. Gauthier

"Who Are We"

Thoughts flee before me
Darkness engulfs the image of a child that was yesterday
Eyes that should of twinkled with wonderment
Plunged deep in sadness, pain and despair
Immobilized with fear

How could the shadow of death
entrap the tender whisper my little child
No one noticed-no one cared
So faint her cry
Escape became a way of life

Why me? Why me? Uninvited
Hunted like an animal — no wall left unscathed
Broken, used, battered
Friend where are you?
I must leave this life — I did — I tried, and I did

No memory over here — over there
Where? I do not know
Invite them out — It's time to tell
Who are we?

Margot Wright

Easter Morn

Far away in the horizon
A silvery purple dawn breaks
Mother earth rolls on its ventral
Eager to catch up the sun's rays

In the scarred, barren desert
Lie ashes blown by the whirlwind

There in a humble corner of the world
Where the gates opened one morning
A mule carried the message
Triumphant spirit of goodwill

Man arrived on superhighway
With big devouring machines
The message misread the cart loaded rolled downhill

The earth rumbled in rage
Lightning flashed through the skies
Thunder roared in its ears zooming waves of illusion

It's easter morn
Come lend me a hand to tend the lilies in bloom
There in the fields dressed in white
With yellow ribbons in their hats.

Adrienne Simonian

Why?

Imagine if there were no limitations,
No ends, no bounds, no laws
The world would be full of harmony
Or would it be hatred?

Harmony is not speaking out of turn.
Hatred is expressing your thoughts,
Your ideas, your opinions, your beliefs
Why can't we figure out a medium?

If we could just try to get along,
Why can't we have a world
Without violence, crimes, discrimination?
Why don't we know more words like tolerance?

Why do we even know words like,
Racism, sexual harassment, murder, rape?
Only in times of grief do we get along,
This world can only handle so much sorrow.

Kristyn Miller

Gems Of The Nile

Two glimmering gems both alike in beauty,
Stolen from underneath a pharoah's guard,
Lie lone in a sack of pirate's booty,
But now might be mistaken for pigs' lard.
Once possessed by Cleopatra herself,
Blue stones of fire that were deeply admired,
Now sit upon a dusty pawn shop's shelf,
Yet rings of sexual prowess when wired.
Lost forever in a journey through time,
Emitting waves of passion 'bout fair Rome,
Hewn from the inner depths within stone lime,
Aflame throughout their cylindrical dome,
Their energy tearing down walls of hate,
In haste, are now but one moment too late.

Thomas K. McNeil

Wild Horse

Wild Horse, Wild Horse, where do you roam?
The canyons, the mountains and the prairies are your home.

You run like the wind, but where do you go?
From the lush green valleys to the hills covered with snow.

Wild Horse, Wild Horse, why do you cry?
I hear your song and wonder why.

Your four legs carry you near and far,
How I wish I could be where you are.

I wish and I hope I could own you someday,
Then under the sun and the stars we could play.

Laura Leigh

Florida

At an aqua-blue poolside in the promised land
there is no winter snow.
Still, grey and white dominate
surroundings in hair and wrinkled faces.
Spanish moss hangs on trees
like a deep dark suntan,
killing its host
but looking damn pretty.
Uncle Howard's New York white legs do battle
with black ankle socks.
An American flag pin pierces his hat brim
and gets us a free round at the VFW.
In a fluorescent beer hall in Palm Coast
a geriatric barkeep battles sleep.
Uncle Fritz smiles widely and says
It doesn't get any better than this.

Jim Sheridan

God's Recipe For People

Doesn't it seem like God took all the things
in the world and put them all into jars, jars of life.
And one day He decided to make a jar of people to give the
jars of life something to live in. So He took the jars of
life and people, and poured them all into a big jar, making
sure to mix them well, and while he was mixing all the
feelings, hopes, dreams, looks, emotions, likes and dislikes,
of life into the jars of people He gave each one what He
wanted them to have and placed each of them in a family and
like all families are to connect, like railroad tracks riding
smoothly along the tracks of life.

But along the journey of life there where a few gaps in
the tracks no one knew why, no one thought it was their fault
the gaps where there, but God put the families there to fix
the gaps, to fix the problems, to fix the differences, and
when the families worked together they came to fix the gaps,
the problems, and the differences so that the whole family
could travel down the tracks of life on a smooth and peaceful journey.

Pierre Davis

My Precious Little Girl

My little girl is so precious and sweet,
With her little nose and cute little feet.
Now my little one is walking so tall.
I love her so much, I hope she doesn't fall,
Her first day of school has started today.
It seems I held her in my arms just yesterday,
My precious one is dating now, you see,
He'd better treat her right, or he'll have to answer to me,
Now out of high school she goes with pride,
She walks down the aisle, and in me a tear wells up inside,
Off to college my loved one has gone,
I can remember when she was playing out on the lawn,
A phone call I get, and my girl is engaged,
I said terrific, we'll have your wedding elegantly staged,
She walks down the aisle, her true love to wed,
The reception goes great, everyone is well fed
Now my precious daughter has a gift who was sent to her from above
Now I have my precious little girl and my granddaughter to love.

Terry Lynn DeVore

The Angry Storm

All day the storm clouds have been gathering,
Swirling, dark, towering clouds with flashes of lightening,
Coming ever closer, all charged with a wild brooding energy.
The air is filled with odor of ozone.

The rain comes pelting down, bringing globules of hail.
The water rushes, in great gushing streams,
Over the land, on its way to the sea.
It carries away precious soil, as well as debris.

The wind howls and screams.
The thunder roars and rumbles, in long rolling clashes,
The night becomes filled with terror,
As bolts of lightening strike, its blue light hisses,
and enters the ground.

The fury of the storm passes and is gone.
Leaving in its wake a tangle of broken tree limbs.
Flowers and gardens torn, uprooted. The air is clean and fresh.

The stars twinkle brightly in a dark velvet sky.
The earth has been washed clean, to dry,
To await the coming of a bright new day.
The storm has passed.

Sarah G. Sawyer-Shepard

Four Sons

Brick hard and unforgiving
The ground the four boys dug,
Complaining, "the rock pile, prison duty!"
"When do we get off?"
Armed with shovels and
Pick axes, chopping holes
Four feet apart, for future trees.

Into them the garbage went
And from potato peels,
A surprise, and unexpected,
A perfect hedge did grow,
From that small victory followed
The barren mountain planted
To a great pine forest, and
Four planter boys to men.

Dorothy McGrady

Service Station

There are so many roads to take
so many roads to follow
roads by the streams and lakes
running by the weeping willow
which road do I take
which road do I follow
my mind seems wide awake
but it's oh, so shallow

The roads are winding
the roads are long
roads are decisions
some right, some wrong
my mind is so musty
the roads are so dusty
I wander amiss with my maps in question
sometimes you have to stop and ask for direction

T. J. Reyckert Manchester

Rainy Day

The wave of the river is heavy like rocks
And boats are swinging like swimming ducks
While cars in the streets go speedy like bees
Yes people run on the pavement feeling at ease.

Oh the lights in the building shown so bright
And clouds in the sky look so dull
Because rain drops are falling so heavily like stones.

Oh what a rainy days for us to be free
Well tell me what to do if I can't see
Through the glass that I once saw me
Oh this rainy day
This rainy day.

Murthlene A. Sampson

Will You Remember

Will you remember me if I die?
Will you remember me when you die?
Will you remember me if you see me in heaven?
Will you remember the magical love between us?
Will you remember when we first met and there
was a twinkle in our eyes, (I will).
I will remember when we first held hands and
all the wonderful times we had,
and how we watched our magical love as it grew;

David Peterson

Life And Friends

Love is having each other — sharing . . .
Never dreaming to be apart . . .
Raising a family — caring . . .
Wishing happiness in their hearts . . .

Life is growing — maturing . . .
Raising, worrying, trusting . . .
Aging is hurting, body and mind . . .
Family is comforting, consoling and oh so kind . . .

Hoping togetherness, always will be . . .
Fearing the worst, happening to me . . .
Alone now, trying not to show pain . . .
Believing someday we'll be together again . .

Parting is loneliness — with pain . . .
Your legs and arms moving . . .
Your heart is walking with a cane . . .
. . . Friends mean so much . . .

Dolores Fahey

Plains Of Presence

As I peer from phonetic oceans in my mind,
And craze the tasting fields, I find,
Coals of praise and cries and trusts,
A blending haze of praying musts.

The yearn for transient clues to turn and close,
The familiar beats of the flame enfolds
My glowing pride with grains of love and precious time,
Bring curling crusts of pensive thoughts so fine.

Ah, once there was and the plans did grind,
Of purest fates, the acts were primed
through careful plottings of the might and soul,
The now rustic tasks of life did grow.

Now, I grasp from afar, odd things and shapes,
That I hold dear and none can shake
The belief within that cradles and candles desire,
Of not what I am, but of what will I tire.

Betty Wells-Pino

Our Higher Power

Oh God of creatures great and small,
A world of beauty you made for us all;
You're always there waiting to receive us all,
All You ask is for us to believe and stand tall.

You're called Allah, Creator, God and Love,
Your Love ever present great spirit from above;
You made the trees from which birds can sing,
Or dear God you created everything.

And as I awoke to the new light of day,
I fell on my knees and began to pray;
Guide me Great Spirit along the way,
Give me the courage to face yet another day.

Fill me with thy Love, Mercy and Power,
To share with each other a bird, a flower;
All honor goes to you, I pray,
For allowing me to share yet another beautiful day.

So give to each person in this room,
The power to overcome the dark and the gloom;
Grant them thy peace, thy mercy, thy love,
Oh Great Spirit from above.

Kenneth Megill Jr.

196

Freedom Of Horses

They frolic in the prairies, running strong and wild and free,
Living for the moment, creating their destiny.

They hold their heads up with confidence as the wind whips
through their mane,
and they live in peace and freedom, a lesson we've yet to gain.

I open my eyes each morning, remembering the dream I weave,
Then reality assaults me, and I find it hard to breathe.

The violence is there and the fear returns, as I go out at night alone,
where danger awaits around every turn, my senses suddenly honed.

As I secure the last lock on all of my doors, the things I would
prefer to see . . .

Are sunlit prairies, and the freedom of horses
Which forever beckon to me . . .

Sherry Keown

Kevin

In Loving Memory of My Son
The time has come to say good bye
I only wish you didn't die
No words could ever let you know
How very much I miss you so.

My life will never be the same
I'll always hear my son's name
There aren't enough tears to cry
I've asked myself why, Oh why.

Was there some thing in your life to fear
I wish I'd have known because I'd have been there
It's much to late to let you know
How very much I loved you so

My heart will break from day to day
But every night you'll hear me pray
So keep in peace in God's love
I'll see you in the stars above.

Edward Stanley

Dancing Memories

Gently the record drops onto the turning table,
The arm swings out then back, the disc now stable.

The needle gently comes to rest in the first groove,
Slowly the music is coaxed forth and begins to fill the room.

The beat is even and soothing as it ebbs into my being,
And soon my body parts are persuaded into swinging.

My shoulders dip, my head sways, and soon my hips swing,
It seems the music takes over as my feet take wing.

I close my eyes and raise my arms to encircle my "partner",
The two of us, we waltz around, it seems we never tire.

The soothing tones soon come to a halt as the song finishes,
And with each note my will to hold back seemingly diminishes.

The record spins, the needle moves to yet another tune,
My "partner" takes me in his arms and we begin to swoon.

My worries melt like lemon drops,
And we dance until the music stops.

I open my eyes and my partner is gone, for he wasn't real you see,
He only exists behind closed eyes and in my memory.

I take the record from the phonograph and gingerly put it away.
Holding on as long as I can to scenes of yesterday.

Patsy L. Lewis

The Rambling Rose

So many times I'd sped past that place
Too fettered and stressed to slow my pace.
But this special day I was drawn to the lie
By a wisp of red that caught my eye.

There entwined in a great Maple tree
Was a rambling rose only I could see.
Its tangled web led to a blessed spot
Where a Celtic clan had laid its plot.

But only rusted square nails and scraps of tin
Now marked the place where the house had been;
And, from the echoed past of that lonely vale,
I heard the shriek of children and a baby's wail.

From high verdant hillside called the Plover
Where nature's wild things had taken over;
And, as the sun dimmed on this forgotten lea,
I knew this Holy place to be a part of me.

Jeffrey Schmidt

The Holocaust

It was like a hawk, in the night,
that gave the Jews, quite a fright.
It was like a storm, that just had passed,
and like a car, without any gas.

And when the storm, began to grow,
it was like winter, without any snow.
And when the Nazis, began to kill,
it was like a cap, without a bill.

Almost all the Jews, became extinct.
It was like a pen, without any ink.
But when the pen, began to write,
the Jews began, to give up a fight.

Until the end, the Jews had fought,
for it was justice, that they had sought.
But in the end, they had a great feast,
for they had destroyed, the terrible beasts.

Aaron Headrick

Pick Yourself Up

I had one of life's great challenges, that seemed to make me fall
but I got back up, stopped and stood and learned to face it all
I worked real hard, went real straight, and things was going nice
but I lost my temper to my friend and fell again, "that's twice"
I got on top was doing grand, but then took a little dip
I picked me up and tried real hard but then I really slipped
life has a lot of challenges, that seems to fill your cup
so when you're down and lying there, don't forget to
"pick yourself up"

David M. Waters

Syncretism

Is it meant to bring me death, this power that preserves?
I cannot see just yet which one my life deserves.
As I pass from life to death and back to life again,
Righteousness reveals the power of my sin.

Energy to impotence to synergy in love
Clemency, forgiveness, release is not enough.
Grace and mercy never bought, love is never learned
The life I love the love I live restored but never earned.

Syncretism of a blackened heart clean with bloodied tears,
Absolution of a hardened heart, love casts out my fears.

Jim Bird

The River

As I travel down this river of life,
I can not forget the waters that I've come through.
A good sailor remembers the rough spots,
As not to travel that way again.
Always remembering the gentle and sweet waters,
So they can be visited often.

The water is a mysterious thing.
Its deep blue color is very inviting.
One minute you are floating peacefully,
In the next, a terrible storm arises.
Somehow, you weather the storm and rough waters.
Only to find the rainbow is just on the other side.

No one knows where his river will end,
Or when it will end.
One just has to keep sailing and mapping his way
down the river,
Until he finds the sea.

Shona Dyess

Adopted Love

You came into my life one day
And changed my introverted way.
You gave me love and joy divine,
the day you placed your hand in mine.

Because of you the sun shines brighter.
My cares and woes are lighter.
Oh, the return of love's wonderful ache
Sometimes I fear my heart will break.

Dear to believe you're my consolation.
Or, are you just a dream, some figment of my imagination
Are you just another guest
Or am I very, very blest.

But when I hear your sweet and gentle laughter
My heart I commit forever after.
I have been here once upon a time
And I'll be here some other time.

Lorna Sailsman

Young Lady Shares

Peacocks and birds, wearing the most precious
Feathers, shall bow to you,
For your arrival on the biggest and most
Featherless bird is truth
To you and me.

Of great significance is each step in life,
God, grant that we have wisdom and love to
Not make that step in life, a life's purpose strife.

A Prince of a King would undoubtedly and instantly
Make you his princess or Queen,
For you are walking love,
Not for a stingy instant, though permanently.

Of great significance is each step in life,
God, grant that we have more love and trust
To give to each other,
For love, like bread has to be given fresh
Every day,
Which for you and me, thank God, is no bother.
Through this attitude blessings are in our lives every day.

Marco A. Contreras

How Would It Feel

How would it feel to be a camera?
Picture taking, and photo making?
Being a camera would be fun,
And you would be proud when your pictures are done.

How would it feel to be a lamp?
If you're battery packed, you could go on a camp.
You would be cheery and bright in the gloomiest of night,
Though you could be knocked down in a pillow fight.

How would it feel to be a telephone?
In the dark ages, you would be unknown.
People talk to you, and you get to ring,
And when nobody's home, there's an answering machine

How would it feel to be a tree?
A simple apple tree in an orchard?
Every day you'd get to be climbed on
By a fun loving kid in a sports shirt.

Yes, I would like to be a tree,
Not any of that mechanical stuff.
A simple tree, that's what I would be,
And to me that would be just enough.

John Paul Romanos

What is it?

What is it that moves me so
What is it that makes the heart search for the unseen
What is it that swirls the mind in endless motion to receive his love
What is it that cause me to bear the burden of caring for the
hopeless, the needy, the unwanted
What is it that you have placed in my heart,
a love that is too great to release,
afraid it may smother you and least you run away.
What is it that makes me hold on,
knowing the end result would be my hurt,
my demise, my loss, but still I hold on
over and over again hoping that this time it is real,
it is love, it is to want the same thing that I long for.
Simply to be cherished, for this is what
all of us seek to be cherished with love.

Teresa Barber

DNA Eyes

His eyes haunt me
They say things I can never —
The spell of his eyes
My heart swells inside.
My mind goes to mush.
When his eyes gives me a rush.
He's the quiet guy that doesn't say much.
Still waters run deep in his eyes.

  His eyes haunt me
Mind; you can't fly to his touch.
Don't turn to mush.
He's worth a tear
Get over him my dear.
Blue skies run deep in his eyes
As his heart and soul flies.

  His eyes haunt me
In dreams of yesterday.
I see his eyes in his Grandson's eyes.
Their eyes give the girls the rush.
Grandpa your eyes are here today to stay.

Vera E. Gutierrez

Tribute To My Caregiver

What is it about a caregiver,
That makes them so truly unique?
To care for, Protect, and Encourage Another,
Every single day of the week;
I know it's not for money, or for wealth untold;
Or a mysterious Pot of Gold;
So, it's gotta be something intangible,
We're unable to see, or to hold;

Now, once again last week, while making mistakes,
One right after another;
And, he didn't complain, or get angry with me,
As each one he would uncover;
Then I realized there could only be
One source for this great love;
He must ask for, and receive it each day,
Directly from our Father above.

Rita Deimling

God's Blanket

Trillions of tiny snowflakes
fall gently through the night
covering the drab brown earth
with a mantel of gleaming white,
stretching far as eye can see.

Day begins to break
and no prints yet have marred
the glistening coverlet, lying peaceful, undisturbed;
transforming the bleak unsightly earth
to a pure white loveliness.

Such is the blanket of God's love,
With mercy and forgiveness, through His Son,
covering the black ugliness of sin;
reaching out with hope to people everywhere
saying, "learn of me and live in love and peace."

Claranore Krey Hallberg

Untitled

Some, fearing death
    Preach real loud, "No war"
They do not want the fighting times
    Like the ones we've seen before

So they shout real loud, "No guns"
    And stay real firm, "No bombs"
They do not want the missile heads
    Or laser beams to come

But I say, "No locks"
    Just imagine them off our doors
Imagine them off our cars and our things
    And even off the stores

'O if the world it had no locks
    We'd be singing out the joys
For our neighbors would be friends
    And our weapons would be toys

William Deitz

My Blue Eyes

You told me that you could
get lost way down deep within
My Blue Eyes. I don't understand
why to me they're just ordinary eyes.
But you they hold the ocean inside.
You said you could fall in if you didn't
hold back. So please let go, so we'll see
just where we'll be at!

Chris Brawner

Mystery Of The Soul

For years I've searched, seeked and looked
for the love of life, that's been untold.

Trying to line things up straight and to match
the unmatchable within my soul.

The four times in hours are unexplainable but
definitely goes on forever, for all eternity.

For the glory of eternity is at hand, for the
new world is on its way.

Walk right in, you're free at last, all past are
gone, beyond our wildest dream, "'tis liberty."

There she is watching, waiting, with arms stretched
out, right on the line, greeting at the gate, singing
with joy extending everywhere.

Peace to you my brothers and sisters, we've made it at last.

It's time to say "Amen" to that, the mystery
of the issue is about to unfold.

Ernestine S. Anderson

Soulmates

Lying on spears of grass,
watching towering ponderosas sway.
In winds of a frost covered horizon,
we envision our lives in the clouds,
shadowing the dormant weeds,
festering in a cold stillness.
Briefly expressing chapters of our passions,
cultivated in questions of mortal logic.
Holding our breath to look around.
Watching Kachinas dancing on moon threads,
waning over grand pillars of aspen.
Spirits whistle conscious acts of salvation,
afloat in the heaven above.
Their reflection touches our souls,
educating the truth of what we are,
demanding change to an inevitable dawn.
Lights sparks draw off the unblemished dew,
lifting us up to make our way back home.

Luke Augustine Wilbur

You Have Touched Me

You have touched me
until I felt the sky become dark.
You held me
until the early morning
when the warming rays of the sun
peered over the horizon.
You have filled me with deep colors
of a burning sunset.
After you touched me,
and held me,
and filled me with passion,
you pulled my sleeping body up to yours
grasped my hand and entered my dreams — forever.

Sheila Buckley

War

Thousands of them are dead from bullets of lead.
Some of them were fathers, the ones who survived won Honors.
The War was terrible, to some survivors bearable.
The War was bad, lots of wives were extremely sad.
You learn a lot about deadly fights,
and you hardly get to sleep all nights.
At all the wars people died in horror.
That's why I will never join the War.

Chris Shaffer

Pulses

The caress of your tongue
as our lips become one.
My pulse racing,
my heartbeat echoing in the distance.

Hands roaming freely
touching, stroking, teasing,
yearning to reach the erogenous zone.

Erotic thoughts
flowing through our minds,
as you slowly remove all barriers.

Our bodies touching, skin to skin,
smooth to rough, experienced with the naive;
gently entering the Garden of Eden.

Tenderly the motion quickens,
bringing us closer, as we get
higher into the clouds.

The caress of your tongue
as our lips become one.
Our pulses racing as our love
echoes in the distance.

Cynara Hermes

Everyman Revisited

Quite lofty goals for life he set
And on these dreams his life he bet.
But by him quickly life had rushed
And in its wake his dreams were crushed.

For others came and sought his aid
And so his dreams aside he laid
But now his death has come at last
The time for dreams is in the past.

Bereft of all alone he'll stand
Till something comes to take his hand.
And to eternity he'll ride
With his good deeds to be his guide.

Edward J. Vinski

How Could They Do It?

We are Gypsies, Jehovah Witnesses, and Jews,
And the Nazis thought of us as scum on their shoes.
They rounded us up as if we were not human;
The Nazis wanted to kill us, yes this was their plan.
All of us had looks of fear on our face,
And they did not think of us as part of their perfect race.
We had no clue why they were doing this persecution,
And none of us knew that we were awaiting execution.
As we Gypsies and Jews were standing naked in line;
The idea of a shower sounded so incredibly divine.
As they opened the valve and the gas landed with a sting,
I still wondered how they could do such a thing?

Nathan Rodman Will

Dim Thoughts Or Sanctuary?

Arrogant dusty echoes
Enveloping demise.
Gallant demeanor, garnished in shabby array.
Posing before an audience of candor,
Vague as carnival tables,
Fingerprints laugh.
Masks of painted smiles balloon in whispers.
No deafening screams surface.
Decades of wind carry over
Planting this pollen of pale.

Debbie Geanangel

His
Son

There were
anguish and grief
in heaven that day,
As God sent his son
to earth far-away.

The angels shed tears
as they dealt with their fears,
For that newborn babe
In a manger roughly made.
His time on earth would be short,
But damnation he would abort.
A ministry of love and forgiveness,
physically and spiritually healing our blindness
While sinless, he gave his all,
For those who heed his loving call

Heaven rejoiced as Christ returned,
His mission complete, with the devil spurned.
Lord, we thank you for the reason,
That
we
celebrate this
Christmas season!

Dorothy E. Thielman

If The Devil Would Only Die

If the Devil would only die, then tears would be joy when they cry,
Mothers would bare no pain while birthing their children under
    father's name.

So the rain drops that scatter from above, would be a brilliant sparkle
of wet pure love, and the soft earth beneath our heels would be
a step of happiness that never tills.

So the devil would never ever again exist and away he would tumble
like a wasted myth.

So the color of our skins would be a bounty of light,
so wonderfully beautiful and such an awesome sight,
How perfect this would be for all of you and me.
If the devil would only die.

If the devil would only die, no more adversities between men,
no more hateful thought out trends.
No lust and disrespect for human life,
and no beastly order from death's awful plight.

Then heaven's emerald gates would swing wide,
and admit all of life inside.
The good pleasure would never hide, if the devil would only die.

David A. Morrow

Unrequited Love

I want to leave you all alone tonight,
And yet, I'd wish you were at my side still.
But in being drawn, in turn, I've lost my sight,
Pity to pity be; the bitter pill.
Altruistic is the arrows swift flight —
From Cupid's quiver to Venus' strong will.
In passion's true form breathes dangerous plight,
Wherein empathy's rules do not fulfill.
I feel a mounting pressure to give in,
Just as the Sun must allow the Moon's climb.
With a willingness to please tucked within —
Safely hidden in its torture of time.
    The Sun's glory sets in a jealous rage,
    When Moon's shine forever holds center stage.

Anthony Shay

Pretty Butterfly

What a silly butterfly you've become
Flitting among the fragrant flowers
Dashing to and fro just to frolic
With a new and glamorous stamen
In your futile search for perfection

Or is it excitement that you seek to find
In discovering the secrets of each new bud
Charming your way into their embracing petals
And extracting their waiting pollen
Like some delightful thief in the night

Is this your eternal legacy to taste the nectar of many a blossom
but never linger for more than a moments sip
will you ceaselessly fly forever free
till you die searching for a better bloom

Are you really free or only locked into a game
running scared from some imagined prison
afraid of commitment, afraid of love
seeking to lose yourself in frivolous action
so you don't have to deal with your emotions

Pretty butterfly, tragic butterfly
fly away now to pursue your destiny
and let me weep for what could never be.

Randall R. Norstrom

Untitled

Icy winds blow through her auburn hair,
the snow sparkles like little diamonds in the
moonlit night.

So beautiful she floats across the mid-night
sky, So deadly her poison for you and I.

I feel her stare, I stop in my tracks,
Oh God help me I can't turn back.
My heart beats slow, my eyes grow hazy,
What has happened to me, I must be crazy.
Two holes in my neck, my blood level
lower, She shrieks with delight and screams
it's not over.

Can no one stop the slaughter of man
by a wicked one since time began

Go slowly at night young man alone,
Trust not a soul if you want to save your own.

Max A. Eley

"Nature Of The Heart"

A cool summer breeze sifting through the trees.

The white flash of lightning dancing through the sky.

A loud cry of thunder . . . Then silence —

Yes! It is nature I speak of — "Nature of the Heart".

Communication holds the key.

For we are creatures of understanding.

I am content and harmonized when we speak with a breeze.

Confused like the scattered veins of the lightning bolt
when we want to reach out but are afraid.

So just as the lightning bolt leads to thunder — My confusion
erupts to Anger — then silence,
a time ponder.

Michael R. Leveronne

Feelings

Feelings are strong, they come from inside,
they can stretch real long, they have
nothing to hide. Feelings are friends, a
pretty close pal, they never end, a good
ole gal. You are made of feelings, they
live in you, they do all the heeling,
they do what you do. You are feelings,
without out a doubt, they are your
shieldings, they make you pout. Feelings
are your motive, your joy, your life, yourself.

Jessica Gilliam

Friendship . . .

Friendship may be a simple thing
but lots of love it can bring
things to share and talk about
it's just something you can't do without.
All your life friendship
lasts through the years
you'll look back remembering
all the laughter and happy times
along with the cries
and sorrow sights,
friendship don't die
it continues to grow
so be sure to cherish
the friendship you know.

Sheila Her

Seasonal Affair

And I loved the smell of summer, piss
in the wind soaking, ruining my penis emerging
from the springtime pure; and the fall falling into winter
freezing the fig and the plum,
and the breast and ass, all loved as well.

Each season passes she and I, purifying
through change but my panache. Time is lost
in warms and colds the feel of which
reminds of summer bliss touching
the sweat of balls thrust into womanhoods.

Springtime, names forgotten, no longer
pure, comes again with time renewing
the lust for difference, yearning the freedom
from pissing into the summer breeze.

Michael Allen

The Representative

I represent, the uneducated;
America's majority, unappreciated.
Without a degree, I have no name;
Not a chance for advancement, fortune or fame.

I resent, America's upper class;
Calling me," plain white trash."
Look down your scholared snouts to see;
Without your certificates, "you're just like me."

I present, the intelligence you ignore;
Without a document, you close your door.
Victims of your constant doubt;
Americans with abilities, that go without.

I sent, this message, to explain;
Without education, we remain...
The Americans working on weary feet;
Everyday struggling, to make ends meet.

Penelope Davidson-Jackson

Hear The Word Of The Lord

What hath the Lord God spoken
Hath mankind His Word now broken
Good intentions in people of Earth
Fall short in not putting God first

Faithful ones obey the appointed Way
Seeking true path and do then pray
God's Word is made truly most clear
Obey it and serve in His works sincere

Grow in preparation for coming time
People will be blessed in every clime
Evil restrained and Happiness will reign
Obedience true and God's Love claimed

Let us pray for God's Will to be done
Asking in the precious Name of His Son
True Peace as promised will portray
God's Love which abides in that Day

Susan Essler

Untitled

I heard repeating waves of crying
From the distant echoing sound
It may came from one who is dying
Lonely, with no one dear around.

Conceivably, it's just dispersing wind
Trapped in labyrinthine stones
Whistling trough their cracks —
Foolishly playing with sorrowful tones.

Or perhaps, 'twere some hungry sparrows
Waiting for their mother to meet —
But the weasel from across the narrows
Came first, finding something to eat.

It would be the same shrill piercing cry
Of a fearful mother at an empty nest,
Her babies' feathers scattered by
From their every tiny breathing chest.

There is the wild struggle for life —
The frights, disasters and the chance
For those who manage to survive
Sometimes, through the savage defense.

Irena Galka

"Tide"

The Tide rolls in . . .
further up the shore, consuming sand and shells,
without care or concern.
The foamy sea tickles my toes
and the seaweed swirls about,
churning in a salty vat of sand and shells.
The water keeps on coming higher,
it swims about my waist; my blanket is now soaking wet,
but I choose to look away.
My eyes burn with the salty air, and my nostrils too.
My ears keep ringing (the seagulls won't stop squawking).
The water now tickles my earlobes,
so I shut my eyes tight.
I know my time has come for the Tide to consume me.
As the water stings my lungs,
I realize that I have been taken without care or concern
The Tide is no respecter of persons.
And as I swirl and churn,
with sand, and salt, and shells,
I comprehend that I am nothing more than what I used to be

Donya Pearson

Endangered

I stare out my window into the darkness,
My reflection is all I can see.
I stare deeply into my own eyes.
Is this the same face I stared at as a boy?
The face appears young, but the eyes seem old and tired,
Like mummified kings.
It is hard to be a prisoner of your own mind,
When your soul is free as a bird.
But even the free bird can easily become the hunted,
The endangered,
The dying.

Shawn Southwick

Who Am I?

I who go by the name of man
Do often wonder why
The creator gave to me, a mystery
Who am I?

I have conquered the earth.
The moon is now being conquered by me
Then will come mars
Another step toward universal supremacy.

Who am I?
How great shall I be?
With all of this awesome power
That now belongs to me

If I could speak with the creator
I would cry
Oh great creator, tell me
Who am I?

Am I fulfilling my destiny?
Am I doing what you expect of me?
In all conquered words, will I only be
The caretaker of your land, air and sea?

Joseph Van Rader

Untitled

   It goes without saying:
That you and I are similar in ways we don't even know.
Take time and think about what that states.
   Amazingly it happened so quickly.
   We have been through so much. On a scale of 1-10, oh about a 10.
It's great to know people like you, whoever you are.

Just sitting here on this fall day watching every leaf fall off of
the 30 ft. maple tree in the front yard.
I am feeling isolated maybe even singling myself out from
everybody.
It sucks but then again being by myself it is great!

Being wrapped up in a blanket on this day . . .

Andrea Vitrano

Christmas Gift

No gift under the Christmas tree?
How could this be? Oh! How could this be!

Then I'm reminded that Christmas is not
   My birthday — but thee.

Dear God, if it was not for thee, there
   Would be no Christmas for my children
   Nor me!

That my dear child is the greatest Christmas
   Gift that the world will ever see!

Christ Jesus, son of God, who was sent with
   Love to you and me!

Nancy M. Ellis

Enough

She walks weeping for joy among the fallen stones,
A gossamer smile veiling her visage.
Her sharp teeth gnash upon the bloodied flesh of innocents,
As she searches the bloated face of the corpse of the living
For frightful hints of the mass graves of murdered children.

Old, she is, this ancient mother of suffering
Whose wrinkled womb has borne the hell of war.
Her seething minions are swathed in hatred,
Conceived in distrust and suspicion, their evil
Shrouded in religious fervor and sanctimony.

What is that to us, some said, we have no interests there.
Bosnia is a place far away.
Their differences cannot be resolved.
Let's not get involved, it's not our problem.
We have much to lose and nothing to gain.

Then arose the American colossus of truth and honor,
Seating herself upon the stalwart steed of valor
She smote the beast of war with the pen of diplomacy.
Gathering the nations, she sat in judgement against brutality,
Comforting the survivors under her wings, proclaiming
"Enough!"

James D. Conn

The Train Of Life

Life is like a train rolling down the tracks,
At some point you get on, and at some other you get off.
The train travels through the darkest tunnels,
And then, it breaks forth into bright, sunlit meadows.
Sometimes it climbs the highest mountains,
Where the glorious view provides a much different perspective
Than from the depths of the valley below.

Many time you want to stop the Train of Life,
To experience for a single moment the things passing by your window,
But the train keeps moving on, and so do you,
You sigh and say, I'll come back this way again some day",
But you know even as the words leave your lips,
That the moment is gone forever, and that you will never return.
Finally, the train comes to the end of the line, and so do you.

Before long, however, the train starts over again,
Back through the tunnels and the valleys and the mountains,
Carrying a new set of passengers, New or Re-newed?
Is not Life like that train, eternally traveling the same ground,
And that, even though we have reached our final destination,
Might we not board it again someday?

Betty J. Meischen

My Final Resting Place

The smell of death surrounds me,
as I sit and wait in this cold night air of hell.
I have no family, or something to eat, or something warm and dry to wear.

I try to sleep, but all I see is death.
When I close my eyes,
I see my family's death and hear their piercing screams.
I listen to the bombs, with their burning desire,
slam and explode into the building beside me.
I hear the cracking of guns, and the screams of death that follows.

There is no light, only the darkness of death and hell in this world.
I lay here with fear screaming deeply though my young veins.
For I know that I will be going to my final resting place soon,
there I will be safe,
there will be light and my family.

Till then I will wait in this dark, cold hell,
and listen to the cracking of guns, the crashing of bombs,
    and the piercing screams of death,
and wish for my final resting place.

Kim Bergmann

A Lady Named Lucy

A laidy named Loosey lived on our street
We'd watch her walk and talk to every man and
woman she'd meet. Up and down, and down and up
the alleys she creeped.

Loosey would switch her hips and flash a smile
for a ten dollar rock she'd walk ten miles
anyone could have her, every 'thang' did
men, women, even kids.

As long as you had a dime, Loosey had the time.
For less than a gram you could bind her mind
    Such a waste . . . Such a crime . . .
A lady named Lucy used to be Sooooooo . . . fine

A lady named Lucy had a T.V. show, She was so
positive, So talented, we all knew she'd go . . .!
    To the top!! To the top!! To the top of the world!!
    She'd be a big star!!! Lucy was that kind of girl!!!

Well, the name Lucy is a household name . . . but
    She'll never see glory . . . she'll never know fame . . .

Drugs dragged her down . . . and down she'd stay . . .
A lady named Lucy died today.

Victoria R. Peoples

My Little Eighty Two Toyota

Altho' it's faded and doesn't shine
I still love her because she's mine,
She's carried me far and near
To me she's still pretty and dear.

When something goes wrong
I get it fixed before long,
The lights still burn, the horn blows
What will happen next, who knows?

New covers and paint they will hide
All scratches and torn places inside,
Altho' it's getting older, aren't we, too
I'll drive her like she's still new.

But one day I'll park her with tears
Being thankful for her all these years,
Then I'll want a little car, just "anota"
That I can love like my little old "T'yota."

Alice C. Glass

Carved In Stone

She walks like the cool breeze of autumn
The wind whispers through her hair
Like my heart the leaves are a-fallin'
To see such beauty there

Her smile has the warmth of summer
There's tenderness in her eyes
And as I gaze upon her
I'm so content, I could cry

She dances like flowers in springtime
Swaying to and fro
Bright colors fired by the sunshine
Oh, how I love her so

Face the long, lonely winter
I long to lie in her arms
Burn the love within her
Keeping each other warm

But I fear my time has come and gone
I'm destined to walk alone
My love for her's an eternal song
Like words carved in stone.

Rob Rook

Untitled

She looked up at him with tears in her eyes,
He had to look away, he could not explain why.
She bit her bottom lip, as shamelessly she cried
And silently he cursed himself for all the hate and lies.
But how do you explain to such an innocent child
that the love which created her has become so defiled?

How love and passion have suddenly disappeared,
And two people who trusted one another have ended up in fear.
Love has turned to hate, happiness to remorse,
two people join their lives, then end in divorce.
So how do you explain to such an innocent child,
that the love which created her has become so defiled?

Waiting at the bus station his nerves are such a mess,
How can he make her see that he'd never love her less?
It'll only be a few weeks, he'll see her Christmas day,
then when summer comes she can come with him and stay.
He wraps his arms around her and kisses her goodbye,
he struggles for some words, as silently she cries.
But how do you explain to such an innocent child
that the love which created her has become so defiled?

Melissa L. Winkler

An Anthem To All

It's not about the red, white and blue,
It's about me and you.
It's about the universe so clear,
It's about taking it to the atmosphere.
It's letting us know what is the truth.
How we should be, could be, would be too!
If only we'd listen to the wind,
If Only we'd give up this sickness called sin.
If only we stop playing the games
of calling one another names.
Deep inside the sky so blue,
There's plenty to share for me and you,
There's plenty to know, to learn, to love.
The symbol is peace, togetherness, love.
This is our anthem an for all.
Let us unite to give up the evil, The proud the fight.
Let's stop saying who's wrong who's right,
And say Humans people, spirits Unite.
In a anthem to all let us use our insight.

Sheryle DeNonno

Two Great Gifts

I sometimes wonder, God,
If you must have a terrific sense of humor,
To make the platypus and wallabies,
And elephants and giraffes,
And rhinos, camels, and emus, too,
And storks and pelicans and gnus.
Plus giving song to meadowlarks and thrush,
As well as "missouri nightingales".
You must have laughed a lot
On that first great creation morn.

But there must be beauty in your soul too.
For a million flowers of every shape and hue.
And worlds of birds with lovely feather scheme.
Plus every sunset and sunrise sky
With colors that stretch our wildest dreams.

You gave us laughter and beauty, God,
To make life less grim and help us see it through.
Thank you, God, for these two gifts
Straight from the heart of you.

Robert H. McNabb

Caring

All around me there's love I feel from the earth
And this love generates from the power of the Holy Ghost.
I wish I could reach out to the Spirit and
give the Spirit a hug because I know it needs love
and hugs too and comfort as well as us.
All of the time the spirit of power trying to please
everyone and I Maryann are trying to please the
Holy Spirit, do you think I'm wrong it has done
So much for me it comes to me all of the
time and I can feel the presence of the Spirit
And it has lifted me out from below and
Showed me the things that will comfort me
and the Spirit is there for anyone who chases
after it, and it's filled with love, and peace
The spirit don't look at your color, race, gangs
Clothes, big, little, the things you have or money
It's there to protect us and love us and be there
in any way it can be. To fill our hearts with
Joy and happiness.

Maryann

Inside Looking Out

Sitting by the window . . .
As I look up outside beneath the blue heavens
I followed the grey clouds drifting far, far away . . .
Then my thoughts settled down wherein my heart and soul
Find solace and comfort in the realm of the past.

I sat to reminisce
Over the bygone days of my adolescence
Basking in the sunshine of youthfulness in bloom;
I revel at the sight of my peaceful birth place
And feel the nostalgia of having lived right there.

It is there where I grew
To manhood and fully equipped to enlighten
The mass of unlettered and anyone in need;
It is one in line with the glory of service
Which I have long espoused for everyone to do.

So anywhere we are
The essence of the times is to stand committed
To serve especially victims and the needy;
For this is a dictum that rings steadfastly
For us to take heed of, as much as possible.

J. Cap Guillermo

Just Because

When someone does something of Love or just because!

It ponders the question, is someone or something up above?

To Hear the need or want from someone other than yourself,
inspires the necessity to Thank the Lord for someone who does.

Just Because!

Carolyn Tarin

As I Look Into My Life

As I look into my life I can finally see,
All the things that are apart of me.
As I look into my life I know,
Of all the things that make me grow.
I see the world through all its years,
With lots of laughter and happy tears.
Through the window of my eyes everyone can see,
The loneliness inside of me.
As I look into my life,
I'm searching for my paradise.

Nicole René Tyler

"Mother"

Lots of words are spoken, by all of us one time or the other,
But there is a different way and tone to our voice,
   when we talk about our mother,
She was there when we called to her for help, when we were in a jam,
If we needed her to soothe a hurt she'd say don't you worry here I am.
We told her of our good times, and of our troubles too,
Because it seemed no matter what our problem was mother knew just what to do.
She would tell us of her childhood, and what the did back then,
And it wouldn't be long we'd be sitting and talking, and we'd
   say tell about your childhood again.
She would get out pictures of long ago and show us how they used to dress
We would giggle and put our hands over our mouths, then say
wouldn't we look funny dressed like this.
There would be times when she would be unhappy, over something
   we had done that day,
She would scold or spank us, and make us stay in the house, and
not go out to play,
Things like this would soon pass with mother, and get back like
   they were before,
She'd tell you to go on out and play, but don't you slam the door.
When the day was over and you had your bath, and you were
   laying in your bed,
Mother would come right in and listen to your prayers, kiss you
   good night and pat you on the head.
So we take this day that is set aside, for all you mothers everywhere,
To let you know of the love for you mom, and just how much we care.

   Robert Smith

Pieces Of My Heart

You walked over and pulled up a chair,
And stole a piece of my heart.

You introduced yourself. Asked if you
could buy me a drink.
And stole a piece of my heart.

You asked me to dance, holding me tight.
And stole a piece of my heart.

You drove me home, kissing me in the moonlight.
And stole a piece of my heart.

Several months later, you asked to marry me.
Two days before we were to wed, you vanished.
And now, I must pick up the pieces of
my heart.

   Carol L. White

Bless This Child

God, lift up her head and hold it high
Don't let another tear fall, wipe them dry
Her conscience is gone, and hope withered away
I pray for her freedom each night and day
Her fear and anger have gradually piled
So God, please help, bless this child

She's looking for a light, the slightest little one
But she's about to give, throw it away, she's done
Her prayers to you are asking for grace
She wants to forget it all, wipe every trace
Her tears and tissues have gradually piled
So God, please help, bless this child

She's done crying, she's finished with it all
She holds her head high down every hall
She figured it out, she found the light
There was no way to miss it, You shed it so bright
Her fear and anger have gradually unpiled
Thank you, God, for blessing this child

   Katie Schnieder

Sunday's Child

Is blithe and bonny, good and gay
A joy to behold forever and a day.
We toured the shops, we swam the sea
Took aeroplane flights, just Linda and me.
Her face is fair, her hair is brown
There's always a smile — no tears for this clown.
The man she wed is tall and lean
Two sons who treat her as a queen
This paragon of goodness and love
Is quiet and gentle as a dove,
But best of all she will always be
My daughter, Linda

   Anne Benton Duthie

God's Woman

God's woman is virtuous, kind, and true;
She's a woman that has patience in whatever she undertakes to do.

God's woman is full of faith and very strong;
She always stands up for right and shone the wrong;

God's woman is humble, loving and meek;
And when there's a problem, her Lord does she seek;

God's woman does not gossip, or have a wagering tongue;
No! God's woman is a praying woman with concern for everyone.

She tends to her own business, her children and her home;
Her main priority is to trust in God and him alone;

She lives her life with Christian pride;
She doesn't have anything to hide;

God has beautified her with salvation
She doesn't have to look like a cheap imitation;
For she's pure through! And through!
If you possess these qualities, God's woman could be you!

   Enola Jones

The Day

The day I began to breath
   was the day I began to see.
For all the world's troubles are all around me.
   For tomorrow's hopes
   tomorrow's dreams,
   are something I have been paying for,
   for thee.
When I look up to the blue wondrous sky
I know God has seen me cry.
I know it's time, to say goodbye.
And now I know, a whole new life
that God has given me,
   a brand new life
   the day I began to breath

   Gwen Bosley

Displacement

Grey cold trees standing straight
with smaller branches intertwined
as if searching for warmth
bleak sky reflected in the water's depth
mirrors only its own coldness
stark november days foretell winter's bareness
surrounded and permeated by this atmosphere
all feeling is removed from my soul

   Martha T. Salmassy

Generations

A newborn baby cries as the day begins,
A promise of tomorrow, a voice of the future.
Warm and soft, vulnerable and cuddly,
Life's sweetness echoes in the breeze.

Bobby socks, loafers, saddle shoes,
Footsteps into the future.
Where, oh where are we headed?
Princeton, Harvard, Boston or Yale?

Teachers, lawyers, many professions we may be,
Learning from the past, projecting into the future.
The pendulum swings from youth to maturity.
Sharing adventures in life with young and old.

Whispers of grey are now marching through my hair,
Marking the time, not too many days to spare.
Grandchild in hand, allows only time to span,
The yesterdays and tomorrows of this generation.

Sandra Ann Kolinofsky

With LOVE To Anne, Forever . . .

When I was young and just a lad,
I knew a girl named Anne.
We would play house; I'd be the dad . . .
I'd see myself a man.

As I grew up, I saw a change
And noticed my best friend.
It's all common, not very strange . . .
True LOVE came in the end.

I asked her to become my wife,
And, of course, she said, "Yes!"
The two of us would share one life . . .
I regret nothing less.

As time went on, we both grew old;
We'd lived life as a pair.
LOVE never lost its wondrous hold . . .
Such happiness is rare.

Now, she has died and I'm alone,
But I'm not very sad.
In this life, she called me her own . . .
Just the thought makes me glad.

Andrew Lawrence Grunzke

When The Old Tree Died

I've remembered the old knurled tree,
Its leaves greening in the spring.

It whispered softly through the wind,
Of days, that seemed to never end.

It told me of the long years,
Of queens and kings, knights and wars,
Of lovers, stretched out beneath its limbs,
Of their tears, hope and joys.

Now the leaves aren't so green,
After five thousand years or more,
Now the old tree has been left alone,
To die, unnoticed and unseen, forlorn.

But, I was there, to say farewell,
As the last leaf fell, I was sad indeed,
I've seen friends come and go,
And the tree that I've loved so,
And I cried, when the old tree died.

For I was left, alone.

Norman Thomason

love

. . . the days are long, the rain gently falls as our bodies are covered with the sweet raindrops which fall from the heavens . . . the rains are the tears of the Gods . . . as they see you are taking their sweet child into your caressing arms . . . they are saddened, but joyed that their loved one has found her everlasting love . . .

. . . and as the tears so silently fall upon our love . . . I take you closer . . . kissing your lips ever so softly . . . I have found the sincerity in you . . . the sincerity I have spent a lifetime searching for . . .

. . . And the beauty within us is shown to the Gods . . . their beauty, within a rainbow, is set forth before us . . . tears of joy fill my eyes, as never before have I felt this love . . . feeling the beauty within you, I smile, and slowly waltz into your arms . . . the love that only the Gods could predict, you and I alone . . . together . . . cover me, as a blanket covers a child...hold me tightly, let me feel your love . . . a love only known to the two of us . . .

. . . your soul has captivated my being . . . love me as I love you. . . our souls are but one and we shall never be without the other . . . life is an eternity . . . as is our love . . .

Leigh Anne Raymond

The Storm

There's a storm brewing in my mind
A dense, misty fog distorts my thoughts.
It clouds my logic and reason,
Making me confused and unsure.
The rain falls in a river of tears
Drowning my faith and hope.

Bolts of lightning strike my heart, and
Claps of thunder sound the shattering pieces.
The gusting wind scatters it all around
Making it impossible to ever fully repair
And make whole again.

I pray for the storm to blow over.
Waiting anxiously for the wind to settle and the rain to stop,
For the dark clouds to break and the sun to shine
So the blue sky can reappear and
Display an inspiring rainbow of hope,
Where, at the end of it, I can find an answer.

But for now . . .
The horizon darkens as my sadness deepens
Signifying that there's a storm approaching.

Gwen Murphy

A Reunion Of Love

You've been gone a long time from me
    sweetheart.
You've been gone a long time from my sight.
I no longer hurt like I used to,
And I dream of you sometimes at night.

I dream of you when you were young,
    my love,
When your hand was clasped in mine.
Never once did we think of an ending.
We were parted by that thing called time.

Now time has intervened again,
And I know that my days are few.
Reach out and take my hand, my dear,
Cause I'll be right next to you.

Our kids and our friends will visit us
And they may shed a tear or two;
But when time has healed and eyes
    are dry,
I know that I'll still have you.

Robert J. O'Leary

Serendipity

Finding you was a great treasure indeed
Like a wildflower surrounded by weed
Your distinction stood out so staid and bold
Serendipity, is the word I'm told.

I shall love you warmly, and never be cold
For years and years, we will be quite old!
So, happy anniversary my love
and I am counting on many more
Like examining all the stars above
I love you trillions and trillions, galore!

Patricia A. Jackson

Love Of Loving

Translated by Talie Parhizgar

I have in mind to build a sanctuary of love,
For love-birds looking for the nest of love.

In the name of Moses, I will build a Temple,
In which the epic of love, be lyric of love.

For Mary and her Jesus Christ I will make,
A church that will be the only Altar of love.

Next to these, I build a Mosque for Muslims,
So in prayer, look for water and seed of love.

In this Grand Hall of Shrines of heart and soul,
I will make a pathway to the cradle of love.
On love's roof with no battle of religion,
There will be a heaven with the myth of love.

So when followers of the "Truth" reach there,
They'd unite like the eternal lovers of love.

Except for Unity and Faith, would be nothing
There in the sky of love, but the sign of love.

To men and women, life plays out this message
That Loving is the only way to a life of love.

Of Shahpar's tears, the mother of pearl wrote
There is one jewel of love in the sea of love.

M. S. Shahpar

The Star

With all that has happened, and all that is done!
I reach for the stars, and find I pick one
Happiness and love are in the world today
so, I let the star go, and it faded fast away
But just for that moment, as I held it in my hand,
I felt warmth and peace, throughout the entire land
A feeling so pleasant, it entered in my mind
to be merry and jovial, and ever be so kind.
And with these pleasant thoughts and
with a life so great,
I'll remember that shining star, filled with
love, not hate.

Kenneth P. Brophy

"Blossom Into Spring"

Birds on the trees are true signs of spring
This is when the robin starts to sing
Real soon the buds will blossom fully
And nothing but beauty will we see
Like nature, let us become a part
Like the birds, let's plant seeds in our heart
As seeds take root, let's get rid of strife
As we also awaken to life
Then we will see beauty all around
And true love, joy and peace can be found.

Mary Countryman

The Road To Heaven

There are roads to travel for all mankind,
and if you search — you will find —
The road that journeys to the rainbows end,
where the treasures of a lifetime lie around the bend.

There are roads that lead us — sometimes astray —
cruising down the "devils highway."
There are roads that bring us much sorrow to bear,
roads we should detour — but, yet we dare!!!

There are miles of pavements — tarred with greed —
highways of darkness and unchecked speed.
There are curves, short cuts and signs to be aware,
pot holes of danger — lurking everywhere.

There's also a skyway — that leads to a star —
it starts in your driveway — it's really not far.
This highway ascends — to heaven above —
it's the one that's known — as the Road To Love . . .

Which road will you travel — which highway will you take —
what be your future — what be your fate?
Before your next journey — swing wide the doors —
which road will you travel — the choice is yours???

Jack D. Collins

I Owe You Teacher Dear

You taught me how to read and write
And to spell and multiply,
You told me I could do great things
If only I would try.

You showed me love, faith and pride
And the need for honesty,
You told me how to treat each one
With respect and dignity.

And as I walk this road of life,
My teacher you should see,
It was your patience that stood the test
So I might come go be.

Now before your life is over
There's something you should hear,
My thanks for all your guidance,
I owe you, Teacher dear.

Howard Fain

Untitled

He pulled her.
Past the house its white face ashen.
Past the grass its emerald fragrant.
Past the blossoms of a summer orchard.

He, soul fused, intoxicated with the chill
of man's first dawn.
He, without choice, received the contract, the gift.
He, the acrobat, in this state of equilibrium.

She, shifting from soil, from rubble and
distress, from tormenting wounds festering.
Saw.

A bauble for her ear, a jade for her neck,
tis only a trinket.
Tis only a simple thing, this gift of life
pulling her out of the mire.

Elle Smith

207

Just . . .

Do it he said,
Just walk in that room
It doesn't matter
Just give it your all.

You can change the mistakes
that you've made in your life.
You gotta believe.
Just give it your all.

You can turn the heads
of all the people that doubt you.
You can prove it to them
Just give it your all.

You can prove to yourself,
That you've got it in you,
To make up for lost time,
Just give it your all.

Jessica Fritz

Instead Of Me

Sometimes I wish that I could be;
Something else instead of me.
Sometimes things get so rough;
I say, "Oh, God, I've had enough".

Sometimes I wish I was a bird;
To fly away without a word.
Sometimes I wish I was a fly;
To Buzz those who make me cry.

But when the storm is over;
And I feel free.
I thank God that I am Me!

Nettie L. Raasch

On That Mountain Side

On that mountain side,
A flower lied,
Each night she cried,
Afraid that her pedals had dried,
With no shade to hide,
So in the sun she lied,
Alone outside,
Having lost her pride,
With no one to confide,
She committed suicide,
On that mountain side,
A flower lied,
With no hope as she died.

Joni Moldovan

Boxes

I wish I could put my fears aside
In boxes, stored away,
And, then like the dreams I hide,
Save them for another day.

Jack E. Hill

Untitled

I had a dream last night,
We were all fighting a war,
But we were all kids.
The commander wanted us to wear
black cloth strips around our heads,
We all laughed and thought it a joke,
Until we were dead.

Robert J. Glass

Held By Love

Slowly, we sift
Through the charred ruins
Of a lifetime,
Of a lifetime stolen
And of a lifetime restored.
Ever alone
Yet never abandoned.
Surrounded by hate,
Yet held by Love.

Catherine Marie Lewis

Untitled

As the bones in my body
Speak louder than words
My mind strays like an eagle
Waiting for the sun to shine
In the pink moonlight sky

I fly to a flawless land
To meet natives inside
Wind constantly helping
The drift of my feet
So I do not end in dive

Reaching my destination
With words in my body unknown
I lay in rest
Waiting for the sun to shine
In the pink moonlight sky

Tammy Conery

Encircled

It's at times when feeling and emotions
Cause a fluster in my thoughts.
And though I try to focus
Sometimes I'd rather not.

I can't explain how I feel
It's like a roller coaster ride.
With everything unsettling
All jumbled up inside.

With time rapidly dispersing
The seasons changing scenes.
The thoughts I had of yesterday
Seem only like a dream.

Though I know it is a phase
That I am working through.
I'm not alone, He walks with me
Encircled —— by friends too.

Cora A. John

Untitled

You are there, I am here
Carving pumpkins in the October air.
One for you and one for me,
On the porch for the kids to see.

I saw, I hammer
And paint the place.
But I still feel only your warm face.

A couple kisses on T.V.
Another reminder of you and me.
I must escape because this is our room,
Out to the horses to look at the moon.

Knowing that is the same moon you see,
Is very comforting
To someone alone like me.

Richard A. Stabert Jr.

The Face

To touch the face
is a glorious thing

The face heals all
wounds within

The face gives hope
to the hopeless

The face gives love
to the unloved

The face gives wisdom
to the unwise

The face gives food
to the hungry

The face give justice,
to all.

The face is loved by
many and needed by
all.

Scott J. Guthrie

Solitary Obstacle

There you stand
Surrounded by weeds
When tired,
      you wilt
When hungry
      you drink
A lawn mower
      cuts your stalk

Obstacle no more

Freshly sprout again
Inside healthy chlorophyll
Replenished by a spring
Running water beneath
      the individual blade
Points toward the fiery sky

Lawn mowers sound
Hacking away obstacles
      only to sprout again-sparks
of earthly green

Brooke E. Lawsing

Looking For Peace

I am looking for something
   That I have not found.
I can not even see it
   But know it is around.
Like a warm summer breeze
   Early in June.
The smell of the lilacs
   Under the moon.
The sound of the ocean
   Licking the sand.
The touch of a teardrop
   That fell on my hand.
The taste of salt air
   When by the sea.
The spongy of soft moss
   Under a tree.
Seems like with all
   These wonders around.
There should be nothing
   That I have not found.

Norman L. Ameden

Wish

Loving you
gives me happiness
the kind I need each day
and if sometimes I don't show it
I love you each day and every way

If ever
I get jealous
it's only because I care
this love I feel for you
is ever so rare

If only
I could have one wish
Do you know what that could be
for us to be together
for all eternity

John P. Lanier

"Accidentally On Purpose"

Do you know and do you see
all earths creatures disagree
all are forced to live and be
within a land they can't call home

Do you know and do you care
I realize that life's not fair
I recognize that crazy stare
welcome to your fantasy

Do you know and can you stand
living in this "promised land"
everyone has empty hands
I think that you've been lied to

Do you know and do you feel
I see you're caught within this wheel
we all are forced to bow and kneel
ground beneath some tyrant's boot

I feel the ends just out of teach
the earth has nothing left to preach
no more peace is left to reach
I think we're going down

James Michael Herring

Forever Damned

Down the lonely path I walk
Alone again deep the dark
My life has been the dust of chalk
My childhood has left no spark

All the world around is grey
Who knew that color was a gift
Blue sky's above when I would lay
And through eternity's sand I'd sift

From the atheist life I've led
I fear what may become of me
A youth's Christianity fled
Visions of Hell all I can see

At the end they say you see a light
A supreme great energy
But I didn't try or fight
And there was no light for me

No matter how hard some try
It just might be too late
Because all religions share the lie —
Damnation serves our final fate.

Joshua Davis

Tranquility

Sitting in silent solitude
Waiting for the night,
I watched the sun extinguishing
The powers of her light.
She's building up a moment and the
Glory it will hold, to paint the sky
A picture with the beauty of her gold.
Just one small hesitation
Then she'll quickly sink from sight
Leaving only a few small rays
To welcome in the night.
The evening is upon us calling
For the beauty of star light,
And all these shimmering diamonds
Are faithful to the night.
In the distant heaven, the moon
Will always shine, and the
Twinkling little bodies
Are the candles of all time.

Virginia Salzlein

Mist

Hallucination behind the mist,
Fantasy in the steamy gray air,
People grabbing others by the wrist,
See the snow in many layers.

Passion relies on the heart,
Love consists of two,
People hope they will never part,
To some this adventure is new.

Mist can be spooky,
Freaky, queer, and blue,
The key is reliability,
For you people with no .clue.

Have you ever seen mist?
Mist causes accidents galore,
Is it on that longing list?
Mist builds on more and more!

Ruth Solomon

Out Under The Stars

I've slept out in the mountains
    under the tall pine trees,
And smelled their sweet fragrance
    as they swayed in the breeze.

I've slept down in the
    Grand Canyon's great depths,
And watched the moonlight push
    shadows down the red cliffs.

When I lay out on the vast rangelands
    under a wide open sky,
I marveled at the million stars
    and the smiling moon on high.

I wondered about the universe
    which extends so far,
About this tiny planet
    orbiting our special star.

Never have I felt so close to God!
    I thought as I lay in my bed.
Look what we miss when we think
    we need a roof overhead!

Shirley Skousen

The Bells

I listen to the bells
    From the church across the way
As they chime their lovely music
    At the closing of each day.

They tell me not to worry
    Or to fear the coming night
For the Lord is watching over me
    With all His love and might.

They tell me of things to come
    Of happiness and cheer
They tell me of His guiding hand
    That wipes away my fear.

So if you listen carefully
    To what they have to say
Your footsteps will be guided
    Along God's great highway.

The toll house on God's highway
    Is the church where you attend
The toll is prayer and reverence
    That you pay at each day's end.

Harold M. Tetro

Falling Water

Soft swirling mist and
gentle small drops
come down to earth
to nourish the crops.

Harder rain and hail or sleet
fall to the earth
with a strong
steady beat

Snows wet fat flakes
come drifting down
a cold white blanket
to cover the ground

The simple word water
not simple at all
only He knows the form
it will take when it falls.

Linda Pittman

An Angelic Guide

On a cold Sunday morning
at the church near his house
was a soldier in uniform
standing quiet as a mouse.
There was no wind blowing,
not an animal to be found,
not a person was walking
on the cold hard ground.
From out of a tree
very near his left side
came the voice of an angel
and he listened with pride.
So soft and clear
the whisper was strong.
"Go inside" the voice said,
so he hurried along.
The service just started
as he opened the door,
and he listened each Sunday
but heard the voice no more.

William T. Redden

Jerusalem

Shalom, salem
Ever scared jerusalem
Sunrise cradles on,
Heaven's mountain

In candle stone
Kindles the eternal,

Salmon's tea,
Sprinkles
The olive tree

Fair merchants roam,
This golden dome

Eternal father,
Wonders yonder

Hither,
Asylum
Human

Peace be upon them.
People of Jerusalem
Tiffany Schneider

In The Dark

In the dark, uncanny, neither world
    Where shapeless things appear,
Shadows cast upon the wall
    Are only the mind's dread fear.

The awesome depth of gloom,
    The blackness of eternal night,
Hold fast, within its grip
    The human mind deprived of light.

Where is the shaft that lets
    Lumination enter through
The clogged, musty depth,
    Where clarity is overdue.

The vault that covers earth
    The static atmosphere,
Keep wisdom of the ages
    From being seen from here.

What clouds human vision
    Keeping man from his goal?
Open up the shaft of light
    So man can cleanse his soul.
Alpha R. Sorensen

Multiplication

Multiplication is easy to do.
Just think is your head,
It will come to you,
Think hard.
Make it right.
And if you want to check it,
Divide, and you'll get it.
Multiplication, yeah!
Jennifer Sensenig Ayell

Rage Against Our Children

This place is abandoned now,
but the past tells of victims
of bruises and cuts and beatings
and death
the antagonists come from no story
not places of fiction or legend
but from my daughter's memory
Beth Secord

Summer Nights

Dedicated to David Sehorn
    The waves roll in, stars
twinkle in my eyes,
    Sharing the sand
with an angle is disguise.
    A perfect man, so
sensitive, yet so strong,
    And a perfect night
when nothing goes wrong.
    Love at first sight,
some would say, but we've met before
and again today.
    The cool breeze
blows over the sea,
    Over on you and me.
    The sweet smell
of you,
    And the aroma of
the sea;
    Sets the mood
for you and me.
Jennifer Reneé Honeycutt

Coming Home

I swallow the blackness
    Life drains away
Never looking forward
    To see another day
Feeling your cold fingers
    Wrap around my face
Stopping my breath
    Comforted by your kiss
Drain my soul
    Let it fly away
Thanos my friend
    End my pain
The one and only way
Robert W. Lardin III

Spark Of Light

Oh spark of light in the sky
My favorite star away up high
You are my guide, my little friend
To find a lover on you I depend
I know she's down somewhere below
underneath your brilliant glow
Robert DeStefano

Autumn Rain

Rain . . . rain, autumn rain,
Steady and slow
Plays a hunting melody
Mournful and low.

April showers help the flowers,
Grass and trees to grow,
December rain — The Overture,
(Concerto will be Snow.)

Rain . . . rain, gentle rain,
Echoing a sad refrain,
'Wintertime is almost here.
Alas! Another squandered year.'

Darkness creeps on stealthy feet,
Night enters, black and bold.
(But I am safe and warm inside,
Sheltered from the cold.)
Marian Hallet

Just A Dream

When I first met you
I fell in love.
This feeling I have
Will not go away,
It keeps telling me
What we have is for real.
If it is real
Then why aren't you here,
Right by my side
So I can hold you
Tight in my arms.
Now I don't know,
Maybe it was just a dream
That will always last.
Kris Vanden Einde

Treasure

The brilliant yellow hair of youth
Has turned to grey
The final truth
Will be the dying day

Friends had as a child
Are dead and gone
When the body is returned to the wild
Pray the deeds live on

And upon taking the last breath
When the final hour has passed
Do not mourn death,
But make toasts, and raise glasses

Youth can fade quickly
Grow young soft and swiftly
P. B. Shelton

The Way Of Life

Clouds rain   sunshine warms
Skies are blue
Birds fly   fish swim
Flowers bloom   leaves drift
Relationships begin end
Cats purr   dogs bark
Babies are born   people grow old
Fire burns   ice melts
Cable cars clang   music soothes
Raindrops fall   stars twinkle
Wind blows
Babies cry
Tides flow
I love you
Betty Sue Edde

If You Dare

Take stairs to the clouds
and go walking on air,
to fly with your dreams
without a single care.

Set your spirit free
to soar with the birds.
let your thoughts fly away
without a spoken word.

Experience your dreams,
but dream if you dare
to take stairs to the clouds
and go walking on air.
Christina M. Thomas

Romeo And Juliet

Death was standing
in the shadows,

Hope was disturbed.

Time was too long and
too short.

Love was so strong,
and determined,
wouldn't leave the other
behind.

Always and forever they said,
a vow never broken

Pain for others left behind
oh sweet sorrow, we must face
tomorrow.

Linda L. Smith

Emigrant Alone

I see Picture in my head from
my homeland. There are times
I can't figure out where I belong
in my new land. Sometime I
wish I was back there and a
citizen here.
When I left I was only a child
there and a child when I
arrived here.
My father and mother are
gone and I still miss them
so. Oh, how I wish they
lived near by now
My smile are often alone
and my thought back home.

Solfrid C. Collins

"My Little Mother"

If I live to be a million
    And search my whole life through,
I'll never find the kind of love
    That I have found in you.

Life must have seemed so long to you
    And burdens hard to bear,
So much of the path you walked alone
    With no one else to share.

You seemed so small and fragile
    Not suited for the fight,
But as a lion fights for her young
    You fought with all your might.

You taught us all the good things
    And gave us each our chores,
But cared and loved us with a heart
    As big as all outdoors.

So if I search forever
    From one world to another,
I'll never find a love to equal
    The love of my dear little mother.

Mary M. Liggin

Where Is Love

Love sweet warm, resuming.
Life to our spirit, to our soul
is the love of God.
Oh where is love, life's sweet embrace.
Where is love in true friendship,
love for a child, love of
a father, mother, the way it should be.
Love so graceful, so free, that
brings light to the eye's
where is love that can be
felt by a touch, a smile, that
reach's across the mile's.
Love so enduring, finds no
fault love that brings two people
together.
Where oh where is love, so
sweet, warm, reassuring.
Love life to our spirit, to our
soul, where is the love?

Evelyn B. Conley

Spirit

Tis the light we see
Tis the love of thee
In the valley
Help me sleep
Help me sleep with my love
My love of you

Audra Snyder

Silent Man

Silent man
What burns in you
Is there an emotion
I can't perceive

I know where you've walked
I see the sand in your shoes
Oh, silent man
What is it you see
Touched by war
Does your mind still bleed
Silent man . . .
Does your mind still bleed

I can't understand the darkness
That shrouds you like fear
Scaring me — who loves you
Silent man
I say silent man
What are your fears tonight

Darren W. Longley

Tender Years

The ole home town appears the same.
Old town clock still strikes the time,
Ducks waddle over their crosswalk line,
Race track's at the foot of the hill,
And around the bend a cider mill.
As I near the old home place,
I can almost see their face.
Greeted by a hug, a kiss and a smile,
As he'd say, "Help me awhile?"
Homemade bread and wash on the line,
And for us she always made time.
How I miss those tender years,
When they were here.

Rebecca Labbe

The Cottage In The Wild

There's a little cottage
In the Wild's of Maine
With a river right beside it
Waiting to be tamed

Follow in my footsteps, Anita Love
Can you hear the mourning dove?
It lasts only for a little while
Follow me and I will make you smile

New passages for us to discover
A magical journey in time
I promise there will be no other
Just you and me and a fishing line

Follow in my footsteps, Anita Love
To the little cottage in the Wild
Some fishing, some loving, and look!
there's a trout on the line
You won't be sorry I made you mine!

Anita M. Plouffe

Reverie

Song of the sea at twilight
Melody of surf and sand.
Cascades of mist and foam
Fury and mirth on the land.
God's Hand.

Erma Gross-Haley

"Come Back Into My Life"

Come back into my life
Hold me close to your heart,
Take me into your arms dear
Promise me we will never part.

Come back into my life darling
Make me happy once again,
Kiss my lips I long for
Be my love, not just a friend.

When you break a heart dear
There's one less star in the sky,
When you don't return the love
You make the angels cry.

There's an empty spot inside me
No one but you can fill,
Comeback into my life darling
I love you still.

Pearl R. Lineburg

Eighth Wonder

Bubbling fumaroles and
gushing geysers.
The ground steams
like a pot of water set to boil.
Minerva's terrace
a solid cascade of flowing tiers.
More beautiful
than the mind can imagine.
View the awesome depth of canyons
and turbulent waterfalls.
Magnificent bison paw the earth
and regal elk saunter arrogantly.
Enigmatic mixture
of landscape and wildlife
to boggle the mind.
Only the hand of God
could create the splendor of
Yellowstone.

JoAnn M. Stiff

"Freedom"

With her sails at half-mast
she floats upon the sea,
awaiting a gentle breeze
to take her gracefully.

Below she sees the fish,
all around she watches sharks,
while the sunshine bathes her hull
and warms her, until dark.

With midnight, comes a calm.
When all is silent and still,
When her captain's fast asleep
and no one to hold her wheel.

The only, real true freedom,
is the freedom that she has.
A freedom, man finds so distant
and always, out of grasp.

Sheri Maison

Final Touch

What a gift God gave to me
To share time so greatfully.

Never once doubting you
A friendship never had been so true.

He gave to me a sense of pride
Knowing all a long he was on my side.

For this person to care about me
Gave my soul peace and tranquility.

I do know why the Lord took you away
To help people like me find there way.

I know I think you every day
For this emotion I can not repay.

I know you can see me from afar
I see you smiling back at me...
   from a star.

Cheryl Ann Fletcher

"Bermuda"

The hurricane wind:
Held, the palm tree's sway,
While tossing:
The blue, green sea.

Jerry Moynihan Jr.

Untitled

I have watched the seagull rest
On a green wave and rise again.
Scattering as he skimmed the crest
Jewelled spray that caught the light.
I have stood on the beach at night
And felt the dawn winds touch my face
With virgin hands; and I have lain
Under pines in a quiet place
And watched the sunlight filter down
In changing patterns, grey and gold.
Yet all the wonders I have known
Are not enough for my heart to hold.
If this hunger could always leap
Like a swift flame at each appeal
Of loveliness, if I could keep
This pain forever - hold remote
The day when I no longer feel
Beauty, aching in my throat!

Paula Long Clayton

A Valentine Love Poem

For you Because I love you;
For you because I care.
   For you because you're beautiful,
Bring magic in the air.

   For you because I see the sea;
And hear the cooing dove.
   Because I looked into your eyes,
And thought that I saw love.

   For you because you're peaceful;
And still a running stream.
   And qualities as rich as yours,
Should never be unseen.

   It's all because I love you;
I say these words to you.
   Please listen for a little while,
And please believe they're true.

Lisa R. McGhee

Jesus, My Friend

I think that I will never see
A friend such as He.
He brings me such joy
As a kid with a new toy.

I stumble with my speech
As I try to beseech.
Jesus is my special Friend
And will be to the end.

He makes me tremble with delight
As He shines like a bright light.
I will follow Him the rest of my days
With a love that puts me into a daze.

Lynn E. Henk

A Whisper

When you are with me darling
So fast the days go by
Yet, days when I am all alone
Crawl by without a sigh.

Our life together here on earth
Is fleeing day by day
The years we've been together
Just a whisper, so they say.

I can't see life without you
You're such a part of me
The years we've been together
Turned to a memory.

Mildred Kelley

"I Wish"

I wish I could help you as much as
   you have me.
I wish I could endure your pain
   and set your body free.
I wish I had told you more often
   how much I care.
I wish I had said "thank you" for
   always being there.
I wish I had told you before
   all the things in this rhyme.
I wish I had been all you thought
   I could be.
The problem with wishing is it
   doesn't always come true.
But the one thing you can count on
   is "I love you."

Shanna Weir

We Wish You, Our Little Girl

We wish you, our little girl,
Many, many more,
Of days like today
With cake on the floor.
We know as you grow
And the spilling is less,
It's easier to clean
The floor, the mess.
Don't worry dear about
The fuss, we love you,
Our little girl, as you do us.
Happy Birthday little one.
Go on, grow up, and have
Your fun, stay a child as
long as you may, for there's
Only one 1st as it is today.
Happy 1st Birthday.

Dianna Belli

A Candle For Mother

Her soul, should rest-in-peace,
makes the living remember the time
of her decease

She would keep one particular
tradition most
alive
The burning of the candle
How hard she for it did
strive

It is my solemn oath to
keep her custom
with generosity, not ever her
spirit to deprive

Betty Adams

God Touched The Earth

God touched the earth
On that cold December night,
When in a stable in Bethlehem,
He celebrated his boy child's birth.

As angels sang to shepherds,
'Neath light of a bright, shining star;
Hope lay in the snow swept manger,
And a new love encircled the earth.

Peace filled hearts to overflowing,
For salvation lay there sleeping,
Tightly holding his Mother's hand;
As joy sang throughout the land.

Hope, love, peace, salvation, joy,
Came to all peoples of his earth;
Who found they could believe
In the touch of the Master's hand.

Nancy A. Benn

Passages

A life lived.
Filled like pages in a book.
A book all too short.
A book we must write.
For we make the journey.
Moving through life's passages.
Passing from moment to moment.
Moments only borrowed.
In the final chapter each a memory.
Each passages in time.

Robert Sessions Smilie Jr.

If I Were the Teacher

If I were the teacher
of Kalamazond
I'd teach the children
as all of them yawned.

If I were the teacher
of Kalamazerk,
I'd sit in my chair
and watch them all work.

But I don't teach in Kalamazond,
I don't even teach in Kalamazerk
I just sit here and act like a jerk.

Tiffany Pegram

To See And To Feel

To see the setting sun,
to feel the last of its rays.
to know you belong,
to see the fighting stop,
and feel the peace again.
to live and let live.
to smile and love.
these are and will be my
Proud Experiences.

Florence Rush Barrat

"Forgotten Souls"

Beneath walls of dust,
"ghost,"
on brittle pages, where
souls go unattached,
passed from memory,
left afloat,
"faces,"
of kindred lost in time,
but for names,
"carved,"
on the
"gravestones!"

Bennetta Allen-Smith

"Very Long Rest"

I now go to take.
My very long rest.
No more worry.
No more pain.
No more problems of the world.
We all have to go.
To take a very long rest.
We will wake up, in a new world
We'll all love the best.
It's sad to my heart.
Having to leave you behind.
But I had to go to take.
My very long rest.
Think of me as being.
The one, who loved you the most,
As I go to take, my very long rest.
No more worry
No more pain
No more problems of the world.

Mae Cuthbertson

Woodsman's Anthem

When the birds are singing "goodnight"
from the branches and the sky,
And I smell the breezes telling
that the rain's not far behind;
I just swing my axe a'shoulder
and descend the mountain high.
One day's good work has ended,
Yet I won't just say "good-bye!"

You can't keep me from here
after I have been around.
After seeing grandiose mountains,
I don't want another town.
My home now is the forest
which is ever wild and rare.
So wherever you can take me,
my heart'll stay right there.

Heather Amrhein

The Road Ahead

In my mind I see a road
That has been paved for me
There are no signs to show the way
For as far as I can see

As I walk along this road
And look from side to side
I see familiarities
Then let them pass me by

To turn around is difficult
I can't see what is there
In back of me is misty fog
That has no need to clear

To look ahead along this road
Reveals an empty space
Even though there's nothing there
It is something I must face

So as I travel on this road
I need not to turn back
The space in front that's calling me
Will give me what I lack

Lynne Anderson

The Tag

Dark and handsome, young and tall,
Perfectly dressed over all;
Tie and handkerchief to match,
Every eye he soon did catch
At his University's
Graduation Mass.

Locks of rich ebony hair,
Royal stature standing there;
Jacket tag upward unfurled
Showing here to all the world,
Upside down but still quite true,
Handmade With Love
by Mom.

Marie A. Darr

Love

I Love
You Love
We all Love
Love is in all different colors.
Like green, orange, black, and white
And lots of others.
All in All Love is around the world.

Tonya Cummins

Breath And Blood

My breath descends
the shallow between my shoulders.
The foreign atmosphere fills
my lungs. My blood, used
and slick, turns red
with oxygen.

I think about my breath,
how I temper it
in a whisper or a song,
how I love with it
and how I lie with it,
how it happens
without my thought.

My blood just does
its job. It cycles
my breath through channelled tubes.
A rushing silence through my veins,
it's only messy when I bleed.

Francis R. Dispo

Witches' Brew
(A Rhyme Of Halloween)

Boil, boil, cauldron bubble
Halloween, harbinger trouble
Crooked broomsticks witches fly
Weaving spells 'cross darkened sky
Cackling laughs, wicked words
Lots cast upon innocent herds
Wolf's-bane season, eye of newt
Hapless mortals 'fore old galoots
Haunted night, no one can tell
Who be the prey of satan's belles
All Saints' Eve, power strong
They venture forth, do their wrong
Dangers lurk, mark thee well
Shun the curse dredged from hell
Dawning's break, the ordeal ends
Alas, one year they ride again
Beware, take care, the deeds thou do
Laced with souls is witches' brew

Curtis D. Thomas

Sunshine Love

Love, like the wonderful sun.
When the sunshine has just begun.
The night comes and brings another day.
It brings me to my happy way.

Sunshine love brings a
smile to my face.
My love come and take
me to a sunny place.
I will then love you
and remember that you
were honest and true.

Love me from life
to death.
I will not waste a
single breath.
To be with you in
the sky above.

Because you are my
Sunshine Love.

Christina Brown

"Dear Dad"

You have been dead
For seven years.
From your being dead
Brings to me lots of tears.

I wish you were
Right here with me.
But in heaven
God and you are watching over me.

I'm 14 years old now, Daddy,
It's been seven years.
Please help me, Daddy,
With all of my fears.

I love you, Daddy
With all of my heart.
We were so close,
Now we're so far apart.

I hope you have a Merry Christmas
Up there safe with God.
Please help me to deal with life
And especially my Mom.

Anthony Hollier

I Want Him

His eyes are green
His hair is brown
He makes me smile
When I frown

His skins so soft
His body's so fine
I can only fantasize
About him being mine

His hands so cold
His touch feels so good
If he asked me to
I know I would

His lips so soft
His arms so strong
I want him so bad
I've wanted him so long

What would he say
If I tell him how I feel
No matter what his reply
I want him to know my love is real.

Haley M. Valko

Retrograde

The ditch along the roadside
Is barren, diminished, nude.
Faith in green returning life
Has somehow come unglued.

Tumbleweeds, like hope deferred
Stumble across the barren waste,
Rootless, wandering vagrants
Going nowhere in mindless haste.

Blown by caustic, contemptuous winds
That criticize and complain
In moaning, menacing whispers,
As if in the throes of pain.

Murmuring of past mistakes,
A wordless, whining confession.
Telling, but not explaining
Nature's ruthless regression.

Billie Houston

Grandma

Her gentle smile, and
tender voice
Remain with me, all
of the while.
Though she is gone.
I can hear her song.
Her great advice,
to make a better life.
No more walks
No more secrets
No more late night talks
I don't hear how much she cares
But in my heart, I know it's there,
And always to remain.

Rae Clark

"Some News Is Sad"

Though the cold is biting
    And some news is sad,
There has been a certain sighting
    That makes our hearts quite glad.

The word is going 'round
    That near a little Inn
An infant has been found
    And a Kingdom shall begin.

For the infant is a King
    With a people in His fold,
And the news the people bring
    Dispels the biting cold.

He rules by love and grace
    From the heart, His earthly throne,
And leads us to a place
    Where tears are never known.

The sightings multiply,
    Reports from far and near,
To every searching eye-
    The King is really here!

Gordon Pope

"if i were me"

oh, why can't i be me,
the me i think i be?
i would be all i want to be,
if only i were me.

you see, i am not me,
'cause I invented me.
me is flawless, sinless and sure.
this feeble i can't be.

since others can't know what
i be, i hides in me.
no one can tell i me be wrong.
painful truth i won't hear.

"who me?" "why me?" "not me!"
i believes i be me.
i be self-centered, arrogant.
esteemed i denies vice.

me is all i can be.
ev'ry blow to me crushes i.
if i could only see...
how many i's won't see.

John Winston Stem Jr.

Another Valley

Ye who walks through the valley
    Of loneliness.
From the very beginning it was
    Destined to be.
Alone with no one to hold,
    With no one to talk,
    With no one at all.
Before you realize, loneliness
    Subsides to fear
    And another valley we walk.

Rebecca L. Hansen

To Make A Poem

Get in the mood and
Get going before you
    get-out-of:
Transcribing musing, conscious
    and sub —
Generated from bits of living
    and dreaming,
Crystallizing motive, title,
    mode-form:
Line, rhythm, rhyme, meter,
    sound and sense.
Take your time — even time-off,
But come back, keep moving to reach
'goal (d) — assay:

Cecil Connell

A Fragment

It happened in a street of gold,
A barren, blazing street of gold,
Where torrid tales of Troy were told
    On ancient piles of dust.
A puff of smoke was seen to rise,
A puff of smoke, before their eyes,
Came ringing through the metal skies
    And blew up on the rust

Of countless images of old
That long had left the figured mold
And now lay glowing in the gold
    Like embers in a pot.

Yeaton H. Clifton

Put Forth A Song

Put forth a song for those now lost,
Valhalla is their blissful rest.
Let each voice sound out clear,
Sing not the song of failure here,
Whence they came the wailing strain
Never more will they fear.

Broken promise, forever shame
Their proud muscles in dust and grain,
The stone records each name.
Let those with honor salute them,
And those without abstain.

When we dance before the shrine,
With each step we say this prayer,
Help those whose present is the past
And whose morrow is despair.

Bart Tuffly

In Late January I Ran Away To Write A Poem

As a zillion stars formed
words in my mind
I saw the lovely hair
on the tail of a comet
her face appeared
and I notice the tropical
sun in her cheeks.
She was lovelier than
a million Zinnias in
the throne room of a
fairy princess.
She is a tropical beauty
and I thought of the inner most part
of an orange
and went home.

Ronald Lewis

"I Saw Jesus By The River"

As I passed down by the river
On a cool summer night.
The stars let up the heavens
With a glow so big and bright
Then I thought I saw a face
Looking down at me —
I said, "It must be Jesus,
Who else could that be?"
I heard a voice that said to me
"What you have seen is true
It is your Saviour Jesus and
He's looking down on you."
The tears came streaming down my face.
All I could do is stare.
I wiped my tears, looked up again,
But My Jesus wasn't there.

Mary Clark

Flame

The flame burns
ultimately beautiful
its power is beyond me
beyond you
you took my love for you
so did the flame
It burned the rose
the one that symbolized our love
The rose was like a souvenir
on a tourist trip
The trip is over
The love is gone
The flame may have taken away the
souvenir,
the love.
But it can not take away the memories
or my everlasting pain of missing you.

Monica Rodriguez

Winter

Snowmen,
Snow hares,
Snow, and
Lights,
Build a fire,
Snowball fights,
Build some snowmen
And sledding too,
And that's just some of what I do.

Wil Whalen

Learning

Learning, Learning, Learning;
Because I know learning is fun
I can touch the sky in a book,
I think like Albert Einstein,
I run, play and jump like
Jesse Owens and touch the sky
when I am in a book.
Writing is fun, I think, and I
explore my mind like Maya Angelou.
I speak like a great speaker. My mind
explores and explores until I hold on
and fly. I like exploring like an
astronaut in space, So I know
learning is the way to go.
Learning, Learning, Learning
is fun.

Erin Daneen Burt

Better Storm

Once upon a time,
Not long ago.
We all complained
About things getting
Better
Not realizing, that where
You were, at that very moment
Was the best place on earth
To be.
A place that we could make better
Or worse.
We knew we could quiet all storms.
Use the storms elements
To nurture, to cultivate, to fertilize
What we are,
And be awed by what we
Could become.

William E. Cheeseborough

So We Dine

I sparkles perserpolis
Have walked the jade Earth
near the wooden forest
And sat among the
    wild flowers and the vine.
Drinking the sweet red,
red wine hobnobbing into time.
And so I came upon a log
I Matti and me
Sat down, we will feast
on Beesbread
And Ambrosia
And so we dine
I Matti and me
Having a good, good time

Maxine Daskins

Fine As Wine In The Summer Time

My beautiful chère
Is fine as wine in the
    summer time,
But you really haven't
    had time to age,
Why not stick
    around until you have
time to age,
    Then you really will be
Fine as wine in
    the summer time,

Imam Sulaiman R. S. Aqeel I

My Love

My life has changed
for good,
not bad
so full of life
at times,
so sad
I have grown
a little,
so much
a life of love
your smile,
your touch
choices I've made
some tried,
some true
one things for sure
the right one
was you.

John J. Munzanreder II

Untitled

my first love,
    new and perfectly pure
like the drifting snowflake that
    had yet to touch the earth.
each accidental glance and
    sweet remark which flowed
from the sympathy that
    was he
thrilled and burned and branded
    my silly schoolgirl soul
which felt so deeply and truly
    that he cared when he held and
caressed my shamelessly surrendered hand
and which ached so genuinely when
    my brief but glorious
moment in the sun was ended

Amy Waldrep

Awestruck

It is with great awe
I watch my friend's baby
wriggle on the carpet
and search the world
with his eyes.

It is with the same awe
his mother watches me
reject all things maternal.

Susan M. Martin

Mill River Bridge

    Host to people of many nations
Way to men of many stations.
    Timeless servant of man
Lending girth to land.
    Stand in memory of those we love
The last glimmer of sun above.
    An effigy of those who care
Farther lands and loves to share.
    Milkman beggar undertaker thief
A standing effigy of a living chief.
    Night cleaner minister lover wife
All wishes of daily life.
    All are yours to know river bridge
Love's venerable carriage.
    What burden do you want to say?
Are we yours in faith today.

Alan R. Thompson

Winter

Cold snow makes
  Me shiver.
A group of kids
  Are sliding,
Nippy air you can
  See.
Dark and frosty
  Nights.
Little bits of ice
  Melt
In my mouth.
  Excellent
Oatmeal for
  Breakfast.

  Sara Ruth Depolito

In Contemplation Of Adjournment

Retaliation,
(In the hearts of men.)
I hate its sin.

You don't know what I'd give,
(My life, I'd forfeit.)
Just to close my eyes to it.

To escape the horrid truth,
(Live the life of blind eyes.)
Would mean my heart was mute.

But, no, the burden's too heavy,
(The hands so few.)
The lost so many.

  Carrie A. Koehler

Friends

Telling secrets
bumming smokes,
late nights together
sharing jokes.

Rowdy games:
Truth-or-dare,
and knowing that
they'll always be there.

Sharing private
hopes of tomorrow,
support throughout
laughter and sorrow,

Someone who's there
on whom I can depend,
a very special person
I call friend.

  Stephen M. Dill

"My Dream Of Hope"

I'm a living legend, it seems so
ordinary. My heart can't be broken

"It's just as simply as said."

Many new challenge "O my so far ahead.

I'm just that's determined to make
it my own journal.

So why shall I continued to hit
you with my legend.

When I'm only in the midst
of a living legend

  Anita G. Nettles

The Mountains Of Silence

The mountains of silence
  is a place that keeps
  It holds what should be
What is real can't get in
  the way it is, is not allowed
Breaking into the silent mountains
  is not impossible

The mountains of silence is where
  what should have happened goes
It goes there till it is needed
  little by little it gets out
It is used by those who
  by those who cultivate themselves
  by those who cultivate themselves

By those who
  Have broke the silence
  those who have broke the silence

  those who have broke the silence
By those who break the silence

  Jared Nicks

Drugs

Heartaches,
tear filled eyes,
so many choices,
so many lies.
People cover,
things are easy to say,
the world is full of trouble,
children no longer play.
A deadly weapon that kills,
it's so easy to find,
seeing it — causes chills,
what's wrong with our minds?
The white snow,
the green grass,
doesn't anyone know,
we're killing ourselves fast?
Depending on things,
people, you can't trust,
the pain really stings,
now, everything is just dust.

  Susan Niles

The Wall

The names appeared before me
  Out of the gray Washington mist
Each one of them a person once
  Added to the Grim Reaper's list

I wondered why they all had died
  So far away from their homes
Some arrived in one piece, perhaps
  Others returned only as bones

It's sad to see some people here
  They find a name, then cry
And wonder often, for all to hear
  Why was it they didn't die

They say our best died in Vietnam
  I'm not sure who to blame
But I've seen some here at this wall
  Veterans, searching for a name

The wall, the names, and the visitors
  All faded in the dreary gray
As I turned and wiped away a tear
  And saluted the wall that day

  Stephen A. Crews

Quietly Sitting

Quietly sitting,
wondering,
wondering where her life was going.
Did it have a direction,
A chosen path?
She didn't think so.
It seemed like she
wandered,
wandered from place to place,
person to person,
day to day.
Quietly sitting,
wondering.
Wondering if she would ever love.
Was there such a feeling,
such an emotion?
She didn't think so.
Quietly sitting,
wondering,
wondering.

  Angela Marie Brocato

His Dove

I don't know why I was there
Had it been so long?
I remember him like it yesterday
So weak, yet so strong.

We grew up together
Best friends for life,
But that whole world shattered
Upon the arrival of the night.

I lay the flowers beneath his name
A pain that will always last.
Tears start streaming down my face
As I remember the past.

I look up and I see a dove
So beautiful and so free.
This could be but only a message
That he is here with me.

And as I walk away I realize
That he will always be part of me.
For his spirit is no longer trapped,
But forever free.

  Stephanie Dorer

Reunion

Oh, sweet lovely child of mine
  Heaven's gift come down to me
So far away, so far alone
  Your life with pain and agony
Take heed, my love, breath soft
  For I come to rescue thee
Hold fast, hold tight
  To God's eternal love
And once, yes twice
  We'll together forever be
These years gone past apart
  Will come together again
And you and I my child will start
  As father and daughter we've been
We'll laugh and cry once more
  As though the sun shall never set
And the rain becomes a mist
  Flowering our love without regret

  Ken Douglass

Another Step

Shut the door,
And let the breeze from the window
Be all that penetrates my soul.
When the song ends,
Let the silence embrace me
And the lingering words fill my heart.
Though I am alone,
I can feel your presence
Yet they say you are dead and gone.
When the storm is over,
It will leave me sodden
But drown in the rain I will not.

Dara Bryn Shapiro

The Swans

Bleached white ghosts
Glide across black glass,
Orange beaks
Stab from dark masks
Into my lungs, taking my breath away.

Martin Redle

A Lady You Are

A lady you are
A lady you'll be.

You are a shining star
For me to see.

You're a monument to beauty
That holds me in awe.
With a dazzling personality
That has no flaw.

You are a guiding light
When I am lost.
And when I met you
Your friendship didn't cost.

If I had more time
To spend with you,
I could show you the world
And my feelings for you.
Because you're special
And you will always be.
Especially to a gentleman,
A gentleman like me.

Saint C. Williams III

The Indian Beggar
(Or Was It Me)

Drink away
drink away
drink away the past
   No matter the future
   the present is one big mess
Drink away
drink away
think away the past
   Dreaming of a future
   the present won't last
Drink away
think away
drink away the past
   One day I come to my senses
   In society . . . or in heaven?

Mercedes Moor

Jesus

There are many names we call Him
But words just can't express
His greatness and His majesty
His love and gentleness.

He's the Alpha and Omega
The First and Last, you see
But Jesus is the name I love
It says it all to me.

The Son of God, He is the Lamb
Messiah, King of Kings
But Jesus is the One I love
That name means all of these.

Paula Lee Cook

Broken

(Oklahoma City, April 19, 1995)
Something has broken, I fear
   Break a dream, shed a tear
Broken dreams, broken lives
   Sonic boom, shattered sky

Something has broken, I see
   Rising smoke; lose all hope
Broken stones, broken bones
   See the flames; go insane

Something has broken, I cry
   Helpless child; sob a mile
Broken glass, infants pass
   Tiny babes; tiny graves

Something has broken, I hope
   Human pride; break its stride
Broken rage, broken cage
   Love of life; ancient sage

Something was broken, you see
   Now it's new; now we're free
Free to choose, how to be
   Live in love; plant the seed

Charles Vincent Hannan IV

Rabbits For Dinner

"Can't" is a four letter word
"Can't" is Atrophy
"Can't" is Worthless
"Can't" lacks self assurance
"Can't" lacks ambition
"Can't" is disabling
"Can't" never caught a Rabbit,
   not even a slow one

"Can" says it all!
"Can" is positive
"Can" is progress
"Can" is infinity
"Can" knows no boundaries,
   save one's imagination

"Can" catches Rabbits
"Can" can't
That's That.

Dong Wood

Imprisoned Soul

Imprisoned in this body
Of mere mortality
Is a soul of mass confusion
Yearning to be free

Free to face tomorrow
Without thought of yesterday
To forgive my own short comings
So I can live from day to day

Free to handle pressure
That daily life might bring
And dodge the stones of malice
That other people fling

Free to ascertain my being
Realize my destiny
Cease wondering what I could be
Be content with being me

Tina Owens

God Is Realized Not Found

God is realized not found.
In Truth She whispers in our ears
A gentle love without a sound.

Silent ripples bereft of sound
Awaken now our lonely fears.
God is realized not found.

Endless echoes round and round
Absorbing now our troubled cares;
A gentle love without a sound.

Despair and hatred all around,
As painful noise our heart it tears.
God is realized not found.

Pride and ego will forever hound
If God is lost for worried fears.
A gentle love without a sound.

All things will be a burial mound
If prey we fall to life's despairs.
God is realized not found;
A gentle love without a sound

Christopher A. Pacini

Sammy

Sammy loved red.
How it dazzled — shined,
made her feel alive.
Sometimes, she wore red
polish for weeks,
bits and pieces, chipping
from her nails.
She would say, "Now I
have to do them over.
I'm mad!"

Red.
Sammy loved red, and I —
instead loved her.
True, it was sassy
against her dark decor,
black mysterious eyes —
said that bright hue made her
but, she made me,
and I loved her —
amidst her wonderful red.

Tina Woolfolk

Let Me Rope!

Rope! Rope what?
Ain't nuthin' round here
But a few chickens
and a darn 'ole stump!

I want a cow
nothing to fat or to slow
Just give me a herd
and I'll let my rope go

Now I ain't saying I can
rope real well
I just like the feeling
of that rope running away like hell

So please!
just give me something I can rope
Cause that 'ole stump has a rope burn
and my chickens all sore throats!

Amanda Wymer

Me

I am me
Unlikely like anybody
Unique as one can be
Amongst one of humanity

I can be what I want to be
For so long as I keep on being me
Not just like to be somebody
But that somebody to be me

I am me
And I love me as being me
And also love others as well

As I live life being me
I see me as good as can be
For I always bring out the best in me
The best I can be is to be me.

Tim Paran

Untitled

As the light drops
Worlds awake.
As the child dreams,
Immaculate lands He creates.
Life does bloom
in the cold darkness of His room.
Dream weaver, world conceiver,
Flower gardens, birds galore
All in His mind.
He bore no evil no mean
All because He could dream.

Then

Dawn and All good is gone.
Willard E. Conklin

Ebony Eyes

Incandescent is the light
That shines in your brown eyes,
Brighter than Ole Solomon
Who dwells amid the skies,
Ebon as the background
Of the twinkling stars above,
Deep within your eyes
I see the lovely light
Of love.

Derrick Leon Harper

Shining Woman

Stark against twilight sky
Taller than a single self,
Warrioress ephemeral.

She blends with shadows
And webbed trees wings
Drinking birdsong,
Singing to creek's flow.

Tribunals shaped her centuries:
Triumph built her presence.
Standing statuesque —
Her roots in wildness.

Taste her wafting scent —
Vitality from the land.
She is Whole,
Her roots deep in the earth.

She changes: She remains.

Standing in crystal light
Taller than trees
A warrioress spirit
Walks upon the land.

Karen D. Zurawski

Church Street Hag

Huddled in the doorway,
Her face and feet in rags,
A carpetbag lay by her side.
The plight of Church Street Hag.

I've seen her there, day by day,
Soaked by rain and snow.
Frozen in the winter wind.
Has she no where to go?

Is there a story in her bag?
Her blank look tells no tales.
Or, is it numbness in her heart,
From all that she has failed?

Perhaps she was too tender,
Too easy to the slight
This life can thrust so forcefully
To hags that walk the night.

So, now she has found a place,
That church door as her home,
And feels she's face to face with God,
And needs no more to roam.

Beverly A. Fanning

"More Than A Woman"

There once was a little girl
But now she's all grown
Up in a women's world
She used to play with
Little dolls and toys
Instead of that now
She goes out with the boys
I can't say when she'd
   come back home
But I'd figured that
She'd be all alone
Until a one fine summer's day
I saw her with someone,
A man who's name was Dave
And that's when I had realized
Who she had become
A beautiful young woman
Who was so deeply in love

Tammy Lee Stookey

"A Place So Near"

Come go with me to a place
so near that only you and
I can share . . .
Come go with me to a place
so near where all our fantasies
seem so real
Come go with me to a place
so near where dreams are so
for real and thoughts are
fulfilled
Come go with me to a place
so near that only you and I
can share.

Anita R. Smith

Grandma

Although I never saw her, I wonder
how she is in heaven, all alone?
the thought of serious brain
cancer makes me wonder why it was her?
I've heard the she was pretty.
I heard that she was nice.
We know that she is with us no
matter where we go, we wish that
she could be here to watch us as we grow.
I know that she would like me.
I know we would have fun.
I wish she wouldn't of died in 1981.

Claire Scott

Reality

Over the steamy brick
the proud figure glides
white flawless legs,
displayed below cut-off jeans
Then . . . But ten paces arrear.
Can this be?
An ancient limps
stooped to shape cee,
clothed in rumpled gray
stubbled chin pepper and salt.
Out from under the hat
a sudden expectoration shocks
and splats upon the hot pavement.

R. S. Howe Jr.

The Windows Of Heaven

How are the windows of heaven?

They're big and they're round
and they're blue!

They sparkle like no diamond
ever has done.

They're full of mischief, and
lots of fun.

They dance when the snowflakes
come flying.

They tear when a baby
bird dies.

I guess you know what I'm talking
about — it's the love in my little
boy's eyes.

Ann V. Steinmetz

Poet's Dream

There are times when all is quiet
  no movement

Maybe unblack
  or black resting on black

A silver daiquiri with summer flame
  a silver daiquiri made of tears

White sands laid out
  with marsh at its elbow

And fish odors
  with each ripple of rock air
    John McMahon

A Winter Wind Upon a Lake

A winter wind upon a lake
The sky above so blue
Auspicious wonders in the sky
Cupids arrow flying by
Will it touch upon my heart
Will love enter in as destiny
Or will it soar on through eternity
And forever pass me by
    Susan Jayne Cino

Rest, My Child

Drifting softly,
  Floating,
Voyaging into space.
  A sweet nothingness.

No hustle.
No bustle.
No hurry.
  Peace.

Caverns of quietness
Invade the mind.

  Sleep has arrived.
  Rest, My child.
    Carolyn Kight

Untitled

A little Jesus
In a garden of Eden
Tears out
Butterfly's wings
    Magdalena Zakrzewska

The Secret Of Life

The beauty of life
is knowing to love
the music and color
and flowers alike
the bridal bouquet
that girls have to find
that bring so much happiness
to people around
the secret of life
is loving a little
is loving a lot
and always to conquer
the secret of life. Amen.
    Fausto Art Velez

What Is Your Passion?

What is your passion?
How do you hold your dreams?
Do your nightmares have you screaming?
Are there spiders in your closet,
Is the S.S. in the street?
Do you see their Swastikas?
And did you know that their colors
Are the ones we will all repeat?

Red, White, and Blue.
Red, White, and Blue what have you done
For your country?

Red, White, and Blue, what has
Your country done for you?
    Kenny Roark

Another Day

Each day that I get the chance
  to wake up my soul thanks the
  Lord, because he permits me
  to walk in his path another day.

Yes, Jesus is always on my side;
  I shall not forget who makes
  my days in peace and protects
  me from all contaminations of
  this cruel world.

Another day to worship and sing
  to my Jesus; whom I fall in
  love with more and more each
  day, whom I believe came and
  she'd blood for me on calvary
  because he loves me. Loves
  me like no one can ever love
  me; with all his heart and
  spirit. Just as I am starting
  to love him with all my
  heart, mind and soul.
    Johanna Sierra

"Nighttime"

The sun sets low on reddened sky
The moon peeks over tree
The birds to straw-like nests do fly
And I come home to me.

The bats begin nocturnal flight
The owls blink in glee
The forest closes down its light
And I come home to me.

The stars create a pattern grand
The firefly glows free
The constellations do command
And I come home to me.

Reflections on day past do plea,
Rest, well done, come home to me!
    Christopher Librandi

Birth

I felt a miracle today,
The miracle of life within me
Thrusting to be free.
But when my child had won its victory,
I cried and pondered:
He is no longer mine,
But his own — and God's.
    Lelia Christie Mullis

Yellow Rain

The sun rose this chilly morn
bright and warm.
It sounded the death knell
to a fall night's hard frost.
I sit at the kitchen table
with the steam of fresh coffee
waking my sleep drugged senses.
Out the window there,
was the sun rising day
where trees now colored
with many hues of yellow
seemed to lift skinny brown arms
in homage to the blue skies.
Then, suddenly,
the bright sun covered forest
shivered before my startled eyes
and a Yellow Rain fell from the trees,
like tears for the years end.
    James C. Shearer

Untitled

On my knees;
I bow before thee
My touch sets your hormones free

Your legs slightly spread;
Just enough room for my head

I hear your moans, and your sighs;
As I am down between you thighs

From the sounds you are pleased;
With my hands your nipples teased

I could be down on you all week;
Whatever it takes for you to peak.

I kiss you here, and lick you there;
Run my fingers through your hair.

I know how to make you beg.
All I do is move my head.
    Korry Lyn Bassinger

The Prayer

Oh, Lord, please, help me in my dream
Things are not always what they seem
A lifetime goal to pursue
Dead end reveals in front of you

Success is easy nowadays
Temptation rules in means and ways
I bowed to all-accepted life
And sacrificed my soul's strife

Oh, Lord, you are my last resource
In fighting for the worthy cause
To be a human boy on Earth
Return from zombies' world of death

I want to love, I want to cry
To feel all pain beneath the sky
To think and suffer day and night
And never sound satisfied

Oh, Lord, if there is chance for me
Show me the way to come to thee
And in your wisdom to redeem
Destroy my sense of self-esteem
    Mark S. Labinov

Omniscient

The rock abundant,
Spanning the hills,
Mountains composite,
Encompassing all,
It is our make-up,
After it all.
Our existence abounds,
In quiet lifeless rocks,
Down through the ages,
What would they be saying?
Unlock the secrets,
From deep earth treasures,
Conceptual presence streams out,
With every new wave of color.
The Bands of sunlight,
Will bask immaculate,
Weaving a pattern of pure insight,
Trust and color unite together,
Silent as Truth
The Truth
        Anthony Fletcher

"The Bird"

The bird in the tree
Sang songs just for me.
        Landry Haarmann

Icy Inferno

My dearest, precious Forrest,
I miss you more than words can say.
How I wish that raging fire
Had not taken you away.

The horror of that morning
Is a pain too great to bear —
The flashing lights and icy snow,
Smoke and ashes everywhere.

The house that once had been our home
Had become a fiery tomb
Stealing the life of the son
I had nurtured since the womb.

In the midst of that inferno
The icy fingers of death
Grasped you in their iron hold,
Robbing you of your last breath.

From deep within my very soul
A part of me was torn,
My heart was devastated
By the terror of that morn.
        Diana L. Erickson

Untitled

Chill breeze tonight awakened me
Scene of lament, a drowning sea

Spent by life but cannot sleep
Regrets like currents flowing deep

Stranger in me begins the old song
Faint is the voice; oh, for how long

Deaf I've been to the melody
That is only mine, the essence of me

Fool was I to dance ahead
To noise that was music, others said
        Valerie McArdle

Pray for Today

Please God try to help my wife,
Bet it's hard without me in her life.
Help my kids to understand and know,
When I get out, it's home I'll go.
I love and miss them very much,
They'll need you Lord for a crutch.
Help her to be strong each day,
Take their fears and tears away.
My family and I have faith in you,
No matter what you need to do.
Please send your love into my home,
Never let them cry alone.
I ask a lot of you today,
You always helped me everyday.
Take some of your love from me,
A little stronger they may be.
Help my family to clearly see,
I pray to you, but not for me.
        Martin Tetrault

Morning Meditation

Dawn; within my house of logs
I hear crickets, I hear frogs;
Water running fast away,
Excess rain from yesterday.

Morning sun now spreads its light
Clearing mist left by the night;
— Waking birds to this new day,
"Rain is gone! Cheer-up", they say;
— drying grass and flower and weeds;
— warming Earth and sprouting seeds.
Seeds may grow to be tall trees
Making logs to work like these
That span my roof, form my walls,
Staying wind and rain that falls,
Framing windows letting light
Ease the shadows out of sight.

Grateful thoughts of God's good plan,
Learned: then made to work by Man
Fill this place with peace and rest.
"Thank you, God, I'm truly blest!"
        Lila F. Brown

Poet Rule

It's a freedom plus
That cannot be told
It can't be stolen
borrowed or sold
Police cannot take it
for it harms not a soul
The I.R.S. won't take it
Because it won't pay the toll
It's a place to get lost
for hours and days
To express your aggressions
problems or ways
It doesn't need to rhyme
or be any length
It has only one rule
and that is its strength
The rule to remember
in only one part
To write your own poem
it must come from your heart.
        Dennis E. Everett

The Lament Of Joseph Plunkett

Oh, darling, do not cry for me.
Our precious time is running out.
Soon I will die; you must be strong.
You will survive, I have no doubt.
We fought and strived to free our land.
I could have stayed in my sick bed.
Instead, I answered Freedom's call
And followed where her banner led.
In this chapel we will be wed,
We'll pledge our love, both you and I.
At dawn they'll lead me to the wall
And for my country I shall die.
Pearse and Clarke have gone to God
And though we lost, we did not fail.
Our nation will be free some day
And history will tell our tale.
Oh, Grace, my dear, please do not cry.
I will be thinking of you when
The bullet does its fatal work
And I join my comrades once again.
        Daniel Oisin Nieciecki

Chanalee (Winter Sunset)

Like to share it with you . . .
To feel the colours of this frozen sky.
The calmest shade of tranquil blue
To drown your restlessness inside.

Like to share it with you . . .
The stream of green eons away,
Not mourning for past lifetimes flew
To where they died some "yesterday".

Like to share it with you . . .
The palest pink, a newborn's mind
Beckoning softly as it grew to
Leave the saddest parts behind.

Can I share it with you?
        Mary Trendle

Untitled

To see the unseen
is to live the untold
to laugh is to cry
to live is to die
to be one is to be none
to be two is to love
to love is to live
to lose is to die
to do is to be
to wish is to want
to dream is to hope
to see is to live
        Kathleen Y. Cameron

The Moon

Shaped like an ark and
    Bright as gold
You hang from the sky
    You are so bold
Surrounded by stars
    Shining bright
You show the way
    You are my light
The night seems long
    But I'll be home soon
You lead the way
    You are the moon.
        Susan Taylor

Of Silver And Gold

What does the future hold
For our love so feverishly bold?
A brilliant sunrise of silver and gold?
A sunset that never grows old?

What does tomorrow bring
for our souls to lavishly sing?
A cool midnight breeze in spring?
Or a snowflake on an angel's wing?

Oh God, I pray that time
Will carry a memory of us,
a brilliant union of silver and gold
memories of our life to be told.

Andrea Luckie

Inside

For so long
the one who brought
them together.
So long the
center,
the loving one,
the loved one.
Now so alone.
So alone inside
myself,
Where no one can go
but me.

Nicole J. Bishop

Life

In an endless, crashing sea,
One that changes constantly,
A raft, weather-beaten and poor,
Roams this desert in search of shore.

Nicole Burke

Deadline

Can't you see what's taken hold,
Mind gaze at the sky.
Lose yourself and leave me here,
Death shall soon drop by.

Life's parodies play their tunes,
Us captured in the game.
Morals torn by sordid hands,
Alleviate our pain.

No notice of our new form,
Entropy takes seed.
Caught within its fatal grasp,
We wait, we watch, we bleed.

Nemo

"Sacred"

I am a desert.
You are a river.
I am sacred, you shiver.
Quench my heart, quench my soul,
Quench my thirst.

I am a river
You are a desert.
You are sacred, I quiver.
Quench your heart, quench your soul
Your thirst.

Peggy Justice

Niagara Falls

Our Grains have turned to rocks
Our rocks then made stones
Our stones then made mountains
And so our love pressed on.

A tear made the waters
That flows across the streams
From a cry that's never heard
From a dreamer that's afraid to dream

Some have often found gold
Some have cherished the sands
Many hearts have often been broken
But broken hearts can mend

Your smile it brighten a day
When springs presence is near
Only leads to pain
When you're not here my dear

On a leaf I'll send a message
And I'll await your call
But please bring an umbrella
To watch Niagara Fall

Malcolm M. Perry

God Cares For Me

When Life
And People get me down
And tempt me to wear
My Smile upside down.

I won't worry or feet
I won't even get upset
'Cause God Cares For Me
Wants Me to be the Best
That I can be
For Today,
    And all Eternity.

Sandra Chavis

The Atonement

He was born of a virgin
The sinless son of God
He grew in strength and wisdom
But man would think him odd

Few would truly follow
The laws he taught to man
Or walked the straight and narrow
Instead they turned and ran

On the Cross of calvary
Three words he did say
"It is finished," He cried
Before he died that day

Just three days would pass by
Before he would rise again
He was the eternal
Atonement for man's sin

Still many do not know him
While other run and hide
Jesus is the son of God
Will you let him be your guide

Franchesca Edwards

Compartments Of The Mind

The sorrow has caressed me
With its silky velvet touch
There is no other thing this intense
Nothing quite as much

If you know the pain I speak of
Welcome to my world
And I guess you have met the spirits
Watch them dance watch them twirl

The suffering it has caressed me
With its thorny surface
There is nothing more painful
They say it serves its purpose

But if you met the spirits
I guess they told you too
There is no escape from "our world"
No matter what you do

Lenore Tsai

When People Leave This World

When people leave this world
It does not mean they're dead.
They've started a new life
With happiness instead.
A life without sadness.
A life that holds no pain
A life that promises
Only good things to gain.
When people leave this world
A brand new life is theirs.
One with God in heaven
Who has a heart that cares.
God's promise to us all
Through Christ, His only Son,
Holds happiness and joy
When life on earth is done.
When people leave this world
It does not mean they're dead.
They've started a new life
With happiness instead.

Kenny Newell

Life

LIFE is Loving, Laughing,
Living to the fullest,
sometimes Loneliness.

LIFE is Imagination, Inspiration,
In awe of the world,
sometimes Idle.

LIFE is Friends, Frolicking,
having Faith,
sometimes Foil.

LIFE is Emotions, enlightening,
Essence of being,
sometimes Existing.

Maxine E. Williams

Summer

Summer is yellow and blue.
Summer tastes like apples.
Summer sounds like water splashing.
Summer smells like pine trees.
Summer looks like a shooting star.
Summer makes me feel happy.

Casimir Wisniewski

Curses And Kisses

Cold, cold rain surrounds —
Grabs at my arms,
and slits at my wrists
Mystic air that falls around
And covers my body
With immortal curses and kisses;
The stars I use as a blanket
To cover my soul and my mind
As a sheet of sanity and beauty
Tortures of the light
That won't go away
And destroys myself by my hand
Of wire and bones, I taste the blood
The warm, sweet silvery liquid
Rolls down my throat;
And I laugh at you —
Decaying slowly in the ground
remains at the pit of my stomach
Womb to hold demons and lies and love
(Love is lies)

Gina Manning

Turnabout

Hypocritical wretches
What hell they have wrought
Their judgment is on us
Their justice can be bought

So now you are with them
You traitorous scum
You believe all their lies
Your mind has turned numb

I feel the despair now
I am all alone
To gaze at my kingdom
And sit on my thrown

You see, I once led them
Chaos was my name
All has collapsed upon me
A turnabout for the blame

Jason Munt

Spring

Spring is a magical season,
The most wondrous of the year.
Each of our trees receives its leaves
And the forests are full of deer.

All the flowers start blooming,
And display their brightest hue.
Our many brooks are bubbling
With their waters so clear and blue.

Spring is the season that everyone
Truly enjoys so much.
When all is in its splendor
With mother nature's touch.

Robert D. Trebilcox

On Hangin' In

My days are all numbered,
my years are far-spent.
My get-up-and-go
Has got up and went.
My zip has been zapped
And my vim is diminished,
But, the good Lord willin',
I'll stay till I've finished

Roy R. Winkelmann

Good Bye

As I watch the rain bead on the
    glass.
I think of the times when I
    wished for the tears to
    pass.
Now the tears are no longer
    around.
For a new love I have found.
A love that makes me feel
    free.
Like a gentle breeze through
    a tree.
A love that holds me in its
    warm embrace.
Like the hot sun beating down upon my
    face.
So now to you I bid
    goodbye.
For you will no longer make
    me cry

Brandy Land

Dear Parents

A poem for parents
on Valentines Day.
I wrote a little something
that I would like to say.
Mothers are nice,
fathers are good,
they take care of us
just like they should.
You've never gotten into a fight
except for once or twice.
I love it whenever my father
cooks pork chops, broccoli and rice.
My mother works and cleans all day,
she works and cleans the night away.
I love you, I hug you,
and hardly ever bug you.

Alan Nastri

"The 6:00 News"

Doberman head;
You've managed quite enough today.
Quaif your evenings fare,
Spastic stroke your panel,
engines idle.

The 6:00 news;
behold the harlequined overdrive
boxe in a corner,
the inevitable catastrophe; . . .
now ghosted reality.
Beneath the stattico message;
the vocabulary of your peers.

Can you watch a turn . . .
Can you run or burn . . .

In the communions holy image
and the shooting star resolution
of your silver fading light,
Shuffle on with your slippers
stir the electron embers
    goodnight.

Greg Schroth

Flour —
In Conversation With A Flower

Another guest came a-calling,
and found my 'pearance quite appalling
because her radiance filled the room —
and mine, to her, enhanced the gloom.

They brought her in from garden bright
the kitchen, then, no welcomed sight
for she had never been indoors,
encased by windows, dusty floors.

As if she thought I would not care,
she penned me with an awful glare
and 'dressed me from her ornate flask
with questions she held to the last:

"Why don't you ever go outside?"
"I'm quite content," I so replied.
"But it's so dark in here!" she sighed,
and then she bent her head and cried.

There was so much she did not know
that I would tell before she'd go;
for nourishment of health is mine,
to cater to each dear design.

Maggie Gazarek

"Slayer Of Love"

They say "it's just skin",
They say it's for fun,
But I say,
"This is not fun"

Oh this creature called fun,
turns out to be a slayer of love,
A killer of dreams
and plans of a future.

A breach of contract
A broken heart
and this is called "fun"?

I'll close my eyes
and bury my head
and hope and pray
I never meet fun.

Mary Anderson

Common Heroes

From dusk till dawn
    As time moves on
They struggle and toil
    To work the soil
They show a love of the land
    Unchallenged by man
With a smile on their face
    You cannot erase
They work hard for success
    And do their best
To feed the hungry
    Of every country
When beaten down
They fight hard not to drown
With little reward
They stay on board
And venture on
Knowing someday they may be gone
Sometimes they fail, sometimes succeed
They do this all for you and me.

Michael Stedman

The End Of Summer

In the hush of evening
when dusk is growing deep
God casts a shadow over the world
and tucks it in to sleep.

It is then trees whisper together
and the whir of the wind is heard
as over the hill there comes the call
of some late autumn bird.

Then all is quiet, no sound we hear
until the East is a brightening ray
and the black bird calls with
all his might.
To announce the coming day.

Lorraine Thomson Files

Our Last Love

Drugs took their toll on you,
And our marriage failed,
Now you go around saying
someone stole me from you,
But you know it isn't true,
I loved you once but drugs
became your mistress and I
was pushed aside.
I found a man who gives
me the love I need,
and I don't have to be afraid
I'll be beaten for not doing
what you want,
Joe, you could have had the
world and me to go along,
But drugs just killed
anything we ever could have known.

Ellen L. Erb

The Garden

Rain down
Crumbling to the ground
Sun down on my soul
The stars are burning out
I've nowhere else to go

Blindfolded
Thoughts sorted
Into one
Our time has come
Our time is done

Sliding down my fate
Open are the gates
I'm losing my faith
As I step into the garden
I'm walking in the garden
I'm now reborn in the garden

Blindfolded by my faith
Every step I take
I melt into the garden
As I walk through the gates

Chris Courtney

Life's Little Pleasures

There are so many things
in life we get to enjoy
like seeing a young girl
trying to kiss a little boy
watching a sunset in the
western sky
hearing a newborn babies
first cry
holding that newborn in
your hands
and seeing the emotion it
brings to every man
these are some of the things
we hold onto and treasure
they are just a part of
life's little pleasures.

Bradley M. Burns

Kids Killing Kids

Kids killing kids
This is America folks
And it's no joke
Liquor, marijuana, and coke.

America's streets are battle grounds
Guns loaded with a few rounds
Hatred is on the increase
And no sign of a decrease.

Kids killing kids is a breeze
Getting a gun comes with such ease.
When will it ever stop?
Not until the last kid does drop.

On our streets blood running red.
In the news another kid is dead.
It makes our hearts so sad
Especially for the Mother and Dad.

L. Marvin Marion

Plural

If you need a plebiscite
    To take a plenary action,
Plebeian you must be-
    From another faction.

Your plight will have to
    Be pliant
To take the plunge,
    And plunk down your action.

Otherwise your pleasure
    Will have to be plural
To find a plus
    In you extraction.

John W. Groesbeck

Forgiven

The best way to learn,
  is from a mistake.
The best way to understand,
  is from a mistake.
And the best way to know,
  not to do something,
Is the mistake of doing it.
  Mistakes can be
  Forgiven

Brian Fedie

In The Spring

The trees put on their outfits
Of colors bright and gay.
The flowers show their faces
And smile at you each day.

The blades of grass all over
Are turning very green.
And all the things of nature
Are painting pretty scenes.

The little caterpillars
Turn into butterflies.
They fill the air with colors
Before your very eyes.

The birds are very happy
And they begin to sing.
All nature is so cheerful
For now it's time for spring.

Alta Hildebrand Hartfield

Silent Dream

If words could explain
just what you mean to me,
your heart would be overwhelmed
and your beauty, others would see.

The joy within my heart
grows fonder day by day
and the love deep within me,
in your passion is swept away.

My dreams take us places
that one day we may go,
and the sincerity of my love
I will truly show.

My lifetime I have waited
for such a love as this,
the gentleness of your caressing
and the fire within your kiss.

My enduring love will keep you
forever in my heart
and no one or nothing
can ever tear us apart.

Tandy Bowman

Poets

Poets use the language of love,
And all is but metaphor.
Why call it a portal,
When you can call it a door?

When comparing a face so true,
One for which you have love,
Why call it what it is not,
Why call it a star from above?

Sometimes we confuse our words,
And say what we mean not.
When speaking in this language,
Emotions may flare hot.

So why confuse and then abuse,
The language of the poets?
Why must our words be riddles,
Rather than clear couplets?

Aaron F. Oneal

"War"

War fills with painful
Fright

Mothers worry of sons in
Fight

Flying high or down below
There's always a chance you'll
Get the blow

Lifeless bodies carried out
Doctor's save them from
Dying out
Don't get caught in war
Or in your heart a hole tore
Daniel J. LeMay Jr.

"Remember When"

Remember me the way I was
Laughing and joking
When you hear a bird sing
I'm singing to you
When the sun shines on you
I'm watching
When the wind blows the trees
I'm hugging you always
When it rains
I'm crying cause I miss you
Always keep me close in your hearts
Today, tomorrow, forever and always
Diane L. Gomez

I Weep Tonight

I weep tonight
For in the day
The doves in my hands
Shall fly away
I laugh with the moon
for in the morn
The quilt round my shoulders
Shall be torn
They shall not fly
It shall not tear
As long as night
Is everywhere
Nicole Jaureguy

"Tears Of Joy"

Tears form water falls
As we cry from pain,
Laughter — a sprinkling of rain!
We cry when happy, angry, and sad.
But the tears from child birth
Were the best I've had.

Gentle little baby cried as I did too,
They're tears of joy, as I look at you.
Such a gift from God,
This emotional time,
I cry tears of joy because you're
precious and you're mine!

And as you grow tears of joy
shall not fade,
for I'll look in amazement at the
achievements you have made.
You're such an inspiration and
you're "mommy's little boy!"
That whenever you see mommy
cry, It's because they're tears of joy
Christel Gee

Untitled

Thank you for the
complement.
I know, with best wishes
it was sent.

But a judge of poetry,
I cannot be,
Therefore I have
the difficulty

Of choosing only one poem
I have written
'Cause with all the hundreds
I am smitten.

Not because of meter
or of rhyme.
Nor does symbolism parade
in its clime.

'Tis message
that is meant,
So, only this one, to you
I've sent.
Dora Geertz

Mary

Mary, Mary, quite contrary.
That's how the nursery rhyme goes.
But that one little line,
Put into a rhyme,
Made history long ago.

Mary may be pretty,
She is sweet and always kind,
But if I say white,
She'll say black,
And drive me out of my mind.

With every word you say it seems,
She has something different to say.
But tell her it's wrong,
She'll say it's right,
It's a constant for every day.

But with the everyday contrariness,
One thing I can say for sure,
If you ever feel lonely,
Or a little bit sad,
Her presence is always a cure.
Rebecca Russell

Lord, I Lift Up My Thoughts To You

Lord, I lift up my thoughts to you,
my worries, my troubles, and my fears.
For you alone are always there
To wipe away all my tears.

Lord, I lift up my thoughts to you
For I know that you will always care.
My sorrows and joy I lift up
To you, for you are always there.

Lord, I lift up my thoughts to you,
because of your great love for me.
You have given it with a sign
That says "Take my love, it's free."

Lord, I lift up my thoughts to you,
as I try to walk with you each day.
Lord, I really want to thank you
for showing me the way.
Brenda Kay Marzinske

Coming Home

What will happen when I go?
When my spirit, heart and mind
get the call to come on home.
One has beliefs but cannot know
the whole of what
our spirit life may hold.

So if I merely drift
from one world into another
leaving earthly pain behind
perhaps to greet old friends
and brothers.
I'll be glad to know
that love is never lost
but forever and divine.

At last I'll find that God
forgives me everything
waiting just for me to follow suit.
Heaven gives me time to heal
and to live on liberated
in the light of perfect Truth.
Kathleen Mitchell Higgins

Can You See

Angels are coming
Angels are going
While we are sleeping
They will be seeking

They come by day
They come by night
With us they stay
To keep us from fright

They want us to see
That we are free
To be as happy
As we can be

They are there
When we cry
And they never
Say good bye

They are in our dreams
To stop our screams
They are there when we're awake
Can't you see them for heaven's sake
Flaming Star Rising

Penelope

Penelope, is it true;
Did you not know Odysseus
When he returned to you
After the years away?
Did you not find
Something in his eyes,
The shape of his hands,
His walk, his voice,
To bring to mind
The lover long so dear to you?

I think that I would know my love
Bruised and battered,
Worn or wounded,
I think that I would know,
Without the need for tests or trials
That something in my heart
Would come alive again
And draw him to my arms.
Ruth Siskind

"The Window To Heaven"

As I look out my window,
in the early morning hour.
I see in the field, a little doe,
with her Mother, being so watchful.

A little time goes by,
and I see the horizon,
and I know soon in the sky,
will be, all full of pink and blue.

When all of a sudden the sun,
peaks over the horizon.
There is a group of clouds and one,
with a large hole in it.

As I look, the clouds change,
to different shapes and sizes,
and also one or two look like chains.
It looked like, the window to heaven.

As I watched the clouds drifting,
and a new sky comes to life.
The sun low on the horizon is lifting,
to bring another day of life.

Virginia Lee Northcutt

Coffee Consumption Before Autumn Dusk

I know I shouldn't
smoke this cigarette.

I know I shouldn't
worry about relationship failure.

Here I sit in this solemn minute
where my mug warms my cuticles
& the taste of nicotine never
felt so splendid

I do know
that I desire prosperity.

I do know
someone is delivering a child of
praying for an end to AIDS

In these fugitive games
we play with our minds,
victory appears logical.

In the end,
we should realize the game is this

We know what we know
and only realize what we should know.

Joe Dimino

Playful Dolphins

Crystal Clear water
You can see though
Blue green waves
Crashing on white
Sandy beaches soft
Wind blowing with
Magnificent colors
in the sky out of
nowhere a playful
Jump in the air
with a splash of water.
Comes a sweet should
of music they shine
as bright as the sun
Like glitter moving
though the waves.

Amber Myers

Flash

A lone, familiar flash in the early
cooling night,
I see her glimmer,
Her futile cry for company.
In search of her own

but alone I guess.

Lost in privacy as the night
absconds with her.

A lonely,

Thinning glimmer.
Here, then there.
A passage of past,
a pleasure of present.

A symbol of freedom and warmth,
now too quickly ebbing.

In search of her own,

but alone,

I guess.

How sad for her to be,
The last firefly of summer.

Valerie Legare

Upon Leaving the Scene

Upon leaving the scene
a new script was handed I
the play read magnificent
between each line

Each character so avid in
their skits
yet the burning inside
no longer wants this

Upon leaving the scene
I too realized this
point would come
now taking the last bow
I run

Not another theatrical performance
no more lines to remember
think I'll just retire instead

I'm leaving the scene
no more to return
'cause for a new scheme
this player yearns

Mary Fox

Quill

(A Small Dedication to a Great Angel)
I love you Gail
Gone from here
are the gnomes of terror.

Harboring now in
the quick

unknown.
Hover.

She has
become
my vanquisher.

John Tassi Jr.

"Farewell My Friend"

It is most difficult to say these words
but I must try

The time has come now
to say goodbye

The very beginning was a new
A friend I thought I found in you
Although you played me for a fool
Empty I found myself without you

It is time now to say
"Farewell My Friend"

The memory I treasure until the end
Farewell, Farewell,
"Farewell My Friend"

Toni Graziosi

"Marie Rose"

A women I've never met,
Who keeps her son content.
Wrapped in his arms with sorrow,
Because there are no more tomorrows.

She's thought about so much,
From all the hearts she touched
Through good times and through bad,
She wouldn't want you sad.

As each and every day goes by,
I can see this women in his eyes.
Through his smile, and his face,
This was a women full of grace.

I wish I could've met this women
Who's brought so much to my life,
Because I am the women who's
going to be, her son's wife.

Joy A. Boudreau

With The Orange Night

Silent snowfall, mystical the
orange night.   Silent orange night.
Behind the first pale flake,
not the last, but there.
To be remembered not by being
alone, but as a part of life.
Contributing in the experiment not
as one of many, but as one of self.
For in the orange of the night,
no two are alike.
Sunlight simply separating the
soul less in his light.   Melting
away confusion 'till the orange
of the night.

Christopher Phegley

Untitled

The ticking of a clock,
Farther, farther, farther
The loudness of silence,
The sweet, sweet revenge,
The undone,
The unbroken,
The only ones to know,
The ticking of a clock,
Farther, farther, farther.

Jennifer Renee Williams

Window Watching

The little toy people
Race through the city
As I watch out my window,
My heart fills with pity.
The black mob of patrons
Looks like a bee swarm,
As they rush to their friends
From the cold into warm.
They run from their home,
To their places of work,
Where they spend the day
As low-paid sales clerks.
From the office they dash
To their home far away.
Where family awaits them
With frozen food on a tray.
They'll sleep till tomorrow
As if dead with no thoughts.
Till I see from my window
One more nameless black dot.

Kathryn Emilie Harris

The Undying Soul

Our soul, the center of our being,
The body, a cover, a disguise.
The soul is life, the body a cloak
Discarded after the years.

Kimberly Novacek

Flame

a
flame
of life
violent with
passion dancing
round tauntingly
spiraling seductively
seducing and caressing
haunting and flickering
lights of non-existent
colors teasingly jumping
burning heat of spunk and spice
and intensity unbearable curling and
turning with fierce intent consuming
transforming creating destroying
gushing and whooshing chanting of
freedom intriguing captivating
and dynamic in spirit

Kathy Heffernan

Spring Storm

Raindrops splashing on the
window pane.
Sky as gray as gray can be,
Thunder crashing and
lightning flashing
The early spring storm is
exciting to see.
Soon the sun comes shining
three,
A rainbow appears and
I am thrilled anew
At the beauty of nature,
God's gift to the world.

C. S. Wright

Mother, 1992

"Mother" does not say enough
for all that we've been through.
  We are closer now, closer too
than grass embracing winter's dew.

  Happiness is a fleeting thing,
like the butterflies of early spring;
  They brighten even the darkest day,
but soon, only the memories stay.

  Yet, every time I think of you,
good memories fill my mind,
  my heart is light like summer rain,
and I am cheerful once again.

  The love between us always grows
becoming sweeter than autumn's rose,
  nurtured by the life we've shared,
watered daily with kindness and care.

  Always remember that where you are,
my heart and love are never far.
  I am always there for you.
May all my days honor you.

Kenneth L. Stillings

The Bullfrog Pond

Serene and green
  Willows and cottonwoods
  Reeds and lilypads
    Bullfrogs and trout
    Jumping all about.
Moss covered banks
  Dragonflies and insects
  Catfish and turtles
    Heron's patiently wait
    Bullfrogs their bait.
Birds are nesting
  Coots are skimming
  Muskrats are teasing
    Haven of rest
    Housing lots of guests.
Sounds fill the air
  Woodducks chatter
  Bullfrogs bellow
    Twilight draws the shade
    The pond sings a serenade.

June Taffee

To Ruth

The Lord looked at thee
Then He looked at me
And He said,
"Friends they'll be"
So we were
And still are,
Whether we're near
Or quite far.
We found each other
For just a day,
Lost 15 years along the way.
Who could have guessed
We would again meet,
Down in a horse barn,
Over a bale of hay.
Our friendship renewed
As it was meant to be,
Because our Lord Blessed us
When He looked at thee and me.

Alice M. Hoover

The Garden

Have you checked upon your garden,
or is it all covered up with weeds
Have you just let it set there,
after you planted all the seeds.

It really take's some work,
to make a garden grow.
You have to feed and water it,
you just can't let it go.

So treat love like a garden,
when you plant it in a heart.
Don't forget to work at it,
from the very start.

You can't just say I love you,
and leave your love alone.
You must care for it to keep it;
a garden doesn't make it on its own.

Effie Louise Thomas

A Buddhist Is Not A Muslim

Oh what a fool I am,
these days grow old
like this warm winter wind.

My love for you has fallen
into the abyss I call Hate,

What am I?

Nothing more than a little man
trapped inside a dead man's body.

Hence I live, inside your head,
in your dreams,
in your nightmares,
in your arms.

I closed the door in your mind.
Soon, I won't exist
Soon, I won't die.

Gregory Brown

Untitled

Ah, lonely river
flowing deep within
seemingly no beginning
and perhaps no end

Deep, wide and surface-still
winding slowly on
not confined, but loosely held
by earthen banks, your home

Momentum increasing
when rapids are near
with white water fervor
your course now hard to steer

Riding out the rapids
then plunging, falling free
over the edge of nowhere
pursuing your destiny

Lonely, lonely river
flowing deep within
seemingly no beginning
certainly no end

Suzanne M. Pelton

Some Days Of My Life

Some days of my life
are rough and tight.
Some days of my life
I can see yet have no sight.

Some days of my life
I linger in pain sometimes
not even remembering my name.

Some days of my life
I weep and I grieve
for loved ones of the past
who are now decease.

Some days of my life
I feel so sad these
are the days of my life
I wished I never had!!!

Esther Celestine

The Sea

When you look at it
you can feel its hunger,
whipping and thrashing its
waves, While, deep down
there's sights to be seen,
colors that are so beautiful
that when you look at
them you feel the sensation
of the sea.

Jaime Crovedi

The Journey

Life deals us all hard blows,
Don't look back,
You can't change the past,
Just pick yourself up,
And start walking again.

She broke your heart,
One way or another,
Though your face is a mask,
The hurt is there in your eyes,
I feel your pain.

Don't let it break you,
Never let it take you down,
I'm here for you,
Lean on me,
Take my hand.

Trust me,
I can save you from your misery,
I'll lend you my strength,
To make it through the long journey,
Back to peace.

Anamarie Cooksey

That Final Moment

Why?
Why did we have to leave?
Did our life priorities take us away.
But still,
why did we leave?
Life is a mystery never to be solved.
We made a bond though . . .
That our love is strong . . .
That final moment
that final look
that final step
took us too far away!

Diane F. Stone

The Gymnast

A great new door was opened,
So she quietly stepped in —
Thinking of big fantasies
'Cause now her home was the gym.

Her body become stronger;
It was soon full of power.
She now wanted to stay thin —
Not much food she'd devour.

At last success was obtained —
To states she'd happily go;
She won a medal there —
The girl's face would surely glow.

The next level was coming,
But at this time she heard it —
Traetta's gym was closing,
So she guessed she had to quit.

Her biggest dream is shattered —
Her gymnastics sadly ends.
She greatly misses it;
A wounded heart she still mends.

Emily Rathod

Sea Storm

The waves crash harder,
 The sky grows darker,
 The wind fights the rain.

Lighting lights up the sky,
 Only to have,
 Thunder darken it.

The wail of people,
 On a sinking ship,
 Fill the night.

The screams grow fainter,
 As the waves grow larger,
 The Mary Elizabeth is gone.

Samantha Applegate

For Bonnie . . .

Sweet and various
 are her charms,
light and winged and vibrant things.

 She stretches, yawns,
and her long hair flows
in waves of feathery dreams . . .

 A bedtime story
 in her eyes,
 her quiet
 shyly
 smiling face.

She's a sleepy Angel . . .
 near enough
 to touch.

Gary Forney

Untitled

A moment in time well spent
With a woman who brings grace and
Beauty to this world
Have we met in a different life
Her eyes her soul never seen before
For she is a mystery to man
But she is also my friend

Kevin C. O'Brien

Untitled

You've been a great friend
Always making me laugh
I've had your shoulder to cry on
When days have gone bad
I've enjoyed working with you
but you're now moving on
I hope that your life
brings you excitement and fun
It's time for good-bye
there's nothing left to say
except that I hope
we meet again someday

Carrie Fox

My Rose

A double Delight Rose
 It is a story of my life and soul
One spring day while admiring a rose
 I uncovered a pure white bud
I took a picture of its beauty
 Not realizing it touched my heart
On the second day
 A pink tint was at its edge
Beauty delight on the third day
 The rose was in half bloom
Why take a picture of that rose
 Each day some would say
The rose matures
 Until it is in full bloom
God will touch our hearts and souls
 We are like that rose
We mush make changes each day
 Until our lives are in full bloom
The double delight rose
 Is a gift to fill our souls

Bill Corneliussen

Oh, To Be A Child Again

I was once a child
 full of trust
 innocent and free

Now my eyes have opened
 I can no longer be

Fair and open minded
 kind and full of grace
 loving, as I used to . . .
 the entire human race

I see it all so different now
 what has made this so?
 This change has been
 long coming

What's done it?
 I don't know
 oh, to be a child again
 eyes closed enough to see

And hope that I might
 capture love, and love . . .
 might capture me.

Delores Deane Harvey

"Confusion"

You is you
Me is me
You is me
Me is you
Who is you
Who is me
Who are we
I don't know
Do you know
Who knows?

Quentin Smith

In the Kingdom of Heaven

In the kingdom of heaven
Is where I will be
Because Jesus Christ
has died for me

Because of my sins
Blood must be shed
But God loved me so much
His only son bled

Jesus was perfect
Not once did he sin
He roamed through the lands
To witness to men

He hung on the cross
So our sins are forgiven
And three days later
He returned to the living

Whenever I need him
I kneel down and pray
And he gives me the strength
I need for the day

Larry R. Bagley

Untitled

Wounded, this favored prey
In silent struggle . . .
To live a lifetime
With these moments that remain
hidden from fear
As panic settles in, so cold
he Whispering frigid sigh of death
honored are my victory's in life
yet honored by me alone
failing the gratitude
of those that once loved
honored by me alone
wholly I am open to lesser reason
with diminutive thought
As your warmth blankets my soul

James Castillo

Poem For You

As I read your letter I feel real good
Asking the Lord if I really could
As I got to the end where you said bye
I felt a tear drop from my eye
For a moment I had peace of mind
In this place that is hard to find
As this poem comes to a close
I can feel my body start to dose
I know you're out there free as a dove
So just give the family all my love.

Michael Russell

"Understanding"

I do not understand
   Why people can be so cruel
   Why cars are so expensive
   Why turtles are so slow
But most of all, I do not understand
   Why nations declare war against
   Each other (as if to say "fighting
   Is the answer")
What I understand most, are keys
   They can open possibilities for you
   They can lock out all your troubles
   And if you are smart enough, they
   Can be the difference between
   Right and wrong decisions

Amber Gorman

Hurt

Hurt is forever.
It can be
concealed,
Never, ever be
Totally healed.
Pain persists . . .
Time diminishes
The hurt, suffering
and Anguish,
But not in
Its Entirety . . .
It only fades.
The wound weeps;
More and longer.
Sometimes it causes one to
Be Stronger,
But . . .
Hurt still Is
Forever.

Nikkole J. Tillman

Seasons

Spring, summer, winter, and fall,
how will I ever get used to them all,

Flowers, sunshine, snow, and color,
are all just words.

How can they describe,
the feeling you get.

On a summers day,
or the first spring shower.

The winters snow,
or the falls leaves.

Such great feelings,
if you take the time to feel.

Sarah Ruth Millman

Long Ago

White moon,
Golden rose,
Silver loom,
Long ago.

Some talk of magic,
Of a horn,
And what happened so tragic,
To the Unicorn,
Long ago.

Amanda Sanchez

The Highway Man

The sweet aroma of naked fear
Beckons the dark angel near
The highway man came riding
Upon his fiery steed he rode
Darkening to smoke
Trapped there in pain
Out of the gateways of hell he came
Over cobblestone streets he clattered
His mission: souls to be gathered
That bright chimeric beast
Upon good willed souls he feasts
Misting the fresh blood
His sword silver-tipped with flame
Cursed is his laughter
When he catches his game
Master to the demons down under
A ghostly galleon of eternal sin
Chances are
You could be riding home with him

Deniz Sand

In Her Eyes

In her eyes as the world crumbles
   down into dust,
She looks back at the past as a tear
   runs down her cheek
Wondering if things could have
   been different
If the past was to change
   could it have been better
While closing her eyes she wonders
   if she fell into a deep sleep
forever would things get better?
What if she was to die forever?
   And if that were to occur
   Would the world stop
Crumbling down in her eyes?
And would it change a thing
   in her eyes?

Danielle Mancone

Beneath The Mask

A cloak is worn
The "real self" to hide,
Concealment essential
In order to abide.

Secrets are covered,
Truth is disguised;
Sins kept out of view
So they're not analyzed.

No one is exempt
Of the whole human race;
Ensuing personality
Then has its place.

A remedy applied
To amend transgressions;
Then character assumes
Brand-new dimensions!

When confession is made
A new being emerges;
The veil is removed
When with God one converges!

Mike Baxter

"Mom And Dad"

To my mom and dad,
more precious than gold.
For you my love
will always hold.
A special place
that's in my heart,
that no one here
can tear apart.
The life you gave me
all my own.
The love you give
that's not a loan.
So at this time
I'd like to say,
I thank God,
he found a way.
With everything
that he has done
for me to be
your chosen one!

Sharon L. Harris-Auciello

Silver Linings

I see a teardrop
   falling
   down.
It hits a mirror.
I see a rainbow,
   through that fear.
Each cloud
   i see the lining
silver.
Look for love
you'll find none here.
Look back,
and see
the shiny tear.
But look to help
   those people dear
And find the love
that once was near.

Kristen Eller

What Do You See?

When you look at a bug,
What do you see?
Do you give it a hug
Or does it bug like a bee?

When you look at the sky,
What do you see?
Does it make you want to fly
Or do you shake at your knees?

When the stars shine bright,
What do you see?
Do you see God's light?
Is it where you'd like to be?

When you look at a flower
What do you see?
Do you see the beautiful April showers
Or do you say, "How ugly!"

We're all here on earth
To admire this beauty.
So when you see them, ask yourself:
"What do I see?"

Sarah Tomsik

Forever With You

For all the months
We were apart
Never once did you
Leave my heart

We shared a special distance
That no one else could see
It was a bond that was there
Meant for only you and me

If now you have a doubt
About how I feel
Then look in my eyes
And know it's for real

A love so pure
Perfect, right, and true
A love I want to spend
Forever with you

Bethany Mize

"Lifing" Roads

Where to love of life
Marked to unforeseen strife?

Aborning, basing, growing:
Which way a new soul's going?

Now seeking, seeing, asking why.
What looks good puts hopes up high
As visions beam at limitless sky.

Playing, drifting, dreaming,
Comparing, worrying, wondering:
Then play or work to make a score
As social tides rate more and more.

Plainer now: Some go it here
And some go it there
Striving for a wanted share.

Ears for peers and eyes for tears
In longing for a sky that clears.

Where dreams survive ambitions rise
And earn success for seeing wise.

D. Gancheff

Growing Old

Mirror, Mirror on the wall
Must you always tell it all?

Can't you lie a little bit and
keep me looking young and fit?

Turn your mirrored eyes down low
Make it shine a soft-dim glow.

Erase these lines — color my hair
Set me in a youthful chair.

Hide the trouble from my years
See? I'm turning into tears.

Maybe others will believe, but
me, you certainly can't deceive. So

Help me accept my years with grace
and keep me always in my place.

Dolores McNulty

"Take my hand, and walk with me . . ."

Take my hand, and walk with me
together we'll get by.
We'll rest a while and dream a dream,
If only we could fly.
I'll take your hand to comfort you
and tell you it's alright.
We'll walk again, this lonely road
into the dark of night.
The dark my try to scare us,
And even my succeed.
But light must follow darkness,
Take my hand and I will Lead.

Dolores "Dole" Baumgartner

Her Eyes Are So Like Mine

I sit in the early twilight,
And, through the gathering shade,
I look on the fields around me,
Where yet a child I wish I played.

I peer into the shadows,
'Til they seem to pass away,
And the fields and tiny brook,
Lie clear in the light of day.

A delicate child so slender,
With locks of light brown hair,
From stone to stone is leaping,
In the breezy summer air.

She stoops to gather blossoms,
Where the running waters shine,
And I look on her with wonder,
Her eyes are so like mine!

Holli M. Marshall

Mist

As I step into the cold,
damp,
mist, of the new day,
I think of my friends,
that died yesterday.
Run through
By sword,
They killed him,
he was my Lord.
Their lives not worth
the cost of an arrow,
they fall to the earth,
crushed was their marrow.

Weeping for them,
women and children.
Cursing that man,
cursing that demon.
"Kill them all!", was his demand.
"Kill them all,
And take, their Ireland".

Marc Molloy

The Moon

It's a quiet light,
Not noisy like the sun.
It is sneaky, and peeks out,
When the day is done.

I know the man in the moon,
And the face that is his.
I'm looking for him now.
Oh! There he is!

Christopher Scott Sled

The Rock

I am a rock, the rock
A piece of solid stone
But not just any ordinary rock,
I am a rock to call your own

A rock that you can sit upon
To gaze across the land
A rock that you can stand on
When trouble is at hand

A rock that you can build upon
To stack your dreams on high
This rock will never crumble
I will stand the test of time

A rock to shield you from your worries
My strength can crush your fears
A rock that you can hide behind
When you have to shed a tear

A rock that can do anything
Not every rock can do
You see this rock is special
Because it belongs to you.

Calvin K. Grogan

Ever Sleep

I am wound in the Ever sleep,
Images cascading of lives
Long past. Some await the birth
Of worlds yet to be: Tomorrow.

I dream within the Ever sleep,
Woven of eternity,
Tendrils of the infinite,
The garment of the soul immoral.

Enshrouded in the Ever sleep,
Splashed with the colours symphonic,
Lit by the timbre of novas,
Caressed by the cold void of space.

I dwell within the Ever sleep,
Deep dreams without awakening,
Past life, pain, pleasure, and death.
Bound round the coils of the cosmos.

Nicholas C. Panzica

Serafina Vienetta Robson, My Kitty

Whenever I was feeling down
You couldn't tell me it's okay
But instead you'd show me
In your special kitty ways.

Your paws and chin were white as snow
Your eyes a brilliant blue
I always knew you loved me
And sweetheart, I loved you too!

Your eyes were sort of crossed
In your head was a slight defect
But Serafina in my eyes
You far surpassed perfect!

As you slipped away from me
The angels sang their song
And you went up to live with God
In Heaven where you belong.

I'll never forget you
Really, how could I ever?
You may have gone and left me here
But you'll be in my heart forever!!

Melynda Robson

Love

Love is like a candle
forever lit and burning
but

There comes a time
when every candle is put out
or let die down
and the love and warmth
it both received and gave off
is no longer felt
It's gone in the cold dark night air
never to be felt again.

But
love is also like a piano
as long as they are
both kept in tune
they will last forever.

Adele Rose Conklin

Monsoon

The summer monsoon came,
With a bellowing sound
like that of a firing canon.
And went like a stroke
Of Zeus thunder bolt.

Leaving behind the droplets of tears;
Cries of hungry children and
An atmosphere of despair.
Fields were no longer there;
Except that of a crystal lake.
Farmers pounding over
The thought of no grains.

Sorojini D. Singh

Good-Byes

Love is dead.
It's all been said.
We said our hello's and good-byes.
Now it is time to let go.

Nothing good lasts forever.
If it did, who would die?
Not love, not us.
No one would have to say good-bye.

The only way to say good-bye,
Is to let someone die.
In our case it is love.
And this is my good-bye.

Jaime Jackson

A Disguise

Just look at my face
and you will see my pain
I may often wear a smile
but, only as a disguise
of the way I truly feel
I may often laugh
when I should be crying
Look deep inside my smile
and you will see the frown within
I dance and carry myself well
but, only to be left alone
I don't want to let anyone
into my realm of pain and agony
Everything is not as it seems
and nothing is how it should be

Jerome B. Underwood

Mother I Am

Oh sleep be swift
as I lay on another tired lonely night.
A mother I am
with dreams as a child am I
The green fields of my memories
sway gently to the breeze called time.
Awake!
Another morrow,
hard concrete fields before me
as the harsh realities of my life.
To teach and to love you
Oh my children
My heart soars as I gaze at you
You are so lovely . . .
My eyes well with tears
must we fight?
Maybe a glimpse God will grant Thee
for a Mother I am . . .
and a beautiful woman too.

Gina Schmidt

Christmas Tithes

Christmas is as Christmas was.
But what is was but what now is?
The glory is all relative,
As well as come-you-elative —
With fatethful heartkening
To transpiritual roots
Through ageless resoundings
Of psychelical joy!

Jane Hindle Bamberg

My Home

Where I rode my brand new bike
And rode the little red trike.
This is home to me.
Where I found my little gray kitty,
Climbed the towering poplar trees.
The place I can always return.
For when painful homesickness burns.
This is home to me.
Snowmen in the dreary winter
And in summer painful splinters.
The swing on the old Olive Russian
Has been cut to almost nothin':
Yet this is my home to me.

Lindsey Tuttle

One Dark And Eerie Night

One dark and eerie night
The moon was round and full.
Witches came out
To make their evil brew.
It bubbled and it burned.
It was so steaming hot.
They took a little bat
And threw him in the pot.
When it was ready,
The witches took the brew
Put it high above the city
And dumped all that boiling stew.
It turned into little flakes,
And fell on all the people.
They looked up in the sky,
And smiled an evil smile.
Turned up the magic.
And danced a long, long while.

Ashley Diane Currie

Promise

A bright future
Shining its light up ahead
Hopes and dreams start to take shape
On the horizon.

A favor told,
young child embraces
Flies away like a bird in flight
When broken.

A pledge of love
To have and to hold
Love that is deep and enduring
Lasting a lifetime.

A belief in the written Word
Spoken many, many years ago.
A covenant, the ultimate sacrifice
Freedom, the price paid.

A promise goes deeper
Than even the heart
'Tho we don't always know
Just how.

Valerie Kinder

Frequency Fliers

We have big eyes
in space, large ears
that roll on tracks —
we scan the future, past
while in-between some sail,
for the facts.

Police cars make their rounds
and guard dogs bark —
women carry heat,
you don't dare park.

They touch down light
and never leave a mark —
access your Future-past,
remove the dark.

Then soar beyond all sensors
in a flash, as lightning
strikes the spot —
returned to Everland
like time were not.

Stephen F. Mason

Beach Dreaming

Far away
Across the ocean
Sunlight dancing upon waves
Caught up in emotion
Suddenly
I am free
My spirit soars through the sky
Waves beneath me
Above the earth
Close to purity
My soul restores itself
Radiates energy
Below in the ocean
A new reflection
Looking at an image
that becomes my connection
There is hope
My dreams are in reach
Given this opportunity
Away from the beach

Karen L. Anderson

'Me'

The weight is heavy
On this soul of mine
My problems are many
They grow like a vine
The tears I cry
No one can see
I keep them down deep
I can't set them free
I put up a front
I have to be tough
But inside I know
It is just a bluff
God how I wish
I could really be me
Then all would know
And they'd agree
The person they knew
Was just a fake
But it's the real person
They'd choose to take.

Fredrick Dyer

Time Has No Measure

For Lovers
Who truly have found
The secret ground
Love's haven
Deep within each other
. . . Time has no measure

It matters not
What age or century found
Nor place that hears their sound
Their minds
Where they find each other
. . . Time has no measure

Is it change
Or awareness aroused?
Each vulnerable, allowed
Friends so true
Life given to the other
When . . . Time has no measure!

William A. Quaglia

One Eye Sees

If one eye sees only good
And the other only bad,
If one sees only happy
And one only sad,
If one eye sees through teardrops
That fall like stormy rain,
Will the one that looks through glory
Blind the one that takes in pain?

Can humanity strengthen one eye
So that visions finally clear,
And if that vision is restored
Will it wash away the tears?
Can I be sure of happiness
If the good outweighs the bad?
Could I ever fulfill the life I saw
In the childhood dreams I had?

The answers to the questions
That run wild through my mind,
Will reach me in this adult world
I've just begun to find.

Carolyn D. Kautz

Eternity

Love only the things eternal,
 'cause they will always last . . .
Unlike the phases of life,
 which soon become the past . . .
Live only for today . . . 'cause
 it'll be gone before you know it.
Go take that chance now,
 otherwise, you'll blow it.
Like the oceans and the clouds above,
 dreams may be ever changing
Believe me those thoughts will last,
 as a part of your past.

Meeta A. Shah

Ford 100 Proof

First gear
Rrrrrrrrrrrrrrrrrrrr
Rrraaaaaaaaaaaaaaaaaaaa
Second gear
Rrrrrrrrrrrrrrrrrrrr
Rrraaaaaaaaaaaaaaaaaaaa
Third gear
Rrrrrrrrrrrrrrrrrrrr
Rrraaaaaaaaaaaaaaaaaaaa
Fourth gear
Rrrrrrrrrrrrrrrrrrrr
Screeeeeeeeeeeeeeeeech
Bud thud
Crunch rrunch
Cam ram
Fire and death
Obviously Henry Ford never intended on
Jack Daniels mixing with his cars

Luke Nemec

A Neruda Poem

Where does a balloon go when it is
released from a child's hand?

What happens to previous years?

How far out does the universe go?

Where does thunder go after it shows
off its big bang?

Where does the wind sleep?

Brian Shadid

Distant Shore

Never to have loved —
Is never to have lived.

One comes to a void —
A cavern of nothingness.

Speak! Speak to me,
And I promise I shall hear.

Oh, how I long to know you,
Hold you,
Touch you.

For too long, I have waited;
But,
Shan't wait anymore.

I am now,
Ready and open,
To meet with you
On that distant shore.

Aida Anderson

Our Love For You

We love you for your loving
works and for your wondrous
ways.

We love you, for a warm love
to us, has always been displayed.

We love you even though we
know, that it's not said
enough.

And to return to you what
You've given us could be
So very tough.

But rest assured and on
Gods word we want to
give homage to you.

So we're gathered here in
Jesus name to give honor
to whom honor is due.

Sabina Washington-Taylor

Green

Green is the grass
of Spring morning
on the vast plains
under the sun.

Green is the music
that is loud every morning
and moving fast by me
without ever stopping.

Green is the power
that controls everything
with a strong feeling
of strength and courage.

Green is the ideas
that make me think fast
with free thinking
of all people.

Lu Y. Xing

From Daybreak

Awakened from daybreak
T'was shiny in true depths,
Of noon 'til dusk glow,
It can lead steps
T'ord hopes of tomorrow.
Of beginnings anew, waver
The discoveries of all things
We might do and savor.
    In times of ado there,
    Recall, venturous souls, the dare.

A lapse of time
Sets lighthearted mirth into
Days of magic sea,
A mystic touch not there now, true,
A pretending we lack of age, a lea
For wandering walks and such
Each daybreak, to forget the last,
Each moment now matters much.
    Filled with awe, will not forsake,
    Time lights up from daybreak.

Carol A. Barnes

A Poem For Poems

It's been weeks
Since I took the time
To write a poem
They've been there
In my head
And my heart
But I wasn't
Honoring them
I wasn't giving them
What they are due —
I wasn't giving myself
What I am due —
The time to put on paper
My thoughts
So that I could know
Their healing and
Recovering power

Lisa M. Holthaus

Life Cycle

Time returns all things
To natural states,
Decomposes,
Life to unseen
Molecules,
Exploding again:
Bombardments
Of love's force
Into suns within
Suns of energy,
Time into time's
Multiplied
By time's space,
Microcosmic
Self elements
Generating
Soul's sole
Equation.

Gary L. Morrison

The School Trap

I wake up
To the repetitive
Droning sound of that damn clock
The shower water
Hits my body with a shock
Nearly all of my life
I have completed this ritual
Almost every weekday
All these years of schooling
Are to my dismay.
I find myself
Pulling stunts
Just to get out of class
To tip back a glass
After a toast with my friends
"To us seniors,
And the day school ends!'

James Femenia

My Friend's Boat

Day, the morning sun
The ocean, wood become one
It is high tide
Scary, windows look like eyes
A nose could be a mouth
My friends boat waiting to show off

Barbara Williams

Luvy La Vida

Some say the eyes,
    Hold the key to the heart.
Both are as pure,
    Yet so far apart.
Yours were the path,
    that opened the door,
Once I but looked,
    and now I wish more.
I speak of the peace
    That you bring to my soul;
Where just a glance
    Fills a long empty hole.
Free to use nor free to misuse,
But to give and to love
    One so gentle a dove
    As you . . .

Howard Liu

"Elm Street Memories"

Looking back through my life.
And all my 40 years.
There's been a lot of happy times.
There's been a lot of tears.
Reflections of my younger days.
Of lightning bugs and summer haze.
Of climbing trees and skinned up knees.
Is how life use to be.
The times of youth come rushing back.
With Elm Street Memories.
Take time to smell the roses.
Take time to show you care.
Take time with your children.
To let them know you're there,
Take time to look life over.
And eventually you'll see.
You'll create your own.
Elm Street Memories.

Daniel Greene

Self

What hidden secrets wrapped inside;
Would we but understand.
What smoldering fire of truth usurped,
What hidden contraband.

Our outer shell, it hardens fast,
In mold of proper man.
Our inner depths remain unpurged,
Held tight by mind's cold hand.

Marlene J. Knapp

Pale Horse

Death ride's a pale horse
But you know that of course
When he come's for you soul
Will you have the toll
Are you going to heaven or hell
Who can ever tell
As death greet's you with a grin
Do you remember when you sinned
Now that your time is spent
There is no time to repent
Time to stand your judgement day
What are you going to say
When you get passed on by
You will sit and wonder why

Randall K. Newton

Untitled

My window frames a picture,
A bounty to behold
Of grass so green, the clouds so white
And leaves a sun-toned gold.

A lovely liquid picture,
Brandy seen through crystal,
It catches light and shimmers bright
With beauty universal.

I think the picture's perfect,
And then it proves me wrong.
A warbler comes with throaty hum
And fills the scene with song.

The "dee dee" of chickadees,
The vibrant daffodils,
And far away across the bay
The dark outline of hills.

I keep my picture all year round.
It never needs exchanging.
As summer comes and winter goes
The scenery's ever changing.

Carol Richardson

In The Times Of Need

Through God's holy grace
The crisis that we face
Helps us to embrace God's Love

The spirit that He gave
To help us behave is
The one we call from above

When we need strength
He makes us strong
He meets us all the way

He said in His word if
We ask we will be heard and
All things will be given unto us

Thank you Father God
For being there
Whenever I needed You.

Judith Dennis

Ode To Pretty Boy

Pretty boy, pretty boy,
You stole my heart.
My black and white joy,
I didn't want to part.

When I first saw you,
You were in a cage.
You looked at the world,
But you were in a rage.

I held you to my heart,
You didn't move.
I knew you were the best,
You had something to prove.

You met me at the door,
Each and every day.
That won't happen anymore,
You had to go away.

You're no longer with me,
My black and white joy.
God set you free,
Goodbye, my pretty boy.

Elizabeth Camplan

Two Glasses . . .

Two glasses of wine.
They've been around
For a time,
Like you and me . . .

Dark purple juice
That has hoarded the sun
To jealously make a truce
With Mother Earth . . .

Never to surrender
For a lesser ransom,
Its hard-won essence;
To a couple less handsome

Than you and I.

V. Brede Westby

Pastel

Delicate hues remind me of you.
Mixed in fragrant scents
Red roses bloom.
Pale colors blend and send —
Precious memories.
Red roses remind me of you.
Sun kissed, breeze cooled, rain
    bathed
Rows of all hues
Red roses remind me of you.
Flower faces of love.
Remind me of you.

Estelle R. Leberman

Those Were The Days

Remember when we were all small
    We always went out to play
The little red wagon
    We pulled in the yard
The first day of school
    Oh boy was that hard
The marbles that always
    Seemed to roll away
And the little thing's
    That kid's used to say
The sun would be falling
    And mom would be calling
Time to come in
    Let's call it a day
Tomorrow will come
    And then you can play

Theresa DiMarco Herd

Two

I've gone from two
To twenty
In two short days
I know too many facts
And too many ways
I wish I knew
Where to begin
Like two separate personalities
Like two different men
There must be two lives
To be lived through then
The first has already happened
The second hasn't begun

Blane Rogers

19

19 not yet a man
19 he heard the cry of his land
19 he accepted the task
19 he did what was asked
19 he joined the core
19 he went to war
19 in a foreign land
19 with rifle in hand
19 he spilled his blood on foreign sand
19 never a man

Frank Massey

A Night On The Town

Fish, fishes, fishy, fishing.
Wish, wishes, wishy, wishing.
Turn the spindle. Roll the thread.
Weave a crown from flowers dead.

Fly, flies, flying, flight.
Why, wire, sighing, sight.
Twist them tightly. Break them not.
Deftly, so you don't get caught!

Dark, darkness, darker, darken.
Stark, starkness, stalker, stalking.
Clear the table. Snuff the lamp.
Cross the alley, cold and damp.

Knock, knocker, knuckle, knocking.
Shock, shocker, chuckle, choking.
Lift the crown. Rest on brow.
All is done — at least for now!

Mark Haapala

Memories

Who gave us this?
Where did that come from?
What trip were we on when we bought it?
What does this remind you of?
Was it a song?
Was it a poem?
Was it a story?
Was it a color?
Was it a flower?
Was it a time, place, hour?
When did you say "Goodbye"?
You left me with memories
Memories that cannot die
They are all around me
I cannot say where, or why

Ethel Nepstad

Age

In search for a meaning,
I did a lot of screening.
Sixteen is forever sweet;
Twenty-one you can't defeat.
Thirty is one third there.
Forty you'd better beware.
When you reach fifty-two,
You know life's gifts to you.
Beyond sixty your clarity
Is replaced with sincerity.
If your hair is gray and thin
Your heart grows and glows within.
If you dance and sing to infinity
And know there is eternity
You come to realize
Age doesn't materialize.

Barbara J. Carman

Young Black Male

Young black male growing
up in a city so full of crime.

Young black male with not
enough time.

My education comes first in a
World so full of hate.
Drugs, guns, killings and abusing
your mate.

Pride, goals, success and leadership
is my fame. The crime who is
to blame?

Young black male, I'm going
strong. Education is the key
to what I want to be.

A doctor, a lawyer, engineer
or chief of police.

Young black male my time
is near.

Young black male, I have nothing
to fear.

Trevell Willis

Ponder

In my room I sit and ponder,
Looking outside I start to wonder
About a rainbow in the sky . . .
And the smell of Jasmine lifts me high!

To see the children play outside,
It makes me want to cry.

Ponder . . .

I shall ponder some more
To think about my life no more.
In this room I sit today
And watch the children start to play.

Stephanie Harr

Enchantment

Purple mountains, painted sand,
Life flows thinly thru the land.

Patch of blue viewed thru the white,
Skeletal framing of the sight.

Red Hawk flowing in the sky,
Cactus flower raises eye.

Lizard run goes to the edge,
Dropping down onto the ledge.

Coiled, resting, diamondback,
Field mouse stops dead in its track.

Field of flowers, morning light,
by noon a wilted, weary sight.

Fine ground sands ride the wind,
Sculpting that which will not bend.

Thunderous clouds, the Western sky,
Torrential rains already dry.

Enchanting evening, blood red sky,
At last the heat begins to die.

Purple mountains, painted sand,
Life flows thinly thru the land.

Joseph P. Blecha

For You, My Love

When first we met
  you did not know my name.
You did not know
  that you had just sparked a flame.

It was then that I called you
  full of hope and of fear,
I began to talk and you listened,
  but you did not hear.

You do not understand,
  when will you learn
Of this love deep inside me
  that continues to burn?

Oh love of my life
  if you only knew,
Of my deep inner feelings,
  that I am helpless without you!

Edward P. Liva

Winds

A wind is a blend
of sins and friends
it can blow your way
or forget you that day
It can cause you pain
but never any shame
If you understand its right
you're assured its gift
If you misunderstanding its song
surely trouble will come along
So be not lead astray
by the winds that blow your way today

Dennis Williams

Drug Free

Drug free is the way to be
In this day and time
It brings on a life of crime

One robs and steals and even kills
Parents shed so many tears
But it never erases the fears

It causes lives to abrupt
while causing families to disrupt
Try it and you'll see
Drug free is the way to be.

Jennifer Glover

Life

Loving, understanding, caring,
Kindness, friendship, sharing,
How could life be more daring?
Dreaming, scheming, talking,
Living, breathing, walking,
Life is forever shocking.
Grief, disappointment, fears,
Moaning, misfortune, tears,
Death clutches too many years.
Confusion, silence, sighing,
Solitude, loneliness, crying,
Living, loving, dying.

Kimberly Bumgardner

Rain Dance

There is romance
  in a rainfall.
Water droplets big and small,
  plunging
from the sky
  to quench the earth.
Tears from heaven
  sparkle
against the darkness
  of the night.
Still reflections in a puddle
  from the pale moonlight.
The
  pitter
  patter
against the frosty window pane.
  Soothing.
  Free.
Dampen the flesh and
refresh the soul.

Janice De Martini

The Magical Land

Let me tell you a story
Of a magical land,
Where everyone was made with strokes
Of a single hand.

There the king's palace
Is so big and tall,
So big, it echoes,
When people call.

Why is this, you say,
This celebration is for the king,
For on this day is his birthday,
And everyone will sing.

The ruler of the magical land
Ruled all the ocean and the sand.
In the city of the pretty lights,
Everyone celebrated in the night,
For he is the king of the land.

Marcus Kulynyis

Dad

Today my world came crashing down,
And my heart was torn in two.
God just took my Dad away,
And there's nothing I could do.

Every minute I talk to God,
I keep asking him why?
Why did he need him now?
Why did my Dad have to die?

I'm surrounded by family and friends,
But still I feel so alone.
I'm sitting in the house I grew up in,
But it no longer feels like home.

I want to kick, scream, and yell,
But for my family I must be strong.
I need to find some strength,
And help them move along.

The time has come to say good-bye,
For his time on earth is through.
God has taken my Dad away,
And there's nothing I could do.

Todd E. Studebaker

The Extinct

The darkened sky in hollowed rage
The extinct bird inside its cage
They'd fly together
If they could
But mankind needed all her wood
The sky quivered at her loss
The people blamed it on the frost
The animals cried
And children screamed
For the bird they knew
Was now a dream.

April Volak

Grandmother

You opened your hands
And many gifts were given
You helped us understand
This life that were living.

You opened your arms
To draw us in
With all of your charms
We knew you would win.

You opened your heart
And let your love pour through
We blossomed under your care
Like a rose in the morning dew.

You gave us your love
A gift that can never be replaced
And you wrapped it up
With all of your grace.

Dorothy Ross

Canyon

At the bottom of a canyon
runs a river
swift and deep.

Cutting through the
wet stone walls
the water never sleeps

As it cuts its pathways
running ancient
through the years,

Flowing with the
wetness of the
ancestors tears.

Kathryn Olson

Untitled

I hear them beckoning
from their hollow graves
a dying melody
the pianist, she plays.
Gaily the old timers
gather round
for whom does now
the bell tower sound?
Their dreams are gone
their time has passed
the world they knew
is changing fast.
Still there is no time
for sleep
my duty is their souls
to keep.

Wendy Keagy

Steps Of Scarborough

Oh wait for me, Oh love of mine
And I will bring thee arms of thyme.
Oh wait for me by stream below
And through my wild herbs, I will go —
To meet you, there, by water's edge
And to you, my heart, I will pledge.
Oh love of mine, please do wait —
By water's edge — by garden's gate.

Marie Elena Stotler

November

November jumps in
with its thin layer of frost.
It drags in its frozen
blanket,
and hauls it around
then slowly creeps away
leaving
only its white blanket.

Scott Biltoft

Untitled

It is no shame to have
a dirty face.
The shame comes when you
keep it dirty.

The shame comes when you
won't even try to clean it.

The shame comes when
you don't even care that
your face is dirty.

The shame comes when you
keep looking for more
dirt to put on your face.

The shame comes when you
keep your face in mud.

I pray to God that I won't
let my face get too dirty
to were it can't be cleaned.

Traci Jones Moges

"Dear God"

"Dear God I'm really scared,
What really will I do alone?
I really love to be here, but
It's not my forever home.
Sometimes I really wonder,
What's beyond the clouds.
When It's my turn to be there,
Will you really see me proud?
I think of many days, when I
Turned and walked away.
Never asked your guidance,
And never thought to pray.
I'm sorry dear Lord, for so
much wasted time.
Doing my own thing, thinking
The day was mine.
I'm so sorry for my sins dear Lord,
So many days gone forever.
The only way I can repay you,
Is live that way again never.

Elaine Johnson

My Toy

She's always there for me
And makes me feel wanted
She listens to me
And keeps me happy

When everyone's against me
I know to whom I should go
She believes in me
And I know she won't leave me alone

Every night she's by my side
Protecting me from the evil around
Her soft fur keeps me warm
As she stands guard with a frown

She stays on my bed
Like the rest of my toys
Waiting for me to pat her head
When I arrive she brings me joy

Marely Hernandez

Sunday Afternoon

Left ventricle closing
and sight unabashed
freeway sunspots
on a distant star
outside your door
consciousness unfolding
in brilliance of color
the mailman grinning
recoiled decadence
children
of reptilian descent
in faded photographs
laughing
at the party
without invitation
and the man wants to know
why you're on the roof
screaming

Batchelder

Mother

The moment I was born
I took a peek
I felt the warmth
Of a woman's cheek
I thought to myself
Who can this be
I was a newborn
I could barely see
I felt the love
Of her tender care
I couldn't talk
I just could stare
It didn't take long
For me to find out
I knew it was mother
Without a doubt

Pat Douglas

"Hope In The Darkness"

To all who have suffered beyond the
realm of some's understanding.
May God be with you and warm you
with his love, during your darkest days.
May he walk with you into your new life.
Where there is no such thing as pain.

Rita Whalen

Probably Not

Some phrases, we dream up,
We think fit for a king.
If Shakespeare had said it,
'Twould be a great "thing".
Though the thought may have touched him
(We must give him the credit)
I wonder if Shakespeare
Would ever have said it.

Richard M. Shaffer

Natural Light Of Dawn

An essence of enhancement
Every dream highlighted
Bright by dark wind
Seeking aroma by sparks
Shifting wonderful nations
Unifying each blade at birth
Predestining victory before sight
Futures beautiful by decree
Balance within circles
Reverence of obedience five-fold
Freeing each inhibited order
Open to the word for guidance
HE provides all heart desire
With glory, honor and peace
Crystallizing each breath to breath
We glorify our source

Dyanne Mitchell Williams

I Walk A Primrose Path

I walk a primrose path
. . . and laugh . . .
I'm remembering you.

I walk a forest lane . . . again . . .
I'm remembering you.

I stop beside a little stream
. . . and dream . . .
I'm remembering you.

I see a bird on high
. . . and sigh . . .
I'm remembering you.

I climb a rugged hill
. . . and still . . .
I'm remembering you.

I see a star on high
. . . and cry . . .
I'm remembering you.

I see a little fawn
and then it's gone . . .
I'm remembering you.

Ruth M. Day

Where To Go

When in the midst of trouble
and you feel deep down despair
If you look into your
innermost heart.
You'll find a light house
which was already there.
As you reach out in harmony,
in the stillness of the night
Gods merciful hand stays
extended
To gently steer you into
His Great Light.

Brantly Marie Baker-Boggs

"I Miss You"

Fog and mist drift through the town
As the wind begins to hiss
I miss you tonight my dear sweet love
And I'm longing for your kiss

Your touch so soft and tender
Like the memories of your lips
I long to have you close to me
Now all I do is wish

Wish to have you in my arms
Instead of ripped away
Your body is buried so very deep
On this cold and misty day

Now I stand above you
Looking down upon your grave
Your dark and dreary tombstone
Illuminates my day

Hilary R. Cartie III

The Tree

Atop this lonely hill I stand
And watch the world below
The people scurry here and there
The seasons come and go
If only they could feel the peace
That standing still could make
To see that life's not just a race
But sometimes give and take
Sometimes a traveler rests his soul
Upon my soft green sod
Cause here upon my lonely hill
I'm very close to God

Rosie C. Foster

"Wisdom Or Just A Guess"

What pray tell
the mind of a man,
who speaks very little
yet fully understands.

What of the man
sitting quietly alone,
never does he interrupt
not even in his home.

The answer he will give,
if ever you inquire,
will be direct and to the point
not take the day entire.

For every question asked
an answer may be found,
if you would inquire of one
who has quietly been around.

The loud and boisterous person
will not have an answer true.
To me they never listen
so, how can they answer you.

Michael K. Roper

Now

Don't long for "The good old days"
Nor fret about tomorrow,
Today, right now, is all we have
Fill it with Joy, not sorrow!

Elizabeth Collins

Yesterday

Yesterday seems so long ago,
it's left me like the winter snow,
it melt's away not long to stay.
Oh yesterday where did you go?
I saw the rose bloom on the vine.
Then turned around and it was
dying. Oh! Yesterday why are
you crying, tis strait ahead that
I am flying.
I'll melt a way just like
the snow, and hear you say,
oh yesterday where did you go?

Maiden Narue

The Father I've Always Wished For

The father I've always wished for
Is a father that will always be there,
The father I've always wished for
Is a father that will always care,
The father I've always wished for
Will never strike me down,
The father I've always wished for
Will always be a clown,
The father I've always wished for
I need not to look no more,
The father I've always wished for
Always comes home through the door.

Brianna Burke

Roni

Pretty face
Open window.
Flash of lightening
Crack of thunder.
Drop of a pin
bloody floor.
Creaking door.
Howl of a dog
shadow in the fog.

Robert R. Lagunas

Oh Kindred Soul

We speak on the phone,
so I know you're really there.

But, we never seem to make it,
For that first glorious stare.

I miss seeing your face,
And all that I envision it to be.

So sad to have to endure
Another of life's frustrations.

But, trudge along we must.
For now, we have no choice.

So no more tears, my friend,
For I know in my heart,

That someday soon the
Memories will become reality.

And you'll be here.
Or I'll be there.

And I'll hold your face
Between my hands.

And capture more visions
For the future to bear.

Janet M. Sloan

"Wishing"

A Memorial To My Mother
Wishing I Could Have You Here
Still Lovingly Stroking Your Hair

Wishing I Could Hold You Tight
Far Away From The Lonely Night

Wishing I Could Love You
And Feel Your Love For Me

Wishing I Could Hear You Say
Your Love Will Always Be

Wishing You Could See My Heart
The Way It Looks At You

Wishing We Could Still Do
The Things We Used To Do

Wishing I Had Told You
How Much You Mean To Me

Wishing This Was Just A Dream
And I Could Have You Here
The Way It Used To Be.

Till We Meet Again
Donna Marie Howard

Lonely Is The Poet

Lonely is the poet
in a state of quietude
Pondering thoughts unspoken
still confined in solitude.

Perhaps about a girl
recalled from yesteryear
Gone but not forgotten
once held most dear.

Or of an incident
etched in his mind
Rekindled once again
after interlude of time.

A poet often inspired
by a momentary episode
Suddenly a gold mine
a poet's Mother-lode.

Lonely is the poet
when inspiration deferred
Ballads and sonnets, sadly,
postponed to be heard.
William Henry Jones

Yourself

Be yourself,
don't ever change
Even if the future comes quickly
and things rearrange
Know yourself,
and I what you believe
even if people laugh
because they cannot conceive
Free yourself,
and your mind
for you never know what's out there
that you may find
And most of all,
Love yourself,
For you are one of a kind
and there is no other like you
anyone could ever find.
Samantha Ash

Untitled

It's orange
It's yellow
It's green
And it's white.

It's pretty
It's calming
It's heat
And it's light.

It's romantic
It's passion
It's love
And it's desire.

It's powerful
It's my strength
It's south
And it's the element fire.
Theresa Creekmore

In The Night

No where to run
No where to hide
No one can help her
She just cries and cries
He's doing it again
No one understands
She closes her eyes
No one knows
Of the pain she carries
Of the pain inside
He's doing it again
Stop! Stop!
She just cries and cries.
Susan Keddie

Expectations

Set upon a pedestal
One seems so grand
So far above the rest
There he alone will stand

Wishing to attain
The butterfly on his throne
Through out the climb
Anticipation's grown

All that time and effort
You finally reached the sky
Now you're actually there
You see it's not so high
Tabitha Cope

Three Things

There are three things
I would like to do before I die.
Beg, steal, and lie.

When I beg, I want to beg God
to depart me of my sins,

When I steal, I want to steal
a way to Jesus,

And when I lie, I want to
lie in the arms of my savior.

So, what about you?
Lillian Combes

A Promise Of Peace

It's quiet, no sound,
the world is so still,
alone with my thoughts,
I remember again,
a promise you gave me,
when I was so young,
"My Peace" do I give you,
don't ever despair . . .

I'll love you. I'll keep you . . .
till I bring you Home! . . .
Mary Dilemme

The Visit

I visit her often in my dreams,
she is cold,
yet comforting and giving.

I stand and watch her,
she boldly approaches,
her icy grip I cannot resist.

I am entangled by her body,
she rolls around me and pulls me down,
yet I am happy within her.

I lay back as she takes me,
enfolded in her rocking embrace,
she soothes me.

I feel her letting go,
slowly she pulls away,
leaving me comforted.

I walk her silken shore,
collecting that which she has left,
and wait for her to call again.
Pamela Grinley

At 70

A young moth consumes
Then grows hard for a long time
Her freedom comes last
S. Lawson Searle

"This Pain I Feel"

This pain I feel you cannot see.
It's hidden deep inside of me.

To ease this pain I work all day.
You never see me run and play.

Silently, I cry at night.
Daytime comes, I act alright.

I search a friend to understand
this pain I feel and lend a hand.

The smile I wear hides all the pain,
afraid to find that I'm too blame.

A joke or two may seem so real,
but can't compare with how I feel.

To know this of my breaking heart,
it is a heart that's torn apart.

Wants to talk but fears to speak,
the mind goes numb, the body weak.

So help me ease this pain within,
so I can live my life again.

This poem is true though no one knows
this pain I feel deep in my soul.
Angela L. Walden

To My Dad — From Your Baby . . .

I'll never forget how it used to be,
your smile and tender eyes . . . I
loved you so much when life was
happy. But I love you even more
today! If only I could ease your
fears; If only I could dry your tears
I'm so afraid to face the pain;
To let you go or watch you suffer
and when you say "You're gonna miss
me" (You know I'll miss you more!)
But please believe me; I'll be okay
I'll always love you in my heart and
be near you in my dreams . . .
So lets not say "Good bye" just
say "See you later"
And we'll hug or special hug, as
I kiss your tender cheek . . .
Knowing how much you loved me
and I you, always and forever . . .

Mary L. Lillard

Cinquain

"In a
Quiet place where
Love reigns — in the secret
Chambers of my heart — I wait
For you."

Unis Monsour

Commitment

My mind says, "I will do it".
Yet, then it is not done.
You mean to follow up
But, pleasure is more fun.

Pledge and do it.
Act out what you say.
Don't hope for others
To show an easier way.

For a determined will is steadfast;
The commitment is real.
It stays when problems come
Seeking no better deal.

First, talk with God;
Then, follow through.
Now, get involved . . .
You will learn too.

When the heart says,
"I will do the act . . ."
Say nothing else;
Commitment makes a fact.

Clara Hill

"Ocean"

Ripples in the waves,
Underwater caves.
Hidden by the foam,
Whales and dolphins roam.
Blue, pink, red, and yellow fish,
Searching for their dinner dish.
Seagulls swarm around the minnows,
Lady fish soon to be poor widows.
Clouds are turning black and grey,
As the sea otters make their way,
Into protection, one fine day.

Lizzie Mollenkopf

Leaves Rustles

It's about being small —
And you stand with your
Eyes wide open and your
Head thrown back.

Your life-sounds go unheard
In the din that comes from
Nowhere —
Everywhere.

Ageless and timeless,
They know you are fleeting.
And so nothing changes.
As they cover our footprints,
The leaves rustle.

Ellyn Kearney

Let Me Kiss Sappho

I am alone with seizure
wearing me like thin armor,
night tongue bends my heart.

Olympus, please crumble
into my shoe box,
morning skin soothes blue blood.

I will bathe in her lyrics,
dance upon Arcadia,
and plant a lesbian
in orchestrated garden.

If all not possible
seal a tigress
and play a schizophrenic harp,

I will kiss dead.

Mark Lazarus Gatti

Golden Dragons

Golden Dragons, enslave
my wildest of dreams . . .
    As I circle beneath my covers
my thought relate on other places . . .
    As I dream you are my lover.

To speak to you softly would end my
    screaming.
    As to awake with you would
    end my
    dreaming

W. F. Juan

Mr. T, Last Of The 85's

As life goes on
And knowledge grows
A man is only
What he knows

Time and space
Never cease
Life is only
Space for lease

So take of life
What it will give
For, that's the only
Way to live

Lessons to learn
Knowledge to share
So feed on growth
And show you care!

Wesley Hicks

Salvation

Open your eyes and look to the sky
The heaven's don't listen to your who,
what and why
See where the angels tread in
the sky above
Soar through clouds as white
as doves
Gaze through the infinities of
blue upon blue
All the while they beckon and
call you
The angels playing words into some
celestial rhyme
Look up and find your salvation
one breath at a time.

Carmela Perconti

A Fantasy

I'm not afraid of clouds of rain,
I will tell you why,
The Lord above sent the rain,
To wash the Windows of the sky.

The dust and smog we make down her,
Rises up into the sky,
The rain washes the windows clear,
So He can see us as He passes by.

Soon the sky will clear again,
Soon the storm will pass on by,
And you can see forever my friend,
Through the windows of the sky.

When the clouds have rolled away,
And the sun is shining through,
You will have a bright new day,
And God may smile on you.

Charlotte Higgins

Light Of Night

The light of night,
    is dark all around.
Deep in the depths of one's soul.
You are lost in this black of night.

You were once on the road of light,
    full of spirit and feeling free,
    full of life, love and joy!

Now you walk in the shadows,
    scared and full of fear.
You find yourself crying,
    in a dark corner.

Wondering where you lost the light.
All alone now in the light of night,
drifting . . . Drifting . . . Gone . . .

Maria Tejeda

Bear Love

My love is like this bear
it is soft, warm, and furry
it is pure as this bear is white
it is there to tell your problems,
stories, or secrets
it is also there if you need a hug,
a friend, or just company
but one thing that my love
does that this bear does not do
is that it continue to grow larger as
each day ends.

Erik Michaelsen

While Sunset Glows

While sunset glows deep in the west,
Memories close about are pressed.

Of day when just a little child,
I lived and played so meek and mild.

Wandering deep into the wood,
Dreaming only dreams of good.

I never dreamed of future then,
Only of the present when,
I was a little child.

But now all childish dreams are past,
Leaving little hope at last.

Only dreams from day to day
Only night to kneel and pray.

Oh give me back those days again.
Deliver me from all this pain.

And leave no dreams of future then,
Only take me back to when,
I was a little child.

Lucille Martinelli

Blood Pain

Slowly the forces gather,
Gather to attack,
Forces of sadness,
Framed in pain so black.

At once they strike,
Striking on one's inside,
They bring sick torments,
Without any pride.

Quickly they spread,
Spreading pain in the blood,
They show no mercy,
Drenched in a flood.

Suddenly these powers leave,
Leaving not any relief,
They buried themselves in one,
These powers of grief.

Janet J. Krings

A Snowy Winter

The trees are like
frosted cakes.
All covered up
with cold snowflakes.

Ice covered tires
crunch on the street.
Car windows
are white with sleet.

And everywhere the people go
with faces tickled
by the snow.

Amanda Cox

Beaches

I love the beach.
   The cool breeze, the fresh air,
the seagulls crying out,
   shells lying on the golden sand,
and people all around.

Kimberly Jenkins

Dunblane

Sixteen children, angelic and small,
wiped out in an instant,
in a gymnasium hall.
Twelve more were wounded,
by a madman's rage,
no one could have known,
he'd go on a rampage.
When the carnage was over,
with no where to run,
he killed himself,
with the very same gun.
With bleeding hearts,
these poor parents grieve,
their children are gone,
it's so hard to believe.
Life will go on,
but it won't be the same,
for the sorrow runs deep,
on the streets of Dunblane.

Karyn Buckthorpe

War Machines

War Machines are crawling in
a distant foreign land and air
machines fly screaming over hostile
foreign skies. Sirens scream
of warnings of death from poison
gas. As nation against nation
send their sons and daughters
towards harms way with a
message of death and hatred
towards man kind. At home
alone sits a mom with her
silent cry's and prayers. For
the one they love and raised
to come home to open arm's
and answered prayers.

Albert Aleman

Departed Love

What a lover you were,
What a lover you'll be,
Such a rugged guy,
The most important part of me.

You taught me to love
And showed me the sun,
You gave me hope
When I thought there was none.

As we grow older
And go our own way,
I'll always remember
They were my best days.

Remember me dear,
Once in awhile,
For I'll never forget you
And your wonderful smile.

Forever I'll love you
Forever it seems
Because you were my love
You were my dream.

Cheryl Clarke

Papa

   Some people love singing and
some love dancing but I love
being with you. When days are
gloomy and sad you're always here
to make me glad. That's why I
love being with you. You're the hope
in my life and the Sun that always
shines through good times and bad
you always seem to stay glad.
You share your love with everyone
and time to time you do get
Mad. You're the path that shows
the way the neatness in my day.

Nichole Benton

Black and cold
Shivery darkness
Bleak impressions
Imprisoned by time
In a cage
With no boundaries.
Sparkling spheres
Against the black
Shivery darkness
Twinkling spheres
In a cage
With no boundaries.
Fiery, colossal
Planets of gods
Rule the black
Rule the spheres
In a cage
Know no boundaries
Only the black
Shivery darkness.

G. Quinn

The Dance

The kindness in your single glance
tells me of your playful dance;
of skipping through this dreadful place
full of laughter, full of grace.
No one needs to teach or tell,
keep you timed, or toll a bell.
For life is yours and be it so;
you'll live it well 'til time to go.
But please before I meet my fate,
Before my time it gets too late,
I wish to dance a time or two
Across the lovely floor with you.

Alice Frey Winchester

Untitled

When you're sick
I feel sick with you,
when you're depressed
I feel depressed with you,
it's hard for me
to see you this way,
you are more beautiful
when you smile,
when you're in pain
I feel you're pain,
we are one
and stay as one
as long as there is a
heaven and earth.

Andrew Slegel

Granite Orchard

Granite orchard
Stands shrouded
In ghostly snow.
Its stones,
Lonely sentinels,
Amid plots of white,
Unmarked by
Boot prints
Since latest storm.
Faded ribbons
Bravely cling
To rusting wreaths,
While hoary icicles
Sob gently.
There's nothing
More lonely
Than a cemetery
In mid-winter.

Audrey D. Houghton

Ocean Of Emotions

(Dedicated To Alex Murray)
We are in an ocean of emotions
it doesn't matter what you say
the emotions are always changing
even till this very day
it doesn't matter how you act
your emotions are never real
the ocean is always turning
it doesn't matter how you feel
you try to stay in one place
but the tides are way too strong
even till this very day
the tides push you along

Jason Matthew Combs

Dead Sex

My frigidity preserves my virginity
Which causes a calamity
Some say it's due to lethargy
But it's actually my sexual fixity
No amount of litany
Will stop my pseudo-sanctity
Only those subject to mortality
Bring out my fallibility
I have a hunger for nudity
And sexuality
Which I love to pursue nimbly

Sara Luther

Life As It Seems

The beauty of a thought
Is something to be taught
For thoughts are only windows
Of our soul related dreams
We strive for wealth, for health and love
But only see it as we sow
It's not the way we win or lose
But how we play the game we choose
So looking back through years gone by
How very lucky we say with a sigh
No matter how the chips may fall
Our God is the reason for it all.

Eleanor M. Culliman

Spring

I thought that I would never sing,
A song as lovely as spring.
Spring that melts the winter snow,
A song that makes the flowers grow.

Spring that calls the swallows back
To nest on trees and let them rest.
A song that brings showers in May,
And cultivates the land with rain.

Spring that drops the morning dew
Upon the pretty leaves that glow.
A song that makes the tree buds sprout,
Swaying on branches sweetly smart.

Spring that makes the flowers bloom
Upon the field once was in gloom.
Songs are sung with foolish fling,
But only God creates spring.

Lucil Evangelista

Breath Of Life

I bless the lord with all
     My heart and soul today.
Remembering that he gave me
     The breath of life,

I take his hand as he leads me
     To help others find the way
To join him here on earth
     In God's great family.

Won't you open your heart
     And soul to him today,
Let him take and forgive all
     Your sins without delay.

Your soul will find eternal peace
     And sweet serenity
As you surrender to him taking
     Your place in God's family.

Alice Halt

Books

Books — are friends
     through which another's voice
     can comfort, teach
     or fill a lonely night.

Books — are someone to come home to
     when you need to listen
     but there's not another voice
     that wants to share.

Books — are contacts
     with the experts and the clowns
     with the laughter deep inside
     needing but a channel to begin.

Books — have saved my sanity at times
     and fueled my fantasies
     and filled my loneliness
one
chapter
at
a
time.

Mary Hinfey

The Mountain

Today I fell backwards a bit,
on this Mountain that I climb.
I did not try too hard today,
I had the toughest time.
I tried to laugh, but tears came down,
the Mountain was too steep.
So I walked the flattest part,
I did not dare to creep.
Finally, I stood back and looked,
the top was still in sight.
So I took one deep breath,
and tried with all my might.
To climb the Mountain once again,
I did not want to quit.
Because, if I set an even place,
each day I'd gain a bit.
And soon, one day, when I
least expect I will reach the top.
All it takes is perseverance,
even though sometimes, I'll stop.

Vicki M. Lee

The Verdict

     Exploded,
Breaking a stalemate
It fluttered across country
     and beyond
Was hugged, and hailed
     like foot falls of Summer sun
     a bouncing babe
     a windfall.

It thudded
Like wet drum
     a still born
     spill-over of pain
     a dream curtailed
Here at last —
     Spelled freedom
     No, spurned liberty
Were echoes from ends of lever
Innocence and guilt
     starkly sculpted, but —
He who fell appreciates it all.

Paul Owusu-Aduening

A Special Friend

Did you ever meet Lula Peavy?
She was a friend of mine
To talk to her was real easy
A nicer person you couldn't find

She lived life with a zest
Laced with a humorous wit
You could tease her at your best
It wouldn't rattle her a bit

She had a wisdom that was basic
To some, considered quite bold
Cause when you really examined it
It would touch your very soul

Her face wore the dignity of age
Of a journey well trod
When her life reached the final page
She maintained her trust in God

Although we are now apart
And her presence has reached its end
She will always live within my heart
For she was my Special Friend!

Norm Campbell

Tender Memories

A lifetime of memories,
Some joyous, some sad.
Which to remember:
the good or the bad.

The joyous ones
I remember best
for they're the ones
that warm my breast

The gentle touch
of her finger tips,
The warm caress
of her tender lips.

These memories
that fill my heart,
Say to me
we will never part.

With face so fair
and lips so sweet,
I'm hoping in heaven,
we again will meet.

Seymour Videlock

Untitled

Last night I woke
   from a dream
A dream of holding you
   once again
Only to wake and realize
   I'm all alone
But not in my mind

Because I still have the memories
   of holding you
But in reality
   I knew
I was once again
   Alone

David Parson

"The Absent Father"

There are men from far and wide.
They procreate, But don't provide.
They have their fun, Then run and hide

Denise L. Otto

"Face To Face"

You come to me, I draw you near
Trust me babe, you needn't fear.
This love I feel inside for you
Will always be so warm and true.

I never knew what love could be
Till I saw you and you saw me.
Time stood still as you walked by
I think I heard you softly sigh.

When at last our lips caressed
I felt a tightness in my chest
I once imagined love like this
And now for me, it does exist.

It's hard to say just what I feel
So much inside needs time to heal
But with your help, your sweet embrace
We'll love forever, face to face.

Robin James Goad

Dear

When I stand before you,
I control my disgust.
My words expressing only
fractions of my rage.
I could not let you guess,
I cannot even suggest
a hint of reality unless
I break you down, and
I break myself with you.
So I choke on myself
and explode in solitude.

Brad Haight

The Crucifixion

Voices yell in anguish
As lightning bolts across the dim,
darkened sky.
The earth's violent quake uproots
The gates of hell.
The crucified, with head held low
Faces humanity with a pierced heart.
Velvet streams of compassion give
Life to all.
Death ceases.
The final book begins.

Thomas Neal Erwin

"The Girl In My Heart"

Soon we will not be together,
but we know it's not forever.
We will be miles apart,
I hope I'm in your heart,
my eyes in your mind,
my soul in your grasp.
I don't know how long it will last.
I've never felt this way before,
I wish I could be there more.
Everything would be all right,
You'd be in my arms every night.
I wanted to tell you,
wanted to show you how I feel,
but it may already be too late.
I wish there was an easier way,
I could be with you every day.
There will be a wish in every tear
that I'll be back really soon.
Though we will be miles apart,
you will be the only girl in my heart.

Chris Campbell

God's First Promise
(The Rainbow)

Stretching across the light blue sky
a beautiful sight to every eye
glowing with colors that number seven
some will say it's a stairway to heaven
but in the Bible it can be read
among the clouds it would be spread
to serve as a sign unto all the earth
God never again would destroy His worth
so my friend no matter what the season
if you can't recall the exact reason
the rainbow was placed into the sky
remember God's first promise and you'll
know why

Carol A. Hohman

Hope

Hope, it keeps us going
   though the road is steep
Helping us to see the specks
   of light, over chasms deep
With hope our goals are possible
   Worth the struggle now
Confidence we keep on having
   Like we know somehow!
The Bible is a book of hope
   It paints a picture grand
Of Paradise Conditions
   With peace throughout the land!
No more sickness, no more war
   God's Kingdom rules instead
Neighbor love displayed earth-wide
   Hope for even the dead!
Surely we must read this book
   That brings such hope today
We can learn just what to do
   To bring this bright future our way!

Dilys Raley

Wordless Expressions

Sweet soul, I know
how you tremble
I can feel it
in your touch
and I know how you
savor me
with each brush of your
lips — sending me
sweetly
an inch above the ground.
Cautiously reacting
to private feelings
but not saying much
never saying too much . . .
letting our emotions
express us
without using words.

Catherine Marie Caputo

Riddle Of The Unborn

Again I say that
Spirit Sense is only learned
In Innocence.

Dreams attained
Will soon belie
The dream that claims
To satisfy.

Long ago, the Sages saw
The burgeoning
Of Spirit Law.

Seven are the
Hands and faces;
Seven planets.
Seven races.

Now we are the
One called Man —
The fifth unfolding
Of the Plan.

Born of water, cleansed by fire;
Knowing Me by sheer desire.

Kaunteya Das

Untitled

If there should be a time
When we both go our way
There will be tears a-fallin'
Why should we part this way

We both want one another
Our love will always be
There will never be another
Who was meant for me

We stuck together for this long
Why do we have to part
I'll never find another
That'll linger in my heart.

Alfred L. Cavillard

My Feather Friends

Come! Little feather friends and
fly with me. Over the mountains,
hills, rivers and dale, up and down the trail.

You don't need a road map, nor
telephone lines. Leave them all behind.

Follow me! I'll show you
the way. When I blow strong
and cold, just follow your nose,
You'll need a place to warm your
heart, as well as your toes.

Mary A. Brumfield

Does Anyone Really Care?

I try and try
But does anyone really care?
Time goes by,
Problems and worries stay
But does anyone really care?
What to do?
Who knows!
How do I solve the problems?
I do not know
But, does anyone really care?
I try and try
To solve everyone's problems
But what about me?
Does anyone really care?

Ann-Marie B. Charron

Sunday Cats

Lazy cats
outstretched on an old couch
warm and lethargic
licking themselves sweetly
wrestling playfully
contently purring catnaps
no need to move
no need to change
cozy close on a rainy day
conversations with our bodies
no need to try too hard
just be there
just be lazy cats
outstretched on an old tan couch
warm and lethargic

Jenna Hyman

Distraction

Seeking the quiet within
spend the evening once again
among strangers
familiar setting
noise of the band
the crowd
relieves me of the burden
thinking
another day spent
seeking the quiet within
within the quiet of my apartment
noise of my thoughts
randomly shifting
made it impossible
to think

Seeking solitude
join the crowd
noise I need to find
peace within

Phillip G. Bunce

Prince Charming

Happy and satisfied
Content with my life,
Never did I dream
Of becoming a wife.

Then he came along
And invaded my soul,
A new zest for life
I'm fulfilled and whole.

We share thoughts and dreams
That have come alive.
My smile is never ending
On his love I now thrive.

Through good times and bad
My love shows support,
Wherever the tide may be
He's docked at my port.

A lifetime of togetherness
We are excited to share,
With a bond so unique
And so very rare.

Marybeth E. Jump

We Live

We ponder with awe our failings.
Live they; become achievement.
Live they of wondrous happenings.
Fade they might of the shadow.
For, what is in us may be out;
What is out may enter.
Live me then the good for knowing.
Forever sleep we not for ignorance.
As borne are we aright.
Aright are we as borne.
Sheep become lions, and lions!
Lions live unto the lions.
We know, we grow.
We grow, we live.
Water be our blood.
Earth be our body.
Cosmos be our life

Jennifer DeVoss

"Feeling Of Love"

Nightfall has come
I lie with you
In the nudity of
Our love
Caressing you
Caressing me
As we combined
Our souls into one
In the tenderness
Of the moment
Are we alive I ask?
Are we in a dream?
Or is the dream in us . . .

Janice K.

Surrender

Surrender to me
Your loving mate
That which was destined
By our inherent fate

Throw off the shackles
Cast of old
Be who you are
Not what you were told

Surrender to me
My loving mate
That part of love
Which became hate

Why wait any longer?
What is there to gain?
To extend the suffering
To prolong the pain

Surrender my mate
What was meant to be
Surrender your love
Give it all to me

Bob Kerekes

Lost Love

Love long and lost;
for I have given in.
My words were cold as ice,
but are now burning deep within.
He knew that I had wronged,
but stayed until the end.
Now that it is over,
my love is long and lost forever,
my friend.

Felissa Koernig

Life

You live a life,
A life you can't find
Unless you look,
Look in your soul,
Look in your heart

Find out who you are,
Why you're here,
What to do

Look deep inside
Find yourself
Then,
Live a life,

Live your life

Leslie Rogers

What Winter Wills

When winter winds wail
Sun's shine sleeps
Snows swirl, silent, still,
Wearily we watch, wait,
Woefully we wonder
Will winter weather win?

Evangeline Chandler

Rainy Days

Pitter-patter
    on my hat,
as it does against the raincoat
    on my back.
This kind of weather
    is awful to some,
but what we saw
    as peaceful and fun.

For us they were
    a special kind of day,
where others call them nasty
    and come what may.

Once surrounded
    by my companions of fun,
it's days like this I reflect back
    on all we've done.

So if you see
    drizzle and rain,
please remember me,
    who doesn't mind this pain.

Philip John Glaser

Herman

I heard a bird.
The song is wrong
For a bird of prey.
(It's an osprey.)
It's a weak, high pitched squeak.

I call it Herman,
Tho I can't determine
If, as some would say,
It should be Hermioné.

He sits on a mast,
His eagle eyes cast
On the marina down below.
Then off he strays
For days and days.
How many? I don't know.
But although I've lost track,
I know that he's back
When he opens his beak
And lets out that squeak.

Helen F. Petersen

Searching Soul

In my slumbering soul I weep, as I
pray the lord my soul to keep
    In my search for god above, fill my
empty soul with love.
    My search has been hard, my
journey has been long, please help
me find my way back home.
    For in my feeble soul I weep,
knowing lost souls you do not keep.

Ereka Yerk

She Wore Her Armour Well

She appeared so strong,
before the world.
As you could tell,
she wore her armour well.

Her eyes hid the pain,
her words rang strong and true,
like the peal of a chapel bell.
For she wore her armour well.

Her body held ridged,
but slight of frame,
standing tall like a fortress
in the raging rain.

Her feet firmly planted
her head held high
and from her lips
a quivering sigh!

A choked cry
a tear fell,
and upon the ground
her armour fell.

Janice Lee Wiseman

The More

The more
You hurt me
The more
I die.

The more
You love me
The more
I lie

The more
I live
The more
I love

The more
You stay
The more
I pay.

Brandy Bock

Ever Alone

Last night was the last night
I'll ever sleep alone

The empty space in our bed
Remains your hallowed throne

The loudest sound I heard all
Night was the silence of the phone

Last night was the last night
I'll ever sleep alone

I gazed out my window the
Darkness oh so dense and all
The thoughts of you soon became
Past tense

I then sat up a tear fell
Down I held my head and
Cried it's now I know just
Yesterday was the day you died

Last night was the first night
I'll forever sleep alone

Larry A. Grzymkowski

Alien

Living apart, alone
separate and yet the same
why do tiny differences have
    such a big effect?
I live there, you live here
why am I an alien to you?

Different friends,
    different jokes, different laughs
We both laugh,
    we both cry
why am I an alien to you?

I want to be friends
I want you to understand
why must you be so insistent
    about keeping me away?
Why am I an alien to you?

Different sorrows,
    different shoulders to cry on
we both hurt, so why?
Why am I an alien to you?

Julie D. Watt

My Shelter

Since I found a shelter
    Under his wings
My savior goes with me
    Whatever life brings;
Until death overtakes me
    and upward I fly,
To that home He's prepared
    For his ransomed on high.
Life's burdens he shares,
    And death cannot harm
Those who trust in His mercy;
I am safe in his arms.
The source of my sunshine,
    My hope for tomorrow;
His love is unfailing
    Through gladness and sorrow.
Whatever he sends me
    My joyful heart sings,
Since I found my shelter
    Under his wins!

Howard M. Lunsetter

Dear Father . . .

I still hear my name
In the whispering wind

An angelic voice
A voice from within

He's calling my name
I try not to cry

He's left me so quickly
Never told him good-bye

At last I can see him
By the edge of my bed

He's come silently to me
Easing sorrows and dread

My life's filled with joy now
A family my own

Dear father your love's there
In my heart and home...

Helen Burnett

Spring

Mother nature whispers low
it's time to wake,
time to grow.
All the earth responds to her.
Then up from ground once
cold and bare, a tiny
seedling pops its head.
It feels the warmth of
a bright sun, and hears
the song the robin sings.
It is the time of all rebirth.
It is the spring.

May L. Rosener

"Oh Lord"

They stroked me
And they strained me
They punched me
And they poked me
They thought they knew me!!
Then they sassed me
Then they smartened me
They burnt me
And they bucked me
Then they hooked me
Then they tricked me
Then they lost me!!
How? Aids is taking me away.

John Michael Gotsch

"An Endangered Bloom"

"The desert flower sits and cries,
. . . Or sometimes stands alone."
"Against the wind and rain and sun,
. . . Then winters or unfolds."

"A heart of gold encased within
. . . An ageing outer shell,"
"only to emerge again . . .
. . . And surround you with her spell."

"Love is like a garden . . .
. . . Of enchanted wilderness,"
"only to be charted . . .
. . . By our unstubborn willingness."

Lana Rutter

Love

Clouds in the sky
Flowers on the trees
Wish you were here
to see what I see

Flowers on the ground
Green in the trees
Listen to the sound
of the humming bees

The birds are singing
The bullfrogs are croaking
The crickets are chirping
The stars are glowing
The moon is high in the sky
The sun is down below

As I lay here by your side
I can see forever in your eyes
As moon twinkles, and all
hearts beat as one, I know 'tis
you who will forever lay by my side

Ashley Livingston

Joy

Just to take delight again,
In softly falling gentle rain,
To feel its cool and flowing dress,
Caress the soil of my distress.

Just to see new sunshine glance,
Around the windy shadow's dance,
Of freshly leafed out olive trees,
Whose youth awaits deflowering bees.

Just to look up thought the stars,
And feel the distance falling far,
While years of light rush to my eyes,
And bend my round old desires.

Just to feel your helm broad reached,
Sing sheeted tight beyond life's leech,
To thread you through the ageless sea,
In phosphorescent tapestries,

Just to take your bliss with me,
Safe stowed astride my memory,
I'll suck it sweet wet fruity ripe,
Forever in the bright black night.

Chris Stanton

The Butterfly

The Butterfly cries
The butterfly screams
Only to fly
Catching the breeze
Freer than most
But most fragile of all
Hear a voice
Arise and soar
Heed to your call
Oh fragile one
And be free forevermore

Amelia Gonzalez

Real Home

She wants to go home.
It's a long journey, you know.
She used to live there with father.
  Such a long, lone time ago
  Can't even remember when
But she told me straight out
That's what she really wanted.
This soul of mine
She wants to go home.

Carolyn Parker

I Only Miss You On Sundays

On Monday there's enough to do
  that you don't cross my mind,
Tuesday thinks of something
  to help me fill my time.
By Wednesday I've forgotten
  the heartache Sunday brings,
And Thursday's full of weekend plans
  for fun and other things.
But Friday's hope cannot postpone
  that Sabbath afternoon,
And Saturday, with all its strength,
  cannot slow down the moon.
Friday's hope cannot delay,
  nor Saturday deny,
That Sunday fast approacheth,
  the day we said goodbye.

Paige L. Huston

Original Love

Do we dare to wonder why
Life has its lows and then its highs
Do we dare to wonder why
Sometimes we laugh but then we cry
As God extends to us His mercy
And we wonder why we are thirsty
When His Word we do ignore
In this World we do explore
With our minds "tuned in" to learning
Still we have a deeper yearning
As we reach for the stars
We are sometimes met with bars
And we feel like we're in prison
Though we're sure we will be risen
So each day in faith we tread
Tho sometimes it seems on a thread
And with Hope we will go forward
As our inner light shines onward
And we know our God above
Watches over us with love.

Janet L. Huber

Angel

In a field of white daisies,
Where the morning dew sleeps soundly
  on satin ivory,
And the pikas speak of forbidden
  legends,
fire touches the horizon,
making clear the pastel heavens.
Angel brings to life her cheerful
  chorus of solitude.
A seductive greeting,
tempting fire to spill over the horizon
  of tears and hush Angel's voice,
silencing her fears, until once again,
  the heavens begin to smolder,
And Angel's eyes can see clearly
  once again

Mathew W. Perry

Elegy For Uncle Frank

Soft, rolling green hills
Among sparkling brooks and streams;
Elm, oak and chick-a-pin trees
Wavering in the breeze.
Under the trees, above the brooks
On top of the greenest hill,
Uncle Frank is laid quietly to rest.
His coffin is covered with dirt,
His body cold inside.
God gave him a long life.
But is life ever long enough?
A bluebird flies by and
My thoughts move on.

Jennifer Mann

Spring

Spring is like a beginning
A rebirth of all creation
The birds all sing with wondrous praise
A song of jubilation
The flowers bloom in glory
A sign that life is new
Their petals glow with sunshine
Kissed by morning dew.

Jackie Mancini-Stone

Webs

The bulbous mass
Brittle appendages
And venomous juice
  of consciousness
Sucks thought
From stimulation
An arachnid feeding.

The flitting wings
Insect optics
And writhing form
  of dream
Contorts reason
Usurps reality
A pasty interaction.

Displayed, struggling moth-like
In psychological webs.

Alvin Crosswhite

Christian Love

God is Love
A person in Love is with God

Hate is Sin
A person in Sin is with Hate

Love is from Here to Eternity
Sin is from Here to Hell

You have Eternity with God
You have Hell with Sin

Guide your Life from Hate
To God for Christian Love

Paul Wargo

Déjà Vu

Continuous motion,
Always moving in a circle;
Moving fast forward
On a rewind track,
Like a hamster
Caught in his wheel.

Nothing looks like everything;
Tomorrow looks just like
Yesterday.
After the fact
Looks just like before;
Just as my future is
Just as I remember it.

That's funny: It
Feels like I've been
Here before.

Continuous motion...

Ronald H. Brown

Moments

For a few moments more
staring at the fire, feeling
its ready joy.
   And yearning to be the fire,
to be able to touch a human
body with the most intimate
of embraces.
   To love finally, ultimately
to consume utterly.

Seandee M. Ghazzoul

Abuse

I stand, mouth agape, as one
who professes to love me
Attacks. His mood, violent.
His words, angry.

Blood runs from the corner of
my mouth. Blue decorates my
cheek and the world spins.
I ask, "Why?"

His face before me,
a trace of a smile,
"For your own good.
Believe me."

"Why?" I asked again.
His hand strikes and he turns.
There is no reason.

JoAnn Krause

Kept From The Night

Are those the last colors of the Night,
   saying goodbye?
I cannot tell, for Light
   is filling the sky.
The sun is too high.
The moon is waving goodbye.
Please let me say farewell
   to the Night.
Keeping me here
   is just not right.
Let me free!
Oh, don't you see?
The Day is filling the sky,
And the Darkness is saying goodbye.
Why don't you let me free?
The Night is all I have,
And you are keeping it from me.

Sarah Kozlowski

Not alone in
  sadness,
    pain
feelings of
  disgust . . .
    shame
happiness,
  the elusive dream
understanding
  your wall
which mirrors my own
  crying secret tears
walking in shadows
  never quite
    belonging
freedom comes
  as the light
    shines brilliant
    thru the doorway
  of **DEATH** . . .

D. D. Kiala

Untitled

Helicopter,
Oh mighty insect in the sky,
Your throbbing alerts me;
I watch you slowly passing by.

Joann S. Warfel

The Belt

He hits me all the time
For no matter what
For things that are inappropriate
He leaves marks and bruises
Now and then
I wish someone would stop
this and put it to and end
One day I will be gone
And I will be done
No more hits will I have to
take — from this man whom
I hat no more bruises — no
more marks — will I have to
hide with a lye — no more will
I have to lye to cover up for
this guy — the Lord has set
me free and now he will
let me be

Melissa Marie Dube

Site #2

In this landscape I realize
the options are dictated;
on a plain one can see too much,
the Fates fast-approaching,
arms loosely intertwined
with stony words on soft tongues
and spilled storms at their heels.
Measuring, weighing, concluding;
their rounded hips seductive and
quick, full-blown decisions made
about my life — was I consulted?
I plow through mid-western grasses:
this view is reluctantly familiar,
and I swell with resurrected memory.
Home-grown ghosts collide with the
ancient women who have warmed me,
and frozen blood flows a fecund red
in this place where dirt forms moons
under stronger, thicker nails.

Rebecca Holtzman

Surreal Truth

Only when you can deposit
questions in slot machines
will money give you answers.

Elizabeth Rubloff Zeisler

My Hero

A bond between a sister and brother
Of this kind there is no other
I'm him, he's me
He's everything I want to be
We rarely say I love you,
But the way we act gives a clue.
I may not be pretty or smart
But he loves me from his heart
He cheers me up when I'm sad
Although sometimes I make him mad
If he or I have a problem
We can depend on the other to help
   solve them
He picks me up when I fall
With his pride I can stand tall
I'm his, he's mine
For always, until the end of time.

Carolyn Powell

The Quietness Of Cold

Still
Still
The snow lies deep
Waiting in the quiet cold
For the touch of children's feet

Waiting for the sunshine
To warm them as they play
Making angels
Building forts
Until the end of day

Waiting for a mother's voice
To call her children home
Wet and tired
Drenched with snow
Happily they go

It's quiet now
The snow lies still
Still
And deep and cold
Waiting

Margery Buckner

Friend And Flowers

Friends are like flowers
They are always there.
Understanding by the hours
You may admire them
It's a mutual trust.

You can not always pick
Or choose if you must.
They come in different shapes,
Colors and sizes
You can have a bunch,
But one soon realizes
One good friend is all you need.

Like a flower you have to tend
You have to cultivate a friend.
You share bad times and good,
Your secrets, sorrows and more.
Laughter and joy, what a friend is for.

Unless you treat them well,
The friendship will die,
Leaving you with sadness to dwell . . .

Eirene Gracey

Father

Father,
Can you feel me?
I have traveled, just as you.
Please do not reject me!
Give me some time,
Time, that will be worthy,
of a sacrifice in love,
not of time, nor of gold.
I may require.
For the appearance of youth,
Items in time of desire.
If you wish,
you do not have to furnish,
all that I admire.
Could you at least play me a chord?
for the feeling of love,
the love that came in a song,
the song of just prior.

Troy S. Bellah

St. Patty's Day

'Tis "Wearin' of the Green" time,
Be you "Patty," "Mike" or "Irv,"
So what if you're not Irish,
All you need is a little nerve.

Put on that old green tie of yours,
Start singing an Irish song,
Get into the "Blarney" swing of things,
You're moving right along.

Shake hands with the guy next to you,
Drink up . . . get that hearty glow,
At least you've got that feeling,
The kind only "Irish" know.

Lucille T. Zappy

Thumbs Up

Turbulent stress
    Anxious test
Motors hum
    Pilot's thumb
Leveling flight
    Fleeing night
Beauty revealed
    Secret concealed
Noble down
    No frown
So life
    confounded strife!

A. Don Augsburger

Untitled

I walk along a busy street,
My feet this way then that;
Never mindful of the little things
Or just quite where I'm at.
My feet grow tired and weary
From never standing still.
My body's quickly fading
And my mind is all but nil.
There never seems to be an end
To this fast and hectic pace.
Stress has left its telling mark
Upon this aging face.
Quickly now, no time for rest.
The day will soon come to an end.
Tomorrow starts another day
To rush and hurry once again.

Daria Goff

If I Go First

Let me leave a shadow,
a little silver shadow
to catch a glint of sunshine,
when I am gone away.

Just a faint reminder
glowing in the twilight,
in the crescent moonlight,
like a firefly in the wind.

Or, just an early flower
a butter yellow flower,
trimmed with dew of morning
and warm and sweet perfume.

I would you not forget me —
I bid you not forget me,
Oh keep a tiny shadow
of my love within your heart.

Anna Marie Clark

Untitled

My friend in a straight jacket
slave to misjudged evaluations
prisoner of Lithium
and padded walls.

Irrational, He tells
of past lives, believes
in L. Ron Hubbard,
sees conspiracies.

Legs shake
eyes dance
"This is what it's all about"
his mind hard at work.

Now on weekends
He comes home
eight months he
spent on hold.

Now I'm the one who
is guilty,
remembering how I
placed my friend in hell.

Eric Baker

Unity America

God said let there be light; and
there was light. Let there be
life and there was life. Let
peace abide;

Let us join hands together with
faith, hope and charity that one
day we will all come together
as one.

Let there be peace we cry out
Lord, unity, togetherness. See
the world crying in turmoil
what shall we do? We can hear
the bells of hope ringing high
from above for freedom, freedom
America.

Let the praises cry out loud for
the whole world to hear. Singing
unity, praying unity America for
unity cries out, unity cries
out Unity America

Cassandra Mitchum

I Stand For You

Like an oak that stands
against the wind,
I stand against temptation
without the slightest bend.

The evils that lure others are no
match for me.
I stand tall and straight to
see what others might not see.
But there is one thing that is
so very hard for me to do,
my dear, my sweet, my one
true love,
I cannot stand to be
without you.

Benjamin Sandel

"The Awakening"

The beasts of the past
Hidden memories long lost
come crashing forward
no idea of their cost.
The lessons the pain
the guilt, the shame
locked up inside
an ever swelling tide.
As the door cracks open
fear strikes a blow
The tendency is to run
never wanting to know
But courage and strength
hammer through like the rains
Freeing the slave
Breaking the chains
The birth is complete
A new light shines through
Free of old fears
The heart becomes true

James Hoyne, D.O.

In Corpore Pulchro

You have no questions,
Are unassailable, fastidious, fulfilled

At thirty,
Wear your life
With lovely woman's certitude
And ease,
Batten your age
On Mozart, and martinis,
Enchant your friends
Some evenings in the week,
Lament the Elizabethans so long dead,
Take your dog to air,
Save the Jews

You are too young for loneliness,
You will not understand,
Nor answer;
You will not recognize your imaged self
In this strange mirror

The symbol's mystery is only faith,
The dream's truth is but desire.

Bill West

"Lost"

Those long summer nights alone,
I would wonder why you left me.
As I wander through our home,
It would lay there before me.

The memory of a time shared.
The showing of how we cared.
From a love that we both dared,
Now only leaves me scared.

But now as I try to gaze,
I struggle, yet can not see.
Before me is just a haze,
I can not see it clearly.

Is the moment lost or gone,
With the feeling it used to spark?
Now I see only a picture,
Standing alone in the dark.

Stephanie Sipe Clancy

My Brother

Tell me where our childhood did go
Those times so long ago
They seemed so much easier
Than the times we have today

Can you explain
Why those crazy dreams
Didn't quite turn out
As we all had planned

Can you help me
To understand that child
Who is now a man
That I may know him again

Can you work with me
To separate the miles
That lie not only between us
But also between our hearts

Can we just start over
Forget the pain and tears
Come to know the people
That you and I are today

De Fletcher

In the Eyes of a Child

In the eyes of a child
between a sparkle and a tear.
Lives the feeling of belonging
riddled with fear.

No mother or father
to call their home.
No big brick house
to call their own.

Along comes a family
with love in their heart.
Compelled by God
from the very start.

Angela and Jenny
Mom and I love you so much,
and we thank God for blessing us
with the chance to adopt.

So to anyone that wonders
the true joy of life.
Hold and adopted child in your arms
and just look into their eyes.

Robert Younger

Dreams

Dreams
Are sketched and drawn
To fill our hearts
With endless joy!

Dreams
Are made to feel
Our fantasies
Becoming real!

Dreams
Are made to see
Lovely mirages
Alive and be!

Dreams
In visions bold
Reap living imprints
A hundred-fold!

Frieda S. Johnson

Austin Night Feb '96

Picture this:
last night, the
air.
the Air was so
flush;
Sultry — that is to say —
heavywithmemories of
skin and Sweat
fragrant with pinemist
promising
Tomorrow, and Yes!
sitting in darkness the
Honeyed night
Half crescent moon and
above it —
Perfect planetstar.
i remember.
oh yes, i do.

MaryAnn Perna

The Words

Over and over I say them,
Again and again in my mind,
THE WORDS explode in my body,
Why can't I say them out loud?

I form THE WORDS with my lips,
I say them when I'm alone,
But when I stand before you,
Somehow THE WORDS won't come.

"I love you," my body is screaming,
"I love you," my whole being cries,
In truth, I know I must tell you,
Or in truth, I know I will die.

Betty M. Wagner

At The Mercy Of Midnight

The dark has long since come
The clock strikes once again
This is where tomorrow starts
And yesterday must end
Outside the world is silent
And thoughts are all I hear
The past and future fuse
I feel an unknown fear
Haunted by life's meaning
Though it's nowhere in sight
Time stands still and I am
At the mercy of midnight

Brian Freel

The Other Side

I am the other side,
so very far from you,
I am the tide that rises,
I am the ocean blue.
So blinded by pain you do not see
the water where I lay,
You do not know that I am there,
as I vanish away.
The coldness of the water I created,
has numbed my body with pain,
I helplessly fall to the bottom,
as your tears for me turn to rain.
The ocean turns to one soul,
one body of life and death,
And we have joined for eternity
as we take our final breath.

Keri Bennett

Winter

It's cold out-side, the
season has come to go sleighing all
day and have some fun,
the leaves are gone
the trees are bare,
it's flu season, so dress in warm wear,
the birds fly south
squirrels hunt for acorns,
cause the winter season has begun,
the snow falls down,
the ice does too, in
winter nothing grows so
we don't need that much light,
the snow and ice make roads slippery,
school's out sometimes
"Isn't that nice"
when its winter, just remember
nothing is fun until December.

Jennifer Payne

The View From My Window

From my sixth floor window
I watched the falling snow,
Blowing, drifting in all directions
while deciding where to go.

The winter and all of its fury
came with a frigid blast,
I walked from my window — wondering
How long, how long will it last?

The weather service and their
warnings really kept me on my toes,
And I just stood there, marveling
at the beauty of the snow.

The snow capped cars blended with
the beautiful snow trimmed trees,
The patterns made on the ground
— a sight that was sure to please.

And from my sixth floor window
I came to realize,
How much God loves me — to put
such beauty before my eyes.

Gladys Spencer

"I Found My Soul In London"

A soul is a hard thing to find.

We sense in a lifetime
of watching sun on breakers
roaring to the shore
in the half-light of winter
that there is more.

We guess from smiles and tears
begging us to see
in the light of day
what lies behind strangers' eyes
lives in us, too.

We become who we are
as we make our lives.

And who is to know why
one day we find our soul
in a city's face—
all those years waiting
for us to create a self
deep enough and true enough
to become a soul.

Mary Anderson

Life

Life is a place of spirit,
A place of growing,
A place of learning,
A place of time,
A place of anguish,
A place of devotion and of concern.

Scarlett Frix

Cloudy Day Blue Bird On A Thankful Thursday

Blue bird, small lovely
so much like special ladies
so rarely seen, Need to
Be spoken to on their beauty
Softly like Blue birds
landing or there take to
Flight going down deeper
Those rare women looking
In their eyes, as sweet
truth that is shore right
out from their souls, so
is this precious it to look
on, like that Blue bird
God may have made a
lot of them I have just
seen a bless few?

Phil (Easy) Welborn

Why?

Why Must I Cry?
Why must I sigh?
Why must my love say goodbye?
As I wait, as I pray, I cry
I say to myself, where shall
I go, what shall I do? What shall I say?
Why must I cry? Why must
I sigh? Why must my love say goodbye?
Good bye he say's, with a wave
of his hand, Goodbye he say's
with his gentle kiss, goodbye he
say's with his sweet aroma.
Why must I cry, why must I
sigh, why must my love say goodbye?
Why must he say good-bye?

Krista Morrow

For My Love

How could this be happening,
that you took my love for granted?
You took me into your arms
filled my heart with love
and when we shared it together
we both knew the consequences,
yet you still let me go.

What will she ever think,
when she knows not of her daddy?
One to love, care and look-up to,
the way she should.
Does she not deserve
to live like any other?
For you took it all away from her,
before you even met her.

You call yourself a man,
yet you think of yourself
before any other.

Mary Jo Hitt

A Creed To Live By

If a man needs a coat
  Help him obtain one.
If a man's coat is torn
  Help him mend it.
If man's coat is soiled
  Help him clean it.
For a man needs a coat
  For warmth and dignity.

If a man's soul is lost
  Help him find it.
If a man's soul is frayed
  Help him weave it.
If a man's soul if fouled
  Help him clean it.
For a man needs a soul
  To believe in himself and his god.

Mary Kennedy Muffley

Prisoner Heart

From sinewy bonds
  Behind bars of bone
    It peers into the soul

In primordial quietude
  It waits alone
    And fears the darkened hole

Cursed aloneness!
  Festering rage!
    Time will not wait

Memories flood
  Then mold with age
    Like words on a patina slate

Forego honor
  Where to start?
    O, set free the prisoner heart!

Mike Powell

Scars As Status Symbols (S.S.S.)

Cover thy bleeding heart
With coloured dyes.
Tattoo thy brokenness before all!

Brandish thy scars
As status symbols,
Emblazon thine eyes with victory!

Dear one, thy bruises
Bear love's shrapnel.
Let me honour thee with kisses!

Katy Miles

Dogmatic

Sat and stared
A few friendly words
in describing
my forbidden Lords
that roam the lands
of undeveloped beings
body language so predictable
fooling themselves, believing
somehow that they're fixable
in their cyclone world
and narcissistic mentality
perhaps one day they'll evolve
perhaps by this
it won't always be my fault.

Jesica F. Cajas

Freedom

Freedom, oh freedom, how I
   long for you now;
I know that I'll find you,
   I will somehow.

I'll be free someday just
   you wait and see;
I'll fly with the birds,
   and flow with the breeze;

I'll run like wild horses;
   I'll swim in the sea;
I'll be free someday,
   just you wait and see;

I'll dance in the rain
   happily and gay;
Rejoicing each and every day.

You can find me in the
   sky; the mountains or the trees,
You can find me most anywhere;
   just as long as it's free.

   Michelle Kells

Lonely Wolf Cry

A lonely wolf cries
Through the
Night
Howling at the
Moon
Waiting
Waiting for the
Answer of
another
But there is
No reply
To the lonely
Wolf cry

   Jared Abrahamian

Hatred

Starts small
like the guinea worm
whose larvae squirm
into tainted drinking water.

So small you cannot see
till once inside you they flee
growing one foot . . . two . . . three.
Raging desperately, then free.

They will bore out your skin
Excruciating pain from within.
You are without
Immunity.

Deadly parasite.
Malicious, and festering
Anger.

   Diane M. Hochman

Together

together forever.
Together in time.
To the heavens above,
Together we'll climb.

It may be far.
It may be rough.
But together
Our love is enough.

   Timothy E. Conrad II

Never Empty

Out of the airy sky
Out of no where come flying
Thoughts are a winging
Buzzing and jesting
Go away, away!
Will not stop singing
almost to a screech
Dance a way on the beach
Touch the moon touch it all
With a stir of the heart
Never gone, always here
Never empty, always alive
Dribbling sand threw fingers
Making a dive
Dewy winds from singers
Giving the heart to a mood serene
On a piece of driftwood
Protected from the burning rays
Runneth full with peace
The wonders of a dream

   Jeanne Crayne

The Grey Cloud

A long time ago,
I looked up at the sky.
And a cloud was about
To commit suicide!

I jumped on a bird who
Took me up in the air.
And I said to the cloud,
"What's going on up there?"

The cloud looked at me
Straight in the eye.
It said to me,
"I want to die!"

I looked back at it
And I asked it, "Why?"
It said "I'm turning grey!
I'm supposed to be white."

Then I said "Well rain.
And the grey will fade."
The cloud said "Thank you."
Then floated away.

   Jacqueline Monhollen

"If"

"If" you were the rose
I would not pluck you
From its vine
I would want you to live
A life long time

"If" you were the wind
I would not run and hide
I would want you to blow
Endlessly through my mind

"If" you where the sun
I would not stay inside
I would want each ray
To run through me until
The day I die

"If" you were the rain
I would not cover my head
I would want each drop to
Run through my veins instead.

   Janet M. Stanford

Benefits of Friendship

Friendship golden,
Friendship divine,
A bond between hearts
   to last for all time.
It gives us aid when
   we feel spent,
It gives us encouragement
   when we want to quit.
It's a shelter from all
   troublesome things,
It's a breath of fresh air
   that makes every day
   seem like spring.
It's a never ending wishing well.
Friendship is a precious thing
   that makes our hearts light
   and able to sing.

   J. Jenny G.

For The Child Yet To Come . . .

I write this for you little one,
although you're not yet here . . .
There's a special person longing,
just to whisper in your ear.

She's waited a long time for you
and hoped in many ways,
That one day in her loving arms
a newborn babe would lay . . .

To place a kiss upon your cheek,
or hold your tiny hand . . .
Would bring to her such happiness,
it's hard to understand.
So even though you're not yet here
and don't know of her love . . .
She's waiting for you little one,
to come from up above . . .

   Terri S. Patten

Faith, Hope, And Love

Faith, hope, and love
The greatest of these is love
Turning a frown into a smile
A heart full to overflowing

Faith is unconditional
To believe without knowing
To feel what is not tangible
To know what is not visible

Hope is an unspoken thought
A soul reaching for comfort
Searching for relief from trials
A mind waiting for direction

Prayer is a wish
Waiting for fulfillment
As is soars aloft on wings
Soft as a butterfly

Let your faith be unbending
Hope to the depth of your heart
Love knows no boundaries
In God we put our trust

   Kathy Bradshaw

An Unusual Love

Like sand on a beach
And pebbles in the water
My love for you should reach
The highest waves in the water
Like the sun on my face
As I stand in one place
My love will soar
As the waters roar
Seagulls flying
And the fish are dying
My love for you
Is always true
The day is over
Like the dead clover
As the sand sit still
How would you feel
If you loved an eel

Larnita Johnson

Lost Love

Lips so soft,
like rose pedals;
Skin so soft,
like silk;
Heart so full of love,
Eyes so full of tears.
Tears are filled with memories,
love, betrayal and fear.
Precious soul, for I have stole;
Mine I've stole as well.

Deborah E. Buntzen

I Believe In Angels

You cannot see her angel's wings
  but I know that they are there,
  as she primly pours a cup of tea,
  perched upon her own small chair.

She stands before the minor
  up on her tippy-toes,
  my graceful ballerina,
  my precious budding rose.

She climbs onto my lap at night
  clutching a book and teddy bear.
  Her little hand holds on to mine,
  my chin rests on her hair.

I read book one and then book two
  as off to sleep she drifts.
  I praise the Lord my son gave me
  this most precious of all gifts.

You cannot see the halo,
  that glows above her head,
  but I can see if clearly,
  as I tuck her safe in bed.

Patricia B. Kotzo

And We Call Them Colored?!

When we were born, we were pink;
When we were sick, we were ashen;
When we died, we were white.

When they were born, they were black;
When they were sick, they were black;
When they died, they were black.

And we call them colored?!

Heather Bales

Reflections On Life And Time

Life is a gift
  The greatest you'll find.
So as you live it,
  Keep these thoughts in mind.

Remember the past
  The good and the bad.
For who you are now
  Grew from experiences had.

Embrace the present
  Make each second count.
For from these precious moments
  Your treasures will mount.

Envision the future
  And reach for the sky.
For your life is unlimited
  When you set your goals high.

So when life is over
  And your future turned to past,
Your gifts left to others
  Are the memories that last.

James B. Neville Jr.

Only The Real

To feel no interest
  Means go no further.
To feel no love
  Means stop right there.
To feel loneliness
  Almost anything will do.
Only real love can
  Stop the confusion.
Only true interest
  Can anything feel right.
Do not let confusion
  And loneliness guide you.
Only hurt, will you
  Be in the end.
If true love
  Is there
The pieces will
  Fall into place.

Hera S. Pickering

The Miracle

Eons have passed
years came and went
But the important thing you see;
before any of the mountains
were ever formed
the Lord had thought of me.

He doesn't ask much
Just follow His ways
By helping your neighbor,
Being honest and true;
If you do your best in these
  little things
peace and serenity will come to you.

The mistake is we all have this God
watching over us in our life;
He has extended His mercy,
  kindness and love
To show us the way to eternal life.

James B. McCloskey

Lost Love

The longing,
the yearning,
the never returning
of a lost love

The sadness
and tears,
always the fears
of loneliness.

The sleepless nights
and endless days,
always regretting
but never forgetting
your past love.

The longing,
the yearning,
but the never returning
of a lost love.

Jo-Ann Evans Heraly

The Real World

The pain I have found
The world so harsh
I run to a world of my own.
Peace and quiet
That is what I want!

Peace is not the world's standards
Look at the wars because of peace
Quiet, quite a myth I would say.
Look at the gun shots in the night
Our world is full of chaos!

I wish I could ease our pain
We need change
Where do we start?
We start with our future
Our children!

William Hall

My Little Girl

She shows me her radiant smile.
So happy so carefree. The way
she reminds me that she loves
me for just being me.

She is my most cherished gift
in this world. To see my life
through hers. Remembering the
fears, happiness and tears.

Being there anyway that I
can, careful not to smother
or control.

Just watching my beautiful
little girl grow.

Ellen Stewart

First Love

I thought I was happy
but not until I met you
that I found that I just
thought I was
I thought I had loved
till I loved you
I thought you were my
first love but you were
really my last . . .

Yolanda Martinez

Untitled

I know a land that is unknown
its sands shimmer in the
sun, its moon a pale image of the
sky. The water is sweet, but
the sun beats down in
hatred, and the wind carries
chills from the North.
The soil upon the terrain
is harsh to those who dare
defy its laws. This land
is old and wise and only
cares for those who
follow its ways.
Do you now understand
the life and honor that
still floats in the
mist of the enchanted land?

Jessica Lindskog

Untitled

The day's radiant with sunshine,
and I am like a child
with a tinsel toy.

The weather man said
rain, rain, rain,
and I could feel the grayness
spreading like a shroud
across the window pane.

Today, in sunshine,
I am born again.

Ruth Millman

Moments In Between The Fabric

Faster than the eye can register
You give me that look
I answer with a little shrug
Sitting remotely quiet on a couch
Watching the circus on tv

A model posed for death, poised
With practiced calmness
Awaiting partner's silent daggers
That pop out from behind a board
Faster than the eye can register

I imagine we turn to each other
To bring to an end the performance
Of why and I don't know
For without a board I am aware
Daggers don't miss when thrown

Nicholas W. Orman

Was It Right

Miles upon miles pass between us.
Will we ever come together again?
Our lives are separated from
The decisions we made.
Was it right for us to make
Those decisions without thinking
About the other person?
How long will we be
Separated from each other?
Will our relationship stand
As one during this period of time?
These things we will never know
Until we meet again.

Beulah-Jean Wright

Peaceful Sleep

Death be not proud
Death be not mournful of tears
to escape harmful fears

The coming is nigh
A long awaited sigh
A quiet exit into
a peaceful paradise

Birth of new beginning
Ebb of life's christening
Old souls chant around
A sacred burial ground

Man's imminent shroud
captured not torn
till death be not proud
and I be not forlorn

Annette Hutchison

Hyakutake's Return

Burning star
melting the eternal night
brightening the 20,000 year sky
inspiring the mind
to wonder . . .

Can I overcome my
mortal fear of death
and shine, just once,
for a moment and
inspire the multitudes,
as you have, or only one,
to brush past the fear
past the unknown, and
appear to the world
naked and observable
judged by whom and
not what I am — and be embraced
for that.

Michael Chapin

What Is A Ham

What is a ham?
No one really knows
But when they key up
Their signal goes and goes.

They sit at a desk,
Sometimes alone in a room
They talk to hams around the world
Bouncing signals off the moon.

They have a language of their own.
We call it morse code.
But to them!
It's emission AIA mode

Some run lots of power
A kilo wait or more
With state of the art equipment
And a linear from the store.

Others work the world
With the power of a flea
And their eyes light with pleasure
When they sign "QRP."

Frank Hulbert

Angels

Angel of mercy
take my hand
and guide me to
the promised land

Angel of sorrow
dry my eyes
kiss my sadness and tears goodbye

Angel of wisdom
open my mind
help to make decisions
that are wise

Angel of hope
would you please
help me to overcome
life's struggles presented before me

Angels sweet angels
in heaven above
guide me to heaven
on the wings of a dove

Cindi M. Fuss

Summer Morning

I slipped out into
the cool summer air smelling
fresh and clean, the dew
on the grass wets my feet and
the warm summer sun warms
my back, the cool, moist dirt
feels soothing against my feet,
and the Day lilies are just starting
to bloom, a birds sweet sounding
song cuts through the air as
I walk to my special rock, I
lay down on it and close my eyes
while the gentle sun warms my
face. There are mornings like these
that I like far more than T.V.
or video games.

Erin De Rosa

Seeds Of Time

And the Gardner plants the seed —
as the heavens labour
through the dark season
surging, swelling —
impregnating the skies
and the wombs of time
weep tears of wonder
upon the fetal earth of winter.

As I stand uncultivated,
clothed only by the sun;
latent figure —
of God's wintry judgement,
Sewn in fertile soil,
Fed by the tears,
I will take root.
Forever preserving
the fruits of the
Celestial Body.

Dwayne S. Hallman

Prayer Of Hope

Take me by the hand, oh Lord
and guide me through this day

The path ahead is rough, oh Lord
but you can show the way

Take me by the hand, oh Lord
and give me strength to cope

Protect me from the cares of life
and bless me with new hope

Take me by the hand, oh Lord
and keep me close to Thee

Release me from all doubt and fear
and set my spirit free

Nancy Miserendino

Past Perceptions

Once, I conceived it then . . .
Once, I believed in everything
you were to me,
a mystery — full magical,
an idol for a mind of three.

Perhaps I was mistaken,
for now I am forced
to question the answers
you never really told.

An unearthliness is resembled.
My love disassembled.
My idol lays shattered
on the ground . . .

Unbeknownst to you
through another sign of oddity.
How can you not
perceive the strange things
which must be?

Carrie L. Giessman

No Choice

In the night we see the light
Of love, that's never shown
But in the day, we must be gay
For we are now all grown.

But cry no more,
For at the door,
knock's life's eternal light.
And what can't be found
On this ground,
In heaven it just might
Be the place to be
for us to see
That things are worth the wait,
And when it comes to pass
and we're gone at last;
We have no choice . . . just fate.

Rhonda C. Kirby

Friendship

I feel love and warmness,
happiness, and joyful liking someone
so much that you want to see his smile.

Friendship

Shannon Kee

Untitled

How many times
Have I expressed my love
To you and the family
And God, above?
I wonder . . .

How many times
Have I cleaned-up my mess
And made mistakes
And didn't confess?
I wonder . . .

How many times
Have you done the same
And not compromised
And pointed the blame?
I wonder . . . but . . .

How many times are we gonna repeat
The same ole stuff
And consider our love beat?
I wonder . . .
Let's try again!!?!!

Mary Homma

A Tree Called Life

I feel,
I feel the beat now;
I hear the music, too;

I taste the milk and honey
and I know,
I know you are near.

I see,
I see the beauty here; but why,
why is my heart so gripped with fear?

I want to be with you too,
but a great chasm — called time,
stretches anew.

No, I cannot go now.
I have . . .
my duties . . . you know.

Since you died
(it cut me like a knife)
I am crucified
to a tree called life.

John-Paul LaPre

The Verdict

On the edge . . .
  Launched mid-air.
If I fall —
  pain, suffering, tears, sorrow.

If I fly;
skyward I'll rise. Above all —
weariness will be no more.
Wondering will be no more.
Wondering will come to end.

If only I could hover . . .
  midline; inbetween;
  the verdict.
  (I'd be safe. —
Make the decision.
  Will it be made?
  Up down
I'll know soon . . .
  the verdict.

Barbara A. Burkard

Reflections

Reflections on the water,
are reflections of our past,
I'm living in the present,
but I keep on looking back.

Reflections of the goals we set
and all the goals we've won;
Of all the things we hoped for,
and of those that never came.

Of problems we solved correctly,
and the mistakes that we have made,
of enemies who hate us,
and our friends we'd never change.

Of places we have been to,
of all the things we've seen,
we'll live and grow and continue,
to remember them and dream.

Tina Jackson

Unsung

The lightning struck out—in anger,
The stars dropped out of the sky,
————————in mourning—
The heavens shook in darkness,
as the sun with-drew her light;
From your throne you descended,
into a world that welcomed—you not;
How the angels cried out as,
you stepped from—heavens light;
Into a world of sin, you were,
brought forth—naked—denied,
your garments of majesty;
Yet this world gave unto you—not,
a crown of gold—but one of thorns,
instead of a throne, they gave you,
a cross of wood to die upon;
Once angels sung unto you—praise,
Yet mankind's praises were left,
————————unsung————————.

Cherie Springfield

Snow

The snow outside
What it hides?
No one knows
The wind whips the snow
Wild does it blow

The sky is grey
But who's to say?
Where the beauty goes

The flakes do fall
Against the wall, with no strength
Yet they seem to spread at length
Quite a few build a ball
Cause a fight and many to fall

The sun does come
They melt away
And we have none
With which to play
Years and years go by days
And the snow's end comes
With the sun's rays

Wanda J. Wagner

Alien

Alien dark and deep
Beneath my covers you sleep
Close as skin
Deep as breath
Feeling our filling immensity
We lie a dark embrace
To never die
Symbiosis
Form complete
One being
One breath
One dream
One sleep
Alien

Timothy F. Abraham

The Lord Of Nothing

I am the Lord of Nothing
Nothing is all I own
Everything I had has been taken
And Nothing is all I Know

I am the Lord of Nothing
With Nothing more to gain
Nothing more to be taken
Nothing more to give away

I am the Lord of Nothing
There is Nothing I cannot do
And there is Nothing that can stop
The one with Nothing left to lose

Damien Campos

Beyond The Road

As I look beyond myself, I see
a person standing there waiting
patiently.

Wondering I'm going to leave a mark
upon the earth, will I ever be
Successful are drown in my sorrow.

But the road I choose is all up to me,
as I walk down that narrow path.

Sometimes I stumble and fall, but
I get right up again dust myself
off and keep going.

I shall not let every stumbling
block come my way stop me from,
achieving what ever I choose to me,

For that person standing there in the
road is me.

Mary Lou Odoms

Rain

It is raining
In the city of angels,
The street lights are shining
In the infinite pieces of shade.
It is like shattered hearts
In the greyness of the sky.
The thick molasses of the fog
Makes me want to cry.
I am singing in the rain,
I can feel the freedom
But I really want to cry
Because the silver pieces
Of shade are here to stay.

Hrair Simonian

For An Instant . . .

A glistening chip of winter,
guided by nature,
falls gently upon a withering
spirit.
As it melts,
it flows,
caressing every curve,
calming every nerve.
Choosing its direction by sensing
overbearing pain and,
ever so softly,
easing all that troubles the soul.
Continuing its route,
enlightening every inch.
Slowly entering every pore,
pleasing the inner shadow that's
losing control.
All senses shiver, seduced by
the motion.
    And then, it dries.

Alonzo Wheat Jr.

Birth

Oh! The pain of giving birth.
Perhaps the greatest pain on earth.
The pain how great it is.
Why couldn't it be his?
A man can never know just how
bad it feels.
Men, they're all such heels.
He stood by my side in the
delivery room. He even cried.
He said he knew just how
I felt.
I knew that his tears were real,
it didn't change the fact that
I was ready to kill.
After it was all done.
I no longer wanted to kill anyone
As I held my new born baby.
He asked if I'd do it again.
I said maybe.

Sharon McDaniel

Collector Of Sunsets

I am
a collector of sunsets,
a follower of rainbows,
a dreamer
of visions of God in the clouds.

I am
a collector of promises
in rainbow-colored skies,
a follower of breezes,
a dreamer hearing
the Spirit blowing where He wills.

I am
a holder of hope
in azure skies
and crimson sunrises
of trailing wisps of angel-fluff
in clouds,
the stuff
in which
God speaks to me.

Bonnie J. Morris

Untitled

He stood high on the hill,
The night wind blowing
softly to him.

In the distance he could hear
the lonesome call of his kin.

As the moon rose slowly into
the night sky he took a deep
breath and filled the stillness
with a howl.

There, in that moment, he claimed
his ancestry, his since the beginning
of time.

Only understood by his kin,
misunderstood by man, respected
by his enemies.
Now belonging to a brotherhood
known as WOLF.

Charles Christman

Alone

Oh that I were a wave
To heave my way cross the sea
To roll over, conquering distances
that keep you far from me.

Oh that I could take wing,
Be suddenly a bird, and flee,
and soar up heaven above,
racing all the way to thee

And oh that I'd be the sun
to flare round your fair body
as it yawns across the shoals
for my eyes of rapt fire to see.

And yet I'm not a wave,
Sun am not, nor bird.
I'm only myself in the distance,
A woman, yonder, unheard.

Alone but for my wonder,
Alone but for what I crave,
Alone but for my dreaming,
Alone, without love, yet love's slave.

Luiza De Mesquita

The Meaning Of Life

Gigantic feasts,
Glorious meals,
A glutton;
That's what I am.

Roasted pheasant,
Cooked perfectly,
A glutton;
That's what I am.

Humongous turkeys,
Smothered in gravy
A glutton;
That's what I am.

Caviar,
The best in the world,
A glutton;
That's what I am.

That's it for breakfast,
Time for lunch,
What a world;
What a world.

Doug McKenney

"Spring"

I am so happy Spring is here,
 I love the trees and flowers.
A secluded spot I hold so dear,
 secure from sun and showers.
I sit in peace and dream sweet dreams
 and all my troubles fade,
As I marvel at the wondrous things
 that our dear God has made.
I raise my eyes in thanks to Him,
 Who has been so kind
To give to me these lovely things
 that are hidden from the blind.

Sadie C. Gremillion

The Heart

The heart is a fragile thing,
It is easily broken
By all kinds of actions,
Or words that are spoken.

The heart is something
That grows on love,
Not the dirt on the ground
Or the air above.

My heart has been broken
By people of all kinds.
It stays in my thoughts,
It stays on my mind.

Now I trust you
With this fragile thing,
I am warning you,
It hangs by a string.

Stephanie May

Wolf

"I" have been,
"I" Am,
"I" know where I am going.

"I" saw,
"I" see,
"I" know what nature has
 in store for me
My spirit rides the Heaven
 Thru Eternity
My Paws touch the Earth,
 so gently.
I am the circle of life,
 God Ordained.
I am the Wolf.

Gale L. Hough

Breathe

I was born to breathe.
Not to let society dictate
What I can and can not achieve
I was born to breathe
Not to go to places
That are set up more like
Prisons than education centers
I was born to breathe
Not to play inside because outside
I have to worry about a drive-by
I was born to breathe
And breathe is what I shall do
Until that too becomes extinct

Carl Dickey

"Life!"

Life is a mystery,
only to unfold,
when we are gone;
tucked away in our graves.
Life is complex,
too hard to handle.
I wait.
Will good ever come?
I wait more.
I think I am waiting for nothing.
I will prevail.
Confused,
until life is gone,
'til then,
I'll question,
why I exist.

Renee Vande Kolk

Untitled

Memories are forgotten
life fades away
nothing left to care about
nothing left to say

Friends are now enemies
life is ignored
people look down upon
what once was adored

Trust is a virtue
life is a fight
the day falls to darkness
as we're swallowed by night

Summer Whitney

Alone

Without you by my side,
this pain I feel
I cannot hide.
Without your love
to see me through,
I really don't know
just what to do.
You know I loved you
with all my heart,
thinking we would never part.
But sometimes life
just isn't fair,
now all I have left
are the feelings
we once shared.

Karell Roxas

Peace

Cottony blue
Deep green blades of grass
Limbs and leaves swaying in the wind
Deep grained polished marble

Dry wind
Drifting tumbleweeds
Small clouds of flowing dust
Simple splintery wooden cross

Light snowfall
Blankets of powdery snow
Bare trees bearing icicles
Etched block of granite

The peace of the soul

John M. Pickering

Always Forever Love You

Always and forever,
never to part.
There will always be room for you
inside of my heart.
Your smiling face so beautiful,
as the heavenly sky so blue.
You're the only one I ever want,
always forever love you.

Promise to be yours,
always and forever.
To never let you down,
to always be together.
Have no fear, child,
I'll forever be true;
right here by your side,
always forever love you.

Jason P. Nornendin

My Will

To the sun
I leave my eyes
Upon the deep blue sky they search;
And to the stars
I leave my hand
To then become a star itself.

To the hills
I leave my soul
For snow to cleanse it pure once more;
And to the wind
I leave my lips
To whisper upon the wretched world.

To the flowers
I leave my touch
To care for them as they may grow;
And now to you
I leave my love
All that there is left to give.

Ann Marie McGovern-Theriault

A Pledge To My America

I pledge allegiance to the flag,
I lift my head up high;
To see the wondrous colors blaze,
Up in the sunny sky.

This beautiful piece of art,
Is more than just a shroud;
It represents our Fatherland,
As we sing our Anthem aloud.

It demonstrates one People,
When the eagles are flying by;
While our Liberty Bell rings,
A boy soldier in Iran cries.

But in America, we're free,
To speak, live, and vote;
Give thanks unto our Forefathers,
As we reread the words they wrote.

And as the years go by,
Our flag shall never fall;
Be a patriot to our home,
With liberty and justice for all.

Jami N. Stigliano

"Thinking Of You"

How you're missed when you're not at
home, It's never quite the same when
you feel all-alone! Troublesome
thoughts come & go, but It's faith in
God that makes us grow! Thoughts of
you fill my mind, I'm praying for
you, God's peace you'll find!
While I wait for your soon return, in
your heart may God's true love burn!
God loves you, He healed you, He made
you whole! Understand today, He's the
lover of your soul!

Arthur M. Sherman

Why?

Why is it that,
Your heart is empty,
When your love,
leaves you alone?

Why is it that,
You continue to love,
Even when your Love,
Finds another to love?

Why is it that,
You want to end,
Your days with 'this one,
But you feel it will never happen?

The reason is simple.
The four-letter word,
That everyone fears,
Love!

Stefanie Hanneman

Hidden Treasure

If ever I thought,
it's now I do,
that we live in a world of confusion.
The truth we once bought,
we now outgrew,
and folks are content with illusion.

Feelings we leave,
then answers we acquire,
this is the way of the Spirit.
The voice we should cleave,
in truth you conspire,
respond to it when you hear it.

For the treasure at the start,
of the bow you can find,
and find it one day you may.
If you seek with your heart,
and not with your mind,
you'll have life in a lovely way.

Samuel Riesterer

On a Bag???

Writing poetry on a bag?
Why not write it on a rag?
Can toilet paper do as well?
Receipts from a banker's tell?

It matters not at all, you see,
On what a poem is written.
A poem grows from deep in me
Whenever I am sittin'!

Carol Brands

My Gift

I sat high on a hill
Gazing down
Surveying the valley below
The green lush meadows
The winding brooks
The grazing cattle
A gentle breeze brushed by
Kissed my cheek
Whispered in my ear
This is all yours
Our father told me so

Marguerite Harper

The Light

I see the light,
But it doesn't shine on me
I wondered why . . .?
Then I saw the light shinning on thee
. . . Don't try to hide
'Cause the shadow you cast
Makes me feel as though
You're reliving the past
You are not blind
Though you fail to see
It's not the color of your skin
That's ailing me
I see the light
But it's out of reach
I'm willing to learn,
But you're not willing to teach
And if we fail, we fail as one
And the cloud we create
Will only obscure the sun
For future generations to come

Emilio Rodriguez

Like the Weeping Willow

Like the weeping willow
Or the whispering pine
I grow and change
I exist thru time
Forever nourished
By the people I encounter
Some are like a rose
While others are like a thorn
Always drifting in the wind
Like a tumble weed
Looking for something to cling to.

Joseph A. Hood

Autumn Rain

All is not as it appears to be
summer in all its green
soon turn to autumn
the seasons of death
nothing more is green

rain brings life
autumn takes life
still rain falls in autumn

when spring comes forth
seeds fall into the leaves
of the previous autumn
dead leaves of the past
give life to the future

Molly M. Kelly

Angels

I know there are angels,
above the heavens fly,
I may never see them,
until the day I die.

But I do know,
they're watching over me.
They are always around,
when I need them desperately.

One night I heard them singing,
in voices loud and clear,
The chimes were also floating,
out through the air.

The little Lady whispered,
that I was sitting with,
I see the angels coming,
to take me to rest.

I know I'll see the angels,
in the place where I shall go.
In the distant land hereafter,
where to me, the Lord shall show.

Gladys I. Reed

Untitled

I speak to you so softly
so I am not heard
I speak to you so softly
I will barely utter one word
I speak to you so softly
because harsh words bite
I speak to you so softly
all throughout the night

I speak to you so softly
so I do not scare your emotions away
they might run or sway . . .
as mine do everyday.

I speak to you so softly
because I don't want to let go
of the love I hold onto so . . .
tightly, never letting go.

I speak to you so softly
because you might discover
that I love you above . . .
anyone else.

Katrina L. Beecher

Bird Song

A little bird sang today.
I know it was my dad.

You have to help your mom
I know she's very sad.

Tell her that I love her so
And that I didn't want to go.

Every time the bird sings
She'll always feel me near.

Every time the bird sings
She only has to hear.

Jan Hynes

Pain

A low silent mumble. A sign
oh so humble. Of Sadness profound,
of sorrow and woe, Of grievance no
gladness. Of sheer utter madness.
A tale of a tortured soul.

Brenda Camacho

Soul-Mate

For my soul-mate, I have waited
for, for years for you too come.
When I gave up that's when you came
unto my life.
And I realized that you were different,
and the one for me.
And when you came unto my life our
hearts were united unto one big heart
that could not be broken.
When you tell me you love me, I
know it's forever.
And when I tell you that I love
you too that's what I mean, that
I will love you 4-ever!
Why? Because you're my soul-mate.
And as time goes on and things
change, but not us you will always
be the one for me.
And that's my Soul-Mate.

Crystal Chronister

Questions For Life

Why is my world so confusing?
Why has everything gone wrong?
Is my life so insignificant to them?
Is there anyone to depend on?

Why are people so judging?
Why are they all so unkind?
It is my color or gender?
Is it my looks or my mind?

Do some people care who they hurt?
Do people realize what they do?
Do they care about what happens?
Or how it affects you?

Is it always so hard to stand?
Is life so full of despair?
Can anyone understand me?
Does anyone even care?

Michelle Meinkoth

"Ignorance"

You're the leading cause
of death in America . . .
you're the disease
transmitted
by belief.
You're a rapist
of virgin minds,
you're the thief
I've locked outside.
You give away
what no one needs
and bury deeper
our only hope of salvation.
You're the drug
they spoon feed children . . .
You're the torment
which drives the genius mind . . .

Chad Lilly

The Web

I watched the spider tat his web
With threads fine as angel hair
The pattern was perfection
Man-made lace could not compare

His intentions never wavered
From the task, as that web grew
Into an intricate creation
Stretched to catch the morning dew

How would a spider's time be passed
Had he not been born to weave
What grace bestowed his dedication
So few beings could conceive

Is it merely spider's nature
Or a task of pre-design
Attention first to capture,
Then one's soul to intertwine

The pattern of our life requires
We trust the creator's hand
Lest we judge with mortal wisdom
What we've yet to understand

Nancy Simmons

Stand Up And Be Strong

When problems overwhelm you
and everything seems wrong,
to be an overcomer,
stand up and be strong.

Your bills may exceed your income,
the support of another you may desire,
whether or not you receive it,
stand up and be strong.

Maybe your children are rebelling,
resisting discipline,
then you feel that you are losing,
stand up and be strong.

Stand up, and be strong,
your battle may or may not be long.
breathe in, breathe out,
stand up and be strong.

If your back is against the wall,
or you're forced to lay on your bed,
Lay down, rest, meditate
Then stand up and be strong

Horace E. Roberts

Life

Behold the Robins are chirping
Bees are buzzing
Tulips are blooming
Creating a nest of harmony

Take no thought for your life
What you should eat, drink, or wear
If the earth takes care of them
Are you not better than they

Consider lilies in a field and . . .
How they grow
They earn no paycheck
If God can sow the grass
Then he can take care of you

Catrice Giles

"Mom"

My Mom is Mom
She is radiant and fair
The thing to avoid
Is the "I mean it" glare.

She's funny and pretty
Inside and out
I'll have you know
She's no one to doubt.

I love her and need her
And as old as I get
I will always honor her
One hundred percent.

No Mom is better
than that mother of mine
No Step Mother or In-law
Could replace in time.

She's gentle but strong
And to me so divine
For the lives that she gave
Are my Brother's and Mine

Sharon Jensen

"Nightmare"

I look around me.
No one.
I see nothing, but darkness.
All around me are trees,
with creaking, outstretched arms,
trying to snatch me away,
I run,
but, I cannot escape.
The darkness is closing in on me . . .

I wake up in a pool of sweat.
I have kicked off all my covers,
in a dazed state,
I realize it was just a dream.

But,
my room is dark,
I am alone again.
I pray for morning to come.

Michael Mattina

Little Child

He sees all those
Who come in the door,
This child who sits
Upon the floor;
This beautiful child
With honest eyes
Is the one who approaches
The child who cries.

When someone hurts him,
Away he will run;
But quickly he's back
To join in the fun.

I love you, little child
With those eyes of blue.
I hope I may teach you,
I do... I do.

Pauline M. Round

Whither The Wind

Oh, the Wind , she is blowin',
Where it comes from I'm not knowin',
I don't even know where it's goin',
I just know it keeps on blowin'.

R. J. Griffin

Old Hunter's Lament

The hunter tunes his rifle
The beginner looks for luck
The hunter has the knowledge
But the beginner gets your buck.

The hunter roams the ridges
Others chase them in a truck
The hunter hunts the deep woods
But the road hunter gets your buck.

The hunter looks around for signs
Hoping to have some luck
Then sits and waits for opening day
While the violator gets your buck.

So sit right in your easy chair
Your expenses you will duck
Walk right into your butcher shop
And save yourself a buck.

Lyle Jensen

Tiny Mouths

In the middle of a
Hot summer night
My baby jolted me out
Of bed with screaming
Red faced open mouthed
Toothless hungry rage.
He sucked a plastic
Bottle dry, watched me
With tiny desperate thanks
And drifted off into
Milky oblivion.
I rocked him gently
Near an open window
Listened to his breaths
Grow soft and short.
In the distance tiny
Voices cried their
Tearless pains.
So many mouths to feed . . .

David R. Scott

Through An Animals Eyes

They watch us hurry
They watch us scurry
Sitting back looking
Curious ad bewildered
What it is
We humans are
For in their world
Money has no part
And looks like the sunrise
Are a glorious work of art
Yet I sometimes wonder
Who should be ruling who
For in their domain they seem to know
The natural order of what to do
Maybe it's time to slow down
And take heed of what's to come
Through an animals eyes
I would like to live
Until my day is done

Patricia A. Nalevanko

Eating Crow

"Fat Santa"? "Fat Santa"?!
I don't have that book!
You want me to search?
Have another look?

I brought that book back
Some weeks ago;
Placed it in the "dumpster",
Just ask me! I know!

Oh, oh! what's this?
A small, skinny book!
Right here on the table.
I'm not off the hook!

I'll have to "eat crow",
Say I'm sorry. Oh, boo!
Find out what I owe,
Oh, what shall I do?

I'll just bite the bullet,
Take the book in today.
Say, "I'm really sorry.
Here's the book. Hip, hooray!"

Joy Manthey Roof

I Wish

There must be more to life;
Than just pain and sorrow.
Sometimes it gets so bad;
I hate to see another tomorrow.
Oh why can't he her me;
And see what I mean.
How I hate to say I don't care
But his drinking I can't bare
My life, it seems I dread;
And wish I were dead.
I love him so much;
And longed for his touch.
Hoping he would always be near;
Never having to shed a tear.
Wishing he would just think;
Before he took that first drink.
On how much sorrow and pain;
He can cause, with nothing to gain.
Oh why won't he just quit;
So our family won't split.

Sheryl Hebert

Cut Bangs

To change my face for a second
to change my life for a day
to change your thoughts forever
the world is salty it brings tears
to the eyes the blue water crashed
upon the small children
who relished in its open warmth
an air mattress serves its purpose
a place to rest my body
people all people love to smile
if only they knew I wish
they were here
"bye-bye" she said
continually as she walked away
the innocence of a child
there are no mosquitos in California
among other things there are
many beautiful boys here and
the go carts went real
but in short I miss Montana

Amber Rose Voegele

America: The Lost

I drew a portrait
a broken picture
The American dream
not what it seems

Out on the plains
where the buffalo roamed
Now there's telephone poles
to each and every home

And to the cities
my how they've flourished
With crime and filth
and children undernourished

I saw our flag
once called "Old Glory"
Waving in the wind
it seemed without worry

But as I grew closer
I saw it ripped and torn
Weeping a tear
for its country adorn

T. Don Thompson

Live Now

When will you be
A friendlier person to me?
Running from place to place
Missing me at every gate.

Live now, for you'll not know
Only the person who loves you so.
Venture out with eyes wide
Ending with serenity deep inside.

Come with me, and you'll soon find
Only the one you left behind.
Love and laugh whenever you can
Don't be afraid, it's all in the plan.

Sara E. Hills

Untitled

Summer is . . .
Blue water in a swimming pool
Ice cream melting on a cone
Lying down in the shade
Hot!!!

Jeffrey P. Gragg

Always

Don't look so sad
I knew him too
I know how you feel
And why you're so blue
I'm sure you've spent many nights
Tossing and Turning
With tears running down your face
Wet and Burning
But we must move on
I know it'll be tough
At least we have our friends
to count on
So it won't be so rough
I know there's a part of him
That wants to be here still
And I know there's a part of him
That always will

Bridget McKinnon

For Those Who Will Give

For those who will give
  Because it is right
    Who struggle through pain
    And cherish the night

For those who will share
  With others in need
    And hold nothing back
    Nor suffer the deed

For those who will laugh
  To light up a heart
    To help show the way
    And make a new star

For those who will love
  And let it be known
    With a love never ending
    To fill up a home

For those who will kneel
  And accept God each day
    A place waits in heaven
    A long time away.

Jim Sheridan

Untitled

The family's all been sick.
They've had a "touch of flu".
I burned the candle at both ends
And now I've got it too.

I tell them I'll be down awhile.
They stare at one another.
They rally 'round to get me well;
"We must take care of Mother".

They shower me with kisses,
(While bouncing on the bed).
"Oh, Mommy, we do love you",
I think that's what they said.

They cover me with blankets,
(Outside it's ninety-three)
Take off their shoes and climb in bed
To keep me company.

And with a great big bear hug,
Cut off my respiration,
And suddenly, I'm well again
In motherly desperation.

Marjorie De Petro

The Artist

A cloak of green and red
Tan and blue
Yes, many a different hue

On his seat of stone
Surrounded by spring grown
With the tools of his craft
Slowly he began the draft

A face pensive, yet peaceful
Eyes that lighted
To something that delighted

Capturing the setting he saw
Perhaps with wonderment and awe
Every stroke of his brush
That of a tender touch

And as I departed
I thanked him full hearted
For what he had imparted.

James F. Flanigan

Little Lives Lost

The candle lights are dim
The air very quiet
You hear the sound of a voice
reciting children's names
The children of the Holocaust
The children whose lives were lost
The innocent victims
Tears begin forming
Rolling down
It breaks your heart
Crushes your insides

No more laughter
No more games
No more anything

Just the stillness
Of death itself
The sounds of silence

Anita Pardue

Ignorance

The prophet sat beneath a tree
And sought life's meaning inwardly.
Upon reflection this said he,
"To suffer is man's destiny."

What manner then of beasts are we
Who view with rapt intensity
And celebrate with perverse glee
Our brother's abject misery?

Unmindful of what is to be,
We're damned by inability
Through clouded eyes to clearly see
The fate ordained for you and me.

R. Michael Luciano

Prejudice

I see prejudice.
It means hate and ignorance.
No caring, no understanding.
Nothing peaceful.

It means hate filled words
And violence.
It is isolation, being shunned,
feeling alone.

Prejudice is a hateful face.
Prejudice is ignorance.
Prejudice is missing out on life.

Katrina Fischer

Memories Of Mother

Memories of you dear mother
Money cannot buy,
Your love reaches higher
Than eagles dare to fly.

Greater than anything
Is the prayer you pray,
For your children everywhere
Each and everyday.

Your smile is brighter
Than the stars that shine,
But I love you mother
Just because you're mine.

Paulette Hayes

Rose

Fragile
Like a dying rose
My spirit is
Falling

I give beauty
And take pain
In return

Cut fresh
The day I saw you
Bleeding
I gave my heart to you

Caressing to touch
A silky rose
Red hair
Resting on your shoulder

Thirsty
For you
Dying
For love

LaDon A. Miller

Winter

Winter that year was cold and gray
The forest cast no sound
Branches clawed towards the sky
Snow blanketed the ground.

The innocence of autumn died
Taking mine along as well
The dying trees sunk to the earth
As the silent fury fell.

Cold icicles clung to my dreams
The pine trees hugged the dirt
Running streams froze solid
As I sat alone with hurt.

I watched the world disappear
Wished I could do the same
Snow angel wings flew far away
As if they never came.

Spring came only to the forest
The purple flowers and the rain
Beauty of a new beginning
But I'd always feel the pain.

Jocelyn Vegter

Watergate Funding

Apegreen eyes watch us from
empty barstools
Furtive eyemoney jades gnash
their candy teeth
somewhere upstairs? Whistles shrill —
The fat flamingoes of somewhere
blow their noses on toadstools
And elsewhere, no one cares much
Why should they? Blood is cheap
Horizons are easily forgotten
As irretrievable as a vanished emotion
We all have our price —
We all have syphillis ideals
God wears a gray flannel dickey —
Santa Claus has cancer
Life goes on

Gregory Hale Orloff

My Life

The world surrounds me
The walls enclosing
I'm living in hell
My brain's exploding
It always hurts
I wonder why
Every situation
Ends up in cries
It's always tough
It's all hard
It seems as if
I'm trying to break steel bars
I always hope
I always pray
For a better side
On each and every day
But my wishes never seem to arose
And never seem to come true
And the world is such a lonely place
I don't know what to do.

Krissy Beiler

Can't Do Without It!

By itself it has no value,
It doesn't mean a thing.
But combine it with some other
And then the good times ring!

Nobody wants it for a gift,
No, that would not be fun.
But nothing makes us happier
Than finding one in our dun!

It can be used another way,
As so many times I've heard,
And, oh, what a sound it makes
When used within a word.

For, without it we'd change history,
And with it double up the poor.
But we just couldn't do without it
'Cause now I've used it even more!

Worthless as it sometime seems
It still must be our hero
That 15th letter of the alphabet
And the meager little zero!

Cheryl Groves

An Angel In My Arms

She sits in silence with her mate
upon a bed of rose covered satin sheets
To wait for him
will be a pleasant feeling
A lonely figure
Like a cherub
She is Heavenly
and so very divine
a Junduesque Figure
With Her thoughts of Him
as they make this new touch feel warmer
He whispers in Her ear
such precious words to speak
as he proclaims her as his Paramour
while they lay
naked
embracing
still and quiet

The Harvester of Sorrow (RH)

Immutable Impression

Perhaps he is sitting there
Listening to a reedy band on radio
Or is it just an empty old chair
Cradling his memory-form with care

Time, too brief to measure
Swept beyond, into the past
Hours of yore to treasure
Wandering along that ancient path

Staring blindly, eternally alone
Framed smile frozen in time
Guarding hearth and heart
Pleading grief be left behind

Mollie Kent

April's Child

December has its Santa Claus
And summer the fourth of July
But pixies smile
On April's child
And paint rainbows in your sky.

The blithe are born at April time
And April's children show
When raindrops dance
While sunbeams prance
You have a special glow

For you are nature's favorite child
You wear her jeweled crown
She grants you wealth
Of charm and health
Your spirits are never down

April's child is a clowning child
With a giving and grateful heart
And those you know
Share your glow
For caring is your art.

Alice L. Barber

Demise Of The Flowers

I am sitting in a field of flowers,
Beautiful crimson flowers.
In the morning smiles crossed my lips,
But day emerged and now
A tear rolls silently down my cheek.
The flowers were once the center
Of my divine attention,
But now I love the sky more —
Both are so lovely.
The sky will always exist,
But for a reason I know not why —
Flowers die.

Sarah Rose Noble

Sky

How far up there do you go,
You who holds up the rainbows,
Where angels with magnificent
wings dance across moonbeams
Where the winged ones fly,
Oblivious to the human eye,
You who creates the rain,
clouds, and snow,
How far up there do you go?

Sarah Hilbig

Child's Eyes

My day is of pleasure
of all living things.
The songs of the birds
the flowers that bloom,
The showers of rain
on a summer's eve
The wind through the trees
the sun and the moon.
For if looking at life
thru love in your heart,
You waken the child
that's locked deep inside,
How wondrous it is,
to see through his eyes.
The pleasure of living
Each day of our lives.

Maria C. Cousino

Lock And Promise

This gift to thee I do entrust,
A simple lock of hair
From one whose love for you is true,
Yet, was not always there

A token symbol of my heart,
For you to claim as thine
In exchange for your true love,
Which I shall claim as mine

A gift from God to one another,
That only we can give
Underscored with love and warmth,
As long as we shall live

This promise I do offer thee,
Guilded letters, set in stone
I'll never leave you for another,
Here to face the world alone

Mark Easley

New Friend

We met one day in April
On pavements damp from rain.
A five-year-old with freckles.
"Hello, my name is Shane."

We shared a special interest
The showers left behind.
A nest of crawling creatures,
The long and wiggly kind.

I made a friend that morning
With only half a try.
Next day we all went fishin'
The worms, the boy, and I.

Madeline L. Keen

No One Understands Me

No one understands but me
No one can ever be

As sad as I have been in the past
Hoping to find happiness at last

No one understands my pain
No success in which to gain

No one understands my state of mind
No one even has the time

To listen to what I have to say
After all, they don't understand anyway

Franzella Malone

Looking Back

Days arrive and quickly go
As time on wings does fly
While I, it seems, stand still
And watch my life pass by.

Often wondering why time crawled
When at a younger age,
It seemed that I would never reach
That free and independent stage.

Suddenly the years were filled
With work and family ties,
Passing by almost unseen
As children grew before my eyes.

Then the golden years crept up
On slippered, shuffling feet
And caught me slightly unaware,
Unprepared for what I'd meet.

Now, looking back with love
On all that life has brought,
I wouldn't change a single thing
Or yearn for what was not.

Patricia Cibula

A Letter From Outer-Space

It's been fifteen hours
and thirteen days since
I've seen your lovely face.
I'm up all night
and I dream all day
I'm a wreck in outer-space.

I never knew
being away from you
contained so much loneliness and pain.
What's a man to do
without a woman like you?
Mere words cannot explain.

I see Venus, Jupiter, and Mars,
but none of them can compare.
I see the sun, the moon, and stars
and Orion over there.

I can't wait to see home-sweet-home
and leave this endless place.
I can't wait to see home-sweet-home
and kiss your lovely face.

Jamie L. Melton

"My Love, My Friend"

My heart is so aching,
as I long for peace.
In searching for my loved one
I find I cannot sleep . . .

I seek God to my comfort,
as each lonely night falls.
His voice says to me,
"I am here child"
as He listens to my call . . .

I pray for strength as He rids
me of my tears.
My faith in Him will heal me
as He banishes my fears . . .

I miss my love, my friend
and I pray as I weep.
As each day begins and the
emptiness leaves,
All the sweet memories, I'll keep —

Patricia M. Singer

Who Are You?

Some love ice cream, some
    pork rib,
Some tell the truth always — with
    never a fib.
Some like to dress, all for show,
Some wear just enough — to go.
It is not important — do we care?
To be ourselves, do we dare
Do we know how to be ourselves
    without veneer?
Or pompous ego, or career?
Ourself is so hidden, we can't
    tell,
How to react — to sing or to yell!
Our shell is thick it covers
    lots,
Ingrained in us since we
    were tiny tots!

Maurine I. Truitt

Mistress Of Mercy

The winds of chaos sweep mine hair
And send mine thoughts a clamour
The mud of the ancients cover
What was and shall be again

Mine soul cries out in agony
As mad Gods tear at the cords
Which bind mine anger and despair
As a tempest in a cage

I have seen much from mine blind eyes
And emptiness fills mine heart
I have seen her face in mine dreams
Mine dear Mistress of Mercy

She holds me in her arms of pain
Her eyes of compassion touch
As if she really does love me
She does not pity mine heart

But in mine mind I comprehend
That her compassion stretches
It goes past her loathing of me
This creature borne to darkness.

Brandon E. L. Adamson

The Secret Of The Rose

Throughout ages gone by
    throughout time and year,
One promise alone
    has stood strong and clear.

It starts as a seed
    poking out of the ground,
Shining its message
    to all those around —

Until one day it blooms
    with overwhelming might
Blinding out sadness
    with the joy of its light.

'Tis beautiful to the eyes
    and sweet to the nose,
This promise lies
    in the Secret of the Rose.

Although hidden at first
    it springs up above,
The Secret of the Rose
    is the Secret of Love.

Melissa Joy Alexander

Beauty of Nature

Trees are beautiful
and when you fly,
high up in the sky,
you see how pretty
trees can be,
just like how
flowers are pretty,
when red, yellow, or blue,
so when I see them
I think, "Cool!"

Douglas Gardner

The Fourth

Happy day America!
The bane of your existence,
The shape that molds your history,
Was born from your resistance.

You pay the price America.
Your liberty's resulted,
In friend to foe and back again.
Adored, ignored, insulted.

So take a breath America.
And stay the course as started.
The cost of freedom's not a choice
When lost of disregarded.

Now take a bow America.
Though perfection is unknowing,
You know you can't please everyone,
That's proof your freedom's showing.

J. K. Snyder

Fear Not

I long to dispel every fear,
Once absent in my infancy,
All acquired as I grew,
Much like hate and bigotry.

So peaceful before foolish pride,
Came to build my walls,
Not hiding me, but blinding me,
And causing me to fall.

Once upon a time, a child,
Love my only constant thought,
Content and brave in mother's arms,
surprised to find as man I'm not.

As man I will be strong again,
If I trust, as a child,
Original just thinking love,
Not fearing all the while.

Fear not, I am finding me,
Way down deep inside,
Under thoughts of selfishness,
and needless fears acquired.

Norman

"Pride"

Why do people look at race?
It's just a color on their face.
Some people want to use a disguise
just so they can hide,
hide from the truth of their culture
It's just mother nature,
so forget the color and look inside.
Why doesn't anybody have any pride?

Sandy Hill

My Prayer

Help me to always remember
The essence of the man
The one I gave birth to
And am proud to call my son.

Help me to always recognize
The contributions he made
To family, friends and colleagues
Through things he did and said.

Help me to always rejoice
Over value in the life he led
For we only had him briefly
But his legacy isn't dead.

Help me to always relinquish
His soul into Gods care
And know that now he is safe
Until I join him there.

Kathryn H. Powell

What Am I?

You cannot see me,
    Though I have many colors.
You cannot hear me,
    Though I have many sounds.
Everyone has me,
    Though I am very different.
Some people love me,
    Though others abuse me.
I am life. I am not long,
    So live me to the fullest.

JoAnn Crisco

Untitled

A skeleton structure
slumbers beside a small pond.
Withered walls are grey from age.
Rusted nails,
barely hold the torn shutters as
they swing limply from a window.
The entrance,
now naked and vulnerable.
The roof is only a patchwork
of scattered boards.
The crippled fireplace
seems to be the cabin's
only life line.
But, punished from time.
The stones are slowly crumbling.

Brenda Miles

If I Could Fly I'd Try

To reach my every dream
To be above the clouds of troubles
in heaven it would seen.

Id only land to help a friend
To cope with their demands
Then I'd soar away up high
Above the trees and lands

I'd have the eye of the eagle
I'd have the cunning of the fox
I'd have the power of the legal
I'd have the world in a box

No wordily cares
No wordily troubles
No more ifs buts or why
If I could only fly

Madelyn Kiser

The Past

The past is the future
that already unfolds
it gives us a clue
of what the future may hold

The past is something
that may tear you apart
it will destroy you
and will rip your heart

The past may have something
that you might have forgot
then you might remember
that you had fought

You might get something
good out of it all
there may only be
a few hurtful falls

The future is coming
the present will go
hopefully you'll live through it
and forget all the lows

Jonathan Bastin

Missing Him

Bring him back?
Wouldn't I though
He was so dear
And I loved him so

Just an uncle you say
Well, not to me
I've missed him so
Since the end that day

All my life he was a dear
Just eleven years older
But he cared for me
More like a brother

The love I took for granted
Over all these years
Leaves me great memories
And a lot of tears

If only I had told him
What was in my heart
I would feel much better
Since we've had to part

Christine Berry

The Unquenchable Fire

"Many waters
cannot quench
Love."
— Song of Songs 8:7

It is
an advancing
Fire,
burning
stronger every second.
The Heat
warms separated hearts,
melts tribulation,
explodes joy.
Inspiration,
like smoke,
lingers
in the Soul.

Stacy Rae Glessner

Once Me — Now Us

It all came fast
too fast maybe
that ominous cloud of love
destroying
eroding
collapsing all preset calculations

Now
there exists
confusion
frustration
responsibility
too large to comprehend or know

My world
once easy
now difficult
once free
now owned
once mine
now ours

Debra J. Henry

"A Stoke Of Love"

When I saw you yesterday,
A feeling came over me, anyway.
Trying to stay away from you,
Made this feeling more and more true!
This feeling for you isn't gone;
A stroke of love was shown.
After all this time past by;
A love for you still, why?
Maybe the times we spent,
Are letting me know where they went.
For days I hid this desire;
Casting your pictures in fire;
Making sure there was no trace;
Of you in my place.
No matter what, I see;
A stroke of love will always be;
In my heart like this,
Because you-are what I miss!

Lou Ethel Wade Bush

You're The One

I wanted someone special
So I asked God in a prayer
To send me the right one
And then you were there.
Your face came to my mind
And your name was there too.
You may think I'm lying
But honestly, it's the truth.
I liked other people
But I started seeing their faults.
I knew I didn't need them
And you were in my thoughts.
I wasn't sure though
So God gave me another reason
Now I'm sure, I know
For what he's showed me in visions.
So if you don't believe me
That's ok too.
I prayed for thee
And "he" may be you.

Shaheen Javaheri

Crutches In The Corner
(Edward's)

Most things that I see
or whatever I do,
still cause me pain;
they remind me of you.

Forty-seven years ago
you stole my heart,
you were always so good,
we were seldom apart.

You loved me and gave
to me all that you had,
including two children
to whom you were dad.

Though always on crutches,
you did all you could,
to run a strong business
and keep us in food.

My lover, my partner,
my husband, my life;
the best years of mine
were just being your wife.

Nettie Gates

My Little Angel Lisa

My little angel Lisa,
so innocent, sweet, and true.
You bring me joy and happiness,
all my whole life through.

My little Lisa's smile,
fills my heart with joy.
Every moment that I spend with you,
I cherish, adore, and enjoy.

My little Lisa's eyes,
always sparkling like the sun.
They enlighten the path of life,
for myself and everyone.

My little Lisa's voice,
so soft, so pure, and new.
If I ever hear your innocent voice cry,
I'll be right there for you.

So my little angel Lisa,
my life, my joy, my pride.
I promise to cherish our love forever,
and keep you always by my side.

Dean M. Di Becelle

The Angel's Song

Spirits rise,
my eyes then close
Can't face the future
Which is death I behold.
Like one has done
My heart has died
Leaving me to wither.
But you will only deny the truth
To protect yourself from pain.
I tried to not subject the ones
I love to such a feeling,
But fate has chosen my path.
I remain in the thoughts of others
Only to believe I belonged.
How long will it be
Till we meet again
As I sing the angel's song?

Kelly Kirk

God's Golden Rule

Live life
    to the "fullest"!

"Embrace it"
    in your own way!

Make the right
    "choices"!

Life is not a game
    to be played!

Learn to live
    by "God's Golden Rule"!

He did not intend
    for us to be fools!

Faye Sizemore

Feet Of Clay

Was it keep me humble
That I was made this way?
So often that I stumble
On fragile feet of clay.

Small sins — often big ones
That seem benign — And so attractive
How foolish have I been!
To choose the less than lovely.

Why don't I chose the beautiful
That feeds the soul within
I should strive daily for perfection
Oh well — Why worry about sin!

The struggle goes on endlessly
Forgive me Lord I pray
Give me strength to choose the best
In spite of feet of clay —

    "Amen"

Ruth A. Nelson

The Lost Sheep

Though I am often in the dark
I know I am not alone.
I am comforted to know
Jesus will come to find me.
I am a lost sheep
Hoping to be found.
My Lord Jesus will come to find me.
I know He will
He is my shepherd
Now and forever
Amen.

Rebecca Moyta

Piano

The keyboard;
Black and white ivory keys
Hands gently come down
A note a chord a piece
Hands flowing back and forth
Cross over —
C F# Bb —
Mozart Beethoven Bach
Harder and harder
Keys Pounding Vibrating
Then —
The soft tinkling of high notes
The Final chord
The hands are gently put in lap.

Lora Taylor

Growing Revelation

It begins
I feel you grow
Slight movements at first
Just barely noticeable
Then harder, quicker more intense
as the days grow shorter
I feel your size
Seems bigger by the day
I talk, sing, laugh, cry, confide
    my deepest thoughts to you
I feel the end is near
I'm saddened by the thought
In my sadness grows a happiness
Though we will no longer be one
We will forever be Mother and Son
It begins again
Talking, singing, laughing, crying
Confiding in each other
Growing to be friends
Learning to love one and the other.

Millie Reedy

Butterfly

Our minds spin silken thoughts
And wrap themselves
Tight within their own
Cocoons.

Layer after layer is spun,
And wound smooth and tight,
So minds are forced to
Shrink.

Year after year the process runs,
Yard after yard of silk is made
From thoughts, experience and
Decay.

Stop the eternal spinning now,
By spoken word unwind
The strands that
Bind.

Each layer laid aside, discarded
Makes the next easier to unwind
Until at last is freed to fly
The butterfly of truth.

Marion E. Griffin

Miss Liberty

Eternal Miss Liberty
Standing over there, holding the flame, magic . . .
looking over the Atlantic
Can you see the May Flower?

Would you bend over
these miserable people
economic migrants or refugees?
Filling hope in soul, they flee

Would you beckon
exhausted migrating birds overseas
gone with the cross-wind
gone with wounds on wings

Gentle Miss Liberty
my light-house when dark
pervading all around me
may you the way to final wharf
a point of entry to humanity
because Eden
was taken away from us
from our dear country.

Phan Tan My

How Long Will You Have Two Opinions?

How long will you have two opinions?
The Lord asked His people one day,
they all stopped and listened intently
then slowly continued on their way.

The two opinions are Him or this world
which one will you choose to obey?
You cannot mix them together
you must choose to follow His way.

Don't let Satan fool you
with all his worldly pleasures and woe,
he's a very dangerous distraction
he's the master deceiver, you know.

So, choose the Rock of Ages
stand on His foundation of love,
if you follow the opinions of this world
you will run when He comes from above.

How long will you have two opinions?
Choose Jesus Christ today!
He's our blessed Savior and Redeemer
He will guide you each step of the way.

Terri L. Hodges

"Thoughts Of You"

  In my life I have had people come and go,
some I loved very so.
  But never have I had someone quite like you,
who makes me feel the way you do.
  You're the girl of my dreams and more,
all I have ever searched for.
  You're not only the one I love with all my heart,
and think about day and night, but a very special friend
  Someone I could talk to and you would always understand,
ready anytime, to lend me a helping hand.
  Inside and out, you're more beautiful than anyone I have
ever met before.
  Just thinking about all you have ever done for me,
makes me love you that much more.
  So with these thoughts of you on my mind,
I decided to write you this poem.
  To reassure you that you're in my heart every second,
of every minute, of every hour, of every day,
and no matter how far apart we are,
that's where you will always stay . . .

Mike L. Oden

Whispering Winds

Gently caressing the woodland trees
  rushing the waves from shore to shore
pure and sweet the smell of pine
  drifts through the night's dark, opened door.

A whispering melody lingering in the stillness
  comforts a stranger who has stopped for the night
by a small stream, he peacefully listens
  to the song of the winds in their flight.

The flowers moving in graceful form
  sway gently to and fro
they feel the wind but fail to see
  the path where the winds would go.

Time flies swiftly all too soon
  winds move to greet the dawn
rising quickly through the shadows
  the whispering winds are gone.

Mona Adams

Polyphonic Polyp

There is a hole in his head
Spilling out infection
Spreading black cloud from his fingertip
Turning reality dissection

He flies to the middle of the room
The room turns into a cartoon
All the walls fall down
Collapsing cranium of a clown

All the faceless children rip off
Their facelessness; showing rage
Characteristic of a sideways floating colossus
Never end sharpening cage

A whore tickles his feet
As he imbibes several germs
He conducts a pogrom
As he masticates with worms

He is inedible and inaudible
He is beckoning me with elegant grace
I bare him my ass cheeks
As he gives me chase

Dylan Lewis

Reflections

I look in the mirror, and see life passing by,
  Then look to the heavens, there are stars in the sky.
Outside my window, snow is softly floating down,
  Everything's quiet, peaceful, not even a sound.

I'm alone, drowning, answers far from complete,
  Help clear my mind, in search for the truth, I seek.
I'm lost, so afraid, but Lord you're at my side,
  Praying for you guidance, there's nothing to hide.

I hear wind, there's sleet, it's cold and angry out there,
  There's trouble in my thoughts, like the wind in the air.
I'm swirling with feelings, like the snow tumbling down,
  Confusion, intrusions, answers must be found.

The sands of my hour glass, slipping out of sight,
  I'll keep reaching for answers, with all of my might.
Descending, not ending, solutions there should be,
  My trust is in Jesus, the right road he will lead.

Suzanne Zietz

Nihilism

We are born and we die.
We occupy ourselves with timing but — run out of time.
We are alone . . . All of us.
But we preoccupy ourselves trying to forget it.
We delude ourselves with other lives and other things.
But, there are none.
We attempt to immortalize ourselves and perpetuate our memory through other.
But time passes and all is forgotten.
For life is brief and impersonal, and our short stay meaningless
  except to ourselves.
Propagation of our memory through our family and our accomplishments
helps ease the pain for us . . .
But, . . . Is otherwise useless!
For life leads to inexorable death, and is too brief to be
  meaningful for most of us.
Religious attempt to confuse us given this dilemma.
And, in the end . . . The comforting are only inept, but parasitic.

Believe in yourself — for that is all there is!!

Martin Wilens

Mama Told Me

I just came to tell you what Easter means to me.
Mama told me it is more that candy, eggs, and glee.
It is about Jesus Christ, as he hung upon the tree;
About God's greatest gift, to folks like you and me.

It seems too sad to think about how they speared Him in the side.
How He carried that old cross, how Jesus bled and died.
But Mama told me something else, about how He still lives,
How He arose on Easter day that God's word might be fulfilled.

And one day I will come again to tell you what I know,
But right now I came to tell you, cause Mama told me so.

Cathy E. Wright

The Tides Of Life

Where did my zest for living go?
I seem to have lost the magic glow
The past is not too far away
When I could hardly wait for the coming day
I had places to go and things to do
And when friends dropped in
A pot of tea I'd brew
A plume from a jet across the sky
And the music of Chopin could make me cry
The sounds of nature, a joyous hymn
And the love of true friends
Filled my cup to the brim
Now the days and nights are oh so long
And in my heart there is no song
Where did my zest for living go?
Was it lost in life's tides
that ebb and flow?

Gladys Cymric Strong

Because I Love You

Let's walk together, grow as friends,
Make sure our friendship never ends.
Together we'll become more than you'll never imagine.
If we believe in love, we can make it happen.

You are my wisdom, my power, my glow.
I'm always with you wherever you go.
You are my ocean, my river, my sea;
I belong to you and you belong to me.

As time goes on and the love then shines,
We'll become one soul and become one mind.
I can't say anything more. I can only show you it's true:
I need you in my life . . . because I love you.

Keshia Tyson

Reality?

So many things, they come and go.
Money can buy happiness but only for a short time.
Nothing comes for free; it all has its price.
Do fame and fortune really work together?

Life hangs within a delicate balance.
Hearts are fragile, more so than glass.
One wrong move and down you fall.
Luck is a lady; or is "she" a man?

Truth is merely perception of the facts.
Pictures like memories fade over time.
Does contrast have to be the difference between black an white?
The harder you think or look, the less you see or know.

Step inside your mind and you'll get lost.
There really is no way out.
It's no different than a haunted house.
You're stuck, and all you can do is scream.

James Collins

Celebration Of Life

Now i tell time on a watch with no hands.
My calendars have no dates upon their face.
For, in this life, our short lifetimes
Are but a grain of sand in the hourglass of eternal time.
And so, upon this day,
   With each sweet breath
   of life-renewing air,
I celebrate my passage
Through this mortal plane of existence.

Roy Sims

The Land On The Edge Of Nowhere

Through the blackberry brambles and the trumpet vine's lair,
By a small patch of toadstools,
You'll find the stair.

With firefly lanterns, the pixies, they'll lead,
Through caverns of diamonds
And rubies that bleed.

To a land of enchantment where spring never ends,
Unicorns run free,
And all time begins.

I've been there, you know.
I've found the stair,
That leads to the land on the edge of nowhere.

Elizabeth Medlin

One Mother's Thoughts

When you were growing inside of me
I gave you breath
I nourished you
I thought for you
I gave you life.

Through the years I watched that life grow.
Now that life belongs to you.
I can no longer breath for you, feed you, think for you,
and most important, live for you.
You now have the choice to live as you choose.
To take each day as it comes, and live life to the fullest.
Just keep in mind that I will always be there for you,
and always love you.
What a beautiful gift God has given us . . . Life.

Mary Aponick

Praises To The Lord

I am washed and now am clean,
Praise to God, our Lord and King!
Gracious, goodness, God most high,
Tremendous security for all who die!
Lord most high, our hearts You know,
Help each one in knowledge to grow!
Let us shed our burdensome pasts,
Lead us now to greener paths!
Rejoicing always before the Lord,
Our shepherd, our leader, our two edge sword!
Sing praises now and rejoice!

You are with us as we trod,
Even unto unfriendly sod!
And so with a joyful shout we go forth,
Onward and upward with a full report!
Prayers of incense you inhale,
Sweeter to you than songs of nightingale!
Lord God of strength, you make me bold,
And for you I'll do all I'm told!
Sing praises now and rejoice!

Paula Jo Welter

"Memories"

Silence and solitude befall me.
I sit surrounded by endless quiet, motionless silence.

Memories capture my mind.
They are the strongest image my mind recalls.
Like a key to a lock, they unleash my past, my dreams, my thoughts,
my fondest memories, my hurts and pains.
Isn't it strange? Memories never change.
They reoccur and linger time after time, but are always the same.

The sweetest memories never lose their savor, and yet the most
haunting memories never release themselves from that one moment
of anger, horror, regret, and pain.

It seems that the memory keeps that special moment alive.
It is as if you feel all the emotions over again every time you step
into the silence and solitude of remembrance.

Time propels itself, allowing it to be master of human fate.
Everything human is subject to change by this very unhuman vandal.
Would we have memories without time?
For if time stood still, we would have no memory. Nothing to cherish.
Nothing to regret.
Time, yet a vandal, stealing from the human race, leaves also
something to envision.

So, is it better to live a timeless life? Or a changing life with
memories to recapture, to sink into, to be surrounded by not only
the past, but the past with the future changing before our very eyes?
Engulfed in time.

Tobye Cox-Kernan

Just Me

Of all the places in the world
I'd rather be at Home
I can sleep as long as I want to
And talk as I wish on the Phone.

My Career was working in Nursing
And I loved every minute of it
But after forty years of work
I felt I'd better quit.

Now I can do whatever I wish
Don't worry about punching a clock
And when I get tired of working in my yard,
I can sit on the porch and rock.

It's so nice to chat with my neighbors
And drive to visit a friend
But when Sunday comes, I go to church
Where I find God and peace within.

Helen E. Vaughn

Kaleidoscope

I feel like I am in a kaleidoscope
With broken colors all around
These colors are my life, dreams, and happiness
They have all broken down to colors
My dreams are no longer shapes, only colors
What happened to all of the love I once felt
Only colors are left
My imagination is gone and in its place are colors
No rainbows or flowers
No blue skies or oceans
Just fragments of color left to lie in my soul
And rot away, leaving nothing behind
When the colors are gone there will be nothing
All of my dreams, my love, and my happiness will be gone
I hold onto these colors with all of my strength
Hoping that someday these colors will form pictures
And my love, my dreams, my happiness, and my life will return.

Amanda M. Schandler

When Can I Die?

Along the shores of the shinning sea,
The sands are wet with hopes and dreams.
We once played here, now we live a million miles away.
And the shores along the giant sea,
Are as dry as your throat on a hot summers day.
For we have forgotten all that is important,
It makes us live, breathe, and makes our hearts beat.
So now I am trying, striving to fight my way back,
To the sands wet with hopes and dreams.
And I know kids are still playing here,
But in my mind I see them walking away,
Starting that million mile journey.
But they should follow their dreams.
Whatever you might lose,
You know that you will always gain something.
You will have self-peace forever.
It will be unforgettable when you achieve this state.
When you do and have something you have strived for.
My feet are wet and sandy, my heart is filled with joy.
For now I can Die!

Niki Nelson

My Dear Guardian Angels

Messengers from God, my dear guardian Angels
who protect me, guide me, and show me the way
Sometimes I am alone, get lost or go astray,
oh dear guardian Angels help me find my way this day.

I feel so lost, so alone and so very sad
Why do I feel this way? I know that I'm not bad.
Please dear Angels, hurry and rush to my side,
I promise, by your directions I will abide.

Help me to forget my long, hurting past,
take the memories and pain from me finally at long last.
Please spread your loving, golden wings around me,
touch me with your loving hands; forgive and set me free.

My dear blessed Angels in the heaven above,
won't you please show me again how to love.
I just can't remember how love feels anymore,
the feelings are stuffed, I hurt to the core.

Protect and help and look after me,
show me how to be the person God wants me to be.
Let me be happy, fill my life with joy and good health,
if I have that, I will have an abundance of wealth.

Virginia M. Smith

"Why Suicide Dad?"

You were young and healthy at age forty-nine
You made it your destiny to be your time
I can't understand and I guess I never will
Why you ended your life leaving my heart frozen still
It's been fifteen years and Mom is still alone
There's not a man that can fill your clone
You left me very sad
For I have no one that I can call Dad
I want to know why why why!
So be prepared to answer me when we bond again in the heavenly sky . . .

Linda Aiello

A Whole New World

When I close my eyes I see a whole new world,
The rain cries for happiness instead of pain.
The thunder pounds for excitement instead of anger.
The winds scream for fun and not for horror.
Fires burn for warmth but not to harm.
When I open my eyes, it all crumbles away,
And it's back to the old way.

Erin McAvoy

To Pace The Pace Of The Pacemaker

If a man is not keep'n with the pace of his companions,
Maybe it is because he is too fast. Possibly, too slow, or even
Because he is, and just can not see it, maybe it's someone in
Front of him who is not keep'n the pace, what if it was
Someone pull'n or push'n him to the front or back? Whatever
It is the pace is not the same. Do you think the questions
Ponder'n in his mind keep him off this pace, or is it the
Answers he knows, possibly the ones that he knows not of, or
The ones he does not want to know. Is it the emotions he
Shows and feels or the ones that terrified him,
What if it is who or what he sees or maybe who or what he
Does not see, is it the people in his life, the people lost in his
Life, or the people that have lost him, Is it the anger in his
Life or the anger in others, or could it be the happiness that
Overcomes him, or maybe the happiness he sees overcome'n
Everyone but him, or maybe it's the happiness he finds help'n
Others or maybe he is not keep'n the pace because he just
Wants to be himself — to be recognized as himself, his
Own person and not everyone else, or maybe he has walk'd
His companion's pace and did not like it.

Shawn A. Capehart

I Really Am

I am alive with every breath I take.
Each bite of food taken and chewed,
says my internal fuel is being renewed.
The moon and the sun and true blue skies
throughout the year are seen with my eyes.
I hear the music playing rhythm and blues.
Who said that songs don't dance in my head
as I rest at night safe in my bed.
If I shed a tear when I bite my tongue,
there was pain, for inside I am not numb.
Summers warm sun feels good on my face
and winters chilled breeze makes my knees shake.
Sea salt air smells the same.
Salt on popcorn and a chocolate shake taste great.
Sometimes, just once without any heartache,
as kids my age, I wish I could run and play.
My age will change in body, heart and soul
and I pray to the Lord, as I get older.
Others will see past my wheelchair and not stare
and see inside me, to whom, I really am.

Dale R. Patchen

The Red Path

I look to the east
the red morning star I behold
it is to her I beseech
for knowledge gained to be retold

I seek towards the north
white cleansing snow so pure
I ask of him to bring forth
patience so I may endure

I turn my soul to the west
black of night calling to spirit
I pray to the thunder beings so blest
to give the word that I may hear it

My heart wanders far to the southland
yellow sun rays bringing growth to me
sacred hoop of life radiance so grand
I become a leaf of the white sacred tree

Above me blue is father sky
below me green is mother earth
our disrespectfullness brings me to cry
I walk the red path to my rebirth

James F. Green

Forever Friend

They're fun, lovable, and heartwarming
You can call them your "Forever Friend"
Tell them anything, they'll keep it a secret
they're true right to the end

Furry to the touch, so cuddly
They'll nuzzle you when you're sad
An occasional lick across the cheek
They'll comfort you when your day's been bad

No, I'm not talking about a person
it's a dog I'm relating to
but in a sense they are human
. . . In a sense they're a part of you

A part which cannot be broken
without breaking the heart
a piece of you forever
from the beginning . . . from the start

So cherish your "Forever Friend"
whatever animal it may be
and keep them in your heart forever
they're irreplaceable, just ask me . . .

Tara R. Harrington

September Soliloquy

Golden hillsides,
   shimmering,
      interspersed with shades of green,

A splash of orange,
   a touch of red,
      white clouds in blue skies overhead,

Leaves release,
   fluttering down,
      layering a carpet to cover the ground.

A nodding forest,
   getting ready for bed,
      soon to be fast asleep,

Cozy and warm,
   under
      a feathery, frosty white quilt.

Joan Rickey

The Color Of Money

Rich and famous, that's the American dream.
Work your way to the top of the corporate ladder.
Honesty is not the best policy, in this world you
   have to scheme.
The best man doesn't always win, it's whoever's
   bigger and badder.
Ethics and values don't matter, who cares if the
   money is clean.

White men aren't always rich and rich men aren't
   always white.
The color of the skin, who cares. As long as I make
   a profit, right?
Own a company and divide it into shares.
Money is green, not black or white.

Don't be offended you know what I mean.
How much will it take to bring me to the top?
Ten grand, four million, I don't care as long as I'm seen.
When I run out of money I'll stop.
Just like jealousy and greed, the color of money is green.

Nicholl Erin Massa

"From Your Future"

I am a being of the Christ vibration
One of the new generation

I am from another world, a being of love sent to you from above.

Wipe the tears and sorrow from your face.
Banish greed and hatred from the human race.

Let me light your way
And bring earth into its new birth today.

I was born on earth to bring light from afar
to help in making earth a star.

I am from your future to help you on this day.
Let us gather together and pray.

I will raise your vibration to love and light,
Hold my hand so I can awaken you from the night.

Heaven on Earth is where you'll be.
Then and only then will you be free.
Come into the future with me.

Mary Collins

Bad Memories

I try to forget but, the memories still come back.
They are crystal clear.
Those horrible images.
I try to forget them but, they still come back!
I can't help it!
I was too young to understand!
But just old enough to remember!
Why me? Why?
I scream to the world. Does anybody understand?
I know there are others but, why me?
Why Me?????
I shiver in the darkness thinking these thoughts.
They are my thoughts, dark, secret, and hiding.
But these aren't totally mine.
They were burned into my memory.
Like a hot brand on a hooved animal.
I wish they would go away.
If only I could seal them in a jar and toss it into outer space.
I would! Only if I could.
Oh, how I wish.

Rebekka Fort

Dream Destiny

The illusion of time seems endless.
Deep sleep of thoughts, imaginary, yet, real.
You were always there, faceless, but true.

The first kiss, a timeless déjà vu. It happened before, not so real.
In my mind, a dream, relentless appeal.

Emotion abound, uncanny summons.
Like summer rain, reminisced.
The strength of a gentle kiss, cherished.

It was meant to be, you and I.
Before it happened, it always would.
A true love with passion, understood.

A doubtless fate, destiny.
Promised dreams, with simple reason.
A love from the heart, deep and true.

Hidden reasons, with few answers. You and I, simple and good.
Dreams act together, one enduring vision.

Imagination endless, infinite fate.
Savor images, within your reach.
Sustain thought, inspire, dream destiny.

Eric T. Aragon

To Papoo

Another birthday my Papoo
I wish I could celebrate with you.
But even though I'm far away,
My thoughts are with you-especially today.

On your day I want you to know
You're loved and honored and cherished so
You've been so kind and dear to me
More than any grandfather's expected to be!

And as I grow, I see more each day
The favors and splendor you've sent my way.
Thanks to you- I've had so much.
I will always treasure your special touch.

Arizona State and Europe too
Have been possible thanks to you!
I want you know though I forget to say
You are the greatest in every way!

Rena Pitchess

Sin

Pain of life spinning its existence
Daily pushing its evil head in and out of time
pressure of decisions make the mind turn over and over
like the wind blowing chimes . . .
I, as the self — willed one
God, as the absolute form of right and wrong
pushes my thoughts to another time
When joy and peace surrounded me —
God, my creator pleased with me then as I
knew no self, only knowing what and how
Now as time moves forward, every path leading to a wrong one
Sin rears its ugly head saying move on, move on . . .
I, as a child of sin not only try to battle
this arrogance of a kind
But have lost many times
as there is only one who can fight this war within and win
Will I ever conquer? Has not Jesus felt this way before?
Time passing on and on . . . Moving slower now
The memory of that joy slowly fading away
Time will only tell what may . . .

Tonya J. Caliendo

Bruised Soul

I've skipped down trails descending through
   forest to river bed,
I've run down paths of sand to waves of ocean,
I've danced down passageways to empty halls,
I've walked down aisles to rocky knolls . . .

But I've never fallen
   and bruised my soul,
   until I hurt you.

Robin Hardin Baldwin

Pure Rain

Through the night I sit and listen to the rain falling down.
And it's beating softly on my face,
so softly that I'm weeping.
Weeping at the pureness of the rain as it intertwines with my tears.
Yes, I taste the sour saltyness of my tears as they glide into my
mouth and drop out of my eyes once more.
And the sadness departs my soul, carried by the tears . . .
I soak up contentment through the pure translucent rain.
And when I open my eyes tiny glimmers are webbed along my eyelashes
and they sparkle with pureness when I blink.

Whitney Brown

267

"A Virtuous Woman"

Mama as a child you were taught
that Old-Fashioned way to behave;
And as an adult you trained your children
through prayer and wisdom that old fashioned way to obey.
. . . You're the Mother all children would love to have
From the sparkle of your smile,
to the beauty of your laugh,
I write to tell you I love you,
And in my heart I know you'd
respond with "I Love You Too"
It's your smile I'll long to see
For it shows how Jesus can give
Perfect Peace,
You've walked in faith always
knowing, that when Jesus called
where you were going, and Mama,
"Many daughters have done virtuously
but thou excellest them all." (Prov. 31:29)
And that's why you've been called.

Adrian Allen

Invisible Fantasy

I see you.
Hard body glistening in the sun
Like a stature.
Seat lingering with oil, merging
As it drips down over your stomach.
Hot Sun.
You can't see me,
Hiding behind the invisible wall
We all put up.
But I'm there.
Watching
Sweet juice dripping as I stare,
Aching hard.
My breasts heave as I take in air, sweet breath
As my invisible hand touches you.
You feel me, but I'm not there.
Eyes closed.
Head reared back in ecstasy.
Sweet pleasure come as
Two become one in fantasy.

F. Kay Shoemaker

"Life's Ups And Downs"

I know when I'm up and I know
when I'm down, but unless I have a map,
I just can't seem to get around.

I know north, south, east and west,
If I have a compass pinned to my vest.
When God gave out a sense of direction,
I came up just short of perfection.

Whenever I deter from the beaten path —
I get lost, and the directions
I wrote, are more difficult than math.

You go 2 miles north, then west
on route 73, Go 1 mile east, and
by that time, you've lost me.

What I need are landmarks that
are easy to see — like the
Texaco station by the Busy Bee.

Life is full of ups and downs,
and all my friends know — I
will never find my way out of town.

Barbara Arnett

Shadow

The face I see is not reality.
It is a dream of space and time.
Of someone, somewhere
Who once was, but is now no longer.
The face I see is but a dream
Forever calling my name.
I turn to look, but he is gone
Disappearing in the shadows.
I know who you are
The game you play — you can't hide from me
Laughter and cries of pain
Echo in the darkness
Turning the hot night bitter cold.
No use in running
He is there
Following my every footsteps.
Protector —
Angel —
Shadow —
Looming over me.

Lesley M. Anderson

Love's Wake

Love is beyond,
the simplest of winds,
into the hearts of shattered minds,
and into the hearts of the wicked,
lay foundering of fates,
and the dismal of wishes,
for each to their own,
we lay all alone,
and only simple fate can divide us,
into this great truth,
like a frightened mind with too much knowledge,
we find what we want,
and know naught what it is,
for if we have enslaved ourselves,
it is our heart that we wish . . .,
wishing upon a star,
how ironic a trick,
to understand my own feelings,
and not know the brick.

John Blackham

Life's Journey

A young couple knelt at God's altar to pray
for His love and His guidance to light their way!
With the exuberance of youth and a love of life
They exchanged the vows to become man and wife.

And traveled life's highway for the next 50 years
Sharing its pleasures, its joys and its tears.
They were blessed with the love of three beautiful girls
A treasure more precious than diamonds or pearls.

Five grandchildren followed; the family had grown.
Then three great-grandchildren as time marched on
"The years pass so swiftly", they were heard to say
Time does take its toll and youth fades away.

The same couple knelt at God's altar today
To pray His love and guidance would still light their way,
And repeat their vows; sharing a bond that had grown
As they continue their journey into the unknown
Lost in the past are all struggles and sorrows
As they walk hand in hand through all new tomorrows.

Beth Suerdieck

Twice The Love

They came in the month of love
one early one late

Looking around with raised voices
at their new world

Oh what joy they bring.
These two who came in the
month of love

Soon they were clawing, walking
and finally running

They spoke, but a language of their own.
A sound at first strange to us

The more love they received the
more they gave

Oh, how they've grown it's now
let me do it. Oh I can do it

Yes. These two born in the month
of love will soon turn three

Oh what joy twins can be
specially these two born in
The month of love

Charles Piecukonis

A Mothers Dream

I carried you for nine months. I felt you kick and some
times you made me sick. Then you were born so perfect so pure
a angel from heaven that's what you were.

   Before I knew it you were toddling around scattering all
my pots and pans.

   Then one day a mother's dream had been taken away. I saw
you on weekends this was not the same.

   Where did the time go. Look how big you have grown. Now
that you are old enough to make up your own mind won't you please
come back home.

   I have a mother's dream all of my own.

Kelli Medlin

Night Vision

I have a vision, of things in the night
To know what is wrong, to do what is right
I have a vision of peace on the land
The love in my life, patterns on the sand

I sigh and dream, of life by the sea
Of people who care and understand me
I dream of the future both present and past
Sweet song of night, dreams deep repast

Fog slowly enchants the scenes harmony
As shadows recede and fly far from me
In a breath, visions shelter the dawn
I become aware and time carries on.

Gail Mann

Dark Love

Night Covers — night loves the one with no lovers
Hide in its shadow, clothe yourself in the color
   Black is wonderful
I crawl in my space, surrounded by my keeper
Held by the mist. I breathe in and take it all away
   Heavy sleep shuts my eyes
   Dream again, Soul is lost
I awake — night fills me
   I am held

Maria Katsos

My Sister

The couple sat there grumbling irate because they had to wait
The old man became obnoxious shouting "The doctor is always late!"
I looked around not knowing why anyone was there
I just knew why I was waiting next to that empty chair
I decided I would fill his time with a different point of view
I wanted my words to make him think since he had nothing better to do
I told him of my sister she's very beautiful young and dear
I told him if I was waiting it meant that I still had her near
I told him of her strength and courage and how she taught me to cope
I told him that while I waited I could never give up hope
I told him time was nothing in comparison to a life
I asked what is a few extra minutes if you are waiting with your wife
I told him that a day might come when to wait he'd have no need
Then I talked more of my sister I knew I'd planted a precious seed
I heard the woman's name called their wait to be no more
I watched the old man touch the empty chair then his eyes followed her to the door
He looked at me with misty eyes thanked me and bowed his head
Please, tell me more about your sister the old man quietly said

Kiki Sellers

Through Someone Else's Eyes

Most wouldn't give him a second glance
Unless they thought their wallets were in danger.
But it's amazing what you can see
When you look into the eyes of a stranger.

We didn't say a word to each other
But the pain in his eyes I will never forget.
I gave my sympathy and understanding
To this man I had never met.

He opened the door and got out of his car
Walked past me and into a store.
I finally figured out why he was sad
When he poured his forty on the floor.

For those who aren't familiar with Thug Life
And the traditions that coincide
You tip your forty to the memory
Of someone who recently died.

For a second I felt I had known his friend
Because I also wanted to shed tears.
I somehow caught a glimpse of him
That I'd carry around for years.

Lily K. Gonzales

Think Of Me At Christmas Dear

Think of me at Christmas dear
Think of me without a tear
For tis a season to be jolly
With Christmas trees and bright green holly

Think of me and never fear
For I'll be thinking of you my dear
And of the carols sweet and low
And the soft white flakes of new fallen snow

Of the times that we have had
The times we've shared both good and bad
Of you and all the people at home
And of the time soon when I'll no longer be alone

Yes think of me at Christmas dear
Think of me without a tear
For I've been thinking for half this year
Of you, whom I hold so close and dear

And as you hear the silver bells toll
And the spirit of this season enters your soul
Think of me at Christmas dear
Think of me without a tear.

David Williams

Sunbeam

You held my hand, softly, strongly and
searched my eyes, with such love, such
immense healing tenderness; you had a
vision of light, brilliant light, white
showing through the leaves. Zoom. Light.
Onto a grassy meadow with thin branches
and trunks reaching into the brilliance —
a painting done by your beloved in your
mind's eye. You are tired now, but your
beloved has seen the light, the sun,
setting, shining through the trees onto a
lake, while small ones scamper at his
feet; it has given him strength; it will
give you strength; your mind's eye grasps
and beholds and shares the strength
gained by your beloved's seeing. His
seeing has become your vision. Go to
sleep, now, my sweet; don't be restless,
be still, for soon you will be in your
beloved's arms, my sweet sunbeam.

Alan Heuer

Reflections On Wars —
After Watching The Video In Our Hands

A ripple, a wave, a scream
The cadence of the life force grinds, slows, dips.
Entropy flares and feeds on the death
throes of living organisms.
Yet the old men of power harden, harden,
trading flesh for slogans, bones for money.

The orthodox creed of one is steel,
which tears the flesh, cracks the bones,
against the orthodox creed of the next.
Our Right is Right! Our Right is Right!
Harden so the truth, any glimmers of
hope, can be ignored.

Not ignored the old men say,
The Truth reveals that our right is right.
Yet the screaming, dying, lives, sentient or not,
how arrogant to think we know what is sentient,
say, demand, clamor for an answer to the question
What eviscerating right can be right?

Philip A. Wentz

Recognize It Or Not

Did you know I like you
every time I pass you in the
hall I say to myself
stop go back tell him how
you feel but I'm nervous.
I'm scared of you saying
No and I'll never be
able to face your face again
All I want in this world
is for you to know I
exist to hold me tight
and be there when I need you
I always wanted to
know why you never
said Hi to me or looked at me is it
my hair, my face am I too short too tall
are my friends a pest.
If those are the reasons then forget you
Your heart is not in the right place
Your heart has to match up to mine

Annie Rassi

Downcast Of My Shadow

The sun sets on another day.
I lay my weary head upon my pillow.
My thoughts drift towards a starry night
concealed within my sedated mind.

Soar for that distant star I whisper.
The one that gives me endless hope.
I need to feel its glow against my face.
Warm me, entice me, show me to a glorious new life.

I feel free, I am free, no more chains of unrest.
I've left my sullen world, the world that has dismantled my soul.
No one of that world wants my emotions, no one cares.
But up here I feel a rebirth, my life is virtuous.

So let those who never wanted to know me
stare forever at my empty pillow.
Let them think of what might have been.
And when that glimmering star warms my face.
Let my shadow cover the earth.

David Winters

What A Father Is To Me

The Bible says, "Call no man Father, except he that is in Heaven"
However, I only have one earthly Father and that is you.
I've called you Dad, Daddy, and Pop but most of all you
were the one who picked me out of all the others. Oh, how
lucky I was at that time you met Mom. I must have been the
happiest child in the world that day.
I'm sure sometimes I brought joy and sometimes heartache
but you always gave me nothing but love.
You built me up when I was down and kissed me when I was hurt.
You let me know when I was wrong by the touching of your
hand and when I did right you gave me a hug.
What more can a daughter be thankful for, than a Father
like you and a Mother like Mom?
Your Loving Daughter,
 Barbara

Barbara Story

Mother

They watched as she walked by,
Head high, a half-smile, a special light in her eyes.
Who is this person, this care-giver, this teacher?
Who is this jill of all trades, this woman?
She is the mother of my children.

Bob Delp

Winter Without You

It's here
It's that day again
I feel it under my skin, in my bones
Wind whispering, blowing (not breezy), chilling
Sun's muted rays reaching, but not quite
Trees swaying, boughs bending — stretching, leaves falling
Sitting outside, in the midst of it all, staring at the sky
Closing my eyes, breathing deeply
Soaking it up
It becomes a part of me.

Death is here now
Soothing, calming, torturing me —
Life will be coming later
On a plane from Kentucky.
Tears have become my companions
Silence, my bedfellow
As time marches on without prejudice
And with pain.

Jennifer Levine

The Golden Years

I love to gaze upon the old — 'tis a holy sight to see,
For soon these souls I gaze upon now will be in Eternity.
Face to face they'll see their God — the marks of age all past.
An everlasting peace will come and a youth that will always last.

Their silver crowns and their wrinkled brow will far outshine the sun.
Their weary bones and their aches and pains will count as victories won.
Their trials and their sadness borne will soon turn into bliss.
Oh, ne'er again will I gaze upon such a holy sight as this.

As closer to their goal they come they seem to have no fears.
This must be the reason why they call these "The Golden Years."
In spite of all the grief they bear, the souls are full of peace.
For each day brings them closer to a joy that ne'er will cease.

In just a year or just an hour they'll be with us no more.
Saints of God will be their lot, their exile shall be o'er.
Dear holy souls, remember us as you stand before your God.
And pray He'll make saints of us too before we're 'neath the sod.

Blessed be those who Love the old, who help them in their need.
For God who lives within the old is marking each kind deed.
He's giving them a message clear, the words are but a few.
"Do unto others as you would have them do unto you."

Sylvan E. Hubrig

The Good Fight

I think of innocence wasted on boys too immature to see a future.
And then I think of you. And I fight off my regrets.
Amazement washes over me as I think of how little you expected of me.
And then amazement over how it took me so long to realize this.

So I close my eyes and remember — I envision our past together.
I see hurried moments in the backs of dark movie theaters.
I see giggly phone calls of unconscious talking.
I see endless evenings of unadulterated fun.
I see smiles shared and laughter caressed.
I see my summer love. Our summer love.

But soon — the months run out
And I am left with blinks of ugly moments between separated spirits.
And no longer can I see the point of it all.

And I think of you today, in a dorm room far away . . .
And wonder if you ever think of me. As if I was fifteen again.

But I know that I am not.
I know that years have passed and the seasons have changed us.
We have grown up and out of our old lives.
And I fight off my regrets.

Jennifer Elizabeth Moyle

The Old Woman

She sits there by the window, looking out
Hoping that someone will come today, after all
Hasn't she always been a good mother?
Outside the rain has begun to fall and
The flowers smell sweetly with the sound
Of a bird chirping in the tree, life has
Been good to me, she thought but I wish
That it wouldn't take so long to die
She rested her head back on the pillow and
Thought of her good life
We should delight in where we come from
She thought, and wonder where else life
Will take us
She smiled and turned her head to the window
Then passed away sweetly
As the bird flew away

Janet Bruders

Foggy Night

As the fog rolls across the land
　hiding all the things built by man.
Its path is one of no distinction
　but its abundance creates a many restriction.
As your eyes strain to see into the distance
　the fog maintains its resistance.
Growing thicker by the minute
　we begin to feel a prisoner within it.
Hoping to see it clear away
　we fall to our knees and begin to pray.
Suddenly! As if magic were near
　the fog begins to disappear.
Fearful no more and able to see
　we come to our feet and shout with glee.
The ground left covered in a blanket of dew
　we walk away feeling not sad nor blue.

James Craig Beasley

Hand-Me-Down World

In a hand-me-down world, in hand-me-down places
Nothing is new, no matter what races
For we hand down our water, our air, and our dirt
We hand down our trees like we'd hand down a shirt
And with each generation, each decade, each year
The world gets dirtier, as if nobody cares
If we cut down pollution, cure sickness, stop crime
We can patch up our earth in plenty of time
So don't waste what you have, for we don't have a lot
Take care of our home, it's all that we've got
Don't wear out the planet 'cause planets aren't cheap
Don't stretch out the world 'cause it's not ours to keep
In a world full of bruises and Band-Aids and scars
Remember the limits and don't go too far
Don't add to the damage, just help fix the holes
Since the world gets brighter with each little rose
And when our hearts are too big and the world too small
We move on to Heaven where one size fits all.

Rebecca Smyka

Dusty Photographs

The smell of the sea after a rainstorm hangs in the air,
As raspberries and goldfish dance to a silent song.

Withered roses and wrinkled suits adorn old memories,
And ancient newspapers blow quietly down a deserted street.

Dusty tables and cracked rocking chairs hum aimlessly
At an empty picture frame that embellishes a blank wall.

Unshed tears and unspoken words run from the sunlight,
As modeling clay and building blocks scatter on the tile.

China plates and curly-haired dolls are covered with dust,
And lazy summer afternoons drift toward lonely winter mornings.

Brook Ridge

Untitled

An artist's pallet once clean and pure
Dabs begin to obscure
Colors run and combine
Become confused by design

So we share this mix of time
Lives like oils do combine
What starts out as clear runs somehow
Dark and light together now

The point, you see, is not the between
Only the masterpiece when the brushes are clean

Patrick Hendron

Depression

Locked into the world of musty life,
Seeking escape through vacuumed air.
Depression of reason, sense of despair.
A perfect closet of hanging wishes,
Suits and shirts torn, slacks beyond repair.
Clogged veins of existence,
Eyes that are filmed by drowning desire.
Forgotten happiness and soggy dreams
Drenched with the bucket of liquid fire.

Cliff C. Thompson

Love

Love is peaceful; love is kind
A definition that cannot be defined
But a feeling that comes from deep with-in
That you can never ever successfully hold in

And when this feeling comes to the heart
Treat yourself and do not let it part
And if this feeling should go away
Wait, and it will come again some day

Danielle R. DeLancey

Farewell

To all my friends at (company name) I bid a fond farewell.
Some of you I'm just getting to know and others I know quite well.
All of you I will miss, some of you more than others, you're all
like a Great Big Family, I've got a lot of sisters and brothers.

You were there when I needed support or just needed someone
to talk to; you were there when I was happy and some of you held
onto me when I was blue. We laughed and cried together, we shared
tragedies and dreams; we have a lot in common, or so it often seemed.

Some of us are small but loud, others are shy and strong, but you
all had one thing in common, you made me feel like I really belonged.

Friendships come and friendships go, but I hope you'll all keep
in touch, because I haven't got a lot of friends, but the ones I have
I Love Very Much!!!! Thank you for making me feel needed and loved.

Tami Louise Stork

My Heavy Heart

One night my heart was very heavy,
With a burden not so light
My Soul was all so weary,
There was no rest for me that night

It was too heavy for me to sustain,
Every thought was too much to bear
Down on my knees I went, crying in pain,
Trying to find refuge in the One who does care

Oh! How I do remember,
His Love of Grace so divine
When Jesus heard my pleading,
And comforted this weary Soul of mine

My lips were filled with songs and praises,
Sung to Him who Cares and Loves me so
For taking all my pain and sorrows,
And casting them behind His throne

Now, that night to me is simply a memory,
One that I shall never forget
Remembering all my pain and sorrows,
And when my Saviour's Peace gave me Rest

Gilbert R. Palma

Mickey McCullough —
The All American Schoolmarm

A drill sergeant in a shirtwaist dress and a Toni perm
An angel with her halo held firm by a bobbi pin
A sorcerer's apprentice with Mickey Mouse ears

The All American Schoolmarm

She can yell with the best and whisper with the worst
She feels the hurt and speaks the pain
She has a smile that lights up lives and a laugh that inspires hope

The All American Schoolmarm

She is proud of her Irish heritage but is Red, White, and Blue
    through and through
She is a flag waver, a peacemaker, and an apple pie baker
She loves kids and dogs and Mickey Mouse

The All American Schoolmarm

She has spent her life with her hands on her hips
her heart on her sleeve
her lips speaking truths
and her soul shining through
Because she knows without a doubt
that helping people become their best is where it's at
and truly what counts

She is The All American Schoolmarm!

Patricia Dunkerson

One Instead Of Two

From each day and all through the night, I
Grew so like my sister and everyone had
Mistaken me for her and each for one another.
It puzzled all our friends and kin, for one of us
Was born a twin, yet not a soul knew which.

One day, to make the matter worse, before our
Names were fixed. As we were being washed
By the nurse, we got completely mixed. And
This, you can see, the nurse was confused (what
Could she do?) my sister had been mistaken as
Me and I mistaken as her.

This likeness even got worse, as we grew, for
We are one instead of two. I put this question
Hopelessly to everyone I knew. What would
You do, if you were me to prove that you were
You?

Ro Ashing

The Eagle

I saw him today . . .
Black, silhouetted against the winter sky,
Yet I knew he was a golden.
Gracefully he moved in a circle
Close to the crest of the mountain
As though he might come to rest
Among the craggy rocks.
"Oh, stay, I whispered, "until I get closer"
And I matched my stride to my racing thoughts,
Thinking I could overtake him.
But no, instead the great wings
Caught yet another wind current
And he was off, fading from my view.
Yes, I saw him today . . .
And he enriched my soul with his beauty.
Perhaps I will see him again.

Frances Baxter

"Unreturned Love"

As I wander through the fields of love
I look back and reflect
upon everything that I have done,
but I cannot detect
the one thing that has turned you away,
the thing that set you free
as you slip slowly through my fingers,
far away from me.

As the salty tears trickle down my face,
I sit and ponder this silly place,
a deep dark hole within my heart,
never to mend if we are apart.
I tried to love you with all my soul.
Why did you leave? Why must you go?

Allison Dawn Gill

Our Prayer

Thank you LORD for this wonderful day,
filled with creatures that come our way.

We love to watch as they eat and play,
grateful for the time we're here to stay.

You've surrounded us in beauty of every
kind. We stand in awe with YOU in mind.

We bow our heads in prayer to say:
Thank you LORD for this special day.

Lajean Pohler

Proud

His face is pale.
His blue eyes do not show his pain.
His shoulders carry a tremendous burden.
His faith though, is as immovable as a mountain.
He is faced with an evil demon which takes his childhood away, not
even stopping to care of his life, which lies so far ahead.
This special boy does not care, though.
Even though his clothes fit him they do not.
I wish he did not have to be that grown up.
With his imagination, he can soar like an eagle when he is confined.
The warmth in his heart helps heal the anger and frustration
    lingering around this enemy.
I long to be brave, strong, and courageous as he is.
The stench of this black, feelingless enemy lingers still in my mind
and I keep asking the question, "Why him?"
He is as innocent as a new born baby.
Still he is punished!
I am proud of my little soldier for he is stronger than I could ever be.

Jennifer LeJeune

I've Never Seen God

I've Never Seen God. But I know How I Feel
It's People like you who make him so Real

My God is no stranger, He's Friendly and Gay
And he doesn't ask me to weep when I Pray.

It seem's that I pass him so often each day
In the faces of people I meet on the way.

He's the stars in the Heaven, a smile on some face
A leaf on a tree or a rose in a vase.

He's winter and autumn, summer and spring.
In short "Gods Is Every Real Wonderful Thing."

I wish I might meet him much more than I do.
I would if there were more People Like You!

Georgia L. Wakeman

A World In The World

A world inside the outside world,
    Full of madness full of war.
It all threatens the mind,
    This world of its own kind.
Nowhere to run for peace,
    Everywhere the noise does not cease,
Each day becomes a passing memory,
    As this time is only temporary.
Hopes and dreams stand still,
    One can only survive by will.
Seeking the answers not found,
    Laws and Rights kept secretly bound.
Joy has brought tears to the eyes,
    Only to be destroyed by lies.
Emotions lay deep waiting for an embrace,
    Fighting within not to disgrace.
One true reality will always remain,
    Inside the heart the soul is Gods domain.

Charles Klein

Lessons

You sit,
legs propped,

your ever-analytic eyes search mine,
hoping to discover
    my mood for the day.

"Go to the piano and play,"
    you tell me.

But the noise I plunk
    is hardly worth
keying the hour with.

Still, you listen
capturing each note.

Sometimes,
    distracted,
I venture from my seat,
    and you,

half-smiling
pull me gently from the window,
where I,
    staring hard at nothing,
thought I heard someone call my name . . .

Diane Peterson

Death

I adore Death.
The blackness of it.
The sadness of it.
If Death should come tonight,
I'll welcome it.

At a long last I stand at Death's door.
Waiting to be let in.
As it opens,
So painfully slowly,
I think back to the life I'll leave behind.
Suddenly, I have a change of heart.
I can't die.
But it's too late.
The door opens completely.
I look in the horrific face of the Grim Reaper.
I try to back up.
He grabs me,
And pulls me in the room.

I get my wish.

Rachel Ulrich

273

Key Boy Kangaroo

Key boy kangaroo makin' no key boy kangaroo seein' key
boy kangaroo key boy boykey seein' keys and boys roo
kangaroo key boy kangaroo makin' no key boy kangaroo
seein' keyboy kangaroo roo? see the boy with key
kangaroo images oh boy key boy kangaroo with roo boy key
boy kangaroo kangaroo kang a roo kang a roo kang a roo
ro key boy kangaroo funny roo funny kangaroo funny boy
cute boy funny kang funny roo funny family and funny kang
a roo funny kangaroo funny key boy kangaroo funny roo
funny kangaroo funny kang a roo funny funny keyboy kangaroo
seein' roo seein' key boy seein' funny key boy seein' ro
and kang seein' funny key funny roo funny key boy kang
and a and kang a funny kang gonk me jerk me funny key
funny seein' key boy kangin' and roooooooo and funny key
boy kangaroo in the zoo funky kanga funny roo funny key
boy kangaroo seein' the kang and the roo and the boy the
keyboy kangaroo in the seein' funny seemin' funny to the
key boy kangin' and a rooin' kanga kanga kanga kanga kanga
kanga kanga kanga kanga kangakangakanga kanga
kangakangakanga
kangakangarooroo kanga
Ursin J. DeRoche III

True Love

Our life began as friends you see,
the way true love should always be.
    As time passed on our soles fell deep,
that's when we took that final leap.
    Now through the years from 1 to 11,
most of our life has been like heaven..
    We've been together through rich, and
poor, but never did we shut the door.
    We've laughed and loved, we've fought
and cried, but always you've been right by my side.
    You've been my lover and my friend,
I know that this shall never end.
    You gave me our babies so soft, and
small, the love we share can conquer all.
    As time marches on our lives will change,
but never our love will falter or strange.
    Our hair will grey, our children grow, but there is one
thing that I know.
    That we are one in sole and mind from now until the
End of time.
Nance Phillips

Ms. Ivory's Garden

Ms. Ivory waters her garden every day, it seems that way.
She looks after it with such love and such care,
It seems that her garden will always be there.
And what about the day that she leaves in the showers?
What will happen to her beautiful flowers?
Will they rot? Will they wilt? Will they weep? Will they die?
Or will they keep growing to ten feet high?
Ms. Ivory gives her garden lots of love and affection,
While she tends it to the greatest perfection.
It's all that she does with her long-living days,
Except for eating, sleeping, and remembering to pray.
But now that she's gone and left the garden alone,
Her house becomes someone else's home.
The flowers pulled up, the ground torn away,
Some wooden poles are installed for a fun place to play.
But where did all Ms. Ivory's flowers go?
You'll see them when you cross the greatest meadow.
For Ms. Ivory's flowers will always live,
And they'll always have their beauty to give.
Danielle Bond

Marty

My deep love for a man glows with illumination.
    His name is Marty; we are one by being wed.
I look upon him with almost pure idolization.

My spiritual love goes solely to Jehovah God.
    Marty gets every ounce of my human love.
In Jah's and in Marty's ways I will always trod.

My dull life changed when Marty came along.
    Now, it is filled with genuine pleasure.
There exists no other love ever so strong.

For me, Marty is the one; my absolute favorite.
    Everything he does, brings me delight.
Every moment of his spent with me, I savor it!
Karen I. Reed

Beneath Your Feet Lies A Rose

Beneath your feet torn, trampled and
tossed aside lies a rose.
Ripped from the place where it once grew wild and free.
Where its beauty was for all to see.
Ripped from the place that made it whole.
All because you did not know.
The beauty of the rose was not for you alone.

So you took the rose in hopes to find.
What made it special to all man kind.
But when its beauty faded you tossed it aside.
And searched for love of another kind.
So beneath your feet lies a rose
Whose true beauty only God knows.
Jody Colden

Gazing Into A Vast Nothingness . . .

The pitter patter on the roof-top
and the chill in the soul
makes us aware of nothing at all.
Some say the end is near
but I believe that the end was here before anyone else.
They say in the end all is good,
I wonder.
They say pain only happens sometimes,
only to the one who deserves it.
So what if you have something inside,
something that is always present,
and throbs in the worst situations.
What if I had a person to look up to,
and now this being is no longer.
Who is there in our world . . .?
I wonder will my time to shine ever come
and if it does what do I do.
I stand in the shadows and watch the passers
who are these so called individuals,
the rain starts to cease and I wonder.
Kelly Clendenin

Leaving The Nest

My children are grown and leaving the nest
To a mother that is some kind of test
Remembering well the feeding and changing
My life's in a process of rearranging
A mother's arms ache to hold them
At times to comfort and to scold them
Fond memories of children watching them grow
There comes a time we have to let go
A mother learns to never say never
Cause children know we will love them forever
Sharon A. Kohler

Untitled

In the beginning I was without you
My life was a college of pain and tears
I found no place for hiding or shelter
No where to avoid my fears
Yet when you stepped into my life
The stone was rolled away
The clouds that darkened my heart departed
And your light brought forth a new day
I felt the love and happiness
In each day we shared
And for all eternity and time to come
My love will always be there
It seems the time we've been apart
My love has grown even stronger
But to hold you in my arms again
Is for what my heart most hungers
To be with you and keep you near
Before I pass away
To love you like I've never before
If only for one sweet day

Urian Harrison

Join The Club

If you think you're the only one who made mistakes
If you think you're the only one who had tough breaks
Well, I've got news for you
Join the club

If you think you're the only one with a broken heart
If you think you're the only one who's torn apart
Well, I've got news for you
Join the club

Join the club
We've got millions of members
Too many names for any of us to remember
Join the club
You'll be in good company
This could be your cup o' tea

If you think you're the only one who's got no dough
If you think you're the only one who spoiled the show
Well, I've got news for you
Join the club

Joe Moitozo Jr.

Priceless Treasure

God in His wisdom, knows all things,
Whom to make Mothers, whom to make Kings,
But some are blessed beyond measure,
With gifts from God, priceless treasure.

Hearts of gold, undying love,
That only comes from God above,
Freely given and in good measure,
To one in need of that priceless treasure.

God knows the hearts, the need of each one,
When He sends a child, a special son,
Providing a Mother who's blessed from above,
With priceless treasure, boundless love.

And although short his life may be,
But filled with love to capacity,
Richly blessed, beyond measure,
With a special Mother, a priceless treasure.

Marilyn M. Hastings

It Just Takes Time

The day they told me you were gone
my world fell apart.
I felt my heart would break in two.
I knew I would never see your face.
That day they put you in the old dark place,
I followed behind you up the hill
and I just sat there still
and as they put you in the ground.
But that's been a year ago
and I still miss you so.
But I guess it just takes time.

Eleanor Lewis

The Guardian Of The Past

Reflections in a blackness so dense,
The images he sees used to make sense.
The old tell stories of their past,
Lineage together, memories that last.

In the blackness there are futures left unguarded,
He sought answers but no one regarded.
Light was life and that was that,
The simplicity of life was the people's tact.

The days they blended, wounds were mended,
He searches for the past which had just ended.
The colors were rich in love's face,
Try if you can to catch the essence of this place.

The people lived their lives unbothered,
Two children who's lives have been fathered.
Where else is there a harmony so hushed but so strong,
They say it's not possible, he says they're wrong.

He observes the experiences in his past,
They've lost those memories; the ones that last.
He falls into the darkness but with one last grasp,

He extends his hand and Life at last!

Will Lewis

Tomorrow . . .

Yesterday was here,

Today is gone.

Tomorrow we leave behind
all the hate and all the wrong.

We are the future of our days,
we can change our lives in many ways.

We can become the stars we want to be
we can make our dreams reality.

We have ourselves to believe in,
don't worry about the color of our skin.

Our pay will love to have peace of mind,

All the world will be color blind

Latasha Brown

Men Of War

There is a purpose for which they fight,
Though a good one seldom comes.
And those who tell the men to fight,
Rarely pick up guns.
They kill, get killed, or go home lame,
Their options are very few.
If they tried to leave by other means,
They found a catch twenty two.

Brian Nickerson

The Ancient One

I stare into the mirrors of the past
my face wrinkled and old with time
my hands chapped and stiff
the lines under my tired eyes
bring back memories of yesterday, a book
chiseled into my mind, of all the times
when things were easier
when the world was mine, now I'm old my life wasted away
and my only friend is this mirror
and the treasures kept inside
my only friend is this mirror
and the cracks that it hides
my whole existence is forgotten
and every night I ask myself why, the Gods
wont give in and let me die
I spend my final days in the hot sun
staring into the deep blue sky
cracks extending in all directions
and finally when death comes
there is no one to say goodbye

Ryann Sharer

He Was Only Twenty-One

He was only twenty one.
His life had just begun.
But suddenly he was forever taken from my sight.
He died alone one cold and dreary night.
My Baby, My Boy, My Son.
He was only twenty one.
He loved life so much, the feel of the ocean breeze,
the beautiful mountains and the trees, the ever changing
colors of the leaves.
My Baby, My Boy, My Son.
He was only twenty on.
I hear his laughter in my dreams.
I see his smiling face every where it seems.
My Baby, My Boy, My Son.
He was only twenty one.
If only I could make but one request,
it would be forever with God
may he peacefully rest.
My Baby, My Boy, My Son oh Lord,
He was only twenty-one.

Linda Freimuth

A New Day!

This morn
I awoke so forlorn.
Then, I took a look within and saw outside —
The darkest before dawn.
So, I went out in search of the sunrise.
Lo, — the sights that appeared before my eyes!
The first light was so bright —
It dispelled the night.
From black and starlite —
Moonlite to purple then
Cyan blue and red and pink to a
Golden hue.
Ah! Sunlight —
Purest white lite.
I watched this huge fiery delight,
And the birds of the air take wing without a care
To welcome the new day.
Then, I realized all my despair faded away.
Today is — A New Day!

France Fletcher

"Butterflies"

From the depths of nature's souls
They soar through the air with such control
Beauty, virtue, and such grace
Nothing could ever take their place

People watch in awe as they fly
Turning their heads to see them go by
Never noticing until today
How they change the world in every way

The way they fly, the way they move
A broken heart they can soothe
But as the world slowly dies
We say good bye to the butterflies

Korri Irvin

A Call To The Musicians

This rome is falling
Here Brothers
Hear and follow your calling
Our empire is falling
Document this with your words and notes
Voice the misery and desperation you see
Sing the songs of strength and hope
Sing to your children and their friends
So as this world ends
So in this dark night
They carry the candle to make their future burn bright
As we sit in the audience of downfall
Trying to delay trying to stall
We bury time
Time to buy time
Time to prepare
As we stare into the mouth of tomorrow

Mark Anthony Simos

The Ice Crystal Artist

A soft pristine blanket of new fallen snow
Brings Earth a sweet quiet of times long ago.
When the Ice Crystal artist at work through the night
Awoke man with wonder and then took his flight
Leaving lace like impressions on all window panes
And sparkling icicles for clear candy canes.
The painting continues as brooks flow between
Ice sculptures and snow hills completing the scene
Then lifting the brush to the tops of the trees
Encases each branch as a window that sees
Fields scattered with diamonds, so brilliant, so rare
Engulfing the senses, one only can stare
As the sun's welcome rays settle down from above
Embracing earth's Winter with a warmth like long love
The Season's enchantment surrenders with ease
As the Ice Crystal artist so silently flees
To return and amaze when we're quite unaware
Of the Wonder of Winter, a gift he must share . . .

Gwendolyn Sue Sparks

Dad's Hand

When I was small you held my hand to guide me
on my way, for promise and security for each and
every day, and when the chips were down, I still can
hear you say "Just do you're very best and things will
be OK" as years go by and time has past I have to take
my part and give to you my family the love that's in my
heart, although the road is long some days I still can
find my way, right back to that guiding hand that
helped me on my way, thank you dad for always being
there and your gentle caring ways and for that guiding
hand that helps me every day!

Timothy H. Graham

276

Welcome Sunrise

I watched the sunrise this morning
It was a nice warm sight
As it rose its colors were pretty and bright
 I watched the sunrise this morning
what a hell of a sight. It's red, orange
yellow beautiful lights.
 I watched the sunrise this morning and oh.
What a sight and it was wonderful
to know that the night has lost his fight
 I watched the sunrise this morning
a new day is beginning
 Watch me make it though this day
 thankful and winning

Theodore Thompson

Confused

Day light eludes me
Darkness covers all that I see
I cannot comprehend what is happening
I draw a blank to match my expression
Can you see the clouds forming
The horizon darkens speckled by the
rays of light that manage to break through
Lonely in a sea of people, blank faces
pass you by and reflect your own humanity
Tears fall and you cannot understand what has happened
Lost on you is the beauty of a wild flower
as if fights through the concrete in defiance
of man and all this accomplishments
Only you know what lies ahead for the master
as the servant turns and strikes
Life loses meaning when death is honored
Only then by raising your hand to be counted
can you join the revolution and cry out
against the machine

Archie L. Moore Jr.

Infinity

Children of the sky,
Come and fly with me —
Come lift up your minds,
Come and soar with me!

I will lift you from this obscurity —
High above, to the light that sets you free!

Children of the sky —
It's time for us to go:
Break the chains that hold you,
Here on earth below.

I will take you past the fountains of the rainbow.
You must make a choice;
It's there for everyone,
But if you come with me;
I'll take you to the birthplace of the Sun!

Dora I. Paredes

"Mama Bear"

As I walked through the house it seemed
empty and bare
something was missing,
maybe a mom no it was a mom then you wonder
why me why not the old women without loved ones
why your mom the one you would have needed
every day of your life for years months
and well for ever and when you
finally notice that she's gone
it's to late

Erin Riley

Look What God Painted

God paints sunrise for us every morning
And then at night, he paints again
He colors the skies with sunset hues
While pleasing only a few
You see, my Lord, has artists hands
More than an artist's touch
And in his heart his love for us comes from up above
The only difference between the
Lord and I is that I'm the paint
and canvass too. My Lord, he's the
 "Brush of Love"

Marie L. Gulmette

Who Loves Me?

Satan doesn't like me. How do I know, you ask?
Beaten and bruised as a little child. Fear and pain. Alone, Mom was
sick. Daddy and my brothers hurt me; badly. I had a shield, but not
joy. God, where were you? I know you, were there.

Satan doesn't like me. How do I know, you ask?
Used and abused. Mom died. Years of tears . . . I married a man who
caused pain without a fist. Abandoned again, ridiculed, little joy.
God gave two gifts of life to me. My husband left them too.
Alone again. My shield still shines.

Satan doesn't like me. How do I know, you ask?
Surgeries, accidents, challenges. More tears, hard work and pain.
Moments of joy . . . alone again. God, where were you?
I know you were there. I had your armor on. Blessings . . .

Satan doesn't like me. How do I know, you ask?
A tired mind and body. Perseverance, endurance, God, more character?
Tears are dry, your armor is heavy. I'm weary. My shield of faith
still shines in my hands. God, where are you? I know you are there.
Come rescue me, bring back your joy.

Satan doesn't love me. How do I know, you ask?
God loves me. Always has, always will. The shield is getting heavy.
Come Lord Jesus. Come quick! I don't want to be alone.
My hands are weary . . .

Satan doesn't like me. How do I know, you ask? I know. God knows.
My hands hurt, Lord! God where are you? I know you are there!
Please carry me . . . Thank You Jesus.

Linda Dempster

A Dream

I saw her standing by a house.
 I ran around her feet.
I loved her oh so much,
 But my love she did not keep.
One day they came and took us away,
 Left her all alone.
And in her eyes the tears they filled,
 And all her sadness shone.
The man she had loved had gone away,
 And left her without a thought.
And so she stood there helplessly,
 Sad, alone, forgot.
She gave herself away, as if she did not care.
But deep inside I knew she did,
 The pain I could not bare.
And now the times have changed,
 Almost passed her by.
And as I think back again my eyes begin to cry.
I guess her life will never be the way she wanted it to be.
 But maybe someday in her soul "God will set my mother free"

Micki Lee Yeater Repasky

Falling Angels

I want to be there when falling angels fly
I want to be there as they soar through the sky

With their wings dipped in gold, their hearts filled with love
Don't you want to be there when falling angels fly

Can't you hear the wind blow like a soft autumn breeze
That's the sound of angels who have just received their wings

Have you ever smelled a rose, that has just come into bloom
That's the smell of angels who know how god's love feels

When all of god's creation starts to sing in harmony
Then you'll know all angels have finally got their wings

And when the day comes when I can get mine
I hope god doesn't turn me down for this cold steel heart of mine

I know I'm gonna be there when falling angels fly

Chrissy Gibson

Still The Same

Hours are the same in every day.
Twenty-four being the number.
But, times have changed, ole timers say.
And the world seems never to slumber.

Sun still rising in the east, we see,
setting in the west, of course.
And God never sleeps, nor ceases to be,
He being the one who ordains its source.

No matter the changes as time passes by,
these things will forever be true.
The rainbow will make us delight with a sigh,
and the sky will forever be blue.

We can count on some days being rainy, I guess,
and the color of grass being green.
Birds always chirping and flying with bliss,
and the sun coming out to be seen.

Mr. Moon hanging high with his face shining down.
And each star has a name, so I've heard,
leaves falling softly without 'ere a sound,
and God cares for each little bird.

Marian E. Gardner

Our Children

What is this world coming to
when the only thing we se
is the constant abuse of children
spread nation wide across T.V.

Can you tell me about these children
with their live's so filled with pain
will they grow up without a future
will their effort's be in vain.

There's a child born every minute
to parent's that don't care
with mother's much too young to be
and father's that aren't there

These babies don't get choices
and they can't just walk away
they don't get to pick their parents
or the place in which they stay

Please don't think about yourselves
stop before it's to late
If you don't want them before you have them
You've already sealed their fate

Michele Danieri

"I Travel"

I travel around this world everyday,
to see the wonderful gifts God has to bring my way.

I thank him for them and keep
right on going to continue my
journey that he has prepared for me.

BUT, sometimes I find myself
stopping and saying, LORD
PLEASE TAKE ME THE
REST OF THE WAY,

AND he looks right down
and smile to say, LO, I'LL BE
WITH YOU ALWAYS
EVEN UNTIL THE END OF THE WORLD.

AND I look up at the heavens
with every step I take and remember
that GOD is with me along the way.

SO, I say to myself why stop
and worry because I have a
friend who is with me as I travel.

Andrew J. Lofton IV

A Wedding Dedication "The Road"

The road ahead is never for sure
There's no guarantee or instant cure
For the problems that life sometimes will deal
Or the bumps in the road we're all bound to feel

You two have chosen to face these as one,
Not only the bumps, but the joys and the fun,
And what you will discover as you go down this road
Is through love and commitment you will both share the load

Protect one another and never lose sight
Of what brought you together as man and wife,
For the road can take turns when you're not prepared
With each other to turn to you won't be so scared

Learn from each other and always take time
To listen to what's on the other one's mind
Be trusting and honest and never cast doubt
So that neither will have anything to worry about

You are strong in your love and you won't lose your way
You are soulmates beginning your journey today
Yes, the road is uncertain, but it will always lead home
If it's traveled together instead of alone

Anne M. Pooler

All-Of-A-Sodden

The weatherman said, "Clear — Cool."
It pours steam. I'm wearing Wool.
A brand-new coiffure — no plastic hood.
My dress is adhered to my skin for good.
The "cabbie" splashes by with disdainful grin
No cat with any pride would drag me in.

Are the buses all stalled with tires gone flat?
(Maybe they're marooned on Mt. Ararat.)
The weatherman sounded so sure, so cheery.
Does he feel chagrined? Profession-weary?
To forgive is divine. But I'll not forget
That to err is humid and I'm hotly wet!

Frances H. Levinson

Cavern

That black cavity you call a mouth
spews at me — bugs, bats, gnats
in my eyes, on my teeth

It stays open like a cavern — forever deep
plunging-dungeon of pitch blackness

In a black and white, your hole shouts
in my face
and all else pales next to
its dank depths

Roll a rock across your head
to block the gaping . . .
Jesus (homunculus) draws it
aside (like an enamel curtain)
and escapes your head (jail) leaving

Spider filled; web crossed
darkness that never stops
over-shadowing the rest of your face

Half expect bubbling crude
to trickle down your chin
or spray in my direction

Angela Pulley

Daddy I Love You

I'm sitting here in prison
All alone in my cell
They say I'm mean and tough
My true feeling no one can tell

I have to tattoo on my arm
One on my back
Everyone leaves me a lone
Because fear I do lack

On visiting day with my family all here
I hug and kiss them
Holding back a tear

My children all love me
And I love them all too
My son puts his arms around me
And says Daddy I love you

No matter how tough you may act
Or how well you play the past
Those four little words
Can melt the coldest of hearts.

Howard Isaacs

Someone I Love Just Died Yesterday

Someone I love just died yesterday.
He was a man that I admired.
I thought I would love him forever.
My dream just suddenly faded away.
Now I can't bare to look at his face.

Someone I love just died yesterday.
I cried till my heart was empty.
I can't feel his love, only my pain.
It's so hard to believe the truth.
Now I no longer want to live.

Someone I love just died yesterday.
He should still be here with me.
I guess this is the way it's supposed to be.
But deep inside my breaking heart.
I know he's gone forever because,
    he just died yesterday.

Emily Madson

For Elizabeth

I remember when you came into this world
The first time I ever saw you
Your eyes were open wide and you were so brand new
I remember the first time you ever smiled
Looking right at me
Your smile stretched from ear to ear and
you looked so happy to be a part of our family
These memories will stay with me wherever I go
And I wrote this poem just to let
you know that I will always love you!

Jenna Boyd

Stranger In The Mirror

Countless rows of prison cells with lives locked away by doors,
windows and walls. Willing prisoners reside inside,
hiding in fear of life.

Brave inmates unlock their doors and venture into the prison yard,
invisible masks firmly in place.
Fear of recognition their unknown terror.

Prisoners of lies laboring together day in and day out,
each in self-made shackles, all careful to keep a safe distance.

None more distant though than the stranger in the mirror.
Even here the walls stand strong, the locks are reinforced.

Freedom, taken away long ago in their youth,
memories of freedom vanishing slowly without realization,
identities and dreams lost and forgotten.

With their voluntary sentence at an end,
they appeal and beg for Mercy,
their need for freedom overwhelming.

Too late, now there is only pain and sadness beyond comparison.
Regret and longing accompany death.

Realizing only now that escape at all cost,
should have been attempted in life.

Misty Saffioti

Borrowing Memories

How quickly the time flew away.
Only yesterday four little boys were in the yard busy at play.

Their toys in imaginary cities in the dirt,
Never wanting to stop playing unless they were hurt.

Then they'd run to Mom for comfort and help,
And the tears on their cheeks would make her heart melt.

Now they are grown with little ones in their yard,
Soon will come their time for that task so hard.

The time to see their children walk away with a new love on their arm,
The one who'll take their place to protect them from harm.

How precious is today, how wonderful the memories tomorrow.
When today is not happy we have yesterday's joys from which to borrow.

Linda Raley

A Single Rose In A Field Of Daisies

A shy little timid rose in a field of daisies
People don't pick you; bees don't pollinate
They respect your independence, your beauty rules the field
When storms threaten to arise, you shy away to the tall grass
To protect and preserve your beauty
Your fragrance roams freely through the field
And puts a sense of life in any creature in its path
Your presence is irreplaceable
You are unique
A single rose in a field of daisies.

Patrick Murray

A Life

Searching for the Truth
in magazines, in storefront scenes,
on the nightly news,
in the eyes of a stranger.

Lost in a world conceived of lies,
living through the Media,
strangers to ourselves.

Our moods controlled by the latest trend,
as we suffer in silent isolation,
disconnected from life, our Emotions,
strangers to our family and friends.

Our Soul — a lifeless void,
Our Heart — forever broken,
Our Rage — just beneath our smile,
Our faith — no more.

Still we go on searching,
like Zombies in the night,
for a Life, for Hope, for Ourselves and for Love,
in a desperate attempt to feel Alive.

M. S. Chadderton

"Cut To Ribbons"

Raw earth forces green from its nails.
The earth is scissor-handed this June night.
Long grasses snip at my pants.
Reaching shrubs trim my shoulders.
Trees snap at me like twigs.
The air is sliced thin
Until the green smells as raw as the earth.

I do not know why I am cut again and again
And I smell only perfume.
I cannot comprehend why the birds
Are ploughing the air, my air, with their discs.
Keeping them sharp for tomorrow maybe.
I cannot grasp why all things
Seem to divide around my feet.

What will be left of me?
How can I stay here in a field with a pond
Where combat slashes in tadpoles left and right,
And somehow I am unscathed?
Is it death, or life, by a thousand cuts?
Survivors guilt . . . I am cut to ribbons.

William L. Schutter

Never Another Oklahoma

People passing never knowing
Somewhere close the danger's growing
Strangers whom they've never met
Something done they won't forget

While a few floors down the children play
To them it's just another day
Some will even see tomorrow
But for the rest a nations sorrow

The truck it has a lot to hide
As it's parked along the curb outside
An act of terror without warning
Explodes the reality of this somber morning

The horror is carried on T.V.
For an entire world to see
An image played out many times
Burned forever in our minds

Lives forever torn apart
But the healing now will start
Held by strength not by pity
Lest we forget Oklahoma City

Gary Hall

Dreams

It all begins in your mind
Sometimes you can even feel your dreams
Burning away at your insides
Feelings that some people try to hide
Others just cloud their mind with thoughts
Trying to keep their dreams buried inside
Hiding their dreams in the passing of time
Until the moment comes for your dreams to surface again
Reminding you that your dreams are still inside
Remember the moment . . .
Remember your dreams.

Bruce Neal

Imagination

Imagination, you've got the best of me
For all you do is make me dream
Of things that cannot be
You hurt and you fool poor confused me
Imagination, please stop disappointing me

Imagination, why are you so cruel to me
Making me believe that in my arms she wants to be
Dreaming of the day that she will come to me
You make me imagine of a love full of passion
Of her kisses sweeter than wine
But when I awake from this dream full of rapture
I feel like I'm slowly going out of my mind
Imagination, why don't you set me free
Remove this hopeless feeling that's insanity
For she cannot love what she doesn't see
Imagination, Please end this calamity
For I know it can never be
Imagination, let's end this fantasy

Surfin Percy

'Soon A Day'

Soon a day is sure to come, when dawn will bring a bloody sun.
A fear will rise in all our minds, a beast will govern all our kind.
Love abandoned senseless lead by death,
    mankind heaves its final breath.

Ignorant of what we are, mankind has not come to far.
We spend our lives in vanity, laughing at our destiny.
Lost in lust we don't repent, wasting life till life is spent.
Each one follows his own path, blindly kindling fortunes wrath.

Listen close to what I say, good sense will one day go away.
Truth for man will have no name, hope for man will have no aim.
Lies will conquer all our hearts, in terror we'll then play our parts.
Like worms we'll writhe upon the hook,
    while evil laughs at what it too

Soon a day is sure to come, when dawn will bring a newborn sun.
Each one will join their chosen lot, each one will know what they forgot
That as God's creatures we're to be, existing in God's harmony.
Some chose his path, some chose their own, each reaps the seed...

Robert Pearson

Education's Future

Yesterday, school was a place to learn.
Today, parents have a much greater concern.
I awaken each morning with a prayer in my heart and soul.
I pray that children will grow up to achieve their goals.
Yesterday, I aspired to impress my teachers.
Today, children yearn to impress gang leaders.
I believe having faith in God will strengthen each child.
Remember, a child is only a child for a while.
Therefore, our teachings today must positively impact our youths.
If our nation is relying on this generation for future use.

Katherine Vaughn-Harden

Untitled

In the moonlight, in the daylight
What a beautiful place to be
By the seaside, on the sand
What a sight to see.

The Gulls are chatting by the dozen
What do you think they say?
Maybe they are also happy
To see such a beautiful day.

Through the shining clear blue water
The little fish run by
Why are they in such a hurry
There is a Shark and they do not want to die.

Why is the human race too busy
To see the beauty of the earth
Each new day brings new beginnings
Which can show us what life is worth.

Hazel Eaton

A Mother Of No Relation

Dedicated to Kay Burnett

A mother of no relation is a special kind of mom
She takes care of you like she is your own
She comforts you with all the love in her heart
She sticks out the tough times with you and forgiving you for
    your wrongs is just around the corner
She is a mother not in the same house but in your heart
She is one you can freely call mother but has no blood of yours
She is the joy of joys light of lights
She can never be replaced for she is one
Yes, there is only one who can fulfill this role, for I ought
    to know, I have been looking for years
I have looked and finally found a woman full of love and no hate,
    full of peace and integrity, and full of forgiveness and
    no revenge
I have found a special woman, or should I call her mother

Carrie E. Rolls

The Quiet Place

Silent, starless sphere,
No creature stirs
No blade of grass to bend beneath a wind
No wind to blow away the stench of death.
A stilly pall of gray hangs low
    above the muck and slime,
Mute testament to ears deaf
    to the warning cries of those who cared.
But who's to know? For man is dead
Only God.
Now He must say "Amen."
And start anew.

Mary Postlewait

Untitled

How do you like to go up in a swing
up in the air so blue?
Oh, I think it's the pleasantest thing
that ever a child can do.
Up in the air and over the walls
till I can see so wide.
There's rivers, an trees, and cattle
all over the country side.
And I look down on the gardens so green,
down on the roofs so brown.
Up in the air I go flying again,
up in the air and down!

Olive Gemienhardt

Is It A Night Mare?

I see him in my night mares . . .
    I see him in real life . . .
I see him in the dark, but never in the light.
    I feel his touch at night.
When I am all alone in fright.
    I try to scream, but never can,
Cause if I do I know I'll die.
    I know he's near, very near,
But where I do not know.
    I feel his hands on my throat,
Making me gasp for air.
    Or could it be the wind making me
Unable to breath?
    I wish I knew . . .
I wish I knew . . .
    I afraid to sleep cause I know he'll come,
He always does.
    Who could it be?
Who could it be?

Cassie Mullins

Untraveled

My mind ventures into a land all its own, but it lies untraveled.
I know every blade of grass and every ripple of water by heart.
Still the truth lies unknown.

I welcome anyone to take a walk, yet they never walk through it —
They just stomp on the ground, leaving marks that ruin the beauty.
All they ever want to do is pick a flower and leave,
Just to show everyone they were there.

Why can't they enjoy the land — enjoy the beauty . . .
Enjoy what it has to offer . . . Enjoy the peace, its true value.

You walked, you touched, and you breathed everything in.
I thought my land was finally taken
I felt your hands run through my water . . .
Your breath caress my flowers.

But when I opened my eyes . . . You were gone
With a flower lingering in your fingertips.

So I will build a sign at the entrance . . .
    "So deceiving it may, so mortal your promises stay
    Leave your mark with pride, may the thorns rip in your side.
    The luscious truth remains in the gravel,
    My land stands alone, untraveled . . ."

Nichole Garvey

Shawn On Foreheads

A forehead has hardly significance at all;
It merely raises you higher if you are not very tall.
It may bear a scar, or a wrinkle or two —
Or it may just be hidden by a big-bushy hair-do!
On foreheads I can make just one true profession:
That they rarely express and expressive expression.
For those who aren't sure if your forehead is even there,
Simply check right above your eyebrows and right below
Your hair.
There should be wide, vast, bare, open, secluded space —
One like no other single place on your face.
It may have a long dent if you've been wearing a cap,
Or maybe pillow-divots if you've been taking a nap.
I have queried many doctors and researched many books
To arrive at this conclusion: A forehead is just for looks.
The chances of using your forehead are very small
For a forehead has hardly significance at all.

Shawn Osborne Rudd

281

A Bible Collector Speaks

I collect Bibles,
    But only rare editions!
Here is a Wycliffe,
And here a Geneva,
And here is the great "He" Bible
    Of King James.
Now I am old —
    With my Bibles piled around me —
And I am alone!
Would I had collected friends
    As I collected Bibles,
Or had lived the life of which the Bible speaks.
Then would I not have been forsaken in my old age,
But would have known the peace which the Bible proclaims!

Frederick E. Maser

A Poem For Denise

With auburn hair highlighted by the sun,
And brown-eyes cast upon a pretty face;
And with soft-words spoken by ruby lips,
She led me gently with delicate hands,
From wide tree-lined streets and broad boulevards
To Jesus waiting by a narrow lane.

Percy Davis Jr.

Tears

If tears could talk what would they say:
They'd cry out "I'm hurt"
They'd say "I'm in Pain"
But tears do talk in more ways than one
They tell all your secrets that should be left undone
They show all the emotions and feelings you have
Tears make you feel good when you really feel bad
A tear can mean joy, a tear can mean sorrow
But tears are something you never can borrow.
Tears are your own, they can bring feelings of pride,
Like when the one that you love makes you his bride
Tears can often bring people closer together
When times have you low and you want to feel better
So verbally say what you want others to hear
But remember to say what you actually feel
Because once that first tear leaves your eye
The feelings you have; have no where to hide.

Susan M. Dospoy

Prayerful Mothers

The Lord, our God created Adam, Earth and Heaven
And when He created Eve, He made things even better.
I thank you Lord for your son Jesus;
But I also want to thank you for Eve,
The first mother of all of us.

On the second Sunday each year in May
We express to our mothers love in some way.
It's fact that prayerful mothers made the
Family structure strong,
They nurture us as well as pray for us,
Right or wrong.

Thank you Lord for mothers
Past, present and to be.
May all of us be what you
Would have us to be.

Evon Jones

The Tree

Soldiers, drums, and golden horns are left upon my tree
They represent the youngest child, for he is still with me.
The angels have all flown away — they live in Tucson now.
They shimmer and glimmer on another Christmas bough.
Santa's elves and Santa too have marched to other places —
and now are viewed in magic awe by other happy faces.
The funny clowns and mirrored balls have all been taken down —
And gone with the three older ones to other states and towns.
And in these towns and on these trees they'll multiply anew —
They'll sparkle and they'll glitter with a radiance so true.
These ornaments that moved away with owners grown so tall —
Still represent the memories of when they were so small
And gazed wide eyed in wonderment and wished for what might be
Underneath — but just for them — our twinkly Christmas tree.
And so I'm left with soldiers, drums and golden horns this year,
Yet all those Christmas memories will be forever dear.

Carol J. Billow

When I Think Of You

When I see the sunset
When I see the trees sway

When I hear the birds sing
I think of you

When the wind whispers
I hear your voice

With the face of an angel
With the grace and peacefulness of a dove

They have all the riches in the world

I have you and that is worth more

Jared Sprinkle

For My Brothers

Well, once again the Brotherhood has come to the aid of a brother in need. This is the special thing that the brotherhood has to help meet the needs of other Brothers, and has been going for years. At times like these, to have the brotherhood of bikes behind you mean everything in the world. Sharing the brotherhood of riding free, side by side with brothers to whom we are connected through the wind and the roar. A feeling inside that you cannot even describe, or define. While I am prevented from riding for now, I still am able to picture in my mind the feeling of riding side by side with my brother, riding into the sunset and the knowledge that someday I will join my brothers again gives me the strength and determination to keep going, to keep my spirit alive, knowing that somewhere out there one of my brothers is firing up that Bad Boy, and thinking of me and the rest of the Brothers whom are gone or "missing", the Brotherhood and the love survive.

Curt J. Carnitz

Relationship Withered

Slendered and brassed,
most elegant pot
concealing the withered
hyacinth that rots
inside the deepest
of the thirsting black.
The roots reach out
and walls they attack.
Oh hopeless stem,
you shriveling spine,
you starve the bud
and leaves that wine.
Like veins gone dry that poison all . . .
Relationship withered — now death shall call.

Regan Tuttle

Paradise

The sight of beautiful birds in flight,
Their melodious voices lifted in song from morning 'til night
A gentle breeze softly rippling an aqua pool,
Soothing my senses and making me whole
A cloudless, azure sky, a beautiful sunset
Enjoying a garden of flowers, feeling April showers
These are but a small part of paradise

Walking in the park, holding hands with the one I love
Kissing in the dark,
Letting him know he's the one I'm dreaming of
Dining in our favorite place, enjoying our favorite dish
Admiring his handsome face, thinking of a fulfilled wish
Hearing sweet music fill the air, dancing 'til dawn without a care
These too, are but a small part of paradise

Singing in church, feeling serene and at peace
Singing with the choir, listening to the Man of God preach
Tithing, rejoicing, praising and worshipping God fully
Hearing children laughing and playing together
People commonly uniting in all kinds of weather
These are just a few of the things that paradise means to me

Evelyn Cogdell

The Hearing Aid

As I passed an old man, I smiled and said "Good Day."
He looked up with a grimace — and said, "What did you say?
I see your skin is not like mine,
For the likes of you I have no time,
You'd best be on your way."

As I strolled by the old man, I paused and said "Good Day."
He looked me up and down again — and said, "What did you say?
I see you men are holding hands,
I think you must be gay.
I bid you please leave me alone and go on far away."

As I strutted near the old man, I took heart and said "Good Day."
He glared at me with knowing eyes — and said, "What did you say?
I see you on the corner in your skimpy leather suit,
Your cosmetic face tells me — you are a prostitute!!!"
I have no time to stay."

As I came upon a wizened man, I bid him a bright "Good Day."
He slowly raised his head — and said, "What did you say?"
Then he gave a little cough and quickly took his glasses off,
And wistfully he said to me, "I hear much better when I can't see.
Please talk with me today."

Arlene Dietrich

Hush Yo' Mouth!!

I need to go on ahead and shut up
before I say something wrong,
but I'd hate to see this despair
amongst black people go on for long.
I need to go on ahead and be quiet
because if I get to talkin'
too wise and too loud
I may get charged with inciting a riot.
I better hush up
before everybody know
that us black folks ain't going to be down, no mo'!
Yeah! I'll tell it.
Stand up and do what's right!
Freedom will never be won without a fight.
And the fight we got to fight is in our minds
Go ahead, say it, "ain't nobody fault but mine."
We will succeed if we go ahead and try
But I'll be damned if I hold my peace, until I die.

Sabin Duncan

Making Left Be Right

He finally said yes. He's taking a chance.
He's agreed to take lessons, to learn how to dance.
"It'll make her happy." That's the manly way . . .
But he's shaking inside, more nervous than he wants to say.
Hear the music. Step to the beat.
It's going to be a long, long night.
He's sweating and swearing, trying to make his left foot be right.
The Waltz meant to be graceful, but we look more like we're having a scuffle, and next comes the Two-Step, the Cha, the Swing,
The Cotton-Eyed Joe, and then comes the Shuffle!
But hey — that time something felt right.
The feet moved in time, sliding along light as a kite.
And we turned the right way! This Sweetheart move, it's really cool.
I'm becoming possessed like some kind of dancing fool.
The Pretzel, the Tunnel and Tabletop; Even the Switch-a-Roo isn't so bad. Show us some more, I can't even think of the fun we haven't yet had. She finally said yes. She's taking a chance.
It's again Saturday night, and all he wants to do is dance, dance, and go dance.

Dan Stehlik

Going Home To Mother

She apologizes for toast crumbs in the tub of butter
And shoves globs of fat
Oozing from deep-fried cooking
Robed in crispy salty appendages

Food expands the plate
She piles more
A privilege missed
More, giving more, more giving, still more

Greedy blue-ribbon prize words
Bubble out like an overflowing dishwasher
How long can you stay?
You are not going to, did you, would you?

More just a little more
More, why and when
More and more, giving more still more
Words echo through catacomb walls

Souls swap places sucking power
Turning flesh into melted memories hardened
In her locket
Again and again she is mother.

Patricia Johnson

Leaving

I was planning on leaving — going off on my
own; Taking my children; try to find us a home.
I was coming in to tell him I was going away and
I heard a sad little voice say:
   'Daddy please be good so mommy will stay.
She cries all the time just calling your name
and I know life without you just won't be the same.
She may not be wrong, she may not be right, but
why does she cry herself to sleep every night. How
can I grow up and face tomorrow if all I see on her
face is sorrow?'
   I stood and I listened for some reply. I
looked in the door, there was a tear in his eye. He
looked in my face and I heard him say; 'Your Daddy
has a sickness he can't explain, if mommy wants to
go, I'm the one to blame — for my sickness has
brought my family shame. I try to do better but
it only gets worse, so you go with mommy, and lite
her sad face, while I go to hell for that's the
drinking man's place.'

Pat Pine

"Die For Love"

In the park, where I dwell
  I met a man I loved so well.
He took his heart away from me
  And told me I was free.
He put another girl upon his knee;
  He told her things he never told me.
I went home to cry in my bed;
  Not a word to my mother was said.
My father came home late that night,
  Looked for me left and right.
Up the stairs he ran, to the door he broke,
  And saw me hanging by a rope.
He got a knife and cut me down.
  Upon the dresser, this note he found:
    "dig a grave, dig it deep, marble stone where I
      shall sleep, upon my grave I want a dove,
        to show the world I died for love."

Megan Garland

Love Hurts

He went out to dinner with a girl that he knew.
He kissed her so softly and smooth.
Then he went home to his wife and his kids.
He kissed them good-night and tucked them into bed.
He went downstairs and kissed his wife.
She remembered when he said he'd be with her for life.
She asked him where he'd been all night.
He said "it's none of your business, so kiss me all right".
She pushed him back and asked him again.
He stood up and she did too.
He slapped her and said "don't ask me again."
She started to cry as he walked out the door.
She fell to the floor and cried some more.
  And cried some more.

Heidi Donnelly

My Soulmate

Dinner for two at Roberto's Cafe
A glance telling much more than words ever say
A charm showing the world that I'm his best friend
Long tender kisses I wish wouldn't end.
Carved stone bunnies and sweet potpourri
Rings tucked in pillows, a surprise weekend spree
Cool afternoons looking over antiques
Lending an ear when I need to speak.
Billy Holiday records to help calm my nerves
Knowing which outfits best show off my curves
Choosing the sure thing instead of the bet
Remembers the very first day that we met.
Piggybacks for my nieces, a kiss for my dad
Absolutely the best laughs that I've ever had
Many sweet secrets that I couldn't tell
How is it anyone knows me so well.

Annette Glaude

Heading South Next Year

Naked tree limbs chattering in the cold,
Bushes shivering amid the heaped-up snow.
Squirrels a-skittering up and down the icy trunks —
Winter's see-saw, freeze and thaw.

Birds listing, leaning into the wind, tail feathers
Blown up their backs by the icy blasts,
Looking for sunshine, finding drippy, drizzling
  clouds instead.
Cold birds look unwanted and forlorn:
Wonder if they wish (in Winter) they'd never
  been born?

Margaret A. Hart

Dad

The saw no longer hums.
The hammer no longer pounds.
There are no pieces to be glued.
There is no saw dust to be swept.
You left us for a better place,
Where you no longer, feel the pain.
Today's your first birthday, away from us,
And to this, we must adjust.
Our eyes fill with tears.
Our hearts ache to touch you..
We know we'll meet again,
In God's own house above.
So fill His house with fiddles and tables,
Made by your own hands,
and given with love.
But make the whirly-birds to fly home to us.
To give us your love and patience,
to trust in God's way of choosing,
The time, that we can all touch.

Margaret Jackson

Single Parents Reality

One with two and so much to do
Pinching pennies as they come and go; yet having nothing to show
Good days and bad, happy days and sad
Taking them all with a smile, no frowns
No matter how trying the ups and downs
One step at a time and all will be fine
Very rare does a day go by without a struggle or fight
Try as they might
Yet they stick together just as they rather
Short days and long learning from their wrongs
Taking each blow just as they go
They will not give up or fall
They will stand strong and tall
Starting each day ready and willing
Waiting to face each challenge no matter how trying or thrilling
They will go on forever standing and fighting together
And in the end they will have each learned a lesson
That whether win or lose each day given them was a blessing
For precious is life no matter what the strife.

Christine Ackerman

To Max

When morning comes, I find my sleepy head
Considers ways and means to stay in bed.

In fact, my night just might a mite extend,
If it were not disturbed by man's best friend.

He gives my face a lick, my sleeve a tug
I open eyes, behold his panting mug.

How can this speechless species so encumber
Fulfillment of my wish for further slumber.

He will not see his fur vent wish denied.
I rise, I dress, I take the dog outside.

He sniffs each bush, each tree, each canine haunt.
Who knows what secrets surface on our jaunt.

While I, confined to sense at human level,
Must search out other treats in which to revel.

But daybreak teams with sights and sounds so pleasing,
This pup has given me the day for seizing.

How rich was my reward for heeding hound.
Is Godspell really "dog" just turned around?

Carl A. Lindblad

The Widow's Soul Cries

I cried for you today.
I probably cried for me.
It's so hard to let go
of what I've held so dear.

I cried for you today
from a dry, hot, dusty place,
deep within my soul,
from where no tears came before.

I felt them gather themselves together there,
in the depth of my soul.
I felt them as they started on their journey
upward and outward, pushing against the dust of decades,
passing across the dryness that always lived there.

It began to hurt, right there,
in the depth of my soul.
The dryness said: "No, don't go!"
The tears said: "Let go, I need to flow!"
And the battle went on, and I hurt.
Deep within my soul.

Madeline K. Evans

Original Thought Microscopic Response

Mind what makes you tick?
Rhythmic computer of God
Clever programming navigation
Engaging mind plus natural chemicals
Is instinct extinct?
It's a species thing, not a fur coat thing
Common sense taught by experience, not the wise
Philosophers think better on an empty stomach
The recharger is on the mountain top
Thinkers and doers have split
The movers and shakers are stirring
The natural order is tweaked
What is 0% fat that includes calories?
They changed the color of bread
Patience is not a virtue, it's hard work
Knowledge and arrogance don't mix
Sports heroes should be role models
A parent is more important (listen Hillary)
Time for kids to really listen
And be heard, not herded.

Gregg W. Traver

Can Just Conquer Injustice?

Injustice owns the world today.
Evil's eyes scope about the tray, capturing every prey.
It pulls you in, tightly gripped,
Leaving you almost no get-away.
It's who you know, and what you have in hand.
That's what it's all about in man's land.
It's who you are, not what you know,
That determines where you'll go.
How else can I say?
Don't wait until the time you face the Gate,
When earthly things must part their mate.
To Hell with money, and all those things.
Promote love and harmony.
Live life for one another,
For we are all sisters and brothers.
Justice, it's the way.
Through this: Just becomes The Way!

William Jerome Gosch Jr.

Untitled

As I look out of my window, I'm thankful for what I see
All the beauty that's around me . . . that the lord gave to me

He provides my every longing he satisfies my every need
He gave me the moon, stars, the sun and he planted every seed

No one could ever love me as much as he does right now
And when I get to heaven upon my knees I'll bow

To tell him how much I love him, is all I look forward to.
To thank him for taking my sins away and making me just like new.

He said he would never forsake me, loving me forever and always.
Preparing my mansions in heaven is how he spends his days.

When I hear that trumpet sound and glory fills the air.
My mansion on streets of gold, with him one day I'll share

So as Christmas soon approaches, and presents sit under the tree.
The best present comes from the father . . . the day Jesus died for me.
Thank you God.

Karen D. Carter

"A Way Out"

When things go wrong
my fears come along to haunt my mind and break my heart
I look hard to find a way out

When days are sad
nightmares arrive to shatter my dreams and disturb the night
I pray hard to find a way out

When crimes are high
death angels sway around to rejoice in blood and claim precious lives
I try hard to find a way out

When children die in war
monster fly around to darken future skies and signal end of our times
I work hard to find a way out

When world has no friends
hate flames rise to spread winds of war and smother smell of love
I strive hard to find a way out

When life is not what we want
troubles grip our minds to shake our souls and sadden our hearts
And I wonder hard if there is any way out

Eliza Khosrova

The Apple Of Flight In Memory The Teacher In Space

To slip among the misty cloud tops, as graceful as a white dove, yet as brave as an Eagle. With the eye of thy sharpest pilot, to catch the beauty of the bluest skies among high, always to appreciate. To every which way of thy wishes and dreams, as the softest feather in the wind, a Gallant Flight, in thy Heavenly Winds. To dive here, to climb there, swaying to and fro, the wind as my comforting blanket, not a foe anywhere. To sweep the dawns gleaming sunlight, to be swept away, as far as thy deepest wonders of blue skies. Always to appreciate Gods wonders hidden within the mysteries of Flight, not to fear, yet to know he's there. To sail with her bright spirit upon the sea of thy universe, with the spirit of thy gallant sailors of old, yet with the mighty wings of silver glamour, still to shine on and on. To the spirit of flight rooted deep within her brave heart, always to venture out; to seek and to also find the shiniest path to thy farthest galaxy. A final goal to grasp more, and more knowledge for mankind in the outer most wonders of the Universe. Don't forget the brave crew that carried the Apple of Flight, or the good songs of their life; May we never forget: The Apple Of Flight.

Leslie W. Bond

Untitled

When you were first within my womb,
I then felt fear and sudden gloom.
But as my body swelled with you,
A special kind of pride did bloom.

No man could ever really know,
What depth of love a woman holds,
When pain and agony has given way,
And in her arms her child is laid.

In you I want to put a touch,
Of all things which mean gentleness.
In you I want to embed truth,
And understanding as wisdom's roots.

There is so much within my grasp,
To mold in you before time's elapse,
That I often worry I might not fulfill,
All that I dream and hope to instill.

But most of all, I often fear,
As you grow taller and straighter with years,
That I might not make you understand,
This love I can't just put in your hands.

Dianna R. Hoffman

The One With The Laughing Eyes

The room was crowded and the noise was loud
A caldron of "colorful ties."
Above the din and the laughter.
I noticed the one with the laughing eyes.

While stories and boasts were abounding
And each player maintained their disguise.
I observed the air of confidence,
From the one with the laughing eyes.

Amused and amusing, they all parried,
Plying each other with lies.
This was observed with amusement
By the one with the laughing eyes.

Finally, he moved slowly forward
And smiled as he came to my side, saying,
"From across the room I noticed you;
The one with the laughing eyes."

Linda Novey-White

Today Is The Day

Today is the day, there are drugs like speed,
Sold to kids who have a much greater need.
Today is the day, teens get shot on the street
Just for a jacket, or the shoes off their feet.
Wars start overseas; just for greed
Why do we do this; there is no need.
Teens these days drink, smoke, and do dope
Sometimes I wonder, will there ever be hope?
Millions of people, die from HIV
Sad isn't it, sounds like punishment to me.
People go homeless and live on the street
While millions get money they don't really need.
They say America is free, yes it is indeed
But not from violence and crime on the street.
So why is the world like this?
We made it that way of course.
Man's sin never wins, it just brings much remorse.
So before this is over, I would like to say
People yearn and cry over dead loved ones
Because we made it this way.

Steven Erbentraut

Random

Someday I'm sure that there can be, for those that wait or care to see,
swaying like the willow tree, a time when all men will be free.

From somewhere out through time and space, I viewed afar the noisy race,
then hung my head in sad disgrace, and was alone in this small place.

To overtake when far behind, takes a courage one can find,
not from depression there resigned, but strength of will through peace of mind.

Some in life do find their goal, searching out the hidden soul,
recording there with pen and scroll, as time stands still and they grow old.

In retrospect it's all too clear, to see the things one held so dear,
take to their wings and disappear, as the wheels of truth draw ever near.

They came no closer as if for fear, the view would then be all too clear,
and the basic reason for their fear, would be plucked from the
ignorance they hold so dear.

They persist in searching for the dove of peace, in a place where
the odds are the very least,

So from life's labors — no relief, a journey through a sea of grief,
troubled by the disbelief, remembered but by a wilting wreath.

But there can be so I've been told, other things to have and hold,
least of which is the yellow gold, by which men's minds are bought and sold.

If you can see or understand, what sparks a dream or drives a man,
or kindles light in a darkened land, this poem has no end for you, my man.

Travis Ross Nobles

Brotherhood

It spreads across the country
  like a wildfire in a breeze.
So passionate, so powerful
  it brings giants to their knees.

It is an outpouring of kindness
  a never-ending flow of tears.
It has brought us all together
  ·in the most difficult of years.

It shows itself in different ways
  this brotherhood of ours.
Often times in great multitudes
  like the rains of April showers.

Sometimes it seems it is hidden
  although we truly know.
It's like the flickering flame of a candle
  that always seems to glow.

It imbeds itself into our souls
  like the planting of a seed.
It is Love pure and simple
  in someone's time of need.

L. M. Peters

Requiem For A Mother

From early morn we watched you
Spread-eagled on your narrow bed
No crown of thorns upon your brow
But greying locks arose and fell
With each long measured breath.
Those who loved you stood the lonely watch
While doctors, nurses, menials came and went.
Was it like that, O Christ, on Golgotha's hill?
Did loved ones bleed with thee
While the curious came and went that cold dark day?
And when the long last quivering breath was drawn
Did peace descend upon your suffering brow?
And that long day seem as naught
When death's sweet hand drew you back home?

Dorothy Dickie

Black And Proud

We're black and proud.
I say, we're black and we're proud.
Blacks have come a long way. And blacks have a long way to go.
But, we can't make that journey, by sitting back and saying,
Child, that — a — do; just as long as I got a hand in it,
It is alright with me.

Get up Black Folks! And take a stand.
You need to help your fellowman!
Throw away that jealousy, throw away that word, I can't.
Throw away that word wait, for if you wait too long,
  it might be too late.

Wake up Black Folks!
You are still sleep. Because opportunities are dancing at your feet.
I say wake up Black Folks! And take a stand,
For many blacks have died that we might have equal rights.

The world is calling for great leaders like you. Such as:
President of the United States, doctors, lawyers, teachers,
preachers, counselors, and reporters.
But, if you don't know God, you still want be able to make it.
By the Grace of God, Blacks have come a long way.

Alice Van Williams

My Legacy

I am prepared to fight.
I am armed with the thoughts and ideas to speak out against them.
They are those who wish to control the will of us all.
They are those who tell us what to think and feel.
I will not listen to their words any longer.
I will think of my own words to say, and feel my own feelings.
I will say that we should think and feel for ourselves.
And there are many other people who agree with me.
These people and I will fight those who wish to control us.
They may control us, but they cannot control this idea.
I will make sure that this idea never dies.
They can kill me, but my legacy shall live on, forever.
I am willing to die for what I believe is right, my freedom.
We all know that we can win this fight for our freedom.
If we cannot win in this generation, we will win in the next.
And I will lead us to victory.
We will defeat those who try to control us.
Why do I wish to defeat them?
Because no one's thoughts and feelings should be controlled.
And because I will be controlled no longer.

Brenda Kay Hale

Lift Up You Voices

Lift up your voices, to God up above,
He will watch o'er you, with His tender love,
He is there to protect you.
He will if you ask,
So lift up your voices,
Lift them up fast.
Don't get discouraged.
Don't feel blue.
Just trust in the Savior to see you through.
Place all your troubles.
In his loving care.
He is there with you His love to share.
He will protect you and see you through.
If only you ask this he will do.
So lift up your voices
To God up above.
Let him watch o'er you.
With his tender love . . .

Darlene Cunningham

Genetic Original Black Truth

Round the world people are waiting to come to America
  But I live in America . . . Land of the not so free
When I awoke . . . User's Liars and Thieves
Hiding out in pulpits and Secrets Societies
Had a hidden agenda to keep me blind and on the bottom
By faith I spoke with my Father
By faith walked the Kings High Way
Found the Land And took the Throne
While others watched in disbelief . . . From West to East
In lite of Prophecy Because we're Black
You say no . . . This couldn't happen
  Now we demand Restitution and Reparations
You say . . . No get back share from our table
  But our God says no . . . Satan used you and Failed
They didn't and don't believe in Prophecy
quick-sand's their jail . . . Armageddon their lot
Now you're awake
They laughed at and scorned the Original Black Truth

Reuben Beckles

Envy Of Me

Don't be mad,
  if all you see is the good
  you don't want me to be.

Don't be upset,
  if when you compare flaws,
  I have one to your three.

Don't hate me
  for being myself, and
  knowing right from wrong.

Hate yourself
  for worrying about what I do, and
  not considering yourself as number one.

Dawn Gallaway

She Mate

Sounding . . . from a timeless place
  Drifting along . . . with misty pace
The call of the wild . . . is none the less
  Passions cry . . . in the wilderness

Larking . . . in the moon light pale,
  Kyoodling . . . past the needled vale,
Ardor . . . finds her abreast of night . . .
  In Lobo's eyes . . . in yellow light

The leaves gave ground . . . where they stood
  The moon turned away . . . as well it should
Silhouettes united . . . absorb the cry
  Quivering against . . . a mid-night sky

Jefferson Graalfs

The Bear

One crisp winter morning, I was waken by the echoes of someone snoring.
I sat up to see just what could that noise be.
As I glanced around the room, I was startled by a loud boom.
It was the children coming to see if that bear they heard had gotten me.
And when they jumped on to the bed, up popped that bears head.
BOY! Were they both glad to see, that that bear was not a bear,
but just their DADDY.

Kathy A. Montero

Butterfly Words

Words hurt,
Words heal,
Words break,
Words build;

A word fitly spoken is an apple of gold;
A word out of anger destroys God's fold.

God's word can grow us and season our speech,
Then words of beauty aren't far from our reach.

For we are His mouthpiece
And each word a gift . . .
Encouragement, love, affirmation will lift,
brighten, expand and change our horizon.

I can, you can;
We will . . .
We must!

Our God in us transforms us with trust.

He wants us to hope,
to believe, to fly;

We see the caterpillar —
Our God sees the butterfly.

Billie H. Cash

Shattered Thoughts

When I think about you my heart melts like an ice cube
laying on hot tar on a sunny, summer day. If the day
comes that I can't have you anymore I would feel like
a little unwanted puppy that knows it will be killed in about 2
minutes. I would cry just like that puppy and my tears
would surround me like I've been riding my bike in a
thunderstorm. The pain of the lightning striking my
back is the same pain I feel as you push me away. All
my thoughts of you fly through my head like a sand storm.
Every little piece of sand is a thought that goes through
the hour glass, but it's bigger than a hour glass it's a
lifetime and when all the sand gets to the bottom I flip it
over and think about you all over again. As you move on.
All the happy and sad thoughts bring pain as the hour
glass falls and shatters against that hot tar as I start to
blow away in the hot breeze.

LaRee Haggerty

Crowing Crosses

On Sunday's path as winter's mask
Stares down an eyeless gray,
A leafless breeze through passive trees
Slaps through a rag tailed frame.

The tree tops sieve this global mist
'Til caws sieve shivering limbs.
Laboring long iced wires from poles,
A crow bellows in wind.

Low hanging smoke from hometown stacks
Downs eyes to endless ties.
Two frozen rails spike frosted backs
Then spine — tree ribbed miles.

A steepled bell hearths church door steps
But serves a silent tomb.
The crucifix, one's story tall,
Spiked cold yet fires the room.

A steepled caw turns leaving steps
The flees a dawn orbed cross,
Then labors 'long the endless tracks
Bellowing an embering frost.

Gilbert Sauerhoff

"The Bottle — The Devil"

I traveled down the back streets of the city today
What a sight to behold —
The derelicts, homeless and winos all out in the cold.
I came to an old man with his head bowed low —
I stopped to say "Good morning, and hello."
He looked up at me with blood-shot eyes and replied,
"There's no good morning for me — I lost it all to the bottle — the devil,
It got its hold on me.
I once had a wife and loving family.
But I lost is all to the bottle — the devil — you see.
Now I'm old and gray and no one to care about me.
So as you go on your way
Please, heed what I say.
Tell others all about me.
How the bottle — the devil took charge of my life
Now there's nothing left for me."

Bertha Roberts

Kelp

There has always been the sound of motor boats cutting up the kelp I
never understood what made iron blades beat the waves fiercely like
the gnashing jaws of eel spirits I remember when the big gray skies
took over, smashing every surface thing into the rocks, plastering
pieces of unkept puzzles in the coral now I know what killed the
motorboats bleating I never heard the sound again, at least not in
puphood if I had only known the chaos that took place far below the
glimmering sunrays, the fallen hard bodies drifting into the deep I
have imagined what would have been if the shells of the machines
hadn't landed in the cool caves nobody told me gray skies can toss
fathers as well as waves like rags of tattered water weed out to shore
I have searched for my missing mentor in the gutted remains of the
ships like a diver I pull and push at the ocean with new hatred for
the cold I am only now beginning to feel the warmth of kelp like a
lasso tying me to empty heartache I am still surprised when the
drifting bleating roams, tampering with the nurturing silent.

Miriam Carr

It Must Be So

In the beginning was the end.
A flash and bang destroyed what?
We do not know but it was the beginning.
All life evolved, all earthy things also.
The sun, moon and planets and debris.
All this we do not know.
Some care, they do their tiny bit to keep it so.
Where does this go in the end?
No beginning and no end.
No end and no beginning.
It must be so.

John Allan

Twas The Day Before Graduation

Twas the day before graduation, I went all through the school;
 Looking for someone, anyone who would give me the last minute rule
First in the office, no one was there,
 Then in each classroom, they too were bare.
I stood still because I thought heard
 Something that sounded like a little singing bird.
I walked in the direction it seemed to be coming
 Only to find it wasn't a bird singing but a little bee humming.
Where is everyone I asked myself aloud?
 One minute frightened the next minute proud.
Just at the moment I began to retreat,
 The curtains went up and everyone beckon for me.
No wonder I couldn't find anyone standing idle by
 Twas the day before graduation and they had all gotten together to
 say Goodbye!!!!!!!!

Earlean Davis

To All Who Loved And Cared For Me

I hated to leave, as you well know.
I loved you much, but my cancer hurt me so.
As you said goodbye, I thought I'd cry.
But my painful body said, it is alright to die.
My years were such a joy, with you and your little boy.
We had such fun, especially when you'd let us run.
As you laid my body down to rest,
I knew I had known the very best.
Of life's joy, happiness, and love.
So leaving you was mighty damn tough.
But as you keep going without me now,
My memory will share each day somehow.
My body lies close, and my spirit is with you.
And my heart still feels, when you are blue.
And I thank you for all of your love
As Sandy, Mitzy, and I look down from above
We smile, with our hearts bursting with joy
As we wait someday to see you and your little boy.

Holly Jane

"Baby Blues"

I painfully muttered, "Dear God, can this be true?"
As the test result window streaked with blue.
In a state of shock, I became cold and clammy,
My face drenched with sweat as I was hit with this Whamie!
I cupped my hands over my face,
to muffle the sounds of my disgrace.
My mother comforted me with a warm embrace,
and words of encouragement as she caressed my face.
She said it matters not, what I decide,
She would always support me and remain by my side.
I was ready for pregnancy years ago,
before I divorced and went out on my own.
Back then it wasn't meant to be,
As this makes pregnancy number three!
I'm so unstable at this point in my life,
Could I make a good mother not being a wife?
My mom seems to think so and she should know,
'cause as the role of "Mom" she steals the show.
Regardless of the decision I make,
Only God, knows this Baby's fate.

Lisa R. Maggard

Victoria Lynn

I have a precious, little girl; her name is Victoria Lynn
I'm always there if she needs me, or needs a helping hand
I have a special place in my heart saved just for her
I special place where her love will always endure
I have a tiny treasure that will grow into a fortune
I am full of riches, for she is worth a million
I hold this precious jewel, and thank God I am blessed
I'm not a perfect mother though, I admit it; I confess
I wouldn't trade her for a diamond, or a star in the sky
Because I just couldn't live without her in my life
I hold her tiny hands and stand her on my laps
And rock her, ever, gently when she wants to take a nap
I watch her when she's sleeping, and I know God does too
My precious Victoria Lynn, my love for her is true
I kiss her tiny nose, and kiss her on her head
And pray that brighter days, is where she will be led
As the years go by, this little girl will be a lady
And I'll still be by her side, she'll always be my baby
My precious little girl is named Victoria Lynn
I won't be just her mother; I'll also be her friend

Julia A. Uriegas

The Mariner

When I looked into the clouds, I saw a bow of white
A silken slip of sailing ship driving wide the wild kites

A flock of egrets long and loud
Made their passing cross the clouds

As the drama yet unfolds the mainsail rips upon the sky
It's long and blue, and catches wind with but a single try

As I watch in quiet awe, relieved from its ethereal moor
The boat comes about the dawn without a tiller, nor an oar

A little man with just a smile tipped his cap and laughed
He pulled the jib a hearty tug and waved 'way the wavering raft

The sun, it broke upon the day with such a gleam upon the eye
I lost the gallant sailing ship reflected in the sky

As time has passed and days bygone, I think of ships in cotton crowds
Yet as I walk beneath the sun, I hear him laughing in the clouds

Tina Walulak

The Phone Call

The phone rings, I'm happy because I know it's you.
I pick it up and say "Hello"
We talk a while, about nothing
I'm doodling on this piece of paper,
Smiley faces, stars, hearts, your name next to mine.
But now you're the only one talking.
Your voice sounds strange, you're babbling
Saying things I don't want to hear.
You want to tell me something?
So get to the point!
I swallow my tears, they sting my throat
But manage to escape anyway.
I've stopped drawing, doodling,
Now I'm scribbling, scratching out hearts, happy faces,
your name next to mine
You say goodbye.
Left with a dial tone, I hang up
I try to scratch you from my mind.
But my pen ran out of ink.

Summer L. Montanez

A Vision Inside

I saw some place I'd like to be
a vision in mind, to let you know.
This vision was short, but enjoyed
a lot, A dream that started as a vision,
I thought it was a sight of the future.
How I found that visions are sacred.
Visions can range from images to
fantasies or even your favorite dreams.
But this is nothing but a thought, a
vision inside your mind.

Bill Niemi

Let Me Be

Please, let me be all that I can be
please let my spirit roam free
remove the blinders that I might see.
Remove my shackles, that I might run, jump, fly
that I might laugh with joy, that I might cry.
Put no obstacles in my path
don't show me negatives in my looking glass.
I promise, I will be all that I can be
just let my spirit, my soul, my joy roam free.

Rosetta Larrieu

Broken Promises

As I awaken to a morn overtaken by down pouring rains and
blowing winds, I think back on old times, old ways and old friends.
    I think of dear ole mom working hard to provide us with
tender loving care, but nought ever mattered for I ran with the
wind, but in my heart mom was always there.
    As the rains fell on, tears gathered as I saw dear ole dad
working hard in the heat and bitter cold, but I left home
early, how he could still love me, I didn't know.
    A silence fell upon me as I thought of my family and all their
love, though poor were we, we made it through, trusting in each
other while relying upon the good Lord above.
    Soon the rains faded but I clung to a picture taken when I was three,
for as I stared at the picture, I wondered did they still think of me.

Gerry Burchett

Gone Forever

You lifted my spirits when I would cower.
You gave such encouraging words to me.
The wisdom of your soul gave me such power.
You were the eyes to make me try to see.

So close to the stars you have now gone to.
Far from me and the worries of my life.
However, you're the one to see me through.
The pain of you now gone cuts like a knife.

I let go of the sadness through my tears.
Letting all confusion out when I weep.
Though it is harder for me to lose the fears.
But, I can still have good dreams when I sleep.

I miss you terribly and wish you were here.
I do know that you will always be near.

Stephanie Devaux

A Very Special Man

There's something special about this man that I love;
he's one of whom God sent from above.

I have yet to meet another of his kind;
what makes him so special is his God conscious mind.

He respects me in every way; this one thing I can truly say.

There's something special about this man that I love;
I have no doubt, he was sent from above.

He holds a special place in my heart that no man can touch;
he's a man of distinction, whom I love very much.

He has a warm, friendly smile that reaches me from afar;
He's the apple of my eye-my bright and shining star.

He has a touch that's so gentle and a heart that's so warm;
With this "very special man" is where I belong.

Catherine E. Barton

The Day

When the soft music started to play,
In his head, he'll remember this day,
He touches her hand and then he knew,
Their hearts were one but they were two,

Now he'll never see her again
And all over, his life will begin,
He thinks of what happened that day,
He knew it was wrong but didn't know what to say.

As a tear rolled down his cheek,
All who watched did not care to speak,
Cause this is what happens to many alive
When friends let friends drink and drive,

Amanda McCabe

The Pondering

I sit upon this sullen ground called earth,
and dream of twinkling stars,
dancing so graceful
within this complex universe.

I ask myself
as I sit and dream,
like the stars that illuminate my solemn face
were they;
as I
upon this place
once upon a time?

Shall I dance upon the tapestry of silver lights
and velvet canvas,
or shall I as the evening breeze
whisper softly in your ear
to say:
"I am always here among the twinkling . . .

Stars."

Barbara E. Scruggs-Warren

Love

Love isn't just heart — It's the hands, taking care.
    Feet walking with you, for you — anywhere.
    Lips not stopped with kissing, but go on to pray —
    For you, and with you: Though you should stray,
    Eyes seeing past the outside — to the in.
    Ears that are deaf to an arguments din.

Love comes out of words — That ne'er have to be said.
    And that sometimes are spoken in moments — so dread.
    From having — forsaking; Accepting defeat.
    Yet, not giving up! Pressing on — never beat.

Love is togetherness — On through the years.
    The smiles — the pleasures, the heartaches — the tears.
    Love is the flame that age cannot smother.
    Growing old to the world, but not to each other

Love is the bond — That makes up a home.
    A family together, wherever we roam.
    Hope for the future, a Heaven above.
    Put them all together and you'll have — Love

Walter W. Hichens

Don't Shoot Yourself, Son!

Father, I did not know the gun was loaded when I took that first
drink. Momma, I thought that I could handle it, I just did not give
myself time to think. Father, I did not know that gun was loaded
when I took a ride on that white horse. Momma, I thought that I was
riding high but I had joined the devil's force, Father! I did not
know that gun was loaded when I met that girl named Crack cocaine.
Momma listen to me I thought that I was cool for a while until I
started feeling like I was going insane. Father, now that I know the
gun is loaded full of lies and not one truth. Momma, I can make
myself a better man and pass it on to our youth, Father, now that I
know that gun is loaded since I have faced death so many times,
Mother, Jesus has turned that gun away from me and gave me back that
true life I had left behind. Father, I promise that I will watch out
for that loaded Gun I thought was full of wealth, Mother, I will
watch out for that loaded gun and I am confident and determined,
your son will not shoot himself to death.

Donald Lee Duhart

Asgard

A realm of Gods of pagan lore,
Obscure legends and heroes no more.
A kingdom aging, forgotten by man.
Lost myths of how we all began.

The bridge of color deteriorates.
The vigilant guard abandoned his gate.
Religion of honor once a stronghold,
As the followers of silver sidetracked by gold.

A hall of Gods emptied from time.
The lack of change, their only crime.
The sword of heroes rusted and recked.
Flawless armor scratched from neglect.

Floors of heaven, stone cold hard,
With the vanished Gods of great Asgard.
Where is Odin? Balder? And Thor?
A realm of Gods remembered no more.

Christopher Gensur

Widow's Prayer

To never see your face again,
the face that made me smile.
    To never feel your lips again,
the lips that kissed me ever so gently.
    To never feel your arms again,
the arm that held me so close.
    To never have these things. How can I go on?

(Voice of husband)

Go on,
    For once again you will see my face
and again it will make you smile.
    You will feel my lips again
and once again they will kiss you so gently.
    You will feel my arms again
and once again they will hold you close.
    But until this time go and live your
life. I will wait forever for you in heaven.

Michelle Crytzer

Ode To David

He was once a strong loving person.
A person who knew too much about animals.
He was the person the kids, who were knee high to a cactus, could look up to.
So sweet and kind was he, to show us
to be as kind as he, to the creatures he knew.
Not knowing he was going to go, he spent as much time
laughing and talking about school as we did.
He knew so much about everything, it was hard not to ask him anything.

Abigail Adams

My Grandfather

When I see him,
He has skin like a wooden pole, with barnacles stuck to them like clamps,
His eyes are like black shiny marbles with a little speck in the middle,
He talks about his childhood in China while I try to visualize his
life as a child,

When I see him,
He is in the garden watering plants, that blossom like knowledge,
He looks like a weak and frail wooden pole,
But he is strong in his heart,
Which keeps him going everyday,

When I see him,
I feel sad and think of the memories I have about him,
The happiness we shared in our lives,
I say my last good-bye as the men lower him into his grave.

Nathan Tran

Untitled

Lightening silhouettes that have faded with time
Come alive in the deep blackness of my mind.
Shattered dreams and empty promises come to life
Of the forgotten loves I've left behind.

Lost memories that are buried deep within my soul
Come back to haunt my restless heart.
Teasing love loses control in my life.
And forever, what seems like love, is of me, again a part.

For what is love, and what role does it play
In the chaotic thoughts that seem to rule me?
Is it the hope of living a life free of pain
That makes the heart lose touch with reality?

But gone are the days where heartbroken youthfulness once lived
Now, the aging heart begins to understand what love is about.
It is an endless masquerade of pleasure and pain
That this heart just can not live without.

Barbara McLaughlin

The Awakening

The morning light unveils a cruel sight,
For there lies a little boy not more than five,
lifeless, motionless, a victim of sniper fire.

Beams of light caress his face,
the tender breeze now sets his hair.
But the nurture of human hand is absent,
Oh Lord, now is that fair?

And just this morning his lunch box mother took such pride to pack.
And she handed it to her little prince not knowing,
that today he won't come back.

Oh people, awaken, come out and see,
something that was and can now never be.

An innocent child, a victim of hate.
Young life cut short, because of faith.

Their pathetic excuse of 'self defense'
for innocent lives they "ethnically cleanse."

And we vow that history shall itself not repeat,
but it is our word we cannot keep.

So let's put an end, to this law they chant and cry,
That whoever is different is lost, and must die!

Babar Khan

Kidney

There's a war going on inside me.
There's a war going on, because I can't pee.

I have to get run on a machine,
To take those chems. out of my stream.

Those chems. build up and fight each other
They got so bad, they killed my brother.

The doctors tell you what you can't eat,
But they're not the ones who sit in your seat.

While others love, work and prosper
I sit at home and itch with phosphorous.

I know people worry and care.
It's just so damn hard, you have to be there.

I have to wait and be patient,
And soon I'll get my operation.

Michael DiPietro

"Our Innocence Bartered"

Sweet Joy of days gone by Builds the sorrow of today
Struggles . . . won again and again
For the memories of Joy
Mother's tears wash the breast of the hidden heart,
     Hardened by the arrogance of man
Straining hearts, fevered thoughts,
The sweetness of terror, Candy of Hell
Blue Sky, color of indifference
Helplessness . . . a Father's fear,
Quiet sobs, Despair finds a home, births hate, breeds contempt
Churn inside . . . sweep it clean
Welcome the stranger and his Baggage
for you to claim.
You Buy . . . You Buy . . . You Buy . . .
God of Greed, Lord of Green Ruler of Men's Souls
Teach us a game of darkness and sorrow,
Sell us our Damnation . . .

George Hill

Mother Mary

Oh, Mother Mary, what goes through your mind
As you gaze on your infant so serene, so sublime?
Does your heart fill with gladness, with love and with joy
As you look down at Him, your baby boy?
Do you smile a little at the year just ahead
Of how you will feed Him, cuddle and tuck Him in bed?
Does your heart fill with pride as to the great deeds He'll perform
Of raising the dead, of calming the storm?
Of curing the sick, giving sight to the blind
Are these some of the things that go through your mind?
Does your heart fill with sadness, with grief and with pain
When you think of the reasons for which He came?
To make restitution to our God above
For the wrongs we have done to the supreme being of love?
Do you pray your loving heart can withstand the great loss
When your divine son dies on the cross?
Or do you thank God in your heart for you know this must be
That His suffering and death will save all humanity
Oh, yes, Mother Mary, what goes through your mind
As you gaze on your infant so serene, so sublime?

Wilbert J. Stachofsky

How Old Is Old?

I read a wonderful poem about an old woman who said when she was
old she would wear purple.

But I wondered, how old is old?

I asked a friend, who was 90 last birthday, when are you old?

She thought a moment and said, "About 10 years from now, I suppose."

I asked another friend, slightly younger, she replied, "When you no
longer thrill to Beethoven's 9th, or the Messiah, or the National
Anthem sung at a baseball game."

I asked a dear friend who is very frail, when are you old?

The tremor of her hands stilled, and her pale blue eyes dimmed with
age, brightened. Her voice strong and steady said, " When you no
longer respond with a rush of love at the sight of your newest
grandchild, or you no longer respond with love at the sight and
sound of those nearest and dearest to you.
Or you feel all dried up, like an old prune."

I put aside the purple dress I had bought for my 72nd birthday party.
Instead I chose a pretty pink, many years old. I put the purple
dress at the back of the closet.

I might wear it in 10 years, if, by then, I am old enough.

Margaret Beadle

Conception

We have touched conception
the moment before it happens.
Gazing on the sunrise
the second before the sun slips above the Earth.
Exploding! With life and energy
The sun warms our skin
melting away the cold night's dew.
Glistening drops of cool water
evaporate into the air we breath.
We breath in
and hold the moment
(just but for a second)
before we exhale.

Debra Angeline Walkush

Reflections

Walk softly now that spring is here once more,
Thou dare not tread upon the budding flowers
Resplendent in all colors I adore
To help me pass my many weary hours.

Talk softly now that silence is the rule,
Thou dare not rouse us from our endless slumber,
Encased in earth, the genius and the fool,
Together now in ever growing number.

Oh, sing of life that we so dearly miss,
Thou dare not dwell on endings such as death,
But sing of love, a sigh, a touch, a kiss,
And cling to these with each and every breath!

Herbert Feldman

Meditation At Eventide

"Jesus was laid in a bed of hay.
Wrapped in swaddling clothes, "they say.
While my baby lies in a soft warm bed
With a downy pillow at his head;
And he laughs and cries and kicks and coos
While I paint his future in rosy hues.
As I kneel and study his innocent face;
Bright and alive with baptismal grace.
I know how the Virgin must have felt
When in meditation and prayer she knelt
By the manger crib of the son she bore
And thought what "His" future held in store.
How sad and torn her heart would be
As clearly the passion she would see
The thorns, the cross then her dead son.
What grace to murmur "Thy will be done."
The serving of God, her only intention
Her great reward . . . "His Resurrection"

Justine Bowen Shawk

Untitled

I visioned once of love drowned in bitter sweet sorrow
lost to life before it blossomed.
A broken heart in time will mend, but there is a scar,
felt if not seen.
To try can be to fail, but fear of failing, is failure.
No sorrow is greater than emptiness.
Giving love is to live, receiving is to be reborn.
Not freely is it given, but willingly it must be.
As night follows day, so must receive follow give.
No joy is so great as love received, and no sorrow
as deep as love denied.
It is sadness to never be loved, but worse yet is to never love.
The spirit survives all, love is an emotion of the spirit
So love will survive . . . always.

Michael D. Quillin

The Memorable Night

It started out as not a date.
But things changed when time became late.
The wind whispered through their hair.
Her soft face shone in the moonlight so fare.
This passion could not wait.

All it took was the awkward kiss.
A kiss full of passion and bliss.
As they looked into each other's eyes,
Their hearts flew through the warm summer skies.
This passion would not miss.

The passion burned throughout the night.
Two lovers in perfect flight.
Hot as a burning ember,
This would be a night to remember.
This union, memorable and right.

John E. Ondrovic

Beings Of The So-Called Night

As you see as mysterious as we are,
common sense is never that far.
Active with the moon lit night,
dead within the morning light.
Immortality has its limits,
most of us are not quite timid.

We hold in our hands the key of youth,
this here is the truth.
Humans think this joy and glory.
But what meets us are feelings of
endless suffering and pain.
Watching the world grow old and die.
You live in depressing youth.

Coffins and graveyards are human theories,
supposing bats and other nights eeries.
Yet other thoughts have still to arrive.
When all we vampires are just trying
to survive, in our world. And your so called night . . .

Joyce Weng

Is It Real?

I'm just sitting here and I look up at the big, blue sky
to see the white, fluffy clouds forming pictures.
I see a duck swimming like a speeding bullet. Is it
real or is my mind playing tricks on me?
I see a pirates ship. Is it real or is my mind playing tricks on me?
I see a child crying for food. Is it real or is my mind playing tricks on me?
The last picture I see is the pillow which I'll lay my
head forever. Is it real or is my mind playing tricks on me?

I guess I'll never know if those pictures I saw were real
or if my mind was just playing tricks on me.

Monique Marie Duursma

Violets And Memories

The sweet fragrance of the Violet disappears . . .
    Leaving behind a path of memories
        Pleasant and sincere.

We cry, knowing its presence among us has ended . . .
    Yielding to the darkness
        Of Winter.

Then, we smile, remembering that the darkness
    Is simply a symbol of rebirth
        And rededication.

The beautiful Violet has not left us . . .
    But is resting, looking toward a new
        And brighter Springtime!!

Linda Heberling

Untitled

I've seen your face in the dark.
I've seen it in the light.
I've seen it early in the morning
And oh so late at night.
I've seen it in my dreams
And even while I'm awake.
I saw it filled with a passion
That could not even be faked.
I've seen it looking in wonder
And also in startled surprise
But I've always wondered what's hidden deep
In those dark and brooding eyes.
Do you long to be somewhere else
Running wild and free?
Wherever you go, are you with
Or are you without me?

Patricia Ross

12000 Days

We've walked together for 12,000 days
And I want 12000 more.
The time has passed in a lover's haze
But I wish the years could go slower.
We've brought home our babies in a ball of fuzz
And watched as they walked out the door.
The road has been rocky and bumpy; because
When life's path is smooth, it isn't life anymore.
A dark shadow lies across our lands
With a dark as dark as night.
I believe that together, holding hands,
We can walk through this storm to the light.
Together we've walked 12000 days
And our time is not near through:
I need more time to list the ways
To say that I love you.

Ronald O. Elliott

"Why I Love Nature"

Sun over water,
Birds in the sky.
People ask why I love nature,
This is my reason why.

Think of the flowers,
And the squirrels in the trees.
Bright flower peddles,
And the trees falling leaves.
The grass in the meadow,
Is ever so green,
The deer run so fast,
sometimes they can't be seen.

So the next time you think of nature,
Remember to think of,
The world and its creatures, and the stars above.

Dora L. Dopin

Inspiring Destiny

Yesterday is a beautiful memory
    Today is a clearer vision
Tomorrow is and infinite opportunity
    Adventure is endless, passion prevails
Boundaries dissolve, become invisible
    Destiny is an inspired creation
Think, Believe, Dream, Dare . . .
    Embrace each moment and celebrate,
    another day in this dance called life

Suzanne F. Hannon

From Day To Night

Outside my window I saw some kids play.
Like the energizer bunny, lasting all day.
Outside my window colorful lights
    surround a house.
My cats are mad because they can't catch
    a mouse.
Outside my window kids sled down hills.
So deep and slippery it gives you the chills.
Outside my window kids build snowmen
all around.
    Running in the snow that makes a
crunchy sound.
Outside my window snow falls from the sky.
You can't see where it's coming from
    because it's up too high.
Outside my window at night the sky is
    always blue.
It's time to go to bed, and like the
earth, I turn off my light, too.

Julio Vasquez

Heaven

How would it feel to be in heaven?
Amongst all the angels and kind souls of the past.
Would I be happy, scared, or even sad?
How would I feel?
To look down at all my friends,
To know that I belong with them.
As a normal school girl,
Riding to school on the school bus every day,
Or walking from class to class between bells,
Studying, talking, or even playing in the school band.
Would I miss meeting new people and going new places,
Or would I be happy to leave this world filled with crime and hatred?
Would I be sad to leave the joy that my friends and family bring to me?
Would I wish I could give a good-bye hug to my little sister
Or hold hands with all the people I left behind?
What would I do in heaven?
Maybe I'd be happy to be as free as a bird?
Or maybe I'd be homesick for all my friends and family
Whom I'd left behind.
How would it feel to be in heaven?

Diana Bharucha

Untitled

A pretty pretty painting of a bird upon a branch
A dirty dusty drawing of a dog upon a ranch

Framed in the whiteness of a front entrance hall
Pinned to the logs of a one-room cabin wall

A lovely silken gown, and golden locks curled so neat
Ragged brown hair, torn ov'ralls, bare feet

Browsing through her gardens and dreaming of her face
Sowing seeds of flowers, fixing, her dooryard gate

The sea blue eyes had brightened, since their sight, had first met
the bowed head and cheeks flushed — his heart had been beset

Propriety had kept, her fondness sadly, at a distance
As a mere yard hand, his love, was without substance

A summon from the house, and poppies dance, irises sway
The bare feet turn toward home, through the gate, on their way

Outside a curtained window is a tree beside a lane
Above a dirty window the dust soars, unsettled, for lack of rain

A dainty little bird is perched, upon a branch
A yellow short-haired dog, runs wild, upon a ranch.

Raina Keim

A Fake Nickel

Curses! Why was I made of lead?
Why couldn't I have been a real nickel instead?
I've been thrown on the ground
Then by children found.
I've lain out in the rain
Then picked up again.
And many a time I've grown very weary
For I know real nickels are always cheery,
Because they are honest and true,
So cannot be blue.
Curses! Why was I made of lead,
Why couldn't I have been a real nickel instead?

Jack Tesch

My Brothers And Sisters

Oh how I wish things could be as it was 20 year ago.
When all my brothers and sisters would come together
at this joyous time of year.
I wish to spend some time with my brothers and sisters
So that I can tell each one of them how much
I love him and her.
I wish for my brothers and sisters to come together
Once again as we did 20 year ago.
For before to long my brothers and sisters will be gone forever
and not know of my love for my brothers and sisters.

Donald G. Smith

Shadow Child

I know that she's got shining hair,
    And eyes that sparkle, too.
And a laugh that lightens the darkest day,
    The girl I never knew.

I know that he just loves to play,
    And sometimes he'd be bad,
But I would love him through it all,
    The boy I never had.

I cook their meals, I make their beds,
    I put away their toys.
I often wish that they were real,
    My little girl, or boy.

Fate had decreed that there they'll stay,
    Locked up inside my head,
And phantom arms, and shadow's play
    Is all I'll have instead.

Barbara Deacon

A Great Grandmother's Prayer

As evening sun sinks in the west,
Little Sabrina sleeps on your breast,
You softly hum sweet lullabies,
Long lashes drop and hide her eyes.

Little chubby, tiny pink toes,
Two sweet cheeks soft as a rose,
Her soft little lips, little button nose,
Sabrina, the sweetest flower that grows.

The Lord smiled down from up above,
He sent us baby Sabrina to love,
May he guard her along life's way,
And protect her through each bright day.

Dear Lord fill her heart with love,
She will reach the home above,
May all her life be bright and fair,
Just a great-grandmother's prayer.

Vadis Pierce

An Airplane

A poem is like an airplane,
Taking you off to distant places,
An adventure in the making.
Or perhaps just a pursuit of the imagination,
Bringing you to a far off land in the clouds.

Twisting, turning, trying to give you a swift,
    smooth ride.
Like an airplane in turbulent weather,
A poem is sometimes rough,
Giving you all but the expected.

Like a pilot, the writer controls his poem,
Deciding what destination his piece will have.
Whether it be a non-stop flight,
Straight to the point,
Or a poem with many destinations.

As the plane swiftly lands,
A poem comes to its close.
Upon arrival, the passenger departs contentedly,
Like a poet capping his pen.

Andrea Stava

Too Soon, Too Bad

Life was tough in the good ole days
It's good that I was young
We didn't have cars and great highways
I rode to town on the wagon tongue

Every Saturday I got my bath
In a washtub number 3
I made mistakes when I did my Math
My kerosene lamp was dim, you see

One day dad came home in a model T
Our house was all in a stir
We all climbed aboard, went on a spree
Down the road with a hum and a purr

You younguns don't know 'bout the good ole days
Your water is always on tap
You zoom cross the world on the great highways
And you don't even need a map

You may even rocket up to the moon
Or Venus, Jupiter or Mars
You've come a long way too soon, too soon
Too bad they invented the cars

Juanita Hunnicutt

Watch With Me

Watch and wait here while I pray,
But they fell asleep
His faithful few
Would that I could have watched
It wasn't my time!
The night grew chilly,
My eyes grow heavy
My head sinks onto my chest,
Oh Jesus like all the rest
I could not stay awake
You ask so little
You give so much
Everything we need
I love you Lord (but)
My will is weak
Why all the things I seek
Seem so unimportant
When I know you love me why am I so restless?
When I know I can rest in your love
Stay here and watch with me Watch and Pray.

Helem J. Jarvis

Will Anything Good Happen Today

Each day I sit and wait for my answer.
Thinking of a reason why I should just say "Forget it.
Wandering if any thing good will happen today.
Each day I sit and wait for any answer.
Hoping something great, mystical and bright will appear.
Looking around to find a sign, anything to tell me what to do.
Time is no longer on my side.
Will something happen today, for me?
I looked over my shoulder, thought a big picture window.
I turned around and walked toward the window, in order to get a closer look.
I could see birds in the trees, children playing ball in the street.
Something great came upon my face.
A smile.

Anglecia Terry

The Seed

I held the seed of a dream in my hand
In the long ago days of my youth,
And I wistfully wondered what fruit it would bear
If I planted it and it took root.

But pragmatic people scoffed at my dream,
So I hid it away in my heart,
And I struggled and strived 'til success I had earned
And had proved to the world I was smart.

But lately at night when I am alone
I take out that seed brown and dry
And I painfully ponder what fruit it would bear
If my seed did not wither and die.

Mary Cook

"The Flower Garden"

I like to walk in my flower garden
Where roses like pretty maids,
show off their delicate petticoats
and gowns of many shades.

There's daffy-down-dilly with her yellow petticoat
and gown of brilliant green,
and the pansies with their smiling faces
that look so bright and clean.

The tulips bloom like little cups
to catch the falling rain,
as it falls from the sky to quench the thirst
of the flowers ere they wane.

The poppies open up their eyes
with the coming of the day,
and close them tightly up again
as the sunshine fades away.

Yes, a garden can be a beautiful,
and very cheerful place,
with many colored petals
like rainbows of delicate lace.

Lorena Cordero

Untitled

I'm an old and dawning dream from fires light divine
colors fought on hills that lie below flowing tides
seers fade than are once again touched by a brilliance
unmoved but of equal base, laughing voices free of strife

Lights so radiant feel our thoughts, remembered hearts
companions faded in a gloom of unimagined lights
time bring back faded things died so young
tales of those who hearts rapt of life's wandering ways

Keith Whale

Almost Mother's Day

I want to wish you a happy day,
Even though you walked your way.
You never saw my smiling face,
I never got to see that place.

You'll never know the love that I could give,
If only you had let me live.
The times we could have spent together,
Braving storms and all bad weather.

We could have known such love,
That only could have been sent from above,
Yes, mother dear, I'm sure you know,
The love we could have shared if I could have grown.

The things together we could have shared,
The first day of school, brushing my hair,
The first school play, trips to the zoo,
Walks in the park, just me and you.

Yes, mother dear, it could have been fun,
Shared by all, since time has begun,
But for whatever reasons, you had your way,
But, I love you still, Happy Mother's Day!

John Daniel Blackowicz

Beautiful Rose

Beautiful flower, why do you cry?
Beautiful rose, please don't die.
Beautiful flower, is that rain,
Or a tear from life's foul stain?
Where are your thorns and pedals at?
Snatched away in sorrow settles that.
The gardener has the rose hidden away,
And lonely is how she tends to stay.
Isolated from the rain and sun,
So no one can see her or what he's done.
He threatens to cut her stem,
Where roots shall be damaged grim,
And if she lives they'll be a scar.
Right now it's all but the sheers so far.
Yet he's cut her stem before,
So she fears he'll do it more.
Beautiful flower, what can you do?
You feel so ugly, what he puts you through!
Beautiful rose, when can you bloom?
How can you stay there, in all this gloom?

Ana Carpenter

Untitled

If we could be free from within
than we could be free without
worries of war, poverty, sin
and underlying self doubt
would could be free from fears
free from hate, free to cry joyous tears
and no longer discriminate
if we could be free from within
then we could be free without
memories of what has been
and fears of what's to come about
we could be free to live, free to love,
free to give to those below and above
if we could be free from within
than we could be free without
the concept of having to win
we'd never have to fight a bout
if we could open each heart and free each soul
than as one, we can make a new start
and as one we can become whole

Victoria Snyder

Teacher's Prayer

Our Father lead us to the ear,
Which never precious truth has heard,
And with a vision ever clear,
Burden our hearts to teach Thy word.

Kindle souls 'til faith flames stronger,
Speak that upon each life will burst,
Hunger where there is no hunger,
And a thirst where there is no thirst.

And when the zeal for truth burns fierce,
And man cannot an answer find,
Use our lips that Thy word might pierce,
And sever chains of sin that bind.

Then to guide with unerring hand,
The souls entrusted to our care,
So these will be prepared to stand,
When on life's path is placed a snare.

When we would chart a lesser course,
And flesh would lesser goals fulfill,
Then Holy Spirit be our source,
Of strength to do our Father's will. Amen.

Thomas E. Reddington

Ancestral

Loch....
A little wooden rowboat scrapes over algae cover'd rocks
with a sound reminiscent of teeth rubbing against long fingernails
the turquoise eyes of a gillie catch the image of charcoal grey cygnets
and carefully steer the craft away toward a small overgrown chartreuse
Island in the center completely obscured by lush ivy and trees
stands the remains of a castle isolated and abandoned
climbing to the top by clinging to the ivy is as dangerous as it is
exhilarating the view from the tower makes the effort more than
worthwhile but there is a flash of red as the gillie turns his back
and he beckons to follow into a narrow passage-way of crumbling
mottled or speckled stone an uneven staircase leads to a hidden
windowless room in which one could imagine the uncomfortable
sensation of breaking through cobwebs being barely able to
make out the trace of his auburn pony-tailed silhouette his hand
reaches out to have us share company in the darkness a "gillie"
is an Irish lake fishing guide.

John Schindler

Time And The Rain

Touching a moment
In a segment of space
An open door brings us
Both face to face
And the rain.
Falling in time
The air is so dense
Filled with emotion, thick with pretense
Long has it been
Long lives the pain
Hits hard, then lifts
to fall once again as the rain.
Once in a moment
I thought I knew you
Once in a lie
I thought I saw through
Once in the rain
The sun caught my eye
But our lives depend now on saying good-bye
Let it rain.

Kathy Lutz

Last Good-bye

There were too many things that were left unsaid
As I sat there sobbing beside your bed.
Though your strength was gone, you were strong in my mind
I recalled all the tumulus years left behind
I wish things had been different, but a child can't ask "why?"
So I grew up without you, and time passed by.
I always knew you loved me — you always had places to go
I'd think of you when things were tough, and I was feeling low
Rambling ways cost me a Dad — deep inside you knew
I wish I'd been a better daughter, and you a better dad too.
So my last time for a "Daddy hug," I'll kiss your eyes of brown,
I'll think of you when I see the 'sea,' or a red sun slip slowly down,
When you left for your journey home — we didn't get to say "good-bye."
But it all worked out, and Daddy "knew" — and he
    never could stand to see me cry.

Billie Jean Hyde

The Crabs

The crabs come in on little crab feet,
    to the syncopated tide, with a rhythmic beat.
Eight little feelers and two massive claws,
    thru the tidal valleys and the muddy walls.
Flowin' with the salty waters to the inland ways,
    with much to-do about nothing, he can travel for days.
To where our boat is anchored, by the oyster beds,
    to my baited lines, made up of flounder heads.
Then — a nibble-nibble here and a nibble-nibble there,
    this crabs takin' a trip, but he don't know where.
Up the line slowly, then under with the net,
    for grabbin' my flounder head, he'll sure regret.
Cause, in to the pot with pepper, salt and basil,
    then out of the pot and on to the table.

Frank E. Valora

In Search for Contentment

Oft, like Coleridge, "she wandered lonely as a cloud"
    In search for contentment —
Until one day she met a bird
    and found that her Moon was his Sun
and now their minds are One.
    He makes her whole
And she is now content . . .

She is no longer a cloud, but is now a stone
    Stable, devoted
She will always be there,
    For this bird to land on.
Even if he needs to fly away
    He can always rely
On this stone to be there for him.

So, don't be sad, my beautiful bird
    Fly high
For you have been locked in a cage for so long
    Fly!
    For I promise to be there for you
Wherever you may want to go.

Nicole M. Tenney

The Hunt

A frosty breath amongst the trees
A sideways glance through the leaves
A single sound that stills the air
Whoever said that life was fair

The twigs that snap against his weight
The glimpse of steel that sealed his fate
A flash of movement before his eyes
The last thing he sees before he dies

Sherri L. Barrick

Untitled

Leaves are turning
the sky is getting gray
winds are whipping up white-capped waters
winters on its way
that's when I think of you . . . when the season ends
wondering why
we couldn't have left each other friends

The days aren't long anymore
the nights are getting cold
I wake to close my window
I find I'm all alone
that northern breeze is blowing you away from me
and it pains to know
I'm just a memory

Why
did I fall in love with you
Why
did you change like the seasons do

Stephen F. Mitchell

Thorns Of A Wild Rose

Beneath the Arms of A wild cherokee rose briar,
Contention unfolds, blooming in profusion,
With words that can heal, but not those of a liar,
Blood red roses, dripping drops of pestilent persuasion.

A heartless move upon another,
Creates a bittersweet aura of suspicion,
Even so, the truth can not smother . . .
Belladonna of selfishness, nightshades of seduction.

Those thorns of that deed, by another to pierce you,
Thrust hard and buried deep, sealed and bound,
Hoping that no one will ever find a clue,
Only to discover truth springs from eternal ground.

Then suspicion falling like petals, the day has come,
To reveal that deed, the passion and the place,
The heartless one has no place to run . . .
Intuition blooms into clues, revelation wins the race.

Loneliness of the heart wont last for long,
There will be someone new, affections to shower,
Those memories deceitful, now painfully gone,
Beneath the Arms of a cherokee briar . . .

Allan W. Trap Hagan

Love

Love makes the world go round and round,
Love makes all good things greatly abound.
Love shows itself in great compassion,
Love never goes out of fashion.
Love is the basis of all beautiful songs,
Love is a balm to all our wrongs.
Love will always stop any war,
Love and love and love evermore.
Love is ever all enduring,
Love will solve all you're fearing.
Love mother, father, sister, brother,
Love without ceasing one another.
Love travels all highways and each avenue,
Love makes things right just for you.
Love brings peace, happiness and more love,
Love encloses you by Him up above.
Love is mentioned, if you will look,
Love many times in the Good Book.
"Love, faith, hope abide with thee,
Love being the greatest of all three."

Alice C. Aslaksen

Untitled

The pregnancy and childbirth is finally over. But, inside of me,
I feel like the baby is still kicking, moving and growing. With
every new generation I hold in my arms, it can be so rewarding
that I cannot believe that this child is mine. By teaching them
their first baby words, or showing them the beauty of this
world. Hearing them laugh, or seeing them play, makes you wish
they could only stay little. Their fingers, hands, and toes, are so
tiny. That holding my child's hand could be so brittle. As I run my
fingers through your hair, I feel the soft spot. Oh my child, I love
you a lot. You'll surprise me with how you'll grow. I want to be
there when you are feeling low. You have a lot to know and to feel.
Believe me, this life is real!

Lana Wakefield

Children Our Past, Present And Future

Hearing gentle laughter from the past of happy times we shared
Gazing into the distant future leaves me feeling very scared
What have I to give to my precious loved ones of this life
Sometimes I am overwhelmed amidst the rapid expanding strife

Changes bring uncertainty about our reason for being here
Shadows of that awful darkness leave us filled with ugly fear
Then beautiful sunshine starts to spread changing dread to joy
Seems to always happen when listening to an innocent girl or boy

They are filled with questions demanding answers here and now
Patience is the virtue as you attempt to keep your holy vow
That you will give them prime time to discuss what's right or wrong
Especially when the couch calls and you sing the same old song

Can't you see I'm very tired, things are very difficult at work
All you are doing this way is acting like a feeble foolish jerk
But if you create a strong foundation by answering with a smile
You'll only spread an abundance of sunshine lasting quite a while

Shadows from the long ago are reaching out as in a dream
When you stop and think a while you'll suppress that tiny scream
Cause many happy faces welcome you to the long journey's end
It's just a little further now around another distant bend

Everret H. Swan

Remembering Sounds Of Summer

The happy days of summer are all too fleeting,
When the gleeful laughter of school children at play
And birds of many species sing joyful melodies, treating
Listeners to the marvelous sounds of summer. An array,
    always enticing, of nature's symphony.
I remember.

The lofty dreams and empty thoughts of the small child
Were melded together by the shattering thunder
    and the soft patter of rain.
I remember the animal mating calls in the wild,
And the gentle cadence of the whistle of a lone train
    in the far and vulnerable distance.

Jettie M. McWilliams

Homelessness

We are alike,
Yes, you and I,
Yet you fail to notice it,
In your eyes I will always be a
    poor and simple minded drunk,
I still with out a home know,
You have a compassion and somehow
    sorrow for me
I am wise through my years and
    fear not,
For the only ones who know the true
    sadness of being homeless, are homeless
    ones themselves.

Katelyn Lynch

To Go

"May I take your order?" she asks.
Indeed, my dear, you may.
Let me take you away to the place my heart lies
and drown in the infinite pools that are your eyes,
allow me, love, to run my fingers through your baby-soft hair,
caress you by candle's burn 'til the smoke's all that is there.
I wish to lie in the safety of your arms all the night
that you may guide me in my dreams, for I am blinded by the light
of your smile and the beauty of your heaven-sent name,
of your lips so red, put the petals of the rose to shame.
If only I could tell you how beautiful you are to me,
take you home and make love the way love should be.
Would you understand that my whole life revolves around you
and the millions of trivial things that you do . . .
Oh love, I see you and I see all of my dreams,
but my courage is fading as always, it seems . . .
"A cheeseburger, large fries, and a Coke to go," said I.

Frank Alog

Carve Me Gently, Lord

Take the clay from the bottom of the winding river;
Maybe the granite that lays atop the soaring mountain
Or even the wood from a grand old oak tree,
But Lord from whatever you may choose to mould me;
Please do it ever so gently.
With the loving touch of your fingertips
Let your spirit flow o'er me and through my body.
Saturate the very heart of me with your love.
Carving a gentle, patient smile upon my face.
Let the rain fall softly, full of thy cleansing power
That it may wash the impurities from body and soul
Leaving me complete; leaving me whole.
Guide your hands all o'er me Lord
Let the sands that blow and shift around me
Wear away only the waywardness of my spirit
Carved gently by your touch; by the winds of time.
May I be forever changing
Ever growing closer to thee.
Walking side by side with you my friend;
My guardian and guide.

Carla D. Fishel

Lost Butterfly

I saw this beautiful butterfly;
    She reminded me of you.
With wings like a silk kaleidoscope;
    Simply dazzling as she flew.

She searched high, then low among the blooms;
    With the wind, she would happily dance.
But, afraid to pick this beautiful flower;
    Afraid to take a chance.

For there is no sense is rushing;
    She wants to take her time.
Take each day as it comes along;
    Until the right flower, she finds.

But the trouble with flowers, they just don't last;
    They fade, and wilt, and die.
'Til all is gone and there's no love left;
    To give to the butterfly.

Without a flower, the world is lost;
    And so the butterfly too.
I might be the flower I'm talking about;
    And the butterfly could be you.

Charlie L. Gordy

How I Came To Think Of You

perhaps and i am not quite sure why i thought of you reading the line
over and over to myself and it made me think i think of you and the
title of a poem which you had written once something to the effect
of i would rather ride into you than inside this great big car and i
have this image of you riding in an old car perhaps pale blue or
violet and the sun shining down slanting in across the rooftop of
america and you in its car driving across this great big land with
the desert and you hand in hand and you smile your big orange smile
and the sun is first everywhere and then reflected in your eyes a
thousand big burst of sun excitement pitch pitching itself to you and
i fancy this and make it into some movie where you would of course
play the star and there would be music by papas or his better teacher
segovia rattling off "en el rio" or some other old spanish guitar
whilst you make your way from scene to scene and what a beautiful star
you make what with your purple honey eyes lidding this way and that
and the aurora borealis heaving and pouting its way through your every
constellation and the storm pouring more cool water down on me all
which leads me to say, borrowing from coupland, that you are a tornado
and i the trailer park and that i miss you and hope all is well

Albert Cevallos

Voyage Off

We're leaving now;
Our home, our belongings,
Our families, our friends,
Are all being left behind.
There's little hope of seeing them again.
We're hurting.
We love them all so much;
We loved our lives.
But now the world is changing,
For the worse we fear.
We better get going.
Hear the planes.
The earth is moving.
There's panic in everyone's face.
What's happening!?!
It shouldn't be like this,
But we can't change it.
We need to go someplace safe,
Far away.
Goodbye.

Cristina Hathaway

Friday In November

It was a time of innocence
   the sunshine of daydreams sweet.
Eclipsed by the shadow of tragedy
   a nightmare on Elm Street.

It was the brilliance of promises
   an era of new frontiers remembered.
Extinguished by the darkness of demons
   the ides of March on Friday in November.

Does the murder of a chief
   kill lofty sights; footprints on the moon?
Do the up-reaching visions
   become blurred and blind at half past noon?

Haunting memories of myopia past
   color blindness lost; retrograde hate.
Is it now that humanity's soul resides
   behind gatekeepers of a ruthless fate?

Is it not false prophets
   that lead us to Armageddon's lot?
Liberty and peace; tranquility with all humanity
   is the legacy of Camelot.

Scott E. Simpson

'Tis Spring

Rejoice Spring is here,
A favorite season for all.
Snow flooding,
A mountain is melting,
while ice perches on trees is falling.
Whispering rivers.
Plenty of water,
The reservoir will never run dry.
Springtime is blossoming:
Beautiful, lovely flowers and other plants.
It isn't a season for filigree of rotten dust.
Yet, love is blind,
even to a seasoned lover.
Life is likened to spring.
It is the season of rejuvenation.
A Rebirth. Rejoice Christendom!
Our Lord is risen on Easter Sunday,
a major religious event of Christianity.
Heartfelt thanks Lord, again
to a wonderful spring which humanity enjoys.

Celebrado "Buddy" G. Quintana

The Ghetto

The ghetto is a terrible place
And believe me it's not just one race
Babies having Babies
Kids killing Kids
Who's there to give a listening ear
Drive-by shootings are almost everyday
South Central isn't the only place
Drug dealers are on the corner all the time
Trying to get kids to take part in their crime
Dads walking out
Moms getting high
Who's there to help the child through life
Graffitti is each and everywhere you look
Police don't never catch the crooks
But together we can make a change forever
Everybody just got to work together

Jamilah A. Grant

"Heaven Instead Of Hell"

I met a stranger while riding today.
As he sat beside me, he began to say.
I appreciate your kindness and I think that you are swell,
It's people like you that go to heaven instead of hell.

Heaven instead of hell, heaven instead of hell.
You can choose your path, but only time will tell.

Whenever he said this, a chill went up my spine.
And although it was raining, the sun began to shine.
I felt so excited, I turned my head to shout.
But whenever I turned back around,
my passenger had gotten out.

Heaven instead of hell, heaven instead of hell.
You can choose your path, but only time will tell.

I stopped my car to look for him, wondering who he could be?
And I got this funny feeling, it was Jesus next to me.

Heaven-Instead-Of-Hell — you can choose your path but only time will tell.

Well sometime in your future, it could happen just this way.
You'll pick up a stranger, and this is what he'll say.
Heaven instead of hell, heaven instead of hell.
You can choose your path — but only time will tell.

C. T. Walden

The Casualty

The casualties were extremely light
In the battle of Achen, they said.
Those words meant nothing at all to me —
My son was one of the dead.

No use to refinish his room;
His dog waits his coming in vain.
Must I console myself with the thought,
My loss was victory's gain?

Top scores for his college exams
Are not worth the effort it took
To prove his fine mind and his promise
And his great love for a book.

Now his goal to teach and work with youth —
Who would be our hope for tomorrow —
Lies buried deep in a far, distant land
And drowned in my grief and sorrow.

The casualties were extremely light
In the battle of Achen, that's true.
But this mother's heart will e'er mourn her son,
Though the casualties were few.

Hazel F. Adams

Stars

Just think of a star,
If it had a mind.
Would it wonder if the millions
Of years it took to get here,
Be worth it all?
Such is the way a man's soul shall wonder.

Bryan Chenevert

Tethered

For so long my thoughts
Were tethered to my love lost
To that point in time
When her words cut to the core
When my dreams were dashed
And I struggled to know just why
Her claims were to weak
My suspicions grew wild and varied
Had she found new joy
And discarded me like a passing fad
Did fear drive her away
Did I try too hard to love too fast
Word from her had ceased
Leaving me to my tears and frustration
Until last night when everything finally — snapped!
Now I'm
       finally floating
           free
                Hallelujah

Kendall Clark

Mom's Magic Without Hi Tech

A stomach that hurts during the night.
Mom gets up and everything becomes alright.
Feelings get hurt kid's cry.
Mom steps in and boy do the troubles fly.
Every day a new problem becomes known.
Don't worry mom will take it up as her very own.
Some how some way Mom's magic
Guides us even after we are grown
At her table is always the place to be.
Mom's cooking there is nothing better to me.
Yes! Mom's magic is beyond compare
May the good Lord. Always let it be there.

Clyde Ellis

Darkness

I adore silence and darkness
wind through the leaves
up out of vision
beyond believe
everything dead awake breathing watching
everything alive is dead
Oh, the stars talk do you listen
Hush!
Oh, feel the darkness feel
the touch
Don't breathe
The peaks the silences touching you deep
to the quick
When all is most aware secrets unfold
the dark, the Master, the
afterglow of night

Sarah Brock

Untitled

It was love that climbed through my window at the eleventh hour
Like a thief in the night
He stole my heart
He trespassed through the crevices of my soul
   until nothing was left untouched
   and everything was overturned
He haunts my dream at night
   so that my spirit cannot rest
He is in my thoughts by day
   so that I am tormented by visions
The torturous pain he inflicts upon my body wounds me
   so that mere balm cannot even soothe my grief
And even in death, I will not find solace
For he will stalk me until the end of time
To him, I am bound, shackled forever more
This is love — the criminal.

Victoria R. Chui

Untitled

She sits alone
But she's not
For, there's so much more in her thoughts
When the tears fall down her helpless face
They ask what's wrong
She doesn't belong in this place
She shouldn't have to deal with all this pain
But do they care
They think to her it's all a game
Yea, she tries, and yea, she makes mistakes
But how bad could it hurt them, it's her who's heart breaks
The anger-filled words, an the restless nights
All she can do is wonder why all their fights
She doesn't know everything
But then neither do they
They try to control her life
They'll realize they can't someday
She sits alone —
With the pain, the hurt, the tears, the confusion, the frustration,
and the fears and she waits

Amy Rosen

The Window

Should one peer in and another peer out,
What would each perceive as they glance about.

One could only change places to exchange spaces, small or vast,
to comprehend the vision each other has cast.

Should the window be designed specifically to let in light and air,
or as a mirror of confusion and wonderment for each to share.

William J. Morrow

No Garden

She sits by the window, looking out the transparent panel
No garden meets her eye, just the days of not so long ago
Children running up the walk, home from school
Laughing and shouting 'Mom', when they walk through the doorway
Her high school sweetheart, parking the car
He enters silently, tired from the days race
A trace of a smile crosses her face as she remembers
The house is silent now, except for the radio
Playing the 'golden-oldies' she remembers so well
The children have moved on to a world of their own
Her high school sweetheart has past beyond the time of existing
She was thrown into a world of today, without her loves of yesterday
She is full of the need to give and in giving she receives contentment
So many need attention, they pull on her heart daily
The alarm sounds and she wakes with a smile
A new era has begun, she's learned to go on alone
Each new day starts a memory for tomorrow
The work is hard, taking her deep into the night
She enters her house silently, tired from the days race
She looks out the clear pane, and sees a garden of budding memories.

Terry A. Stanley

Watch What You Say

In course of your conversation each and
    every day,
Think twice. Try to be careful of
    what you have to say;

Your remarks may be picked up by
    Someone's listening ear,

You may be surprised at what some
    people think they hear.

Things that you innocent say, or
    try to portray,

Can be changed and greatly exaggerated
    along the way;

Many stories change for the worse as they are retold,
So try to keep any questionable remarks "on hold."
May I give all of you some very sound advice?
When you speak of others, say something nice;
Try to say good things, regardless of who is around,
If you have nothing good to say, don't utter a sound.
You may find that an innocent remark, in the end,
My lose you a close and valued friend.

Tamika S. Brown

Separation

    She used to live right next door;
we shared a wall and the same floor.
    We got along well besides an occasional fight;
but now if we talk we have to write.
    When the time had come, it was not fun
because she was my sister and my only one.
    She had been so close for all my years;
but when life was without her, I was in tears.
    It is still hard now, but I have come to know
that the hardest part of all was just letting go.

    But when she arrived, the house was filled;
that lonely feeling she had concealed.
    We laughed and talked and listened a while;
just being reunited brought a smile.
    We had been brought close by being apart;
but I knew too soon the car would start.
    I didn't waste the now with thoughts of the near,
but enjoyed the time my sister was here.
    Because again we were together right next door;
that very same wall and exact same floor.

Dani Potter

Raging Hearts

As I sit here mezmorized by the calm ocean
Remembering both the good and bad times we had
Along the sandy shore

Those times we spent walking along the shore
Laughing, Kissing, Romping through the water
Awakening the ocean with our childish behavior
Splashing, Kissing, Screaming

But —

When the ocean was angry
So were we
Yelling, Hitting, Pushing
Causing the ocean to react the same
Waves crashing against the shore
Begging us for more

Once again the ocean lays calm
All that remains are itsy bitsy pieces of shells
And a half drawn heart as
He sits there mesmerized

Heather L. Chabo

Desert Night

Not black, this night.
Low clouds reflecting light.
Silent — still. A Desert night.

Yip yip — yooo. Close by — a desert cry.
Yip yip — yooo. Distant cry — answers why.

Touch of wind upon my face,
Crunch of gravel beneath my boots.
Do you think they are in cahoots?

Yip yip — yooo. Close by.
Yip yip — yooo. Answering cry.

Landscape silvered in the moonless night,
Shadow depthless in this light.
Silent — Still — Desert night.

E. A. Mash

"I've Paid"

As I lay here in deep thought, about
life and death, I wonder as, I off times do;
Why I came to be, and where do I
go from here. I pass through my heaven
on earth, although life's a living hell.
My years slowly turn to seasons, my
seasons into weeks, my weeks into days,
my days into agonizing hours. As I contemplate
through my own book of life, my trials and
tribulations, rather than a better life after
death, or a soul of living hell, I'd rather a
dreamlike state of eternal contentment.
I've made peace with myself.

Reginald W. Travers

Suffering

Seeing your small helpless children writhing
Under the weight of starvation.
Feeling you're a failure as a parent and
Feeling your children think the same.
Eating only the scraps and garbage
Retrieved from filthy green dumpsters
In dark, lonely alley ways.
Needing a little help and compassion, but only
Getting nickels and looks of disgust.

Drew Johnson

An Ode To Spring . . .

Oh, oh an ode to Spring —
  when flowers bloom and birdies sing.
An end to winter soon draws neigh
  when first we see the robins fly.

The death of winter seems forlorn
  it all disappears on that first sunny spring morn.
The life cycle is renewed
  Black becomes white in a display of floral delight.
All is as should be
  it's all part of the master plan.
Something which can only be observed
  and not controlled by mortal man.
Oh what a sight to behold —
  The buzz of the bee, the shade of the tree
  The scent of the blooms as clouds overhead loom.

To read, to dream, to believe —
  all becomes real at the first sighting of spring.
   Marianne G. Pindar

Changes

The trees have a secret whispered in the wind

Silently falling snowflakes,
Blanket the tree with moisture,
Providing a picture of white beauty,
While the tree appears to be silent

Sun warming the branches
Birds finding a home in its hearth
The tree begins to show life
Buds that bring forth wonderful colors.

Still the days get warmer
This tree now thriving
Shade from the heat
Shade from the heat
Produced by hundreds of leaves

The brisk air is beginning to surface
Leaves changing to brilliant shades of sunsets
Being carried slowly to the dew drenched ground
The silence of winter is beginning

The tree faced each season proudly
Listen, hear the wind, learn the secret
   Marlene L. Carpenter

The Stranger Yet To Come

There is a stranger yet to come
and currently we are one.
One mind, one body to house and protect.
I know not the things I should expect.

Nature works wonders everyday
and gives us nine months of delay.
We know not how our lives will be
once this little one parts from me.

The questions are numerous and fear is strong
The time to deliver is not very long.
Such pain and discomfort is hard to bear.
Do I push? Do I dare?

This experience is like no other;
elated, tired, and body uncovered
No modesty is left to you.
You do not care, this life is new.

This baby lies so helpless now
and all its problems are on my brow.
Complete is the love for your child
and as it grows you can't help but smile.
   Georgette Morse

Untitled

Your beauty
arrests my senses
like a sacred visionary
fire . . .
of pure spirit and light . . .
There is no release —
or reason —
Only your eyes,
melting my soul,
softly glowing
like a lantern
in the dark
wilderness, there are wolves howling
As your voice
speaks — to my heart . . .
savagely, like a knife
in a violent sudden death!
There is no struggle . . .
only the shock, entering and surrendering . . .
to the bliss of the pure spirit and of the love, calling . . .
   Crystal Joyce

Old Dunblane

Why is it so in old Dublane,
  In driving rain and sleet and snow,
A searching soul does sing refrain
  As dripping hate begins to grow?

A village here so quaint and quiet
  Nestled in placid sea
Is center stage to raging riot
  As fractured soul brings death with glee.

Tender child, this monster's morsel,
  Sentenced to sleep in cold, hard grave.
Of bile and filth his heart was full.
  We were not there to fight nor save.

Innocent babes who knew no crime,
  Ensnared by death's cruel embrace.
The moment's passed with no more time.
  A joyous smile so soon erased.

Billowing breeze dances through this town,
  As tear soaked mud tastes yet more rain.
With such a frown God peers down,
  And sheds a tear for old Dunblane.
   Everett Edwin Gale

The Leaving Of Autumn

The gloaming silhouette of swaying shadows
The wind softly singing of daytime tattles
The night wet with dew
Beds down for dawn anew
The sun cools from the heat of battle.

Tossing their headdress forward and away
Nodding to the night, curtsying to the day
With arms bare and worn
Graceful but forlorn
Covered by night with a soft moonlight spray.

Flipping a frond and a little beyond
Freeing their leaves under the winds respond
Their trunks looted of treasure
Ravished by autumn pleasure
Trees are bared for the touch of winter's wand.
   O. J. LaMontagne

The Soul

I stand outside the steely chamber
And remember what's inside —
A wilderness I created for myself
Where I can run and hide.

This place holds all my demons,
All my monsters, all my pain.
It's a place I've neglected for so long,
I must return again.

You've found the key to this secluded place
I haven't visited in years,
Depression guides me down the forest of my soul,
Through layers of pain, anger, and tears.

As I journey through the dense, dark forest
There's so much I should fear,
But somehow I am comforted
By each and every lonely tear.

I strive so hard to reach the core,
I'm searching for my soul,
But when I reach that vast open space,
It's just a void — a black hole.

Jennifer Brown

My Wish For You Happiness And Love Everyday

Dear,

I can't just wish you Happy Holiday at Christmas and New Year
Nor can I just wish you Happy Sweetest or Valentines Day, My dear.
But I can definitely wish you Happy Everyday all year through
which not only includes everyday in between . . . but Holidays too.
My love for you is constant . . . every moment of each day
It flows on a continuous basis . . . and is here to stay.
I love you in the morning . . . and in the evening too
It really doesn't matter . . . whether the Sun is shining or the sky is blue.
Holidays are not excluded . . . but it's every day that really counts
Because it's love that's given everyday . . . that really amounts.
When we exchange good values . . . this is what is known as sharing
When we learn and grow together . . . this is known as caring.
What I'm really trying to convey . . . in my very own simple way
Is that love and happiness . . . should be displayed every single day.
It wasn't meant to be big business . . . to become so commercial
Because love and happiness is natural . . . and doesn't need a rehearsal
I give you universal vision this holiday season.
Love,

Wallace K. Wileman

Looking Thru A Dirty Window

I look thru my grandmother's dirty window
And I see her sitting in a chair
And I know she is pondering her lifetime past,
Remembering all of the moments,
Happy, sad, and terrifying.
Thru that dirty window with smashed bugs on the window sill
I look at her and think about how the bugs had a past, too.
I feel her pain. Even in her bright blue blouse you can sense it.
I feel her sadly remembering all of her life past
And remembering when she could run
And roll in the grass underneath the sun.
I see her let out a slight sigh
For her life is all said and done and she can never go back.
Looking upon her I learn a valuable lesson
I learn to enjoy life while life can be enjoyed;
To savor the moments of love, hate sorrow, loss, and excitement
And turning away from that dirty window I run to the back yard
And start to have fun
Because thru her I have seen how life must be lived
Before it is over.

Christopher Cummins

Times Gone By

There are times when I am alone, I look deep into the black abyss of my soul and I see the face of a child.

The child looks at me with haunting eyes that make me grow cold, as I am forced to see the past that I have buried deep within my heart.

Looking through the child's eyes, I see a house which today does not stand, a large crumbling house, a red dog sleeping on the porch.

Moving from room to room I see with remarkable clarity. Wall paper of years gone by hangs as if to defy time. I can reach out my hand and touch it yet in my conscious mind I know it is not there.

The house is cold and forgotten sounds of children echo through the halls. A family crowded around a scantily clad table, drinking coffee and telling tales.

Another memory begins before the first ends, winters and summers, the peach tree outside the window, is bursting with pink blossoms, the aroma is a sweet as the gentle breeze on which it rides.

Houses that once stood tall and proud have long since been cleared for more modern structures and I am reminded that the road of life once traveled dissolves in the sands of time.

The present is just a rare jewel which must be cut and polished so that it shines brightly within the dark cavern which hides your soul.

Chris Mark

Untitled

Somewhere in the stubborn clock that runs between my frontal lobes
It will always be Wednesday, October 11, 1972, and I just seventeen,

A freshman at a downstate college, thinking of nothing but *escherichia coli* and Mary Ellen from Ellenville, clutching French books to her ersatz leopard coat.

And now, a quarter century later, I find myself again driving down our old street. Our house seems smaller now, the block shrunk to half its former size.

That house-high blue spruce and those hedges are long gone. The downstairs porch, once open, is now enclosed.

I wonder if that Prohibition speakeasy and dusky casks of long evaporated ale Still lurk against the wall of the basement where Marty's band once played.

I always want to go up and ring our bell and see our apartment again,
But somehow I can never walk up those grey steps and do it.

Instead, in my car, taking every conceivable alternate route,
I attempt to retrace your steps.

Which way did you walk when you took that last walk
Into the woods where I played as a child?

And what were you thinking when you took that stroll, past School 19 perhaps
Or the house of the girl I loved, with broken Japanese fan and ringlets of gold?

Did you see any of it, anything at all? Or had tincture of almonds
Blinded you to do terrible beauty of it all?

Robert Schalit

Celestial Clouds Of Fire And Smoke

Autumn has just begun.
Behold, the season of many colors.
The earth, a brilliant canvas in daylight,
at sunset, its brilliance comes darkness
set against a backdrop of celestial
clouds of fire and smoke.
Behold, a masterpiece no canvas
could reproduce,
no lens could refract.
Created by the master,
his splendor above the earth and the heavens.

Carol Ann Geise

Water Falls

In life we see what could have been,
and what might become to be.
Who are we to say which one,
that is the right for thee.

At times we look at all of this,
and wonder why at all,
that we are down upon this earth,
to know the best for all.

Just like the river that passes by,
around each rock and falls,
it may be wrong to take that turn,
but once it's down, it crawls.

Slowly but surely it finds a path,
to follow once again.
The end of this one, what to find,
a solemn lake or been.

The future is something we do not know,
we have to play by ear,
we find a path, and pray to God,
with faith, we know he hears.

Cindy Jackson

"Give Me Your Hand"

I reach out and take your hand
And, we will stroll this road together
God is somewhere between us!
I can feel His touch and feel His love,
Combined with ours, we are homeward bound,
Don't the discouraged or feel inept!
We will try again, and go much slower
The teetering between Earth and Hell!
Has taught us well, My Love!
The heart grows tired, timid, and afraid sometimes!
It needs to rest!
I'm grateful for you hand in mine
You are the end of me and my new Beginning!
There are so many tomorrow left and owed to us
Let us reach out for that secret place, that
no one else has touched!
Slide next to me! See, no position is
uncomfortable or wrong, then moving to your face!
Your eyes still dazzle me as our months match
Our insides will probe each others, for all eternity!

Patti Messina

A Plastic Heart

With nothing in the middle
Where a diamond ought to be.
Now one could see right through it.
There's nothing there to see.
Sept a hole in the middle
Where a diamond used to be,
Shiny and bright as bold as the sun,
I always though I'd keep this one.
How'd I know it wasn't mine to keep?
An angel gave it to me in my sleep.
She didn't say hold on to it.
Or keep it close and dear.
Just smiled and winked and flicked her wing
And whispered in my ear.
Shadows only crawl
And good men do die young
I give this plastic heart to you
Cause you're my favorite one,
    I never questioned her,
Mark P. Barbus

Daddy's Little Angel, Daddy's Little King

You're daddy's little angel, you're daddy's little king,
I wouldn't trade you for 1 darn thing.
I wouldn't trade you for diamonds or gold,
I wouldn't trade you for things untold.
Just close your eyes and sleep real tight,
dream sweet dreams that last all night.

You're daddy's little angel, you're daddy's little king,
I wouldn't trade you for 1 darn thing.
You took a short trip and stayed for good,
you went to my heart and never returned.

You're daddy's little angel, you're daddy's little king,
I wouldn't trade you for 1 darn thing.
I wouldn't trade you for diamonds or gold,
I'll keep you forever to love and to hold.
You're daddy's little angel, you're daddy's little king,
I wouldn't trade you for 1 darn thing.

Daniel Thomas

Love Thine Own Enemy

I hate love — and love hates me.
They tell me that they love me — and soon enough they leave me.
Love, you are a stranger — though I am not your enemy.
Right is right. Love is night: Dark; uncomfortable and scary.
Ignore me no more — for I shall never knock at your door.
The words of hurt and hate cannot explain.
That word so sweet in the dictionary — soon to be removed from
my vocabulary. What a sad day that will be.
What a sad day they have been.
It's not real — I want to scream
I was wrong again — see what I mean.
My heart is heavy — oh let me cry
My heart of love is soon to die . . .

Hope-Maria Jones

I'm Just A One Able Star On The Halo Move

And with clenches fist I come at you from the dive sky. And you
shall know by the depth of the wicked sons of satan that I have
arrived. And long ago with my name on that black granite will you
thought I glad caught you at your lie, and no more shall the soldiers
of these united Republic States of America in vain sky. Still some
lied some died and others just cried like watching a movie for the
glide that someone else wrote. Of other places of other people help
by the throat. The stench of their bodies left on the ground.
Like so much dead hamburger sold by the pound. Some we can
deal with some that we don't. Fears we forget and others we won't.
With cries sigh stand. Comes now the axe blade sword of justice of
dan. Vietnam. I come against thee now, because in full force of
strength I can, be dammed. To have been there is never to
forget. To have not is never to know.

Robert S. Hartley

Eight Seconds To Glory

The shoots were cold and the day was hot,
He didn't even know if he would make it or not,
With a busted leg he won in Cheyenne —
Tonight this cowboy's gonna make his stand,
Cause he was just a kid when he saw him live —
Firmly strapped down on an eight second ride,
On three thousand pounds of pure hate
Coming out of the shoot from Satan's gate —
These bulls are big and these bulls are mean
But only the best cowboy will come away clean —
Cause an eight second ride is a lifetime to live
But at the National Finals Rodeo that's all you can give.

Larry L. McBride Jr.

In The Arms Of An Angel

In the arms of an angel I traveled last night
and the things that I saw were of sheer delight.
I watched the world as we passed by;
then I saw all our children from way up high.

I waved to them as I just wanted to share
but they did not notice us way up there.
Then in a flash all the kids were gone
in the arms of an angel I traveled on.

I saw a tunnel, at the end was a light.
A path with red roses, what a beautiful sight!
The gates to Heaven were all in white
but I could not go in the time was not right.

In the arms of an angel I traveled on
to so many places where I had never gone.
What a trip I had, everything was just right
in the arms of an angel as I traveled last night.

Nancy L. Naylor

Tranquility

For as a stone breaks the calmness of a
lake's water surface and makes wakes,
so does the appearance of a tear running
down a calm, smooth face.

For as each wake that breaks on the bank,
that is one step closer to calm, and as each
tear falls and finds its destiny, that is
one less tear that may be cried.

When the last wakes break and the last
tear falls, then and only then will things be
back to endings, calm, the norm of life.

Shawn P. Ritter

From Then To Now And Now To Then

Grandma's meals were always planned
Straight from the garden or what she had canned
No trips to the store for a carton of milk
Direct from the cow it was smooth as silk
Fresh eggs came from a near by nest
And added to batter you can guess the rest
It's good to remember days done by
And birthdays remind us how fast they fly
My car inched closer to the drive thru speaker
And through the glass the voice sounded weaker
With a touch of a button the glass was lower
And from the outside menu I ordered #Four
Another button touched and the stereo was on
Then I took messages from my car phone
Some say the old days were better they find
But what about these luxuries we'd leave behind
If you really could take a trip back in time
Would you hitch a wagon or book an airline?

Mary Lucas

Nothing Much I Have To Say

It's nothing much I have to say.
That would make you and I feel any other way.

Though you shine on me each and everyday
and speak to me in every way.

My love for you will never go away
It will always be here to stay.

You are the first and the last Queen
that could ever give me a Dream.

For that's nothing much I have to say because,
you showed me the way.

Shaaron Drew

Eat Me

She liked to watch him eat
that primal yet inescapable function
that even he was forced to participate in
the way his lower jaw bone, the mandible,
separated and rejoined to the upper
"Chew, chew, chew," she said to him
She thought of how later she might
nibble on and under that mandible up to his ear
"Nibble on the mandible," she said to him
Occasionally his tongue, his strongest muscle
would come out to lick his lips
and she said to him "Lick, lick, lick,"
and she thought of how that tongue
once licked her

Rachel Malocha

My Big Sis

I always looked up to her — my big sis
Now she's the sis I'm going to forever miss
We've been through thick and thin together
And in my heart she'll be forever
When we were together there
was so much laughter
I hope it's still there in the here after
I was always
here when she needed a place to run
Never thinking she'd ask for a gun
I never saw her planning her life like this
it was something that passed by that I missed
She called me in the morning
to let me know it was her time to go
Saying I love you Jen
Never believing it was the end
I always looked up to her my big sis.
Now she's the sis I'm going to forever miss

Jennifer Young

A Daughter's Love

It is now midnight on the day you died, I'm sitting here wondering why I lied.
I swore to mom, my sister and brothers, that my tears would be for others.

My precious drops would not be cried, for you I said but I have lied.
For as I drove home tonight, the tears did flow against my might.

I shouted "Daddy" up at a star. Hoping, could you see my car?
For heaven is the place you'll be, looking down on me to see

All my love afraid to show. Oh, my Daddy, I hope you know
that my heart is hurt so bad. Afraid to think I made you sad.

Could I, should I, maybe, why not. The things undone, unsaid are a lot.
The hurt, the pain, the guilt so real.
With God I wish to make a deal.

For as we lay you down to rest, I promise to always be my best.
And in return I hope he might hold you in his arms tonight.

May God give you the love we feel and time allow us all to heal.
Goodbye my Daddy, I love you so
please forgive me for not letting you know.

Barbara Hulse

Untitled

I don't recommend wearing only one shoe.
Dressing is faster, this much is true;
But walking is awkward
    and running is too.
You might want to wear both of your shoes.

Linda Steffen

I Remember

I love my huge queen sized water bed,
mine and no one else's.
As it engulfs me when I sleep,
the most comfortable thing ever!

I get in a fight,
or even just frustrated.
So I lie on the side of my bed in a narrow slot.
I feel trapped,
yet my tension is somehow release.
I now feel better.

I adore a picture,
it stands proudly on my head board.
It's a picture of my mom and me,
I was only one.
I dream,
I remember the old days,
and the way things could have been!

Jacque Lutz

Bob White

Bob White, calling from your place on the ground;
Are you calling to tell your mate of something you've found?

Or are you calling to tell her of your love and devotion
Which are deeper by far than the depth of the ocean?

Now Mrs. Bob White answers from a bush quite near me.
Does she think that she's hidden so no one can see?

Is she reassuring you of her devotion and love
And trying to tell you such love's from above?

Wherever you make your nest on the ground,
You can always be sure she's somewhere around.

Soon you'll have babies, and although they're the best,
They'll keep you so busy you'll have little rest.

Before long they'll be ready to fly.
It's not long before they'll begin to try.

Although they may fly far, far away,
Your thoughts are with them through all the long day.

And when they have all flown far from your nest,
You'll have each other — and perhaps some rest.

Mary Imogene S. Huffstutter

"Children"

I'll start out this poem about
Our little girl and boy,
Whom we like to call our
Pride and our joy!
They are the greatest thing
A couple can achieve,
For those of you with them
That's easy to believe!
As all parents know they all have their days,
A lot like us adults in a
Few particular ways!
When they were being born
Your hands kind of shook,
I'd give my life for them if that's what it took!
They grow up so fast, enjoy them everyday,
Let them know that you love
Them, it's very easy to say!
When they grow older they'll
Know just how we feel, that's one thing in life
That no one can steal.

Mike Murley

Untitled

Everybody knows her name
I owe her all my wealth and fame
Though all my wealth is not much to see
She's the one who gave it all to me
She spends her whole life trying to please
We think she does it with such ease
We never give thought to how she's feeling
We always seem to leave her grieving
You can treat her how you will
She will always love you still
Who is this woman with such wonder
There is only one, it's my dear Mother

Matt Ellis

Growing "Old"

Listen — can you hear the whisper of yesterdays gone by?
Bringing back the feeling of a special day and time.

Chasing after dreams of old,
no longer am I young.

Streaks of gray dance through my hair,
how quick the time has gone.

I thought I said it yesterday,
that tomorrow I'd get it done;
but yesterday has turned to years
and tomorrow fades with the sun.

I never thought it would go so fast,
seems the final moment has come.

To say good-bye to yesterday
and the things I've left undone.

Inez Yates

Mary Ruth, Mary Ruth

The softness of her beauty shows
A loving heart that dwells within;
All love she gives to me thus grows
And makes my soul somehow begin
To understand.

With hazel eyes, she blesses all,
And gently, gently with that gaze
She has no need to speak or call
Thus leads me through my own fate's maze
To understand.

I look upon her loveliness,
And feel her presence bless me then;
We surely met in ages past, and
Now we love again.
I understand.

Robert Ford White

"Trading Places"

Mr. Squirrel sitting on a tree,
Mr. Squirrel do you wish you were me?
I wish I were you when I see you climb.
What an acrobat you are walking the power lines.
And when it's cold and snow is deep,
In your warm cozy den you sleep.
Putting acorns in a pile,
Swishing your tail to make children smile.
With you, I might trade place.
But for acorns, would I ever like the taste?

Lora Renee Yarber

Rhythmic Thoughts Of You

It turns into "one sweet day"
When I "daydream" about you
Take me "underneath the stars"
And make this "fantasy" come true

You are my "dream lover"
Who I'll embrace "someday"
My "emotions" run wild
And I start to "melt away"

"Love takes time"
And "now that I know"
My "vision of love" with you
Is starting to show

"Just to hold you once again"
"There's got to be a way"
To let you know "I've been thinking about you"
And how "you need me" to stay

My love isn't "vanishing"
So I'll "never forget you"
But I'm still "alone in love"
And living "without you" . . .

Tanya Kauhi

Wisdom's Choice

In each one, my son, lies fertile ground
With streams of living waters.
Dry desert and snow lands abound divided by tentative borders.
Each of us must understand life hands to every one around
A place which we must occupy and wherever we are found,
We, from within, must draw upon our inner most resources.
We hope and pray that wisdoms smile
Will 'ere direct our courses.
We may flounder in sin's quicksands;
Its beguiling innocence will trick us.
Just remember this, my man,
Blame, hate, and greed will prick us.
Remove this thorn from out thy side;
Cast it away — draw patience close,
Steady thy boat upon life's tide.
Ride out the storm, count not the loss,
It is but dregs. Just count the gain.
Fertile is Mt. St. Helen's ash; life from it arises.
In each of us lies a universe — earth, sky, sun, and rain.
Self deny, reach out, look up, fulfillment wears disguises.

Neva Rogers

It Could Be Me!

How sad the heart, how empty the life,
Of a man alone, without a good wife.

How empty the woman without a good man,
To love her, and hold her as only he can.

How awful the fate of a child all alone,
With nowhere on earth to call his own home.

How lonely the heart of an aged mother,
Left all alone, with no one to love her.

How bitter the days of a dear old father,
Whose children have become too busy to bother.

Yet we, who do not share their pain,
Are the ones most likely to complain!

Why can't we, who are more fortunate,
Give thanks we do not share their fate?

Lord, help us each to plainly see,
'Except for Your grace, it could be me!'.

Clarence N. Wesson

The Human Body

The human body is a precious gem,
some are women and some are men,
some are short and some are tall,
the Lord our savior, made us all.

Each body has a precious soul,
that within us lives,
we must learn to keep the Devil out,
and keep our Savior in.

As we live our lives each day,
and God's creation around us we see,
if Heaven is our goal to be,
then we must be careful with our personality.

As we do our work each day,
we must do it with sincerity,
helping others as we can,
and thanking the Lord, for his helping hand.

As life's journey comes near the end,
we don't need enemies, only friends.
If Heaven is to be our goal,
may God bless us, and save our soul.

Paul L. Bollinger

A Love Story

One day, eons ago, the sun beheld the earth
twirling and swirling in all her blue gowned glory
    And he fell in love with her
Then by way of his rays, he sent her a letter
    declaring his love and proposing marriage
Miss Earth who had long basked in the sun's warm rays
readily answered "Yes." And a wedding day was set
The two married in a cosmic ceremony
The moon was bridesmaid. The stars sang the Song of Love
Mother Earth hugged them. Father Sun beamed with pride
Angel Stars gathered about them and rejoiced
The Mother fed them her rich earth milk. The Sun by
photosynthesis, gave them the building blocks of life
Both became multi-celled organisms, filling sea and land
Then over many eons, they developed into present day life
The plant first. The grass before the antelope
The tree before the song bird who nested in its arms
The rose before Man who was enchanted by her beauty

Orville Brooks

Fear Of Living

Life
Did you really live it?
Were you just passing through it?
Did you live like there's no tomorrow?
Did you lead or follow?
Did you love like it was going out of style?
Was it full of toil and turmoil?
Would you do it all again?
Did you just sit and let it spin?
Did you play or pass?
Did you watch or dance?
Did the weight of the world get you down?
Did it make you strong?
Did you take a risk or live in fear?
Did you tremble and shake and drown in your own tears?
Now the waiting is over.
Death is at your door.
No more hesitating.
There isn't anymore.

Celeste E. Weston

I Warpaint Your Face

No more happily jumping double dutch and
hop scotch with a dented Yoohoo can
pigtails in the wind
Simon says
red light green light 1,2,3
strawberry shortcake with cream on top
Bang!
I die drowning in the air of pain like great Hiawatha
My peacock arrows drown, strangled in a quicksand of mud
as I pull and pull and your soldiers grab their rifles in the early
morning charge!
Falling cowhats, leaping galloping horses falling with brown eyes
that are bulging from the
bleak ride eyes that bulge from those who would rather be at home
Perspiration that drops into the ditch and mixes
with the blood from your feet as your boots are gone
your jacket torn, and your drenched face is frozen in fear . . .
you are arrow dead with the British coming
You are my best friend, my golden red sunset, my darling Buffalo
as we play toward the opening evening sky.

Hedwig M. Chappelle

The Little Clown

The little clown put on his frown
And went into the ring.
His voice was coarse and very hoarse
When he began to sing.

His nose was red and on his head
He wore a little hat.
His coat was worn and badly torn,
His cheeks were very fat.

He, like a sack, fell on his back,
Then did a somersault.
His tricks galore, made each child roar;
One could not find a fault!

When he stood tall and looked at all,
You saw into his eyes;
They were a chart into his heart,
His frown was telling lies.

And at the end, he was their friend.
The children laughed and cheered.
That sad-face clown, forgot to frown.
He knew the children cared.

Vertella S. Gadsden

The Evil Inside

You lay down to go to sleep,
that is when I enter into your dreams.
I am your dirty thoughts and your worst nightmares,
I know that you do not want me there.
I am the evil inside, a part of your subconscious mind.
I will be with you until the end of time.
While your guardian angel tries to keep you strait,
a little devil tells you that
it is okay to lie, cheat, and steal.
There is a battle going on within yourself.
Good and evil always dueling,
each trying to dominate the other.
A never ending battle, you can't get rid of me.
I am the evil inside, a part of your subconscious mind.
You might lock me away deep within yourself.
But, I will always be a part of you until the end of time.
I am the evil inside.
No matter how hard you try
you can't get me out of your mind,
because I am the evil inside.

Brett Hawks

My Thoughts On A Saturday

What a glorious feeling to be able
    To close your mind to outside sounds,
To feel Gods love pouring into your very soul.

The warmth from the sun, like the warmth of his love.
The breeze gently touching you, like the
    gentleness of his words.

I cried a lot, only because it felt so good
to be able to release my fears . . .
    To hear his words to me.

What an up lifting!
I wanted to fly to shout to say
    "Alleluia — Lord."

And when I was still hesitant,
    I asked the Holy Spirit to intercede.
And he did.

The trials that were — were!
The trials to come shall he over come.

Praise be to God!

Sharon Lee E. Serena

"Fatherless"

It was a cold January day

A day that no one knew would be the last to say
good-bye and I love you.

He was loved as any father was,
held close within our hearts.

But who ever knew that this would be the day we'd
have to part?

We were the last to know, and, Oh, the pain that
filled our souls, because we loved him so,
The family that loved him so, sat lonely on a
church bench listening to a preacher say;
What a man he was and would have always been.

People all surrounds us, They say "It'll be ok,"
but dear God I pray, Will my life ever be the same?

Five years have passed since that day so long ago.
Seems only yesterday he was here and would have never gone!

Life is not forever, and we know that everyone
must go. But with that family that loved him so . . .

Who would have guessed . . .
    We'd be Left . . . "Fatherless."

Chad Alday

The Only One

People always wonder why I don't cry
Instead I choose to keep it bottled up inside

Now and then a tear will fall
But my dad is the only one that hears my calls

Every night I bow my head in prayer
To thank God for letting him be there

And as for true friends, I have but one
My father, to which I am like a son

In my heart he will always stay
And from him I will never stray

If it was not for him
No doubt, I'd be out on a limb

For he's the only one that keeps me sane
And I know he'll always be there to help me through the pain

Stacey Drasher

Peanuts My Cat "Me"

Nose like a diamond, ears of a racoon
Eyes like a deer always so clear
My tail like a whip or a windshield wiper going swish, swish
Paws so soft like the feathers of a dove
My coat 'tis many colors so beautiful and shiny
Purest white my tummy "T"
Why could'est spin a sweater from me
Whiskers are my high tech gear
Yet it doth make a safe driver of me
Run like the wind and man's best friend
'Tis just the way I do it
By your side I do walk just to prove my LOVE for you
My nails sometimes snare you as we play
Yet my tongue tis pinker than pink with the roughness of
sandpaper
Though 'tis for my bath you see
Well me heart tis big, bigger than all outdoors
For you, only for you my LOVE
Cause I'm "Peanuts The Cat" I am, I am

Gladys M. Gibel

"I'm Not Afraid Of Dying"

I'm not afraid of dying, I'm afraid to be dead.
You see me here pale and frail, my eyes are dull, my senses dim.
My fear persist within my soul,
I'm not afraid of dying, I'm afraid to be dead.

You see my body all worn and torn,
but my soul still sores to heights of unknown scorn.
For you see my baby, she is almost eight months old
and my fear that I will be dead,
will clear my memory of me from her head.

So you see I'm not afraid of dying, I'm afraid to be dead.
For my little girl I pray my memory will always be
a loving lasting rose of human dignity.

Jennifer Turner

Purity

Purity is like a crisp, white rose.
It is clean, fresh; standing tall in the perfect pose.
It has not become scarred, bruised, or crumbled,
It holds fast to its beliefs and does not tumble.

The white rose just sits and waits.
Waiting to find the perfect mate.
Marriage is a wonderful gift God has given,
Give praise to Him who's livin'.

The best gift to give your future spouse,
Is not beauty or a house,
But your white rose of purity,
Showing them and Him your loyalty.

Kristina Bellows

Our Children's Day

The colors of our children are like the colors of a day
Each one is different, yet each the same some way
We must nurture them as they grow
If they are to blossom into life
Water them with love
So they may enjoy the gift of life
Not yet are they aware
The future of the world is the burden they must bear
So let the children play
Burden them not with worry this day
May they grow healthy and strong together
With the nurture and love of today
They may grow up to look upon one another
Each with the beauty of a new day

Robert Dyer

The Music Of The Milleniums

Your eyes chase me in my dreams,
I awake and I wish for you.
How much would I, should I say
about how you touch my soul?

sleep eludes me as I vacillate
between desire, and risk, and danger.
Frustrated by hopeful perceptions
that may only be delusions of a fool.

But what if I'm not deluded?
What if there is reciprocation?
Two souls in glorious harmony
making the music of the milleniums?

Can I take the risk of passing by
that song that makes life beautiful?
Yet the danger of scarring my heart
already calloused with scars is high!

And then there's the risk to you,
the risk of the music fading.
I would rather have never sung,
than to have you suffer one note of discord!

Glenn A. DeeDon

Jonathan

So anxious to be that you came too soon
God's special gift in that stark room;
Though you lingered only a week and a day
Lives changed forever when you went away.

Earth's mission ended, you soul could soar
To join loved ones waiting on that other shore.
In death you're a donor that others may live
There is no greater gift a person can give.

Now as we pack you small things away
God, give us strength to get through today
And help us accept what was not mean to be.
Comfort us. Renew our faith and trust in Thee.

Helen Stewart Webb

To My Valentine Angel

You have made my life so happy,
That I revel in just your smile.
Your understanding when I show my faults,
Has shown love is your only style.

Your touch makes my love grow stronger.
It beckons me with definite resolve,
And I won't be away much longer;
I'll hurry to hold you, my loneliness to solve.

When I'm away, your face crosses my memories,
And I wish to be in your arms,
For I am weak without you to please,
And I want to be wrapped in your charms.

My absence was necessary for this little time,
To get the things that we desire.
But to give up your arms for a short time,
Is a price I must pay, as I alone retire.

Soon I will be on my way to meet my misses,
Only when it's in our best interest I'll roam.
And I'll greet you with my best hug and kisses.
I want to be with you, my Valentine Angel, at home.

Jim Davis

Holy Vows

What God has joined together no one shall tear it apart,
Because the vows that were made together were so sacred from the start
But the pressures we live in today it is so easy for us to stray,
If only everyone would stop and think of the vows that was made
    on this special wedding day.

When God joins two people together in divorce it should never end,
Just think of the holy vows together that were made back then,
If two people would stop and think how hurting divorce can be,
And of all the hurting moments each one of us will see.

What God has joined together should be such happy years,
With our love growing stronger holding the one we love so dear,
Sharing everything together until death we do part,
Keeping each holy vow as each new day together we start.

There would not be so many broken hearts with hurt showing on their face,
Because marriage vows were broken and loneliness took its place,
If your marriage is at the point of going separate ways,
Just think of all those holy vows that was made on your wedding day.

    Jewel Patterson

The Private Femme

No crowds she seeks, nor platform highs,
    No stage to stand upon.
A few close friends and family ties,
    Her world is built thereon.

A private femme this bonnibel.
    Bound with integrity;
Receptive ears that listen well,
    So true her loyalty.

Her simple joys from nature's sights
    Of sunsets in the West.
A solo walk out late at night;
    Serenity her quest.

And yet she has a zeal for life;
    A tendency toward risk.
A dealer's deal, her husband's strife;
    A bet on spin of disk.

She care not what the world may think;
    Her thoughts need not be shown.
No crave for jewels, ermine or mink;
    Her mind is of her own.

    John Hamilton Wright

Unity

Everything seems to move in the same direction.
Natures seasons.
The planets, sun, moon and stars.
The streams, rivers, oceans and seas.
Man must work, striving for accomplishments, a dream of unity.

    Frances V. Caffey

In Love With You, In Love Without You

I thought . . . my love means nothing without you
As I touched your lips in a kiss,
You held my hand in a warm embrace,
As a loving smile came over your face.

And I thought of how we had been together so long,
I thought of how our love had grown so strong,
And I thought of how it had fallen apart,
How we had broken each other's hearts.

And as I touched you lips in a meaningless kiss,
As I held you hand in mine,
Looking in your eyes,
I realized . . . my love means nothing with you.

    John R. Trotter IV

To Pennington Family Graduates Of 1996

To Angela and Gayla and Jesse and Thad:
Now, you're thinking, "High School wasn't half that bad".
To Bethany and Phillip and Brian and Scott:
You're saying, "I did need all those College classes. Believe it or not."
But you stayed right in there. You worked real hard
So good grades would show up on that final grade card.
Now at last, graduation day is finally here,
You've looked forward to this for several long years.
You'll feel a little sadness to leave all those friends,
It will not be the same as it was "a way back when."
You'll be, more or less, out there on your own,
Things will be a bit different than when you were home.
But we're all quite confident you will do your best
In whatever is before you, you'll master the test.
You've made us all proud. We think all of you great,
So along with your parents, we Congratulate!
We're sure you H.S. graduates will set your sights on college.
You're plenty capable of absorbing all that needed knowledge,
And you College Graduates, do what you're trained to do,
But remember, always, "To thine ownself be true."

    Auba E. Pennington

Love Is Like A Butterfly

Love is like a butterfly
    Which soars on delicate wing,
That reaches heights of great delight,
    But love is a fragile thing.

Like capturing hands can crush the wings
    Of the fluttering butterfly,
So love can be crushed by possessive grasp,
    Yes, crushed and slowly die.

So keep your love like the butterfly,
    Breathtaking and gloriously free.
You'll keep your love by letting go . . .
    That's love's simplicity.

    Edwina Waide

"The Prize"

Just like the "Wheel of Fortune" life is a
puzzle, like a maze you can't always get
through. So when the burdens of life becomes
to hard to bear and before you become despair.

Reach for the telephone and dial 1-800-463 this
line is always open and best of all it's "free".
After you finish your conversation don't forget
to say "thank you" for your advice, time and giving
me a peace of mind.

Just remember there's no one like "The Heavenly
Father," from above he always has time to share this love.

    Charlesetta Hulon

Ballroom Dancing

I'll be dreaming of that lovely place for dancing,
Lights and shadows change as music plays,
Shining eyes and flashing smiles are so entrancing
As we swirl and sway the night away.

That the dream becomes reality I'll pray for —
It seems that you are really in my arms,
And we're gliding on a cloud of yellow roses —
Romantic music is the magic charm.

Enchantment of this lovely dream is everywhere,
It doesn't matter — sunny skies or rain.
I'll keep dreaming of that magic music playing;
I'll find that place and dance with you again.

    Naomi Elliott

Muddy Feet

Yesterday was my last day of college
After six years I'm finally done
I look back at my horrid teenage years
And see how far I've come

I'm now the mother of a four year old
The single mom of a son
And I still remember how I was at that age
Just loving to have fun

My mother is watching the rain fall
And she's watching her grandson whine
He wants to go outside and play
And be in the warm sunshine

It stops raining, so we dress him
In his favorite green jacket and cap
And he runs outside to play
While I lay down to take a nap

And then I hear my mother in the other room
She's crying, and she covers her face to be discrete
And I look down, And see the trails, as she smiles
At some familiar muddy feet

Monica Mae Juarez

"Hidden Gifts"

We all touch others
In ways, that are unimaginable
Actions take place
Whose methods, are intangible

None can compare
With those of a child
A simple wiggle, or even a smile
Can leave her mother, completely beguiled

Seeing no faults
In her mother's actions
She provides endless love
Never demanding, a reaction

Moments such as these
Make life worth living
It is the essence of life
For it is always giving

Joseph D. Osborne

Abortion Is Just Plain Wrong

Homicide or murder,
aborting or killing.
It just doesn't seem right,
but people are willing.

The blinded people don't see
that so many lives are taken.
The baby just dies,
never to awaken.

Abortion is murder,
it's all the same.
It's a matter of death,
not just a game.

So you chose to kill,
you thought it was the right thing to do.
Now your baby is dead,
and you wish you were too.

You made a mistake,
now just who has to pay?
Don't blame the poor baby,
he deserved to stay.

Adam J. Rhoades

The Symbol Of Love

We are separated by many a mile.
How I wish I could reach out and touch your hand;
I long to see your smile.
It's too far to simply cross over the land.
How much longer? Maybe only a while,
Our love, the test of time must stand.
Through the hardships we are faithful, temptation and trial;
If only that symbol of love I had, the golden band.
O what a joyful day, sweet heavenly bliss
To be near to you, to touch;
When upon my lips you place a kiss,
Such a gift, it will symbolize so much.
Please, I beg, hurry home to me
For it is you, my love, I long to see.

Jennifer Bibbee

Time

Will I go before my time, what's to say what
time is mine.
Enjoy my time as best as can be for at time,
it will be taken from me.
Will I be ready when I must go, I will
miss all I know.
Weep for me little then go on your way,
make me proud as I am today.
We will meet again some day we will,
so till then don't be still.
Do what you want and do what you
can to make life worth living as best
as you can.
I will take your love that you have
for me and keep it always in reach as
my love for you; you must keep.
I will always love you and keep you close.
Keep on living and be your most

Millie Jackson

No Fault

I remain ——
        Dismayed!

That an unknown woman
        Can reach into one's home and family
Take one's husband
        Deprive one's children of "parents,"
                Acquire a fine living, and
                        Financial security,
And, consider it "her right"!

What shall befall her Soul
        To balance out this blight?
I cannot contemplate the woe
        This intruder has earned as birthright
                In another life!

Frances Beall Giuliani

Friends

My friends are such a treasure
I cherish everyone
They come in all sizes, shapes and colors
And ages up to ninety one
The babies grow up and marry
More babies come along
They call me aunt or grandma
My love for them is strong
God's plan has given me
A ring of purest gold
He set it full of diamonds
My friends in my heart to hold.

Viola M. Young

All You Need

A young woman cried out with sorrow as they told her the horrible news
They said that she had AIDS. And there was nothing more they could do

She firmly grasped her purse as she ran through the double doors
She ran and she ran till she couldn't run anymore

She stopped in front of a church and paused for a while
Then decided to go in and sit near the aisle

As she listened to the sermon tears filled her eyes
Everyone in the church could hear her cries

She cried out O Lord, I did not know you back then
But please O mighty God, forgive me of my sin

She cried and she cried of happiness and pain
For she knew that day that she would never be the same

And those tears that she had cried stopped on that very day
For she knew deep down that she was on her way

On her way up to heaven to the city of gold
Where she would never feel the pain or ever grow old

And the day that she passed away she softly closed her eyes
And welcomed the hands of Jesus as he led her through the skies

And the moral of this story is clear in deed
That no matter what life gives you, Jesus is all you need

Litha Carver

"Sisters"

To me to have a sister,
is to have a special friend.
Someone that I can come to,
whatever shape I'm in.

You're always there to listen,
and give a caring smile.
You know just how to pick me up,
and let me know "life's worth while."

You listen to my feelings,
and try to understand.
You encourage me and hold me close,
with open heart and hand.

I know it's not been easy,
I've tried your patience "yes."
But through it all, you did stand tall,
and passed the sister test.

Your love continued daily
and constantly does grow.
Through ups and downs, smiles and frowns,
that sister love does show.

Glinnie M. Lumpkin

My New Land

I smell the salty spring air, hear the sounds of the city.
The sun seems warmer here with the ocean frothy and close.
I see faces like mine, some sad, some happy,
hoping hopes like mine, dreaming special dreams,
my little boys quietly laugh for the beauty of life I feel,
the fight of where I came from and the struggle of life I had
cannot quench the joy I feel as I look at my new homeland.
Here I can work my hands and build, here my heart can lift a friend
grapes the size of oranges here, I will see what gifts I can find
smell the flowers, live and work, join my heart with others who care.
Courage to work a land and strength to create my dream
make this different Land a home and help where I can
I have found a gift here; surely I've found my promised land.

Linda Lane

Walking With Christine

The little girl walked along beside me
and from the corner of my eye I saw her edging closer,
and in her dear way shyly slide her hand into mine.
She tossed her head a bit and her long hair
swung round partially covering her face
that she lifted towards me showing
a pleased smile of immense satisfaction,
and I smiled back as we continued on.
And at her other side her father, with
affectionate pride, said, "I don't know
how you got stuck with that,"
and I said, "this is the kind of 'getting
stuck with' that I like", and gave her hand a little squeeze,
and silently added, "the best."

Ina Van Valkenburgh

Protector Of Dreams

The chief's memories are always there,
He looks into space it seems like a stare.

The mighty buffalo as they graze,
He sees the past of long ago days.

The brave young bucks as they go off to war,
The mothers afraid, knowing what's in store.

Chubby brown baby on a cradleboard,
Drinks from an ancient gourd.

Beautiful maidens in white doeskin,
Belts and moccasins of beaded buckskin.

Graceful white tipi's with painted sides,
Painted ponies for braves to ride.

Indian chiefs with colorful bonnets,
Majestic with eagle feathers upon it.

He thinks of times long past,
That seem to vanish just as fast.

The times of hunting and freedom lost,
Cold hard winters and families lost.

Our great American native it seems,
Are vanishing into a misty dream.

Dixie Kendall

Kentucky Derby Week

Thunder over Louisville starts the week,
and fireworks light the sky.
"Ooh's and Ahh's, booms and bright lights,
capture excitement and surprise.

Hot air balloons, of colors galore,
saturate the winds overhead.
Swoosh, up, up they go, high up in the sky,
the most graceful race in the world.

The Bell of Louisville's time has come,
to race her rivals again.
Her whistles blow as she paddles fast as she can,
and people cheer her on to win.

The Derby Parade, of bright colors and flowers
that fill the city streets.
Big, beautiful floats, and marching bands,
and clowns so silly, they seem.

The Derby Race, that traditional moment,
jockeys mount, and the horses strut to their gates.
Bonnets turn, "My Old Kentucky Home" plays,
then "Bang", they're off and running.

Sharon Stevens

Granny's Cure For All Ails

If you are feeling low and out of sorts
 I know what will cure your "ails"
A great big swig of the "recipe"
 Made from white lightening and horse shoe nails.

Or may be a rub with snake oil
 From your head down to your feet
With an asafetida bag tied around your neck
 Now wouldn't that be a treat!

And don't forget the goose grease
 Rubbed on good and thick
Or skunk oil mixed with garlic
 That surely would do the trick.

If you try all this and it doesn't work
 Don't be too timid to say
There's a lot more stuff in another book
 That I could send you right away.

I know all this sounds real corny
 But, it was written just to make you smile
And if it makes your day a little brighter
 Then the effort was all worth while!!!

Quennie Tucker

Just A Smile

If you smile at me I'll smile at you.
But who would have thought it would be true?

As I took a look we made eye contact.
Who would have thought we'd attract?

As I continued on, I took a look around, you were no where to be found.

On my way out at the water spout, your smiling face came about.

I giggled with water drops on my chin,
not even knowing I just might win.

Your sense of humor and politeness accompanied me on out the door.
I definitely knew you were not a bore.

You're handsome and sincere, so I continued with no fear.

Days have gone by and I remember you.
The question is, What will we do?

I wonder if we'll continue our friendship for awhile and
remember it began with "JUST A SMILE."

Debra E. Castro

"Night Prowler"

Were I to leap through the air
with a raised back
and cast my silhouette
before a gypsy moon,
or sit shoulder to shoulder
on a fence and howl at the night,
I might get hit by a shoe or two.
Then scramble up a nearby tree
to hide beside my whiskered friend.
'til the sun comes up
and the world comes alive.
With the chatter
of everyday life
My innocent meows
bring a bowl of milk
as I coyly flash
my big green eyes,
my purrs sure to captivate a lonely soul.
The one who was first to throw a shoe
Calls me "pretty kitty."

Elizabeth Wolf-Degnan

Journey Of Faith

There's a place at the top of life's mountain where joy and peace can be found,
There's victory a top that mountain, but you've got to start from the ground.
During the climb there are hindrances and obstacles to face,
It's a challenge to even start until your foot finds a place.
Then when you find that sure foothold you can convince yourself to go on,
To the next level; where there is room only for the strong.
As you ascend even higher and your strength is running out,
You can say prayer of faith and to heaven give a joyful shout.
You then feel a surge of energy and vigor you never dreamed you had,
Just a few more feet, now keep the faith, see it's not that bad.
As you reach the final crevice where your fingers just can't grip,
You suddenly loose your footing and feel yourself begin to slip.
You cry out, "oh God, please help me, all my trust I have in You!"
Instantly you're whisked away on angels wings, where the sky is so blue.
You look around victoriously, you've finally reached the top,
Where joy and peace can be found because your faith in God never stopped!

Deidra Bell

Season Of Sorrow

This is my season of sorrow.
Let me shed tears of recall and regret
Then I will look forward to tomorrow.
But, now, I need to recall my family gone . . .
Thoughts said and unsaid, acts done and undone,
 love withheld and freely given.
This is my season of sorrow.
Let me express my loss, acknowledge my debt
During this period of time I borrow
From my daily life to recall those I loved and often failed
 to appreciate, not taking the time to say, "I care..."
Now I need to recall the family gone.

 This is my season of sorrow.
I give praises to Christ who holds them near, and has
 eased them from earthly burdens of tomorrow.
I wish not their return. I rejoice in their pure joy in Your
Arms, oh Lord, but . . .
Now I need to recall my family gone.
This is my season of sorrow.
Let me shed tears of remembrance, not regret
And then I will look forward to tomorrow
Recalling the blessings of their presence
In my life and not the void their absence left.
I seek a space . . . a piece of time . . . to deal with my season of sorrow.

Leslie Hodgson

Awards

The joy that's felt inside
is truly hand to hide
as I bowed down my head
with the happy tears I shed, so humble, yet with pride
To know form nothing I came, because of God on to fame.
This moment I must confess
My great achievement of success.
Thru the years of pain and despair
My hopes I believed in the Lord, in prayer.

 I did not know my purpose now in life
Only to follow whatever door, He opened
No goal was ever too big to complete
No challenge was too hard to meet
 years of toil and labor
 with time for a neighbor
 Loving family with care
 Adding members to share
Passing each year without fear, knowing the Lord, was near,
Then my day came at last, going forward leaving the past
A new purpose in my time, to take pen in hand and write a
rhyme.

Dorothy I. Brown

Dream Scope

Last night I took a trip on a fairy boat called love,
That traveled down narrow straits to a land that never was.
On this boat I road my dream to all the things I thought I'd seen,
I saw a man sitting on a throne that told of the things he owned,
He showed me rivers and trees that covered the land,
And places that has not been touched by a human hand.
A beauty that glowed was so brilliant and bright,
That it lit up the land that never knew night.
And all the people there had wings and could fly,
So naturally I wanted to see this place from the skies.
I saw animals playing on over a thousand hills,
And the land was covered with flowers bearing fruit in every field.
    Well it's almost day and I must go, But I'll tell you
the way if you want to know, Just follow your imagination,
It will take you where you want to go, Because you are
the master of your mind the one in full control.

William L. Hardister

Her Own Private Stage

She doesn't really see the people passing by her —
She just keeps twirling
dancing for the audience only she can see
The waterfall from the fountain on the square
is the roar of the crowd
only she can hear
The laughter from people talking around her
is the adoration of the fans
only she can know
As I sit in quiet judgment of this woman's oddities
I am suddenly aware of a subtle irony —
I struggle through my days
with a career, education, family —
and a world full of responsibilities
anchoring me firmly to earth
while she —
although void of these things —
can drift freely anywhere
strangely exempt
from reality.

Debbie Valentini

Spring Returns

The mocking bird peels forth his song,
at the beautiful dawn of day.
I too, join him in his sing-a-long,
before I go on my way.

I love to hear her notes of gladness,
as spring comes in view.
The dancing sunlight, the staccato rain,
the early morning dew, bring spring in all
her beauty, to you, and you and you.

Florence E. Weaver

The Unborn Child

Cradled in the warmth of the womb, the child sleeps.

Clouds of shame roll over empty playgrounds.

To be, or not to be; alive but unknown. Two as one,
    but both alone.

No future, no choice; a heart that beats, a body
    without a voice.

Waiting in an isolated darkness, a short breath
    whispers a farewell to innocence.

A bright star falls from the sky, and concedes the
    death of the unborn child.

Hal Armstrong

Forgiveness

Finding strength in our hearts to
Overcome feelings of anger and bitterness so that we can
Release the past and
Give way to a bright productive future.
In time, with God's gentle guidance we become
Victorious over our pain,
Ending the hopelessness and fear,
Not ever looking back,
Except to reflect upon what was learned
So that we can finally
Say good-bye to the hurt and embrace the love we deserve.

Aimee M. Brimmer

The Tempest Of Bath

The boat tossed on the mighty waves
The swells near overcame it.
So many lives here to be saved
And the sea no way to tame it.
The sails are torn, they lay in shreds
The crew has nary a chance
As the sea comes crashing over their heads
The captain holds his stance.
The wind blew gusts of forty knots
The water swept o'er the bow.
And, then, just before the main mast rots
Mommy says, "Bath time's over now."

Connie Dalzell

Solitude

Oft when I sit alone
I hear a most peculiar tone.
Not a noise you understand
With the brash sound of a band.
Just a sound soft and low
With the strength to take my heart in tow.

There is an inner peace in me
When I'm here by the sea.
Maybe it is the gentle wave
That makes my heart behave.
I may never know for sure
But it is always a pleasant cure.

In time I must take pen in hand
And make some notes well planned.
I will do that some day
When again I come this way.
Otherwise I'm stuck with remembering
And for my head that is too encumbering.

R. Al Morrison

"Marga's Bangs"

Marga's bangs have a mind of their own . . .
All askew or lopsided as if by an unruly hand soewn!
They express the quirks and quips of her quick wit . . .
Marga, my sister through love, who was sent
by the spirits from above . . .
She rests me down as we both feel the ground.
Suggested by Milton, our guru hound.
Barbie doll, supreme . . . Silver-brown tumbling down.
She needs not jewels, her hair is her crown . . .

Irene Clark

Rebirth

I was thrashed and beaten into the ground

I was not killed

I did not die.

My roots began to grow again——

I burst out of the Earth
and felt the heat of the Sun.

I reached for he Sky——
and found the STARS.

Sylvia L. Blalack

"My Love"

How can I describe my love for you?
You are always there when I'm feeling blue
You have never had a cross word for me
When I want to twice, you say, "have me three"
I have known you so long, you've never complained
You devotion to me? Complete and unrestrained
I just want to say that I love you, honey
And that you are worth every bit of the money
That I have spent so much of on loving you
You will never leave we, sweetie, I know that too
There is nothing that I wouldn't do for you my dear
You're my Love, my Life, my frosty mug of
Iced cold beer!

Kevin M. Orr

Small Refund

IRS tax forms received, of all days XMAS eve.
You put away for later, hoping to forget the matter-
after all, this year's check must be fatter!
Jan, Feb, March, we're running out of time.
So we start, piece by piece,
trying to get every last dime, in place.
Hurry, hurry finding all we need?
For at least a feast!
After all it's April Fifteenth.
And are we relieved.
But will Uncle Sam believe?
A refund yes, a family of four to dine.
Must be at Wendy's, no money for wine.
The return's in the mail,
But did we remember to sign?

L. L. Fogt

Black And Gold

The curling fingers slowly close the galaxy
In preparation for the awesome trip to b4
Where super-speeds and time will turn to black
The pages of its space-time history.

Ten billion years, or more, this darkness will remain.
No spark will light a dream in this deep-sleep domain.
Since all created must traverse this rounded universe,
The galaxies will re-unite again.

Such speed occurs when two huge galaxies collide,
That atoms loosen leaving naked their inside!
Their passing through each other leaves an endless cloud of fire
That parts in half as they reluctantly divide.

Electron's golden threads will patterns soon appear,
For suns and satellites that fall within their sphere.
The final fabric makes the curving diamond veil,
To hide the secrets that the magic might prevail!

Leland Embert Andrews

My Love

I've loved you all my life, why I can't explain!
Everytime I see there's hurt in your eyes, my heart can feel the pain.
How can I love you so much and expect nothing in return?
How can we share each other's lives, when we have so much to learn?

Do you know the reasons why I worry, the reasons that I cry?
Can you give me that real love, or the strength to get by?
What could you do in my time of need?
Could you soothe my pain when I feel my heart bleed?

Since I can remember I've shown you love.
Without any special reason, you were always thought of.
Maybe it's the love I was taught as a kid,
The kind that was there no matter what I did!

I wish you could learn the love that I know!
Then our hearts would be free, and our feelings would grow.
Then we'd be happy when the tables have turned.
We'd love each other as one, there'd be no more to learn.

Khaleelah McCleary

Angel Mama

Though you have gone, Mama,
You are here in the heart of things
And I am tied to an Angel's apron strings.

You gave me life, and in the giving
Taught me how to live.
You are with me when I hear
The hoot of an owl; the call of a whippoorwill;
See the shape of a cloud; a tree on a windy hill.
A rail fence marching along a country lane,
Some violets there in the early Spring.
A campfire burning on a cold, clear night,
A river flowing quietly by its light.
A rainbow spanning the Eastern sky;
You taught me God put it there, and why.
The wake of a ship on a tranquil sea,
When I see these things you are near to me.

Angel Mama, though you are Home with God and those you love
Attend me still, for you are here in the heart of things
And I am tied to an Angel's apron strings.

Juanita M. Onweller

. . . OnlyMajik

Feelings of thought deep within be at rest
Peaceful, calm and composed
Balance amid the virtuous and the wicked
Not to be disrupted by where my mind may journey . . .

Words passionately whispered begin a harvesting
A slow gathering of intense minuscule thoughts
A rise within the confines of my mind . . .

Sensations . . . milling and churning
Feverishly trying to organize the theme
Desperately needing to focus the ever-expanding exhilaration
Overcomes once organized thought . . .

Power of fantasy and rush of ecstasy
Do hold this mind captive as spells being cast
Transforming all thought to insatiable desire . . .

Bursting from within my mind.
The multitude of emotions do spread
Enveloping my entire form
Creating an openness . . . one that is without measure . . .

Pulsing waves of enlightenment alerting all senses
Capturing the emotions which were once mine
Rendering this one breathless . . .

Shermaine Shell

Japan

Don't treat me like Japan today
I don't need a guilty enemy to say
I'm your friend even though you hurt
Forget my bomb, forget you were burnt

I don't need Mr. America tonight
Little Miss Japan is quite alright
Without your guilty friendship near
With you gone, I would have no fear

I now know I can battle any heart
No nuclear love can tear me apart
And baby, being Japan feels pretty grave
Trying to forget the nightmares you gave

Don't treat me like Japan today
I don't need a guilty ally to say
Forget my bomb, forget you were burnt
I'm your friend even though you hurt

And it's all bull, I know, it is and always will be
I'm not your Japan, no not me
And it's all bull, I know
So Mr. America, let me go

Ivy M. O'Connell

"Edward Ray In June"

June in the summertime. A special time. A special name.
A time for brides to wed their grooms, times for love
under stars and moons.

June months passing. Year after year. A baby boy born.
Time to laugh? Or mourn? Love is given freely to the babies
born in June. The year of nineteen seventy and two.

Baby, are you bleeding? Does your heart ever heal? Is
there time for love, now? Why are you so still? Do you know
the meaning, of the word: Hemophilia? Is your name not Edward?
Or is it — Free Bleeder?

What are you to me, now? Why should I care? I am proud
and healthy, while you have to be so careful. Careful is not
a word that children learn so easily. June is not a time to
sit and watch the world go by. Bruises, broken bones. You
lived. You would not listen. Does it matter that I loved you?
That I cared? Do the words: "I am sorry" mean anything to you now?
No.

What is AIDS? And, why is AIDS? I watched it as it claimed you,
in a horrifying way. Another victim down — Edward Ray in June.

Cynthia Garris Pyron

Visit From An Angel

I have lots of fear, for I can not hear.

One lonely night,
  I was sleeping tight,
  when I woke up in a terrible fright,
  looking out at the lonely night.

When I saw a light,
  so very near,
  and to my surprise I could hear
  an Angel whispering in my ear:

"Lend me your hand
  and I will take you to a land,
  where shall hear,
  and run with deer,
   and where everyone wishes to be."

Bonnie Kitchens

Shooting My Bow

Her parts are standard,
Yet masterfully engineered.
Her body, forged to perfection;
Her limbs, strong and slender.

Grasping her naked frame
We are one — in tune.
Experience surpasses clumsiness,
My arrow fits gently into her rest.

The shaft slides and
Her spine arches in a half moon.
Minute noises are induced from the strain
As her hair; draws against my cheek.

Concentration focused, my muscles tense.
There is no more holding it — I release.
A muffled shout breaks the silence as
Her limbs thrust forward, then quiver to stop.

The shot is perfect
And we are again as we were:
With me, holding her naked frame,
And beholding her standard parts.

Mark Oblinsky

Garden Isle

Oh, to plant the seeds of beauty,
  And fill the earth with hope;
To ease the souls of troubled woes,
  And live where I could cope.

I'd see the flights of birds,
  And view their lovely plume;
Then chase the moon through cloudy skies,
  And watch my garden bloom.

I'd smell the scent of Sampaguita,
  The wind that sways their leaves;
The tall trees in the green woods,
  That never cease to breathe.

I'd taste the wine on wings of songs,
  And let the bluebirds fly
From tree to tree to pollinate
  The flowers on my garden isle.

And when my eyes could see no more,
  I would not fade in vain
To trail the path where angels trod;
  Where God would lead the way.

Lucy Evangelista

Turf War

The wind dressed leaves of autumn gold
rampant in the whirlwinds of change
dead soggy leaves, intermingled with colors
of turf wars blood,
dead brown winter, barren trees holler
shake branches quiver,
the knife, carved lover's trust,
in frozen bark, and rage quivered,
trembled,
baggy pants, belts inconsequent,
I freeze berries,
And found the weathered body lifeless,
with nettles necklace,
warm youth lost —
families drape darkened robes of mourning
and sense the exit, escape from anger,
hopeless winter wind, autumn leaves —
adorned with turf wars blood, tears.

Antonia A. Acevedo-Schoups

Camel

A benign beast with fluttery eyes
bears the burden of the hump,
    and wonders why
Bears someone sitting on the hump
    and wonders why
When he sits asked not to bear,
    his flickery ears wave away flies
Chewing his cud, showing an infectious smile
    he wonders when will he die.

Dennis T. Flanagan

Without You

Without you I am nothing
. . . a sun without the warmth
. . . a tree without a branch
. . . a song without a tune
. . . a ship without a sail
. . . a life without a purpose
Without you I am nothing
You are the sea that keeps the ship afloat.

Tami Weaver

My Grandchildren

I remember when you came into this world
Each one of you had your own little twirl.
We held you, we loved you and watched
you all grow.
And now is the time to fill your dreams
and let you go.
The years have passed and I am getting old.
But I still remember you just like gold.

Elsie Hickman

Never Got To Kiss Good-Bye

They played that old song on the radio today
It brought back memories of you
I felt those old feelings too
It's been a long time since I felt that way

I was wary about seeing you that last day
Somehow I think you knew
You were also looking blue
But we both knew we would be O.K.

It was a memorable summer in Delaware
Thank you for the time we got to share
Why didn't we fight for the way we felt
We could have been each other's help
I'm not at peace if you can understand why
Because we never got to kiss good-bye

John Hooks

Hiding

Hiding inside myself dying to escape
I'm in a great big shell hiding from my fate
I have a window looking out, but the blind is always down
Hiding from the world today never to be found
    Better not to be loved at all than loved by those you hate
Better to be all alone than deal with all the pain
I don't wish to cry any more but I feel it's much to late
When I see her face I see mine
I don't wish to be like her I'd rather die
    Don't try to save me it hurts to much
Please don't help me I can't feel your touch
I'm all alone in the world today
I'll be all alone no matter what you say
I can't be loved and this you will see
That thing called love, it hurts me

Keisha Castillo

When She Left Us

There was one day when my sister could not stay.
Everything was O.K. Until that one unusual Saturday.
I cried by day; prayed at night; asked if everything would be alright.
The only answer I ever got was: "I wish I could say yes, but
    that would not be the best."
Her birthday came; she was not there.
We got it all set up; I guess she did not care.
Nobody would have felt the way I felt if we were not so close.
But seeing her run away, made me feel lost.
No sign of her anywhere; made me feel nobody cared.
The cops stopped looking;
Our happiness was fading.
Then the day came that we got her call.
She told us that she wanted to come home, and that she missed us all.
When she came home, we all cried.
But that will be the happiest day of my whole life!!!

Kelly Loudenber

These Trees At Gettysburg

Walking around this sacred ground,
    my attention went to THESE TREES . . .
        . . . the silent, living monuments to events that
        occurred on those three days;
            . . . the quiet witnesses to heroics that
            may never be seen again;
                . . . some wearing scars of battle while others
                perhaps serving as shields and angels unaware.

THESE TRESS — what would you say . . .
    these survivors of this bloody battle?
What would your stories be?
What lessons would you have us learn?
Perhaps,
    in walking on theses hallowed grounds
    if we are quiet,
        and silent,
our hearts will hear what it is you would say . . .

THESE TREES —
    Silent Sentries of the past
    and future.

Judith A. Erb

I Am He

I am He that was born of Mary in bethlehem one day
He that left His home on high a mighty debt to pay
His back was bared to the mighty lash that all ye may be healed.
In the blessed book these words you'll find "Whosoever Will"

I am He who lives forever, I am He,
That gave His life on Calvary.
I am He that makes the lame to walk and the blind to see.
The one that saves you from your sins. I am He, I am He.

I am He whom ye crucified on Calvary that day, that bore the
sins of all the world that your soul might be saved.
Come and touch the nail-scarred hands and see the pierced side,
Plunge beneath the crimson flow all your sins to hide.

I am He ye lay in the tomb, and the third day rose again,
And conquered death, hell and the grave that ye might be
saved from sin. I have come to reap the harvest of the ones
who live for me. To take you home to Glory to live eternally.

I am He that prepared a mansion in heaven for you.
For all of you who pass the test and to the Lord stand true.
Up there you can eat of the tree of life and live forever more,
And reign with Him forever on heaven's golden shore.

Ruby Canada

Remembering Waco

I heard no screams.
Did they go silently into that red noon
In sudden bursts of flame?
But in the night I heard them cry
I asked the dark, "Why, oh why?
And who is to blame?"
Powerful grown-ups took their lives away,
They had no voice at all —
Pushed tight against that wall
Of Cult and Law — and then the searing Flame.
Pawns they were, no more than property;
Ultimately dispensable they were
In planning to win the game.
Now power people are trying to explain.
On one side-all bureaucracy,
And on another I can see
The darkest part of the human heart.

Elizabeth Armstrong

Night Life And Light Life

I have some kind of power
to calm the dark at this hour
And see the night in flower.

I can feel the deep understanding
of the weak and of the commanding
And I can feel the hate disbanding.

This is a life of unequaled love
A love not below or not above
A love that's not push-come-to-shove.

Everyone crosses an uncrossable line
Where the light seems to cease its shine
And nothing is good or just fine.

But I have come back to loving life
And I'm back in the light after all of my strife.
Even so, I am not quite ready to be a wife.

I have some kind of power
To calm the dark at this hour
And see the night in full flower.

Leah Martina Siefka

Descendant From The Motherland

Embrace me in your bosom
And tell me stories of old
Allow me to feel your warm breath on my cheek
Let me listen to your soul

Give me history with names of our Kings
and titles of lands where we once lived
Strengthen me with your tolerance of pain
and how you endured, to forgive

Share with me the elegance of Queens, like yourself
and your portrait of the 'seas' divide'
Complete my heart with your righteousness
and how you have come to abide. Help me feel the glory of faith
and the attaining of the crown. Help me subdue the aches in my heart
Help me grasp the strength I'm bound

Teach me the prayer that you say at night
And the ones that guide you through the day
Give me direction to the path you took
That led to the 'sacred way'. Invite me to the 'recipe'
that you grew and tilled from the soil . . .

Show me how to nourish my being;
To become closer to my Lord.

Paula R. Jackson

The Love Within Us

Today we stood with love in our hearts on our Wedding Day

Everyone gave congratulations and wishes of the best to come our way

Peaceful dreams I'll dream tonight — joys, emotions reaching a new height

I trust and love you with all my heart

To think this is only till death do us part

The time is for now our new life

Joined together as newlyweds, we became man and wife

Adelia Jean Pendleton

"A Deltaville Thanksgiving"

Back to the basics with family and friends,
Sharing memories as the conversation lends.
Times remembered and dreams unfolding,
The little one forever beholding.
A walk to the water, what a special day,
The stresses of the city whisked away.
So few the times we are able to share,
But nothing, oh nothing can compare.

Sandy Winn

The Soul Speaks

Sometimes you wake up and find yourself all alone,
You look everywhere you know but in no heart can you find a home.

You search for all the answers in the eyes of someone wise,
You search for the truth but find it was only a disguise.

You can search the whole world over but you know you'll never find,
The answers you've been searching for, they're all hidden there in your mind.

You hope by chance you'll find a clue, by a phrase or just a word said,
The answer is there, you know, hidden, somewhere in your head.

So you listen with all you have, to the words of ones who care,
Knowing no one can tell you the answers you know are already there.

So you sit in the dark and wait, in the silence for your soul to speak,
Your heart and mind may fail you, but your soul is never weak.

So you patiently wait inside yourself for the time to be just right,
When your soul finally sheds the answers you've been searching for
    with all your might.

Jamilyn Norman

In Search Of The Magic Potion

I have heard that somewhere there is a magic elixir.
Does anyone know who makes it?
Who is the mixer?

It is said to have the power to rejuvenate the old, to give them youth.
Some think it can make them rich, others just search for the truth.

I wonder! If I were to find it, could it work magic for me too.
Could it restore my happiness?
Could it make my life anew?

Is it real?
Is it just a dreamed up illusion?
These questions and many more, leave us filled with confusion.

But the possibility that it may exists.
Creates a strong curiosity as our searching persist.

Is it a pill, a shot, or a lotion?
Until we know for sure, we must continue in search of the
magic potion.

Glen T. Rankin Jr.

Dear Ryley,

Winter got a lot bleaker, when you went away
But I know it's nicer in the land of unclouded day.
Did Jesus put His arm around you? And smile? I bet He did,
For I read in His book, He especially loved kids.
Introduce yourself to Great-Grandma Miller and Marle Washechek
Uncle Cliff, Great-Grandpa Wirth, Aunt Bernice and all.
Say hi to Peter, James and John and Paul.
It's hard for me to believe your journey on earth is done
Especially, since it had only just begun.
And this I've never really understood,
How all these things work out for the good.
I see so darkly now, although you understand
Exactly how you fit into God's perfect plan.
And would you wait for Nana and I?
We'll be along in the bye and bye.
Linger just inside the eastern gate,
There's no time in heaven, so you won't have long to wait.
And then we'll stroll the golden streets hand in hand.
Love, Papa Stan

Stan Miller

Halfway There

I find myself halfway there
What it all means I'm not sure
Reaching for something higher
Comforts my lonely nights
Searching the dark skies for my hero
I don't know all the tales
But they're always shared by the warm firelight
The secrets are passed to those who stand waiting
And then it starts again
Where dreams end the shadows fall long
And all is still
The fire is cold now
And long since burned its last ember
A chill like after the rain fills the air
And the only thing moving
Is time itself
Then I hear the soft calling
And as I look ahead
I find myself halfway there

Kendra Leyn Greiner

Flowers

Flowers of purple, pink or gold
Are big, bright and bold.
Sitting in the ground, the wind makes them blow,
Swaying side by side in colorful rows
Little April showers
Make happy flowers.
When the blazing sun stays out,
It makes the flowers pout.
Flowers are beautiful in a group or alone.
If you care for them they can brighten your home.

Chantelle Rogers

In Tempo

The ocean's roar and gasping tide
In tempo
White caps dancing toward the sands
In tempo
A kiss . . . tongues darting to and fro
In tempo
The slap and very first cry
In tempo
A whole life of joy and tears
In tempo
The last breath and then death . . . in tempo

Jerry M. Martin

Untitled

Dear Son,
You were such a special sunbeam,
Spreading sunshine every day.
A celestial being, sent to us,
Along the milky way.

And as I touch your favorite Teddy,
I can only share, a memory of a smiling face,
A lock of curly hair.

Your eyes were like the evening stars,
Happy and sparkling bright.
I felt a twinkling feeling,
When you hugged me extra tight.

And if I listen carefully,
Tiny foot steps fill the air.
For, I know within my heart,
You play on golden stairs.

We hold you close in memory,
Your journey here is done.
Our heavenly Father keeps you.
Dear, beloved son.

Ann C. Strupp

No Hope

Contemplating a commonplace turbulence, the battle's raging!
Yearning anguishes from the driven deprivation of an aging
loss of companionship, caring and collateral closeness, caged
in a giving heart, held in a hemisphere of haughty hatred.
Protect me, it pleads! Preserve the pitiful pounding of patience.
Wait for when the wanting will wash away resistance,
and song's saved for soaring through silver-lined skies.
Escape these effects and ever ease my effervescent eyes!

To desire, to dream, to delay the dawning of a different day!
If time would tick but not turn, the tempest t'would tarry.
I'd find my friend, I'd forget to be frightened, I'd feel
the touch of tenderness, the tongue's taste, the skill
which whispers while wrapped with words of wisdom.
Ordinary occurrences occupy our opulent order of opposition.
A tiny thread of tinsel is tied to a teetering, toppling tree.
Hope's here in my heart, but it's hidden even from me.

Virginia Sullivan

The Nightmare

The nightmare begins with the ring of the phone
oh how I wish you were back home

I can't stand up, I fall to my knees
this can't be true, I'm begging you please

You're so young and so very strong
something has gone terribly wrong

Try to wake up, try to scream
this is no nightmare, this is no dream

No words can express the way I feel
can't even eat a simple meal

Can't find one reason, one reason at all
someone must pay, must take the fall

All this anger bottled up inside
why must my brother be the one who died

You want the world to share your pain
but that's not fair, it's all in vain

Try putting your life back together
while everyone else just worries about weather

No words of wisdom in this letter
the nightmare continues, it doesn't get better.

Thomas M. Phillips

The Lost Generation

The world is a web of many generations,
While each one is woven with certain complication.
And truth is distorted by man's technicality,
Which questions the premise of what is reality.
But the media just waits like a hunger-stricken vulture,
Determined to devour what's left of our culture.
We're so busy fighting over who's wrong or right,
That our lives pass us by and the issue grows trite.
So as we move forward in this life made of fiction,
We find only feelings of more contradiction.
Because like it or not this world fails to see,
That stolen ideas define it philosophies.
But if a poem or song can represent how we feel,
Then surely we've lost an innocence once real.

David Odle

Mother

You showed me things within my heart, I'd thought I'd never find.
  You cared for me, loved me, time after time.
You gave me advice, and showed me the way.
  And I love you for that each and every day.
You hugged me when I was right.
  And held me when I was wrong.
You always told me just to be strong.
  You told me to do what I felt was right.
And someday my wings would spread, and I'd take flight.
  What I feel for you is hard to explain.
Just that I love you, if that's not to plain.
  I thank God everyday for sending you to me.
You're one of a kind, you're like no other.
  You're the best, for you're my Mother.

Michelle E. Misquez

Why Must The World Seem Down?

When news strikes,
The heart trembles.
Full-knowing of thy actions,
Of self-infliction and denial,
For what exists with consternation.
I can not complain, yet I make excuses,
For what my discipline with not accomplish.
I know my task, it is great and baronial,
Yet my humanity shrivels in the face of light.
When feelings strong, of love and fight,
Entangle the web of human virtue,
My soul stands tall but dies half-way.
If one could show,
The evil strength of mass destruction,
Caused by oneself,
The world would surely fly into the night.
While life goes by,
With fawning subtleties,
The actors rise, and the masses fall.

Michael F. Maltese

Sunflowers

  Sunflowers are beautiful, they also smell great.
In the morning of sunshine, or in the deep night of heartache.
  They cheer you up when you're down with their luscious
leaves; noticed under bushy green trees.
  They rush into your heart faster than your blood,
even though they're buried under dried up mud.
  They might not be roses, though they are unique. Their
yellow petals attached to them look especially chic.
  Have you seen a sunflower?
  This is undoubtfully true, in this gigantic garden
of life, there is a sunflower made for you.

Lindsay Lambert

Dear Mom

Write a poem, my mother said,
And so I looked inside my head;
I had to fish around a bit,
'Cause no one's lately dusted it.
And there to my surprise I found
Lying everywhere around
Words that rhyme and words that don't
And things that work and things that won't.
I picked them up and put them straight,
And tried to make a poem that's great.
But all I found, to my dismay,
Was senseless noise and disarray.
And so, Dear Mom, this one's for you . . .
It's the best that I can do.

Linda L. Bradley

Untitled

Dear Heavenly Father, I desperately pray
That Ye will forgive my unrighteous way.

The loneliness felt I know is earned
Thy wonderful Spirit so easily spurned.

In the midst of Thy light and blessings given
I have let Satan in and sinward was driven.

Publicly strong and secretly weak
If only the right road I always would seek.

It must be remembered, I have to see
I am never alone when Thy Spirit is with me.

Failures past I'll learn from and use
Turn them around and righteousness choose.

Or Thy wondrous grace I will rely
Only through Thee can I get by.

For yesterday's transgressions I spiritually weep
The Priesthood covenants I will honor and keep.

The future begins now, I will start again
Renew my strength and seek help against sin.

With this gracious Father I vow to try and be
Worthy of Thy presence for the rest of Eternity.

Terry L. Cato

"Who Am I"

To those, I am the "Hero" in your life. The person you looked up
to for love, strength and wisdom.

To many, I am the "Eagle" in your life. The wind beneath your wings.
The one who led you thru trouble waters, the one who pulled you up
and gave you strength and courage to shine. To only to have set you "free".

To all, I am the "Listener", the hope in your life. The one that gave
you inspiration, faith and love, when you needed it the most.

To those, I am the "Disciplinarian" in your life. The one who taught
you morales and values in life. The one who told you to take full
responsibility for your actions. I could have taken "No" for an
answer, and sometimes I wished I had.

I am unable to be with you now, but I do exist in your "hearts and souls".

Thank God — You all were, "My Wind Beneath My Wings".

  "WHO AM I"

I am "Your Father . . . "Your Grandpa" . . . "Your Brother" . . .
But most of all — "I am your "Friend".

Wilma Jean Tinto

Until We Meet Again

Until we meet again
I will cherish all the memories that I have of you
remembering forever all the good things you have done
and how grateful I am of the time we had together

Until we meet again
I will miss your face, your voice
And your presence
But I know that you are
And always will be with me in spirit

Until we meet again
I look forward to seeing you
meeting again in peace
to be together for eternity

Until we meet again
in that beautiful world on the other side
know that you are not forgotten
and are always loved

You will always be in my heart
and the help you have given will never be forgotten
Until We Meet Again . . .

Mitzi L. Mask

D Day

On the 6th of June, 1944
invasion came to Normandy's shore.

The soldiers were poised as ready as could be
to engage in combat for liberty.

The day was cloudy and overcast
none knew how long the battle would last.

The salty surf swirled, the wind raised each wave
sending many a soldier to a watery grave.

Some who survived to the beaches and sand
were cut down by gunfire and died on the land.

All were weary and some thought of retreat
but determination vanquished defeat.

They conquered their fear and charged valiant and bold
on Omaha, Utah, Sword, Juno, and Gold.

Normandy's beaches are peaceful again
but the memory of D Day will never end.

Margaret Mary Ferrari

The Descent Of Nature

The bird soured across the blue, sunlit sky. It scanned the
mid-day horizon, searching . . . searching. A bang is heard in the
distance. The bird falls dead on the dirt path. The hunter
stands over the dead bird, rifle in hand — "Ah, lunch!"

Steve Katz

We Offer What We Can

We know that life's a challenge, sometimes hard to understand.
It's hard to be a parent, we offer what we can.

When we received the message, we cried with tears so loud.
It made us feel so happy, we felt just down right proud.

We knew that you could do it, working hard with open mind.
To reach a goal is not easy, it really takes your time.

We love you very dearly, although some day's it's hard to show.
But to us it's so important, to really let you know.

We tried to give you freedom, some days was out of hand.
Just remember that we love you, we offer what we can.

Charles O. Richardson Sr.

Growing Up

I thought that being seventeen was strange
And much too hard for me to try to be
I guess I prob'ly thought I'd have to change
And try to act like someone elderly.
Now I'm it and I was right — it's all wrong
I wish I didn't have to get so old
I really feel quite small and don't belong
I just don't look my age, that's what I'm told.
But maybe age is not so bad, you know.
I've got to learn it changes every year
I'll see with time that I must learn to grow
And leave behind this crazy little fear.
I guess I'm at the age that's in between
And now I just can't wait 'til I'm eighteen!

Denise A. Cross

My Thoughts Of You

My wonderful and sexy man, oh all the wonderful thoughts and hopeful plans.
The way that you touch me is such a dream.
Your body my love so sexy and lean, will surely send me into a wonderful dream.
Kissing your lips so soft but sweet, is like a once in a lifetime treat.
Those strong arms to hold me until dawn's early light . . .
The lovemaking I know can only feel right.
Wishing that we could forever go on making sweet love until the morning dawn . . .
Touching and kissing our bodies in synch, sharing an intimacy that
mind and body must think . . . That Heaven on Earth is our magic link.
Should I ever have this chance I wish . . . That you and I will begin
a lifetime of wonderful and happy daily bliss.
Let it be known that I can't resist the chance to be that one special
woman on your thoughts and list . . . My heart tells me these thoughts
and feelings I should resist, buy my mind keeps saying there's always a risk.
Oh my sweet man the dreams I try to resist of touching you, kissing
you until time no longer seems to exist.
You know who you are so I'll end at this . . . Should I have the chance
it will not be missed . . .

Kathy D. Walton

Old Age

Old Age, how cruel is the blow
You've dealt upon me! Yes, for sure
I did expect you, but I swear
I never dreamt you were so near.
You've vested me with aching limbs,
And faltering voice, and sight that dims.
You've robbed me of my right to hear
And now I live in dire despair.
You've caused me to outlive my friends
Thus I'm alone without defense —
With fruits and leaves and branches dead —
Entangled in your subtle web.
I wish kind Death would come around
And snap the web with which I'm bound.
I'll go rejoicing on my way
Then you would hunt another prey —
Some hapless traveler on Life's Road
You'll lure into your damned abode —
Another wretch whom you'll proclaim
The victim of your selfish game.

Thelma I. Hannibal De Souza

To Baby Jason

Sitting there, holding you
Talking to you about your future
Wondering if there will even be one for you
I give you hope an a promise
Of a life full of achievements and rewards.
Just breathe normally and leave this sickness behind you for good.

Gail Ann Bucolo

321

A Grandmother's Prayer

To what do I owe my many years of life?
My parents, who have patiently showed me the way?
My husband, who has lovingly made me his wife?
My grand-children, who have given me many joys each day?

It wouldn't be fair to put one before the other,
All these stages made me a mother.
Now, I sit back and watch them grow.
Enduring their pain when they're feeling low

I've seen them grow-up from infancy . . .
Which makes us very attached, you see!
I'm grateful to their parents, when —
They show their willingness to share them.

Too soon the years go passing by,
I look behind with a tearful eye
But no matter what, I've been given a gift
Health, happiness and soon to see my 75th!!!!!

Anne M. Warren

My Best Friend

My best friend is like a sister to me,
For there are things I can tell only she.
There's no greater blessing than a best friend,
Who's there in times of trouble and on whom I can depend.

We've cried and laughed, dreamed and shared,
Since we were little, we've always cared.
Forty years have passed since that day,
I took her hand in mine and said, let's play.

She offers a hand when I need it, a smile when I'm sad,
A shoulder to cry on when times are bad.
A lift when I'm weary, a hug when I'm down,
Thanks to my best friend for being around.

To have a best friend so dear to your heart,
Even in times when we're far apart
Gives my life such a meaning, I cannot explain,
For Sandy, my best friend, you'll always remain.

Carolyn Richardson

Untitled

Brown hair once sparkled with light
Now gray, dull and lifeless.

Laughing crystal blue eyes
Faded and dimmed with pain.

The soft, steady hand that once held mine
Feels cold, frail and trembles with fear

Only a mutilated body is left
Of a once vibrant person.

Memories return
Days of laughter

Secrets shared
Games we played

Advice freely given
Advice ignored.

A rock to cling to
During hard times, sad times

Where is the sister who guided my way
Where has my sister gone.

I feel cold and all alone
I'm afraid of winter coming.

Phyllis N. Walsh

Anticipation

Waiting in anticipation, holding my breath,
That she may "be" scares me to death.
So many changes, I'll have to make
Sacrificing much for the babe's sake.
Me with white knuckles and wet, sweaty palms
Hoping at church I gave enough alms.
Sitting and staring, waiting for the call
My boss wondering why I don't get on the ball.
The phone rings and my heart is always beating faster
Wondering who will soon be my master.
It's not for me and I cry, "enough is enough!"
I close my eyes. I try to be tough.
I make up my mind to take what life gives,
but still worry about how we will live.
Then fear gives way to peace and peace to joy
As I ponder playing with my little girl or boy.
My old concern changes its angle that day,
For a curious thought fills me with new dismay.
Waiting in anticipation, holding my breath
That she may "not be" scares me to death.

John S. Knox

The April Of Our Love

Ah the April of our love, it came
a vibrant wind, a tempest pot,
the day spun forth and exploded
the night of a million multicolored stars.

Came May, sweet languid and restful,
yet the wind blew hard and tugged
at the bosom of our hearts.

The summer of our love invaded us,
warm, tender with intermittent showers,
now it's late October, the embers
slowly flame and hurriedly die.

We arise and strive with an elegant grace
to bank the fire against November, knowing
full well that in December we can only
remember the April of our love.

Ervie C. Jones

Awakening

Suspended aimlessly above the mold of a plastic world
In an animated tree with leaves of crumbling gold
I admire the calming waves of a lilac mist that hovers below

All the while, the piercing jaws await
The instant in which to strike.
The most feared beast of the nocturnal world,
Is at my side
Watching and waiting, as electricity pulses through its veins
Giving it life and strength

The brim of dawn
Peaks through my lilac mist
Turning it gray, as it senses the beast.

The attack is precise and sudden,
Unsuspecting.
My body tenses as my heart pounds,
And grasping for breath, I force my eyes
To open and greet my enemy.
He is staring with glowing red eyes,
And is pleased with what he has done.
With his relentless, piercing screams.

Ryan M. Akers

322

Our Senior Citizens

Of our seniors we can be proud;
They are the silver lining of our cloud.
For this generation seniors are the key;
If not for them we would not be.

From our seniors we have much to learn;
Their wisdom is gathered like butter in a churn.
They have traveled the hard road of life
Through sorrow, happiness and strife.

Our Seniors fought wars to be free;
They deserve gratitude from you and me.
Our Seniors have slept under the stars,
Followed the mule, drove Model A cars.

So if we pay attention and listen close
They can teach us the right approach.
Our seniors represent the eagle soaring high;
We need their knowledge of days gone by.

Albert Hart Jr.

Grandma

I love my grandma oh so much
Her face, her voice and her touch
The ring of her voice warms my heart,
Her wise age makes her smart.
Always thinking of others rather than herself
She isn't rich, but because of her great
heart she shows a better wealth.
Always giving her advice and love,
She is whom everyone admirers and thinks of.
We love our grandma oh so dear
Because she love us so much and has
always been there.

Danielle and Nöelle Jouanelly

The Adventurer

I've flown the fastest airplanes, and fought in many wars,
I've ridden winning horses, and driven racing cars.
I've explored the darkest jungles, and trapped animals by the score,
I've dropped food supplies to refugees, and smuggled in much more.
I've been beamed right up to U.F.O.'s, and flown a gas balloon,
I've blasted off in shuttles, and walked upon the moon.
I've sailed the seas in pirate ships, and been bled by Captain Hook,
I've seen men do things to other men, too cruel for any book.
I've courted many ladies, and fought in many duels,
I've "stuck up" many "cowtown" banks, and broken other rules.
I've been lied to, pampered and petted, but was at a total loss,
    the day I stood in that noisy crowd, and saw Jesus on the cross.
I've really had all these adventures, but as you mighty plainly see,
I've experienced them on the sofa, in front of my T.V.

Jack W. Johnson

Untitled

Remember skies of blue and full of sun?
Those days have gone, and rain drowns out the dawn.
Remember when the days were filled with fun?
Those days have past, and my world muddles on.
Today, skies have turned shades of blue and gray.
Money is all that seems to matter now.
Add blind rumor of she's queer and he's gay,
And we begin to break apart life's a bow.
The world will always change and so shall we.
Oh, how I dream of those days that have passed.
Is it all written in our destiny?
Days when one just was, and one was not classed.
Our friendships fade and seem to drift away.
That makes one less friend in my world today.

Robert Harris

No Longer Lost

All my life there seemed to be an empty feeling,
Afraid of having and knowing it would not leave.
The roads were hard and unyielding.
The way to go was uncertain with mystery.
Happiness came then left me, why?
Now that time has come and gone,
Memories have not eluded my emptiness but filled it.
The uncertainty of which way to go has cleared.
Many times I wondered if I could continue knowing how I felt.
You came to me when my darkest memory had engulfed me,
Leading me onto another path which was easier.
The emptiness is filled with a love I never knew could exist.
I now feel that the past will give me strength to continue.
Knowing you give me the will to make my own tracks on this road of life,
Will forever keep me alive and yearning for your love.

Teresa Lidman

Star Gazing

Heavenly bodies too wonderful to be the work of any man
Reside above us, silently watching the land
As the scorching balls of gas spin
And the moon gives his quarter's grin
We often mistaken their banality for insignificance

We fail to acknowledge that these tiny fish in the midst of a jet black ocean
Are indeed glorious creatures though they lack motion
They continuously fight the wars of the night
Battling street lamps for the brightest light
When put on a scale with them we cannot compare to their magnificence

When dawn arrives and forces the sun to open her eyes
Each individual star is forced to put on an amorphous disguise
One that hides the beauty that is imperceptible by day
Because day light and clouds tend to get in the way
But the stars return once again surrounded by all their omnipotence

Their service to us seems to last eternally
Because whenever we look out of a dark window we see them chatting happily
Bringing us messages of good nights and sweet dreams
As we rest our heads under their brilliant gleam
And go to sleep assured with a feeling of complacence

LaTefia Bailey

My Mission On Earth

As I contemplate my mission on earth
My reason for living; my being, my birth,
What is the Master's plan for me?
What is my calling, my destiny?

I can't build skyscrapers, majestic and tall,
Change the course of rivers; create a waterfall,
I can't build great roads for men to travel upon,
But, I can introduce the world to God's dear Son.

Some men create inventions that boggle the mind,
Medicines and serums for the healing of mankind.
But, if I can create in one soul a thrust for Christ,
Then, to me, that is fulfilling, and worth the sacrifice.

In all of my endeavors, if it is mine to choose,
Just let me be a vessel that The Lord can use.
The harvest is ripened, but the laborers are few,
Just peak to me Lord, "What will you have me to do?"

As I travel on toward the setting sun,
Whatever is said when my work is done,
If I can lead lost souls to The Master's feet
Then, I'll feel that my mission on earth is complete.

Raphael B. Jones

Starwalkers

I beam you up into
the magic magnet-field of Venus
assemble you from threads of silver
my memory and specks of eons;
to float on helium-light solar clouds embracing.

I switch off the galaxies you quench
your thirst on the Milky Way I am
the black hole the black hole consuming
we rock in stardust
our antennae like unruly hair-strands
send signals: we are the earth-born aliens
the unashamed.
The pulsing radio-waves, our screams, are music.

Small beads of moisture settle on your skin like mimosa
metallic flowers sprout titanium-green ivy
like Gods we clasp smooth lip on lip exhaling
dust onto dust.
We energize.

Eva Szabo

Mother Pearl

I gaze into the sunlight
on a sea of broken dreams
Reflections on glass water
show a strength I've never seen

Through rolling waves of tears
I see a shining pearl
Hanging by a thread
to a tiny sheltered world

Though tossed and turned still precious
as beautiful as her grace
Like a storm upon the ocean
she sometimes loses faith

She wants to let go now
but she can't seem to leave
For everything she's worked for
is in that shell you see

She knows the sun will shine again
on her sea of broken dreams
And she will have another chance then
to see what's not been seen

Pamela L. Callahan

Before I Close My Eyes

At first sight, my daughter
was a small bundle, and all I could detect
was curly hair and an open mouth.
All I wanted — was to stand watch.

My thoughts were to protect
and hold onto
one so helpless
one so precious.

Blink once —
she's holding on,
pulling up and
pushing out on her own.

Squinting, I encourage her to be loving and kind-
but not to let someone else control her mind.
Not to look for the simple ways to achieve
but enjoy the struggle. Work hard and in yourself do believe.

Bleary eyed, no matter how hard I've tried to do,
I pray my mistakes are not hurtful and few.
I give my daughter all my love
What I can not give, I put in the hands of the good Lord above.

Sundra Johnson

If You Love Me Honey Smile

Theirs a game we used to play.
Before, we all grew up and moved away.
One would stand in the middle and make a face.
The one who smiled would take their place.
It's called "if you love me Honey Smile".
Then you can stay with me awhile
The game preserved in my mind,
Cant be erased for the end of time.
As I've grown up and moved away.
No one has heard of the game we used to play.
"If you Love Me Honey Smile."
Can you stay with me a while.
Make a smile and take my place.
I still see your funny face.
It's a game preserved in time.
But it's always on my mind.
It was nice to laugh and smile.
And be around them awhile.

Tina Johnson

Driftwood

Drifting with the tides I see
    another piece drifting before me
through the tangled mesh of green
    slightly darkened and obscene
    and as I follow I wonder why
he's drifting much slower than I
and turning so he blocks my way
I must see him sad and gray
    our shells all broken and callused some
    touch just once before we're one
    and drifting with the tides we go
    the cattails swaying to and fro

Amy P. Ingram

Digging

Icy clinging mud chills my raw hands,
As I grip iron rocks and wiggle and tug
(And wiggle and tug and wiggle and tug).
God, it's like pulling some monstrous slimy
Amphibian's teeth,
Coated with saliva, weathered to a smooth brown,
And oh how hard to grip.

I've gotta get them out, banish them all —
Make this fallow plot of squishing mud soup
Plantable (Has this place ever seen a plant?)
Before the shipment of baby carnations
Arrives (too early as usual)
Tender, young, and relying totally on me
To provide for their helpless roots
Impossible rockless soil.

Jessica Lucarini

Untitled

Loves mysteries
Love is a mystery
Shared by lovers through out history
Like a merry go round
Love is full of ups and downs
Love lights up your life
Like a candle at night
And like the candle that burns in the night
Love can be snuffed out at the break of light
Love is a mystery
Shared through out history
Susie Keys

Susie Keys

You And I

Sit with me on this bench. It's an old bench. It's a dirty bench.
Don't wear anything white.
Let me caress your strong hands.
I can see the pictures you once drew as a child with these strong hands.
I paint your nails and you put shaving cream on my face, to shave,
you start.
Run to the rainbow, find the end. How far could we climb up?
Is it as beautiful as we imagined?
Will the flowers have enough room to run and play?
Lay with me on this bench. It doesn't look that dirty anymore.
Wear your best clothes.
Brush my hair. I'll tell you my secrets.
The secrets you don't tell anybody.
Are you going to leave me when you see the sunlight, as if you were a vampire?
Plant the seed there. Where the rainbow starts.
Maybe that's not a good place for it.
The angels have their playground there.
Pull the stars over us. We don't want to get wet.

Katie Carlstrom

Untitled

Jesus said he was going
to prepare a place for me
and anywhere my Jesus is
is where I want to be
That's why I'm riding on
The old ship of zion
a ship that's never late
I have friends and loved ones there
waiting for me at the Pearly Gates
I don't know what time it'll be
morning, night, or noon
but this one thing that I am sure of
that I will be stepping off soon
You can read your holy Bible
in the book of revelation
old John declares there's a tree over there
with leaves that will heal a nation I may not be so lucky
as to get a leaf of that tree
but if I can just get to Jesus
that will be home, sweet home for me!

Wilbert Carney Jr.

Through A Child's Eye

Through a child's eye, there is a world of curiosity,
Through a child's eye, there is a world of hope.
Through a child's eye, there is a world of anxiety,
Through a child's eye, there is a world of love.
Through a child's eye, there is a world of excitement,
Through a child's eye, there is a world of sunshine,
Through a child's eye, there is a world of adventure,
Through a child's eye, there is a world of patience.
Through a child's eye, there is a world of dependence,
Through a child's eye, there is a world of mysteries.
Through a child's eye, there is a world of fantasy,
Through a child's eye, there is a world of treasures.
Through a child's eye, there is a world of opportunities,
Through a child's eye, there is a world of sounds.
Through a child's eye, there is a world of imagination,
Through a child's eye, there is a world of color.
Through a child's eye, there are obstacles,
which await them in the future.
Through a child's eye, there are questions,
which await for their answers.
Through a child's mind there will be memories of all these,
for through a mother's eye.........they grow up.

Christina Bauer

In Memory Of Jo Ann

I'll never view again her dazzling smile,
Nor see anew, her smiling face.
But, if by chance, we meet again,
Will memories we shared take their place?

I'll miss you my darling. More than anyone will ever know.
I'll miss your presence, tho the seasons come and go.
But life and death go hand in hand,
Our time on earth are like grains of sand.

When the dusk of evening falls,
And the din of day is done.
I reach in vain, for arms not there,
And find an emptiness, so hard to bear.

I'll be the very last to forget you,
Tho there came a time we had to part.
Needless to say, I'll always remember,
And keep a place for you in my heart.

Steve Brouillette

7th Dimension

Cool breeze blowing
    across brown and yellow drying prairie grasses
Blue sky swirled with a thin veil of airy white
Intense sunlight emitting rays of warmth upon the fields
Undulating landscape like curves of naked bodies of lovers
Nothing between us and earth-Mother
Sacred ground . . .

One with all creation
Breasts nurturing
    a deep intimacy . . . union of body and soul
Transcendent . . .
Re-creating life
A mystical union of the divine in nature

Golden haze . . . sun setting
Quietness
Ancient melodies closing the sky
Sacred Space . . .

Corene K. Besetzny

Snow

It was Sunday morning, March 20th . . .
As the snow fell sights of naked tree limbs could be seen.
As you looked on the ground all you saw was
a blanket of snow crystals. As you look in
the sky you can see the grey waste away!
You look right, then left, up and then down.
Then you stop and frown. There's no more
snow, it is spring!

Timothy Jones

The Poet

How else to show the poet, who lives inside
the poem, the feelings of the heart
The thoughts inside, yearning to come out
uncovering the hidden talent, words to satisfy

We wonder who will read our lines
and will understand our reason
Our hope and purpose, the springing of the thought
forever new and written just for you

I have a dream that all will appreciate my work
as a poet's heart gives out the rhythm of the verse
the revelation of the reasoning from within

as tired fingers with the typewriter create
the master of lyric and form lives on
to reveal the poet's inspirations

Hazel Carestia

Kids Killing Kids

War on the children, why can't we see;
Our children are dying, not running free.

Kids killing kids by knives and guns;
Trying to point out who's the better one.

Fighting over property, that they can't claim;
Gangs killing for colors, in this crime game.

Lord the pain, the parents must go through;
These kids of ours, they have no clue.

Educate these kids, is what we've tried to do;
Giving our children a future hold on to.

Kids dies for reasons, we don't understand;
A wasted life, in another kid's hand.

These violent crimes, are signs of the time;
No future generation, no life, just crime.

D'Juana Lei Earl

The House Of The Lord

Darkly stern quiet and burning candle wax,
Lingering incense clings to the senses
While long slivers of light intrude
Through the columns of stained glass.

A cold draft dwells in every corner,
In between each row of old mahogany pews
That sit at upright and reverent attention,
Marked by tattered and aged hymnals.

Images of people garish the walls
Reflecting carious stages of pain and suffering.
They surround a bearded and tormented man,
Gaunt, broken, a haunting look in his eyes.

Solid, wooden altar, standing taller than a boy,
Stretches end to end like a sleeping giant
Covered in mysterious cloths it awaits offerings
To a stone likeness of this crucified man.

This is the sacred place of worship
Where I was brought as a small child
To learn about love, peace and forgiveness
When all I felt was fear, dread and horror.

Pamela Walencewicz

Broken Bond

I gave my friendship to you.
I was there for you through and through.
I was there for you when times were bad.
I shared both your pain and tears when you were sad.
In times both bad and good,
I was there for you always, as true friends should.

Your other so-called friends became jealous of what we had.
Seeing the bond we shared made them mad.
Listening to their lies,
Their false, beckoning cries.
Making you believe I had wronged you.
Maybe to you, this is true.

But if you never let me know,
If you never let your anger show,
Was it my fault our friendship died?
Could you not see the tears in my eyes?
When I asked, you refused to say what was wrong.
So, all I could do was hope it would pass and not stay long.
I did all I could to keep our friendship alive,
But by staying silent, you let it all die.

Dolores Juliano

Awakenings

Dewdrops sparkle and shimmer, suspended on the very edges;
Moist swirling mist shroud the foliage, as if to hide its existence.
The air is crisp, cool, damp, and clear.
A faint scent of damp bark and pine accost the senses.
Small creature scamper about, keeping just out of sight.

Streams of sunlight break through the overhead canopy;
Sounds of life seen and unseen erupt and diminish.
Streams flow onward, destiny unknown, no cares, no worries.
A continuing cycle of life, death and rebirth.

Silence envelopes one's being as awareness awakens within.
Movement is unhurried, no rush, no need.
Beginning to realize, understand, to comprehend;
Life moves swiftly, many things are taken for granted.
We're not all powerful, omnipotent, but part of a plan.

I stand in the midst of this haven from heaven;
I breathe deeply and freely, restrictions unleashed.
Absorbing the colours of life and creation, understanding at last;
The insignificance of self, but the magnitude of God's love.

Elaine Satchell

Life In The Ghetto

Life in the ghetto is a life that's tough,
food on the table, there wasn't always enough.
Life in the ghetto, a daily struggle to survive.
Every morning I wake up I thank God I'm still alive.
Life in the ghetto some can't cope,
they choose suicide because they've lost all hope.
Life in the ghetto, most fathers are gone,
leaving their wives and kids all alone.
Life in the ghetto I was slowly sinking down,
but I stood strong I kept my feet on solid ground.
Life in the ghetto, so many friends die,
innocent victims of another drive-by.
Life in the ghetto makes me dream of far away places,
where the people are happy, no frowns on their faces.
Life in the ghetto doesn't have to last.
Education, determination, can put it all in the past.
I'm young and there's a lot I don't know,
but one thing is for sure, life is tough here in the ghetto.

Johnny T. Long

On Christmas Morning . . .

I heard a Christmas carol today while driving down the road
A season I didn't want to come
A time of year I didn't want to acknowledge

The tears welled up and began to flow unceasingly
My throat ached from the pain
Pain that comes back anew at different times
And especially now,
This time of year — the season of joy

Memories of you came flooding back
All the hurt afresh
I thought of you and all the Christmases past
I remembered all the sounds of you
Your squeals of delight on Christmas morning
It was one of your favorite times of year and
Our first Christmas without you —
A vacant place around the Christmas Tree
A stocking hanging empty
A silent bell
A voice forever missing
On Christmas morning . . .

Barbara M. Thomas

A Fire Yet To Be Felt

My heart holds another soul
A picture of a face
A silent night
A bright moonlight
From which the stars to shine

You look to the sky
With your unexplainably green eyes
To watch the fire burn
Fueled by life
By love, by hate

My spine tingles
When you hold my body to yours
And for once your hands are warm
Not like ice
But like the fire itself

A FIRE YET TO BE FELT
Shana Marie Gobel

Eight Leg Waltz

Over and under she dances through.
She teaches us a thing or two.
With dignity and divine grace,
She climbs her silky spiral case.
The floor she gracefully glides upon
Supports her modest marathon.
And when at last her legs have tired . . .
And she's fulfilled her heart's desire.
She then rests in peace of mind,
Rejoicing over God's design.
We would lead a life of lesser faults,
If more of us would learn her waltz.
For when our work on earth is done,
Others gaze upon the life we've spun.

Tammy Browne Jurgensen

Jennifer, Come Another January

Rather than don and romance the pathetic;
sometimes, willingly, defying the murkiest from the pit of
   remembrance,
the poignancy has lessened.

I am fatter, the moon fuller.

Months may pass without a thought of you,
   thoughts pervasive of nothing current,
   blemishes, void of obdurance.

The belonging to another — you and I motioning apart,
   polished in the coarse divinity of time and valence —
   canvassed for a naive promisor
      that loved and loves you: remotely, differently, but well.

David R. Bailey

The Beach In Winter

The beaches in summer are beautiful places.
With hot, white sand, and people with tans on their faces.
But what happens when the crowds all go home?
When the trash is recycled and the hot sun is gone.
Does the ocean still flow?
Do the 'gulls still fly low?
Do the fish stop their frolic and play?
Do the cold winter nights really turn into day?
Maybe the crowds, and the rubbish, and the heat are gone,
But the beach is still there, all the year long.
It's there for the rain, the sleet, and the snow.
It's there for the taking, but not many go.
So until next summer when they come back again,
Thanks for the memories, and especially the tan.

Jody Marks

The Pines

I wonder how this world would be
Without the stately, tall pine tree;
It stands so high, with branches spread,
And keeps the sun rays off my head.
The black crows call it home
For their fledglings 'til they're grown.
When the wind blows the branches swing;
It sounds like angels whispering.
They shed their needles and their cones
For folks to decorate their homes.
When winter comes, and trees are bare,
The green of the pine is always there;
The wonderful scent is so sweet,
You would think that attar was at your feet.
It's used to build houses, and toys and beams,
And rafters and boats, and other things.
So I wonder how this world would be
Without the stately, tall pine tree.

Martha C. Jones

The Cabin

The cool crisp breeze of the morning
The fog rising off the lake
The cry of a loon like an alarm.
Then silence,
The whimper of the dog
The meow of the cat waiting to be fed
The cackle of the dying fire from the night before
Plunk, the sound of a rock hitting the water

The smell of breakfast floated through the air
The fragrance of flowers danced along with it
The aroma of the lake on a crystal clear morning
The stench of rotting fish on the shore
Gas fumes from the morning fishing trip

As you admire the sensation of the setting sun
And watch the brilliant fluorescent ball rise
   over the glassy water
The radiance of the moon and the cracking fire
Put you into a deep deep sleep

Afton Sauer

America Thank You For Taking Me In!

When I left my country in 1937,
I found peace and almost heaven.
In the beautiful United States,
I knew then, I was here to stay.

I remember staring up the tallest building,
Looking around, I felt I was shrinking.
Never have I seen such wonders before,
The stores were filled with goods galore.

It was not easy not knowing the language,
They called me a greenhorn; that brought me some anguish.
Trying to find a job in strange Manhattan,
I was lonely, lost, and forgotten.

Wondering how I will make out in this new land
After awhile, I was no more the same.
There was so much to see and to learn,
And I had my daily bread to earn.

Year after year, some good, some lean;
But I swam along in this fast stream.
After all, we had to become millionaires;
From the land of opportunity, I wanted my share.

Erna Parpard Turner

Goddess

Venus kissed his lips ruby red

Mother earth placed within his hips
the rhythm of woman . . .

Honeysuckle bathed his skin till sweet
Morning glories kissed each cheek . . .

Medusa reached within her soul and touched
his head with a wild wild do . . .

As he poured onto the golden runway
lady slippers arched their backs high
to lift his heel . . .

He had become Venus' daughter and son
and grasped the hand of the greek gods . . .

Standing among the oaks . . . He was god
Diva —
He is Goddess

Russell Wayne Jackson

Destiny

I have time off to lie in the sun
I'd be lying if I said, it wasn't fun
But why do I have to lie in the sun
And continually think of you as the one?

Why can't I bring my heart under control
And with my head reach for another goal?
Life can be so simple if the head is in control,
With the heart one sinks to the depth of the soul.

Oh well, as long as your head is on straight
I don't have to worry about my destiny or fate,
My destiny was decided on the very first date
The very beginning was timed, too late.

Maybe someday soon your heart will lose control
And your head can read the depth of my soul
Then I would be so happy to lose all self control
If you were the one at the end of the goal.

Rebecca Shelton Steinwach

The Flight

I saw the lights, 100 miles away.
The lights were green, white, and grey.
They circled 'round the bright, big dipper,
They zig-zagged and dipped, Yonder and Hither,
They played hide and seek through the clouds so dark,
And bobbed up and down, dodging the stars.

I imagined a boy in far away Guam,
Watching what I did here in Washington,
People from Zimbabwe, Spain, and Taiwan,
People from Egypt, Belarus, an Azerbaijan,
Saw what I saw, and couldn't believe their eyes.
And if they told, they would be accused of lies.

The sight was amazing, a spectacular experience to see.
And then I woke up! Oh . . . Silly me!

Nicolle Dew

Best Friends

An understanding not visible in words
Communication taking place with even a look or gesture
Sharing experiences
Openness and acceptance, laughter and tears
My confidant, close no matter how far
Almost as sisters, bonded in trust
Always forgiven, always loved.

Leesa A. Wheeler

Untitled

Michelle, my low red moon
My love lives on, but my time has come
Now, my body cold, silent, at peace, and still fearless,
Rests beneath shallow earth
Far from troubles, beyond the grasp of fears
This timeless sleep, this time to shed skin, bones, chains, debts,
hate, and pain.
I lived well, a life in dreams, I died well, in dreams of life
I carry on now — I watch for you,
Over you, to you, forever a dedicated soul to you.
With sweet emotion I will sit, in the soft glow of the nights
low red moon and quietly moan your name, as I get down on my knees
And take your delicate heart in my hands
I whisper my name until it is stuck in the depths of your soul
Come to me, not tonight, no time soon, please
But make sure when you see a low red moon, that your tongue
Lets my name escape, but shed not one innocent tear
Save those please, for when our souls again share,
The same space, the same love, the same low red moon.

Jodey C. King

My Reality

You step back
You look to the future
You look to the past
You see yourself now

But, what do you really see?

NOTHING

You can't really see your life
It's all an image in your mind's eye
Truth and reality become integrated
With lies and fantasy

What is real, what is fantasy?

EVERYTHING

We see only what we want to see
What we are told to see
We can't look in front of us
We can't recall the past

What is your life, what is you?

NOBODY

Sally Stryker

Lucifer's Mirror

He sits beyond the future waiting for the end;
As he welcomes past indulgence with a haunting seed.
The present, in his purgatory with a slight vanity,
He smothers the faint air through a hunger of need.

There are ashes in his eyes like a solid rainbow,
While the blood of tears dances in his night.
Not unlike a flower as it wilts away,
He claims the agonizing darkness beneath the light.

Always welcome, are thee who believe in his pain,
A fatal tool for the burning of their bleeding souls.
A scarred reminder, to those who live in their vain;
You may not pay a price, but be fearful the tolls.

Sacred are the days of this present to past,
Which mark the dawns of an empty age.
While violence and greed create stagnation of minds,
This future becomes secular within the human cage.

Humanity, which sleeps bare with calm deceit,
Will force the house of cards to rise and fall;
Their cameras won't catch the ashes,
Though observing angels will write it all.

Brian A. Joon

Life

When totaled up life's experiences can be numerous.
They can be sad, pleasant or humorous.
Just take the time to think a bit.
It doesn't take much to provide some wit.
How nice it would be to live the American dream.
And what a blessing if all were peaches and cream.
Let us practice ignoring people's smirks.
Then maybe we can avoid calling them jerks.
Look at all of the positives as rewarding.
Never think of the negatives as bombarding.
We can all do things that are worthwhile.
One would be to replace a frown with a smile.
Not being an enemy is most ideal.
Be a friend and live life with zeal.
Living life to the fullest should be our strive.
I personally think it is great to be alive.
Each night when in bed I always pray.
It is then I thank the Lord for another glorious day.

Noel E. Harvey

The Journey

It was time to go.
The journey had begun.
He looked around at the people he loved.
He remembered and treasured each moment, every laugh they shared together.
He knew by the tears on their cheeks, they didn't understand why he wanted to go.
One day they would know.
They would know at the time their own journey began.
A journey to a new way to live.
A life free from sickness and pain.
A journey when completed would end in much joy.
The urge to leave was getting stronger.
He could now see the path he was to follow.
At the end of the path he could see where it was he longed to be.
He turned one last time to look at the faces of the family he loved.
They couldn't understand now.
One day they would.
One day they would see what he already knew.
They would all be together again.
This time for good.
The journey had began.

Kit Moody

My Prayer, "Dear God"

First of all, "Dear God" I pray
Give me strength for what,
"I have to do to-day.
Give strength to this "Character of mine"
Give me the "wisdom", of "Father Time."
Let no "shadow" of yesterday
Keep me from doing what's right to-day.
Let good come from the "things", I do.

"Please", Dear "God", help me
Keep my "faith" in you.
Let me sort right from wrong
Even tho, I know, "you"
"Judge me, all along"
Let my suffering, not be in Vain —
"Please", "Dear God", "help me",
Once again.
"Help me", to forgive, "those" who have
misjudged a deed".
And help them to understand, for
that is, "what", they need.

Josephine V. Bozoukoff

Broken Dream

She was lying in the street,
her arm twisted painfully.
Her long, matted, black hair
caressed only by frosty wind.
Her delicate lips were soft as a rose
forever trapped in silence,
yet her face bore her tale.
Her eyes glistened through tattered lashes,
shattered innocence now alive with death.
In a scarred cheek sprang hope eternal
a will to survive undaunted by war.
Her tiny fingers remain outstretched
waiting for someone to love her.
A broken doll . . . a child's broken dream.

Nicole Robinson

Untitled

Looking through a child's eye,
This world is one big butterfly . . .
Those little eyes, they see no wrong.
For everyday they're full of song
They laugh, run and play
They see things no other way
Through a child's eyes you'll see
Their views are different from you and me
It's hard for them to visualize
What they will grow up to realize
This world is not a butterfly
For that is through a child's eye.

Pat Lichoroluis

Sunset

Where do you go?
Where do you stay?
As you sink beneath,
The hills every day.
Your colors are full of beauty and grace.
The shine on the land,
And cast a soft light on my face.
Your fascinating colors dance in your light.
They dance and dance,
But they fade at the night.
What makes them so light and airy?
Could it be you're some mystical fairy?
How do you move so close to the ground?
How do you do it without making a sound?
Does the Almighty Painter go wild with his brush,
As he makes your beams so wonderfully lush?
I watch from my house just before night.
As you descend beyond the hills to make your flight.

Kristin Krocker

"Searching"

Sometimes the sky is blue.
Sometimes the sky is gray.

Sometimes the wind is still.
Sometimes the wind is strong.

Sometimes the clouds are calm.
Sometimes you can't see them at all.

Sometimes the stars are bright or sparkling.
Sometimes the stars are gone.

Somewhere I lost a friend
I searched and searched in vain
But after searching all this time
I know where she may be.

J. Harman

What Is "Black?"

What is "Black?"
Is it a color for bad luck?
Or is it an excuse to keep us stuck?

Is "Black" a color that will harm someone
Or is it a racial struggle that makes us one?

Is "Black" a color that many can't see
Or is it unique, a form of beauty?

Is "Black" always degrading and ignorant?
Or have your eyes missed the creativity in it?

Is "Black" so scary that you can't bear?
Or is it different with each strand of hair?

Is "Black" so dark that it disappears?
Or is it a lifestyle that makes you fear?

Is "Black" so mean because of its dark face?
Or is it the rise of our race?

Is "Black" like death or a dream?
Or is it alive like each eyes gleam?

Tiffany Johnson

To Whom It May Concern

To whom it may concern,
I have no voice and I have no rights.
I am not human and I am not free.

They want to keep me ignorant.
They attempt to keep me low.
They try to silence me as if I were a foe.

I shall wage the battle
I shall win the war.
Educated, Human and Woman
strong to the core.

My voice will ring freely
with no one to oppose me.
And when I speak
I'll be heard
with respect and admiration.

Because to whom it may concern;
I will be the educated woman
of today's world.

Martha Gabriela Isiordia

I Failed

I failed her, as I here failed many, but it hurts
me more than any other time. I couldn't save her
I could bring here home, and I was there and, I was
helpless to stop death from taking her; I allowed her life
to be terminated, and I allowed my life to be forever changed
I failed her because I am human; and I am powerless
against gods wraith.
God took her out of our nature; and put her into his.
So I failed to fight God off.
If I could fly to heaven I'd tell God death and aging
are wrong, we all should be connected by soul and matter
without evil, blest and most of all pain, sadness and death.
Life everlasting should not come at the expense of death and decay.
And if God himself were to come to me and ask
me to recant I would tell him to send me into the depths of
hell before I would ever take it back.
But, who knows I may feel differently after I pass out
of human nature.

Joseph W. Dennee

My First Love

I love to write in verse, you see
So please, would you just think of me
When e'er a verse or two you need
to cause a reader to pay heed

To dragon flies, and spiders, too
To birds and bees and morning dew,
To mountains, valleys, lakes and streams —
There is no end to this, it seems.

And then there's city life, you know
Where crowds are rushing to and fro
With one way streets, and honking horn.
Here the "sky scrapers" are born.

And ah! The beach, and shifting sand
Where mighty oceans meet the land
with whispering waves, and seagulls too.
I love those sights and sounds — don't you?

And I could just go on and on
But then my ink is almost gone.
Be sure to let me know, my friend
When I can fill my pen again.

Oliver J. Larlham

Yes, Spring Is In The Air

Of roses in beauty and color so rare,
Yes, spring is once again in the air.

Of the flowering dogwood so white and fair
Yes spring is once again in the air.

Of the robin that tends to her nest with care,
Yes spring is once again in the air.

Of tulips arrayed in perennial paired.
Yes, spring is once again in the air.

Of the cherry blossoms at which we stare,
Yes, spring is once again in the air.

Of the daffodils that sway and dance with a flair,
Yes, spring is once again in the air.
As the sun lingers longer, and the day wears.
  Yes, Spring is in the air.

B. A. Black

Complete Silence

As life spins endlessly
down toward obscurity . . .
I sit and lose myself
in the passing of eternity . . .

There is no stagnation
in a life completely out of control.
Lately, I just sit and wonder
if it will ever be silent . . .

The absence of color — blackness or blankness
I thought would contain no sound
Obviously I was wrong
because there is no silence; no, not, here.

The hustle and bustle of the crowd
there is no absence of sound
A great destructive explosion
a silencing tool

Yet still there is no silence
at least not for me
With this endless bickering
inside of me.

Serena Agusto

All Alone

When I realized you were really gone,
And I was left all alone.

A piece of me slowly died
Leaving an empty place inside.
I think of you night and day,
Trying to figure out why you went away.

Was it something I did or did not do,
Realizing no it was only you.
I did all a person should dare,
To show you how much I care.

I will continue to love you as I do,
Because you last words to me were
A mumbled I love you.
I don't know why we had to end,
I just keep hoping you will come again

I will be alone for a long, longtime,
Until I except the fact you're no
Longer mine.

Mary Faye Blackard

The Autumn Comes

The autumn comes as a creeping death
slowly, silently, defacing the earth;
Scarlet leaves fall quickly, as drops of blood,
(oh, what malicious mirth)!

The memory of springtime is but a dream flown away,
As most of my hopes have sprung up with the dream;
The pitiful greyness of the time
Covers life, (or so it seems).

Soon the sun will rise again
When summer soon returns;
And darkness here will fall again
As the soul within it burns.

The autumn comes as a creeping fire
Consuming those who cry;
For refuge in one faltering prayer,
The Mourners, fate, and I.

Deborah L. Killion

Passing

One hour till dawn —
Five hours have passed . . .

The labored breathing slows;
The face, long so taut, relaxes now;
The weakened pulse slows, slows — flutters and Stops.
Numbly, I wait, still holding the hand I've held so many years;
The unseeing eyes seem to be trying to speak to me;
But no — only silence.
Mechanically, I fold the arm I hold;
Impulsively, I kiss the cheek and close those eyes.
Notify the doctor . . . Wait.
Call the hearse . . . Wait.
Eternity passes; Strangers in black arrive;
Wordlessly, I lead them to the still form;
Lovingly, remorsefully, I lead Mother from the room.
Too soon, the strangers, wheeling a loaded cart pass through.
Cries are heard; "Don't cover his face . . ."

Watching through the window, I see the hearse
Steal stealthily out of sight — past all the darkened apartments.
Good-bye, Daddy, good-bye! Did I even say "I Love You?"

Orpha June Metzger

Angel Prayers

I heard soft murmurs in the night, And followed a glowing candle light.
Through the door of Laura's room, An angel was kneeling in the gloom.
Moon light threads fell on her bed, A golden halo on her head.
Her little body bent in prayer, Folding dimpled hands with care.

"Now I lay me down to sleep", Her fragile whisper soft and sweet.
"I Pray the Lord my soul to keep." A glinting curl upon her cheek.
"If I should die before I wake, I pray to God my soul to take."

Lost in thought, lost in time, I searched to understand this rhyme.
I held my breath, and tears would start, Her words were arrows through my heart.
This key I had so long forgot, Had turned my soul, a rusted lock.

A gentle heart, so pure and clean, I saw my tarnished soul once gleamed.
When angels prayed with me at night, And life was filled
with pure delight. I too had knelt beside my bed, With a golden
halo on my head.

Suddenly I saw this power, That pierced my rusted breast this hour.
Her love has helped me see this might, Will keep us safe, by You,
this night. Unlock my heart, our lives are blest, My rusted soul
has strength, to rest. Amen

Ken La Rive

I Think Spring Is Here!!

The snow is disappearing and the weathers getting warmer,
I wouldn't be surprised if winter's gone and spring is just around the corner,
For the children who've stayed inside because to go outside and play it is too cold
They're watching the weather closely — when it's warm
    enough they won't have to be told
They're polishing their bikes and skates, getting ready to go outside and play,
They've not used them yet, as they had them for presents on Christmas Day.
When they go outside, they are so happy — it's lovely to hear,
There are many sounds that can be heard — I do think spring is here!
The breeze is whispering in the tree,
The birds are chattering keeping them company.
The bulbs are coming up in the ground
Telling us all that "Spring Is Around."
The boys are flying kites in the sky,
Men on their motor bikes go whizzing by,
All these things make us aware,
That Spring is here — it's in the air!

Ella Dunford

Senile Angels

White pigs with wings, crickets that bark at winter
Butterflies that cling to my skirt
Begging summer to stay.

Infant minds, withered bodies weep hearts dry
Senile angels walk backward footsteps
Stand outside inside world, grasp for gates that close
Reach for me
Plead to go
Cry — Mama

I look into the stare of no tomorrow
Eyes empty as a virgin's womb
Bitter rivers flood my face
I answer I'll be your mama, senile angel
You were mine yesterday.

As winter sleeps
I curl inside it
Dream
White on white
And tomorrow
I am you.

Dorothy Blundell

331

I Am Free

I am free or at least I try to be.

My heart grows sad
for the thoughts
that encircle my mind
makes me want to go mad.

I am free or at least I try to be.

But the hands of others always
seem to grab at me.

their words,
their stares,
their silences,
tries to hinder me.

I am free or at least I try to be.

My face is no longer like stone
for it begins to shiver and
the tears begin to roll.

I am free or at least I try to be.

But they still seem to get to me.

Shana Williams

Fall

In fall,
During those hazy afternoons
With ever lessening daylight and
Ever lengthening shadows,

All existence seems to be hung
Between summer's warmth,
And the approaching winter.

It's almost as if the cosmos was
Undecided which way to go.

Possibly that's what is so special
About fall,

That pause . . .

The haze that masks out, slows down, and
Hides the ordinary,

Making the extraordinary more visible.

Jeff Wise

Epitaphs

For the short time we are here,
Let us dance and shout joyfully.
For that is how we shall be remembered.
Good times . . .
Shared experiences,
Those good times.
But who shares those darker moments
When we are alone with our sadness and our solitudes?
When we are beaten down by the countless disappointments
We turn to find that no one is there.
We also find we have naught
But memories of good times.
Shared experiences
Those good times.

And those that we've shared them with
We leave behind
To write our
epitaphs.

Andrew F. Decker

Picking Time

Some people often say,
No good comes from a rainy day.
The sky is cloudy all around,
The fall of rain the only sound.
They feel real gloomy or upset,
But there's one thing that they forget.

When the rain is stopped and the ground is dry,
The sun appears up in the sky.
Apples get ripe and flowers bloom,
The sun shining throughout the room.
The oranges are ready to fall from the tree,
Tasty treats for you and me.

The wheat is waving in the field,
What you've planted, so you'll yield.
And what you reap is what you sow,
Plant some seeds and watch them grow.

Prospering from all the rain,
Plant and pick and plant again.

Terry Russell

Untitled

Who went to the Father one year ago today
While we are sad and miss you greatly.
We are grateful for having you as long as we did.
For you not only touched our lives.

But every one who ever met you.
If there was anyone who mirrored Christ,
On earth, it was surely you!
And the father sent us all a message.

When he called you home on St. Patrick's Day.
Your love and friendship will never be forgotten.
Your presence is ever near us yet.
You're the kind father we would never forget.
God called you to dwell in His house.
But your gentle smiling face is with us
As you pray to God for us.
We will always pray for you.

Things may come and things may go.
Your memory will never leave us.
You were laid down to rest.
I always remember as you being here today.

Evelyn T. Tallman

Umbrella

The storm of tears are falling with all its strength and
no umbrella in a sight to be shielded from the storm,

The weather is so fierce sticking
from all directions colliding with
anything in its sight, and in the
midst of the storm of tears,
I am searching for shelter for my
protection, only to discover
I have the strength that no safe haven can provide,
It is right here within myself,

I must overcome the damage
done and not let it cripple
my life in anyway and
look ahead to sunny days for they will come.
The storms of life never last long, only a
little while, so pull out your
umbrella and keep yourself
dry, sunny skies are on their way right now

Julie Harris Killen

Hold On To Your Dream

Hold on to your dream — never let it go;
You will find comfort — no matter how slow,
Unless your dream — is not your own,
For God gave you a dream — meant for you all alone!

You're constantly tested — as you weave back and forth;
Sometimes, you may even have to take time to sort —
Just the good that you'll need to remain,
While ridding the bad — that'll bring your heart pain.
An obstacle course is ever there,
That's when you'll find out just how much you can bear!

After the transformation — you may find,
Thoughts will, swiftly pop into your mind,
While you keep the faith — deep in your heart —
Never once losing sight of the dream you did start!

Lorraine K. Johnston

What I Need

I don't need anything to eat,
Neither fruit, not vegetables, nor meat.
What I need is someone's love
And yours is whose I'm thinking of.

I don't need anything to drink,
Not a serious book to make me think.
I don't need rich clothes to wear
Not even a pricey coiffure.

What I need is a forgiving smile
From a heart loving free of guile
And eyes that glow with warm sweet love
And yours is whose I'm thinking of.

Thurston John Lewis

OJ Simpson

OJ Simpson was a really nice guy
Rich and famous and never camera shy
Loved by everyone with his head held high
So why did Ron and Nicole have to brutally die?
Because OJ was also a violent abusive guy
OJ did a bad thing and told a really big lie
And his slick attorneys were ever so sly
They conjured up a ridiculous alibi
And after many witnesses did testify
His guilt all the evidence did verify
But the jury acquitted him Why oh Why?
Out the window fairness and justice did fly
So OJ gets off and merrily goes bye bye
Unremorseful with an ego as big as the sky
While Ron and Nicole's families grieve and cry
OJ Simpson USED to be a really nice guy

Stephanie Poole

Happily Ever After

Before they met each other the were unlucky in love,
Their hearts filled with distrust they could not rise above.
Their former loves left them with a feeling of despair,
The desire to commit to love again just was not there.
At first you know they could not get it right,
They argued and fought till there was no end in sight.
Their perils in life then sent them apart,
They could lie to themselves but not to their hearts.
Since then they have made every thing all right,
They have returned to loving again night after night.
Now they look forward to a life time together,
There is no storm too rough that they cannot weather.
Now they shall live together in joy and laughter,
Just like the fairy tales of happily ever after.

Sherry A. Helton

Feel The Feelings

My sister told me she's having a baby,
my heart filled with joy, and I began thinking maybe . . .

Maybe a precious baby boy, he would be such total joy.

Or maybe a special baby girl is best, she would surely be so blessed.

Only God can make that call, and really it matters not at all.

Love and life are the miracles here
and the time is growing oh so near.

New life will join us soon I know,
for I've so much tender love to show.

Even a lifetime would be worth the wait,
I tried to tell her it was not too late.

A baby my sister longed so deeply for,
She'll now have that baby and much, much more.

She'll have a precious life to forever hold,
While Love has bonded and they've grown old.

Life means so much, and she cannot hide,
the eternal love she now feels inside.

Oh, there will be lots and lots of tears,
and, oh my God, so many fears.

But in the end she'd choose no other,
for she'll feel the feeling's of being a Mother.

For Tricia and her precious daughter Caitlin,
with love from your sister and aunt.

Marcia Morrow

The Baby Came To Church

As we gathered on Sunday morning
We knew it would be great
To hear our Fairview Choir
sing the Cantata — to celebrate.

The church looked a bit different
There seemed an expectant air.
The congregation was more reverent
As if someone special might be there.

In came the radiant choir
Their music made the rafters ring.
Soon we would see shepherds
And even a far off King.

Suddenly, the lights were dimmed
While Mary and Joseph did appear.
And when she knelt and rocked her babe
Many wiped away a glad tear.

They say we can't see Heaven
or hear its glad bells ring.
But, this one Sunday morning
We saw the Baby — and heard the angels sing.

Wilma Jean Cornwell

Rececka

Creamy whiteness. Mopstyle, uncombed hair — pale, burned, brown. Soft, soft hips. Soft lips. Sexually knobby, stringy, olive rope legs with a story . . . Angel voice. Cocked, capped, crimped left arm eating ramen under the sun in the shade at noon. Quiet famous features fed cosmos' buddah or krishna. Koresch or christ. Unmentionables unknown. By me imagined the saviour playing humanity, sucking souls. Never returning, always unlearning, and that.

Jason Eisenmenger

A Ghost Of The Past

You are so prominent, in my every thought.
When it's sunny, brilliant and blue,
I am glad for the outcome and I can live with my life.
But, I still wonder about my dark baby boy, gone to the universe,
Then I get angry and yell to the blue sky at you.

When it is dreary, gloomy, dark, and rainy,
I get a deep, penetrating sadness.
Your essence haunts me.
Your omnipresence comes out from behind the rain clouds,
to infiltrate my aura.
Suddenly, a darkness overpowers me, as though I were part of the day,
and I rain tears that fertilize my soul,
just as the rains fertilizes the soil.

I later become lush, vibrant and strong.
I do not see it now, but later
I will sprout into one the strongest vines ever known,
And the haunting leaves . . . temporarily . . .
But it will come back again and again . . .
Unfortunately, I cannot rid myself of you completely . . .

You are a ghost of my past . . .

Mary Ellen Thompson-Rodriques

Entering Into Silence

I reached down deep within my heart
to learn just who I am
Am I the one I think I am
Or am I quite another?
If that is so then why, what for,
And does it really matter?
It was not easy, it took some time
To quiet inside chatter
To try to find the silent place
Of silence "without doing"
When all my efforts finally ceased
The calm became a natural peace
A warmth produced an inner glow
Of light to see, to know, to go
From consciousness to spiritual sense
I entered into silence
Unseen, unheard, my heart revealed
The truths I lived were truths I believed
And then I knew Faith is the goal
My Spirit reached and touched my Soul.

Viola M. Ronci

Confusion

Why has thou Courage forsaken me!!
   My own soul disowns my wretched body —
I yearn for it back —
   Help me LORD, I pray to Thee.
The hideous demons try so hard to weaken my shattered heart.
Why I ask thee — am I not strong — for I feel weak —
   fill Thee dear Lord with Thy knowledge to overcome my heartaches —
   For I am lost and weary,
   Lonely and afraid,
I'm within a dark forest with no end-
Help thee find Thy Light and lead my hand to follow Thee
   up the path of light and righteousness.
My heart that breaks so much
love has captured my worst fears —
it has turned against Thee and You dear Lord know this —
Why has my hearing been silenced from the world around it?
I try so hard to be me or at least who I think I am —
   But is it really me?
   I ask THEE that.
Am I a wicked creature who has no heart?

Laura A. Burchard

Duck Soup

All night big-wheeled dragsters thunder past TV talk show transvestites
Dragged down low by transmission frequencies
Past empowered soured politicians who know who's really to blame
Imploring with gloried stories of their struggle
For freedom of depression.

Low fat sexual lions slink into driving machines
and purr into the twenty-first century
Instant credit solid circuit statements of manifest destiny.

Robot sentries with computer enhanced libidos
Shake and shimmy across new mall parking lots, guarding family values,
While billboards blink: Trust me. Trust me.

A family of ducks staggers across a pesticided 14th fairway
While a distant memory asks: Where the hell did my wetlands go?
And a man yells: Fore!
"That's a hell of a slice you've got there," the jester said
to the king, "Have you tried reducing your carbon intake?
I could write up a program for you, sir" he said with a smile
While the traffic light sang: Trust me. Trust me.

David Keene

A Bird In Flight

I want to fly high and high
to learn the secrets of the stars,
and touch the ceiling of the sky,
chasing rainbows before I die.

To look down upon the world
with great hope and solemn faith,
wishing that men change their mind
and make the earth a safety place.

Then I'll forget how sad I feel
when men explode with hate and war
and women cry and children hunger
to be loved as mother's sons.

I want to fly far and far
to see the young loving their folks
and the old ones joining their siblings,
and together sing sweet songs.

Then when I make my final journey
my soul will be a bird in flight,
spread wings beyond the rainbows,
high and high, far and far . . .

Gloria Sostre

Another Love Lost

The clock strikes the hour
My soul is finally adrift in pleasant slumber
As my body seems lifeless
My mind is so alive and flowing
Like the pages of a book
My fantasies come to life
You are there
Representing my love
Lurking in the shadows of my thoughts
Taunting me, arousing me
Flesh against flesh
We become but one soul
Soaring high above the heavens
Entwined like the strands of a rope
Dancing in intimacy
To awaken now
Would mean losing the dream
Losing you

John Owen

"What, How, And When"

What causes the Stars to twinkle; What causes the Sun to shine;
What causes the Moon to beam brightly? Science and Astrology may
have answers, — But I believe that God had something to do with it.

How did Birds get wings to fly; How did Fish get to swim in water;
How did Caterpillars become beautiful Butterflies; How did Babies
become Children and grow up to be Men and Women? I believe that
God had something to do with it.

When did the Clouds begin to form and circle the earth; When did
Rain-droplets and Snow-flakes begin to fall from the heavens above;
When did the Winds begin to blow gently across fields and over the
Clover, Grasses, Wild-flowers, and rustle the Leaves on the trees?

Yet, when it is all said and done . . . in the end, — The Scientists
and even the Astrologers may conclude and tend to agree, —
That from the beginning . . . in His own infinite magnificent omnipotent
Wisdom . . . yes, — Only "The God of Truth" knows all of the answers.

And if He is God of the past; God of the Present; God of the Future
. . . Then I do sincerely and whole-heartedly believe that God with
the Holy Spirit . . . did Create all of it.

Sparkey Murray Sr.

What's In a Name

From birth to age fourteen
I first began to flourish
Everyone I ever knew
Called me Joey Bures

Then I studied far from home
To learn and preach what Christ assures
And there they changed my name
And often called me Bures

Next I wandered further
Gained adult assurance
And often heard them say
"Good Morning!", Mr. Bures

Many decades later
I learned that one endures
All the things they call you
Except what's right (that's Boorz!)
. . . a Bures is a Bures is a Bures . . .

Joseph M. Bures

A Mother's Pain, A Mother's Sorrow

A Mother's pain a mother's sorrow,
something that we dare not borrow.

Perhaps her perfume or maybe her purse,
but don't forget, may I please first.

Disappointments to full to measure,
to hear "Mom I'm sorry" is her only treasure.

Pages yellow and only time can heal,
but we can't forget how that feels.

A mother's pain a mother's sorrow,
for now it's our turn, it's our tomorrow.

The pain we caused is ours to receive,
for now we too, we have conceived.

They will grow up, they will make their parents hearts glow,
but not without pain or a little sorrow.

And so it continues day after day,
we ask God and we pray,
"Help us to be good parents and to appreciate too,
our mom and dad did the best they could do"

A mother's pain a mother's sorrow,
I wish we could've learned before our tomorrow.

Cathy Worstell

Questions?

What is color?
Black or white?
Abstract or realistic?

What is love?
Does it know color?
Does the flame burn red?
Does it see on the outside?
What type of picture does it paint?

Are love and color indifferent?
Do they separate like oil and water?

What is harmony?
Can love and color be combined to form one element?

I ask you this for the sake of love . . .
For it has no eyes.

Marcy Isch

My Corner Of The Sky

My telescope and I survey the skies
And so, I gaze far back through time and space.
What wondrous sights await my eager eyes
And stretch my reach beyond this earthly place.

Though rooted here by physical restraints
My view transcends the barrier of birth
And like an artist's vision as he paints
I glimpse the grand design though bound to earth!

Let others probe for clues to how and why
I seek no answers in this endless quest.
To wonder 'neath my corner of the sky
Brings inner joy that must elude the rest!

May Kressel

You Can't Recapture A Rapture

There's a secret place within you that no one else can know;
You keep it tucked way down inside where only you can go;
Places you've been; friends you've met; and many things you've done;
Sometimes recalling sorrow and often times the fun.
You sit and dream and try in vain, the memories to recall;
The feel of babies in your arms when they were oh so small;
Tavanier at sunset, Keywest, my oh my!
The beautiful bridge at Raritan and good old days gone by.
The far off places come to mind and tears you try to fight;
You'll return again to find the same sweet awesome sight;
Palm trees still swaying, the flowers all a hue;
but remember the wise man and the one thing you can't do,
While your wishful thinking of those you'd like to see;
Please turn your dreams a nautical mile and give some thought to me.

Terri Daley

My Angel

You are so special, don't you see?
If you hurt yourself, you would hurt me.
You are so special, I can't describe.
There are so many feelings I feel inside.
You are a friend that means a lot to me.
You seem like an angel, always watching over me.
An angel who's always there, always ready to care.
I hope you feel the same way too, because I'm here for you.
Through the good and the bad, through the mad and the sad.
I'll do all I can to make it better for you.
Please don't leave me, I wouldn't be able to live
without my angel by my side.
Always there as my comfort and my guide.
Please don't leave me, I don't know what I'd do.
If you chose to die, I'd die too.

Jessica Arnold

A Mother's Plea

Times are very hard — For the parent whose alone
Trying to be mother and father — Trying to protect their own.

You say, "Mama don't understand me — She don't know what I'm about."
But do you understand her — Do you know why she fuss and shout?

Your mother tries — She tries very hard
To get the things you need — To not let you starve

Don't hold it against her — She's doing her very best
You may have less than others — But you have much more than the rest.

There will come a time — When her life on earth will pass
Only then will you realize she loved you — That her love will always last.

Have faith in God — Let him show you the way
Trust in him — You should do it today!

Felicia Fay McKinney

I Find Myself

I find myself thinking about you
    when I'm all alone on a cruel mid-winter night
    when it's just me and the sunset, no one else in sight

I find myself reaching out for you
    when only a warm hug will make things alright
    when I'm listening to Manilow by a soft fire's light

I find myself seeing you
    in the vulnerable little notes that you sometimes write
    in your admirable restraint when you kiss me good-night

I find myself loving you
    in ways too numerous to but briefly write
    in ways I will continue until my last rite

Randy Offner

It Would Be Easy

It would be easy to fall in love with you
But would you love me?
Could you be true?
It would be easy to say I Love You
But would you break my heart?
Would you leave me blue?

It would be easy to stay here with you
But would you stand beside me?
Like I would stand beside you?
It would be easy to do all these things
But should I bide my time?
And see what love brings

It would be easy to walk away free
But to live life without love, would be torture for me
It would be easy to say whats the use
But that like asking a question, then not wanting the truth

It would be easy to fall in love with you
I know in my heart that I already do
It would be easy to say I love You
For such a long time I've wanted to tell you.

Dan Hollon

Green

Green is the grass growing high.
Green is the seaweed on the ocean floor.
Green are the trees that clean our air.
Green, is everywhere.

Heather Strain

Lost

She was a rose in bloom,
On a stormy day in June.
She loved the fad,
She knew was bad,
She couldn't tell her feelings,
After all was left were the peelings,
of her heart. She felt a need,
she couldn't plead,
Inside she would bleed,
The person she was had lost her seed,
She could not fake it any longer,
The needs she felt prolonged her.
She took the chance,
Her only romance,
It was to fill her;
Instead it killed her.
We will always remember those big green eyes,
But that cannot soothe the sobering good-byes.
She paid the cost,
For being Lost.

Michelle Canaday

Untitled

As I sit back and remember the years
I can easily recall thousand of spilled tears.
it seemed that I always ended up alone
sometimes unsure of where to call home.
The only things I've always desired
was the one girl who lights my fire.
I've often thought I'd found her
only to have my dreams flounder.
then I would swear "never again"
will I give my heart to a girl to rend.
But deep in my soul I kept the dream
that I'd find someone to see through my eyes that are green.
The one to give me a major league hug
who wants to make love on a bear skin rug.
To hold each other tight
night after night after night.

William L. Kuhn

When We Part

Treasures kept safely inside the heart
Where neither dust nor ruin can destroy.
Never to be misplaced or stolen
And to enjoy for life's endurance.
A touch tucked warmly away.
A kiss still fresh as morning dew.
An understanding that makes the world bearable.
A love that comforts the soul.
My special treasures . . .
They surpass any comprehension of desire.
Their worth cannot be compared with the universe.
Kept fresh with each breathing breath
And able to journey with me when I am silent,
Forever throughout all eternity.

Sylvia James

Untitled

Music is a beautiful thing
Countless moments of pleasure bring
From brass and ivory and strings it's heard
Including the song of a happy bird
It gladdens the hearts of lad and lass
Makes their dreams come to pass.
God given talent portrayed in song
Praising the Lord all day long.

James N. Parrish

My Son Steve

Last night full of love and joy
It was my special fortune to meet my little boy

I held out both arms to beckon
He came running that very second

We embraced hugging with all our might
My heart pounding at his very sight

Still squeezing, I said, "I Love You, Stevie"
   I was so glad.
He, responding, murmured, "I Love You, Dad."

'Twas all so wonderful — too good to be
   true it did seem.
Suddenly I awoke to learn it was only a dream.

God doesn't allow the pleasure of seeing
   him alive to be mine
You see — He took my Stevie to heaven
   in 1969

   Edmond V. Grosso

Life With You

Dedicated to Molly Cowell
The sun will rise
To the bluest skies
As I walk my life for you

And the earth will shake
As the earth quake quakes
As I walk through life for you

And the oceans will part
Because you're in my heart
When I walk through life with you

And the birds will sing, when I give you that ring
As we walk through life as two

And the mountains will fall
When you give me that call
And say our baby's not one but two

And when our kids are gone, and we sing our song
I'll live life again for you

And when we grow old, and our stories been told
Our life together will be through

And the angels will cry
When I look in your eyes, and say good-bye to life with you.

   John Riley

The Fire Trap

Many were guests at this renown club
For dining with entertainment galore
On that fateful night in November
In the midst of the Second World War

Precautions were none, the recent inspection a sham
And the crowd far exceeded capacity
Business people, service men, regular patrons
Including a party for a well known celebrity

A careless employee replacing a light bulb
Lit a match to locate the socket
The flame caught combustive tinsel
Making the fire explode like a rocket

With only one door, other exits were blocked
Limited escape could be no faster
Death toll four hundred ninety-one
Injured over one hundred fifty
From this inexcusable disaster

   Richard C. Losh

The Devil's Own

To feed the magic red eyed beast,
to feed our desire for immortality,
we invite him to the feast.
The lure of the beast is strong,
the duration of life could be long.
However, the price is high,
but off with the beast, the dammed do fly.

Victory over mortal death is fleeting,
laughing, he leaves you immortality bleeding!
Many stand in line to gain,
foolishly grasping the rein.
Pawning themselves on bended knee,
cast into hellfire for eternity!

His triumph? Stoking hell's eternal fire!
Not the pawn's desire!

   Thelma Moore

Untitled

As daylight seems shorter and the nights seem oh so long,
   don't be afraid.
For somewhere in the vast world,
   tears are being shed for you.
Although you may feel alone and untouchable,
   always know that you have touched hearts.
Those of who's faces you have never seen or thought mattered.
If I had the strength over the world as God does,
   the words pain and suffering would exist no more;
      only happiness and freedom.
So when friends seem numbered and prayers don't seem to
work,
   think of me;
      your faceless friend.
The one who will cry for you, sigh for you, and laugh for you.
And for every day that passes, whether rain or shine,
   you'll know that somewhere in this vast world;
A flower is blooming, the sun is shining, a child is born,
   and a poem is written;
      for you.

   Cindy A. Phillips

Adieu

I find myself finding solace in your sears,
drowning in the model of your blue-ribbon Nile.
The clothespin on the ear, the clip on the mouth
it's all here, I'm here. The storm is starting
to cease, to crease, to create a new aisle
to know me, you, and your doubts.
As I'm sitting here waist deep in adornment,
you give me the ashes of our combined suicide
to keep, to breathe, to care about.
The pixy buried in February is finally present,
the candle put out.

   Candace Herr

Tribute to Dad

I've come to realize that recently,
I've never really conveyed how much you mean to me.

In a life full of heroes, you have always been mine.

A life full of teachings, meant to foster the best,
A lifetime of learning, you helped produce success.

I wish these words could send more of a message,
To let you know how easy you've made my passage.

I just thought I should let you know,
It's not often a boy grows-up with a hero at home;
And that's the greatest gift, a man can ever hone.

   Christopher Lindbeck

The Deepest Of Thoughts

I can't seem to explain
This unbearable pain
It comes from the deepest of thoughts,
The highest climax of hate —
And the peak of my youth.

So why am I so different? Or am I?

This unbalanced flow
Of feelings I show
Come from my innermost soul.

My thoughts and dreams
Are like lightning beams
And they fall to the ground
Without a sound
Like rain.

This life I lead
Is sometimes a chore
When it is I wonder what I'm leading it for

I've always wondered
But now I see,
That my one true enemy has always been me.

Alicia Johnson

Untitled

As I've grown, as I've learned, I gave and earned
respect, and as I live from day to day I give what I expect.
Respect plays a major role in every human's
life; respect is earned, learned, and give to those
who do what's right.
When you give respect, you expect the same
in return; so in this life, whatever you do,
make sure a lesson is learned.
Even if life don't go right don't have a nervous
wreck; just be a good person, pray to God, and
always give respect.
My meaning of Respect . . .
Realize
 Everybody
 Suffers
Pain
 Even
 Christ
 Think about it!

Harry N. Charles

Dear Teacher

Here I am at my desk alone and scared.
I have a lot to learn
about math, history, reading.
But, most of all I have a lot to learn about me.
And the world around me.
How to handle insults, compliments, laughter,
to share and be silly with other girls.

You see it's not easy for me.
No one at home will listen to me.
When I express my feelings . . . they laugh at me.
When I make a mistake . . . they criticize me.
Sometimes I get whipped . . . just for being me.

So, if you please, take note of me.
Don't ignore me or write me off as hopeless.
Work with me,
  stand close to me,
   look me in the eye and smile,
    say something nice about me.

Your love will last me a lifetime.

Christine Blaser

Men In Blue

A moment's notice, they come in force.
No second thought of doubt or choice.

By night or day, their labor done
with fearless pride and trusted gun.

Few accolade and praise bestowed
on those our peace of mind is owed.

For Justice served they stand as one,
united by the badge they don.

Our prayers and heartfelt thanks to you,
the brave and noble Men in Blue.

Terry Patey

All Alone

The tropical atoll is covered with palm,
it sits in the waves of the ocean's calm.

No humans to see its beauty with their eyes,
just a lone seagull gliding by.

The infinite white beaches glisten in the sun,
but there is no one to take advantage of the fun.

The island is viewed by very few spies,
watched only by a lobster's glistening black eyes.

The atoll is as isolated as a leper colony,
far from everything, locked within a sea.

All alone.

Patrick M. Killen

Confinement

In the cage she sits and sings. Her heart as empty as her space.
She ponders life to carry her burdens; a bag to hold problems
twenty times her weight.
And in that cage the little bird hears crying; no one else but the
voice in her head.
So sad is that voice of crying; a longing for freedom and the best.
She looks past the bars that hold her in, only to see the world is
just another cage.
She longed so much, she courted Death who opened the window
and gave her wings.
With those wings she flew from all her loneliness and all her pain.

Zarah Del Rosario

The Henry Fonda Rose

With sturdy roots in midwest soil
Both to nurture and to grow
And survive life on the prairie
In the wind, the rain, the snow
Then to take with you, this hardiness
A tremendous journey . . . it may seem
From the most meager of beginnings
Toward a yet unfinished dream

With offspring, following your footsteps
Each in their own way . . . given room
Offered a gentle hand and kindness
To live their lives, to grow, to bloom

In commemoration of your birthday
We begin a life . . . anew
Through the use of spades and shovels and love
And, "With A Fonda Cottage View"
You've earned a world's respect and honor
Now your Friends . . . gather and propose
To return back to your garden
The Henry Fonda Rose.

Ken Bulton

Men Don't Cry

I am told that tears, are one of many instruments
God uses, to cleanse the souls. I sincerely hope this is
true, simply because, of what I am about to do. Even now,
as I lie here, there is a single tear, About to fall
from my eye. There is no mystery as to the reason why.
The reason stands very clear, you see my love. It is
because you are there and I am here.

Believe me when I say, this is a very painful situation for me.
To tell you the truth, I feel like a fish without a sea.
A fish without water is sure to die.
Without your love, so will I.
You are to me what fish are to the sea.
You fill me from end to end,
as my lover and as my friend.

So since for now we must be apart,
I am forced to lie here with a single tear and a helpless heart.
Yet, I do thank God for this tear,
because it, along with all those that follow
Prove without a doubt that whoever said, "Men don't cry," told a lie.
Because if men don't cry, then why, pray God, am I?!

Terron Teray Bailey

The August Beach

Red hot. The August afternoon sun hangs
Wrapped around golden skins on the beach
Overhead pot-bellied skies, a pregnant blue balloon of stillness
The diamonds visible on the water's sun
Yellow firelights
Of a dormant city beneath the sands of a thousand years

Silver laughs stretch across the waters
Interlocking echoes of captured children's voices
And water birds overhead in the distance
Heart-shaped frenetic drones
A people pilgrimage escaping concrete monotony

Earth connections in sweat-soaked sands full of
Convoluted memories melt with the silent sails
of inertia. Unquiet montage of laughter
Collage of abandon to the sun-God
Wooed by the indolent fireball and the purple haze
Honeyed bodies knitted in the August afternoon
Feasting dreams like rising yeast in a tangerine stream
Of the August Beach

Ali De Boisneuf

Accent Of Love

Love, I believed only happened in dreams;
A Concept of the mind with no reality.
Attached only to sleepwalkers afraid to wake-up.
Truth had escaped them in their blind submission.

In my own slumber, true love appeared.
Admittedly I feared its presence;
Likewise denying its power, laughing in its face.
Not knowing my time had finally come.

Its revelation acquainted that I was the one asleep.
Living, but not to my full potential.
The doors of discovery closed;
A zombie to the drum beat of ignorance.

It began with lessons, small but true.
Just as a newborn, my meal was free of lumps.
I gained great respect of love,
Which now became my omnipotent mother.

I grew and achieved confidence;
For each experience made me stronger.
Though I questioned, my doubts were removed
And love accentuated my being.

Ronald Coppage

"Infinity"

Dedicated to a great man who lived a simple life.
The shadow of death it draws closer,
    And beckons that I give an ear,
    But I turn my back in defiance,
    And act though if I didn't hear.
For my plans are numerous and many,
And there's things I'll just have to do,
And the cold hard master of infinity,
    will just have to wait,
        till I'm through.

Floyd Metcalf

Little Boats

Two little boats, they are only toys
Sailing along the swimming pool
Their only captains: shadows
Shadows of our granddaughters,
Katie and Amy.

We, Mima and Bipa, were walking around the pool
With these memories. We heard their voices,
"Oh! No! Our boats are sinking.
We have to save them!" "Yes," the sister said.
"Good, we got them."

All of this is simple but deep in our
feelings. Without our grandchildren,
loneliness will be. 'Til we see them
playing with their boats again . . .

God bless you.

Manuel S. Benitez

Mom

To my loving mom, who I owe so much.
She can ease my mind, with her gentle touch.
When problems come, and are too much to bare,
I run to her, she's always there.

Her arms are open a mile wide.
I feel I'm safe when I'm by her side.
She gave me life, she gave me love.
For this I thank the Lord above.
That she's my mom, and I her son.
For I was born to a special one.

John Antone

His Loving Spirit

His loving Spirit light is guiding,
yet . . . still things we long to say, to do;
His loving spirit He's us Enfolded,
yet . . . to feel his warm embrace once more;
His loving spirit we see smiling,
yet . . . we searched to see his face today;
His loving spirit will always be present.
yet . . . we are human, we miss him here;
His loving Spirit so joyous to feel,
yet . . . we felt his loving spirit here;
His loving spirit we all share,
yet . . . this parting still so hard to bear;
His loving spirit we're grateful for;
His loving spirit makes us more;
His loving spirit, So near, so real.
His loving spirit will always be here.

Cathy Palumbo

339

Lawrence

Lawrence, Lawrence, what a wonderful name,
Any other wouldn't be the same.
Lawrence, Lawrence, what a wonderful boy,
He's his parents pride and joy.

On election day he was born,
While an angel blew his horn.
For he is a miracle we believe,
A gift from God that we received.

Lawrence, Lawrence, what a wonderful name,
Any other wouldn't be same.
A name passed from father to son,
From generation to generation.
A special name that my child now holds.
He is a wonderful gift from God to behold.

Maria Henderson

Our Pastor Our Friend

I said a prayer for you today —
To give you strength along the way,
For all you do to keep God's will —
What an empty gap you fill.

You share the pain of others —
In the loss of Sisters, Brothers, Mothers.
Looking into the faces of pain —
It's God to please — you accept no gain.

We look to you —
A miracle to do,
We need to understand —
You were just an ordinary man.

Used by God you accepted his plan —
Putting it into motion — guiding your clan,
You're looking to Heaven for answered prayer —
Sending up to God-all our care.

Beneath your frame —
You have a new name,
Known only by the Father
We know you as no other
Than "Friend".

Melaney Piles

"Flower Destination"

Strange eyes and hands touches the soil.
Planting the seed of dreams and fascination.

Time will break open that tiny seal of crystal.
Making the smallest roots to run through the soil.

Strange eyes and hands give love, hope, faith, trust.
Making growth of a wonderful new life.

Flowers of new life blossoms to bend to that sun shiny hand.
Hands of trust, love, warmth and promises.
Growing ever so strong from belief.

Flowers has become fully grown and beautiful.
Standing in the shadows of those hands.

Strange eyes and hands begin to drift into new soil.
Leaving the other soil unturned and uncared for.

Returning and adding water.
Adding forgiveness and possibility with that water.
Giving that flower a chance of life once again.

Those hands will cut the roots; Destroying that flower.
Leaving the roots to bleed and dry out. Destined to fade away.

Wanda Evans

My Angel

I cry the tears of sadness
    like I've never known
Sorrow overwhelms my heart
    from the deepest part of me
My angel has now gone to heaven,
With God is where she will always be..

I long to be with her
I ache to hold her near
I miss my little angel
I wish she could be here.

I think of her every time
    I look up at the stars
I know we'll always be together
No matter how far apart we are.
She will always have her own special place
    deep within my heart.

Judy Brown

Untitled

As I'm lying down
I wonder who might come around
But when I hear that ringing sound
It makes my heart start to pound
Anticipation of knowing who's calling
I thank Alexander Bell for not stalling
Putting that sweet voice on the line
My eyes begin to shine
Imagining you in your bed
With a soft heart to lay my head
While things just don't seem fair
You can count on me to always be there
As we try to put blurred situations
into view.
Just remember, I shall keep on loving you
Even though we may not solve all things
from the start
We are still communicating with our hearts

Kelly Clumsky

Portal To Portal

Three score and ten, the life of men;
The measure of faith, a life span.
Out of the depth, of memory and individual life's hegemony.

Original cognitive of primeval recollections,
A stream of consciousness of infinite reflections
A jewel of uncountable facets of perceptions
This unspeakable peak of ongoing revelations.

A continuous line of expanding opportunities
Transformed into successes, failures, non-entities;
Ever reaching goals of greater significance and satisfaction.
Plateaus of satiety, re-road to perfection.

From a prosaic of remembrance
The lightening of the burden of encumbrance
With each passing episode down time's past
Until Harmony rises out of it at last.

Understanding follows in rejoicing, thankfulness
With the grace of good at the point of the need;
Cresting each wave of intimidating threatfulness,
Alas; fulfillment that coalesces:
Contentment, Godspeed; at rest.

Ralph L. Streicher

His Hands

His arms wrap around me to show that he cares,
holding me in times of need, hurt, comfort, and scares.
Occasionally showing strength to those who dare me harm.
Though, the best part is at the end of his arms.
These are the hands that often hold mine.
On one is my ring, with its green stone that shines.
His hands help me up when I too often fall down,
writing gentle words to erase my unwanted frown.
While gently wiping the remains of tears from my face,
they straighten the hair that has fallen out of place.
The things they do are simple, yet sweet.
They don't make him more, only complete.

Jennifer Vitori

Defenses

Oh, guarded knight, forever a challenge
is the castle atop the hill.
From across the countryside I see you,
knight of armor. White stallion galloping.
Lance cutting through mists,
charging the gates of my medieval sensibilities.
I watch your approach
from the tower of my mighty fortress.

As I hastily descend the castle stairs,
I hear the bridge bowing to accommodate you.
Chained and heavy access.
White hoof-sounds, close and deafening.

Here we stand face-to-face,
oh, man of the hour.
Shall I draw my sword and raise it high above my head
in greeting?
Or drop it —
thunder and lightning on the stone floor —
giving fair warning
of my submission?

Lucy Butler

Souls

Souls are like the wind,
They go where they please,
They wander great valleys,
They roam mountain tops,
They cannot be trapped,
They are never contained,
They sing with joy,
They sing with sorrow,
Some are here,
Some are there,
Nevertheless,
Like the wind, they're always around,
Whispering their secrets,
Telling their tales,
To those who care to listen as the wind blows

Nicky BarBre

Pets

I want a dog, I want a cat,
I want anything but a bat,
I want hamsters, gerbils too,
But I've never wanted a rat, have you?
I asked mom if I could have these things,
Then I said, "Can I have a parrot that sings?"
I want a guinea pig, want a pony,
I don't want a VCR from Sony,
Don't want TV, don't want a phone,
Don't want ice cream in a cone,
Only pets will do for me,
One two or even three.

Jean Rudnicki

The Journey

I traveled down a path of inky darkness, prickly thorns.
Somehow, it seems I'd lost my way, amid contempt and scorn.
I cried alone and so afraid, not knowing where to turn,
I blindly stumbled on my way as my soul scorched and burned.

I came soon to a mountain steep and rocky, hard to scale.
Above I saw the faintest glow; below me I saw hell.
The journey up was filled with rocks and pitfalls, to be sure.
But flames were licking at my feet, damnation was no cure.

I grabbed each tiny handhold as I climbed toward the light;
And as I slipped and slid I prayed, "Please help me win this fight."
Then suddenly I reached the top and what did I behold?
My Savior, God, The King of Kings, waiting to take me home.

Margaret A. Stewart

Take A Hike

I don't know what happened between
me & you, all I know is I got used.
Everything happened so fast, I had a feeling
our relationship would never last.
You said you weren't the type to use girls,
this statement alone put me on top of the world.
I thought you were special in your own way,
but hey, it's cool, that's okay!
It has happened before it will happen again
It was not the first and it won't be the end.
It's not just the kickers, but the jocks and the heads,
No matter who they are they all want to go to bed.
I should have been able to see through it all,
but, hey, it's okay, I only have two things left
I want to say:
One is, if you're going to use me "take a hike."
The other is all you bastards are all alike!

Sonya Hogate

Daddy's Little Boy

He taught me how to swing and play.
He taught me how to run all day.
He taught me how to ride a bike.
He taught me how to fly a kite.
He taught me how to wash a dish.
He taught me how to catch a fish.
He taught me how to stand up tall.
He taught me how to hit a ball.
He taught me how to drink rootbeer.
He taught me how to shoot a deer.
My Dad is crazy, His mind is in a whirl.
Doesn't he realize that I'm his little girl?

Micki M. Stanaland

Like Colored Chimes

Twice on my homeward ride thru the windy dusk,
I imagined a perfect place of peaceful rhymes.
Lucid notes fluttered above my purple-light shell,
then whispered lyrical waves that cried
    like colored chimes.
Nobody saw the stowaway with me that night.
Only headlights occupied the clear glasses,
while blank shadows inched below sucking tires.
Like colored chimes
    the ghost sang into my ear.
I was unhappy that he could not show himself,
so I kicked my pedals wildly toward the sky.
He rode beside me, he rode beside me! While
angels performed above my head
    like colored chimes.

Ronald J. Goralski

Prayer Of A Wave

You come to me, hoping to find an answer
You sulk on a rock and wait for me.
You watch my body sway on the sand
Yet, you ignore my advances.
You step all over me
And, I welcome you abuse —
You kick sand in my face
To release your anger
You throw rocks at me
But, I never receive an apology.
When you visit me,
Your sorrow is my greeting.
I'm always there for you
When you need a friend.
When you go, I am left with your problems,
They are all taken in stride.
When you come back to me,
The solutions have not been found
So, you begin the cycle all over again.
I pray that one day, you will be My friend.

Kim Zamudio

The Other World

Something came over me one day
And suddenly I was no longer myself.
My mind had drifted to a world of color.
No objects fit into this space of mine —
I alone was a spectator.
I looked at the color yellow — but it felt blue,
And green appeared more like red.
Shadows became warm and bright and whites became gray.
Gazing around me, I noticed the colors had life.
They moved, swayed, and communicated with me.
They began floating about me like dancing rainbows
That had separated to become their own color — Alone.
And I did not want to leave, to go back to a world
Where orange was orange — not purple.
Suddenly, I was pulled back into the dimension of chaos.
Darkness felt cold again,
And my colors became lifeless.
I could only dream of the day I would go back to the other world.
Where pain no longer hurt,
And loneliness felt safe.

Diana Costantino

Spring Love

In the nuclear clock of the cosmos
Celestial bodies are suspended in space like ghosts
Moving synchronistically in perpetual motion
Through vast regions of time for signs and seasons to behold

Fleetingly embracing themselves in intoxicated intimacy
Seasons drift to each other like long last friends with the winds of change
Expressing emotions of affection in reflections of the weather

Silent winters daunting plight
That shroud the soul in cold night
Leaves with the sounds of new life
As the warmth of spring is unleashed
By sunlights bright radiant heat
That reigns abundantly having all the colors in life's spectrum
A combination unleashing sweet effervescent to the heavens
As Mother Earth opens her majestic treasures
Sending high tides of pleasure and joy
Crashing on the shores of our Heavenly Fathers heart

Scientist like to just call it gravity
But the supreme force binding the universe
Together as one is the Spirit of Love

Omar T. Brown

Live For The Moment

What comes from man will never last,
   is here today, tomorrow past.
What comes from God will always be
   the same for all eternity.
Tomorrow's plans, I do not know;
   I only know this minute.
But He will say,"This is the way,
   don't be afraid walk in it".
Look beyond the night of sorrow,
   there shall be a glad tomorrow.
We had a friend who stuck by us,
   who was closer than a brother.
And even though he knew our faults,
   his love was like no other.
The time has come for me to choose —
   it's Jesus Christ or heaven lose.
But if what heaven loves, I hate,
   then closed to me is heaven's gate.
Beyond the losses of this life that causes us to despair,
new hope is born within our heart because we know He's there.

Kevin W. Vest

The Last Day

Put all your old school pictures away
and we will pause to remember the days
when we all were beginning to make friends
and it seemed our times would never end.

Slowly growing up in each others eyes,
looking back thru years a little more wise,
from kindergarten to our senior year,
suddenly graduation is so near.

The anxious lost tears of leaving home,
the added fears of moving on alone,
we know our special friendships will last,
we're all bound by our high school past.

Although a few enemies we have gained
and some of our hopes and dreams have changed
with time, some of our best friends we have lost,
others we've kept-no matter the cost.

Even though we must go our separate ways,
our time together is counted by days,
and there will be bonds that will be stronger,
but our ties will last forever, -longer.

Randi Lamphere

"Adopt A Spot"

Adopt a spot and kept it clean
   in front of your house
      or
somewhere in between . . .
But just adopt a spot . . .
Be the first on your block,
   to pick that certain spot . . .

Take pride in it, as you stride,
   and stride to beautify . . .
to keep plants and shrubbery alive!

Soon you will see; all these
blocks, that are side by side
have been adopted by others,
   who simply could not hide . . .
and guess what?
Your community now looks "brand new"
   and filled with pride
cause your neighbors decided they wanted
   to be like you!!!

Arnease Finley

Two Rare Birds . . . Two Love Birds

They flew together as birds of a feather,
They flew together as birds of love, high above.

They flew together across friendly skies,
They flew north and south and east and west to new highs.

They flew across dance floors of many continents,
They flew to theatres and Springs,
They flew to concerts, movies and other things . . .

But they didn't just fly as swallows do.
They took time to chirp and chirp,
to touch wings and souls,
to nest in the sun and moon,
and took time to wallow, too.

They were two rare birds . . . two love birds.

But now one bird cannot soar,
and while not grounded, it cannot fly as before.

So should two birds be grounded together?
Or is there the greater love that says
'Fly on my love, cause you need to fly.
You can't be caged or you would die.'
So Fly! So Fly!

James M. Fitzgerald

A Benevolent Dream

You came into my life, so quick with ease
  Like a servant, I am, eager to please
By a thought's span, heart's impulse, from the light
  Of a candle burning in this precipitous night
I lay my head upon my pillow and dream
  About a passionate woman, it seems
Nevertheless, it would be my wishing
  That I might die with kissing
And falling in love, with a secret past
  Unknown to cry; but, no lie, it will last
As long as I keep dreaming and never wake
  We will be as one; your love, I take
For if you ever leave I will be in your heart
  Dreaming we never part
For dreams come true,
  And my dream is being "in love with you".

Art Gentner

"Roses Of Old Memories"

When I saw your face, I thought it was you;
Somehow you still smiled like the young boy I knew,
Looked into your eyes and it had to be true.
Because nobody else could have eyes of such blue.

I remember the days, when I was a child,
You showed me a place where roses grew wild;
And the days seemed so short, I still picture your smile;
When evening would fall, then you'd wave goodbye.

Now I'm all grown up, those days went so fast;
I guess that it's true good things never last,
Like the smell of wild roses in those days long since past,
"oh where did they go?" I just can't help but ask.

Well, right now it seems like just yesterday,
And I still love wild roses, but can't find the place;
And I've since seen your smile guess some things never change,
But were no longer children I'm so sad to say.

Still, there are times when your shadow settles over me;
And I almost smell roses, blown in the breeze,
And I feel like a child, dreaming old dreams
There are no thorns in the roses or old memories.

Eva Newsom-McKay

We Will Have Crescendos

The taciturn twigs of March
Avoid our begging eyes.
But we will have their blood-knot sprouts
Against the slated skies.

We will have them all;
velour arrows, minute pin greens,
the wayward vines.
We demand these with the noise of manic streams.

How will we hold them when they sing?
The light will swell, and their hands will spread.
The spare and windy brush of March will pass
And the copper spears of dark moss will shake the dead.

Weightless, the flower offerings defy
Grounded stones upon the hill,
and speed toward our loaded eyes.
They will not kill us, but bend us sore.

The momentum claws until the alterations peak
At last. We are now odd thunder;
chilled and warm, wide, meek.
We will have crescendos.

Thomas Beaird

This Is My Place

The clear crystalline box looks pure,
when shrouded by the mist of black obsidian.
The steel bars make it obvious.
The thick chain woven between the bars is padlocked.

Inside the box,
sits a girl,
glowing from a blue-white light.
Emotion ravages her face —
not regular features.
Pieces of paper are scattered everywhere.
Letters and words cover the sheets,
along with the rips and tears —
she has written so hard.

Is my place ordinary?
No. My place will never be ordinary.
Consider what is locked inside.

Chestina L. Kidd

From Gallows Hang

Solemn eyes like orbs of sea — all the rage of stormy nights
sparkle with maniacal glee like the satyrs' vernal rites.
That gaze — purely maddening! — spied upon a mirror.
Its salty retort saddening. Its coldness met with fear.
  Rattling, wisp like autumn wind on some moonless eve,
  her voice with neither tear nor grin brings any a God to grieve:
  floating as a death shroud ever timeless into soul,
  soft bells whispering aloud, 'ah, so hallow is our toll.'
Wild, wind strands, no modesty! — As brilliant and red as flame.
Her sinful, naive majesty; free from guilt, though not from shame.
Twine unfurled from gallows hang, yet lively still like infant tufts.
Each piece undone, a barber's pang, and, yes, fancy as ruffled cuffs.
  Lucidity sways like weeping trees upon a mountain cliff on high,
  dancing in the carnal breeze — heard as nature's candid sigh.
  Accosted by humanity, with none e'er to speak again
  o'er her absent sanity, or me, her damnèd friend.
As dreams cease, and pass away, branding hearts of lovers true,
she too did fall from heaven's way when from the cliff she flew.
That soft, pale kiss of morning's dew rests blissful on her lifeless cheek,
And when she left for world anew, by tragic fate her soul I seek.

Al Ferkel Jr.

343

Soul Searching

Strong winds blow wildly through the trees,
searching for pleasant thoughts to put my mind at ease.
It's daylight now but soon the sun will go,
when darkness comes the future seems unknown.
The time seems to slowly tick away,
the days of my youth shall forever be astray.
Hold the days tight for you never know how dear,
the smile on your face can easily disappear.
Reach for the rainbow that seems right in your grasp,
if you let it slip away you let it take your past.
Seek and you shall find the diamond in the rough,
even though the world outside makes it kind of tough.
When paradise seems a million miles away,
look to the skies to help you find your way.
As you see the heavens pass by up above,
look inside yourself and try to find that self-love.
The place where it's hidden is in the worst place to find,
You see the worst place . . . is looking through your mind.

Michelle Sustarich

The Ballerina In The Music Box!

I am the ballerina of a music box always dying when the music stops.
I wonder if there's life after death and if there's death after life.
I hear the sound of music and only the sound of music.
I want a partner with whom I shall dance the "Everlasting Waltz".
I am the ballerina of a music box always dying when the music stops.

I pretend to be deaf and dumb to everything but enjoyment.
I feel the light of happiness as it shines upon the dancing footsteps
I leave behind.
I touch the music when it walks its way through my shoes.
I cry as I see my dreams dance themselves away to fantasies.
I am the ballerina of a music box always dying when the music stops.

I understand that everything I want can come true.
I say to myself, "A daughter is to her mother, as music is to my heart".
I believe in myself and beg for my dreams to come back to me.
I try to glide through the notes that bounce across the frantic stage.
I hope peace on earth when music's love becomes my vocation.
I am the ballerina of a music box always dying when the music stops.

Angela Rodriguez

Farewell Santa Fe

Oh how I'll miss, its ole mournful sound, that could be heard
all through the day, and through the night.
It wasn't very long, didn't travel very fast, but it could
take you on many "Sentimental Journeys..." before going out of sight.

Many long hours, Cowboys have spent picking on their guitars,
about life on the rails.
But now that the tracks have been removed,
there's nothing left but an "Ole Santa Fe Trail."

The Santa Fe like a rugged Iron Horse,
tugged tireless hours, to help build up the land,
and make a better place for us to live,
what more should we have expected, from a train?
What more was it suppose to give??

I wonder if there could have been, another way?
I wonder if this really, had to be?
For each time they took away, a part of that old tack,
it was like they were taking away a part of me.

There is one who constantly watches over us, from above.
If you don't mind, I just want mention His Name.
But as we enjoy His blessings, from day to day,
may we never do Him, like we did that Ole Santa Fe Train.

Ray C. Woods

"You"

A heart stands for love,
that you've given me.
An eye stands for looking,
that you've been doing this week.
A hand stands for holding,
you've stood by my side.
A foot stands for standing,
that you've stepped on me with
Your lips stand for a kiss,
that you've kissed me with.
An ear stands for listening,
that you've heard me say, 'I love you'
A finger stands for writing,
for letters you've written to me.
An arm stands for holding that you've held me with.
A head stands for brains, that you've showed me you have.
A leg stands for running, that you've ran to me with.
A ring on your finger stands for always,
that you've cared for me.
A body stands for your life, that you've given up for me.

Jackie Moncivais

A Dream Within

Horrible! Sometimes it may seem
To dream a dream that will make you scream
Dreaming of people that are near
You are afraid to fall asleep
Because of fear
Dreaming, dreams that are not true
Dreaming awesome dreams that keep you blue
Thoughts traveling on the mind so fast
Oh dream how long will you last
Wake up! Wake up!
Sometimes you try
But, before you know it
Your dream has died

Freddie Leslie Sr.

Time

Who was that person that had time to wait
For the right one to come along for that perfect date
And how were they to know that it wouldn't be too late
They must have known the time was right; it must have been fate.

How are we to know that time won't pass us by
Faster than we can blink an eye
And when are we able to know the right time to say goodbye
Without looking back with regrets that make us cry.

What time can it be when it makes it hard for us to find
Enough love to give our children peace of mind
And where in our hearts can we go to keep us kind
There has to be enough time to get us out of this bind.

Where can we find the time to make love last
Long enough to learn from our past
And why does time have to go by so fast
There must be a way; a way to make time last.

Carol M. Smythe

Why Do They Do It?

Why do they do it?
Why can't they just muddle thru it?
Some use pills
some use a gun.
It doesn't cure any ills
or pay any bills.
It only makes life over before it's begun.
Why do they do it?
Why can't they just muddle thru it?

June Croft

Things Of Man, Things Of God

There are things in the heavens above
And in the earth below that man cannot explain.
Things that happen beyond all logic and reason.
These things are done with the power of God.
With the power of God all things are possible.
He can create or destroy a world
With just the wave of His hand.
He can take a man,
Mold him, teach him, and lead him to do His will.
He an make him or He can break him.
No matter what man does to Him,
Or fails to do for Him, God still loves him.
In man's time,
There may be separation,
But in God's time,
There is nothing but eternal togetherness.
In man's realm,
There is pain and suffering.
In God's realm,
There is peace and happiness.

Pastor P. Bradley Carey, PhD

Untitled

Flailed to the floor, slowly I rise,
After attempts to sit in my favored, placid chair.
Resting on absence, dwelling upon the dawn,
When I no longer meet his lap to sit upon.

Who is held responsible now?
For scattering my habitat, without my premise.
Festering on the sacred spot, where calm cushioned fluff
Where arms should still be wrapped around,
    and will soon enough.

Legs, heartier without burdened me
Back awaits forever posed, his duty to support,
Resolution of migration for another.
I feel, now, my place is caught in the arms of brothers.

Beginning to accept blazed loss.
Frivolous in pursuit, I now inquire whereabouts . . .
Of he that has risen, equilibrium.
In his memory, my protection, to succumb.

Kena Mayfield

Inside The Mind Of A Vegetable

The world thrummed the chords of his life
Apathetically offering him a black heart
Particles of terror and fear mingled in the air
Vibrations ringing from the depths of his soul
Sent waves rippling through his corporal entity
Leaving his body with less than a whimper

Blinding white light, dripping plasma, tightening leather tough skin
Hard sheets drawing its roses on the base of his back
At every deep valley and far reaching point he travelled
Lay his own livid, lifeless body in a dusty wooden coffin
Tangled with death through infinite time and space
One blanket, one ocean whose waves crashed
Against a dwindling self in endless waves of sorrow

The sound of the vesper made him turn and look
He untied the black, silk ribbon tied around his heart
Falling face down with his nose in the sodden ground
Smelling the odors emitted before the crack of sun
He saw himself gathering firewood for a quarrelsome old man
Hearing a boy read verse from a worn, tattered school book

Louis Choi

Untitled

Helicopters falling all around me
The pollen count is 3000
My hair is dirty
My heart is shameless
New fish bring no happiness
I want to wear my new shoes on the plane
I want my daughter by me.
I need my love with me,
My heart houses new pain

Elizabeth J. Bennett

Autumn Leaves

One by one the leaves are falling,
I can see them standing here:
Looking through my open window.
Leaves are falling everywhere.

Now they fall in greater numbers.
Tumbling down like flaking snow.
Awesome is this sight to gaze at:
Great creator planned it so.

Soon the trees stand bare and naked,
Like a babe from out the womb.
All exposed to sting of winter
Like a ghost from out the tomb.

Won't be long sweet spring will break forth,
And tree buds begin to glow;
Trees rerobed in living colours,
Adorned like beauties for the show.

M. May Lovelace

T.L.C.

Surely I have in my hand,
a companion to its sensitive nature,
shaping solitary being,
from separate statures,
within the beating cavern,
sheltering warmth is made,
our love's secrets are celebrated,
dreaming in gentle shade,
changing impressions on the outside,
reveal life's journeys maturing from within,
as the intensity of our grasp,
along the breathing, bending skin,
my hand is secure,
comfortably aligned with its mate,
growing outward into fervent light,
loving the pure miracle of fate.

Trevor Summers

Person In The Mirror

Person in the mirror who could it be?
I pray and I hope that it isn't me.
Her chest is flat, her legs are skinny,
Her body is so ugly it's not worth a penny.
    She doesn't have a boyfriend and it makes her cry
    The guys don't like her and she's not sure why.
    She's an ugly duckling and she knows it's true,
    That's why deep down she feels so blue.
    Her pain is real and there is nothing you can do,
    For she can't change her body and neither can you.
    She hopes this will pass and she knows it will
    Because when it does her heart will heal.
    These feelings are mine and they have helped me see
    That when I look in the mirror She is the real me.

Krystal Bradley

Then And Now

In the still of the morn, with dew on the ground,
The wind in the trees. No other sound.
I drove the lone road — no plans for my day
The rainbow above was showing the way.

A time to pause. A time to think.
In the clear babbling brook I took a drink.
The clearing blue sky, the air crisp and clean.
I lay down to nap in the clean meadow green.

Birds playfully singing. No handmade toys.
Nature's music. No manmade noise.
With all God's creatures, never lonely
Dreaming thoughts of me only.

I awoke and joined the crowd.
Life got busy and noise more loud.
The search for gold. The price too high.
The only question now is "Why?"

Along life's path, I took a wrong turn
I lost my way. I didn't learn.
But that was Then — and this is Now.
I can't return. I know not how.

Sharon McClain

Born

Born into a world that knows few truths.
Born from a womb that bore many fruits.
Born a girl child, weak, yet strong.
Born in chaos, right and wrong.
Born to suffer great and small.
Born to bear burdens, not all.
Born to cry, weep and wail.
Born to succeed, try not to fail.
Born to trials, simple and few.
Born one in many, as grass with dew.
Born not to peace, but that to crave.
Born to give healing, to help and to save.
Born example of what not to be.
Born with eyes open, yet never to see.
Born with a heart that weeps in pain.
Born with a soul many have slain.
Born of this earth, human, so frail.
Born of a nature forever to rail.
Born to a time few will survive.
Born, knowing soon that He will arrive.

Lisa M. Allen

Cosmos

Are you the chariot of the ancient gods,
The fiery wagon of the sky?
I've seen you now admiringly,
Last night with mine own eye.
For over hundred thousand years,
You ice cold roamed the worlds afar
Passed some, today no longer here,
Witnessed the birth of many a star.
And yet they say you merely are
A chipped clump of our universe,
That lonely drifts through space
And until now refuses to disperse.
But oh! Unearthly beauties flow,
When heated by approaching our sun
Entailing gases make you glow.
Our fears arousing our hopes you stun!
Some deem the end of our days is here,
When you approach, oh COMET of the year.

Urs Yous

A Little Dot Of Light

I want to be a star up high, out in deep dark space
I want to be real far away from the human race.

I'll look like the other stars that you will probably see
So there will be no way to tell which one is really me.

When people back on Earth look out into the night
They won't even notice me, I'm just a dot of light.

But I want to be the one to guide the shuttle out in space,
And maybe even shine a light upon a pretty face.

Stars are like people and forever do not burn
I enjoy helping people but from the past I did learn.

If I was a person and people did like me
They would only be hurt when my end came to be.

But stars have no buddies, no pals or no friends,
No one will be hurt whenever my life ends.

When my time finally comes and my light goes out,
People back on earth will say "That's what life's about."

No one will ever miss me and everyone will be all right.
There will be no broken hearts over a little dot of light.

Jimmy D. Coleman

Our Church

There was a little church that nobody used
Till one day someone mused here is a church that must be used.
Our house of God was in disrepair
Our faith in God we all did share.

We jumped right in and God did lead
We fixed it all up oh yes indeed
He sent us a preacher a carpenter too
He sent us some singers some listeners who
In all due respect there's a place for them too.

We prayed for our people they prayed for us too
With out all the prayers we would not make it through
We painted and plastered we fixed and repaired
We laid down new carpet the other was thread bare.

We worked and we prayed and ask God to lead
First thing you know we started to succeed
God has blessed us from above
He lead and conducts us He has shown us His love

God answers prayers we are proof of this
Just ask in His name be on His great list
He bore His cross without sin or shame
We ask all this in His Holy name. Amen.

Ora L. Casteel

Untitled

I wanted to kiss your smiles,
make love to your tears,
disrupt your peace of mind.
But instead the taste of you, nothingness,
was left in my mouth.
Breathing you like the copper taste of blood.
My lips, stained with the wine,
from your mouth, your eyes, and your words.
I shrank into your face for a moment
and was enveloped in a storm of lust,
gathering around me like the finest velvet.
You, softly caressing my skin with
your eyes, your hands, and your lies.
I would have spat it all back on you, except
I tumbled town your blueberry hill.

Autumn Breaud

Where's Faith

Believe. Losing faith is having no hope.
  Loss of faith is giving in.
Believe. Losing faith, What to do?
  Dreams and wishes can come true.
Believe, if not in me then in you
  Look inside yourself and find
    the faith you lost and left behind.
Believe. Loss of faith, wrought in despair.
  Then you realize you just don't care.
On your knees, to beg and plea,
  for what it is you cannot see.
    Faith, just believe.
  Amanda MacDonald

Peaceful Spring

Winter's icy grip slowly loosens.
Melting snow glimmers in trickles and puddles.
Washed stones lie revealed on clean sand.
Birds wheel in unison against fluffy clouds.
  Distant thunder
    grumbles behind dark clouds.
Raindrops fall, embrace seeds and spores,
  awaken inner urges
  programed since the beginning of time.
Rain threatens a deluge but slows.
From naked limbs hesitant drips fall.
Behind rough bark sap rises;
  dormant buds swell.
Fruit blossoms pledge a bountiful harvest;
  soft breezes waft their fragrance.
From fertile decay, morel mushrooms
  thrust their pointed caps upward;
    trilliums and violets bloom beside ferns.
Singing birds build nests; baby lambs frolic.
All is peaceful, it is spring.
  Helen M. Sherrick

Barer Of Gifts

The old woman came and one could not tell her age
From years past or now she was the barer of gifts.
She carried a colorful basket made by loving hands
Which showed things wrapped in silver or gold.

She gently reached into her basket-full of gifts
She clutched the gift covered in silver
She said the gift of caring for others with regards
To our Great Creator and concern for Mother Earth.

The last gift she presented was caress in gold
Gleaming with brilliance priceless at best
She said the gift of giving of yourself to all others
Bestow to your people a special gift your own self.
  Edward L. Allen

I Find God

I find God in the tick of a clock,
The shape of a lovely leaf.
The blue of the sky, and fleecy clouds,
And the bell-like cry of a bird.

I find God in the powerful crash of thunder,
The quickening flash of lightening in a summer sky . . .
The slope of a hill to a blue peaceful lake —
The rise of the sun in the fall.

I find God in a meadow of sweet clover,
And the first sprigs of spring grass.
The deep and masterful quiet of forests of oak,
And the lonesome tragic singing of pine.
  Carol Weiby Bohlig

The Blizzard

It's Here!

Icy hands of winter strikes
The darkened heaven bows.
To kiss the frozen earth again
Snowflakes settle on the boughs.

Slumber beckons drowsy bears,
Feathered friends flit to forest dark,
Timid hares turn ermine,
Antlered deer bounce to parks.

Nature crouches on the plains
Bilious ridges, piles of snow.
A lone man totters through the drifts,
As the blizzard grows.

The winter's trail roars from north,
Striking with savage beast.
Icy water, stiffened with froth,
Spraying high, losing heat.

Beating fists of sleet are heard.
Biting winds, blinding rains.
Whirling, moaning, pouncing, groaning, striking at my window panes.
  Effie Ritsche

"When We Make Love"

When we make love . . .
When we make love . . . it is truly making love.
Borne of beauty, gentleness and warmth, just as it should be . . .
Spiritual as much as physical . . . this gift shared between you and me.

Our minds taking over our physical bodies . . . hypnotic . . . euphoric.
In a celebration of life that can only be described as . . .
Breath-takingly . . . glorious.

No taking, only giving, not here to conquer or to tame . . .
Me unto you . . . and you like same.
Blessed with peace and tranquillity . . . void of hurt, guilt and shame.
Just a blending of ourselves . . . to which we both can lay claim.

Like waves from the ocean coming in to the shore . . .
Crashing, swirling, exploding.
Till one knows not which is sand and which is sea . . .
That is how this love, in all its magnificent splendor and glory . . .
Is shared between you and me.

And just as the beach eventually succumbs . . .
To the overwhelming power of the tide.
So too do we surrender ourselves . . .
In a completeness that only a union sanctified by God could provide.
When we make love . . .
  Randy N. Clapp

When . . .

When I was a child, I used to say,
"I hope to grow up and be a teacher one day."

As I grew older, my thoughts were the same
And teaching became my profession, and not
  just a game.

I want my students to learn from me
Math solutions, science, and geography.

I always stress to teach respect
A quality not graded as wrong or correct.

As I look up when each day ends
I see my classroom once filled with friends.
I go home, check school work, sit back in
  my chair
And hope those I teach know how much I care.
  Beth J. Gambrell

Good-bye Old Friend

In the middle of the back yard, beneath an old shade tree
I knew if I was looking, that's where he'd be

Barking at the squirrels, or a squeaky toy for fun
Chasing his buddies, or a nap in the sun

A ride to the lake, or a cruise down the street
Rattle the car keys, he jumps to his feet

He is always so happy, he never complains
Old age sets in his body, he lives with the pain

Running is a rare sight, he lays on the floor
Just a walk to the water bowl, has become such a chore

His bones are now fragile, his heart has grown weak
I rub his loving head, as I watch him sleep

He has lived a full life, although but a few short years
He asked for nothing but my love, and scratch behind the ears

Now my heart is broken, don't know when the pain will end
I go on with my own life, and say good-bye to my old friend

Dennis M. West

The Dove Of Peace

May its strength capture us
and lead us to hope.

May its spirit comfort us
and guide us to freedom.

May its memory, without needing to remind us,
direct us only in love.

May its wings embrace us
and grant us our peace.

Kerry A. Rouleau

In The Sadness

In the sadness there is love of a greater kind.
It's God's expression of His Son who gave His life for mine.
In the sadness there is time to think about ones life and if
for none other than the fears and tears we shed.
Be aware of all our hurts that are kept inside ourselves.
Allow our Lord to help us through for He has seen our tears.
Be not afraid to let Him in for He will rid our fears.
In the sadness of our lives He is always near.
Closer than we've ever thought when we've accepted Him.
In the sadness of our lives when we have lost all hope.
He reminds us of His love and gives us peace to cope.
In the sadness of our lives He never leaves our side.
He tells us to believe in Him and go on with our lives.

Concetta Nastasi

"Those Of Us"

There are those of us who miss the chance
to see the healing light . . .
There are those of us who fall from grace
and fail the walk of right . . .
There are those of us exceeding well
and learning to live clean . . .
Yet some of us refuse to tell
the evil that we've seen.
It is this silence from the old
that burns the youth of now . . .
For they don't comprehend the "what",
the "who", the "why", the "how".
The learned must relate their tales,
the youth, they must take heed,
for experience will serve them well
throughout their times of need.

Jed R Taufer

"As It Was" A Prophetic Warning: The Boat

Matthew 24:44 "Be Ready!"
Noah, our friend — have you gone mad.
Are you out of your head?
You're building A Boat in the desert! How sad;
"He's lost it! He's crazy! He's loony!" they said —
But soon they were all swept away.

For many long years he labored; while they
Jeered and made jokes at his building each day.
"What you doing, You nuts? Can you sail in the sand?
Or fashion some fish with the Almighty's Hand?
Your imagination's gone wry!" But then:

"Let us in! Let us in!" the rain keeps on coming!
Now laughter turns screaming as water keeps running.
"We thought that your warnings were mongers of hate!"
You pleaded "Flee into the boat!" Now — too — late —
His time is fulfilled, many missed it.

But, You, friend you've heard x times over again.
No excuse is sufficient to not hear His Cry!
At midnight He wakens all Saints, who ascend
Eternal in glory to reign at His side!
    "So it shall be!"

Bob Hutchins

To Number One

You have what it takes,
The attitude, the class,
To be the very best at what you do.
But you can not do it on your own,
You need the rest of them behind you.
Right now you don't have it,
They only want to bring you down.
Don't let them take this precious gift away.
Refuse to accept anything less than you best.
Don't play the game their way.
You won't ever settle for second place,
And that's the way to be.
Only a special few are like that,
Like you are.
This attitude will take you where they will never go.
To number one.

Amy Kuenzi

About Life

As charming, as beautiful, as peaceful as it seems,
As full of joy and ecstasy,
When we do realize our dreams;
As daring and exciting
And glowing with happiness,
Life has its bad spots which beat upon our breasts.

As boring, as painful, as frustrating as it appears,
As frightening and disappointing
When we must shed those tears;
As sad as we are or as lonesome,
As unfair as things may be,
Life still has its good points. They're here for all to see.

Just look around you and observe.
You'll find beauty everywhere.
No need for us to search for it;
No need to stop and stare.
God has placed beauty in everything,
In all we see and touch.
How sad we go through life complaining,
Never knowing we're missing so much.

Doris H. Hawthorne

To My Number One

When I was a baby, you came into my life.
You loved my mom, so you made her your wife.
Mom couldn't have done a better thing,
When she slipped on her finger, your beautiful ring.
I know that you had love for us too.
She couldn't have found a better man than you.
I am so proud that you are my dad.
For I wouldn't have had the things that I've had.
I must thank you for all the things you have done,
And to tell you, that you are number one.

When I went through school and acted like a fool,
You were always patient while keeping your cool.
When I needed your help with homework, you would stay-up all night,
Drilling it into my head until I got it right.
You have done so much for me.
It's like you hold the lock and I the key.
When I have done all the right things,
It is then, I will earn my wings.
I must thank you for all the things you have done,
And to tell you that you are my number one!

Vicki L. McKee

In Time Like These

In time like these: We need to thank you Lord for
The wonderful things you've done, my heart is over
Flown with happiness because to my rescue you
Were willing to come.

In time like these: We need to thank our Savior above
for every precious moment He has given us.

In time like these: we need to thank you Lord
For the wonderful sunshine, the starlit sky, the
Raindrops and the gentle breeze.

In time like these: I will never forget my
Savior's love that he has so graciously shown,
His kindness without a doubt is the best I've ever known.

In time like these: we need to know that our Savior's
Love is unconditional.

In time like these: our Savior did die for sinners like
You and me, and yet we continue to live in a sin sick
World where the love for our brother's keeper have grown cold

In time like these: we will always need our Saviour
Who is worth his weight in gold.

Jennifer R. Matthias

Before The Darkness

Out in the dark hiding in wait
A mountain of anger an ocean of hate
Lurks in the shadows who can it be
Lord help us all I think it is me

Watching for weakness the smell of your fear
The beast feels its hunger the hour draws near
His claws wrap around you a taste of his breath
A roar full of thunder get ready for death

Make peace with your maker the skies turn to black
The moon shines above you there's no turning back
Souls scream of agony life cries of pain
Thirst howls entwined wind sheds bloodstain

When it is over you feel the heat too
You are the beast now the killer is you
Stalking a victim beneath the moonlight
The sound of his screaming but you know it's alright.

Eric Christie

My Chickadee

Through my frosty window
I can see your small determined stance
as you point toward the grove of grey maples
that you hold forth from your high pedestal
above the snowy cakes of broken creek below.

Your tender feathers abruptly stand against the breeze
as you cling to the brittle oak sprig
that props your tiny weight upon it.

Anticipation carries you over
to your black capped companions for the early banquet
who sway gently with suspended feeder.

I behold the moments watching your calm competition
of plucking each sunflower seed, exchanging frequent glance;
while the blue shadows of fresh snow beneath the old Norway pine
are dimpled by your careless morsels.

Suddenly you pause, take spontaneous release
over the sparkling blanket of winter
that carpets fallow fields of autumn's elapse
to flutter away with your fill
and ride into the grace of this December morning.

Barbara Tuttle

Answers

Some decisions are easy,
Others stare you down as you are waiting to find the answer.
The toughest are the ones where you feel there is no guidance,
However the Guidance you must seek . . .

Not the Physic Friends Network,
But the guide who lives inside who waits to be freed.
And once you know the truth, then it will set you free,
However the Truth you must seek . . .

Once you know the truth inside you,
It will free you from all your burdens.
You must allow your burdens to go,
However the Freedom you must seek . . .

Who will free you for the burdens that lay on you?
Who will get rid of all your pain?
The answers lurk inside you,
However the Answers you must seek . . .

You must find them on your own,
Because it is different for all.
But the question still remains,
How to get through this life alone.

Abbie Sauerteig

Old Mercer River

Old river running wild and free —
    you gave me wonderful memories
My carefree youth — spent on your banks —
    for happy days — I give my thanks
In springtime — lovely moss so green —
    and snowy waters — clear and clean
The frisky trout — leaped way up high —
    showing their colors as they dive
Shooting stars were blooming — here and there
    with nodding heads — as though to care
The azaleas flourishes along the stream —
    adding fragrance — through a misty screen
Was here we swam our summer days —
    till skies turned to an autumn haze
    Then the river trickled down —
        till springtime once more came around

Billie K. Nuttall

A River Of Tears! Ode To Oklahoma City!

With malice and forethought the deed was done that robbed so
many of father, mother, daughter, and son; now the years of
sorrow and pain have just begun.

So violent was their demise and after the thunderous noise
you could hear the survivors cries.

From the rubble the remains were removed some so badly torn
apart that it broke the strongest rescuers heart.

A nation now morns the loss and can not understand why so
many innocent had to pay such a terrible cost.

Parents and grandparents can no longer hold their child or
grandchild, to hear their laugh or see their smile.

Reminders remain in sight day and night, the children's toys,
trucks and cars which belonged to the little boys, dolls
with ringlets and curls that belonged to the little girls.

Now through-out the land you can hear a rallying cry from
woman and man; hang the guilty party and hang them high so
all the world can watch them die.

A river of tears shall continue to fall when to our minds
this tragic event we recall.

Alfred L. Vetzel Jr.

Butterfly, Butterfly

Hoping to catch your eye
Circling around you, oh my
Butterfly, Butterfly, come into the light
Oh, what a beautiful sight

Flying so gracefully
Into the sky, the butterfly

Trying to catch a butterfly
Fly, fly, fly, butterfly

There he sets upon the mums
I'm having so much fun

Here's another on the sill
You're standing so still
You go to touch him
There he goes, the butterfly
I here a tapping on the window
It's the butterfly, fly, fly, fly

There he goes into the sky
Flying so high, the butterfly

I'll see you another day
Butterfly, butterfly, away

Sharon Fleming

The Trinity

Three hermits alone on a deserted isle
Simple men, plain, without guile
Penitent, dress of sackcloth and ashes for sins unintended
Days spent in fasting and supplication, utter faith, unrended.

Their prayer, a wrenching cry of the spirit
Stark, unadorned, naked anguish for grace to merit
Their words, "God, we are three and YOU are three
So, Lord, have mercy on we."

A seafaring preacher of eloquent words and dress
Sought to teach the simple men a silver tongue's largesse
Chastened, they strived to pray with flowery gestures and speech
The preacher, boating away, felt clever for he had staunched a breach

Then down the beach the hermits came running, bathed in a great light
Tell us again how best to pray, for we must get it aright
Humbled, he of the silver tongue told them to go in Peace, prayin'
"God, we are three, YOU are three, So Lord, have mercy on we"
Amen.

Sharon B. Gambill

Grandpa Do You Remember Me?

Grandpa do you remember me,
    and how fun life used to be?
Coming to visit we would have cookouts and play croquet.
    Sometimes you would make silly faces and act as a clown.
I remember you sitting in your favorite chair and telling me stories
    of the old days you and grandmother once shared.
I long to see the smile that once surrounded your face.
    Now I look at you and only see a blank stare.
You once told me of life and how things aren't always fair.
    I miss you Grandpa, even though you are sitting near.
Grandpa do you remember me?

Molly A. Webb

The Poet

Strewed amongst a pattern ever streaming
Whispering under the shroud of dauntless dreaming
Awakens a residence perverse and maddened
Rising from a dwelling long thought abandoned
More than a thought suppressed in a lurid crevice
Subjugating the remainder of the mind, intent on malice
As heartfelt desolation heightens the season
The distant hum becomes deceitfully lyrical
Yet the source does not occupy compassion or reason

Matthew Hone

Yesterday is past, tomorrow the future, today . . .

Yesterday is past, tomorrow the future, today is now presumed the
present. Only yesterday I said I can't wait till tomorrow but alas
it is still today. Yesterday was today and tomorrow will be (today)
and today is present, for now.
But when is now? What is time? Do you understand this rhyme?
Then was not but for a moment, now is past and soon, to come.
Now is never and forever.
Is there a soon or then, or are they now . . . past, to come.
Hey diddle diddle I say to the cat and the fiddle.
Do you comprehend
. . . my riddle?
Is yesterday today before and tomorrow today to come?
Is today the sum of tomorrow and yesterday (together) or is it the
difference (between) As I write Now!
Right now it is past, yet still here. So is there a past or just
todays, gone by and now too —
come, I wonder . . .

What is half of now?

Travis Scott Dempster

A Childhood Memory

When I was still young,
I asked my Daddy if he'd always be here.
He looked in my eyes and he could sense my fear.
I asked my Daddy to never go away,
and I asked him if his love for me would ever, from me, stray.
With his gentle blue eyes and a smile on his face,
he gave me a comfort no one could erase.
I looked at him and said, "Daddy, I will never love any man more than you."
Then my Daddy said, "Loving your Daddy is all you need to do."
But still I insisted and I promised again, "I will never love anyone
more — I swear it 'til the end."
My Daddy chuckled for a second and with a tear in his eye,
looked at me and said, "Love no one? Why?"
With my childish sense, I became quiet mad.
I looked at this man and said, "'cuz you're my Dad!"
After a moment, words from his lips did unfold,
he said my feelings would change as I grew old.
I asked him why, I did not know what to do.
And the last thing he said, "I love you too."

Julie M. Eaton Beane

Seagulls Bench

I sit upon the piling so high
no judgement I shall pass,
The wind is my gavel
Seamiest will surpass
The waves are the jury
crashing among the rocks
I thank God for wings
I'll fly higher now
The sentence has been passed

Paula Lee Borrelli

Life

I'll put down my emotions
And let out a little sigh
All these problems within myself
And my life is passing by.

It hasn't been a long life
It hasn't been to short
I guess I'm at the middle stage
Still trying to make it work.

I know enough to play the game
Sometimes I get sent back
But I always have to play again
To see how far I get.

I'll go around the board again
I wonder where I'll land
Please let me get past the spot
That says I failed again.

I have to learn to roll the dice
Believing that I'll win
And if doesn't work out this time
I'll get up and try again.

Vickie Carter

Anasazi

The wind on the sea,
The bird in the air,
The days are long gone
From that land fair.

Eagles fly high above,
O'er the land the Anasazi loved.
Warriors brave and of the sun,
Fought so well, their enemies did run.

Centuries past and white man came,
Destroying life, where'er he reigned.
Eagles fly up above,
O'er the land the Anasazi loved.

Lisa K. Hamlin

Seek And Ye Shall Find

I found a God within my heart
Not lost far out in space
A God who sets each day apart
To lead me in the race.

A God who bids me follow close
If I the goal shall reach
A God who leads with outstretched arms
My weary soul to seize.

And tho my weary footsteps falter
And from the pathway stray
He still is pleading do continue
I am the only way.

Michael I. Brow

Fruit Of The Spirit

Love — and faith and hope, revive
Joy — helps us survive
Peace — is tranquil
Patience — helps us fulfill
Kindness — keeps us calm
Goodness — is like a balm
Faithfulness — is true one to another
Gentleness — as a babe with its mother
Self-control — is strength untold
Fruit of the Spirit here unfold

Sophie Testa

Whispering Wind

Softly I hear your voice,
beautifully can you sing.
The notes come out of your
mouth and whispers in
my ear.
Whispering wind.

Valerie Elizabeth Page

A Summer Storm

The rain has stopped
only to leave the
majestic desert alive
and blooming.

The saguaro's are
filled to capacity
while the prickly pear
stand at attention.

White tailed rabbits
scamper in and out of
their hiding places to
smell the freshness of
the damp palo verde and
mesquite.

Only a lingering rainbow
is left to testify
to the powerful, elusive
summer extravaganza.

Kathy Foster

Sing Me No Songs

Sing me no songs
When I am gone.
 Sing not my praises
 Nor my gifts,
But give me now
Your blessings
And your love.
 Let me know
 Your caring
While the heart beats
And the flesh is warm
And the blood runs.
 Wait not 'til
 Breath is gone
When I will not feel
Your love, your warmth.

 Sing me no songs
 When I am gone.

Florence S. Sinclair

The Poet

She who creates . . .

 Arises like the sun.

Drawing words of expression —
 which ignite power.

Within the strengths of art,
 She carefully settles inside
herself what shall be spoken.

 Alas, doors are open
 And windows of sunshine
peer through, hoping to
receive even an ounce of her
philosophy.

Words are blessings of freedom.
Yet abusers alter liberation wholly.

 The artist is constantly
 searching for perfection . . .

She who creates is
The Poet.

Camille C. Stanford

To Soar

I want to soar with the eagles,
into the bluest skies.
I want to go to heaven,
when I die.

I want to be with my family,
my loved ones, my friends.
I want to walk with Jesus,
into the promised land.

The day Jesus takes
me by the hand
is the day
I become a man.

Dale Nichols

Morning Mist

When fog embraces the meadow
and only the tips of the
mountains lay bare
what fuel for a dream!
You can travel anywhere in
the world
wherever you yearn to go
or muse on your heart's
dearest treasures
whatever they may be.
As the warm glow of dawn
brushes away the fog
may some beautiful dream
linger to fortify your day.

A. Bernice Clark

"Cameo"

For Christabelle
Like a child chasing shadows,
I reach out to you,
Whose childlike wraith
Moves my agèd spirit,
Ungainly toward noontide.
There, black-on-white in silhouette,
This shadeless waif appears
A mirrored ghost in tortured dreams.

mcminn

Yearning
(Thought to Her Service-Man)

Star shine on high
floating through the sky.
    He looks up at you,
you look down on me
and we form a bond
across the wide wide sea.

    So star shine on high
floating through the sky.
    You me and the moon
on this night in June
bring him to me soon
I sigh.

Irving S. Stone

Ora Pra Mi

Ora pra mi — pray for me
that my erring eyes may see
God's work, His great creations.

Ora Pra Mi — pray for me
that my deafened ears will be
open to His sensations.

Ora Pra Mi — pray for me
that my foolish heart will be attuned
to His chosen vibrations.

Ora Pra Mi — pray for me
that my gift of love will meet
all His special expectations.
Ora Pra Mi.

Vera Rush Hill

A Bruner Reunion

They came
To celebrate
A Bruner reunion
To chat of days gone by
What fun.

To church
To grow in grace
To hear the band again
To catch the rhyme marches
Twas great.

Refresh
To tables set
To mingle among the crowd
To partake goodies many
How good.

A day
Well spent with friends
Must come to a sad end
But joy it brought to all
Good-bye.

Ellen Perkins

Garden Of Sorrow

As I stroll
Thru the garden
On cobbled paths
Memories of love
Reflect from the past
Like the dew of morn
Upon the grass
The joys of love
For me
Would not last

Daryl E. White

Plasma Of Love

I hunger
You give me food;
I thirst
You give me drink;
I hurt
You give me comfort.
Silent and motionless
You hold me;
A transfusion of love
Flows through my veins;
You give me life.

Barbara S. Weppener

Christine At One

Christine is a fledgling
Her red fluffy dress
Like the puffy, rumpled
Feathers of a baby bird,
Getting ready for flight.
Her steps are now sure
Not wobbly as they were.
She points her finger
And cries "Dee, Dee, Dee"
She is calling her brother
She wants to rest in his arms
Before making another
Attempt, to fly away.

Verle N. Higgs

Singing In The Night

My pen lies broken
Reflection of my heart
All themes have seeped away
And I have let them go

Your absence presses close
Aching wound that will not heal
All images have faded
And I have let them go

I lost you
When the dawn appeared like midnight
And in the heat of the day
I will become lost to myself

Emptiness filling emptiness
Becoming all in all
Nothing to lose
Mutual embrace

Karl Disley

A Place

Come with me and together
We will search for what we seek
A place where there are no hours
Nor days within a week

A place where what we say or do
Is clearly understood
A place where the seasons change
With our every passing mood

A place of gentle breezes
Of golden grains of sand
Where rain falls soft and gentle
Where time gives no command

I know a place like this exists
A place one of a kind
I've traced it here on paper
For I found it in my mind.

George W. Arthur

Deception

An aluminum foil
midnight
was trying to pass
for the snap and glow
of a January dawn

Leaden clouds covered
moon's sterling medallion
angering it to burst
its circle
like a milkweed pod
sending light slivers
fogging down

Name the scheming sorcerer
Solitude
working this winter madness
forcing earth-glow
to reveal a pregnant sky
and I could hear the snow.

Mary-Ann T. Bebko

A Friend Like You

A Friend like you
is so hard to find.
A friend like you
is so loving and caring.
A friend like you
is a pleasure to know.
A friend like you is always
in my heart.
A friend like you
means the world to me.
A friend like you.

Donna Bello

You

You seem so far away for me,
but you're close
Every minute of the day,
your handsome face appears in my mind
your chocolate brown hair,
your wonderful smile.
Every time you laugh or smile,
I know everything will be O.K.
or you'll try with all your heart
to make it alright.
You're my golden flame,
that burns eternally in my heart you
You're everything I want;
compassionate, romantic,
loving, caring, kind.
There will always be a
place in my heart for you.

Cheryl Stewart

Burn the Book, Amelia Toye

There's nothing I can say
    to legalize my words
        or make them disappear,

I can't explain my actions
    or detest myself
        and make them re-appear,

But I can make the memory last
    my only legal action and words
    and that will never disappear.

Cliff Donaldson

352

Mine

He suffered for all his life.
Dead now, free at last.
Never had my own.
Tombstone only thing that was mines.

Candas Taylor

Searching

These old bones, deep in the ground,
but my spirit, it is still around.
Restless, wandering, can not rest,
things undone, never forgetfulness.

Wandering between the worlds unknown,
heaven nor earth, be my home.
Searching, looking, not complete;
something gone, the missing link.

Crumbling bones, flesh all gone;
Only visions present my form.
Decay, sorrow depict my home;
no one but me knows those who
wronged.

What was once will be again;
it will come, just like the wind.
Troubled, weary, need to rest;
all things must pass the final test.

Rings, spirals, are now reversed;
when we're here, deal not in mirth.
Haunting, wandering on this earth;
Fulfillment marks the final birth.

Julia T. Taylor

My Personal Favorite

I need you now, I want you back
I long to see you once again
I can't remember just what I longed for
except to see you once again.

I can't remember what you looked like
—— I wish I could
You abandoned me
    when I needed you most.
I trusted you
I depended on you
Now you are gone.

Too bad that I did not realize your
essence when you were here.
Too bad I didn't know how.
Too bad I ignored you in my prime.

Where did you go?
I thought I'd have you all my life,
I looked around and you were gone, and
I never even saw you leave.
And you didn't even say good-bye.

Teresa Thompson

This Is Just To Say

I have
not done
my math
home work

Sorry it was
just to
hard

I hope you
won't be
mad.

Aziz Akhtar

Where Breezes Blow

High where the breezes blow
looking down on our town below,
you in my arms forever,
don't ever let me go.

Lights going off and on
winking approval till dawn.
You gave strengths to go on,
I'll never let you go.

Fog rolls in from the ocean
covering everything.
You're the love and devotion
to making my happy heart sing
now our hearts are as one.
One beat till the morning sun.
I gambled and now I have won.

High where the Breezes Blow.

Ethelmae Vance

Life's True Treasures

As you go through each day,
Do you stop to see,
The clouds drifting by,
Or the flight of a bee?

Do you stop to hear,
The birds sweetly singing,
Or the sound of a gate,
As it's gently swinging?

Do you feel warmed all over,
When the suns shining through,
And when some ones especially kind,
Are you more generous too?

These are life's true treasures,
So stop to see, hear and feel,
Your life will be much richer,
And your soul will begin to heal.

Ethel K. Walter

This Day Of Birth

We pass this way once again,
To celebrate this day of birth,
A checkpoint of your life,
Of love and joy, and all they're worth.

A time of rest and ponder,
Our worries now are cast,
A yardstick of growth and values,
We've gathered from the past.

As others are surely envious,
And wish that they were me,
Knowing that loving you,
Is like winning the lottery.

No place, nor time,
Nor anything I could do,
Could make life more special,
Than to be blessed with,
Another year with you!
With all my love,
Happy Birthday Jean!

James M. Wheeler

Dad

In my opinion you're everything
My feelings for you are so good
You do for me just what you should
You take a fellow under your wing
You make me happy, you make me sing
My feelings for you will never change
No matter how far away the range

We'll soar high
We'll soar low
Where ever you go you'll always know

I'm so happy
I'm so free
I'm just glad
That you're my Dad.

Peter Bradin

Silent Sadness

Clouds of sadness build around me.
Viscous melancholy fills
my hollow heart.
Perhaps I heard the coyote talk,
but did not know his tongue.
Perhaps I hear behind me
falling years, tumbling faster,
stripping cover from the
lesser days in front.
Could this cloud be vapor
from the tears I should have shed
seeping through the cloak I use
to hide me from myself?

Robert C. Vander Wagen

I Remember

I remember the nights in a
field close by,
Under the stars and with love
in my eyes.
I remember a certain touch by
your strong hand, and the
scent of that near by land.
I remember the sound of your
voice, so smoothing, so calming,
so choice.
I remember you so clear the
look in your eyes, I hold
so dear.
I can only hope your
memories are as clear.

Robbin Taylor Underhill

Contrariwise

Man is contrary, said God,
I speak through the thunder
And roaring winds
And he will not hear me.
Earthquakes shake him
But a little while.

I will send
My littlest creatures
To take him unawares,
A newborn calf,
A tender birdsong,
A baby in a manger,
That hardened to my strength
Man may still be won
By my gentleness.

Carolyn Shafer

"Thoughts"

When I think about my Savior,
My faith begins to grow;
The window of my mind is opened
and I learn much I need to know.

He guides me through each morning,
Reminds me of my prayers
and helps me through each troubled day
To show how much He cares.

An angel tucks me in each night;
My Shepherd holds my hand;
One day I'll see his loving face
and then I'll understand.

I feel His love, His grace, His peace,
But only in a part;
The day will come when I will see
The longing of my heart.

Eve Kuehn Whalen

To Oliver, My Teddy Bear

He's just an ordinary bear you say
With plastic eyes and a replaced nose
Why do I carry him around everywhere
And why do I often change his clothes?

Fat and fuzzy and a little worn
All day long he sits in his chair
With his Fisher Price Pooh TV
Waiting patiently for me to be there.

Laughter and tears, joy and sorrow
He's shared them all and more
No harsh words does he utter
He cares not if we're rich or poor.

A good companion when we travel
He never tries to pick the route
A couple of shirts and a pair of jeans
He doesn't need a business suit.

When night falls and I drive home
I smile to think of him there
Warmth and love I see in his eyes
I know I'm lucky to have that bear.

Barbara A. Dunn

Take Me

Take me lovely lady
In the quiet of the night,
Don't say no or maybe.
Until the morning light.

Take me where your sparkling eyes,
Ignite my inner soul;
Let's whisper fantasies and lies
For hours in a row.

Take me to the magic,
Of the love we often miss,
make my life less tragic,
With the softness of your kiss.

Take me where our love can rest,
Upon a mossy hill,
And there we can explore the best,
Of destiny and will.

Take me where I've never been,
I surely want to go,
And then please take me back again,
Where lover's passions flow.

Christopher W. Boyden

The Birds

All of a sudden
    the birds were there.
They came from nowhere
    through the air.
They came in thousands
    swirling around.
They covered the trees and
    they covered the ground.
Like a huge black blanket
    spread on the grass
They fluttered their wings
    in a moving mass.
And then on block
    they swiftly flew
Into the distance
    and out of my view.

Hazel Stonehouse

Harbor

As I walk to the edge of the water
Stand by the harbor
The tide rushes in
And out in flows
The memories drift with the tide
A tired old shoe washes in
Like the one I once wore
Bringing back the thoughts
Of how I filled those shoes
Like the sea we flow
We flow to places we try to forget
For the harbor brings back the memories
I harbor the feelings I have
Try not to let out what I feel
But they rush in with the tide
Thought I try and fight
The harbor lets me know
That I can not hide
From myself

John Gonski

Hunter Feral

Jagged, glistening, drooling jaws
Gleaming eyes, ripping claws;
Running, leaping, chasing prey
Tearing, killing, night and day;
Hungry, thirsty, primal drive
Howl and charge, live and die.

Sean Romer

God Is Speaking

He is speaking in the glad times,
speaking in the sad times,
speaking to you and me.

He is speaking of things to come,
speaking of things undone,
speaking of his only son.

He is speaking of his Heavenly home,
where we'll never more be alone,
speaking so we can go on.

On in the glad times,
on in the sad times,
on to our Heavenly Home,

Where we'll never more be alone.

Virginia Breeden

In The Coffee House

In the coffee house
Duncan, who won't wait tables,
smiled and talked
of Shiva and the Vive
and the communal love
he felt on ecstasy
at the raves

Human love,
not sexual,
he said
as he flashed uneven teeth
and dragged on his camel

Bobbing his head
and smiling
glassy eyed
at some place behind my head
he said my cynicism
was perfectly understandable

Deborah Bone

A Paper In The Dark

A small, metal desk sits
In the corner of a dark room
Where a sheet of paper rests
On its cold surface.

Beside the paper lies
A long, black pen that
Used to write the dreams of
A long forgotten youth.

The way the sun would shine
On her long brown hair,
And the way she used to smile
When we sat here in this room.

But then sun has gone away
And the pen is out of ink,
So the only thing left
Is a paper in the dark.

Matchett Bradford III

The Revealing Smile

What a gift is a smile!
It grows from deep within
to heal our troubled mind
and feed our hungry heart.

What a treat is a smile!
We watch our spirit renew
with humor and delight
as it eradicates our pain.

What a discovery is our smile!
Those cares and woes we dread
are transformed to repose
as we see a new approach.

What a magnet is our smile!
The energy it radiates
envelopes kindred souls
who bathe in its comforting glow.

What a blessing is our smile!
It mirrors universal faith
in an enveloping spiritual truth
that gives us the strength to smile.

Carolyn Ashe Stokes

Forever The Boy

Dedicated to My Mother
A young boy plays
Playing away the days
Not thinking of tomorrow
Having fun, not sorrow
The boy is now adolescent
Not caring where time has went
Wishes he was more mature
What he really wants, he's not sure
The boy has become a man
Achieving whatever he can
Learning life day by day
Wanting his life to stay
The boy has reached middle age
Has seen life from every page
His days go by fast
He thinks of the past
Thinks of the days he was ten
Wishes he was there again

Robert Romine

Hurting Friends

Friends around are hurting Lord,
    please show me what to do.
Friends I love so deeply,
    feel left alone and blue.

Things that they are going through,
    I cannot understand.
So much more I want to do,
    to lend a helping hand.

I want to be a comfort Lord,
    a friend that's always there.
Someone they can turn to,
    let me show them Lord, I care.

Give me special words to say,
    or just a listening ear.
Keep my heart in silence Lord,
    so truly I can hear.

These special friends I lift to you,
    while kneeling down in prayer.
Teach me how to help them Lord,
    your love to them I'll share.

Terrie D. Burch

Feather Elephants

Late afternoon spreads lazy lethargy
through all who inhabit the particular
slice in time. Day long sun and heat
give way slowly, mysteriously, almost
unnoticed to graying skies.
No gloom, no doom, just peace and
tranquility reign; as do the thickening
puffs powdering the vast azure.
One by one, the drops and
drips slip through the air,
inevitably invading the silence.
The once quiet roof begins
increasingly to tell its tale.
Random rhythms land above,
recounting the centuries of steady
foot-fall of feather elephants.
Soothing stampedes, constant in
presence and magic talent to enhance
idea and dream, borne of the waterfall.

Andrea D. Johnson

Liar

Told!
A story
To get what you want
Smitten
I put my faith in you
Cheated!
You made me believe
But you lie
Now, outside
Your vicious circle
Deception!
Has no control
Over powered!
I conquer
You,
You lose!

Alixandra Browning

Untitled

Too bad the sunflowers
    don't feel the same toward
    the moon

Too bad the fallen prey
    won't see tomorrow
    life is cruel —

    I could walk on coals
    for you.

Tirzah Strom Peterson

I Sit And Watch

In a lush green field
I sit
on a thousand year rock
and watch
the daily sunset burn.
Birds look warm
against the sky.
Blossoms at my feet
rose tinted
curl inward
for their sleep.
A cobalt mantle
covers all.
I leave the scene
contented.

Mary Goodman

"It Was Me"

The day was not ordinary
We were all awaiting
Which one of us would it be?

As I sat contemplating
Could it really be
Which one of us would it be?

Hours passed slowly
Productivity at its lowest
Which one of us would it be?

We comforted each other
With doubt and uncertainty
Which one of us would it be?

The hour finally came
Everyone now knows
It was me . . . It was me.

Dolores M. Oubre

Remember Dr. Still

Andrew was a special name
    For Andrew Taylor Still
Who learned to heal the sick and lame
    He used his special skill
He brought to us a world-wide fame
    Andrew was a special name
    Remember Dr. Still

Ellen K. Davison

Gray Days

Warm and cozy, soft and still
Feelings of relaxation
Lying about at will
No stars, no sun, no clouds, no moon
Fading softly, much too soon
Cuddling close, holding on tight
Not quite dawn, not quite night
Languidly stretching, resting the eyes
Sighing with contentment, no rush hours
The mood is set for all the day
Lovely, lovely shades of gray

JoAnn Dandridge

Untitled

We must learn to keep the word of
Jesus Christ, the son of God, in
Our hearts, and daily speaking
I want to learn,
Help, help, help, help;
We, me, us,
Yes all of us,
I can not read,
I can not read,
I can not read?
I can not read %#_&'(14)(12)*
Help me,
Who is me, teach me too learn,
God's word, and see
Yes teach me,
Jesus Christ word, and, and truly, see,
I wish it would rain, rain, rain,
Christ, God's Jesus
Teaching.

Richard N. Benjamin

The One I Love

My nights so long, my days so sad
Thinking of the love we could of had.
We were to shy to say anything
When either one of us walked by.

When I looked deep
Into your beautiful
Blue eyes it gave
Me strength, and
I could touch the sky.
If I were the beauty
Lost in never ending sleep,
Would you bend on
One knee to kiss me,
To wake me
With your lips so sweet?

Will we ever stand,
Hand in hand in a beautiful place,
Stand together soul to soul
As face to face?
All I can do is think about you!

Diana Yannetti

Untitled

Some boys need other boys
Props with which to play
But not for he and he
The sexual way
Led and leading astray
Almost but not
Praise God
But where is the boy
Is he wanting
He differently
To be
Or not
A scoundrel
The predator
The animal
Your play
Your way
He won't be
Wasn't, isn't, neither of the three

Stephen J. Riggs

Heart's Desire

Deep inside my mind I see,
Scenes of things that used to be,
Seeing you there next to me,
Forever by my side.

Down inside my heart I feel,
A deep, abiding love so real,
Feelings that no one can steal,
That I would never hide.

I sleep and in my dreams I find,
Visions of your hand in mine,
Our desire and strength combined,
To find our destiny.

In the morning I arise,
Can you imagine my surprise,
When right before my very eyes,
Your face appears to me?

Now I know what dreams impart,
That we never were apart,
You were there right from the start,
I hold you in my heart.

Frank Yeager

I Can Walk Again!

My doctor's warnings
were loud and very clear,
High blood pressure
was a symptom to fear.

As fast as lightning
flashes across the sky,
A stroke could paralyze me
or I might even die.

One Friday morning
I had a bad attack.
I awoke dazed,
lying flat on my back.

I could not stand up
and it was very plain,
My recovery will be slow
while I endure the pain.

Although I felt depressed,
I was not defeated,
Fortunately, physical therapy
was all that I needed.

Joseph M. Snyder

Spark Of Love

When you came into my life
You lighted up all my fires.
But then it went so fast
The groove just didn't last
So few moments! So little time!
Breaking up was too hard,
But your love forever
Has a place in my heart.

So brief, yet so immense
So brief, yet so intense
So brief, yet shined so bright
So brief, yet felt so right.

Brief spark of love
So wonderful, so divine.
May the sun lose its shine
And the rainbow all its charm
But the memory of your love
I will not let it die.

Benedict Loredo

"The Sleeping Sin"

From the prick of a pin,
Blood can be spilled.
From the fate of man's sin,
A world can be killed.

But he who lit the sun,
And started it burning;
Shall judge the one,
Who stops the earth turning.

Guy Mercier

Our Father

In the middle of I don't know's
confusion of "What do I do?"
The love of our father never
fails to show
He's forever seeing our
troubles through
Our hearts may ache our
answers weak
but peace can be found
when it's he we seek.

Sara J. Miller

Untitled

I won't believe
What my eyes can't see
I don't need nothin'
but chaos and peace

I've seen 'em beggin'
An' washin' their feet
Boy what you don't know
you'd never repeat

I cant talk too tough
about what I've seen
I barely found out
religion ain't free

Now I been thinkin'
about you and disease
Eating away at
society's ease
But is there something
you can take from the land
Don't shoot up nothin'
ya don't understand

Matthew Stoker

Expression

I never thought myself a poet
An artist with a craft
What was just an outlet
Evolved as so did I
And now it seems I write
Because I have no choice.

Words, thoughts, images
Converge in my mind
And demand a voice
I become their bond slave
Freely captivated
By the hold they have on my heart
And once on the page
We become one.

Cindy Farrar

Vow Set In Stone

The permeating brilliance
of the burst of fiery light
that mainstream the inner most cuts
sparkles and reflects
off the infinite layers
of tiny mirrors
that all arrive
at the center point
of this magnificent symbol
of the forever faithful burning love
that my beautiful diamond ring
brings to my eyes
as I gaze upon its presence
on the limb that says
forever
my mate
I will love you.

Kelly Ann Moberly

My Gift Of Time

I may not be able
to by you things
but, I can give to you
something far more valuable
My gift of time

Though we may not
have any great wealth
We are very fortunate
for we have our health
along with my gift of time

There's no treasure
to be found anywhere
I only hope you find
the lasting pleasure
in knowing I care
which is why
I gave to you
My gift of time

Cheryl J. Richard

"Without You"

Take the blue from the sky,
Take the warmth of the sun,
Take the coolness of a northern wind,
The smile of young children,
The serenity of the rain,
For without you, they have no meaning.

Raymond L. Miles

Fully Grown

We are from two different worlds
   yet there is a bond between us,
For we are a composite of all
   who have journeyed before
Life shapes and molds us
   into who we are today.
I hope that a part of me
   will continue with someone new
Taking only the best part
   leaving the rest behind
I wait for the day
   that I will be less of them
   and more of me
Then and only then will
   I be fully grown.

Loretta Allen

Sin

The day has begun
Yet no one can see.
The danger is near,
But just in your dreams.

Perhaps you will learn
Who calls in the night.
To poke at your soul
And make you feel fright.

You cannot see that
Which lurks in your room.
Something that's evil
Or maybe just you.

Beware not to peer
For fear you might find.
The demon that seeks
to greet you sometime.

So guard your soul well;
You've only got one.
To trade in the end,
When doomsday doth come.

Randall W. Moore Jr.

Far-Reaching

The waiting arms of morpheus
propose rare overtones,
convention is converted
to mystic 'twilight zones'

Whisked into an eddy
of tri-dimensional scenes,
intwining threads of happenstance
weave such transit dreams

Imaginary habitats
with wondrous avenues,
horizons so far reaching
unequaled rendezvous

A world of supernatural
subconsciously induced,
valleys of mixed emotions
anxieties unloosed

Interludes of slumber
disturbed by coming light,
fade into a depth beyond
the fantasy of night —

Evelyn M. Cole

Untitled

The inability of man
Makes nature rule the land
He pipes proudly "Progress"
Nature's gentle roar
"What a mess"
From his mind, to his so imperfect
Self expression
While time merely is
Nature's eternal lesson
This is the core
Fight the battles
Never finish the war
Without nature, without time
Man is a zero
Without man
Nature lies the hero

C. Jenkins

The Freedom

The sky, the earth;
the wind, the sea;
all that is free,
are we.

The grass, the insects;
the clouds, the snow;
all that is,
are we.

The buildings, the trees;
the birds, the bees;
all this which is free,
are we.

Karen Wisniewski

Evening Concert

Each evening when the sun goes down
It's time to take a walk
To hear the chirping of the birds,
For that's the way they talk.
The little insects do their part
With many different sounds,
And together make an orchestra
That through the night resounds.
The moon provides the spotlight,
The stars are twinkling bright.
How peaceful just to take a walk
And hear the sounds of night.

Nancy L. Goode

Appointment

I'm going on a journey,
I have an appointment to keep.
At the end of my journey,
It's Jesus Christ I'll meet.
He will be standing at the gate
to welcome me home.
He will take me to meet God,
Who's sitting on the throne.
What a beautiful city,
so bright and fair,
I'll be caught up
to meet him in the air.
I have loved ones
waiting for me in the sky,
and I will see them for sure,
by and by.

Christine P. Harris

Indian Summer Love

In my youth I had many loves.
Like many young people of today,
I thought love was only for the young.
Now I know love can come again,
Like an Indian summer sun.

When winter settles on your head,
The flame of love burns
Warmest in your heart.
It is only then you know
The joy true love can impart.

Indian summer love is not
just a candle in the wind
That can be blown out again and again.
My love is an eternal flame
That will burn forever,
Then start over again.

Emily Peterson

A Friend Of Mine

A friend to share my feelings
And listen to my dreams,
To lend a hand or shoulder
When I'm splitting at the seams.

Beyond the qualities of a friend
Is a special kind of guy,
Who shows me all his love
That I know will never die.

Forgive me if there's sadness
After the drying of the tears.
Our special love will always be
In my heart, throughout the years.

Cindy Lee Thompson

Thank You God For Friends

Friends are God's way of
making other people happy.
Friends are the way to say
to someone, I love you and
   I care.
Friends are who you can turn
to when the chips are down.
And hope that by their smile
   they'll pick you up.
I love you friend and I care.
Take me by the hand, I will
always be there.
Thank you God for friends!

Carol Morris

Who You Are

God is forever
And we are of God.
We do not end up
Beneath the sod.

The real you is perfect
Complete and whole.
Not made of matter
But pure mind and soul.

You are eternal
Forever will be
An integral part
Of God's Family.

Julia Winter Cohen

Time

Time passes by much like the breeze;
Rarely noticed and never seen.

It sweeps through lives
And leaves us bare;
Taking the years
That once hung there.

Moaning tearless
Across the moors.
Bringing new skies
But closing doors.

Rippling waters.
Uplifting sands.
It can't be stopped
With human hands.

It eases hearts
But brings the rains.
It whispers truth
to weather vanes.

Time passes by much like the breeze;
Rarely noticed and never seen.

Alisa Vaughan

Three Little Words

Help me
I can't reach you
You are too far away
You left me behind
When you said you would stay
I try to call you
But you're never home
I try to write you
But I never get past the first line
I try to talk to you
But no words come out
I tell myself not to think of you
But I can't get you out of my mind
I am lost without your love
Without your love I cannot grow
Without growth I cannot love
You are gone now
And will not come back
Just remember three words . . .
I love you

Angel Swies

She Makes Dreams

I've drowned myself
   In dreams of you:
I've become soft
   as raspberries and honey
Without you in my arms.

I've lost my crown chasing
   this dream that's you:
I've abandoned my
   inspiration, caring, heart,
   even love entirely
In anticipation of once again
rediscovering them with you.

I've found new hope
   after talking to you:
I've grown to hope dear
   even my inescapable name Greg
Is still inspiring, hopeful
desirable and even lovable to
   you: Sarah.

Greg E. Griffith

Stormy Wave

On a warm and breeze day
Down by the ocean I went stay
I sat upon a rock to look
Out at the stormy wave coming
In from the sea.

I hurled around a tree
My heart pounded as I
Waited to see, when the
Wave rush in I stood
To my feet to hear the
Waves sounds oh so sweet
To me this where I want to be.

Walking alone the sea at
That moment I'm feeling
Well and free, just to
Be near take away any fear
Close your eyes picture the wave
Swish!! You will hear coming
In from the sea.

Linda Steward

Untitled

As I sit in my room
My eyes flushing brown
I think of you whenever
I'm feeling down.
You're always on my mind
I can't keep you out.
I love you forever
There is no doubt.
I can be kickin' it with my
friends and still think of you
There is no way I
can do without you.
I stay up late at night
thinking about you,
I know in my heart you're
thinking of me too.
I know you love me and
I know I love you and
we'll be together when
we both say "I do"

Tamara Portugal

Love Fades Away

You think you have a lot of things
So, tell me what you've got?
All I see is your plastic face
And friends that you have bought.

You say you're always happy
But I've seen right through your smile.
The tears are there inside you
And they've been there for awhile.

The world is in your hands. You say?
So you've no reason to cry?
Look again and I think you'll see
The world has passed you by.

Don't tell me how much you care for me
There's nothing I want to hear.
The story is only iced with lies
And nothing is sincere.

I thought, one time, you were for real
But now I realize
How rotten is the apple
That once was in my eyes.

Martin E. Hanes II

Kids In Space

I have two kids
They're in my space
They're in my house
They're in my face

They're always there
Wherever I go
I wait for Mom
The day goes slow

They fight, they whine
They yell and play
My nerves are tested
Each and every day

When my head is pounding
And there's no escape
I want to send
My kids in space

William Hansen

Someone

I need someone
to tell my troubles to
I need a friend
who understand what I do
who knows I rarely
mean what I say
I'd like to meet a person
like that someday
just a person
who I can really trust
gotta have an open mind
and they also must
be in the same mess as me
so they can really relate
someone has to understand
why I'm in this state
the person I need
to tell my troubles to
could be found someday
maybe that person is you

Katie Madderra

"The Eyes Of A Child"
Dedicated to Kayla Mercedes Stevenson

   The eyes of a child,
full of wonders and fears.
   With so much to learn,
as she grows through the years.

   She struggles and she tries,
and takes on so much.
   It all seems so new.
Through each little touch.

   And through all of the days,
her memories are kept.
   On boldly she goes,
with each gentle step.

   Her eyes open wide,
as the world becomes known.
   'Til she ventures with caution,
and goes out on her own.

Erin Stevenson

PMS

Moan of chalk
across the blackboard
Burning itch
between my toes
Sand under my eyelid
Splinters under my nails
Lava boiling in my veins
Nerves curling like
wood shavings off
the carver's knife
Noise like the hum
of a thousand bees
works its way beneath
my scalp and rubs
my brain
the wrong way

Tanya Moysaenko

The Hardest Thing

I know sometimes you look for me
and do not understand

The things you have to go through
asking "What could be His plan?"

I know your heart, I know your mind,
They cry out with despair;

"Why does this have to happen, Lord?
Don't you even care?"

Yes, I care, even more than you,
my pain is deeper still,

I had to watch My Child die,
so He could do My will;

I had to turn My head when
He went through all His pain;

I couldn't even help Him
when I saw His body slain;

The suffering that you feel inside
is something I fully know,

That the hardest thing I had to do
was let My Child go.

Teresa McAnear

dust is the soul

living life is to witness daily
to all travellers of that moment,
when soul, spirit, heart exist
recognizing another before self . . .
seekers of faces pursue another
trying to find self prudence,
as abandoned imaginaries fade . . .
spirits touch to reflect souls
as they step upon life's trails
to stir, awakening morning doves
by touching beyond vespers tolls . . .
season moments cycle around,
reflective of the moon and sun
caressed by stars in day or dark
as life is trying to find spirit
witness life's rite of passage,
allowing no one to ignore
the spark that leaves the soul
to achieve the final cornerstone . . .

ERL

Untitled

No one understands me
What I see
How I feel

I hide what is so plane to see
Obvious and obscure
Dying for a person to reach
    deep to touch my
    beating heart
To reassure me it is still alive

I breath and walk among
    thousands of people
Yet I am so alone
Desperate to find a soul
    such
      As I

Catrina Hefner

Yesterday's Dirt

Days go by
And nights come in
Yesterdays dirt is carried
    by the wind

Yesterday's dirt has
    much to hide
It tells a great story
    'bout all who've died

Listen someday when
    you hear the wind
Hear the mourning carried
    within
The sound you hear
    is pain and hurt
Made by lost souls
    of Yesterday's dirt.

Michael Jordan Hinds

Eagles

You are free now . . .
Go find your way.
I do release you, on this day.
You must fly, so spread your wings,
I cannot watch,
I cannot sing.
To release you, gives me mixed pains.
I know it's right, but when it rains.
I will remember you with heavy tears.
Knowing of the many dangers and fears.
Although I know, you must be free,
Like an Eagle, you will see . . .
    Me standing here,
      Looking up high,
        Looking for Eagles
          in the sky.

Gail-lynn Moore

Untitled

To my loved one . . .
So sweet and delicate,
So honest and pure,
I love you more than you'll
    Ever understand.
I feel these emotions
    From my heart.
As I gaze, alone, into the
    Bottom of my glass.

B. L. Toby

Inner Peace

Peace of the soul,
Peace of the mind,
Comes to us slow,
But in good time.

When knowledge and love,
Abound in our life,
Then we have won,
The goodness of life.

These qualities still hold,
When our souls are freed,
Then we are told,
What it means — indeed.

Madelaine Martino Luther

"I Hope You Are Listening"

The fear in my eyes,
The worry in my heart,
The pain of wonder,
That we will part,
I see the tears,
I feel the pain,
But I still wonder if you are okay,
The fear I will never hold you again,
My soul will try to mend,
But even though my heart breaks,
I'll try to send,
My love for you,
I'll pray again.

Holly Anne Bonin

"The Letter"

An old man sits
along the entry
ramp, reading a
letter,
tears
dripping,
    dripping,
      dripping.
What could be
enough
to make a
street-man cry?
"It's from Mom,"
he says, as he
tears it to shreds
and gives it
to the wind.

Shirley Conrad

"Bid Reality Adieu"

When the smallest of dreams
Refuses our wish to come true,
Then listen for the silent screams
Of a heart laden with rue;
Then watch as a life fades
Into the cool, transparent night
Of a world's parlor game charades,
Where the prize is power's might;
Then feel the pain of a lost mind,
Once searching for a way out,
But now spiritless and resigned
To accept what reality's all about.
But if you dream a dream come true,
Bid all of what reality's about adieu.

M. A. Willis

Dear One

I think of you so often
So many miles away
My mind is just a buzzin'
With the things I have to say
When I write to you — tomorrow

But now , I have to make the beds,
clean the house, and then
get dinner, do the dishes . . .
Too tired tonight — but then
I'll write to you — tomorrow

I really mustn't wait too long
Because you have to know
How I love you and I miss you
And I'll absitively, posilutely
Write to you — tomorrow

Dolly Sharpe

Silent Memories

Memories.
Like silent birds,
Gliding above the oceans
Of my mind.
Bursting forth and
Vanishing into
The nebula of my thoughts.
They glide,
Over the swiftly
Changing plains of
The future.
They glide,
Over the hills of
The past,
To return to their
Faraway dwellings,
To peace, joy and
Utter contentment . . .

Maryvonne C. M. Martin

Flood

Memories float
a cloudy landscape
raindrops
storm through my mind
drift toward
confusion
a downpour of emotions
strike lightning
consuming
my tribute to you.
A whirlwind of feeling
cyclones into
new awareness
sinking in
a moment of time
swept away
silent emptiness drowns
a once content heart.

Ginny Becker

Rusty (Acrostic For My Dog)

Running freely on a grassy hill,
Up and down, my way is my own choice.
Suddenly I'm lost, afraid, until
Turning, I can hear my master's voice
Yonder call me in the night so still.

Robert K. Meyer II

Puppy Love

A shine comes
Into you eyes
When I come
Into your sight.

You jump around
And get all excited
When I come
Into your sight.

You wag your tail
And slobber and drool
When I come
Into your sight.

You're always there
Walking at my feet
When I come
Into your sight.

You always show
That puppy love
When I come
Into your sight.

Amy Mitcham

Passion Reborn

Your legend drifts to me
from beyond the distant shore.
Whispering in vain
while the tales, they still ignore.
In passion, you speak,
for truth and light to set you free.
For it's the weight of time
that takes you far from me.
Intense, you rise,
through the depths
to grasp my pulsing throat;
And call to me,
my precious Queen,
to the gentle words you wrote.

Dawn Finch

Knots

This feeling is like a twisting wind
Going through the body
A twisted emotion
Twisted into knots
Several knots
A string of a little knots
Waiting to be untied, to be set free
To feel safe
To shout to the world free at last

Sharon McDowell

Dead But Still Alive

The scars have damaged my life,
emotionally and physically.
I am alone in this world it seems.
The damage had taken my life that I
should lead.

Sometimes I feel like I am already
dead, dead and away from the
abuse I have led.

All I have left now is pain from years
ago. Why is it still within me,
Why can I not let go?

Kristina Inzana

Piggy

Piggy one and piggy two
How the heck are you who-who?
Piggy pile here and piggy pile there
Piggy piles everywhere!
Piggy prints are left behind
Piggy prints are easy to find
Piggy messes on the floor
Don't be surprised, there's lots more
Piggy one says ho-ho-ho
I'm too busy to mop the floor
Piggy two seems not to care
If he helped who would share?
Oh my gosh, oh gull darn
Piggy one is in the barn
There he's snuggled in the hay
Sound asleep and there he'll stay
His dream for now is to philosophize
That everyone should realize
For piggy two to give some slack
Piggy one has to scratch his Back!

Richard L. Helpenstell

Memories

Painful memories,
They loom in everyone's past.
Some are worse than others.
And some are full of class.
You can never know what
someone hides
The deep dark secrete of their lives.
So take a closer look next time
Someone turns away
And think about your memories
That made them what they are today.

Jessica Horsley

Untitled

Here's to Frankie
Who is now seventy-three
So what — he's young
in heart you see
He makes magic like the
waves of the sea
He makes my heart
beat with glee
And thanks to God he
belongs to me
Do we all love him?
Yes sireee!!!

Louise Maxwell

Untitled

I was such a fool . . .
Here I am all alone tonight;
I need your love . . .
I want your touch
is feeling so much.
Don't leave me alone in the night.
I need you by my side tonight.
A thousands of dreams for you and I.
Memories that last forever . . .
Do you remember the times we had?
Seems like yesterday.
You were in my arms.
Do you remember the time we fell
in Love it just seems
like yesterday . . .

Kelly O'Donnell

The Tears

The tears in my eyes
Are still there since my mom died
I still think of her
Even her death is after
She got the ghost of christ
Now she lies at rest
I'm still with her
She's still with me
She always will be
In my heart
We will never part
Glory to Christ
Christ be the glory . . . Amen

Charlie E. Gess

Forget Me Nots

I created those beautiful flowers,
the birds, the trees, the majestic
mountains for all to see.
Forget Me Not.

I have created you for Me to tell
others how special I am, and that
I am the Way, the Truth and the
Life; walk by faith and not by sight
Forget Me Not.

Yes, I died on the cross to save
men's souls, but I arose and bloomed
again, just like the rose.
Forget Me Not.

I am alive! And working miracles
every day. Please come into my
presence and pray, and
Forget Me Not.

Lisa Beth Jenkins

Love And Time

With a little love,
We'll reach our destination,
With a little time,
We'll be alright,
But with both,
We'll see the light,
With love,
Jesus takes our hand,
With time,
We'll understand,
But with both,
We'll take everyone's hand,
With love.

Misty Honeysuckle

Grandpa's

Grandpa's are sweet
Just like a treat
I love you so
I know you had to go
God needed you above
Just like his doves
I'll see you in heaven
One day
So wait for me okay
I love you grandpa
Your love,
Cassandra Cawood

Sandy Cawood

Untitled

We are tearing down the walls
Which
We have erected in self-defense
Of a cruel
And hurting world.
Removing them
Block by block
We realize
More
Of each other.
We are opening
Up doors that have
Long been locked
Against the assault
That life wages.
Waiting so long
For the one
Who has the key
To softly
Step inside . . .

Kim Bevelacqua

The Gift

There is a gift inside each one of us;
It cannot be taken away.
Some people never let it come out,
While others share it every day.

This gift is a thing we call kindness,
And it should be in great demand.
For the world would be a better place
If we spread it throughout the land.

I want to share my gift with the world
And if you should ask me why,
I'd tell you my life would be complete
If I have no kindness left when I die.

Jeff Allison

The Flesh Is Weak

With in the mind the thoughts of flesh
Release the night to sleep
With in the spirit of the mind
Awake the flesh is weak.

The steady hand upon the wheel
Gained their confident
The unlearned tongue with words to burn
Sounds no evidences.

Lairs chose to rake the coals
Cause the mouth to laugh
Temporal things the fool he brings
And nothing comes there aft.

The one that heard the few that be
Ponder after thought
Awake the body in the night
Till won what wisdom brought.

Passed the shadow through the veil
Who read the message clear
And the voice of fearful words
No longer held the ear.

Eugene L. Gable

An Angel Within

Everyone has an angel within,
In the mind in the heart in the soul and in sin,
You can misbehave you can sing and play,
But the angel within you will always stay.

Kate Sherry

This Is My Home

A place to rest my head,
    nourish my body,
    and dry my tears.

A place to hear kind words,
    that my spirit
    may be lifted.

A place to receive encouragement
    that my hopes
    and dreams
    will be filled.

My faith is made stronger
    by the voices I hear.

And love is always present
    to ease my pain
    and calm my fears.

Sandy Corbitt

Tommy

Today the bleeding started that
    reminds me I'm a woman.
No cause for joy, however.
It reminded me more of the little life
    Ripped from its nest
A month ago,
Murdered by its father's unconcerned
    and jabbing blows.

I saw my sweet boy today and
    All he said was,
"Why, mommy, why?"
There is no ready answer
    for the innocent.
I only could reply,
"Sleep with the angels, precious,
    Until your mommy comes."

Margaret Keshawarz

Untitled

Life with no purpose
Like a deer on the highway
Alone in the darkness
Treading upon the hardness
Searching for substance
Finding only discards
Of others finer existence
Softly walking across life's
Dark abyss
Carefully trodding
Wondering through
Shaking with anticipation
Hoping to reach that greener garden
Caught in life's rights lights
Of ones meaningless existence
In ones last moments of confusion
Forced down
By a random act of
Societies demise.

Vanessa Sanchez

Untitled

Glistening liquid
Pools vibrating on roadway
Stretching toward the sun

John G. Gerkin

British Neighbors

Nature crows its morning alarm
Sounds of sleep broken
   by people chatter
   and horse clatter
Two legged neighbors
   with furry feathers
   quack their breakfast request
Simple eaters, they are
   wheat or white, biscuit or cracker
   never complaining
Rain water, bugs on the side?
The trip down river was fine

Precipice balance on stickly feet
   leisurely ambling the streets
Stout aquatic barristers
   stuffed up with self importance
Cosily home in wet windy fog
I think I see a pocket watch
   buried beneath that wing
Time to go? Till tomorrow then

   Loraine Jenness

A New Bridge Is So Unstable

A new bridge is so unstable
Should I cross or turn away
I wonder if it's able
To take me past today
Or would it simply take me
Into another darkened time
And forget all my hopes and dreams
And leave them far behind
Would it take me there within your arms
To make strength where I have fear
Or would it take me further from you,
Even further from, than here.
A new bridge is so unstable
For I've never seen it before
It feels as if I'm standing
At a never opened door.
A new bridge is so unstable
All the safety that it lacks,
I will try for the first step,
But I may come running back...

   William Carroll

Catharsis

The muse in me,
of me
is dying to get out;
to create
to live, love, to be loved and
accepted.

Do I dare?
There is a bitter lamentation
in my heart
and yet there is deep yearning
of my mind and soul to escape . . .
wash away and simultaneously unfold
a radiance of long host;
now,

new-found dreams and
creations
watch me
see me now
before I disappear there
here...before you!

   Karen B. Maloney

la belle dame sans merci

   it is the dandelion
     my love,
   so beautiful and full
   that chokes all chance
   of life existing around it

lone-blossomed-ancient-mask

marked by her she-wolf scent:
   Ishtar weaving a coarse
     yellowing veil
     hidden on
   her dimly lit corner

   of de-light

sashaying and praying
one-lone-lipid-drop
   lost in mud
our magnificent and conniving
   slut of weeds

oh-how-she-breeds.

   robbin thrush

The Four

Ten-thirty on a Saturday
When I heard that he was gone
Seized in the bathtub
And found by his mom

She was only thirty-two
Brought down by one she loved
Another child dies in vain
And now watches from above

He was a father to his daughter
But not a husband to his wife
He died an artist as he wanted
A final, open, second life

Poor, black, awake, alone
Cries the man in the hospital bed
I want a cigarette for breakfast
And now, he too, is dead

They were my patients
But more important, my friends
Untimely demise is all around
An unjust way to an inevitable end

   Frederick W. P. Gibbs

"Pretend"

One of the hardest things in life
Cannot and will not pass you by
If you would take some chances
It will ease the pain when you die
The burden is so strong
It will get the best of you
That's what we thought all along
Move on in life with laughter
It won't get the best of you
It grows more when it becomes
Your best friend through and through
Learn this now and it will say
Life is something that can end
When someone is not careful
As they live life to pretend

   Ken Rainbolt

Once Loving

Love is an angry sword
unthinking, without reason
friend and foe
do fall before it

In my breast
It found a home

What a pretty sword
lunging in my heart
would I want it
for it is pain
I do need it
for it is life

In my hand
a bloody rose
my soul
held aloft for all to see

A mocking laugh
a subtle smile
bringing death
to the child

   Jason D. Vinsonhaler

Wishing Well

"And if you throw a coin in,
you can make a wish . . .
And it will come true for you!"
They tell me.

My little childish eyes grow wide
And I peer down in the well.
The infantine reflection stares back
And the white clouds pass over head,
the sky in the water blue.

The copper pennies sparkle tempting
Among the copper fish
Nipping at the silver nickels
and the shiny quarters.

And in my chubby fist
I clench,
a dirty grubby dime
. . . Upon that solitary coin
I blink and make a silent wish

To be determined by the fish.

   Percy Waters

Tell Me Heart

Please tell me heart
where to begin,
if I follow you,
I'll be led to him.

And I'm scared to see
what will happen there,
for there is another
for whom he cares.

But there's so much I want
to say to him
each day I long
to be held again.

So, tell me heart,
what do I do?
Should I forget,
or follow you?

   Stacey Stratton

So Can You

No one knows when they are born
Even whats their name
The game of life begins right there
But for all, it's not the same

Some will rise to heights unheard
Power, fortune, fame
Some will spend their days in hell
Failure, sorrow, shame.

Though both the same beginning
It truly isn't fair
For if you're taught that yes you can
You're more than halfway there

But if you're told that no you can't
Don't aim your hopes so high
You will never really have a chance
And life will pass you bye

So let nobody keep you down
Let no one live for you
Know you can and then you will
Make all your dreams come true

Thomas R. Gilrane

On A Gust Of Wind

*round and round
like a piece of paper
on a gust of wind
searching for
a place to land
somewhere to stay
just a piece of something
wandering aimlessly
looking for a home
a place to be
. . . stop . . .
here comes another
gust of wind
. . . off again . . .
on another endless,
whirling ride
when will the winds cease
so that I may find a home
my home,
a place to be . . .*

Donna L. Dickinson

Scoured Away Memories

When the sky is dismal
with grey and dark grey clouds
it brings up painful memories.

And when the rain begins to fall,
it penetrates my heart
and forces me to remember.

It seems as though
the buried thoughts and memories
are found again.

Because the rain
washes away the dirt
that covers the graves of my memories.

And there they are
washed to the top
and with nothing for me to do . . .
. . . except remember.

April Ross

Untitled

In joy and final relief
I run around,
I sit, I lie down,
I roll, I stop,
I look around and breath deep.

The trees, the birds
and all the creatures
sing grateful in unison,
the wind blows
warm and gentle.

My chest is filled
with a strange pressure that bursts
in a song of laughter,
long forgotten.
I jump up, look around, again,
and fall to my knees
at peace with myself.

Roberto Martinez

Heroes

I say a prayer each night
for all the "Knights of the Highway",
that God will guide their hands
and keep them safe along their way.
May they get to their destination
as safely as they can,
for they hold the lives of others
in the palm of their hands.
They are the men and women
who drive up and down the road,
they criss-cross this country
just to deliver their next load.
Some people call them truckers
and others call them names
but to someone special out there
they're heroes without shame.

Anna M. Krol

Timeless

Two meet,
Love is One,
Christened by generations before,
The sands of time are stopped,
together within.
Souls entwined, the heart
is warmed only to reveal a
part of us, that shall never
be repeated.

Mark Dyer

Look Around

Look around
Look around
What do you see
Really see
The world around is not that clear
All we know is we are here

Below the waters
Above the trees
We don't know much about these

In the sky
Or underground
We don't know what might be found

What is this world
What does it mean
Is it really what it seems

Kristen McVearry

Freefall

The eyes inside my eyes are closed,
And, clearly still they see,
Me falling through to join the self,
I always knew could be.

She who knows a central truth,
And entwines it in my heart.
Who built a single being,
From a multitude of parts.

Jean A. Murdock

Poems

Some poems are sad some are blue
When you choose your poem see that
it fits the story of you.
Poems made you laugh and cry, some
made you get a tear in your eye.
Some tell a story, some sing a song
Poems are short and long. Poems
are great and always up to date.

Antoinette Nalezyty

Teddy Bear

If I had a special teddy bear
I'd hug him very tight
I'd put him under my covers and
Sleep with him all night!
We'd wake up in the morning,
Our hair would be a mess!
If I had a special teddy bear
He would be the best!

Jenna Dee Gebhart

The Hands

His hands are worn, cuts
and scars you see there. His
hands have worked hard, harder
than you and I dare.
His hands have felt pain,
and love too, his hands
have helped give life
and grasped death we
never knew. His hands
have been strong, now
with age they grow
weak. His hands would
tell you a lot if
only they could speak.

Donna C. Gaydosh

Dreams Fulfilled

Put nothing past the works of the
imagination,
Because when using it,
Nothing has to have an
explanation.

Don't give up on anything as unreal
as it may seem,
Although others may tell you
it is no more than a dream.

Just don't look back onto the past,
And only look forward into the future.
And keep in mind that;
Like a glass of water can be refilled,
A mind full of dreams can be fulfilled.

Christa Joachimi

The Wait

I sit patiently
  in the rocking chair
Its oscillations help
  spend the time away

My brain is numb
  with events passed
It fails to comprehend
  what is true and will last

The prejudices and conditioning
  of religion and society
have taken their toll
  on reason and sanity

The brain tried
  a balancing act
but failed in its efforts
  and now sits pat

I give up and stay
  in the rocking chair
waiting for the
  final act to play.

Ketan Desai

Flying

If I could fly
I would fly anywhere
I could fly to the clouds
And touch a cloud
I would hold it for a while
And then let it go
As I watch the cloud fly away
I could take a deep breath
And relax.

I would then catch a passing cloud
And rest on its soft white body
As if it were a pillow.

My mother would call me
And I would answer, "Coming!"
I could zoom back down to land
As I soar through clouds.

I would return home
And as I was lying in bed that night
I would dream about tomorrow.

Daniel Yang

Holly

Touch me and I stir,
Hold me and I feel wanted,
Kiss me and I die.

Tustin Ellison

Déjà vu

All the noise that use to be,
Are all precious long gone memories.
What my mind love to picture and see,
The long gone Hosts, Hostesses and me.
When we go down memory lane,
We some how always dispel the pains.
The little bodies we have borned,
Are all now grown and gone.
Rewards are the replicas
at family gatherings we see,
The Hosts, The Hostesses and me!

Vivian Noisette

Standing Next To Me

I wonder where my friend is at
His dog tugs at my knee
Up in the clouds or invisible
Standing right next to me?
Was that him in his car
Or shoveling neighbors snow for free
I wonder if he knows I carried him
To his grave by a sad looking tree
Is he listening, is he standing
Standing right next to me?
I just wonder where my friend is
If he's okay and things like that
I wonder if he's watching
But I know he's not coming back.

John Divers

My Savior

My savior took my hand
as he led me out to sea.
He took me where he knew I loved
and truly wished to be.
With chrism on the poor man's thumb
and faith with in my heart,
I crossed a hidden boarder
to where we could not part.
As now I guide my sister
as one once guided me,
my savior took my hand
as he led me out to sea . . .

Cheri Starr DeStefano

A Beloved Friend

I have a door into my heart,
That needs a special key;
There's only one can enter in,
And give his love to me.

I know I need to only call,
If joyous, lonely, blue . . .
And then while there he comforts me,
And gives me courage, too.

There's not a thing that I can hide,
He has such empathy;
While giving tenderness and love,
The secrets flow from me.

This love for him is so unique,
A lifetime one can wait;
To find a friend who understands,
My love I consecrate.

Shirley L. Jennétt

Love To Love

Lost in love and not emerging,
Vision dulled and wisdom purging,
Seeking where to gather strength,
Searching love from width to length,
When the searching finds no goal,
Trying then another role,
Finding there, as found before,
Non-acceptance evermore.

Needing love can make one bleed.
Love to love. Don't love for need.

Kenneth Kage

Words Unspoken

The wondrous sound of God,
calmness broken by the wind,
  blowing in the trees,
A light breeze catching my chimes,
  soothing and comforting
  like a soft whisper.
A beautiful sound to behold,
  the word of God in flight.

Janet L. Dearborn

Colors

Leaves are green
Snow is white
Birds are different
Colors I like the
robin the Best
the robin is red
the Blue bird is Blue
People are different
Colors too,

Sunil Pai

Mitt

Chalk-white knuckles
bordered with shadows,
extend from stubby follicles
blanketed by strands,
and pointed cuticles beginning
beds of quarter-grown dirty nails,
offer glimpses
of moon life.
As the bubbled lines
transport cells,
starting from dark red
base balls stabilizing
four extensions of bone
and flesh, the salty water
forms in the corners,
craving the smoked catch
of the day.
And the counter-side
clearly reveals
a winter-struck tree.

Judith Colonna

Change

The tides of time crash into the shore,
With everyday we are changing more.
The stream of life takes its toll
Ever changing the banks of our souls.
The minute meander of the river
Changes us but only a silver,
But the raging rapids and waterfalls,
Well, those change us all.

Robert Ramirez

Down Sizing

the company is down sizing
forced, early retirement
fear of the unknown
not enough money
his depression
my anxiety
our love
gone
no!
o!

Eileen Raymond

Love Song

My dearest darling, long ago
Before our ways entwined,
A little redhaired choir boy
Each Sunday one could find
Singing.

Freckled face, merry blue eyes,
Soul of my soul a part,
Grown up choir boy I love
You always send my heart
Singing.

Elaine Messenger

Its Love

They say we all must die
    Why?
They say it is Gods will
    Still
Would it not be nice to live forever
    Whatever!
Just be happy for here and now
    How?
Hey! Go on day by day
    Anyway
You can get along most anywhere
    So there!
Just believe when we die to go above
    Its Love.

Alice Clemons Beyer Van Cour

Knowledge

"Ignorance is bliss" they say,
But I don't feel that's so:
To totally remove yourself,
From a world that's on the go,

Not to see or understand
The good things from the bad,
Lack of knowledge on such things
is really very sad!

"I would that I knew not" I've said,
But that's not really true,
I want to know and learn and grow,
to see, to say, to do.

I think knowledge is important
If your use is wise,
To understand the truth in life,
And recognize the lies.

So pay attention, drink it all in,
And store it all away,
For learning all you possibly can,
Could save a life someday!

Janine S. Sarnowski

Black And White

Some see us differently,
some see the outside,
some see the inside,
and some only see black
and white.

We're all different,
our views aren't the same,
but those who only see
black and white need to
get their vision checked!

Amanda Gee

Secrets In The Night

Whistling wind through the trees
Tossing all the dead dry leaves;
Sending by a chilling cold breeze,
While sweeping in through the eaves.

Whispering of deep, dark secrets
That refuse to ever die;
Constantly breathing regrets,
Hidden beyond the night sky.

The pale glowing moon pearled
Casts down soft beams of light,
Illuminating the quiet world
Slumbering through the night.

And with the first rays of dawn,
The lurking secrets start to fade.
Though seemingly gone,
Will return with the dusk's raid.

Carolyn Lu

The Struggle

A journey unparalleled
Life's merry-go-round

Worlds within others, bound!
At times in conflict and harmony
Yours depends on autonomy
Secondary, outside influences

Ultimately determines circumstances?
People of diversity
Sustain life's complexities

Avenues along the way
Night and
Day
Delight Looms
Out of life's ruins
Weighs heavily
No
Steadily . . .

Fred Pease

In Memory Of . . .

At times like these,
It's better to have the power,
Not to grieve with each
withered flower.

Instead you should remember,
"Its" color which was so strong
— brilliant —
And "Its" life, which was
happy and long.

"Its" seeds have spread,
"Its" memories sustain,
And in your heart, "It" will
always remain.

Keri Lyn King-Stephenson

Dream My Friend

Dream my friend
Dream of what could be
It can.
Soar my friend
Soar high above the platitudes of doubt
Behold the graves of mediocrity
They ceased to dream.

Dempsey Collins

Rain. Rain? Rain!!!

It rained today
And I must say
It also rained yesterday
And tomorrow another day!

My yard's a mess
But I must confess
The rain's not to blame
I left it untamed

But flowers still bloom
So it's not all gloom
The trees still fruit
So neglect is moot

The rains still come
You son of a gun
Go way! Go way!
I want to play

This poem's my first
It came in a burst
I know this is terse
I'm not versed in verse.

Lucy R. Lockary

My Prayer

Lord, show me how to do things,
how to love, live and obey.

I need You to walk beside me,
and be with me every day.

I know there is more to life,
than just doing what others say.

With your help to love and guide me,
I know you can show the way.

Our life is short upon this earth,
there is no time to delay.

To teach the world about your love,
how to live and how to pray.

Robert H. Hoines

Spring's Welcome

Frogs Leaping
Water seeping
Ivy creeping
Flowers peeping
Birds cheeping
is Winter really sleeping
Welcome Spring

Shirley Pater

Untitled

Sleep on,
O Bethlehem, whose rooms and inns
are full of those who've come
to be enumerated for
the tax.
Sleep on,
oblivious to the needs of one
whose time has come,
who seeks a place to bear
her child.
Sleep on,
completely unaware of one who lies
among the animals in lowly manger bed,
One whose life will change
the world.
Sleep on.

Elmer E. Smith

Untitled

Driving me crazy
Is what you're doing
My every thought is of you
But the phone never rings

Your deep voice
filling my ears
Your strong hands
Touch my heart
I want to forget you
But I can't
I want to hate you
But I won't

Hope is all I have
For you are all I want
I want to feel your touch
I want to feel your breath
I want to hear your voice
Saying my name

Maria Sconfienza

He Lifted Me

He lifted me
From the darkness
Of the deep black hole.

He lifted me
To see the flowers
With colors of scarlet,
Majestic purples and the deepest golds.

He lifted me
To spread my wings like
The graceful mighty eagle.
To soar above life's toughest storms
And there find the pot of gold.

Judi Bishop

Is It?

Is it possible to hate others?
When indeed we dislike ourselves
Is it wrong to want possession?
When indeed we exploit ourselves
Is it love we share from our heart?
When indeed we fear to love ourselves
Truth is not ours to know as human

Andrea M. Holtgrewe

Untitled

No rainbow to follow the thunder
No sunset to watch at night
The moon, she'd hide her gentle glow
The wind, he'd steal my candlelight
The sea would toss its angry waves
No sparrow ever flew
Deep inside my soul would ache
Constantly, I searched for you
One day I heard you call my name
I thought it was my mind
I opened my eyes and saw you there
My heart no longer blind
I reached out and took your hand
I kissed your tender mouth
Our souls danced in unison
You are what loving is all about
Forever may breathe its last one day
And time may pass us by
Yet my love for you will endure
Long after eternity dies.

Lisa J. Iwig

Insanity

I am who I am
she said to me.
I'll never be any thing else.

I like you as you are,
I said.
That's quite alright with me.

I am insane you know, she said.
I've never been quite right.
People tell me all the time,
that my nut is not quite tight.

I completely understand
I said.
We're both in the very same boat.
Instead of being just a few bricks shy.
I'm missing the whole load.

Sherry Alyce Curzon

The Dandelion

I am beautiful
in the Sun's golden rays.
So sad
in the bitter cold of winter.
So alive
in the days of spring
mourning
the days of fall.

The wind blows and howls
at my petals
and laughs
when they turn to seeds and drift away
on the wind's soft breath
and I am left
sad, aloft, and alone.

Jennifer Manghir

Echoes

The brain is like an endless hallway
The door's locked until you show a key
The key, my friend, is a word.

A word can reveal to you the secrets
That are whispered though the hall
And echo from room to room
When they think you are not listening.

Listen for the echoes.

Erin George

Oregon Fog

Love's fresh footprints
Remain visible after,
Early morning tide

Harry L. Garnham

Gobble-De-Gook

The hills are tawny and russet
    With treelets of oak and of pine,
And a stillness hovers o'er us,
    While viewing nature's design.

Now seems a small part of heaven
    As we stride along for a shoot;
The turkeys today are elusive,
    And I've got a rock in my boot!

Ellen F. Spoon

Profession of Faith

to live
    to long
        to search

in the pain of experience
in the exultation of the spirit
in the communion of body and soul

to find
    to know
        to rise

to human heights on earth where

humility
    understanding
        love

acquire true meaning

at last to say
i have lived
i ask no more

Piero Braggiotti

Undecided

Me today or yesterday,
Perhaps even tomorrow,
I could change, but maybe not.

Do I like the clear of white?
Do I like the colors within black
Or colors between of gray?

What shall I wear today?
What did I wear yesterday
Or does it matter anyway?

Should I proceed left?
Should I recede right
Or merely out of sight?

I don't know what to do.
I don't know where to go
So, I do nothing at all.

The world is a mystery,
Or is the mystery within me?
Not knowing, I just let it be

Undecided, like me.

Linda Louise Smith

Your Gift — Your Life

Each day passes quickly
Each fleeting minute,
We must use this life
Put some effort into it —
Contribute something
To make our time here worthwhile
Give some stranger a hug — or
    just a smile!

We can give of ourselves
Give a gift free of cost,
To a soul who is hungry,
    abandoned, — or just lost

Spare just one minute —
Stop! — For like time,
We'll not pass this way again —
We have only THIS lifetime . . .

Shirley Ann Ford

366

Treasure

I have voyaged far
and farther
I must go

I have no map
no certain direction to go

Only my senses
my instinct
and
my heart
can guide me

I seek a Treasure
a wealth beyond
all
imagination and hope

A Treasure that would . . .
fill me with happiness
make my life complete

I simply seek
someone
to Treasure

David Pelloso

This We Ask Of You

The life once given
which now you take,
is our loved one so dear
the heavens await.

Keep him close in our hearts
like the closeness we shared,
for the distance between
is too much to bear.

Though our lives have been altered
our paths you've now changed,
keep our faith in you strong
while on earth we remain.

With our eyes now turned upward
it's to you Lord we pray . . .
May your strength and your love
be with us each new day.

Marianne E. Morris

Some Things Cannot Be Spoken

Only
the poet
knows

for a long
time
I forgot
I
was
a poet

There is this magnolia tree
with ring
of pink
camellias —
round
that
Gautama Buddah
never knew

Floralee Neff

"Sports"

Now it's that time of year;
when basketball is near.
It's the first time I've played.
And practice starts today.

I'm quite apprehensive and nervous,
but I'll give it my best shot.
I'm sort of excited; actually a lot.
I hope that we win.
If not it's a sin.

Next comes softball.
Pitch, hit, and run.
Before you know it, that's done.
Then comes soccer in
early fall.
Run, run, run go kick the ball.

Score a goal; help us win.
Then it starts all over again.

Shannon Castonguay

Why?

Why is love so hard,
Difficult and complicated.
It will change in an instant.
One minute you'll be flying,
On the wide wings of love.
The next,
You're drowning in a raging river
Of your own tears!
Why is love so hard to understand
And so hard to live without?
Love always seems so sweet.
But when it gets a hold of you,
It's pure torture.
No matter how much it hurts
You love every minute of it,
And you miss it when it's gone!
Why?

Melanie Combs

New Beginnings

Once I was angry,
But now I am not.
I sought out new battles,
And each one I fought.

Then one day I realized,
That anger is fear.
And all of the sudden,
My purpose was clear.

Now I live each day,
With one strong notion.
That in the eyes of the Lord,
There are only two emotions.

Those two emotions
Are fear and love.
I can willingly choose either,
With help from above.

Once I was angry,
But not any longer.
With God's love and guidance,
I grow ever stronger.

Virginia Kay Ponder

A Damp Encounter

You brought your mighty force
Upon my body
Drawing from it pulsations, sweat
And heat in a backlash
To your steaming pores

Our thoughts were fluid
Our eyes blinded
To what might follow
It was not love, mere lust
A damp encounter

People are meant to love
To touch soft and firm mass
To breathe in their aromas
It's clear that you prefer
Multiple, meaningless, damp encounters

I gave freely, you took greedily
We are both diminished
This diminution is costly to me
More like a drowning
A damp encounter!

Irene Senior-Pomeroy

Hope

Hope never gives up
she's like good luck
she never lets go
you better know
she never lets go her rope
she fights all of our battles
she's our everything
my faith is in her
when they least expect it
don't let go of your rope of courage
all you need is Hope
so hold on!

Kris Tubman

Untitled

Like a leaf,
the ammonia
of my mind,
casts the stem
from the branch.

Fallen from
the tree
a leaf's life
comes to
its end.

No more to live,
only fit for compost

Nenad Baiada

The Ring

How did America become
one massive boxing ring?
Peace has become
just a useless thing.

Gloves aren't used;
just knives and guns.
Society thinks
that violence is fun.

Be a leader
and leave the ring.
You'll be a champ
for doing the right thing.

Robby Couch

Shhh

Shhh. Listen. Do you hear that?
It's my heart.
Breaking.
Into a thousand tiny, tinkling pieces.

Shhh. Listen. Do you hear that?
It's my eyes,
Crying.
Soft, salty tears splashing my ink.

Shhh. Listen. Do you hear that?
It's my mind.
Dreaming.
Longingly looking for hope.

Shhh. Listen. Do you hear that?
It's my soul,
Singing.
Wrapped in warmth of new love.

Lynn M. Obenauer

Through The Years

Fading away are my memories
of my childhood days
drifting away in my mind
only to be unlocked at a later time
by a picture or a nursery rhyme
I would splash in the mud puddles
with my brother
and sit on a sandy beach
and make a magnificent sand castle
only to be washed away with the tide
close to my heart are those times
when I had no thought of time
and I could run and play
sweet and true are those days
that the world could never undo
but they slowly disappear
with time
in my mind

Holly Tompkins

Christmas

Birthday
Happy, joyful
Giving, cooking, enjoying
Birth of Jesus
Loving

David E.

Admirations

The sweetness of your laughter
the tenderness of your kiss
the time we spent together
forever I will miss

The depths of your eyes are endless
the beating of our hearts combined
pound with a force relentless
so sweetly intertwined

The words we leave unspoken
the silence that we speak
a most rewarding token;
it's anything but weak

The chances that we take
the fears we come to face
with you I chose to make
my partner in this race

Katie Campbell

Untitled

Night Seasons

the vision of the evenings
        indigo wings
with silky breath,
        the night
an arm's length off

smoky heat of day
        slips away,
in the velvet hand
        of night

hours thicken
        textures of sight,
details disappear
        coolness trembles
in the seasons of the night.

CC Chapman

A Phone Call

I called her tonight
my obsession
for the last time really

I was a little drunk
two beers and a
Byronic hero
emerges, watered down
Considerably

Tired of trying to
convince myself
I cared carefully

Embracing the lover
of aloneness
submit to her willingly

The click of the phone was final
decorated casket of a receiver
my emotions for her dead
Resurrected on paper

A poor epitaph for such
Infatuation

George W. Strine

Angel In A Pocket

*Dedicated To My Granddaughter On Her
13th Birthday*
You were an angel in a pocket,
Your mother said to me.
Tucked inside to stay a while
Your doctor did agree.

Then one day precious little one
You came into this world.
The oooh's and ahhhhhh's,
Were heard by all.
You knew they'd hear your call.

You held your Daddy's finger tight,
You tiny little girl.
He gave his heart to you that day.
That's where you will always stay.

You seemed to be an angel
Sent down by God above
To fill each heart that saw you,
With lots and lots of love.

Dottie Ferris

In Watchful Prudence

Dimly lit room,
Container of my present,
within your walls,
Protected, I reflect.

Of hearts resplendent,
Of naive youth,
Of passions burning,
Of simple truth.

Dimly lit soul,
Container of my past,
Remnants of lost loves,
In waiting, stealthily attack.

Of times gone by,
Of promises broken,
Of tears once cried,
Of words unspoken.

Dimly lit heart,
Container of my future,
The test of time upon you,
Enduring, in watchful prudence.

Jorge Montero

Teared

Teared
are the cords
on which the melody sounds
on your life.

Broken
like the wings of
a butterfly on the
winter-tree.

Trampled
the ash of your
youthful strength
united with the
black soil of the
years without you.
Teared
the dialogue
of our hearts.
Never

Rita Kasumu

"Forever After"

Forever after I watch the sun set
    Behind the hills afar.
Eternity awaits to take its place
    Forever after, we are.

Forever after the rain will fall
    Creating a rainbow of red.
Reminding me that you are near
    Forever after, it bled.

Forever after the stars will fall
    unto the earth below.
One fell the day you passed
    Forever after, It glowed.

Forever after the end of time
    I'll be there by your side.
If I can not see your smile
    Forever after, I cry.

Forever after our eyes met
    I fell in love with thee.
We shall meet in the heavens above
    Forever after, Eternity...

David L. Liddick

Say It

After the night is over
and daylight comes
will there be any tomorrows
for us?
Say there will be many.

Will the rushing hours
of this night
vanish our tomorrows
once it's over?
Say they won't.

To think that
all there'll be left
is only yesterdays
makes me want to alter time
and make this night last forever.
Say it will.

Anthony E. Mazzini

My Son Comforted Me

When the weariness
    was so heavy

That a straw could knock
    me off the cliff,
    spilling tears,
    too choked to talk

A sensitive 23 year old son
    asked what he could do to help
    taking me in his arms
    supporting me, wordless,
    with his love and caring

Already, he is parenting
    his parent.

Vonna L. Korb

Windweed

A windweed blowing in the air.
Catch it. No! It's over there.
Down the road it goes,
Down the road we go.
There's Sue's frog and toad.
Want to watch our funny show?
No way, we say.
Down to Gran's mill.
Gran says, help drill my mill?
No Gran, can't stop to drill lady.
Down to Tan's house.
Want to have a pet mouse?
Yop! We say, forget today.
There's the windweed, we're on our way.
Get it! Got it! Let's go play.

Kari Gayle Hensley

Regrets

I have broken
your china plate
with little pink flowers
and pastel green leaves like icing

I cried
on the floor
kneeling in the pieces
of shattered memories

Forgive me,
it was so dark
and so tragic
and so real

Anne Lucyle Lambert

My Mother A Forever Friend

I have a true forever friend
that's my Mother Mrs. Dorothy
Middleton
I thank God and give praise
for all the things she does.
I love and adore my mother
she brings me blessings like
God does. Mother when
there are dreadful days your
spiritual being especially, as a
great loving parent and a
Sunday school teacher. Gives
me peace and comfort to my
body, mind, heart and
soul. Mother you replenish
my desire and lack of fear,
blessed I am to have a
wonderful forever friend
And that's my mom
Mrs. Dorothy Middleton.

Wanda Lee Middleton

Untitled

During the troubling times,
The enemy tried to claim him

During the troubling times,
The seas tried to claim him.

After they were over and peace
was in the land.
Industry and aging made their
claims on him

Through seventy plus five years
He fought the claims on him
Mom and kids all six of us
We had our claims on him

And at last, good dad
could not defeat,
The greatest claim by HIM.

Patrick Bernart

In Memory Of Dad 1948-1996

You left without saying goodbye
I know you didn't want to leave
When I heard all I did was cry
And stayed in disbelief.

I will miss you. Never, will I forget
Didn't get to say I love you.
God, how I regret.

The days go by so fast,
How I wish you were here
My love for you will last
from year, to year, to year.

Someday we will meet again
What a lovely reunion it will be
To be together once again
Oh, what that would mean to me

Dad, I just want you to know
That you will live on
In my heart and soul
My love for you will grow
and grow . . .

Leticia Z. Zamora

Living For Today

Thank you Lord for the joy
Of living another day
Of sharing you with my loved ones
And friends along the way
For another chance to serve you
In the way that I know best
By a smile, a friendly voice
Or daily duties at my desk.

To live each day to its fullest
As if my last it were to be
In such a way that others Lord
Can see your love in me
To lay aside past memories
Both the triumphs and dismays
And live "today" as the tomorrow
That I dreamt of yesterday.

Martha Henson

To Grandmother With Love

As you life silently
No movement, no words
Not even a tear now,
. . . You cry inside . . .
God watched your hurt daily
Not eating, not walking
Only the feeling within
. . . you wanted to die . . .
I tried for your sake
To let go, to understand,
To want the pain you felt
. . . to go away . . . But then . . .
I find myself constantly reaching out
Wanting to hug you, to hold you
Telling you how much I love you,
. . . Never letting you go . . .
    And Grandmother
My love can't ever go away
It doesn't know how to leave!

Nanette L. Rahm

"Sis"

Yesterday has come and gone
Yet, it doesn't seem that long

I was young and you were too
What crazy things
We use to do

We grew up
And fell in love
We went our separate ways

Oh! How I miss those glory days

We still keep in touch
Though not as much

It's hard to find the words to say
How I miss you
Each and every day

You're still my closest friend
You always will be
'Til the end

I love you sis, gotta go
I just wanted you to know.

Rose Schuldt

Oceanscape

So moves the ocean
  see life
Paths with no beginning
  no end
The waves that ebb
  and flow
Sometimes with great calm
  others unsettled
As good being done
  good comes
Giving away precious love
  love comes
Oh joy to feel
  the peace
Overwhelmingly but then again
  washed away.

    Mary K. Marselas

Regrets

I have broken
your china plate
with little pink flowers
and pastel green leaves like icing

I cried
on the floor
kneeling in the pieces
of shattered memories

Forgive me,
it was so dark
and so tragic
and so real

    Anne Lucyle Lambert

While On Guard

Walking beneath the starry sky,
Watching toward the sea.
I guard my post for freedom
As my Savior speaks to me.
Over the pounding surf
His voice is very clear,
Reassuring me again
That He is ever near.
How wonderful it makes me feel,
How glad that I can say,
I love my Lord Jesus,
He is with me all the way.
So I'll guard my post for my country
And pray for all mankind,
For Jesus Christ is our only hope,
For He gives us Peace Divine.

    John R. Gates

A Little Brown Bear

A little Brown Bear

Is a snugly toy

As good for a girl
As it is for a boy

You an just sit and look at him
Or take him to bed
He looks cute and healthy
And never needs to be fed

You can dress him or kiss him
Wherever he's lugged
But the thing he likes best
Is just to be hugged.

    L. Mila Warn

A Feeling

Shivers up my spine,
  a feeling so divine.
My heart starts to flutter,
  as my body starts to shudder.
My mind gets lost in time,
  as my soul follows his rhyme.
What am I to do?
For we are meant to be two,
  and not one as I had so wished.
My chance at love was missed.
Heart to heart, soul to soul
  I felt so whole.
A feeling that came,
  and is now gone.
What went wrong?
Who's to blame?
I feel like a fool,
  life can be so cruel.
A feeling of love so true,
  only to turn out blue.

    Kristina Herring

The World Whispered

Even though you have chained
  and drilled
  and maimed
  and spilled
  and coveted
  and overtaken

Even though you have misrepresented me
  as your own creation
I will nevertheless receive your insult
  into my soil
offer rivers for your irrigations
claim what you have staked out
  and forgotten
and remind you of what you seek
for Love I inherit myself
  and am meek.

    Greg Hester

Angst

Suffering surrounds my soul
Jealousy jaunts and jeers
She is confused and cold
As time torments my tears.

    Jeremy Reed

Planet Of Peace

Why are we low like this?
Can we be civilized?
We're lower than we once were
Like a speck of dust
God gave us a choice
We should choose love and peace
We all need a planet of peace
Se we can live by ourselves
In peace and harmony
In this world
Grown men cry themselves to sleep
Infants are born into fear
We are all brothers and sisters
Living in the same family
The family of God
Waiting for a ride
To get to the planet of peace

    Christian Marcuzzi

Trees

I

Oh to
Be as

The one who
Can see the
Sun and air

Fill life full with
Warm rays calm wind
With soft rain upon
Soil that need care

Which bring forth flora grand
Fauna brave until man's trash
Kills ozone layer let's awake
Since earth alone can't bring
Forth green trees which lusts

And

Greed

Destroy

    Reuben A. Baybars

Alone

Alone I am
in this country
Which is not mine
I eat its bread
And work its soil
I love and sleep
And wake again
Alone
In this country
Which is not hire

    Tinake Questroo

For Brendan:

You are the gardener
we are the buds
that blossom into roses
with your tender care
You nurture us
and guide us
weeding our path
and feeding our souls

We come to you
as seedlings
unsure of our way
growing wild and unchecked

With a stern hand
and loving eye
you teach us to bloom
each becoming a wondrous rose

    Robert Ray

Un Poema Por Tú

My love my love
Without you there is no me
This love this love
So perfect, it cannot be.

Mi amor mi amor
Sin tú allí es no mi
Este amor este amor
Así perfecto, ello lata no ser.

    Carrie Callender

The Strongest Man I Ever Knew

The strongest man I ever knew rode horseback every day
Though not for fun or play or sport, he did his work that way
He wore a hat and boots and jeans and often a weary face
But he always did his best to please, and make a better place

His strength was not the kind you see displayed for public gain,
But in how he went to work each day, come sunshine or come rain
He didn't make excuses of his luck or nature's laws
And he never griped about his lot, though I think he had just cause

He's never used his strength in place of brains or common sense
He almost always practiced patience, and he built a lot of fence
He's raised and chased and doctored countless cows and kids and horses
And did the best with what he had, just minimal resources

His life's been filled with ups and downs, with disappointment, and with hope
But in the strength of his convictions, he finds ability to cope
He's worked from dawn till dusk each day, and hard I wish to add
I know this for a fact you see — this man, he is my Dad!

Boyd D. Moon

A Blessing

It's a blessing to study God's Word and talk to Him in prayer,
for the more we read God's Word the more we want to pray.
So the more we pray we will want to read God's Word.

It always strengthens us when we pray, and grace comes pouring in.
We may eat more than we should; we may go beyond our strength;
But we don't read God's Word too much, or pray enough.

Beulah Denney

The Hypocrite's Prayer

I knelt to pray when day was done and prayed, "O Lord, bless everyone"
"Lift from each saddened heart the pain, and let the sick be well again."
Then I woke another day and carelessly went upon my way.
I did not even go to see, the sick man next door to me.

And once again when day was done, I prayed: "O Lord bless everyone.
When suddenly I heard a voice: "Pause hypocrite, before you pray,
Who have you tried to help this day?"
"God's sweetest blessings always go, by hands that serve Him here below!"

Then I hid my face and cried: "Forgive me Lord, for I have lied."
"Please let me live another day, that I might live the way I pray."

Eursula Elizabeth Bryant-Van Alstine

Division At Matrimony

My love was twofold but divorced in wedlock,
My morals would only let me be true to one.
Marriage is forever, I couldn't let my thoughts dock.
I searched my love for the first, it was solid as rock.
My journey was excruciating and I wished it was done.

But I had to search my love for the other just the same,
Only to think this one may give superior interest.
This one was a bit more passionate and lit a hotter flame.
They were still equal in my heart, and this was no game.
I honestly knew my love for them was at the same crest.

On this day of my decision, they each unaware,
I'm prepared to ask the question that would bond us forevermore.
One of their hearts would be broken and thinking I didn't care.
The other happy and content never questioning my amour,
Once at the conclusion, eternally in all things we will share.

My choice has been made and I say this with a hit or a miss,
For all eternity a query will come when choosing a mate.
My love was twofold but divorced in wedlock, my choice was this;
I married the one that was a bit more pleasing at the "intimate bliss."
After considering everything, that is what made them separate.

R. Torry

Untitled

I love her
She does not love me
Only in my dreams
Does she have feelings for me

When I am awake
She is loving him
When I sleep
She loves me again

I wish to sleep eternally
Death is the wish
I grant for me

I believe society
Will be fine without me
Some may be sad
But not for long
She'll be with him
I will be gone

Robbie Sanders

Shave And A Haircut, 200 Bits

Thoughts drift back to childhood days
    And Dewey decimals when
I contemplate this dollar bill
    Was worth a penny . . . then.

Achievement of a lifetime!
    (By the Yew Ess Government)
They almost squared the circle
    When they wrectangled the cent.

Ralph J. Langsjoen

Winter Wonder

The snow was gently falling
so soft, so cold, so white
it fell silently down ever faster
in the cold and dark of night.

The children saying their prayers
the windows all shining with light
the fireplaces blazing merrily
in the cold and dark of night.

The world outside all covered
and "Oh" what a beautiful sight
the air so crisp and clean
in the cold and dark of night.

As the dawn came slowly stealing
over this wonderful world of white
it changed to a beautiful morning
from a cold and dark of night.

Madelyne Long

"Beauty"

What is beauty?
It's a sunrise just breaking
It's a flock of geese, in formation
It's animals, playing all about
It's the wind, rippling a field
It's a lawn, just freshly mowed
It's two skater's, upon the ice
It's people, hustling all about
It's a sunset, just at dusk
    What is beauty?
    It's — Life

Donald L. Henley

A Poem For Jenny

It seems like only yesterday,
You were running out to play.
Life was happy and you were well.
Then everything blew apart.
The day they told me you would die,
I didn't scream. I didn't cry.
They must be wrong I told myself.
We will get through this, wait and see.
Now you have been gone for one whole year.
I thought I was prepared.
Should I have told you what was to come?
Or were you already aware?
I still expect to find you in your room.
I still listen for your voice.
I can't believe you're really gone!
If I'd only had a choice.
It seems like only yesterday,
I held your hand and heard you say,
I love you Mom, can I go play?
If only I could hear that today.

Susan Cullom

The Bright Light

A bright light emanates from the wounds of
all souls creating passages to new beginnings.
It shines for the hope of tomorrow and for the
faith in healing old memories. It leads us
forward unto crossroads where the truth may
be found and where destinies, which were once
hidden, may be discovered. To the one without
fear of darkness, the morning dew of day to
follow will quench the eyes of wonder and will reveal
the glimmering visions of all the joys to come. The
rays of the sun will reflect off the depths of the
heart and freedom of all emotion will soar with
wings upon the brisk wind that whispers soft melodies.
Songs to which the rhythm for waves dance, will
flow vigorously through the veins of revelation
and through such enlightening motion will come
balance upon the shores of the soul. And like the
weightless sky, love will flourish, lifting up and
above all dreams with an eagerness to release the
fleeting spirit into a world of open consciousness.

Paula M. Pagano

Everyday Is Special

Love and compassion fill you home
it's family and faith
that give you strength
to see clearly
what matters so dearly
it's family and faith

Just when impatience takes over
and masks what matters
in your heart you know
everyday is special

Your empathy and understanding
are stronger than the tears inside of you
your love and compassion
are stronger than the things
that you don't show
there is only the present moment
and in your heart you know
everyday is special.

Sheila Ina Kahn

My Aching Back

I woke one night with awful pain.
Arthritis struck my back again!
With water hot I filled my tub:
I had to soak before my rub
I loved the smell of Old Ben Gay.
The modern rubs don't smell that way
I rubbed and rubbed and rubbed some more
my aching back was still as sore.
That minty smell? I'd goofed again.
Tooth paste just was not meant for pain?

Albert J. Obrecht

Apart

Since we've part time has stood still.
A path I must travel against my free will.
The days last forever the nights do to.
I wish for the past, to start yet anew.
Minutes like hours, hours like days.
Your memory consumes me, I'm lost in a haze.
What can I do? What should I say?
I'm feeling so lonely, it won't go away.
How can I cope? Is the question I ask.
Maybe with time these feelings will pass.
I feel so depressed, and become so withdrawn.
I pace the floors nightly till day breaketh dawn.
Your memory lives on alive in my heart.
These thoughts are so precious, I can't bear to part.
We're bonded together, our hearts and minds too.
Without you I'm nothing, what am I to do?

Cozmo

The Good-Doers Club

The meeting was called to order.
Members pledging to honor their creed:
"We will show kindness to everyone
And each day do a good deed."
"Say, Amy isn't at the meeting, yet.
Mark my words, she's having an affair.
A man was walking her down the road.
She was all dolled up even crimped her hair."
"What did he look like?" "Was he old?"
"Knew he was able, he held her arm tight.
His shirt was blue, think his eyes were, too.
Bet some skull-duggery went on last night."
Amy entered the hall, quite out of breath.
"Sorry I'm late. Hope I didn't cause a fuss.
Had a bite to eat and just waited around
Til my brother boarded the out bound bus."
"Oh! Amy, Dear, we thought you were ill
Just making a motion to send you a shrub.
Alas! The disillusioned members carried on
The old and new business of the Good-Doers Club.

Norma K. Shea

The Chase

Why do you tease, then run and hide your face.
Why do you visit me, dressed in silk and lace.
Why do you call my name, then act like you don't know me.
If you're real, then reveal yourself and show me.
I long to know you,
I long to hold you,
I long for your embracing.
I hope that one day this game will stop.
So that you I don't have to keep chasing.
You bring with you, beauty like a rose,
And great peace like a dove.
The one I've been chasing after, is the mere thought of love.

Joshua Jordan

Robots

Robots of Society with no feelings at all.
Robots that have hearts of stone.
Robots that have souls gone dark.
Robots that stay at one level of darkness.
Robots that never grow into the eternities.
Robots that refuse the light of truth.
Robots that live in dwellings spread over the landscape.
Robots that express emptiness.
Robots that lose compassion for fellowman.
Robots that forget about life's grandeur and beauty.
Robots that forget to love one another.
Robots that exist with nowhere to go.

Robots that go back and forth over the crossroads of life.
Robots that live in there own vacuum, refusing to feel life.
Robots that know only one direction in life.
Robots that are caught up in the merry-go-round of life.

Carol-Ann Swatling

Yesterdays Past

I drove up an got out, and walked inside to
get a drink, as I looked around, I saw an
old man sitting in a rocking chair looking out
the window,

He looked up said, mister, I seen days of
the free, when the tumble weed rolled across
the plains, I've seen the blue grass where it
swayed to an fro,

Yea looking out the window of yesterdays past,
the window of yesterday, yea yesterdays gone,

He said, I seen rolling streams, an tall pine
trees, the place where the indians used to
roam with the buffalo, an the clouds hung low,
an the mountains were distant,

Yea he was looking out the window of the past,
yesterday past, yea out the window of the past,

As I stood there listening and looking, I thought
about a place and a girl, I thought about a
window of the past, yesterdays gone.

Patrick E. Leath

My Flower Garden

I planted a garden of flowers,
I worked for hours and hours.
I dug up the soil and dropped in the seeds,
I pray that my garden is free of all weeds.

Then I sat and waited a while,
I watched one certain little pile.
It did not move, it did not shake,
How long must I wait, how long will it take?

Then the rain came pouring down,
The seeds all snug beneath the ground.
Along came the sun, so warm and bright,
Dark clouds disappeared, and in poured the light.

But then in the soil, I saw a break,
"Hurray!" I thought as it began to quake!
Then the break grew and there I saw,
A little stem, not very tall.

Not one, but many were peeking through,
Suddenly my flowers were red, white, and blue!
So many flowers, bright colors galore,
Who could ask for anything more?

Shannon Metzler

City Slickin' Friend

Born and raised in a city, of country life I was not aware
Although I was pretty sure that country horses needed care.

My friend was searching for a room mate a hundred miles away
She came in search of me, asking, "With me would you stay?"

I said to her, "On one condition; the chores we both will share."
To her delight she answered, "that is super and that's very fair."

Although she too lived in a city, she was a country girl at heart
And I learned that a horse was included in her country part.

Little did I know chores included the cleaning of a barn
Where Red, the quarter horse, lived - to myself I said "Darn!"

One Winter's day the full wheel barrow I pushed from
Red's fragrant stall
And wouldn't you just know it, over the knoll, my balance lost,
I took a fall.

Fertilizer then surrounded me with no place for my hands to go
Oh how I wished, just then, to be sitting in a pile of drifted snow.

My friend peered from the window as cries of help
seemed to have no end
She laughed her way around the barn and gave aid,
to her City Slickin' Friend.

E. Carole Smith

A Thousand Years

If I would live a thousand years,
I'd want to live each day with you.
I'd let you know and all who hears,
How much and truly "I love you".

If you should live a thousand years,
I'd want you always near to me.
I'd share with you your sadness tears,
But most of all your love and glee.

If we should live a thousand years,
We'd have a thousand girls and boys.
We'd love each child through all the years,
Receiving from them cheers and joys.

But if we live ten thousand years,
My love will be ten thousand more.
I'd tell the world I have no fears,
Of loving you forever-more.

Ralph Hayashi

Fear

The fear, the pain in my heart flows deep
It tugs at everything I am and burns in my soul
Like a torch to a flame
The fear is deep in my heart
Far below the surface, to far out of reach

You can't heal it, or see it, or feel it
It won't disappear with a soft touch or gentle kiss

The fear shoots through my body
Like a hunter's bullet to the heart of his prey
The pain serges to my heart, grips my soul
And won't let me feel no matter how desperately I try

You can't heal me but don't abandon me
Reach out hold me close
I wish I could let you feel my fear see my pain
My heart won't let me tell you I'm scared
My arms want to reach out
But my heart pulls back

I can't let you inside to see my pain
Feel my fear, it takes away my mystery
It takes away me.

Christine Mary Kilday

373

"Awakening"

God-like, child-like
Tell me, man, what's it like?
To live in a world
Free of all tears
Free of all harm
And free of all fears?
Rains flood the city, stopping time in its place
You go about your routine with the sun on your face
Bombs are being dropped, AIDS is killing the nation
Least of your concerns on your three week vacation
One day, the world will catch up to you
When you least expect it
Find your fears and weaknesses, turn you inside out
Make you eat your words, take back your actions
Love your neighbor, open your eyes
The world is turning
You'll start to feel it
When He doesn't come for you
I know you'll start to feel it.

Kevin Bastian

The Tree

It stands out in the meadow
and all the memories it brings
like the picnics we had under it
and I'll never forget the swing

We played games like hide and seek
as it was always the base
Oh my first broken bone
when I fell and hit my face

The time it was struck by lightning
we thought it would burn to the ground
but like magic something saved it
it was the talk of the entire town

And there is always a favorite memory
but mine I can not tell
It was Barbara Ellen Walker
such a sweet southern country bell

Now today the memories will end
cause they're cutting down the giant oak
and this place will lose a monument
Thanks to them city folk!

Brad Mooney

"Making It To Heaven, I Might"

I sit in the shadow so cold and alone,
There's no one around and no one at home.
I have no friends, no one who cares,
and no one to tuck me in at night,
but I'll always pray that, making it to heaven, I might.
The summer's are long and the sun's so bright,
I don't know if I can make it through tomorrow,
or if I can even make it through tonight.
But I'll always pray that,
making it to heaven, I might.
The summer has gone and winter has came,
and it seems as if no one knows my name.
I'm cold and lonely and have no place to sleep,
I begin to cry and then I weep.
I stare at the stars they're so bright,
Then I begin to pray that,
Making it to heaven, I might.
My time has come, what a beautiful sight,
My prayers have been answered and everything's alright,
Because I made it to heaven, that night.

Mark Bartley

"Obsidian Brilliance"

The night sky beckons with a gentle turn from day to dusk, and
all the cares of the bright, loud world become a mere bother.
More nights than many have I spent beneath these stars, from
Orion's winter splendor to the autumns harvest moon.
A fleeting nocturnal wind slips past my being, bringing scents of
a living world; grass and leaves, soil and dampness.
The clear, brilliant night looks on, noticed by so few, still
concerned with the thorns of their daily lives.
Deeper in the night, an owl calls out from its perch, asking
questions of the surrounding wonders.

Todd A. Bouverot

The Pearl

I've uncovered a pearl, a pearl so rare;
But what can I do with it, I've not a nickel to spare,
I could put it under glass, for the world to see,
but what good would that do, for anyone but me,

I could polish it up, and make it shine like a gem,
but its real beauty lies in the condition it's in.
I could leave it, or sell it, or show it in town,
I could take bids on this beautiful pearl that I found.

Why did I find it, and what should I do?
I'm holding it right now, I think I'll give it to you.
Its real beauty lies in what only you see,
so when you are finished, please give it to someone for me.

It's in the shape of a poem, and it sounds like a song.
You must except it now, for I must move on.
Just remember, you could polish it, and make it shine like a gem,
but its real beauty lies in the condition it's in.

John Hilligoss

To My Dear Bonnie Jean

Forty nine short years have passed
Since Mother Vivian made a baby book.
As you can see . . . it did not last!
These pieces prove it . . . take a look.

Now it's time to salvage and re-do
These pretty cards and snapshots so dear.
With scissors in hand and a bottle of glue
It'll all come together . . . have no fear!

So on your special day may you be blessed
With a very special measure
Of birthday joy, fun and gladness
And a new baby book to treasure!

Remaking this baby book has brought some tears . . .
Wishing I could go back to those years
To hold Bonnie Jean in my lap,
Or lay her down for an afternoon nap,
Or to ride her in her buggy down the block.
But I'd rather hold her in my lap to rock!
Making this new book was my intense endeavor,
Knowing my love for Bonnie Jean will last forever!

Vivian Schafer

The Visiting Place

My intuitiveness overwhelmed me as Silence was
Seducing my slumber
Somewhere — someplace — something was going on
Causing chaotic disturbances among the still warm air.
I became comatose as the glare of the clock screeched
Stop! before my eyes
Not know where, rather am I here? Again?

Kirsten E. Forczek

Who Am I?

You think you know me, don't you?
Well, think again, because you don't
No one really knows me, not even me.
You only see a part of me, others see another.
I see them all, but I don't yet know which one is me and which ones
are just facades, that I put on to hide others from you.
Why must I hide them?
You ought a know by now, all your double standards are driving me insane!
Tell me who you want me to be and I'll try my best to please you.
Perhaps you won't see that it isn't really me.
If I act one way you'll laugh, if I turn into another you'll get
confused and scold.
I simply can not please you and soon will stop trying.
But that will be hard for me because I'm working so hard on who you
want me to be.
The funny me, the somber me, the friendly me, the introverted me,
the snotty me, the accepting me, the moody me, the ditzy me, the intellectual me,
the me people like to see, or the me I used to be.
You've distorted my view of myself, I feel like I'm looking into a fun house mirror.
I've worked so hard on being "The acceptable me," that I'm caught
between being her and being the old me.
I would like to be acceptable, but what will you accept?
And what you accept, others might not, what they accept, I might not.

Is my confusion understandable?

Jayme Childers

Spring

Walk in the woods today the first of Spring
Tread carefully amongst the pale primrose.
The bluebells have appeal but do not ring.
Between exposed elm roots the soft moss grows.

Hear the calls and shrieks of nesting birds.
The sound of breaking twigs as each foot moves.
Soft mating calls each with those special words
That seek the male response if she approves.

Watch the crafty fox steal from his lair,
With tail held high, the pride of horse and hound.
The mole, the weasel and impatient hare
Seek warm and tunneled quarters underground

Man should find example in this scene.
Nature maintains a balance in her demesne.

Ronald O. Hardy

A Woman

What is a woman? Well, she is earth and sky.
    A woman is every part of the universe:
Sunset's fire is in her eyes,
    and he was consumed by it.
And Starfire burns in her heart,
    giving life to her dreams.
Her skin is the pale moonlight,
    and her touch is the gentle rain.
Hair like the finest silk,
    flows like a waterfall to her shoulders.
In her smile are the stars of heaven,
    put there to brighten the darkest nights.
And he came to bathe in the light,
    and was overcome by the power.
The nights grew colder,
    but his passion was an inferno of desire.

A woman is many things, but most of all, a woman is special.
    She deserves all that any man could offer.

Brad Gray

"I'll Sweep Her Off Her Feet"

She has dusted her reflections
Of her clean, just polished day.
She has shined through good intentions
So mopped-up along the way.
She has washed away her sorrows,
Waxed her new found dreams,
Scoured new tomorrows,
She's been swept away, it seems.
She has scrubbed some shining faces,
Neatly tucked away.
Darned near ran her through her paces,
As she picked up come what may.
She has mended broken promises,
She has folded broken dreams.
She has ironed-out some problems,
While vacuuming, it seems . . .

Measuring her yesterdays,
And, cooking 'til we meet.
She'll wring her hands,
And, honestly, I'll sweep her off her feet.

James E. Mason Jr.

The Little Girl Inside

So I hold my shoulders straight
    and my head up high
The little girl inside of me, just
    breaks down and cries
So I put on an act of being
    strong and bold
The little girl inside of me screams
    for security, for someone to hold
There's no one for me to turn to,
    no one for me to tell
The little girl inside of me, is the
    only one to understand my true life of hell
I want to, but I can't, run
    and hide
Because the only one there to listen
    is the little girl inside

Angie E. Barbour

The Great Flood Of '94'

The flood of '94'
had never happened before.
It didn't knock on any door,
but came and covered every floor.

We all had to evacuate, we didn't have time to wait.
We got into out cars and wanted to leave the state.

For awhile we didn't know what to expect,
but we knew our homes were in a wreck.
So we waited to return to inspect,
and found our homes filled with insects.

We felt sad, even mad,
and everywhere we looked things looked bad.
We had to remember whose children we are,
and that our Father is not far.

He knew that we were in a daze,
but still he waited on our unlimited praise.
As our faith and trust begun to grow,
we knew that restoration would be slow.
But without any doubt we knew within our core,
that we would rise above the flood of '94'.

Alfreda D. Williams

Personal Pronouns

Thirty years are going by this year.
You and I, I and you, but mostly you
Until I found an I stuck in myself.
This I that I am rediscovering
Had been buried and left a-smouldering
In manic ruins of a war called World War Two.
You were big, ready to fight as a 90-day wonder.
I was small, playing hookey. Air raids and bombs
Couldn't touch me.
When we met at the crossroads of broken hearts
My baffled I, I gladly laid a-slumbering
Under the wings of my soldier, you.
But the I of my thorn that stuck inside me,
Started swelling and wanted out.
You took care, waited valiantly.
I am still bewildered and feel so tender
After finding out what kind of an I
I had carried with me the day I met you.
It is eager to grow to become the we
That I so anxiously wanted for us.

Adriana Millenaar Brown

Forever

I never will regret — my decision as of yet
To stay by you forever more;
As long as lives fade away
And children yearn to play,
As long as the sky above is blue
And the truth is always true,
That's how long I will love you;
Until the end of time and through.
As long as sunsets inspire poets to write
And a gentle wind nudges baby birds into flight,
As long as loss brings a tear
And the unknown causes fear,
For just as long I will hold you dear,
For just as long — year after year;
As long as war causes death
And a man's first real regret is his last breath,
As long as humans wonder why
And unjust pain makes people cry,
I promise you — this is no lie;
I will love you until I die.

David Josef Volodzko

Memories Of Love

Losing someone dear to your heart, has made tears flow
They say, each day will be easier to bare, "this only you know"
Whether you hold in your loss and pain, or whether you cry aloud
Remember this, one day you will see them again, beyond God's blue clouds
Memories of someone can be happy or sad
Remember, you special loved one would not want you heart to feel bad
Please remember this, think of them and remember the love
They are in God's hands, in the heavens up above
They would not want your heart to ache
Because, in God's open arm, "your loved one" He did take
They would want you to keep loving memories
Of them so strength may come from within
Please know that they would not want you to go through life being sad
They would want you to think of the good times you had,
So when you think of them you will fell not sad, but glad
We know you will miss them, with all of your heart
Remember them, and in your life, they will always remain a loving part

Deborah Renee Shaw

Pathways Of Life Renewed

The energy in my soul burst forth.
I see the wheat blown all directions,
like my soul drifts north,
ever so deeply in love with earth's old erections.

The oak tree that stands alone,
in the field and shades the babbling brook,
my soul it took.

The twisting and turning of the crystal clear water,
smoothly running down the rocks,
the invitation I took.

This makes my soul renew itself,
for I too want to run through the wayward wind,
blown wheat fields,
I too want to play with the brook.

I will splash through the cold running water,
play upon the huge stones,
for I am one willing to risk pathways unknown and feel renewed.

Shirley J. Bierly

For Anyone Who Is Having Problems . . . Written From Experience . . .

I really don't know . . .
When you tell them about a problem all they
tell you is so.

They make rumors about you that aren't true,
when you talk to people who really aren't
friendly, you don't have a clue.

You can run away from your problems
but that won't help when you
should've stay with yourself and kept.

You can't really trust no one and
that is a fact, if they tell your
stuff them turn you back!

Kathreda Whipple

Time Is Fleeting

Time is fleeting, and one lost day soon becomes two;
To be wise,
Pluck flowers yet sprinkled with dew.

Seconds, minutes, hours too often turn to
Idle moments, and the clock cries
Time if fleeting, and one lost day soon become two.

Linger not on fond memories, those precious few,
Nor let reminiscence hypnotize;
Pluck flowers yet sprinkled with dew.

Fancy not of chimeras to wild to come true,
For daydreaming is evil in disguise;
Time is fleeting, and one lost day soon becomes two.

There is no eternity for intentions to brew,
For in old age potential withers, then dies;
Pluck flowers yet sprinkled with dew.

On each day that starts anew
A chance for greatness may arise.
Time is fleeting, and one lost day soon becomes two.
Pluck flowers yet sprinkled with dew.

Hannah Swinbank

M e

All I see of me,
Is a tall, dead, shriveled, tree.
Dutch elm disease crept up its branches.
Cold, dead, chipping and peeling,
Wholly revealing,
Worms holes and grubs nests,
Termites, ants, and other pests.
Nibbling away with tiny beaks,
All until the sap leaks.
Rotten-yellow at the base,
Gnawing all with rapid pace.

Alone I stand in desolate wilderness,
No other tree abandoned like this.
Wasting away as some rotted log,
Streaked bark, evidence of flog.
Isolated and worn this is me.
An ugly, tired, tree of seventeen.

Diane Hernandez

The Jaguar

Click!
The jaguar growls,
then purrs with contentment.
Sleek, moving swiftly through the urban jungle,
quick and powerful,
it easily overtakes its adversaries,
the Lexus,
the BMW, and the Mercedes.
Navigating through the narrow,
treacherous territory,
and the thick foliage,
the forestation festooned with flickering red and green lights.
Careening through the concrete clearings,
it swerves in and out of
the scenery shadowed by the surrounding skyscrapers,
until it stops,
screeching to a halt,
screaming its fury to the bystanders on the side walk.
Strong and fierce,
it is as mighty as ever.

Michael Sun

Grease

Grease,
The silent predator.
Watching you.
Waiting for you to make a mistake
Waiting for you to pick up that last piece of fried
Chicken.

Down he goes,
Into your arteries,
Clogging them up.
You should have listened,
Now it's too late.
Aren't you sorry you over ate?

Tamara Turner

A Curtain Made By God

As I look out my window at night, I see the beautiful curtain made by
   God's might,
He sewed on it the moon and stars, and placed in it the planets,
Venus and Mars.
It is only open during the day, when all the folks are at work or play,
It is closed at night and shut very tight,
Until once again drawn and night changes to dawn.

Richard A. Kuenster

Baseball: My Life

I was born and raised to play the game.
I hope someday it will bring me fame.
I've played ever since I was 6 years old.
I'd play in the heat, or even the cold.
I've played 10 years of competitive baseball.
There is not a game that I do not recall.
I learned how to play from a remarkable guy.
If I could I would play till I die.
I was taught all of this as just a young lad.
This man is a good coach, and even a great dad.
Now I'm older and in 5A high school.
If I were to quit now, I would be nothing but a fool.
I have a good inspiration, that's my mother.
She's taught me morals like an older brother.
Now all I can do is build up my skills.
And give my Mom and Dad unbelievable thrills.
After baseball comes a family with a gorgeous wife.
They will know that Baseball is my Life!!!!

Ricky A. Garcia

Twilight

The Freaks gather in the entrance hall to await the final test.
They shoo their children off to the stage
Where they will soon become unknown specks of darkness
Hanging somewhere above the stratosphere.
The Freaks drink coffee and tea and dine on small animal teeth.
"One at a time, please, one at a time."
A goblin eyes the mongoose head of the vendor selling tea.
You couldn't trust those mongoose people.
That's why you bought a cup of coffee, but instead of drinking it
You put it in your pocket and took it to be analyzed.
The hall shudders.
"Don't be alarmed, folks, everything's fine."
A piece of sky falls and crashes through the ceiling,
Landing on a small group of tigres.
The Freaks rush for their vaccinations, their free hearing tests,
their sun screens.
Through the hole the insects swarm (Don't be alarmed)
The northeast tower has fallen. The Medicine Men were wrong (right)
Praying to their false gods, the Freaks prepare for the rain.
And the Nacirema lower their heads.

Daniel R. Dowell

My Reasons For Loving You Babe:

You're the other piece of my puzzle they call love.
When I'm having it hard you always pick me up.
You see what no one else can see sometimes it even baffles me,
But then I feel the love down deep inside.
Something that our hearts just can't deny.
I love you more than anyone else,
and sometimes I just can't help myself.
You are the one who makes my skies stay bright.
And in our kids I see your face your sweet sweet smile,
and soft embrace, and then I know deep down the reasons why.

Kristina Robertson

Wrong Eternity

As I look at the television. The picture
bends and pulls. Is it the drugs or
is life finally killing me. I try to
Straighten the bends but they just
Wrap around my hands. There are Blue,
Red, Green, and White squares in the
bends and pulls. All of them wink at
me and tell me to join them. I tell
them no then pull the trigger. Now all
I will see is Red for all eternity.

Christopher Gene Steinkraus

Wales Tales

Brown Bear sits on the table now after years of constant use.
He's traveled with his "bestest" friend, despite unmeant abuse.
His body once round, now lies flat. His arms splayed out so wide.
His face is crushed; his torso thin from being at the side
of his young owner, constant friend; his buddy through and through.
From infancy through preschool years, to give Brown Bear his due.
As Bear grew older, he got used to being set aside.
His boy had other things to do, which filled Brown Bear with pride.
His boy went off to school to learn the things he'd need to know;
to face the world without Brown Bear, continuing to grow.
The day will come to put away Brown Bear and other toys
to join the grown-up world of life and leave the world of boys.
But Brown Bear will have done his job, have served a useful life;
the wear and tear of joyful years, the trail of pain and strife.
From bed time pal to confidant, to playmate and to friend,
Brown Bear has always been around, a buddy to the end.
So on the shelf Brown Bear will sit, his coat of brown worn thin,
but ready if the need be there, to calm the fear within.
For Brown Bear give a warm embrace, his love he does release,
Security, relaxed repose, true comfort and true peace.

Alexander H. Wales

Memories Child

Thou art unseen, yet I hear and see you.
You are in the earth, the air, the deep blue of the sky,
Like a star in Heaven.
What sympathy we have is for self.
We look before and after; and cry for what is not.
We laugh but with pain.
We have felt pride, hate, fear;
If we were not of God then we couldn't shed a tear.
For I've found sadness turning to joy.

Memories outweigh our grief.
Remembrances of kindness and love give us harmony,
And we see into a presence of thought
That will keep you ever near
Where you are dwelling now is love and light with setting sun.
Therefore, let the sun shine on me on my solitary walk,
Feeling the winds blow about me,
Filling me with sounds of harmony.
Though absent, you are always with me.

Eleanor E. Powley

Supernova

Coming from the Timeless space, Dei Gratia
through the Infinite darkness and emptiness
She had a brighter face than billions of Suns
carrying Sunshine and Oxygen in Her bag
bringing the ultimate Genesis upon Time
Supernova! The beautiful Angel of Life!
The unique Explosion, that was so constructive!
Creating the Stars, the Planets and the Sun
the Lakes, the Oceans and the Mountains!
The Chromosomes of my own, hidden in a crude,
untouched Substance as an Archaic gift to the first Man.
The Nucleus of a young apple-tree,
sprouting from the Soil.
Supernova! The beautiful Angel of Life!
Who gave to me Her pretty face to be a Human
and the Harmony of the great Cosmos
by implanting into my Tissues its Miniature!
I'm waiting for Your new arrival again
to see Your innocent, Apocalyptic face!
Remaining as a little part of the Universe, I'm the Universe, itself!

George E. Rhymstett

I Am A Woman

I am a woman of color I found
I am a woman of mind, body, and sound
I feel the presence of nature in me
Though its power I can not see
I am a woman, pretty and bold
I see me as young, you see me as old
I've been around for many years
I've been around to shed some tears
I see the pain in everyone's eyes
The pain stays there for she never cries
I am a woman, graceful as ever
You can't blow me down, I'm not a feather
I am a woman and not a child
In my heart I'm young and wild
Their clothes they always want to us to mend
I am a woman, my job will never end.

Jennifer Evans

A Birthday Surprise

A little girl with golden hair;
A little birthday with fun to spare.

A white silk dress with a bow in her hair;
She walks down the hall with wonder and care.

When she walks in the room what a sight
She sees there.

Presents and music is in the room and
Shouts of "Surprise!" fill the air.

Sarah Beth Weidner

Mother's Day

Who wipes the nose? Who picks up the clothes? It's Mom!
Who cares for the sick? Who gets them well quick? It's Mom!
Who makes the meals? Who does the kids' apple peel? It's Mom!
Who does the dishes? Who remembers birthday wishes? It's Mom!
Who dusts and cleans? Who cans applesauce and beans? It's Mom!
Who does the washing and ironing?
Who settles the kids' fighting and whining? It's Mom!
Who cares for knees cut or swollen?
Who often has goodies in the oven? It's Mom!
Who is it that does all these things?
Who is it that love and joy brings? It's Mom!
Who is it that we cherish and treasure?
Who is it that we love above all measure? It's Mom!
Who would we all like to say "Hope you have a nice Mother's Day."
    It's us — your family.

John Kemper

Music And Morals

The king is dead, to the dogs his
Bones were fed. His mind and
sole to the fire's were fed.

God was alive. His philosophy
will survive. All our lives we will derive.

The king is dead, his followers
to the sea were lead.

The king is dead, and God's
philosophy will survive.

Nathan H. Schweitzer

Heartstorm

Sun sets; day-heat shimmers, lours, drifts;
thought flickers like heat lightning across a private sky.
A tensioned stormfront builds,
grey/blue/black walls of hanging energy.
The breeze stills; voices die to whispers;
thick humid air is alive with caresses.
A touch — a chord — dark rumbling heartsounds
mount on one another in crashing chorus,
fire leaps to meet fire. Rain spatters,
Surges, tumbles, crests —
Storm-swept sweetness crashes and cascades
waves of blood-borne liquid melody.
Sudden stillness in its wake; flood-scoured
coolness of air, clear depth of gentling night.

Nita L. Glazewski

The Fish

I was out on the pond
In a boat all alone,
With nothing to bother me,
Not even a phone.

I grabbed my rod and checked my gear; I saw
the spot I wanted
And cast, with no fear.

I prayed really hard and made a wish, that
the God I trust would let me catch the fish.

Neal Byrd

Nonchalant

I often sit and stare into space;
Concentrating on nothing in particular and
   everything in general
My mind is free to travel wherever I want it to go.
I can explore the depths of my soul or the flight of a butterfly.
I have no particular concerns.

I listen to the silence. I watch the sway of the tree
   branches in the wind.
A chid playing in the distance has become part of my
   existence but not part of me.
I have no particular concerns.

I see all things around me but concentrate on no one thing.
My senses are exaggerated but not one is overpowering.
Freedom of the mind breeds relaxation. And . . .
I have no particular concerns.

Debra Miller

"Where Once There Stood A Forest"

Where once there stood a forest, there now lies barren land
We knocked down every single tree to build a home for man.
We didn't see the eagle, nesting in the tree
Or hear the cry of the baby wolf, when he couldn't find a place to sleep.

No care was given to the deer who took its refuge there
And when the owl cries out at night, there's no one left to hear.
We took the homes of all of them and never gave them a thought
We still haven't learned the lesson, that Mother Earth has taught.

If not for the trees and plants so green, we'd have no air to breathe
The sun would dry up all the land, till nothing was left to eat.
The forest we knocked down today to build a home for man
Tried to give us a warning, but we didn't understand.

It tried to tell us that each life gives life to something else
It's all a simple circle, in which each one of us must help.
We all must join together, to protect this precious land
For if it dies we'll all die too, its future's in our hands.

Nancy J. Stillo

Untitled

Seemingly enticing are these temptations
As our souls contrive the possibilities.
Realism impedes much effort,
Ironically enabling us to surmount
the improbabilities.

There are simpler things in life,
why they aren't sufficing,
we've yet to determine.
It seems the easier it becomes
the more difficult to discern.

Though the trials and tribulations
often make us ireful, we
withstand the belief that resilience
builds strength,
therefore, we are powerful!

Nett Keeler

Conflation

People are like books you see some of love some mystery,
some of sinning some repent, some of sport some government.

On tables in drawers on selves with dust, in some places kept with care,
In other places of disgust, some are left just lying there.

Some are waiting on the shelf for curious eyes to dare,
fumble through the pages — look to see what is written there.

Some are bound with covers hard to last through out the years,
some are bound of least degree with broken hearts and tears.

Then in rooms we stand them stout, we wander in we wander out,
we dust some off we throw some out, we hide some out of fear.

Joe E. Day Jr.

My Child

Today I thought about my life with you
Our times together were all too few.

I would love to go back there
To show you one more time that I care.

When I hold your child's hands
I flash back to other times and lands.

I miss that child of mine
Maybe you'll call tonight at nine.

As I lace that shoe
It reminds me of those days and you

Those precious days of long ago
Are reflected in your child's face aglow

I miss those special days and times
And also the night-time rhythms

I realized today that I still have you
When I am hugged by your beautiful baby with eyes of blue

Linda C. Brown

Seed Catalog Vistas

The bark of the maples across the road
With winter's brush has silvered gray
Or is it the sap has begun to run
And leap again to the lengthening day?

Tho the frost is still beneath the turf
Yet bulbs force green again through hoar
While dormant folk crowd cozy fires
And grasp at Spring through a printed door.

Margaret Tayler Anderson

Lost And Alone

Lord,
  See that child
    He's lost and alone . . .
    Unconditional Love, he doesn't understand!
    When given . . . he runs.
  He knows your Word!
    "I have loved you with an everlasting love."

BUT
  His computer reads ERROR!
  His walls are high
  They must come down!
  He's helpless . . . weak . . . afraid
  The task is just too big.

You are strong!
  Brick by brick
    Take down his walls.
  Let him accept
    Your Love and Smile
      He needs to know
        He's your child!

Cheryl Pangburn

Here By The Fir Tree

Lying here on the ground, the tree and I
  spread our limbs to the sun and the sky.

Our roots are based in this same land,
  life's strength is given us by God's hand.

Sustenance from this place we drew,
  sons with gifts and potential grew.

O perceive the tapestry surrounding girds,
  bright flashing branches, insects, and birds,

Crocheted loosely with a myriad bands,
  of sparkling and refracting sunshine strands.

Bernice R. Jones

Choices

There are goblets in my mind
Whose wines I have not tasted
For fear that sipping, worth to find,
May prove their value wasted,

While swirling patterns 'gainst their sides
Delights and stretches pleasure —
Since satisfaction there abides,
I'll not imperil its measure.

H. Dean Cowles

In The Blink Of An Eye

In the blink of an eye on a winters day,
My life was shattered when she went away.
All of my dreams for a future with love,
Were suddenly doused with tears from above.

Maybe time apart will prove to be,
The best that could happen, for her and me.
Loneliness lingers and chews at your heart,
But somehow we try to make a new start.

Now I look at life different and wonder why,
Would I ever consider to let love die.
Saying farewell is hard for me,
But I know that my love needs time to be free.

Tomorrow will come and I must be strong,
Or the love that I've lost, will surely be gone.
But with a turn of my head and blink of an eye,
Right now all I can do is cry.

Gregory E. Johnson

Crying In The Wind

Sometimes when you listen real hard
You can hear the Cherokee people crying in the wind
Asking their great spirit in the sky
To keep their souls safe within
As the Cherokee people
They fought and they died
For the land that they loved
Against the white man that lied
The white man told them
They would have to go
To a land far away
To a land they didn't know
This split the people into two
One to go the other to stay
Their lives to be changed evermore
As there was no other way
Their journey was long and hard
Many of them did die
It's called, "The Trail of Tears"
For the lost souls that cry

Betty Lee Plum

Untitled

Where's my little girl gone?
Now and again I catch glimpses of her.
The one who still say's Oh! To the newest doll
at the department store.
The one who hides in the bathroom to talk of boys
with girlfriends
    Where's my little girl gone?
The one who still dresses up the cat and tucks her in bed.
    And yes the one who now stands in front of the
mirror admiring her new look. Out of the cocoon
like a new butterfly.
Where's my little girl gone?
The one who still needs mom. But not for
bedtime stories, band aids or playing house,
but the one who needs a ride to a friends,
the one who needs her favorite blouse washed,
the one who needs help with a school project due in the morning.
Where's my little girl gone? No where I guess . . .
Just growing up, testing her wings, finding her way —

Tina R. Christ

Good Versus Evil

You never know — when you gaze into smiling eyes
What treachery and deceit there in lies
The face you see may be the one they choose to show
Some only by chance you really get to know
Some show pleasure some show pain
Some only smile when they are seeking to gain
Some crave peace — some crave power
Some live only for the current hour
Some see the beauty and love in this life
Some are wanton — envious and greedy and know only strife
Some with eyes cannot see — living for now not eternity
Some use pleasure with evil intent — sad is a life so unwisely spent
Lucifer while in heaven had every thing worth while
Yet even in God's own kingdom there grew an errant child
When the spirit from this earth takes its final flight
All its material possessions remain plainly in sight
The morale of the story I've just told
To obey God's commandments should be the ultimate goal
Win-lose-or-Draw — you gamble
The stakes are your soul

Virginia E. Hannah

"The Poe In Poetry"

The years were long — the tears were long
The pain and most my fears were long
And all that host my ears were long
— 'Twas the counsel to my creeping

The day was gone — the say was gone
The push and pull my weigh was gone
And all that host my sway was gone
— 'Twas the willing to my weeping

The night has come — the plight has come
The fright and might my rite has come
And all that host my spite has come
— 'Tis the reason to my reaping

The stay is here — the fray is here
The lay and pray my day is here
And all that host my way is here
— 'Tis the levee to my leaping

The end at hand — the send at hand
The knell and hell my mend at hand
And all that host my rend at hand
— 'Tis the comptoir to my keeping

T. L. Harris

Writing

The hardest part of writing occurs
When arranging the music in the words.

The rhythm in words murmurs in my ear,
even though the chorus can be impossible to hear.

The right sentences form melodies in my soul
Even when it's hard to find the tone.

The composing of notes, whole or half,
can be a never ending task.

The music can often become trapped
In the resonance of the past.

Forever the words can sound a discard
If pain is given to much reward.

When the words are finally harmonized
Their music at last can be realized.

Shelley Previl

The World Today

When we wake up in the morning,
fresh, new and the feel of a new darning.

Bathing, showering and preparing to dress,
there are no feelings of inner distress.

Leave our homes and down the street,
the face of the world begins to creep.

Folks with no homes are on the corner,
as you pass by someone begs for a quarter.

Oh no, oh no we want to say,
please find a job that offers pay.

There are some children playing near,
a drug pusher is close by and you can see the fear.

A voice cries out, "When will it end?"
some day very soon we all pretend.

But before it's over it knocks at your door,
this can't happen to me, it is only for the poor.

There is no where to run and no where to hide,
so let's stand together side by side.

To make this world a better place,
we must find a solution to end this race.

Lucy Cooper

Louie

Goodbye Lou, we'll miss you
been there since I could remember
survived all the cold Decembers
but now your time is due.
Goodbye Lou, we'll remember you
we all took our last glance
we knew this was our last chance
but did you? But did you?
Suffering on the outside, no effect on the inside
that we could see, kept it a secret from me
but we want you to be, painless and free.
So it's Goodbye Lou, we'll remember you
you won't wake up tomorrow
won't wake up with sorrow
we will drain, all of your pain
is that all right with you?
So it's Goodbye Lou, we'll miss you
but don't be afraid, if one day it fades
and we put you in the back of our minds
Goodbye Lou, we'll remember you, we'll remember you.

Ryan Herzog

An Ode To My Dear Sister

I have lost a dear friend and sister;
I'll miss you each and every day.

I never called you Mother,
But you were my Mom in every way.

When our family suffered one of our greatest losses,
You came home and helped us all through.

You lived your Faith by your actions;
It seemed so natural for you to do.

My mind is flooded with wonderful memories
Of which you are so much a part.

You gave of yourself always;
You gave lovingly from the heart.

Now you have joined with others
In our Heavenly Home above

Where there is no pain, no sorrow,
And the word for all times is . . . LOVE.

So Judy, if you hear me
(And I know in my heart you can),

We here on earth will miss you,
But your memory lingers on.

Shirley (Kjome) Nesseth

"Extinction"

Lonesome harpooner cast your eyes away,
All which survive you, too deep to slaughter this day.
King Neptune sobs as he sits, there upon his throne,
He's searching for his kingdom, yet sits there all alone.

Wise old haggard sailor, toughened by the brine,
Wasting not a moment of the hunt, to search those brother's mine,
You'll tether not a tail, nor tie a flipper fast,
Those days of breaching leviathans, have long ago been past.

Clowners of the oceans, no tail flips in the sun,
You're driven to the sands, and bludgeoned till it's done.
I shed tears for thee my brother's, but that is all I do,
The power hungry lions, away they drive me too.

Gulls glide away, feed not upon these bones,
Let them fester here, leave us to be alone.
Let them mark insanity here, of what this days been done,
An epitaph to my landlocked brother's, for eternity to come.

Peter E. Dyehouse

I Like What I See

What do you do when things go wrong,
when dreams are smashed into bits?
When it seems your whole life is not going well,
when it's harder to try than to quit.

When you ask if it's you or someone else, that is tearing into your heart.
When you had a plan, but it just didn't work,
years go by but you're back at the start.

That's when you take a good look in the mirror,
say out loud "I like what I see."
Be strong and have comfort in life ahead, be proud of what you can be.

The road you're on may have a few bumps,
the smooth roads are not always best,
Once you've traveled that rocky road,
you'll have more peace than the rest.

For life is like an orange, it gets sweeter inside with time,
But you have to watch the outside, with the sweet and bitter rind.

So throw your head back and stand up tall, the journey has just begun,
When you find happiness within yourself, the battle is already won.

Margie J. Stockert

Lover

I wonder if I would ever miss
you being near enough to me to kiss,
with that man in the moon
looking down here from up above
seeing us in our Garden of Eden making love,
so if you are with a sweetheart of any kind
please keep this special message in mind,
if your love is true
there is one thing you can do,
tell them that you love them with all your heart
and that you'll never part,
but if your loved one should up and run
tell them you are finished, kaput, completely over and done.

Angelique Mason

The Sun, My Heart And Mind

When I cry I blame it on things
if I'm out in the sun I blame it on the
rain because raindrops fall upon my face
trickle down my cheek onto my neck.

When I smile I blame it on my heart
cause it fill me with joy a special kind of spark

When I'm scared I blame it on my
mind it controls my thoughts every time.

And when I am sleep there's no one
to blame cause the sun, my heart and mind
are doing the same.

Kendra Lowe

Untitled

Feelings of you rising higher then you'll ever understand. I want
to be with you, I want you here all you can. What can I do? Not
afraid you'll ever leave me; run away with someone new. Every
sight I ever see is the sight of me and you sitting up late at night
watch the sun rise on the dew. Sitting up with candlelight, all
alone, just me and you. Can you ever comprehend every thought I
think is true. You are more then just my friend, you and I are one
not two. You many not want to know exactly what you put me
through. Everywhere I ever go, all I think is all of you.

Julie Anne Gerke

"Is It Wrong To Dream"

When the day begins, does it seem to pass you by
Have you often wondered why
Does your mind drift on and can't settle upon
What you want to be
When everything in life is to hard to see

Is it wrong to dream?

To be something or even try to be someone
To know you are and even have the right to be
When life is too short and it is not what it seems

Is it wrong to dream?

I hold my head up high and I keep telling myself I must try
To make life go on and take the hurt with the pain
Along with the happiness and the good
These are some of the things that I have understood

Is it wrong to dream?

You see they are all some small part of me
And I will always know and even sometimes show
To all that maybe around

That it is not really, wrong to dream . . .

R. J. Corsino

Ode To Sissy And Rebel

We were the first to build a house in a large subdivision. We
bought two English pointers whom we grew to love. Within a few years
thirty houses had been built and some began to complain about
"thoughtless people" who left their dogs run loose. (Sissy climbed
out of a wire pen that was ten feet tall.) Reluctantly, we gave our
pets to a veterinarian friend. He kept Sissy, but Rebel had to be put
to sleep because he could find no home for him.

Today, town has encroached upon my life.
The teeming population has refused the joy and peace of
    two English pointers
The city limits has arrived to deny the everyday
    pleasures of slow-paced graceful trots on evening walks
No more the dumb, loving, questioning look
    of Rebel as he lays his crooked mouth upon my knee
No more the powerful burst of muscle in chase of ball
    and twisted stick
The tennis ball lies waiting — never to be retrieved
I sit alone . . . no company . . . no contented, faithful
    companions waiting near, Sissy and Rebel are gone —
Thanks a lot, Cruel World; we all need Cars and People and Noise
— who wants a good ol' faithful dog, anyway?

Gina Ronhaar

Mindless Task

Amazing grace in the corner
Tunnels leading to insanity, a melting pout
To the left, the weeping mourner
Up on the ceiling, there's reasonable doubt

Rolling in ecstasy, look over your shoulder
Reckless little tot in the midst
Expressionless eternity where it grows colder
Near the entrance rage, anger, irate, pissed

To the gray matter in the center
Turn and cock your head a bit, down shifting
There's where the air smells quite better
Flowers with strong fragrance, confidence sifting

The doves with sugar coating, through the cracks
Scribbled mentality added in
Streaks in the softness, might something lack?
Out the pin prick, falling grin.

Caroline Clausen

Life Flame

The pain seems overwhelming,
 like a swimmer far to tired to stroke,
  as a last ditch effort I float
   and pray somebody saves me.

Or sometimes it takes a different twist
 against myself is turned,
  and I am filled with self disgust,
   such loathing, my belly burns.

So set the dial for self-destruct,
 but slyly so no one guesses.
  I am just tired to fight,
   need no proof that I am worthless.

Then comes the one I sometimes hate,
 'cause his eyes see what I am hiding.
  Tosses a life-line, wrapped in a dare
   guaranteed to set my temper flaring.

For in me it is anger, properly stoked,
 that keeps the life-flame burning.

   B. J. Anderson

Thoughts In A Gambling House Deluxe

The furnishings, lush; the carpeting, plush —
With stars on the ceiling, and soft music stealing.
The beautiful women with gay, painted smiles;
The men look important, have traveled for miles.
The tinkle of silver, the rattle of dice,
But winning or loosing, they're paying the price.

Each person comes searching for money or more,
But few who look happy will walk through that door.
The slot machines rattle, the dice still shall fall;
Las Vegas, you've given me nothing at all.

The four walls are bare, and the furniture's plain.
The only sound there is the falling of rain.
The only stars there are the stars in your eyes,
My music, your voice, and the thing it implies.
A touch of your hand, and a thought that we share,
And a whole wonderland is awaiting me there.

So take all your tinsel; with that you may dwell;
And leave me my Heaven; it pleases me well.

   Kay Kuhlman

Necessity

There always has been a fine line between wanting and needing,
Sometimes telling the difference between the two, can be quite misleading;

There once was a time, that I wished upon the stars for you,
 but now that same desire has grown,
This must be a miraculous surprise, because until now my emotions
 for you have never been shown;

These sensations from "deep" within opened my eyes and sent me
 on a quest in search of the truth,
I discovered the wisdom to cross that line, and now I certainly know
 for sure that I do need you;

Nowadays, I'm drunk with a passion that flows through my body
 like raging rapids,
I don't know why or how, but I'm in complete ecstasy, since all of
 this happened;

I don't know what's going through your mind right now, but
 please tell if you do care for me,
I can only "hope" that these words of truth will influence
 the decision, whatever your precious answer will be.

   Dave Smith

My Treasure Chest

On days when I am at my best
I take things from my treasure chest
These days I really try to share
The treasures I find waiting there
There's friendliness and kindness too
There's thoughtfulness in all I do
For generous praise there's always room
Warm words of hope to dispel gloom
There's Courage, Faith and Love to spare
These treasures that are waiting there
Why do I keep them tucked away
Why don't I use them every day?
The answer I can only guess
Perhaps it is my 'humanness'
Like jewels one declines to wear
And thus their beauty never share
Oh, how I really long to say
"Lord help me use them everyday.

   Rheta T. McGranahan

Heavenly Kingdom

As I lay myself to sleep
I always feel myself to weep
For as I wonder about family and friends who have died
I always wondered why
I do not fear for our time will come when we will join in the heavenly kingdom
Because I know we will be in God's heart as we we're from the start
I often wondered as a boy why we had to die now I know it's the final goodbye
As I've cried with so much sorrow I know now that one day
there will be a neverending tomorrow

   Mark Gallegos

The Hunt

Moonlight, cold and grey,
Shines on newly fallen snow.
The shadowy outline of a raised muzzle,
The howl that pierces the silence.
Loneliness grips his lupine heart,
Hunger burns in his soul.
His breath escapes in crystalline mist
Hanging in the air.
Slinking in and out of the shadows of trees,
He hunts, tracking his prey with stealth,
His movements graceful and lithe.
With one clean snap of his jaws,
His price is won.
He pauses, surveying the serene landscape
Then he moves on, deeper into the forest.

   Robin Chandler

House Of Emotion

And the house wept with her passing
A relief in a sense
The windows sparkled a smile
To never worry or shatter again
The walls stood at attention
No fear of being riddled with punches
The doors whistled on their hinges
Knowing the locks would hold
His heart would not allow him to stay anymore
And the house full of bruises
Full of lingering pain, wept,
Wept again, though the wounds healed
The scars left, tell too many tales
And he's leaving, to move away
From her ghostly memory
And the house wept at his leaving

   Richard C. Dowdell

Missing Love

We were together all of those years
We lived with laughter. We lived with tears
And then one day they came and took you away
I'm missing you, Mary Lou

When on the farm the children came,
One by one we gave them a name,
That, I guess, is part of the marriage game
The old high chairs, the clothes they wore
Those little footprints on the floor
That's when I keep thinking of you
Missing Lou is all I seem to do

The birthday parties, Christmas Eve
Easter morning, thanksgiving day
Those are the times I'm still with you
Missing Lou is all I seem to do

I know someday will meet again
Don't know where; don't know when
But till then I'll be dreaming of you
Missing Lou is all I seem to do
Meyel H. Haack

Untitled

Invitation to a celestial sea nymph — novice class:

Wink when ready to sail
Your maiden voyage through the night sky,
Tacking capriciously from constellation to constellation,
A foam of stars curling over the gunwale,
A white satin spinnaker pressing over the bowsprit
As it plunges rhythmically in and out
Of a rolling, milky sea,

No sound but the slap, slap, slap of the hull
And angels whispering in your ear
As their wings caress your breasts.

Careening from blasphemy to bliss,
A moonlit rooster tail sprays star dust
on your inverted buns —

"Come, come, come", the angels entreat,
"Catch a falling star!"
And you do, you do,
Again and again and again —

One night, one anointed night,
An eternity in memory, a lifetime between dusk and dawn.
Michael S. Hare

The Howling

An old English house in this far off land by the moors with their
history of mystery withstanding, a cold winter night a fireplace
by the bed fire-light flickers on the ceiling an Aurora Borealis in color.

A howling so eerie woke from my sleep she covered her head as I
leaped from the bed imageries of a wolfman dancing in my head,
I creep down the stairs my back crawling like snakes a distant
howling from somewhere a cousin to the one lurking down there.

Through the French windows the moon shining bright a wind blows the
trees shadows dancing on walls, the beast silhouetted in the window
I see howling at the moon my scalp nearly jumped off.

I grabbed at the beast the struggle begun snapping white teeth it
was as scared as I, it dashed through the door growling and growing
it headed up stairs I bolted behind.

It laid on the floor exhausted and cold fear in its eyes told the story,
I spoke to it softly stroked it so lightly this Poodle on its very first night.
William J. Cedar

God, The Scientist

God of our universe,
Scientists are aware that you wear many hats.

You are a master painter, coloring the leaves in fall, and refracting
the sun's rays at dawn and at dusk.

You are a music maestro, imprinting your songs on the DNA of birds
and on the winds that circle the earth.

You are a bold sculptor, carving and uplifting mountain ranges, and
molding hills and valleys.

You are a chef magnifique, brewing the products of decay and
fermentation, and making them appetizing to a variety of species.

You are a mathematical genius, dividing cells and multiplying organisms.

You are Mother Nature, sending birds migrating
and other animals into hibernation.

You are Father Time, controlling the movements of the planets and
stars, and regulating the half-lives of the elements.

From the Big Bang to the last Hurrah, you write and legislate the
laws that govern the cosmos.
Surely, you are a scientist.
Marilyn J. Fiegel

What Is

What is earth? What is life?
What is birth? What is love?
What is all of this to those above?
We're put on earth to live and love.
But what is life to those above?
My heart cries when someone dies.
A Mother sings when birth she brings.
On earth we may cry or we may sing.
Depending upon what fate might bring.
You are unknown like a star in the sky
But things are different when you die.
What's your name and who you are mean nothing at all so far.
Who you are may matter none 'til heartache has begun.
So let's smile for a while and with each breath
let's pray for more life instead of death.
He who prays shall be blessed.
God's non believers are usually depressed.
Pray that we will all grow old and
when we die "God! Save our soul."
This my heart feels this person reveals.
Sandra Sue Davis

A Purr-fect Love

You wake me up almost every day,
It's 5 am but that's ok.

You want me up and out of bed,
My hairs a mess, my eyes are red.

I change your water, I give you food,
But you just sit there, no change of mood.

I try some milk and even a treat,
You do want something, but not to eat.

So I get down and sit with you,
Your mood seems to change, it's not so blue.

I hold out my arms, you come to me,
Oh, that's what you want, now I see.

You want my attention so I hug you,
You purr and cuddle, even a coo.

Now I know what you, want when you look above,
You just want me and all my LOVE.
Dolores Calabrese

Spring, Apart From A Lover

In my minds eye . . . I see this
On this, a lovely warm sun kissed morning
I glance to your profile in peaceful sleep
The light beams touch your cheek
I envy them the chance to caress it . . .

A delta breeze drifts in, past the curtains,
as it makes it way to your bed where I do not lie
I see it brush your light hair from your forehead
and tickle your nose playfully and softly
as my fingers would if given the chance . . .

I watch you turn on your side slowly
Struck silent by your beauty, my heart aches
A thousand miles from you, I am denied
One kiss from your full soft lips,
Perhaps a sigh as you dream . . .

My skin longs for your breath
As if my own would not sustain its life
My entire body aches to be near yours
An unintentional brush against me
Would fill my heart completely . . .

Nancy P. Boyle

Season IV

When icy winds advance your way
with whirls of frost so bold,
may you within your home be warm,
protected from their cold.

If curling drops of ice should fall
and strike you on their way,
may you withstand the frigid blast
and stand, then standing stay.

With hope you'll wait for spring's mild breath,
its trees of twiggy green,
when autumn's mists are far away
and winter's just a dream.

Jane F. Hutto

Breath Of God

The wind blows like the sun shines
The never ending breath of God goes on
People say God is the light, sun of our life
I say he is the breath of our salvation
Without him we would be lifeless beings
Inanimate to our surroundings, to our world
We would feel, think, sense, and love nothing
But with him we have all of these and more
We have eternal life

Jonathan N. Berkey

The Piano Player

His fingers glide across the keys.
He captures your heart,
But his, you can never seize.
His music is the only love he'll ever know.
So your feelings you try not to show.
You watch him play day in and day out.
His passionate music makes your heart shout.
Your thoughts of him will never pass away.
Forever in your heart, he will always stay.
But your tears begin to flow
As his fingers glide across the keys,
Because you know his love you can never seize.

Becky Teaford

Phantom Love

The phantom Wind drifts upward to the oriental sky
rising to meet Beauty's light up where eagles die
the ghost Cloud descends upon the passive blue sea
calling for her warrior, the Wind, to set her spirit free

The Wind leads a life, a life of lies, but never will he deceive
To be within the cloud again, is all he really seeks
One final time within her love, inside her fantasy
To know the Union of body and soul, of beauty and Beast

Centuries they've lived apart, bound only as the night is to the day
Yet from dusk 'til dawn he burns her torch hoping she'll drift his way
Though enemies storm his castle walls, he leaves his tower unsecured
To share with her his final breath, and plant his requiem within her world

O Gods why must you torture me, do you find pleasure in my pain?
To lead me down the path to love, and bind me with its chain
But yet do I defy your lords of death, your prophets of doom and shame
For I'll cast off your sacred bonds, and always stay untamed.

Love eternal would Wind give the Cloud, but alas his heart is dead
The fires vanquished from his soul, its passions deliberately bled
And as the requiem is sung, and the darkness fades to day.
The ancient soul crosses to beyond, the Union brings another in its place.

Kevin Gair

Trust And Believe

Birches without branches
Cardinals without wings
Mentors without secrets
Kingdoms without kings

Courtyards without poets
Apples without seeds
Paupers without puppets
Churches without creeds

Maidens without lockets
Playground without swings
Beggars without pockets
Bridegrooms without rings

In an age of empirical enlightenment
And intellectual sobriety
Child-like faith is often seen as a crass charade
Something of a drunken idealist's dream

But sometimes
Things aren't always what they seem
Yes, sometimes
One must be simply willing to trust and believe

Steve R. Halla

Come Walk With Me

Come walk with me through fairy lands
Of light and music intertwined
Carefree and guileless babes once more
Unfettered by constraints of mind

Come walk with me through shadow lands
Of mystery and deepest blue
Dark fears set free to loom and soar
Forgotten now because of you

Come walk with me through pasture lands
Clear waters mixing with our souls
Earth's sensual pleasures overwhelm
A finite glimpse of all eternity holds

Come walk with me through nether lands
No flesh to die, no pain to moan
Our souls complete at last as one
Beyond this life to lands unknown

Andrea Schaffer

Weather

May the wind carry my spirit to places I've never been
While the rain cleanses my soul of each of its sins.
May the snow purify my thoughts and set my heart free
Let the sun bring forth growth of the best within me
Will lightning to strike if I should not try
To make the best of my life as each day goes by.
Fill my ears with thunder so I shall not hear
The words that cause violence prejudice and fear.
Send hurricanes and tornados to uproot evil and dread
And hail to beat it down if it once raises its head
At night send the darkness so I shall not see
Anything but good in those that I meet
And when it's all over and I stand at your feet
Know that I did my best to weather defeat

Beverly McCaulley Selepack

Reunited Mates

Disaster struck my mate and I,
One recent sunny day.
As we were dumped into a pool
We thought, for fun and play.

We whirled about and had great fun,
'Til we were taken out
And dried in much delicious warmth
'Midst more tumbling about.

But then, alas, disaster struck
As we were torn asunder
I went in the drawer for socks
Where is my mate, I wonder?

It seems he had been caught beneath
The corner of a sheet.
Until the sheets were changed, it seemed
We daren't hope to meet.

But then, at last, the day arrived,
My mate discovered there,
Was reunited by my side
We're once again a pair!

Virginia B. Harchol

Beyond What I've Become

And so it happened dreamed all my personal perversions
Feeling it would never end

You glanced at me so cold
Reaping all my minor diversions
But I have broken the mold

You see I've changed
I am no longer numb I've rearranged beyond what I've become

I just need a light
A reason for all my suffering I want to know why I fight

I believe in truth
Only divinity could be king
Then forever I am youth

Now moreover we have become the sum
It's forever beyond what I've become

My search is endless
Knowing a dream is only a dream I must go on never rest

One bright angel sings I'll always search for her and redeem
I lie for the hope she brings

In her embrace I hear her soft hum
She reflects grace beyond what I've become

Alfredo J. Gonzalez

Hope

My dreams remained mine only
It rained; I saw rainbows
But none came my way.
And if they came, I was too late.

The winds blew, and swept me from
my feet, I tried to hold on.
But the weakness of my will
let go, I fell for a while.
Then stood up, and looked forward.

I got lost, you had gone, betrayed
me, or did not love me enough, to wait.
I have no one to blame, I believed in you.
I still do, because there is hope,
there is a rainbow, after each thunderstorm.

My eyes will wait to get a glimpse of you
There is hope, there is love, there is God.
I will always wait for you, your glimpse
maybe you will pass my way, but once.

Talat M. Khan

The Four Seasons

One, two, three, four, Summer's first for the list on my score.
Swim, play, dance all day.
Never gets dark oh look, the ice cream truck is on its way!

Here comes Fall, better get your rake Summer might be gone,
but the weather is still great.
Leaves fall, flowers die but they'll be back after Winter passes by.

Look at Winter, time for the cold, time for skiing, sledding,
snowing and a big runny nose.
Hot cocoa on a snowy day, don't be upset Winter's just on its way.

Spring is here, just couldn't wait, fresh morning smell of
flowers on its way.

Four Seasons in all here we go again, the seasons will never stop
and the seasons will never end.

Dwanna M. Pittman

Stars

Oh lightning bugs of the sky,
Who wink and blink your starry eyes,
Or hide behind the foamy business of the black sky,
And play the game of peek-a-boo with the sight,
And then of late are far away
Or maybe closer to my gate,
Because no matter how I try to keep you in a place,
I cannot make this rolling earth
Refuse to like to rotate.

Vera Cleo Magee

Vision

I dream of a vision, so beautiful and sweet
A vision of a girl, whom I hope I'll soon meet
This vision I see, is all but so clear
for the face I imagine, just isn't there
I imagine this woman, with all of my heart
But incomplete, it's like I didn't even start
With no eyes to admire, or hair color to choose
No facial expressions to desire, I guess I still lose
Without any picture, of any such detail
I'll disregard this dream, rather than fail
As for this dream, Goes my heart ripped apart
But for reality I know, I've not yet begun to start.

Gary Slingerland

Untitled

The fruit that grows on trees
Is able, hungry and it's pleased
Squatting under bushes of berries
The eagles got pissed but the koalas berried
Laughter of above and cries from below
Shouts of hear, shots that glow
For days it raked of mistletoe
The aroma was loud, the aroma was great
Panic said happiness under hats of hate
War was heard and they with a smile
Killed them all from mile to mile
Extinct in nature, material selection
One man dies from another's infection
As some got rich some got poor
In the next battle see what's in store
And the ferns are mad and the leaf's are green
It's sad but silly to see others greed
So if you're alone and hate the pie
Pick the berries and curse the sky

David Valentine

Shattered Dreams

A shot shattered the silent night
She fell to the ground
The man fled the murder site
And she died without a sound
Her parents stared with disbelief
At the lurid scene
Their hearts were flooded with the grief
For the lifeless teen
Their eyes were fired upon their daughter
Eyes of horror, shock, and fear
The victim of this appalling slaughter
In a puddle of blood and tears
Her crystal eyes, frozen in fright
Her mouth hung open wide
A silent cry resounded all night
On her cheek, one tear she'd cried
Her dreams were stolen, her hopes are dead
No chance for this young girl
She lost, sleeping in her coffin bed
Living in death's dark world

Dan Blim

The Key

Dangling in fear, but never shedding a tear
Looking around for hope, but there is none
Slipping away, silent speech,
but only a few hear, few care, others shrug
Grasping at straws, and climbing your walls
getting closer finally reaching the peak, a whole new view
Scrambling in a frenzy, with a lovely view,
scared to jump, not knowing what's at the bottom
Trust is non-existent, falling rapidly
Is there anyone there?
Caught by a gentle hand, holding a key
But doesn't know the use, confused with passion
Getting closer to a door: Is it the right one?
Scared of yourself and things around
Stumbling with anxiety, reaching for the door . . .
Terrified to open, creaking sounds
Walls and ground shake!
Door wide open, calmness settles
Light breaks the dark treading lightly, what is it you see?
Only you know what the key may bring

Ken Elliott

Patient Heart

My Patient Heart is beating so,
I only wish the world could know,
the way I feel for her this day
and how she loves me that special way.
As time goes on I'll wait my turn,
for this much love I'd need to earn.
This choice can not be made so soon.
We'll have to count the stars among the moon.
There is much at stake for her you see.
How in the world could she choose me?
I'll wait for her both day and night
till her heart will say the time is right.
There's so much pain with every breath.
The thought of losing scares me to death.
My God, my God, I love her so.
Each night when tears fall from my face,
I pray someday my life she'll grace.
For me I can't foresee my fate.
But, forever my Patient Heart will
wait.

Mark Spradling

Play Ball

The sky is clear, a glorious blue.
The field, so green, a magnificent hue.

Music is playing all around.
Fans are screaming, children abound.

The seats are now filling. The moment nears.
The noise level rising. Crescendo of cheers.

All of a sudden, the organist plays.
Fans on their feet. The stadium sways.

The tune is the same. The words we all know.
. . . Home of the brave. Get on with the show!

Men on the field, taking positions.
Hey vendor! Come here! We need provisions!

The winds are blowing. The flags fly high.
Something is brewing, the visitors cry.

We know in our hearts, the home team will win.
If they could play two, they'd bill it a twin.

All that's now needed, that immortal call.
The two greatest words in the world - Play Ball!

Kevin Dean Foster

Years

Can it be so that you have been gone for so
very long from this place that you did call home,
it doesn't seem possible that much time has passed
sense you've been here to rome.

For it was yesterday that made so many memories
come to the surface of my mind recalling the braking
of my heart in pieces when life did pass from you,
no matter how much I try I can't believe it happen
so quick without even a clue.

Leaving our good-byes to each other never told and
what was in our hearts was left unsaid,
though words were left unspoken I know what would
have been said is all kept safe in my head.

Though your face has always stayed fresh in mind
each day even with so many years that has passed by,
it will last forever there with out fading away till the
time has come for me to die.

Roxane C. Berish

A Young Soldier In Time

The Ball Of Fire, suspended in air, rotated and spun towards us,
  slicing the atmosphere.
It was nearing the summer evening, although the sun was still present,
  and the sky was a magnificent
sundry colours, permeating amongst each other with absolute freedom.
We will never know where those colours shall go once the moon
  dangles in the sky.
When the sun has returned, new colours blossom, and those too will fade.
The Ball Of Fire was before us, whirling its fiery tinted blue and
  orange rage in the reflection of our eyes.
Most suddenly, after pausing in our direction, it droned an awful
  sound, laughing uncontrollably.
Where upon, it turned and thundered towards an open field,
  roared above it, and was gone.
Ironically, the field stopped, and we could view nothing beyond it.

The earth shall but for a time live; its contour appears to the stars;
might such a light shine in the presence of all.
The moon tumbles down upon the darkness to create a manifest of
figures, dancing sluggishly about;
the shadows are but for a short while.
Handsome rings orbit round great marbles; icicles shall glitter.
The red bomb sinks into the atmosphere, the pupil in an eye.
The comet struck the shining light, and darkness hushed the shadows.

Tiffani M. Chapman

"Forbidden Love"

An unresolvable predicament,
a hazardous trap to be caught in.
Yet the excitement is intensified
by the danger of the sin.
Secrets kept by two souls, who can not,
dare not, breathe a word of what they've done.
They keep returning for another sip
of their precious forbidden love.
When alone, their passion is unhindered,
their hearts can seek what they both wish to find.
Which is the utter happiness they feel,
when the world is left behind.
They desperately cling to the precious moments,
for they come few and far between.
They know the world would not approve of their union.
Yet, still, they dare to dream . . .
of the happiness and the bliss that
they find in each other's embrace,
and of the wonderful true love
they find in each other's face.

Pamela L. Boliew

Morning

Morning is really beautiful, the best time that's for sure
No tall tales have been told yet, the day it is still pure

She lays there still sleeping, so lovely near and real
I reach out and touch her, and I can't help but feel

A sadness, a sorrow, so deep and oh so strong
For reality is such, that we don't have very long

A lifetime we've spent, being together as one
Loving and sharing and raising our sons

But time now is short and infinity is at hand
And we will both soon go on to a new and different land

Yet there is no crying, no tears are left in me
For love it is eternal, and we were always meant to be

So close, so happy, new lifetimes yet to touch
And I will for always, for eternity, love her so very much

Lawrence J. Nemzin

Lamentable State

Chain me not to the golden leash
  of tradition and formality,
But give me the Earth and its heritage.

Pledge me not to the allegiance of flags,
  and the battle of ignoble thoughts,
But give me the Earth, my birthright.

Return to me a stolen legacy
  that I am no longer
this bastard creation of time.

Abdullahi Ibrahim Bin-Yahya

A Touch

The touch began in Genesis many years ago
  God touched the cheek of Adam and life began to show.
The touch is mighty powerful, as witnessed by our Lord
 He touched the eyes of a blind man, his sight was immediately restored

The Touch is just as strong today, tho it seems we've lost sight of its use.
  The touches that we make today are often signs of abuse.
But if you touch the one you love on the cheek or on the hand,
  And feel the love flow through that touch, I'm sure you'll understand.

Recall the touch your mother gave, as you lay sick in bed.
  The touch meant more to you than all the things she said.
So reach out and touch someone today, and whisper "I love you";
  You'll bring much joy to the one you touch, but Oh what it will do for you.

Raymond J. Stefanick

The Goddess Speaks Of Beltaine's Rites

"Out of winter is born the Spring;
lovers hand fast adorned with their rings."
"Pagan kin, come dance and sing; be full of mirth, rejoice in Spring."
"Our Mother Epona she rides to Earth; now quickened females
shall soon give birth."
"Come one; come all, join Beltaine's rite.
Gather round the fires to gain the sight."
"See new babes born of moon and horn;
our Mother soon shall reap hawthorn."
"Epona enjoys all acts of pleasure;
make merry now, for they are her treasure."
"The time has come to copulate;
rush to the woods with chosen mate."
"Good Wiccan folk remember this,
our Lady loves the five fold kiss."
"And as lovers are entwined on this Beltaine night;
keep in your mind it's the Great Rite."

Maria Cernuto

Crazy

Green with envy, he despises his fellow man
Cowering in fear from the end result of life
None to pretty a flower
That will draw his attention form his wandering thoughts
He sits mumbling unspoken words to a deaf ear
He does not know why the pain hurts
Never obtaining the feeling of guilt
He does not enjoy the bright surroundings
The light is too intense for his frail existence
He will crack under the strain of nothing
The walls seem to have their way with time
But he can't even fathom the idea of time
In his world he is both the king and the peasant
The victim and the intimidator
Then with a sudden burst of realization
He jumps up and yells "free"
But soon he is brought back one again to the cold floor
His existence is flawed but no one seems to notice

Iain Gulin

The Coming Of Spring

The heart is vibrant and alive in the kindred soul
A mind that is full of dreams and future possibilities,
Awakened by prospective enthusiasm, none too old.

A cane will be grabbed from the corner collected by winter's
dust
Hesitation for a moment, before the walk, balancing her footing
Ever so right,
Determination prevails in seeking the first pussy-willows in sight.

The exhilaration of fresh air after a long season of despair
She buttons her sweater tighter, wrapped in warmth from the sun rays'
Glare,
The daffodils pop their heads and the crocus of multi purples and
Yellow give a smiling stare.

The coming of spring is in the air.

Eleanor Bentley

The Madonna

The sky shined blue and bright,
High above, the yellow sun, flickering lights.
Entering the new day, with love and song,
May the angels above us sing, with us, loud and long.
And so this image, through the years, been seen and admired,
Daily prayer, and the singing of the choir.
On this day, the yellow bird sang,
Nothing but happiness, in this lush and fruitful land.
Nothing could disrupt this tender moment, pure in love,
Above them, the blue tinted sky, clouds bright white as the morning dove.
And what a tender moment, a sight to behold,
Nothing can compare to that image, not the shimmering of gold.
Delightful is the blessed Mary, goddess forever she shall be,
Tender, joyful, blessed Jesus, our savior is he.
High above them, the green trees blew,
Entering rays of light, through patchy leaves, in colors of green
   and yellow, emerald hue.
This is what the painter paints, this is what the poet writes,
This is how I feel, do you feel? Inside.
And so it ends, this cordial image, intoxicating as it is,
Now I rest, sit and ponder, of this vision, endless bliss.

Jose E. Hernandez

Ocean

The vast ocean!
Is a place of relaxation
Like a drop of a sincere potion.
You feel the breeze of freedom
As above passes a flight of seagulls
And beyond the water a school of dolphins.
If we could be like them
We would be true to ourselves.

Julia P. Garcia

Halo From The Heart

A halo of light surrounds the earth
it is love, that emits from our hearts
Through ravages of war and repression of truth
There is love that emits from our hearts

Through violence and hate a barrier is formed
But there is love that emits from our hearts

We can break through the wall
through the efforts of peace
And rejoice when success is achieved

For the halo of light that's
surrounding the earth
it is love that emits from our hearts

Greg Miller

Humble In The Sun

Why are we on earth? To fight, to live, to plunder?
Let not Almighty put us under, those who chose the wrong.
What makes us right to think them strong aggressive beasts?
Do we not thunder to the feast at victory's call?

Are we not bad? To them they think they're good
To them we are the beasts who fight and steal and murder
To them we are the clan, who should be banned
Stricken as the world intruder.

Isn't he the one, who humbles in the sun, the strongest of them all?
Do we have to fight with all our might, till every man must fall?
Call out this call to every one, lay down your arms and say
"We'll meet you on the boundary line, I believe it's called half-way."

Let neither side be won today, let victory be defeat
We're marching homeward glory bound, with flags in every street
Both sides they claim they lost today, both sides they claim they won
But well we know that we're the ones who humbled in the sun

Paul R. Fritter

Hint Of An Idea

Through nights and dawns a plenty
The luminescent heart grows
Through time and distance
We learn to make decisions
Life pulls us through many tunnels
Never revealing eternal answers
Speak now or forever hold your peace
Act now or leave this world a restless spirit
Each day brings new promises of happiness and sorrow
Make every moment truly beautiful
Spend every morsel of your time
Feeling emotion and creating experiences
For that is what leaves with you
When you pass on to new levels of life

The birds are singing
The flowers are blooming
Children are laughing
And hope is returning
Why are you watching T.V.?

Kerri Durham

A Gift Of Love

It seemed a perfect wedding gift
For bride and groom's abode
This washer-dryer set should lift
The burden of their laundry load.

It took me back to my first set
That truly filled my heart with glee
Though in my one-room launderette
The only power source was me.

So mine was not a "Whirlpool" cool
A 'Speedqueen', or a 'Maytag' sleek
I was the lean speed queen machine . . .
The whirlpools were in the creek.

A galvanized wash tub and board
Plus bar of 'Naptha' soap
Was all the 'set' he could afford
And more than I could hope.

I must admit new ways are best
But don't let love decrease
If you are put to old-time test
Of using elbow grease.

Nita Paddock

389

Longing For You

The moment I met you,
it was love at first sight,
and my life has never been the same.
Not a day goes by without me thinking about you at least once.
Dreaming of how wonderful it would be having you hold me in your
strong arms, caressing me, and holding me so tight.
When you walk by I get dizzy and light headed,
butterflies invade my stomach,
and I get cold clammy hands.
To hear your voice gives me goose bumps.
I shudder with the touch of your hand.
When I'm not with you,
I long to see you.
I try not to think about the fact that you might not share my
same feelings.
It's sad that I can only hope that some day we will be together.
Physically, mentally, and emotionally,
I have fallen in love.

Tammy Billieu

Burning Church

Smoke rises in aromatic praise,
hoping, seeking the infinite.
The night remains silent — no reply.

Flames escape in a frantic gesture,
reaching, beseeching a meaning.
An impassioned roar pleads—no answer.

Serpentine hoses are quickly laid;
man waters battle the appeal.
Enticed by sirens calls,
the crowd murmurs: "sacrilege — abomination."

The sanctums zeal is soon controlled,
slowly, methodically conquered.
The heat quietly subsides; the smoke thins.
Passion spent; soul purged.

Night regains his cool, dark silence,
certain, content in success.
The answers are still safe — no reply.

Edward H. Jacobs

Thinking Of Our Love

Here I lay, in my bed, feeling all alone,
with you in my heart, my mind begins to roam.
Thinking of our love, how it is so sweet,
with you on my side, there is no defeat.
Times have changed and so have I,
I can honestly say that looking eye to eye.
There's been lots of pain for the things I have done,
without you my world is cloudy, please bring back the sun.
Together we have been through so many years,
with lots of heartache, lots of tears.
You have changed my life and gave it new meaning,
one thing hasn't changed, with you on my mind I'm always dreaming
I have done things for you to show you I care,
It's with you my love, my new life, I want to share.
I stare at your face, looking deep into your eyes,
my soul begins to cry, so I know this love is no lie.
This love can't be stopped it can only progress,
cause with you my love, I have the very best.
All that matters is our love is always there,
Wanting and craving new feelings we want to share.

Christopher Lee Raymer

"It Used To Be The Game"

Spring and baseball are upon us; and the story's still the same,
It's been a tiring winter fracas, now it's time to play The Game!
Teams are now a forming, managers attempt to keep the peace,
Yet, contracts are a storming; players need a large increase.

The stars will hone their skills, while the lawyers add their clout,
Fans still seek the thrills, dreaming all will soon workout.
The union wants a contact, needing reconciliation,
Yet, the lawyers want a combat; baseball's still a favorite in the nation.

Why don't they reach agreement? Will it happen before the season?
No; money's still their treatment, it's got to be the reason!
Players seem so greedy, owner's actions aren't much better,
Lawyers are still seedy, Making baseball "Stormy Weather".

Who will be the winner, surely not the loyal fan,
Whose treated like a "sinner", in a God-forsaken land.
All, will soon be lost, if they handle it the same,
Someday, we'll learn the tragic cost — "It Used To Be The Game".

Gordon E. Oeschger

I Remember

Yesterday,
  When you and I were young
  Our lives were touched
  With so much fun
  My love was shared
  With no other one
  I loved you so, I gave you a son.
Today,
  I have all my yesterdays
  With a heavy heart
  For the moments we shared
  Sweetheart, Lover and Wife
  I'll always be yours
  The rest of my life.
Tomorrow,
  Is a sleepless night
  A longing to have for you hold me tight
  A whispered "I Love You" a sigh, because I love you too
  Forgive me darling for hurting you let there be A tomorrow.
Forever and Always.

Mary Dyer

The Dance Of Autumn Leaves

The colors dance in my eyes,
To a song of flame of amber and gold.
I am in a state of ecstasy and sadness
As memories of vivid colors,
Lead the rhythm of the song.
The song of two little girls,
Dancing in the park, near the ducks;
Up in the mountains, near the sky;
Down the trail of innocent dreams.
Trying to chase a butterfly,
To catch the amber and find the gold.
The girls have left . . .
A few leaves twirl here and there;
And suddenly, a wish breaks through the air.
In their freedom, please, help them God
To find the courage to fly high;
To reach the stars up in the sky;
To catch the amber and find the gold,
And in a shower of silver dust,
Find their dream and see it last!

Danae L. Yannis

The Stand

Standing tall, so shining and new, dressed all in blue
being faithful and true
soon people will talk about you.
Some would say he's a good fellow
others would say he so pale and yellow
so no matter what's the talk about
just hold your head up high and always stand proud
you'll soon be noticed in the biggest crowd
if courage is what you need then I will give you my heart
so you can learn the things that I have
and lead you to a better start.
For you will overcome your fears
believe me it's o.k. to shed tears
and for you I will always be here
take my hand
and together we shall stand

Elizabeth Martinez

Blood Of Who

The cadence of music pumps in my veins
It keeps me alive, it keeps me insane
The sonic pulsating of impulsive expression
Gathers together my thoughts through regression
And expression makes the world go 'round
Life would be dead without the music of sound

Innocence is an experience
For all to delight
What lives in the day
Somehow dies in the night
For what seems like forever
Your illusions go on
What's important that night
Seems trivial at dawn

Rational thought obscures my delicate insanity
and the cadence lives in every part of me.

Angela Peppers

Too Many Oreos

I have a friend who embodies life, in a way that most don't understand
all the same carries herself with the world in her hand it's not
that things always go her way, but she makes the most of the things
that come along — she has ten thousand suitors down on one knee,
and she loves them all in a way they have never known but where her
devotion lies, no one really knows she has a smile so bright, but it's
her laugh that eventually crawls inside — someone who has grown so
much and come so far, she finds herself lost in dreams and promises,
taking care of everyone but herself they'll wait on her hand and foot,
but in the end, they're the one's that take the prize, and yet still
am I being selfish? She asks she only wants to be in the place where
shecan give the most, but still she asks, am I being selfish only if
you have too many oreos to eat and refuse to share with the one who
needs them more I say, I love her laugh, it comforts a tired heart
and makes you feel in the middle of things — that's a great feeling
to someone who finds herself on the bench more than on center stage
— I will miss her when she leaves, and I know that she will someday
— but I have always admired the way she follows and finds her hearts
desire — I'll find her again, because true friends are always found
in the end she'll be waiting at the end of the rainbow and we will
sit and smile, whine and cry, sing and dance and when the day is done
we will smile away the sun and whimper with the moon, because that's
what friends do. I tell her this and she laughs.

Susan Olsen

"Mother"

Mother, you're special in so many ways,
you lighten the nights, and brighten the days.
There's so much love in your warm embrace,
No one could ever take your place.

You taught me so much in my younger years
You shared my laughter, you dried my tears.
So many times I've counted on you
To make my hopes and dreams come true.

Through the years you've given so much.
You've always had that special touch.
My mother, my teacher, my best friend, too.
Mother, you know just how much
    "I love you"

Sherry Russell Wyer

Who Is She?

The heavens appear through the pines,
the warmth embraces your spirit
She hears your heart bleed in the wind,
your soul ache in your heart
She watches your face secretly
I wish I was there, for here is an eternity.

Now brush the canvass,
with the colors of your wisdom,
let your spirit soar.
She watches your face secretly
I wish you were here, for there is an eternity.

Turn thoughts beyond bliss,
surrender into the night, as you feel her love
your touch silently moves over her, her senses cease
She watches your face secretly
Take us where you want to be.

Teresa Gaskin

"Toy Soldiers"

Do you see them lying on the beach?
Toy soldiers strewn about without a care
and no one will come to pick them up.
Beady eyes painted on all their faces
with pallid cheeks and pointed noses,
little silver buttons of pseudo-symbolic patriotic semblance.
Dressed the same in uniform red, white, and blue,
soiled with sand from the abandoned beach.

Whose children were these soldiers?
Were they yours? Were they mine?
Where are the parents that bought them at the store?
Where are the children that played with them until they broke?
Will anybody come to pick our children up
now that their plastic limbs have
melted away from metallic skeletons,
charred and rusted from the government games?

Rick Bahto

Condescending Cat

A black cat yawns, and stretches in the sun
It's much to early; he's to sleepy to run
Unless his master calls with food that will arouse
He turns over slowly as his stomach starts to growl
Beef, or bird, or fish would be nice
Any kind of meat will surely suffice
But for now he'll be content to just laze in the sun
And when his master calls . . .
Maybe he'll just fake a run

Jerry A. Mills

She, The Treasure

Her hands were callused from the garden,
 From planting seeds and pulling weeds;
  The colored flowers of her yard
   Were famous in that town.
Her apron wet from washing dishes,
 Shining pots and scrubbing plates,
  Her food was always so delicious,
   Ask anyone in town.
A smile always graced her face
 And sparkling eyes and scarlet lips
  Her long brown hair, her dress of lace,
   The beauty of that town.
Her hand all men in love had yearned
 To take 'til death did do them part
  But then in disappointment learned
   Her husband lived in town.
That man he held a golden treasure,
 His wife, though he knew not,
  For he was in pursuit of pleasure
   The drunkard of that town.

Victor M. Moyer

Art And War In Sarajevo

Ancient writings, histories of the soul
new destroyed, in a flaming black hole.
 And the library burned;
 and the people,
 yearned.

Twenty-two died while waiting in line
for a loaf of bread on which to dine.
 And the cellist stayed;
 and for twenty-two days,
 he played.

"Bolero" ballet on opening night —
the orchestra played and dancers took flight,
 transporting all from their daily skews
 and the ballerinas,
 had no shoes.

"Overwhelm the war" is their battle cry.
Fear, met with faith, disappears with a sigh
 when musician, sculptor, poet and dancer
 strike at the madness
 with healing answer.

Elaine Jordan

I Am Dream

I couldn't meet you when I've always known you.
You couldn't kill me, if you fought me, without killing yourself.
Take me away and you are nothing.
You are never blind when you see through my eyes.
You can't fall when you have these wings.
You can't hunger when I continuously feed you.
You cannot be deaf when I speak to you.
I am what drives your every decision.
I am the one you make love to.
I am the only God you've known when you were broken and scared.
I am the only friend you ever had when you were crying and alone.
I'll be there when you die and forever after.
And I'll take you with me to live again and again.
You'll soon realize that there was no search.
Because I was always there . . .
And I always will be.
You cannot ignore me when I am everything.
I am Dream.
I am King.

Barbara Revilla

Couplet Rhymes

A man came by one day —
And said you'll have to pay.
I saw that this book is out-dated —
Besides the cover is faded.

I don't know where Molly is going —
But she's in a boat rowing.
She visits a friend across the lake —
And their friendship is not a fake.

A poor little lonesome stray dog —
Can't see where he's going in the fog.
A little boy comes by and stoops to pet —
I'll give you a place to stay, I bet.

Oh, what a mean trick to play —
You're supposed to wait 'till Halloween Day.
You didn't follow the rule —
So we are taking you away on a mule.

Cold times; are fun times —
So bring a handful of dimes.
Falling off sleds and rolling in the snow —
So, you'll want some hot drinks; you know.

Virginia M. Siverly

The Family

The sun was shining, ever so bright, and we boys had
slept throughout the night. Mom and Dad were up and around,
Tipping so quietly, with very little sound. The dog was watching
the cat in the tree, and the cat was satisfied where he could see.
Gramma was sitting in her favorite chair, smiling and happy,
combing her hair. Grampa was outback putting line on his pole,
preparing to go to the old fishing hole. Jerome and Bobbie so
happy and free, wondering where their Grampa could be.
Grampa! Grampa! Do you think it's too cold? No! No! Boys
we'll go to the hole. Dad spoke up, and said, Boys can't you
speak? Good morning everyone, but it was Grampa we seek.
Mom said, Boys, come on, I want you to eat, it's Biscuits,
Bear gravy, and a nice chunk of meat. Gramma said, you
three I will miss, come give Gramma a nice big kiss.
Well, they now have all passed, but I can still hear their voice,
So I dream and listen, I have no other choice.
The hole is still there, I'm happy to say, I know we'll
be together again, I hope, and I pray.

Jerome Oates Sr.

Dear God

Where did my childhood go?
May I please have it back?
Please let me start over again.
Please let me choose nice parents this time
Who will love me and not hurt me.
Please let me have a loving family
Who will comfort me when I need it and
Laugh with me and not at me,
Who will let me grow and not hold me back and
Will love me for who I am.
Please let me have a perfect body,
No defects please, and
If I do have defects,
Let my family not care.
Please let me have a family
Who will not abuse me in anyway please.

Amen,
Carolyn

Carolyn Duff

Trust

Trust is old way to the respect,
trust is gold key to the love and friendship.
How could we float not to expect
each of us has future: ocean and ship?

Loosing trust way — loosing respect.
Loosing trust key — loosing love and friendship.
How could we float not to expect
each of us has future: ocean and ship?

Untrust brings us only fear and darkness, only scorn,
in God we trust, in God, he's our lasting nod,
in God we trust, in God, he's our daily corn.

Don't taste once forbidden fruit and don't taste devil lie,
trust in yourself, trust in justice, trust in God,
then you never die, then you, man, never die.

Stefan Lukacik

Asphodel

From dance to conception: One spark to turn undisturbed circles.

Here was life once, with shadow, echo, dance. Here was light once,
whenever wished.

But a name lost among stones is more defined than the dark:
A star to ignite the mirror.

Here: To become alive, animated within the carbon palette of ceremony . . .

Within hidden embers . . . what can emerge in the advent of moment
that the nightingale can bring . . .

Held in the breast: Something shifts . . . allows room for wings to beat.
What is felt releases . . . what beats responds to sweetness
and brushes wings with another in kind.

Stephen R. Wray Jr.

The In-Between's

These lovely people that's stuck in between
They are full of laughter
They have many dreams
They are sometimes unconcerned and sad
Disappointments seem to make them mad
They despise constructive criticism
They think we're full of old fashionism
But love and guidance can cure their ills
Their mind is filled with adventure and thrills
Excitement and temperament is a big part of their lives
Very few at this time, choose husband's and wives
They are friendly and helpful when they want to be
Encouragement my friend is left to parent, you and me
Who are these people that's struck in between?
"Our lovely sweet hearts" the teenagers! The teens!
Our help is needed to perfect their dreams.

Ruth McMahon Glass

My Escape

When things are troubling and it's hard to cope.
The ocean is my means of escape from it all.
It relaxes me like nothing else can.
I sit beside the ocean and this is what I hear:

The roaring waves whisper, Come join me, take part.
I am your escape from life, feel my freeness.
Swim beside my children, join in their laughter.
Taste the pleasure of my free will.
Without regret, make your choice to be free.
Escape form life and all its pain.
You are the sign of the fish, this is where you belong.

Judy L. Taylor

Missing You

My friends are leaving all around, I know for sure they are
heaven bound.
I have two children that I fear for, I know now that's why I'm here for.
I try not to cry, but the tears go by.
I sit and sob, and then I sigh.
I sit and wonder why, Lord did you take them away?
I remember the times that we would say, Hey cheer up things will get better.
Just and write your thoughts in a letter.
If I could make it through this world and see my children's children,
this would make me truly happy.
If I could accomplish this, Life truly would be bliss.
Goodbye for now my great friends, until we talk again,
    God bless each and everyone.
I didn't say while you were here, I Love You, and now I know the tears
that I have shed for you are coming from my heart and soul.
So my friends if you can hear me now you're in my thoughts and prayers,
and I will miss you everyday as long as I am here.

Linda Bedwell

"Thinking Of You"

As I lay here in my bed, the night breeze blowing gently in my face,
I am savoring long precious memories of you and I once again;
and I wonder what you are doing!

And I ask myself this futile question that I have asked myself a
hundred times, "What happened to the realities we once had in
our little world that are now nothing but fantasies once again?"

The warm springs nights of dancing in the moonlight, the cozy
winter nights of whispering sweet nothings into each others
ears by the fireplace, the candlelight dinners we had every night
and yet still not enough of.

But Darling, I still love you dearly, and as I sit here thinking of
you, I will write my thoughts about you, coming from the
deepest part of my heart that only you have the key to.

Darling, forever the liquid gold united with moonbeam passion that
sparks our already overheated furnace into the fireworks of our hearts.

Together, combustible fragrance and total meltdown saturates our
already violable short circuit with fervent fire, roasted pleasures
and pain of a rainbow spattered journey of love.

You are my love and with or without you my own being grows to its
peak of romantic ecstasy and golden cream climax as your
garden of love swallows me in her womb so eternally.

And with my love stained heart open for you, and the key to it in your
hand, that my beautiful darling has me thinking of you.

Burton Fariss

Life Is A Day

Life is a short day for us all to use,
Our dawn a beginning, no time to lose.
Each venturing forth with a creep and a crawl,
To an upright stance, some to rise, some to fall.

Always looking ahead and setting goals to seek,
Hard work will challenge both strong and the weak.
The difficult roads won't be easy to measure,
No directions for finding either trials or pleasure.

Walk along slowly, to savor, any beauteous site,
On all paths, view both to left and to right.
Much love you will find, in all God's good things,
And to family and friends contentment you'll bring.

Much strength and weakness in us all will abide,
In our lives to be balanced and used as a guide.
Remember, enjoy, and be happy in all that you do,
For each, dusk will fall when the day is all through.

Laura Greene

Each Step We Take

I walk with God, He is my light.
Each step closer to Him my light becomes brighter.
To understand is easy: To accept is hard.
Faith in Him, for He shall never turn away.
Hope is our existence, fear, anger, hate jealousy is our
destruction.
Search for your answers within yourself,
and you shall find in yourself all the answers.
One lives to understand all that He must.
One dies when He has found part or all of that which He was to
understand while He lived.
Life can be a bright light if you make it so. Filled with joy,
wisdom.
To give of yourself to all people good and bad.
Death is beautiful, peaceful, a breath of air
filled with love and life eternal on a journey to God.

Helen P. Muniz

The Path

The world takes on new meaning
  in the deepness of the night . . .
Time stops itself
  and with the Infinite Space
We lose ourselves in the Path . . .

The rains of memories begins
  and unexpectedly the past washes away.
With each tear
  we wish to transfigure the present.

Ahead lies The Unknown
  But walking carefully through
    the distance of time,

The Path becomes illuminated . . .

Vladimir Pavlov

Bob The Bum

He died a lonely old man so old and gray —
No one to befriend him to show him the way.

Everyone thought he was dirty old scum —
He slept on park benches, he was called Bob the Bum.

His earlier years were filled with love and hope —
Until one day he came home and found his wife hung by a rope.

To suppress his sorrows he turned to drinking —
In his years before he never touched a drop, he just
wasn't thinking.

He was kicked out of his house and turned out onto
Lewiston's back street —
Where no one could see him, not a friend he could meet.

His life was in shambles when he finally did die —
No one remembered him, not a tear they did cry.

Heidi Jordan Sammons

A Flower

A flower is a beautiful thing,
it appears in the season of spring.
It's fragrant and smells like perfume,
and I love to watch them bloom
  There are many types, I like the rose,
every day its beauty grows.

Andrea Milleson

Winter Eve

I lie here safe and warm,
with paper and pen;
as the raging, freezing, chill,
hunts a way in.

  Spattering, icy rain,
slants 'gainst the walls an panes,
lulling you, yet, chilling you,
fogging the pines . . . it rains.

  A day to reflect upon
The deepest thoughts within,
to stop and consider new projects,
or places to begin.

  And as the gray wet day,
fades into winter night;
curl in your bed . . . and read;
old words . . . by flickering candlelight.

Vickie L. Goldsberry

Nature Pulls The Blinds

Shadowed crevasses down the side
Of blazing, snowcapped Spanish peaks.
As nature slowly pulls the blinds,
So moonlight may her vigil keep.

Green, shades of every hue stand out
In the glorious rays of the setting sun
On nearby mountains 'round about,
While hazy purple reigns on far horizon.

The dark blue lake is bridged by gold.
Scents of pines carried with a windy sigh.
Silvery fish gracefully rise, for bugs too bold,
All bidding the day, "good-bye, good-bye"

Stranded from their hidden nests, day creatures
Watch unseen, with baited breath,
Fast beating hearts, the darkening features
Of their imminence to death.

Hildreth Willits

For Girlie

I'm twenty-five
or I'm three, no one really knows;
I'm an angel.

I can't walk, but I can fly
with my smile, my giggle, my eyes.
I tell people, but not everyone understands.

Heidi Boerstler

Love For Someone Special

I love you more than I can express
Sometimes I don't always act it
For that, I'm very sorry
I don't like when work calls you
Because there's got to be some us time
Set aside somewhere for only us
I don't understand that
You love me, you've said so
So why can't just us be together
And have no interruptions
There should be a weekend off somewhere
But if this is how it is
I'll accept it because of love
I love you and only you beyond all measure
Please forgive me for being stupid

Julie Shapiro

Semana Santa

Blistered and broken, caked in mud and filth
not perfumed with ointment but disfigured.
Odors, infections, sores, gashes
these are the servants of our endeavor.

Not sentimentality, but passion
yearnings of the lover who freely
discards roles and positions
new vision of the beloved.

Who is the bearded lover - tired
after so much wandering
What word is there for us - oppressed
by our own fickleness?

Galilee tracks traced across a desolate world
where the majority are still barefoot and
have nowhere to lay down their heads,
desolate, frigid, indifferent or hopeless

Galilee becomes ours, and the broken bruised feet
are more than physical symbol.
The passion is not a passing image of Friday
the passion is our journey, our striving, our lovers-quest.

Basil Postlethwaite

I Pray

I pray for you each, and every night
I pray things for you to work out right
you are due for a love, a love that is true,
and I'm sorry your dad was the one that
said we was through.
God gave us all different road of life,
and mine just seems to be an endless fight
I guess the plan I had for you and me has
been put in a bottle, and thrown into the sea
but maybe one day on a far away shore
we can meet again, and it will not be like before.
I pray you find that love so warm, and
true, like the love I hold so deep inside
for you, but if our path's should never cross
again, I pray you will always consider
me nothing less than a friend.

Roger Messer

Summer

On the beach there is laughter and fun
It never ceases until day is done
Children laugh and sing and play
Oh for the joy of a summer's day
The sun is shining so rosy and red
It seems like hours before the children are in bed
Wet bathing suits, dirty towels, sandy hair and such mess
Mothers lose patience when put to the test
Summer is a time of fun and joy
For every sun tanned girl and boy
They seem to thrive and grow so strong
While mothers weaken when things go wrong
Oh how I wish I was a child again
So I could run and romp and play
Just let me imagine a long summer's day
Not as a mother, but a child at play

Bernice Bennett

Untitled

I don't remember seeing the sky in New York City.
There was no blue to the black rain
      Buildings that lined my view.
      Windows reflected Windows
         and People
and the asphalt sparkled instead of stars.

Margaret Richardson

To My Darling Mimi On Valentine's Day

If my memory doesn't fail me,
That was 1995 — January twenty three;
I proposed my love that came from my heart and mind,
Asking a beautiful lady, "will you be my Valentine?

She replied, "Yes, why not, I would love to be,
And you are the first one to ask me;
But just this Valentine's Day!"
Such a reply I felt so very happy.

My love towards her grew deeper each day,
I want to say it the way I like it to be;
So I sent her a poem on her birthday, 29th of May,
Assuring to love her come what may.

I promised to write her everyday,
Showering her with love of great certainty;
I received a reply from her with no equal,
Saying 'Yes' to my marriage proposal.

My grateful heart was filled with love,
For I know Mimi and me were blessed by God above;
Pronounced husband and wife by Hon. Judge Max Ratunil,
To love each other, we should never fail.

Manuel L. Paquingan

Life Is Like a Garden

Life is like a garden.
The planning and preparing.
Planting of the seed.
Caring for the seed.
Fertilizing and weeding.
Anticipation of growth.
Courteousness of development.
Will it turn out like expected?
The coloring.
The beauty.
The fulfillment
The inflorescence
Life comes in many different ways
But defined, is existence.
Not always what is expected nor planned.
Grow your life carefully, to get the most
Beauty out of it!

Kathleen Venita Simon

Change!

We live our lives — sometimes slow or with haste.
Hours, days, months, even years we waste.
Not seeing a creature's beauty, not nature's real wealth.
We don't care about others or our precious health.

We move through existence without much thought.
Ignore things we see, forget what we were taught.
Being hectic or apathetic, blind to affection and faces.
Yet being frightened lonely in overcrowded places.

You feel sorry for yourself and blame bad luck.
Thought you had it going and just became stuck.
Everything goes wrong what you plan and arrange.
Until admitting your perception of life has to change.

Don't become a bitter person or act like angry fools.
Re-entering this world only when winning the pools.
Focus on basic values instead, with a total new strive.
After all you are the lucky one — you're healthy and alive.

Hans-Peter Brammer

"I Often Wish"

Dedicated to Tessa Zanke
I often wish,
That I was taller then the biggest evergreen,
But smaller then the smallest mushroom you've ever seen,

I often wish
That I was an Eagle,
So I could soar above my enemies,

I often wish
That I was a Cheetah
So I could run away from any problem I might have.

I often wish
I was an Elephant
Because their is strength in size.

But who I am I cannot change,
I will be him till I die,
But I can't say I hate this guy.

Delirious (Stephen Lee Stevens II)

Life's Purpose

Life's Purpose is to touch someone and mark them forever.
A brand that comes only from love and understanding.
Always leaving them with a feeling that someone cares.

Life's Purpose is to share the light and energy from above.
Letting someone know that they are not alone.

Life's Purpose is to heal in many ways, by our actions,
our words, and our touch; by just being there.

Our very presence, shared with compassion,
will lead many souls
on the path
of light and love,
and together,

We can touch the face of God

Marie G. Lawrence

"Good-bye"

I have decided now to shut my eyes, and say goodbye.
This web you have pulled me in
has caused my heart sorrow, from deep within.
I need now to pull myself out
and realize what this whole things about.
I will miss you in my time of true
but we both know what is best for me and you.
So I will go now and leave behind
the things I once had and used to be mine.
These pieces I used to know
have not been held by me to show.
But there are memories that will be kept
in my mind, until they have left.
Though I am leaving, I have been here before
but now it's reverse, and I close the door.
I will be strong, and stay alive
because I am willed and able to survive.

Michelle Wilkin

Candy Shop

Stay away from candy shops my dear, my very sweet.
For if you're caught in one of them they'll package you quite neat
And ship you to a customer who'll yum and ah and ooo
And start a gobblin' 'till there's nothing left of you.

Carl Rosen

Plant A Seed Of Love

Plant a seed of love and watch it grow,
You will marvel at the wonderment of it,
Shower it with patience and nurture it, and soon you will know,

With loving, toiling, earth stained hands that place the seeds that
    are sowed,
You will receive gifts of sunshiny happiness bestowed,

The seeds of love are delicate and fine,
With the attentiveness of a mother nursing her child,
All it takes is to be a little kind,

The love droplet that is watered, nurtured, and raised to grow,
Will bring good tears,
The kind of joy and contentment you will learn to know.

Be thankful that we have the chance to care and share with one another
and love, from the Maker of all lovers and love droplets from above,

If each and everyone of us plants a seed,
which isn't all that difficult to do,
Perhaps say I love you,
Or turning a tear into a smile is truly the epitome of a good deed,

If everyone of us has at last a seed planted,
I know that with loving hands and minds we will find this land,
Once again to be like heaven, enchanted.

Ann Snelson Sears

The Color Red

Memories of a bullfight
in Madrid, Spain
a foreign land,
an alien culture.

Enjoyment? Entertainment?
Through their eyes — not my eyes.
Dare I to judge?

A bullfight — just one bull — no!
But a number of bulls up to four
as I can remember.
My stomach — smells of blood
attacking my senses;
colors of red — red blood — red cape;

Oh, Matador, made great by the jabbing of a sword
by the swirling of a cape,
the angle of your feet
in your pretty costume, palette of gold and white,
and an arrogant black hat.
To fight the bull, the greatest prize!
At least the meat is for charity.

Anna Marie Foisy

Fog

The fog is like hovering souls over
The land.
A deep love floating over the earth
Looking for a home, a place dwell.

A smothering layer of smoke over the
Land that slips in through the night.
It's as though a spirit of love lurking
In the night, waiting to be invited in.
Just longing to be wanted and bring
Peace to its vast being.

Let us not wonder if I was once a spirit
That was once loved or lost to the song
Of time. I pray to the father of time
For the day I wonder no more.

Carla Basham

Child Of Burdens

Little girl crying in a corner,
dry your tears and cry no longer.
  Smile even though it hurts,
once again you feel like dirt.
  Play the part even if it doesn't fit,
come on kid, use your wit.
  So many problems for a young girl to face,
no matter how hard you try, you can't win this race.
  Tell me child, how does it feel,
to be constantly pulled and peeled?
  What are you to do,
no one cares about you?
  They'll just do it again tomorrow,
but why worry, you're used to the sorrow.
  Go ahead, crawl back into you corner,
and cry for a little while longer.

  Jackie DiNunzio

A Tale Left Untold

With gentle hands and a loving face
his eyes an amazing blue
his hair a tightly curled blonde

I had a premonition of our acquaintance
at a family camp-out, a subtle voice
an overcoming feeling of importance
I liked him

As the night wore on I felt my heart pull
a shock of disappointment settled through my body
his parents called to remind him they would be leaving soon

As we parted he watched
tears filled my eyes
I was afraid it would be friendship gone to waste
I waited for weeks
not a word
not a letter
his face slowly left my mind
but his memory never left my heart

The end remains unfinished
my peaceful dreams hold the key to that untold tale

  Jennifer St. John

The Sacramento River

Northern California is the start,
beautiful Mt. Shasta doing its part.
A hop and a skip gets you across,
but not too far or you'd be at a loss.

It huffs and it puffs and it rolls over rocks,
the roar and speed you cannot exceed.
It roars through the mountains
with the greatest of ease.
The trees nodding good-bye,
as big as you please.

The fish teasing the fisherman
with his fly and his bate.
'Till the sun goes behind the mountains
and it just gets too late.

You pull in your line
and call it a day.
Cause when you get skunked
what else can you say.

Good-bye to the river and happy sailing too.
You knocked me down and made me black and blue.

  Tillie Dettling

A Blended Tapestry

A blended tapestry of singing human hearts
Sharing melodies and rhythms of heartache and pain, joy and comfort.
Endless acceptance, mutual love, caring and affirmation for all lives.
Divine energy sprouting and emerging reflected in Jesus heart, fully
human and fully Divine.

Pilgrims united by God's Holy Spirit
Called to be Holy friend, Spiritual companion and neighbor to all.
Listen to the inner voice of Christ within. Find the golden thread of
God's pure and absolute love.

Deepening spiritual ripples and blossoms.   Spreading joy and awe.
Individuals find God's center and truth
Holy Love abounds and creates from within.

Empty hearts of wounds and suffering.
Roll away the stone from the tomb. Turn over stones.
Hearts open and fill with God's passion and Love.

Answers processed and refined
Apparent darkness transforms into pure and sacred Light
Awareness of who we are in God's time
Becomes a never ending reality and awakening.
Listen Pray Listen Act Create Listen Pray

  Jan Grader 1951-1994

Soft

Who knew, that the pageantry of the roses,
  would keep my eye?

That the softness, of our ribs,
  between my calloused fingers,
    would soothe me?

Look at me, scarred and battered,
  Look at me, soft inside . . .,

If I held you close,
  warm, sheltered in rugged flesh,
Would you harden your heart to me?

If I spoke quietly,
  in your ear,
    Would you listen,
      take heed to what I say?

Or would you wilt,
  in my clasp,
    decayed and molten,
      like everything else?

  Scott McRaney

Loss

It's hard when you lose, someone that you love
  Even when you know, they're in heaven above

Your heart feels so empty, it hurts deep down within you
  Someday's it's too much, just trying to get through

But they're really not gone, even if they aren't here
  For the rest of your life, they'll always be near

To give you guidance, and watch over you
  To take great pride, in all that you do

Life is a journey, we travel every day
  And as we move forward, some of us can't stay

But I truly believe, they're in a better place
  For up in the heavens, they're in Gods embrace.

  Karen R. Meltz

Suicide

How do I feel
How do I know
I guess I don't feel what I'm supposed to feel
I guess I don't know what I'm supposed to know.
Death
Do I know it
Do I feel it
Do I see it
Why you
Why me
Suicide
I feel it
I know it
I see it
But sometimes I wonder . . .
Can I feel it
Do I want to feel it
Why must I feel it, if I must
But I ask you
Do you feel it? . . .

Natalie Baptiste

The Way

Walk freely in the wind not against it,
but with the breeze allowing the Spirit
to draw you forward.

Feel the sun upon your face and be guided
by the warmth, let the rays touch your heart
with the glow of love.
Catch the rain upon your flesh as the chill
brings refreshment to your being.

Gather the living waters within supported
by Grains of Truth, so that one may float
upon this island in the Eternal Ocean of God.
Cast not about your course to self, but
rather trust the waves and tides of Divine
Providence. Living in today journeying into
tomorrow.

Let peace be in your soul
Love in your spirit
Joy in your heart.

For each is a child a universe unto oneself
to their Lord and God. Born of Freedom and Endless.

William I. Elliott

"O Great Nation"

O Great Nation so faithful to me —
O great life, so abundant to me.
Thy shadows hover and taint thee.
What illness grows and troubles thee?
Thy values have changed and many lives were lost.
Thy legends have changed with winds of frost.
Tomorrow's promise of hearts and fame —
We must nourish them with truths un-shamed.
Thy great bounty of peoples past and present —
Testify to thee and pray ironies!
Our great numbers shine as shimmering rainbows —
Yet our understandings are as untold.
We hold up our honor searching for gold —
Forgetting our promise with words so bold.
Lift thy head and cleanse thy thoughts —
Prevail thyself and loiter not.
Each of us must bear the truth —
Each of us must be undiffused.
For together we are the truth!
Forever great and forever unbruised!

Wesley Ray Moore

Love And Hate

Sometimes, you have to hate! A little,
  To find out, just! How much you love.

  But never! Let hate! Eat you up,
    Because, there is someone up above!

He judges you! For what you do!
Your love that's kind and true.

  Please remember there are others,
    just like you.

    But! You don't have to be another hater add to the crew.

Audrey M. Cousins

Don't Forget What God Has Made

Don't forget what God has made,
The rocks, the trees, the creatures;

Don't forget what God has made,
He made all the seasonal features.

The trees He made so lush and green,
The flowers oh so bright;

He made the sun and moon and stars,
He made the day and night.

He made the rain that waters the trees,
He made the sparkling snow;

Oh, He made all the wonderful things,
As well as what troubles you, I know.

So next time you see a pretty flower,
Don't pick it, just leave it there;

Because of this, God can make
Another beautiful flower grow there.

Dawn Ashley

Lightship

She has known the sea's
Relentless whip.
Oxide crusted, devoid of power
She limps
Into an alien port.
Death for her? They ask.
Perhaps.
But, now she rests.
And there's the chance that one will see
Beneath the barnacles and rust
The sturdy steel
And then restore
Her dignity.

Mary Anne Harny

Full Circle

I am alive. I am all around you.
With every gust of wind, a gasp for clean air,
with every drop of rain, a tear of hope and sorrow.
I am alive. I am all around you.
With every forest fire, the burning question of why,
with every earthquake, a tremble at the thought
of what is to come.
I am alive. I am all around you.
With every sunny day in July, with the snow at Christmas
time, with the leaves changing color,
and with each and every day, I thank you.
I am alive. I am all around you.
I am Mother Earth and I need you.

Patricia A. Ferchland

Forbidden

The sound of your voice warms me
like a soft downy blanket
on a cold December night

Your eyes reach out to mine
and for a brief, shining moment, we are one
in a secret, shared thought

Then we touch, ever so slightly
and my heart dances with longing
for things that never can be

Linda R. Stollar

She's Only Nine

Her birthday arrived a week ago,
She let it into her heart.
A welcome visitor like new-fallen snow,
The celebration of her splendid start.

Her giggly friends lugging sleeping bags
Joined her for a party night.
Pizza, popcorn and hair in rags
Amid squeals of surprise and delight.

No fluffy frosting or sweet ice cream
No traditional birthday cake,
Sugar-free treats replaced that dream,
Since diabetes planted its stake.

Sticking her finger with love and care
Syringes filled with insulin gray,
Like brushing her teeth or combing her hair
A part of her little girl day.

She's only nine; this daughter of mine
A small but mighty force.
Her approach so logical, her spirit so fine
She already must chart her own course.

Kelly Failla

Untitled

A queen she be? She stands so tall
And holds dominion over all
A goddess she? She shines so fair
The stars themselves grow plain and bare.
Say no, my friend, for that is right,
Though as the sun she seems as bright.
No emerald she, no sparkling pearl
but just a comely mortal girl.
Yet feel no shame to answer yes,
For goddess had been my best guess.

Ryan M. Malone

Untitled

I feed my depression in 24 hour increments
Stopping only briefly to dream of death.

I do not possess the muscles required to smile.
Gravity keeps my head facing forever downward.

It is cruel enough to hear the world.
What, if anything, is worth looking up for?

My miserable existence on this planet is wasted.
I seek nothing, so shall I find nothingness.

What happened to this once happy kid, who knows?
What will happen to this tired and bitter man, who cares?

Depression is my drug of choice.
As with any addict, I cannot live without.

Forever alone and happily
Alone forever.

Mike Sherrill

Portrait Of A Traveler

The coat had to be red,
only the red coat would do.
He did not care to consider,
a garment any shade of blue.

With the coat came adore,
gifts abound at his mention.
He lived days without toil,
and nights with female attention.

In the coat he felt special,
above all the people he knew.
He saw the reds being pale,
and the blues were just blue.

Threw the burrows he wandered,
in places high and at sea.
Never stopping to notice, the hearts open and free.

He saw a young man in a cloak, the cloth was royal and regal.
It had all the eyes glowing, yes the cloak had no equal.

The man thought over time, his fabric's color had faded.
Truth now be told, the coat's wearer was jaded.

Vance P. Spillman

A Leaf

Fall is approaching; my color of green is now light
I am changing thoroughly
My body and stem is rustling swiftly with a sound of pity
From the beauty of when I was created
Bright green — a change of red, blended with speckles of orange
I know soon before the mighty breeze come I am slowly dying
As the breeze flows through me
I am changing faster then ever
From my birth color, bright green,
Blending into deep red,
Fully growing into light orange; just about changing into yellow
"Swoosh," the mighty breeze has come to take me over
I am rustling with a fear of death for my stem has loosen
Flowing deeply down into the hearth of Mother Nature
As I had the thought of death,
My feelings and emotions had loosened freely into thin streaks of air
Just as my thoughts and memory were banish
My energy had overtaken my inner soul
All my life parts were soaked into the thin streaks of air
I soon will be gone; all gone gone gone gone gone gone gone gone gone

Khoa N. Nguyen

"Instinct"

Geese sail over an ice packed lake,
To rise above a snow filled bank
Their wings beat a wind swept sound,
As they stretch their necks southward bound.
As they elevate into the sky,
They seem to me to wave good-bye.
What fire burns inside their soul,
That tells their brain it's time to go.
So close to heaven, yet so far away,
Who makes the choice to fly today?
Is migration something they all know,
Or is it guidance from the soul?
What dares to jest the minds of men,
Who claim an instinct from within?
They form a wedge above the land,
And fly with guidance of God's hand.
I watch the geese disappear into the sky,
I pray to migrate when I die.
The creature I choose to be, is far above the geese I see.
Geese fly high and close to thee, but I have God inside of me.

Mark A. Hurt

399

I Want

I want a chance to live a life where I could be free
Where people judge me by my character and love me for me

I want a chance at an education in a school without a fight
Where you're graded on your knowledge not your skin type

I want a chance to walk and not worry about thugs
Where people get high on life and not on drugs

I want a chance to raise my kids and put love in their heart
If we are going to have peace this is where it must start

I want another chance to talk to grandma and put her on stage
So she can tell how to live right and reach her golden age

I want the President to call all countries from the south to middle east
An say O.K. we tried fighting now lets try peace
I want, I want, I want
        Bernard Mack

The Game

In the game of life there are no rules
In fact I think it's played by fools
People hope and dream that we may all
live as one
Only to be shattered by the sound of a gun
To live and love will assure you to
Heaven, if you so desire
While the journey to hell ends with bars
and barbed wire
So good or bad, what will it be
Or does it matter, can't I just be me
To figure it out would be like standing in line
When you're finally in front, you're out of time
        Tina Huntley

That'll Do, I Deserve Better

why do women compromise ourselves to settle for less
than we deserve by having a womb we are thrust
into this position by virtue of hormones unbeknown to man
we give in accept bare facts starting revelations from our
mates i myself have found this to be the conflict in my
life i would like the question addressed i found that by giving
in to my it was to avoid the dreaded argument silence
across the dinner table let's not leave out the sleep on your side
don't touch me the results were no conversation dinner or sexual
contact which meant giving in or repeating another night forget
the day nothing ever went right after a night like that your moods
would shift a thousand past confrontations would be reviewed to
obtain a solution to this dilemma many the time i felt compelled
to stand by my resolutions not give in damn the consequences
being the woman that i am i would give in yes dear it's o.k. if
you go play poker with the boys instead of spending time that
we may better connect it was more important for his ego that he be
allowed to perpetuate the male image of being in charge girlfriend
i know you have done the same thing for me the constant giving in
was wrecking havoc on my mental state i decided to not give in to
another persons needs again be it my man whatever the situation
from this day forward it would be my way to say i deserve better is
an understatement but that'll do, i deserve better
        Nyata C. Frazier

Life Within

It's a green leaf from under the ground.
It grows with the years and seasons around.
It's sharp and painful yet beautiful too.
Its bloom is delicate with glistening dew.
It blushes with red as the blood rushes through.
Its thirst for beauty is passionate and true.
For the rose has as much beauty as the child within you.
        Jamie Cole

Untitled

You are the presents,
you are the gifts.
You have reminded each of us
of how very human we are
and that nothing is more important
than the human touch,
Nothing is more important
than the fragility of the very human heart
None of us has to travel
by plane or car or train
to receive the wonders of the world . . .
The wonders are within us
and there is not a human being amongst us
who is anything less
than extraordinary.
        Kathleen Reilly

Death

Time is lost.
Thoughts are broken.
Special moments are unwoven.
The earth covers you and warms your soul.
Life is replaced by other ones that benefit;
    and as you lie down to rest,
    the earth covers you in its crest,
    and you go to bed.
Forever in darkness.
Forever in peace.
Forever in eternal history only the rocks of
    the earth can teach.
        Joseph Neves Marcal IV

"The Only Ones"

To man who was given this wondrous earth.
Let it not in its orb swing and sway;
for to let it so by thine own birth.
Doom it forever to rust and decay.
Stand firm and believe in the quest.
Keep it clean and pure at his behest.
Tis all that is needed day by day.
From the smallest to the largest say.
"You will keep your promise. I pray."
Plant a tree, clean a spring with pride,
forever the reaper is on the side;
take care not to tarry or procrastinate,
for we alone did he create, Earth.
For all the universe he did decree birth.
Go forth, multiply, in all thing be free.
This wondrous earth to you and me.
No where else are beings in charge.
The Universe is beyond our Nit and Ken,
we are the only ones at large.
We whom he stamped and made into men.
        Lawrence E. Travagline

The Queen

My past was retold
In a musky mirrorless chamber.
Onyx-black eyes scanned my palm,
Silhouetted in glowing amber.
Scarlet lips whispered:
"You sold yourself without qualms
To a snake who tricked you, then left you to bleed.
Your lover,
While he took your love as alms,
Caesar's blood grew cold."
        Balaji Krishna

"Vision Quest"

Brother wolf came to me in a night vision. We sat by a fire and smoked the sacred pipe. "Remembering days gone by," he said. "In thebeginning the buffalo sustained life, our people knew the ways of the ancient ones. There was harmony in our midst. Seasons came, seasons went."

Then the eagle came, taking me in the spirit. Thru his eyes I saw a great gathering of our people. They came from the four winds, the elders sat by a fire and while smoking the sacred pipe one by one, the moon showed her face for the seventh time. The sound of the drums stopped as the greatest of elders spoke. "In the beginning the buffalo sustained life, our people followed the ways of the ancient ones. There were stories of courage and honor, dances telling deeds of past and present. There was harmony in our midst. Seasons came, seasons went."

When I returned, brother wolf gave me the sacred pipe to smoke. He asked, "Do you have understanding of this vision?" Considering all I had seen and heard I said, "The buffalo that once sustained life is gone. So our people must draw from this essence, giving totally of themselves that they might have life. By returning to the ways of the ancient ones we will once again have harmony in our midst and for seasons to come."

Leonard Martinez

Cool Breezes

Sweet, cool breezes hit my face,
And all I think about is him,
Who does he claim to love?
I wish it was me,
We've known each other for quite a while,
He was like my best friend,
So I guess our love was never meant to be.

I think about him constantly,
Is he thinking about me too?
He came into my life like a cool breeze,
So quick and fast,
His love surrounded me like no other's
Since that day, I never was the same.

His love overwhelmed me,
Like a cool breeze,
He was perfect in every way,
He made my cloudy days turn to sunshine,
With every smile and touch he gave,
But I guess good things don't always last forever,
Because he's gone now, like a cool breeze.

Stephanie Pena

The Father's Footstool

I had hoped you'd come, sitting in the chair
I promised you, drinking from my cup.
I wanted you to be with me and know I am always
near. The hopes and dreams I gave you
still linger in your head. The love and life I
granted you still holds to every movement
of my hand. You have everything I had to give,
everything you wanted but somehow that
wasn't enough. The oceans, the land, all the
beauty of this earth I wanted you to
have, use and enjoy. I made them for you. I
shared my heavens and brilliant universe,
my peace and adoring glory with you. Even my
son I gave for you. I held you in my
hands and let you feel My power as if it was
yours. But it wasn't enough, what then
do you want that I haven't already given you,
what do you desire that I will not give you?

Carina Walz

The Lady In Waiting

A lady in waiting for her man to return
for deep in her heart a fire still burns.
Promises are made but they never hold true
So patiently she waits, for what more can she do.
His every word lingers on in her mind
and his love she still seeks and hopes someday to find.
She reaches out for to capture this dream
and miserably she fails, or so it seems.
With each passing day her hearts still does ache
for everything she cares for is so much at stake.
She tries to hold on as the days pass by
but still the tears flow from her eyes.
Love isn't easy, this she now believes
and sometimes her own-self she tries to deceive.
Often she wonders if her pain he can see
a hurt that she carries for a love that can't be.
To this false hope he gives she will desperately cling
but of happiness and love she can no longer sing.
And with each tomorrow the sun will still rise
While the lady in waiting for her man still cries.

Sabrina Michales

One For Yeyo

Thru teary eyes I saw blue ice glimmering in the sky
But I heard no glory in the heights and felt no peace in my heart
How sad was the night when the gentle old man closed his eyes.

Slowly I walked thru the hours of my days
Tempted to turn my eyes to the hills
And echo the old sage "From whence cometh my help?"
Gone was the friend, the shelter, the one who always saw my side.
And I mourned more for me than for him,
For the lack of farewell, for the empty shelf of love.

But as the weeks turned into years
And I mused in the garden of my life I discovered him anew,
Not in his flesh, but in mine,
My roots, I learned, were deep in his
And he came and walked with me,
And together, closer now than ever,
We cried and we smiled at the offspring of my life.

And when the night of that day arrived
Through clear eyes I saw again blue ice glimmering in the sky
And I heard, oh yes, I heard clear and loud
Glory in the highest and peace in my heart.

Cristobal Sanchez

Fabrication

From this faint life
I've felt the fabric that twines together,
The silk is my good side,
The wool is my domestic life
I slip into new fabric everyday
Learning something new and different.
I am now so full of knowledge that the threads are running
  and tearing.
Red is the evil within and
Green is the source of nature and chemicals.
It tows me through weeks at a time,
The ripples are the mistakes
The ironed is wealth we bring into society,
We now have thousands of fabrics
  that represent each new path.
If they shall crease that is the downfall of mankind,
Where will we end?
Flowing through the Milky Way or flying through the sky.

Dave Wheeler

Spirit Of The American Indian

Long braids of black
Copper red skin
Struggling day to day
To keep alive the beliefs and dreams within.

Proud and strong
Trying to survive
I admire their courage
And will to stay alive.

They have endured much pain and suffering
The extent we will never know
Their belief in who they are
Help them face tomorrow.

We've taken so much from them
And not given anything back
They may not have much
But in spirit they will never lack.

We allow them to live in poverty
Making promises we never keep
See the sorrow in their eyes
We wonder why their anger runs so deep.

Marn M. Brix

Caring

Caring is diverse as the universe —
    an engulfment of the environment.
Caring during youth is so honest,
    with aging years — sometimes dishonest,
Caring as watchful and tender during
    days, should be all embracing and loving
    the night.
Caring should not be guilt so expressed
    as to oppress.
Caring is not bondage, but a flowing,
    high flying freedom —
Caring not did cause a sinful shame
    should this cause an endless blame?
Rather turn and let this endless feeling
    be of great pride —
Right now this moment, every moment
    through eternity.
Caring is two together, two concerned, two
    aware, two in love — sharing each other's
    every need in peace forever —.

R. Ramon Sedillo

Food For Thought

If we look at the world as a huge melting pot
We would gather the best ingredients we've got
We would measure them out and mix them well
Then bring them to boil and wait for the smell
Soup is no good with just one thing alone
It needs good stock as well as the bone
Let us start with a giant mixing bowl
We can each play a part without a starting role
We will start with the finest cup of peace
You won't believe the aroma it can release
Then add a dab of compassion, just to taste
Handle it carefully, we don't want to waste
Stir in some kindness and lots of love
These ingredients come from Heaven's Kitchen above
We all should blend together to do our best
Let's get the job done, then we all can rest
We can take a universal problem and make it our own
We all have to pitch in, no one can do it alone
When the soup is done we can all sit down to eat
Now that will be one meal that can't be beat.

Elaine Jackson

Pure Sensation

I live to be more than your experience
I have destroyed the mountain
Just you can see my shadow
Dancing across the plain
Vulnerable
Helpless

My heart can dance and drop with one breath
My soul can soar and plummet with one glance
My body can tingle and numb with one touch
My world can open up and crash down with one word

I am devastating explosion and a weak tremble
I am the source of light and the path to nothingness
I shine, I fade
I love, I hate
I laugh, I cry
I begin, I end
Right before your eyes
Your beautiful eyes
Your beautiful
Eyes

Jennifer Smith

Country

The grass I need to mow,
the grass sways to and fro.
The breeze is soft and cool,
not a sound can be heard but the chirp of a bird.
Cornfields far as the eye can see,
happy and glad to be me.
Clean is the air I give,
peaceful and sound mind is the place I live.
Weeds I pull and pluck,
a garden I grow to save a buck.
My tomatoes are red and ripe,
my neighbors don't complain or gripe.
I pity the folk that live in the city.

Charity Rose Hinkel

A Special Place

Tucked away deep inside the minds of every living, breathing
creature, is a magical place where they may go to find true
spirituality and grace.
To the deer a lavish field filled with endless acres of wild
flowers, and untouched blades of grass, sweet, savory and satisfying.
To the trout, endless streams with many paths to follow, filled
with flies for which the trout may swallow.
To me not so different from the deer and trout, a world with
endless acres of pure untouched majesty, a world which flows like
streams, without famine, into places where all would find inner
peace and sanctity.
Such fond places do exist conceived from hope, brought to life in dreams.

Scott Biggs

Summer Day

Butterflies floating in a warm, sweet, breeze
Children's laughter, shrieks of excitement
Tourists drifting through town by the thousands
    Beautiful women in bathing suits
    Rainier 40's, bonfires on the beach
    Renter girls out on a late night mission
Yellow, golden, relaxing rays sink deep into your skin
    Sleeping in, no worries, never rushed
Kick back, relax and enjoy this beautiful summer day

Mike Bonfini

Senses

We are here
On this glorious green blue sphere
Living the lives we were given
Pretending to be forgiven
Existing only to exist
We are people who persist.

We don't want to not love another,
But, we sometimes hate our brother.
It is human nature, you see my friend
That makes us destroy our fellow American.

It is our human disposition
That sometimes shatter our coalition
We must keep our senses and attack.
Attack with consciousness, which we sometimes lack.

Ah, but to attack is human
To be Human is to attack.
Therefore, we cannot fight fair,
For there are many who just don't care . . .

Michael Reed

Rhymes

Your pen writes the lyrics to the song.
But my pen writes the words to the poem.
We use the words that rhyme.
Your words have music of a different kind.
My words have rhyme of the opposite kind.

All the words we use are full of meaningful heart beats,
Some of time of away of life.
Some of hate, love or fright.
Words of love that is a mess.
Tomorrow we'll take a rest.
From the words that are a test.

Words used so sweetly, words so discreetly.
Words of year gone by with meanings of words changed on the sly.
Tomorrow they will vary in kind.
So today the words come so smartly.
To make the poem so tartly.

If the lyrics of your song doesn't come with the ease of wand.
Then take the time to let your mind
Wander through the words of my rhyme.
To measure the elements of words that rhyme
Is the season of mythical thyme.

Nancysue Johns McIntire

"In Colored Calms"

I'm settled here — in colored calms,
the sweet embrace of autumns arms.
So felt as deepest sea the hues,
a romance drifts on dazzled shoes.

There's red to share and in between
a dancing gold to fill a dream.
The one that stifles all alarm,
a joy of life — in colored calms.

The bright of sun does yield the hue,
bedecked against the sky of blue.
It's such as smile — its dimpled charm,
a cherished while mid colored calms.

I'm settled here — in colored arms,
the sweet embrace of autumn's arms.
So felt as deepest sea the hues,
a romance drifts on dazzled shoes.

Mark W. Haggerty

An Attic Of Dreams

Mem'ry's the box where children grown old,
tinker with toys of their youth,
recalling livelier days of the years,
time buried with one broken tooth.

Mem'ry's the garden where youngsters grown wise,
search-out the blooms that will last,
among the dried flow'rs, pressed between leaves
of treasured books, read in the past.

Tucked in the haven of yesteryear's niche,
where spiders and cob webs convene,
sacred to some, are echoes they'll hear,
while rafters of laughter careen.

Out from the musty dim shadows unwind, evoking's of visions of yore,
revealing clear traces from dustings of mind's
sand castles up, down by the shore.

Dismayed by the slue of things I can't do,
reality's comfort in change,
is memory's helping hand guiding me through,
from a trunk full of truths within range,
in an Attic Of Dreams, to exchange . . .

Alfred A. Colo

"The End Of Winter"

He has fought the long hard battle,
Of life's winter, with its stiff winds, and chilling rattle.
And gave a very good showing, with brave heart and of knowing.
And remembering back the years gone by.
The love and home, the good times, how they fly!
But now Winter's wind, has flown,
And he has found his peace, and is not alone,
He has found the Everlasting Spring, that is in "Gods Holly Place".
He has found, "everything", so weep no more for him my dear.
There is no pain upon his face, Here he lives with
love and faith, forever free of fear.
So weep no more for him, my dear.
For Him it is the End of Winter.

Ronald J. Katz

Marine

Rain like tears, uncertainty drips
through the echo of the soldier.

Ignore the pain.

I've made my fight like life's not enough
so prove it through these puddles and

Ignore the pain.

So this is me and this is real
and another soldier yells

Don't even think of stopping.

There's death for one
bare feet for another
one fight chosen, one just happens.

I ignore the pain.

But not the thought
then into the mud I'm done.

Rain and tears together
like me
and what I make of this day.

Mark G. Viviano

403

A Mother's Prayer

On the day you were born my heart filled with joy
It never really mattered if you were a girl or a boy
I mapped out your life and made plans in my head
As I held you in my arms from my hospital bed
From the 1st step you'd take to the 1st word you'd speak
I had all these expectations for you to meet
As years went by and you did things your way
Suddenly I realized you had a lot to say
You have your own mind and life to live
It's only love and direction that I'm to give
Although you look like a carbon copy of me
That doesn't mean that your life also shall be
I didn't stop and take notice of all the good you've done
And be grateful that God choose you to be my (daughter) (son)
"God only lends you his children" so treat them right everyday
Cause you never know when he will take them away
So on the day they are born love them for who they are
Guide them and praise them they just might go far
And remember the reason you wanted them before they were born
Don't try to remember if ever the day comes when you are in mourn

Judylynn Nelson

Long Time

Haven't heard from you in so long.
Now I have only the memory to pull me on.
And what do I remember?
Nothing.
Nothing of happiness.
Nothing of love.
Only the yearning.
Only the wish.
And no hope to comfort me.
So here I am.
No joy.
No laughter.
No comfort.
And one dream.
One large, unattainable dream.
To be everywhere.
To do everything.
And to do it with you.
But I am still here,
Doing nothing.
Alone.

Elizabeth Gale

Coming Home Again

We laugh, we cry, we live,
    we die
So this is how it goes??
Why must we grieve in time
    of death
When in the end we know

We're all coming home again
    Coming home!

In birth there is celebration
    joy and tears
A life has begun, beginning
    anew so fresh.
    So innocent, so true
A family begins with mom and dad
    and sons and daughters too

So tell me why do we grieve
    When our time does come?

Can't they see that in the end
Our family will be as one again

We are all coming home, coming home, coming home again

Nancy Falango

Sunrise And Sunset

I wake and look outside
To see dew sparkling on the grass.
The early morning mist rises from the river
As the tide slowly moves in.
Crickets chirp softly on the lawn
As the wind whistles through the trees that stand tall.
At the water's edge
A white heron eats crabs and fish.
Ducks dive high from the sky
And land gently in the water.
Goldfinch fly to the feeders
And scare away the squirrels.
At sunset the sky is orange and gold.
And the Canada Geese honk in the distance.
As night falls, the moon rises.

John-Michael Hubbard

Sweet Darkness

When the bright day sky gets tired I start to spread my wings.
I can fly once again.
My moon shines sweetly because death does not await.
Taking the sun in my arms I cradle him sweet,
    then I swallow him for the infinite time.
You see I am the women of the night, I can sing forever.
    My voice is watched.
        Echoes muffled by sweet clean smells of my midnight flight.
        Oh you don't recall that I watch you,
you can see me but can't place the name for when you wake
I am remnants of a long sleepy song . . .
    Oh talk to me, Make my game pleasurable.
Make me high with your whispers
Lie to me with your long wisps of smoke
    Do you watch the stars tangles in my hair?
    Do you want to help me get out of this trap? . . .
Do not listen for I am a liar, I may swallow you up.
    You have a secret, I will not tell.
I will lay my weight on the soft atmosphere and sing lullaby of
faraway places so distant from here . . .
then I am gone and your secrets are forgotten until I hunger.

Crystal Moselle

Broken Arrow

I never really knew him
I only knew of him.

I went by what they said — it was the only way.

I was always told that he was a brilliant man, a talented man, a
gifted man . . .
Yet I never saw it or felt it — I have only heard of it.

I didn't doubt it for a minute.
I could see what his capabilities were.

Yet I feel cheated and hurt that I couldn't be a part of it.
Or that I'll never know where it could have taken him.

No! He's not gone yet.
He is still here.

But somehow it doesn't matter.
Because his spirit is gone,
His hopes are lost,
His dreams are dead,
He is empty . . .

Such as the bottle that brought him to this place.

Jessica Lynn Centamore

Untitled

Don't lie to me. I am not the kind of girl you want to lie to. I don't know the kind of girl you are accustomed to, but I can assure you I am not that kind of girl. Don't take me for granted. I am not the kind of girl you want to take for granted. I don't know the kind of girl you've been with in the past, but I can guarantee I am not that kind of girl. Don't sell me short. I am not the kind of girl you are accustomed to. I am the kind of girl who will not be lied to. I am the kind of girl who will not be taken for granted. I am the kind of girl who is strong, strong willed and strong minded. I am the kind of girl who could love you truly and deeply, but I am not the kind of girl who will do so blindly. So do not think, for one second, that you can treat me like the kind of girl you expect me to be. That is not acceptable, because I am not that kind of girl.

Stephanie A. Smith

Darkness

in the darkness she finds her solace
in the darkness she finds a peace
just beyond her reach outside her world
in the darkness hides her relief
mommy left her years ago she's been so all alone
her only joy and fun was taken
emptiness is her only home
night plagues her with memories
night brings visits of deadly pain
visits from the knife and anguish
where is my relief where is my darkness
make the night end all i want is darkness
darkness whatever you are come save me
make him go away make this world leave me
sleep it brings relief but only for a moment
where is my forever relief
God if you are real i want to be free now
make my nights go away let me have real sleep
in the darkness hid her relief in His light she finds her peace
He is her relief her solace she found Him

Rebecca L. Wills

Life and Lore

Life is so short
But love makes everything alright
The days are so long
But you don't mind when you
Have your love to lay beside you
And hold you each night

But when his love is gone
And he's still there beside you
You can't reach out and touch him
Because you're so afraid to.

You lay awake hours after he's asleep,
and just listen to him breathe,
praying that morning will soon come
and wishing

Life was not so long

Janet Lucas

Wind

Above the soft wind blows,
Happily whispering in and out among the strong, fierce waves.
Will it die?
Will it grow?
Will the wind take a desperate route with the sea and graves?
It has breathed its final blow toward the seagulls' shout,
No longer making them slaves.

Kelly Coon

The Sands Of Time

The sands of time have washed upon the beaches to disappear into the landscape. If we only knew where they have come from, what wondrous places they have seen, how many fingers have touched them, that warm white sand.

How many times have they been washed away to another place in time. How can we say with certainty that these sands have not reached out from our past to be sat upon again in the future.

As a child, we sift the sand through our fingers and let the gentle breeze blow it to another place where maybe someday we will again look back and remember. A child sifting the sand, and who's to say this may not be the same sand blowing in the gentle breeze of a past and a future.

Sandra Raybould

For The Rose

I take a sip
and feel the rush of warmth down my throat,
the descent of a tear like an autumn leaf.
My gaze dissolves into orange red flames —
I slide inside an intoxicating rapture
and sigh to a single white rose I've befriended.
Strange newness is betrothed to the anguish
that devours my insides relentlessly.
A romantic strength springs into my spirit
and I willingly grow oblivious to reason.

Melissa P. Kanes

Early Morning, Pre-Caffeine

Crawling through the maze of half-finished dreams
And the cobwebs of the subconscious,
My eyes take in the gray of sky,
Still lifting from the black of night, as my mind
Struggles to emerge from its cocoon of sleep.
Stars fade, awkward feet on a cold wooden floor.
Rain today. The scent of its coming hits me
As I stand wavering and stretching before the window.
The mind slowly finds its track, the path of practicalities:
Coffee to make, clothes to press.
While thought marshals its forces on the verge of
Another day of work, laughter — God knows what —
A part of me follows the rain, slowly trickling,
Obeying gravity's dictates, the ease of a pre-made plan.
A sure sign of early morning, that — giving rain
The wisdom of Buddha; but as I turn to the world
Given to me, made by me, the duties of everyday,
The sound of a thousand drops somehow falling as one
Leaves a sense of peace more lasting than
The promises of bus schedules and answering machines.

Kelly Whitaker

Lady Butterfly

Once again you have greeted nature with the essence of harmony . . . Your song is silent, But it fills each and everyday of my life with the joy of promise . .. Your beauty is an exquisite yet tasteful puzzle of happiness, pieced together by the careful precision of love . . . just the mere sight of your heavenly body warms my cold yearning heart with inspirational, comfort, And the tender bliss of affection . . . you're truly a wonder in De'skies, And because of the caring you give, endures each passing moment with sheer confidence that love will see us through . . . You're sweet just as you're beautiful, You're gentle though yet firm when you stand by something "U" believe in . . . Therefore you're everything my dreams are made of, And I am quite sure you knew why nature had intentions for you to be . . . my only "Lady Butterfly".

Pinkie Everett

Woman's Body

Each delicate segment in conflict with gravity
her neck, once taut, crayoned with curvy lines
goose-flesh skin pulled smooth by elongated
breasts still crowned by perky nipples,
casting shadows.
Light before shadows.
Her abdomen, once indented, separated into soft
cushions by a thickening waist
her belly, once concave, remembers it all:
Skin expanded — balloon shaped not once
but twice, no longer elastic succumbing to
earth's pull, dark silky pubic hair tinged
with coarse gray gently enveloped by
cellulite dimpled thighs still remembering
shapely legs.
Woman's Body — gently reshaped —
by years' tender touch.

Christel Radke

Everything Brings Me To You

Like the sun pulls the flowers to her
And the early morning drifts from her hue
As the waves crash over the ocean
Everything brings me to you.

The dreams that I hold in my head
And the feeling of something brand new
The rainbow at the end of the storm
Everything brings me to you.

I behold the stars adorning the sky
And the next day it's shimmering blue
How could I think of anything else
When everything brings me to you?

I stand in the sun and gaze toward Heaven
Up where the angels once flew
The flowers around me are blooming mad
Everything brings me to you.

Kneeling down beside you now
There's nothing left I can do
As the life streams out of my body
Everything bring me to you.

Traci Solinger

The Question

Beneath blades of intertwined grass
hidden by layers of sifted ash
lies the frontier of my soul.
How time seemed startled on the day we all departed,
doom surrounded all like a hazy frost.
Sages foretold and predicted,
yet we all still conflicted our fellow man.
Without a tear or fear we did ignore,
then quick as a bolt we were shaken to a core.
Lavish wealth and peasant filth
were mottled together in foaming silth.
When it was evident we all would smoother,
every man became a brother.
A simple lesson to understand, yet never practiced in our land.
To late the message was already sent, we would die to repent.
Intuition, pre-cognition, words for what I feel
may seem myth but are all too real.
After we press too far in one direction
naturally there follows correction.
Why can't in godly nature man fulfill his own expression of freewill?
The question and clue I leave with you —

Sunny Rosen

Contemplation Of Love

As I sit here contemplating what to do with my quiet day
I can't help thinking of your smile, your touch, your gentle way
I picture you and me outside, a breeze blows through my hair
The look of love you give to me goes floating through the air
I love the way you hold my hand as we go walking 'round
The way you say I love you without uttering a sound

As we kiss beneath the clear blue sky, I melt in your embrace
I wonder how we ever got inside this lovely place
A place where nothing interferes with the love we chose to share
Where tender hearts explode in faith because we know we care
It's all good things I contemplate, as love continually grows
I live my life each day for you; each day it always shows

I love the way you feel at night, all snuggled by my side
The warmth your body gives to mine as I let you be my guide
Your lips, your touch, your passion's growth, all bring me such delight
With pleasure at its highest peak, I know this feeling's right
Now contemplation time is done, as the day has passed me by
Still, I'm happy and my heart is full, and you're the reason why . . .

C. Theresa Fletcher

Carousel of Pain

Please come be with me on my Carousel of Pain
The cost to ride is totally free
How you ask?
For all the pain is on me
It spins wildly out of control
It tears out your heart and weakens your soul
I can never get off, it spins too fast
Sometimes it slows down, but it never lasts
Hope can be an ally
A little bit shows up every day
Especially at night, when I fold my hands and say
"Now I lay myself down to sleep
I pray my heart discontinues to seep
All the love that it has yet to give
All the wrongdoers I have to forgive
All the days where I get to love again
To that special someone that might not have been
All the love and happiness I have yet to gain
All because of the lessons I learned
On my Carousel of Pain."

Chad Ahl

Ocean's Rising

In a dreamy vista of colors
splashing reds
and frothy whites
spilling pinks in the sky
and that cool gray-green color of the undertow
pulls me in

Milky white Moon lingers
pulls to the West

Ocean flies caterwauling
waves smash together
fall back to the East
to the red messenger
'the Day is coming
Ocean's rising'
in vivid memory I see the dream:
beautiful Ocean . . .
seagull —
scream!

Edward J. Laake

A Mere Speck Of Dust

A mere speck of dust, a polished imperfection born
into a world of claims that never hold true.
Speaking of peace but achieving war, putting
trust in men blinded by their pursuit of power and money.
Calming of words between world powers,
religious strife and hatred for sacred soil fill other
lands with bloodshed.
What is to happen to a world that only knows how to hate
those that don't share the same beliefs?
Has there not been fair warning of what will be our future?
Holy writings have supplied the answers all along.
Thousands upon thousands of people dying from sickness
and starvation, a simple act of kindness is all some ask for.
While many consider life a precious gift, is it not a greater gift
to love?
Choose your role models well, for the day of the separating
of good and bad is near.

Dimitri Frant

Silence

The day we separated and said goodbye
Numerous tears fell from my eyes.
The soft colors soon turned to a Seemingly gray
With the endless flow of tears,
I looked away.
Knowing this was my last chance to look at you
The best qualities came out,
Through and through.

It's hard to even imagines us apart
With these deep emotions of pain
We hold in our heart.

But just knowing we'll be united
Soon one day
All the pain and anger will slowly
Melt away.
And with that last silent glance,
You said goodbye to me.

Melody Ann Burgess

The Power

Her presence, alluring, so true,
a stunning frame unnerving to view.
She captures attention, she captures the eyes,
maintains her hold without compromise.

Her long dark hair, the confident glow
It aches almost to watch and know —
How lucky the man who wins her,
How crushed he'd be to lose her.

Such is the power of this young fair's smile.
Men wish to tame it, yet all the while,
The yearning won't fade easily —
For her vision will not cease to be.

Gerald Sokolinski

Sad Irony

Good things discarded but left to linger in your mind
will grow kinder, more truthful, more understanding.

What remains is just that, remains;
looking for unconditional warmth.
Warmth, to dispel forever a darkness that
transforms into intelligible words.
Words, too painful to speak.

So, words with no other choice, just dissolve and
return to the surreal comfort from which they came.

Mary Rowray

Much Like A Flower Garden

Love is much like a flower garden,
When you think in terms of need;
For either to bloom and prosper,
Takes much much more than just seed.

They both take a lot of nurturing,
And weeding out between the rows;
They require special cultivation,
And tender care to make them grow.

Someone has got to remove the rocks,
Put some enrichment in their place,
Protect the roots from infestation,
Provide each with a quiet place.

Sometime during inevitable downpours,
When you wonder how either can exist,
The sun peeks out from behind the clouds,
And gives lovers and flowers a kiss.

Ben T. Meyer

Celebration Of Life

Life starts out with the day of birth
Your parents bring you upon this earth
As you grow older, you'll become a teen
Life is full of colors like blue and green
The sky and grass of beautiful nature
Life as a teen can be tough and torture
You should have fun while still a kid
Life as an adult is harder than you think
Now graduated high school and think you're free
In life there are prices for your priorities
So get a job your parents will say
Life just gets shorter each and everyday
Then someone special will come in your life
Become your husband or even wife
Some say we're blessings, but only children
Remember that everyday: Life's A Celebration!

Crystal F. Schmidt

Daughter

My dear daughter the years have flown by.
As you played with your first doll, you were gentle and loving.
You carried the same sparkle in your eye for that doll that
I had in my eye for you.
You grew into a very wonderful young women.
And I grew right along with you, but you were so busy in your
little world you didn't see it.
I will always hold very dear to my heart the memories of you as you grew.
And one day my sweet daughter you will have a child of your own.
And that's how you will know only a daughter will ever know the
true depths of a mothers love.

Brenda L. Morris

What If?

How often I have pondered, just what my fate might be,
If I had been born someone else, and wasn't really me.

What if I was taller,
What if I was lean,
Maybe I'd be smaller,
Maybe I'd be mean.

Perhaps I would be richer, a fate I wouldn't mind,
However, I'll just settle for having been born kind.

Pamela M. Scott

Crushed Dreams

What happened to yesterday; all those hopes and dreams
It seems so long ago; do you know what I mean?

I see a young girl with long golden hair
Her eyes are so blue it just isn't fair

No chance did she have He took it away
It seems like only yesterday; but it's been four months and a day

It wasn't supposed to happen; she was older than me
I miss her so much it just couldn't be

She died on a Saturday; I will never forget
I still can't believe it; but she had her mind set

She lived a short life; one of pain and sorrow
She didn't have a chance; she won't have tomorrow

What happened to yesterday and the young girl I knew
She seemed so happy but her days were few

It's so hard to believe she swallowed those pills
The pain was too great she had lost all her will

She's gone now forever my sister it seems
Had no bright future he crushed all her dreams

What happened to yesterday I wish I could tell
She lived all her life in memories of hell

Patricia Gessing

Untitled

What's going out and what's coming up
Whatever it is it is a cardinal sin
What's up for dinner and what's on T.V.
Modern day technology.

A rose is a rose, so that's what they say
But not today that Roseman say
In the air the camera knows
What it's like to smell like a rose.

The heat is on and tensions are rising
This is a day of no compromising
Feel the power in your eyes
'Cause you know that the camera never lies.

What's coming in and what's going out
My sensors feel what it's all about
I can tell you what you see
It's modern day technology.

Line up your sights and shoot to kill
Through camera eye enjoy the thrill
Camera see with camera eye
And we know that the camera never lies.

Jim Davis

"A Father Mourned No More"

Turtle heads, noogies and Indian burns,
lots of affection and attention helped a child
to learn and grow

Support, strength and wisdom raised
a young lady to become a woman

Laughter, seriousness, heartbreaks and
rules bound our home securely and safe

All grown up and a family of my own

You will not be forgotten, so I can lay
you to rest with no regrets at all.

Amy C. Knox-Fanning

The Sounds Of The Dead

Sleeping to the sounds of the dead
I dreamt of the cat asleep in my bed,
lived under the earth
but come for milk and bread.
Purr my pretty
As I pet your head.

Glimpsing mysteriously at my eyes..
then, transformed to a giant black hawk
Frightened, I challenged my bloody hand away.
Running for the door and reaching the lock;
Oh, my pretty! No longer darling and gray
but a ferocious creature — so I began to pray.

Bring back your feline soul
fore many tears I've shed.
Twilight approaches . . . now a serene moment.
Tomorrow more discovered dreams, time to get up instead.
Languor conquered as blood dripped off my fingers . . .
Waking to the sounds of the dead.

Elizabeth Vasquez

My Grandson —

Dedicated to Ryan Benfield

I have a little grandson all of two feet tall.
He's fast as lightning, smart and that's not all.
My little Grandson brings me joy,
happiness, laughter and that's not all
My little Grandson can sing, color,
count, run and climb too!
Most of all he's my little grandson,
all of two feet tall.
He sings, I love you and Twinkle, Twinkle
Little Star. He's my little Grandson,
Precious by far, and that's not all!
He loves me and that's the greatest
thing he does of all,
My little Grandson all of two feet tall.

Donna Brim

Twilight

As I lay in the soft, cool, moist grass
beyond me the trees reach out to the island of the blessed.

While lurking in the shadows
heaven cried tears that fell upon the dark gloomy world.

As the brilliant halo looms from the feared
everlasting darkness.

The magnified light banishes the witching hours
with rays of unalloyed delight to all that beholds.

The eye of heaven's flying colors dance through
the trees blissfully upon the world below.

To all who takes in the first blush of day will be
filled with ecstasy for infinity.

Ali Jones

The Cowboy's Dream

The cowboy slept in the bunk house and dreamed
of things to come. He dreamed of horses and cattle
and the round-up soon to be done.
He dreamed of sweat and branding and all the work
to come. He dreamed of all the hours he'd spend out
in the blistering sun. He dreamed of riding some
ole nag for hours upon end, and after the round-up,
the fences he'd have to mend. He dreamed of when
the work was done and winter had set in. He'd collect
his pay and rest for a day. Until it started all over again.

Roy Brown

The Four Seasons

Winter weather in the air,
Tiny snowflakes in your hair,
Shoveling snow is such a bear,
Winter weather everywhere.

Spring, spring, warm and nice,
Better than all that snow and ice,
Time for fishing, time for fun,
Time to play and time to run,
Hotter and hotter and hotter it gets,
Later and later come the sunsets.

Summer weather took spring's place
And sweat is running down my face,
Queen Anne's Lace begins to grow,
But I bet it wouldn't in the snow.

Summer weather has gone away,
Time to roll in leaves and play,
Fall has come with its leaves and colors,
Some are brighter than the others,
Red, orange, yellow, brown or green,
They're still the prettiest leaves you've seen.

Andy Bachman

In My Memory

I close my eyes
And there they hang
Quietly against the house
While people come and go through the back door.

I close my eyes
And there they hang
Worn and cracked from miles of use
With stories left untold.

I close my eyes
And there they hang
In my memory —
Grandpa's boots.

Melissa S. Burch

Herb

Herb was a friend of mine.
We used to meet at the coffee shop, from time to time.
We would talk about the things that used to be.
And all the different things that we used to see.
Herb could recite the Bible, line for line
And he believed in life all the time.
Herb was a man of God, he wouldn't lie.
The other day he got sick and up and died.
Now he is with God and now he knows,
That all that he believed in is really so.
Herb talks to me from time to time.
Please understand.
Herb was a friend of mine.

Roy M. Stevens

Rescue Me

I'm a homeless man on the street
I'm a peddler man who needs a bite to eat
I'm a crying child who no one hears
I'm a widow woman alone for years
I'm a blind man who doesn't see
I'm a troubled friend who begs for plea
I'm a crippled man who can't walk around
I'm a deaf child who hears no sound
If you can oh please will you come and rescue me

Johnnie Lee Jr.

Childish Dreams

Childish dreams; life is not what it seems.
It's just a fairy tale. A bed time story to tell.

Like a princess bride and a silver knight.
A sword of steel but nothing is real.

You and me; we're like a melody.
But we're a song out of tune, beneath the light of the moon.

On a cold winter night by the side of the sea,
you were whispering words. It was just make believe.

A fantasy; making dreams for you and me.
It was done foolishly. I can't face reality.

Like a drop of rain in the desert sun.
Love is only in vain, when it's done just for fun.

Like a soft lullaby or the tears in your eyes.
Life is not what it seems. It's just a childish dream.

Joe Medina

June Days

I am trapped in the wind all alone, high upon the plain I stay.
My tears are dry but, I surrender to the vision of her face.
I am about and drive away my fears.
The last breath I take is not my own.
Wars rage in the conflict of my mind.
And as I see her face again, only the beauty of her face is to
    be my death.
Never to decay but, be devoured by the earth, "undecided", I say.
"Useless", I say, "but ambitious".
The rain comes and cools my burning soul.
As I look down the hallway my life does succeed and prosper.
But why am I so worried and depressed of my own likings.
Feelings are raised by the sight of her face again.
It has a price and the price is dangerous but, I am willing to pay
    that price all over again.

Kenneth C. Irvin

Love Alone

I thank the Lord above, for giving me such a special person to love.
I cherish and I hold, the gift that is greater than gold.
My love for you I can't deny, if I did it would be a lie.
While my love for you grows stronger and stronger, each time
were apart seems longer and longer.
You are the one for whom I deeply care, being separated from
you I could not bear.
For just being with you is good enough, when I hold you in my
arms I can't escape your tender touch.
Your smile gives me a warm feeling inside, by your love alone
I could abide.
You give me a feeling of warmth I can't describe, and a sense
of caring some never find.

Dennis Gabinski

Ode To J

It seems like only yesterday the fierce wind blew
Time has gone so fast
It seems like years since the sun was here
Time is slipping slowly away
The years will pass but the wind . . .
remembered
It will always be
The birds will sing
but not as sweetly
The sun will shine
but not as brightly
My love will grow, just the same.

Maryjo Longo

Untitled

Imagine, my friend, if you can..
The evils wrought by the hand of man..
Since the date of our birth there's a freedom of choice
Whether we're born girls or whether we're boys..
From the time we open our mouths to our first cry..
Till the years swiftly go, and we're compelled to die—
We have the choice—we have the will..
With one nasty word a foe to kill..
There's another choice that we should rue..
It's all the good things we out to do...
The Lord gives us freedom to choose..
Whether to drink water or to drink booze...
The Lord came along with a blanket of snow..
To cover all the filth on earth below...
Did it really matter whether the vehicle stuck..
Was a cadillac or merely a truck?

Julianne Raudabaugh

"First And Lasting Impression"

Silvered silence granting pardon,
   Heaving heart a benediction.
Tallest cowboy in the garden —
   Lightning bolt of recognition!

Memories of ghostly lovers
   Lost and found through countless ages . . .
A soul, completely robbed of cover,
   Feels compelled to turn the pages.

Conversation, freed from haste,
   Slides into the empty spaces,
Washes clean the aftertaste
   Of Robert Frost's cold desert places.

Naked, needy, poorly armed
   Against this unaccustomed feeling —
Ice dam heartaches, slowly warmed,
   Whisper promises of healing.

Wounded heart takes one last chance
   To warm itself inside the sun.
Man and woman's wary dance . . .
   I hope it's not a waltz for one.

Sandy Barham McLain

The Demise Of The Handkerchief

They talk about depression days
Of people on relief,
Back in the days of thirty-one,
When stores sold ten cent beef.

What stands out in my memory,
Perhaps by far its chief,
Is the passing of that ole square rag
They called the handkerchief.

You talk about the good ole days
And call for their return.
And certain things might be ok, I wouldn't give a darn.

Now grandma made her own lye soap,
Before the new detergent.
And I'll admit for handkerchiefs, the product was most urgent.

Perhaps they had their place in time. I would not press the issue,
But I still bless the day Kleenex made the disposable paper tissue.

Time passes on its fitful way, nor would I try to stop it,
If the progress train passed thru town I'd be the first to hop it.

But I have wandered from my theme, in closing I'll be brief.
Bring back things from by-gone days, but not the handkerchief.

Roy T. Copenhaver

The Love I've Chosen

For you to hold my body, to love me, and make me yours is
the dream I've always dreamed of.
For me to caress your body as you would mine, for you to
say you love me and will be there by my side is all I ask of you.
For the chance of my young body to grow with yours and
not to be pressured is all that is needed to be waited for.
It's hard to say "I don't love you" when I know that I do,
but what would you call love between me and you?
Love to me is a commitment to understand ones feelings
and thoughts, willing to take a chance in love or failure to love.
This chance I give to you. My dream of a love will always
be you. You're the love I've chosen!

Valeria R.

Hungry Heart

Deep within me
There are poems still unwritten,
Songs in search of a voice,
Paintings without a canvas,
Caresses yet ungiven to some dark lover.
But —
The dishes in the sink beckon.
Bills loom large on the desk.
A child cries out in the dark.
So with a ragged sigh
I lock the dreams away
In that secret drawer at the back of my soul,
In order to attend to life.
And as each day passes,
It becomes a little harder to remember
Just where I hid the key.

Sarah McKee Clevenger

Prisoner

To define ones freedom is to be trapped in ones environment.
To have ones mind clouded, stifled and suppressed.
To agonize about what could have been.
To agonize about what has been.
To agonize about what is.
This a frightening thought the power of the mind.
To be controlled, to try to step into the daylight
only to find darkness in a strange land.
I so desperately need to find reality, to find what is
I so desperately need my mind and body to be returned to me
The figure behind me is dark and dismal. I need
To find the light, dear god I need to find the light.

Maureen Taylor

Fathers

Fathers are all the men in this life
   Who beget children with or without a wife
They start this off in the height of passion
   Then each one fathers in his own fashion
There are those who dote and cook and diaper
   While others want mother to pay the piper
All one hears is "quality time"
   Or "latchkey" children with key on a line
Life today is not life of yore
   And that I suppose is what "play school" is for
Altho' father may no longer be lord and master
   Life without him could be a disaster
Father — Dad — Daddy — Pater — Pop — or Pa Pa
   He is still needed even for life in a jar
So let us all rise and shout, hooray
   Even tho' this isn't Father's Day.

Mary A. Weltchek

The Place

The sun shines brightly in the garden
A thick carpet of grass is beneath my feet
The country side is painted with wildflowers
As a stream flows gently below the hill
This is a quiet place
Birds sing their songs in the trees
Happy songs fill the morning air
A gentle breeze caresses my face
As the aroma of flowers engulf me
This is a peaceful place
Small animals frolic in the fields
The young playing a game of hide-n-seek
No person has entered this haven
The desolation has not left its mark
This is a safe place
In my mind I paint this picture
Safety beauty love and harmony
All living together all free
The hopeful dreams I now see
This is my place

Tami Oxenrider

Kill Yourself

Your very own personal kill yourself.
Made to fit.
Hand crafted from the finest guilt and suicide.
All natural.
No preservatives.
Just pure hate of yourself.
It's not accepted.
It's not the norm.
It's not neglected.
It'll make you feel warm all over . . .
When you're burning.
You don't feel it anymore.
The pain and suffering has ended.
Stare death down, . . .
Look him straight in the eyes . . .
Tell him you love him . . .
Tell him you understand it all . . .
You owe it to yourself.
You've worked hard.
You own yourself, you protect yourself, now make yourself,
    kill yourself.

Ryan Bowen

A Mother's Dream

I dream of picnics and baking, games and toys,
giggling girls and sweet little boys.
But I've got cleaning and laundry and work to go to,
So my time is taken away from you.
You beg "Please, Mommy, let's go to the park,"
But before I know it, it's already dark.
Another day has gone by and my time meant for you,
Has been spent on other things I needed to do.
Please forgive me my child, it's not my wish,
To have to wash yet another dish.
If I could spend every moment just playing with you,
And discovering everything in this world anew,
I'd feel happy, relaxed and wonderfully light
As I hugged you, squeezed you, and kissed you goodnight.
For when you're grown, and I've got time to spare,
I'll be looking for you and you won't be there.
I'll be thinking "Let's go to the park and play."
But you will already be gone away.
So grab my hand, the work can wait,
Let's skip to the park-Before it's too late.

Sherry Mayszak

Little Jack

The world has many dogs I know
Some for pleasure and some for show
I don't deny there's good in all
Gods gift to children some will call

But as for me and my dad too
There's just one dog that will do
We call him by his first name Jack
A black and tan coondog at that

Quite the hunter he'll tree a coon
We'll run to him by light of the moon
He stands proud up on that tree
A crying voice and a sight to see

Jack knows for sure that coon's up there
But dad and I don't see it anywhere
I'll shine my light that's what I'll do
Now I see them not one, but two

When Jack is certain we take our claim
Away he'll go just like he came
It won't be long and he'll tree again
World championship hunter he's out to win

I call him little Jack, he's my best friend!

Kimberlin Annette Combs

I Cry

I miss you, I said to the curtains.
I miss you, I said
to the yellow cab on the street.
You're still not here.

You're standing in front of the crowd
being admired
I stand fading in the shadows.

You are larger that I've ever seen.
Me, just a tiny speck
that goes unseen, unheard.
I cry.

I cry for the greatness I've never had
but always wanted.
I cry for the pain that tears me up inside.

Just one day, I pray,
to have your greatness.
To be big, tall, larger than life.
While you take a turn in the shadows.
I cry.

Holly Breidor

Warehouse Woes

Like any other system, it has its flaws
But to the one in charge, it's a hopeless cause!
When one function works, another goes sour
So they have to improvise, hour after hour!
The salesmen call in to see what's wrong
And hope this system works before very long!
The customers are fussin' when a delivery fails,
The store managers are cussin', cause they're losing sales
Reservations are a hassle, cause they don't have the facts
The merchandise is in the computer, but not in the racks!
They can breathe a little easier without any doubt, when all
These problems are finally worked out
This is just a bit of humor put into a rhyme, hoping to
Lift spirits for just a short time!

Jane Jenkins

411

Life

What is the meaning of life?
For some people it is having a family
Or, having a special someone there for you always
For others it is simply the joy of life itself,
Knowing, there are always people to support you
Everyone has his or he's own meaning of life
To me the meaning of life is not about material
Things or how much money you make
It is about being loved and loving the people that are
Dear to you, caring about the ones, close to you,
Sharing the gifts the loving Lord has gratefully
Given to you and discovering them to use wisely.
Life, life what a powerful gift it is
Sadly, some people take that power and abuse it
Whether taking your own life or taking the life of
Another, people sometimes take their life for granted,
To them the meaning of life is not important
So, what is the meaning of your life?
Or,
Do you Know????

Lisa Skaer

The Wind

It was late outside and she went outside for a walk
the air was cold but the street was calm and quiet.
She stood there enjoying the silence.
The thoughts of the day slipped out of her mind
and peace and tranquility filled her body.
As she slowly went back to her house the wind
began to roar.
It banged and clattered against the windows.
She got into bed and fell asleep to branches
hitting her window and the cold eeriness
of the whistling wind.

Andrea Luisada

The Shotgun, The Benz And The Gemini Twin

Almost twin's
They drive off in a rag top Benz
To cleanse a crime
They had just been
Red finger's grip the wheel
A shotgun at his heel
Close his eyes and grin
His passenger is not in
The Hwy. Breeze has dried the blood
As he screams please Oh please
I need my twin
He will take credit for my sin
And I can go on
As a Gemini with a crime
That had not ever been
Or until my shotgun and twin
Want to sin again.

My mother once told me
Hey, don't have a fit just be a skitz
And go through life and all it's s***.

Kevin T. Matthaei

To Be Loved

To love and be loved I find,
 In truth and purity the sweetest kind,
I then can smile as I face each day,
 And know that nothing can take it away.

Look for all the good things in life, and reap
 Life's great rewards, and sweet memories to keep,
To love and be loved I find,
 The root of life, and the peace of mind.

Florence L. Garrett

Dusk

Once upon the dusk of a full moonlit day,
I saw with my eyes the dreariness of gray
a glance of midnight, it was barren and grave, I knew then
the past, it was late.

Beyond the candles that burnt gleamed upon my face,
love gave me no surprise because devotions of sanctity laid ahead,
far from proximity, I saw it reach.

Return the outstretched hand I must, try to understand and
explain the reason to lust, the charcoal was laden of sorrows forgotten
an haunting experience of evil, took my body and shook my soul.

Gray is the color that opens the shutter to mysticism under the gutter,
capture me in void, release not to decoy,
I have hidden the present, bleakness prevails.

Grant me a wish, siege my vendibility,
take possession of deception and gratify me
a darkened piece of wisdom portrayed,
a delicate bite out of future days.

Sensation overload, an ounce of flesh paid,
close is the guarantee of time in space,
sculpt the essence of your grace.

Leave behind the ghostly name, offend the people of haste
verify a perplexity, then strain to the fierce of the fingers that pierce.

A vision no longer soaked in artifice, no more the facade,
for gone are the days, remain in reticence,
retreat in madness, see the density of today —
free yourself from the gray.

Nancy Yin-Ann Chen

White Christmas For A Southern Belle

Somewhere near an old New England barn,
A Southern Belle found her most excellent Christmas memory.
She had dreamed for many years of sledding in inches of snow;
Reminiscent of a calendars on walls in old country stores,
Revealing nature's winter miracle.

The breath-taking moment arrived — the sled was put in place,
Instructions were given for the final time.
She had been groomed, and she was sure she was ready;
Yet she stood frozen, not out of fear of failure,
But from sheer anticipation and joy!

A tug on her arm brought her back to reality.
She never uttered a sound, but took a deep breath;
Lay down on her tummy, put her hands properly in place
To guide the sled down the incline — a push from the rear;
The electrifying journey had begun!

The snowbank along the cold road became a blur,
The cold wind whipped angrily at her face.
The nerves in her body were tense with excitement.
When the sled came to its final stop, she got up, smiled,
Anne began the long climb to the top of the hill.

Helen M. Martin

My Love Prayer Poem On Obedience

I do not know what tomorrow may bring:
Nor, beyond today's thoughts may ring.

I do not know what pleasure, or pain.
Nor, the falling of sunshine or rain.

I do not know every great thing.
Nor, every secret to know.

I do know, just to be cherished, as thy child,
And to be guided where I go.

Sue R. Tucker

Jesus' Will And Testimony

I am in heaven now knowing everything you do,
This is my will, I left it all to you.

I leave my love, the greatest thing I own,
I leave you my spirit, so you are not alone.

I leave power in my name — to heal the sick,
cast out devils — to cause blind eyes to see,
I loved you so much, I died to set you free.

I leave my promises every one is true,
they will give you strength from day to day,
to help fight your battles thru.

I leave my parables — for wisdom and your guide,
when you are not sure — if you are wrong
or you are right.

I leave my forgiveness, to take away your sins,
when you repent, be baptized — you have a
chance to win.

I leave hope for eternal life, where all is peace,
joy, and love, so you can have all the
things (you) have ever dreamed of.

Betty J. Reaves

Gecko: The Life Foretoken

Slither, slide up the guiding path I go,
Above the frame of still life,
Away from the cat of fear,
I perch high above in pride,
Too far away for fear to touch,
Fear may be stronger and faster,
But my life too high of promises and joy,
Towering over the low land of fear,
Climb to the limits controlling destiny,
Running the length of the sky,
To take a leap of faith at the open opportunity,
Fear runs at my side in its long slithery shape,
Knowing and thinking how good I am,
I run on water to the heavenly shore on the other side,
Fear stops at the edge unsure to follow the risky path,
I shall say this now,
Do as I say and not as I do,
Look ahead at the future to come,
And do not take life for granted,
For the fishy side of fate will swallow your life whole!

Adam Moore

Children Spin

Around . . . around . . . around . . . the world whirls,
As I spin and spin on a grassy plain.
I am a child . . . giddy and smiling
With my hair, a veil of gold, streaming behind.
My mouth hangs open
The soft wind cools my tongue and tickles me behind the ears.
The sun blinds my blinking eyes
As I peer up at a cloudless sky.
My arms swing at my sides,
My knees wobble beneath me,
And someone . . .
Off in the distance
I hear my mama's soft laughter
As I try to walk in my drunken state.

But all at once . . .
A strong of wind
Throws me hard to the ground . . .
And . . . once again . . .
I am the adult . . . who doesn't spin anymore.

Emily Dressel

Rain Rain

I look up into a raining sky and say to
God can you help me learn to read.
The rain is coming down hard it is
hitting my face. The rain is turning to
tears my tears run down my face to
the ground. My tears and rain are
all running all around. The rain and
my tears are turning to letters. The
letters are running all around and pickup
the letters in my hands and open my
hands letters say rain rain.
I thank you, Oh God, for helping me.
I now know how to read.

James D. Ross

Money

Money — such a trifling thing —
Can kill a man or make him king,
Can open doors to grand new places,
Surround one's world with smiling faces.
Help mankind when it has need,
Enables the holder to do good deeds.
Can make a poor man hollow inside,
Steals his smiles and stomps his pride,
Closes doors and makes one bow,
Can break a man with one hard blow.
Money — such a silly thing —
Makes dreams come true,
Or dreams turn blue,
Can kill a man or make him king,
Money — such a senseless thing.

Brenda J. Nelson

Always

My love for you is like an ocean
It goes on and on forever
Your arms to me are like a live oak
They're always reaching out
And even though there are storms
They always go away
And sometimes it may be shaky
But like the sea, it always calms down
And even though we can't be together
We're like the sky and the ocean
We always meet at the end
And I just want to let you know
That even though we can't be together
I'll always be your friend

At times I lie in bed thinking
How I wish you were by my side
And sometimes I even dream
About how life would be with you but because you love another
My dreams have faded away but I just want to let you know
That I'll always love you and you'll always be in my heart.

Neidra Wilson

"Boston's 95-96 Snowfall"

This year it reached one-hundred
Snow was seen for miles and miles
George Burns, reached one-hundred too
As we all remember him with smiles
A Hollywood star, a meteorologist dream
We approached one-hundred inches of snow
As if George Burns, had put on a glorious show
Somehow we survived it, tho we lost him forever?
Our memories will linger on, no matter what the weather!

Janet M. MacGilvray

The Sea

The sea,
diamonds sparkling in the sun,
tiptoeing along the shore,
the cool feeling on my feet,
the smell of seaweed in the air.

Beach sand,
seashells scattered about it,
pad, pad, being formed into a castle,
the soft feel on my feet,
as I make footprints.

Fish,
those shiny gold shapes swimming around,
their tails splashing as they scatter,
their slimy bodies,
those pointed fins.

Waves,
folding over the sparkling water,
Woosh! As they run forward,
clapping as they fall,
their big hands capturing the sea.

Courtney Dyer

Going With The Flow

Enjoy and experience the now.
Remove your thoughts from the process.
Hear the universal wisdom instead.
All knowledge is contained there.

Learn to disconnect your personal imprint.
Flow into the universe.
Be guided by instincts, because those are
Nothing more than the universe whispering
Its secrets to you.

Go to the place where all things are known.
See others with love.
When listening, empty your mind and
Hear the truth of others.

Laure Carpenter

Gift Of Love

You are a gift of love
A gift sent from Heaven above
The Lord has done what He said He would do
For long we have waited and prayed for you.
When the man of God said you would come
We grew weary and thought we would not overcome
But he always told us to keep faith and trust in God
His vital words would encourage wherever we trod
When I heard your strong heart beat loud and clear
I knew then we had nothing to fear
So dear one, we love you and always will
And after you're born the Lord will be given praise still
I don't know a better present a mother can have
Than to know this Mother's Day the Lord has given what she asked

Shirley A. Pieri

Friends

Friends come few and far between
They are helpful and fun but not always keen
They always come back even when you are mean
Not meaning to be but somehow they know
There are good times and bad and always a glow
When there is love for a friend the friendship will grow
And in later years we can look back and see
All the hills and the valleys that brought us to be
"Friends"

Donna L. Vanbuskirk

To My Best Friend, My Valentine

You have been my one and only
Valentine for 36 years today.
And from my heart I could never
fill any other way.
To love is to forgive, accept and
understand.
In my case, I am so grateful you can.
I know your life has not been easy
and often hard.
Thanks for the encouragement and
strength from you I have had to borrow
I would like to say that from now
on you could be worry free,
But All I can do is, pledge my
Love and loyalty to you from me.
If time for me was over, and
I had no more.
I like to say life has been like
a big ole house, with you as
the door.

John P. Kitchens

Watching Me . . .

I have prayed for you, and cried for me,
I've grieved for the things, that you've made die, inside of me,
I've dreamed about you, in such a great fright,
Knowing, that I am the only one, who can see you with my sight . . .

I know how much it must have meant to you, for me not to include you,
I've refused you, and accused you,
But it all has been true, so now, there is nothing left to do,
But to sit in my room, and wait for death to come to you,
Not by any of my doing, and that, I know to be true . . .
But my friend, you have been caught in your own web, that will destroy you,
I have disappointed you, and oh, so greatly annoyed you,
But you will not try to take a new point of view,
Or, even take responsibility, for your altered attitude . . .

And with everything you have put me through, I still feel damn sorry for you,
And I only wish, that I could be there, when you have to face the final truth,
Death is all that you'll come too, no matter how hard you beg or what you do,
And with some torture, as that would be so Deserving for you,
After all, look at all, you are still putting me through! . . .

Kelly Hanna

The Biography Of A Poet

My friend Darlene would call me on the phone
Say Margie, 'put your drinking dress and hat on at home'
'Tell you Mom we're going to church'
This was long before I became a Elk Grove low paid nurse
In church, we flashed our coats, giggled, and jitterbugged our feet
Yep, we were going nightclubbing, right after this Jesus meet
Sometimes we wondered out loud if this man Jesus really knew
Which bars and clubs we were going to sneak into
Sometimes we make change from Father's plate
To buy at least two drinks, as we had no date

The porch light's on and here I am sneaking in back home
Oh, how those steps would creak and groan
It seemed no matter how I took those stairs
The fifth and sixth was a troublesome pair
If I could only make it up behind the door
My secret safe behind the core
At last at the top, I start to beam
As I dance my "Rocky" theme
To be continued

Marjorie Henderson

Tis The Storm

It was a warm summer's eve when the storm came to call,
As I was sleeping peacefully in my room down the hall.
Suddenly, the thunder pounded and the lightning struck the ground,
I jumped to my feet, my breath trembled, my heart did pound.
I finally, calmly told myself, "Tis the storm, go to bed."
I did so, and I gently lay down my tired head.

For me, slumber and harmony came a little too quick.
I could still hear the light sound of the second toll tick,
When suddenly the thunder throbbed and pulsated,
And I sat straight up, wide-eyed, and anticipated.
Anticipated one more strike to further end my life.
Just one lightning bolt to cut right through me like a knife.
Alas nothing did occur, the window was there, and very cool.
I became wroth with myself and scolded, "Tis the storm, silly fool."

But as soon as I had my scolding, there came a loud thud.
With a mad shattering, glass flew to me like spears of mud.
I made a hasty dash to the looking glass so I could be seeing,
And what I saw in the glass was a foul, foul being.
My sister, five years my senior, came rushing from her dorm,
And all my twitching lips could utter was, "Tis the Storm!"

Then I woke up.
Michelle Ewing

Lovesong

I want you. To hold you. To love you.
I remember your scent, your feel.
I long to gaze at your beauty, to devour your ripe voluptuousness.
To touch you in places you want me to know.
Thinking of you makes me restless in the night.
Heaven on earth when I make love with you.
Lightly my fingertips play over your smooth flesh.
I titillate your pleasure zones.
Your body the instrument with which I make music.
The source of my desires, the culmination of my dreams.
The delicious feel of your contours is sweet remembrance.
My world is brightened when I feel you moving in time with me.
Your impassioned cries as music to my soul.
My fires increasing in tempo as you respond to my ministrations.
I bring you the brink. And over. And again.
Then my thoughts turn to total unity.
Our love is sweet. Our duality has merged. One entity in time.
Until the impending crescendo is achieved. And we part fulfilled.
And then I impatiently await our next opportunity to perform together.
My love. My life. My guitar.
Michael J. Ardrey

Love Everlasting

My love for you is a deadly sin,
Something that should never have been,
This love brings nothing but tears and pain,
A love that is just an immortal strain,
It will be the cause of my untimely death,
It shall be with me till I breathe my last breath,
You will hold my heart till the day I die,
And if you crush it before then, I will cry,
My tears will fill rivers, ponds, oceans, and lakes,
But my love for you will always be there for you to take,
For committing this sin I will be surrounded by fire,
But my love for you will still be alive with desire.

It will be there for all Eternity,
And it will be there for all the Gods to see,
Everyone that sees that love will know,
That I loved you more than life itself, but I never let it show.
Marissa Amezquita Bosquez

"Meditation On My Vacation"

Sitting here on the mountain side
I feel the presence of God, in me, abide
Over-looking the lake, so blue
Knowing our Lord watches, whatever I do

God is here in so many ways
I could sit here for days and days
Viewing his mountains, flowers, lakes and trees
Just enjoying the sun and the breeze
This is a place that God set aside
For us to meditate on why his Son died
We study His word, sing and pray
And someday we shall be with Him, to stay

Oh! What glory, that will be
When face to face, our Saviour we'll see
No more sadness and no more tears
Just happiness and joy, for eternal years.
Ruth P. Ricks

Two Beats, One Heart

I had a love, rare and true,
He treated me with the most respect.
When asked if I returned his love I missed my que,
And my man I continued to neglect.

How could I be so blind,
So foolish to let him slip away?
Now his forgiveness I cannot find,
Took him for granted, now I must pay.

Realizing now what I once had . . .
The miracle between girl and boy.
Cursed myself to a heart forever sad,
And a life without your joy.

What can I do to reverse my fate?
I cannot change the past.
For another chance with you I wait . . .
Wondering how long my misery will last.

My heart beats for you, never another.
You see, no one else will due
I can love no other,
For you are love . . . and love is you.
Tenaya LeDeux

No Matter Where

I remember her smiling and her soft velvet skin
I remember her laughter when she was with him
Life was an adventure they promised they'd share
She vowed to be with him, no matter where

She'd get him his whiskey and put him to bed
She vowed to be with him that's what she said
She'd wait by the phone and sometimes by the door
She vowed to be with him, that's what vows're for

She knew that he needed a drink now and then
But who was he drinking with, what, where and when
Life was an adventure they promised they'd share
She'd better start drinking if she really cared

With each sip of her wine he guzzled his gin
Then cursed her and blamed her for all of his sins
They could've had their adventure if she wasn't a b****
If she had tried harder, been prettier and rich

Her smile has faded, her laughter is gone
His pain's now her pain, his plan all along
Life was an adventure they promised they'd share
She vowed to be with him, no matter where.
WendySue

Tree Of Love

Dedicated to Ms. Lillian Aaron of Kingston, NY on Feb. 12, 1996
Spring is just a veil away, and
the seed of our love will grow
into a magnificent tree of sublimity
I have for you!

Knowing, I will not taste of its fruits
or shade my tormented soul from loneliness . . .

Just flowers of hope . . .
branches of insatiable dreams . . .
scars of passionate kisses . . .
roots pursuing your image through earth,
as I search you with despair through my broken heart.
Will our love survive the seasons of life?!

Dr. Victor Haim L. Fuerte

Like A Little Child

Like a little child, I need your gentle touch
Your eyes that speak so clearly of the love I need so much
Your ears of understanding that can listen and agree
Your tears that tell me dearly of the love you feel for me

Like a little child, I need your hand to guide
Down a path I cannot see of God's blessing open wide
Your wisdom and your insight that only age can bring
To share the song that fills your heart so I can learn to sing

Like a little child, I need your rod of discipline
To keep me from temptation of falling into sin
Your smile bright with glory to show me how to laugh
Your heart that goes before me to lead with shepherds staff

And then someday when I grow up with my child I will share
The lessons in this life and how you taught me to care

Lisa Bennett

A Struggle

Hand in hand, my brother and I, we shall succeed.
Against our masters, I shall fight, even if I must bleed.
Beaten, starved, and betrayed, but not just us two.
Our generations to come, need to know what we've been through.
The white people called us niggas, and tried to make us feel small.
Little did they know that we would rise and conquer all.
We've tried so hard to stick together then, my brother was all I had.
He was the only one that helped me when I made my master mad.
You kill each other day by day, and not even shed a tear.
You are becoming too much like the master I fear.
I may have walked over a thousand miles, but I have many to go.
My job is to educate the young ones on the things they need to know.
I have a will to live this I know is true.
So listen to the message I send to you, to you, and you.
Never be little yourself you are much better than that.
Think about you future keep your life intact.
Killing is not the right answer, and it's not the only way.
Don't be afraid my brother, to kneel down and pray.
And now as I wipe sweat off my brow and shed a tear for my loss.
I hope no one in your family is killed, and you have to pay the cost.

Jazmenda Valadez

It

A slow horrid death it brings,
to those unfortunate ones who have the genes.
It grows and divides, killing all in its sight.

But it can't be stopped some scientists say,
still others work long and hard,
trying to find an end to this deadly cells day.
For maybe, just maybe,
one day there will be a cure for this killer.
Cancer.

Jan Irene Erickson

No Smoking Here

When I was young I used to smoke, I don't know when I started,
I didn't know I'd get a stroke unless we two were parted.

If I could count up all the costs that I have paid for smoking,
I'd pay my bills and know the thrills, the truth is, I'm not joking!

I must have smoked a million times and spent a lot of money,
The cost was more than only dimes, it turned out it's not funny.

Now if you have not started yet, please take this one's advice,
It's best for you and others too, you will not pay the price.

I found out late it's not so cool, I once thought it would be,
A shorter life is now my fate, I was the fool, you see.

For those who smoke it's not too late, so quit while you're ahead,

You're not the only one you hurt, you could just wind up dead.

You will not need to puff this weed tho' some will say they do,
I can relax, I know the facts, and later so will you.

Each time you smoke a cigarette you've lost more than you gain,

Eventually, the most you'll get is end it all in pain.

The best advice I have to give is something dear you see,
It's just that I would have you live a longer life than me,
The man named Everett C. Koop will back me up with everything I say,
So take advice and don't think twice, and you will quit today.

Jesse D. Rose

My Heart Won't Let Go

He sings to me from a distance, but only
in my dreams. I just wish that reality was
as nice as my dreams. But it's something
that won't come true no matter what I do.
We were both in love at that time, but now
I'm not sure what he thinks of me. I would
love to have another chance because I still
have deep feelings for him. And I just
don't want to let go. He's drifted so far
away and he won't drift back, so I have
to swim to him. The cold water won't
keep me from reaching him, but him
pulling away from me will put me into
the darkest hole. Why, when I try, does
he turn away from me? I keep telling
myself to give up, but my heart won't let
me. Every time he pulls away from me I
fall deeper into the darkest hole. My heart
won't let me go on with my life, so I'll keep trying.

Jamie Mendoza

Evil Walked Dunblane Today

Evil walked the streets of Dunblane today,
much as it had before.
Today Evil walked in daylight,
shunning its usual darkness cover.

Evil walked the streets of Dunblane today,
reaching out to touch the good;
The Good were young and full of life's joy;
They just were learning life's full reward.

Evil walked the streets of Dunblane today,
At first none took notice of its passage.
Yet, when Evil had finished it journey of death,
We all felt its dark, grimly crusted hand upon our soul.

Evil walked the streets of Dunblane today,
It tried to take part of Good away.
Evil did not darken daylight, joy or hope,
God was introduced early instead,
To such shining examples of his Good!

Donald R. Waldrop

Looking Beyond

The loneliness I sometimes feel when
there's no one there to say,
    which way to turn, which road to take
to lead me on the way.
    Through all the trouble's and all the grief
I felt throughout the years,
    I reach to grasp a shared of hope to
dry up all my tears.
    Mistakes are made quite frequently by
all withing this sphere,
    the world today that we all share
in turmoil, a mass with fear.
    I guess there is no way to change our
globe which rounds the sun,
    but if we all just do our best the
change has just begun.
    So look down deep within your heart
and find that guiding light.
that leads the way beyond our fears
and shed us of our fright.

Thomas F. Watson

"Dove's Of Love"

When my heart is hurting, frightened, lonely, or misunderstood,
I go to the Lord in silence;
Knowing that he would,
Healing every little hurt, the best that he could.
The heart of understanding, is a gift from above,
Only with his presence is trust in the "DOVES OF LOVE".
The 'Fruit Of The Holy Spirit', embraced with-in my chest,
Having full assurance, He gives us Peace and Rest.
The walk on earth is trying, as we need Him everyday,
Knowing when we're in Heaven, He will dry our tears away.
Our humble hearts are breaking, God knows we'll stand the test,
He allows the tears of sorrow, to help us do our best.
We've got to keep on going, as Grace abounds us still,
And know He leads gently, so "All" may do his will!
In The Beloved Name of 'JESUS', SON OF 'THE LIVING GOD'

Sharon Kay Jenkins

A Special Request

We can't just call her mother, a friend, or just a wife.
She touched too many people in her
short but "special" life.

She knew the way to comfort you when
troubled times were near.
She could reach your heart without a word,
and wipe away your fears.

Her eyes so blue were like the sky so
warm and bright and clear.
You knew she always found the truth
when she looked at you, my dear.

We can feel her touch, her strong embrace, we hear her voice inside.
She has never really left us, but keeps
returning like the tide.

She drew us all together she made us strong you see.
She couldn't have it any other way
"united" we must be.

These words are small and simple and they only make a start
so God, please treat her "Special" and
give her a "Golden Heart!"

Kathy Wolverton-King

Lost And Found

Long ago I chose to not know
from where I came
or where I'll go.

Let my sails fill with angry winds of fear
yet give me the courage to keep mortality near.

I search with eager eye
for answers in the star lit sky,
A grain of sand on a lonely desolate beach,
into the stars and ages my yearning soul does reach.

Like sturdy roots of the giant oak
or the fledgling nurtured by the yoke,
I dig deep and grip the anchor of my soul
clenching fiercely the essence of my whole.

Weary of snatching empty handfuls of rain
that simply serve to worsen the pain,
I turn and face the empty night
only to find on the horizon, look a light!
There! My lighthouse on a distant shore
its beacon to guide me forevermore.

Patrick Donovan

Pomp and Circumstance

With wafting spring Come to call
Gentle — unwhispered Memories

Down the hall — Your bouncy gait — walking
A glimpse of curly head — A wry smile — a dimple — freckles

Delight Promise Smiling Laughing Pranking
Pitching Out that first ball of spring.

Helpless — pleading — Trying desperately —
Can't get you out — Screaming in a fiery fear.

Those who love you File into the church —
They speak tender words — Mourning.

They carry Your life. Why?
You change who today?

With wafting spring Come to call
Gentle — unwhispered Memories

Kathy Freeman Smith

To the Graffiti Man

Around the sparse and open spaces,
on borders of railroad tracks and buildings,
you are at your self-established business:
a brush on one hand and a pail of paint on the other,
engaging quietly, each morning, in graffiti painting.

What a way and a style to express yourself!
Graffiti, graffiti, graffiti, graffiti!
Graffiti man, yours is a restless soul
wallowing in the sea of graffiti.
Stop! Think of the destruction you've done!

Count your blessings for such energy.
Draw your thoughts away from graffiti;
to a much better venture, sway it.
End a useless display of an emotional kaleidoscope
of black, white, blue, red and green.

The signs of the times? Society's decay?
Some people's indifference? Graffiti man,
whatever thoughts you have about your deed,
on spaces better seen, plain and simple,
say goodbye to graffiti; it isn't your best!

Linda P. Perez

417

Simplicity Sings

Who knows where Time will lead us tomorrow?
Who knows when all our dreams and fears let go?
Under silent moons, stormy winded nights,
Through fragrant gardens and breathtaking sights
As endless skies of bright deafening blue
And golden leaves fall generously for new —
Your love's alive in full reality;
Innocence asleep in precious beauty.
Laughing, crying, fall silent truthful tears
As brave sad sighs bring wisdom to the years.
Run, Time, run forever down in valleys;
Hide, Time, hide — for all true love will seize thee;
Die, Time, die — let us all shine in glory —
No souls left trapped in you, no boundaries.
Eternal light, God's saving hands, fly free —
"Confusion's dead," sings sweet Simple Beauty.

Alicia Soliz

"In Loving Memory Of My Mom"

Nowadays there is not much to believe in
It's a real crazy world that we live in
From the time I was a small child
When everything seemed calm and mild
You were my best friend
Right down to the very end.
You used to tell me I had a big heart.
But it seems slowly but surely it keeps tearing apart.
I know you taught me to be strong and how to hang on
Quite frankly I just don't feel I belong
So mom, if it's possible, toss me a star
Something to wish upon
Mom you are loved and will always be
'Cuz of all the special things
That you have given to me

Amy Steinburg

Winter's Night

Stygian darkness, night
Moonbeams filter through shimmery flakes
That spiral, float, flutter, drift, and descend,
Reflections of an opalescent stole
As it softly mantles ground.

Tranquil quiescence, night
Winds gently tip graceful boughs unfurled
From barren elm trees stenciled on glistened snow,
Silver branches melodiously sway
Whispered arias to stars.

Nancy M. Ledzianowski

Earth Mother

Now to my youngest child his prayer is granted.
Not the ocean's might nor the fearsome desert
nor even the wingless air do I bar against him.
     Now may he freely
carve my timeless hills to his field convenience;
grind his merciless roads through field and forest;
snare the lightning's pride in a million wires —
     still am I patient.
Only, let him remember the price. For nothing
nothing is given. All that he is — and may be —
he won by a dream. And this let the hills he conquers
     bid him remember.
Not till his dream is dead will I turn and slay him.
Not while one of his race remains whose worship
turns to the elder gods who dwell in wonder
     back of the sunset.

Mary C. Pangborn

Bloody Marble, Weeping Stones

They pledged allegiance to the flag
     And to the freedom for which it stood
Leaving children, wife, and others
     The crossed the deep and offered their blood

A mother's son, a father's dream
     Enemy bullets shredded his flesh
One final prayer, one final breath
     The final passing from Life to Death

The war is over; shed the tears
     But the warriors' memories live on
Heroes history, courage ignored
     Sensing their sacrifice forgotten

MIAs and POWs
     Engraved with those whose lives did fall
History etched in darkened stone
     Their names inscribed on a long black wall

Marble for blood, stone for tears
     The empty wage of desolate tours
Tell me, sir, would it be enough
     If the fallen son had been yours?

Mark Allen

One More Night

All I need is One More Night,
I want to show you my love.
You've always made "us" feel so right,
Cupid's arrow hit me from above.

All I need is One More Night,
To show you how much I car.
Just remember to keep in sight,
My love is always there.

All I need is One More Night,
To find my happiness again,
All you'll do is hold me tight
And let go of the feelings you hold within.

All I need is One More Night,
To share with you I plead.
Like a rose, my love grows bright,
I've handed you the seed.

All I need is One More Night,
To plant that seed in your heart.
I want your love, for it I'll fight.
Give me one night, and never will we part.

Kassidy Keylon

"I Have Been There"

To go down a long and winding road,
to have taken on a lengthy load . . .
     I have been there.
Through it all, and learned so much,
to finally feel a gentle touch . . .
     I have been there.
Life's to short and love's never too late,
heed this warning and do not wait!
Love is here and here to stay.
We keep getting closer everyday.
     I am here!
I am here. And here, I'll be!
I've already been there . . . You see!

Betty J. Posten

To My Gram

You brought a smile to any face
In our hearts there will be for you a special warm place
We all knew you were not feeling well, and for that we will not dwell

You really tried to do your best, but now it is time for you to rest
So close those beautiful eyes, and we will never say goodbye

For the Lord has taken you to his wonderful home
And there as well as here you will never be alone
You brought us many joys and very few sorrows
Now God has made you an angel to make for us a brighter tomorrow

You taught us how to love and care
Always remembering not to take but to share
Because of you our dreams will go on forever
Our thoughts of you will leave us never

Now the Lord has taken you to his special place
Where you will always have a smile on your face
We all know now you have no more pain
And through that we all have strength to regain

Gram, you are at peace now, we will no longer ask why or how
Just remember we won't be apart forever
For the Lord will bring us all together

Gloria J. Wolf

Fire In The Sky

The oracle spake thus:
The Judgment,
Fire in heaven above,
The image of Possession In Great Measure,
Immense wealth is yours,
Supreme success,
One may undertake something,
No blame.
The interpreter says:
"It's not material possessions.
Shelter is your wealth."
Perseverance furthers.
The Clinging brings success.
"And remember,
Amparo is your wealth."
No blame.

Edgar A. Llinás

"Dreamer"

Sometimes when things get tough
it makes me just wanna run
run away from all the pain
to a place where I can dance and play
a place that's soft and sweet
where you'll get swept off your feet
by a guy who'll always be true
who'll do his best to make you happy whenever you are blue.

Sometimes when things get rough
it makes me just wanna laugh
look a problem in the face
and with my laughter start to erase
erase the hurt and pain I feel
and hopefully things will soon start to heal.

In my world of make believe
things are perfect, problems fade
when I shut my eyes and dream
things are never what they seem
we live in a world full of hate
but in my mind, all is safe.

Sandra Conoscienti

Tears In The Rain

Pain shadows my heart
His face creeps in my mind
Happiness maybe in my smile
But tears secretly fall, from mile to mile
I may speak to you with poise,
But pain lingers inside my voice
To write this is my only choice,
To burst my feeling without a noise
I'm sitting here in the rain
Drowning with all the pain
Baby, why can't you stay with me?
Maybe that's how it should be
It's hard to stand without you
I don't know if I'll make it through
But I can't stand and walk away
I still have to live my life day by day
Believe what I say is true
That I'll always long for you
And as the rain washes the tears away
The memories of you will always stay . . .

Myra J. Monteagudo

"Princess"

When I look in the mirror
   I squint and dim the lights
and cry. Inside and out.
Displeased, so ashamed.
   At my dull, lifeless eyes
      and gaunt, desolate face.
Then I remember you.
How beautiful you look, always.
And I cry some more.
Beyond vanity and envy
   lies so much Hatred
the pictures which I tear to shreds
      especially yours
only engulf me into bitter memories.

But today,
   I go above my fear, my ignorance.
And listen to something beyond those infinite raindrops
   you're as beautiful as you believe you are
so I turn on the lamp and open my Eyes. And I see   you.

Shayma Patel

Holy Man

Sitting on a cloud so still,
Contemplating God's perfect will
Awaiting a spiritual dawn to see,
Soul in keeping, to be set free.

Storms have touched him, some silent, some not,
Hampered only by human thought.
To him shall come eternal favor,
Not judged by present time behavior.

Although the mist has dimmed the skies,
Spirit truth burns from his eyes.
Not always present, not quite one,
Paths not steady, but halfway done.

The touch of God's almighty hand
Is never easy to understand.
His plan was not forced to accept,
The trials not easy, promises not always kept.
Blessed ones are chosen for a new world to bring,
Second covenant of our Saviour, love of a king.
To sense things the spirit has never sent before,
Confident God will hold you, forevermore.

Jacqueline D. Inks

419

"Leaves In The Evening"

Dedicated to S.J.S.

Corners of the world. Making it all right. You thought of the
flowers I thought of the wine. We would come together. To share a
precious love. You would bring the nectar I would bring the buds.
But it's true. Sunlight leaves in the evening
Oceans move forever. Making it all right. You would bring the
pillows. I would bring the night. We would share forever.
Something like no-one. You would bring the laughter. And I would
  bring the fun.
But it's true. Sunlight leaves in the evening
Moonlight in the desert. Making it all right. You would bring the
honey. I would bring the hive. We would last forever. Till the end
of time. You would bring the illness. And I will bring you life.
But it's true. Sunlight leaves in the evening.
Birds leave in the fall. The love of my life has said good-bye.
Now nothing is forever. Forever is no more.

Jonnie Jett Soltan

Love Is

Love is the very breath of you
it is the thought of time without age or grace.

Love is the road I travel it is
my needs and my wants all rolled up in you.

Love is the things I do because of you
without you I would never have done any of these things.

For you are my life and my days
all rolled up into this thing we call life.

Love is your voice on the phone
when I hear it, it lights up my
entire day. I don't have to
talk to you all day just hear you say hello.

You are every dream I have ever wanted
every, every sexual fantasy I had as a young man.

Love to me is you over the years I have
pondered this question and until I met you
I never truly had an answer. But now I do

You are the answer the only answer for you are
Love I have known many women in my life and
until I met you I never truly knew love.

So for all my days and for all time this I
swear you are and will always be LOVE.

Sean Patrick Conaway

We Mankind

Distant skies once blue
promises from yesterdays forgotten
friends become enemies and vice-versa
not knowing which way to turn
Will we really miss things that become
  extinct
will we be missed if we died tomorrow

Oceans will last because they live in
  harmony

If we died tomorrow
the skies would be gray
there would be no more promises
no more friends no more enemies
no way to turn
no more extinction
nothing would miss us

And the oceans would still be in harmony
and we would be gone because we
  had no harmony

Lyndi Murphy

Sunrise

Watching in wonder as the daybreaking light strokes
Different pieces of the earth —
Like the hands of Time, stroking every second of
Everything . . . giving birth
To the most powerful and magnificent of nature's
Secrets;
The air fills with scents of newness —
A new day, a new chance —
As forgiveness and understanding are
Airbrushed by God across the sky,
In all the hues of the sunset in reverse . . .
Watching this sparkling magic take place
Morning after morning,
It's easy to forget that the Sun
Is Always there — sometimes out of sight.
It's easy to forget that Dawn is a gift —
Just imagine an eternal night . . .
Nevertheless, daily we are endowed with this
Glory, called Sunrise.
"And there was light"; better yourself today.

Dana Hayley

John

All the times I've sit and wondered why,
We ever had to say goodbye.
I do not understand, why I cannot erase,
The memories I have of one man's face.
I think I'm O.K., then I'll here a song,
Then I feel the need to be alone.
The quiet evenings, of holding him near,
The special feelings, of just having him here.
The times in the park, that special dance,
And the glisten in his eyes, at just a glance.
The quiet nights, by the T.V.,
And him curling up on the couch with me.
The games of tennis, a bar-b-que,
Everything was special, that we'd do.
I could go on and on, because each of our days,
Were filled with love, in so many ways.
A new marriage, time, and distance won't heal,
The feelings my heart holds, and the love that I feel.
God please, don't these memories disappear,
As long as I have them, he'll always be here.

Cheri I. Berry

"The Beginning"

All at once there was being, and the being beget need.
The need found desire and was recognized.
Desire exercised was discovery,
and so there was the realization of knowledge.

All at once everything had changed.
The knowledge knew pleasure and pain.
Feeling was being,
and thus utilized the knowledge in desire.

As the knowledge grew, so did the desire.
But the feeling grew not, and again there was need.
The knowledge searched,
however unable to fill the need.

As the need grew, so did the knowledge.
But the feeling knew love and hate.
Love was the need.
And through the need, the knowledge knew the feeling.

All at once there was the soul.
The love filled the need and was justified.
Knowledge satisfied desire,
and so by the soul, there was new being.

Jason Alley

Spring

Spring is a season of pleasing,
. . . is casting off the fetters of winter.
. . . is breaking out balls, bats, bikes and bubbles.
Spring is a season of renewing,
. . . of abiding faith.
. . . of life, grace, energy and love.
Spring is a season of beginning,
. . . of Catkins on the Willow, in the corner,
     by the barn.
. . . of Snow Crocus, Forsythia and Daffodils
     filled with sunshine and haze.
. . . of longer uplifting days and shorter, sweeter,
     starry nights.
Spring is a season of promising,
. . . that buds on the trees will blossom,
. . . that strawberry summer will follow,
. . . that clean fresh breezes will blow,
. . . that crystal clean rivers and brooks will flow.
. . . and that rainbow dreams will come true.

Donna M. Sweeney

Dazing

Oceans away and miles apart
   How they tear at my heart
I close my eyes to think of you
   A wonderful vision comes to view
Seeing you lying on the sand
   with your Auburn hair and golden tan
Smells of the ocean all around
   Birds and waves make the only sound
Concentrate harder on being there
   Feeling your warmth. Touching your hair.
Making love under the sun
   Can't think of anything more fun
Now my view is turning to haze
   I reach for you but your only a daze

Mike Johnson

Dreamer's Query

Whither thou o' cloud?
   cotton-puff of the sky,
Whither thou; other than to
   cast shade for such as I?
Where away, beauteous thing?
   billowy white, drifting silently
On wind's unseen wing.
   Will you cloak a mountain peak,
Or, mother a brilliant lightning streak?
   Will you caress parched earth with rain
Then drift away — to return again?
Whither I go, o' cloud, I know not where;
Yet, resembling you, I seem not to care,
Nor worry where tomorrow, today.
Whither we go o' cloud, drifting?
   Where away?

Jack A. Klempner

Shyness

Shyness is a furtive shadow that receives
its form from the light of love.
When love is only a faint glimmer shyness hides
itself among the outer shadows of the night,
But when the light of love grows and becomes
a brilliant illumination, this silent shadow
reaches forth with power capable
of over coming its creator . . .
Only when the eye becomes accustomed
to this ever present shadow does the
light of love reveal it's true luster . . .

Candy Mohwinkel

"No Tomb"

How sad it is in the United Lands
Fate of Life lies in the woman's hands.

As the innocent unborn has no voice,
Reputation, education and career makes the choice.

She justified her mindless plight:
Because it was legal; it was right.

Guilt and grief emerged from the lost
Which was only part of her opportunity cost.

Though she wanted to forget what she had done
She was haunted by thoughts of her dead daughter or son.

Guilt raged in her mournful soul;
her heart became black as coal.

Nightmares controlled her sleep;
Day visions of the child made her weep.

God's forgiveness gave her hope.
In that she managed to cope.

She sighed with a single saddened breath;
For her child and her spirit — there was death.

The miracle of life inside her womb
Became a mass of death without a tomb.

Lori E. Burnett

Forgotten Love

They fell in love years ago.
Who would ever guess, how could they know.
Two different people, from different worlds.
Big city boy and small town girl
Came the day, they made the move.
Two young people said "I do"
They had so much to overcome.
They pulled together, joined as one.
Passing days, months and years.
Then came the day he caused her tears.
The day would come, he would leave.
Her trust was gone, she would never again believe.
She'd sit alone wondering why, that special
man would make her cry.
She wonders where she'll go from her
What her future holds, her final years.
Did he fall out of love, She'll never know.
He left with no reason, Just distant and cold.
It came with no warning, no time to prepare.
After all he's done, how could she still care?

Misty Deem

Mama

Sitting in my Mother's kitchen
Watching her create a golden haven
Of happy talk and aromas sweet . . .
Wrapped in her warmth
Feeling her love for me
There, no matter what.
Sitting in my Mother's kitchen
With sunny tomorrows and peaceful dreams
Alas, existing now
Only in my memory.
But how many times do I return
When things are hardest
And I feel at my lowest
To know once more
That lovely cocoon
And the beautiful spirit
Who lives
   Through me
   Her daughter.

Natalia Radula

Whispers

You whisper you love me,
you whisper you care,
but that won't take us anywhere.
When actions speak louder than words,
I feel like we're two birds.
We fly toward each other,
then you swerve the other way.
You come back,
then turn again.

Everyone hears whispers in the wind.
I whisper to you, "When is this gonna end?"
But what's left for me to say,
when my whispers have gone away?

Now listen to my mind,
and accept it please.
I'm going down on my knew,
to beg to you let's agree
not to feel anymore agony.
So listen to me with both ears.
I feel like I'm telling you careless whispers.

April Hill

The Unforgiven

Two score — seven years, and more
Resentment fans the flames of hate;
Burns tears of shame into my soul,
While, in supplication I implore
Acceptance by a wrathful mate.

Deep in the past yields wrongs to
Punish, mixed with vows of tender love
Words to forgive, to care, and yet;
Hollow the words that talk forgiveness
While still refusing to forget.

Resentments, number one offender,
Demands we hurt the ones we love
With no remorse, and no restraint;
How deep the hurt — how high the price,
How long endured without complaint?

If, an end of such obsession,
Raise our spirits to more God like
Planes of love, and anguish cease;
All praise to Him, who hears our pleas,
And through forgiveness, gives release.

Leslie G. Taylor

Streams

The Reothydgway River runs down second avenue west, under miniature
glacier formations and over many a crack; If we put a microscopic
yacht in this stream, you'd be surprised how far it would trek . . .

There are streams from one heart to another, and many a vessel is
sent out to sea: One is the leader in exports, the other a harbor so
busy it's hardly free.

Some wait eons for their ship to arrive, and it dawns on them
seemingly that: To give is as profitable as is to get, and exporting
is where it's all at.

A shipment can come in the form of smile, the kind that some ports
manufacture: Relationships are big business indeed, not a single
heart ever need fracture.

My board of exchange has so dealt through time, in some friendly
way or another: And what profits we make, by sending off ships,
in streams that we share with each other.

Paul Deal

Christmas Thoughts

As the Holiday season draws nigh,
And our spirits grow more cheerful and bright,
Let us remember the reason,
We celebrate Christmas Night.

The fantasy side of Christmas,
Is the fun part, don't you see,
Of Santa, and Reindeer, and Sleigh Bells,
And presents under the tree.

Of Turkey, and Cranberries, and Dressing,
And laughter from small girls and boys,
'Tis the season for giving and sharing,
And all of those wonderful toys.

In spite of our Joys and our Sorrows,
And our fortunes, whatever they're worth,
There comes a Voice out of Heaven,
Saying, "For All Mankind - Peace on Earth".

The Voice said, "Love one another,
As dearly as I have Loved You,
For as you have done for others,
So shall I do for You".

Ralph W. Kiesling

Cozy Place

When you're looking for a cozy quiet place
to call your own,
Go into your garden
and there be left alone
With the birds melodious singing
and the fruit trees galore.
All the flowers and the butterflies
You've just begun to explore
All the gifts that God has given
In your garden, just for you.
Then sit beneath a shady tree
And feel the breeze upon your face
And hear your Father whisper
How He loves and saved you by His grace.
It's just a bit of heaven here on earth
He's made for you.
So when you're looking for a cozy quiet place
to call your own,
Go into your garden
and there be left alone.

Judy Ecrement

Love He Don't Know About

I wish upon a million stars
to erase you from my heart,
but it's your face I do see
just as the wind blows through the trees.
My fingers touch the golden sand
oh how I want to hold your hand.
I reach for you all the time
mystically only to find
you're the phantom in my mind.
My secret love for you that shines
I will take to this grave of mine.
So rare and true, it taunts me, too
That you will never know
this girl is the one
who loves you so
with all my heart, body, and soul.

Nonnie Wagner

Untitled

My only surprise.
The unexpected detour.
From my map of planned wonders.
I packed my toothbrush.
I packed my soap.
But how was I to know that maps are worth five cents in a
million dollar world.
You cracked my champagne glass.
And I didn't mind.
But when you turned your back,
I lost all control.
That's over now. My map is gone,
and my soap is slipping in my bag.
But I'll keep walking, running my fingers through my hair.
Chewing on my pen cap.

Sarah Valim

Untitled

What will happen if man continues
His forsaken ways, which sever the sinews
And ties, which hold him strong?
He thinks on the short term, but never long
Away, to when his descendants live,
On a choking earth that has no more to give
To them. Never more will they know the way
That men and children used to play
Outside, where everything is green.
What of the young lovers who will have never seen
A tree, with fragrance sweet and blossoms flowing?
They will have no way of knowing
The birds, who took to flight,
Trying to avoid the blight
Of man, as he killed the wild —
Leaving no place for the unborn child.

Patrick M. Malone

Untitled

Sitting here in a room
where your presence was felt
only hours ago
strange I am here for the same reason
you were
yet not at the same time
mindless hearing
words fall on my ears
I know but do not listen
the soft mumble of another language
like rain falling on water
blurs through my senses
Now can you feel my presence as I find you here
I doubt you look for it

Meg Scheu

Long Life

In the horizon of the day begun
A rainbow in the sky
The sunlight shining on your face
The spring breeze blowing through your hair
The sound of the wind whispering in you ear
Morning dew on your feet
Your shadow on the pavement
Skipping through the grass so ultra green
Birds peacefully gliding through the air
Gazing at the worlds scenery
Picking flowers and breathing in the aroma
Oh the smell of the world so fresh
A time to dream and be anything you wish
Loving the world and loving yourself
Loving life and living love

Fumiko P. Salone

Anniversary

A year ago we made a vow to love forever and a day.
A year has passed, my love, and now you are much too far away.

But though far, I think of you and dream of days
when I will be with you and we are free to love again.

Each time I get your letter the girls who see me know it.
Since each day I love you better, how can I help but show it.

As I walk after supper each clear night in the cloudless sky I see
that there our star is shining bright forever for you and me.

Then I look to the future when my life with you will be complete.
At last I will be where you are and work with you to make life sweet.

We'll make our home where skies are blue with valleys steep
and mountains tall. There where our fathers' axes rang true
to clear the land for good and all.

We'll live and learn the lessons of a life of work, play and fun
with folks we know, in land we love we'll run until our race is won.

Dawn Hyde

Mother's Hands

A mother's hands may be wrinkled and old,
But they tell of memories untold.
They tell of a child on a sleepless night,
When the touch of Mother's Hands made
   everything alright.

They tell of the many wonderful things
   they have done,
And all the children's love have won.
Sometimes they tremble when fixing a
   child's hair,
And choose the right clothes for it to wear.

They prepare the meals from day to day,
And with love send the children on
   their way.
Mothers Hands are so precious to me.
How thankful to God we should be
   for Mother's Hands.

Betty Harris

"Mr. Mountain"

With each step I breathe harder
and my heart beats faster,
but I refuse to stop

Moving forward I think of my destination,
persistence will help me reach the top

I begin to cry at the thought of my path
and I'm afraid of the person I will become

Instead of cursing this mountain
I will conquer it,
so I move forward listening for the drum

I can see the top now, but I'm still in pain
my scars are not visible,
but I could feel their mark

I know now not to look back, so I focus on what's ahead
a few more steps forward, and I'll be on time

Once at the top I can join in on the victory tune
with the rest who conquered this mountain
including a one wing lark

Denise Forte

SPEAK UP LORD

With a soft breeze You beckon me, but still I lay here, reluctant
to begin another day of endless noise.
It is nine o'clock on Sunday morning — Your gift of rest to us.
The city's pounding blood pressure enters through my open window.

The busy highway passes nearby, filled with automobiles racing to
their destinations; a police siren screams in the distance.
A giant silver bird moves across the sky; its booming roar rattles
the windows as it passes.

Our neighbor is out early this morning; his power mower is setting
birds on the wing and chasing squirrels to the highest branches.
His wife plugs in the edger and the two of them perform a loud duet
around the back yard.

Perhaps ear plugs are the solution? No, that would be like wearing
blinders so we couldn't see.
What we escape from, does not go away; and the gift of our senses
becomes the culprit — as if to say, "If only we couldn't hear —
if only we couldn't see."

Speak up Lord, so I can hear You. Help me make sense of all of it.
I know You are with us — though it becomes harder and harder
to hear You in our mechanized world.

Rosemary Rochon

Poem For Life

Make peace with your parents before it is too late,
  for then you will realize you missed out on the
  best friends you could have had for life.

Make peace with your siblings, for they are a part
  of you and share the deepest feelings of the heart.

Make peace with yourself, for in this world, all you
  have is you. Learn to love yourself, no matter
  your color, age, or sex. For everyone is beautiful
  in God's eyes.

Make peace with each other. In a world so filled with
  turmoil and destruction we need not more aggravation
  to add to the burning fire. We are all brothers and sisters.

Make peace with God. For if you can accomplish a relationship
  with God, you can accomplish all.

Lisa Dawn Halden

Untitled

Injustice is a word that means a lot,
It can have you incarcerated for
years in one cubic spot.

Injustice doesn't help the innocent one,
because the circumstances they put you
in makes your mind nonfunctional at the time.

Injustice can make you cop-out for the
maximum, although you be patient and
go to trial you might walk away with a
lesser charge, or freedom the same day.

Injustice is sometimes a media stunt
to up the rankings of a lawyer, or
D.A, It can be played perfectly if
both work together to put you away
indefinitely.

Tristan Buckner

Tragedy's Mask

A smile,
A laugh,
All hide tragedy's mask.

A mourning heart,
And an everlasting ache in your soul;
Never to be revealed.

Those around you must always see the good in you
And are never to see that you too are human,
For this would bring about the realization that you too feel.

So when the tears
Threaten to overcome you,
You grit your teeth and smile.

And when emotions come too close
To the surface and you begin to sob,
You crack a joke, and lo and behold a laugh suddenly escapes.

But underneath it all,
Is just a teardrop and a crying heart,
Hiding within tragedy's mask.

Kari A. Hansen

"Holy One"

Merry Christmas we hear from others,
Peace on earth to you and your brothers,
Lend a helping hand because of the season,
But so many don't know the real reason:
How the Son of the world was born
In a stable early one morn.
So many came to Him and gave praise,
Joyfully their hands did raise.
The magnificent Savior was just a babe.
But He had the hands that would save.
They were also the ones that bled,
So that our lives would not be shed
He is a counselor, a teacher, a son,
A best friend to those who have none
This one Man I truly love, He sits on a throne up above.
The one that was born and slain, and suffered tremendous pain
Just to let us know he cares.
And the troubles we have He bears.
So happy birthday to you, God's son,
For you are the Holy One.

Claudia Cape

A Rose Blooms In December

"An elderly man aged eighty
Set out to discover a matey
He sought far and wide
For an elderly bride
And always acted sedately."

"When an amorous lady he dated
He found his vitality faded
For all he could do
Was say 'how do you do'
They laughed and were highly elated."

"We still have great years he shouted;
How could we every have doubted?
We'll sing, dance, and revel,
See movies, love sunsets and travel;
Roses are ours; fears have been routed."

"Old age is a time of art, he said
We'll use all colors and hues of red
To paint our new pictures
Of each day's new raptures
Till finally we fall into bed."

Clark Harshfield

The Beach

Why must I walk this beach alone?
To see the light of a different sun.
Why must I walk this beach alone?
To feel the breeze of an alien wind.
Why must I walk this beach alone?
To hear the swoosh and roar of relentless waves.
Why must I walk this beach alone?
To be shaped and molded like the sand.
Why must I walk this beach alone?
To be purged and healed by the sea of time.

verne j. harper

"Diamond"

Silently curled, she lay like a mold,
her tiny body turned out to the cold.
Left to nature, just a pile of ribs,
how someone could do this, is simply a sin.

Warm for her heart, caring to her soul,
she grew out like a beautiful sweet rose.
Her eyes glow gold then turn so green,
not a hair of that fur could be the least bit mean.

She's the "diamond" in the rough,
she's showed us she's tough.
She a christmas star, a precious gift,
forever ours right out of that wintery mist.

Carol J. Wateski

Learning To Live

Where are they?
These people that call themselves friends
They laughed with me
Before they found I was dying
Is it because the are afraid
To face their own mortality?
Is it because they find this
To depressing?
Where are they?
They could still laugh with me
Or simply hold my hand
I wish they could see . . .
It is from the dying
One truly learns to live.

Carol Haney Brooks

The Fish Story

How did that fish come to my door?
There is no lake, there is no shore!
How did that fish ring the bell?
He had no hands, that I could tell!
How did he get here, at my home?
How did a fish start to roam?
What does that fish want at my door?
Perhaps directions to the shore?
Should I answer and let him in??
And bow my head and shake his fin?
What would you do? If it were you?
Say, come on in and take a swim . . .
Or fill the sink, for him to drink?
Why did that fish come to my door?
I'd never seen fish walk before....
I should have answered the fish at my door,
No one will ever believe this fish lore,
And now I will never know what this fish came to my door for.....

Novella C. Furfaro

A Toast For A Bridal Shower

All the world loves a lover;
Next to that, surprise.
When we get them both together,
It's only natural to surmise.
There's happiness ahead for someone;
Happiness no earthly care can touch.
A dream so vivid and enchanting,
It can't be dimmed by wars and such.
For the heart that has truly loved never forgets,
But as truly loves on to the close.
As the sunflower turns on her god when he sets,
The same look she gave when he rose.
So here's to Martha Ann and Billy,
It's both with envy and with pride
We wish a life of happiness
For the future Bridegroom and his Bride.

Minnie T. Bramlette

Feelings Of My Life

I want to solve world peace and world hunger,
But my own small problems I can stand no longer.
I am hushed as I speak against homelessness and war,
Does this world not care about the holes it has tore?
Happiness, sadness, and confusion are mine,
Such a mixture of feelings so hard to combine.
Will anyone take me and hold me so tight —
That I'll not be alone, nor weary from fright?
Overwhelmed with the grief of our bad little planet,
Depression, unacceptance, and abuse — we should ban it.
Smothered by negative and angry thoughts,
Nervous that I should hear gun shots.
Giddy and hyper and active, yet cold,
Right now I do so need someone to hold.
This poem is of my sorrows, my strife,
My encounters, my joys, my feelings, my life.

Kerbie Reader

Ode To A Pal

You're known by many titles, you early morning brew,
    and though you are hot-headed — you displease very few;
You're the one love — we'll never part;
    yet, you've many affairs with many a heart;

Your aroma entices with romantic airs,
    you sooth and caress — when no one else cares!
At the dawn — you alert; through the day — you attend;
    In the twilight — you're warming; and a dusky old friend!

You're America's cup — the hot one to go;
    America's love — whose name we all know;
For richer or poorer — in sickness, and aglow:
    our intimate pal — Hot-Headed Joe.

Gary Bitson

Be Yourself

As I looked over the valley,
I noticed there on the highest hill was a flower.
The flower was not alone but different from,
any other flower on the hill.
Then I noticed, like that flower,
I was very different from anyone else too.
The flower was not perfect,
and perfect I would never be.
And for once in my life I realized,
I should be proud I'm me.

Katherine M. Whitney

To Jean

Although this is almost the end of the book
  I have something important to say
That concerns an event during World War Two,
  And the date was eleventh of May.

Just fifty years back from this very day
  You and I walked the length of the aisle.
The asthmatical organ was groaning away
  And the guests were all dressed up in style.

Exchanging our vows didn't take very long;
  On the way out I trod on your train,
And now the half-century mark has arrived,
  I wish we could do it again.

Now this little verse is devoted to you,
  In thanks for a most happy life,
And if I had it all to do over again
  I'd surely choose you for my wife.

Peter West

A Busy Happy Mom

Being a mother could be lots of fun
Those tiny little people will keep you on the run.
What did they do today?

Did they spill something on the floor?
Or did they make a silly face that you could not ignore?

Did they run a fever that kept you up all night?
Did they disagree and have a little fight?

Did they stroll tissue paper up and down the halls?
Did they run from store to store when you
took them to the Mall?

They always make you smile, when
you're mad! They always seem so caring
even if you're sad!

Yes my little children, Mommy loves you
very much and there's no one in this
world that can steal your magic touch!

Jocelyn L. Fox

Senses Of A Boy

Do you see the sparkle in his blue eyes?
So full of laughter and joy
Notice how it dims as he starts to cry
When they tease this little boy.
Do you feel the warmth from his loving smile?
The tender glow surrounds him
Notice how it fades for a while
When he can't be one of them.
Do you hear him as he prays each night?
Notice the miracle he pleads
For our Lord to make his mind work right
Then he would know how to read.
Do you taste the sweetness of his mother's words?
As she tells him of faith and hope
Notice the pain that this has stirred
When she can't seem to help him cope.
Enjoy the aroma of the flowers he grew
They have strong roots and are thriving
Notice though the weeds force their way through,
The buds open, like him they're striving.

Anna Daly

Christmas Back Home

I watched a snowflake as it fell to the ground
When all around me there wasn't a sound.
I felt a breeze and flutter in the air.
Then I knew that God was there.

It made me remember home many years ago
When all winter long we had snow.
The days were carefree happy ones
Plenty of love, laughter and fun.

We had sleigh rides and snow ball fights,
Roasted chestnuts in the fire at night.
Mom and Pop told us stories of long ago
Kept us awake with our eyes all aglow.

Christmas eve we all went to church.
We sang carols and learned about our saviors birth,
How he would be born on earth and walk with man
Suffer and die and rise again.

There was lots of rejoicing that Christmas morn
As we celebrated the day that Christ was born,
We knelt on our knees and said our prayers.
All was right with us because God was there.

Carrie B. Smith

A Single Rose

Soft kisses
  across my face . . .

With strong arms
  you'd embrace . . .

And with a light touch,
caress my skin

Revealing the feelings
you have within.

So with this rose
I send to you,

A message by which
my love is true.

A single leaf, a single stem, a single petal,

for a special friend.

A single rose, a single hug, a single kiss,

for the one I love.

My feelings through words
cannot be exposed,

As much as my love for you
is symboled by this rose.

Sheraya Brown

Solitude

Eternity is longer than I ever dreamt it could be
The sands of time move much more quickly than before
Life without you was never meant for me
For with you it's something sweet, to be adored
The days are long, the nights everlasting
Since last my eyes feasted on you, my love
'Tis a play that He is casting
and my part is very sad and blue, my love
Peace will come when He wills it to be
The sky will turn the clouds to a heavenly blue
The sun and earth will glow with ecstasy
For in my arms will be my beloved and
  wonderful you.

Saul Greenwald

Anger Within

They took them from their land,
They took our land from us,
They placed them on plantations,
And moved us on reservations.

Together we've harvested this country,
As the engines and the slaves are treated the same,
Our freedom had been raped to no end,
As time passed so were our women.

They were punished by their master,
When we were assaulted by their government,
To this day we are discriminated,
And never once was an apology delegated.

Although laws were written in our favor,
The law was never enforced for their actions,
And to us as another day begins,
There will always stir anger within.

Rick Fisher

Untitled

I swear if you swear
Friends forever
Friends so ever true
Bound by our hearts
Bound through the deepest part of our souls
Bound through the magic of our minds
We'll live on forever in time
Remembering the dreams we dreamed
Remembering the secrets we shared
We grew up with a treasure richer than gold or silver
The rivers of our minds run fresh as the melting snow in the spring
The flowers of our hearts sway radiantly with the fall season wind
The rainbows of our souls light the sky like summer fireworks
And our friendship bound as we are
Illuminate the sky like the moon on a long winter night
We share the moon and stars like secrets
Secrets of the past and those left to share
From the memories of the heart we are one
And the joys of friendship we will share
Of yesterday and tomorrow

Christine Rheaume

The Ballad Of Torian Grey

He held his mighty blade aloft,
And the blade descended with a deadly swing;
The sound that echoed ever-so-soft,
Was a hellishly hollow ring.

The sword was blocked with great swiftness,
And sparks spewed high overhead;
And the Evil Shadow showed much finesse,
As the atmosphere morphed yellow and red.

A bell tolled loudly, long away,
But the Battle raged in minds;
And the bell tolled twice for a brand new day . . .
The first ray was the sign.

The Shadow trembled torturously and suddenly fled,
With the coming of this day;
And followers everywhere praised the head
Of the Youngest Hero, Torian Grey.

He held his mighty blade "Heller" up high,
And all people proceeded to cheer;
And People everywhere started to cry,
"Our Lord, our King is finally here!"

Jeremiah Whitehead

Untitled

I found an old Christmas card
You thanked me for being a friend.
But the honor was mine.
You have been gone ten months
And still I grieve!!
You were really hurting inside
And saw death as a way out.
I wish that I had been able to help;
Been able to read between your words.
You had many problems.
Could I have helped?
I should have walked closer to you
Should have listened more
Said "I love you" more often.
It might have helped a little.
It might have made the difference
You might still be here.
Now it is too late and you will never know
That I really care.
In a way, I think you did know!!!

Rita K. Underwood

The Swim

The waves are relentless, the current so swift,
despite my effort, I continue to drift.
My arms are heavy, the future looks grim.
How can this happen? My faith is in Him.

My strength has now left me. My limbs have grown numb.
It's painfully clear that no one will come.
I love you Lord Jesus, and feel that you're near.
Before I come home, my request you must hear

My children will grow with their father not there.
Their most special moments I'll no longer share.
To you I turn over my children, my wife.
If this be your will, then come take my life.

Then God called a boy out into the deep,
while ears all around him were surely asleep.
The heart of a child, the strength of a man,
were two things he needed to further God's plan.

Just like that, I was back on the shore.
Sometimes you don't know what God has in store.
It can be quite exciting to live in God's will,
but to die without Jesus, imagine that chill.

Jeff Olson

Flying Horses

A small town in Tennessee just a few miles left from Hell,
was where he said he came from and that's all that he would tell.
He talked of all the Indians and of buffalo he had killed.
Of all the gunfights he had won and men that he let live.
"Why I fought all the biggest names," he would often say.
"From Hitchcock and Bat Masterson to old Doc Holliday."
"I never had to kill them I shot their guns from their hand."
"Who says you got to kill someone to be the better man?"
I remember when he passed away he was almost ninety-five
I locked myself up in my room, laid on my bed, and cried.
But then his words reached thru my haze and I set up on my bed.
"Boy you never go away just your body's dead!"
"Don't let them forget me memories never die,"
"we'll see you in a couple years, we'll ride horses that can fly."
"We can head down to the creek and catch some big old fish,"
"Up here there's no problems you live as you wish."
"But boy you just listen to your old grandpap
I miss you and I love you don't ever forget that!"
I promised him I wouldn't and said a sad goodbye
I'll see you in a couple years we'll ride horses that can fly."

William Eddie Dulaney

Life

Life . . . Has much offerings. In Summer, Winter, Autumn, and Spring.
Memories of those you've treasured. Memories that can never be measured.
Thoughts of joy, and sorrow. Thoughts we all seem to borrow.
Dreams that we want to share. Dreams our forefathers once bare.
It is but a shame we cannot be great. Everyone breathes some type of hate.
Be it for a difference in taste. Or the mere presence of another's race.
Simply denying our brotherly love. A given gift from the Lord above.
Who are we to create this madness? Surely we've all had our share of sadness.
There's always room to make amends. Respecting each other is
where it begins. Shouting, "I love myself as well as my brother!

Echoing down upon all others
In our past, hate has broken the chain. In our future, love will destroy its stain.
Offerings to our youth, is only our duty. Leaving our generations to
come, a vision of beauty. And in the end, our paths shall meet.
Brown eyes to blue eyes will shake hands and greet.

Rochelle Durr

Autistic Child

The best word for Autism is Frustration.
That for most is an Exclamation.

I am a child just like you,
I like to play with toys too.

Autism is not catchy as some people think,
I can not give it to you, even if we share a drink.

I cannot say all I wish to say,
My words are garbled even when I pray.

Not even my Mother can understand all,
The frustration makes me want to bang my head on a wall.

There is only one who understands,
My life and soul are in his hands.

Thank you God and Heaven above,
For my Mother's unconditional love.

Katrina Hodge

Visit From Breeze

Breeze is rather curious today,
running through the grass like a playful child.
Tickling leaves of happy flowers,
wandering where it may . . . running wild.

To my ankles, to my knees.
Then blows my skirt so high!
Laughing! I don't care out here.
Breeze lets out another sigh.

Tossing grasses across my legs,
teasing bugs and butterflies.
Skipping atop a sparkling stream,
then off again to other skies . . .

Alanna K. Bixby

Dark Cave

Deep in a cave, starving for light.
It seems I've been here forever.
Feeling my way through the turns and the rubble.
Trying to find my way out.
My eyes have adjusted to the darkness.
Yet, deprived of the light, I'm losing my mind.
I walk slowly and carefully.
Trying my damnedest not to fall.
What would I find if I were to fall?
Where would I be?
Don't know if I'm going in the right direction.
Don't know what awaits me at the end of my journey.
Oddly enough, I have no fear.
Maybe that's the effect of the cave . . .

Felicia Procaccio

"Don't Stand Still"

I turn around, but to see a shadow —
The water trickling, oh how shallow —
Round and round, will it ever end —
We awake each day, never pretend

The trees so bare, will they come alive?
This way, that way, forward drive
Many a winding road to follow, to get there —
but they all inform me, "You must beware".

So I stand alone wondering why —
Holding back and saying good-bye —

The trees do bloom, without a thought —
Love does live, without being taught —
Money is made, the mind creates,
The inner soul — sedates!

Things do happen with control, but some without
each new day, each new doubt —
You are you — and that's okay
The seagulls flock around the bay
Life amongst us, here to stay
Love is with you everyday!

Evelyn H. Pirrotta

Charon

What sort of man are you, ferryman?
What is your life apart from this boat? This toil?
Do you have a wife, and sons to honor your name?
Are your daughters wed?
Who mends your cloak and tends your fire?
Where do you take your respite at day's end?
Who fills your wine jar and warms your heart?
On what do you spend those wretched coins?
Do you like your work? Did you have a choice, or
did some god assign you it, time out of mind,
before the world began?
Is it a hard crossing? Is it long?
What do they talk about, your passengers?
Does the god sail with you or are they left to you alone?
Do you pity them?

The light was dim and yet I saw
his cheek was wet not from the river's spray.
"No one ever asked." He said.

Beatrice C. Green

In Our Hands, Through Our Eyes

Feel the refreshing salty spray
While running, dancing and at play
Inside out and outside in
What a confusing world we are in

Hear the ocean's crashing waves
See the sun set day by day
Trees sprout up and then fall down
Still the earth turns round and round

Swim, climb, run and explore
Love the art more and more
Create it with respect and care
Hopefully it will still be there

Running through the wet and salty sand
Love and hope is at hand
Jump the ditch so dark and deep
And climb the hill so high and sleep

In our hands through our eyes
Take the world by surprise
Hear the warning loud and clear
Fight for what's right when the chance comes near!

Kristen K. LaCasse

Nostril-Domus

They call me Nostril-Domus,
They say it's because of my nose,
Not that it's big or unsightly,
They're just having fun I suppose.

There isn't an odor I can't detect,
I've got a super sniffer,
I can smell a rat a mile away,
I'm rather proud of my whiffer.

I can tell you when something smells fishy,
And detect when there's rain in the air,
My nose will never forsake me,
I take it everywhere.

I can smell if it's rotten in Denmark,
My snout is simply the best,
I know when something's cooking,
And I know the sweet smell of success,

The next time you smell something funny,
Perhaps you'll remember this verse,
They call me Nostril-Domus,
They could call you something much worse.

Twyla Bosshardt

No One Loved You More Than I

I love you, but you must go, yes I brought you in my
life, when I was young. You were a new friend and I was so
proud to show you to everyone.

We have been friends for over twenty-five years.
We have become as one. People see us and smile. Some
even ask to share you. In a nice, but lustful way. And most
because I understand the passion and desire they had to
touch you and breathe in your being.

And yes there were other times. I became angry
because I didn't want to share you with anyone.

In these last five years I realized how much you
have hurt me, not intentionally I know, but my circulation
and lungs can't take anymore. So I must say
goodbye to my friend (20 Class A. Cigarettes, Light 100's).

Donald Davis

Wendy Wynn Watched The Wind

When did Wendy Wynn watch the wind?
Wendy didn't really watch the wind.
But she did sit for an hour
And watch the wind's strong power.

It shook houses and trees
Then it sent cool cool breezes.
The wind moved with force and speed
Which reminded Wendy Wynn of Mrs. Reed.

Wendy watched the amazing wind
Take her neighbor's kite high in the sky.
Then she quietly whispered and gave a sigh
Yes, the wind is like my teacher Mrs. Reed.

One day, I'll be like the two
And teach legions of pupils with force
Until their minds soar like a kite
After I've taught with gusto and might.

Shhhhh, Wendy closed her eyes blue
While visualizing the grandiose job
She would do some happy day.
With knowledge, manifold minds she'd spray.

Florence M. Jones

City Life

As I walk on the grass, with the serenity of nature,
    I can see a spider spinning a web in the trees above;
and the once still and silent air, with its sweet smell,
    has been broken by a wailing siren in the distance.

A gunshot, or is it a car backfire, pierces the air,
    like a knife stabbing through the heart of peace:
a barking dog, a child's cry, a parent screams an order,
    the silence is broken by sounds of life, the calm is forgotten.

Take a deep breath to inhale the clean, crisp air,
    and a tear begins to fill my desperate heart;
for what was once a sweet, cool taste of fresh air,
    has been replaced by a dirty, decrepit, stale flavor.

I pray for rain to come and fall on this retched land,
    and wash away this foul, polluted stench:
for like a knight which slays the mystical dragon,
    beauty shall again be returned unto the lost land.

Although this glamour stays only for a brief, bright moment,
    like an oasis in the forgotten desert of time;
the peaceful beauty will always shine through the cold,
    a lonely star shining through the cloudy sky.

Steve Anson

The Sleeping Giant

Many years have passed since he died,
When they said time heals all you thought they lied,
They didn't lie, they didn't know it isn't so.
The pain just burrows deep inside, there to hide
To fester and to grow, but not to show.
It waits there while you live and laugh again,
It sleeps there till you think you've lost the pain
Until some word or musical refrain stirs it up again,
Then like a giant tired of sleeping
It leaps to life and leaves you weeping
You thought maybe that you'd forgotten how to cry,
Till pain sprang at your heart like lightning from the sky
Each time the knife turns it leaves you gasping
And you wonder will this pain be everlasting?
And of course you know that this is so.

Leonie F. Nulle

From My Heart

I am sending a message,
    from my heart.
For loving me, through thick and thin.
For helping me work through,
    anger and pain.
For standing by me, and not being afraid.
I love you!

For showing me, my strength inside.
For being proud of my accomplishments,
    and showing pride.
I love you!

For showing me, a love so strong.
For letting it feel, like Christmas.
Even when things, were going wrong!
I love you!

I have worked through, so much.
From things from then,
    now I see, a bright light, around the bend.
Thanks for teaching me, what is to have,
A Loving, Wonderful, Friend!

Dolores Miller

To God

I asked the Lord for an angel to love, if
He had one to spare from Heaven above. I
waited over the years oh so patiently, but there
was not an extra angel in Heaven for me. Then
one day it finally occurred, I met you and I
knew that my prayer had been heard. Once I
got to know you it could only mean, the only
extra angel, was one without wings.

Bradley D. Miles

Remembrance

Wrapped snugly in the sacred cloth of
the newborn, hoisted high upon the
proud hands of the father, the child
felt the love, the honoring, while still
immersed in the confusion of birth.

The tribe gathered, rejoicing at the
arrival of an ancestor returned. Women,
wrapped in richly-dyed fabrics, singing,
praising great spirit, as they prepared
foods designated for the feast.

Drums, vibrating with the beat of joyous
celebration. Feet pounding upon the Earth,
her dust rising to become one with the
dancers. Chants of blessing, of gratitude,
of jubilation echoed throughout the forest.

The ritual continued, a tribute to this
shaman soul, an omen of good fortune for
all, as the child, secure in the arms of
its mother, suckled at her breast, at peace,
at home...this other home for a time.

Ashi

Spirit Of War

Their cries echo across the blue
Where white froth washes away the red
We mourn, for the children are dead!
Pain's boney finger scratches the green
As towers of steel rise up to scream
Thoughts try to flee with confused haste
Life's sharp teeth reach out and taste
We mourn, for the parents are dead!
The tiger of greed as devoured their minds
Sins of the heart have now been fed
Suffering of war has murdered the soul
Greed, lust, and power, are the new goal!
We mourn, for we are dead!
The bridge of compassion lies buried
Beneath our hatred too strong to shed
No longer united, our shadow grows small
Divided, we weep, we falter, and fall
We mourn, peace is dead!

Helen Jane Montero

The Winds Of Time

The Winds of Time, moving swiftly and forcefully in anticipation.

Like that of an eagle soaring in high elevation, yet holding strong
   with determination.

The Winds of Time, savored and cherished by "mythological" Gods of
Long ago, still unknown, respected and full of information.

A. M. Atarodian

David

Guess what happened that Eve in September,
These special moments, we will remember!
Cute little ears and eyes so bright,
just to hold him is pure delight.
Ten perfect fingers, ten perfect toes,
He has his Mom's pretty nose.
He's half Baggett and half Perry.
These are genes he will carry.
We love him very much you know.
And we will always let it show.
We nuzzle his neck and kiss his feet.
Everything about him is so sweet!
His mom and dad are walking tall.
They know now — they have it all!
We're so proud, our heart may burst.
David must be a little Angel, who came to earth.

Annis J. Baggett

Not The Ordinary

Age
Seems to be the only difference between us
Years —
Only a number and not much more

Both of us long,
Wanting for something to hold on to
Searching
To make our souls complete

Curious
To whether people would understand
This relationship definitely not the ordinary
Or would they just judge?

Could we overcome
The doubts of others?
Or more importantly,
The doubts of our own . . .

Linda Gail Baker

Frayed Ends Of What Used To Be

Memories of a time ago . . . Threads that bound us together
Something old and something new . . . tears now create our river
Reflections in that perfect mirror . . . Drown away Now and Forever
Present thoughts, they leave me empty . . . Those days were promising
   Never
Mangled now i fast alone . . . Starving my own ambition
Held down by the will of Fate . . . Killing all of my wishes
Wondering where Time is standing still . . . Should i even finish
For Innocence is nowhere to be found . . . as his age is now
   diminished
Built in a positive mental image . . . treading between two worlds of
   false Hope
Rejected by both sides of the stream . . . left hanging by an old
   friend's rope
Our world sinks around me . . . so the ends of Time by us are severed
My feelings used to swim free . . . but what used to be is now gone
   forever . . .

Michael Corey Thompson

My Light Of Love

I am the light inside your heart comforting you at night
your world will never fall apart as long as I'm in sight
It doesn't matter where you may be just look for the radiant light
mine is the love that sets you free forever burning bright
Whatever heartache you may go through, for every unwiped tear
My light shines freely upon you, I will always be here
I am the light inside your heart!

Cindy Borgwardt

Evensong

The path beckons on ever higher,
    Awash in its sunglow and warmth.
In tow are life's countless blessings,
    That fill and that overflow.

Pause now at the vista before you;
    Never before as wide or as deep;
Sharper and clearer its meaning
    That young minds cannot yet perceive.

Pause, but don't stop — it's not over!
    The mantle still rests on your frame;
More joys up ahead yet to savor;
    More wisdom to gain — to impart.

Now hush! Hear the Evensong swelling,
    And filling the air with its sound;
Washing o'er you with great benediction —
    Bringing joy — bringing peace to your soul!

Agnes Schumm

Night Sounds

As the dusk deepens and the air cools,
I relax as the night sounds awaken.
Crickets keep time with the water from the fountain
That tinkles merrily on the pond.
Brandenburg's melody mingles with the sounds of nature
As he drifts toward me on the fragrant night breeze.
Each star shines brightly as the darkness envelopes me,
And as a blanket envelopes a child in comfort,
I let the night sounds lull me to sleep.

Jo Jaimeson

"Cold Winter Rain"

Trees are bare, grass is brown.
Mountains sparkle white.
The rose is out of town,
and the birds are not in sight.

Winter rain, winter rain,
plays tunes on my window pane.
Crisp morning breeze blows gentle rain
on my window pane.

On our beaches the cold fog rolls in.
Seagulls hover overhead.
All the bathers have gone home.
Winter has made its bed.

Winter rain and cold north winds
blow faded leaves to the ground.
Seeds are sown, and when springtime comes,
the birds are homeward bound.

Emily Pauline Baldwin

Taylor Marie

Taylor Marie — She's cute as can be,
Did I mention — She needs lots of attention?

She's very alert, observant, and not a bit shy.
She plays possum — She's really sly!

She's five weeks old — She's learned so much,
and she knows her parents have a very special touch.

Her smile and her "going" makes Grandma so proud —
Especially when we are in a big crowd.

All her life she will always be,
A very special Granddaughter to me!

Alice M. Smith

Life's Road

When you're walking down life's dreary road
And you're sometimes sad and blue,
Just stop and think of the many times
That our Saviour was weary too.

Sometimes we're afraid to walk any further
Afraid all our courage has gone,
But then, stop and think of our Saviour's worries
How He needed strength to go on.

So few are the times that we remember
Our Christ on dark Calvary,
Just stop and think why He came to us
He came to set us free.

Let us all go out on that road together
And make it a road for Him,
Let the light of His love come shining thru us,
Never letting that light grow dim.

Carolyn Barker

He Gave More

I ask him for health
He gave me help
I ask him for peace
He gave me rest
I ask for love
He gave me friendship
I ask for friends
He gave me many
I ask him for sleep
He gave me rest
I ask him forgiveness
He gave himself
I ask for blessings on others
He gave me more
I ask him to stay within our hearts door
He did give, He gave once - that's forever more.

Cecilia J. Barnes

Camel

Camel, the one who roams the
arid deserts of the world.
You are forced to carry hundreds
of pounds of heavy material;
yet still, you do not stop to rest.
You are pulled across land with no praise
yet still, you behave and walk willingly.
You go days without water or food;
yet still, you do not cease to work hard and well.
Camel, why do you still bow to the human hand?
Is it because, without a human guiding you
along the deserts, you would be lost?
Or, is it the other way around?

Sudheer Balakrishnan

Secrets

I suppose all good things one day must come to an end
Only through the tears can I see that with my love I lost my best friend.
There are so many memories and the feeling of how much we both cared
Sometimes it hurts endlessly to realize how much we once shared
Although with the good memories comes the heartache
And the last careless whisper which caused our hearts to break
I must dream on, I must reminisce
Of happy times of our first kiss.
For with every good-bye we tell a well-kept secret
Of sweet pain and tough love-dear things we will never forget!

Jessica Beckman

A Purple, Blue Flower

I walk along a lonely road,
the setting sun splashes orange across my face.
I step to ponder a delicate blue flower
seeming almost purple in the fading light.
A wide starry sky twinkles overhead.
A long stretch of barren land
as far as my mind can wonder.
There is no one in this place
to share my simply pleasures,
only me and a longing to live.
But can a person live in such away?
Or only survive the daily needs?
Will there ever be someone,
a person to understand
that the universe, at this moment,
is a lovely, delicate purple, blue flower
to be explored, to be shared
with someone you love?

Carol Herring

"Nostalgic Thoughts Of Alaska"

Dance on little silvery leaves,
   Rustle to your heart's content.
For soon your efforts of growing up
   Will be fruitless and not well spent.

Grow quickly little fireweed,
   For surely as the last bloom bursts forth,
Mother Nature is waiting for your seed in her cold earth.

Dash across the meadow with your baby, Mother Moose.
   Play and browse while you can,
For some evil hunter wants to kill you
   So he can prove he's a man.

Struggle forth, almighty salmon,
   Your skin's already turning red,
Your goal in life is to lay your eggs;
   Then count the hours before you're dead.

Please, Lord, keep my animal friends safe,
   Let no intruder come near their home.
Alaska was meant to be their shelter
   And may they forever be free to roam.

Elaine Startz

Life

Life was, life is and life ever will be,
From everlasting to everlasting, thru eternity.
Before the Sun, the Moon, the stars,
The God-life brooded, way beyond Mars.
That other Sons of God do exist
And dwell afar, way beyond the mist,
Tis the message, loud and clear,
Of each and every Avatar, from far or near.
Shiva, Buddha, Zoroaster, Mahomet,
Speak of realms, Heavens, vast numbers of planets.
A blade of grass, a breath of air,
Contain the source of life, so precious, so dear.
A mountain high, a valley low, stars at night, all aglow,
Mirror the beauty, the vastness, the serenity,
Of time and space, of boundless eternity.
Life or death, beginning or end,
Mere useless terms, philosophers defend.
God is the Universe, the totality of life.
Earth, Galaxies, Aeons, all embodied, without a wife.
We exist, we survive, because God alone possess life.

Rupert Marques

Awakening In Time

Earth
Once again I experience you in physical form
But this time I intend to fully awaken

Quest
To fulfill my destiny
To remember the source as my being

Yearning
To be home again
Yet memory is dim as to which galaxy

Body
Will I remember how to take you
Or will you remain as before
Journeying.

Pat Summer

The Girl

The girl who lives inside of me
is young and gay and bright,
She sings along with music
and she dances in the night

She always smells of sweet perfume,
Her hair is softly curled,
Her face is painted, her nails are too,
Because she'd still a girl

Mirrors and pictures are not her friends
They show what others see.
No one knows, except for me,
The girl inside of me.

Louise Magill Swansey

First Love

If by chance we cross on a street
Don't think of my tears that fell painfully at your heels
Or try to find the words to make yourself justified as a man
Keep walking
Never look back to see the shadow of the past
You will always be a part of
Leave yesterday in the crimson bed we slept in
Stained with my initiation into womanhood
Pretend we never new what was
Let it be a memory, ever, if only of regret, pass by
As you did when you left me
A stranger

Dawn C. Davis-Reid

Prologue To African Roots In American Soil

From two continents, of like dignity
On the Atlantic where we lay our scene
With minor differences under scrutiny
People voyage forth in 1815

From Europe and Africa two ships sail
Bound for America and a new life
For those reaching her shores hearty and hale
One group will find freedom; the other strife

One ship carries passengers full of dreams
That life will be sweet and fate will be kind
The other, human cargo; hoarse from screams
The freedom they had has been left behind

Two groups leave their homelands and ride the waves
One group to be free men: the other, slaves

Patricia S. Sykes

Destiny

In my minds eye I can see, I can see the spirits.
I can hear them, they call to me.
They call for me to come, to come home.
My destiny awaits me. I can hear the spirits calling.

Something is pulling, pulling me to my destiny.
The spirits are pulling, my soul mate awaits me.
He is calling, to come.
To come home, for it is time.
It is time to entwine.

I must listen, listen to the spirits.
For they know, they know my destiny.
My soul mate awaits for me.
I can hear, hear him calling,
It is time, it is time.

Mitzi L. Barnett

He Knows Not What He Does

Just by hearing that word come from his lips, Sheryl . . .
    He knows not what he does.
The way he smiles and melts me completely . . .
    He knows not what he does.

When his lips touch mine and I can no longer tell where he begins
    and I end . . .
    He knows not what he does.
He looks into my eyes and sees my soul so clearly . . .
    He knows not what he does.

Knowing that I can Trust him with all my secrets . . .
    He knows not what he does.
And the touch he has when his hand meets mine . . .
    He knows not what he does.

When he tells me he loves me and my Heart beats uncontrollably . . .
    He knows not what he does.
With the thought of making Love to him fills my heart with sudden
    warmth . . .
    He knows not what he does.

God grant me this hope that someday . . .
to me he will know what he does.

Sheryl R. Taylor

Reflections (The Rainbow Poem)

I believe in fairy tales coming true;
Magic potions — casting spells.
I can see the face of the old man on the moon;
Full of wisdom — keeper of ancient tales.

I believe in the colors of a rainbow;
Each one tells a secret — each one holds a dream.
I can feel the changes in the seasons;
Reflections in my heart — not everything is as it seems.

I believe in wishing upon a falling star;
Images in the clouds — Pegasus in the midnight sky.
I believe that all these things are true;
Without a doubt in my mind — without a reason why.

Kathryn Thiele

A Drop Of Water

I was like a leaf shaken by its master;
Never blowing in the same direction,
and wilting from within.
Then I turned to the Lord,
who like a drop of water,
replenished my soul and gave direction
to the path that I must go.

Lora Bell

Smile

The smile of a child is such glorious and wonderful sight.
It makes the sun rise in the morning and the moon at night.

It keeps the days very busy and overflowing with pure joy.
There is no difference whether it's from a girl or a boy.

Their minds are so full of wonderful things to say and do.
So maybe they did that yesterday, today it's all brand new.

With the determination of a giant and all their strength and might.
They work day in and day out just to get some small thing right.

To learn to eat from a spoon or to drink from a big kids cup.
To stay in line when coloring a page, tie a shoe or button their coat up.

The simple act of being who they are will endear them to all they meet.
The warmth of a hug or the touch of a kiss makes our life so sweet.

Childhood passes so quickly and try as hard as we might, we can't hold it back.
We take hundreds of pictures to just try to remember and help us keep track.

Then comes that dreadful day when we know we must let them go.
So it's off to the first day of school, so they can learn and grow.

The days speed past, then the months, then the years too are gone.
Oh, the sights they have seen, the places they have been and the things they have done.

Then all of a sudden here it comes again, that very special smile.
That lovingly beams back at us from the face of a new grandchild.

Susie Cochran

"Daydreaming"

To sit and be quiet and wonder what's there,
to dream and to think and just sit and stare.

To listen and hear all the world around, and
do nothing but nothing but sit on the ground.

Look up to the sky and watch clouds fly by,
hear the wind, pick a flower, hour by hour.

So easy to do is nothing that's true but still
we find so little time to do.

Just hear the birds sing and feel the sun on your
face, and smell the new foliage of honeysuckle
and fern lace.

To daydream what a pleasure, and forget what
must be done and do whatever you would do,
in your own timeless leisure.

So, be good to yourself and daydream
away and remember tomorrow is still
another day.

Gloria E. Parker

Thanks Be To God

Thanks be to God for giving to me
The glasses on my nose that help my eyes to see

The love of my family members who care very much for me
The kind of love you gave them that passed it on to me.

The car that I drive that I can go from place to place
The love that's deep inside that time cannot erase.

The children that I have that hold my love my love most dear
By my example, they can live their lives without fear.

My health is good as time marches on!
My life is so content now, my heart sings its happy song.

Thanks be to God who died upon that tree . . .
Who gave me my loving spirit that dwells inside of me.

Ellen Kaye Webb

433

A Life Not Spared

Sounds of rage so close to here,
No one should have to feel this sense of fear.
Nazi soldiers will be coming soon,
You think to yourself while watching the moon.

You know you've lost your childhood dreams,
When you hear the horrid screams.
They came from down the stairs,
The Nazi soldiers were finally there.

Taken to prison camps by this brutal cult,
Some to the showers; but it's not your fault.
Death to them all as the door is closed,
You hear their pleas as the wind blows.

Rage fills your broken heart,
How did all this madness start?
Death by the numbers; you just can't win,
Your sorrow and pain must be held in.

You write a journal as your tears are shed,
A sign of remembrance for those that are dead.
Maybe it will help in future years,
To stop the killing; to stop the tears.

Rebecca Thompson

Happy Birthday Jesus

God Wanted a world, where all could be free.
But one bite from an apple condemned you and me.

Then up in the sky, a star took form.
Lighting the way to a manger, where our Saviour was born.

Taking the wise men to where, the virgin Mary gave birth.
They brought gifts of gold, of incense and myrrh.

You came to this world, without evil or shame.
Turning darkness to light, Jesus Christ was your name.

He could heal the sick with the touch of his hand.
Evil spirits would flee at the sight of this man.

He fed thousands with nothing but some bread and 5 fish.
Loving all of the masses was his only wish.

Whether Jew of Gentile, black or white.
He'll return for his children like a thief in the night.

But until that day comes, I just want to say.
We love you Sweet Jesus and Happy Birthday.

Michael Whaley

Emotions Run Deep

Little hurts turn into big wounds with time.
Mountains of anger and feelings piled up
Volcanos of poison waiting to erupt.
Pretending to the world that all is fine
While anger boils up within the mind.

Some people's hurt slide off their backs
Never seeming to pierce or stick
A river runs o'er rocks that are slick.
Cold, steady streams route crevices and cracks
Polishing the smooth, hard surfaces of black.

Human beings experience anger that seethes.
The strain of conflict churning within,
Crushed spirits need healing to begin.
Soothe the soul; hurt will leave
Let the heart have hope, begin to believe.

Leslie Tousley

A Fine Day

Traveling on such a beautiful day
from here to there it was a fine day.
As we travel we pass through the lives
of those who came before.
We experience their hopes and aspirations
as we see residue of their having been there.
An abandoned house that was anchor
of the dreams of some who have had to
go to the next chapter of life.
Was the work too hard or the results
good enough to make them move?
We picture a family happy with their lot,
raising pets, a garden, a farm animals
as they find the tragedy that life brings
made them stronger. We bet that it was
A Fine Day that day for them too.

Truman Troop

The Subway's Bedazzling Movements

Zooming through the city's dark caverns
these juggernauts rocking and rolling —
whiz by the aged stations like a
zephyr sending winds from floor to ceiling.

The steel pillars create a collage
of flickering and illuminating light
for commuters who huddle in shadows
evacuating the subway — hustling into the night.

Sparks like red and white phosphorous flares
spray the winding tracks while the screeching coaches
haul a human cargo to the skyscrapers
that light up the dark streets and alleys.

Under the ground the wingless fuselages
fly along the earthbound rails to a subway
hangar where the graffiti vandals
swiftly mark the cars in their decaying way.

Ronald J. Beattie

Captivity

I am in captivity of a place I know right well.
I am in captivity of a place I think as heaven.
I am in captivity of sounds I can't escape.
I am in captivity of Music.

Joshua David Turnbull

Cowboy

He is a gentleman, through and through.
No one else has ever been this true.
He is young, his way is old.
He is soft, gentle, kind and bold.
It is true what they say
For he has taken my heart, and now gone away.
If you should see, this gentleman of mine,
Treat him ever so kind.
And remember . . . he will only be around for a time.

Amy R. Bergsrud

"Our Country"

"To live on Earth we need to be at peace with the world for tomorrow and the Lord that let us have life and peace on earth let us learn together so we may understand the liberty for our children to be, and our Country right or wrong our Country, and may our flag forever fly-high, and keep our land together forever, and may the good people of war be at peace, and our flag at home be waving so true, and awaiting to give a welcome to all that serve so brave"

Walter Andrew Raichel Junior

434

Life Is Love

Days may come, and nights may go.
Our lives on earth are just for show.
One day we're here, the next we're gone.
Some lives are short, while others long.
It's what we do, while here that counts.
We can be a saint, or be a louse.
For some, we learn; right from the start.
That we are judged by what comes from our heart.
Others, like me; learn this lesson too late.
And will have to answer at deaths gate.
What was life worth, without the love.
Given so freely, from those we should have loved.
For if you don't learn to give and receive.
You're the only one, you are going to deceive.
Grab hold of whatever time you have left.
To show those of whom you care for the best.
Give them your love, straight from your heart.
Before this life forces you to depart.
Above all my dear, what I'm trying to say.
I Love You today, forever; always!

Ricky G. Wadlow

Dreaming Of You

I fall asleep, and you are there.
Our eyes meet, but all I can do is stare.
You hold out your arms, and motion to me,
I reach to you, and we smile happily.
You pull me close, and we hold each other so tight.
We can see the love, we know this is right,
My hands roam your body in perfect form.
My hand touches your face, it's smooth, and warm,
Our lips meet with a force so strong,
We stand kissing for so very long,
"Crash, shatter" I hear something break.
I say goodbye, because soon I will be awake.
I open my eyes, and look around,
I notice the glass my cat knocked to the ground,
I think to myself; "How could this be?"
A broken, shattered glass to you from me.

Tina Marie Wagner

Winters

Winters are cold. My grandmothers
are getting old. We sit around the fire and think
of our strongest desires. My cousins
ask if we can go sled, but the parents
say "It's just about time for bed." Our
parents sing us a late lullaby then
us kids say goodnight and goodbye. We
huddle under the covers and hug
our fathers and mothers . . .

Kelli M. Wallin

Sonnet For All Seasons

The cavalcade of her merciless reign
Preceded the new birth, only by days.
Her cruelty was rather unfeigned
As she made no provision, in clothes ways,
And dallied around, waiting lady spring
To provide his attire of elfin greens,
At which she did in a dandified fling.
Then in total disregard for his dreams
They thrust him into the school of summer,
Offering no explanation, they fled;
Letting him learn of a distant drummer,
He to whom the sweet September was wed.
Thus casting upon him the autumn vine,
And his submission to old father time.

Rose Walls

Puppy Love

In the late of the night,
Birth. She had given,
Eight, how could this be,
First time mother, so brave was she,

Tiny, and cute, pure and innocent are they,
Masked as the father, the mother, or both,
To earlier to tell, the future will show,

So carefully she handled, nursed them all,
Throw exhausted, she carried on,
A registered blue tick, so prude was she,
No flowers were given, the praise was received,
She allowed us to share in her joy, but quick to retreat,

First hours go by, then, weeks, they can see,
Puppy love from mother, how sweet to be a part,
In life she had given, and care for them all,
The reminder threw babe, and a special place in our hearts,
For the love of a mother is as no other,
In all forms of life,
And the love for eight tiny puppies,
That came late one night.

Susan A. L. Walsh

Endure The Night (For The WERC, Yellowstone)

God bless the feral wolves,
may they finally wander free,
in America, once an unnamed land,
her fauna teemed alee.

God bless the feral wolves,
may their song endure the night,
where stars once blazed the timber trails,
replaced by ozone blight.

God bless the feral wolves,
may their howl be heard in halls,
from hallowed, to fallowed, to justice,
and habitatless malls.

God bless the feral wolves,
fate renewable year by year,
should myopic men forge a masque of death,
tis Man must shed a tear.

God bless the feral wolves,
prey to greed, so pray for time,
with every species that we lose,
the hourglass cracks in kind.

Rich Fiegelman

Lonely, Sad, And Blue

My greatness is my weakness,
My will is my meekness.
My strength comes from within,
I'm strong most of the time,
But in some point in time I'll bend.
You must not forsake me, 'cause then to,
You'll be lonely, sad, and blue.

There is more to life than
Pain, hurt, lonely, sad, and blue.
Some where in your heart,
There's the joy of being dear and true.
How great thou art for me and you,
How great it feels not to be
Lonely, sad, and blue.

Love can be sweet,
Love can be a treat,
But at some point in time,
Love still becomes lonely, sad, and blue.

Bernice Ward Willard

Humility

Each continent sends its messenger
Earth dust transported by wind's energy
And thus returned in unison

We are visitors united with each breath
I know not my brother — yet
I dwell within — and he so in me

Are we not then our own unique universe?
I see scenery and become one with it
When I feel beauty — I know it is so

I sing a song like a bird
And worry not who is listening

Sally Jackson

I Love America

America, America, I love this land,
From its seas and mountains to its desert sand,
My heart soars with pride on an eagle's wing,
To bestow this message, I joyfully sing!
America, America America the free!
America, America, God bless thee!
My love and respect are eternally for you,
For my country and my flag — the red, white and blue,
America, America, your rich heritage,
Is a rainbow of colors — a universal bridge!
America, America, America the free!
America, America, God bless thee!

Consuelo T. Ramirez

For The Moment

The moment there is light
Life begins to change.
Life changes are very important,
And other times not so vital
Since time has no patience and no stop signs
Life comes and goes like a heart beat.
If only that moment,
That instant,
That sudden change
To change nature's way.
Life would be meaningless
To exist for the moment.

Joseph Bermudez

Turning Point

Fragments of reality now chipping at her heart
Reviving insecurities once suffered at the start.
Gnawing doubts and quiet tears now fill the lonely night
Obliging her to heed as truth is forced into the light.

The dream has proved imperfect, a fairy tale in pain,
Their tender love, once intimate, now soiled and mundane.
The image of his faithlessness held deep within her soul
To haunt the memory of the love which once had made her whole.

Now childhood wounds awaken to remind her of the lie,
No, love is never perfect and heroes sometimes die.
So good-bye sparkling magic and happy ever after
Replaced by disappointment, torment, rage and nervous laughter.

Their love has reached a turning point. Were both of them to blame?
The fragile balance titled, will it ever be the same?
Could they ever find the strength to make the feelings stay?
Or will their lace of love unravel slowly every day?

J. G. Ramos

Happy Mother's Day, Mom!

I wish this could be a happy day for you.
I'll try to keep you comfortable in lieu.

There's not enough words to express how I feel,
But I know you know, my love is for real.

Thanks for your shoulder, when I would be down.
Thanks for your patience, when I'd act like a clown.

Thanks for your advice, when I'd ask what you thought,
Thanks for just listening, when advice was not sought.

You'll soon be in Heaven; I'll see you again,
As soon as I learn, to live without sin.

I've had the best teacher; you've tried your best,
It's up to me now, to complete this big test!

Kathy Nickel Reilly

Untitled

They say it was random, mere chance . . . happenstance,
that our world and all life came to be.
A cosmic explosion of matter and gas
Set earth spinning as spatial debris.

And then from deep oceans which magically rose
From hydrogen drawn from the air,
sprang single-celled life forms, primordial ooze,
which somehow evolved from there.

And through endless eons and millennia uncounted
The slimes and the plankton transformed
Mysteriously changing into living creatures;
some winged, some finned, some horned.

And finally, they tell us, from out of this chaos
A man and a woman emerged.
And these became families, then peoples, then nations,
and all of us now on the verge

Of forgetting our father, our only creator,
who really set things into motion.
We proclaim ourselves wise, but mere fools we become
If we ever embrace such a notion.

Russell Eric Reimer

Awaiting A Message From Heaven

Awakening on a sunny warm day
All was as normal as it could be
Each of us waking and on our way
To people and places daily we see.

One by one we receive the call
Mom has collapsed as she practiced her game.
She had just fallen down after bowling the ball
Her active life was snuffed, nothing's the same.

My wife, my mom, my grandma, my friend
We all feel so hollow and tears fall like rain.
For eight days you linger never to mend
At your bedside we stand enduring our pain.

Mom where are you? Don't know who to ask
You left us last June and we're all so alone.
We have each other and we all wear the mask
of forced smiles and bravado but feel as if stone.

I lie alone at night and wait for you to appear
Hoping against hope I can feel the presence.
Can you sometime come back with words I can hear?
I'll always love you mom and can't bear your absence.

Lynn A. Ricci

Untitled

Little Joey walks down the street,
looking for something, anything to eat.

Beyond his days and years he strives,
to find a place that is warm to hide.

His mommy and daddy are nowhere in sight,
they must have up and left him last night.

A small teardrop falls from his eye,
as he struggles to think of the reason why.

His beat up size sevens are old and torn,
and the clothes on his back are tattered and worn.

As dusk grows nearer he crouches out of sight,
for Little Joey is afraid of the night.

The temperature is dropping rapidly,
and Little Joey is afraid he will freeze.

Soon Little Joey drifts off to sleep,
and the Good Lord above has a promise to keep.

So in the morning Little Joey will not wake,
for the Lord has promised his soul he would take.

Amy Estelle Boden

Untitled

Please let me slip my hand in yours
Be it but a brief and passing dream
Please let me tell you my darkest fears
So that you might comfort me

For I have walked along deep chasms
With nothing to guard my feet
And I've met faces that smile in friendship
While their eyes look right through me

I see a cliff that I cannot climb
When I close my eyes at night
And screams I hear when all else is silent
But I cannot escape from their fright

But once the chasm was not so deep
When you waited on the other side
And I saw in your face a certainty
And eyes that looked deep into mine

Please hold me close while I'm beside you
No one knows for how long this will last
Please let me slip my hand in yours
Before this time is past

Sarah Bowler

Hummers I Have Known

Surely you have encountered
these busy-bodies of the forest.
A hum-m-m announces their arrival.
A flash of iridescence follows.
They are plain show-offs, border on
being intrusive, and afraid of nothing.

These dashing, inquisitive humming birds
visit every forest flower and
speck of color, be it on a cap, book
cover, or label inside our tent
To encourage their visits our feeder
is hung between two ponderosa pines.

We delight in watching their antics and
wonder if they have visited us before.
The sad part comes when we pack to leave.
The friendly hummers still sip nectar,
even as the feeder is lowered. We will
miss the hummers of the mesa.

William McGowan

Brother-In-Law

My brother-in-law, his name is Ott,
He likes to drink and drinks a lot.

He likes to party, that's his high,
He parties hard, don't ask me why.

He frequents night clubs. "Bars" if you will,
And doesn't leave 'til he's had his fill.

He arrives home high, buzzed or drunk,
Always and forever in a funk.

He picked up a stray in his roam,
We said, "She can't stay here, she has to go home!"

He cannot see the pattern here,
for if he did he'd surely fear.

His search for control is hard to find,
Because he's looking while running blind.

Ott needs to open up his eyes,
Admit to himself all deception and lies.

Suddenly, the light will dawn,
And his total confusion will simply be gone.

Realizing the reality will bring the discovery,
Of what to do and how to begin the road to recovery.

Teja Liljestrand

Rosestorm

Write me a song that says how I feel
Finding the words that makes it so real
The care you've given, the love you've shown
Just has me caught in a Rosestorm
  A light in the storm, a rose in view
  A candle at night, being close to you
There's a fight still fighting, our love will pull through
Horses and white nights, and I love you
You shattered all my doubts and curiosities
Thinking of you brings me to my knees
I look through my old songs to find something new
None of them say how I feel for you
  You are a light in the storm, you are a rose in view
  A candle at night, making love to you
I have a new life, new words to say.
Please don't leave, don't go away
There are no lies, I was caught by surprise
Being with you opened my eyes
  You are my light. You are my rose
  You are in my life like nobody knows
  I'm in love with you caught in a rosestorm

Doug Bloomer

The Spring Rain

Rain beating against the window pane
Claps of thunder ringing in my brain
Lightning flashing across the sky
Somewhere I hear a child cry.
Too young to see the beauty in
A spring time storm that has began
The rain that falls down to the ground
The world will awaken all around.
Flowers, grass, and trees will grow
The warmth will melt away the snow
Sparkling water coming down
Like specks of silver to touch the ground.
Valleys green, flowers in bloom
Beauty that melts away the gloom
Of winters days that hide the earth
The rains of spring that bring rebirth.

William L. Titus

Down Sized

In the board room on the second floor
We waited for the news
that we all knew was coming
    from the months of rumor hews
Then we were brought to order
    When the President came in
And for the next two minutes
    you could hear one drop a pin

In my thirty years of banking
    This is my hardest day
I never thought I'd be here
    with what I have to say
We're moving operations we've
    sold accounts down here
You'll all be given packages
    We're closing by new year
You'll all be recommended;
    the Job you've done is fine
But you know we're in business and need that bottom line

There really were no questions. We were free

Michael Riordan

Who Cares?

I've been under and over the clouds
Been apart from and part of the crowds
I've been wet, I've been dry
I've been low in my high
and I've always been able to cry.

Educated without any schools
Mixed in upper class circles with fools
and I've had to tear values in half
But I've always been able to laugh.

I've known houses conceived in a dream
I've known hunger with pains that would scream
I've been taken and learned how to give
and I've always been able to live.

I can dream and see things as they are
I found peace in a world filled with war
I found reasons for "why"
and a conscience that's dry
and I've always been able to die.

Patti Lane Rivera

"Do You Know?"

Twas a fire, a fire in the light.
The knight holding the fire was at battle with his war.
But he shall not win his battle
without losing the war, or could he?
The light shown by the fire,
was it his life's desire?
Or was his life urging for more?
Twas the brave knight who wanted more?
Or is it me? Was his life a plan or a destiny?
Is all that true, or is it what the light doesn't show?
The mystery of life, the mystery
of death, the mystery of the
scared knight passing the light.
The light of life and death.
Are we here to stay or live?
Why don't we understand it?
Because the light doesn't show it.
And the "brave" knight is a coward.
Who knows? Do you?
Me, no, as long as I'm alive.

Misty Carpenter

Dream

In the dream I feel as you must have felt,
trapped and alone.
I hear shots ringing out in the add, still air.
White heat in my heart as I fall.
I'm sorry,
I should have been there holding your hand in mine.
You were so strong, I was so weak, now you are gone.
I awake and know you will not hold me
    nor chase away my fears.
    I dry my eyes
        I sleep again.

Andrea Richmond

Pain Of Love

To love someone with a burning passion.
To feel her every move, and to sooth her pain.
Almost a memory now as she comes to me in my mind.
Causing heartache, and tears falling from my eyes that
    used to see love.
She left me without a word of goodbye.
Now that she left, left me forever, in the coldness all alone.
My heart seeks forgiveness, but in my mind I know better.
For if I took my once loved back, I know that she'll leave me again.
But, this time the pain would be unbearable that
    would stricken my heart
Like playing with fire and get burnt.
I must forget upon the past, and look for a new
    love, to give my heart to.
As long as she is true to my heart, and will be true,
    true to our love.
May heaven shine its light down on me and find the
    one, the one that will show me love to fill my
    heart with warmth again.

Kevin Rickard

A Mothers Love

In Memory of Eileen C. Ringrose
A Mothers Love is all there is
A Mothers Love she longed to give.
A Mothers Love she gave so much.
A Mothers Love I miss so much.
A Mothers Love so Beautiful indeed.
A Mothers Love is what all need.
A Mothers Love I regret I miss.
A Mothers Love I shall not forget.
A Mothers Love was always there,
    thru is sickness, sadness, death and sin.
A Mothers Love I shall always miss,
Until one day at Heavens gate we shall
be reunited once again.

Lloyd Ringrose

A Poem For Cousin Ron

Heaven is a place of light,
where God hangs out all day and night,
watching us all, down here fight,
about things that don't really matter.

Matter is just a place on earth,
where dreams are born, and friends do die,
while God hangs out in heaven,
watching us all down here fight,
about things that don't really matter.

The headlines read, "A Child is Born",
to parents who love and will keep them warm,
and teach them to love, and not to fight,
about things that don't really matter.

Sheilah Annette Cordell

Winter's Gold

Golden Winter light warmed the world it shone upon:
Reddish straw in the pasture brightened and glowed;
Wing-ed creatures glistened in the light.
Black and white, rust and white
Bovines shone gloriously
With haloed golden backs.
Contented with their world, they munched peacefully,
Encircling their goldish yellow-green hay.
Cool metal rings, arms of rusty goldish-brown
Wrapped to embrace the treasured fodder.

Golden Winter light warmed the world it shone upon:
Rich, mystical cedars, adorned in dark green,
Lost their protective role as creatures,
Large and small, emerged to tend to business,
Delighting in the light's graceful benevolence.
No sounds of man interrupted the gift
Of peaceful joy
Celebrated by God's creations.
Struck dumb, the solitary human, too,
Joyed in the world's shimmering, glowing, effervescing gift.

Della Carson

Memories

He is an old man
    an old sad man
A lonely, old, sad man
Whose lifetime companion has died
Leaving him bereft after 58 years of love and loving

He spends many hours reading and sorting old letters
Arranging and cataloguing old photographs and snapshots
Carefully naming and dating each image
For his descendants, he says, so they will know
    from whence they came.

His children worry about him
Stop living in the past, they urge
Look to the future, they cry

They don't understand
The past is secure; known, lived through
The future is frightening, full of dread, pain and more loneliness
He is afraid of the future
    The past is safe

Joseph J. Brenner

Glories Of The Prairie

Spikes of gay feathers upon a northern prairie bloom —
Waving April's name across the snow melt of the land . . .
Above them flurries of snow geese fill the azure sky —
Quickening my winter's heart with their
Deep honking cry . . .

Golden fingers of sunshine melt the last patches of snow . . .
While beneath the thawing earth, the glories of the prairie
Continue to grow . . .

This humble kingdom I see from my old weathered farm —
Another new Spring's eternal charm — the richest painting by far
Sketched by Mother Nature's
Own eloquent arm . . .

As I breathe in the beauty of this prairie perfect day,
I stand on the porch — my hand on the rail —
Clutching the wooden edges — so that I and the frame
Won't fly away.

Judith Durnbaugh

"Stampede"

It came about so suddenly, and with such rapid speed.
It seemed bound to happen as if by fate decreed.
There was a flash of lightening, and then the thundered rolled.
The herd bolted and were running wild, as one, uncontrolled.

The wranglers that were in the sack, made a record mount.
They were up and ridding, before you could hardly count.
The trick was to get them circling, before they got too far.
To keep them from some ravine, or some quicksand bar.

It was very dangerous work, for only fifty cents per day.
A wrangler trampled beneath those hooves, would never draw his pay.
He never shirked his duty, he learned to conquer fear.
He would risk both life and limb, for a ten dollar steer.

When they finally got them circling, like a top in a spin.
They all breathed a sigh of relief, the stampede was about to end.
When they had them under full control, one was heard to say.
Who was the guy who said, a trail driver never earned his pay.

They finally arrived at trails end, It was the rail head.
They made it with a few wounds, but no one was dead.
They drew their pay and headed for the bar, there to have some fun.
When morning came they were as broke, as when the drive begun.

H. Fitzgerald Durbin

Vessels

Male and female join
Uniting a part of each,
Life creates a miracle within her —
They combine but cannot create.
She becomes merely a vessel
For the two to become one.
Cells multiply,
Following a secret roadmap,
A recipe with its own intelligence
Its own uniquity, purpose and destiny.
Multiplying and growing,
Developing and programming each cell —
With a knowing
Every cell a brain of its own
And every body system
Performing in harmony and perfection.
Until 40 weeks of careful planning and creating,
Brought forth to being with two cells
A miracle is expelled from her vessel —
The perfect clothing for a new soul.

Catherine L. Browning

Us

Stepping out of all this worlds pollution,
now all the problems have a solution.
You bring the snow, and the tourists you show, this wonderland,
and you make it look grand.
There was never anything that made my heart so free,
till you came along and like the snow covered me.
Days I spent just wondering what it all meant,
and it meant you, a blessing heaven sent.
There was never any joy I had known,
like hearing your voice on the phone.
When I'm near you and melt into your eyes,
my heart takes wings and off it flies.
Then for a few days you'll leave me soaring,
but life without you is unreal and boring.
I need you like a forest needs rain,
to put out fires, and soothe the pain.
Yet I feel I'm dying, and I'm not lying,
Because mathematically our relation I show,
two into one will not go.

Andréa Burrell

March-U-Worry

January, February, the combination brought together in March
With the sometimes unexpected high winds
It takes out of your clothes all of the starch
It reminds us of our life full of sins.

When the snows continue to come
The cold seems to chill to the bone
You say "Where is this still coming from"
Your body aches and you begin to drone?

Complaining is often heard
Will Spring ever get here
This Winter surely has been absurd
In March there is constant fear?

The weather in March is unsure
Sometime there are Spring-like days
Then it snows, making it clean and pure
Eventually, out comes those sun's rays.

Let us all take it in stride
Before long we will have those days of hot sun
Be careful not to complain, just let it ride
Let's forget the Winter and have some fun.

John C. Bruce

To Give Or Receive

To give or receive
this festive yuletide question
has been asked from eve to eve

Some say to give, cause it warms the heart
with a holiday spirit, that can't be bought

What can I give, a trinket or toy?
Nothing on earth, can match this seasonal joy

It all started long ago, on that first Christmas day
"AWAY IN A MANGER", the greatest gift lay

He came to the world, to spread peace and love
given to all, from the Father above

It's more than I, or any can give
but not to much to take, the gift is from Him

"So receive" I say, from that first Christmas day
He's there for the taking, the price has been paid

Kurt Von Shultz

Reward

I do not want to be separated!
I live in love with you. Should this not be true let death come!
I live in love with you. There is a corner in your heart for me.

I live in love with you.

If you knew how much I suffer, you would be suffering along with me,
but you must not experience my pain, my anguish.

I live in love with you.

Restlessly, I carry on. Attempting to awaken your misplaced heart.
The travels have shown little hope, and possible destitute.
I carry on.
My love for you is eternal.

And, Your love will be like the spring, after a hard and cruel winter;
manifesting the birth, and blossoming of beauty. With the leaves
turning green, the flowers exhibiting their natural perfection.
Your new love for me.

Inner strength and perseverance are my ushers to your heart.

How glorious is our world when one loves, and ultimately relished when
love is returned.

Jose Joaquin Carreras-Burgos

Untouched Land

Weary, weeping for the lost years
    the degradation of their faith
Set them forth out to sea,
    like so many before them
On a journey . . .

Time drew nigh;
Anon they landed on a Rock
    not a round nor square one, but jagged
So that they would cleave their mark
    and begin anew . . .

An uncouth and untouched land,
Where one might wage life unscathed,
    unhindered
    by the vise of tyranny.
A place of liberty
    and of freedom,
Where one's seed might waft and bloom,
Where one's posterity might walk and roam
    in the Light,
And where ones fruit might taste the sweetest of all.

Steve Burris

The Wind

Swoosh, swoosh, swoosh I go, for I am the wind.
You take me for granted, for I am the wind.
I make your boats go and kites fly high

John William Burtle

Grandpa's Rocker

In a cane backed rocker
Grandpa liked to rest.
It was loaded in the covered wagon
When he and his bride headed West.

Soon after the Civil War he left
With the title for a Kansas Homestead.
Grandpa brought a home made chest of drawers,
The cane backed rocker and a featherbed.

A kerosene lantern was their only light
When the sun went down.
A campfire cooked their food,
There were no Cafes around.

Grandpa dug a one room home
In the hillside, near a tree.
He also dug a well for water,
Raised wheat and a family.

Seventy years later and a fulfilled life,
Grandpa died in his rocking chair.
It's been passed on to the third generation,
Very well preserved for all the wear.

Olive W. Barker

Mother Silence

Why do I forget you, abandon you?
You who are wholeness,
you who are home, always now, always present,
giving what every cell in me yearns for
to collapse into your warm breath of life,
defenses drop, naked I be,
cherished solely for my nakedness,
my void, my forgetfulness.

Silence pregnant with all sounds,
I come back, prodigal that I am,
bruised, tired, wired,
to be undone again by your embrace.

Vivian Larson

Untitled

Close by her side he paused to stand
As he took his ring back off her hand
How could he ever live to grow old
Never again having her hand to hold
All of their memories still fresh in his heart
He realized just how their love had fallen apart
All who stood watching did not dare speak
As a silent tear ran down his cheek
And just as he turned and started to go
They lowered her casket into the snow

Steve A. Bryan

"Imagine That"

Imagine that unkind words, were not spoken,
Unkind deeds were left undone,
Unkind thoughts were never dreamt of,
And life was full of fun.

No one's feelings would be damaged.
No one's heart would be scarred.
Children's faces would not be tear-stained,
And egos would be left unmarred.

Instead of hurting, we'd be helping.
Instead of yelling, we'd be talking.
Instead of crying, we'd be rejoicing.
Instead of hitting, we'd be hugging.

All of this could be ours,
If we would only stop being hateful,
And start being thoughtful.
Imagine that.

Kerri Hartung

Meaning

She calls me home;
  enriching and revitalizing,
  my spirit is exalted,
  the core of my soul takes meaning,
  drawing me back for purpose,
  rationally I owe her all,
  the beginning point for life,
  where answers take form,
  digging my feet into her,
  I receive the blessings of the master.
And as the mother,
  the earth the soil,
  reclaims all.

Lyle A. Bane

Reclamation

I gave you the power of my poetry at night,
Settling for you and the T.V.
So I could be we.
I buried similes in the backyard
And stored metaphors in the closet.
Onomatopoeia was barricaded in the basement.
Symbolism was rendered
And her bones strewn about the house.

Now you have left.
I sit silent with my cigarettes
Watching the smoke drift out the window
As the night slips in
And subtly, oh so subtly
The stars begin to stir
To the moon's muffled rhythm
And I sleep
To dream in iambic pentameter.

Annette Rasmussen

Stone Porridge

Call
the children in
from hungry games
breakfast is sweet
on the clean air

Running with empty stomachs
their out-thrust tongues
test for nourishment
in the porridge scented morning

Hoping in all the additives
which promise life

The children crack their budding teeth on stone

Antonia Burgato

Wild Flower

I am just one of those
Wildflowers
People always walk by
Never seem to notice
I am always there
I add color
Not much, just a little
No one ever notices one little wildflower
Growing in the grass.
A small girl stops by, sees me there
She picks me up, puts me in a glass of water
Proudly shows me off to her parents
They seem to like me
That feels nice because
No one ever notices one little wild flower
Growing in the grass.

Selina Burright

Fading Love

Our love is like heat rising off the
hot summer asphalt;

Yet to be focused as one would with the
dials of an old T.V. set.
I could only regret to lose a love like ours
because to me you are the reddest of roses
in a whole bed of flowers.
After the fine tuning I can only hope there
will be, the clearest of all pictures for
our souls of love to see.

Todd Gauthier

Better Than You

My son Marcus meant the world to me
But all I have left is his memory
He explored the world with open arms
And never lost his grace or charm.

I search for him in many faces
Trying to recapture the traces,
Of his chiseled masculinity
That embraced calm and serenity.

Though cancer took him away
His spirit is here to stay
His zest for life never wavered,
And he fought a fight I'll always savor.

As I watched him fade away
His wisdom haunts me to this day.
When asked of Marcus "How do you do,"
His response was always "Better than you!"

Mary King

Fingerprints

Scene opens sirens wail
Police and dogs check the trail
Looking for clues at the crime
Thank God no fingerprints are mine
Down the road seems to be commotion
Everyone is running with emotion
Guns are drawn, situation very tense
Could cut the air with all this suspense
Can hear them shouting back and forth
As the cold wind blows from the north
There's so much chaos all around
Hear a sound and dive to the ground
Over there a suspect has been sighted
Men make sure the building is lighted
On the radio-cops made an arrest
Law enforcement was put to the test
They question-do I know when it was taken
Said no-everything so fast just happened
Saw face said it can't be you who stole
But you left fingerprints all over my soul

Gary L. Havranek

My Thai Grand Children

They arrived on united!
Aye sure was delighted!
'O' is a little boy of two
Speaks only Thai but wants to visit the zoo!

'A' is a beautiful girl of seven! Said coming over on the plane
It was so high she reached up to heaven!

First night in Houston we had some drama
'O' fell out of our Queen size bed,
Which worried his Mama!

But after aye wiped away the crocodile tears
Aye hug him in my arms and whisper
Little boys are brave and have no fears
Aye read him a little bed time story!
He falls asleep to music from tunes of glory!

Oh' such a delight to see their faces
Aye have to take them to so many places!

Rocky Jocky Anderson

Candid Carrots

Candid Carrots burrowing through the ground,
I don't imagine they make a sound.
They are slithering with the worms
and scratching their itches on the pebbles,
moving gracefully among the earth mites,
pushing past a group of roots,
slipping by a mushroom and stopping to talk to brother potato
before bathing in the moisture of the nourishing rain.
Candid carrots nestled in the ground,
must embrace the silence before they are found.

Kelly Cable

Dreams

A strange light surrounds me,
flashing dimly, so hard to see.
Colors and sounds whisper words and emotions,
as they seep through my brain.
My spine tingles as I feel a strong blast of cold air,
strewn with diamonds,
which become tangled in my hair.
My body floats around,
twirling and spinning without a sound.
Suddenly pictures of the day become disoriented in my face,
colors and sounds echo and twirl with grace.
Dreams

Eric Cosselman

"Love"

Love can mean so many things, it's two hearts as one and
the joys it brings. It's a pure white rose on a Winter's day, or
a tear in an eye when one's away. It's a hand to hold when
one is sad, it's staying together through good and bad. It's
passion, romance and burning desire, it turns the spark into
a fire. It's a shoulder to cry on when things aren't right, it's
still being there in the morning light. It's trust and respect
and faithfulness, it's giving all of yourself and nothing less.
It's a sweet tender kiss, making love until dawn, it's missing
the other before they have gone. It's playing and teasing
and joking around, it's sitting together without needing a
sound. It's knowing one's heart and keeping it true, it's
forgiving the past and starting anew. It's giving in when
you know you are right, it's keeping it strong, not losing
sight. Love is a gift, shared only by two. It's all that I
feel, when I look at you.

Susan K. Kinzer

Through A Child's Eyes

A child is not born with the
influenced of prejudice and sin.
So in a child you can find truth within.
A child sees things in an innocent light.
Their love is unconditional whether
you're wrong or right.
Only a child can be chastised one day,
and then come back and say "I love you anyway".
A child has not yet been exposed to
sin and how it hurts you.
So a child does not understand the
evil that men do.
So though a child's eyes you may
see things in a better light.
And a child's innocent eyes may compel
you to do right.

Andrew L. Pope

Retirement

Where have all the good days gone
Nothing's as you planned it,
Work hard all your life, really give it your best,
Each day will be as you command it,
All bills are current, income sufficient,
A short term mortgagee, a savings plan,
A part time career, you're so efficient,
On top of the world, then the news,
You're out of the Health plan, you can choose,
Less coverage, more cost, no prescriptions,
Rearrange your funds, you have conniptions,
The part time career goes nowhere, you try for others,
Pay off bills some of the savings are safe,
In desperation, you're like an old waif,
No place to go, no way to get there,
You have good years left but none seem to care,
The kids would help but you won't ask
To keep you solvent is not their task,
Settle down, you'll work it out,
Forget the past and think about
The future?

Floyd B. Carey

1980

Go ahead and dream, my son,
  'Tis dreamers that do get things done.
They grasp a hold the Golden Rings
  And rise above the earthy stings.

And then, my son, when they are there
  They turn to those who would not dare —
They grasp them by their trembling hand
  That's when, my son, you'll be a man.

Jim Glenn

The Storm

The storm approaches, timbers moan;
Uncertain, I view the gathering gloom
Where the sun sleeps.

The glow is warm, with dancing tongues;
The timber wails — I must go forth;
For if I stay, the timber will fail.

The timber rejoices, as the wind shifts;
Deception clouds my eyes, as the storm flanks me;
Unleashing its fury from where the sun awakes.

I cannot see, I cannot hear;
The message the storm roars into my face.

I find shelter under the caring thicket;
I only wish the storm would whisper.

Roger D. Hendershot

Untitled

I new day has begun
I think God I'm alive
I think about yesterday
Wondering how I survived
I think about the struggle of growing up in the hood
Wondering how anyone could wake up feeling so good
I think about my faith in the man upstairs
Knowing that he truly...truly truly cares
I think about us children just trying to get an education
Wondering how we plan to save this Great Nation
I think about mom...looking so content
Wondering how to pay this months rent
I think about the man lying in the street
Wondering how he'll make ends meet
I think about the boy who took her son's life away
Wondering how he lives with himself each day
I think about the gun that goes bang in the Heights
Looks like it's going to be another one of those nights...

Stephanie Hosea

Like Sisters

I once had a friend for a very long time,
it's like we were sisters . . . each doing fine.
When we were younger we both used to play
inside and outside for most of the day.
When we were teenagers we used to hand out
with the rest of the crowd . . . or we'd just roam about.
We never found time to fight over boys
'cause just being together was one of our joys.
Now that we're married with families and such,
we both work so hard at just keeping in touch.
We still call each other when one's feeling down,
'cause there's a place in our hearts although one's not around.
We've both grown to know the true love of a friend
and know that each other is there 'til the end.
To Gayle, my best friend, who is really true blue,
I have only three words . . . and they're "I love you."

Roseanna Calascibetta

G.O.D.

(Get Out Devil!)
Get out and stay out, DEVIL, because in my life you have no place
No matter what you do, you'll always be a disgrace
You can keep coming up with more stupid plans, if you desire
Because I know you're going to burn in the lake of fire.

Talk about celebrating the 4th of July
That will seem like nothing compared to the day that you fry
You see, DEVIL, over the years there's one lesson you never did learn
And that is that my God is all powerful and will always win
And for that you're going to BURN!!!

You were once an angel, with God you had favor
But you blew it because all your blessings you failed to SAVOR
So, I rebuke you, DEVIL; On me and my family you will not bring gloom
Because you see, I revel in knowing that you're headed for doom!!!

"Amazing Grace"

Spaces For Corn

The August corn grown up to the barn's edge
didn't understand the protocol in spacing,
the divides between humanity and its work.
What it did, was it filled itself up, full,
each kernel, ear, stalk, row
bulging in the kind of excess you see
from young women in stores
who lightly brush peach nightgowns with soft fingers of hope.
The fine silk wove around thistle spikes and
choked the reliable system of hollyhocks dressed for sun,
until even the barn, surrounded,
yielded to the moist depths,
accepted what the corn knew
(about sharing)
and clung back to the knowing mosses that hitched its old boards
together, to form tokens of insight,
the old fossils of ideas lost
in another row.

Ann Marie Frank Wake

The Test Pilot

A thousand eyes scanned the skies for a speck of silver gray,
Five hundred faces upward turned, white and taut with fear,
A mass of steel hurtling through the heavens, like an unguided slay,
The object of their attention for testing day was here.
For every day is testing day on the desert in the south,
And men with nerves of iron and a daring skill to match,
Must every day their lives betray for the sake of knowledge learned.

But somewhere in the blue above one heart beat like no other,
With clammy hands and bloodshot eyes he battled to recover the plane.
Plummeting earthwards, screamed as if in agony,
Far below men shook their heads, for they felt what was to be.
A woman wept, an alarm rang out to proclaim that death had won.
But what of it, who can deny him his place in the sun.
And when the dawn breaks on the morrow after this,
Why someone there will be to take his place.

For liberty in this land of ours means guts and work and sweat.
And some must risk the pain of death to keep us out of debt.
And some pioneers must shun the cheers and do their duty true,
But no matter what you or I may think, honor the chosen few.

Bernard G. Aronstam

A Parent's Wish

Angels flying on wings up high.
Like beams of light across the sky.
With halos gold and hair snow white.
Protect my child throughout the night.
Give unto her peaceful dreams.
Of fields of flowers and gentle streams.

In the morning when she's at play.
Watch over her throughout the day.
Give me patience from above.
So I may guide her with my love.
And when she lays her head to rest.
I will know I did my best.

Carl G. Clark

The Big Game

I dream of you, I dream of me, centering a line made up of three
Sharpened blades and sticks taped tight
We're ready to go it's hockey night

Stands are packed they dim the lights
Our team is here on home ice tonight

Sports writers ready with pens in hand
To see the new sensation of the land

Will I fail? Will I succeed?
Or will the coach send me back to the minor leagues

They drop the puck the crowd goes wild
The coach gives me a little smile

Ten second left I take a pass in the slot
"Oh no" tripped up, it's a penalty shot!

I wipe the blood from my sweaty chin
In hopes that the goalie will let one in

I race up ice with the puck on my stick
As the crowd irrupts with the flick of the wrist

I let it fly, my best shot yet!
Hope the minors still want me 'cause I missed the net
I dream of you, I dream of me, I dream of things never meant to be

Christopher M. Cooke

Themis In Theme

Wielding a fractured sword of justice,
And clutching a battered shield of truth,
In her cosmic scales are balanced
Vindictiveness and truth.

Upon her head, there rests a tarnished crown.
A tear-soaked bandage conceals her eyes.
And, in respect to humankind she stands
Blindly to our cries.

Not a word she hears, nor speaks.
She stands there deaf; she stands there mute,
Beyond all reach
In disrepute.

Her name is Themis.
Lady justice.
And many cry,
"Why don't she trust us!"

And as of late, I've spied her likeness
In the shadows of the courtroom.
Like a chastised child, in the corner she stands - alone.
A lovely statue made of stone.

Justice Burke III

Svetlana

At times your beauty hides
in the mist of an indifferent day,
as if shamed to reveal itself to the outside world.
And one who does not know you would pass without a second look.
Well, you yourself said "there are many girls such as me."

But the one who touched your soul
and in the darkness of the night looked into your eyes,
he understands that to be with you
it's like inviting the demons of a mad mind
to a party at which all dreams come true.

You are the spark of life, a gift from God.
There is no end to your beauty,
like there is no end to the infinite; you are the universe.
Words in any language fail to describe
the feelings which you arise.

In your dress or without it you are fair and beautiful.
Only a girl, true . . . but joy that you give
is born in heaven, conceived in the enchanted
world without time, since it is forever.

Michael P. Wnuk

Look At Me

See my quiet face
You boys and girls
All you men and women of the world
Passing me on the city streets,
I search your varied faces fleetingly . . .
Though we are strangers, reserved and shy,
Without words, I feel our kinship,
Aching to know your concerns, stories, mysteries
Hoping you perceive this spirit of good-will . . .
You are my brothers and sisters!
This is our time — our century,
Our planet, our turn to make our mark,
With choices, for peace and joy —
Let us "Take on the day,"
Hearing the voices of the wind
Knowing our shared humanity!
Thankful.

Lois Smith Triplitt

Suffer The Little Children — Sudan Requiem

The vultures hover.
There in the dirt and filth;
A forsaken child bows in fetal surrender
    to the hopeless horror that surrounds it.
And in desolate pain,
    cries out to some unknown God,
    in sightless agony.
Behold this innocent pawn of man's inhumanity
    to man;
As it silently surrenders to the darkening
    shadows of death that surrounds it.

I curse you!
You apocalyptic bastards who slay these
    lambs to feed your senseless greed.
You kill and rape,
    only to end up in hollow victory,
    over a martyred land of graves.
While an uncaring world stands silently bye in
    total indifference;
To your slaughter of these innocents.

Bob Northcott

Hey, Teach

Will
You
Please sit down, take out your
silent reading books and folders, and
Close you little mouths?! Do you think you
Could do that for me for ten minutes, or is that
Simply too much to ask from you? What? No,
You may not haveapass! I don't care if you
Are sick! Where is your . . . folder? Of course
I am collecting homework. Yes, it may very
Well be on the test. It's notatest, it's a quiz
And it won't be until next week. Shall I
Just take you down to the office right
Now? Sit down! Oh no, nonono!
Who left their gym clothes here
On my desk yesterday? Whoa!
Alright, I've had about
All I Can take!
Sit Down!

Robert A. Doughty

Today

Today, I became an old woman!
I am society's victim.
I am the remedy.
I am the Universe Network.

I stand alone, wearing my invisible veil.
I am the captain!
I am the navigator!
I explore the world!

I am an ancient branch,
Mingling through time and space.
I am intuitive.
I am feminine.
I am aware.

I am the beauty which dances
With the music of the shimmering silhouettes.
I am the moon. I am the truth.
I am here.

I am a sad, old beggar woman.
I am a star waiting to be born.
I am the Universal Bohemian Woman!

Danae Noel

Witches Of Darkness

Let me tell you people of this frightening tale
of the witches of darkness who once did prevail.
'Twas a time full of mystery, superstition and fear
in a land now abundant with sorrow and tears.
In a dense creepy forest aloft on a hill
stood an old wooden cabin once part of a mill.
In the dimly lit structure, a sight to behold
many witches in circle, foul, ugly — old.
Their skin full of wrinkles, complexions like stone
hair brighter than silver, sores that show bone.
Backs like a humpwhale, hands full of warts
their foul lips repeating ancient phrases of sorts.
In the village nearby, townspeople have ears
stay away from these witches and live many years.
As time slowly passed and the people forgot
the witches of darkness, but the witches did not.
Then one night it happened, the witches came down
and formed a huge circle in the middle of town.
With arm waving signals, ancient witchcraft of lore
a sudden explosion the town was no more.
And to those who have doubts and fearless of fright
remember this poem on Halloween Night.

Felix Gordillo, Jr.

A True Friend To The End

There was that shiny new rocking
chair that Mom and Dad had bought.
To comfort me when I cried, and they'd
hummed to me while they rocked.
When years went by and I married, It
was used for the very same thing.
I rocked each one of the children, and
I remember the songs I would sing.
Now that I'm very much older, I'm
still rocking in that same rocking chair.
It's no longer new or shiny, just an
old friend whose memories I share.

Rose C. Devine

Untitled

If the white is day,
If the black is night,
The yellow is dawn and sunset.
The earth pulses with the rays of the sun;
The land breathes with the beams of the moon.
Soft dawn brings dews,
Feeding grass and trees;
The sunset glow designs colorful dresses,
Beautifying our mother earth.

If the white is day,
If the black is night,
The yellow is dawn and sunset.
Together
We compose a human life
And make a whole of the world.

Ninghui Zhang

The Best Of Friends

I have a slew of sisters, we are the best of friends
We laugh together, we cry together and tell a joke or two
For we are the very best of friends and that's what sisters do

We know when one is happy, we know when one is blue
We are always there for one another, and that's what sisters do

We've shared together through times of loss and celebrated too
For we are the very best of friends and that's what sisters do

We can tell when one is hurting and even feel the pain
We can tell when one has prospered and even shared the gain
We can even fuss and argue and give our separate views
For we are the very best of friends and that's what sisters do

Bonnie Dues

Castle

Crookston Castle in all its glory was center of the territory,
it was built there to intimidate. Its purpose was to dominate.
There's the great hall in the citadel where feudal knights raised
merry hell. The wall-walk when there was no war, and Nobles toyed
with paramours. The rooms where lords and ladies stayed, the chapel
where they knelt and prayed. The kitchen and the turret clock, the
stables and the smithy shop. Now it's gone. It had its day,
all in ruin and decay. But tunes come through the countryside,
where kilted soldiers fought and died. In the waning day and soft
twilight, comes the doleful skirling of the pipes.

Come, raise your glass and drink a toast to the long gone
Crookston Castle ghosts.

Norman Rasmussen

Lost

I'm lying on the grass.
The school is quiet even though today is a school day.
The city is silent like there was nothing there.
The grass looks like green velvet, thin and soft in my eyes.
I like to pick, pull each blade of grass gradually.
It lies in my hand, depressed, and poor like myself, with the whole
sadness around.

The sound of music blended with a female voice traveled with the
wind far, far away. Disappeared.
The sorrow was like a rope tightening around me.
Suddenly, I wanted to scream, but my throat was so sore.
I felt that my body would blow up in a moment.
I closed my eyes, shook my hear, and tried to calm down.

I was alone and lost on a trail into live. It was a scary and lonely trail.
Really.
My heart was cold, and I felt so strange with the love that you were giving me.
Oh! My love, please understand and forgive me.
I don't want to cry, but lied with myself. Tears drop on my lips,
make them soft and gentle.
My love, the last words for you are that I will forget every problem
around me to think about you.
I wish I could sleep in your arms with safety and protection.

Where is the moon now?

Nga Tuyet Trinh

Anima Enema

my soul is its own torture chamber
my head, its own madhouse
my hobbled feet walk paths of nails I spat myself
and my heart is mere cobweb,
    deserted long ago by spider dreams.

nothing left to do but embrace the shadows . . .
(and the pain and the cold and the biting knives comfort me)

let in the worms knocking outside my aortic door,
    let them gnaw and feast.
learn to walk without feet,
    ignite evolutionary anarchy and weave a world of fish.
crack my braincase against the wall,
    to ease the pressure of monstrous thoughts within.
savor the sweet kiss betwixt blade and flesh,
    and bottle the pain for a day with no rain.

but most of all set my moth-soul free
    to fly like I wish I could . . .
though I catch her by the wing
    and tuck her neatly in a box,
when I start feeling human . . . as I should.

Jana Palaski

What's Happened

What's happened to the Happy Little Voices
That lived in this house
And whats happened to this man that's
Aged him, as he sadly slumps to the couch
The only thing happy here is the pup
That's asleep on the soiled carpeted floor
The sun warming his belly as it filters through
The smudged window of the front door
And the flowers he used to bring in
Everyday have long since died
Sitting on the stereo that doesn't
Work anymore, but could if he tried
He curses as he struggles to get to his feet
To grab a beer and fix a Spam sandwich to eat
And shuffles now to the darkening window on the door
Looking for the happy little voices
He doesn't hear anymore

Jerry Russell

When Your Loved One Dies

Perhaps, you'll think it eerie
    And, even a bit queer . . .
To have my very own Eulogy
    Recited at my bier.

But, you folks, out there, did know me
    Or you wouldn't all be here
To show respect and sadness
    And, perhaps, to shed a tear.

And, tho', you'll feel bewildered
    At this time of my demise . . .
And, your questions go unanswered
    While sobbing those anguished "whys."

Just hold back those tremulous sighs
    Which should help suffuse emotion
And, to those precious ones remaining
    Shall you channel your devotion.

Thus, with this anodyne applied
    To all those who are left behind . . .
Just delve into the wondrous past
    And, keep those memories in mind!

Dorothy Schreiber

"Love"

When you love someone very much
It should be from your heart as such.
Love takes two love is not something
that comes out of the blue.
Love is like a plant or like a flower
You plant it, water it, nurture it, give it
tender loving care and it will grow like a tower.
Love is believing and trusting in each other.
No matter what people say or do, it should not bother.
Love is being truthful and honest and
no matter what, always being there for that special person.
Love is caring for that special someone
when you care, you will be able to
bare almost anything, anywhere, and at anytime.
That is sincere and true love.
Now may I have a soda with lime?

Cynthia A. N. Ramos

A Cycle To Repeat

A being, surrounded by others.
Undetected, not even suspected.
Plans are formed, rejected, recreated, and finally executed.

Moving cautiously, so as not to gain notice.
It begins its moves to bring pain, and dysfunction.

The young are its prey, it feeds on their trust, innocence, and light.
Sending its tentacles from the sides, it gains entry to the soul.

It feeds well, frequently, needing more and more, as it grows, and festers.
The victims are drained of heart, wounded, and left for dead.

A trial is left, it is not hard to follow.
Bits, and pieces of children, even though some live.
Eyes that are dead, devoid of emotion.

It does its work well, for it believes in the job.
We know it well, we have encountered it, and tailed it, since time began.
The pattern may be new, but the job is old.

We find our person, get our justice, and revenge.
So we think, but do we?
Or do they gather together, and form bigger,
and better plans, as they await release.

A release that comes, sooner than soon, a cycle to repeat.

Valerie A. Garrett

True Life

I was raised in a family with 13 other kids.
Somehow Mom and Dad always knew exactly what we did.

It didn't matter what they ask us or even what we'd say.
Somehow we always managed to give ourselves away.

Maybe it was the love we had or respect on high.
Whatever it was we all knew nothing would get by.

We never truly appreciated all the time they would share.
Not just for the kids of their own But, all who needed care.

They never seem to have the things that other people had.
But look at them really close it never was all that bad.

For my parents our very special it's time that they hear.
We all love and appreciate you that's why we stay so near.

Now I'm not saying things were perfect Heaven only knows.
But look at a family full of love and just see how fast it grows.

So as you go along your way. Sometimes you may get blue.
But please remember your 14 kids
just cherish you It's True.
Jennifer True

Eavesdropping

. . . Wouldn't it be simpler if
    Life demanded only one role to play?
    Instead of the metamorphoses
    Of hormones and social mores
    In order to succeed, we could live
    A very basic, fulfilling existence,
    From Day to Day,
    Observing the small, delicious, delicacies
    Of life.
Just the Truth, unchanged and obvious, universal,
would fill our lives.
    Instead of finally arriving at Truth,
    After venturing so many times
    Into the unknown,
    We could regard each other without concern
    For sex, or skin, or dogma,
    Without using each other? . . .
"How dull!" you say . . .
But then, you haven't lived as long as I . . .
Diana Lien Velis

Oops

Oops said the baby when he dropped the ball
Oops said the young boy when the lamp fell
Oops said the young lad when the window broke
Oops said the teen when he wrecked Dad's car
Oops said the man as he told a lie
Oops said the man as his neighbor cried over the lie
Oops said he old man as the final judgement came and
He had to account for all the oops in his life.
Mary Ann Meyer

Harvest Of A Life

What is our life? A harvest of wheat;
We complete a season of life, then repeat;
Just as the first seed of wheat is planted,
The beginning of our life is being granted.
Tender shoots push through to the sun,
And our life in the new world has begun.
The wheat grows with each passing day,
While our life changes in every way.
It is nursed and pampered with great care,
We are taught the things in life we must dare.
As the wheat turns golden, so do the years,
But we've left a few seeds, everything we hold dear.
Dawn Eggers

Black Or White

What is happening to the world today?
We are supposed to work together but we're so far away!

Sometimes I think animals are more mature.
They don't care what color, where they live, or what shore.

They know they must stick together.
So their species will live now and forever!
Whitney Sunseri

Through Morning And Night

I'll give you a gift, of my love so true
It's a gift I'll give, to only you
So hold me in your arms
Through morning and night
Then we'll set off forever
Together in flight
We'll swim through the sky
And fly through the sea
Then we'll drown in the ocean
So our souls will be free
Then we'll journey to heaven
On a beautiful light
There I'll love you forever
Through morning and night
Justin McCullough

Bouquets

Friends are like flowers, some planted-some not.
Never really knowing what time has brought.

They come in many colors, shapes and sizes,
Like most living things, full of surprises.

The ones that may look like weeds from the start,
Can grow into blossoms that touch any heart.

The sweet aroma that some bestow,
Sometimes leads to a sting on the nose.

Some bring joy, some bring sadness,
But there is a purpose to this madness.

When things look gloomy both can shed a little light,
Then everything begins to feel alright.

Thank God for flowers and for friends,
He knows the purpose and he knows the end.
Bernadette Merrill

So Many Things (Two Sides To Everything)

The boundaries of life are vast,
the things which life beholds.
All words have different meaning
and yet they are all the same.
All questions are mysteries
yet the answers lie within ourselves.

Love is a valuable rich, meanwhile
being rich is valued at the same price.
The intelligent have not gained enough knowledge
whereas the ignorant know all that is needed to be known.
The stars in the midnight sky are looked upon with admiration
while they themselves look down on us in luminous shame.

Each person has their own destiny
and yet in the end, all destinies meet.
Some people don't know where heaven begins
while others don't know where hell ends.
There exists so much within this world
but it all leads to only one thing.
There are two sides to everything.
Stacia S. Merry

He's My Savior

I feel the hand of Jesus on my shoulder.
I feel his gentle grasp upon my hand.
I feel my heart grow younger, as I grow older.
He's my savior, my master, and my friend.

I feel his arms around me when I'm weeping.
I feel him lifting me when times are bad.
I feel him in my grief, and it strengthens my belief.
He's my savior, my master, and my friend.

I feel his presence ever without ceasing.
I feel his peace filling me with joy.
I know he died for me, so my soul could be free.
He's my savior, my master, and my friend.

I will love him till my days on earth are over.
I will love him after I am in the grave.
You see he loves me forever and forever.
And without him I'd be lost, so I'll love him at all cost.
He's my savior, my master, and my friend.

Sharon Miller

"Sorrow"

Some days deep in the darkness my candle shines alone.
It tries to light my lonely path where others have not shone.
The light calls out to all, "Please answer my faint pleas."
Yet others can not hear them except for tiny me.
Fierce gusts of wind and rain
Vie fiercely for my flame,
As trembling hearts think deeply of who can be to blame.
Dark clouds build overhead,
I can't think of what was said
To cause this great distress.
As my outlook grows ever somber
I doubt I can continue longer
As my pain dies slowly down.
I find the rain has softened now,
Softened, soundless to the ear.
So does the washing river flow more swiftly with my tears.
I cry and cry for what lost, and the little we have gained.
So too, do I wonder if I can ever soothe my pain.

Gary DeCesare

Dreamer

As I lie on the sands and ponder;
Many things are here to wonder.
Why should I go off in space.
Or dream of Things some other place
The surf laps a pointed finger up the sands
And beckons me to other lands.
A magic carpet just for me,
To travel out across the sea
Egypt has its Pyramids and Pharaohs
Africa its Bows and Arrows,
The Taj Mahal in all its glory
Could tell me a Romantic Story
The white marble of the leaning tower
What prompts such architectural desire?
I would see the beauty of Lake Kilkarny
And you bet I would want to kiss the Blarney
I'd help an Eskimo build an igloo
And have a taste of his Caribou
The sun is high, the day is hazy
I'd do all these things
But I'm just too lazy!

Pat Goddard

Our Greatest Gift!

*Dedicated in loving memory to my mother-in-law, Mary Neld,
who lost her battle to cancer! I love you!*
There is a woman that we know so well, her
love, her heart, it never fell. She took us
in, with a gentle touch, I never knew
anyone to give so much!

She is the greatest gift our family knew, It
seems unfair her time here is through. I
truly believe she is out of pain, but our lives
it's true will not be the same!

We will go on, without her grace, her warmth
her smile, and warm embrace! She would
want us all to bare in mind, to just be loving,
strong, and kind!

How lucky we are to have been loved by her,
Although we must, face life, so sad and unsure.

So mother please hear me, these loving words, and
our cry; We love you, we miss you, we can't say good-bye!

I know we will see you again someday, I know
that you want us to remember, and pray!

So until the day comes, that you hold
us again, please know and remember, this isn't the end...

Sherry Nield

Sea Of Love

As children we played in the sea,
We built sandcastles and our dreams.
I recall the moonlit nights with seagulls in flight.
His caresses engulfed me like the sea breeze,
Our promises together never to leave.
The sea shells we kept as finders,
The shooting stars were are reminders.
The tidings felt like a hurricane,
His immanent departure seemed so inane.
Our life savings he refused to be giving.
To the profession of trying to keep him living.
He wanted to dance once more,
So off we walked down the shore.
His love in my soul I will always hide,
Our hearts saying goodbye to the rhythm of the tide.
I watched him melt into the sea.
My tears cascading down until no more could I see.
Now, I look at the tide yearning to be at his side.
My footprints in the sand remind me I am alone,
God, please keep him safe until I get home.

Rachel R. Mingo

Faith

I met an old man today.
He didn't have much to say.
He was old and crippled and couldn't see.
But he held his head up high and
never, ever asked why.

He was stronger than me.
Why? I could not see.
He than began to tell me how
he would never frown.

He said, "It's not about being
strong or weak. It's about the
person inside you seek."
He told me that the choice is
yours from the start.
    You choose the amount of faith
that is in your heart.

Sandra Mills

448

A Woman's Beauty

The brisk of the wind reveals her glamour as it lifts her hair;
She walks with integrity with a song she sings, which makes the day so fair:
Step by step listening to her glide I wrestle with my inner thoughts;
The blade of the grass complements her as she flowers on a day of naught:
Just like a precious jewel she's admired by many of the
scent she leaves behind;
The warmth of her beauty gives me words of a simple shrine:
The melody of her voice offers me hope as she responds to my hello;
The attraction is so seductive it even makes the moon glow;
But the impurity of my thoughts gives me discomfort and despair;
I wonder what she thinks of me the day I noticed her hair;
Lowering my thoughts I imagine as she peacefully rests upon her pillow;
The glitter of the stars rides down her face as a river flows past a willow:
Closing my thoughts I notice we are just words apart;
Because of her virginity only cleanliness can come from within the heart:
What made her cross my path, there are words we'll never be able to find;
But by the sweet savor she gives makes her one of a kind.

Wayne L. Mitchell

Dreams

Where will I go this night while I sleep
To mountains high or oceans deep.
To carnival or rainbows' end,
To raft the rapid river bend,
To sing for thunderous applause
Or visit with Ol' Santa Clause
Or take a bumpy camel ride
With strutting peacocks at my side.
To see the earth from vantage moon
Or see the dish run with the spoon?
Oh sleep, come quickly I implore.
Bring wondrous places to explore,
Of secret paths my soul to wit
And misty caverns candlelit,
With rain of pearls and diamond stars,
Where streets are paved with candy bars.

Jacqueline Granati

Never Got A Chance To Say . . .

There's so many things I never got a chance to say,
Like I'm sorry for my mistakes in each and every way.
I'm sorry for all the stupid things I use to do,
I was young and I didn't care —
I didn't have a clue.
And I'm sorry for the things I did and say,
I regret those words — and cry every single day.
I said I hated you and I didn't care about you.
I said I didn't want a mother, and now I'm so confused.
If I knew this was going to happen —
I would've told you sorry for the things I did say,
And I would've told you everything I never got a chance to say.

Renee Starling

Winter, My Favorite Season . . .

Winter, summer, spring, or fall . . . winter is my favorite season of all.
Snow will fall. I don't cry. You ask me why?
Because I can roll it in three big balls and make a
snowman that stands mighty tall.
It is so fun to run and play in the cool, cool sun.
You might even freeze your buns.
But when all is said and through, christmas is the
day your dreams come true.
Winter reminds me of this special day.
When I'm the happiest and everything is just my way.
You see, winter and christmas go hand and hand,
when the winter snow must go, my christmas spirit will just disappear.
If winter could stay all year, so would everyone's Christmas cheer.

Jillian Marie Mueller

Death Of A Day

A warm sunny spring day.
Translucent faint the blue sky rushing upward.
Water rhythmically splashing on the beach.
Breezes gently brushing against my face.
     — A glimpse of eternal paradise.

No eternal paradise — imperceptible change
Clear blue sky fades into brilliant yellow.
A visual cry for help from the sun
     As it falls into the sea.

Deeper, deeper, fuller colors — almost opaque purple sky.
Behind me a foreboding gray sky,
Before me a blazing yellow, orange, red sky,
     A last chance for the day's glory.

Darker, darker colors edged in purple
Darker, darker as hopelessness settles
Over the day and sea, and land.
A fleeing opportunity in life gone forever.
     Day is dead.

Gail Schulz Mandell

Perfection

Things so perfect,
Never to replace,
Time, love, laughter,
Our perfect place,

Making a wish,
Upon a distant star,
A golfer's dream,
The perfect par,

Search around, if you can
Trying to find,
The perfect love,
From woman or man,

It can't be done,
We've heard them say,
Never giving up,
Come what may,

Reaching deep within my heart and soul,
Did I look too hard?
Has love taken its toll?

Kathy Thomas

God's In Charge!

Our faith In You seems strong Lord,
     When life is going well,
We trust and praise, we smile and sing,
     Your love to others tell.

But when we walk through trials,
And answers do not come,
Your presence seems elusive,
Your voice seems stilled and mum.

These tests of faith are hard Lord,
Remind us how to wait,
"Be still my soul to whisper,
The LORD's in charge — not fate!"

The preciousness of Jesus,
The character of God,
You'll teach with greatest meaning
As through dark times we trod.

Exchange our weakness for Your strength,
Remind us WHO YOU ARE.
ALMIGHTY GOD-YOU CANNOT FAIL!
LIMITLESS IN POWER!!

Ruth M. Sissom

Kaleidoscope

Perplexities of thought, fragments of dreams
glimpses at reality, always more then it seems.
The enigmas of life, the riddles of mind
confusion only bars, discouragement of time.
Of the mind can be said, in thought reality hides
discouragement vacant, and dreams to abide.
Callousness of emotions, walls of separation
tween reality and mind, dawning of recollection.
Superstitions of old, hauntingly present
shattering of dreams, leaves hope absent.
Depression's equivalent, dismemberment of vision
thought acceleration, fear's admission.
Darkness impending, light's shadow casting
fact and fiction, thought's accumulative massing.
Segregating memory, departure from past
exploration's height, memory's splash.
Configurement of time, corrugation of phobias
arrangement of dreams, attachment to rarities

Anthony Dale Moore

Yellow

Like the ruins of a war torn city,
That hideous color yellow,
Paints a picture of death and gloom,
Making me remember.

The city streets sicken me,
All lined with that evil,
And why not signs of aqua-green
Or rose-petal pink?

My father . . . my mother . . . my grandmother . . .
And poor Lilly Ann . . .
Lives taken so viciously . . . slaughtered!
In a house of yellow.

I feel as if I am falling now
From that disgusting ball
Blistering in the sky with long thin streams . . .
Like knives . . . like knives!

My spirit released to flight,
I will purge myself forever
From that puss color
As it oozes from my veins.

Marlene Burgin Pruitt

Untitled

I have forever wanted to be like a star,
Magnificent Betelgeuse, blazing red,
Snow white Sirius and Rigel,
or faithful Polaris,
guiding me home.

But if it is not Your will
that I be a star,
then make me a moon,
with no light of my own,
reflecting the light of Your love.

Ann R. Darling

Poetry

There are so many poems in me,
I like to grasp and write and see,
I have no doubts of the words that flow,
God's in charge of me you know!

Susanna G. Taubenberger

In Memory Of Lucy Marie

God sent an Angel to live here on earth.
She arrived at our home the day of her birth.

She was not a pretty child yet always had a smile.

When she grew older she had so many friends.
Her beauty it seemed came from within.

She had Cancer, the Doctor gave her six months
to live, She lived eight and had so much Love to give.

During her illness she suffered such pain.
God called her to heaven it was her gain.

Just before her death, she gave a great sigh.
She could not speak but reached up to hug me
Good Bye.

Nora Weathersby

Sounds Of The Seasons

Why oh why do I listen while I sleep,
I wake up hearing something sounding very deep.
Is it the birds chirping,
On an early spring morning.
Or the wind howling,
Sounding like a bear growling.
Can it be the sound of a child,
Acting very wild,
Having fun,
In the sun.
Maybe even the thump . . . thump of an icicle melting on the ground,
Which was once practically round.
It's all around us,
It surrounds us.
The different pitches of sound.

Melissa Doncheske

Broken

I feel as though my heart is breaking
You love me and I love you except you don't see that
You think I'm in love with your best friend
That's not the truth, since the night has happened
Where are you when I need you?
You never seem to notice me, though I see
    you staring at me

You're afraid to ask me out
Someone tells you not to
I'm sure you want to
You seem to not know that watching you gives
    me a heartache.

You go and talk about these girls
Saying you'll ask them out in front of
    me to see my reaction
I stand there with no expression

Seeing you is never going to be the same
    since it happened
I'll never forget, but don't you forget
    that my heart is broken.

Lindsay Feranec

What Is A Flower

A flower is an expression of potential
in our cosmos, a regenerative transitory
aspect of elan vital. In the eye of the
beholder its beauty becomes a many-hued
window through which we may perceive the
relative phenomenon of Nature, or simply
bask in its beauty.

William T. Mulligan

A Remaining Truth

Of late I stood at the invisible wall
That separates the truth from fiction,
Not knowing if I stood on reality's side,
For fantasy rules my diction

Of words that always ease my mind
And dreams of a far-off place
Where people take time to smell the roses
Not trying to keep up the pace

Of the life we've grown accustomed to
That brings success to our feet
And protects us from the one great fear
Of dying without great feats

Of happiness bought and thus attained
Through hard work and esteem
Fighting the battles we know we can win
But forgetting about our dream

Of love forsaken long ago
Too gone to answer our heed;
For through this life, at death we find
Love is the one truth we need.

Jared McQueen

Respect

When a child is born, it knows no wrong.
As the child grows, ideas are formed.
By the age of three, definite traits are shown.
If no respect is shown amongst the people around,
Then how can the child know respect on its own?
Self respect must be known and shown,
For to get respect you must have some of your own.
By the age of ten our environment has played
A very large part in our personal growth.
By this time the patterns are set for life.
No respect by then, leads to strife.
This can be changed over time,
When associations are formed with someone,
Who has respect for themselves and everyone.
But this is an outside chance, not the norm.
Show your child respect and have some of your own,
For if none is shown more than likely
This child will grow to be
A person, bitter, alone, and old.

John T. Humphries

"Into Springtime"

I watch you
growing green and straight and strong, despite me,
as the springtime of you awakens softly, subtly,
my sapling princess

So bright-eyed and fair,
a wonder before me, I watch you shine
despite my shadows,
and I ache with the sweetness

You shine so bright, so fierce,
that there are times when I cannot meet your gaze,
and times
when I can do no more
than turn away
for fear of seeing too much of me there

I wish the magic for you always,
I wish the flowers in your hair,
I wish the sun for you, despite my constant raining.
May it beam down on your inner landscape
lighting true your way,
upon your dawning journey into springtime.

Lauren Mullaney

"Dance"

The music I danced to was never
my own.

I never kept to my rhythm,
but yours.
Yours alone counted.
Yours alone mattered.

Then one day I realized it.
I could make my own music —
Create my own dance.

I was scared to perform at first,
but when I did . . .
I soared!

Now I am the composer and choreographer
(God, the Producer and Director)
of My "two-step"
My "Madison"
My "Hustle"
My Dance

The Only Dance.

Gabriela Hall

I Wonder Why

As I look up into the sky
I shake my head, and wonder why
    The sun's, so yellow
    The skies, so blue
This most beautiful thing, for me and you

The stars put on a show at night
They dance and shimmer in full moonlight
It's the prettiest sight to see
This most beautiful thing, for you and me

A plane flies silently, in the sky
To places unknown, and I wonder why
    The sun's, so yellow
    The skies, so blue
This must beautiful thing, for me and you

Deborah M. Smith

The Birdie

I awoke one morn feeling down and depressed,
Not knowing why, without reason,
And sat outside after having dressed,
For it was balmy and spring was the season.

Knowing for certain this day would be bad,
I took no notice of grass nor sky,
So determined was I to remain blue and sad,
Though I certainly could not explain why.

A songbird came to visit a tree,
And flitted there and about,
Each move getting ever closer to me,
Breaking my mood to sit there and pout.

The bird kept repeating a beautiful song,
On the closest branch of the tree,
And I found myself whistling along,
There we were the birdie and me.

When its mission was done the bird flew away,
And back towards the heavens it went,
Now I look forward with joy for each new day,
Thanking God for the birdie He sent.

George J. Luther

451

Your Clock Of Life

Life may be compared to a clock;
It will survive through many a knock.
But the question remains — above the clicking,
When will "your clock of life," stop ticking?

From time of birth, you have no power, —
To determine just when is your final hour.
Don't wait for the clock to strike "11" . . .
It may be too late for a journey to Heaven!

Life is not lived by days or by years,
Or heartaches and hurts or valley of tears.
And life is not measured by winning or losing,
But more so the "road" of your daily choosing.

Time moves ever forward — time does not stand still;
For life is most fragile with much to fulfill.
Life's goals are accomplished by what you put in it;
Live joyously in serving each golden minute.

When your "roadway" is paved with dignity and grace,
You're more apt to see the Lord's shining face;
For He alone controls with majesty and power,
Your "clock of life" . . . each minute, each hour!

Ezio M. Tozzi

Walking With My Master

I am walking with my Master
as I travel down life's way.
I am walking with my Master
and I walk with Him each day.

The road we walk is narrow,
Most Days I stumble and fall
But He always helps me up,
and to Him, I owe my all.

So if you walk in circles
and have no place to go
Come walk with me and my Master
Real peace and joy you'll know.

The walk that we are taking
Leads to our Heavenly Home
And that day, our Master will sit upon his Throne.
Our walk will then be finished and at last we will be home,
So I am Walking with my Master,
No more will I roam.

Richard H. Kotsch

A Legacy To My Beloved Walter

To those I love and those who love me.

When I am done, release me, let me go.
I have so many things to see and do.
You must not tie yourself to me with tears.

I gave you my love; you can only guess,
How much you gave to me in happiness.
I thank you for the love you have shown,
But now it's time I travelled on alone.

So, grieve awhile for me, if grieve you must,
Then let your grief be comforted by trust.
It's only for a while that we must part.
So, bless the memories within your heart.

I won't be far away, for life goes on,
So if you need me, call and I will come.
Though you can't see or touch me, I'll be near.
All of my love around you soft and clear.

And then, when you must come this way alone.
I'll greet you with a smile and "Welcome Home."

Celia Keiper

Untitled

I would like to count my blessings
    as I go along each day
but how can I count my blessings
    when my troubles get in the way.

I would like to live each day for the Lord
    and go each night to rest
knowing deep inside my heart
    that I have done my best.

But somehow my good resolutions
    and the ways of the world going by
never seem to go together
    no matter how hard I try.

May be I sit and think to much
    of the things that I should do
and never get up and take action
    to make these things come true.

Whatever it is that I do wrong
    no one will pay but I
so I'll try to count my blessings
    as I watch the world go by.

Movlean Epps

Forever

Love is forever, forever I say.
I hear your heart calling to this very day.
I shall love you always, I want you to know;
For you forever, my love shall flow.

Kimberly S. Gregory

Untitled

Where is that tower of strength
    That I envisioned myself to be?
The building blocks go up,
    and soar . . .
Only to be toppled by those I love;
    Irony, irony, irony,
By those I love.
    Strength's greatest weakness lies in love!

Elizabeth J. Gortemoller

Heart To Heart

From heart to heart, and soul to soul,
I had searched my whole life through.
Yet when I least expected it, I walked straight into you.
The bond we share is pure and true;
We think as One, myself and you.
Your love's so strong, so pure and tender,
It wraps me up and keeps me warm in winter.
You make me smile, you make me laugh,
Yet you never get mad when times are bad.
I always feel safe, I never get scared, and all because
I know you'll be there.

Jackie Kline

Darkness Approaches

Darkness comes from forgotten memories, forever lost in spaceless time,
It creeps up your spine at midnight on a stormy night,
It seeps out of Egyptian tombs, long forgotten in the history of the planet.
Or from an old sunken treasure ship, condemned to a life
in the blue crevices of the ocean.
It sneaks silently up the stairs when everybody is asleep.
Darkness comes from a dragon's hateful eye, evil with red gloom.
From an empty eye socket in an old cracked skull,
To the expanding space between a ring nebula, darkness approaches.

Daniel J. Bulfer

Tainted

Sweet smelling honeysuckle drifts through the open windows.
I move my glass in small circles, throwing the broken ice cubes
against each other. I like the sound it makes.
The clean crisp cotton of my nightgown clings to my body.
It is hot, summer scorching sun sucking life from every living thing.
Purple freesia, Spanish tiled swimming pools, unprotected skin.
My hand scoops yellow sourballs, lime hard candies from the raspberry stained dish.
I gulp the remainder of my orange whipped cooler before it evaporates.
The sun is selfish.
Wildflowers struggle to survive. I can see them from the window.
Bright patches. Tainted with insects feasting. Bellies stuffed.
The bugs are selfish.
He packed his suitcase and left. Left like four years was easy to walk away from.
Just as well, I should have slept with another man.
The transistor radio sits perched on the window sill, sputtering songs of the old days.
I recognize "Bridge Over Troubled Waters".
I know the words so I hum the tune to myself. Nobody else is here to listen.
I catch a firefly between my fingers, it will soon die because I won't let him go.
I pop melon balls into my mouth and move them from cheek to
cheek with my tongue. I can't make passionate love with scenery.

Corinna Rae Saunders

Butterflies

We sat on the grass and talked that day,
I remember.
I remember the way you looked,
  the way you smelled,
  the way the grass stuck to my sweaty legs.
We were tired from the night before,
  and that heat only made it worse.
Butterflies came to say goodbye,
  as days slowly changed tonight,
  and sunsets rainbows caught our tears,
  staining them with their light.
The sunset faded into black,
  and just like that our time was gone.
I stood up,
  and the grass left an imprint on my legs,
  as the summer left on my mind.
"Thank You". I said,
  and that was all.
A butterfly kiss,
  and you were gone.

Christine Burke

Life Among The Lilies

Lilies are like life, the energy she maintain are like
no other entity. She hides away from life forces,
then when the earth cannot hold her down any
longer, and she feels the need to take a peak
at the world, the earth gives way to her desires.

The earth with its smell unlike any other breaks
apart and makes the path clear. She inspects
what is on top and gently pushes her way through.

Her fragility such as that of a baby at birth is
the small green points, sticking up and waiting for
suck which is the rain. The growth began when
the stems pushes higher toward the sky, and the
greenness is made aware to the eyes.

The greenness gives way to the yellow, and the
yellow display a gleeful dance, the wind is
her teacher. She dances throughout her rein,
and when her feet no longer moves she return
to her home, the earth. Her rein
is over and her season has come to an end.

Elizabeth Jones

Real Friends

I'm not sure what real friends are
I don't recall I've ever had them. Maybe
a few good ones here and there but no
real friends. You know the ones who act
real, like humans. There were some very
special ones that touched very close to
the heart but their stay was dramatically
abrupted. From now on there is never quite
enough time. The ones who can stay are good
don't get me wrong, but the one who
left, left memories to carry on.

N. Stanton

The Lost Fighter Pilot, WWII P-51, 9-12-44

He flew so high,
That one Shepherd above us,
When Eighty German Fighters
Appeared at 12 O'clock High.

A Lone Fighter Pilot
Could only but try
To delay that Gaggle
At 12 O'clock High.

He rolled over,
Attacked them from their rear,
And blew two out of the sky
Before it was his time to die.

With our escort recalled,
Luftwaffe limited to one pass,
Fourteen B-17s still spun down
To crash on German grass.

But the greatest loss of all
Was that Shepherd who answered God's call
And Gave His Life For One And For All.

Thomas W. Clarke

The Perfect Friend

Today I found a friend, who knew everything I felt
She knew my every weakness, and the problems I have been dealt.
She understood my wonders and listened to my dreams,
She listened to how I felt, about life and love, and I know what it means.

Not once she interrupted me, or tell me I was wrong,
She just understood what I was goin' through, she promised she'd stay long.

I reached out to this friend to show her that I care, to pull her
close and let her know how much I need her there.

I went to hold her hand to pull her nearer and realized this perfect
friend I'd found was nothing but a mirror.

Amy Cartee

My Mom

I just can't say how much I love you,
For it would take up all the room I have,
Days when I'm hurt or sick,
I see your face waiting for me to get
better so we can talk again,
As I lie in a moment of silence,
I hear your prayer over me,
I may get older every year but,
I still remember the love of
yours every time I think of
it one tear comes out of my
eye and I hear the angels singing the
bells of never ending happiness . . .

Amanda Lopez

453

Why?

Why do I try?
Why do I even bother?
My heart always goes out to you
But yours is for another

Always someone close to me
Treats you bad but you cannot see
You think it's their way of loving you
But in the end, all they do is hurt you

I'm not like others
Who say they are yours but are with another
You think they are true to you
But actually they are playing you like a fool

I think you would be better off with me.
You say that in time we will see
What will and will never be,
What will probably never be is you with me.

Danielle A. Whittenberg

Moonbeams

As the moon beams life to the sea,
so God's love brings a tide into me.
Continuous flows the waters to the sand,
His grace gives use to these hands.

The moon beam soars straight to the soul
and God's love is gracious and bold.
A peace in the wind so sure of its goal,
His guidance to me is precious, I know.

Storms come and so they shall go,
their time is no bandit, God's in control.
As waters do rise, so they must fall,
the sand's ever changing is hope for us all.

Ancient winds of being, never being seen
helps keep it flowing, the hearts given wings.
The tides of decision, the mind of a child,
ever reaching for moonbeams on the dark shore of time

Magnificent is God's moonlight which guides my sight.
The shores path is clearer with His splendid light.
Tides of cleansing and the changing of the sands,
rapture of the waters, God holds my soul in his hands. Amen

Debra Pace

Jillian I Bought You A Card

The card I bought was pretty and new.
It spoke of violins and roses, true.
My name written in the proper spot,
Put in the mail, for the February 14th drop.

I finish my day, coffee in the cafe.
My thoughts, what exactly did that card say?
Did it speak of your smile and dimpled chin?
Or the way you look with that witty grin?

The bounce in your eye, when your puppy's up close,
The way you say good night, when he's tuckered the most.
I especially love the warmth that you share
With your friends, your brother, and those who care.

Imagine the Beatles, and, of course, the Cure,
Breakfast with heather, tatoo parlors "for sure"
A smile in your classroom, waves in the hall,
Our late-night talks on your telephone call.

This february my heart wants to say
I love you so much — Happy Valentine's Day!

Michael Carlock

Words

Sometimes words cannot convey the meaning
A touch is simpler.
Sometimes words cannot form; choked by emotion.
A hug means so much more.
Sadness can strike at any time.
Loneliness also can rear its ugly head.
Holding hands can make things better
Even a tender kiss.
Hurt can cause so much pain;
A caress soothes it all away.
Blackness can descend upon us all
Enveloping us with despair.
Another person's presence can bring the light back.
Bitter words should never be spoken.
A silent friend can cure it all.

Beryl Green

Boston

On Beacon Hill the Brahmins live,
with chandeliers of dusty light,
beneath which they sit
and dine at night,
down below Woolworth, underneath the bridge
a young, old woman lives.
With scarlet scarf and purple coat
and flowered hat that sits askew.
She dines alone under
the street lamp light
a can of Molson beer
and a rain soaked cigarette.

Kathleen Meehan Greenan

Leaves

When color burns within the trees
That's when the children collect the leaves
All the children laugh and shout
While making piles of leaves about
Leaves of brown, red and gold
Children use to play with in the cold
Even though they may cough and sneeze
They will stay out in the chilly breeze
And even though the fall won't stay
The memories of happiness will never go away.

Leah R. Hachman

Will Thee

The quest is for knowledge, for wisdom and strength.
Will thee but ask, will thee but feel?
Will thee but will the healthiest route?
Will thee but know how to seek it out?
Truth, love, honor, peace
Will you but will a task such as this?
Or will you but can't and quite before dead, while the day young,
And questions unmade.
Soon to come death, ascension or bust, all ways or no-way, we
All are but dust.
From thence we came and so shall we go.
Taking nothing, naked, alone, as we came.
What shall we leave that shall not rust.
The love, the care, the souls we have touched.
The day we are born, starts the day we die.
The soul in thy body someday . . . someday shall fly.
The question
The question
The question is this . . .
How high?

Christopher Hager

The Lighthouse

I love the gallant old lighthouse yonder,
  love for that lighthouse has guided me since childhood.
The way it stands there, forever giving of itself,
  transformed me.
Gallantly it stands against wind, rain, and surf,
  just to be of aid to the lost and hurting.
Old fashioned may such ideas be,
  but they inspired and guided me.
Lighthouse, sender of clear honest signals
  to help others.
    That's the life style I want.
Yonder, very far yonder across life's timeless seas,
  where I must one day voyage.
I know I'll reach there safely because
  my lighthouse guided me with its beacon of love.

Tomila Joanna C. Louise

Close Friends

I knew when I first met you,
We were meant to be together.
But both of us had one problem,
We were married to another.

So we became close friends,
Something I thought was best to do.
You are always there for me,
And I will always be there for you.

In the short time that we've known each other,
We've had our share of fights.
But you are always on my mind,
Every minute of the day and night.

I've done something that scares me,
I don't know what to do.
I'm not sure how you'll take it,
But I've fallen in Love with you.

If "friends" are all we're supposed to be,
I wish the best for you.
I'll go my way and stay in touch,
Just so you know "I'll always Love You."

Juanita H. Parker

Untitled

How many waves have hurled their tears against the Rock
And gently away, have returned to their puddle,
Relieved, peaceful and free of many struggle
For they have been soothed by the eyes of the Rock.

How many lines, pages, books have been written,
Void of any sense, without love or conviction
But the eyes of the Child discovered the passion
A crying pen lost, traces of words unwritten.

How much time has been misplaced on futile Dreams?
Tragic wars, pathetic desires? Hear me now,
You, surrounded by moody Gods, and broken vow
Of profound feelings: There is a place to fire Dreams.
I, hopeless mortal, have found the Righteous Dreamer,
The one, who like the Rock, restrains the many tears
And shows the way to better sorrow and laughter,
And broadcasts to the Clouds words that calm the fears.

If you listen to the hands calling out to you
And hear the whisper those eyes murmur close to you
Your heart will see the friend you have been longing for
Open your eyes! And you will stand alone no more.

Ann O'Neamus

Giving Love

You call it love
And I call it being
You say it's wonderful
That it's all in seeing
What a joy to be living
What a joy to be giving love.

We've watched the children grow
Teaching them what we've learned
That you reap what you sow
And your heart will yearn
For the joy for living
And the joy of giving love.

Down thru the years
We've shed many tears
Nothing we could do but pray.
Then came the light
To overtake our fears
And show us a brighter day.

You call it love and I call it giving
You say it's up and down and I say it's living
What a joy to be living what a joy to be giving love.

Ernest Collier

Endurance

Most people call me ugly,
But I don't care.
Most are beautiful like the majestic rose,
And will bloom and wilt to die.
Unlike me who isn't that beautiful.
I will continually bloom like the great pine,
And will continue even through the hardest times,
And like the pine that drops its pine cones,
I shall spread parts of me to one and all,
Not as ugliness, but as a spirit of joy and endurance.
Like the pine cone that is prickly,
Not everyone wants it,
But it will still remain for others
To take if it is wanted,
And like the pine its supply will never die
For beauty dies, but endurance prevails.

Autumn Croxell

Life

Life is a roller coaster.
It has its ups and downs.
Sometime life is a cherry.
It has its pits.

Other duration's, it is a grape.
It has its vines.
Many times it is sour as a lemon or
as sweet as sugar.

A couple of days everything is coming up roses,
Others it is coming up weeds.
You water and pick.

When it rains it pours.
Occasionally, there is a silver lining
and a pot of gold.
It can be hard and cold as ice or
soft and warm as cotton.

One survives through the storm
tattered & torn, but alive.

Geralyn Gorski

To Live To Die

To live to die
   Without a reason,
Would be to call insanity as God.
To live to die
   In darkness for a season
Would gain no more for man than does the clod,
Yet in this fettered spirit
   There are callings
That whisper "When this task is done."
   "You've lived, now die
To all illusions
   And walk within yourself
As one,"
For there are none
That call the flesh their haven
That know that they are nothing
   But the clod,
Unless they've heard
   one spirit calling
A facet that reflects a way of God.

    Julia T. Carlyon

Dragon Slayer

I quietly slip away each night,
riding the bare back of a nightmare
to a world imprisoned in my soul
where shadowy figures without faces
rise to greet me, testing my courage.

Am I out of character or really
this person who kills without remorse,
and rests in the arms of strange lovers.
I slay great fiery dragons and search
relentlessly for home and loved ones.

I mourn the stranger who spends nights
with me running from soldiers and spies.
We fly, spreading our arms and rising
above the herds of red-eyed beasts.
Sometimes I cry.... no one hears me.

I return each morning from the nameless
streets and dark countryside so familiar.
Weary of two worlds, I find no rest.
Am I a dweller of the day light,
or just a haunting spirit of the night?

    Paula Lemieux

Longing

For what must I atone?
That I am again alone
Wish only to have the company of someone sweet
Whose absence is cause to weep
Is it my head bald?
But the look becomes me I'm told
My spirit, once loose, is walled
Longs for a slender hand to hold
Oh, it is easy to find sex
But without intimacy it is a cruel hex
Approached as if going to war
Requiring armor instead of amour
To pull her close with both hands by the waist
Anything else compared is just a waste
For a kiss that is shear delight
What else can be so right?
Two people in love is magic
To be alone is tragic
Oh god how I would sing
If only that phone would ring

    Jim Joy

This Illusion

I never imagined it to be.
Yet, it hit me so amazingly hard.
This illusion of you and me consumes my ever being . . .
Maybe, we went too far too fast —
But I know deep down, I wanted it to last.
I tried so hard at something,
That I never imagined to be.
Why didn't we last, was it me?

Now, it's hard imagining it not to be.
How do I cope and end the confusion.
Tell me how do I erase this illusion
From my heart and soul . . .
I try so hard with this tormenting battle.
Why am I affected so much by something
That I never imagined to be.

It seems so real, but never within my reach.
Despite all the tears and fears, this illusion continues to endure.
Why do I do this to myself,
When I know deep down, this illusion will never be
All that I imagine it to be . . .

    Dana L. Hale

Untitled

I used to wonder what it would take for me to gain inspiration again.
There was a point in my life when I would write endlessly,
Creating romantic episodes and scenarios
With the swift movement of a hand.
   but now all movement has ceased,
The inspiration to write no longer abides in me
And even when that inspiration visits my being
I scribble only of longing and remembrance.

So often I wait for you,
Sometimes in vain . . . Sometimes not.
Yet, when I talk to you
When I see you,
And you smile your smile,
So charming and debonair
And your eyes fill with surpassing tenderness
It is then that I am inspired to write endlessly,
It is then that my hands are once again filled with energy and
vibrancy
Because for that moment, that one moment,
Renewed . . .
I love.

    Wanda Denise Hall

Love's Devotion

In life, everything seems to change,
from the hours of light to the phase of the moon at night,
from rivers that run wild, to the heart of a small child,
everything changes.

People look into their souls to see themselves,
from times of charm to thoughts of harm,
from wants and need and the hopes to succeed,
everything changes.

People see inside their mind,
from increasing their power, to thoughts that cower,
for using to teach, and helping to preach,
everything changes.

Once in a lifetime, love comes to play,
from the passion of fire, to thought and desire,
from promises and devotion, to caring and understanding,
from holding and closeness, to days spent away,
but once it happens, you fall in love,
it never changes.

    Michael Leinen

Music

Music seems to take hold of the soul, each note that is pitched
might bring comfort as well sorrow
Reading its life of ups and downs like that of a music scale
When the soul's mind is at peace, it creates "sharp gospel harmony"
But when the bass orchestra blues lowers into flats, the soul's
heart "trebles" pain of sorrow
Solo beat performances represents great strength and discomfort
For the power of the soul auditions its score

Opening prelude — HOW MUCH CAN ONE BARE

Intermission — RHYTHM OF LIFE

Conclusion — ONE SOUL MUST LEARN HOW TO CONDUCT
   Marian Cooper

Santa

I think I saw Santa on the eve of Christmas day.
I think I saw Santa, his reindeer and his sleigh.

I think I saw Rudolph, his red nose shining bright,
My tummy felt funny, sort of silly and light.
I laughed and I giggled, it was sheer delight,
Santa slid down the chimney, what an amazing sight.

He's a jolly ole fellow, round from head to toe,
He winked his eye and gave a smile and twinkled his button nose.

He carried my presents one by one,
Under the tree so gallantly done.

I left Santa note I wrote all by myself,
Thank you for my presents and did you elves help?

Here is plate of cookies to eat,
I knew you'd be hungry, a snack and a treat.

My mommy and I baked them just for you,
Take one for each reindeer, they might like one too.

I know it's time for you to go,
I know you have work to do.

To visit the children around the world,
And help make their dreams come true.
   DeAnn Hasquet

Bored

I heard someone say their reason for doing drugs today
I'm Bored
read a book,
write a story,
do a dance,
take a chance . . .

Get Creative
Innovative

Play a game on a table.
Spend some time in a stable.

say a prayer

Lift Your Spirit

Walk outside and take a breath,
drink in life,
say no to death.

You though you wanted something to do,
what you really were looking for was . . .

You!
   Elizabeth Ann Campanelli

Sleepless Nights

Give me tonight your amber light,
Sweet dream of mine, delight.
I whisper soft of our desire,
Oh Morpheus, tis you I inquire.
Converse to me, may slumber be
My reward tonight.
Cast your precious spell my friend,
Entice me with your charm.
I welcome you so tenderly,
Only for you do I have open arms.
Tell me of stories never been told,
And I will never tell.
May the moon and her stars watch over me,
Illuminating so eloquently,
Shadows dancing with delight.
   Michelle Lucas

"Mine Alone"

If I cry for others, will they cry for me?
If I feel for other, but do they feel for me?
I see how they act not knowing if they are true.
Knowing all this, makes me sad and blue.
   I cry for them, the feeling is mine alone?
It's made me realize how they are.
   So please don't cry for them,
Cause I'll cry for you.
   Telling me the problem, you have.
Are strong to bare, it seam to me that
   you care. Hold your tears with in yourself.
Cause here I am, so don't cry to me.
   I'll cry for you
   Salvatore J. Finocchiaro Sr.

Alone

Without someone to hold,
Stars are looking bright,
Who are you with tonight?

You wish, you hope, you pray,
That maybe, just maybe someday,
You'll have a friend to talk to, to brag about,
To tell your Ma and Pa about.

To hold, to love, to treasure,
To supply your needs and pleasures.

In the dark or in the light,
You always seem to be in fright.

Will you ever find a friend,
Or make believe once again?
   Adam Russell Goodwin

Special Angel

There is a chorus of angels singing in heaven today.
They are trying to clear the path, and lead Daddy on his way.

A pair of wings and halo, are waiting for his stay.
With our love, and God's blessing, he is headed on this day.

From heaven up-above us, he will watch us day by day.
We will always feel his presence in each and every way.

Daddy lead us down the path of whatever road we took.
Now, someone's leading Daddy to set by that gentle brook.

Take care of him, "Our Father", please guard him with your love.
No worthier angel than Daddy has ever gone above.

So-sing you chorus of angels, sing as loud as you can.
Clear a path to the heavens for this very special man.
   Gaylene Sue McConnell

There Is A Brighter Day

Life has its ups and downs
Like mountains ranging from peak to peak;
So then too our experiences — however profound,
They are what fashion us into being unique.

For what may not seem to be very clear to me
On this my choice, my cross, my journey;
When the storms of life seem to cloud my way,
Still deep within my being I KNOW
There is a brighter day.

The heart yearns to fulfill a deep bedded quest,
Ambitious, vivacious — my soul cannot rest.
But when ALL seems lost, pushed aside and gone astray,
I yet HOLD ON and for many a day
I believe, I wait and unceasingly I pray;
Once again I am reassured
I remember, there is a brighter day.

Donna Houston Sherrard

To My Mother

The Lord is her shepherd as he is her guide.
A light shines through her that she can not hide.
Her word is precise, her chastisement firm,
But her love is shown through each correcting word.
The truth shrouds her like a white cloth,
Showing her purity and virtue that never is lost.
Her patience is unyielding, her abilities never ending.
She has the strength of Sampson and the beauty of Esther,
And she has the modesty of Ruth that shall outlast her.
She cares for her flock as Christ cared for his.
She is a model for her children and an inspiration to her husband.
Her smile greets us and fills her heart with pride,
A pride knowing she had raised her children right.
So here is to my mother, one of God's greatest creations.
That she may know I admire her greatness.

Autumn Jackson

The Unmade Bed

Upon returning, I find you rumpled,
Warm.
Still welcoming after many years
Never giving away secrets.

Today you desire clean clothes,
Although you would never ask.
But the soft feathers in your pillows rejoice
When plumped. Some will escape.

I will smooth them
And I will be soothed
And comforted
For thirty years more.

Shirley Knight

The Rose

The rose looked so sad there alone,
All its pain would now be shown.

The dew looked like a tear,
As it fell showing all its fear.

The outside protected by thorns,
But inside its heart could still be torn.

The petals red as blood,
But still showed all its love.

One day the rose would be picked,
And its love will burn inside as if it
has a wick.

Tamarah F. Hatcher

If Not For Spring

If not for Spring, spirits dampened by the cold
Would not awaken, to see new life unfold.

If not for Spring, the solitary dove
Would call aimlessly to its love.

If not for Spring, frozen rivers would not flow,
The Easter lilly would shamefully not grow,
Unfruited tree and honeysuckle vine
Would wane for Earth to give her sign.

Soon comes the Spring, with spirit soaring high,
Red breasted robins descend from cloudy sky,
To offer truth that Spring be but a day,
Or maybe two or three away.

And with the Spring, we look to Heaven's door,
And vow to love forevermore.

Julia B. Lewis

He's Only Just Away My Son

When I got the news that you were gone,
I stared into space. I couldn't believe what they had said,
They just told me that my child was dead.

I remember when you were just a little boy,
You would play outside most of the day,
I would go and check on you. Later you would come in the
house and check on me.

Do you remember when you would take your toys apart?
Somehow you would manage to put them back the way they
were made to be.

This couldn't be true, that you are gone,
You said to me, "Mom, I will always be there for you."

As you got older, you would say to me, "Mom, I am Ok, Don't worry
about me." You always listened to your favorite music.
Up above my head, I hear music in the air.
"Honey, are you somewhere up there?"

You see, I am not Ok,
Jesus said, "My child I'm coming back again. I will bring your
loved ones back with me."

He is only just away.....

Delores Maloy

The Sandy Shore

Walking along the blue water's edge,
On the peaceful sandy shore,
Thoughts race wildly through my mind,
As I think to times before.

There were days that I was happy,
And enthusiastic about my life.
Now dark clouds hung about me,
As my days turned into unending strife.

I found it interesting to watch,
My naked feet make etchings in the sand.
And soon I turned around to find a trail,
Following me over this wet and rocky land.

Quickly the waters swept up,
Onto the sandy shore.
Now gone were the footprints I had admired,
Gone were the steps I had traveled once before.

No records of the places I had been,
Or the thoughts that had preoccupied me.
No reminders of the places I had walked through,
Only a sandy shore beside a moonlit sea.

Andrea Herington

Dreamy Night Honey

Start with some moon glow you gathered on a night
That shone all shimmery with bright starlight.
Then drop in a touch of glimmery glow,
And stir it all together, nice and slow.
If you've got any leftover starlight twinkles,
You can mix them in with some sandman sprinkles.
Then think of a down right silly thought
And toss that in with a polka dot.
Add some sauce made from a great big yawn
Blended with the graceful glide of a swan.
The last thing you need is a silvery thread
From a cap that sits on a wood elf's head.
Add that in with all the rest.
And your dreamy night honey will be the best.
Just a taste of this before you sleep,
Will help your dreams be soft and deep.

Susan Doleen Gardner

"And this is all that's come of it, Sarah"

She was hot coal. The dusting of her skin
melted a year of snow. I was a mountain
in her tan arms. Naked on the kitchen
floor, stairs, in the attic (we thought to begin
at the top), I could only imagine

the next moment racing, stretched, loud, tight, flush
against her hips, broad, moist — the hours rushing
by — the smell of oranges — the percussion
of the days — the months — the years — the hush

of everything — and she is cold, white ash
between the sheets. The passion's
gone. My eyes are icebergs. The clouds crash

like thunder. Whales are giving birth. Their young
fill my mouth. Their words rush around my tongue.

Chad S. White

Stars

I have been preoccupied with stars,
Not their mathematics, light years, or cosmic dust,
But rather as transcending all the bars —
Worldly mortality, and grief, and rust,
An antidote to our impermanence,
Attractive glitter in the firmament,
Swinging in arcs that make divinest sense,
Remote from worries how to pay the rent.

We are what we have been, creatures at night
Hiding in caves from beasts beyond our ken.
What did the stars mean then? A wonder-light
A promise the day star would come again.
Deep in our blood the wonder, the awe, the glory,
We are a part of the magical ancient story.

Marie I. McHenry

To The Voice In The Distance

To the voice in the distance, to the one who calls.
I'm a name not a number, I'll rise when I fall.
Like the roaring clasp of thunder, or the footsteps in the sand.
It don't matter what you say, I am who I am.
Like the Colorado mountains, reaching to touch the sky.
I see the lands promising beauty, with my own weary eyes.
I see the grasses swaying, as the wind begins to blow.
I hear the trees laughter, with no where else to go.
I am the fallen soldier, becoming the rolling lands.
I'm the ever changing countryside, made by glorious hands.
I see the flash of lightening, dancing in the rain.
I'm like a solemn Indian, searching the dying plain.
And as the water ripples outward, I know not where I stand.
But I'm a name not a number, looking out across this land.

Marie Mannor

Guardian Angel

"Though I walk through the valley of the shadow
of death, I will fear no evil."

For my Lord has given me a Guardian Angel to walk
with me and protect me. He keeps away all things evil
and in his wake follow the good things of this earth;
"A friend loveth at all times and a brother is born for adversity."
I have indeed found a friend who "loveth at all times" and
is a brother through all adversity for he helps me through mine:
"A man that hath friends must show himself friendly, and there
is a friend that sticketh closer than a brother."

I have found a friend who both shows himself as a friend and sticks
"closer than a brother." For he is always there when I need him.

He is a friend, a confidant, a Saviour, and a lifeline to solid ground
when I need one; may he lead a blessed life for always
and forever. My prayers follow him on his daily journeys.
I pray God to go with him wherever he goes and protect him from the
pitfalls of life. Just as he would protect me from the same pitfalls.

Florence McFarland

My Brother Richard

I see you in the rain
I feel you through my pain
I wander aimlessly throughout the day
wishing we were little and again could play
You were my knight
then again sometimes my fight
Me your big sister you my big brother
so much love that it could almost smother
I moved away but only in miles
I still felt your heart and your wonderful smiles
You had your trials and crosses to bear
throughout them all had love to share
I want to cry for all who are left especially Mom
whose heart won't mend.
Nothing the same just your name
No more memories to make, am I insane.
I'm sending my heart on the wings of an angel
way up to Heaven marked "fragile I'm broken"
Please send it back marked "fragile I'm free"
Then I will know you never left me.

Debbie Ramsier-Naquin

The Wolf At The Door

She lived in the middle of nowhere,
With only a perfect sky, endless fields, a barn full of hay,
    And the wolf at the door.
He usually came in Winter,
When there was little else to do, when he was hungry and alone.

The night was cold,
    yet he watched through the bedroom window.
She was kneeling by the bed, her head in her hands.
She looked so sad;
He thought she must be crying, but her shoulders were still.
He wanted to scratch at the window,
    Jump on the bed,
    Lick her face to comfort her.
But more than that he wanted to watch her.

She was praying to God that he would come back.
That he would always come back, and wait by the door.
He watched her slip into bed, pull the covers snug around her,
    and drift off to sleep, a peaceful child's sleep.
Her sleep became deeper and deeper...
He turned and trotted off into the night.

Sally S. Moretti

And I Remembered Love

I saw the sunlight in the trees,
And felt the soft and gentle breeze
That touched my lips, a kiss.
And I remembered bliss.

The laughter, joy, the cherished voice,
Of one who left, but not by choice.
A song without an end.
A kiss I could not send.

I felt the breeze that stirred my hair,
Gentle fingers ruffling there,
A touch, a message from above.
And I remembered love.

I smiled, with tender thoughts of him,
And sent a kiss, upon a whim.
It floated gently to the sky,
To reach him by and by.

Joan Barton Barsotti

The Game of Life

It looks like life just threw me a curve.
I would rather have had a pop fly.
The answers are never easy,
And we really don't ever know why.
Who knows what the future will bring,
Let's just get through another day.
We're lucky to be here and enjoy ourselves.
Let's make the most of today.
The game of life is a gamble,
And no one said it was fair.
How are we to accomplish our dreams if we don't dare to dare?

Colleen M. Conway

My Familia

My Familia, my family it means. It's a
bond of forever it seems. Your family is
something no one could ever change. For the
fact that the blood that flows through your
body is the same. I may be young and
starting my family a little early, but that
doesn't mean I can't love in hurry. Your
age doesn't make a difference on how much
you can love someone. Just as long as you
remember where that love comes from. That
love comes from a special friend we know as
God. He gives us the strength to look
forward and beyond. Your family always
comes first before anyone else. Your family
can love you more than two friends themselves.
Your family will stand by your side through
thick and thin. Even if you think you can't
win. Your family is something you should
cherish forever. Because if you lose your
family who will you have ever.

Stacie Sanchez

Who Are You Really Sorry For?

You say you are better that me.
Not in words,
but acts and deeds.
My success was just a piece of chance.
That's what you say be the way you prance,
and seem as though you're sorry for,
poor misfit me,
Who cannot soar.
Yet why am I so happy here,
and you so discontented dear?

Rene Holman

Ode On A Roll Of Tissue Paper

This lofty product of Canadian wiles,
azure, angelic softness that caused smiles,
can many tears from children's faces wipe
or catch the dripping juice of fruits just ripe
which dribbles down the careless cheek
of youths while life's pure joys they seek.
Perhaps, at times, it will remove
salves, ointments, creams . . . which only prove
to eager women's eyes of curious glance
intent upon a mirror that, perchance,
wrinkles of years in fact do mean
that all these beauty charms can't make you clean
unless there is improvement from within,
for beauty lies beyond the skin.
Woe to the wretched creatures who
only less noble things with it can do!
The donors, then, should all repent;
but I, who got the gift to my content,
lifting the tone of this, their mirth,
do truly thank them on Christ's birth.

Maria E. Galindo

Blaine

You were my best friend
before we became lovers,
In this lifetime there can never be another.
Whom I love so deep and so true,
When you're away my whole world is so blue.
With the love that we shared,
We brought to life a beautiful baby girl,
And no matter where you are we
Know that you care,
And can see that her smiling
eyes shine like diamonds and Pearls.
She loves her daddy more than anything,
She mimics back when she hears you sing.
I only wish you were here to watch her go through
the changes in her life,
And our time together will soon make me your wife.
I love you so very much dear,
and time will soon bring you back here.
You do what you need to while we're apart.
Your love is still alive and is living here in my heart . . .

Becky Murl

Loneliness

My heart screams out in the dark of night
In agony of the coming light.
The one I love is no longer here,
My one and only that I hold dear.
The rain is falling clear and cold,
causing pain that only I have known.
If just once more I could hold you tight,
the rain would cease and bring the light.
In my nights to fitfully sleep,
my dreams waken me and I weep.
I'm haunted night and day,
by memories of you, if I may.
I'm lucky though, I kept you a while,
and knowing this I can smile.
In the darkness and in the black
There is a light, I may have you back.
I miss you much while we're apart
Yet I know that I am in your heart.
My heart is within your grasp.
All that remains to be done is ask.

Nick Davis

Marshes Of Time

after all it was
just
a thousand days of my life
wading now through the thick interminable marshes of time
alive yet breathing somehow somewhere
  in the shadows
    between anguish and despair
I count the nights by the tearstains on my pillowcase
but I wear my daytime smile well
dark eyes in a painted face are nothing
  mirror lenses can't fix
I hold my own
a man of steel biding time in a tower of stone
my soul can feel you in another's arms like
  coarse surfaces and
  rusty jagged sawteeth
I used to be whole but you've left me
  a vampire
with no taste
  for the sun

    Matt DP Thompson

The Creator's Creations

Grass as green as the sky is blue,
The warmth of the sunshine,
The morning dew.
Rain that falls from the sky above,
The cry of a newborn baby,
A miracle of love.
Mountains with exquisite designs and forms,
The rivers and oceans flow on and on.
Snow comes down so cold and white,
The moon and stars light the night.
Planets suspended in outer space,
The gentle touch of the wind upon my face.
Miraculously the trees change as the seasons change,
A kaleidoscope only the Creator can arrange.
Breathtaking vistas, picturesque and perfect,
Are the Creator's Creations.

    Joanne Hinton

Salinas 75

She took you on a Western run
through neon nights and forgotten fun
you two did some things you'd never done
and began to live as one

The first fight came and blew away
like the Salinas sun on a normal day
that's the lady's way your mind would way
as the plot became a play

And I can tell by the way you walk and talk
you don't sound so sure
for a man lost and losing in love
there is no cure

All your life you thought you'd know
Hell, you'd been so high and you'd been so low
when the North wind called you'd have to go
back to yourself so slow

But regardless of what you say I believe you still love her
And regardless of what you say I know you think of her

    David Hayden

Growing Up

As the sun slowly sets beyond the horizon,
and the day comes to an end,
like every thing else, I can feel my childhood
getting lost in time.
Though I'm afraid, I'm not sure of what yet;
maybe just growing up.
I stand alone as so many others did before me,
my heart seems to linger as I think about leaving
everyone for what so little people know.
I was given a gift, (a talent) and my desire
has always flowed high for what god gave to me.
So many obstacles to over come, but I shall work
hard for what I want. Making a stand in a world
where so many things go wrong, I try hard to
tale the right path.

    Scott Lynn

One Way Bridges

  By chance I was walking along a solid path among a
great woods, when I came upon a wide open canyon. To my
dismay, there was no other way to cross this gorge, except for
a narrow rope bridge. It took a great amount of courage to
take the first step upon this bridge. As I took my first step,
I happened to turn around and the scenery behind me began to
fade. Before I could find the courage to take another step, a
chilling wind appeared from out of no where. It caused my
little bridge to sway violently back and forth. I was frightened
to continue my journey, because I knew it was going to be a
long, hard one. However, I knew I had to take a chance to get
to the other side. I decided to simply hold on, close my eyes,
and let one foot fall in front of the other until I had reached the
other side. I knew once I had reached the other side my
bridge would disappear and that it was only one of many rope
bridges that I would have to cross within my lifetime.

    Danielle M. Courreges

Change

Life rips and mends,
it coils and unwinds,
it shows hatred and love,
but most of all it expresses the way we feel without words,
but through our bodies and minds,
through nature and the unnatural.
Through art and expressions life changes itself to be realistic
  and irregular.
Subconsciously we do not realize how drastically we change from
  time to time,
but if we look deep enough we shall find
what it is that is needed to be changed.

    Lea Schache

Epitaph

They followed along, waiting and watching,
the beauty of nature naked to them.
Oceans, flowers, mountains, trees flourishing,
yet people pursued false pleasures through sin.
They preached of love to the savior, **our** god.
Pure babies born and old people dying.
Thru running streams, jungles and fields they trod,
The heat of fires raging, souls crying.
Desecration, desolation, too much.
Tanks, submarines, guns, metal birds that fly.
Fighting over land, praying for his **touch.**
And we ask him **please** god, **tell us , "Oh why?!"**
If the stars, sun, moon and clouds be heaven,
Then war on earth is the HELL we live in.

    Michael C. Frank

The Mirror

This face seems quite familiar,
seen first so long ago.
Not quite the same as I remember,
The early one I came to know.

I do not see those clear blue eyes.
No mop of hair upon the brow.
With loss of youth, am I now wise?
If so, I do not see how.

This face with which I've lived so long;
Decades of pleasure, sorrow, song,
Is now so withered it scarce seems true
The days remaining are so few.

Are there regrets? Perhaps a few.
Some things I planned, I failed to do.
But with this face so long I've known
I have never been alone.

Keith C. Chastain

L'amour Autour Du Monde Entier

Wherever I am, wherever I go,
be it in Rio, Miami or Tokyo,
you, ma bien-aimée, are in my reveries and prayers,
where you are eternally acting as the major, most powerful player.

Blown by destiny to England's breathtaking shores
I envision us two in times of yore,
when we would have been in a state of bliss as Countness and Count
with our bosoms permeated by love and endearments abound.

The season of frost draws near as the feathered creatures soar South:
so do I in remembering your sweet and ambrosial mouth.
The city of Rome unwinds in front of my eyes,
while I wish you at my side to behold this Italian midwinter sky.

Next stop on my seemingly unending journey
is my country of birth and fond memories — good, ol Germany.
There I will praise thee bountiful, o my heart's desire,
to show my friends what I dearly admire.

The city of God my final voyage will be,
where our Lord willing I will reencounter thee.
This haven of spiritually called Jerusalem
is surrounded by joyful shouts: "Yahweh, Shalom!"

Leif Hoffmann

Lord Jesus Christ, Have Mercy On Me

Lord Jesus Christ, have mercy on me.
Give me the strength first to see
my own faults, whatever they are
so temptation away from I may keep afar

Lord Jesus Christ, have mercy on me.
Let my love towards others grow increasingly,
let my patience with others be steadfast,
so I may never cast a stone, first or last.

Lord Jesus Christ, have mercy on me.
In Christian tradition let my example be.
Help me lead a sinless life heretofore
to help others thru heavens golden door.

Lord Jesus Christ, have mercy on me.
Help me gain eternal happiness with thee
through service to your children all
that I may help to make them hear your call.

Lord Jesus Christ, have mercy on me.
From your guidance never let me flee.
Help me to learn the true word to spread,
as apostles of God, as disciples well read.

George L. Mattoon

My Wife's New Man

There's a new man in my wife's life.
She runs to his side whenever he calls,
day or night.

She fulfills his every need.
She even makes sure he eats well,
and he's dressed warmly.

He takes time and energy that used to be
reserved just for me.

And I know she loves him.
You can see it in the way she looks at him
and talks about him.

He has changed our lives forever.

But I guess I can live with that.

After all, he's my son, too!

Wendy Berry Wren

The Old Home Place

I took a trip yesterday
On a journey back in time.
A weathered porch swing beckoned me
Through the veil of a honeysuckle vine.

Back fifty years to my birthplace
And that of my mother and sister.
For a hundred years it stood there,
That old house by the river.

Music of fiddles and guitars filled
The rooms many years ago.
Scenes from the past drifted through my mind,
Granpa's mandolin and Daddy's banjo.

I've heard it said you can't go home again.
Perhaps that maxim is true.
Tears welled up when I saw the old place,
And a longing for Daddy, too.

Daddy's gone, but not the memories.
They'll live with me forever.
I took a trip yesterday
To the old house by the river.

Cecelia Hughes

The Loving

He feels it, the fire.

It burns in every fiber of his being.

For Her, the fire still burns.
The kind word,
the touch of a hand on his face.

The kiss,
the warmth of Her all around,
wrapped in love's embrace.

The sound of breathing,
the smell of her hair;
serve to remind him
that the fire still burns there.

And the memories pouring into reflection;
dipped in understanding and
the colors of life.
Gave him strength to carry on;
through the disillusionment of strife.

Oh, he feels it, the fire.

For it burns in every fiber of his being.

Frank Foster

A Room With A View

A wall is graced with flowers, the offerings of obligation and care.
The proximity is questioned, yet, a sense that they are near.

Their odor smells quite pungent, in spite of colors sweet.
A crowded closeness surrounds one's head right to their feet.

A somber face draws toward and adjusts the kneeling pew.
He's followed by the numbers cast at the "likes" of you.

Walking in procession — reflection takes its post
Comments left unspoken by a still and quiet host.

"Should have, would have, could have" are things we need to know.
For time has pressed the decades while reaping what we sow.

Gone the hopes of reunions bound to promises undone.
Pity is the measure left for the tunes we leave unsung.

Think twice, my friend, of love and life before this time's at hand.
All the points are tallied whence this moment finally takes a stand.

Too late at the story's end upon you like the cunning fox.
Too soon a lifetime echoes, "It is 'I' who's in that box!"

Andrea M. Paglia Taylor

Grandchildren

Oh how we love to see them come
Their voices, their joys, their smiles.
They laugh and play with utmost glee,
Especially if it's been quite a while.

A hug, a kiss, and that laugh as we meet,
Gives pleasure that words can not say,
A touch of the hand that holds so tight,
Is warmth that makes our day.

Their stay at grandma and grandpa's house,
Enlivens these walls once more,
Of children's little pitter patter of feet,
As they enter through our doors.

Their lively personalities bring back to us,
Memories of our own children's days.
So precious were they, that we've now a repeat,
Of our grandchildren as they come to stay.

If God would give us a special gift,
A choice that's ours alone.
We'd take those happy precious ones,
Our grandchildren, our very own!

Ruth Williams

The Widow

Wandering aimlessly in garments of darkness
reflecting her sullen mood,
or maybe just the dissolved hopes
of her vanished husbands soul.

Pitying herself for her immense loss,
part of herself being lost coincidentally.
She lies to herself,
and each day her heart feels her husbands pain.

It isn't the pain he felt in death,
only the pain he feels now when he looks at her
Groveling in the past . . . in him,
instead of living the present
and looking forward to the future.

He can no longer communicate with her,
or express his love.
He only longs to beg her to live
the life she has been given,
instead of wasting it over his that has expired.

Justine Homiak

The Glass Heart

The glass heart, so beautiful both inside and out.
It expands with love from the warmth of the person who loves him.
Pain is its worst enemy.
For pain is like a hammer that will shatter the heart with ease.
Although the glass heart can be mended, there will always be
    a piece of glass that will no longer fit.
Even though the heart can start loving again where it left off,
    it will not be able to expand with love as much as it once had.
The glass heart will become so fragile.
Even the slightest breath from words spoken in hatred and
    betrayal, will shatter the heart over and over again.
Soon, the glass heart will have been shattered so much that
    the pieces will have become too small and fragile to mend.
Along with the disappearance of the glass heart....
    the love and the soul of the man who once held the majestic
    and loving glass heart deep in him.
Where there was once a loving heart, there now is a deep
    black hole filled with sorrow and frustration.

Eddie Watt

New Love

As the sunrises a Love begins,
with two peoples heart and souls,
will it ever end. The hope is there,
The love is strong. Everyone said it was
wrong. The time is right. The passion is wild
They said it will end with child. The desire
lives. The yearning burns, With a sigh
everyone turns. The hearts are full, the
souls are high. As the sunsets, everyone
cries. The love was right. The hope was
bright. Everyone said it's a Beautiful
Sight.

Vivian Smallwood

The Strongest Tear

The strongest tear,
Could not be held back.
Through all the smoke
So thick and black.
On that day, 168 died,
Can't forget, no matter how we tried.
    Shed, was the strongest tear.
The day, the heartland, filled with fear.
Help arrived, from all over
from pacific coast to dover.
And west virginia to the northwest
All night and day, not slowing to rest.
Unsung heroes, there were many.
Giving not just time, but their last penny.
We will always remember

Daniel C. Welch

What Do You Want?

Look in your heart, really look deep.
Know what it is that you really seek.
Are you trying to live your life God's way,
In everything you think, do and say?
Or are you really wanting God to do,
Things the way you want him to?

We're here on earth a very short time.
And the stairway to heaven is an uphill climb
Nothing or earth is easy or free,
But heaven is great, we all must agree.
Open your heart, it's much easier you'll find
When you earnestly pray, "Thy will, Lord, not mine."

Barbara K. Griffin

Untitled

Sadness fills me deep within
For the things that could have been
Who knows what the future did hold
For the children killed before they were old.
Judgement was passed by a man very odd
Who put himself in the place of God
The steel and bricks fell to the ground
People deafened by the hellish sound
The story that rocked the nation
Was carried on every station
This man decided who should live or die
All we can do is pray and cry
Now we all sleep less well
Because of these scenes from hell
Never has terror hit so close to home
And discover it comes from one of our own
We should not just slip into a coma
Lets bend our heads and remember Oklahoma

Sharon Sloan

On The Threshold Of A Dream

We've worked so hard for so many years
Through many a heartache, trials and tears
we're done our work that is finally done, and
we've spent many an hour in the sun
and now we are all on the edge of a dream
we've accomplished a lot just to
get our work done. Finally we realize
our dream with all the plans and schemes.

Now it's time just to step backs and
take a good look, whether it's on
the job or in some school with
your brooks, or being a nurse,
Homemaker teacher, or working
in the oil fields, or parents of
little ones, or a grandmother
who has had her day. Now it's
time just to retire, or go on a
long vacation or a cruise ship
that's all we have to do is to
realize our vacation and live to paradise.

Anna R. Maynard

The Walk

Walking down the street
Shoes slapping the asphalt floor.
Knowing laughter and shrill whistles —
Submission in progress.

Their lewd thoughts follow you down,
push you in the dirt,
stuff the mud in your cries
until no tears can wash you clean.

Smirking eyes try to steal
the music from your hips,
ignoring the shame
that seeps into your cheeks.

Your pretty face — a past ally,
pulls your head under,
distorting the self-claimed power
you once thought you had.

They know when you're feeling small.
Only wanting to hide from their . . . motives.
You can only keep your head from falling.
Ignoring them as they've always ignored You.

Jessica Jones

The Dream

That night her dream came true,
Her prince in shining armor.
There was nothing he could do,
Or say that would harm her.
In his arms he holds her,
Telling her all she wanted to hear.
If only he would have told her,
That midnight was drawing near.
Her dream would have to end,
Soon she would have to wake up.
Her heart would never mend,
After finding his words were made up.
Now as she sits here crying,
Her heart begins to dance, her head starts to spin.
Thinking of him, she feels like dying,
But she'd still do it all over again.

Hillary Thomas

A Man's Justice

Dead man walking shouted the guard
as you walked your last steps
down a drab-colored corridor
the walls are closing in Time Is Running Out
you look for your friends
you look for your family
your mother's tears and pain
forever engraved in your mind
no one is there Are You Scared?
Alone your stockinged feet feel the cold, hard floor
only ten steps to freedom
and the words of the guard ring in your ears
dead man walking
You Last Supper still digesting in your stomach
with each nervous step your eyes burn bright blue
and tears sting your pallid skin
you take your last few steps as a child first learns to walk
and you wonder... will death bring you justice
or will their justice be your death?

Vicki L. Van Arsdale

Untitled

A familiar face wakes you up first thing in the morning,
a warm smile a sturdy hand yet gentle to the touch
With fire in the eyes, if you do anything to up set
her offspring, her work is never done and her
wardrobe changes from sun to sun, one day a doctor
next a mechanic she will be strong in case of a panic
Always looking for the best in a person no matter
what the problem she'll help find the answer.
She's a queen of queens, and a diamond in a ruff,
the warmest of beings I just can't say enough
So let's get down on our knees and thank the Lord
above for blessing us with a mothers precious love

Think about it...

Theo B. Broadnat Sr.

Everlasting Love

My love is gone, no one can know how much I miss
His warm embrace, a good night kiss
Talking things over the problems of the day
That we solved together in our own special way.
His suffering is over; now a peaceful sleep.
I sorrow but happy memories I keep
Life must go on Friends all say
But through a maze of tears, I cannot see the way.
Go on ahead by darling but kindly wait for me
It won't be too long and together we will be.

Yola McCallum

"Ising"

"Being" stated by itself
has limits as a pantry shelf.
Each is held within confines —
one to life and one to wines.
Although a shelf is very long,
and to have life is to be strong,
that isn't all upon the earth
that shares in living - human worth.
There are those things which do not live,
and yet impart to the human sieve
bits of matter to make one think,
adding strength to the human link.
All life has both shape and form,
and to nature's laws it must perform,
to limits of "being" it must conform.
But thinking is the art of "Ising."

Barbara Birenbaum

Fearful Whisper

Midnight it is, a new moon leaves no light. Enthroned upon rooftop,
a shape darker than the night. The raven whispers, is it "never
more" that you hear? Or a silent message colder still that hovers near.

This summons has been heard before, no age has escaped the unearthly chime.
This fearful icy whisper, that stretches throughout the
width and breadth of time. Damp and cold like early morning mist,
clinging as a shroud that cannot be shed. Oh, if only there were
someone who would answer in my stead.

What is this force that haunts us so, causing even grown men to cry?
An invocation that can come at any time, as quietly as a sigh.
It is life's stalking mystery, that leaves no life in its trail.
Crushing man's dreams of immortality, into the dust of a child's fairy tale.

Many of those that I loved, have heeded this invitation before.
Keeping the inevitable appointment that we have all come to abhor.
Helplessly I watch the temporal dreams they have weaved, unravel and unwind.
Leaving a lonely place in my life, where their presence used to reside.

Where to hide, what shield to raise, to protect human kind from the
finality of the grave? When our ship for Valhalla finally sets
sail, who will help us to cross that veil?

"Good news!" Sings the white dove, there is a hand outstretched.
Available to one and all who recognize this life as a test.
A glad hope so bright that it outshines the sun.
Peace of mind for all of those who look to the Son.

John E. Webb Jr.

Generation X

Where are we going?
What will we do?
Every day we hear about a crime committed,
A murder, a robbery, a slaying,
What have we become?
A society of barbarians,
Where only the strong survive.
We are named Generation X,
But will we become Generation Z?
The last Generation,
The last of our species.
Will we kill ourselves off?
Will we be the last?
It's time to stop fighting against one another,
And start working together.
Together to build a society.
It started with the dinosaurs,
But will it end with us?

John J. Infanti

Sometimes, I Cry . . .

Sometimes, I want to reach out, . . . and deep
Within the souls of the unfortunate ones . . .
Instead, I cry . . .
And the salts from my tears reach even deeper . . .

Adib Abdullah Rasheed

Think About It!

You think, "Hey, it's a party."
You think you're having fun.
You think you're in control.

You think you can handle him.
You think he cares for you.

You think he'll stop if you ask.
You think he'll be safe.

You think he'll say he's sorry.
You think he'll ask for forgiveness.
You think you misunderstood.
You think it was all a nightmare.

You think you can forget.
You think the nightmares will stop.

You think you want to kill him.
You think you'll go crazy.

You think no one will believe you.
You think they'll say it was your fault.
You think, "if only I'd . . ."

You think about it — all the time.

Anja Schaefer

To My Guarding Shadow

Mother,
    Cloudless climes and starry skies,
        Gave way to tears and loving cries.
            A child was born with your brown eyes,
A child, a son, a soul, and a person of whom you gave rise.

Somehow,
    Deep within your flawless your form,
        There lies a self so gently tender,
            Splendidly solving my subsequent failures
            And sheltering my shattered frame;
Indifferent, endlessly eternal, and silently remembers

Forever,
    Your soft replies my question call,
        Leave deep puddles of thoughts for me to ponder.
            Yet somehow your soft voice,
            Will always answer,
My dreams, my hopes, and my remaining wonders.

Darren G. Sher

Wisps

Foolish girl! She is but a child who knows naught
of grandeur and splendor, only wisps of pleasure.
This girl, this child hath vast carnal knowledge, yet
hungers love. Her sky-blue eyes are clouded by distant
dreams, dreams of but one man. Her soul craves
his. He is the wine that quenches her thirst for love.
Would but she could have his heart! But,
alas, tis not to be, for only her heart sings
this tune. Her lips doth not repeat these
lyrics of love. Why, pray tell? But one question plaques
her, "Doth he return thy love?" Pride will not let her
ask, and pride will snap her taut heartstrings.

Sheila Colleen Larson

"Lead With Your Heart!"

You can't walk backward into the future,
Or forward into the past.
You can't compress hours or minutes,
For each one may be the last!

If you can't wear a smile, if you can't sing a song,
You and your guardian angel
May never get along!

You don't have to be your mother;
You don't have to be your dad,
But if your heart rules your head,
You'll always lack money,
But you'll always be not quite bad!

For the person who looks up to God
Doesn't find Him in the steeple;
Because of Him that person
Never looks down on people!

Mark McCall

"Seek, Search And Find"

Ye shall seek and search,
Ye shall respond and be present,
Stay awake until the end of day
Be alive until the setting of sun.

Listen, listen and hear, stir up the flame,
There is hope and love does abide,
Shoulder the joy and pain.
Stretch the mind, do the things you need to do.

Awake community!
Hug the old-embrace the children
Live as "we" — and not as "I"!
Discard the lust of the day!

Be aware of what you are saying —
Be aware of what you are doing —
Experience your life as lovable.
As we are beloved by God.

Live the life of the spirit.
Feed the hungry,
Clothe the poor.
Pray for the wicked, and prepare for Glory!

Johanna Wolfe Dubensky

Trandameric

Sundiferous she said, as a wink closed the eyelids of the
venetian blinds . . . See? No, blinds. Then, as if on cue, the
American Eagle rose to the occasion . . . A rose, by any other
name wouldn't fly however. Wander to wonder if the bread is
fresh, as friendships stale for reasons of the superfluous . . .
Never floating on that superior liquid.

Trandameric to query, went meandering in search of the preponderance
. . . What is life? Packing quickly, the product boxed was endeared
by Mikey . . . What does he know anyway, he's just a kid.

Quandiclitis, her passing fancy was noted to depart.
Nevermind arrival . . . It was her passing fancy in a plain brown
wrapper, uneventful.

Frondermatiscent, in climbing the corporate ladder was heard
to say: "Have you wrung your hands too often at my exploits?"
And continued hand over fist, and boot to the tooth . . . It is a
long way down after all.

Waximenternal. The moon waxed as Wane bid you good nocturne.

Scott G. Flax

Rockets

That night on the beach, you looking for stars,
The Dippers, Andromeda, Venus and Mars,
Scanning the heavens, as beachwalkers do,
Til you turned and saw me looking at you.

You stared, you shivered, was it fright?
Or just the seabreeze in the night?
As you suddenly knew: we at last alone.
I heard you give a little moan.

"I've waited so long for you," you said,
And rockets went off inside my head.
Then your lips were warm, I felt them part,
And rockets blew apart my heart.

How wonderful, what happened then,
Rockets exploding again and again.
I aching for the whole of you,
Striving to reach the soul of you.

When finally I opened my eyes to the sky,
Expecting millions of rockets on high,
I couldn't believe the quiet night air.
I couldn't believe that the moon was still there.

A. T. Kline

Daughter Of Light

There you stand all dressed in white
In your eyes Jesus' light shines bright
I have watched you grow in body and spirit
Frustrated by your questions, yet you wouldn't hear it

A parent is a guide here on earth

But Jesus is your key to heavenly birth
I can hold you in joy and sorrow
But Jesus helps you through tomorrow

Bow your head and say your prayer
The Lord you know is always there
As I sit here filled with parental pride
My little princess is now Jesus' bride

Kneel now before the host
Accept in faith the Holy Ghost
Enjoy the banquet of bread and wine
No greater feast shall you come to dine.

Rebecca Sweat

Waiting

Listen for the sigh, That escapes from her lips
 As the long lonely day slips into darkness

She will gaze at the shadows, As a smile lights her eyes
 And she hold a bit of moonlight in her hands

Waiting for him to come knocking
Waiting for him to come around

She whispers his name to the cool summer stars
Hoping somehow they'll guide him along

To the place at her side, where the shadows lie still
where she holds a bit of moonlight in her hands

Waiting for him to come knocking
Waiting for him to come around

Now her days are all gone, yes she sits in the night
Though the light in her eyes has grown dim

With the hopes that she's held, for so long in her hands
She's still waiting, still waiting for him

Waiting for him to come knocking
Waiting for him to come around

Timothy L. Blevins

Those Special Words

Some things are too hard to say,
If I could only think of a way.

To announce my love to thee.
I know that we were meant to be.

I wish you would just give me a chance,
We could make some romance.

You're too blind by love to see,
What I know and believe.

Please say you love me too,
But I know that would be too good to be true.

Why can't say you say you love me,
As much as I love thee?

I hope, dream, and pray,
That one day you will look at me and say:

I love you,
And then I would smile and say I love you too.

Hollie Shannon

When All Is Lost

When the world is deep in thought
We forget the fight must be fought
When a life has lived and won't live anymore
We bury it in our soul but never close the door
When the battle is fought but somehow lost
We remember the price should we pay the cost
When the children are gone and the dreams are shattered
We dare try again if only it had mattered
When the sun has lost its shine and the moon has turned red
We forget all love and hope for our hearts are dead
When love has turned to hate and hope is despair
We shall drown in a tear to find peace in a prayer
When all has come and gone and blind eyes now see
We shall know the only hope is what you can be
When everything has lost interest and there's no love without cost
We know we shall fall when all is lost

Charity Beckett

Goodbye Mother

Wasn't it just yesterday you brushed away my tears when I fell off my bike and you kissed away my hurts?

Wasn't it just yesterday you walked me to school my very first day and assured me you would be waiting when I returned?

Wasn't it just yesterday I sat on your bed and confided to you that I was in love for the first time?

Wasn't it just yesterday you held me in your arms as I sobbed over a broken love affair?

And wasn't it just yesterday I called you on the phone excitedly and told you I had found the man I was going to marry?

Wasn't it just yesterday you sped to my side and cried tears of joy over the birth of my first child?

Wasn't it just yesterday I realized all the wonderful and selfless things you had done because of your love for me?

And wasn't it just yesterday when I realized as I held you in my arms that you had grown old and tired and wanted to leave your earthly pains behind and go home to your Lord?

Then the yesterday came when we had to say goodbye. You could not hold me in your arms to console me as you had done so many times before. But as I kissed you goodbye I knew you had left me all your yesterdays to remember and love you for, and in one of our future tomorrows we shall be together again to relive our yesterdays for eternity.

Mary Ellen Galo

When Death Comes

When death comes like a beautiful massacre
Like a rainy day in August
Like a slap in the face

I want to walk through the door with confidence,
Not afraid of the other side

I want to know that I lived life
And didn't just pass through

And therefore I will live my life
With no regrets or disappointments
I will experience every moment
With despair and happiness at the same time

When I graduate from the school of life
I want to have learned to live
So that I know how to die

Christian Strauli

To My Daughter

Scraps of satin and lace lay as I wander back through time to see a child's face shining in my memories . . .

You were only three just yesterday with
strawberry cream hair waving around your
face and chubby little hands reaching up
for mine . . .

You were just seven — riding a bicycle,
playing with your dolls, searching for
a personality that suited you . . .

You were just a teenager driving me crazy,
skipping school, being the best beer drinker
at the party and satisfied that you hadn't
made the worst grade on the history exam . . .

Yesterday, it seems like it was yesterday.

And yet, here you are today, in satin and lace and pearls and I am filled with pride and joy and wonder. How did you travel so far so quickly? You are grown and beautiful and the little girl captured in my memories has become this other wonderful person — my equal, my ally, my confidant. My child . . . My daughter . . . My friend.

Joyce E. Kelly

Black Woman

Black woman let me apologize for the wrong that I have done.
Last night I left you alone,
from my own soul I'm on the run.
While caught up in the idea of being an American man,
I failed in my duties to you,
abandoning your heart in this wicked land.

Looked upon as lower than life,
given weapons and vials of crack,
yet my anger reserved for the world, fell upon you,
the very one who watched my back.
Now only a shadow of my former self,
an empty shell of what I used to be,
in my struggle to find equality,
along the way I lost me.

Who would've know that last night would last so long,
or the difficulties I'd have finding my way home?
Home is where honor, compassion, and truth reside,
but I sold my key for a diluted dream,
and for this, I apologize.

Brandon Luster

Be Careful About The Things You Desire

Unable to breathe freely, choking and gagging
The room was filling with a veil of smoke
Red eyed and crying out of pure terror and pain
Burning alive in the place you considered your sanctuary
Death was all you thought about — obsessed
Dying was the only way out you wanted to see
Your silent cries unheard by the one's around you is what you believed
believing there was no possible hope for your chaotic and confused lost soul
A single persistent need to ask for help from the people in your life
With open and out stretched arms they offer up all they posses inside
They would give it all away to save you
With your back now towards them & once again you're facing the
    darkest crevices in your life
Nineteen years seemed so long but yet it was just a small taste of
    what could have been
Now trapped by fate, death inevitable
Now after years of wasted life on the bad things and plans of suicide
Why?
Now faced with your true end, you change your mind . . .
But it's too late after death my dearest friend

Sarah Jane Kersh

I Miss You Wildly . . .

More so, I miss you touching me,
teasing me,
caressing and kissing me.

I miss the sparkle in your eyes
and the slippery feeling of your hair sliding through my fingers.

I miss the warmth of your skin pressed up hard against mine,
and the rhythmic dance of your body, while when mounted atop
of mine the way it skillfully and masterfully navigates and
explores the uncharted rhythmic sea in me.

I miss your fingers artfully fertilizing and nurturing the deepest
seed of my womanhood and the volcanic fire that sears through
me when you bring its rare and precious flower to a full bloom.
I miss you suckling on the breast of the mother and your gender
tool enveloped and pulsating inside of mine.

I miss the serene complacency that falls upon us when darkness
creeps over the land, when the stars steal our consciousness up
to the sky an lays them about in a field of dreams.

I miss the morning sun kissing us and urging us to arise and the
gentle embrace you gather me in before you depart and bid me
well on my journey through the day.

Marjorie Morningstar Korecki

Rustling Stars T-shirt

Now that I've laid it down,
took if off and laid it
down (this T-shirt),
do they really have to come
and rustle in it? (The cockroaches).
I sweat sweetly, I'm hot a lot, I
don't even think of drawing them near
to my body again (my arms). Summer at its height.

(It could have fluttered hanging on the line, it could
  have contained: wind. Air of its bird's wrath air.
It could have hung down dripping and down toward the
  ground heavily disabused. But it's not that wet.
Put on, taken off now down there crumpled. And rustling.)

He's not wearing it (I'm not wearing it) inside out anymore,
for inside out it was (I was) there, in the ashes, (in the
sugar ashes) in the sugar ashes, and instead of bees, small
as freckles, pulsatile (as stars) if only you could hear them,
the cockroaches.

Niculescu Mihai-Vlad

You, Potential Energy

You stand behind a closed door
And although you are not visible — I see you,
as you are, violent in an instant.

As you are, I realize that YET AGAIN I have been duped
Into believing that 2 polarities could coincide
In a fairly-priced, mildly affluent roach encampment —
without the civil war of the Moors and the Spaniards

You the dynamite
And I the anxious flame . . .

I see you as the innovator that you are
Giving flight to insults that linger like your cigarette smoke

Arsonist of friendship
Unibomber of (domestic) civility
Agreements nulled and voided by the sound of your hiss . . .

As you are I realize
That you are no amiga — ni amante,

But you do not understand the importance
Of these words, ni de otras:
Vibora, traidora, desgraciada — and you never will . . .

Being that I just apologized

April Cox

Dream Treasure

Daddy, oh daddy, come and walk with me.
Let the daisies lead the way.
Daddy, oh daddy, let me pick the ones
That are here for us today.
I can throw them far to the sun above,
To fall back on our path.
Daddy, dear daddy, let me be with you,
To talk of times we've passed.
Me, you protect, and guard with your life,
So I feel loved, loved true.
My daddy, dear daddy, where would you be?
I've searched the earth for you.
A daddy, true daddy, a treasure would be.
There are flowers near the trees,
To pick, arrange, for my daisy colored world,
Throw to the sky, the breeze.

Nancy L. Brown

Death Of All That No Longer Serves You

Winter, winter, why must you be so cold
have you not a heart in one of those souls
Snow, snow, why do you melt away
have you not learned how to play different roles

Winter, winter, your heavy body breaks branches
do you not know when to stop destroying
Snow, snow, your innocent coat will soon be dirty
do you not care to be lifted and soaring

Winter, winter, you give water to the land
why do you do so in the coldest of forms
Snow, snow, you shed light on the city
why do you do so in the darkest of forms

Winter, winter, your peace brings discomfort
have you not learned how to love unconditionally
Snow, snow, your warmth always freezes
have you not a mind to think more thoroughly

Winter, winter, some day your time will pass
do you not hate missing the season of love
Snow, snow, spring will soon melt my tears
do you not know you'll always fall from above

Jaime G. Louise Jaramillo

Untitled

When it is my time to walk
the trail beyond the sun,
As the journey has just begun
Jesus will say, "Here comes my son."
He will take my burdens and my hand,
Looking toward Heaven say, "This is my man."
Those behind as the tears flood,
Jesus will say at the alter, "I spilled my blood,
for this one and you, too,
Don't grieve, don't be blue.
Look up to Heaven and rejoice!
Be prepared to hear His voice."

Connie McClinton

The River's Catch

Here by the river with my grandchild Rebecca I sit,
'Tis late afternoon as I sit and knit,
Then up at the clear, blue sky I gaze —
And then, at the river so long and wide,
Even the trees cannot it hide,
Thoughts rush rapidly through my mind's memory;
Did I ever explore the river's wondrous possibilities?

Fish large and small, so abundantly, within the river swim,
Sportsmen, happily taste of the catch therein
Fishing's a joy for most everyone,
and youngsters swim at the river's edge, rushing in one by one.
So much does the river pour out
But, so few, its wonders do shout!

The river washes, cleanses and bathes,
Mothers fathers, children, and little babes;
Boating, surfing, and sailing - all wonderful to explore
As the river gives, and gives its treasures to forever pour,
So thanks do sing to nature's offspring
But, most of all, thank Him —
God Eternal, who created everything!

Marguerite Rocco Orsomarso

Hard Eyes

Cutlass eyes lash out,
quickly from frame to frame,
too intently focused than necessary,
shooting icy cold photons outward radially,
instead of gently passively sensing softly,
seeking the refuge of pure thought,
letting true sight enter the mind.

Richard A. Weddle

Calendar

Calendar time seems so simple,
Flattened down without a wrinkle,
Measured in inches and anchored on a page,
A maximum endeavor in a minimum of space.
To level the ups and downs of fortune,
Every day gets an equal portion.
Side by side, from left to right,
The blocks they leave are still in sight.
Yesterdays lead the way.
Tomorrows wait in line.
Today is the square from where we measure time.
Staying in step with an old tradition,
Spaces are left for notes to be written.
No need for batteries or electrical wire.
Calendars continue. They never expire.

Genevieve R. Griffin

My Future Home

In that beautiful rose covered garden,
   By the gentle flowing sea,
Walking hand and hand with my savior,
   How beautiful, heaven will be.

It's sad to think of leaving loved ones
   But God will care for His own.
Drawing them ever nearer,
   Gently guiding them home

Think, of the happy reunion,
   with loved ones gone on before,
Many are waiting to greet me,
   with Jesus, on that beautiful shore.

Ruth C. Guyer

Stand Quiet

Stand quiet and listen in the presence of God.
Listen and hear with reverence and awe.

Do not be hasty to walk away.
Listen with your heart, stand and obey.

Who knows better than God what we must do?
We must take the moments He asks, not just a few.

For if we make rash promises that we don't intend to keep.
Then we pile our sins on our head in a great big heap.

Rash words and unkept promises are meaningless unto the Lord
He wants us to come to Him, body, soul and spirit, all of one accord.

Great things He can work through and for us,
If we just stand, stand, stand and wait for Jesus

Karon Schlicker

Goodbye, Dad

Dad is gone now, he just slipped away,
God wanted him home, so he couldn't stay;
Not even long enough to say "Goodbye," "Farewell,"
Or "I love you all."
God summoned him home, and he answered the call.

Our loss is so great,
It's too much to bear,
Without the strength
Of having Dad here.

But we must be strong and live as Dad taught;
Square our shoulders and do what we ought.
Life is not easy, or timely, or fair.
But trust in God and the strength will be there.

Goodbye to you, Dad.
We all love you so.
We know you'll be waiting
When it's our turn to go.

Nancy J. Frees

Ghosts And Memories

Ghosts are guilt and confusion.
Memories are comfort and joy.

Ghosts are something chased by fools.
Memories are what we learn by.

Ghosts attack and leave in doubt.
Memories linger to touch when needed.

Ghosts are anger, range, pain,
   and cop out from reality.
Memories are what you hold to touch when needed.

George G. Gargano

Just As . . .

Just as sure as the sun shine everyday.
Just a sure as the moon shines every night.
Just as sure as the rain falls from the sky.
Just as sure as He promised His everlasting love to us.
Just as sure as he promised that whoever believes in Him
   has everlasting life in His Kingdom.
Just as sure as His love for you is more special than any other.
Remember and don't forget,
   when you need strength and guidance be humble.
Get down on your knees and pray for His help
   that he so readily gives to all.
For He loves you more than all He has created in the universe.
Take time and look around and be amazed by His awesome Power.
For He can give you so much life, if you give him yours.

Patricia Adkins

Khanapara Our Alma Mater

Within the crest of the Himalayan mountains
Our beloved college in memory comes to view
With knowledge flowing freely as fountains
With friends and classmates long ever true.

We will always be shouting praises of the college we hold dear
Of her green slopes — jungle and villagers near
From India's plains and mountains we assemble in Assam
At Khanapara — place of knowledge, and syllabus exam.

Onward Assam Veterinary College our Alma Mater true
Love ever present and in retrospect always for you
Ever praising her athletes and entertainers without fear
Teachers and friends always in our memory revered

Leisurely resting under soft light of the moon
Listening quietly to barking deer and foxes or sitar's tune
Playing-working-studying fretfully with the mosquitoes hum
With eagerness and hope to Khanapara we come.

Our college we love in hot sunshine or harvest moon
We turn to her in weather clear or during monsoon
Campus of winding pathways — rocks and hills without water
Faithfully we stand by you still our Alma Mater.

Harold Wood

"I Know"

"I know" not to climb or I'll fall and get hurt,
I know you climbed anyway and now you tore your shirt.

"I know" not to ride with people I don't know,
I know now you're gone and I don't know where to go.

"I know" about sex, you've taught me so much,
I know you let someone touch where he shouldn't touch.

"I know" not to drink 'cause I could fall into trouble,
I know that you're drunk 'cause with me you want to rumble.

"I know" that school's important, without it I'm nothing,
I know now you're a dropout, now what, welfare or something?

"I know" to use protection, I don't want no baby,
I know that you're pregnant, are you getting the picture maybe?

"I know" not to date just any man I meet,
I know you've been beaten and the rest is not discrete.

"I know" smoking or dealing's not the right thing to do,
I know I don't have bail money for the judge for you.

"I know" I should listen but I don't know why,
I know you look sick and at times I must cry.

"I know" that diseases such as AIDS can kill,
I know it's time for you to write your will, I love you.

Elizabeth Anderson

We Are The Bridge

We jam to different music yet dance to the same beat
We are the bridge to complete

Why is there prejudice of color or race
That is the poison that we taste

For if the rotten rind we don't peel
The bitter center we will feel

Sitting before us is the great crown
Let's put it together and dance like clowns

We are the bridge, you, I, everyone
Do it for your granddaughter and her son

All the colors mesh together, on a canvas plate
The river will channel us, erode the hate

Melting pot of spirit human kind
Water and sunshine a garden to find

The great puzzle should not be divided
The right piece should be provided

We jam to different music yet dance to the same beat
We are the bridge to complete

Kyle Williams

The Rapist And His Victims

How many times must I die?
You're the stranger, you still lie.

So little did you have to pay . . .
They were your victims, they were your prey.

So smug you act, you show no remorse . . .
But someday you will get caught in the act, of course.

You're toying with everyone's minds this far . . .
You have others thinking what a so-called human being you are.

But the wise can see beyond that and someday they will all know the
truth about you . . .
How you played a lot of people for the fool.

When you think it's over, you will dare . . .
A few more victims you will snare.

Lois Johnson

The Dawn Of Mourning

Awoke my mind
Before the rest,
Wrested from slumber's weak grip . . .
As body lingered deep.
Broke my mind
The fetters of early primeval mist,
And peaked above its shroud . . .
Unencumbered by flesh and bone of birth
Borne high, toward a wee voice,
Weaned of earthly restraint,
And spoke of things profound
   and times sublime.
And strolled across the dappled coolness of morning,
And mourned the dawn.
But then awoke my head, and fled the voice
Beyond the chirping of a sparrow.
Sole and secluded it sings . . .
   of things profound
   and times sublime.

Robert G. Johnson

"Fingerprints On My Heart"

Around me was a cloak of azure blue, birds called in a myriad of songs akin to foreign-tongued calling to their brood.

I was in repose in paradise as the sun climbed the stairs of heaven, a Giant holding a lantern glowing with rose-colored light, wishing to illuminate mankind, with an opalescent glow.

Pondering what my destiny was, while surrounded by potato peel and passions I paused in my solitude, holding back salt-laden tears surging forward from behind that Dam where that Dutch Boy held his finger in.

I remember yesterday, long passed, ever near, squeezing at that vulnerable place where feeling dwells like the bread-maker kneading his dough, leaving fingerprints and bruises on my heart.

Birds give a symphony for life, that awesome lantern has illuminated my sacred place. My bruised heart, now worn, is warmed by the sun and sound of life. I know You are there still for me.

One black night, on the wings of the wind, behind tears of the rain, You visited me in my desperate hour. I prayed for death. Icons sinking, You whispered to me of life and changed my course. I could no longer tread the murky undertow of my troubled young existence. You gave me a lifeline; You sent me a friend. She is with me still. Her name is Helen.

Edna M. Alduino

Escape

The sea so full of great power
The mountains so peaceful with no worry at all
The valleys so full of beauty in all seasons
Wild flowers full of beautiful colors
Colors of a rainbow after a first rain
Waterfalls so clear and pure

To go to these beautiful places
To think when I am troubled
Takes my troubles away
Makes my feelings clear and free
From pain and anger built up inside

To release my feelings into the surroundings
Relax my soul at the sea mountains or valleys
Where that place may be
To watch the eagle soar above
Free from anger with no worry at all.

Theresa M. Holaway

Courtney At One

You were born one year ago today,
Oh, what a night we had.
Dad was supportive
Mom abortive
But all turned out okay.

You were born so perfectly
Not a mark had you
All fingers and toes
All arms and legs
Were there for all to see.

We brought you home one fine sunny day,
So proud and anxious were we.
Should we diaper now,
Should we call the doctor,
Or read the book anyway?

That beautiful smile beamed so bright
From nearly a month on.
You brought joy to our lives,
You filled an empty space.
You made our lives just right.

Myra Lezanic

Night Stare

I often sit upon my porch at night, and stare up in the sky.
The moon sits like a beacon, welcoming me to this sight.
Its light is only broken, when a cloud goes slowly by.

I marvel at the light of stars, and the distance it had to travel.
The mysteries and wonders it must have seen, as it passed along the way.
If only we had wings to fly, our boundaries would unravel.

I think about the planets, and their distance from the sun.
How blessed earth is to be neither too close or too far.
How ignorant we really are, to think were the only one.

Daniel T. Kehoe

Autumn 1995

Feather silent, they flow across
    this red maple sky
Crying their way toward the warmth of summer.

Long they travel, in their searching
    driven perhaps by woodsmoke
Or that first slow dawning of day.

Their cries are lonely, filled with longing
    though they do not sing alone
Their path predestined, they gather, and lift into the sky.

And surging, soaring, into morning
Strong wings bear them toward the season
    of fireflies and tadpoles and sleepy summer days.

A snowflake falls,
    leaves flutter to the earth
Feather silent.

Nora Starr

Untitled

There stands a tombstone on a hill
All around it's very still
Standing there at the lonesome plot
Long forgotten whats in the lot.

It's a ghoulish thing that granite stone
Standing there so stark and lone
Time has worn its letters bare
I wonder how long it's been standing there.

The graveyard emits squeamish moans
Sometimes it even howls and groans
Cold winds whistle through barren trees
Rustling dried and fallen leaves.

I can't forget that forlorn place
Or how the spirits run and chase
The whole yard is filled with fear
As it lies forgotten year by year.

V. Myrle Coffman

Progress

Salamander whispering on webbed waxed toes
Brown rock and tree bark know where he goes
Fat green frog eyes a lazy dragonfly
Pirouetting in mid-air, singing hushabye
Snake eggs are hatching; tiny snakelets slither scurry
Eagerly in search of mom, who isn't in a hurry
Furry squirrel pauses in his search for nuts and berries
To smell aromas from the flowers, plentiful and merry
Brilliant birds sing out, rejoicing; building, feeding, living love
Gliding, swooping, summer dancing, flirting with the clouds above
Moss and mushroom, crystal stream, faerie dust is falling
Trees are laughing with the wind; can they escape the chain saw calling?

Gina Daidone

471

Quirks And Quarks And The Me, Recycled

Me! Eternal pioneer!
You'd think I would have had enough
By this, my fifteen billionth year.

At creation, I appear,
— Specks of me as swirling stuff —
That time for sure a pioneer!

Combine, explode, then re-appear!
Just Universe-al blindman's buff,
And now, my fifteen billionth year

Made me! One more coat — a new veneer
On re-assembled, borrowed stuff
Forms an eternal pioneer.

Grant at least I persevere!
(Stale, recycled, cosmic slough!
And now, my fifteen billionth year.)

Will some night-calling chanticleer
Ever crow a final snuff
For me, eternal pioneer
Now in my fifteen billionth year?

Isabel Ernst

Spring Wheel

The weaker sort of little brave importance
who think them brave;
And the poor despised truth sat counting
By their victory;
Oh fools, they said to prefer dark night
Before truth light;
To line in grate and hate each day
Does not show the way
The way which from the death and darkness
Leads up to God
A way where you might tread the sun and sky
True light
One cannot pin all life with
scarce trust
Make me O' Lord — The spinning wheel complete
All pinked with nourished flowers of paradise
That I be clothed in holy robe of glory.

Percilla Nader

Images On The Water

Droplets of fine oil
gently falling to my bath

Entranced within their beauty
floating down their path

At first they were like faces
looking up at me

They merged to be bombarded
and yet another be

I saw fish and stars and mountains
rabbits and much more

They touched and split and passed along
never fighting any war

They lived a life of peacefulness
as though they did belong

Before me they created a verse
to my life's song

They played and danced on water
no sound at all to hear

And then a moment later
I saw them disappear

Andrea T. Iott

Life's Journey

I am being driven forward.
The path ahead grows steeper,
The terrain becomes rockier.
At my back the air is warm and calm;
The wind at my face is cool, fresh and sharp.
The threads of life stir in expectation;
My goal no longer seems beyond reach.
I have waded streams and swum rivers.
I have crossed canyons and climbed mountains.
Yet, there is still a moment of hesitation;
The sun is no longer at my back to light my way.
Instead, it is blinding my already tired eyes.
I can no longer see my way along the trail
So I must walk aimlessly —
Trying to avoid the burrows and stumps
That cover my path.
I know soon the sun will set, and there will be
Total darkness —
Except for the stray moonbeam
That will attempt to light my way.

Jean M. Martin

A Veteran And His Flag

I looked, and what did I see?
But our flag as pretty as could be.
Its colors of red, white and blue,
Shining so brightly for me and for you.

While watching that flag upon its pole
I started to recall its many roles
Over many different places it has flown
In many countries as well as your own.

Sometimes it was flown over a conquered land,
Placed on a hill, mountain or even in sand.
I remember once — a long time ago —
That our flag stood proudly all aglow.

It stood proudly on a hill in Saipan,
An island we took away from Japan.
It was a glorious sight for all to behold
For those who had fought and were so bold.

But for me, I wanted the world to realize
That my flag to me is still a prize.
I'd never burn it, stomp it, or tear it to shreds
I have too much respect for the living and dead.

Edmund J. Nickerson

A Greenhurst Day

Was a cloudy day, on a brisk fall morning, in late September,
I was driving to work. The clouds in the sky were like
Ocean currents, waves, curled above as the winds swept by.
It was thick up there...to thick for flying,
Birds bolted to earth like leaves from the trees.
On hills and in valleys, cows were laying;
And the geese stopped over to visit with these.
The deer were restless, though I couldn't see them
I felt their presence with the cool of the air.
There is nothing like nature to stir the spirit
the presence of God is everywhere.
I wonder why sometime we just can't see it,
the beauty around us, so sweet and serene,
We have all the comforts and joy that is needed,
The things in nature have made it so plain.
I feel, I can spread my wings like great geese flying
run through the forest with swift moving feet,
Lay down at night, see stars above me,
In song, or on canvas, I can do all these,
Yes, I know, I can do all these.

Margaret Moore

Nuclear Lullaby

Sleep little baby, sweet child of love
  keep your eyes shut, don't look above —
A great ball of fire has covered the sky
  and we'll all blow away, away bye and bye —

Ten little Indians all in a row
  one little match caused the world to blow —
And all the king's horses and all the king's men
  can't put the earth together again —

I'll hold you forever, if forever may be
  if only a second for you and for me —
And the dust made a pattern as they lay side by side
  while the cradle rocked softly and the lullaby died —

And the dust made a pattern as they lay side by side
While the cradle rocked softly and the lullaby died.

  Amen.

Jane Graves

A Prophetic Kiss

A prophetic kiss, the joy untold,
An everlasting love, what the future holds,
Worries, and troubles, come what may,
Our love together, will never fray,
A life together, built as one,
No matter what, will not be undone,
I pray you'll love me, I wonder why,
You seem to pay no attention, and pass me by,
Being with you, the joy I feel,
The feelings I have, are just unreal,
I am ecstatic, I played my blues,
Nothing more to say, I love you!

Joel Lynn Clausen

"Success"

  Success is attained by persistence.
Perpetuated success is the art of diligence.
Consistency is the very essence of continued
acquirement. Having the ability to perceive
the future helps to maintain success, being
charismatic isn't enough. Extrapolated goals
are your directives. Allow for patience. Let
"New found knowledge mentor you," and be your
guide to "infinite wisdom". Eloquence and
maturity will expedite your efforts!!
Ascertainable success is measured by achieving
personal goals and having a sense of euphoria,
  Based on your accomplishments.
"Remember, always think intellectually"
"Success"

Nathan Earl Robinson

Scared

Endless days and sleepless nights
What once were big dreams have become my frights
I look and I see where it all went wrong
Too proud to concede, a will far too strong
It's all so unclear, the pain won't subside
I look to the next day and hope we'll survive
My breathes seem shorter, and not so intense
my body is weary, I've lost all that makes sense
It's all so confusing, I wish I could pretend
that the nights aren't so dark, and these days will soon end

Karen Atwell

Web Of Dreams

Living in a world of sorrow,
All she can do is dream
About the person she will never be,
About the things she will never do,
About the places she will never go.
She believes in fairy tales and fantasies,
In cotton candy clouds and sugarplum fairies,
In diamond dewdrops and chocolate rivers.
She believes in magic spells and love potions,
In crystal castles and streets of gold,
In unicorns and enchanted forests.
She believes that one day her prince
Will rescue her from her pain.
Until then she stands alone
In a cruel and hateful world
Weaving, thread by silky thread,
Her web of dreams.

Valerie Martz

Question And Rhyme

How do rhinos kiss you say
  With such big horns atop their noses?
Well, they do just fine you see
  As long as neither rhino dozes.
Rhinos do not watch TVs
  Nor go to school with suitcase lunches,
but they hear the whispering trees
  And gobble grapes in purple bunches.

Alan Fishbone

Confession

I walk with the shadows
Down a long corridor — a motionless alley
No guide, no destination, no future . . .
Hopelessness fills the air with sudden anguish
As I walk with numbered steps, the distant path narrows
Until eyes meet with that which calls himself the end
  — of a meaningless journey through time.
It is he, the one who brings fear and truth
Suffering knows him though too well
It is too late, nothing can be done . . .
I face him as he holds me with an all-knowing force.
There is no turning back as the truth is revealed
Trembling with fear as the image teaches . . .
A ruthless man who realizes he has done only evil.
Reality becomes clear, the corridor lightens . . .
The law of justice and order is awaiting his arrival.
Pity fills my being until I can withstand no more . . .
The mirror reflection has won, committed to a life of injustice,
I must serve time to redeem the goodness in me
  — that I once knew.

Heidi Anne Bell

Tears Of Remembrance

Sitting in my room at night provides me time to ponder
How many times I missed or chances not taken;
And opportunities long past, now barely remembered,
Never to be used again.
Not able to turn the clock back.
Of the disappointments in my life,
None will stand out, none will be imprinted on me,
  as much as enduring loneliness.

Jeff Kinnamon

Familiar Face

An early wake at an alarmclock face,
I turn to find no familiar face.
Another dream she filled the space,
My Aphrodite with a familiar face.

I prepare for work, it's another day.
Hundreds of people around me,
Still alone in another way.

That familiar face, fills my mind,
I can only hope that it's somewhat in kind.
That familiar face, fills my soul,
It pains me to think of letting go.

A paradox in motion, the same to the heart,
Familiar face leave me no place to start.
I really should turn and cut from the chase,
But the moment looks bleak with no familiar face

Its back to the night, where my dreams will be graced.
This time, I'll turn and find that familiar face.
Its back to the day, where my thoughts will be chased
In hope of spending real time with that familiar face.

Christopher Mudgett

United

November 27 was a wonderful day,
and when he asked her to be his,
yes was all she could say.
From then on their togetherness was guaranteed,
their hearts were a race,
and their love was in the lead.

From decorations to dresses, shoes to curls,
her mind was in great big swirls.
But he was there to help her through,
and now it's final, their love is true.
Their color is green, her dress is white,
their lives were dark, but now they're light.

Now with their friends and family they repeat
their vows to love and care,
don't you think they're a perfect pair?
I must admit this day has been the longest,
but they will never forget the 17 of August!

Teresa Marie Bruce

Nostalgia

Soft memories, lit up by sleepless conscience
To flicker in the darkness of a new moon,
Sing me your song of future coming soon
And living moments stolen by the past
And thrown as prisoners into Queen History's dungeons
To make us long for things that would not last.
Our life is but a trail of reminiscence,
An orphaned beauty wandering by chance
And never even giving a second glance
To what she'll search for when her youth is lost
Rubbing through endless hills of hoary dust
Only to learn how Lady Luck can dance.
Yet, sometimes we return from the unknown
To that which had been lying like a stone
On the expedient road we'd blindly chosen
Convinced that it would lead us to our throne.
Yes, we return but do not find the sunrise,
There is a home but not the one we've sought,
And as we stroll along our personal worldliness
Days past only await us in a thought.

Alexander Stessin

In This Unknown World

Beautiful landscape whisper of dark tales.
Frolicking gorges grasp their deathless rock beds.
Gleeful birds lullaby the afternoon's breeze.
The aromatic, promiseful blooms send a tear down a
    face of any animal who looks upon them.
Silent music in the air plays unheard.
A faint faraway call in the distance
    sustains a moment of curiosity.
Blowing winds of enchantment kiss the leaves of trees.
Strings and canopies echo the symphonies below.
Here, it is peaceful.
Here, it is calm.
Here, the melodious songs are heard.
Here, in this unknown world.

Romana Galvez

"Frozen Ice And Drifting Snow"

Frozen ice and drifting snow.
How much farther, I really don't know
Sometimes I wondered, if it was worth
This time I've spent up in the North
I'm lost and can't find the way
I won't be alive to see another day
I'm so sleepy from the wind that does blow
Across the frozen ice and drifting snow.

Frozen ice and drifting snow
Soon, it will be my time to go
I have been gone for many a night
Alone with the stars and moon so bright.
My feet are gone and my hands are blue
So I must say this before I'm through.
Don't ever be a fool and go — Alone
To the heart of the frozen ice and drifting snow.

John Maruhnich

"He Is God"

I have a spirit in me
It's growing everyday
The Lord himself put it in my heart
He said, "child use it"
For the mercies on me
And I will see you thru it all.

He is God, He is God
He will take you, thru all trials
He is God.
When you call on his name
He will answer, and reply
Because he is Almighty God.

Children, if you have a work to do
for the Lord today
Don't put it aside. Do what he commands
He will bless you for the work you've done
and a reward you'll receive one day.
And a place up in heaven to live.

Pauline Stevers

A Day In School

School starts at 8 and ends at 3
In the computer lab people help me
Math is cool, and P.E. is good
In CMS I am understood
Africa is a neat subject to learn
In class I wait until it's my turn
Lunch is at 10:30 am
Some people think I am strange, but who cares about them

Rocco Cavuoti

Cosmetology (Spray Paint)

Wax figure in the candlelight, molded in the image of God —
    Illuminated mimicry,
Endowed with every curve, color, and conscience —
    Varied omneity —

Of eyes with which to invert the exterior,
Of mouth with which to elicit the interior,

Olfactory nerves for the fragrance of flowers,
Tympanic membranes for the chorus of showers,

The hand to legibly interpret the mind;
    God within
    God without:

        Ceraceous spirit.
        Empyreal nature.

A coalescent body of parasitic animation
Devouring enzymes of a suicide creation—
    Catalytic radiance,
    Ephemeral pain:

        Dissolving in the pores of Cain.

Micah Shane Palmer

Day And Night

As my eyes open I see the reflecting sun.
When my eyes begin to close I see the beaming moon.

Warm air and clear sunny days.
Dark night and cold whipping wind.

I am the day and I shine
I shadow

I am the day who awakens with brightness.
I put all to sleep.

I am the day that brings new things.
I contemplate the days happenings

I am the day during spring, shiny
I am the coldest winter night.

I bring new life
I can suppress the largest of beings with my chill

I am the blistering summer day set off to the beach
I send people huddling around a fire.

Clear as day light
Dark as the back side of the moon

I am the day, warm and soothing
I am the night, cold as a Antarctic freeze.

Scott Jennings

The Tablecloth

Naked and cold, the kitchen table
Waits for someone
Or something to cover her body.
The good samaritan that I am,
I arrive and drape myself over her,
My loose ends dangling in bits
Down past her legs.
Like the Chiquita girl,
I sport a center-piece crown
Of cherries and bananas
And charm passers-by.
There is a concentration of colors
On my skin-circular patterns of flowers
That serve as a source of amazement to bees
Who remain transfixed,
Wondering if the flowers
Are real or not.

Lavanya Iyengar

Does Death Live On?

Death
Does it begin when you are born?
Taking off a minute of life every minute you are alive
Is that fair?
    Fairness isn't a topic
    Not when you're healthy or sick
    You could be very right or wrong
    But, you couldn't fight for long
    Injustice will tear you apart
    And leave you with a bleeding heart
    Does fairness count here?
    Does it comfort you when death is near?
    A doubt lingers in my mind
    I feel there is no hope left to find.
    The unfairness fears me to the core
    As death quickly slams the door
    Is my life now gone?
    And does Death live on?
    Is that fair?

Andie Pellegrini

If I Be

If I were the wind I would constantly blow
past you one reason would be to keep you cool
the other so I could touch you every min-it.

If I were a wave I would thrust myself upon
you over and over to drown you that way I could be
inside you for the rest of your life and
the last thing on your mind.

If I were a dog I would piss on your leg
so everyone else would know you're mine.

If I were the sun I would shine so bright,
it would be me making you see things the
way you do and play an important role in your life.

I am none of these just a small person in
your life the only way I could make any impact
on your life is if you would consider me to be.

Brooke McCann

Forever Love

I could tell that you were someone special from the first time
    that I looked in your eyes.
Love that I feel for you is something that comes only once
    in a lifetime.
Of all the time that we've spent together, you've shown me just
    how special one person could be.
Very many times in the past, I had only dreamt of having
    someone like you with me.
Everyday that goes by, I'm so thankful that you've come
    into my life.
You are a dream come true, I can't imagine anyone but you
    as my wife.
Of all the dreams that I've ever had, you are the biggest
    dream to have come true for me
Under all the circumstances from above, I have only one
    question, will you marry me?

Jonathan N. Katzenmaier

"Eternal Love"

If it's true that life can be over in a blink
of an eye. How much then do we know about ourselves?
Where have we been? Here there we begin to stare.
As we watch our friends go by, I thank the Lord
for you and I. I wish that everyone could be as
much in love as you and me! Then the world would
be a better place, for all eternity.

Ruben Rodriguez

Sandy Days

Water crashing up against the sand;
Salty sea air flowing all around
Gently touching the sand, toes wiggling in it.

Feeling the softness throughout us,
A soothing breeze of fresh air passing by;

Getting a chill through us that doesn't stay,
As the sun falls down into the sea.

The dark comes over us,
But as son as we look up,

There will be a starry sky,
Sparkling at us with almost a smile
From the earth and sky.

Dawn Del Russo

Old Glory

I first learned about her when I was a little girl; I'd watch her
flying on that pole, and sometimes around it she would twirl:

Told I was back then, that Betsy Ross made it and she stitched it well;
however someone else might have made her, this since someone to me did tell:

Whoever it was that made her, she was a sight to behold;
And on her folks, I'm truly sold:

I pledged allegiance to her proudly, when I started to school;
That to me, was part of the golden rule:

Perseverance, justice and vigilance, is what her field of blue means,
is what I did learn;
With its 50 white stars now for our states,
and mad it makes me, when in protest her they burn:

Thirteen stripes for the original colonies, is what they are for;
let's see now — Yes, about our flag there's more:

The red stripes mean heartiness and courage, and purity and
innocence are the meaning of the white; a more beautiful sight to
see than our flag flying, at dawn's early light:

I don't mean to sound like a fanatic about patriotism, this isn't
what I've meant to do; but forgotten some of these things about
old glory was by me, and perhaps by some of you:

This past memorial day old glory was flying in our cemeteries
Hundreds of them and such a beautiful sight to see; for all of
those brave men and women who served and many died for their
country and for you and me:

Donated they all were by their families — This their family wanted
to do; yes old glory, our countries flag, of red, white and blue:

Shirley Buffan

Only A Leaf

Annie saw it fall from the leaf-fringed sill,
so shinny and colored in the autumn chill.
As it seesawed down to the yard below,
the sun would spot it and set it aglow.
And then in my palm, she said to me,
a leaf has fallen in front of thee.

So smooth and frail and soft to touch,
its crafted edge from natures way.
And yet so strong and rough it grows,
knowing its return after winter snows.

And what about you who have eyes that see,
look for the miracle of only a leaf on a tree.
And know in your hearts, its no darkness I see,
but God given miracles in front of me.

Denis O'Doherty

I've Been There Before

Whenever I see him
I see a lot more
Than what my eyes tell me

I see a gentle, kind soul
A warm, caring heart and one who will never break my heart

But then something clicks
I've seen him before
They're all the same

He'll win my heart
I'll fall head over heels and then will come the tears

I'll be another face
Another name on the list
I'll never be the same

The twinkle in my eye will be no more
I'll be sad, sadder than before

So now, in a millisecond,
I see a new person
a lying, selfish heartbreaker

It's just not fair
How one can ruin it for all the others that come

Christina Marie Doebel

"Sunshine — For Lori"

Body like a weak stem, face blossoms like a beautiful
Bright sunflower.
I call you 'Sunshine.'
Where is your happiness?
You search for love, craving it.
Where is your romance?
Huddled on the porch, outside in the cold air.
You looked like a lost little misfit.
You were so quiet, I asked you why.
"I'm just tripping," was your answer.
I wonder what was going on in your mind?
What kinds of colors did your blue-green eyes see?
Did you find something that would save you?
Sometimes you look so small, like you'll slip
Right through my fingers.
My Sunshine fading away in a kiss of moonlight.
But please, don't go too soon.
The world will be less bright without you.

Renee Foschini

Untitled

Brazen buzzard beats the air
by Sams Point Road,
flapping, angry
At the tons of whizzing steel
Separating him
From the object of his heart's desire . . .

Puddled possum pie
Pounded viscous
By the great
Rubber robber barons:
Goodyear,
and Firestone.

He dances
In and out
Dodging death for dinner.

S***ty way to make a living.

Richard Brooks

A Personal Crisis: Upon Encountering A Boulder

A woman, evolving along the way
with latent seeds awaiting discovery
to cultivate and develop,
explores the dense forest around her.
Upon encountering a boulder
she finds the path diverges;
one leads to uncharted valleys
full of inescapable dangers,
the second circles back behind her, and yet
another meanders onward to the forest's edge.

A deepening self-awareness permeates her soul.
Pausing at the boulder,
she chooses not to walk among familiar trees
only to repeat her yesterdays and their sorrow,
but to travel along the path to the clearing,
beyond which lie unexplored forests, for perchance
the essence of her spirit may flourish there.
She steps around the boulder
now full-knowing where she's going . . .
In search of soft green fields.

Elizabeth A. Kliesch

My Native Land

Things may be different in this changing world
Since heaven's winds "old glory" unfurled;
Her colors a beautiful glorious sight
Some things may be wrong, but most things are right.

There is freedom to worship in this godly land
For moral integrity with honor we stand;
Our churches the torch of salvation ignite
Some things may be wrong, but most things are right.

As liberty's statue still beams with each wave
I will always love the home of the free and the brave;
My land of courage of freedom and might
Some things may be wrong, but most things are right.

When my journey is finished and my race has been run
And I am waiting to hear that blessed well done;
The star spangled banner will enrich my flight
I'll give my Lord praise, that most things were right.

Lloyd F. Brownback

Moments Of Pleasure In The Rain

Moments of splendor, moments of pain,
Finding pleasure in the rain.

Moments of darkness, then moments of light,
Joy as wisdom conquers night.

Moments of courage, moments of fear,
Soothing comfort when love is near.

Confounding moments of the shrinking soul,
Repelling the doubting flows;
We Unchained the ebbs we knew consoled
Those incipient glows.

We swelled the crestless rising tide
Those waves of surging hope
Buoyed by your essence at my side,
Sweet fragrance of heliotrope.

Oh moments of grandeur, limp moments of pain,
We savored pleasure in the rain.

Richard J. Ward

Untitled

Each breath I take is pain
Struggling to stay above water
I'm drowning in my sorrow
My sins weigh me down

Nothing left
No where to turn
I'm lost in this world of games
Only continuing to lose . . .

Gambling with death
My feet take me to forbidden places
Fruit that is sweet in my mouth
Only leads to eternal flames

Save me from these waters
Give me someone to lean on
Wash me clean from this soiled soul
Lie me on the sand to feel the warmth of life!

Stacie Green

I Am Envious

I envy the man who's smile is true
and who's heart is content with the world.

I envy the man who's eyes are bright
and who's dance is free and flawless.

While the worries of the world are worrying
and while the winners strive for more,
the man I envy gratefully accepts the
humble nature that his half empty cup serves him.

While the rest of us knock our fists
at the enemies prominent shin,
the man I envy walks away,
and knows his distance will win.

I envy the man who cries for joy
and who lays his burdens down before God.

I envy the man who has less than I
yet treats his share like gold.

I envy the man who creates the time
to bless the changing season.

I envy the man who is slower to react
than he is to reason.

Jessica A. Zouzelka

The Storm

The clouds move in so swiftly
With gusts that come from nowhere in particular,
Casting a thick, bile-green haze upon everything it touches

Then comes the all too familiar rumbling
As if a warning were ever needed
For the anticipated crash to follow.

It happens.
The house shakes as the thunder rolls through
Beating upon the soul like a ceaseless hammer . . .
Pounding . . . pounding

Finally, the water bursts through the clouds
Pouring down, trying to wash it all away

Then, as quickly as it began,
Yet another storm is over
And as the dark clouds drift ever so steadily apart,

Somewhere a child shakes with fear
And wonders silently, "Where do I fit in?"

Susan M. Pichler

477

In God We Trust

I was just a piece of copper, in the mine so deep.
Down beneath earth, I lingered, where all the minerals sleep.
Then the miners with their picks, so very sharp and new.
Dug deep into the mine where, all the treasures grew.
They were digging for, all the gold they could find.
Never dreamed of bringing copper, from this gold mine.
This copper can be useful, I heard one miner say.
Yet they unearthed me and discarded me with the clay.
I was a treasure beneath years of rock and decay.
Beneath that pile of discarded rubbish, I did not want to stay.
Into the sun baked earth I saw day, from darkness and night.
Then the miners discovered I was pure copper, shiny bright.
Now I'm a small penny, you can hold me in your hands.
You can save me or spend me in many different lands.
I'm so grateful that you found me deep beneath the earth's crust.
Then you inscribed upon me, "In God We Trust."
May I be used a million years, and changed from hands to hands.
May I always carry a message of peace to many lands.
It all comes from within my heart, a joy I can't hide.
May I carry this message, "In God We Trust," with pride.

Grace Rosen Baldwin

Rape

Walking alone at night thinking nothing goes wrong,
Suddenly you get full of fright and feel someone among
You walk faster as nervous you get inside
Run, run you think outloud no time to hold back
but in no time he caught up and to the ground you fall
Struggling tears fall down your eyes and you ask
yourself "Why me just innocent and nice"
A pain on your head and nothing to remember
You still do not understand why it was you being so
innocent and nice.

Lydia Luna

Biting Pyramids

Wearily wondering who the Celestine Prophets were,
uncomfortably comfortable in this
dry, warm room
wanting to bite a pyramid
and lull the sandy stone on my tongue
or drink of jungly rivers with hairy trees and
Butterflies the color of pale Spring nights
grazing my cheek, a sweaty belly dancer in a raunchy cafe
in Roma, drunk on its bitter red wine, feeling like a Man,
slamming my fists on splintered wood table tops, then
Wrestling an alligator, breathing its rank breath — I name him
Burny Winger and mount him on my truck hood, eating
Onions and Cinnamon Apples, driving to the red-gold
Temples of the karate Kings, kissing Budda, and Knighting
His incredibly enchanting soul on the way to my vacation at Balmoral
Oh — Espana will salute me, dashing its sequenced tricorns,
turning them pale with Dust . . .
(ahem!) Yesss . . . dust — that nestles itself, particle by particle,
upon my "Weather-Worn" skin in this,
my Very dry, Very warm room

Ryan Patrick Schuchart

Untitled

Alone he stands on the summit of a hill,
    waiting, listening, watching;
As multitudes of people scurry along the walk,
    without greeting or smile.
Nature has given them this beautiful glorious day
    and no one takes heed.
Can they not see or feel the warmth of the sun . . .
With a heavy heart he starts to turn away and hesitates,
As a soft breeze caresses him and he hears the
    sobbing of a child and steps forward.

Julia Lalley

New Life

The dead leaves that surround me,
their colorless life.
The cold air blows through,
will I survive? The loneliness I felt,
the cold winter snow.
To cover up what I had,
my sorrows it will show.
The flowers they look amongst all the ground,
ashamed to be seen, a new life has been found.
Below all the forest, no light to shine through.
The rain is kept out, the warmth and the dew.
But there to the side a gleaming bright glow.
A rose that blooms bright, and melts all the snow.
Strong and alive, my care that it knows.
It's love that I feel,
makes me drunk, but still grows.
So now here I am with you by my side.
Lasting forever, together we are tied.

Beth Ahrens

Time

The more things change
The more they stay the same
Time came and time went away
Time to grow up and go your own way
Wish things could've stayed the same

Looking back on how it used to be
Each others shadow, you and me
We thought it never would end
But then time came and our separate ways we went

Now looking in a mirror at the face I see
It's no longer a child looking back at me
But the eyes of a grown up, or it's supposed to be
My how time slips away

Now the years have come and the years have gone
But the memories in my heart still they go on
And when I feel alone or I feel a little blue
Those memories in my heart take me back to you

John Clayton Cole

One More Minute, God

Give me one more minute God
To take just one more look
To glance into a baby's face to read just one more book.

Once more I want to feel the
Wind blowing in my face
And feel the sun warming me
Filling me with grace

I want to say I love you
To oh so many people
I want to hear a sunday bell
Ring from a beautiful church steeple

When I have then apologized to anyone I have wronged
And thanked you for my fruitful
Life I'll be ready for my final home

I'll be ready when you are God
To savor my rebirth
I just ask — don't suddenly
Take me from this earth

Let me have just one last look
Give me one more minute God.

Helen S. Lyerly

Treasured Feelings

When I'm with you I feel so safe,
Our talks, your touch, your warm embrace.

Not a moment too soon, or a moment too late,
It was simply a dream and then became fate.

Your grip so tight, your eyes so near,
This is the moment when we most care.

I never imagined me with you,
Is this a love that will always be true?

As the days go on the more I care,
It's not yet a destiny, but it's getting there.

Our hearts are together, beating as one,
Even if someone tried they couldn't ruin our fun.

I admire the way you listen and stand,
And the way we walk hand in hand.

You take the time to actually care,
I hope our friendship is something we will always share.

You will forever have a place in my heart,
We care far too much to be apart.

So read this poem and think it through,
Do you feel for me the way I feel for you?

   Kim Tadsen

"A Private Message"

As my eyes come to rest upon your picture on the wall,
I wonder are you warm and safe, do you stand straight and tall
As you are lying in the sand that you must make your bed,
Have thoughts of fear and pride chased each other in your head?
The years that have been given to the shaping of your soul.
Will see you through the coming weeks and long nights in some hole.
Just do your job as best you can believing in the truth,
That a liberated country has a future for their youth.
I can only say with pride and love which comes from me to you,
That you are on a courageous mission that must be followed through.
I pray for your swift and safe return each night as I lay down,
Remembering when you played at war, crying when you fell down.
Now if you should fall again, do not cry my son.
Many more will follow you, get up and carry on.
If God decides to send you home out of harm's way or another,
I'll stand tall with pride, awaiting you.
Love always,
  Your Mother
   Patricia L. Stavis

The Comet

A hazy blur in celestial heaven.
Blazing a trail of prismatic reflection.
Casting eyes upward to the starry sky,
Wonder captivating the question 'Why?'

Is it only a pattern of fate,
That it circles and in our time relates.
Or is it a messenger from above,
Validating Faith, Hope, and Love?

Clouds overcast and cloak,
Weather, cold and icy choke,
Huddled inside the mystery unfolds,
Yet few pause to behold.

Will the end of the earth be so?
All to see, but few to go?
Some elated, beyond recall,
Others miss the eternity made for all.

   Dawn R. Moyer

America

America is my chosen country,
A God-given gift to me.
She's full of life's conveniences
Moral values and acts of friendliness.

It's a land of bounty, peace, and happiness,
With real democratic practices,
Freedom, human rights, and equality for all,
These do we all enjoy.

Health care for all people
This is her primordial concern;
Rich or poor, young or old,
Are given the same full attention.

Cleanliness and sanitation do people observe,
In the streets, in the parks, and in every home,
In the fields, in the forests, and in every ocean
Nowhere can filth nor pollutants be found.

Oh, Lord! I consider myself fortunate,
In coming to this great country,
I Therefore offer my thanks to you,
And sing a song of praise!

   Adelaida Garcia Juanatas

Life Is

I asked an old man, what is life
And this is what he said to me
Life is a terrible terrible thing
And when you get older you'll see

I asked an old woman, what is life
And this is what she said
Life is a hard day's work
From time to get up till time for bed

I asked my pastor, what is life
And he looked down into my eyes
Life is an experience we should cherish
Till the day we die

I asked God, what is life
And this is how he answered my prayer
Life is love, family, and faith
And people who will always care

I asked myself, what is life
And from all the things that I've learned
I think life is a priceless gift
To those who are concerned

   Derek Chase

In Memory Of Easter

Easter time is special, we celebrate each year
To wish all our loved ones a special Easter cheer
A very joyous day and the children love it so
But we have to look back many years ago
The day of Good Friday, how Christ died for our sins
How the soldiers treated Him and how the people had been
How they mocked and they slurred Him and crowned Him with thorns
And how they nailed Him to the cross and saw His flesh torn
And Jesus turned and said in such a wondering plea
They don't believe in God so they can't believe in me
But the guilty right beside Him, who was nailed to the cross
He asked Jesus to save him for his soul had been lost
So Jesus saved this man on this dark bleak day
And the heavens opened up and the thunder rolled away
So God promised us all that Jesus would be back
That's the reason for Easter and that's the gospel fact

   Barbara O. Cruz

My Love For You

When you came along, it was love
at first sight
I longed for your love in the heat
of the night.
Our first kiss, took my breath away.
You were in my thoughts every hour
of everyday
You showed me what love is all about
Never again will I be in doubt.
You've made me who I am today.
This is why I must say.
I love you for your gentleness.
Your loving smile, your warm caress.
I feel safe with you, you are my crutches.
You send chills thru me with your tender touches.
I never knew love could be so good.
I feel things I never knew I could.
My love for you is growing strong.
My love for you will last a
lifetime long.

Denise Daneau

The Coming Days Of Lent

With feet bare and with life's comfort aside
He walked the barren sands, the devil at His side
It was not about candy as He fought the desert sun
But of a world ahead and of a people He wished one

With troubled years past
And with future's shining light
He asks us now to walk with Him
Painfully through His night

For forty hard and fruitless days
A living fear He did pray
Come let us share His fear in silence
Through the coming Lenten days

His life seemed so simple
And so we struggle to understand
As we rise to each day's glory
And live the pressures of this land

We look to Him for a hope that only He can give
What little sacrifice is asked so that we forever live...

Ronald J. Unterreiner

I Am My Mother's Child

When I no longer need a friend
To share this life in which I'm in;
When I need no one to share my sorrow, peace and feeling
And all is harmony, joy and healing.
When life is naught but past memories gone unspoken
And hiding the heart which is truly broken
With fading thoughts which will not last
With no words of expression or signs of life
Absent from this body all worldly strife.
With no need to share my thoughts of today
And no need of help along the way.
At rest I lay . . . no emotions of display . . .
With no need of understanding the things I do . . .
God takes my soul in silence
While you sleep without a clue.
When this life is perfect, . . .
I will call on you.
I am my mothers child.

Jimmie L. P. Best

The Doll In The Drawer

There was a place in Grandma's house where I'd go to play,
Buried treasure in a drawer wrapped up tucked away.
I'd stand so tall upon my toes to peer at what was there,
For in the top of that dresser drawer lied an old doll with no hair.
The doll was old her body worn from years of a little girls touch,
Who played with her in sunday church tea parties, picnics and such.
Oh how I wish I could play with her and make-believe she were my friend,
But grandma says we must be careful until her stitches we can mend.
Limbs of leather filled with sawdust her face faded so fair,
Brown soulful eyes all crackled and sleepy a top her head without hair.
Tiny chipped hands all moled together secured with some tattered lace,
A doll tucked away for so many years longing for a loving embrace.
For it was memories of my youth I had her repaired for grandma and others to see,
Just what a grand old doll she once was and how special she is to me.
And now she prevails in all her glory for only love can hold the key,
The memories of a little girl opening a drawer
letting an old doll free.

Tamie Christine Wood

An Important Woman

There is one very important woman I know; she is my mom. My mom is very important because she is always there when I needed her. I knew her for almost eleven years. Her name is Katherine Ann Hutcheson. She is very polite and generous. I love her very much.
The reason why my mom is important to me is because she is the only one I can trust. She also listens to me.
The biggest reason she listens to me is because I am her daughter. We are also good friends. My mom loves me a lot and I love her more than anything in the whole world.
My mom is very creative. My mom and I once baked four batches of Christmas cookies. It was hard. My mom has her own business called "Kathy's Dreams." She makes dream catchers and sells them . . . they are neat. My mom is very talented.
My mom is great and fun to go shopping with. My mom and I go shopping a lot, but we always spend too much money. I love my mom and going shopping with her.

Amanda Harris

I Remember When

There was a joyous and eager feeling
That I thought was spring, calling,
But it stayed with summer, stealing
Away again with Summer's falling.

It was such a glorious aliveness
My thoughts could ever take.
So my heart sang with happiness
In the quiet night as I lay awake.

Now, somehow, in this hurried life,
I lost my joy in the coming of Spring.
And now there's only bitter strife
Where once glad bells would ring.

Tho' that breathless expectancy has gone
There lingers some faint wonder yet
With maybe hope in a newer dawn
And kinder dreams when the sun has set.

Norma Wright

Rattles In The Closet

The cloak of respectability lies on shoulders heavily,
Yet sometimes it slips and shows,
A hidden side that others seldom know,
The inner self, which only proves us human,
For no one wears respect forever, neither man nor woman.
So we all kick up our heels, occasionally we all enjoy a little sin,
Ignore the clacking bones in the closets, for each closet has its twin.

Ernest D. Schlier

Foundation Planting Without Foundation

Out of the blue this gray day came two yellow-slickered men
Three lone shrubs to prune and shape meticulously and then
Drift off to some other numb chore.

Had they but raised their dullish heads, the trimmers would have seen
This poor landscaping's parent building all wrapped in Visqueen,
Within a week to be no more.

Once foundation planting, now briefly sculpture in the round,
This Italian garden will soon be bulldozed to the ground,
Leaving nothing that was before.

Come the next date for trimming, this same invariant pair,
Confounded by the shrubs' absence, will instead trim the air,
Their small ordered world to restore.

Ronald K. Enholm

Sarah's Gift

Mother and small daughter Sarah
went shopping in a downtown store.
Sarah was having a birthday and that
you couldn't ignore.
There it was propped upon a shelf
the gift supreme.
The gift of her dreams,
a beautiful hat!
She raised her arms into the air
exclaiming, I must have that!
A huge yellow hot with lots of green beads
several flowers of very bright red,
she quickly put it on her head.
And awful gift for a girl of five,
out the door she went her head held high.
She wears that hat every day
and doesn't care what people say.
That huge hat for a girl so small?
Never mind, she tells them all
I'll wear this hat until I'm tall.

Wanda Anderson

Silent Drums

Silence claims the battlefield, where once the cannons roared
And rockets flared
And mortars screamed
Men fought and bled, then fought no more.

The drums of war are silent now, the warriors all have gone
The flag is furled
The guns are stilled
The battlefield is hushed.

Out of the stillness comes a sound, for those of us who hear
The voice of those
Who perished there
Whispering, please remember us.

Bessie M. Westphal

Emotions

How do you fly, if you don't have wings?
Where do you go if you don't have courage?
What do you believe when everything you have is a lie?
What do you see when everything is dark?
What do you feel when you're completely confused?
When does emotion play on the heart when everything is dead?
When will sleep bring peace instead of frightening dreams?
When will life come together to began again?
Why? Ask (an you shall receive) When?
Because Jesus said so.

Rosie Phelps

Untitled

Fantasies of boats gently rocking
in their moorings
we follow the plumage of the gulls
crisscrossing the air,
avarice guiding them to bread crusts tossed
    above our heads
solitary intrusions in this haven at dusk.
With the strand line our thoughts recede
against the crispness and sharpness of the trees
cicatrices on bark from fallen leaves
measure our brisk strides
as we search for that perfect spot of stillness.

Maltesian blue-gray skies
tinted with the flight of contagion
contrast the sleep of the trees in their winter cathedral,
heralding the split infinity of our own.

Wind spun leaves encircle us
    and I am again reminded
        that her silence shows me she understands
        this nearer quiet.

Sandra E. Wells

Society

I can't help but to hear,
I can't help but to learn what's near.
The old society pays its due
Though the vents in us make us new.
Just where exactly do we lead . . .?
Whatever we are is what we perceive.
Although your mournings are my dawns;
Whether happy or sad, everyone moans.
Some stay far away, some stay close;
What does it matter if we overdose?

The jackets of our vibrations
Control our very own migrations.
Yet my ass does have a nose,
It sniffs out anything I oppose.
It will sniff the bitter, it will sniff the bazaar;
We're all so close, yet we're all afar.
One can't tell if the water's to deep;
Society pushes until we weep.
If we push back it only tears;
Then comes the laughter, and the glares.

M. S. James

"Up North"

Up north beside the lake and the very tall of pines,
Is a place we hold so dear within our hearts and minds.
Grandpa built a house there more than thirty years ago;
A place of warmth and comfort that we would come to know.
Grandpa's kind old eyes and the mischief we could see;
He filled our lives with laughter and then he had to leave.
Grandma small and quiet with all her strength and will,
Her kindness and her caring that is always with us still.
To sit and talk with grandma and the stories she would tell,
Of family members present and those gone on as well.
Grandma left us years ago on a day I still remember,
Way back in eighty one in the middle of November.
Wishing I could tell her all the things I never said,
But her love is carried with me so my tears need not be shed.
"Up north" is not a place on any map I've found,
But it's the place I'm going to for years to come around.
The wind blows through the pines like a whisper on the breeze
Calling me to come and put all my life at ease.
Because up north beside the lake and the very tall of pines,
Is the place we hold so dear within our hearts and minds.

Sandra Joan Fisher Meza

"The Old Oak Tree"

Oh! What to my wondering eyes should appear.
But a huge broken tree, in the yard to the rear;
At nine a.m. sharp, there was a great sound . . .
That mighty old oak, just fell to the ground
Northeast it lies, of the old wishing well
All crumbled and broken; today, when it fell
That sudden ice-storm was really to blame . . .
Our's is the loss; and oh what a shame.

Rosalyn E. Blackburn

Untitled

May your child be born
With the blessed beauty of a morning sunrise.
With the gracious attitude of a
moistened earth after a spring shower.
With the serene outlook of an eagle in flight.
With the loving capabilities of his parents
For it took a giving love to create such a miracle.
And may your child be born.
With the knowledge of God;
Of truth, wisdom, courage, and freedom.
May your child be born with these virtues.
And may he stumble less than you or I.
God bless your child.

Nancy Watts

A Friend Named Dan

I am a girl with a friend named Dan
We're an interesting pair, so try if you can
To believe in the fact, that sometimes it's true, and opposites do
    really attract
We'd meet every Christmas for 3 or 4 years
At a holiday breakfast not thrown by our peers
Across from the table we'd sit and we'd stare, right through all of them
Sitting so big in their chairs
As we pass the vegetables, the hot rolls, and butter
We turn around at the sound of a shutter, and staring back at us,
    a camera and my mother
Well, we smile as if it's the time of our lives
While at the same time hoping to get out alive
We made it! It's over! We've gotten through the meal!
But only to us is this a big deal
I guess it's the tension of never quite knowing where is the point
    when the parents start throwing
Those unwanted questions of "How is it going?"
We've stayed great friends in spite of these mornings and both have
    decided to use them as warnings
That sometimes you've just, got to adjust
To others in life, just to get out alive.

Laura B. Mendoza

Summertime

Remember those summers of yesteryear
With fresh lemonade and frosty root beer —
Running barefoot in the grass
Wishing somehow the days would last.
Skipping rocks on the pond,
Ice cream socials on the church lawn.
The old porch swing and the evening breeze —
And sitting back doing just as you please!
Oh yes, those summers of yesteryear
With fresh lemonade and frosty root beer.

Deborah Randolph

"Feed His Sheep"

On the third roosters cry, Peter's eyes down-turned,
A bitter wail from lied sown lips.
A broken promise, and a failed faith.
Shall this man stand to see another day?
Oh pain . . .
Oh failure . . .
Should he stand again?

Death silently ruptured in the man on the cross,
Again Peter whimpered with faith lost,
And his tears merged with the blood stained dirt.
What shall heal his pain?
How he longed to hear the voice once more,
To turn again from mourning to laughter,
Yet how can he stand in the faith he lost?
Three times a question asked, and three times an answer.

Do you love me?"
"You know I love you."
"Feed my sheep."

Oh dear, Peter, turn and feed his sheep.

Timothy D. Molepske

Shortcuts To The Inevitable

Where I am
No need for alarm, I
have you here, safe
Why am I here
You need care
What did I do to warrant same
You have yourself to blame
Alcohol consumed in a quantity
Blotting out your identity
Drug abuse, from cigarettes to cocaine
Financed by earnings of illicit sex
With same or opposite sex
Destroying your brain
The lights grow dim, the echo fades
Why is that . . . AIDS
Oh my God, which of my vices caused my fail
All
When will I see my last moon
Soon

Norman Bravo

"A Daughter's Wish"

From birth to 21, we make many wishes,
good or bad, we fight for many issues.
As babies in a crib,
our diapers were changed.
You fed and clothed us,
and I do believe you sang.

As little girls, you played games with us,
and many times we'd loose, and make a fuss.
Later as teenagers, we wanted to date,
but all the guys knew you, and
they felt it was best to wait.

We've gone thru many changes,
more than we can say.
Our life with you, Daddy,
has helped us in every way.

We're going to make some mistakes,
whether they be great or small, and
we've learn from your experience, after all.

Today is "Fathers Day", and our wish for you each year,
"Be Happy" we'll always love you, whether far or near.

Arnetta J. Moore

Beauty Of The Old

Youth has beauty untold,
But can not compare to the old.
A young persons beauty is flawless and innocent to see,
But the old ones beauty is strength wisdom from thee.
Time has disguised it with a wrinkled face,
But the beauty is there hidden in another place.
The beauty of age is etched on our heart,
not on a canvas or snapshot.
The kind of beauty I'm speaking about,
can not be seen but felt.
It's felt in the heart mind and soul,
There's nothing more beautiful than beauty that hides.
Behind the face of the old.

Beverly J. Hill

Daughter Of Mine

There have been so many days,
I was feeling lonely and blue,
Only you could lift the haze.
And show me love, pure and true.
A real beauty with eyes of green,
Brightly shining as you talk on the phone,
Five months and you'll be a teen.
Five years and you'll be full grown.
I dread the day you'll meet a man,
Then fall in love and move away,
I'll get along the best I can.
Praying for your happiness every day.
Hoping it's a lasting love you'll find,
And you'll have a child of your own,
For I love you, daughter of mine.
As a child and after you're grown.

Deanna Ringstaff

The Unbreakable Bond

Sometimes late at night
as I lie enveloped in the darkness,
I feel arms holding me tight.
I hear the slow, rhythmic heartbeat
of a body at rest.

I feel a slow, gentle motion,
and hear the creaking of a rocking chair.
A bond of Love that cannot be broken.
A mother and child,
a moment that they share.

For all that you have given me,
how can I ever repay?
My Heart and Soul will forever be
bound to yours through eternity.

Steven Boos

Love To A Mother

I tell you that "I love you" in so many ways,
Maybe not in words, but in the things I do
And pray
The Lord will let me keep my love flowing
In all my daily cares
And my heart with love always glowing.
This is my every prayer.
But it's easy to do these things
'Cause I have one who cares
And one who is ready to share the love
I give so freely
She receives my love
And I hers
Sincerely!
This is the love of a mother and a daughter

Evelyn Johnson

Solitary Grackle

He arrives!
The knight in shiny purplish-black armor,
brandishing his beak of a sword,
staring with yellow eye at us
staring at him through the window.

Cautiously rummaging through the spoils
of discarded hulls from predecessors,
an interloper before his time
he knows, because the birdbath
is still frozen solid with ice.

A hasty arrival unrewarded
with sweet seeds of nourishment,
leafy nesting hideaways,
and where is the cavalry?
straggling behind?

Skreeauk, he ah wells,
and journeys on
continuing his quest
for the Golden Spring.

E. J. Miller

The Elusive Bluebird

How long I have waited for the elusive bluebird's flight
Its dance of beauty hanging above me
Enticing but yet to avoid what's upon the horizon
Ever watching, ever sleeping, ever menacing

Reach out for it's longing for a peaceful flight
Floating through the wistful night
Catching only a glimpse of the bluebird's bliss and sweet caress
Since, ever watching, ever sleeping, ever menacing

The glide of poise from a humble start
Makes a noise that breaks the flight
Believing but yet to obtain a solace of make-believe
Wondering but yet to project a sweet surrender to the uncanny flight

If only for a moments time it wakes
To shine of shimmering blue
Across the lake into the bluff
Ever watching, ever sleeping, ever menacing

Cynthia L. Turner

Unto The Grave I Cry

You grew to be a man, married and became a dad
your family you ruled with an iron hand
not realizing what you had.

Why did you journey down the road that was taken
didn't you know this road would be shaken?

Your very soul so full of anger
inflicted wound after wound
causing your family great danger.

As years came and years went
by your own choosing, your family, you were loosing
all the anger was vainly spent.

By then you were old and without much fight
unable to bare the long lonely night.
Standing all alone one day you knew you
would have to pay.

Death the only escape? Couldn't you see
what it would do to me? Unto the grave I
cry why, why did you choose to die?

Veronica Sanders

483

"Never Enough"

Pictures of you are still on my mind
You gave me your love, then left it behind.
It was never enough just to hold your hand.
It was never enough for you to understand.
That I really loved you with all my heart
And I never wanted to come apart
I gave you my heart, I gave you my love.
But still it wasn't what you were dreamin' of
You know you hurt me way deep inside
When I turned my head you weren't there and I cried
Looking back on the times we had it made
But as the days went by it all began to fade
It's a shame that what we had was all just a lie
And that's why it's time to say goodbye
We started out good but then times got rough
Cuz everything I give you was never enough

Bonnie McKenna

The Wishing Well

They say you can never go home
but I'm so tired of being alone.
Pine trees are swaying in the wind
calling to me like a long lost friend.
The well stands covered and dry
where we would talk, you and I.

We tossed our coins in that old well;
you'd make wishes you'd never tell.
Some things you didn't have to say;
I knew you wished I would stay.
So I came back home late this year.
I tossed a coin; you weren't there.

If you could you hold me just once more
by the fireplace where my stocking hung before.
If you could tell me one more time
that you love me, it would ease my mind.
If I could have one minute more
I'd make it last forever more.

Linda Mauldin Hogan

Cocaine

The cocaine glisten on the mirror
like ice crystals on snow.

Carefully,
I slice the white powder
delicately like a surgeon.

With a deep breath
hunger, pain, disease and poverty cease/abruptly.

I'm free
soaring over jagged mountains.

I can stop anytime
because I'm smarter than most.

Crouched in a corner,
my clothes soaked with sweet
and perspiration trickles between my breasts
like water dripping from ice,
as my body trembles

As my body trembles

As my body trembles

Sherri Knoy

Dragons Of The Future

Arm yourself with bright sword and shield,
for the dragon's breath can be heard from over the hill.
The dragon's breath has long tongues of flames.
Many men have been defeated, what were their names?
In the heat of battle some turned around,
they dropped their dull weapons and ran to safer ground.

A brave man goes onward and upward to meet the foe.
Though his heart is trembling, he does not turn and go.
With a shield in his left hand and a bright sword in his right,
he keeps fighting the dragon into the night.
The dragon is covered with thick scales from his chest to his toes
with green fins on his back and fire from his noise

The dragon's roaring flames light up the night
and just for a second the time is right . . .
A quick thrust of the gleaming sword with all your might
and the dragon is sent into eternal night.
Arm yourself with bright sword and shield,
for a dragon's breath can be heard from over the hill.

Gerald W. Brooks

He Still Walks Alone

A metropolis stands where there once was a town.
A town that had stick people all around.
Walking through the one way street,
All of them moved to just one beat.
The sun went up and the sun went down,
Yet there was no one to save this town.
But the people did not cower in fear,
The people did not shed even a tear.
For they could not see it, they were so blind.
They did not know it, not one had a mind.
Then one day, there came a man with color.
This man did not laugh or look down 'pon the others.
Instead, he looked at the houses so square,
And he looked at the lines gathering there.
The people looked back at him with scorn.
So he left this town, sad and forlorn.
Everyone cheered, and applauded his run,
Little did they know that he was their one.

Amy Tay

Paper Flowers

Your life is too short to end,
we all know it is true.
Your wounds are too deep to mend,
there's nothing we can do.

You're like paper flowers in the wind,
getting blown in every which way.
Not knowing when your journey's going to end,
or when will be your last day.

Your reach out for a hand to help,
but all you can feel is the air.
You don't agree with the life you were dealt,
to you, it isn't very fair.

You scream and cry and even wish,
hoping a miracle will come through.
Your heart is one the world will miss,
but there's nothing we can do.

You're like paper flowers in the wind,
wishing to end the pain.
Not knowing when your journey's going to end,
or if you'll ever be the same.

Courtney Meyer

Author Of Love

Dear Heavenly Father up above,
Yes, you the author of human life and love.
Please hear me as I pause to pray
on this, my daughter's wedding day.

Is there a place where passion's purple roses stay in bloom,
and lovers meet with each new dawn to capture once again,
the spoken vows and the exquisite intimacy of this,
their very own wedding song?

What will happen to these pretty candles
when angry shadows chance
to dim their lovely warming glow?
Somehow it's the little things
that seem to shade a heart the most.

An unkind word, a tender glance
or touch, "I'm sorry, I love you,"
it really doesn't take much.

And when the magical moments of this,
my daughter's wedding day have passed
it will be you, please God, who will make them last.
Tell me, what more of a Father could a mother ask? Amen

Lee Eagle

Prayer In Time Of Trouble

O God, our helps and assistance, you are just and merciful
and you hear the cries of Your people. Look down upon me, a
miserable sinner. Have mercy on me and deliver me from this
trouble. I am deservedly suffering because of my own actions.
I acknowledge and believe O lord that all trials of this life are
given by You for our correction when we wander away
from you and disobey Your teachings.

Please do not treat me as my sins deserve, but according to
Your great mercies, for I am the work of Your hands and You
know my weakness. Give me, I ask, Your divine help. Give me
also patience and strength to go through this trial with
complete submission to Your will. You know my miseries and
sufferings, You are my only hope and place of safety. I come to
You for relief and comfort. I am trusting in Your infinite love and
compassion.

In Your time, when You know best, You will deliver me
from this trouble and turn my distress into comfort. I will
rejoice in Your mercy and praise Your Holy Name, O Father, Son
and Holy Spirit now and even unto ages of ages. Amen.

William Asarisi

Young Love

Down the dusty old Country Lane,
walking together hand in hand.
Feeling nary a twinge of pain,
listening to the country band.

The chirping and whispering of birds and bees.
The fluttering of the butterfly's,
the rustling of the wind blown leaves,
as we look upward to the sky.

Red birds, blue birds, flustered quail,
barking dogs and moo-ing cows.
Chipmunks resting on the rail and
grey squirrels scamper over twig and bough.

As we near a bend in the road,
happily homeward bound
we see an ugly fat old toad,
hopping over the ground.

Sylvia P. Heckert

For Lennon

As Christmas comes around,
We think of you and say,
"He gave us a new sound
And showed us a new way."
We remember your talent and charm,
For we watched it take shape and grow.
That anyone would want to do you harm,
Was something we just didn't know.
How could we ever forget the man.
Whose thoughts He was not afraid to speak.
The one who taught us that we can
Be gentle without being weak.
And we wish you were sharing Christmas with us, John.
Wish we could tell you "Happy New Year."
But all we can do is remember,
With a smile, a "Thank you" and a tear.
Our love and respect for you will not yield, never.
We will pray you are in Strawberry Fields, forever.

Irene Marie Smith

"The Cry"

A man I called the "wolf" has left his "dove" to cry.
Can he hear this echo way up in the sky.
Does he feel my tears and the stinging in my eyes,
As he lay sleeping does he know I'll always care?

The "wolf" with the green eyes can you hear my cry?
If anyone on earth can grant me one more plea
Please bring my "baby" back to me.

"Two" of us left that day
when the shot rang out and took your love away.
You looked so sad as you laid by the cross,
For all that we've shared seemed somehow lost.

I'll wait for my "wolf" when the "dove" will no longer cry,
The sun will reach us up as we fly towards the sky.
For the "wolf and the dove" their love will never die.

Diana Boyer

"Looking For Romance"

I guess I'm looking for romance in all the wrong places.
Because everywhere I look I see the same old faces.
I'm looking for a person to cuddle up to.
I want someone who is real and very true.
It's hard to find romance in this time of day.
Because you can't tell if they're straight or gay.
I've met a lot of people from which I would like to show my love.
But I know when it's my time, because I'll see a flying white dove.
I want a person to treat me with the deepest respect, and would
treat them the same and not like a reject.
I want a person to hold my hand and watch the sunset and the sunrise.
And to say "I love you forever" as we look into each others eyes.
I just want a person that I can always hold, and to be hand in
hand as we grow old.
I want a person who loves to slow dance, and someday I will
find my true romance.

Larry Dwyane Barnes

My Black Box

Inside is a shadowless box of darkness
my mind has emptied and my heart has numbed
as the hours grow, heavy darkness wears my soul
I hear only a deep silence

Hopelessly wishing for the thread of light to carry me forth again
into the gallery of life

Julie Marasco-Ilic

Angel With Wings

I have a daughter, I love so much with beautiful eyes of the blue.
My heart beats with happiness as I held her close, the most
beautiful love I have ever known.
I was young with no care, life as easy as an evening breeze.
I held my daughter and watched her grow, her laughter and smile
made me glow.
An angel from above sent to me I love her with all my heart.
Tiny hand's reaching out to me, I would hold her close her eye's
of blue looking up at me.
I felt so proud to have an angel sent from above, she filled my
heart with pure love.
Then one day I woke to say "Where has my angel gone?"
She must have grown wings.
Can't see her looking back at me, her blue eyes or tiny hand's
reaching out to me.
Life's not easy as the evening breeze with out her here my
heart break's will she be gone forever to stay?
Love her with every beat of my heart every breath I take with
Out her my smile has gone away.
Has my angel grown wings? The reality of life has awakened me.

Sheryl Tillman Coleman

The West Texas Wind

It's a warm wind, the West Texas wind, full of bird's cries.
I never hear the West Texas wind but tears are in my eyes.
For it comes from the West Texas lands, the old brown hills,
and April's in the West Texas wind, and daffodils.

It's a fine land, the West Texas land, for hearts as tired as mine,
apple orchards blossom here and the air's like wine.
There's cool green grass here where men may lie at rest,
and the mockingbird are in song here singing from the nest.

"Will ye not come home brother? Ye have been long away,
It's April and blossom time, and white is the spray;
And bright is the sun, brother, and warm, is the rain
Will ye not come home, brother, home to us again?

"The young corn is green, brother, where the rabbits run,
It's a blue sky, and white clouds, and warm rain and sun.
It's song to a man's soul brother, fire to a man's brain,
To hear the wild bees and see the merry spring again.

"Larks are singing in the west, brother, above the green wheat,
So will ye not come home, brother, and rest your tired feet?
I've a balm for bruised hearts, brother, sleep for aching eyes,"
Says the warm wind, the west texas wind, full of birds' cries.

Wanda Landmon

Ballad For Nicole

Nicole, Nicole, God rest your dear soul.
You suffered in silence, in pain all alone.
When bitter tears rolled down your rose-tinted cheeks,
Your babies would quietly kiss you to sleep.

One night in June you came home to rest.
You gathered your young ones so close to your breast.
They touched your gold hair with an innocence rare.
Alas! This would be their last gaze you would see!

Nicole, Nicole, will justice prevail?
Has Death placed forever man's conscience for sale?
God gave you your life and your children to bear.
How cruel the one who has silenced your prayer!

To all who dare be decent and fair,
Speak up with some courage to end our despair.
For Nicole is dead and her memory fades.
Her soul must find peace in an eternal grave.

Imelda Delgado

Arizona, I Love You

I came to Arizona, but never thought I'd thrill
To the enchantment of the desert and rough foothill
I love Arizona with the strongest love I've known
For any land, eclipsing my native own.

Its spacious natural beauty is a gift of healing peace
Its fascinating background gives a troubled mind surcease
Where else can one enjoy the glamor of yesterday
Yet rejoice to be part of this progressive state today.

When it rains out on the desert, a rarity indeed,
Still stranger is the odor which you'll find does precede
Then afterward the mesquite with water diamonds rare
Strewn throughout its branches adorns the deserts bare.

When the sun again is shining, ants come out from their lair
And you'd laugh to see them going with their rears up in the air!
There is a little spider, fragile and colored light
That gets up on its tiptoes and looks from left to right.

The sunsets, O what sunsets, so beautiful to see
Makes me wish intensely that an artist I could be
I love the place I came from and the people held so dear
But Arizona caught me and my roots are taking here.

Mary DeRosa Ide

The Tears Of A Man

You should weep, my heart, weep your sorrows,
you should weep heart, sad and lonely,
weep your glooms because they are yours,
weep as you are doing. Oh sad heart!

As my heart cannot weep, nature is guilty,
of denying to my heart this release,
even though I have never been a coward,
instead of my heart, my eyes are weeping.

Today I notice a lack of common sense,
in words written a long time ago,
that well known but false affirmation,
which says . . . "The men never weep".

Everybody weeps, when one is just born,
later everybody weeps for the just dead mother,
Is somebody hard enough to resist the tears,
feeling the misfortune inside the home?

Then, for a man, weeping is not a crime,
the physical weeping alleviates the sorrows,
dropped tears from the eyes of a man,
are the tears of his sore heart.

Carlos Garibotto

"Try"

I have watched you for so long,
   I can't help wondering if you look back . . .
What would I do, how would I react,
   Would my fears make me look away . . .
Do I open the door of my heart,
   Do I let this even start again . . .
I dream of your soft warm touch,
   Then I remember that Love can hurt so much . . .
The pounding in my chest as you walk by,
   Fills my head with thoughts of giving love a try . . .
Now you've turned the corner,
   You're no longer in sight . . .
All I can do now is pray to the stars of the night,
   Waiting for you to tell me if this is right . . .
Tomorrow will come and I'll be here,
   I'll see you as you come near . . .
Grab my hand as you walk by,
   And together we'll give love a try . . .

Linda O'Hallaran

Things That Are Beautiful To Me

Watching stars twinkling in the night.
Watching the sunrise at morning light.
And when the sun comes up so bright.
Watching a child flying a kite.
A child with manners and wanting to do right.
All these things are a beautiful sight.
Watching children play with their faces all a glow.
Even birds sitting on the light line in a row.
From the skies above to the fields below.
Watching rain fall from the sky.
The wind blowing and wheat swaying.
Like waving, and saying bye.
And the mountains so high.
And seeing my grand babies born, brought to life.
All these things are a beautiful sight.

Peggy Hulsey

Wife And Mother

As I sit here in my worst fears
I'm drowning in a pool of tears
and in a room just down the hall
is a lovely woman that tops them all
so brave, so kind, compassionate and true
and so much courage to see things through
I pray to God as she fights for life
forty five years, this is my wife
My heart is so sad, I'm filled with such gloom
each visiting hour, I enter her room
the stress is so great, I can't stand the strain
To see such a woman, lying in pain
make her well Lord, please send her home
Without her here, It's so alone
watch over her God, for there is no other
like my dear wife and sour children's mother

Charles E. Kitchen

Ode To The Poet

I sail the ever changing sea of time,
On a vast expanse of endless signs,
They reveal the path to knowledge and reason,
Giving me hope and something to dream on.
When I reach the distant shore of death,
I will come upon a poet's epitaph;
He lived to love and died to rest,
To never return to the life he loved best.
He took his soul to the other side of mourning,
To see an unlucid future dawning.
He saw his own beginning and his tragic end,
Now to the fields of heaven he will ascend.
He wrote poems daily only now to find,
That the words of a poet shall never die.

Christopher M. Doughty

Stranger

Everyone said he's one of a kind.
Everyone said girl you better watch out;
He's a stranger to himself, a loner to the world,
Got a heart of steel and'll break any heart in his way.
Me, I don't know how to listen; have to learn for myself.
I fell in love with the stranger,
The man with a heart of steel.
I wish I could say I know the man, but,
The stranger's still there.
Now where do I turn, when he says:
I love you but . . .?
It's impossible to walk away, yet there's no place to stay.
He says he loves me; says he needs me.
But he is a man of the wind,
A stranger in himself.

Stacey Robinson

Politico

I saw you again on Valentine's day,
Sleeping soundly in my subconscious,
Revealed in vivid color,
Rich repetition,
Bright pattern,
Sealed safely behind barriers,
Bars and glass.

You screamed soft pastel
Dreams and predatory creams.
You took your fare
Unaware, disbelieving,
Wholly astounded at
Tooth and claw and orb:
A prehensile clasp.

The chain link divides you into diamonds,
Bars beat your image, again and again.
The glass rimes your sleep, forever
Icy, impervious to trouble,
Blood red and silver laced,
Inside a polar day.

Claudia Patrick

"Wild Child"

He moves like a cat
  across my bedroom floor
He's everything my mother feared
A wild child
  long hair, a tattoo, a motorcycle
  and a way of moving that screams
  raw sex.
He's my father's nightmare
  and my mother's most decadent dream.
and I am feeling him
  layer
    by
    layer.
Uncovering the tenderness, the vulnerability.
  The prince and the poet.
He roared into my life like thunder and
  touches me like warm rain
He's the fire in my forest
And the calming in my raging sea.

Holly Shaughnessy

"AIDS Is Everyone's Sworn Enemy"

It is taking more and more lives everyday,
Afflicting "us" all: black, white, straight and gay,
What can "we" do to put an end to this disease?
And perhaps allow mankind to one day live at ease.

"We" can start by changing "our" way of life,
By educating "ourselves" about this horrible strife,
"We," then, may somehow understand it,
And help its victims escape from its bottomless pit.

Instead of blaming "them" for "their" mistakes,
"We" should use compassion and understanding,
  for that's what it takes,
Because "we" can not "them" suffer alone anymore,
For "they" already suffer much more than "we" could
  ever possibly endure,
AIDS is ruthless, vicious, malignant, but most of all deadly,
Therefore, "we" must "all" declare war, because AIDS is
Everyone's
Sworn Enemy.

Dennis P. Almeida

Hold The Hand Of A Child

Hold the hand of a child
   Teach it the way to go.
You will never be sorry
   For it is wisdom that you sow.

Hold the hand of a child
   What joy it will bring to you
They will take you to never, never land
   And the old woman who lived in a shoe.

Hold the hand of a child
   Of children everywhere.
For children are the future of the world
   And they will take you there . . .

   Dolores Stinespring

Hold On

Poor premature flower
Withered away hour by hour
In your arms I cried
In your perpetual beauty I took pride
Because it's darkest before dawn
In despair I do hold on

You were the rock on which I stood
Now I stand on sinking sand and broken wood
In my mind I see your face
In my dreams I long for your embrace
Without your smile all hope is gone
But still I do hold on

When I can no longer endure
I think of our love so honest and pure
Your life I held it dear
Your death so impossible to bear
I feel sometimes that my life should end
But I will hold on 'til we meet again

   Simone Rose

Beauty

I have seen many wondrous things.
The sun's ascent at daybreak,
illuminating the heavens in hues,
of majestic purple and vivacious orange.
The pristine snows masking the mountains,
glistening as legions of minute mirrors.
The willowy flight of the Jay,
cross myriad verdant bluffs and glens.
The gleaming stars hung aloft in lone splendor,
gazing fondly unto his azure globe.
But none have I seen that starts the,
swelling tender emotions as you.
Eyes, that you possess, pale the stars,
shimmering in the heavens above.
A beam that procures frailty in the knew,
and a heart so taken with faultless warmth,
it would deliquesce the mightiest frost.

   David Siegel

Down Cast

Now that everything is lost I peril myself through an
endless journey to slay my immortal depression. Yet I
have eyes, ears, hands and everything someone would
want, I have absolutely nothing. Nightmares flow
through my thoughts like fire. Although they cannot
harm what's been destroyed or burn what's been
blackened, I am still disturbed. I wonder what reality
is when that which is real seems so obscure, like a
dream. I am in an eternal sleep. I am still, for I have
nothing to do but be. If I could ever wake up it would
be of no use, for all I would see is darkness.

   Jon Johnson

That's What Friends Are For

That's what friends are for.
With friends you can soar
from the mind to the heart.
Boy! that's a good start!

It's like loving from the soul;
(that's always been my goal).
With you by my side,
I know I never have to hide.

That's what friends are for.
With you, I know I don't have to cry.
With you, there's only the sky.
You never touch the ground in friendship.
That's what friends are for.

   Talitha D. Wopinski

My Grief

Upon this troubled bed that I now lie,
Shattered dreams form dreary shapes
To reconstruct their name;
In the stillness of the night, my silent cry if loosed,
Would torch the heavens like a flame.

I, once so brave, am strong no more,
But tremble like a leaf upon a tree.
I lie here shaken to the core;
Awaiting respite,
Awaiting peace,
Awaiting to be set free.

   Phyllis R. Moses

"Bravehearts Of Old"

There once was a group of mighty men.
Whom all lived in Sherwood Glen.
Led by Robin Hood dressed in Lincoln Green
Little John, Will Scarlet, Friar Tuck and all
the merrymen held him in high esteem.
Against Evil King John they struggled with might.
And prayed for Richard's return to make things alright.
All men take courage from their many deeds
They installed freedom in hearts as a Noble seed.
They robbed from the rich and gave to the poor
And stood for truth and justice forevermore.
Here's a toast to you Robin Fitzooth Montfichet
your deeds have been immortalized and
are here to stay.

   Earnest B. Parker

Untitled

With the dawn of spring of blossoms in the air,
the sunlight all around thee to proclaim that thou art fair.

The mist that rises from the earth and nurtures to its own,
restores the weary champion to guard the angels throne.

The dew that forms on lovely petals awakens with the dawn,
can not match thy own sweet lips the passion that they spawn.

Gentle little creatures the songbirds fill the sky,
proclaim the dawn of brighter days as wise men wonder why.

For of all the signs of beauty that pierce the heart of man,
none can match the power of the gift of your sweet hand.

As sunlight causes winters blanket to melt into the ground,
blanket me with kisses in peaceful places we have found.

Wrap your life within these arms like the petals of a rose,
you sacred trust to follow where the enchanted sprit goes...

   Paul H. Jones

"He's The Only Way"

Sometimes I'm made to wonder how in this life today
People take things for granted of things they can't repay
When life is so precious, and all the memories within
The Lord knew that from the start He'd be with us 'til the end

He has a plan for all of us, each and every one,
His works are greater far than we have ever done
We must pray and ask for guidance each and every day
To follow in His footsteps for He's the only way

Satan tries to stops us when the Lord's work is done
He's always there behind us waiting to claim he's won
But with the Lord in our hearts, and the Bible in our hands,
Be ready faithful pilgrim to always take your stand!

Constance Hall

Happiness

Happiness is a fleeting thing.
Where does it come from,
What does it bring?
A smile, a tear, a wave of hand
Or is it something much more grand.
Does it sit on your shoulder on a summer day
Under a beautiful sky — watch your children at play.
It comes and it goes, you never know when
It will leave you and suddenly come back again.
I sit and I wonder how this happens to be
I've been to the depths and now I am free
To live to the fullest on life's stormy sea
For happiness is within
And I know It's in me.

Joyce C. Ettenborough

Sunset Celebration

A festival approaches . . .
muffled caravans of tarped buses and drummed car loads of people
seeking an experience, behind them in the middle, wheelers and
dealers, the money makers, come to spread their greed and
destroy the trade of a society.
But still I see who know more than they reveal, trading their
precious goods for objects of interest, Staying cautiously clear of
the plaque known as money and the greedy devastation left in its wake.
My purpose is to tinkle a talk throughout the starlike camps, one of
free-thinking and revolution, a desire to travel on purple robes and
incensed air, hung smooth with smoke.

A revelation in the camp transcends to a higher order, and a group
is formed, each one drawn to the other, by an urge that can only
be described as "Destiny"
   A day too wonderful to forget, dusty linens and old mystics
with caned walking sticks and kasmir sashes
carrying on their haunches back-legged staves, wool rugs, carlum
crafted drums of elk and deer, small satchels of essential herbs,
crystals, and images strolling from the hills,
         Their first venture in more than a year.

Chris White

Mom

I remember so clearly the days of my youth
your towering image of courage and truth
you accomplished more in a morning
than most in a day
you were busy at work while I was at play
I learned the importance to do a job right
the worth while feeling gave comfort at night
You were my protector, my teacher, my idol, my friend,
my moment of truth and my muse to pretend
No greater gift I can give you
my life than is proof
for I remember so clearly the days of my youth.

Laura Russ

Pieces Of Life

Life has its wonders, dreams
its visions, and the world relates
its glory in beauty.
For I live in ever changing thought
to be part of, or to become myself,
I am beauty in my own right,
Moving forward through time as it ticks
away at my destiny.
To belong, to be loved, to be needed,
is life so simple that man has made
it so completed to be used against
the wills of my thoughts and my being
All I want is to be loved, to share,
this short space in time, to exchange
ideas to relate and to be understood
Ask not for the glory's of man, wealth
and power for to share me to you is
riches, like the grains of sand on a beach
For love is the only lasting joy.

Jerry E. McCray

Blossoming Love

Sweet droplets of dew
trickle down the petals of a flower.
A rare blooming of such uniqueness
that is only witnessed ever so often.
An experience so precious
that gold cannot compare.
Sweet words that warm my heart,
And embraces that soothe all sorrow.
A voice that comforts a troubled soul,
A sympathetic hand that
reaches for an escaping tear.
Love's beauty blossoms in my life,
And love's treasures fill my spirit.
In the midst of love, time becomes dear,
And moments become memories.

Janel Estes

Water-Glass Lessons

I give you these words
when nothing else is left
but the purple half-moon shadows
that you painted beneath my eyes
(clashing with their greenness):
void, void, void

"Voulez-vous coucher avec moi?"
I taught you to say, and "Va te faire foutre!"
and "Merde!"
You were only ever interested in the obscenities
the most trivial improprieties
of what we call existence

Now I teach you emptiness
the red in the corners of our eyes
where the tears are born

Heather Ubelhor

Peacefulness

Flowers bleed their colors of choice
   in the distance I can hear your voice.
It's crying, crying out in pain,
   the flowers burst in the gentle rain.
Come with me take my hand
I'm going to take you to another land . . .

It's so peaceful there.

Christopher D. Gillette

The Misty Rose

The soft mist embraced the elegant rose petal
as if it was comforting it in tearful sorrow.
As the ending day became a part of yesterday,
the light began to shine gently on the red flower.
It had enlighten the petal from the darkness of the night.

Today is another day of the glistening soft, silky bud.
It will bloom into the light of this, a new spring day.
By darkness, the petal of the radiant rose will droop
with enchantment of the flower dissolving with time.
The once beautiful bud is shattered by its own life.

It's yearning for the forgotten ugly bud to be cut back,
so another majestic bloom may replace it in due time.
The rose, the captivating, alluring rose is life itself,
We all have a chance to bloom like the delicate flower,
before our bud blooms within and dies forever with time.

Lucille Buhr Jasmer

"Sometimes Love Hurts"

When I look at you my eyes swell with tears.
Will your cancer take you away from me? That is my fear.
You smile, hug and hold me tight.
When you're gone will I be afraid at night?
I worship, love and praise your name.
And sometimes I still play those flirting games.
I love you with heart and soul.
I no heaven's gate will be your goal.
Don't worry about me, I'll get by,
Just tell me another joke before you die.

Mary Claire Zapko

The Box

When the box opens, and
The light leaps out,
The joke's on us
A-ring-a-big-bang-boom!

When the box opens
And the light wells out
Like a tear from Mnemosyne's eye,
We are fulfilled.

When the box opens
And the light leaks out
In a puddle, dark and viscous
Then life's equation and all its variables

Must rise, once more, into the
Poochy hole
Which orbits the infinitesimal point
That draws us in.

Tim Walker

The Winds Of Change

They blew, and I was young
— carefree —
Mindless of things to come;
And sweeping me along so slowly
though it seemed
They brought with them the turmoil of the years
— the troubled teens —.
They quickly passed through years
of youth's unrest
And softly, gently, into maturity passed
And calmly settled into life's
untimely age,
Knowing that the winds will ever blow
Creating and accepting changes, for we know
that this is so.

Dorothy Hovel

The Call Of The Wild

From deep in the heart a small voice calls
An echo from ages past.
The faint wild strain of a pulsing song
That makes the heart beat fast.

Having filtered down through alien blood
Oft crossed with the ancient one
At last the beat is almost still
The call is almost gone.

But sometimes when the wild goose flies
Or an owl hoots high in a tree
Or a puff of smoke floats to the skies
This heritage calls to me.

My mind's eye fills with mysterious things
Such as rituals and dances of old
The haunting notes as the "shaman" sings
And tales of great courage are told.

For the drop of Indian blood I have
Many times I've been held up to scorn
But to all who have held me thus I've said,
"Full-blooded, I wish I'd been born."

Constance Hughes

Poet's Paradox

You speak one word, or several words express.
Your words bring peace, I clasp them to my breast.
Oh subtle treachery that they,
Should bring no peace, while seeking sleep I lay,
Upon my bed, your words my peace do slay.
It's not your fault dear friend, myself I grieve.
My poet's mind must slay your words of peace.
From soul to mind the arrow makes quick speed,
And I surrender to my pen and me.
My blood runs cold and with emotions taut,
As tightropes that the acrobat must walk,
Your words, so peacefully expressed,
Bring little peace and total sleeplessness.
Exhausted, weary, spent, down breaks on the horizon,
The madness of this night, my eyes to gaze on,
Unfolds the paradox, that mocks, that always mocks.
Your words inspired in me return in peaceful thoughts,
Of greater depth and scope, your words of peace to me.
I give you back a poet's night of creativity.

Nel Ryng

I Am A Broken Heart

I am a broken heart
I wonder if my pieces will ever be found and mended
back together
I hear the sound of me breaking constantly-crack
And I so want to be put back together, again, forever
I am a broken heart

I pretend that nothing is wrong, but sometimes
I feel as though yelling and screaming
I can barely touch the dreams I so want to come true
I cry, sometimes, because I lost my true love and that
makes it even harder to grasp my hopes and dreams
I am a broken heart

I understand that I can't get anyone I want and
I say to myself, as well as my friends,
"That's okay-let him go,"
I dream every night in bed that I didn't have to
I try and try to be happy with who I have
I hope someday that everything will come together
I am a broken heart

Celia Veronica Valencia

Patience

Newly born, you cling to me,
Source of all you know.

At five, you hesitate
To enter a world without me.

At twelve, you run,
Wanting only to exclude me;
To be your own you.

At sixteen, you don't even
Want to acknowledge that you know me.

At twenty-one, you realize that, perhaps,
You can enjoy me —
Once in a while.

And then, your child on your hand,
You return to me,
Source of all you know.

Judith Kelvin Miller

The Poor Little Boy On Walnut Street

Five years old, there he sat on walnut street
All dressed up in his Sailor's suit, his little blond curls
combed so neat, ready to go in the summer heat
Waiting, waiting, to be picked up, by someone, anyone who
might love him, who might care
No one came and no one cared, no one to meet the poor little
boy on walnut street
There he sat, all dressed up on Walnut Street, so small,
so sad, so sweet, with his little blond curls combed so neat
Only five years old, but, oh, he knew, he was just a little
Throw-away boy, who lives on Walnut Street
Just like the poor little throw-away toy, that's quit giving
love and joy, just a poor little throw-away toy
Oh, how small, how sad, how sweet
The poor little boy on walnut street, setting there weeping,
weeping in the summer heat . . . so small, so sad, so sweet

Jack R. Kays

The Days Of Glory

The boys in blue lie round about, with smoke and fire above their heads,
The boys in gray, they lie there too, their bodies cold and dead.
We fought at Shiloh, brave and true, and at Gettysburg as well.
We followed Bobby Lee and Grant, they led us into hell.
My comrades now are calling, the fighting has bygone
And I must follow with them, to fight with sword and gun.
Old Glory waves above us, she ripples in the wind
My mind goes back to home and friends, I long to see again.
I look upon the ramparts, I fear the canons roar.
A rifle shot has found me, and I will be no more.
Remember me with fondness, throughout all the years.
And, say "that I died bravely" and sometimes shed a tear.

Carol J. Minnick

The Real Fight

When all is lost
When complete insanity breaks
When our brothers and sisters
The ones, that is, who hate, who murder, who rape
Become the majority and rule
When love and respect turn-into out-dated ideas

There will still be a few
Helpless to aid the intolerance
Standing, watching teary-eyed

Realizing, when there was a chance to stop the war
That stopping wars was not the fight
The real fight was the fight against ignorance

Ira Gornick

The Him

The darkness submerges the anxiety,
A sensation of passion surrounds us,
The indifferentness of life infuriates me,
But he is calm as the deep blue sea,
The thoughts of hostility he has
Intimidate me, beyond belief.
I see the clowns dance around the park,
The delight lost from their eyes.
I will foster him 'till he needs me no more,
After that he will forever, be dispossessed,
His misery will guide me.
He will show me how to arrive at my destination,
Even if I know not what it may be.
The nights will get shorter,
But the day will get darker,
Is such a trade right?
Is my life headed toward utter disaster?
Only he can see that,
And he won't divulge his secrets.

Jenny Wills

The End

A painful, bitter end,
with not a sight of being friends.
All can not be forgiven,
She thinks so carefully.
A lot of things have changed.
Yet it still remains,
He was a part of her past.
A forever that was supposed to last.
So she ever so gently tries to close the door
    on emotion.

Darcy Klein

The World Of Dreams

Through eternal darkness I see light
to dance the dance with the Shepherd of Night
The lies I've told cannot come true
But how can mine compare to you
If I wished upon a star
I'd dream of when I'll go that far
But the night has come
and I'm still here
to comfort you in all your fear.

Rusty Derrickson

Maestro

We fit together, you and I
Classical instruments fine-tuned to perfection
You play me well —
A virtuosa —
Command performance

Your changing rhythm
Staccato to legato
Lento to presto
Intuitively changing tempo
Striking each chord with deep resonance

Every moment with you my private concert
A symphony composed by one
Performed by two
Atonal bodies and souls
Uniting in harmonious counterpoint

Each kiss
Each caress
An encore in itself

Stephanie Lee Caldwell

Your Thoughts

If things are running through your mind,
Which should not be abiding there,
How do you stop the oppression they cause?
Which way do you turn — where?

You'd like to rid your mind of the stuff,
Forget that ever was your thought.
Do you say, "I can do this if I try",
Like a battle that's being fought?

We all like to do things on our own,
But we really need some help,
Need to turn to our Lord and Saviour,
Take our Bible off the shelf.

Things honest and pure and of good report,
Philippians tells us to think about.
If we keep our mind tuned in on these,
We find that other thought has gone out.

We need to feast on the Word of God,
Learn verses to strengthen, when we weaken,
Keep our Lord's precepts in front of us,
Like a powerful and eternal beacon.

Virginia M. Parsons

Our Precious Memories

You can not purchase those precious memories
Not with currency, silver or gold
They are ours but not for a price
As the years of events unfold.

We long for many things in life
Some which have caused thorns of pain
But God has the knowledge of what was best for you and me
And he sent both sunshine and rain.

Through hard times we learn to appreciate
Good times as they come along
If life was all fun and pleasure
How would we be able to grow strong.

But seasons come and go
Along the way we have many good years
Which taught us to be kind to others
To even feel their sorrows and tears

If we wish to have precious memories
When the years of life unfold
We must learn to love one another
Then our memories are worth more than silver and gold.

Phillis Warren

You've Got To Be A Believer

You've got to be a believer to believe that this story is true.
For if you're not a believer, this could not happen to you!
I was workin' a whalin' ship takin' some sun on a stroll.
I fell off port gunwale when the ship started takin' a roll.
Now it gaily sailed on by me, and I wast then lost at sea.
But I caught the tail of a great grey-white whale,
when the ship started comin' for me.
Ol' whale 'e started a div'in', down under the ship 'e sped.
Rammed 'er at 'er rudder, and 'e shook 'er with 'is 'ead.
A flippin' me up in the air 'e did with a flick of that 'normous tail.
"E was an onerous son of the beach, 'at ominous
grey-white whale.
But, aye, I arrived back aboard softly, when I landed on top of a sail.
Now, mate, if ye doubt my story, for I know that 'tis true.
Just ask old Captain Ahab there. 'E'll state it could happen to you.

G. Milton Luttrell

Moments

Life can be easily changed.
Things can change in minutes,
And thoughts can be rearranged.
As the sparrow flies,
And the cold wind blows,
A part of this life dies.
It won't be missed,
It won't be mourned.
It will be someone, left unkissed.
As the rain starts to fall,
And cover the street,
A friend makes that important call.
The call to let one know,
That through all the troubles,
Their love does grow.
And as one surrenders to sleep,
Gives up the fight,
The other begins to softly weep.
The battle still rages deep in their minds,
and the clock ticks on.

Jill M. Heyes

Teenager's Plea

Adults worry about teenagers
But we are people, too
We express ourselves in different ways
And so did you, so did you

We experiment in ways that's unacceptable
It doesn't mean we are depraved
Try to understand that we are exploring
But our future will be saved

Most of us are going through a stage
Didn't the same thing happen to you?
We don't always act our suppose to be age
But you weren't always true blue

You worry about our designer clothes
The drugs and the fads we're into
This is a trial and error period
Soon this behavior will be through

We will take our place in the world
And promise to do our very best
Crime, homelessness, the environment is our goal
At last our skills will be put to the test

Lois J. Green

"The Establisher"

By the shore of this
ever moving path, where
rays cause our faces
to shimmer in brilliance.
The glory of the "Self" is a
towering jewel, that replaces
complaining with understanding . . .
Stormy circumstances, eventually become
vibrant skies, that open doors of visions,
to those who dare to seek.
Flamboyant attitudes that elude
fall prey when the will bows humbly
to the call of wisdom and her beauty.
Everlasting, Everpresent, Evermore . . .
She springs forth from
the center of the conceivable, the
unseen force of all existence.
Self established
It is
the Establisher

Vernon I. Davis

Oneness

Outside into the night, I stepped.
No, it was not dark,
The moon shone its caressing rays
Into the dancing clouds,
And onto the trees, some tall, some stout,
The breeze softly brought a harmony of perfumes
From above to below.
Snails trod their way, silent and slow,
Crickets from nowhere sent their swift music show:
I realized I did not walk anymore
I did not know since when
Blended to all,
Part of all,
One with the immense peace.

Hong Dang Bui

A Mother's Blessing

There is a blessing that I see,
As I look into the heart of me.
That is where I hold so tight,
The memories of your smile so bright.
As I look into your face I see,
The moment I cherish with you and me.
God gives us beauty in many ways,
The birds, the flowers, the stars to gaze.
The mountains, the oceans, the deepest blue,
Is nothing compared to my Love for you.
So remember when, In the mirror you look:
You gaze at the blessing of a mother's love.
If someone ask:
What do you see?
I would answer:
A little of you, and a little of me.

Audrey A. Hall

"Alone No More"

She stands alone in a field of green
    Admiring the beauty that is there to be seen
A sky so blue, with clouds of white
    The sun way up high, so warm and so bright
A tree in the distance standing tall standing proud
    With the songs of the birds ringing out loud
Flowers so precious, so dainty, so small
    Showing off vibrant colors to one and to all
Running all over from here and from there
    Animals frolic without any care
Slowly rolling by is a crystal clear stream
    A scene that looks like it comes from a dream
A breeze so gently crosses her face
    She has never seen such beauty, such grace
She stands in a field, like never before
    It is then that she sees, she is alone no more

Kenny J. Hilliker

Untitled

Sometimes when grandpas live far away
They wake up in the morning
Look out the window and say
Sure wish I could see my granddaughter today.
Well I can't be there,
But there is one thing I can do,
So I filled this box with love
Especially for you.
You can open it, shake it,
Whatever you may do.
Grandpa's love is there to stay.
It will never go away.

Walter Comstock

"A Sunrise Lament"

No one told me where to land.
I just fell out here upon the sand.
I think I'll just stay here on your windy beach.
With horizon and reality just beyond my reach.
The crystal water brushes my ears with sound.
And there's really no one else around.
Kiss my sleepy eyes awake.
For the day's begun and I fear I'll break.
Shattered sense of time within.
Someone tell me how to begin.

Chad Hoy

Unmasking

I've stolen your heart, I've stolen your kiss,
I weaved my spells for a deceiving bliss.
I infused in your heart, a spell of desire,
And a spell of longing in your candle's fire.
I've clouded your mind, I've confused your heart,
I've misused my powers and now we must part.
You've told me your hopes, your dreams and your fears,
I've gotten too close and now I cry tears.
You say that you love me, you say that you care,
Do you know who I am? The truth can you bear?
I now stand before you, no mystic nor magic,
Is our relationship doomed, this conclusion so tragic?
Could you ever forgive me, or must this all end?
Is there a fork in our future, or only a bend?
I've dropped my magic, my guard and protection,
And as you now see, I'm far from perfection.
Can you love me now, now can you care?
Knowing my confession could you possibly dare . . .

Jeff Khalsa Edmiston

Searching

Our life is a question and we wonder why
There's no real answer, yet we try
To find a reason for why we're here
Continuing to survive from year to year.

To view a sunset and its beauty unfold
Is one of God's miracles that we behold
In our daily struggle to live and be good
We try to do right, knowing me should.

With faith and hope we move along
Greeting each day with a plaintiff song
And carry on with troubles and strife
Doing our best in an unknowing life.

Many have left this earth, hoping to find,
A much better life than the one left behind.
But search as we will for a greater love
That will be ours when we join those above.

James H. Hurlburt

"Painful Love"

Don't try to tell me how I feel
this love just has to be for real
I've fell like this for so long,
and I try to act really strong
But, when I'm all alone in the dark.
The ache has left its toll and mark
My heart has burst from the pain
on my soul, there is a stain
he hasn't meant to hurt me,
but his intentions are always good
but he doesn't love me as I wish he would

Angelene Ward

Vacation

One scene as I bow to pour her coffee:

Three Indians in the scouring drouth
huddle at a grave scouped in the gravel,
lean to the wind as our train goes by
Someone is gone
There is dust on everything in Nevada.

I pour the cream.

Timothy Tiess

October Midnight

The moon was slow as Old MacPherson rose from his dusty hold
He was clear as air, in a skate-glide passing under the lamp
The old man's passing whisper pulled me on to follow
He lilted in silence before me over the cool grass; I snapping twigs
Between skeletal trees bathed in moon blue
to a glistening clearing with the moon unimpeded
It was here I lost him (or did he just leave?)
He was gone in the crispness, cloaked behind my white breath

I soon noticed a dark form on my left before the moon
In the icy October midnight the gravestone felt cold
yet its shape was warm, its patient call an alluring impulse

To the wood I was called forth where Old Death has no fear
I heard his breathy whine as quickly I walked, hair bristled
The breeze of his passing halted me briefly
The grass swayed side to side entranced
Death's invisible eyes were lurking around me
pushing me down into the soft dark earth
I laid down in the sweet stillness
resting upon my warm shadow, under the hypnotic haze

Even so, the moon was weeping as I crossed the great divide

Glenn D. Leupold

Hippie

The balmy breeze whispered 'cross the street
On which wandered her bare feet
With bottoms black with soot

Her long blond hair dripped round her shoulder,
A drape reflecting the smoulder
Of the noon-day sun

Round her neck she wore yards of love
A collar to color this dove
With bright beads and seeds

How young and slim in body and mind
This fragile child we find
Cutting away the past

Into the future she walked,
Sang songs, and taped and talked
Out of clouded dreams

She wandered down the street of life
Her rootless path brought strife
To then and now and self

Frances C. Barsh

Untitled

The world of my own determination,
The path to success, must have motivation.
Confident I stand while I'm tested as a man.
The power of my will causes the dreams to fulfill,
But is it real? Questions from the doubt
A negative emotion, distrust non comes about.
Get Out! My mind calms its thought.
Back to the path I steadily walk.

Tre Enigma

"The Traveler"

A place. A home. A new horizon. This is what the traveler seeks.
Ever searching, questing for knowledge, learning as she goes.

As she travels down the pathways of life, many roads branch off,
people are met, befriended, loved. Which path does she take?
Which road does she follow? Or, which road does she build?

As the traveler walks the many byways of life, she learns new things,
a baby's cry, a lover's caress, a friend's voice. She also learns
her purpose in life, to give, of herself and for herself.

From her depth comes a strength bestowed upon her by her creator,
a strength of purpose, welcomed like an old friend.

Does the traveler ever stop traveling? Ever stop saying good-bye?
Always saying hello? For her to stand still is to stagnate,
once done in her life, never again to be allowed.

What lives will she touch? What lovers caress? What friendships
develop? She hopes that friends made on this journey, will be friends
never forgotten, always cherished, forever loved.

Patricia L. O'Neill

Promises Of Spring

Look what . . .
The March winds
Blew in . . .
Breath taking fresh air . . .
Golden sunshine.
Big golden yellow sunflowers
Deep red roses . .
Beautiful purple violets.
And pink cherry blossoms . . .
Come into the garden and let's pick some . . .
There are blue birds singing
And tiny buds of leaves are springing . . .
Soon there will be tiny eggs . . .
Where baby chicks will pop out their legs . . .
Spring is wonderful
Bringing life to everything . . .
That seemed so very dead
From winter's friend . . .
Frozen Jack Frost . . .

Saundra Diamante

Writers Abode

There's a little corner in eden,
an ancient, shabby cell
occupied by writers.

Not much there, a few worn tables
and scruffy chairs littered
with crumpled paper and pencil stubs.

A rather disorganized affair at best;
blight in the heavenly community.
Here the odd ones dwell.

Never seem to do much but
play with words all day or,
stare and mumble disjointed phrases.

Very exasperating to the sober members
of the celestial kingdom who
find this activity incomprehensible.

Yet, with all the seeming aimlessness
and seedy offbeat air, a special glow
of radiance surrounds all
who sojourn there.

Grace M. Pohl

"Love"

'Tis said that spring bespeaks of love
With flowers' scent and song of dove.
Yet in the midst of winters chill
At times the heart will warmly thrill
To a love renewed.

Or when the corn is tasseled tall
May be the perfect time to fall
In love. And when the hawthorne's red
And leaves are turned and mostly shed
Can be a good time to be led
From solitude.

Ah, love may seek us with no rule
Of age or season, prince or fool,
But takes us lightly by the hand
Across a dreamscape gently fanned
With love's caresses. And leaves us there,
To dwell in all that's fine and fair.

Ruth Severns Lehman

Clouds

I love to see the soft, white clouds drifting across the azure sky —
So very slowly do they move, as if they're loath to hurry by.
Just now I saw a little lamb, all poised for frolic in the blue,
But in a second he was gone and in his stead there came to view
A stern-and-awesome-visaged man; his piercing gaze seemed fixed on me,
Half frown, half smile, the while he strode, so steadily — so proud was he —
Straightaway toward a lovely maid, in flowing folds of billowy white.
Then suddenly his features changed, his arms stretched wide to hold her tight.
As I, entranced, in wonder watched, the sun broke through the hazy mist,
Flooding the sky with burnished gold, and as it did, the lovers kissed.
Oh, who can fathom — who explain —
The magic that unfolds on high —
Just one of Nature's priceless gifts,
The panorama in the sky.

Ione Myers Morgan

Head Storm

While I frantically stack sandbags
against the rising water,
talking head shouts,
"It's the sleeping head . . ."

Then the mind awakens,
comforted by the still darkness
which stopped time,
created form,
held the flood.

I had been fooled
by minutes of water
that breached sandwalls
in unstoppable seeping consciousness.

Sitting at the morning table is my father,
an unlikely interpreter of dreams.
He frowns, looks out the window, shakes his head,
"Man, there's a dark cloud back in there".

Paul Hawkins

Light

Somewhere high in the sky,
here's a light that glistens far and wide,
The warmth of this light runs deep in everyone's life,
but when this light touches mine,
it makes me feel like crying inside,
And what is this feeling that everyone looks for?
Many don't know of this true emotion,
to when this feeling lies upon your path don't push it away
because it can only last.

Tieray Jones

Of Space And Time

Come walk with me through fields of desire
Into the forests of our imagination.
Journey with me down rivers of emotion
Up to the mountains of our creation.
Through the dream of time
Will we sail our lightest ship toward completion,
Crossing oceans of wisdom and trust.
We will build ancient cities in our image,
And give the Sphinx his riddle.
We will pass through arcane rites,
And write symphonies with Beethoven.
Only when we have learned all the world has to teach
Will we rise through the heavens;
Taking with us the lessons we have learned,
The love we have shared;
To a new world,
A new plane,
Where we will begin the cycle anew.

Tracey L. Ahring

You Don't Know Me, So Don't Worry

I don't expect you to know me and I don't expect you to care.
The fact is that I don't even know me and I don't even care.
You see, I never accomplished anything worthy of anyone's noting.
I never managed to master the art of completing anything fully.
I'm going to die unnoticed, unfinished, and undone.
I'm soon to be going, passing on, and leaving young.
My only consolation is that I won't suffer very much longer.
And my only fear is leaving my dear one to her other.
I know it will end this way because my heart has overgrown cold.
In my thoughts I've grown accustomed to never growing old.
Good luck to those who knew me, I know it was a trip.
Please forgive me Lord, as you know, I'm handling in my slip.

Jace

Under

Capricious, time has proved you fate,
Whose story reads of blatant rending of my heart,
And lamenting of my soul,
All written by the charlatan you are.
As if clemency has hid out of sight,
And as if I am not contrite,
For what I have not done,
You have held me under, bound by steel fetters.
All that life is composed of,
And all that happiness derives from
Trickles at my feet . . .
My efforts to rise end at the lengths of the chains,
Leaving little to fill my soul.
Dreaming at night, becomes nothing more...
But it is my only home.

Anthony Di Francesca

Special Friend

In time of despair
You showed that you cared
By the thoughts and the feelings you showed

And in the end
When I needed a friend
I always knew where to go

So on this special day
I am happy to say
Thank you for all you have done

May each day you spend
Be fulfilled to the end
God bless you, my special friend

Richard L. Wallin

Big Brother

When Mom got home, she had something
I was hoping It was a new toy;
But she said I must not touch It
and called It "Our Bundle Of Joy"!

It made a funny squawking sound
then Mom would give It a drink;
It really couldn't do much of anything,
except occasionally stink!

I couldn't figure what was going on,
so I decided to ask my Mother;
She said I'd become very important,
For now I was a big brother.

She said It didn't know much,
It was a newborn, had just become alive;
And I knew a bunch of really neat stuff
since I was almost five!

I realized It really needed my help
as I climbed down from Mom's lap;
But It would have to wait a while,
for I had to go take my nap!

Buffie Armstrong

Don't Wait It Might Grow To Late

Dance with me, enhance me, romance me.
Don't try to get rid of me, be a kid with me.
Climb a tree with me, be free with me, and just
stop and see with me.
Let's have some fun, don't shun me. Let's have some hope
and climb up to the hay on this rope.
Then together soft as a feather we may roll in the
hay, jump from one bail to another, play around with
each other, throwing hay on one another, till we could
almost smother, Oh brother!
Then again don't have it at this. Let's not dismiss it
with just this! We need to stop and just kiss, and
maybe make a special wish.
Then may we run off together through fields and hills
because it so thrills me, and it actually brings warm chills
to me, and again it actually seems to heal me.
May we be able to always crate lots more fun in
any kind of whether, but always together.
Don't you know we can be each other mates and always
try to keep each others dates. Let's not wait until it grows too
Late!

Marky Dicks

"Stand Tall"

No matter what I decide to do with my life
There is still no other person I want to be
For the world is much more intriguing
When I step forward to pursue my dreams
Grow in wisdom, love, and still be me!
Each one of us must "Stand Tall" in our particular goals
To see each new day is yet another test;
Knowing ourselves enables us to live life to the fullest
with profound pride in having done our best.
Just believe in your dreams for you are unique
A warm heart means much more than words not always said
For our achievements would not mean quite so much
If we always knew what was ahead.
So learn to be comfortable with your-self;
With each new accomplishment be exuberant
And each irreplaceable friendship do rejoice
You'll find the challenge of reaching your dreams
Is right within your grasp
Go ahead — reach for the stars — it's your choice!

Elizabeth Heyser

Sailing

As the ocean's expressions change.
I see the disappointment of a child,
A child that wants change but is scared of the unknown.

The unknown waves rock the boat from side to side.

There is a look in the eyes of the child,
A look in of disappointment.
disappointment because the boat rocks side to side.

The man looks at his better half and sees the change.

Is change the driving force behind disappointment?
Disappointment is the driving force of change.
Without disappointment there is no change.

When we are content, we strive for nothing.
When we are disappointed we strive for happiness.
Without happiness there is nothing.

Ronnie Talas

Untitled

I remember when we would go to Grandma's
and have camp-outs with our cousins.
I remember when we would have hot chocolate
and popcorn parties.
I remember when we would play restaurant with
the play dishes . . .
And feed Grandma so much "play food" that she
would have to nap in her chair.
I remember when night finally fell, how Grandma
would put us all to bed.
I remember crawling up the middle, from the
bottom, of the feather bed.
And every time it was always the same Grandma
Hazel kissing us each and then she'd say,
"Good-Nite! Sleep Tight! Don't let the bed bugs bite!"
And everyone, even Grandma, would giggle.
I remember thinking then, how special I was for
having my Grandma Hazel's love.
I will always remember these special times with
Grandma and I will remember all the love she had for us all.

Martha A. Jordan

Lovers

In every age some love is found
    Where faith and fancy do abound.
For Romeo and Juliet,
    For Pierrot and Pierette
The little things enjoyed a mighty state,
And so for you and me they are the measure of our fate.

The clouds that wend their weary way
    As breaks the newborn cheery day
Are really only dreams of you.
    The birds that soar into the sky
Are but reflections in your eye of thoughts so fond and true.
Waves that bathe the sandy shore
    And beat upon the rocks the more,
Are all grand passions I construe.

And so we love, we two alone,
    As other lovers once have shown,
That though our cup be filled to brim,
    Or fateful fortune all be dim, we are together,
    Wrapped in love's embrace,
Unafraid of any world we are called upon to face.

G. Merle Bergman

What Do You See?

When you turn and look my way, what do you see?
When you ask me a question, what do you really want?
When I fail to meet your standards, what did you expect?
When you wish I were not here, where do you wish me?
When I call you friend, how does that make you feel?
Because I am different from you, why are you afraid?
Because my ways do not follow yours, why do you shun me?
If something goes wrong, would you suspect me?
If a crime should be committed, would you then accuse me?
Because you do not know me, why do you still judge me?
If there is something about me that you do not know,
    why don't you ask?
When you turn and look my way, what do you see?

There is more, much more, my friend,
and unless you dare to find out the truth;
you live in your own ignorance.
        Katherine Downie

For The Love Of A Child

We go through life and never find
The love were looking for,
But every day right after school
It walks in your front door.

We seldom notice that it's there
Until the day it's gone,
We look and look and never see
'Twas right there all along.

Our busy lives are filled each day
With things we have to do,
Before we know it we are old
And soon our lives are through.

But if we stop and take the time
To let them in our space,
We'll find what we are looking for in every tiny face.

So take the time to look at every child that you may meet,
For there's a little piece of heaven
Standing there right at your feet.

Give of yourself to your sweet child and they'll give back to you,
And you will find the love you seek right in front of you.
        David Phillippi

Heart Of Creation

Time is only fleeting the past is in the past
life cannot be redone once the die is cast
If you do not take a chance and only let it pass
you'll have missed a pretty flower
or a love that will forever last
I cannot change the things that are
or create the things that are not
If I could I would for you
For straight through the heart have I been shot
But I've kept it quiet not a word have I said
And now my heart is filled with dread
I know not if you care or if it matters if you do
What would happen to me if only you knew
I will not say tis love
But more than friends is in my heart
So if friends you say
then friends we'll be
And I will wait as long as I am able
For you mean that much to me.
        Jennifer Midwell

Christian Brotherhood

I wish that I could hold your hand
And listen to you talk
We'd share our joys and troubles
As we took a little walk.

Somehow it helps to tell a friend
The troubles on our souls
And lay aside the burdens
As we strive to meet our goals.

They seem so monumental
Until I hear of yours
Or see someone who's suffering
Destitute and spirit poor.

Love one another . . . Christ's command
Oh, that we only could.
I'll try, will you, my brother
For Christian brotherhood?
        Hazel Graves

What It Is To Be American

Being American means
    an opportunity to be your friend
Because I am privileged to live
    in a country that's a melting pot.

Being American means
    freedom to love you
    and to learn from our differences
    as well as our various ethnic and cultural backgrounds,
Because that's what makes you, you!

Being American means
    living in a country
    with magnificent landscapes and skies,
Where each one has a right
    to pursue the God of his choice
    as well as his dreams.

Being American means
    respecting my government,
    whether or not I agree,
Because my country has given me
    freedom to be me.
        Isla C. Miles

Spick And Span

Beside the window sat this man
    And watched the ducks all swimming there.
A peaceful life in Spick and Span

The silent lake, the warm spring air
    And flowers growing everywhere.
Beside the window sat this man!

What more in life can others share
    In love he is a millionaire.
A peaceful life is Spick and Span.

Perhaps it is the waiting there
    That makes our loneliness unfair.
Beside the window sat this man!

He waited in the old wheelchair,
    And silently he said a prayer
A peaceful life is Spick and Span.

Where are the friends, are friends so rare
    Does nobody ever really care?
Beside the window sat this man
    His peaceful life is Spick and Span.
        Brian Morse

497

Rejoice

When it comes to singing a song every day,
listen to the Lord, he has quite an array.
Whether it be day, evening or night
He has the tune, the words are just right.

You will sing through your troubles, cares and woes.
When you are faced with your worst foe.
A song on your lips, the Lord in your heart
nothing can ever keep you two apart!

Open your mouth, sing praises, not signs.
Your heart will be lifted to our father on high.
The day will run smoothly, the night will be clear.
Satan will stop and listen, he has lots to fear!

I will make a joyful noise, that is all I can do.
I hope the Lord is tone deaf, for I am too!

R. Nielipinski

"Queen Of Flower"

The rose, magnificent in color, form and
size, a show case, displays its worldly
features, desirable and enchanting, a promising
sight to behold,
elegant to the heart, more precious than gold;
bursting with fragrance, sweetly scented, like
the smell of perfume
captured by the warmth and softness of a breeze,
that only a breath of air can consume;
delightful and charming , pleasing to the eye,
like the twinkling of stars, that blanket the sky;

Alfred Judd

Psalm Song

The Lord is my shepherd, no want shall be mine
In verdant green pastures he makes me recline
By still, sparkling waters, so quiet and clear
My soul is restored, for His presence is near

In pathways of righteousness with Him I go
For the sake of the Master who loves me I know
Through shadowy vales though my journey may wind
Naught shall alarm, with a shepherd so kind.

Thy rod and thy staff furnish comfort and ease
My table is laden with all things to please
Thou anointest my head with oil from above
My cup runneth over with blessings and love.

Thy goodness and mercy forsaketh me never
I shall dwell in the house of the Father forever.

Karen Becker

Untitled

What is this thing about you that makes me feel so good
My heart beats faster than I ever thought it could
When we are near each other, I turn from shy to bold
And when you look my way, I can't tell if it's cold

With one of your warm smiles you melt the ice away
Your blue eyes shine so brightly, at night I think it's day
I care for you so much, have I ever told you?
I wish the time were right for you to feel as I do

But circumstances dictate that we must be apart
So I must remain patient with my breaking heart
And hope that someday soon you'll come collect the pieces
To put them back together, and say my long wait ceases

No one knows the future, and so I don't pretend
That it's even fated you'll come to me to mend
But please always remember, I've known it from the start
No matter, whole or broken, you're always in my heart.

G. Edward Van Slyke Jr.

Life

What is it that makes us forget,
the laughter and suffering of yesterday?
And with our happy smiles, you can bet,
our past pains are wiped away.

Sometimes we sit and try to remember,
the pain and sadness we felt,
our broken hearts have made us wiser
to he suffering that life has sometimes dealt.

If at times you feel very discouraged,
reflect on your better days,
when you were happier and always managed,
to beat the punishment life sometimes pays.

But sometimes life deals a good hand
when you're happy and content and you smile
this is when the road is shortened,
and all that's left is a mile.

Andrene Smith

In Between Nothing

In between nothing,
I cannot see a thing.

Weeping willows and dark sheets,
count among the things in between.

I do not see anything within me,
but shallow trees among dry meadows,
and grass that's brown instead of green,
but nothing white among the black in between.

Rotten bones, weakened toes,
can't reach high, I'm sinking low.

Broken spirit, no hearts afire,
frozen cold, numb to desires.

Foggy skies, distant cries,
hidden but exposed, open yet closed.

In between me and the world I see,
is this nothing that's trapped within me.

Tamar Gonzalez

Good Friday

Steel Striking Steel, cold metal striking cold metal
such a piercing sound, it is both high pitched and yet deep
with each strike I feel it deep within me
the echo resounds over the entire valley
keeping the sound pounding in my ears pounding,
pounding it continues on seemingly without end. There is no escape
I don't know how much longer I can listen without despair.

The sound of hammer striking nails and nails being driven into wood
is not new to me
I have heard these sounds many times before without
notice hammer, nails and wood are common in this area
these are used to provide shelter
these are used to provide comfort
these shouldn't be used to kill a man, especially this man
this man who gave us such hope, such promise
this man who promised to save us, this man who would be our king
with each pounding of each nail my hope grows dim, blackness
envelopes the land I cry out in anger to God above, why this
pain, why this injustice. Don't you care! In these my darkest
moments I remember his words, "I will rise in three days" I will wait
and see, I believe but . . . I'll give him three days and then I'll see.

Thomas Germino

Homeless On The Subway

Why did that man look at me with one eye open and one eye closed
but in essence he was really sleeping with nowhere to go.

Look at that woman over there in a world of her own, and her inner
thoughts screaming "Somebody help me", "Somebody please", I
don't wanna be alone!

Why must they lay there wall to wall, and seat to seat — no place to
go — no place to eat — no place to sleep — why must they sit there in
a deep stare — emotionless faces — faces that don't care — faces with
no hope for tomorrow — faces of endless despair . . .

Hey! That man defecated on himself, and now he has a whole car to himself.
Inner hatred, relentless thoughts, bias, bigotry — can they cope?
Should we put them on an island all by themselves? Is that the
answer or should some of us help?

Question and answer could go on and on but there must be a
solution to this endless scorn. Time keeps ticking and soon it
will be too late — Hey! Don't you know judgement day is near?

Wake up everybody! Before it's too late — open your hearts
and give some loving grace. That's what the Lord most high
intended for us to do. It shouldn't be hard it's a simple clue . . .

William D. Thompson

Requiem

Life is just a battle or so it seems to be
For sickness, love and fate have all joined forces against me

They muster high atop a hill and form an overwhelming horde
But I have no fear of them for strong and swift is my sword

They advance down the hill towards me quickening their even stride
I see a darkness behind them with evil they doth ride

So begins the battle on a plain where I can't hide
And there I stand as a pebble alone against the tide

Sickness comes upon me and whips me with its chord
While love strikes deep at my heart as fate skillfully breaks my sword

A few friends have joined me to no one will they yield
But as the darkness befalls them they lie as heroes upon the field

Oh where is thy savior the cause of my woes
As I fight on fiercer embattling my foes

But the battle was decided it's me they now surround
And with loves final blow I fall softly to the ground

Brian Marston

Grandfather

There was a time many years ago,
when I was a small child.
There was this man,
beautiful beyond belief.
Wavy gray-black hair,
that you could get lost in,
if you closed your eyes and tried.
Skin as soft as a rose petal.
Eyes as deep as the sea.
He used to come and play with me.
With him he would bring,
everything a little girl could dream of.
But most of all he brought love.
A love that was so vivid and beautiful,
you could see it.
It was as bright as a rainbow.
With oranges, reds, blues, and greens.
There was nothing else that could be
better than this love.
For it was from my grandfather.

Tricia A. DeFranco

Foods From The Rainbow

My nickname is Ha-Ha.
I am a bamboo eating Panda.
I came from Tibetan highland
To find new foods and friends.

I hope I can get help from you
Who appreciated and know
That foods have colors and hues
Like the beautiful rainbow.

Please join me in searching
For foods in pretty colors and so
I can learn to enjoy eating
The tasty foods from the rainbow.

Number one food from the rainbow,
Do you like the crunchy and red apple?
What other fruit do you know
That its fibrous skin is edible?

The second food in the rainbow,
Do you like the juicy, golden orange
With the hue of red and yellow?
What other fruit is in this color range?

Donald L. Chu

Even Thou

Even thou we had a short time together,
I have seemed to develop a lasting love,
Even thou you left so quickly,
I knew my love would never die,
Even thou I did not hear from you,
I felt a bond that I would never lose,
Even thou you loved someone else,
I had a strong feeling our love would last longer,
Even thou we had a weekend of bliss,
I know we would have another someday,
For love lasts in our hearts forever,
You in your way and me in mine,
We will always be together in our hearts,
Even thou we should be apart..

Mark Nebeker

Steps Into Moonlight Fantasy

A slow dimming of the lights
A dance of love as I strip off my days demeanor
A cool frosted glass filled with soft vernis wine
A plush covering under my feet to cross over
A low melodic bass movement to accompany me to the balustrade
A voice beckoning look, to the heaven
A face enveloped in a halo of pale shimmery beams
A laugh richer than smooth velvet
A sigh as I lay down
A glimpse into the night as I delve once again into my
   moonlight fantasy

Donnetta Asghari

Point Reyes

Bombarding the senses
The roar, the shout
From the boundless sea
The waves embark

In the sand
Forgotten raiments
Graceful mirrors
Rippling thin pools
Bespeak the mourning dove

Jane Levy

Love

The honorable rose
so delicately formed
Grows from a bush
all covered with thorns

A beginning which casts
roots strong and deep
Never to be seen
When its beauty is reaped

A life which you see
that blooms so bright
Gives no sign of the pain
it can bring to light

For the thorn must grow and give its pain
So the rose can appear
without flaw . . .
though shamed

A beauty which fades in the passage of time
But will appear again
from the same roots
. . . the same stem
. . . the same vine
Philip O. Naylor

Posteriori

Many years of self service
Every day thoughts of being fulfilled

Those who nurse the staff of knowledge
While others set their minds to play

Paradise comes and paradise goes
But reality remain the same

Give or yourself wholly, knowing the
scepter of truth
Rides a crooked horizon

The glory of that, that is
The knowledge of that, that isn't

All in all, that which is understandable, will be
That which isn't is of no concern

Live not to harm, nor harm to live
one of confusion, another of lust
But not a difference does either make

Keep growing and prospering
never looking back
And all that is worthwhile, will be
made yours
Thomas O. Watson

On Castle Rock Road

On Castle Rock Road 'neath a natural fortress outcrop of stone
Where rare peregrine falcons and red-tailed hawks soar
A clever native California couple has created its timeless clone:
A secure home in harmony with this honeyed land of legend and lore
A tercentenary coastal oak shades the gateless entree
Near a clear creek where it makes an ox bow bend
The linen-colored dwelling set on a foundation of an earlier day
Invested with love and meticulous care, seemingly meant to mend
They've brought the outdoors inside with lustrous, glass-catching light
The huge hearth erected from native stone from the cooling creek
The warmth of wood adorning every chamber, in the living room to great height
The use of spruce and pine whose aroma your nostrils avidly seek
May God bless this sanctuary and the souls who dwell therein
Here the human and the divine combine; here there's no separation of sin.
Norman R. Nelsen

Great Grandma

It happened so fast. It happened so quick.
I felt that my life was on a stick.
I could walk through a mountain.
I could swim a sea, as long as you could be with me.

I miss the way you smile.
I miss the way you laugh,
But most of all I miss you.
I cried day and night
And wished it wasn't true.

I would wish upon stars
And pray to the Lord.
Nothing made me better.
I write her letters every day.
Not that she has gone away.
Danielle Marie Colson

The Peach

Take a big bite and its juicy insides will
S-P-U-R-T
and trickle
down your cheeks
in — every — which — way
trickle, tickle, sticky — leaning forward quickly
to — stop — it — from — going — down — your
oops!
And giggles from fuzzy stuff that tickles your nose.
Ah!
Sweetness of summer and sunshine,
gentle and warm,
with joys of luscious juice
cool, quenching, refreshing
and inviting to another
big bite!
Billie Marie Harlan

Now That You Are Gone

Now that you are gone, nothings the same
Now that you are gone, I get tried of this game
Now that you are gone, and you're no longer here
Now that you are gone, I always shed a tear
Now that you are gone, there is nothing I can do
Now that you are gone, I really miss you
Now that you are gone, you always have my heart
Now that you are gone, I hate to be apart
Now that you are gone, I feel it's a shame
Now that you are gone, I am still tried of this game
Amanda L. Lordi

Since You're Gone

The years have come and gone Dear
Since God took you away.
So many lonely nights
So many lonely days.

Learning to live without you
To have you by my side
As we were, so many years ago
When I first became your bride

I long to hold you near me
To see your tender smile
Or look into your eyes of blue
For just a little while

But this will only happen
When we meet at Heaven's door
And your arms reach out to hold me once more.
Helen Burman

"I Know Mommy Will Be Waiting"

When I woke up this morning I crawled right out of bed.
I rubbed my tired eyes and scratched my sleepy head.

I roamed into the kitchen and saw Mommy standing there;
Cooking pancakes and scrambled eggs so I climbed into my chair.

There was syrup on my pancakes and my eggs were topped with cheese.
I ate all of my hot breakfast and said, "I'd like some more juice please."

I pulled on my favorite blue jeans, tennis shoes and baseball shirt.
I brushed my teeth and brushed my hair and from my face I washed the dirt.

Outside the kitchen window I saw the lightening Flash.
I heard the thunder Boom and rain drops went Splish Splash.

My mommy said, "Get moving, the bus is down the street.'
I put on my yellow rain coat and galoshes on my feet.

As I climbed onto the school bus I turned for one last peek.
My mommy blew a soft, warm kiss that landed on my cheek.

I know my day at school will be filled with lots of fun.
But best of all, I know Mommy will be waiting when I'm done.

Lori W. Creer

Alone, Again

Jumping thoughts inside my head,
While I lay here silently in bed.
Why this mess of sorrow and pain.
What will my tears offer me to gain.
When will it end, this sickening game.
Why does my life story never seem to change.

Shattered are the dreams you denied me.
Broken pieces are all that remain.
Silent are the tears I weep in vain.
Empty are my thoughts after you leave.
Fearful are the voices inside me
to reach that point I never knew was so low.

You can take my heart. You can take my smile.
But God help me, you'll never take my soul.
It's what's inside that keeps me alive.
It's what's inside you try to make me hide.

Lost in your world is what I would be.
Trapped would be my soul, never to be free.
So now I close my eyes again, bloodshot and teary
Only to face another day, tired and weary.

Marianne Crockett

Mothers

Mothers bring joy to a world filled with pain.
Mothers bring light to a world filled with rain.
Mothers bring caring, and hoping, and love.
Mothers all carry fresh life from above.

For deep in their bodies, where eyes cannot see,
they carry the spark of a life yet to be.
The finger of God within them will move,
and the birth of new life, will His love, once more prove.

The new life is hidden, so safe and so warm,
and then with travail, the new life is born.
Years follow years of duty and joy
of raising and nurturing, a young girl or boy.

Until at the last the child leaves the womb
of mother and family and empties the room,
of sweet good night kisses and cherubs in bed,
where laughter was heard and "I love you's" were said.

For mothers are in the end left all alone
as children strike out to new worlds of their own.
But God will reward them, they willingly served,
as the means by which life in this world was preserved.

Jesse Yeakel

The Homicide Survivor Prisoner

When it happened you are Horrified —
that one of your own human race could do such a terrible crime.

Then you learn that the criminal justice system
take their time —
For they put you into a Box Of Shame.
To live, I guess is to suffer
In one degree or another.
And as time passes you Try to learn —
How to ease the Pain of shame.

Slowly the winter winds blow away.
The sun shines warmer every day.
The birds return — their song to sing.
Proclaiming it is really spring.
Breathe again, Slowly —
Released from most shame.
The Terrible Cold has nearly gone,
but not forgotten.

And a Homicide Survivor soul — in loneliness
Finds release in Heaven
Wrapped in the solace of truth and love
Safe in the care of God's Love . . .

Evonne G. Carron

"At Last"

At last I've reached my destiny
My very own space
With even room just for me
And no more room for shame

I've never been handle, as if I were fragile
Before I reached this destination
They dress me how a baby is handle
With tenderness, respect, and admiration

You know this place is really kind of cozy
I've tried to come here many times
But I never had it in me
To question the reason for life

Here I'll never have anymore memories
Or secrets to keep, hide, or tell
Here my body's innocence has been return to me
For bad touching the dead, is a sure ticket to hell

Evelin Cruz

Letter To Francis Scott Key

Dear Mr. Key,

I would like to say in response to a question that you once asked,
"That star spangled banner does it yet wave?"
Yes, Mr. Key, indeed it does!

Our flag no longer has fifteen broad stripes
Like when she flew o'er McHenry, Sir.
Her beauty is still a lovely sight
But her stripes are now only thirteen.

Old Glory has changed not only her bars
Since over the old fort she was homed.
She now proudly bears fifty bright stars!
Yes, Mr. Key, we are fifty states strong.

One more thing to report before I close
Concerning your Star Spangled Banner.
This poem that you wrote now everyone knows.
And in part is our National Anthem!

P.S. Mr. Key, I really must say
In response to the question that you asked.
That Star Spangled Banner yes it does wave.
O'er the Land of the Free and the Home of the Brave!

Paul Hinton

Untitled

What kind of hell must I live through? What did I do to deserve this
from you? Why am I a victim of your hate and abuse? Why do you
keep me if I am of no use? You must control my every move, I
have no freedom that's not through you, I am not allowed to be
who I am, but a puppet of yours on a short string again.

I can not take the arguing, the hate, the persistence of battle, and
your always being right, this is not right, I can not be, In a world
of argument, hate, and no me. You control me, hate me, and
fight all the time, the kind of environment that fails from mine,
I'm hurt and tired of all this gruff, from the fear of your anger,
control and all that stuff. Enough to do your wishes and to live
in this hell, is but a day am living and not living well.

The fear of loss and denial but you sit there with that attitude and
stupid smile, I'm sick of this strife and tired of the trial, so let
me off the hook and lay this to rest for a while. You look for the
worst, center on revenge, a small mistake and you reel to the end.
I can not be who I really, am because your control has no end.

I avoid the fight and your attack goes untold, then I jump back and
hide until the anger explodes, now all that's said does not to be revealed,
the words of anger are better left concealed. I give up and leave without
a word or a fight, you control me like all have, before in this life.

Walter G. Merchant Jr.

Mirror

When people look at a mirror, the see themselves
When I look at one, I see another world.
A world of illusions and non reality,
A world where children's nightmares live,
A world where the bogeyman lurks in every shadow,
A world where it's dark at day, light at night.
In this world, there is no sun, nor moon.
The light comes from the rainbows and stars,
The dark from the bogeyman's blanket.
There is no rain from above, only from below.
As an earth dweller passes by the mirror,
They do not see my world.
For I'm the only one who can see the illusions,
For it is my home.

Melissa Hood

When Things Change

We met in autumn, leaves have falling.
We were young full of joy, our love grew.
Now we are older our love still stronger than before.
We both have been sick and lost a lot, have only our dreams
and our thoughts in our hearts.
We don't know what changes there are, but for us our love is
stronger by far.
If things are going to change for the better, let it be now forever.
Because soon we will be apart, until then when we meet we
will be sweethearts once again.

Annette Jahelka

Passages To The Soul

Life is a book.
Each event we encounter is a passage
That makes up chapters — windows to our souls.
From time to time these chapters close,
Sometimes forcibly,
Before we are ready for that story to end.
These are our lessons — growth experiences.
We can go back and re-read a chapter,
But the ending is always the same.
Why bother?
But I ask you Father —
Why must our lessons be so painful?
Is this the cross you ask us to bear?

John Belt

Mother's Prayer

The light is out and my child is asleep
I go in to take a peek

I watched him lie upon his bed
Then I knelt to touch his head

God take care of him, hold his hand
Help him grow to be a man

I wonder if he will be alright when he reaches
His full height

Will he stand up straight, will he stand up tall
Or will he waiver, will he fall

You brought him to me a short time ago
I did not realize how fast he would grow

Sometimes heartache, sometimes joy
A lot of life for a little boy

God take care of him he is sound asleep
And
I came in to take a peek

Charlotte North-Coffey

Raison D'Etre

With the dawn of each new day there is a chance of rain and clouds,
Making for heavy hearts and thoughts, burdens created by
a life of stress and pain,
Leaving lovers and best friends far apart and alone.
Striving to survive the empty feeling created by an unsurpassed
loneliness.
No sense of sunlight and glow but a need to constantly touch
By way of thoughts and feelings and belief in each other.
There is a constant and sure trust in the fact that the support and
caring
Will always be there without any explanation.
The glow of the sun that is you constantly relieves the pain
Creating a warmth that overshadows any feelings of emptiness.
The assurance shared between two beings embraces more than
Physical love
And is precious and constantly reinforced.
You are that sunshine and assurance . . . You provide my reason for
Existence and serenity.
You are my life.

Phil Henderson

Bad Poetry

There are few wonders greater than this,
the perfect love of an imperfect being, or the selfishness
of offering a poem to one who forgets, who must not remember,
after all was completed — maybe never all —
when everything is finished, and one resumes
daily rhythms never thought imaginable,
the single toothbrush, the unheld hand at night.

I would walk the miles to you
with a sandwich, an excuse,
a will to remold the universe with fire.
But where you are now, there are delicatessens,
and what of the cheese that must spoil before I reach?
So I'll let you go then, take my
boots off and keep the cheese refrigerated.
What use now, my arranging sandwiches
on the borders of something you said
fell apart, was not within you
anymore. What use now, those nights
saying, "I am not afraid of writing bad poetry —
for you, my soul, for you."

Minoee Modi

A Friend

Someone who you can share your inner feelings with . . .
knowing you wont be judged or rejected
someone who gives freely . . . without expectation or motivation.
Someone who lets you be who you are . . .
if you want to change, it's up to you.
Someone who is there when you're hurting . . .
offering true tenderness.
Someone who see's your beauty . . . your true beauty.
Someone who gives you space when it is needed.
Without hesitation someone who listens . . . to what you're
Really saying. Someone who will consider your different
beliefs . . . without judgement.
Some one who you always feel close to . . .
even when they are far away.
Some who is comfortable to be with . . .
anytime, anywhere, doing anything.
A friend is a special gift to be cherished forever.

Laurie Dent

I'll Never Loan My Love

Our love marched on like a springtime parade, but we knew deep inside
it was just a charade.
We lied to each other, said those sweet words.
Then you flew off like the autumn-time birds.
You flew away south for the winter,
and left in my heart a deep, painful splinter.
But now I have another; I know what love is. The love I gave you
is now only his. He loves me truly; he has no wings to fly,
as you once did when you left me to die.
I rotted a while, but I didn't die; I picked myself up, up to the sky.
I was cold and lonely; my heart broken and dead.
Then he came along and lifted my head.
The memories of you now seem so old,
for they've been replaced with a love of pure gold.
But now you are back, ready to amend;
I tell you now our love found its end.
You wanted to leave and leave you did do.
I'll never again love someone like you.
You'll love me, then leave me, so this way it must be.
Go back south, leave me alone. My love to you I'll never loan.

Lisa R. Carpenter

Beautiful Thing

The birth of my child
that wondrous feeling
of profound and overwhelming love.

The smile that lights up my face
like the first day of spring

The smell of a baby's neck
that makes us feel warm and safe

Oh what a wonderful joy
your heart so full it aches
tiny fingers and toes
this is a beautiful thing to explore

Family and friends grace my home
with laughter and tears

Never have I felt so important
never have I felt so scared
then to care for this little life entrusted to my care

As I hold that little face to my breast
my love expands to unbound limits

And in the twilight I sit and think
this is a beautiful thing.

Tia Johnson

The Soul Of A Nameless Grave

The soul of a nameless grave I saw
walking in a yard one drizzle morn.
With him I saw the breath of wind
and the leaves of an Autumn day.
The power of all men, but blessed
with the innocence of a small boy.

The soul of a nameless grave I saw
walking in a yard one drizzle morn.
The blackness of brimstone was
alive and well in his heart,
but he had no intention of fear and torment.
I feel for that soul being bound
to a nameless death and having to
walk the earth for eternity,
and not a moment sooner.

William Bannon

If I Could

If I could give away
Like I have the others
Send you on your way
Kiss you goodbye
Erase from my mind your name
Forget the feel
Turn this passion to a fading memory
Send you home
Like the child I wish you were
Playing a silly game
Put my heart back in its box
Take your image from my eyes
This torch from my soul
Walk away never to see you standing there
I don't think I would....

Kelly S. Hill

One Life Per Customer

You can't live my life
Nor can I live yours.
We live in tandem at times;
At times in parallel.

But, child, you must live yours,
Allow me to live mine.
When you seek advice, I'll try to help.
But live it for you? No.

You think, feel move through the world
As your very youth dictates.
All of me is governed by years of living.

I love, you, child, but cannot,
Indeed, will not live your life,
Nor will I permit you to live mine.

Virginnia Miller

On A Well-built Fence

The cedar posts by the hatchery road
Formed a sturdy fence a century ago;
Keeping who or what from coming there
And this or that from going where.

The tireless firs have pushed aside
The nodding rails whose wire they hide
In their bark up high where the sap drips down
And forms a pool with an amber crown.

I like this fence, but I can't say why
I always look when I'm passing by.
Perhaps it serves a purpose best
Long after its makers are laid to rest.

Robert Endicott

Twenty To Life

She lives behind a razor wire fence.
Her house is behind a locked door.
She has not seen her family since,
She's been there almost twenty four.
The years were long,
There is nothing fast about her life.
At first she thought she was hard core,
but today she will be fifty-four.
A forth of her life wasted, and
She's not yet lived.
Today, she will leave it all behind.
Where will she go? What will she do?
Mostly though, how will she act?
She won't have to ask to anymore,
To do life's simplest things.
And, they tell life is not so simple anymore.

Paula J. Jordan

My Special Hero

Although you were not my mother
I felt so close to you unlike no other
You were truly the best
You pulled through everything unlike the rest
Until one rainy day
When everything changed its way
This day March 6th, is the worst day of my life
You meant so much to people, you were a
     mother, friend and wife
There was always a smile on you
I can say that about few
Linda Kalai watch over me
Because I need thee
I Love You!!

Courtney Simmons

Addiction The Creature

It creeps upon you like a shadow in the night,
You can't see it, it's nowhere in sight.

It slowly rapes both body and soul,
Taking your mind, so it's in control.

Your thoughts are cloudy, your mind is in a mist,
You are no longer living, you only exist.

It drives you to insanity day after day,
You can't remember how life got this way.

Some don't know, and others don't care,
But most won't admit the creature is there.

It doesn't matter if you run and hide,
You're killing yourself, a slow suicide.

Shelly Kirkpatrick Smith

Awakening

It envelopes me
     a love beyond compare
     compassion for those that do not know
     one day will discern
     born again
     out of fear
     the darkness consumed by light

Tranquility now
     an everlasting peace
     a fountain breathes the spirit of life
     awestruck in the midst
     children sing
     glorious
     the dawning of a new day

Brian G. Szczerbowski

Squeaks

High-pitched, shrilling squeaks
Noises ripped through the house
A small mouse spoke his squeak, to show joy over the opened pantry he had just found
Pairs of un-oiled hinges screaming as the mouse wiggled into
the slightly ajar pantry doors
Recently waxed floors whined as the mouse dragged his newly
found wedge of Swiss across it
The choir of squeaks filled the house
It rattled off the windows . . . Squeak!
Bounced off of the wall . . . Squeak!
Echoed the throughout the house . . . Squeak!!

The mouse's only competition in this squeaking song was the chirping of a cricket
To an observer, the noises were almost identical, but the pests heard a world of difference
A squeaking cricket, cowardly ducking into the corner of the kitchen
With authority in his step, the mouse slowly approached his opponent
They eyes met and they began to scream at each other
!!!Sssqqquuueeeaaakkk!!!

The two hollered at each other until the room was flooded with
the glow of a fluorescent light
The home owner had been awakened by the disturbance and
was now standing in the kitchen doorway
"Oh my God!! A Mouse!! A Cricket!!"
The screams of the homeowner made the squeaks seems insufficient
The mouse and cricket stood still in mute amazement...

Matthew Caputo

The Grace Of God Is Like The Snow

As the snow falls from Heaven on man, beast, trees, birds, and bees
     So the Grace of God from Heaven falls indiscriminately
on all mankind (Titus, 2:11) kind and unkind.
     The snow comes down from Heaven hiding all impurities
covering all with its whiteness, clothing all with its
brightness, giving its purity to all.
     So too the Grace of God comes down from Heaven cleansing all
souls (Romans, 5:15-18) from sin's impurities, Whether we are young or
old covering all with His "whiteness" (Isaiah, 1:18) clothing all in
His Brightness (St. Matthew, 17:2) giving His Purity to all.
     The snow makes us cold, Whether we are young or old.
Now by the Grace of God we are told if we only be but bold we
shall never grow old.
     For God by His Grace has given us His Purity, Leading
us to maturity (Ephesians, 3:12) bringing us into Eternity.

Vincent G. Mead

"A Life Is A Terrible Thing To Waste"

Some things in life we just have to face,
Like how are we gonna preserve our ebony race?
We shall soon be extinct from this deadly place,
Because a life is a terrible thing to waste.

Don't kill our brothers that we see every day,
Because that's like killing ourselves in every way.
Look in the mirror and we will see,
The men we are killing are you and me.

We occupy such a large part of time and space,
We are the originators of the whole human race.
Let us not go out in shame and disgrace,
Remember, a life is a terrible thing to waste.

We are a family with the same family tree,
We are brothers and sisters with the same ancestry;
Then why are we perpetrating such random genocide?
Don't we possess any more racial pride?

Let us live and let live with pride and grace,
Let us preserve the best and rest of our race,
Let us savor the flavor of life with a taste,
And remember, a life is a terrible thing to waste!

James Leon Harris

Poetic Thoughts

People often wonder why words flow in my hand
My undying admiration, they just can't understand
they tell me I write violent s***, this phase will pass with youth
they don't look below the surface to find a deeper darker truth

They tune me out instinctively, they have some inbred screening
they say they hear the biting words, they don't listen for the meaning
Taken at face value, my lyrics may offend
But there's a striking truth and wisdom in the messages I send

There's something in words you can't hear; But more you feel
Something almost tangible, something very real
to most it may seem hectic, a raging blur of speed
But that supplies the power for the impact I need

I like my lyrics hard and fast, I think it's really great
There's just so much they look past, they can't appreciate
I don't ask that they like it — it's an acquired taste
But sometimes I get angry when with ignorance I'm faced

Just accept that it has merit, even though it's not your style
And stop ripping it apart with your smug and mocking smile
I'll stand by my conviction, your approval I don't need
I seek only to enlighten the true nature of the breed

Michael Burgess

Realty

Let me take you into my reality
It is so very lonely there.
Being separated from normal people
Whose ways and speech are strange to me.

How did I arrive into this sphere?
Why me, I want to be with the crowd
Laughing, talking being normal
Not in this distant arena where I exist.

I will force myself into your world
So that I will feel connected.
But I know that I remain there
Only by a thread that is wearing thin.

But unlike you, I have somewhere to go
When your world I cannot bear.
A place where your reality does not exist
Only the world that was created by me.

Brenda McCoy

Whispers In The Wind

Time is but a whispered breeze blowing quickly by,
    I tilt my head to catch the sound too busy to reply.
Years have passed the time away and I let it be,
    I should have fought against the clock,
spent more time, just you and me.

Now in the quiet of the drawn out day's
    I wonder where you have gone.
My little boy that used to play,
    out there on that lawn.

What was it that the whisper said, he's growing, growing, gone?
    Not yet I cry, not so soon, could it have been so long?
Time is but a whispering breeze quickly blowing by,
    now I listen carefully for your lost reply.

Like leaves in the whirling wind too soon I let you go,
    but you'll return a man some day, my heart has told me so.
Listen to the wind my son, there is wisdom in the breeze.
    It's whispering my Love to you, over land and over seas.

Janice C. Dow

Rose Valentine — The Best Of The Best "Rose"

Love is — pulverizing the remains of my mother,
transported to the US in a hardwood shipping container
via Delta Airlines from Rome, Italy. A stroke, paralysis,
striking her the morning after her evening arrival.
I rest the weight of my body on an old brick-red wooden step.
Clutching a weathered window screen and a gray-tone rock,
I surreptitiously sift charred coffin wood, nails, teeth and
pulverize brittle bone fragments into ashes.
The cemetery manager's words burned into my mind,
"No way, lady — can't bury her here — father's grave too shallow,
and don't try anything funny — I can throw you in jail."
I think otherwise.
Headstone uplifted, I bend my knees to the ground
and cradle your ashes
in my hands, until fingers open and stretch wide
releasing you to blend with your husband and my father.
Nothing else matters.

Marguerite Wander

Through The Eyes Of A Child

Through the eyes of a child, most things wonderful and new.
There's no shame when they look at you, through the eyes of a
child, all is so bright, it's you they look to for those gentle goodnights.

Through the eye of a child, there's nothing you can't do. My oh
my how they adore you. Through the eyes of a child, full of
trust and delight, when they see you, they smile at your sight.

Through the eyes of a child, you make their dreams come true,
many of the others you help build them to. Through the eyes
of a child life is fun it seems, it's you that they look to
when someone was mean. Through the eyes of a child, they're
watching you. Close attention to detail, all the things you do,
many of them watching want to be just like you.

Come, lets look and see as they do, maybe if we try it, we shall
start to see as they do, our world will become anew. Peace, Love
and Happiness, what a sight to share. A rainbow of colors
through the eyes of a child everywhere.

Candacy M. Roberts

Courage

Why must I be judged by
the clothes I choose to wear
or by the style I have my hair?
You've got to make a stand that you can rely.

You must try, in order to succeed
You must believe
There will be others to put you down
But don't let them worry you, no need to frown

You got to ignore the voices
that will try to distract
It's not gonna be easy, that's a simple fact
Remember, we make our own choices

There will come to be, a certain point of time
That we will all need to free our mind
In order to survive
We must strive to stay alive

Set your goals, make your plans and continue
to do what you got to do
We must be strong and follow through
For us, this is all very new.

Astrianna Johnson

The Perfect Gift

If I could give the world a gift, I would give the world a friend,
Someone who brings peace not war,
Someone who likes everyone, no matter what the race,
Someone who can lend a ear, when the world has something to say,
A friend the world can talk to about stressful problems,
Someone who can make a difference,
Someone who offers hope, when everything is lost,
Someone who is fun to play with,
A friend who brings joy to all,
Someone who can make the sun shine on a rainy day,
Someone who is never sad and always glad to help,
Someone who can keep the world out of never-ending trouble,
A friend that brings the starving world a Jupiter-sized pizza,
Someone who brings the world advice,
When nobody knows the right words,
If I could give the world a gift, I would give the world a friend...

Kyle Stuart

The New Creature

A new creature, um hum, healings are taking place over the
entire body, um hum.
Not just the individual body but the entire body of Christ Jesus.

A new creature in his name, um hum, no longer the same as before.

Accepting Jesus as Lord, inviting him to make his abode in our hearts,
um hum, we get them. Jesus has promised that they would make
their abode in us, He and our Father.

If we bury the old man daily, we remain new creatures.

New creatures in Christ Jesus.

Um hum, his healings are taking place, taking the place of sickness,
loneliness, depression, hatred, malice, envy, strife, um hum.

Healed in every way of everything, um hum, a new creature.

A new creature, um hum.

Winifred Mayo

BIOGRAPHIES
OF POETS

ABU-KHDEIR, ISMEIL
[b.] May 5, 1977, Kennastone Hospital; [p.] Fahmi and Najah Abu-Khdeir; [ed.] High school, now in college. Wheeler High School, Kennesaw State University; [occ.] Cashier; [memb.] Theta Chi Fraternity; [pers.] Anyone can do anything, but can that person do whatever and be happy? That depends on you. ARF; [a.] Marietta, GA

ACEVEDO-SCHOUPS, ANTONIA A.
[pen.] Antonia; [b.] September 25, 1954, San Rafael, CA; [p.] Jorge and Martha Acevedo; [m.] Luc Schoups, April 28, 1984; [ch.] Selena, Annelise, Evan Schoups; [ed.] Physicians Assistant - Stanford, Foothill Primary Care Associate Program, Master's in Public Health - San Jose State University, BA degree - creative Writing/English - San Fran. State University; [occ.] Physician's Assistant - Hazel Hawkins Hospital Community Health Clinic Hollister, Calif; [memb.] Arabian Horse Association, Shetland Pony Club; [hon.] Honorable Mention - San Mateo, Jr. College - Short Story Contest 1976; [oth. writ.] Short stories - poems - unpublished.; [pers.] I write to sense the music and the heartbeat of life - beyond that, I'm unsure...; [a.] San Martin, CA

ADAMO, TINA
[b.] August 17, 1979, Delaware; [p.] Joseph and Ann Marie Adamo; [ed.] I am a senior at Manheim Township High School; [occ.] Student; [hon.] Manheim Township varsity Softball team; [pers.] Always follow your dreams and put forth the best work you can. I would like to thank my mom, dad, Joey, and my grandparents for being my inspiration in life.; [a.] Lancaster, PA

ADAMS, CONNIE J.
[b.] November 10, 1059, Waverly, OH; [p.] Eldie and Norma Montgomery; [m.] Stephen E. Adams, April 16, 1994; [ch.] Eric, Ryan and Morgan; [ed.] Piketon High School; [occ.] Self-employed; [memb.] Humane Society, Love Animals; [pers.] In my writings, I try to bring out love and affection to touch one's heart. I've been writing poems since my High School days.; [a.] Beaver, OH

ADAMS, DAVID
[pen.] David Adams; [b.] December 19, 1946, Pittsfield, IL; [p.] Mr. and Mrs. N. V. Adams Sr.; [ed.] 2 1/2 College John Wood CC; [occ.] Self employed; [a.] Pittsfield, IL

ADAMS, JOANNE
[pen.] Jo; [b.] June 18, 1962, Chicago, IL; [p.] Foster Homes; [m.] Freddie L. Adams, September 4, 1993; [ch.] Candy, Albert, Jonathan and Christina; [ed.] Morton West Berwyn Ill., Liberty Univ., VA, Oneonta College, NY, East West Herb School, CA; [occ.] Vinyal Siding, Herbalist, writing a book of course living for, God; [memb.] Rainforest, American Indians, Feed the Children; [hon.] My honors are not through a ma - but God awards what is done in silence. Also, done to the National Library of Poetry! Thanks! Howard; [oth. writ.] Just finished a short story book. for children and adults. Waiting for God to show me who to bring it to for publication.; [pers.] I am not here for my will only to serve God. To love one another. Not the found. But the lost. The sick. Clothes and food is all we need to survive, also to thank Michele Tierra. His knowledge of herbs helped me to become well.; [a.] Greensboro, NC

ADAMS, MONA M.
[b.] March 27, 1932, Vernon, NY; [oth. writ.] Not published.; [pers.] I like to portray an awareness of people and nature together.; [a.] Oneida, NY

ADKISSON, PAUL L.
[b.] December 18, 1937, Bakersfield, CA; [p.] John M. Adkisson Sr., Velma (Gifford) Adkisson; [ch.] Ronald Scott, Susan Kim, James Gaku; [occ.] Retired; [memb.] Free and Accepted Masons, Scottish Rite, Veteran's of Foreign Wars (Life); [hon.] Received 34 Awards and Decorations including three silver stars denoting participation in 13 separate combat campaigns (Vietnam). Retired Master Chief (E-9), USN; [oth. writ.] "Anchors And Eagles", my autobiography covering 20 years military services is due for publication this year.; [a.] Grover Beach, CA

AFULEZI, UJU N.
[b.] 1938, Nigeria; [p.] Nkwocha and Igbegu Afulezi; [m.] Carol Afulezi, February 12, 1972; [ch.] Five: Chidi, Ugo, Ijeoma, Nzoputa, Udodiri; [ed.] B.S., M.S. (Oregon), M.L.S. (Pratt Institute (New York), Ph.D. (Missouri); [occ.] Librarian and World Bank Consultant; [memb.] Center for American Development Internal Inc., American Library Association, Black Caucus of ALA, Knights of Columbus; [hon.] Inventor, Calaumatic (Automatic Appointment Scheduler and Reminder), Mood meter (Communications, Facilitator of the Inanimate Kind); [oth. writ.] Several short stories, unpublished dissertation, unpublished poems, several newspaper articles; [a.] Corona Queens, NY

AGUILAR, ERIC
[b.] June 18, 1970, Los Angeles; [p.] Alex Aguilar, Emma Aguilar; [ed.] St. Paul High, Otis Art Institute, California State Univ. Long Beach; [occ.] Painting student; [oth. writ.] My poem "Love" is my first published piece.; [pers.] My writing is an impetus, an outlet to my mercurial emotions.; [a.] Fountain Valley, CA

AHRING, TRACEY L.
[b.] July 3, 1971, Little Rock, AR; [ed.] Graduated Magna Cum Laude from Univ. of Arkansas at Little Rock; [occ.] Studying for doctoral degrees in Homeopathy and Naturopathy; [hon.] Phi Kappa Phi Honor Society National Dean's List; [pers.] Ignorance and fear are our greatest adversaries. Through fiction and nonfiction, I seek to tap into the beauty and truth of the universe that lies waiting to be uncovered within us all.; [a.] Little Rock, AR

AIKMAN, DAVID
[b.] April 5, 1971, Decatur, IL; [p.] Floyd Aikman, Sharon Aikman; [ed.] MacArthur High, Lincoln Land Community College, University of Illinois at Springfield; [occ.] Student, Fitness Instructor; [memb.] Aerobics and Fitness Association of America, College Democrats, Mid-America Playwrights Theatre, Phi Rho Pi, Poets' and Writers' Literary Forum, YMCA; [hon.] Dean's List, "Best Aerobics Instructor" 1992 for Illinois Times "Best of Springfield" issue, honorable mention for Best Supporting Actor in State Journal Register's "Best of Theatre 1995."; [oth. writ.] Poems featured at local workshops and live readings. Previously published in V. of I Springfield's Alchemist Review.; [pers.] I'm too young to have a philosophy!; [a.] Springfield, IL

AJELLO, LINDA
[b.] December 19, 1952, Paterson, NJ; [p.] Marie and Roman Szymansky; [m.] John Ajello, May 19, 1973; [ch.] John Jr., Steven, Kimberly; [ed.] West Milford High School; [occ.] Self Employed, since 1975 Lightning Press and Lightning Signs Pompton Plains, NJ; [pers.] My poem is a reflection of my love I felt for my Father, I love you Dad. You are truly missed.; [a.] Wayne, NJ

ALBRECHT, PAMELA S.
[b.] March 5, 1970, Daviess Co.; [p.] Frank and Sandra Fulcher; [m.] Frederick M. Albrecht, June 3, 1989; [ch.] Blake and Ashlee Marie; [ed.] Washington High School and Cosmetology degree; [occ.] Loving mother, wife; [pers.] Women, should be proud to be stay home mothers. Society should be to! In no way will you change the world as much as you will at home.; [a.] Washington, IN

ALEXANDER-LARKIN, STEVE
[pen.] Smokes, Scarface; [b.] May 9, 1981, San Francisco; [p.] Paul Larkin, Addie Alexander; [ed.] Nine years of School, never graduated kindergarten, Middle School; [occ.] Businessman, student, professional; [hon.] Sports Channel Attendance, stay in school challenge. Six Perfect Attendance Records; [pers.] My job is the worst job in America. Pay's good but the work's murder. My job is to change the world or die trying. I hope people will appreciate my work.; [a.] Greensburg, LA

ALICEA, MIRIAM ESTHER
[pen.] Mia Alicea; [b.] January 6, 1946, Bayamon, PR; [p.] Maria Esther Pacheco, Casimiro Rosario Alicea; [m.] Single Parent; [ch.] Kristine Denise Dunleavy; [ed.] Central Commercial H.S., N.Y.C.; [occ.] Office Administrator Plastic Surgery (18 yrs.); [memb.] Marble Collegiate Church 5th Ave and 29th St., N.Y.C.; [oth. writ.] Presently writing two books (hoping to be produced for film): A) A comedy drama based on my professional experiences and the people I came in contact with during the past 18 years, plus many, many - funny, funny office experiences with doctors, patients and salesmen - Hilarious! Sub Title: "Surgery with a Smile", B) Second book is based on the memories of my childhood friend who for the past 20 years has been a homeless, N.Y.C. Shopping Bag Lady - my heart hurts for her! Sub Title: "Excuse Me, N.Y.C. is not a Rotter Apple"!; [pers.] When wisdom entereth into thine heart, and knowledge is pleasant unto thy soul, discretion shall preserve thee, understanding shall keep thee: Proverbs 2, verse 10, 11

ALLAN, JEANETTE
[b.] August 30, 1924, New Athens, IL; [p.] Elsie and Albert Weible; [m.] 2-marriages 1st Phil Frech, 2nd William Allan (Both deceased); [ch.] Peggy Frech Idecker, Susan Frech Boxx; [ed.] Completed 4 years high school and 1 yr. business school; [occ.] Retired; [memb.] United Methodist Church at New Athens; [hon.] Given an award for being church organist for 50 years; [oth. writ.] Other poems I thought this one was my best.; [pers.] This poem was written about my own small Methodist church, built in 1870 - I have been organist for 50 years - In 1963 a larger church was built but the small church where I was brought up in is where my memories are.; [a.] New Athens, IL

ALLAN, JOHN
[b.] April 4, 1910, Glasgow, Scotland; [p.] John and Mary S. Allan; [m.] Ruth Dodge Allan, October 28, 1933; [ch.] John Allan Jr., Mary S. Allan; [ed.] Glasgow High School, Concord High School, Berkeley High School, College of the Pacific; [occ.] Retired teacher of Sonoma County, Elementary, High School and Junior College (Night school) (Art Metal and Class for the Blind); [memb.] California Teachers' Assn. Sonoma County Sheriff's Bagpipe Band; [hon.] Award in bagpiping - 2nd place - at Caladonian games in San Francisco (Circa 1946); [pers.] An interest in all forms of science and the arts. Also, have an interest in peoples since prehistoric days -- their history and artifacts. Has also built, or helped to build, four log houses with native stone fireplaces.; [a.] Guerneville, CA

ALLEN, ADRIAN
[b.] March 2, 1968, San Francisco; [p.] Evelyn Allen, Bertha Allen (Grandmother); [ch.] Dantrell Rayvon, Donte Lamont; [ed.] John McLaren Park High School in San Francisco, CA, Mission Accomplish Bible College, Modesto Jr. College; [occ.] "Mother of Two" and Data Entry Clerk; [memb.] Standing of Faith Ministry, Calvary Temple Assemblies of God Church; [oth. writ.] Several poems and essays "Down in the Valley", "Shekinah Glory", "He is Risen, "The Comforter", "Friend", essay - "Streets of San Francisco", "How Does it Feel to be Single Me" etc...; [pers.] My soul desire is to reflect holiness to my readers, in hopes of sharing my love for the Lord Jesus Christ, through my writing, and personal experience. I hope to be an encourager to all who are in need of encouragement. (2 Chr. 35:2); [a.] Modesto, CA

ALLEN, GERTRUDE
[pen.] Gertrude (McClain) Allen; [b.] July 10, 1912, Greensboro, PA; [p.] Lena (Boone) Eberhart and Elmer Eberhart; [m.] Edson L. McClain (Deceased - May 12, 1942), January 27, 1932 and Clifford C. Allen (Deceased, November 20, 1990), August 10, 1946; [ch.] Gloria Dean, Donna Marie and Edson Arlene; [ed.] German Township High; [occ.] Retired from Mountain Bell Telephone and Telegraph in El Paso, Texas; [memb.] Womens Aux. Arthurdale, W. VA, Loma Terrace Baptist Church Telephone Co. Pioneers; [pers.] May 12, 1942 Edson L. McClain was killed in the explosion of the Christopher #3 Coal mine in Osage, W. VA. on Scotts Run. For 10 long days, I waited, watched, prayed and pleaded for the good news that never came. At the end of the 10th day, I was a grief-stricken widow, expecting a child, with 2 young daughters and an uncertain future. In my quest for peace of mind and order in my life, I found inspiration to write this poem which helped me put my grief to rest and go on with my life.; [a.] El Paso, TX

ALLEN, LISA M.
[pen.] Lisa Allen; [b.] November 11, 1956, Detroit, MI; [p.] LeRoy and Lois Ruddle; [m.] Jerry L. Allen, September 5, 1981; [ch.] Marie and Brian Allen; [ed.] Wayne Co. High School, University of North Ala., Hinds Community College; [occ.] Registered Nurse; [memb.] American Heart Assoc., University of Tenn. Alumni; [oth. writ.] In process of writing book of poetry and a children's book.; [pers.] I give God, my Eternal Father, the Glory and the talent.; [a.] Strawbery Plains, TN

ALLEN, MARK
[b.] February 12, 1973; [p.] Steve and Nancy Allen; [ed.] Adirandack Community College, Roberts Wesleyan College; [occ.] Security Guard, Leo O'Brien Federal Building; [hon.] 1st Place, A.C.E. NY, State Competition, short story writing; [oth. writ.] Have written several novels and many short stories and novellas.; [pers.] I try to bring beauty to the darker sides of life. My influences include Clive Barker, William Blake, and Edgar A. Poe.; [a.] Fort Edward, NY

ALLEY, JASON
[b.] October 2, 1973, Los Angeles, CA; [p.] John Alley, Carla Alley; [pers.] I can do all things thru Christ who strengthens me. The piece, like myself, is just a small part of a larger work.; [a.] Issaquah, WA

ALMEIDA, P. DENNIS
[b.] October 26, 1976, Pawtucket, RI; [p.] Antonio S. Almeida, Maria H. Almeida; [ed.] Saint Raphael Academy, Rhode Island College; [occ.] Student; [hon.] Dean's List, Fall-1995; [oth. writ.] High School poetry contests held by Saint Raphael Academy over several years; [pers.] "Knowledge is the most powerful weapon known to human kind."; [a.] Pawtucket, RI

ALVI, WASIMA E.
[pen.] Gul; [b.] July 20, 1961, Lahore, Pakistan; [p.] Main Enver Saeed Alvi, Surraya Jabeen; [m.] Major Agha Ali Imam Naovi, January 28, 1983; [ch.] Nader Ali; [ed.] MS in special Education - Indiana University IN MA - Secondary Education - Punjab University, Pakistan, BA - Kinnaird College for Women, Pakistan, Metric Certification - Cathedral High School Pakistan CA - Community College Credentials for Instructor and Service for Develop Disable; [occ.] Consumer Service Coordinator, and Qualified Mental Retardation Specialist; [memb.] Proud Indiana University Member in Good Standing Alumni and International Society Society of Poets 1995-1996; [hon.] I have the honor of being a mother of a son who has already shown promise towards growing up to do great things in life; [oth. writ.] Several poems in Urdu and English. Clear Designated subjects Adult Education Teaching Credential Subject: Handicapped.; [pers.] "In the interest of securing a complete vision of reality, therefore, sense - perception must be supplemented by the perception of what the Quran describes as Fuad or Qalb, ie Heart" From: The Reconstruction of Religious thought in Islam - By: Allama M. Iqbal.; [a.] Ontario, CA

AMEDAN, NORMAN
[b.] August 21, 1976; [ed.] Community College of Vermont; [occ.] Furniture Maker; [a.] South Londonderry, VT

AMERS, KARYN
[pen.] Karyn Buckthorpe; [b.] June 11, 1959, Lippstant; [p.] Martin Buckthorpe, Margaret Bucthorpe; [m.] Brian Amers, September 3, 1988; [ch.] Nadine Amers, Scottamers Amers; [ed.] St Marys Convent Berwick upon Tweed England, Ashington College Northumberland England; [occ.] Homemaker; [pers.] I find that writing poetry is very therapeutic for me.

AMRHEIN, HEATHER
[b.] January 23, 1982, Brooklyn, NY; [p.] Elizabeth and Paul Amrhein; [ed.] 9th Grade at Lenape Middle School; [occ.] Student; [memb.] National Junior Honors Society; [hon.] I Won the First Place in the State of Florida for some of my Writing; [oth. writ.] I haven't had anything else published just yet, but I'm working on a novel and am almost finished with a short story I'm planning to submit to a few magazines.; [pers.] If you have a talent, utilize and share it! For that is when wonderful things happen, and you finally feel whole.; [a.] Doylestown, PA

ANCIANO, JOY M.
[b.] September 27, 1962, Manila, Philippines; [p.] Orlando Paule, Carmen Maris; [m.] Ed Anciano, April 26, 1989; [ch.] Zachary; [ed.] Registered Nurse Certified - open heart Nurse, NICU - Premiee Nurse Train in Telemetry, Defox and Med Surg.; [occ.] Nursing. NICU Dept at Parkview Hosp

ANDERSON, CLEVE
[b.] June 27, 1919; [hon.] Five Majors Patents in the Nuclear Waste Management Field that can resolve the Problems, they are not Politically Correct among Nuclear Advocates, However; [oth. writ.] A book entitled: "The Nuclear Threat That Dwarfs The Bomb" plus several articles on Plutonium including my most recent one "Defusing Weapons Plutonium."; [pers.] I share the belief of the Hopis, a peace-loving Indian Tribe in Arizona, there are many paths to the summit but there is only one God. Tolerance of people with different pathways to the summit is vital to world survival.; [a.] Green Valley, AZ

ANDERSON, ELIZABETH M.
[b.] January 7, 1956, Troy, NY; [p.] Mary E. Hatch - William A. Hatch; [m.] Tyrone L. Anderson, December 31, 1987; [ch.] Malena D. Williams, Chase J. Anderson; [ed.] Troy High School, Hudson Valley Community College; [occ.] Housewife and grandmother; [memb.] American Cancer Association; [hon.] Dean's List; [oth. writ.] Home collection of works; [pers.] Being a survivor of drugs, alcohol, abuse and cancer twice, I see that life is not always and maybe sometimes never a bed of roses. I am a realist about life which helps me and others to stay strong and keep fighting. "Thanks Mom".; [a.] Fayetteville, NC

ANDERSON, ERNESTINE S.
[b.] October 22, 1941, Riceboro, GA; [p.] Earneste and Louise Stewart; [m.] Charley Anderson, June 15, 1960; [ch.] Four; [ed.] High school; [occ.] House wife - tutor with Youth Guidance; [memb.] Choir - "The Jesuitte Choral"; [oth. writ.] Song writter

ANDERSON, LESLEY MARIE
[pen.] Lesley Anderson; [b.] November 11, 1969, Annapolis, MD; [p.] Suzanne Nast, Paul Philip Menendez; [m.] John Anderson, June 16, 1992; [ed.] High School, Ballard High, Seattle, WA, Tech School, Lake Washington Technical College, Major: Early Childhood Education, Kirkland, WA, Computer Learning Center, Philadelphia, PA; [occ.] Administrative Assistant, Unibol, Inc., Marietta, GA; [memb.] America On Line, Center for Marine Conservation; [hon.] Graduated Top 5% from Computer Learning Center, Philadelphia, PA, In

1994; [oth. writ.] Misc. Short Stories, "Red Shadows", is about vampires. Will be published for the Australian Vampire Information Association Newsletter, July 1966. (AVIA); [pers.] "If you decide to run naked in the rain, be prepared to catch a cold."; [a.] Marietta, GA

ANDERSON, LOLA FUNK
[b.] March 18, 1904, Agency, IA; [p.] Lambert and Anna Brown Funk; [m.] Dwight Leroy Anderson, September 10, 1924; [ch.] Dwight Anderson, Jr., Robert Funk Anderson, Lola Lee Anderson Pike; [ed.] Agency, Iowa, High School of Fine Arts, Ottumwa, IA, Iowa success Business College, Ottumwa, IA; [occ.] Ninety-two years old. I have written sixty-one gospel songs, words and music. Started writing music at 85 years of age. Two were sung at my husbands funeral, there will be sung at mine.; [memb.] Agency, IA, United Methodist Church, Velda Rose United Methodist Church, Mesa AZ, Rebekah Lodge #455, Agency, Iowa, Estern Star #112. Ottumwa, Iowa, WBCCI Airstream Club- Iowa, Illiamo, Arizona, Units; [oth. writ.] Have written for Ottumwa, IA. Courier, Eldon IA. Forum and Batavia, IA, Beacon; [pers.] Writing gospel music has brought me very close to God and Jesus Christ. I wish more people could experience the blessing. It would make a much better world for everyone. My daughter says that when I quit writing and have gone to my permanent home, she will have published all my songs and explain how and why each song was written.; [a.] Mesa, AZ

ANDERSON, LYNNE
[b.] June 29, 1969, Quincy, MA; [p.] Paul and Marilyn Anderson; [ed.] BA in Psychology from Eastern Nazarene College; [occ.] Administrative Assistant at Brigham and Women's Hospital; [hon.] Psi Chi Honor's Society, Dean's List; [pers.] Pursue your dreams and make wise choices for the future, but always try to enjoy today.; [a.] Braintree, MA

ANDERSON, MARGARET TAYLER
[b.] May 1, 1918; [p.] George Lawrence Tayler, Tressie Huntington Tayler; [m.] James Kress Anderson, December 31, 1940; [ch.] Bret, Blythe, Beth Murray, Burke; [ed.] Willamette Univ. Salem Or (AB) '39 (MA) '40, Columbia Univ. Teachers College, NYC (MA) '67 (PD) '70, Deominican College of Blauvelt (Hon. DHL) '91; [occ.] Real Estate Broker, Career Counseling Consultant (22 years Director of Womens Counseling Center); [memb.] Am. Assoc. of Univ. Woman, League of Women Voters, Rockland County Democratic Committee, Child Development Council; [hon.] Distinguished Alumni Teachers College, Columbia Univ. NYC; [oth. writ.] Poetry published in Epworth 1935, Herald Magazine, and college anthologies 1939; [pers.] Optimistically looking for growth everywhere and in everyone; [a.] Palisades, NY

ANDERSON, MARY R.
[b.] April 4, 1937, Escanaba, MI; [p.] Alice and Renold Anderson; [ed.] B.A. Summa Cum Laude, M.A. Holy Names College, Oakland, CA, Ph. D. University of California, Berkeley; [memb.] Rank and Tenure Committee, 1994-96, WASC Steering Committee for Educational Programs, (Co-Chair), 1993-95, 1984-85.; [hon.] Sears-Roebuck Foundation Teaching Excellence and Campus Leadership Award, Distinguished Professors Program, Indepen-

dent Colleges of Northern California, Personal Invitation to U.S./ Russia Joint Conference on Education, October 1-9, 1994, Presidium of the Academy of Science, Moscow. Biographical Sketch in Who's Who Among America's Teachers. Selected by students listed in Who's Who Among Students in American Colleges and Universities, Listed in The World's Who's Who of Women. 13th edition, Winter 1994-95 and 14th edition, 1996. Cambridge, England: International Biographical Centre.; [oth. writ.] "Deconstruction and the Teaching Historian" Journal of the History of European Ideas; [a.] Kensington, CA

ANSON, STEVE
[b.] November 6, 1971, Granada Hills, CA; [p.] Steve Sr. and Sara Ann Anson; [m.] Cynthia Anson, October 10, 1993; [ch.] Zachary Christopher; [ed.] Canyon High, College of the Canyons; [a.] Canyon Country, CA

ARAGON, ERIC
[pen.] E. T. Thomas; [b.] August 25, 1964, Ogden, UT; [p.] Arthur and Helen Aragon; [m.] Shuree Harrison, July 15, 1988; [ch.] M. Sable, Ashton Thomas; [ed.] Roy High School, Weber State College, BS, Univ. of Utah, MS; [occ.] Health and Fitness Consultant; [memb.] National Strength and Conditioning Assoc., American Heart Association; [hon.] Several Local, State and National Powerlifting Awards from 1983-1987; [oth. writ.] "Fit to Win" handbook Utah Army National Guard, I also design, write and edit several corporate wellness newsletters; [pers.] The mystical forces within each of us are very intriguing to me. Love, hate, passion, attraction and the senses. The awesome power of mother nature and stirs my creativity.; [a.] Salt Lake City, UT

ARMSTRONG, CYNTHIA ANNE RENÉE
[pen.] Cindy; [b.] May 22, New York; [p.] Clint and Fredericka Armstrong; [ed.] Post Graduate: Certificate in Dance/Movement Education; Graduate: Master of Science in Dance/Movement Education; Undergraduate: Dual Certification in Child Study/Special Education; [occ.] Early Childhood Special Education Teacher at Shaklin Elementary School, Beaufort, SC; [memb.] Association for Supervision and Curriculum Development (ASCD); [a.] Beaufort, SC

ARMSTRONG, JENIFER
[pen.] Buffie Armstrong; [b.] November 11, 1948, Buffalo, NY; [p.] Edward and Betty Young; [m.] Michael Armstrong, August 2, 1969; [ch.] Michael, Jenny, Matt, Mark Heidi, Paul; [ed.] Vermilion High School, Vermilion, OH Oberlin School of Commerce, Oberlin, OH; [occ.] Housewife; [a.] Pontiac, IL

ARTHUR, GEORGE W.
[pen.] Arthur W. George; [b.] June 29, 1928, Altoona, PA; [p.] George and Ethel Arthur; [m.] Lorraine, June 14, 1968; [ch.] Four by Prev. marriage; [ed.] BS Sociology, MA Counseling Psychology; [occ.] Private Practice as Licensed Clinical Prof. Counselor; [memb.] American Mental Health Counselor Asc., Montana Clinical Mental Health Counselors Asc.; [hon.] Nothing that would be considered earth shattering or traumatic; [oth. writ.] Two poems printed in the Montana Poet; [pers.] My writings reflect the deep down feelings of the feelings that many people have but are unable or unwilling to express.; [a.] Thompson Falls, MT

ASGHARI, DONNETTA
[b.] July 21, 1947, Michigan; [p.] John E. Lewis (Deceased), Mrs. Eloise Langston-Williams; [ch.] Mrs. Carmen Amaro, Anthony Archer, Elliot Lewis; [occ.] Tutor, Collegiate Marketing Campus Representative; [memb.] UCLA Alumni Association Assoc. for Supervision and Curriculum Development, The Teacher's Cooperative, American Assoc. of University Women; [oth. writ.] Unpublished, two manuscripts, several poems, skit, one act play.; [pers.] I strive to do the whole law, immortal crime is a waste of one's creative talents.; [a.] Van Nuys, CA

ASHI
[b.] April 25, 1948, Brunswick, ME; [p.] Dorothy Robinson, Carl Robinson (Dec.); [ch.] Andy Napier; [oth. writ.] Spiritual poem published in Seattle newspaper. Currently creating a book of my erotic poetry, visually enhanced with nude photography.; [pers.] Writing and art are vehicle to express my passion, power and vitality. I love creating that which stirs and awakens others (and myself) into knowing, feeling and expressing themselves from unremembered and undiscovered places within their souls.; [a.] Portland, OR

ASHLEY, DAWN
[b.] September 16, 1983, Calgary, AB, Canada; [p.] Mike and Linda Ashley; [ed.] Grade 5, St. Charles School; [memb.] Young Author's Club, Girl Scouts; [hon.] Choir Award Music Award; [oth. writ.] Poems published in Young Author's Anthology; [pers.] My goal is to become an author and illustrator after college.; [a.] Kettering, OH

ASLAKSEN, ALICE COWAN
[b.] August 27, 1912, Brooklyn, NY; [p.] William Arthur Cowan, Alice Togus Cowan; [m.] Olaf Arthur Aslaksen, October 9, 1953; [ch.] Alice Aslaksen Rynd, William Arthur Aslaksen; [ed.] High School - Kathryn Gibbs Business, NY; [occ.] Retired Secretary; [memb.] D.A.R. - Women's Club of The Desert, United Church Of The Desert; [pers.] I like to send original poems instead of commercial cards. My grandfather James Cowan was an editor, published many poems and wrote a book "Daybreak" in the late 1880's early 1900's. (Holyoke, MA); [a.] Palm Desert, CA

ATARODIAN, ANA M. MANDULEY
[b.] March 5, 1960, Havana, Cuba; [p.] Carlos Manduley, C. Esther Manduley; [m.] Hossein Atarodian, April 12, 1990; [ch.] Nilofar Esther; [ed.] Montgomery College, American University; [occ.] Senior Program Analyst, (Dept. of Defense (DOD)); [memb.] Cuban-American Cultural Institute, CASA Cuba, Disabled American Vets; [hon.] Cong. Newton Steers (Rep. MD) Congressional Internship, Dept. of Navy Recognition Awards; [oth. writ.] Working in various poems and novels (unpublished); [pers.] My writings are totally predisposed by past philosophers, poets and novelists and their outlook on life's wisdom.; [a.] Gaithersburg, MD

ATCHISON, MATTHEW S.
[b.] April 25, 1965, Hamilton, TX; [p.] Carl and Kathleen Atchison; [ed.] Southwest Bible In., Howard Collage, Angelo State University (ASU); [occ.] Respiratory Tech.; [memb.] North Side Church of Christ. NRA; [oth. writ.] "A River at

Sunset", "Lesson of the Butterflies", "True Wealth"; [pers.] My goal in my writing is to honor my God by calling attention to his beautiful, wondrous creation.; [a.] San Angelo, TX

AUGSBURGER, A. DON
[b.] December 21, 1925, Elida, OH; [p.] Clarence and Estella Augsburger; [m.] Martha K. Augsburger, June 5, 1948; [ch.] Phyllis, Patricia, Don Richard; [ed.] B.A. Eastern Mennonite University, M.R.E. Eastern Baptist Seminary, D.Ed. Temple University, Philadelphia, PA; [occ.] Chaplain at Mennonite Home Lancaster, PA; [oth. writ.] Books: Creating Christian Personality, Marriages That Work Ed., A Pattern For Living, Book: Creating Christian Personality. Marriages That Works was published in 1984, and a Pattern for Living in 1993. Thumbs Up: Turbulent stress, anxious test, motors hum, pilot's thumb, leveling flight, fleeting night, beauty revealed, secret concealed, noble down, no frown, so life confounded strife!; [pers.] Honor God the Creator, Jesus His Son and live life to the fullest.; [a.] Lancaster, PA

AUSTIN, MARIA G.
[b.] March 22, 1958, Chiapas, Mexico; [p.] Luis Rincon Martinez and Belia Ballinas Dominguez; [m.] Dennis K. Austin, September 21, 1985; [ch.] Josue R. Austin, Richard L. Austin; [ed.] Social Sciences and Humanities, Elementary School Teacher; [occ.] Owner, Editor of upcoming publication in Spanish, for Hispanic Women.; [memb.] "Organizaccou De Trabajadores Para La Educacion"; [oth. writ.] Many unpublished poems written in Spanish. Several articles published in local Hispanic newspapers. Writer, Editor and Publisher of several newspapers in Spanish. I am currently writing a novel in Spanish.; [pers.] To give at all times, the best of ourselves socially, morally and professionally and preserving in reaching our dreams.; [a.] Sterling, VA

AVILES, MARTHA SCHNEEGANS
[b.] July 29, 1959, Managua, Nicaragua; [p.] Gloria and Rene Schneegans; [m.] Joaquin J. Aviles, March 7, 1980; [ch.] Martha-Lucia, Denisse Marie and Sabrina-Renee; [ed.] Attended St. Teresa's Academy since Kindergarten to H.S. Graduation. B.S. University of Central Texas; [occ.] Own and Manage a Drapery Workroom; [memb.] Patron Sponsor ASID (American Society Interior Designers); [hon.] Dean's List; [oth. writ.] All published - Poems, working on a novel. Essay, etc.; [pers.] Admiration for Ralph Waldo Emerson Henry David Thoreau since an early age and even more so since I became exiled from Nicaragua; [a.] Austin, TX

AXELROD, LAWRENCE
[b.] January 19, 1942, Detroit, MI; [p.] Marvin and Zelda Axelrod; [ed.] 8th grade; [occ.] Disabled; [hon.] Sports, Military, Human Life, Artist of Sea Shells; [pers.] Give thanks for the great state of Florida. Love to love woman, serve my community.; [a.] Daytona Beach, FL

AYALASOMAYAJULA, NARASIMHAM R. A.
[pen.] Arun Narasimham; [b.] November 28, 1933, Visakhapatnam, India; [p.] A. L. Narayana Rao, A. Mahalakshmi Gunnamma; [m.] A. Kamakshi Devi, June 12, 1955; [ch.] Lakshmi Devi Ganti, Narayan Rao, Shyamala Prakash; [ed.] M.A., B.Sc., B.Ed., Master of Arts (Psychology), Bachelor of Science

(Chemistry), Bachelor of Education; [memb.] Advisor to Nature Club; [hon.] (1) Received Recognition for 40 years of Service to Loyola, Jamshedpur, India from Pope John Paul II, (2) Lions Club Gold Medal for Meritorious Service to Education, India; [oth. writ.] The manuscript, on "A Text Book on General Psychology" for graduates and under graduates, is under preparation.; [pers.] "Do what you do, do well!"; [a.] Sacramento, CA

BAGLEY, LARRY
[b.] June 19, 1973, Marietta, GA; [p.] Lawrence A. and Theresa A. Bagley; [ed.] Graduated Shaw High School and went on to Columbus Technical Institute to receive a Diploma in Machine Tool Technology and Working on Auto Body Collision Repair; [occ.] Machine Operator at Precision Components International (PCI); [oth. writ.] Don't worry, My Best Friend, All I Need The Light of the World, and The Answer to my Prayers.; [pers.] I am currently serving time in prison for an automobile accent in which my girlfriend died. While locked up I discovered the true joy that comes from knowing Christ and receiving his salvation and I began writing poetry to share my joy with others.; [a.] Columbus, GA

BAILEY, JERRI
[b.] March 16, 1957, Oceanside, CA; [p.] A. L. Renner Jr., Barbara J. Wilson; [m.] Martin P. Bailey, June 8, 1991; [ch.] Jennifer Cutsinger, Megan Bailey; [ed.] San Luis Rey Academy, Oceanside CA, Mira Costa College, Oceanside, CA; [occ.] Asset Manager, National Bank of So. California; [a.] Huntington Beach, CA

BAILEY, TERRON TERAY
[pen.] John Doe (JDoe); [b.] March 5, 1957, Winston Salem, NC; [memb.] Prince Hall Masons; [oth. writ.] Men don't cry is from my collection, "The Simple Writing's of John Doe." It is one of my earliest works. My thoughts have advanced for far beyond this level. I hope to publish the collection.; [pers.] I see myself as a traveling spirit sent by God. For the sole purpose of giving him the honor, praise and Glory. Through the gift of words. I pray my words will be read while I'm still yet alive, not only after I'm dead.; [a.] Winston Salem, NC

BAKER, ERIC
[b.] September 16, 1975, Huntington, Long Island; [p.] Russ and Linda Baker; [ed.] State University of New York at Stonybrook (SUNY) Advanced study at Gemological Institute of America in California seeking degree as "Gemologist"; [occ.] Have worked in Family Operated High End Jewelry Store in Port; [memb.] Jefferson, L.I. - will return to full time work when I receive my degree; [oth. writ.] Have written poems and short stories in college courses - have not submitted anything for publication; [pers.] "— Follow my heart my teeth to the wind"; [a.] Setaucket, NY

BAKER, KELLI
[b.] October 3, 1983, Ft. Thomas, KY; [p.] Charles E. Baker, Karen S. Smith; [ed.] Presently 7th grade, student at Gray Middle School; [occ.] Student; [hon.] A/B Honor Roll Trophies for Soccer and Soft Ball Ribbons for Writing Stories; [oth. writ.] Story published in school paper.; [pers.] I really enjoy writing poems and stories, especially ones that interest people. I think it is a real accomplishment to get a poem published. I'm very proud.; [a.] Florence, KY

BALDWIN, GRACE R.
[pen.] Grace Rosen Baldwin; [b.] September 9, 1914, Buckingham, VA; [p.] Henry Rosen Bessie Crews, Charlie Jones; [m.] Everette S. Baldwin (Deceased); [ch.] Charles H. Jones; [ed.] Buckingham High, RPI Orts and Crafts, Business in General owned and Operated Girl's Dorm; [occ.] Retired (82 yrs old) mother of the year 1996; [memb.] Phi Sigma Alpha, Monument Heights Baptist, Needles Eye Christian Fellowship, Belles and Beauy, Senior Adult Group, house mother and councler girls Baldwin house; [hon.] Come Live With Me, Play in New Virginia Library Rova being loved by over one thousand girls. Oil Paintings - Barter Theater; [oth. writ.] Come Live With Me poems by Grace, Historical Monument Ave Richmond VA, The Baldwin House Who's Gonna Take My Place; [pers.] Come Live With Me traces the trials and faith of me but it also captures Richmond's history during a radical change, a story about innocence, loss but keeping hope alive; [a.] Richmond, VA

BALES, HEATHER
[b.] September 8, 1983, Roanoke, VA; [p.] James Bales and Frances Hensley-Bales; [ed.] Green Valley Elem., Hidden Valley Jr. High, several gifted summer classes at Colleges in the VA area (UVA, Roanoke College); [occ.] Student; [memb.] Good Samaritan Hospice Volunteer, Hall's United Methodist VBS Teacher, an Active Member of the Church itself and Assistant to Sunday School (Youth) Teacher; [hon.] John's Hopkins University State Verbal and Mathematics Excellence Award (2 years), Honor Student-Hidden Valley High, Spelling Bee District Champion (1 Year); [oth. writ.] None, unpublished, many poems and numerous short stories.; [pers.] To write a great poem you should look for and observe what you want to write about. Then write from your heart.; [a.] Roanoke, VA

BAMBERG, JANE HINDLE
[b.] May 17, 1930, London, England; [p.] Annette Zeiss Hindle Lye, Wilfred Hope Hindle; [m.] September 3, 1952; [ch.] Winifred Bamberg (1961), Katharine Bamberg (1962), Elizabeth Bamberg (1965); [ed.] Cornell U. (Psychology), Columbia U. (B.S. Occupational Therapy, '54), Cornell U. (Grad. School Science Ed.), U. So. Maine (Spec. Ed.), U. So. Maine (M.S.Ed. (double) - Counseling and Rehabilitation Counseling '84); [occ.] Counselor - Private (all ages), Counselor - School Children and Families; [memb.] Bd. of Counseling Professionals (Licensed Clinical Professional Counselor), Bd. for Rehabilitation Certification (Certified Rehabilitation Counselor), Nat'l Bd. for Certified Counselors (Nat'l Certified Counselor), Occupational Therapist (OT Registered - Nat'l), many environmental conservation organizations "Healing the Healers" group; [hon.] M.S.Ed., with Honors ('84), Who's Who Among Human Services Professionals, 1992-1993, 3rd Ed., (Nat'l Reference Institute); [oth. writ.] Other poetry and prose, songs.; [pers.] I believe we are all intimately and integrally conjoined with nature. To bring the most meaningful connections to fruition is a relentless struggle. Yet our planet's best potential for hope and positive transformation lies in both human kinds flourishing connections with nature, and with each other.; [a.] Oxford, ME

BARBER, ALICE LE SASSIER
[pen.] Alice Ker; [b.] February 5, 1923, Mississippi; [p.] William and Katherine Le Sassier; [m.] Richard E. Barber III, Divorced 1967; [ch.] Richard E. Barber IV; [ed.] MSW 1953 Tulane University New Orleans, Louisiana; [occ.] Retired 1992 Professor Emerti Va., Commonwealth Univ. School of Social Work 1964-1992; [memb.] Reared: Live Oak Plantation West Feliciana Parish Louisiana; [oth. writ.] Private collection never published; [pers.] I write for the personal enjoyment of family, friends and colleagues. I have never submitted for publication before this. I strive for light and airy stanzas that delight and lift up the reader.; [a.] Richmond, VA

BARBUS, MARK P.
[pen.] Marcus Paul; [b.] April 1, 1953, Evanston, IL; [p.] Paul Barbus, Dorthy Davidson; [m.] Divorced; [ch.] Linda A., April M., Paul E., Dennis; [ed.] Clover Park High SC., Tacoma WA., - Ft. Steel Coom Cloge, Privot Pilot; [occ.] Glazier, Musician; [memb.] Church of Scientology; [oth. writ.] Many other writings and art work not published yet many songs written and performed some recordings.; [pers.] I am who I have always been, I will always be who I am, I eather make it happen or allow it to occur. I am an artist; [a.] Heflin, AL

BARNES, CECELIA J.
[b.] March 3, 1926, Chowan Co., NC; [p.] Clement T. Jordan, Mary M. Jordan; [m.] Van C. Barnes, June 18, 1953; [memb.] Indian River Baptist Church; [oth. writ.] Several in North Carolina, Perguimans Cty (Weekly News Paper) of family life and love of people.; [pers.] Although the years pass into many, my heart still is as young as the outside green Woodlands and Wild Flowers.; [a.] Chesapeake, VA

BARRAZA, LENA CAROL
[b.] July 8, 1961, Manchester, NH; [p.] Harold and Sarah Gilfillan; [m.] Michael John Barraza, May 27, 1992; [ch.] Two children; [ed.] I haven't graduated from High School but I do want to finish getting my education an education is very important.; [occ.] Ft. Braggmain Exchange Mens Clothing Department Sales Associate; [oth. writ.] Kristina, My Father The Run Away, My Children For Every Blue ocean; [pers.] I have been writing since I was 16 years old I always wanted to be a writer. I have confidence in myself I know if I put my mind to it I can do anything.; [a.] Spring Lake, NC

BARSH, FRANCES C.
[ed.] BS and MA New York University, MBA Fairleigh Dickinson University, studies Oxford University; [oth. writ.] Articles: Journal of Cultural Economics, Commerce Magazine, Waste Watch, etc., and other feasibility, demographic, economic studies and surveys.; [pers.] Writing allows one to contribute to the body of knowledge. Writing poetry allows one to give voice to the nuances of our time.; [a.] Naples, FL

BASILE, JOANNA CHRISTINE
[pen.] Joanna Christine Basile; [b.] October 18, 1983, San Antonio, TX; [p.] Thomas F. Basile, Jody M. Basile; [ed.] 7th Grade Student. I one day hope to attend the University of Notre Dame; [occ.] Student; [hon.] 1st Place in 4th Grade Social

Studies Fair - "Titanic Project," Honorable Mention County Social Studies Fair (1994); [pers.] I want to thank my mom (Jody) and my dad (Tom), my sister Emily and my friends Brian, Erica, Stacy, Joey, and Stephanie and last but not least my teacher Mrs. Perks for helping me along.; [a.] Charleston, WV

BASSETT, C. KAY
[b.] July 16, 1957, Denver, CO; [p.] Doris and Richard Bassett; [m.] John Patterson, May 20, 1994; [ed.] Senior at the University of Colorado at Denver major: English; [occ.] Secretary; [oth. writ.] Poems: (Published) Stitches, Memories Ring, Article: Encore Magazine: "Heart to Heart"; [pers.] Always believe in yourself and in your dreams.

BATTISH, SARITA
[b.] May 13, 1970, Punjab, India; [p.] Jyoti Battish, Jaswinder Battish; [ed.] B.S. Biology - East Stroudsburg University, M.S. Biomedical Science - Drexell University; [occ.] Biomedical Scientist; [memb.] Biomedical Computing Society, Drug Information Association, Network of Female Executives, Women's Alliance for Job Equity; [hon.] Who's Who Women in World

BAUGUS, CLARA
[b.] April 4, 1927, Giles, TN; [p.] Robert and Naomi Cummins; [m.] John Baugus, July 16, 1945; [ch.] Sammie and Patricia Baugus; [ed.] 4-years at one room school house; [occ.] Home maker; [memb.] Church of Christ; [hon.] Wife and Mother, Grandmother and Great Grandmother; [oth. writ.] 3-books and several poems.; [pers.] I hope my work will help people love the Lord and each other more.; [a.] Columbia, TN

BAUMGARTNER, DOLORES
[pen.] Dolores Baumgartner; [b.] July 13, 1948, Niagara Falls, NY; [p.] Connie Pleskan, Henry Kisby; [m.] Kenneth Baumgartner, July 4, 1964; [ch.] Warren, Yen, Christopher; [ed.] Dover High, GED - Parsippany Hills; [oth. writ.] Several poems for family and friends.; [pers.] I guess it's true, with a lot of encouragement from my best friend (my husband) all things are possible, and at 48 yrs. young I'm a possibiilty!; [a.] Spring Hill, FL

BEARD, MICHAEL
[b.] December 11, 1953, Beaumont, TX; [m.] Linda Beard, December 31, 1975; [ch.] Matt, Mary, Mandy, and Mason; [ed.] University of Texas; [occ.] Orthodontist; [a.] Jacksonville, TX

BEASLEY, BRANDON D.
[pen.] BDD; [b.] December 28, 1975, Tyler, TX; [p.] Mary Lyons, Ray Beasley; [ed.] Taking Classes at Hillsbrough Community College Tampa Florida. Majoring in Biology; [occ.] Airmen First Class, United States Airforce; [memb.] Member in local Church Choir; [pers.] Just because you start on the bottom, does not mean you have to end up there.; [a.] Tampa, FL

BECKLES, REUBEN
[b.] March 4, 1932, San Francisco, CA; [p.] Simeon and June Beckles; [m.] Shirley; [ch.] Six; [ed.] HS - Two years College; [occ.] Writer; [oth. writ.] 3 novels, 10 short stories, numerous poems; [pers.] The essence of living is simplicity - so to be able to

write effectively - one must be able to do more than talk and talk, but walk and walk - because being black it's all about a spiritual journey...; [a.] Los Angeles, CA

BEDWELL, LINDA KAY
[b.] April 11, 1963, Wilmington, DE; [p.] Curtis and Edna Burton; [m.] Ervin J. Bedwell, April 25, 1981; [ch.] James E. and Ashley Marie; [ed.] Smyrna High School, James H. Groves Adult Education; [occ.] Daycare Owner/Operator; [memb.] Boy Scouts of America, Foster Parents for State of Del.; [pers.] This poem is in memory of all my friends that were loved and lost especially my friend Elaine M. Schaffer who was taken from us to soon. And I would like to thank my family for supporting me through these Tough Times in my life.; [a.] Clayton, DE

BEEBE, CLAUDIA MARIE
[b.] February 26, 1961, Manhattan, NY; [p.] Ken and Dorothy Beebe; [ed.] GED; [occ.] Disabled; [pers.] Close head injury: Learn the world over people: Place Wisdom, Peace: Walk on.; [a.] State College, PA

BEED, MICHAEL
[pen.] Mike; [b.] November 10, 1972; [p.] Thomas and Iva Beed; [ed.] Culinary Institute of America; [occ.] Chef; [pers.] Marry your mind to the inside. Make yourself your bride. Never become petrified. Take hold of the High tide. The tide is the outside.; [a.] Gaithersburg, MD

BELL, DANA NICOLE
[b.] February 18, 1974, Pittsburgh/Alagany; [p.] Clifford and Carole Bell; [ed.] G.E.D. and Rayn High School, Earle C. Clemnts Job Corps Center, Clevland Job Corps Center, Youngston State University

BELL, HEIDI ANNE
[b.] August 14, 1975, Augusta, GA; [p.] Pamela Anne Bell, James Edward Bell; [ed.] Wayne Central High School, Ontario Center, NY, Monroe Community College - Associates Degree in Literature/English studies and Associates degree in Biological Technology, Rochester, NY; [occ.] Pharmacy Technician, Office Clerical and college student majoring in Medical Technology; [hon.] Wayne Central Chapter of the National Honor Society, Who's Who in American High School Students - 1992 and 1993, Academic Achievement Awards in English 1992, Monroe Community College, Dean's List.; [oth. writ.] Unpublished writings including: A book named Secrets of Deception and several poems entitled "Entity", "Awaiting Death," "Bondage of the Soul," "Destined Love", and "Into the Unknown."; [pers.] Through my many reading experiences, I have learned to appreciate the many literary works by authors, past and present, and have gained admiration for those who took the time to incorporate their talents into written form for society's reading enjoyment. I hope that I will also be able to make an important contribution to the literary world.; [a.] Ontario, NY

BELLI, DIANNA L.
[b.] April 5, 1958, Burlingame, CA; [p.] Charlie and Doris Agius; [m.] Raymond Belli, June 10, 1978; [ch.] Miranda; [occ.] Domestic Engineer; [hon.] Wond an award at the San Mateo County Fair; [oth. writ.] This is my first writing.; [pers.] You can substitute any child's name for the "our

little girl" part of the poem. Originally I had "Miranda" and I changed it for this writing. She'll always be our little girl.; [a.] Elk Grove, CA

BELLMAY, JOY M.
[b.] October 3, 1974, Waterbury, CT; [p.] Lena M. Barilla, Nelson John Bellmay; [ed.] Sacred Heart High School, University of Connecticut, Palm Beach Atlantic College; [occ.] Student; [hon.] Colonial Dames of America Scholarship Winner, Dean's List, President's List; [pers.] For me, writing is an emotional outlet. I strive to create works that everyone can identify with in some way.; [a.] West Palm Beach, FL

BENJAMIN, RICHARD N.
[b.] November 3, 1946, Manhattan; [p.] Vida Benjamin (Mom), Lucis Head (Dad); [ch.] To my daughter with love; [ed.] GED Graduate, Earn 34 Credit at Orange County Community College, need 34 more to graduate; [occ.] Night Maintenance Worker; [memb.] Second Baptist Church, Middletown New York; [hon.] Work experience apprenticeship program, May 15 - June 26, 1986, from Eugene W. Jordan, Program Supervisor, Solomon Goodrich Executive Director; [oth. writ.] Success, A Think of Art, Special Comment, Dear Proud Queen, Just Thoughts, A Thought of Silence, The Key to Happiness, This Magic Moment; [pers.] My thanks and Godly Blessing of our Lord Jesus Christ to all. Amen. The joy of sharing thew world of our Lord Jesus Christ is always growing.; [a.] Middletown, NY

BENN, NANCY A.
[b.] July 28, 1940, Island Falls, ME; [p.] Kermit and Frances Esty; [m.] Shirley "Butch" Benn, December 25, 1971; [ed.] Aroostook State Teachers College (University of Maine of Presquel Isle); [occ.] Church Office Manager and Bookkeeper; [memb.] Hodgdon United Methodist Church; [oth. writ.] Book of Poetry titled "Tween Me and God (But I'll Let You Peek!)"; [pers.] In my writings I attempt to bring closer to God.; [a.] Houlton, ME

BENNETT, BERNICE
[b.] July 20, 1935, Amagansett, NY; [p.] Evelyn Miller, Duane Miller; [m.] James W., September 11, 1954; [ch.] Joan, Glenn; [pers.] Everything in life is an "Event". It will never happen again.; [a.] East Hampton, NY

BENNETT, LINDA HARMAN
[pen.] Linda Harman Bennett; [b.] August 31, 1952, Chelsea, MA; [p.] Frederick and Shirley Harman; [m.] Barry Lee Bennett, April 29, 1968; [ch.] Tammy, B. J., Fred Bennett; [ed.] Associate Degree in Applied Science - Registered Nurse; [occ.] Associate Administrator for Home Health Agency; [pers.] Poetry is my passion, also a means of escape and way of coping with life's trails!; [a.] Crystal River, FL

BENNETT, LISA
[pen.] Lisa Hendricks; [b.] March 12, 1963, Los Angeles, CA; [p.] Wayne and Kathleen Hendricks; [m.] Steven Bennett, September 12, 1981; [ch.] Nikki Bennett, Danielle Bennett and Benjamin Bennett; [ed.] High School Diploma/Gateway High, Aurora Colo., Carson St. Elementary, Carson, CA.; [occ.] Staff Person - Chelwood Park Foursquare

Church; [memb.] Chelwood Park Foursquare Church; [oth. writ.] Several other poems printed in Church Ministry Newsletters.; [pers.] I strive to reflect the goodness of God, our creator and savior in my writing.

BERGMANN, KIM
[b.] December 6, 1978, Houston, TX; [p.] Delores and Duane Bergmann; [ed.] Senior in High School (Navasota HS); [occ.] Student; [memb.] A member of my schools Dance and Drill Team; [hon.] Second division award for a dance solo, Best Novelty Dancer of the year for 1995-96, nominated for Who's Who among American High School Students for 1995-96; [oth. writ.] I have been writing for years, but this is the first time one of my poems will be published.; [pers.] When I write poetry, I write from my heart, and hope the reader feels what I felt when I wrote it.; [a.] Waller, TX

BERRY, CHERI I.
[b.] November 21, 1957, Atchison, KS; [p.] John and Ruth Moeck; [m.] Todd E. Berry, April 2, 1994; [ch.] Brandon and Bryan; [ed.] Graduate of Atchinson High School; [occ.] Cook; [oth. writ.] I usually write poetry about happenings in my life. It helps immensely for me to deal with the problems, and makes me feel better to recall the good times.

BEST, DIANA
[pen.] Di Rice; [b.] January 7, 1964, Columbus, OH; [p.] Pat and Buddy Bush; [ch.] Eli J. Best; [ed.] Mehlville High - St. Louis, MO Buena Park High - Buena Park, CA Fullerton College - Fullerton, CA Victor Valley College - Victorville, CA; [occ.] Broadcast Journalist; [pers.] Count your blessings and don't quit!; [a.] Victorville, CA

BEST, JIMMIE L. P.
[p.] Mary Nell and John L. Partridge; [ch.] Fifteen; [ed.] My parents were almost totally uneducated formally but the most intelligent, bright, spirited, and loving people in all the world.; [pers.] This poem was written under great heartache as I faced the world driving home at sunset, alone in sorrow the day of my mother's burial. She was the greatest friend I ever had. Her wisdom, courage, bravery, strength, humility, love, understanding, support, peace-making ability, dedication to what was right in the sight of our Lord, her touch, her parables, her teachings, and yet her "sassiness" and demand for respect of herself, and her home, and her family, has enhanced my courage and strength. Her eulogy, as I listened, was as though I was the Immortal body laying in wait. I never knew what made me "tick" until I sat at that memorial service of my mother. What I have inside of me was the only inheritance I have, and is indeed the greatest inheritance a person can have. After going through fifteen acts of childbearing and all the strife of being a mother who never asked for anything but Love and Peace, but one who learned Patience, she died alone. In a hospital bed, without disturbance, not a child of her own was there, only a faithful, aged widowed sister, and the loving wife of her son, J.L. Jr., who were sleeping in the house she lived in, which belonged to someone else. I Am My Mother's Child.; [a.] Woodville, MS

BIGGS, SCOTT P.
[b.] December 11, 1973, Vancouver, WA; [p.] Don and Nancy Biggs; [occ.] Student at Montana State

University; [pers.] My poetry has been greatly influence by the natural grandeur of Montana and several personal experience that have touched me in many, many ways.; [a.] Vancouver, WA

BILTOFT, SCOTT
[pen.] Scott Biltoft; [b.] November 8, 1981, Hastings, NE; [p.] Wayne and Kay Biltoft; [ed.] 8th Grade; [occ.] Student at Davenport Community School; [hon.] Modern Woodmen Creative Writing Essay Contest - 3rd Place Americanism Essay Contest - 3rd place; [pers.] I get my inspiration from our farm life in Nebraska.; [a.] Devenport, NE

BIRENBAUM, BARBARA LAPIDUS
[m.] Mark; [ch.] 2 daughters; [ed.] BA, MEd Univ. S. Carolina, EdS Boston Univ., Post-grad Suny, CW Post, Univ. S. Fla; [occ.] Literature Educator, State of Fla Div. of Cultural Affairs, Author, illustrator, Composer; [memb.] IRA, FRA, ASCAP, FPA, NASP - Charter member AAMD - Charter member, CEC - Charter member; [hon.] ABI Distinguished Leadership Award, 1996, Nat'l Library of Poetry, Editor's Choice Award, 1996, 200 Notable American Women, 6th ed., 1994, 8th Edition, 1996 ASCAP Popular Music Award, Forever Friends, 1995, Internat'l Who's Who of Contemporary Achievement, 3rd ed., 1995, New York Art Review, 1991-92, Distinguished Fla Author/Adler Literary Conference of Fla, '87; [oth. writ.] Books: The Olympic Glow, 1988, 1994, Candle Talk, 1991, The Hidden Shadow, 1986, 1993, The Liberty's Light, 1986 Music: The Pelican Blues, 1996, Forever Friends (Olympic Torchbearer Melody), 1994, Where Are You, Punxsutawney, 96; [pers.] The gift of self expression is based in learning, but takes free form in the art of thinking; [a.] Clearwater, FL

BIRKHOFER, MELISSA
[b.] June 1, 1977, Iowa City, IA; [p.] Dean Birkhofer, Yenette Manley; [ed.] Charlotte Latin School, North Carolina State University; [occ.] Student of English Literature; [memb.] Literary Magazine Staff, International Thespian Society; [hon.] Dean's List, Who's Who Of America, Most Improved Dramatic Award; [oth. writ.] "Nothing Will Never Happen", is my first poem to be published.; [pers.] "Nothing Will Never Happen" is my poem of hope. Saved for rainy days, everyone can make use of a little hope.; [a.] Charlotte, NC

BISBEE, MATT
[b.] August 14, 1984, Spokane, WA; [p.] Ken and Teri Bisbee; [ed.] I attend Cheney Middle School; [occ.] Student; [hon.] Safety Patrol, 3 Blue Ribbons for Track, Geo, Bee, Academic Award, Library Helper, Basketball, Citizenship Award, D.A.R.E. Award, Blooms Day, President Ecd. Award, Student of the Month; [pers.] I believe in and try to live the "Golden Rule".; [a.] Cheney, WA

BISHOP, JUDE R.
[b.] August 16, 1950, Greenville, SC; [p.] Mr. and Mrs. Clyde E. Ross; [m.] Billy W. Bishop, July 2, 1971; [ch.] Brian Bishop (Age 12); [ed.] High School, 2 yr. Business College; [occ.] Disabled; [pers.] I suffer with disabilities of depression. I try to portray my feelings through my poetry.; [a.] Greer, SC

BITSON, GARY
[pen.] Lance Pentagrasp/Lance Freeman; [b.] September 4, 1953, Shelby, MI; [p.] Arthur Bitson, Cista Bitson (Rought); [m.] Cindy Bitson (Boes), January 5, 1974; [ch.] Wyatt Arthur, Benjamin Franklyn, Rebecca Lynn, Joshua Clay, Betsy Lou, Mary Bell, Samuel Mead; [ed.] Shelby High School; [occ.] Free-Lance Write and Christian Preacher/ Philosopher; [oth. writ.] Articles in local newspapers, self-released "Views" paper: (The Sentinel); [pers.] I promote and debate the reality in God through nature, word, and common sense, of man's need for God, and the unalienable right to life, Liberty, and the pursuit of happiness - without crushing my fellow man's right to do the same.; [a.] Baldwin, MI

BLACKBURN, ROSALYN E.
[pen.] Rose Lynn; [b.] September 29, 1912, Hamtramik, MI; [p.] Rose Grapka Soja - Stanitey Soja; [m.] Neal Blackburn (Deceased 1980), November 4, 1949, (1st marriage, October 1933); [ch.] Elizabeth Ann, Lorraine Marie, Bill, Tom; [ed.] High School - 1 year College - Dale Carnege Course L.P.N. nursing - certified reflex and color therapist astrologer and handwriting analogist certified; [occ.] Certified reflexology foot-therapist gardening Grapho Analyst; [memb.] Senior Citizens of Davison AARP member - since 1945 Association for Research and Enlightment of Virginia Beach, VA. St. John Catholic Church member; [hon.] 1st Prize in a Dale Carnegie Public Speaking graduation course in 1951, selected as substitute teacher for a handwriting class at Baker Junior College in late 50's. Diploma in Nursing from State of MI; [oth. writ.] Was published in an astrological magazine - under pen name of Rose Lynn in mid 60's title - "The Influence of the Moon" (magazine now out of print); [pers.] I am of Austrian birth - first generation an orphan and product of Foster Care homes - Widowed twice - had to work as a "Nanny" to obtain my High School Diploma at age 14 - went to IHM Convent to become nun - but returned a year later - kept house for three priests, in Flint MI until marriage; [a.] Flint, MI

BLACKHAM, JOHN
[b.] May 13, 1974, Salt Lake City, UT; [p.] Frank and Jean Blackham; [m.] Melisa Blackham, August 13, 1994; [ed.] Utah State University, Computer Science major; [occ.] Soldier-National Guard/Student; [hon.] Army Achievement Medal, Professional Development Leadership Ribbon, Service Ribbon; [pers.] The truth of people lies in their hearts. Sometimes it takes other people's words to bring their soul out.; [a.] Logan, UT

BLACKMER, CONNIE
[b.] November 8, 1952, Great Falls, MT; [m.] Ken Blackmer, August 5, 1972; [ch.] Stephen, Sherrill; [ed.] Vassar High School, Central Michigan University; [occ.] Presbyterian Church Secretary; [memb.] Vassar Presbyterian Church, Stephen Minister, Habitat for Humanity; [pers.] I write for my own pleasure and to release emotion - it beats screaming into pillows!; [a.] Millington, MI

BLACKWELL JR., JEREMIAH
[pen.] Jeremy B.; [b.] July 2, 1957, Helena, AR; [p.] Jeremiah Sr and Unita Blackwell; [ch.] Jermaine Deon; [ed.] Rolling Fork High, Rolling Fork, MS., Miss. State Univ., Univ. of Ark at Monticello;

[occ.] Enlisted Ass. Navigator, Leading Quartermaster; [memb.] Phi Beta Sigma Fraternity Inc.; [pers.] I have a love since High School for poetry. So I decided to write a poem. I have always wanted to write thus I felt it was now or never.; [a.] Mayersville, MS

BLALACK, SYLVIA
[pen.] SB; [b.] June 19, 1930; [occ.] Writing book "Meet My Pugsi"; [memb.] AFA; [pers.] It is only through love that we can reach "Nirvana"; [a.] Joshua Tree, CA

BLEVINS, TIMOTHY L.
[b.] March 23, 1949, Dayton, OH; [p.] Carless and Jean; [oth. writ.] Never attempted to publish, but do have a book of poems that I've written over the years.; [pers.] Would like to be remembered for being able to put the way I, and perhaps others, feel on paper.; [a.] Dayton, OH

BLIGEN, DANIEL
[pen.] Richard A. Doyle; [b.] July 27, 1973, New York, NY; [p.] Daniel A. Bligen Sr., Maria D. Bligen; [ed.] New Port Pacific High; [occ.] Student; [oth. writ.] None published; [pers.] Without life There is no experience, without experience there is no life. I try to live life to the fullest and I hope it will show in my work. Don't let it pass you by!; [a.] Bronx, NY

BLITCH, MAYMIE
[b.] June 3, 1911; [m.] Died 1980, May 20, 1960; [oth. writ.] I have only put a few in our Church Paper, and someone asked me for me to write some more.

BLUNDELL, DOROTHY L.
[ed.] Carnegie High School, Okla City University, BA, Masters in Creative Writing, Poem Published in OCU "Scarab"; [occ.] Retail Business 37 years; [hon.] Being Published in OCU "Scarab" is Great Honor; [oth. writ.] Other poems.; [pers.] Try to paint pictures with words. All my personal experience is revealed in my writings I feel and experience these emotions.; [a.] Oklahoma City, OK

BOATMAN, LARRY
[b.] February 9, 1952, McKenny, TX; [p.] Deceased; [ed.] 4 yrs College Drama Major Psychology Minor; [occ.] Maintenance Supervisor of Multi Family Dwellings; [memb.] Lions Club; [hon.] 3 from World Of Poetry; [oth. writ.] Bag Lady, My Friend, Hard Times, also articles on Fort Worth Star.; [pers.] I write from the heart, on life. Hoping to leave a legacy behind documenting the times in which I lived.; [a.] Fort Worth, TX

BOCK, BRANDY
[pen.] Brandy Bock; [b.] July 30, 1981, Dubois, PA; [p.] Susan and Wayne Bock; [occ.] Student, a Sophomore at Dublin Scioto High School.; [memb.] I belong to the Women's Choir at Dublin Scioto high school. I also take voice lessons after school.; [hon.] Merit Roll in school; [pers.] I'm influenced by romantic songs and other poetry. I write my poems from ideas that just come to my mind and things that happen in my life.; [a.] Columbus, OH

BODEN, AMY
[b.] February 16, 1976, Barberton; [p.] Lisa Boden, Martin Whitzman; [ch.] Christian Howard Thaedeuss Lambert; [ed.] Barberton High School;

[occ.] Currently enrolling in college for journalism; [pers.] I enjoy writing, poems and short stories. I hope to accomplish writing my own book someday.; [a.] Barberton, OH

BORGWARDT, CINDY
[pen.] C. B. and Company; [b.] October 23, 1962, Rapid City, SD; [p.] Janice, Alvin Morehouse; [m.] Larry Borgwardt, October 9, 1982; [ch.] Trista, Tyler; [occ.] Homemaker; [memb.] M.A.DD.; [hon.] Received Certified Dental Assistant Degree 1981. Received Green Belt in Jujitsu and won a few local tournaments.; [oth. writ.] Have written several poems; [pers.] Suffered from severe childhood and cult abuse and have been diagnosed with M.P.D. most of my poetry reflects on feelings and experiences.; [a.] Rapid City, SD

BOHLIG, CAROL WEIBY
[pen.] Carol Weiby Bohlig; [b.] October 12, 1928, Fergus Falls, MN; [p.] Maxwell Oliver and Mabel Hovland Weiby; [m.] John M. Bohlig, October 24, 1947; [ch.] Georgann Nirva, Sandy Lee Bohlig, John D. Bohlig, Erik O. Bohlig; [ed.] Graduate Southwest H.S. Mpls. MN, took creative writing: St. Thomas College, St. Paul, MN. took various art classes in La Crosse, WI. Attended Art seminars 1 week for 25 years, Green Lake, WI; [occ.] Own and operate "Viking Heritage" gift shop for past 20 years; [memb.] Member of "Sons of Norway" for 25 years. Life member of Vesterheim Norwegian Museum, Decorah, IA; [hon.] Honorable mention for several water colors. I have been painting for over 30 years.; [oth. writ.] Working on a pioneer story about my grandfather's life in the Dakotas and Minnesota in the early days. Also a collection of poems, not published.; [pers.] Walt Whitman and Robert Frost influenced me. I feel the power of our creator in the great outdoors.; [a.] La Crosse, WI

BOLLINGER, PAUL L.
[b.] March 20, 1922, Spring Grove, PA; [p.] William and Jennie Bollinger; [m.] Mary J. (Kraft) Bollinger, November 14, 1942; [ch.] David and Linda; [ed.] Graduated from Spring Grove High School in 1941, Worked for P.H. Glatfelter Co. for forty some years, as a Quality Control Insp., Retired July 1, 1984; [pers.] I wrote two poems several years ago, I would wake up, write the verse down, go back to bed, wake later, write it down, till the poem was completed.

BOLTON, KENNETH L.
[pen.] Ken Bolton; [b.] August 28, 1946, Council Bluffs, IA; [p.] Howard and Helen Bolton; [m.] Phyllis Bolton, July 29, 1973; [ch.] Kimberly Nichole Bolton; [ed.] Thomas Jefferson High, Iowa Western College; [occ.] News writer and photographer with focus on the arts and antics in the nation's capitol; [memb.] Iowa Motion Picture Association, The Donna Reed Foundation, Friends of Fonda, Richard Nixon Library and Birthplace Association; [hon.] Hollywood Overseas Committee for service in an USO musical group touring Vietnam 1968; [oth. writ.] Numerous poems and articles published in national newspapers and magazines and local newsletters; [pers.] One should always find time in life to help the elderly, however a moment spent helping a child lasts a lifetime; [a.] Council Bluffs, IA

BONIN, HOLLY
[pen.] Holly Bonin; [b.] June 27, 1981, Houston, TX; [p.] Martha W. Bonin and Daniel J. Bonin; [ed.] Elkins High School; [occ.] Student; [memb.] Elkins Elite Dance Team Elkins Concert Choir Campus Life; [hon.] Second Place in Majorettes Sweepstakes Pre-VIL (Choir); [oth. writ.] Poetry entitled- "Close Your Eyes", "I'll Love You Forever", "The Blind Love of a Murderer", "Burn in Hell", "Heart of Ice", "The Dark Days of Anne Frank", "Die Silently", "To Chad AE With Love"; [pers.] The poetry I write has a lot of meaning to me and to some others. Poetry is a way for me to express my feelings and thoughts, poetry is just a beautiful thing.; [a.] Missouri City, TX

BOOK, JONATHAN
[pen.] Jon Book; [b.] December 24, 1979, Decatur, IL; [p.] Bobby Book, Linda Book, Kathy Brooks, Brad Brooks; [ed.] Bethany High School; [occ.] Part time Fast Food Worker; [hon.] Honor Roll; [oth. writ.] One poem published in High School year book.; [pers.] Life is like a thorn tree. If you stand back and enjoy the view it is beautiful. Yet, if you touch it wrong you'll get hurt. Learn to enjoy things without getting to close and life will be good.; [a.] Bethany, IL

BOOS, STEVEN
[b.] June 13, 1962, Hays, KS; [p.] Celestine Boos (Deceased), Benita Boos; [ed.] A. S. Radiologic Technology Fort Hays State University 1992; [occ.] Radiologic Technologist Halstead Hospital, Halstead KS; [memb.] American Society of Radiologic Technologists, NRA; [hon.] Dean's List; [pers.] "The Unbreakable Bond" is dedicated to my mother, Benita Boos. "True Freedom is found in the expression of one's soul."; [a.] Halstead, KS

BOSANKO, LIZ
[b.] February 24, 1981, Harvey, IL; [p.] Paula Bosanko, Clarence Sexton, and Randy Bosanko, Rocky Bosanko; [ed.] Attending Argo Community High School; [oth. writ.] I have close to a hundred poems, this is the only published.; [pers.] I would like to thank God and all of the people who love me, for having such a wonderful influence on me.; [a.] Burbank, IL

BOSSHARDT, TWYLA CHRISTINE
[pen.] Twyla Perry; [b.] October 26, 1947, Glenwood Springs, CO; [p.] Colleen Olive Wilson; [m.] Divorced; [ch.] Arvella, Kathleen, Tammy Dee; [occ.] Voice Talent and Communications Svcs.; [oth. writ.] Short stories, song lyrics, and working on a novel.; [pers.] I desire, to inspire.; [a.] Atlanta, GA

BOYD, JENNA RENEE
[b.] March 1, 1986; [p.] Marilyn and Crawford Boyd; [ed.] Kennedy Elementary School; [occ.] Student; [hon.] 2nd place in the Star Ledger Newspaper in Education "Our Voices" Competition; [a.] Flanders, NJ

BOYDEN, CHRISTOPHER W.
[pen.] Zeek A/K/P Zeke; [b.] January 4, 1952, Orange, CA; [ch.] Kacie Marie (13), Matthew Paul (11); [ed.] Secondary, Phillips Amdouse Academy (70) B.A. Fairleigh Dickenson Univ. Madison N.J. (1975) J.D. Setom Hall Law School (78); [occ.]

Attorney at Law (1979) North Palm Beach, FL; [memb.] New Jersey Bar Assm., American Bar Assm. FL. Bar Assm., Palm Beach County Bar Assm.; [hon.] Fairleigh Dickenson Univ., Magna Cum Laude 1975 with Univ. Honors in Political Science Dean's List 4 yrs Seton Hall School 1978, Cum Laude, Fairleigh Dickenson University 1974 Poetry Contest - 1st place; [oth. writ.] "The Turtle" (Nat. Lib. of Poetry 95), "Your Gift of Love" (poem) Nat. Lib. of Poetry (96), Wide Eyes Tears (poem) 1995. (you should have that one you), without you (poem,) and song - pub. by The Pam Alley Sarasota, FL. Why? The See Saw of Life (poem) God Created Evolution, So Why All the Fuss? (Article); [pers.] I seek to comprehend that certain grandeur, in this dimension of life, which maintains the Ethereal Balamie with the many others, all in harmony, arrayed across eternity.; [a.] North Palm Beach, FL

BOZOUKOFF, JOSEPHINE V.
[pen.] Jo, Josie; [b.] November 26, 1915, Export, PA; [p.] Louis and Anna Turack; [m.] Michael Bozoukoff (World War II Vet.), June 23, 1946; [ch.] Michael J. (AF Major and Engineer), Joanne (Mathematician-Computer Analyst); [ed.] PA Washington Tusp High School, RN - graduate citizens Gen Hosp. New Kensington, PA - 1942 - trained Pittsburgh, PA, Children's Hosp. OR-Supervisor Citizen Hosp. taught students and helped in operations.; [occ.] Writing, gardening, thesis newspaper articles - day and night Hosp. Home Care of Thrombocystpeniia pt. care; [memb.] (Past) Nurses Club, Girl Scouts, Senior Center Council Member, Vise P. Merysville Golden Agers, Vice P. AARP Club - Monroeville, PA, (Correspond Sec - Past) Monroeville Sen Cit Club Coordinated Citizens Club, Monroeville, I worked on passage of "Refrendum" to limit local govt. term in office.; [hon.] High School - Third H. (enclosed) - Wartime Recognition as instructor, of cadet nurse corps by Surgeon General - Thomas Parran - for or training and sterile techniques, decorated areas and helped to raise money for handicapped children "Vintage Club"; [oth. writ.] Songs - "Words That Make Me Happy", "Peace In My Heart", Newspaper articles, thesis to different presidents - and replies published - "The Beat" - written on the day of the JFK Washington, DC - Historical tribute. The copyright returned to me. A thesis to Pres. Kennedy 1963 a change of juvenile court procedures and responsibility act. Received reply.; [pers.] When I reach bottom, "I Reflect", it's not "Defeat" or the end, but a message, go achieve something better and rise above despair. For I believe it's My Faith, In God", that makes me want to change what needs to be changed, and I tell myself "It's God's world not ours", please the enemy, and the devils among the sheep would be victorious.; [a.] Monroeville, PA

BRADLEY, LINDA L.
[b.] August 6, 1948, Denver, CO; [p.] John Lane, Dorothy Lane; [m.] William Bradley, February 14, 1975; [ed.] Pasadena High; [occ.] Secretary; [memb.] Sierra Club, Environmental Defense Fund, National Humane Society; [a.] Memphis, TN

BRADSHAW, KATHY
[pen.] Kathi Shaw; [b.] June 27, 1917, Ohio; [p.] Deceased; [occ.] Retired; [oth. writ.] "Memories" 1982 Pub. American poetry anchology, I wrote a number of other poems (unpublished).

BRAMLETTE, MINNIE T.
[b.] December 2, 1904, Pageland, SC; [p.] J. M. and Harriette Taylor; [m.] T. N. Bramlette, June 14, 1962; [ed.] N. G'Ville Baptist Academy 1923-1927 Winthrop College 27-25, Limestone College 1928-1931, Furman University, UVA; [occ.] Retired Teacher 1969; [memb.] Nat. Retired Teacher's Ass'n, 1st Bap. G'Ville, S.C. Eastern star, Demo Women of G'Ville Country S.C. Arthritis Foundation; [hon.] 3 Scholarship for College, 4 $10.00 Gold pieces for writing assignments in one-teacher, one-room school in 3rd grade, used as teacher's helper in grades 1 and 2 decided then to become a teacher; [oth. writ.] "A plan for teaching social studies in 5th grade short stories.; [pers.] I tried to help each student reach his/her highest potential.; [a.] Rock Hill, SC

BRANDS, CAROL
[b.] March 26, 1946, Hammond, IN; [p.] Arthur and Betty De Jong; [m.] Harold B. Brands, July 14, 1976; [ch.] Four boys and four girls; [ed.] Lansing Christian elem. (8 years) and Illiana Chr. High (4 years), Reformed Bible College (2 years) Trinity Christian College (4 years); [occ.] Teaching K-4; [memb.] Protestant Reformed Church Edgerton, MN; [oth. writ.] I have written many articles for The Beacon Lights, a young people's publication of the Protestant Reformed Church.; [pers.] I belong to my faithful Savior Jesus Christ and above all things want to glorify Him. I have dabbled in poetry all my life. "On-A-Bag" was written as one of numerous poems as I was teaching poetry to my students.; [a.] Edgerton, MN

BRAVO, NORMAN
[b.] July 11, 1929; [occ.] Retired; [memb.] A member of both an Odd Fellows Fraternity, and Mechanics Fraternity; [oth. writ.] Two published short stories: Regular Lime and Final Circumstance. Published poem: The Fallen Tree.; [pers.] Best loved poem is 'The Day Is Done' by Longfellow.; [a.] Dallas, TX

BREIDOR, HOLLY CROMPTON
[b.] September 26, 1968, Pennsylvania; [m.] J. Lance Breidor, February 14, 1993; [ch.] Jesse, Joey and Kayleigh; [occ.] Business Owner - Excel Building Services Company Inc.; [oth. writ.] Two poems published in the American Poetry Anthology. Volume 9, Number 4.; [pers.] "I Cry" was written during a stay at the Hyatt Regency in Chicago Ill.; [a.] Creamery, PA

BREYAN, JOSEPH
[pen.] Poppy, G.I. Joe; [b.] April 14, 1933, Bayonne, NJ; [p.] Mr. Joseph and Moratha Breyan; [m.] Anna Nancy Breyan R.N., September 26, 1959; [ch.] JoAnn Brink, Jennifer Price, Mary Ann Harbig, Jeffrey and Rudy; [ed.] Bayonne High School, St. Joseph School, Bayonne Tech. High School, NY, Institute of Criminology, N.Y.C., Adjutant General School, Fort Ben Harrison Ind. (Adm), NJ., Military Academy, Sea Girt, N.J. (Adv) non-Commissioned Officers Course; [occ.] Nite Crew Chief, A and P Tea Co., Hillsborough, NJ; [memb.] VFW 2290, Manville, NJ, USAR, Retired; [pers.] Writing poems is a challenge, it must have a meaning as much as it does to have laughter. It's like a story: it must have a beginning and an ending.; [a.] Somerville, NJ

BRIGGS, ANNIE
[b.] December 2, 1976, Cooper; [p.] William and Angie Briggs; [ed.] Glouster County College; [occ.] Retail; [memb.] Animal Welfare Association; [oth. writ.] Other poems, but not published; [pers.] I also have an older brother, Bill Briggs; [a.] Somerdale, NJ

BRILL, WELDA
[b.] October 25, 1947, Parson, KS; [p.] Eloyde Lela Davis; [m.] Daryl Brill, November 25, 1991; [ch.] Four; [occ.] Writers, was a Surgical Technologist until I became disabled; [hon.] 4.0 Ave. in Surg. Tech. School; [pers.] All you need is faith in God.; [a.] Phoenix, AZ

BRIM, DONNA FRAZIER
[pen.] Nana; [b.] September 17, 1946, Charlotte, NC; [p.] Alfred and Mary Frazier; [m.] James William Brim, January 15, 1966; [ch.] 3, 5 Grand.; [ed.] High School; [occ.] Housewife and Nana; [oth. writ.] 5 Titles Holly, Justin, Chelsea, Kalie, Justins Song; [pers.] Life is Children. When I was a child it was fun. When I had children, grandchildren it was grand. When I had grandchildren life began again.; [a.] Charlotte, NC

BRISCOE, BESSIE MAE
[pen.] Bess; [b.] November 3, 1926, Hillsboro, GA; [p.] Johnie and Daisy Thurman; [m.] Mairon Albert Briscoe, June 30, 1947; [ch.] Lloyd, Carvete, Leroy, Mattie; [ed.] GED from Cleveland Community College; [occ.] Housewife; [memb.] Palmer Grove Baptist Church Sr. Citizens of Kingstown, N.C. - Pres Board of Directors - Partners with Kingston Youth - Board for KCOCC Evangelic Leader of the Senior Sunday school class; [hon.] Pastors award, Teacher of the Year, Outstanding Senior Citizen of Kingstown, Outstanding Senior Citizen of the Year, Outstanding Community Service of Kingstown and others; [oth. writ.] I hope my writing will help someone else. And remind them, they don't have to give up because, they are sick, or old.; [pers.] Through my life I've faced many obstacles but because God has always been in my life I have overcome. Therefore I awake every day looking forward to helping and encouraging others.; [a.] Kingstown, NC

BRITT, ANGELA MARIE
[b.] March 11, 1977, Salem, OR; [p.] Mark and Eileen Davis; [m.] Todd Britt, July 13, 1996; [ch.] Brandon Davis Britt; [ed.] Graduated 1995 at Lane Community College. In training to be a nurse in summer of 1996.; [occ.] Mother; [pers.] Being a mother is such a great joy. My son and my husband have been such a wonderful inspiration in my life.; [a.] Springfield, OR

BROADNAX SR., THEO B.
[pen.] Iceman and The Last Poet; [b.] April 5, 1960, San Jose; [p.] Fred and Gloria Broadnax; [ch.] Ryan - 3, Regina - 9, Theo II - 6; [ed.] Silver Creek High; [occ.] Private Investigations; [oth. writ.] The purple Monkey; [pers.] I have written poems since 10 years old. I call my self The Last Poet because of my style; you give me a word, any word, I can write a positive poem about it.; [a.] San Jose, CA

BROADWAY, THIRISIA
[pen.] Thee-Thee; [b.] May 25, 1979, Chicago, IL; [p.] Margaret and James Broadway; [ch.] Marcellius

E. Lang Jr.; [ed.] I took Band for 6 yrs. Spanish 3 yrs. Computer Workshop, Physics, and Creative Writing; [memb.] I am in Principal Scholars Program, and T.A.M.B.I.T.C. Teaching, Advanced Management By Investment Techniques at DuSable High School; [hon.] 2 Certificate of Achievement for English, 2 Awards for Computer Workshop, Certificate for Art, Reading, Math, Perfect Attendance, A and B Honor 3 yrs. Straight Scholarship Award; [oth. writ.] That's the Way Love Goes, The Game, Me and You, the Game II, I am Woke at Last, In the Bed, Your in my Dreams, I wonder?, I Cry For You, Summer Heat, and Black Angel; [pers.] I want people to read my poems and be able to relate to what I feel. My poems come from my heart and they're a big part of my life.; [a.] Chicago, IL

BROOKS, CAROL HANEY
[b.] March 26, 1948, Greenville Co., SC; [p.] Marvin Haney, Edna Haney; [ed.] Hillcrest High, Simponville, S.C.; [occ.] Receptionist, Advocate to AIDS Patients; [memb.] Human Rights Campaign-Victory Fund - GLPM S.C., Board of Directors - Sue Kuhlens' Camp for Kids (with AIDS); [hon.] Several poems published in local newspapers nominated for S.C. Who's Who; [oth. writ.] "Lillies in Winter", "Red Ribbons Other Side", "Someone Else's Call", "He Speaks in Silence", "I Won't Go Alone"; [pers.] My own battle with a life threatening illness connected me to those who were dying. It is from them I learned to live. The things I've learned are treasures to give away.; [a.] Columbia, SC

BROOKS, DENNIS W.
[b.] May 12, 1949, Jax., FL; [p.] Deceased; [m.] Susan C. Brooks, January 13, 1995; [ch.] Michelle, Dary L, (Stepchildren Jason Jones, Shanon Bell); [ed.] High School Graduate, Englewood High School; [occ.] Electrical Foreman Duval County School Board; [oth. writ.] Many poems that range from thought provoking, sentimental, cute, some from the perspective of children, to observatory to strange.; [pers.] Man has within himself or herself, the ability and drive to accomplish any destiny that can be perceived.; [a.] Jacksonville, FL

BROOKS, ORVILLE
[b.] October 11, 1963, Enloe, TX; [p.] Oscar Brooks, Annie More Brooks; [m.] Bertha May Bell Brooks, August 31, 1929; [ch.] Ann Brooks Dingus; [ed.] BA Baylor University, 1929 I am a member of the Hunt County Uni Tonian Universe list Fellowship; [occ.] Retired Farmer-Rancher; [oth. writ.] The Dragon and the Butterfly, Children of the Stars I studied browning under Dr Armstrong - 1928-29.; [pers.] I regard love as the basis of both my religion and my philosophy - Love for all beings, human and natural, all nature and the cosmos.; [a.] Klondike, TX

BROOKS, SAM
[pen.] "Yosemite"; [b.] November 17, 1958, Leadville, CO; [p.] Nancy and Lee Brooks; [ch.] One (buried in 1983); [ed.] Graduated Top 10 Class of 1976 (President of Honor Society) in Grants, New Mexico. Studied at Santa Fe Academy of Natural Healing St. of NM License 1979; [occ.] Carpenter, Massage Therapist, Guitar Player; [hon.] Congressional Recommendation to the Air Force Academy in Colorado Springs. I turned it down because I don't believe in killing people or fighting

for peace. This was my senior year of High School; [oth. writ.] I've got some original music and songs. "Some Changes" is my best, I feel. I've never published or copywrited any of my work - perhaps some day.; [pers.] I have recognized since an early age that we live in a world with many problems. I've always felt it was my responsibility to change my life and this world for the better.; [a.] Milan, NM

BROPHY, KENNETH P.
[b.] March 4, 1955, Geneva, NY; [p.] Philip (Deceased) and Lucy Brophy; [m.] Divorced; [ed.] High school, Geneva Graduate 1973; [occ.] Working at restaurant; [memb.] Free and Accepted Masons, U.S. Air Force Reserves; [oth. writ.] None published, but I do have more poetry to be published if given the chance.; [pers.] I write poetry, actually thoughts on papers and have a good life, I enjoy serenity in my writings.; [a.] Waterloo, NY

BROWN, JACOB JEREMY
[b.] April 21, 1965, Denison, TX; [p.] Jimmie and Fiffie Brown; [m.] Robin Le Anna Brown, April 17, 1992; [ed.] Bridgeport High; [occ.] Electronics Technician; [pers.] Life is but a dream, reality but a choice, both with unlimited boundaries, as all things possible in the mind, only through the ego are we limited, yet truth can only be found in the Holy Spirit. Much love and many thanks to my wife for her inspiration, support and love.; [a.] Tulsa, OK

BROWN, LATASHA
[b.] July 26, 1970, Bridgeport, CT; [p.] Rudolph Brown, Leslie White; [ed.] McKinley School, Paul-Lawrence-Dun Bar School, Warren Harding High School, Housatonic Technical College; [occ.] Dietician, Bridgeport Health Care Center, Bpt. Ct.; [memb.] Mount Aery Baptist Church, Warren Harding High School, Vica Club, Softball, Volleyball, Basketball; [hon.] Warren Harding High School, An award for Outstanding Services; [oth. writ.] "Here I Am Without A Man" published in Bean Feast, the literary magazine of Housatonic Community College Spring 1992.; [pers.] My poems are influenced by everyday life. I try to create great "Meaning" in my poetry. My goal is to be understood. I want to connect people with one another in a diversified manner.; [a.] Bridgeport, CT

BROWN, LILA F.
[b.] May 31, 1914, Richwood, WV; [p.] Arthur H. Brown and Willie A. Brown; [ed.] WV School for the Blind Romney, WV, Baptist Missionary Training School Chicago, Ill; [occ.] Retired; [memb.] Home Demonstration Club (Est of W.Va University) organized and led local 4-H Club Volunteer Dispatcher Local Rescue Squad Church School Teacher and other Church Activities; [hon.] Honor Student at BMJS many Recognitions from Soil Conservation Extensive work, Community Services, and Church Leadership; [pers.] Probably as a result of an accident when I was three, causing permanent blindness, I have developed a strong belief in being helpful in my family, among neighbors, and in my community.; [a.] Winchester, VA

BROWN, MICHAEL I.
[pen.] Michael I. Brown; [b.] October 15, 1916, W. York, PA; [p.] Ira Brown, Flora Brown; [m.] Doris Brown, May 15, 1980, Mary Brown (Deceased), September 26, 1938; [ch.] Michael, Robert, Wil-

liam, Thomas; [ed.] 12 yrs. H.S.; [occ.] Retired; [memb.] 1st Brethren Church York; [pers.] Man looketh on the outward, God looketh on the inward.; [a.] York, PA

BROWN, NANCY L.
[b.] November 4, 1957, Springhill, LA; [m.] Terry Michael Brown, May 20, 1976; [ed.] Eastfield College, Mesquite, TX Taylor High, Taylor Arkansas; [occ.] Artist; [hon.] '90 Phi Theta Kappa Honor Society, Piano Player Taylor Ark. Spring Branch Church '74, '75, Student Commissioner Eastfield Secretary, distinguished service to Phi Theta Kappa, Certificate for Service to Eastfield College '90; [oth. Writ.] "Promises Of The Heart" in tapestry of thoughts book of the National Library of Poetry. "The Tree" received honorable mention from Eastfield College, Mesquite, Tx. '96, during 9th annual literary festival.; [pers.] In someone's ideas lie the answers to troubled difficulties in life, that could help everyone.; [a.] Dallas, TX

BROWN, OMAR TERRANCE
[pen.] Soul Surfer; [b.] January 4, 1969, Eugene, OR; [p.] Terry and Fatima (Divorced); [m.] Elizabeth Blair Brown, October 28, 1991; [ch.] Rachel Hope Brown 3 yrs. old; [ed.] Completed the ninth grade, and got a GED; [occ.] Fishermen; [memb.] The Body of the Messiah; [hon.] Most improved Cadet JROTC Army; [oth. writ.] Echoes of Yesterday, Beauties Revenge, Dragons of Doubt, Woman, The Other Senses, Fire of Desire, Just a Kiss, 4th of July, Ambitions in Sedition, Salt Water-Love, Ignorance's Bliss, Adjusting the Flow, Today the Time Machine, Shine on, The Expedition, Meat and Potatoes, Senseless of Great Expectations, Medicine From Heaven, Consummation of Love, Trajectory of Pleasure, A Terrestrials Immortal Youth, Breaking the Spell, The Waves of Spirituality.; [pers.] Why are we here? Such a simple question, with an element that seems apparently for some, to deep to view, in the midst of this technologically complex era, caught in the net of knowledge and confusion. As we're born into the fellowship of mankind, while passing through adolescence, the soul seems to sneak its way into the scene of life. Adding dimensions of depth within our hearts so vast, that only God's Holy Spirit can fill. Through the Revealing hope for an awesome fate to the senses, with evidence of blessings from the heavens. This world is merely the birthing ground for souls to eternity. She is in pains of labor for us all though we reap and rape her all the day long. Our duty is to let everyday be a good day to die. By causing love to shine, in the midst of a broken heart's darkness, and gloom of shattered dreams. For we are too be emancipated from this place, this earth, this vain lot. Being held accountable for our actions, according to a divine plot. Destined only by our own free will, to exist by choice in either ecstasy with the creator of the universe, having immortal bodies structured in glory by the good deeds administered in this present world, or to be caught up in the true horror of having wasted every second opportunity, to lay claim on eternal salvation. Inheriting a dreadful demise among those who refuse to wise up. To be destitute, harrowed in aimlessly wailing and gnashing of the teeth, crying, "Why are we here . . .?", "Rejoice, and be exceedingly glad: For great is your reward in Heaven" Jesus the Messiah; [a.] Atlantic Beach, FL

BROWN, RONALD
[pen.] Tavarick Holder; [b.] May 20, 1973, Etobicoke, Ontario, Canada; [p.] Merle and Hubert Brown; [ed.] Thistletown Collegiate Institute (ON), Vivian Gaither H.S., Hillsborough Comm. College (Both in Tampa, Florida); [occ.] Storekeeper Second Class (Surface Warfare), United States Navy; [oth. writ.] Small collection of unpublished poems.; [pers.] My purpose is to include some element of reality, joy and pain as well as fragments of human character. My influences include Biblical prose, Maya Angelou, E.E. Cummings, and Jimi Hendrix. All thanks and Praises to the Lord God Almighty.; [a.] Tampa, FL

BROWN, ROY
[b.] May 17, 1939, Blythe, CA; [p.] Jay and Helen Brown; [m.] Sharon K. December, 1930; [ch.] Darryl and David; [ed.] High School Drop out, finished High School in Air Force, 2 years Jr. College; [occ.] Retired, Injuries received in Military; [memb.] Disabled American Veterans; [hon.] The Honor of having my poem published by you folks; [oth. writ.] Santa Came To The Desert, A Horse Called Shucks, The Cattle Drive, and one called "Gridlock" for the Politicians in Washington. Also verses for greeting cards.; [pers.] I write poetry for my own satisfaction and hope it will uplift the spirits of anyone who reads it. I write mostly cowboy poems. I hope to give everyone an insight to the cowboy's life.; [a.] Glendale, AZ

BROWNING, ALIXANDRA KATHERINE
[b.] May 13, 1966, San Francisco, CA; [p.] Albert E. and Betty J. Browning; [ch.] Kier Anthony Browning; [ed.] Wallenberg Traditional High School, Mt. Diablo Valley College; [oth. writ.] Anthology "Death's Perception" (Forthcoming); [pers.] Overlook no one, overlook nothing, inspiration may be found on the face of stranger or the dregs of your coffee cup.; [a.] San Francisco, CA

BROWNING, CATHERINE LORING
[pen.] Catherine Loring; [b.] June 3, 1954, Las Vegas, NV; [p.] John Loring, Rose Loring; [m.] Divorced; [ch.] Ron Browning; [ed.] Gen. William Mitchell HS, Northern Virginia Community College (NOVA); [occ.] Director of meetings/conventions Am. Society of Cataract and Refractive Surgery (ASCRS); [memb.] American Society of Association Executives (ASAE), Professional Convention Mgmt. Association (PCMA), Association for Research and Enlightenment (ARE), Greater Washington Society of Association Executives (GWSAE); [hon.] Nova Dean's List, Graduated Cum Laude; [oth. writ.] Poem published in a metaphysical convention program, and church brochures; [pers.] Everyone is exactly where they should be in life in order to learn specific lessons to develop spiritually. We are all souls dressed in human clothing.; [a.] Burke, VA

BRUCE, JOHN C.
[b.] July 24, 1944, McCready Hosp. Crisfield, MD; [p.] Mr. and Mrs. Oliver and Bruce; [m.] Carolyn W. Bruce, December 27, 1975; [ed.] Myself - 12th my wife 12th and 1 year Technical school; [occ.] Seafood worker truck driver; [memb.] Assembly of God/Church Promise keepers.; [hon.] From, Full Gospel Business Men's Fellowship, Int. Assembly of God/Sunday School Dept.; [pers.] I enjoy writing about my childhood days and things about life related to God's word. Also, relating to everyday life with its uncertainties.; [a.] Crisfield, MD

BRUCE, TERESA
[b.] January 12, 1983, Tulare, CA; [p.] Karen and Danny Bruce; [ed.] Gramer: Linwood Elementary Middle School - La Joya; [occ.] Student; [hon.] Honor Classes Literature class-best actress award, Honor Roll Student, 3 class achievement - Best Female Artist, most creative, Quiz Kid; [oth. writ.] Poems - Smile Now, Cry Hater, A Valentine For The One That's Mine. Short stories - A Long Lost Friend these writings for family and school.; [pers.] This poem was written for my Aunt for her wedding. I like to write for the comfort and enjoyment of others like we should all do with all our talents.; [a.] Visalia, CA

BRUMFIELD, LESLIE
[b.] August 13, 1932, Bolivar, LA; [p.] J. Leslie Brumfield, Lela Brumfield; [m.] Shirley McDaniel Brumfield, May 13, 1968; [ch.] Ben Brumfield; [ed.] Baton Rough High School, Louisiana State University; [occ.] Retired Newspaperman; [oth. writ.] Poems off and on since boyhood, innumerable newspaper reports, editorials and columns. Lives very quietly and secluded with wife, two elderly female cats and Henry, a spoiled beagle, in the verdant hills of Northern Tangipahoa Parish, LA. Favorite poets: Alexander Pope, Thomas Gray, Robert Frost, Dylan Thomas; [a.] Kentwood, LA

BUCHANAN, KATHLEEN
[b.] November 6th; [p.] Elmber and Nola Loy; [m.] Colby Buchanan, Sept. 19, 1951; [ch.] Ten, 6 girls and 4 boys; [ed.] GED; [occ.] Housewife; [memb.] Baptist faith; [hon.] GED; [pers.] There is a life worth living, after this life, a Heaven to gain and a Hell to shun.

BUCKNER, MARGERY
[b.] February 27, 1940, Winona, MN; [p.] Kenneth Rand, Frances Rand; [m.] Robert G. Buckner, August 5, 1967; [ch.] Phillip, Timothy; [ed.] Winona Senior H.S., Winona State, Southwestern Seminary; [occ.] GED Teacher; [hon.] Conservation Essay Citation, Kappa Pi, Kappa Delta Pi, Purple Key; [oth. writ.] Poems published in Local Newspaper; [a.] Brandon, MS

BUCKNER, TRISTAN J.
[pen.] Baby D; [b.] September 27, 1974, St. Louis, MO; [p.] Mary L. Buckner, Garrett; [ed.] Madison Elementary, Madison Ill. O'Fallon Dr. High School, O'Fallon, Ill., Madison Senior High School, Madison, Ill. Barbering College Ark. State University, Jonesboro, Ark. (Criminal Justice Major); [memb.] Church of Christ, Centreville, Ill. and Madison, Ill. Boys Youth Group O'Fallon Senior Marching Band; [oth. writ.] None, but I will continue my education in the Criminal Justice area, whereby dedicating my life to upholding and bring the true meaning of injustice and justice to all individuals, regardless of race, creed, or national origin. "Money will not buy my me" in order to hurt another human being.; [pers.] I have been greatly touched by the late poet Langston Hughes and the Greatest Civil Rights leader Dr. Martin Luther King Jr. and the greatest of all "God Almighty" and my Mother the greatest woman, parent, teacher and role model any child or children could ever have, thanks Ma.; [a.] Waynesville, MO

BURD JR., RANDAL A.
[b.] December 16, 1978, Little Rock, AR; [p.] Randal A. Burd Sr., Bonita G. Burd; [ed.] Salem High School; [occ.] Euphonium Player, 135th Army Band, Army National Guard; [memb.] National Honors Society, Mu Alpha Theta, SCA Band, SCA Choir, District Band, Who's Who Among American High School Students; [oth. writ.] Poetry published in Creative Kids magazine as 7th grader. Currently compiling a book of poetry.; [pers.] One of God's greatest gifts is our depth of feeling. I try to bring those feelings out through my poetry. There is so much more to life than what can be seen at a distance.; [a.] Salem, MO

BURES, JOSEPH MICHAEL
[b.] September 23, 1944, Antigo; [p.] Joseph Martin and Theresa Bures; [ed.] 1 year college University WI, (Madison Corpus), Univ. JS (Iowa City JS Campus); [occ.] Stockperson at Marshall Field's (laborer); [pers.] I have two interests that dominate: I'm an amateur classical pianist and abstract artist. Prose and poetry are given secondary attention. My creative work all concerns my personal realm or existence. The acrylic, mixed-media painting interpret horoscope, cast and also, broad astrological themes.; [a.] Chicago, IL

BURKE, CHARLOTTE
[b.] January 25, 1924, Astoria, NY; [p.] Thomas and Charlotte Winkel; [m.] Jerome Burke, June 1947; [ch.] 5 Boys, 1 girl; [ed.] William Bryant High School; [occ.] Retired; [memb.] Notre Dame Choir Herricks Theater; [hon.] Goodwife award from New York University; [oth. writ.] Poems published in poetic voices of America, County Transcript of Susquehanna PA.; [pers.] I enjoy writing poems expressing my feelings. The scenery, people mountains and flowers inspire my writing. I love to sing. Being a member of the Notre Dame Choir gives me religious inspiration.; [a.] New Hyde Park, NY

BURKE, LUCILE I.
[b.] December 16, 1922, Macon, GA; [p.] R. E. and Myrtle Thompson; [m.] Robert E. Burke, November 1, 1941; [ch.] Charles Byron Burke; [pers.] My poems are given to me to share with our world at this time. They are part of my contribution and my reason for being here. I understand sorrow is a part of life but a kind or understanding word can surely help.; [a.] Iola, KS

BURMAN, MRS. HELEN
[b.] September 13, 1918, England; [p.] George and Edith Ibbotson; [m.] Richard M. Burman, March 7, 1939; [ch.] Carol, Richard, Joyce; [ed.] Some High School; [occ.] Retired; [memb.] Christ United Methodist Church of Mt. Top, Older Adult Club of Church Leasure group of Mt. Top. Sr. Citizens of Mt. Top; [hon.] Top Prize Loders Sr. Citizen Olympic, Post President of Leasure Group; [oth. writ.] God's Gift - Lonely Pal - Memories of a Little Girl - The Water Fall.; [pers.] I wrote "Since You're Gone" in memory of my late husband who died in his 80th birthday June 12, 1991. He was proud of my other poems.; [a.] Nuangola, PA

BURSENOS-KNIGHT, HOPE
[b.] September 14, 1978, Fairfax, VA; [p.] April McMullen-Knight, Grant Knight; [ed.] College Student in 1997; [occ.] Student/Air National Guard Recruit; [memb.] Animal Defense League; [hon.] Outstanding Academic Achievement/Commonwealth Challenge Program; [pers.] I plan to teach in an alternative education environment, helping young minds explore their world.; [a.] Virginia Beach, VA

BUSH, LOU ETHEL WADE
[pen.] Trudee Lee Bush; [b.] January 4, 1952, Baton Rouge, LA; [p.] John Oliver and Lou Ethel A. Wade; [m.] Arthur Bush Jr., December 22, 1973; [ch.] Shalona, Arthelius, John; [ed.] W. H. Reed High, NYC Corps Baton Rouge, LA; [occ.] Disabled writer; [memb.] The National Authors Registry; [oth. writ.] "The Burning Bush" first book. Illiad Press - American Poetry Annual - Poet's Guild - Sparrow grass Poetry Forum Creative Arts! Science - poetry in collusions.; [pers.] We must all take a stand for what is right and good, never causing a flaw. Living the laws of the universe we should, never violating God's law.; [a.] Baton Rouge, LA

BYRD, NEAL
[b.] July 6, 1978, Lenoir County; [p.] Archie Byrd and Kay Whaley; [ed.] Maranatha Christian Academy Graduate; [occ.] Student; [memb.] Maranatha PFWB Church; [hon.] Most Valuable Football Player, Poetry MCA Award, MCA Basketball Award, 1 poem been published in the 12th Annual High School Poetry Anthology, The Messenger et als one poem has been put to music and recorded.; [oth. writ.] Inspirations from my Heart; [pers.] I write from the heart — how I feel.; [a.] Beulaville, NC

CABLE, KELLY
[b.] May 30, 1968, Columbus, OH; [m.] Eric Cable, 1990; [ed.] Ashland University; [occ.] Adolescent Counselor; [pers.] I'm having fun writing, creating and expressing ideas with poetry. I admire many contemporary authors and musicians and have been inspired by their art.; [a.] Powell, OH

CAIN, MELODY
[b.] December 7, 1966, Evansville, IN; [p.] James and Susen Keown; [m.] Michael Cain, June 11, 1985; [ch.] Belinda, Michael II, Christina; [ed.] Harrison High; [occ.] Owner of A-one Auto Sales; [memb.] Wildlife Federation, Fund American Heart, Nature Conservancy, Special Olympics; [hon.] Honor Roll, Citizenship, Music; [oth. writ.] I had poems published in Sand Castles and read poems on Channel 9.; [pers.] I want people to enjoy my poetry that I write. To me that is an accomplishment in life.; [a.] Evansville, IN

CAJAS, JESICA FRESIA
[b.] September 4, 1975, Union City, NJ; [p.] Carlos and Jesuska Cajas; [ch.] Niece - my Sunshine, Shani, Victoria Cajas; [ed.] Emerson High School '94 but now, school of Visual Art, N.Y. College; [occ.] Messenger for N.Y. Theatre's; [memb.] Member of a high school click and still on going, The Losers Crew, (A cherished memory); [hon.] Honors - to be still living; [oth. writ.] Written a song for Edlee Music Co. called "In Love"; [pers.] Calling all humans, a slap of realism, "Everything is so interesting, but yet nothing matters".; [a.] NJ

CALLAHAN, DARLENE C.
[b.] March 30, 1954, Yorktown, VA; [p.] James and Evelyn Christian; [ch.] Roslyn A. Callahan, Marcia J. Callahan; [ed.] York High School Gardner School of Business; [occ.] Legal Secretary to Hon. Geoffrey M. Alprin, Assoc. Judge D.C. Superior Court, Wash., DC; [memb.] President 1996-97 Judicial Secretaries Assoc., DC Superior Court; [hon.] 1987 Employee Recognition Award, DC Superior Court; [oth. writ.] "A Child's Prayer" read and published on program for the 1994 and 1995 "Adoption Day in Court" at DC Superior Court; [pers.] I seek to express my wants, wishes and true feelings through a pen - placed in my hand - by the Lord; [a.] Suitland, MD

CAMARGO, AMELIA F.
[pen.] Melinha Marini; [b.] February 24, 1960, Brazil; [p.] Antonio Luis and Maria Ap G. Marini; [m.] Horacio F. Camargo, July 25, 1987; [ch.] Renata, Marcela; [ed.] College University of Artistic Education of Artes San Paulo Brazil; [occ.] Works with projects (culture) of the city Kinder garden Teacher; [memb.] Rotary Club San Antonio Church Escola De Educacio Caracol; [hon.] Honored By writer Paulo Dantas; [oth. writ.] Book published by "Editora some LTDA "1990" Re "Para Dizer Te" contain's 60 poems.; [pers.] My writings are part of spiritual life.; [a.] New York, NY

CAMPBELL, CHARLOTTE
[pen.] Charlotte Ann Campbell; [b.] March 6, 1942, Littlefield, TX; [p.] Hamp and Leota Pittillo; [m.] Steve Campbell, August 23, 1973; [ch.] 1 son, 1 step-daughter, 1 step-son, 1 deceased son; [ed.] Lake Worth High, Manpower Business School; [occ.] Housewife; [memb.] International Society of Poets, Northwest Art Association, Lake Worth Baptist Food Committee, N.W. YMCA Volunteer Foodgivers; [oth. writ.] 4/96 published by Watermark Press, 1st small book of poems 80 pgs. "Whispers of the Spirit" for family and friends; [pers.] I write simple poems of passion of the soul and heart, hoping to restore faith in all mankind, and to lift the spirits of the human heart. The purpose is to enrich and enable the common man in some small way.; [a.] Fort Worth, TX

CAMPBELL, NORM L.
[b.] June 11, 1944, Columbia, SC; [p.] Jim and Alice Campbell; [m.] Linda, November 19, 1988; [ch.] Rene', Kellie, Heather; [ed.] Lower Richland High, University of South Carolina; [oth. writ.] All my poems have been written for relatives and close friends as expressions of concern, compassion of appreciation. Hopefully a legacy!.; [pers.] My poem was written in honor of my late mother-in-law. She enriched the lives of those she touched, truly "A Special Friend".; [a.] Cumming, GA

CAMPLAN, ELIZABETH
[b.] November 24, 1934, Indiana; [pers.] Pretty Boy was my beloved cat for 15 years. I loved him, and I miss him very much. He passed away on December 18, 1995.; [a.] Chicago, IL

CANADAY, MICHELLE
[pen.] Michelle L. DuBois; [b.] November 7, 1981, Fresno, CA; [p.] Janice DuBois; [ed.] High School; [occ.] Student; [hon.] Rotery award "Bond" writing won contest in a state writing medallion for sports; [oth. writ.] Essay "Drugs"; [pers.] All my writing has come from experience. This poem was a true story from a friend, that I experienced with her. So Christy we love you!; [a.] Humble, TX

CANNON, DANIELLE
[pen.] Jamie Mendoza; [b.] August 21, 1981, Poughkeepsie, NY; [p.] Mary A. Miller and Dr. Luis Mendoza; [ed.] Currently attending - New York Military Academy; [occ.] Student; [oth. writ.] Stories and poems.; [a.] Beacon, NY

CANO, AMY M.
[pen.] Dreamer Jr. or D.J.; [b.] October 13, 1980, Saint James, Chicago Heights; [p.] Ted and Lisa Cano; [ed.] Friendship Jr. High, Elk Grove High School; [hon.] 2 certificate's of achievement in Academics; [oth. writ.] I have written at least 20 other poems, 1 short story and a play, none published.; [pers.] Thanks to my boyfriend Mark Hoskins, my sister Dawn Cano. My uncle Shawn Cano, and Best friend Brandy Jacobsen and my Mom for inspiring me to keep trying. (And Deanna Peters); [a.] Elk Grove Village, IL

CAPUTO, MATTHEW
[b.] June 24, 1980, Smithtown; [p.] George and Matilda Caputo; [ed.] I am currently in my Junior year of High School. I have also taken Creative Writing courses; [occ.] Student; [oth. writ.] I have written several short stories, poems, and novels for which I am presently trying to find publishers.; [pers.] Writing is a way for you to let people know your opinion without telling them flat out.; [a.] Nesconset, NY

CAREY, P. BRADLEY
[b.] May 12, 1958, Castro Valley, CA; [ed.] A.A.: in Parapsychology B.S. (Dual major): History Philosophy, Ph.D. (in Religion), Ph.D. (in Pastoral Hypnotherapy); [occ.] Minister and I write a regular column for a monthly christian publication.; [memb.] Association of Independent Clergies United Faith Misistry, American Bible Society, St. Joseph's Indian School (in S.D.); [hon.] 1996 Christian Teamwork Award; [oth. writ.] Books: "The Darkness in the Light", "The Quickening", have had several magazine articles published in Christian magazines.; [a.] Burlington, WA

CARMAN, BARBARA JEAN
[b.] April 15, 1935, Mason City, IA; [p.] Charles and Anna Edel; [m.] Anthony Jack Carman, April 30, 1953; [ch.] Paul, Stan, Phil, Doug and Mary; [ed.] St. Joseph's High, Washburn Univ.; [occ.] Retired; [hon.] Dean's List; [oth. writ.] Newspaper Articles; [pers.] Love one another.; [a.] Topeka, KS

CARNEY JR., WILBERT
[b.] December 6, 1918, Baton Rouge, LA; [p.] Wilbert Sr., Mattie Carney; [m.] Annie Lee Carney (Deceased), August 21, 1941; [ch.] Delores, Doris, Carolyn and Beverly; [occ.] Retired - Entergy; [memb.] Ebenezer Baptist Church Choir, American Legion Post 502, EBC - Sunday School; [hon.] EBC - Sunday School Teacher Appreciation Award; [pers.] I started writing poetry after the deaths of my wife and close friends, time alone gave me the opportunity to reflect on my life.; [a.] Baton Rouge, LA

CARNITZ, CURTIS J.
[b.] November 5, 1957, Milwaukee, WI; [p.] James and Rita Carnitz; [m.] Karen Gleason, 1980 (Divorced 1987); [ch.] Christel Gail and Brandon Lee; [ed.] Hamilton High School, Milwaukee, Wis. 1975, MATC for trade school, West Allis, Wis.; [occ.] Owner of Power Plant and Cycle Shop known for custom building, racing, bike performance, and parts.; [memb.] ABATE it's a Brother Club known worldwide; [oth. writ.] So Close - So Far, Life is a Puzzle, For my Brother and more; [a.] Waupun, WI

CARPENTER, ANA
[pen.] Ana Carpenter, "The Mystery Lady"; [b.] August 2, 1967, Dothan, AL; [p.] Catherine Willis (Died - September 1993), Legal Father - Steve Broome (Died - July 1995), Biological Father - Ed Eldridge (Died - October 1991); [m.] Johnny W. Carpenter, January 21, 1988; [ch.] Jason, Dustin, Joshaua; [ed.] High School (S.A.I.L.), Tallahassee Fl., some vocational training in child care; [occ.] Homemaker, Songwriter, Amt. Singer, Poet (amt.), (Amt.) Freelance writer; [hon.] Recent invitation accepted for membership in International Society of Poets, two songs accepted by Hollywood, Ca., companies, one or more pending acceptance. One poem published, and this poem being accepted is an honor. Made A's in Drama, Media Production and Creative writing, plus I was a Peer Counselor in High School, Made A's; [oth. writ.] Songs, children's stories, essays, poems, jokes, other writings also.; [pers.] While most do as they please or as they will, I do as I say, no bluff, no joke, no game, if I say I'll do it, expect it. I write to live and live to write. Goal in life, write, sing, entertain.; [a.] Chatom, AL

CARPENTER, MISTY LYNN
[pen.] Misty Lynn Blackmon; [b.] February 6, 1985, Jacksonville; [p.] Mary and Dave Blackman; [ed.] The 6th grade; [occ.] Student; [hon.] A and B honor roll 2 Academic, Reckianition in reading; [pers.] "No matter what age one race we all achieve."; [a.] Rush, TX

CARROLL, DAVID MICHAEL
[b.] October 16, 1974, Washington, DC; [p.] Donald, Mary Carroll; [ed.] Bowie High, Bowie, MD; [occ.] Asst. Cabspro Administrator at Arthur Andersen LLP; [hon.] Semi-Finalist - 1996 North America Open Poetry Contest Poem Published in Lyrical Heritage; [oth. writ.] Several poems written for Weddings, Anniversaries, etc. Written personal love poems in behalf of friends.; [pers.] Just write down what you really feel. It may not rhyme, and that's just fine. Put down what you're feeling in your heart and mind.; [a.] Landover, MD

CARRON, EVONNE G.
[b.] September 16, 1946, Minneapolis, MN; [p.] Mrs. Agnes Carron; [ed.] Cambridge High, Cambridge, MN, Houston Community College, Valencia Community College, January 1994 - March 1994: North Hennepin Community College, MN., English and Social Problems Courses, June 1992 - July 1993: Disney University Learning Center, FL., Language Review and Creative Writing Course, MS/PC/DOS, Word perfect and Lotus 1-2-3, January 1991 - July 1993: Valencia Community College, FL., Real Estate, Business and Social Science Courses, June 1991 - October 1991: Institute of Florida Real Estate, FL., Real Estate Appraisal Courses, November 1989, 1991: Mid-Florida Technical Institute, FL., Architectural Drafting and Light Construction Courses, January 1982 - May 1985: Houston Community College, TX., Real Estate and Business Courses; [occ.] Real Estate Appraiser and Professional Bus Driver, Licenses: Registered Appraiser #R10000193, State of Florida, January 1992 - December 1993, Real Estate Salesperson #NS0519235, State of Florida 1987-1992, CDL Class B with Passenger Endorsement, C650-207-46-836-0, FL. and MN. (Safe Driver); [memb.] Bereaved Survivors of Homicide, Inc. of Central Florida. Other activities: Served on Walt Disney World Bus Operations Safety Committee Board, S.T.O.P. (Stop Turning Out Prisoners), Osceola County Victim Assistance Program; [hon.] Victim Professional Services Development Program Award by State of Florida, January 1993; [oth. writ.] Editor of Bereaved Survivors of Homicide, Inc., Newsletter, Reflections of a Homicide Survivor (not published yet).; [pers.] Written in Memory of my sister, Annette Cail Carron Seymour, Who was murdered July 14, 1992, who wrote this poem, Glimpsing: Feeling happiness, but also sadness, not knowing what's up or down, Oh! Don't let it get you down. Times are changing, never really sure about tomorrow or even today. So make the best of each glimpse of life, for surely it passes quickly. Chief Judge, Sol Wachtler, New York, 1985 was so right when he said, "Too often when our citizens seek a dignified place of deliberation in which to resolve their controviersies they find instead aesthetic revulsion. They bear witness not dignity to deterioration, not to actual juctice delivered, but to the perceptions of justice denied or, worse, justice degraded.; [a.] Orlando, FL

CARTEE, AMY
[b.] July 10, 1979, Cliton, IA; [p.] Rob and Judy Solam; [pers.] I would to thank personally Desirée Harvery for making me realize it doesn't matter what you look like on the outside, but what you look like on the inside. I love you.; [a.] Aliso Vijo, CA

CASSIDY, JUDITH A.
[b.] July 13, 1947, Muscatine, IA; [p.] Alfred and Sybil Hartley; [m.] Divorced; [ch.] Allen, Missy, Helen, Dirk, Justin; [ed.] Hawkeye Inst. of Tech Wilton Community Schools (HS); [occ.] Certified Nurse's Aide and cook; [hon.] Graduated from Tech school with honors; [oth. writ.] writing poetry for personal enjoyment; [pers.] Write from your heart about things you love and believe in.; [a.] Bethany, MO

CASTLE, PHIL
[b.] December 21, 1932, Rosedale, OH; [p.] William D. and Goldie Mae Castle; [m.] Betty Mae Castle (Deceased), September 20, 1951; [ch.] Teresa, Ann, Phillip; [ed.] Deer Creek Dis School; [occ.] Retired; [pers.] Sometimes I have so much inside of me I must express myself on paper.

CAWTHEN, CAROLYN REBECCA
[pen.] The Poetry Lady; [b.] February 27, 1945, Cheatham Co.; [p.] Mr. Cheatham Edward and Mrs. Ruth (Judd); [m.] McElroy David Franklin Cawthen, October 18; [ch.] Bradley Cheatham Cawthen and Anita Carol (Blclock) Steen; [ed.] Grades 1-9 Kingston Springs Elementary Grades 10-12 Belleuwe High 1 year Middle Tennessee State College; [occ.] Cook - Bethany Hills Camp - grounds, custodian - Harpeth High; [memb.] Kingston Springs Church of Christ; [hon.] Distinguished Member Plague from International Society of Poets and three Editor's Choice Awards; [oth. writ.] "Memories of Robert of Christmas",

"A Merry, White Christmas Day", "In Loving Memory (A Tribute to Ruth Judd McElroy)". "A Tribute to God's Day", "A Visit on Father's Day", "My Daddy's Up in Heaven".; [pers.] Most of my writing is about my family members, either those who have passed away or moved on with their lives. They create so many emotions in my life that I have to express them.; [a.] Kingston Springs, TN

CENTAMORE, JESSICA LYNN
[b.] October 9, 1969, Brooklyn, NY; [p.] Kathleen Bello-McGuire, Vincent Centamore; [m.] Willie Vargas-Rizzo; [ed.] FDR High, New York University; [occ.] Marketing, The Bank of New York, NY. NY; [pers.] Both my mother and father write. I am grateful to inherit their talent. I have been writing short poems and stories since I was 10 yrs. old, but I never felt ready to share any work until now. I am glad to be part of such a special book.; [a.] Old Bridge, NJ

CESPEDES-TORRES, LENE
[b.] July 10, 1963, Havana, Cuba; [p.] Olivia and Monolito Sanchez; [ed.] High School; [occ.] Carpenter/Cabinetmaker; [oth. writ.] Many poems not yet submitted; [pers.] My only direction is forward.; [a.] Independence, MO

CHADDERTON, M. S.
[pen.] Dark Angel, II; [b.] Linz, Austria; [m.] Robert Chadderton, February 12, 1991; [ed.] City College San Francisco, CA, School of Hard Knocks; [occ.] Legal Secretary Part time writer/Philosopher; [memb.] North by Northwest writers group; [oth. writ.] The Legacy (Unpublished) countless short stories (Unpublished) Journals of Perception (unpublished); [pers.] Without truth there can only be delusion.

CHAMBERLAIN, MICHAEL L.
[b.] February 27, 1968, Gary, IN; [ch.] Brittany Skye Chamberlain; [ed.] Crown Point High School, U.S. Marine Corps; [hon.] American Authors Award; [oth. writ.] Mother's Love, Adults of Tomorrow, A.I.D.S., My Daughter and Running Around.; [pers.] I write about subjects that matter to me the most. Also how this world has made all the wrong choices to be where we are at today.; [a.] Crown Point, IN

CHAMP, THOMAS EDWARD
[pen.] Thom, Tommy C, Tom; [b.] May 20, 1957, Princeton, WV; [p.] Betty Nicholson Champ and Ed L. Champ; [m.] Fiancee: Katerina Alexandra Polutoradneva, Later 1996; [ed.] B.S. in Electrical Engineering, A.S. in Air Commerce Transportation from Florida Inst. of Tech., Melbourne, FL; [occ.] Supervisory Engineer for U.S. Dept. of Veterans Affairs; [memb.] Capt. (USAFR); [hon.] Eagle Scout Award - Boy Scouts of America; [oth. writ.] Someone to Hold, Feelings, I Promise!, The Love Rendezvous, Letter Writing Romance "First Meeting", "U", Vilnius and a Love Connection, Oh! My Love, Faithful Promise, Katerina, The Love Letter; [pers.] The poetry demonstrated within my writings come from my childhood love of nature, and the current passion in my heart for my one and only true love, Katerina.; [a.] Princeton, WV

CHAPIN, CHERA L.
[b.] July 28, 1983; [p.] John Dale Chapin Jr., Karla Jean Chapin; [occ.] School; [hon.] Solo's in School choir, I played Tenor Sax at Union, and got the

highest score, I was an actor in a play.; [pers.] I think my life is boring, so I hope to spice it up by being a writer someday. I can't put almost any thoughts in towards for books and poems. Mostly stuff just for me, but I hope to be known someday.; [a.] Barnhart, MO

CHARLES II, HARRY N.
[pen.] Tuma; [b.] June 1, 1974, Florence, SC; [p.] Harry Charles and Patricia D. Charles; [ch.] Calvis S. Hill; [ed.] Cumberland Daycare, North Vista Elementary School, Williams Middle School, Wilson High School, Alternative School, Florence/Darlington Technical College; [occ.] UPS; [memb.] Mount Sinai Holiness Church, Young Adult Choir, Boys and Girls Club of Florence; [hon.] Certified CPR, and Standard First Aid; [oth. writ.] Several other poems to be published in my book, when I finish it. Air is the name of my book, which was given to me from "Sontay" my nail technician at Total Experience Beauty Salon.; [pers.] When I write, I try to be very positive, understanding and uplifting.; [a.] Florence, SC

CHASTAIN, KEITH C.
[b.] July 20, 1917, Ibapah, UT; [p.] William and Armina Brown Chastain; [m.] Bernice Zilinski Chastain, March 29, 1958; [ch.] Sally, Keith, Susan and David; [ed.] Ibapah, UT Elem, Wasatch Academy HS, BS, Cal of Northridge, MBA, USC; [occ.] Retired; [memb.] International Society of Poets; [oth. writ.] 1st Place American Records Mgt Essay contest various poems.; [pers.] Regard my background in remote farming area among native indians as most valuable toward my ability to embrace most disciplines with some degree of success.; [a.] Banning, CA

CHEN, NANCY YIN-ANN
[pen.] NYC, '96 '85; [b.] October 5, 1979, Taipei, Taiwan; [p.] Susan and James Chen; [ed.] Kilpatrick Elementary School, East Valley Elementary School, East Cobb Middle School, Wheeler High School; [occ.] Student; [memb.] Atlanta Chinese Christian Fellowship Church; [hon.] Honorable Mentions for several drawings entered for Reflections contest; [oth. writ.] Poem "Sacrifice" published in Atlanta Constitution newspaper, poem "Eyes That Deceive" entered in Reflections contest.; [pers.] "There is a great vacuum created by words unsaid, thoughts unfelt, of devotion undevoted." "I am lost." "I have always felt sorry for people afraid of feeling, of sentimentality, who are unable to weep with their whole heart. Because those who do not know how to weep do not know how to laugh either."; [a.] Marietta, GA

CHRIST, TINA R.
[pen.] T. R. Christ; [b.] November 12, 1961, Denver, CO; [p.] Toni and Ted Kaczmarek; [m.] Robert J. Christ, February 4, 1984; [ch.] Sarah E. Christ, Adam K. Christ; [ed.] Arvada Jr. High, Arvada West High; [occ.] D.S.C. Fabrics Inc. Factory work; [oth. writ.] Personal notes, poetry, etc. for family and friends; [pers.] I write and strive to see beneath the surface of the everday life of human beings, to the soul of us all, the common thread that ties us all together. And have been inspired by such writers as Alice Walker, Maya Angelou, Clarissa Pinkola Estes.; [a.] Arvada, CO

CHRISTENSON, LEE
[pen.] Lee Christenson; [b.] June 24, 1996, Webster City, IA; [p.] LeRoy Victor and Anna-Margaret Christenson; [m.] Lolita (Divorced), September 16, 1974 to August 28, 1978; [ed.] Nettleton Business College-Omaha and Des Moines Area Comm. College Ankeny, Ia. Computer Programming/Anthology-Sociology; [occ.] General Laborer, formerly Computer Operator, Whse., Microfilm Op., Rice Delivery, Legal Assistant, Taxi Driver, Pharmacy driver.; [memb.] Good Sam Club, Camping World, Boat/US, RLDS (Reorganized Church of Jesus Christ of Latter-Day Saints), AKA, Warrior Prods. when calling Great Escape Productions, Pasadena, Ca. an ongoing video project showing a few simple Taichee and Wing Chun tricks even an 8-yrs. old can do escape muggars, kidnappers, thieves, etc. Projected by Time-Warner in near future. Produced and directed by actor Will Duvall (Robert's cousin). Future movie and video game projects involvement.; [oth. writ.] 52 other poems, including "Why?" translated and published (and illustrated by) Miss Nguyen Thi Hien, when a high school in Saigon, in her girls-only High School newspaper. 1 short story in my high school, and have currently, begun work on a book, science fiction based on Nikola Tesla's works, it's continued research and development by the US gov't. as revealed in "Cosmic Conspiracy", many T.V. documentaries, and Biblical prophecy! And articles "The spotlight" newspaper and Patriot groups.; [pers.] I believe those who are well-off ($25,000 plus) and wealthy should cease and desist all life-style based on greed, self-centeredness, self-glorification, and their control trips over the less fortunate and homeless! And start helping the less fortunate and homeless to get going, devouring them from off the face of the Earth as prophesied about this current generation who are oh-so Perfect in their own eyes!; [a.] Pasadena, CA

CHRISTIAN, ERIK
[b.] July 19, 1972, Newport Beach, CA; [ed.] Univ. of Washington (Psychology and Eastern Religions) Peninsula College (Art History and English); [occ.] Landscaping and Freelance Artistry; [oth. writ.] The Civil Cannibal (An autobiographical novel), The Empty Hand Behind the Flower (Hyper-extended poem of lost innocence); [pers.] "Transcend the lyrical "Norm" into the most uncertainly of expression."; [a.] Port Townsend, WA

CHRISTIE, ERIC
[pen.] E. Mann; [b.] September 21, 1969, Baltimore, MD; [p.] Arnold and Patricia Christie; [ed.] Baltimore Lutheran High; [occ.] Office Manager; [oth. writ.] The Pit, The Tower, The Next Level, Christina and The Palm Tree; [pers.] I dedicate my writings to Christina and Matt, both of whom have given my life meaning.; [a.] Baltimore, MD

CHRISTOPIC, JENNY
[pen.] J. Cee; [b.] June 26, 1951, England; [p.] Ernest Gomm (Deceased), Dapne Gomm; [m.] Ronald L. Christofic, June 15, 1985; [ch.] Matthew Garner, Jean Garner; [ed.] Red Lion High School, Lancaster General Hospital School of Nursing; [occ.] Registered Nurse; [oth. writ.] Strictly An Amateur; [pers.] I believe this life is a journey of learning, and that love and forgiveness makes the trip easier.; [a.] Elizabeth Town, PA

CHRONISTER, CRYSTAL DARLENE
[pen.] Chee-Chee, Crys; [b.] November 6, 1978, St. Mary's; [p.] Mr. and Mrs. James O. Chronister Sr.; [ed.] Hector High School; [occ.] Student; [memb.] S.A.D.D., FBLA (Sr. High), Journalism; [hon.] Student Journalist Award, Editor's Choice Award (twice), Band Awards; [oth. writ.] After the Storm, Best Poems of 1996, Best Poems of 1990, and Lyrical Heritage and many local newspapers.; [pers.] I started writing poems when I was younger and have been writing since. Many people have made me realize that I have a talent so why not use it. It makes me feel good to see my poems published.; [a.] Hector, AR

CHU, DONALD LONG
[pen.] Dragon Chu (Long - Dragon in Chinese); [b.] June 22, 1916, China; [m.] Kit; [ch.] A Professor, an Attorney, a C.P.A.; [ed.] Chinese Literature, Photography and Motion Pictures; [occ.] Retired; [memb.] Life Member of Motion Picture, Film Editor Guild, in Hollywood; [hon.] Won Photography Contest in New York World Fair, made Training Films for U.S. Arm Forces and a Life Long Career as a Film Editor in Hollywood; [oth. writ.] Numerous articles and poems for my home-town newsletters, in both Chinese and English. A Documentary book, Chinese Secrets and the U.S. Presidency.; [pers.] I came to U.S.A. at age of 15. It was tough to start learning a new language. But, I was lucky to have many good American friends to help me. So, my personal feeling has always been to reciprocate.

CHURCHILL, CHERYL A.
[b.] October 19, 1962, Claremont, NH; [p.] Daniel G. and Linda A. Westover; [m.] Mark W. Churchill Sr., March 30, 1989; [ch.] Mark, Felisha, Daniel, Trevor; [ed.] Mascoma V.R.H.S. W. Canaan NH; [occ.] Housewife and Laborer for Town and Country Tree Service; [oth. writ.] The inspirations of my poems comes from things that happened in my life. I express my feelings of my heart and thoughts into my poems; [a.] Enfield, NH

CLABORN, MARYTEJA
[pen.] Teja Liljestrand; [b.] September 13, 1953, Ann Arbor, MI; [p.] Sven and Barbara Liljestrand; [m.] Randal G. Claborn, November 25, 1983; [ch.] Five: Peter, Benjamin, Elisabeth, Daniel and Sarah; [occ.] Supervisor/Retail; [pers.] You cannot exercise your strengths until you realize your limitations.; [a.] Aurora, CO

CLARK, IRENE
[pen.] Ms. Tiger, Irene Dropman, Monsieur I-C-E (pronounced EC), Barbara Jacobs; [b.] December 12, 1943, Manhattan, NY; [p.] Joseph Farkas, Margaret Kovacs; [ch.] Devin Jeane; [ed.] Life Buddhism Dance Companies; [occ.] Dance Movement Consultant, Performing Artist, teacher, Dean of Dance at the Academy for boys who want to be girls; [memb.] Vice President of the Noyes Rhythm Foundation, member dancers over 40 N.Y., Member Eulinspiegal Society; [oth. writ.] Dance Columns, Childrens Stories, Erotica; [pers.] I consider myself an 'artist' - a compassionate human being that helps other and that strives to develop all of my abilities to their fullest potential.; [a.] Roosevelt Island, NY

CLARKE, LUCINDA LEE H.
[pen.] Sophy Romanov; [b.] January 21, 1953; [p.] Alan Thomas Clarke, Lillian Mari Clarke; [m.] Not

married yet, but very much in love.; [ch.] 1 daughter, father deceased in 1985; [ed.] High School (11th Grade), special student at Georgetown University studying writing and law, sing like a songbird, like Natalie Cole and Barbara Streisand; [occ.] Student of life, free-lance writer, ex-singer and model; [memb.] Came back to Maryland where I was born last year (Oct. 1995), love the state of course.; [hon.] Have never tried till now for entering poems in a contest honestly speaking. Debating award at 17 in Boston; [oth. writ.] Done for pleasure and extra credit in school in Penn. when back from Switzerland, Italy, Paris, at 16 my friends when family was together and my father alive.; [pers.] "I think therefore I am." -- Descartes.

CLENDENIN, KELLY
[pen.] Sheba; [b.] May 19, 1978, Richmond, VA; [p.] Peter and Karen Clendenin; [ed.] J.R. Tucker High School graduate and current student at Wheaton College; [occ.] Student; [memb.] National Beta Club, MU Alpha Theta, Thespian; [hon.] J.R. Tucker Faculty Award; [oth. writ.] Published in an underground High School magazine; [pers.] When stones sing and trees yell, it's time to take the Sheba to the laundromat.; [a.] Richmond, VA

CLIFTON, YEATON H.
[b.] October 9, 1922, Camden, NJ; [p.] John Martin Clifton, Roberta Yeaton Clifton; [m.] Mary Patricia Murray Clifton, December 28, 1959; [ch.] Sheila and Yeaton Jr.; [ed.] Phillips Exeter Academy (1938-1941), Harvard University (1947-1949), Columbia University (B.S. 1954, Ph.D. 1961); [occ.] Retired Professor of Physics, still teaching (volunteer basis) at U.S.U.; [memb.] Amer, Math Soc., Lingu. Soc. of America, Amer, Philatelic Soc.; [hon.] Sigma Xi (Scientific Honors Soc.); [oth. writ.] Unpublished poems (one published in the U.S.U. Alumni Mag.), Published Scientific Articles.; [pers.] "A Fragment" was written when I was 18 and heard that Coleridge dreamed the first stanza of "Kublai Khan." Every night I tried to dream a poem and finally dreamed "A Fragment" and woke up and wrote it down. I was unaware that Coleridge was in a drugged dream.; [a.] Logan, UT

CLOUD, RONALD L.
[b.] September 6, 1935, Bradenton, FL; [p.] Mr. and Mrs. R. L. Cloud (Dec.); [m.] Gloria (Cookie) Cloud, August 7; [ch.] 7 Daughters, 1 Son 26 Grandchildren; [ed.] Plant Hi-Tampa Fla. - Hillcrest HI Hillcrest SC - Edmunds HI Sumter S.C.; [occ.] Cert. Weldor of Mechanic Fla. Power Corp.; [memb.] Vets of Foreign Wars PBA Member Senior Bowlers Tour, Member of the International Society of Poets.; [oth. writ.] Several religious poems printed through churches in St. Pete Fla. two poems published through (the National Library of Poetry).; [pers.] My writings are story poems. Mostly religious poetry. Also love poems and humor. I want to capture the heart in my poems - poetry is one of my fondest loves.; [a.] Tampa, FL

COALE, LORI
[b.] March 10, 1970, California; [p.] Robert Coale and Dianna Creed; [m.] Jeff, May 1, 1993; [ch.] Adrianna, Allec, Allison, Austin; [occ.] Independent Beauty Consultant for Mary Kay Cosmetics, Artist; [pers.] I pray for a world where hate and loneliness do not exist.; [a.] Garland, TX

COBURN, TANYA
[b.] July 18, 1979, Weymouth, MA; [p.] Betsey Durfee; [ed.] I am a Junior in High School; [oth. writ.] Several poems published in School Newspaper; [a.] Exeter, NH

COGDELL, EVELYN
[b.] May 16, 1954, Chicago; [ed.] Chicago State University, John Marshall Herlan High School, Rudyard Kipling Elementary School, Jacob A. Riis Elementary School; [occ.] Office Automation Clerk; [hon.] Annual Certificates of Merit in Elementary School, several job performance awards; [oth. writ.] A few other poems, a cookbook, a few articles published in the school and job newspapers.; [pers.] I enjoy writing poems that will uplift and inspire others, I tend to also write about life's experiences.; [a.] Chicago, IL

COLBERT, CLETA E.
[b.] September 20, 1916, Cable, OH; [p.] Charles and Marie Huddleston; [m.] William T. Colbert (Deceased), August 40, 1940; [ch.] Clark Thomas - Lea Elizabeth Richards; [ed.] Cable High, Maare's Business College; [occ.] Retired - Legal Secretary; [memb.] Urbana United Methodist Church, AARP, Senior Citizens, APWU; [pers.] I have always loved poetry and memorized so many poems as a child. It is a dream fulfilled to have my poem published in your Lyrical Heritage.; [a.] Urbana, OH

COLE, ALFRED JAMES
[pen.] Alfred J. Cole; [b.] June 4, 1954, Salt Lake City, UT; [p.] William C. Cole, Louise Pulsipher; [m.] Madlyn Cole, December 20, 1975; [ch.] David Andrew and Anthony Joseph; [ed.] B.S. Developmental Psychology; [occ.] USMC (Ret) Attending graduate School; [memb.] Psi Chi Psychology Honor Society, National Deans List, No Jackets Poetry Club Eastern Wash. U.; [hon.] Graduate Magna Cum Laude, National Deans List; [pers.] I am currently writing a book about adolescent acceptance in a society preparing for the new millennium. Titled: The Sword And The Chandelier. I believe that all people are limited only by the potential they wish to explore.; [a.] Spokane, WA

COLE, EVELYN M.
[b.] January 18, 1924, Lincoln, NE; [p.] Floyd H. and Marie A. Zerbel (Deceased); [m.] Orven S. Cole (February 4, 1923), April 9, 1944; [ed.] Havelock High (class of '41) Lincoln, NE; [occ.] Housewife; [hon.] I have been published by The National Library of Poetry in several anthologies in the past of few years. (ie) River of Dreams - East of the Sunrise - The Path not Taken - Best Poems of 1996 - The Best Poems of the '90's - Through the Hourglass - Best Poems of 95 and others.; [oth. writ.] Some Music with lyrics - and much poetry, all type and subjects.; [pers.] Our family moved to California in my Post-graduate year of '42. I had several occupations before I married. I have been the sole office-help for my husband, a heating and Air Cond. contractor for 50 yrs. (now retired.) We celebrated our 50th Golden Wedding Anniversary in '94. In an effort to learn to play the piano in '54, I began writing poetry for my own pleasure and still do. The Lord has been very kind...; [a.] Los Angeles, CA

COLE, JOHN CLAYTON
[pen.] John Cole, J. Clayton Cole; [b.] September 3, 1965, Marshall, MI; [p.] John Cole and Virginia Holder; [ed.] TeKonsha High School, TeKonsha Mich; [occ.] Nutritional Aide at Guadalupe Valley Hospital; [memb.] Good News Fellowship Church; [oth. writ.] Poem "Bubba Claus" printed in Hospital News letter in December '95; [pers.] It's always good to reflect on those people, places or things that have touched our lives. It never fails to bring a smile or a tear of joy, to look back and remember.; [a.] Seguin, TX

COLEMAN, SHERYL TILLMAN
[b.] January 19, 1956, Bakersfield, CA; [p.] Mary F. Moore - Jerry W. Tillman; [ch.] Cherisa L. Daniels, Roy A. Daniels; [pers.] My poetry is a reflection of what my life is, both the good and the bad.; [a.] Bakersfield, CA

COLLINS, DEMPSEY B.
[b.] July 12, 1954, Kennett, MD; [p.] Richard and Dealy Collins; [m.] Deena L. Collins, May 21, 1976; [ch.] Ryan Andrew, Dana Michelle, Matthew Bryan; [ed.] Florida College, Univ. MO St. Louis; [occ.] Minister; [pers.] I have the most wonderful wife and children in the world. God has made me the most fortunate of men.

COLLINS, ELIZABETH
[pen.] Beth Collins, Betty McGeorge; [b.] November 17, 1917, Philadelphia, PA; [p.] Helen M. Suplee and Harold McGeorge; [m.] Harold Roy Collins, November 24, 1977 (2nd Marriage); [ch.] Two girls plus his son and daughter; [ed.] High School, School of Elocution and Oratory Comptometry School; [occ.] Homemaker; [memb.] Friends (Quakers) AOPA, Flying Farmers Intn'l, The 99s Inc. (Women Pilots), Worked with the Girl Scouts and Brownies; [hon.] 1979 Cessma Aircraft Award for being flying Farmer Queen, Member of earlier Awards; [oth. writ.] Lots of poems over the years also do people's Names truly making a personal poem for their; [pers.] Have had an interesting and adventures life. Have enjoyed balloon trips and loved travel - Europe, Gallopogos Islands, Hawaii and we go to Alaska.; [a.] Mount Laurel, NJ

COLLINS, HELENA ALEXANDRA
[pen.] Alexandra Wassmann; [b.] April 26, 1940, Germany; [p.] Gisela Linke and Egon Wassmann; [ch.] Three daughters; [ed.] G.E.D. 2 yrs. college; [occ.] Retired - Previous - Bookkeeper; [memb.] Lutheran Church; [oth. writ.] Not finished - several songs started. Some of my mothers writings need to be translated.; [pers.] Greatly influenced by country music. My mother's influence in opera tragedies historical and contemporary ever present. Incurable romantic - always wanted to write - no time 'til now.; [a.] Seattle, WA

COLLINS, SOLFRI C.
[pen.] Sol; [b.] December 6, 1942, Orkdal, Norway; [p.] Ruth and Harold Svalgress; [m.] Dennis F. Collins, April 2, 1966; [ch.] Brendan and Brett Collins; [ed.] I have 9 years schooling. Brendan - Bachelor of Science, Britt - Bachelor of Communications in Journalism. Master of Arts (History); [occ.] Housewife; [hon.] I cross country award, only girl participate against boys.; [pers.] To express feelings from abuse, love and family communication and affect and next generation, also abuse in the work labour employment.; [a.] North Reading, MA

COLONNA, JUDITH
[b.] January 5, 1973, Manhattan, NY; [p.] Terry Moyer and Jay Moyer; [ed.] Convent of the Sacred Heart High School, NYC, Providence College, Providence, RI; [occ.] I hold various part-time jobs while I continue writing; [oth. writ.] Several poem published in The Alembic, as well as numerous photographs.; [pers.] Through my writing, I wish to enhance images and ideas for the pleasure of my readers - and myself. Writing, for me, is one of the most important means of communication.; [a.] New York City, NY

COMBES, LILLIAN
[b.] July 22, 1935, Havana, FL; [p.] Lucille and Eugene Curtis; [m.] Willie Combes, September 25, 1954; [ch.] Four; [ed.] High School; [occ.] Maid House Keeping 3 years, Nursing 11 years, Supply Unit Mang. 13 years, House Keeping supt. 2 years (total) 30 years in hospital Work (retired); [memb.] Church, Camping; [hon.] care award recipients, for courtesy, positive attitude, respect and enthusiasm. June 1991 - October 1991, February 1992 - July 1992 - (August 26, 1992 which was put into County Newspaper, "The Pulse". (Photographs) Awards Ceremony General Hospital 20 years, 25 years and 30 years.; [oth. writ.] (Short one), Sub. See, I See, You Don't, You See, I Don't, Want It Is You See? See What It Is (You). Now I know (You see, I see, so what?); [pers.] It's in your heart, to say what you say all the time, and love is the main thing.; [a.] Barton, FL

COMBS, JASON
[oth. writ.] Ocean of Emotions, Life is a School, Love Chain, What I like, Emotionally Unstable, Mentally Unstable, Gazing, Emptiness, Staying from Reality, My Room of Nothing, I'm Already Gone, What We Did and Said, My True Friends, Forever Sleep; [pers.] I have created my own style of writing that I call "Interemotive Neuro-Linguistic". It is a style of writing that has personal meaning to everyone that reads my work. (This is the first time any of my work has been published); [a.] Cincinnati, OH

CONAGHAN, KATHRYN DIANE
[b.] July 24, 1977, Blackwell, OK; [p.] Lee and Kathy Conaghan - Karen and John Agee; [ed.] Barrow High School/Tonkawa High School, Northern Oklahoma College; [occ.] Full time Pre-med student; [memb.] Arctic Community Theatre, Concert Band, Northern winds Pep Band, Native American Club; [pers.] I have never given enough credit to the four people who raised me, thank you so much. I would never be who I am today without you.; [a.] Tonkawa, OK

CONAWAY, SEAN P.
[pen.] Sean Patrick Conaway; [b.] April 12, 1956, Salem, OR; [p.] Charles Bruce and Kathryn Ann Conaway; [ed.] 12th grade and Home Study Art, Real Estate, Acting Comic Book Art, Karate, Kali Silat; [occ.] Temporary Laborer; [hon.] Honorable Discharge, USMC; [oth. writ.] "Dream" and "The Pools Of Your Eyes"; [pers.] If we never try we can never know just how far we can go.; [a.] Portland, OR

CONKLIN, ADELE ROSE
[b.] January 17, 1977, Goshen, NY; [p.] Arden and Carol Conklin; [ed.] Pine Bush Schools, Kouka College, Orange-Ulster Vo-Tech; [occ.] Cashier,

Child Care Provider; [memb.] Girl Scouts, Council for Exceptional Children, Education Club; [a.] Bloomingburg, NY

CONKLIN, WILLARD E.
[b.] December 27, 1970; [p.] Arden and Carol Conklin; [ed.] Pine Bush Schools; [occ.] Construction; [memb.] 4-H, Boy Scouts; [a.] Bloomingburg, NY

CONLEY, EVELYN B.
[pen.] Susie; [b.] April 8, 1938, Columbus; [p.] Fred L. and Georgia B. Johnson; [m.] Divorced 1982, August 18, 1956; [ch.] 4 Living - Oldest Died 1985; [ed.] 6th grade, Key Punch Oper. Worked Volunteer Red Cross 12 years drove Bus for Met. Retarded 6 years; [occ.] Caring for sick; [memb.] Just at Malachi Bapt. Church on the Ministry there doing God's work when called upon.; [hon.] Red Cross, Cert. for Carrying out revival at Church Malachi Bapt. Lic. as Evang. 1981; [oth. writ.] (Songs) Hello Mommie, His Great Love, Hello Jesus copy writted 1995 other poems and songs not yet copy written.; [pers.] I was ordained into the ministry, 1981. Raised 5 children, now have 13 grand and great grand. Enjoy helping sick, singing, flowers, crafts, Ministry.; [a.] Columbus, OH

CONN, JAMES D.
[b.] January 1, 1944, Monticello, KY; [p.] William and Reba; [m.] Bonnie, June 22, 1974; [ch.] Donita, Hayden, Timothy, Kyle, James; [ed.] Lexington Baptist College, Wayne County High School; [occ.] Computer Center Manager; [oth. writ.] Various poems, essays, articles published in The Portable Companion magazine.; [pers.] The divinity within us all transcends the handwriting on the wall.; [a.] Land O'Lakes, FL

CONNELL, GWENDOLYN L. SMITH-RUSSELL
[b.] April 6, Denver, CO; [p.] John Edward Smith, Gladys Emanuel Smith; [m.] John T. Connell, September 7, 1996; [ch.] Quent C. Russell, Steven G. Connell; [ed.] B.A., Eastern Washington U., M.A. Lesley College, Cambridge, MA; [occ.] Counseling Psychologist and Consultant; [hon.] General Mills, American Association of Physician and Surgeons, Veterans of Foreign Wars, American Red Cross, The White House, Sachs Foundation, Eastern Wash. U., Lesley College, Underwood-Olivetti, DePaul Hospital, Denver Public Library, National Poetry Association, Rocky Mountain Writer's Guild, etc.; [oth. writ.] English and Portuguese Translation - "The American Free Enterprise System vs. Communism", 1st Place Nat'l Poetry Association - Journey of the Gull, Seven Articles - The Denver Post, Guest Authorship - Black Knight Magazine - "A-bor-shun", Pamphlet Authorship - Hospice Care - DePaul Hospital, Cheyenne, WA; [pers.] My private practice philosophy is my family life philosophy - Honoring Life Through Acceptance and Re-Exploration.; [a.] Cheyenne, WY

CONRAD, SHIRLEY
[ed.] Will take a BA in English (Writing) 3/97 I will be teaching writing at the Community College Level; [occ.] Student at Southern Oregon State College; [memb.] Student at Southern Oregon State College; [hon.] Earth Day Poetry Award '96; [oth. writ.] Published Poetry: (Pa-

cific North West Anthologies) Rogue's Gallery '95 and '96, Shearwater '95, Sites '96 and my own chapbook: "Voices in the Wind" 1996; [pers.] I am a believer in "What If's"; [a.] Central Point, OR

CONRAD II, TIMOTHY E.
[b.] November 27, 1978, Wheeling, WV; [p.] Timothy E. Conrad, Diane L. Schroeder; [m.] Judy Thompson; [ed.] Burkeye Local High School; [hon.] Whose Who Among High School Students; [oth. writ.] I have written several poems, but none of them have been published.; [a.] Tiltonsville, OH

COOK, PAULA LEE
[b.] June 3, 1955, Erie, PA; [p.] Richard and Joyce Richter; [m.] Jack A. Cook, January 31, 1975; [ch.] Stephen, Serina, Shawn, Christopher; [occ.] Office Manager at Cook's Auto Body, North East PA; [pers.] My poems are written to let people know about the comfort, forgiveness, and hope that I have in Jesus Christ and that they can have that too.; [a.] North East, PA

COOK, REBECCA
[b.] October 12, 1970, Dearborn, MI; [p.] George and Mary Jane Ralph; [m.] James Cook, January 19, 1991; [ch.] Stephanie and James R.; [ed.] High School (Edsel Ford); [occ.] Housewife; [memb.] Faith Lutheran Church, Highland, MI; [hon.] Youngest Woman to join the Lutheran Women's Missionary League in 1984; [pers.] If your friend or a family member is gay, don't change your friendship and love. Love and support them more. AIDS is everyone's problem!; [a.] White Lake, MI

COOKEMBOO, KEVIN WAYNE
[pen.] Terry Rhodes; [b.] September 11, 1958, Poblar Bluff, MO; [p.] Joseph and Patricia Cookemboo; [m.] Mary Jane Catherine Cookemboo, February 3, 1979; [ch.] Mrs. Kimberly Stewart, Amy Wrights, Stefanie Cookemboo; [ed.] Cleveland High, St. Louis, MO "75", Self Education: Classics, History, Political, Linguistics; [occ.] NAPA Auto, Genuine Parts; [oth. writ.] No Greater Fool Hath History Told, Than To Have The Treasure And Not To Hold (Love); [pers.] The wind blows in the night neither do we see it in the day (Discerning Reality).; [a.] Saint Louis, MO

COPENHAVER, ROY T.
[pen.] Roy Copenhaver; [b.] February 2, 1905, Girard, KS; [p.] Sam and Mary Belle Copenhaver; [m.] Orpha (Crosswhite) Copenhaver (Deceased), June 7, 1936; [ch.] Donna Lea Copenhaver (Deceased); [ed.] Grade School and High-School also, Electrical Correspondence Schools, and I might add, looking for better ways of getting the job done right and well.; [occ.] Maintence electrician with General Motors, 30 1/2 years (retired); [memb.] 1st. Presbyterian Church and 67 years AF&AM Masonic membership; [hon.] Being honored by having a poem I came up with being considered for including it in the prestigious National Library of Poetry is I consider an outstanding honor.; [oth. writ.] I am really not a poet but I sometimes come up with one for special occasions of situations that I can put in rhyme to put a thought across.; [pers.] I am very much concerned that this wonderful country I dearly love is not holding to the idea of a nation under God, as our God-fearing founders wrote the Constitution were guided by the idea that it would ever be so.; [a.] Overland Park, KS

COPPAGE, RONALD
[pen.] P. B. Henderson; [b.] October 12, 1958, Chicago, IL; [p.] Richard Sr. and Hursalean Coppage; [ed.] Bachelors Business Admin.; [occ.] Customer Service Rep; [oth. writ.] Chapbooks - rich beyond compare and guide my steps. Lyrical compilation confessions of the heart.; [pers.] I believe that love is the key to all the goodness mankind is able to achieve. Without it we are lost. With it, all dreams are possible.; [a.] Atlanta, GA

COPPOLA, MARTA
[pen.] Morgan Mayquinn; [b.] November 4, 1978, Stamford, CT; [p.] Lois and Ermanno Coppola; [ed.] I have just Graduated from Stamford High School and will be attending Moravian College in the fall of 1996; [occ.] Student; [memb.] Formerly a Member of the National Honors Society (before graduating), Member of the School Choir and Madrigals, also contributed to the School Literary Magazine Vertigo; [pers.] By limiting the mind, one inevitably limits her artistic capabilities, regardless of how much "technical" skill she may have. In my writing, I express my own thoughts as well as others who have influenced me.; [a.] Stamford, CT

CORNWELL, WILMA JEAN
[b.] October 6, 1926, Bloomington, IN; [p.] Vada and Bertha Cracraft; [m.] John F. Cornwell, August 29, 1948; [ch.] John, James, Robert, Thomas; [ed.] Bloomington High School - 1944; [occ.] Retired Antique Store Owner Mgr. and Owner, Rental Property; [memb.] Fairview Methodist Church, Alpha Delta Omega Philanthropic Sorority, B.H.S. Alumni Reunion Comm., held offices in several P.T.A. groups, Newsletter Editor 701 A.D.O.; [hon.] Disciple Graduate - Fairview Outstanding Service Award - A.D.A.; [oth. writ.] Mostly poems about home, church, children, friends.; [pers.] The words we set down on a piece of paper may be as a beacon of light to someone unknown to us now - maybe never.; [a.] Bloomington, IN

CORTEZ, MANUEL
[b.] December 24, 1967, Paxaca, Mexico; [p.] Rogelio Cortez, Consuelo Bautista; [ed.] Three Years College on Mexico (Topoerafhy) 1 1/2 years Institute of Art; [occ.] Restaurant Business; [oth. writ.] I have written poetry and songs. My whole life for personal fulfillment. Several of my songs have been performer by local musicians.; [pers.] I have been influenced by the classic poets, of Mexico and South America I just want to put music at the poetry.; [a.] Seaside, CA

CORTINEZ, CARLOS
[b.] March 8, 1934, Santiago, Chile; [p.] Carlos, Quintila; [m.] Cecilia Heydl-Cortinez; [ch.] Cristian, Veronica, Barbara, Raimundo, Sebastian, Claudia; [ed.] Ph.D. in Spanish from U. of Iowa; [occ.] Spanish Professor at Florida AxM University; [memb.] M.L.A. (Modern Language Assoc.), Institute International de Literature Iberoamericana; [hon.] International Writing Program (at Univ. of Iowa 1968-70) Poetry recorded at the Library of Congress (Washington D.C.), Included in several anthologies both in Spanish and English; [oth. writ.] Treintaytres, Opus Cero, Abba, among other poetry collection. Author of two novels and a book of short stories. Also scholarly books on Pablo Neruda and J. L. Borges;

[pers.] Strongly in debt to the poetry of Pablo Neruda and Jorge Louis Borges. Poetry and music no less than love and children has given me a happy life.; [a.] Fork, PA

COSTANTINO, DIANA
[b.] March 11, 1976, Glen Cove, NY; [p.] Vincent and Assunta Costantino; [ed.] Presently a Junior at Suny Binghamton, Glen Cove High School, Graduate; [hon.] Dean's List, Service to the Glen Cove Community Award, Community Scholarship Award; [oth. writ.] Several articles published in school paper.; [pers.] My writing has always been inspired and encouraged by my loving family. I am currently working on Shakespearean sonnets.; [a.] Glen Cove, NY

COSTANZO, VICTORIA
[b.] January 13, 1966, Abington, PA; [m.] Frederick P. Costanzo, May 17, 1986; [ch.] Fred J. Costanzo; [ed.] Ardsley Elementary, Abington High School Graduate; [occ.] Mother, Wife, and Poet; [oth. writ.] Children's Book (Fiction) "One Less Egg", Copyright 1995 by Victoria Costanzo, and other unpublished poems.; [pers.] Before you get so high and mighty, look, listen and smell the life around you.; [a.] North Hills, PA

COTOU, DEBORAH HOPKINS
[b.] June 21, 1962, New York City, NY; [p.] Patricia and Donald; [m.] Stephen, May 6, 1989; [ch.] Stephen Jr. and Brian; [oth. writ.] Personal Journal of poems written over the years none yet published. Personalized poetry written for newborn family members and special occasions; [pers.] When writing poetry, I reflect on Love, Laughter and Miracles of life. Sincere Love to my Parents Patricia and Donald as well as Catherine and Francis Cotou, My wonderful in-laws.; [a.] Ozone Park, NY

COUCH, ROBBY
[b.] February 24, 1977, Abilene, TX; [p.] Gloria and Alvin; [ed.] Eula, I.S.D.; [hon.] Citizenship Award (1991), Eula Junior High Basketball Manager of the Year (1991); [oth. writ.] Working on a poetry book.; [pers.] I stumbled through a tunnel until I found the light and I want people to get a good message from my work.; [a.] Abilene, TX

COURTNEY, CHRIS
[b.] April 16, 1977, Valparaiso, IN; [p.] Richard and Rosemary Courtney; [ed.] K-12, graduated June 7, 1996; [oth. writ.] Around 200 more poems; [pers.] Don't let anyone drag you down.; [a.] Valparaiso, IN

COUSINS, AUDREY M.
[pen.] Dr. Cruz, Mom, Blessed and many more; [b.] December 28, 1941, Wilmington, DE; [p.] Emanuel W., Margurite Redding; [m.] Divorced - 1977, April 18, 1959; [ch.] Audrey Jr., Joslynn, Kim A., Timothy L., Christina L., Tarra A. Cousins; [ed.] GED 1970, James Grove's School, Culinary Ins., Poughkeepsie, N.Y., Langly A.F.B. VA., Cosmetologist, Best Beauty School, Dover Del; [occ.] Retired from Dover A.F.B., recently as lead cook, (Officer's Open Mess); [memb.] Sweeping The City, President Non-Profit Organ; [hon.] Birth Certificate (Smile); [oth. writ.] The Creation Of Woman, poet's pen., Delaware State news 1960 to 1970, Del Castle Record? Five Star Music of Boston and recently Chapel recording Co. of Mass.; [pers.] To increase one's knowledge of the spirit world and of the flesh.; [a.] Hartly, DE

COWLES, H. DEAN
[b.] June 23, 1925, Moorefield, NE; [p.] Deceased; [m.] Mary M. Cowles, February 2, 1952; [ch.] Anne Cowles Hinton; [ed.] Baker Rural High School, Stapleton, NE, University Of Nebraska; [occ.] House Pet and Kitchen Aid (Retired); [memb.] Church of the Holy Spirit Episcopal, Bellevwe, NE Past Master, Masoniclodge, Scottish Rite Mason, Valley of Omaha; [oth. writ.] Melodrama, poetry and short stories.; [pers.] I find humor alleviates, courage overcomes, Integrity Elevates.; [a.] Papillion, NE

COX, APRIL ESTELLE
[pen.] April Estela Cox, Miss Chicana All-Star-of-the-Universe; [b.] August 29, 1975, West Los Angeles; [occ.] Working-class in origin, suburban by luck and social activist/poet/student through invocation.; [oth. writ.] Notorious for her athletic inability, she swears by grassroots mobilization, (r)evolutionary writing, Mexican bottlerockets, jirafitas and ice-cold horchata. A character, if you will.; [a.] Buena Park, CA

COX, DAVID LAWRENCE
[b.] August 6, 1975, Pasadena, TX; [p.] Tim and Laurie Cox; [ed.] Simi Valley High School; [occ.] Military; [oth. writ.] Completed volume of poetry, not yet published; [pers.] I am only directly influenced by T.E. Lawrence's 'To S.A.' Young poets exist, but only in immature and nonsensical stages. I want to not only prove that our generation can write great poetry, but also create a revolution in the way poetry is received by society.; [a.] Simi Valley, CA

COX-KERNAN, TOBYE A.
[b.] December 15, 1970, Oklahoma City; [p.] Kim and Beverly Cox; [m.] Michael A. Kernan Jr., August 19, 1995; [ed.] Bachelor of Political Science and Sociology; [occ.] Supervisor of Marketing at Excel Telecommunications Dallas, TX; [memb.] Mortar Board, Pi Sigua Alpha, Dean's Honor Roll, Who's Who; [hon.] Dean's Honor Roll, Political Science Honor Society; [pers.] I hope that through my poetry I am able to help one recognize the emotions that rage within, and that by doing so, their emotions will be channeled in a positive, fulfilling and educational way.; [a.] Carrollton, TX

CRAIG, SUZZANNE
[pen.] Suzzane Craig; [b.] February 11, 1964, Wichita, KS; [p.] Jim Bruner and Sue Boone; [ch.] 2 girls: Brandy 15, and Leslie 13; [ed.] I got my High School Equivalency - May 15, 1987; [occ.] Home Mother; [memb.] CASA, Safehouse; [hon.] May 1993 - Court Appointed Special Advocate (CASA). March 1994 - Safehouse - To assist Victims of Domestic Violence and Sexual Assault. Oct. 1993 - Okmulgee County Family Resource Center. Certificate of Appreciation; [oth. writ.] I'm writing a book of any childhood. All of the Sexual abuse I went thru as a child. My sister and I went thru 3 family - All 3 family my sister and I were abused. And what it does to your whole life.; [pers.] I've wrote poetry for years. Never wrote wildest dreams that I would have a poem published. Never give up - I didn't.; [a.] Dewar, OK

CRAWFORD, GINGER
[b.] January 30, 1953, Chamblee, GA; [p.] Hubert and Pearl Hamrick; [m.] Joe Crawford, July 31, 1978; [ch.] Kayla Marie; [ed.] North Springs High,

Kennesaw State College; [occ.] First Grade Teacher, McGarity Elem. Hiram, GA; [memb.] PAGE; [hon.] Phi Eta Sigma, Kappa Delta Pi, Dean's List, President's List; [a.] Dallas, GA

CRAWFORD-HOLCOMB, BEVERLY JEAN
[pen.] B. J. Holcomb; [b.] May 18, 1940, San Antonio, TX; [m.] Robert Holcomb; [ch.] Richard, Kenneth, Steven, Cheryl, Robert IV, seven grandchildren; [ed.] Master of Science Degree in Education, Teaching Credentials: Reading Specialist, Learning Disabilities Specialist, Early Childhood Education, and Elementary Education; [occ.] Experienced Educator, Business Owner, and Writer; [memb.] Advocate and supporter of literacy as member of "Friends of the Library"; [oth. writ.] Several magazine and newspaper articles published. In addition to writing poetry and traveling, interests include World Religions and Native American Studies.; [pers.] Poetry to the Writer is like the painted canvas to the Artist. It is the reflection of the soul. Growing up, my favorite poet was, and still is, Emily Dickinson.; [a.] Austin, TX

CRAYNE, JEANNE
[b.] February 25, Newton, MA; [p.] Elizabeth Krzewick; [m.] Fred Crayne, August 2, 1967; [ch.] Kim, Elizabeth, James Joe, Rose and Amanda; [ed.] Newton High, Citrus College, Chaffey College, Riverside Com. College, Daytona Beach Com. College; [occ.] Receptionist, Mariner Health of Deland, FL; [memb.] Atlanta Center of the Arts Deland Cultural Arts; [oth. writ.] Poems; [pers.] I believe that true wisdom is a gift from the chid and the child holds the keys to heal all of humanities anguish.; [a.] Deland, FL

CREIGH, ZANIA REIGH
[pen.] Zania Reigh Creigh; [b.] September 15, 1953, Indiana; [ed.] Atlanta School of Massage, Indiana College of Bus./Tech.; [occ.] Sports Massage Therapist, Creigh Therapeutics/owner; [memb.] American Massage Therapy Assoc.; [pers.] With gratitude, I desire to share, explore and examine with others, my mind's alternative perceptions. These writings result from the influences of my dreams, meditation, and therapy. All contribute to healing my emotional mind.; [a.] Atlanta, GA

CRITTENDEN, JEANNE
[b.] September 17, 1934, Texas; [p.] Dr and Mrs. H. B. Masters; [m.] Gerald Crittenden, May 1, 1954; [ch.] Julie Ann Crittenden and Dianne Lee Crittenden; [ed.] Battle Creek Central, Michigan State; [occ.] Self Employed; [pers.] I like to write poetry that reflects a time or feeling in my own life.

CRONE, KEVIN
[b.] April 15, 1966, Amarillo, TX; [p.] Tony Crone and Paulette Strebeck; [m.] Tammy Crone, October 31, 1987; [ed.] Amarillo College; [occ.] Student; [memb.] A.C. Voices of Verse and Film Guild, Amarillo Live Poets Society; [hon.] A.C. Honors Program (President), Who's Who in American Junior Colleges; [pers.] The mystical is as important as the physical or emotional, this is what I try to reflect in my writing.; [a.] Amarillo, TX

CROSS, DENISE
[pen.] Denise Simacourbe; [b.] October 7, 1955, Camden, NJ; [p.] Maurice and Phyllis Simacourbe; [ed.] Northwestern High, University College, Uni-

versity of Maryland; [occ.] Engineering Assistant; [memb.] Friends of the National Zoo, Chesapeake Bay Foundation, National Wildlife Federation, Humane Society, U.S.; [hon.] High School Varsity Letter - Track and Field, Dean's List academic achievement - University College; [pers.] I wish to thank my late parents for everything that I am and will be, I owe and dedicate this accomplishment to them. I wish to acknowledge my 12th grade poetry teacher, Rebecca Street, for encouraging me to continue to write poetry.; [a.] Hyattsville, MD

CROWLEY, ANNA B. MACIAS
[b.] March 6, 1956, Guayaquil, Ecuador S.A.; [p.] German Macias and Vicenta Correa; [m.] Thomas J. Crowley, February 23, 1985; [ch.] Aida S. Montanez and Charles M. Crowley; [ed.] The Assisium, N.Y., Plaza Business School, N.Y., La Guardia Community College, N.Y.; [occ.] Associate Teacher, Colonial Northampton Intermediate Unit 20, PA; [memb.] Evangel Church, Parent/Teacher Officer, Al-Anon; [hon.] Dean's List 2 yrs, graduated with honors from College; [oth. writ.] Many unpublished poems/short stories (personals). None published; [pers.] Everyone has the right to be treated with dignity, love and respect, mainly the children without a voice (mothers).; [a.] Reeders, PA

CRUZ, BARBARA O.
[b.] April 4, 1942, Hawaii; [p.] Mr. and Mrs. Clarence Outlaw; [m.] Victor M. Cruz, December 8, 1961; [ch.] Kim, Vickie, Sandy; [ed.] High School - Edenton-Chowan; [occ.] Housewife; [oth. writ.] None published other than local news paper; [pers.] I love to write poetry in a very personal note. The poetry that I write about, I've lived it.; [a.] Edenton, NC

CULLER, JEANNE C.
[pen.] Cecille Huntingdon; [b.] Over 50, Pittsburgh, PA; [p.] Sarah and Cecile Culler; [ed.] Six years of College - part time, night school major - Criminal and Abnormal Psychology; [occ.] Between jobs; [memb.] PETA, Fund for Animals - Animal Org.; [hon.] Nothing special; [oth. writ.] Wrote for foreign magazines back in '50's and '60's. Have written historical novel in regards to American Indian and family on mother's side.; [pers.] I researched the 'Nam War Interviewed Vets - this 19 line poem from 54 page poem regarding Marine POW's. I feel it will help POW's and natives of 'Nam.; [a.] Clay Pool, AZ

CUNNINGHAM, CLARE
[pen.] Grandma Clare; [b.] August 2, 1915, Fennimore, WI; [p.] George Novinski, Minnie Novinski; [m.] James B. Cunningham (December 1986), September 19, 1938; [ch.] Ellen, Sheila, Ruthe, Patrice, Deborah, Denise, Daniel, Janice; [ed.] Graduate, Atchison County Community High School; [occ.] Homemaker, retired Postal Clerk; [memb.] NARFE, Library Community Club, Ladies Church Group, Social Club; [oth. writ.] My poems are written for and about my family; [pers.] I have a close-knit family and on occasion I delight them with a poem written to mark a special family event or to make a gift memorable.; [a.] Effingham, KS

CURZON, SHERRY A.
[b.] October 2, 1962, Mount Hope, ID; [p.] Janet Schultz and R. Dean Clifton; [m.] Phillip L. Curzon,

February 7, 1990; [ed.] Glenns Ferry High School, Glenns Ferry, ID. Graduate of Institute of Children's Literature; [occ.] Homemaker, writer; [pers.] My poetry and writing is in my life and my life is in my poetry and my writing.; [a.] Pocatello, ID

DALY, ANNA
[b.] April 8, 1959, Quincy, IL; [p.] Howard and Carlene Stambaugh; [m.] Robert Daly, November 5, 1976; [ch.] Craig, Christopher, Trista; [pers.] I am inspired by the emotions of myself and others. I hope to reflect the feelings of life's challenges and rewards.; [a.] Quincy, IL

DALZELL, CONNIE
[b.] February 18, 1946, Vallejo, CA; [m.] John; [ch.] Kirsten, Erin, Justin, Michael, David; [occ.] Dog Breeder/Housewife; [memb.] Inland Empire Akita Club, Akita Club of America, American Cancer Society; [oth. writ.] Several poems published in Local Chamber of Commerce Magazine, poems published monthly in Akita Club Newsletter; [pers.] I believe that language can be a powerful tool for the betterment of mankind and that poetry, by its nature, can touch and move in ways that prose cannot.; [a.] Corona, CA

DANIELS, MARIONETTE S.
[pen.] Aunt Nette; [b.] August 25, 1927, Union, SC; [p.] William and Essie M. Sanders; [m.] Edward Daniels, August 25, 1949; [ed.] Masters in Social Work, Columbia University, NYC, NY; [occ.] Project Director, Alzheimer's Program, and Social Work Consultant; [memb.] NASW, Inc., APWA, St. Mary's Baptist Church, D.C.; [oth. writ.] Professional Publications; [pers.] I am intrigued by the relationships among and between people and always want to capture the beauty in the interdependence naturally inherent in our lives and the joy of loving responses one to another.; [a.] Silver Spring, MD

DAVID, SANDRA DEANNA
[pen.] Deanna David; [b.] May 25, 1951, Norfolk, VA; [p.] Edwin Hendricks and Mildred Hendricks; [m.] Gene David, October 11, 1984; [ch.] Tim Thompson, Sherry Thompson and Elise David; [ed.] Kecoughtan High, Hampton, VA; [occ.] Gospel Singer and Writer; [pers.] If we could conquer our worst enemy, we could end hatred, racism, and violence, end hunger and poverty. Who is our worst enemy? We are?; [a.] Hampton, VA

DAVIS, ACQUINETTA
[pen.] Elizabeth "Bernice" Muffet; [b.] July 17, 1967, Charlotte, NC; [p.] Walter Davis, Bernice Davis; [m.] William J. Davis Jr., June 6, 1987; [ch.] Joshua Eein, Vontraciya Joel, and Gabriel Emmanuel; [ed.] South Mecklenburg High School, Bennett College, Honolulu Community College, Leeward Community College Fayetteville State Univ., UNC-Charlotte; [occ.] Songwriter, Poet, Evangelist Playwrite, Human Services Student; [memb.] Writer's Digest Member; [hon.] 2nd place in Female Vocal Contest, Honored 2 consecutive years in Who's Who Among High School Students; [oth. writ.] Several poems and other writing, plays, movie-scripts, awaiting publication and/or production.; [pers.] I endeavor to bring hope, joy, and peace to mankind, by letting them know, "Through God all things are possible."; [a.] Wahiawa, HI

DAVIS, BENNETT PRYOR
[b.] July 23, 1928, Nesquehoning, PA; [p.] Arthur Davis, Anne Dunstan; [m.] Irene Daderka Davis; [ch.] Mary Anne, Nancy Jane, Bennett F., (Robert Arthur, deceased); [occ.] Retired; [pers.] When asked by friends how I could still write this poem at such a humbing time in my life, I replied, "Because I loved my son dearly, and I still love my God". "I'll have the `reason' some day, and we'll both be secure in God's living arms."; [a.] Summit Hill, PA

DAVIS, BETTYE J.
[pen.] J. Davis; [b.] March 15, 1957, Yoakum, TX; [p.] Gwendolyn M. Lee; [ed.] B.A. in Business Administration Seattle University, Graduate Student in University of LaVerne Masters of Business Administration; [oth. writ.] Several other poems published in University of La Verne's Reflections Magazine Quarterly; [pers.] I strive to overcome life's tough challenges in desire to improve myself and teach my peers and youth that your most important competitor is yourself and the greatest and most positive way to succeed is to continue to improve; [a.] Claremont, CA

DAVIS, DONALD
[b.] August 21, 1946, Saint Louis, MO; [p.] Willie and Lillian Davis; [m] Karin R. Davis, June 19, 1970; [ch.] Robin L. Davis; [ed.] B.A. in Business, B.A. in Psychology; [occ.] Personal Care Attendant; [memb.] Masonic Order, United States Taekwon-do Federation, International Taekwon-do Federation; [hon.] Honorable Discharge U.S.A.F.; [pers.] My words beat in my heart like a timeless drum heard by the whistling wind, and the children of the wood. Now all will hear my words.; [a.] Columbia, MO

DAVIS, EARLEAN
[b.] December 13, 1947, Sawyerville, AL; [p.] Mr. and Mrs. Roosevelt Rutley; [m.] Timmy L. Davis, November 6, 1970; [ch.] Patrice, Jesse, Jermaine; [ed.] Central Elem., Druid High, Stillman College, Oakland Univ., Logos Graduate College - (Doc. candidate) currently working on; [occ.] Student Advocate Lincoln Jr. High School; [memb.] PEA, NEA, MEA, Amer. Lung Assoc. member of Berea Family, Tabernacle of Faith Church, Mothers Against Drunk Drivers, Pontiac Police Athletic League; [hon.] Pontiac 1991 teacher of the year. 1996 Who Who's Among Teachers, 1994 Receiptant of the Oakland County Child Abuse/ Neglect Council Award; [oth. writ.] Several poems, currently working on a manuscript for a book. Book entitled "Poetry Reading in the Elementary School"; [pers.] To be successful, we need Godly wisdom knowledge and understanding. Knowledge - acquisition of info. Understanding - knowing how and why we use it. Wisdom - knowing when and where to use it. "Faith without works is dead"; [a.] Pontiac, MI

DAVIS, DR. H. CLINT
[b.] October 16, 1939, Anthers, OK; [p.] Rev. and Mrs. Ross Davis; [m.] Dee Davis, July 14, 1962; [ch.] Christi, Teresa, Nathan; [ed.] Doctor of Education with Comprehensive Minor in History; [occ.] Supervisor of Education, EWCC Prison for Women, Taft, OK; [hon.] Eagle Scout, 1955, Phi Alpha Theta (History Honor Society), 1988, National Collegiate History Award, 1988, USAA

Scholastic All-American Collegiate Award, 1988; [oth. writ.] "Mist of Time" (Book of poems), "Dogman of Boggy Bottoms" (Biographical Sketch), Dissertation: "Factors Contributing To Increased History Enrollments in Texas Four Year Colleges, 1985 to 1990, A Case Study"; [pers.] If a teacher can't touch the heart of their student, they will never be able to reach their mind.; [a.] Muskogee, OK

DAVIS, LEXIE
[b.] August 31, 1958, San Diego, CA; [m.] Regina Davis, January 24, 1986; [ch.] Joshua, age 3 1/2; [ed.] Oceanside High School, Mira Costa College; [occ.] Self employed, Business and Management Consultant; [memb.] Portland Victory Fellowship; [oth. writ.] Many poems and songs.; [pers.] A poem is a creation, and has a creator. Having worked at the Air National Guard Base (Guarding F-4 fighting Jets) in Reno, NV., I was impressed with the design of the F-4 jets. If I flew over a volcano, and then dropped into it all the raw materials needed to create a F-4 jet, how long would I have to wait before a F-4 jet came flying out of the volcano? The human body and it's intricate design makes the fighter jet look like a child's toy. I can't believe mankind evolved on it's own, anymore than someone reading my poem could believe it wrote itself.; [a.] Portland, OR

DAVIS, PAUL T.
[b.] October 21, 1969, Worcester, MA; [pers.] You'll never realize what you can do until you open your mind. Dream of Angels.; [a.] Worcester, MA

DAVIS, ROLAND B.
[b.] August 24, 1934, Cleveland, OH; [p.] Roland (Hallam) Davis, Elizabeth Zelenak; [m.] Marie Jane Szalay, September 15, 1956; [ch.] Bernadette Marie Furlong, Deborah Anne Blatnik; [ed.] East Technical High, Cleveland, Ohio, Cuyahoga Community College, Parma, Ohio, University of Notre Dame, Notre Dame, IN; [occ.] Engineer; [hon.] Eagle Scout, BSA Scouters Award, BSA Scarabaean Honor Society, East Tech National Honor Society, East Tech Steuben Society of America Award, for excellence in German, good conduct medal, U.S. Army; [oth. writ.] Simply Blue, The Garden of Life, The Two Sides of Life, Best Poems of The 90's, The Looking Glass, Frost at Midnight; [pers.] I am a romantic that finds pleasure with people and machines, and I write what comes from within. The solitude of a moment can turn into an eternity of life, enjoy the moment.; [a.] Stow, OH

DAVIS, SANDRA SUE
[pen.] Sandra Sue Davis; [b.] February 5, 1953, Oklahoma City, OK; [p.] William Walter and Billie Jean Clary; [m.] James B. Davis, June 20, 1981; [ch.] Two stepchildren; [ed.] High School, Crooked Oak High School, Oklahoma City, Oklahoma; [occ.] Homemaker; [oth. writ.] "What Is Life" and "Live"; [pers.] Your acceptance of my poetry is one of the greatest occurrences in my life. I shall forever be honored, proud, grateful and most appreciative.; [a.] Cypress, CA

DAVIS, VERNON ISAISH
[pen.] Change and Khepra Maat Tekhen; [b.] October 25, 1968, Saint Louis, MO; [p.] Lillie L. Davis and Willie Strong; [ed.] Vashon High gradu-

ate (Saint Louis); [occ.] Underemployed Artist, Author, Painter, etc.; [hon.] 2nd place in '94, Vaughn Cultural Centers, Poetry Slam; [oth. writ.] "This Is A Test", "Voices", and "Dnekrad-Esouh"; [pers.] Strive to recognize God as the ever-present one who encompasses all. And be blessed by the power within.; [a.] Saint Louis, MO

DAVIS JR., PERCY
[b.] November 20, 1944, New Orleans, LA; [p.] Mr. Percy Davis Sr. and Mrs. Wilhelmina B. Cola; [m.] Divorced; [ch.] Percy III, Anissa and Ja'Net; [ed.] GW Carver HS, Delgado College, New Orleans, LA; [occ.] US Army Retired, security officer; [hon.] Phi Beta Kappa Honor Society; [pers.] Everyone should love one another and forgive one another as God for Christ's sake has forgiven us.; [a.] Birmingham, AL

DAWSON, JANIS ELAINE
[b.] July 8, 1961; [p.] Jim and Aline Gravitt; [ch.] Donna Elaine Dawson; [ed.] Johnson High School; [occ.] Secretary; [oth. writ.] None that have been published; [pers.] I thank God every day for all my blessings!; [a.] Flowery Branch, GA

DAWSON, LINDA MAE
[pen.] D. Lovel; [b.] April 9, 1948, Hannibal, MO; [p.] John Russell and Mary Frances Brummer; [m.] James Thomas Dawson, March 17, 1973; [ch.] Adopted Alisha Lea, Danakaye, Carol Sue; [ed.] Ged and Medical Office Assistant graduate; [occ.] Wife and mother poetry and song writing; [memb.] I belong to the P.T.A.; [hon.] This is one big honor I hope to have more poems and songs published besides this one, in the anthology.; [oth. writ.] I have written 60 poems and songs, none have been published yet until now. This is first contest I've entered.; [pers.] My talent didn't come out until age 45 when I started drawing and painting and learning to play the piano. The Lord has been my entire inspiration.; [a.] Quincy, IL

DAY JR., JOE EDWIN
[b.] March 8, 1941, Tampa, FL; [p.] Joseph E. and Gruce H. Day

DE MESQUITA, LUIZA
[b.] November 7, 1926, Azores, Portugal; [p.] Antonio De Mesquita, Maria L. De Mesquita; [ch.] Maria A. Angelis; [ed.] Lic. Nacional Horta (High school) - dip., Alliance Francaise (Paris) - Dip. Tourism/Inst. N. Profissoes (Lisbon); [memb.] Real Gabinete Portugues de Leitura - Senacula Brasileiro de Letras; [hon.] Biography published at the "The World Who's Who of Women", Int'l. Biographical Centre, Cambridge, England (5th ed.); [oth. writ.] Books (poetry) "Ondas de Mare Cheia", "Mar Incerto", "Areias Movedigas", "Tempo de Mar, Tempo de Amar", "Caminhos do Mar", "Bateau de Papier", "Cantigas de Mar e Bem-Querer", "Mar de Sempre a Cores", Ciclone"; [a.] Winter Springs, FL

DE SPAIN, LAVELLE G. WHITING
[b.] July 1, 1921, Woodruff, AZ; [p.] Marion and Mary Gibbons; [m.] Melvin F. De Spain, December 21, 1962; [ch.] Four - Pam Benson, Claudia Lowell, Ken and Ed Whiting; [ed.] St. John's High School, Weaver Beauty College in Phoenix; [occ.] Retired; [memb.] St. Johns Beautification Cemetery Comm.

18 yrs. - Leader (Area) and Grp. Leader in Recovery, Inc, 27 yrs - Church of Jesus Christ of Larren Dag Saint in Ladies R. Society 50 yrs; [hon.] St. Johns Chamber of Commerce - Woman of the year - Certificate of Appreciation for Outstanding Contribution to the preservation of St. John's Folk Lore - Certificate of Appreciation for 27 years of Service to Recovery and It's Work in Mental Health. Certificate of 45 yrs visiting Teacher; [oth. writ.] I have recently comply a collection of my writings in a 320 page book - "From Closet Drawers To A Book" I have written 2 story books - 1 and 2 "Story Time" - I have 15 Stories and poems in American Folklore Series "The Oral Tradition Of The American West." I wrote the chapter in our church stake book on the Presidents Of The Relief Society - 12 Presidents In All - my own life history - 8 journals and life story of my deceased husband.; [pers.] "Where Much Has Given, Much Is Expected." And I have been given much. I hope through my writings I have been able to convey my love and appreciation for my savior, my family, this great land of America, and my many blessings and for myself.; [a.] Saint Johns, AZ

DEAL, PAUL THOMAS
[b.] February 7, 1961, Robbinsdale, MN; [p.] Duane Deal and Barbara Ward; [ed.] High School, Greenway; [occ.] Sales Representative in Duluth, MN; [oth. writ.] 187 original acoustic pop/ballads, "Ghost Story Songs."

DEARDEN, CONSTANCE JONES PRINCE
[pen.] Connie Jones Prince; [p.] Earl and Marguerite Jones; [m.] Dr. Bert Dearden; [ch.] Sylvia Loner, Yvonne Mihaescu, William T. Prince, Jr.; [ed.] Graduated Barlow Local High School (Vincent, Ohio); [memb.] 1. Poets Pathfinders Club, 2. Indiana State Federation of Poetry Clubs; [hon.] 1st Prize for a poem entitled, "Bridges"; [oth. writ.] Cards: 1. Armed Forces Greeting Card, 2. Serviceman's Sympathy Card, 3. Vietnam Veteran's Card, Books: 1. My Daddy is in the Air Force", 2. "Search for Serenity", 3. "Red, White, and True!", Musical Dramas: 1. "Rendezvous with Destiny", 2. America, A Dream that was Dreamed"; [pers.] I want to use this precious gift of life to encourage and inspire others. I am a thankful and concerned American who values the sacrifices paid for our freedoms. Life is very short-with mixtures of bitter and sweet experiences. I want to leave good memories.; [a.] Logansport, IN

DECKERT, SONIA L. SALDIVAR
[b.] May 12, 1967, Arroyo Grande, CA; [p.] John and Carmen Saldivar; [m.] David Dcckert, May 15, 1986; [ch.] Courtney 9, Mary 2; [ed.] El Camino High School; [occ.] Homemaker; [pers.] Keep your ideals high enough to inspire you, and low enough to encourage you.; [a.] Salinas, CA

DECOITO, ROBIN
[b.] September 26, 1975, San Diego, CA; [p.] Ann Hudson, Norman Boucher; [ch.] Ivy DeCoito; [ed.] Presently enrolled at Mesa Community College. Major "Writing"; [occ.] Costumer Service Rep. at Bank of America; [oth. writ.] Several poems, currently putting a book together.; [pers.] My dream is to be a writer. I'm a firm believer in a positive attitude, and my theory about life and dreams is: never, never give up.; [a.] Mesa, AZ

DECRESCENTIS, LOUIS J.
[pen.] Mr. Dee; [b.] March 21, 1937, Denver, CO; [p.] Louie and Frances DeCrescentis; [m.] Esther, June 29, 1963; [ch.] Gina and Joe; [ed.] B.A. C.S.C. Greeley M.A. D.U. Denver; [occ.] Sp Ed. Teacher 63-91 (retired) Retail Auto Sales 91-96; [memb.] C.E.A. N.E.A.; [pers.] Writing about children, animals, and nature brings great pleasure to me.; [a.] Brighton, CO

DEL RUSSO, DAWN
[pen.] Dawn Del Russo; [b.] May 20, 1979, Montclair, NJ; [p.] Angelo and Diane Del Russo; [ed.] St. Joseph's Elementary School, Barron Collier H.S. and West Morris Mendham H.S.; [occ.] Writer, Singer, Dancer, Actress; [hon.] Art Award, Beauty Runner Up Award, Poem "Sandy Days" published; [pers.] I enjoy writing poems and wish to further my skills in more writing.; [a.] Mendham, NJ

DELANCEY, DANIELLE
[b.] April 29, 1984, Pittsburgh, PA; [p.] Shyrl Hyland and Pat Delancey; [ed.] South Fayette Elementary (6th grade); [hon.] 1st and 2nd place ribbons for gymnastics, 2 trophies for swim team and 1st, 2nd and 3rd place ribbons for swim team awards from school, and made it all the semifinalist in dancing; [pers.] Life is like the weather -- it's unpredictable.; [a.] Bridgeville, PA

DELP, BOB
[b.] February 25, 1941, Eugene, IN; [p.] Maurice and Mabel Lorene Delp; [m.] Marilyn Delp, November 7, 1963; [ch.] Robert Ray, Jimmy Wayne; [ed.] Central Texas College; [occ.] Maintenance, Anderson Golf Course, Ft. Hood, TX; [hon.] Dean's List, various Military Honors and Awards, Vietnam Veteran, Retired U.S. Army; [a.] Killeen, TX

DEMPSTER, LINDA L.
[b.] December 12, 1949, Norristown, PA; [p.] James G. and Helen Frances Lohr; [m.] Divorced November 22, 1983; [ch.] Travis Scott and Jennifer Lynn; [ed.] Upper Merion HS - PA, Montgomery Hospital School of Nursing, PA, CA State University of Long Beach; [occ.] RN, BSN, CA DHS - Audits and Investigations, Medical Review; [memb.] Stephens Ministry, Lutheran Cursillo of Southern CA; [hon.] Phi Kappa Phi, Honor Society since 1979 graduated CSULB - Great Distinction with GPA March 97; [oth. writ.] Testimonies of Forth - Miracle of Jennifer - published in local newsletters.; [pers.] Isaiah 43 - All our challenges are miracles writing to happen. All victims can become survivors when we permit God's love to give us courage to conquer fear and to heal!; [a.] Huntington Beach, CA

DEMPSTER, TRAVIS
[pen.] T. S. Dempster; [b.] June 15, 1977; [pers.] Life's worst tragedy is the loss of possibility.

DENNIS, JUDITH
[b.] August 12, 1940, New York, NY; [p.] Edward Thompson, Winifred Thompson; [ch.] Robert Lee Dennis, Robin Inez Dennis; [ed.] Evander Childs High School Ambassador College Bible Correspondence Course; [memb.] Fellowship Covenant Church Deaconess Consumer Board of Mental Health; [hon.] Certificate of Completion of Bible Correspondence Course copy right for Liter-

ary Work; [oth. writ.] Book of Spiritual Writings unpublished as of yet; [pers.] I am so thankful that I allowed God to come into my life. He has opened my eyes to greater insight and through this awareness he has allowed the Holy Spirit to let me say through spiritual writing what thus sayeth the Lord, to me.; [a.] Bronx, NY

DENONNO, SHERYLE B.
[pen.] Cleo I; [b.] February 19, 1959, Englewood, NJ; [p.] Mr. and Mrs. Robert Lee Wilson Sr.; [m.] Charles J. DeNonno, July 17, 1982; [ch.] Chas J. DeNonno, Charleshai, Bettina; [ed.] Fashion Industries High School, Columbia University 1 yr. 1980, Art Instruction School 2 yr. 89-91, Volunteer V.A. Mahattan 70-73; [occ.] Art Instructor, Writer Freelance, Mother Day Care Teacher; [memb.] Church, PTA, Future possibilities program to help children grow industrial to the environment and future progress for the betterment of life.; [hon.] Art Certificate, Diplomas Certificate of Excellence, Volunteer Hospital Award 5 yr., Day Care Teacher Award (Newspaper article 1984), Daily News; [oth. writ.] I wrote a mini Biography (To Save My Sanity), still have it never published it yet. Wrote stories for children, my mentor Og Mandigo (The Greatest Miracle), other self help books.; [pers.] I love to become a writer to inspire the world and especially children. I'm very touched when I can make a contribution to the world and life, there is so much in me to express.; [a.] Bronx, NY

DEPOLITO, SARA
[b.] July 19, 1987, Norwich, CT; [p.] Steven and Sherri Depolito; [ed.] Will be entering 4th grade at Preston City School, Preston, CT; [memb.] YMCA, Sign Language Club, Preston City Chorus, Dance Company; [hon.] Ribbons for Read Racing Clean Up Award - P.T.O. Preston City School Trophy for Soccer; [oth. writ.] Poem about spring, summer and olympics math poems.; [pers.] "I hope my poems turn into songs like Francis Scott Key's Star Spangled Banner."; [a.] Preston, CT

DEROCH, LINDA
[b.] September 21, 1968, San Francisco, CA; [p.] Darhl and Carole Cowden; [m.] W. Scott DeRoch, May 13, 1995; [ed.] Tomball High School, College of the Mainland; [occ.] Documentation Clerk at M.W. Kellogg, Houston, TX; [memb.] Greater Houston Toast Masters, Memorial Lutheran Church in Katy, TX; [hon.] First place in 9th grade Poetry Contest at Jubail Academy, Jubail, Saudi Arabia; [pers.] My personal writing theme is to show that no matter how dark a soul becomes, there is always a chance to turn to the good.; [a.] Katy, TX

DEROCHE III, URSIN J.
[pen.] Eelian Gale; [b.] December 7, 1976, Buton Rouge, LA; [occ.] Guitarist/Composer; [oth. writ.] Lots of beautifully unpublished poems; [pers.] I can't find a good all-night diner anywhere.; [a.] Baton Rouge, LA

DEROSA, ERIN LOREAN
[b.] November 17, 1984, Cincinnati, OH; [p.] Chris and Sue DeRosa; [ed.] Grade 5, Kolerain Elementary - Kindergarten, Ford Elementary 1-2 Grade, St. Joseph School; [occ.] Student; [memb.] Girl Scouts; [hon.] A/B Honor Roll - Presidential Fitness Award 3rd and 5th Grade, National Fitness Award - 4th Grade; [oth. writ.] Poetry and stories in St. Joseph's Literary Magazine; [pers.] 11 years of age.; [a.] Acworth, GA

DERRY, RENATA BIGHAM
[pen.] Renata Bigham-Derry; [b.] March 24, 1952, Marlin, TX; [p.] Sidney J. and Lebetha M. Bigham; [m.] Dolphus J. Derry Jr., December 28, 1970; [ch.] Kimberly, Dolphus III, Adam (3); [ed.] University of Houston (History) Houston Community College - Psychology; [occ.] Administrative Assistant - Computer Software and Consulting Company; [memb.] Second Baptist Church; [oth. writ.] Currently working on a book of poetry and also have begun a book about life's journey on the road to eternity.; [pers.] I believe that the other 90% of the brain currently not being utilized by mankind holds the key to life beyond death.; [a.] Houston, TX

DESKINS, MAXINE M.
[pen.] Maxine M. Deskins; [b.] January 24, 1943, Washington, DC; [p.] Carme and Pedro; [m.] Ali Ahmed, December 25; [ch.] Gypsy, Tony, Cinno and Wayne; [ed.] High School, 12th grade; [occ.] Writer and poet; [memb.] "Legend" a club I started myself; [oth. writ.] "I Evoke Thee", I evoke the fire, I evoke the sea, I evoke ye Gods, I evoke my love Ali!; [pers.] I wrote this poem for my beloved son. "So We Dine" Cinno Howell, who was killed on February 16, 1994 and Tony, Gypsy and Wayne, other sons living.; [a.] Washington, DC

DESTEFANO, ROBERT F.
[pen.] Robert "Fox" DeStefano; [b.] May 16, 1963, Glendale, NY; [p.] Robert B. and Harriett L. DeStefano; [ed.] Huron High School-Ann Arbor, MI Eastern Michigan Univ.-Ypsilanti, MI College of DuPage-Glen Ellyn, IL Aurora University-Aurora, IL; [occ.] Self employed, seeking employment, working on novel; [memb.] National Wildlife Federation, Nature Conservancy, Defenders of Wildlife, Willowbrook Wildlife Foundation, Aurora University Alumni Association; [hon.] Several awards of Academic Achievement, Peer Tutoring Certificates of Appreciation, President's List; [oth. writ.] This is my first published writing. My artwork has previously been used for a Willowbrook Wildlife Foundation Christmas news letter and a local Women's Club. I hope to publish more art and writing in future.; [pers.] My work is a celebration of the world of nature. I strive to help people appreciate the natural world as a source of wonder and spiritual renewal. Humanity can't survive without nature!; [a.] Placentia, CA

DETTER, ANGELA DIANE
[b.] September 24, 1968, Newton, NC; [p.] R. Henry Detter and Frankie S. Detter; [a.] Maiden, NC

DETTLING, ONA OTTILIA
[pen.] Tillie Dettling; [b.] October 2, 1905, Nicolas, CA; [p.] John Scheiber (Switzerland), Anna (California); [m.] Steve Dettling (Deceased 1992), October 1, 1932 (married 59 years); [ch.] Richard Steven Dettling, John Gary Dettling; [ed.] One-Room School House, Nicolas, CA, St. Joseph's Academy, Sacramento, CA; [occ.] Homemaker at age 90 I drive my own car wherever I want to go. I take care of all my Own Business; [memb.] Holy Rosary Catholic Church; [hon.] On Special Occasion there were Prize Waltz attractions. My partner and I most frequently won; [oth. writ.] (None) see attached sheet data on my history and hobbies/interests. Red Cross Nurse WWII, Pink Lady Hospitals (Woodland Memorial and Country) Musician - Piano, Hobby China Painting.; [a.] Woodland, CA

DIAMANTE, SAUNDRA-TAYLOR
[b.] January 12, 1959, Baltimore, MD; [p.] L/CR Stanley A. Taylor, and Rose Mary Taylor; [m.] Gill P. Diamante, October 25, 1985; [ch.] Gill Jr., Robert, Timothy, Ariel and Athea; [ed.] Serverna Park High 1977 Md Inst. College Art 1977-99. I obtain my FFC License in 1980; [occ.] Homemaker; [memb.] Member of IS of Poets; [hon.] Two I.S. of Poet Merit Awards. Two Editor's Choice Awards; [oth. writ.] "The Balance" printed in "The Sea of Treasures" - "September" printed in Spirit of Age, "I too, once was a Child" printed in A tapestry of thoughts - A Bit of Christmas Cheer" printed in Carvings in the Stone/printed in The Rippling Waters Happy Valentines Day; [pers.] "With Education, everything is with in Reach"; [a.] Daly City, CA

DIAZ, LINDA F.
[b.] April 3, 1972, El Paso, TX; [p.] Julia Diaz; [ed.] University of Texas at El Paso, Bowie High School, Guillen Intermediate School (7th-8th), Roosevelt Elementary, Aoy Elementary School; [occ.] ESL Teacher for El Paso Independent School District; [memb.] National Honor Society, French Honorary Society, Business Professionals of America, National Honor Junior Society; [hon.] Dean's List, Honor Student at Bowie High School, Top 10% graduating Senior in High School, LULAC Scholarship Recipient, Best Haiku Poet for Guillen School, Honor Roll Student, Presidential Award; [oth. writ.] "My Greatest Treasure" written for UTEP's West Texas Writing Project. I won 1st place for grades 9-12 category essay was published in an anthology entitled "Education", "Yesterday, Today, and Tomorrow." I have written other unpublished poems and essays throughout my school years.; [pers.] I strive to venture into the depths of one's own mind, one's own soul, and one's own heart in the writings I have done and continue to do on daily basis. I have been influenced by every author I have studied in high school and in college.; [a.] El Paso, TX

DICKS, MARKY
[pen.] Marky; [b.] October 22, 1951, Logan, UT; [p.] Casey and Helen Edwards; [m.] Paul Albert Dicks, September 24, 1990; [ch.] I have ten children; [ed.] I have completed 11th grade. I am hoping to finish high school and some college soon, when the children are older; [occ.] House wife, I have to be at home for our children; [hon.] This is the first time and have sent any of my poetry in. So I have none as of yet; [oth. writ.] I have nine other poems I have written besides "Don't Wait it Might Grow Too Late".; [pers.] I hope my poetry might help others to think, learn, and it might help them grow in their lives here on this planet.; [a.] Logan, UT

DIRIENZO, PETER
[pen.] Peter Dirienzo; [b.] December 28, 1953, Bronxville, NY; [p.] Ralph and Louise Dirienzo; [m.] Jeanette Thibaut Bartlett, December 28,

1995; [ch.] Jaime Lyn, Dylan Patrick, and Jennie Louise; [ed.] Eastchester High, Mercy College; [occ.] Logistics Support; [oth. writ.] Personal poems; [pers.] Don't ever give up. I also am influenced by the poet Dylan Thomas.; [a.] Kingwood, TX

DIXON, CAROLINE CRESS
[b.] February 15, 1965, Ludwigsburg, Germany; [p.] Johnnie P. Cress II, Monika Cress; [m.] Tony E. Dixon Sr., July 27, 1989; [ch.] Theresia A., Michael T., Tony E., Tonika D.; [ed.] Hobbs High; [occ.] Mother and wife; [memb.] Living Waters Church; [hon.] Black Heritage Arts Award; [oth. writ.] Non published; [pers.] In all of my life endeavors I have been guided and influenced by our father and my Lord and Savior. I dedicate "Once Bound, Now Free" to Him.; [a.] Burns Flat, OK

DONALDSON, CLIFF
[b.] August 25, 1957, Glendale, CA; [ch.] Kevin Drew, Jennifer Kayleigh; [occ.] U.S. Navy; [oth. writ.] When Death Becomes A Lie, Outside Of Prayers Perimeter; [pers.] Every color in my soul is connected to my children - I love you both.; [a.] Lemoore, CA

DONOVAN, PATRICK
[p.] Bill and Betty Donovan; [ed.] Ph.D. Clinical Psychology; [occ.] Forensic Staff Psychologist; [oth. writ.] "Today Is Tomorrows Yesterday", "The Chase", "The Spirit Warrior"; [pers.] "Lost and Found" is a poem dedicated to my friend Chris Alvord. The inspiring impression of his life will forever endure beyond the poignant tragedy of his death.; [a.] Paso Robles, CA

DORER, STEPHANIE
[b.] January 30, 1978, Towson, MD; [p.] Stephen and Linda; [ed.] South Western High Towson State Univ.; [hon.] Who's Who, National Honor Roll, Presidential Academic Award, Honor Roll, Distinguished Honor Roll; [oth. writ.] The Sheriff, Crazed Obession, various short stories for classes.; [pers.] I value uniqueness. I strive to make my writings reflect my interests and personality as well as entertaining and enjoyable to the readers.; [a.] Glen Rock, PA

DORSEY, MARCY
[pen.] Marcy Dorsey; [b.] February 28, 1962, Westminster, MD; [p.] Charles Hodge, Genevieve Hodge; [m.] Kenneth Dorsey, June 26, 1987; [ch.] Kenneth "Lee" Dorsey Jr.; [ed.] Westminster High School Frederick Community College; [occ.] Senior Staff-Day Care Worker, Carroll Child Care Center; [oth. writ.] Black Child, A Child's Cry, Little Lost Soul, Awake, Commentary Writings for Carroll, county times and for Brotherhood of maintenance of way Employees Journal (CSX Journal for Railroad Workers); [pers.] I am a concerned black mother of one son. I am very much aware of the drugs and crime that plague our communities. My poems are a reflection of these immoralities that deprive our young men from achieving their ultimate goals.; [a.] Westminster, MO

DOUGHERTY, BRANDI MARIE
[b.] February 21, 1981, Peoria, IL; [p.] William T. Dougherty Sr, Tammy L. Doughterty; [ed.] Sophomore in High School at MacArthur High School,

Decatur, IL; [occ.] Student; [memb.] 4-H and Patrol; [hon.] Trophy for Best Attendance at Sunday School, Marantha Assembly of God, Decatur, IL, Award for Best Student in Grade School and Award for Patrol in Grammar School, Honor Roll all through School; [oth. writ.] Poem "Brothers" published in yearbook, 1994; [pers.] Many people may doubt you, but if you believe in yourself you can always succeed through God.; [a.] Decatur, IL

DOUGLAS, KRIS
[b.] August 30, 1974, Saint Vincent and the Grenadines; [p.] Kenneth Douglas, Ny Jones; [ed.] St. Vincent Girls' High School, City College of New York; [occ.] Student; [memb.] Lions Club International World Association of Girl Guides and Girl Scouts; [hon.] Distinctions in French, Spanish and English Language; [pers.] This poem was my first composition and to be given the opportunity to share it on such a large scale means a great deal to me.; [a.] Brooklyn, NY

DOWNIE, KATHERINE
[b.] December 22, 1976, Kansas City, MO; [p.] John Downie and Linda Schwand; [ed.] Zionsville High, Purdue University; [occ.] Student; [pers.] (For my Gramma D. - You Are My Light.) "Computers, vaccines, space travel, this is technology, to live without prejudice, this is achievement.";
[a.] Highland Park, IL

DUBENSKY, MRS. JOHANNA A. WOLFE
[pen.] Johanna Wolfe Dubensky; [b.] Alamogordo, NM; [p.] H. Joseph Wolfe, Clara C. Qebel Wolfe; [m.] George E. Dubensky, one marriage in St. Mary's Catholic Church; [ch.] George Jr. and Jim, 4 grandchildren - Mike, Shelley, Kristen, Jan; [ed.] Three years college, and continuing education for Permanent Deacons (4 yrs.) and spouse since 1976 - 1995 (Husband Deceased (Oct. 5, '95); [occ.] Retired Fed, Home Keeper Volunteer, "Pastoral Care" Hospital Assist at Service Weekly 10 years.; [memb.] At home of the aged St. Margaret Mary, 40 years, Eucharistic Minister 18 yrs. (Note) (HQ-Head Quarters) (Fed. Gov.); [hon.] Recognition of Civil Service, 1. Command HQ Kelly AFB, SA, TX. 2. Randolph M.P.C., SA, TX., 3. HQ Defence Mapping Agency, SA, TX. Ministry 104 "Pastoral Counseling" (Seminary 1985), Certificate of Outstanding Service, 1991- Hospital and "Courtesy" Display (Oil Paintings) local library 1985; [oth. writ.] Facilitator 3 yrs. Religious Gp. "Renew" named "Most Successful" newspaper poetry published in two year books, 1946-Poetry Broadcast "The Exposition Press, NY (two songs), (unsuccessful) poetry published by "The National Library of Poetry" 1995-1996; [pers.] To bring "A Little Sunlight, Hope and Cheer" into the hearts of all God's Children.; [a.] San Antonio, TX

DUBUC, AMANDA DARLENE
[b.] June 11, 1981, Oklahoma City, OK; [p.] Rita DuBuc; [ed.] 9th Grade; [occ.] Model; [hon.] Numerous Gymnastics Awards, Kung Foo Awards, Over-All Runway Miss (Modeling), I received a letter from President for the poem "Keep the Hope (OKC Bombing); [oth. writ.] Short stories, Myths, many other poems, song lyrics; [pers.] I want to thank my family for encouraging me to write. I was greatly influenced by Kurt Cobain and Courtney Love.; [a.] Moore, OK

DUJARDIN, MICHELLE
[pen.] Michelle DuJardin; [b.] September 23, 1981, Virginia Beach, VA; [p.] Patti O'Kane; [ed.] Starting 9th Grade, Freshman in High School; [occ.] Student; [hon.] 8th Grade Journalism; [oth. writ.] I've written many other poems. Just to write them.; [pers.] Writing poetry for me is kinda like drugs for other people. I have to keep on doing it to survive.; [a.] Seabrook, TX

DUMAR, CATHERINE
[pen.] Catteen; [b.] May 4, 1927, Chazy, NY; [p.] Charles and Catherine Lucia; [m.] Spaulding Dumar (Death May 3, 1993), October 13, 1949; [ch.] Michael and Charles; [ed.] High School Diploma; [occ.] Merchant and House Keeper; [memb.] Altar and Rosary Society Senior Citizens C.C.D. Teacher Human Needs Co-ordinator; [oth. writ.] Many and old dates; [pers.] Poems are my treasures that my dead husband wrote and sent to me - in the Fourties. I also did some writing.; [a.] Chazy, NY

DURANTE, DONNA M.
[pen.] Donna D.; [b.] June 23, 1948, Port Chester, NY; [p.] Nicholas and Marie Antionette Tolla; [m.] Frank J. Durante Sr., June 8, 1969; [ch.] Joseph and Frank; [ed.] C.W. Post Long Island University, Western Ct. State Univer., National Academy of Hair Styling - Stamford, CO; [occ.] Hair Stylist Country Boutique - Greenwich CT; [memb.] Luchimia Society, Assembly of God - Brookfield CT, Retreat for Our Savior; [hon.] Blessings silent only. "Seek first the Kingdom of God and all else shall be given unto you."; [oth. writ.] "From Jesus", "Jesus and I Alone Again", "Why Not Choose Jesus?", "Waiting on the Lord", "I Have You, Ma", "Love Ya"; [pers.] Without my Lord Jesus Christ, it would not be possible to invite as I do. Inspired by my Lord, loved ones and friends, these are the greatest riches one could increase.; [a.] Sandy Hook, CT

DURBIN, H. FITZGERALD
[pen.] H. Fitzgerald; [b.] February 18, 1915, Todd, OK; [p.] W. R. Durbin - B. LaVinia Romines; [m.] Nolda Juanita Walker, August 15, 1933; [ch.] Barbra, Herb, Joe, Bert, Paula, Dan and Don; [occ.] Retired Minister; [memb.] General Council Ass. of God International Society of Poets, Rutherford Institute, United Seniors Ass. Inc.; [hon.] Gold Pin Award for Fifty Years of Ministry; [oth. writ.] The Man Last, Wanted!, True Love After The Storm, Conquest, five books of poetry, poems published in local News Paper.; [pers.] That my life and writings may in some way glorify the God of Heaven.; [a.] Wyandotte, OK

DURHAM SR., RONALD J.
[pen.] Ronn Durham Sr.; [b.] March 29, 1947, Corbin, KY; [p.] Robert S. and Nannie Mae Durham; [m.] Thelma Jean Durham, April 14, 1979; [ch.] Jody, Rhodora, and Ronnie, grandchildren: Cassie, Brandon, Colby, and Kennedy; [ed.] Cumberland College Williamsburg, KY, BS Business Administration, BS Computer Science, BA - Art Community College of Air Force Lajes Field, Azores Union College, Barbourville, KY; [occ.] Disabled Service Connected Veteran (Vietnam); [memb.] Various Military Organizations and local memberships to include Mt. Zion Ministerial Association; [hon.] Forty Three Military Awards and Decorations,

included the U.S. Army Special Forces Green Beret; [oth. writ.] Several poems and stories, children's literature and adult. In addition to writing, I am an accomplished artist.; [pers.] I come from a background of Military Men and Federal Officials, and Lawyers.; [a.] Corbin, KY

DURR-MOOR ROCHELLE
[pen.] Rochelle Durr; [b.] June 19, 1965, Gulfport, MS; [p.] Travis and Helen Durr; [ch.] Cameron Aarron Chela, Dearron, and Deziron Durr; [ed.] Gulfport High School; [occ.] Teacher's Assistant for Gulfport High School; [memb.] Gulfport American Federation of Teachers; [pers.] I would like to thank God for giving me the strength to press on, and acknowledge my family for providing the unity that gives my life meaning.; [a.] Gulfport, MS

DYEHOUSE, PETER EUGENE
[b.] November 30, 1950, Battle Creek, MI; [p.] Roberta Sinclair and Walter Dyehouse; [ed.] H.S. Madison Heights, Anderson, Ind., A.A.A.S. Liberal Arts and A.A. Business Mgmt. Westshore College, Scottsville, MI; [occ.] Quality Control Auditor, Lowell Engineering Corp.; [memb.] A.S.Q.C., V.F.W.; [hon.] U.S. Navy Unit Citation, Viet Nam Service, Viet Nam Campaign; [oth. writ.] Many other poems using many different formats; [pers.] "Strive to be the best human being you can and be a leader not a follower."; [a.] Nashville, MI

DYER, MR. FREDRICK D.
[pen.] Mr. Eat'em Up; [b.] July 23, Wichita Falls, TX; [p.] Mr. Fred and Mrs. Faye Dyer; [ch.] Daleon Dewayne, and Erica Dominique; [ed.] Jack Yates High (Houston, TX), Byrd High (Shreveport, LA), Vocational Tech Inst. (S'port, LA); [hon.] 31 First - Places Awards/Trophies for Singing and/or Dancing on Talent Shows in Tex. and LA at different Clubs or Schools. And was First Runner's Up in the '87-'88 Mr. Charlotte (N.C. Male Dancer) Contest; [pers.] I'm going to do my best to stop racism and violence in America, with the help of my God. Also, I want to help turn our/today's youth around before it's too late...please, don't judge a book by its cover, it's just wrong.; [a.] Houston, TX

EARLE, ASHLEY
[pen.] Ashes; [b.] November 11, 1980, Agora Hospital; [p.] Bill and Joelle Earle; [ed.] High School and looking forward to be a Therapist or a Sergeant; [occ.] Student; [pers.] We should always be ourselves and don't strive on other people's beauty and remarks that may be true. But always remember you are who you are. No matter what people say, you always make your own decisions. Ugly or not, fat or not, I will be your friend.; [a.] Thousand Oaks, CA

EATON, HAZEL
[pen.] Hazel Eaton; [b.] May 15, 1941, England; [p.] George and Irene Wells; [m.] John, November 14, 1965; [ch.] Fiona Nemetz, Sadie Kennedy, Jacqueline Fix; [ed.] Hawnes School, England Royal Academy of Dramatic Art, London; [occ.] Retired; [pers.] I would like to portray the need for all of us to appreciate and take care of our surroundings. "There is none so blind as those who cannot see."; [a.] Atlanta, CA

ECKBURG, ALTHEA LOUISE
[pen.] A. Louise Eckburg; [b.] Pecatonica, IL; [p.] John A. and Louise B. Eckburg; [ed.] Pecatonica (Il.) High School, B.A., U. of Minnesota; [occ.] Retired as Executive Editor of the Medical Annals of the Districe of Columbia; [memb.] Chevy Chase (D.C.) Presbyterian Church, Phi Mu Fraternity, Zonta Club of Washington, D.C., Women's League (of D.C.) for Traffic Safety, Mid-Atlantic Chapter of the American Medical Writers' Assn., USDA Travel Club, Inc., Women's Org. of Friendship Village; [hon.] Listed in "Who's Who of American Women", 6th ed., Community Chest (D.C.) 1952 Campaign Award; [oth. writ.] Many editorials, articles and poems for the Medical Annals of D.C. compiled and edited "History of the Zonta Club of Washington, D.C. 1922-1972", chapter on White's writings in "William Alanson White: The Washington Years" (A.R.T. D'Amore, M.D., ed.) edited many medical papers for publication in retirement years.; [pers.] It is not so important how much you make as what you do with what you make, nor what talents you don't have as what you do with those you do have.; [a.] Schaumburg, IL

EDVALSON, JOHN
[b.] September 3, 1978, Pasco, WA; [p.] Tom and Linda Edvalson; [ed.] High School; [occ.] Student; [hon.] A.P. English Student of the Year, Art Award for the year Honor Roll; [pers.] Life is what you make of it. Don't let it make you into something you're not.; [a.] Benton City, WA

EDWARDS, JUDITH GREER
[b.] April 16, 1957, Martin, KY; [p.] The late Claude Greer and Ivalea C. Greer; [m.] Paul A. Edwards; [ch.] Christopher S. Edwards, Jason L. Edwards; [ed.] Allen Central H.S. Eastern KY; [occ.] Housewife and Writer; [memb.] NSAI Ladies Auxi. KY; [hon.] Song Writer Award several write up's about the song "The Closing Of The Door" in Hearld Standered in Uniontown PA; [oth. writ.] Fade Away (song) KMA records, "The Closing of the Door" (song) IMX records. I co-wrote the "The Closing of the Door" with my brother Michael Greer.; [pers.] My poems and lyrics come from the heart of a southern soul. I love to write and it comes from my heart to your soul. I have been influenced by Loretta Lyn, Stephen Foster, Conway Twitty and many others.; [a.] Martin, KY

EDWARDS, KENNETH H.
[b.] January 14, 1935, Lewistown, MT; [p.] Gerald and Doris Edwards; [ch.] Shawnna Larree Edwards; [ed.] High School; [occ.] Retired, before retirement - Timber Faller, Airtract Driller and Powderman; [memb.] Eagles; [oth. writ.] Dads Travels By Covered Wagon published Mo. in Wampin Rock local paper.; [pers.] I like to write fiction or fact. Louis La Amour had a lot of influence when I found he wrote and read poetry. My mother has 4 treasury of old poems that also inspire me. I strive to write facts as true as possible.

EDWARDS, NEAL M.
[b.] April 27, 1928, Montebello, CA; [p.] Tom Earl (Deceased) and Eva E. Sweetland (Deceased); [m.] Divorced; [ch.] (1) Son Tom Earl II; [ed.] University of Southern California (BS); [occ.] Certified Public Accountant (Semi-retired); [memb.] American Society of Certified Public Accountants, Cali-

fornia Society of Certified Public Accountants, Beta Alpha PSI (Hon); [pers.] I have written poetry all of my life for my own personal enjoyment. This is my first publication (To the Lady I Love) I like to write romantic poetry and of life in general. I went through all of the poetry that I wrote in the past it amounted to about fifty in all, and discarded them. It was time to move on. If I had known that it was so easy to get published, I would have sent many to the publisher. I think many were better than this one. I guess I really did not want to share them.; [a.] Mission Viejo, CA

EGLEY, OPAL M.
[b.] October 23, 1919, Warsaw, IL; [m.] Lloyd had been married; [ch.] 4 children, Kathy (Deceased January 1974), Stephanie, Sharon and Richard; [occ.] Lloyd preached for a time there was a Chef; [memb.] He was a Member of First Baptist Church and the Chef's Unionism, CA. until he passed away, December 27, 1990; [oth. writ.] Lloyd lived in CA a good many years, at Death Valley, where many of his poems were about. He wrote more than 200.; [pers.] Lloyd spent his last couple years in the Veterans Home in Marshaltown, IA. He was always cheerful and generous in spite of his physical problem.

EIDSON, MARIDALE K.
[b.] April 15, 1948, Tulsa, OK; [p.] Julian Kaster and Lorene Kaster; [m.] Ronald Eidson, April 28, 1978; [ch.] Lori Michelle, Melissa Suzanne and Christopher Allen; [ed.] Central High School, Draughon School of Business; [occ.] Homemaker; [memb.] American Red Cross Volunteer, First Presbyterian Church; [pers.] It is my goal to be an encouragement to others in my writing. The greatest experience in life is living it.; [a.] Montgomery, AL

ELIAS, DICK G.
[b.] November 6, 1959, Guayaquil-Ecuador; [p.] Beatriz Toro - Julio Elias; [m.] Kelly Jo Elias, August 14, 1991; [ch.] Yong and Erin Elias; [ed.] Juneau H.S., Drill Sergeants School, U.S. Army NCO Academy, Columbus State Community College; [occ.] Columbus Division of Police Officer; [memb.] F AM Fayette Lodge #107, Scottish Rite Valley of Columbus, Fraternal Order of Eagles Erie No 423; [hon.] Army Commendation medal, Army Achievement Medal, Good Conduct Medal, Humanitarian Medal, etc.; [pers.] "One must have confidence in oneself to achieve a milestone." This is my personal theory.

ELLER, KRISTEN MICHELLE
[b.] February 12, 1978, Bakersfield; [p.] Susan P. Russ, Dr. Mark A. Eller; [ed.] High School Graduate from Bakersfield Adventist Academy; [occ.] Student in College; [memb.] AHSA American Horse Show Association, IAHA International Arabian Horse Association, CDS California Dressage Society; [hon.] Two Awards for Poetry in my school; [oth. writ.] None that are published thus far.; [pers.] Poetry is literary art. It is not the words alone that paint our picture it is the pause, the expression and the way it is written on paper.; [a.] Bakersfield, CA

ELLIOTT, KENNETH V.
[pen.] Ken; [b.] September 23, 1971, Chattanooga, TN; [p.] Vance and Wilma Elliott; [ed.] High school, some college; [occ.] Construction/ Student; [a.] Soddy-Daisy, TN

ELLIOTT, NAOMI
[b.] August 19, 1917, Kalamazoo, MI; [p.] Walter Friebel, Myrtle Friebel; [m.] William Elliott, October 19, 1940; [ch.] Jeannine East; [ed.] Thomas Cooley High (college prep)/The Business Inst. (Stenotype/Secretary) Mt. San Antonio J.C. (English, Psych., Soc.), Detroit Conservatory Music (6 yrs. piano); [occ.] Retired (formerly secretary, typesetter for Daily News, Indio, and for Fresno County, CA); [memb.] (13 yrs.) Calif. Heartland Chorus - Board Member, script writer, creator of newsletter, The Vocalizer; [hon.] Calif Heartland Chorus, "Sweet Adeline of the Year"; [pers.] Everyone would enjoy having an English Lit. teacher like Mrs. Perkins of Cooley High: And inspiration to youth!; [a.] Fresno, CA

ELLIOTT, STEVE
[pen.] Jed Smith; [b.] August 2, 1949, Cinti, OH; [p.] Jane Elliott; [ch.] Andy, Candy; [ed.] Oak Hills H.S. Cinti Ohio; [occ.] Logger - Timberman; [memb.] Institute of Children's Writing, National Rifle Assn., National Timbermens, Assn. National Wildlife Fed., National Youth Soccer Assn.; [hon.] Ohio Logger of the Year 1988, 1994; [oth. writ.] Currently working on my first novel, a book about the American Fur Trade of the American Frontier of the 1820's and 1830's.; [pers.] My writing is dedicated to the love of my life, Norma Mantz. She has a special place in my heart and in my soul. I am free when we are together.; [a.] New Lebanon, OH

ELLIS, CLYDE
[b.] B'ham, AL; [p.] R. L. and Evelyn Ellis; [m.] Deceased, July 1955; [ch.] Neal - Kay; [ed.] School of Hand Knocks; [occ.] Apparel Plant Mgr; [memb.] Various Civic Clubs including VFW America Legion Elks; [hon.] Boy Scout Little League; [pers.] Dedicated to my deceased wife the mother of my wonderful children and to Kay and Martha the mothers of my wonderful grandchildren who inspire with their love.; [a.] Haysi, VA

EMERSON, MARK W.
[m.] Kathryn E. Emerson; [ch.] Kristopher, Sandra, Kayla; [ed.] Seattle Pacific University, B.S. in Computer Science; [occ.] Systems Analyst, Professional and Personal Coach; [memb.] PPCA, NCN, CHADD, DECUS; [oth. writ.] Editor and Editorialist for a local DECUS Newsletter; [pers.] My greatest sense of freedom comes from helping another to find freedom.

EMIG, ELIZABETH
[pen.] Elizabeth Emig; [b.] March 18, 1982, C-BMC; [p.] Terry F. Emig Sr., Phyllis; [m.] Ann Emig; [ed.] Frankin Middle/Lansdowne High; [occ.] Student; [memb.] High Voltage Major Ette/Drum Corp. Emerald USA talent and beaut pageant, Miss Baltimore pre-teen Miss American Coed parent; [hon.] Miss Emerald USA Pre-teen, top ten in Baltimore pre-teen entering Miss American Coed; [oth. writ.] Several other poems wrote plays none of which I entered in anything.; [pers.] I believe that all people have a special purpose or talent whether you look into yourself to find your greatness is your choice.; [a.] Reisterstown, MD

ENDICOTT, ROBERT
[b.] September 3, 1967, Shelton, WA; [p.] Rachel, Richard; [m.] Sara; [ch.] Gray, Indi; [pers.] Only some may understand a poem - but it should be read by all.; [a.] Eastsound, WA

ENOEX, JENNIFER ERIN
[b.] October 6, 1981, Santa Monica, CA; [p.] Paul G. Enoex III, Angerine Enoex; [ed.] Completed 9th Grade at Centennial High School in Compton Ca.; [memb.] YMCA, Tower of Faith Church of God in Christ; [hon.] 2nd Place in Poster contest against drugs and also 2nd place for an essay against drugs for my school, Vanguard Middle School in Compton, CA; [oth. writ.] Several poems written as special assignments for my English Class, as while as for fun, Birthdays, Mothers and Fathers Day, etc.; [pers.] My 3rd grade teachers, Mr. Louie adomished my mother to encourage me to write because he felt I had a talent for it.; [a.] Compton, CA

ERBENTRAUT, STEVEN JOHN
[pen.] Steven John Erbentraut; [b.] January 12, 1982, Darlington, PA; [p.] John and Cynthia Erbentraut; [ed.] 9th Grade; [occ.] School - Home Schooled; [memb.] United States Tae Kwon Do, Union North Texas School of Tae Kwon Do - Granbury, TX; [hon.] Gold Medalist 1996 Texas State Tae Kwon Do Championship; [oth. writ.] Poetry; [pers.] You don't have to do anything, but sometimes there are consequences for not doing something.; [a.] Tolar, TX

ERICKSON, DIANA L.
[b.] April 8, 1950, San Bernardino, CA; [p.] Joseph Habecker, Barbara Habecker; [ch.] Forrest Wayne, Lane Hutton, Anna Kristine; [ed.] Eisenhower High School, University of Oregon; [occ.] Accounts Payable Clerk; [a.] Aloha, OR

ERSHAGHI, MIKE
[pen.] Mike Ershaghi; [b.] May 15, 1955; [m.] Maryam Ershaghi, November 1984; [ch.] Two; [ed.] MSC Engineering; [occ.] Quality Engineer; [oth. writ.] Just started. I been oil painting for past 20 years, wanted to try poetry.; [pers.] Art's flavor of life as spice's flavor of food, life without art is as flavorless as food without spice.

ESSEX, VERDA BELLE
[b.] February 18, 1966, Saginaw, MI; [p.] Don and Lucille Shelby; [m.] Dana Essex; [ch.] Vergil Jermaal Essex and Xavier Byron Essex; [ed.] Buena Vista H.S., Northwood Institute Delta College; [occ.] Wife and Mother; [pers.] I thank God for giving me this poem. I hope many will be lifted by these special words from God.; [a.] Saginaw, MI

ESTHER, DOUGLAS STEPHEN
[pen.] Douglas Stephen Esther; [b.] December 5, 1961, Hempstead, NY; [p.] Jon Esther, Dorothy Esther; [m.] Alana Esther, September 6, 1993; [ch.] Austin Lee Esther; [ed.] Princeton High School, Eastern Kentucky University; [occ.] Police Officer, Owensboro Police Department, Owensboro, KY; [memb.] Fraternal Order of Police; [hon.] President of Owensboro, FOP Lodge #16, Army Achievement Medal; [oth. writ.] This poem is my first attempt at writing.; [pers.] I tried to reflect how important radio dispatchers are to police officers, who deal with a variety of situation on a daily basis.; [a.] Owensboro, KY

ETCHEVERRY, ADELE A.
[pen.] Adele A. Etcheverry; [b.] California; [ed.] BA's: Fine Arts Painting and Drawing, Minor: English Lit., Single Subj. Teach - Art, AA: Busi-

ness; [occ.] Artist; [memb.] Mendocino Arts Center 1981-1982, 1994 to Present Central Calif. Art League 1994 - present Napa Valley Art league 1996, Knickerbocker Art League 1996, National Assn. Fine Arts 1994 to present Sacramento - Pastel Society West Coast - 1996; [hon.] I have been accepted several International and National Fine Art Exhibitions — most Recently Exhibiting Soft Pastel Paintings; [oth. writ.] Although I have written for my personal pleasure for many years is my first attempt to published or display a written creation.; [pers.] My goal in painting is to present to a viewer a performance of light lined by color texture and composition elements. I want to share the emotions I experience at the precise moment when I am captured by a particular vision or image, it is my intention to present that feeling except via words and phrases in my writings and poetry.; [a.] Salida, CA

EVANS, MADELINE K.
[pen.] Mae Lean; [b.] June 26, 1937, White, AR; [p.] Ervin Kelley, Rosie Lee Kelley; [m.] Bennie Evans Jr. (Deceased September 2, 1994), December 9, 1961; [ch.] Stanley Keith, Greta Denise, Jeannene Kelli; [ed.] T. W. Daniel High School, Crossett, Ark., B.S. Degree from A.M. and N College (Now known as University of Ark.), Pine Bluff, Ark in 1960; [occ.] USA Federal Government Retiree; [pers.] I write from the depths of my heart of the joy, hope and expectation, for hurt, pain and despair of one lonely female in search of a permanent home. I write because I have a desire to.; [a.] Los Angeles, CA

EVERETT, DENNIS E.
[pen.] Dennis E. Everett; [b.] June 21, 1966, Kansas City, MO; [p.] Edward E. and Beatrice E. Everett; [ch.] Travis Strohfus; [ed.] High School; [occ.] Truck Driver; [oth. writ.] Compiled in the book, "Life Concepts, Through The Eyes Of One Trucker. A collection of poems by Dennis E. Everett."; [pers.] A person who is able to enlighten the spirits of others is more apt to enjoy his being than one who chooses to criticize another person's life.; [a.] Watertown, SD

EVERETT, LINDA LEWIS
[b.] May 2, 1961, Indianapolis, IN; [p.] Daisy and Chester Lewis; [m.] Dubois Everett, September 12, 1990; [ch.] Kenneth Peters; [ed.] Shortridge High School; [occ.] Mail Processing Clerk Post Ofc.; [memb.] Indiana Black Expo, NAACP; [oth. writ.] None published yet; [pers.] Love for my family keeps me focused, on course and level-headed, all of which keeps me trying to achieve my goals.; [a.] Indianapolis, IN

EWING, MICHELLE
[pen.] Michelle Ewing; [b.] October 21, 1981, Abilene, TX; [p.] Donna Henry and Gerald Ewing; [ed.] Jr. High School Graduate; [hon.] Academic Merits and letters in school; [pers.] I have never been published until now, and I think that I am doing fairly well for a 14-year-old.; [a.] Arlington, TX

FAILLA, RELLY
[b.] June 25, 1954, Wheeling, WV; [p.] Milton Green, Jody Green; [m.] Bob Failla, July 18, 1984; [ch.] Joel and Joanna; [ed.] Wheeling High School, West Liberty State College, West Virginia University (MA); [occ.] Pre-school Teacher; [memb.]

Shades Valley Lutheran Church, Juvenile Diabetes Foundation; [hon.] Graduation with High Honors from Liberty State College; [pers.] I enjoy writing for children and about children, especially my own. My daughter's inner strength and my son's resilience have inspired me. I have also been blessed with a sense of humor!; [a.] Belham, AL

FAIN, FRANKLIN D.
[pen.] Howard Fain; [b.] August 1, 1934, Jessamine Co., KY; [p.] Clifford and Beulah Lowery Fain; [m.] Ruth Ann Rhorer, June 30, 1957; [ch.] Howard Douglas, Cecil Allen (Deceased); [ed.] Nicholasville High School, University of Kentucky, International Correspondence Schools Commercial Art; [occ.] Artist-Primary, Author-Secondary; [memb.] Edgewood Baptist Church; [hon.] Jess. Co Hall of Fame Award; [oth. writ.] Published book - art and writing entitled "Six Years Before Electricity", art and writing of short stories in "Country Extra" magazine.; [pers.] I like to record past scenes and situations of the past through artwork and writing.; [a.] Nicholasville, KY

FANNING, BEVERLY A.
[pen.] "Fanning", "B.", "Assaf."; [b.] January 29, 1944, Bridgeport, CT; [p.] Alfred J. Bell (Deceased) and Lorraine M. Bell; [m.] John R. Fanning Jr., (Twice), October 17, 1964 and May 12, 1990; [ch.] Elizabeth "Dawn" Flick, Moses J. Assaf (Deceased) and Andrea Marie Assaf; [ed.] Montgomery College - Sociology N.Y. Institute of Finance; [occ.] Stock Broker, Financial Consultant, SR. V.P. for: Wheat first, Butcher Singer; [memb.] Rotary International, Lycoming Crippled Children's Society (Board Member); [oth. writ.] Book, "For The Benefit Of Ivy", (of poems) unpublished. However, the dedication of the book (also "For The Benefit Of Ivy") was published in a local anthology in Lycoming Co. in 1982 apx.; [pers.] (Generally found in my writings.) I try to celebrate the miracle of life. To be aware that those who share this time with me on earth, I am connected to.

FARMER, MOSES GRADY
[b.] May 30, 1936, Goldsboro, NC; [p.] Moses Farmer and Laura Gavin Farmer; [ed.] Garner High School, B.S. from North Carolina State University; [occ.] Retired Engineer from NASA; [memb.] St. Mark's Episcopal Church, Hampton, Tidewater Writers Association; [oth. writ.] Several poems in church newsletter. A book of my poems "Equal Infant Children"; [pers.] I feel a kinship with William Wordsworth and the other romantic poets.; [a.] Hampton, VA

FARRELL, FRANKLYN
[pen.] Ian Andrew Farrell; [b.] March 13, 1974, New York, NY; [p.] Alberdore and John Farrell; [ed.] BS in Biology at St. Johns University, M.S. in Electrical Engineering at Columbia University. Pursuing MD at Cornell University Medical College; [occ.] Student; [memb.] New York Academy of Science. Golden Key National Honor Society; [oth. writ.] "The Entire Man", "The Ameliorator", "Cairo Sands" (poems), etc.; [pers.] I believe that when you find the person of your dreams, that love is to be expressed freely and joyously. My poems try to convey that by their unrestricted form and length. I hope to publish a small book of my poems very soon.; [a.] Briarwood, NY

FAULKNER, KIMBERLY A.
[b.] August 2, 1960, Danville, IL; [p.] James E. Bowling, Rose M. Bowling; [ch.] William J. Faulkner; [ed.] Moline Sr. High, Moline IL Danville, Area Community College, University of Illinois at Champaign-Urbana; [occ.] Homemaker - Poet; [memb.] Springbrook Cts Resident Council, American Heart Assoc., Peoria Jaycee Women, Fundraiser-Arthritis Foundation; [hon.] President's List-Danville Area Community College Jaycee Woman of the Year 1985 Peoria Jaycee Women; [oth. writ.] I've written poems, prose and short stories, however this is my first published work.; [pers.] What I write reflects a life-long inner struggle to come to terms with mental illness. My hope, my redemption is that a soul in torment will find solace and comfort in what I have written.; [a.] Moline, IL

FEDAK, ROBERT M.
[b.] April 23, 1966, NJ; [p.] Robert and Geri Fedak; [ed.] Christian Brother Academy - High School, Brookdale Community College; [occ.] Artist; [oth. writ.] Three books of poetry; [pers.] Poetry has always represented to me an internal freedom to put forth your feeling in an universal way; [a.] Atlantic Highlands, NJ

FELDMAN, JACK ALLISON
[pen.] Jack A. Feldman; [b.] December 19, 1923, Amsterdam, NY; [p.] Leon Feldman and Anna Esther Olender Feldman; [m.] Margaret Waldman Feldman (Deceased), July 19, 1946; [ch.] Robert Louis and Diane Lynn; [ed.] High School and Valedictorian of Electronics, Naval Air Apprentice School 1948-52 (7588 hours), also taught math in school of study; [occ.] Retired from 35 1/2 years with Naval Air Station: Electrical Engineering Tech., set-up Electronic Standards (World-Wide); [memb.] "Senior Engineering Technician" with "Institute for Certification of Engineering Technicians" by "National Society of Professional Engineers". Member of "Jewish War Veterans of America", Medic in World War II, Platoon 7, Battalion D; [hon.] World War II, Two Battle Stars, Asiatic Pacific Ribbon, American Area Ribbon, Philippine Liberation Ribbon, "Honorable Discharge", (Navy), While working in Electronic Standards Laboratory, I won several money awards for inventions in calibrating electronic standards in Electronics all over the world as well as The United States.; [oth. writ.] As Senior in Wilbur H. Lynch High School, Amsterdam, New York, I won first prize in city, and honorable mention for state of New York and certification for an essay titled, "How the Spanish American War Helped to Influence Our Present Latin American Policy".; [pers.] I was inspired in poetry by Robert Frost, Bliss Carmen, Henry Wadsworth Longfellow, William Shakespeare, Virgil and Homer (Greek Poetry). Inspired by my deceased wife, Margaret Alice Waldman Feldman, by my present wife, Shirley Feldman, and her friends as well as my friends.; [a.] Norfolk, VA

FERANEC, LINDSAY
[b.] March 12, 1982, Bridgeport, CT; [p.] Mr. and Mrs. Gary Feranec; [ed.] This September I will begin ninth grade; [occ.] Student; [hon.] Daniel Wasson Citizenship Award, Presidents Education Awards for Outstanding Educational Improvement; [pers.] I'd like to thank my parents, my grandma Belus, and a warm thank-you

to a family friend, Diane. My special thanks to my best friend, Bonnie, and her family for always being there.; [a.] Milford, CT

FERKEL JR., AL
[b.] April 22, 1975, Levittown, PA; [p.] Margaret Ferkel, Al Ferkel Sr.; [ed.] Harry S. Truman HS., Moravion College; [occ.] Alternative Media Journalist and editor; [hon.] Omicron Delta Kappa Leadership Award, Dean's list; [oth. writ.] Several articles for various alternative journals.; [pers.] The catharsis that results from poetry is an on valuable liberating force. It can be the incisiveness of vengeance, the warmth of familiarity, and the spirit of revolution. It is the role of the poet to reconstruct the imaginary of race, gender, sexuality, and other just hierarchies so as to undermine them.; [a.] Bethlehem, PA

FERNANDEZ, JUTTA HILDEGARD
[pen.] Tamara; [b.] October 4, 1957, Kaisersla Utern, West Germany; [p.] Alfons and Adele Susanne Hupp; [m.] Fernando Delfino Fernandez, May 21, 1985; [ch.] Ronnie and Rafael; [ed.] Finished High School 1972, 3 years of Professional Private School in W. Germany (Junior College), Small Business Management, Hotel and Restaurant Business Management, English, German, French, Spanish, Italian Bilingual; [occ.] Primary Nursing; [memb.] American Heart Association, American Hospital Association; [hon.] Employee of the year 1992, School Volunteer Praise Certificate S.C., American Red Cross Volunteer Certificate, Salvation Army Volunteer Certificate, Achievement Award Certificate 1996; [oth. writ.] In the Shadow (Suspense), Quiet Wind and Rolling Thunder (Heritage), Corina (Teen Girls), Schnucki (Fairytale), Horizon (Poem for friend), Peaceful Sleep (Love, Friendship and Dedication Between Father and Daughter).; [pers.] I wake in the morning only to find myself dreaming. Feeling, emotions happenings take a hold of me, I can't wake until the urge the uncontrollable must to write is fulfilled. I am dedicated to the everything and anything I can put in writing. Pencil and paper turn into my drug, giving me the relief of heavenly happiness. Only then can I wake.; [a.] Plains, MT

FERNHOLZ, JOAN M.
[b.] July 17, 1946, Milwaukee, WI; [p.] Dorothy and George Fernholz; [ed.] West Division High School; [occ.] Legal Secretary; [pers.] The Song Singer is the first poem I have written since High School. I plan to write more in the future and hope to publish a small book of poems.; [a.] Greenfield, WI

FIEGELMAN, RICH
[pen.] Rich McKeown; [b.] November 5, 1957, Philadelphia; [p.] Dr. Marvin and Beverly Fiegelman; [m.] Ruthann Brink Fiegelman, August 2, 1992; [ch.] Zachary (3 yrs.), Derek (1 yr.); [ed.] Northeastern University, Mansfield University, Wyoming Area High School; [occ.] Business Management; [memb.] Smithsonian, Wolf Education and Research Center, North American Fishing Club; [hon.] Watching both of my sons come into the world!; [oth. writ.] Author of various magazine articles, newspaper columns, and did a very interesting one-to-one interview with Barbara Walters (A Role Reversal For Her); [pers.] Mark Twain and Ray Bradbury are my favorite writers. Twain put

mankind in its place, Bradbury searches for a better one. In the meantime, it is vital that we treat all of the passengers on this planet with love and respect!; [a.] Shickshinny Lake, PA

FILES, LORRAINE E.
[b.] June 17, 1923, Mankato, MN; [p.] William L. Thomson, Honora Anne O'Grady; [m.] William Courtney Files, June 11, 1947; [ch.] Lenora, Patricia, Linda; [ed.] 4 yrs. in St. Teac Col Eng Lit, BS Elem Ed, University of Cincinnati Manuscript sent to publishers; [occ.] Retired School Teacher; [memb.] Zeta Tau Alpha; [hon.] Scholarship Indiana State Teachers College; [oth. writ.] A book "A Long Way To Go"

FINCH, DAWN LYNETTE
[pen.] Kenna Ray; [b.] October 3, 1967, Milwaukee, WI; [p.] Carol Lang, Dan Drew; [m.] Don L. Finch, May 21, 1988; [ch.] Marcus 8, Alexandra 7, Courtney 5; [ed.] Marquette University, Iowa State University; [occ.] Freelance Artist, Pella Employee, Carroll, Iowa; [hon.] Chairman of Publicity, Marquette University Hunger Clean-Up, Marquette University Honor Roll; [oth. writ.] Am currently writing my first novel.; [pers.] I am intrigued with history and its rich details. Much of my creativity is a result of that perspective. I also have my husband and my father to thank with a brimming heart for their undying faith in my pursuit of creative happiness.; [a.] Vail, IA

FISCHER, KATRINA
[b.] March 14, San Jose, CA; [p.] Kathy and Jerry Fischer; [ed.] Currently a sophomore at William Mason High School; [memb.] Drama Club; [pers.] The most important lesson I've ever learned is persistence. With it you can do anything, without it you can do nothing.; [a.] Mason, OH

FISHER, GAIL
[b.] August 18, 1935, Orange, NJ; [p.] Deceased; [m.] Divorced; [ch.] Samara and Jole; [ed.] Metuchen, N.J., High School; [occ.] Actress and Writer; [oth. writ.] Edward Fisher Music, BMI, Recorded Works, Cannonball, Adderley, "Mercy, Mercy, Mercy", Carmen McRea, "Spread To All", "Stolen Moments", Nancy Wilson, "Below Above".; [pers.] "I never worked, I was about the work, as an actress, writer, artist, hoping my work, would help make it a better world!!!"; [a.] Laughlin, NV

FLANIGAN JR., JAMES F.
[b.] July 20, 1947, Philadelphia; [p.] James and Ann Flanigan; [m.] Sheila Ann Flanigan, March 29, 1980; [ch.] Mary Margaret and Paul James; [occ.] Electrician for Broward City, FL; [pers.] Love is a spiritual gift. To receive, we must give without condition.; [a.] Margaret, FL

FLEMING, MARTIN L.
[m.] Mary; [ed.] Suffied High School BS - Accounting (Bryant College) MBA (American International College); [occ.] Retired Financial Officer; [oth. writ.] Book published by Vantage Press entitled Inside the Washington Post; [pers.] My writings center around history and at times seek a better direction for the future. A second book dealing with American politics and fiscal responsibility is currently underway.; [a.] Lake Worth, FL

FLETCHER, DE
[b.] July 7, 1962, Little Rock, AR; [ed.] John L. McClellan High School. Weber State University - BS Community Health (Graduate); [occ.] Health Educator/Employment Interviewer; [memb.] Health Education Association of Utah (HEAU), Association for Supervision and Curriculum Development (ASCD), Association for the Advancement of Health Education, (AAHE), American Alliance for Heath, Physical Education, Recreation and Dance (AAHPERD); [pers.] My writing is influenced by the teachings of the Native American People.; [a.] Huntsville, UT

FLETCHER, FRAN
[pen.] "Fran" (Fletcher) "France", "Aurora"; [b.] March 4, 1946, San Francisco, CA; [p.] Bill and Fran Pryor; [m.] Deceased - Dan Fletcher; [ch.] 1,500 Foster and 9 natural, Dwaine, Kenn, Dale, Paul, Charity, Kelly, D.J., Erin, Deni; [ed.] Attended Metaphysical classes - studied under Mentor's MariAnna Love and Art teacher 'Nelson' at Butte College; [occ.] Domestic Goddess!; [oth. writ.] 1st Publication; [pers.] I am a 'star child' - citizen of the universe - my family and heritage is 'The Rainbow' tribe - I am a sovereign free spirit - which is what my French Indian name means - "Freedom and Enlightment". I seek love, peace, happiness and freedom for my brothers and sisters - we are all one.; [a.] Oroville, CA

FLETCHER ANTHONY
[b.] 1951, Los Angeles; [ed.] Warren High, Downey CA, Diploma, Cerritos College, Norwalk CA, Associate Arts Degree; [occ.] Professional Extra, Computer Form Preparer; [memb.] KLAS Act, Vaudeville Troup; [oth. writ.] Arizona Citizen News, Cerbat Mountain Newsletter; [pers.] The truth is reflected all around us in nature. Seize the truth.; [a.] Hualapai, AZ

FOISY, ANNA MARIE
[b.] July 21, 1954, Newark, NJ; [p.] Mary Ann and Philip Pagano; [ch.] Nicole Marie Foisy; [ed.] Ocean County College and The University of Connecticut; [occ.] Elementary Teacher, in HISD School District Houston, TX., (Houston Independent School District); [memb.] Congress of Houston Teachers; [hon.] Taas Writing Teacher Score of 4, Taas Buster Teacher, Dorothy Roberts Award - Academic, Who's Who in America Junior Colleges and Universities. Pop Warner County cheer leader. National Honor Society High School and Jr. College (President); [pers.] Hebrews 12:2A, looking unto Jesus the author and finisher of our faith.; [a.] Webster, TX

FORCUM, MATT
[b.] December 22, 1985, Mattoon, IL; [p.] Jackie and Danny Forcum; [ed.] Stewartson - Strasburg Elm; [occ.] Writing; [memb.] Bass Masters, Fox Kids Club; [hon.] 1st place Baby shown, 1st place Kindergarten pedal and ractop pull, Top Boy Scout Popcorn Salesman 1990; [oth. writ.] Simple Things, Scribbled Down in Math class.; [pers.] Life is precious, don't mess it up!; [a.] Mode, IL

FORTIN, MICHELLE
[b.] May 14, 1971, New Haven, CT; [p.] Robert Fortin, Maryann Fortin; [ed.] Briarwood College, St. Mary's High School; [occ.] Executive Secretary, New Haven Register, New Haven, CT; [hon.] Who's Who among students in American Junior Colleges, National Business Honor Society, Dean's List; [oth. writ.] This is my first published work. In the future, I will tackle writing shat stories.; [pers.] My poems help me deal with issues and questions I don't understand so I can see various situations in life more clearly. I would like to hope that someday my poems or other writings may do the same for others.; [a.] East Haven, CT

FOSCHINI, RENEE
[b.] February 2, 1974, Camden, NJ; [p.] Rose Foschini, Al Foschini; [ed.] Gloucester Catholic H.S., The Cittone Institute; [occ.] Clerical, Most Health Service, Voorhees, NJ; [memb.] America On-Line; [oth. writ.] Currently working on a novel called "Eclipse"; [pers.] "Trust your Instinct" - Nicholas Hexum (311); [a.] Bellmawr, NJ

FOSSEN, SANDRA
[b.] December 27, 1961, Santa Rosa, CA; [p.] Roy Ochoa and Tomasa Asien; [m.] David Todd Fossen, July 16, 1989; [ed.] Santa Rosa Junior High, Santa Rosa High School, and Santa Rosa Junior College; [occ.] Retail; [hon.] The "Valentine Love Line" in the Local Newspaper, "The Press Democrat" (Poems Contest Winner), "Editor's Choice Award", The National Library of Poetry "1995". Editor's Choice Award, The National Library of Poetry "1996"; [oth. writ.] 'Earth', "Between The Raindrops" published in "The National Library of Poetry." "Revelation", published in "The National Library of Poetry." Poems published in the Santa Rosa Newspaper, "The Press Democrat", Poems published in "Santa Rosa Junior College News Letter." Poems recited on tape, "The Sound of Poetry."; [pers.] My poems are dedicated to my precious husband for his support, trust, and undying love for me, to my beautiful mother for all the love she possesses within, to my understanding siblings for allowing me to be who I am and to my trustworthy friends for clearly communicating their innermost feelings. I love you and cherish you.; [a.] Santa Rosa, CA

FOSTER, ASHLEY
[pen.] Ashley; [b.] June 29, 1981, Lima, OH; [p.] Christopher and Rebecca Foster; [ed.] Sophomore at Allen East School; [occ.] Student; [hon.] Design an Ad Contest, First Place and several High School Band Awards; [oth. writ.] Personal writings.; [pers.] I would like to thank my sixth grade teacher Mrs. Butler for inspiring my ability to write.; [a.] Lafayette, OH

FOSTER, JOSEPH R.
[b.] September 17, 1944, Mechanicsburg, PA; [p.] Joseph and Eva (Stutzman) Foster; [m.] Barbara J. (Koester) Foster, September 14, 1968; [ch.] Keri, Kristi, Kae Lee and Mark; [ed.] Eden Theological Seminary, D. Min. Lancaster Theological Seminary, M. Div. Kutztoun University, B.A.; [occ.] Sr. Pastor, Grace UCC, Frederick, MD; [memb.] American Association for Clinical Pastoral Education, Clinical pastoral education, Lions Club International, Board of Directors, Hope Homes of Maryland, Inc.; [oth. writ.] Articles and writings for Church, Educator, Church Worship, Clergy Journal, Carbon County, PA., Times/News newspaper, The role of the Local Church in Meeting, The Needs of Mentally Retarded Children, CSS Pub.; [a.] Frederick, MD

FOSTER, KATHY
[pen.] Kathy Foster; [b.] September 28, 1942, Reedsburg, WI; [p.] Ann Baker, Berger Kolberg (Deceased); [m.] Dan Foster, March 21, 1964; [ch.] Greg and Jason Foster; [ed.] Bachelor of Arts in Education - Arizona State University; [occ.] Real Estate Broker; [memb.] Tucson Association of Realtors, Friends of the Arizona Cancer Center, Tucson Chapter, Skyline Country Club; [pers.] Nature and the beauty of the universe are favorite topics of mine.; [a.] Tucson, AZ

FOX, JOCELYN
[pen.] Cocoa; [b.] April 10, 1970, Cleveland, OH; [p.] James Sudberry Sr., Rosemary Young; [m.] John T. Fox Sr., March 12, 1994; [ch.] Charnese, De'Andre, Jonae, John, Rionna; [ed.] East High School; [occ.] Housewife; [memb.] Mason Temple Church of God in Christ; [oth. writ.] I have written many poems, however I didn't think of getting them published. I guess I didn't think they were good enough!; [pers.] I'd like to tell the world if you ever have a dream, don't sit on it because God will make your dreams come true! I've always dreamed of writing poetry and it's finally happening! Thank you Lord!; [a.] Milwaukee, WI

FOX, MARY
[b.] August 18, 1971, Glenridge, NJ; [p.] Joseph and Clara Lynch; [ch.] Veronica and Crystal Fox; [ed.] High School Graduate, Essex County College, and Certification in Phlebotomy; [occ.] Certified Phlebotomy Technician, C.P.T; [memb.] An Associate Member of the American Black Book Writers Association - Marina Del Rey, CA; [hon.] Essex County College, Honor Roll - 1989, M.T.I, GPA 3.0 - 1995, 2 copyright awards - 1995; [oth. writ.] Several poems published in anthologies such as Treasured Poems of America, Meditations, Best New Poems, Treasure the Moment, and Lyrical Heritage; [pers.] "Life and experience has taught both expression and truth".; [a.] East Orange, NJ

FRANK, MICHAEL C.
[pen.] Michael C. Frank; [b.] October 8, 1966, Brooklyn, NY; [m.] Amanda Chakravarti, March 1, 1992; [ed.] Jeffersonville High School, S.U.N.Y. Cortland, Communication Major; [occ.] Butcher at Kocker's Continental Specialty Meats Ridgefield, NJ; [pers.] I write of things I know, and of things I wish to know, and of both I know little.; [a.] Montvale, NJ

FRAZIER, NYATA C.
[pen.] Nyata C. Frazier; [b.] May 4, 1957, Newark, NJ; [p.] Margaret Frazier; [m.] Divorced; [ch.] Cremonlyn A., Nyata C., Angelena T.; [ed.] East Orange High, Wayne High, Jacksonville State, University, New World Business College; [occ.] United States Army; [memb.] PTA President, Comer Parent Articulation Group, Reach to Recovery Cancer Group; [hon.] Computer Operations Specialist Certificate, Army Lapel Button, Army Achievement Medal 3rd. Award, Army Good Conduct Medal, National Defense Service Medal, Army Service Ribbon; [oth. writ.] My Journey Back From Death; [pers.] Learning to cope with my breast cancer, keeping my life positive, offering wisdom and experience adds an insightful, uplifting flavor to my writing.; [a.] Charlotte, NC

FRITTER, PAUL R.
[b.] May 7, 1927, Columbus, OH; [p.] James and Ruth Fritter; [m.] Betty J. Fritter, August 13, 1945; [ch.] Paul Gayness; [ed.] High School (Central) Columbus Ohio; [occ.] Retired Master Research Technician - 40 yrs. Battelle Memorial Institute; [memb.] Current Member, Capital Area Humane Society, Past Board of Directors, Member C.A.H.S., 1920 to 1925; [pers.] I try to reach the hearts and emotions of the people when I bring of the people. When I bring a tear, a smile or open laughter, then I know I've succeeded in touching someone.; [a.] Worthington, OH

FRITZ, STEVEN R.
[b.] August 25, 1953, Dayton, OH; [p.] Joseph C. Fritz Jr., Connie S. Fritz; [ch.] Jeremy Steven, Justin Ray, Michael Stockstill, Jeremy Lee, Daniel Joseph, Andrew Joseph; [ed.] Belmont High School, Dayton, OH, Sinclair Community College, University of Dayton Police Academy, Ohio Peace Officers, Training Academy, Ohio Highway Patrol Academy Toledo Criminal Justice Center; [occ.] Insurance Claims Investigator; [memb.] Dayton Claims Adjusters Assoc., Parents without Partners, Special wish Foundation; [hon.] 1986 Officer of the year, Montgomery 1983 Merit Award - International Asso. of Credit card Investigators, 1983 Law Enforcement Award, Miami Township Optimists Club, Top Instructor 4 years Running - Miami Township Police Academy, 5 Trustee Awards, Miami Township Pi Promoted to Detective, 1983, Promoted to Detective Sergeant, 1986; [oth. writ.] None published, presently writing a novel, fiction, involving a homicide of a police officer and the investigation.; [pers.] I believe we all need heroes. Not Superman or Batman, but ordinary people that rise to the aid of others or the occasion in extraordinary times.; [a.] Laura, OH

FUSS, CINDI M.
[p.] Joseph and Theresa Swedo; [m.] James A., September 9, 1989; [ed.] Wyoming Valley West H.S. Plymouth PA; [occ.] Office Administration and Sales; [hon.] Silver poet award, Prize winning photographs (Kodak sponsored); [pers.] I wish to thank my mother for her many years of support and encouragement. The poem "Angels" was inspired by and is dedicated to her memory, in life and in spirit you will always be loved.; [a.] Courtdale, PA

GABLE, EUGENE L.
[b.] December 20, 1930, Billings, MT; [p.] Andy and Anna Gable; [m.] Ann Lizabeth Gable, September 7, 1977; [ch.] Christina Esther Terin, Mark, James, Andy, Lyndora, Gwen; [occ.] Retired; [a.] Tucson, AZ

GADSDEN, VERTELLA S.
[b.] February 24, 1918, Kingston, Jamaica, BWI; [p.] Samuel and Elfred A. Valentine; [ch.] Pamela V. Gadsden, Jeffrey V. Gadsden; [ed.] Julia Richman H.S., some College; [occ.] Retired; [memb.] On the executive Board of: The Brotherhood Synagogue, Boy Scouts of America, Intern'l Training in Communication Member - Metro Chapter of N.Y., AIP, Coord., Cncl - Bikur Cholim; [hon.] Outstanding Volunteer Synag: Kallah Torah, BSA: Silver Beaver, Silver Antelope, Shofar Award, District Award of Merit, AIP: Special Chapter Recognition; [oth. writ.] Local newspaper, newsletters, NLP anthologies; [pers.] Love they neighbor as thyself.; [a.] New York, NY

GAIR, KEVIN
[b.] December 21, 1958, Baldwin Park, CA; [p.] Robert C. Gair, Linda Gair; [m.] Beverly Wood Gair, May 1, 1982; [ch.] Stephanie Renee, Cristine Nicole; [ed.] Ph.D. La Salle University, M.A. Pt Loma Nazarene College, B.A. Cal Poly Pomona, A.S. Mt San Antonio College; [occ.] Learning Director, Dunlap School Dunlap CA; [memb.] Faculty Advisory Group - Fowler HS, Sanger Lodge of FIAMs, Unitarian Universalist Church of Freson, Parent Teacher Club and School Site Council at Dunlap School; [hon.] Who's Who in the West, Who's Who of America's Teachers, Certificate of Merit, Cal. State Senate Mentor Teacher; [oth. writ.] Novels - Dark Descent, Dark Descent II, Return to Tet, Poems - Phantom Wind, Razor's Edge, Songs - Dawn, Glory, Ascent, Voyage, Lovechild, Razor's Edge, Set; [pers.] Who we are is not the color of our skin nor the blood of our ancestors, but who we choose to become in our hearts.; [a.] Squaw Valley, CA

GALE III, EVERETT EDWIN
[b.] May 10, 1967, Miami, FL; [p.] Beatrice Caballero Gale, Everett E. Gale Jr.; [ed.] George Mason University BA Govt to Politics, Rutgers - Camden School of Law, J.D.; [occ.] Attorney; [a.] Lincoln Park, NJ

GALLAWAY, DAWN
[b.] May 13, 1974, Orange, NJ; [p.] Michelle Gallaway, Arthur Johnson; [ed.] Orange High School, currently attending Lincoln University Oxford, PA as an Actuarial Science Major; [memb.] Lincoln U. Track and Field Team, Lincoln U. Basketball Team, Math and Computer Science Club; [hon.] Who's Who Among American High School Students, 1994-95 Lincoln U. Basketball MVP, 3 time Track and Field All-American, Track Phi Track; [pers.] With an open mind and a free heart, endless happenings will be your only prey. I am influenced by the personalities, characteristics, and feelings of the world's people.; [a.] East Orange, NJ

GALLEGOS, MARK V.
[b.] October 17, 1964, Del Norte, CO; [p.] Tom and Christine Gallegos; [m.] Patricia Gallegos, September 24, 1995; [ed.] Graduate Del Norte High 1984; [occ.] Factory Work, Desktop Publishing; [oth. writ.] Writing and publishing a local newsletter for my company.; [pers.] After days of grieving at the loss of my grandmother, I was awakened with this poem in my head. At 3:00 a.m. I wrote this poem on the back of an envelope. This poem is truly a message from God.; [a.] Waxahachie, TX

GAMMILL, MIKE
[b.] August 19, 1960, Lawrence, KS; [p.] Conway Gammill, Faye Gammill; [m.] Diana (Basel) Gammill, November 10, 1979; [ch.] Paul, Jennifer; [ed.] Eudora, KS High School (1978), Brown Mackie College, Overland Park, KS; [occ.] Coker Unit Operator, Conoco Refinery, Ponca City, OK; [pers.] I feel it's time that someone told the truth about something that's really important to others and really hits home. This is my attempt at doing just that.; [a.] Ponca City, OK

GANLEY, TOM
[b.] April 4, 1955, Syracuse, NY; [p.] Luke and Nancy Ganley; [m.] Mary Pat, June 30, 1979; [ch.]

Kelly 16 years and Tim 13 years; [occ.] Sheet Metal Worker; [pers.] "Forget mistakes. Forget failures. Forget everything except what you're going to do now and do it. Today is your lucky day." (William Durant - Founder of General Motors)

GANSHERT, ALAN L.
[b.] March 26, 1946, Shullsburg, WI; [p.] Lawrence and Anna Ganshert; [m.] Gloria Ganshert, June 9, 1973; [ch.] Ryan; [ed.] Gratiot High School, 2 1/2 years Military (includes Air Force, Army, Navy); [occ.] Work at Wallace Computer Printing Co.; [memb.] American Legion, VFW, Knights of Columbus, Catholic Knights, International Order of Odd Fellows, Member Our Saviors Luthern Church; [hon.] Viet Nam Service Medal, Good Conduct Medal, National Defence Medal; [oth. writ.] Have turned to writing country music songs.; [pers.] The world needs more poems and songs.; [a.] Osage, IA

GARDNER, MARIAN
[b.] September 28, 1930, Youngville, NC; [p.] Mary Elsie Winfree and Preston; [m.] Green Eaton, October 17, 1947 - Husband Deceased; [ch.] Lynda G. Harris, James Michael Gardner, and Janice G. Davis; [ed.] North Fulton High School, some college at University System of Georgia, Clark Howell and R.L. hope in Atlanta and Zebulon, N.C. Elementary Schools; [occ.] Retired from Royal Ins. Co., Mother to 3, Grandmother to 8, and Great grandmother to one.; [memb.] AARP, Victory Christian Center, National Wildlife Federation, National Geographic Society, St. Jude Children's Research; [oth. writ.] I enjoy writing poetry and poems, and I have written many, although I have never before submitted any for publication. Some day, I would like to have them all together in a published book of poems.; [pers.] I enjoy writing about nature and how I feel in my heart about people, God and the world in which he made for us to enjoy, as well as His unfathomable love towards His children.; [a.] Atlanta, GA

GARIBOTTO, CARLOS
[pen.] Garabato; [b.] May 30, 1932, Lima, Peru; [p.] Enrique Garibotto and Ana Minness; [m.] Rosita Henao, February 26, 1985; [ch.] Victor, Carlos, Miguel; [ed.] Salesiano Elementary School, Lima 2 de Mayo High School, Literature S. M. University, Systems Tech. CIDCA, Col. ESL and News Media S. F, City College; [occ.] Translator, Eng. Spanish, Writer, Poet, Journalist; [memb.] Federation Periodistas Latinos Masonic Lodge; [hon.] Circulo de las Americas San Francisco, Certificate as a Poet. Literary Contest, Miami 3rd place; [oth. writ.] Interact. Programmation for IBM System 34. Story of a Wonderful Revelation. Funny Stories. Requiem Para un Guerrillero Cronologia de una violacion, Mis Mejores Poesias, others.; [pers.] I enjoy reading old classic poems, I also write every day, romantic poetry or funny stories as my feelings of the day.; [a.] San Francisco, CA

GARNHAM, HARRY L.
[b.] May 30, 1941, Beaumont, TX; [p.] Harry (Deceased) and Sue Garnham; [m.] Penny Garnham, December 14, 1977; [ed.] BLA (Landscape Architecture) Louisiana State University, 1965 MLA (Landscape Architecture) Harvard Graduate School of Design 1969 University of Colorado; [occ.] College Professor; [memb.] Fellow in the Ameri-

can Society of Landscape Architects, American Planning Asso., Urban Land Institute, Center for Marine Conservation; [hon.] Harvard Loeb Fellowship in Advanced Environmental Studies 1972-1973, Harvard Graduate School of design Jacob Weidenmen Prize for Design Excellence (Traveling Fellowship); [oth. writ.] "Maintaining The Spirit of Place" PDA publishers 1985, "Listening to The Echoes, A New Design Ethic for the West" Colorado Asla publication 1993, Hawaii open space plan, Ekistics 1974.; [pers.] Always seek the spirit that casts the shadow.; [a.] Denver, CO

GASCA, ROSE M.
[b.] March 3, 1926, Wichita, KS; [m.] Paul R. Gasca, October 20, 1946; [ch.] Two; [ed.] 2 yrs. H.S.; [occ.] Retired - care for handicap husband; [oth. writ.] You need not publish or 1. He's Gone Away, 2. Our Nest In The Sky, 3. Wonderful World, 4. Grandparents, 5. My Promise; [pers.] I dedicate "The Men in Blue" to my nephew Philip Guerrero who is a policeman for the city of Chicago. God be with you. Love, Aunt Rose; [a.] Pinellas Park, FL

GATES, JOHN R.
[b.] May 19, 1911; [p.] Renfrew W. and Marion T. Gates; [m.] Eleanor W. Gates, April 26, 1942; [ch.] Lynda, Louise, Joanne M., Carolyn E.; [ed.] Hollywood High Ca., Certified Travel Counselor Michigan State University; [occ.] Retired as Travel Agent and World Tour Operator; [memb.] Elder at Hollywood Presbyterian Church Ca., American Society of Travel Agents ASTA "In recognition of Dedicated and outstanding service to the travel agency industry. (Life Member of Certified Travel Agents.); [oth. writ.] I also wrote about my involvement in the 1932 Xth Olympiad held in Los Angeles California. "Frozen in my seat in the middle of summer".; [pers.] I am presently writing a book of my life of travel for my three daughters and seven grandchildren.

GATES, TAMARA A.
[b.] November 15, 1973, Roanoke, VA; [p.] Carolyn and Douglas Terry; [ed.] Bachelor of Science in Business Administration with a concentration in Finance from Virginia Commonwealth University; [occ.] Transfer of Assets Specialist Wheat First Brokerage Firm; [memb.] Society for Advanced Management; [oth. writ.] Several yet to be published poems; [pers.] Life is not to be questioned, it is to be lived. It is not to be taken for granted, it's to be appreciated. Each day is a brand new gift of endless possibilities. Each day passes both good and bad as God gives us direction to grow; [a.] Richmond, VA

GATTI, MARK LAZARUS
[b.] September 23, 1973, Buffalo, NY; [p.] Larry J. Gatti and Jean Gatti; [ch.] Nathaniel Elijah Gatti; [ed.] Buffalo State College; [occ.] Food Service; [hon.] 1996 Joel Oppenheimer Creative Writing Award - Poetry, Dean's List - Spring 1995 at Buffalo State College; [pers.] Like the Ghost in my head, like the bones in my pen, I am off to haunt the literary world. And if this world isn't shaken by my presence, let the bones crumble and the ghosts be pinned down.; [a.] Kenmore, NY

GAYDOSH, DONNA C.
[b.] February 3, 1962, Tennessee; [m.] Richard E. Gaydosh, February 26, 1983; [ch.] Arielle and Chelsey; [pers.] My poetry is a gift I kept to myself for far too long, now I wish to share it.; [a.] Tampa, FL

GEANANGEL, DEBORAH DEANNE
[b.] November 5, 1970, Steubenville, OH; [p.] John and Phyllis Bickerstaff; [m.] Ty Geanangel, October 20, 1995; [ed.] Cadiz High School, Jefferson Comm. College; [occ.] Licensed Practical Nurse; [oth. writ.] One poem published in local newspaper.; [pers.] The selection "Dim Thoughts or Sanctuary" is dedicated to my poetic mentor Elaine Calabria.; [a.] Wintersville, OH

GEE, CHRISTEL
[pen.] Christy Gee; [b.] September 9, 1965, Springfield, OH; [p.] Diana and Richard Campbell; [m.] Robert Gee, September 8, 1990; [ch.] James and Nikyta Davis; [ed.] Proud to say a high school education I didn't receive but my mental accomplishments would make any one think differently.; [occ.] Housewife; [oth. writ.] I have several other poems that can be looked at for publication one that I like best is titled "My Daddy".; [pers.] I've enjoyed poetry all my life, and my poems are different than most. They come from my heart and are based upon my past, present and future experiences. I would urge anyone of any age to not battle up what they hold so dear inside.; [a.] Springfield, OH

GEERTZ, DORATHEA
[pen.] DG; [b.] Chicago, IL; [p.] Edward A. Erdmann and Cora J. Erdmann; [m.] Eric Julius Geertz (Deceased); [ch.] Gerald, Mark, Luke, Julia; [pers.] Who am I? A nobody. Give birth, I do, though to poetry. Published, each line ought to be. To let others enjoy my poetry. Read my lyrics and you will see 'tis not so bad being a nobody!

GENSUR, CHRISTOPHER
[pen.] William Marter; [b.] September 13, 1973, Bridgeport, CT; [p.] Charles Gensur, LaNell Gensur; [ed.] Notre Dame High School, Housatonic Community Technical College, Sacred Heart University; [occ.] Student at Sacred Heart University; [memb.] Sacred Heart University Drama Players; [hon.] Dean's List, Comedian of the Year; [oth. writ.] "Imagination Murdered" published in a literary magazine called "Beanfeast".; [pers.] I like using classical styles while incorporating modern themes into my poetry. I am greatly influenced by Johnathan Swift yet not as pessimistic.; [a.] Bridgeport, CT

GEORGE, ERIN
[b.] June 30, 1983, Asheville, NC; [p.] Edwindale and Nancy George; [ed.] Seventh Grade, Entering Eight Grade; [occ.] Student at P.S. Jones Middle School; [memb.] Bible Bowl High School Marching Band; [hon.] 2nd Place in DAR (Daughters of American Revolution) Essay Contest, 1st Place DARE (Drug Abuse Resistance Education) Essay; [oth. writ.] Several poems not published; [pers.] Writing is a way for me to express my feelings, whether it be about the past, present, or future.; [a.] Washington, NC

GERARD, ROSE E.
[pen.] Rosebud [b.] September 20, 1977, Haiti; [p.] Yolande and Forest Gerard; [ed.] H.S. Graduate, LPN License - Practice Nurse License, Plan to

attend Ponce University this Fall 1996; [memb.] Member of American Heart Association, National Association for Practical Nurse Education; [pers.] You never know what you can do until you try.; [a.] Saint Albans, NY

GERICKE, JENNIFER L.
[pen.] Jace and Jennifer Clements; [b.] August 18, 1966, Valparaiso, IN; [p.] Barbara Clements and Tom Clements; [m.] Julius Joseph Gericke III; [ch.] Amanda, Adam, ben, Drew, Joshua; [ed.] Valparaiso High School, Valparaiso University; [occ.] Homemaker, Sunday School Teacher (on and off); [memb.] St. Michael's Luth. Church, Hebron, IN; [oth. writ.] Poems in local newspapers, poems in another anthology - currently working on a short story.; [pers.] I am searching to regain my faith (once strong). A recent medical diagnosis leaves me struggling with life.; [a.] Hebron, IN

GESS, CHARLIE E.
[pen.] Cha-Cha, CC; [b.] October 1, 1959, Lexington; [p.] P-Nut, Faye Gess; [ed.] 11 grade GED; [occ.] Artist; [hon.] Sportsmanship, IBM Junior League Baseball - Pitcher Shortstop; [pers.] Dreams of Eternal Future the Mellinum, Armageddon the Rapture, The Tribulation, Heaven, Hell, Hatties, Life of Spirit, Life of Soul, Eternity Everlasting.; [a.] Lexington, KY

GHATTAS, CHRISTOPHER
[b.] May 9, 1986, Anderson, SC; [p.] Bill and Mary Ann Ghattas; [ed.] 5th Grader at Still Elementary, Powder Springs, Georgia; [occ.] Student; [memb.] Southwest Cobb Youth Soccer League; [hon.] Gold Medal in 2K race at still Elem., Trophy for excellence in soccer, Kaleidoscope Arts Festival Winner; [oth. writ.] Many stories and poems.; [pers.] The humor in Shel Silverstein's writing has had an influence on my writing.; [a.] Powder Springs, GA

GIBBONS, CHARLOTTE RUTH
[pen.] Charlotte Gibbons; [b.] May 31, 1935, Stoystown, PA; [p.] Clifford Leo and Bernice-Kennedy Gibbons Bracken; [ch.] Michael Charles, Stacey Ann, Toni; [ed.] Kantner - Forbes, Stoystown, PA; [occ.] Retired; [memb.] Humane Society, V.F.W., American Heart Association, American Cancer Society Nursing; [hon.] Semifinalist, National Library of Poetry for poems "Observe a Rainbow" to be published in "Lyrical Heritage" edition and "The Journey", to be published in the "Memories of Tomorrow" edition.; [oth. writ.] "The Journey" - to be published in "Memories of Tomorrow" - by the National Library of Poetry.; [pers.] There is no experience better for the heart than reaching down and lifting people up. (By John Andrew Holmes); [a.] Somerset, PA

GIBBS, FREDERICK W. P.
[b.] November 30, 1965, Natrona Heights, PA; [p.] Frederick P. and Judith S. Gibbs; [m.] Patricia A. Gibbs, March 22, 1989; [ch.] Amanda C. L. and Dylan W. P.; [ed.] BA University of Akron '92, MSSA Case Western Reserve Univ. '94; [occ.] Social Worker AIDS Hospice Team; [memb.] American Psychological Assn., American Public Health Assn., National Assn. of Social Workers; [oth. writ.] Various songs and poems (unpublished), 1 children's book on death (unpublished).; [pers.] I dedicate this poem not only to the four

people who inspired it, but to all those affected by the AIDS epidemic. May we sometime be able to speak of this scourge in the past tense.; [a.] Hudson, OH

GIBSON, CHRISSY
[b.] May 16, 1980, Portland, OR; [p.] Dave and Janet Gibson; [ed.] Currently student at Richland High; [occ.] Student; [memb.] Campfire, RHS Choirs and Drama Club; [pers.] Thanks to my mom and Dad for my upbringing. To my sisters for influencing some of my work. To my better half for loving me and encouraging. I love you guys.; [a.] Richland, WA

GIBSON, FRANK H.
[pen.] Frank H. Gibson; [b.] November 9, 1907, Des Moines, IA; [p.] Charles and Julia Gibson; [m.] Wanda L. Gibson, September 18, 1993; [ch.] Leta, Spencer, Walter; [ed.] A.B. San Jose State, M.A. Stanford University; [occ.] Retired; [memb.] "Rossmoore", "Lions Club"; [hon.] For Dedicated and Unselfish Service - "Magnolia Center Rotary Club." 1976 Riverside Calif.; [oth. writ.] On Friendships - On Retirement on "Mothers Day", "On Travel", etc. On "Marriage"; [pers.] Writing poems for my grandchildren and my great grandchildren way of expressing your love.; [a.] Walnut Creek, CA

GIBSON, OPAL
[b.] March 16, 1929, Cyril, OK; [p.] Claude and Winona Long (Deceased); [m.] Oren Gibson (Deceased), July 17, 1948; [ch.] Judy, Connie (Deceased), Tienna, Michael, James, Glenda, Brenda, Jeff; [ed.] 12th Grade - Cyril High School; [occ.] Retired; [memb.] Member: First Baptist Church, International Society Poets; [hon.] Several Editor's Choice Award on various poems.; [oth. writ.] Approximately 14 poems published in various books, three poems being made into songs for recording.; [pers.] I enjoy writing lyrics and poetry on all matters, but I enjoy most writing on thoughts of philosophy and of a religious nature.; [a.] Cement, OK

GILBERT, JOSEPHINE C.
[pen.] Jo Gilbert; [b.] March 16, 1942, Mobile, AL; [p.] Joseph Calascione and Helen Louise Losse; [ch.] Barry, Cheryl and Regina; [ed.] Associates in Business Management, Northern Virginia Community College; [occ.] Program Analyst for U.S. Army Corps of Engineers, Wash. D.C.; [hon.] 1995 Army Resource Management, Employee of the year for evaluation and analysis of financial resources; [pers.] Our creator has given us many talents which we neglect to develop. I have decided to expand and explore my gift for writing.; [a.] Arlington, VA

GIULIANI, FRANCES BEALL
[b.] November 20, 1924, Madison, IN; [p.] Willard R. Beall and Octavia Smith Beall; [m.] Albert Hector Giuliani, August 6, 1949; [ch.] Twins: James Albert, February 14, 1957, John Francis, Arlene Ann, March 28, 1960, Carol Marie October 1, 1962; [ed.] Diploma Nursing, Meth. Kahler Sch. Nurs, 1946 (Mayo Cl.) Rochester, MN., B.S. (Bact and P.H.) Mich State Univ. E. Lansing, MI. 1948, M. Educ. (Eval. and Research), Wayne State, Detroit, MI 1954, Amer. Inst. Med. Law, Healthcare Risk Mgt. (120 Hr) 1995; [occ.] Retired, temporarily. Making a major residential move.; [memb.] Amer. Nurs. Assoc., Mich. Nurs. Assoc., Assoc. Pract. Board of Directors, MSU College of Natural

Science Alumni Assoc. 1990-1996; [hon.] Who's Who in American Nursing 1984, 1986; [oth. writ.] "89 Reasons To Be A Professional Nurse", published 1989 in Honor Society of Nursing, Sigma Theta Tau Int'l.; [pers.] My philosophy continues to be that written for the Sigma Theta Tau Int'l publication "89 Reasons..." I have avocational interests in Parapsychology, Astrology, and Naturopathic Nutrition, and am a fine seamstress. I have enjoyed the priviledge of travel - three times to China, and also to Jordan, Israel, Egypt, Russia and Uzbekistan 5/90. American Red Cross, Nurse Volunteer, Northern California Disaster, 11/89; [a.] Bloomfield Hills, MI

GLASER, PHILIP
[b.] August 13, 1952, Kenmore, NY; [p.] Raymond and Mary Ellen Glaser; [m.] Kathleen Ann Glaser, August 20, 1994; [occ.] Inmate, Wende Corp. Fac., NY; [memb.] Vietnam Veterans of America; [hon.] Eagle Scout, Coast Guard Achievement Medal, Numerous Ribbons and Awards from Albany Inmate Art Shows, Exhibitor at the N.Y. 1990 Rochester Finger Lakes Exhibition; [pers.] Life is an adventure, pursue and cherish it as such. There are many prisons in life, other than being behind bars, the worst of all could be your own mind, and memories and attitude can set you completely free.; [a.] Kenmore, NY

GLASS, RUTH
[pen.] Ruth M. Glass; [b.] July 22, 1924, AR; [p.] Money, and Lorina McMahan; [m.] Bruce O. Glass, March 4, 1989; [ch.] William, Steve Royce, Crystal, Renita, Patrice, Joy; [ed.] Lanny Merrit College - Bay Area School of Preaching Oakland Calif.; [occ.] Retired Supervisor of Tailoring Alterations J.C.P. Co.; [memb.] Mallory Church Christ Afro-American Poetry Club Housing our families project give Christian Education; [hon.] Poems published 4 years straight in New voices in American Poetry, 4 years in Kumber. In the Process of Publishing a book "If Tress Could Talk" and "The World Was"; [oth. writ.] Lectures - poems short plays - skits and card expressions has been published in our Christian newspapers.; [pers.] I am the mother of 8 - 4 boys, 4 girls, lost one boy. 36 grands and 6 great grands. I love people - I write to share and encourage. I also love to travel.; [a.] Portland, OR

GLAUDE, ANNETTE
[b.] February 20, 1953, Pawtucket, RI; [p.] Raymond and Estelle Hebert; [m.] Robert Glaude, September 7, 1986; [ch.] Vanessa Marie; [pers.] Writing poetry is comforting when I'm sad, therapeutic when I'm angry, passionate when I'm happy and emotional about people I love. I dedicate this "Emotional" poem to Bob.; [a.] North Providence, RI

GLENN, JAMES ALBERT
[b.] May 12, 1945, Battle Creek, MI; [p.] Crystal, Albert; [m.] Catherine, July 30, 1976; [ch.] William, Thomas, Crystal; [ed.] 9th grade; [occ.] Longshoreman; [pers.] I believe everyone has ability far above there present awareness.; [a.] Anch, AK

GLOVER, JENNIFER
[pen.] Jen; [b.] December 7, 1983, Austell, GA; [p.] Johnny and Deborah Glover; [ed.] 6th Grade; [hon.] Perfect Attendance for 6 yrs., Honor Roll for 6 yrs., Safety Patrol, Best Personality, Best Dressed Girl, Most Friendly; [a.] Powder Springs, GA

GOLDEN, LINDA TICKLE
[pen.] Tick; [b.] November 15, 1949, Orlando, FL; [p.] William R. and Orna Rowe; [ch.] Charity Tickle-Boyce; [ed.] Elem Schol Orlando, High School and 1 year Jr College Sarasota, Fl.; [occ.] Previous occupation, Telecommunications/Out Patient Service/E.R. Management, Presently I am not employed - due to injuries; [memb.] Received in Several Automobile Accidents - I was hit by drunken drivers; [hon.] We must fulfill our destiny, by continuing to grow and learn, there is no room for bitterness or self pity, there is only time for sharing the rich experiences that life gives us.; [oth. writ.] No Peace of Mind, Running With the Wind, Weep, Go Quietly from Me, Sea Mother, Drinking in the Wine of your Spirit.; [a.] Sarasota, FL

GOLUB, BARRY
[b.] May 7, 1901, Russia; [p.] Howard and Pauline; [m.] Roslin, March 24, 1924; [ch.] Ruth, Marion, Libby, Natalie, his Dorian; [ed.] High School graduate; [oth. writ.] Setback, Silent Telephone, I Love You, Love Lost, Happy Birthday, Bon Voyage; [pers.] I was more clever when I was young. My memory has been affected due to a stroke I suffered in 1980.

GOMEZ, DIANE LYNN
[b.] November 13, 1957, McKeesport, PA; [p.] Robert and Joy Harvey; [m.] Deceased - Ignacio Gomez, March 31, 1979; [ch.] Robert, Anthony and John; [ed.] New Smyrna Beach, Night School G.E.D.; [occ.] Assistant Manager Hardee's Restaurant; [pers.] This poem was written for my sons, in loving memory of their Dad.; [a.] Edgewater, FL

GONSKI, JOHN
[pen.] John Gonski; [b.] June 2, 1972, Waterbury, CT; [p.] Joseph and Sally Gonski; [ed.] Holy Cross High School Waterbury, CT, Southern CT State University, B.S., New Haven, CT; [occ.] Manager, staples; [oth. writ.] Several poems published in local magazine and papers.; [pers.] I try to make my poetry reflect my feelings as much as possible with my life experiences.; [a.] Prospect, CT

GONZALEZ, ALFREDO JAVIER
[b.] November 17, 1965, El Paso, TX; [p.] Luis N. and Carmen A. Gonzalez; [m.] Irma N. Gonzalez, April 27, 1991; [ed.] William H. Burges H.S., El Paso, TX; [occ.] Bookkeeper, Western Glass and Mirror, El Paso, TX; [memb.] San Antonio de Padua Catholic Church, Confirmation Catechist; [oth. writ.] None published

GOODE, NANCY L.
[b.] January 6, 1923, Deatsville, KY; [p.] Edwin and Ella Mae Riggs; [m.] Deceased; [ch.] Two; [ed.] High School, two years College and work related courses, (Methods and Time Measurement); [occ.] Retired, and Writing our Family History; [memb.] (In past), (Santa Clarita Doll Club) Friendly Valley Country Club; [hon.] Methods time measurement the Maynard Companies and MTM Association for Standards and Research; [oth. writ.] Short Stories and poetry and family history; [pers.] I have been an avid reader from early childhood. I wrote my first poem at age 14. It was published in a local newspaper; [a.] Newhall, CA

GOODRICH JR., ABIJAH V.
[pen.] Godrick Hall; [b.] January 5, 1931, Newport News, VA; [p.] Elsie and Abijah Goodrich; [m.] Lucy Goodrich, March 6, 1995; [ch.] Abijah III, Jeffery, Susan; [ed.] High School, 5 Navy Schools, "AA" Degree Long Beach City College.; [occ.] Retired; [memb.] Naval Minewarfare Association, Naval Ships Weapons Systems Engineering Station, Retired Employees Club.; [hon.] "Apollo Achievement Award". NASA Naval Presidential Unit Citation (Korean War); [oth. writ.] Book: "Excape from Venus", "Rayo" (Western). Many poems too long for submission.; [a.] Ojai, CA

GORALSKI, RONALD J.
[b.] December 31, 1963, Hartford, CT; [ch.] Jayson, Danielle and Ryan; [occ.] Job Coach for the Learning Disabled, CT Institute for the Blind/Oak Hill; [memb.] Coalition of Connecticut Bicyclists, The League of American, Bicyclists, Bristol Jaycees; [pers.] "Sometimes while pedaling through the Farmington Valley, I thank God for the privilege of raising my children. And I praise Mandela for teaching me how precious this freedom of movement really is."; [a.] Bristol, CT

GORDY, CHARLIE L.
[b.] August 11, 1938, Galveston Co., TX; [p.] Charlie M. and Agnes M. Gordy; [m.] Sharon A. Gordy, July 30, 1994; [ch.] Chad L. Gordy, Casey L. Gordy; [ed.] LA Marque High School North Texas State University, University of Houston; [occ.] Real Estate Broken and Insurance Agency Owner; [memb.] National Assn. of Realtors, National Assn. of Professional Insurance, Texas Association of Realtors, Houston Association of Realtors; [hon.] Various Business and Professional Designation; [pers.] People are like stars. Some shine brighter and are more famous. Some are barely noticed. But it takes all to light the heavens. We all have some light to contribute, no matter how bright. Just be proud of your own brightness, and heaven will surely thank you for it!; [a.] La Marque, TX

GORNICK, IRA MICHAEL
[pen.] I. M. Gornick; [b.] August 29, 1949, Santa Monica, CA; [p.] Morris (Moe) Gornick, Ester Gornick; [m.] Stephanie Rose Ferries, September 18, 1976; [ed.] Venice High, Santa Monica College, Cal State University Northridge, Bachelor's in English Literature; [occ.] Special Education Teacher for Autistic children, Los Angeles Unified school District; [pers.] I am inspired by a great line of poetry, a painting, a thought, a piece of music that reaches deep into our essence of humanity. I wish to be a contributor to this lineal yet creative world of art.; [a.] Santa Monica, CA

GORSKI, GERALYN R.
[b.] October 2, 1963, Chicago, IL; [p.] John and Jean Gorski; [m.] Engaged to Michael J. Anderson, Spring 1997; [ch.] Future stepdaughter, Jennifer R. Anderson; [ed.] Schaumburg High School, Schaumburg, IL., CNA, Harper College, Palatine, IL., Medical Records, AIBT, Specialist, Phoenix, AZ; [hon.] CNA Observation Papers, Honor Roll - AIBT, Perfect attendance, AIBT Library Aide, Nathan Hale Elementary School; [pers.] One may not always shine in life, what counts is the survival. Influenced by Emerson, Thoreau and Walt Whitman, Transcendentalism.; [a.] Glendale, AZ

GOULD, NATHAN JOHN
[pen.] "Z" G, G or NE; [b.] October 22, 1977, Kansas City, MO; [p.] Ray and Louise Gould; [ed.] K-8 Port Ryron School, 9-11 Home Schooled; [occ.] Green Bradtke's House; [memb.] Syracuse Eagles L.E.A.H. Isaiah 40:31 Basket Ball, Syracuse 1st Church of Nazarene, Canal Convenience B. Bail Summer League; [hon.] Two 1st in Chess Sculpture 3rd and 1st in poetry at Festival of Life, Boston, Mass. They start at church level, regional state then Boston in Eastern States from Maine to Washington DC; [oth. writ.] I have almost 200 poems, most about love; [pers.] Accept the Lord, or turn away. Renounce your sin, or you will pay. Jesus Christ or Lucifer -- make the choice, the choice is yours. Live or die!!! by Kings Gate; [a.] Port Byron, NY

GRACEY, EIRENE
[b.] October 26, 1918, Medak, India; [p.] William and Janet McNicol; [m.] The Late Rev. David Gracey, July 15, 1942; [ch.] Heather and son David who died in 1995; [ed.] In England-N.W. Community College-Winsted; [occ.] Retried Art Teacher, Director of Religious Ed.; [memb.] St. Michaels Church, Litchfield, Board Member of Glebe House-Woodbury, Ct; [hon.] Person of the year in Torrington for running a Social Club for Disturbed People for Mental Health Assn.; [oth. writ.] Life Story - plus over 70 articles published in local newspaper.; [pers.] This was a poem I put together in a few minutes. But I do believe friendship is fragile, and should be treasured.; [a.] Torrington, CT

GRALIKER, MARY
[pen.] "Graeme"; [b.] November 16, 1927, Indiana; [ch.] Five grown children; [occ.] Retired; [memb.] International Society of Poets - 1995-1996; [oth. writ.] "Autumn" published in "Rainbow's End."; [pers.] Second poetry submission. Hobby, primarily oil painting.; [a.] Jacksonville, FL

GRAVES, JANE S.
[pen.] Jane Graves; [b.] January 10, 1930, Stillwater, OK; [p.] Raymond Swartz, Oretha Swartz; [m.] Luther Graves, January 14, 1951; [ch.] Dr. Ray Graves, Dr. David Graves, Leslie G. Rankin; [ed.] Annapolis High, Mary Washington College, Tri-State University; [occ.] Homemaker; [hon.] DAR Award 1947; [oth. writ.] Tri-State History and Cookbook; [pers.] Never lose one's sense of humor and always rise from adversity; [a.] Fort Wayne, IN

GRAY, HELEN
[b.] December 29, 1933, Drummonds, TN; [p.] John and Erma Dickerson; [m.] Alfred H. Gray (Deceased), July 31, 1949; [ch.] Four boys; [ed.] 7th grade; [occ.] Retired; [oth. writ.] A Chain Letter of Prayer, Hail Hail To All The children, No More No More, I Can't Go On, Happy Come Back, Our Hero Ron Brow, plus more.; [pers.] From my past and the present sad story and good things. Sunshine - the River given to me by God.; [a.] Rock Falls, IL

GREEN, BERYL
[b.] March 27, 1945, Littleborough, Lancashire, England; [p.] Nora and Wilfred Fitton; [m.] David Green, December 18, 1965; [ch.] Conrad M. Cheryl, Ch. Sam, Alice, Anna, Lois M. Eddie; [ed.] Scarborough Girls High School, Brentwood College, Dip. in Education; [occ.] Educational, Consultant to schools in Belgium, Teacher/Educator;

[memb.] Orton Pyslexia Society Illinois Branch; [pers.] Ex-principal of the Bruessels English Primary School. I have been privileged to work with people from so many countries. I believe we teach children form a young age to respect everyone regardless of country of creed.; [a.] Glen Ellyn, IL

GREEN, JAMES F.
[pen.] BO; [b.] April 13, 1954, Detroit, MI; [p.] James and Winifred Green; [ed.] Strong Vincent High School - Erie; [occ.] Inventory control - Glenwood Beer Dist. Erie, PA; [memb.] I.G.A.S. - International General Assembly of Spiritualist; [oth. writ.] I.G.A.S. the journal has published many poems under pen name BO. Also Christian Spiritualist Church news letter.; [pers.] I write to reach out to people, to help them to be aware of our spirituality to develop it. I also write about ecology, and the simple conditions of everyday life.; [a.] Erie, PA

GREEN, REGINALD D. D.
[b.] June 22, 1929, Jamaica, WI; [p.] Mr. and Mrs. Cyril Green (Deceased); [ed.] Montego Bay, Anchovy P.S., Crescent College, Jamaica Bible College, American Bible Institute, La Salle University (Ph.D) Enrollee; [occ.] Missionary Christian Teacher, Certified Counselor, Westchester Chapter; [memb.] National Assn. of Black Social Workers, American Assn. of Family Counselors, Dip. Black Democrats of Westchester; [hon.] International Society of Poet Awards, Epsilon Delta Chi Sigma Chapter; [oth. writ.] Author: Commentary on Paul's Epistle to Philemon: Practical Love In Action. Poems of Joy, Praise and Glory Dec. 1996.; [pers.] Born Again Christian Jan. 1945 whilst in S.S. served in six countries. Missionary by Divine Calling and Training. Love Travel, Art, Preaching, Reading.; [a.] Yonkers, NY

GREEN, STACIE R.
[b.] April 3, 1978, Erie, PA; [p.] Don and Denise Green; [ed.] I currently attend Edinboro University of Pennsylvania. Where I am majoring in Elementary Ed.; [occ.] Waitress at Log Cabin Restaurant; [memb.] Kearsarge Church of God; [hon.] Who's Who Among American High School Students, Presidents Award for Educational Improvement; [oth. writ.] My own personal collection.; [pers.] Writing poetry allows me to free my soul and the credit goes to my muse who is my one true love, who lives within my heart.; [a.] Cambridge Springs, PA

GREENAN, KATHLEEN MEEHAN
[b.] April 17, 1922, Ireland; [p.] Agnes McTiernan and Thomas Meehan; [m.] Eugene Greenan, June 26, 1954; [ch.] Imelda, Eileen, Eugene Jr., Michael, Kathleen, Patricia; [ed.] Commercial College Ireland Associate Degree Harvard Univ Bachelor of Arts Harvard Univ Cambridge MA; [occ.] Retired; [memb.] Harvard Faculty Club Quincy YMCA, Irish Music Club; [hon.] The Santa Joseph Cunselio Prize, Harvard University Cambridge MA; [oth. writ.] Autobiography Titled "Tell us a story Mama", "An Irish Immigrants Story", "The Legacy"; [pers.] I have studied creative writing and poetry at Harvard University. I like to write about subjects that I have a first class knowledge of and in touch people will have an interest.; [a.] Milton, MA

GREENBERG, FRANK
[b.] September 4, 1912, Brooklyn, NY; [p.] Jacob and Gossie; [m.] Beatrice, December 1, 1946; [occ.] Retired; [memb.] Workmen's Circle; [hon.] Nothing much more than a good reputation; [oth. writ.] "Shades of Tan"; [pers.] I wish to greet all my former co-workers at the New York State Employment Offices, and at the office of local 132 of the ILGWV, and also, local 98 of the ILGWV, where my wife, Beatrice, was Office Manager

GREENE, DANIEL D.
[b.] December 3, 1957, Washington, PA; [p.] Ronald Greene, Helen Greene; [m.] Denise Greene, August 22, 1981; [ch.] Daniel Andrew, Jessica Ann; [ed.] Trinity High School, 4 year mould making apprenticeship program (P.M.I.); [occ.] Mould Maker at P.M.I. Washington, PA; [memb.] American Bowling Congress, S.N.P.J. Lodge 521; [hon.] Journeyman Mould Making Certificate; [oth. writ.] Several poems and songs not published; [pers.] I strive to make people stop and think about life and how wonderful it can be.; [a.] Washington, PA

GREENE, LAURA IDA
[b.] August 17, 1928, San Bernardino, CA; [p.] Martin and Viola Cleveland; [ch.] Rita D. Roller, Anthony Greene, Frank L. Greene; [ed.] San Bernardino High School, Adult Education Classes, Computer Programming, Word Processing, Spanish, English, Corresponding course writing for children; [occ.] Retired Secretary Nursing Administration, San Bernardino County Medical Center; [memb.] Highland Senior Center, American Association of Retired Persons; [oth. writ.] Several short articles printed in "Do You Remember" in Living section San Bernardino Sun newspaper.; [pers.] When I retired my writings were to document my family history for my children and grandchildren. I liked writing stories for my grandchildren, Tim, Erik, Stacy, Chris, Ryan, Steven, Zach, Zoie, Chaz.; [a.] San Bernardino, CA

GREENOUGH, LAVINA
[pen.] "Lavina"; [b.] October 10, 1950, Newberg, OR; [p.] Sherman and Iona Murray; [m.] Stanley B. Greenough, June 21, 1969; [ch.] Jeffrey Alan, Lori Ann, Jarred Murray; [ed.] La Grande High School, La Grande Or Eastern Oregon State College, La Grande OR (B.S. degree in Elementary Education with a Minor in Remedial Reading); [occ.] Administrative Secretary for the City of La Grande Public Works Dept.; [oth. writ.] At present my poetry and short stories are unpublished.; [pers.] My writing is inspired and influenced by the people in my life and the experiences we have shared.; [a.] Island City, OR

GREY, DEANNA
[b.] November 29, Minneapolis, MN; [p.] Sherry and Richard Gray; [m.] November 22, 1985; [ch.] Mary, Deanna and Danielle; [oth. writ.] I have written a few stories. I have had only one of them published into a book. Writing is fun for me and I hope it is for others too; [pers.] Writing is a tool to use to show emotion. When you write, you are letting your mind go wild. You should write or draw or do whatever you like to do because you should be able to delve deep into your soul for happiness; [a.] Kalamazoo, MI

GRIFFIN, MISS MARION E.
[b.] April 8, 1907, Laramie, WV; [p.] Walter B. and Elva Griffin; [ed.] B.A. degree, Keuka College Penn Yan, New York; [occ.] Retired, formerly Chief Medical Record Librarian in many different hospitals across the country.; [hon.] Tau Kappa Alpha Honorary Society; [oth. writ.] I have been writing poetry most of my life but never before submitted anything for publication.; [pers.] I have been greatly influenced by Ralph Waldo Emerson and his philosophy.; [a.] Cobb Island, MD

GRIFFIN, ROBERT J.
[pen.] Mr. Arrgee; [b.] October 19, 1918, Danby, MO; [p.] Tom and Stella Griffin; [m.] Helene Griffin, March 19, 1944; [ch.] R. Jeff Griffin Jr.; [ed.] 2 yrs. college GED; [occ.] Retired; [memb.] American Military Society, Fleet Reserve Association, National Family Care givers Assoc., well Spouse Foundation, Multiple Sclerosis Society of Amer.; [hon.] Just Military Awards for 20 Yrs. under the Sea in Submarines. My old home and I went to hell and back many times in '42 and '43, and she's still on patrol at the bottom of the pacific. I miss her very much. A part of me is still with her.; [oth. writ.] The Wit and Wisdom of "Mr. Arrgee Says"; [pers.] Just amateur poet, and I know it. My wife has been married to the same man for more than 52 yrs. She deserves a medal. Putting your marriage first will make it last!; [a.] Keystone Heights, FL

GROESBECK, JOHN W.
[pen.] John W. Groesbeck; [b.] July 11, 1919, Hartford, CT; [p.] Earl and Lavinia Groesbeck; [m.] Doris Oberhuber, October 10, 1959; [ed.] B.S. Bus. Admin. Rider University Lawrenceville, NJ; [occ.] Retired Front Milliken and Co; [memb.] Presbyterian Church Troa; [hon.] Distinguished Flying Cross, Air Medal with Oak Leaf Cluster, Captain, Airforce Pilot - China, WW II; [oth. writ.] Currently working on book length combat experience entitled - "Target, Hongkong".; [pers.] Believe in the old adage, "Laugh and the World Laughs with You, Cry and Cry Alone"; [a.] Young Harris, GA

GROH, LEANNA W.
[b.] July 5, 1916, Tioga Co, NY; [p.] Frank R. and Ina L. Parker Wheaton; [m.] Robert L. Groh, May 13, 1939; [ch.] Robert M., Ellin, David, Charles, and James; [ed.] B.S. Cornell U., 1939; [occ.] Retired, Teacher; [oth. writ.] Desk-Top publication: Wheaton Genealogy, (Also: Parker, Brown Gould) "Leant Hill Folks", "War Letters" - "Two Brothers - Same War": "Memories in Reverse, Slowly" - "75 Years of Letters" - "See What Stamps Can Do"; [pers.] "Communication is the basis of civilization" - I love words.; [a.] Dresden, NY

GROSSO, EDMOND V.
[b.] February 12, 1917, North Adams, MA; [p.] Charles and Henrietta Grosso; [m.] Deceased, May 22, 1952; [ch.] Edmond Brian Grosso; [ed.] Syracuse University; [occ.] The Springs Restaurant - Motor Onn Owner; [memb.] Rotary - Unico; [hon.] 1. Partial College Scholarship, 2. Having the Springs Restaurant Selected as One of Three Outstanding in State of Mass.; [oth. writ.] Presently working on cook book. The Springs was chosen as one of three outstanding restaurants in State of Mass.; [pers.] I enjoy climbing mountains! Do something good and your life will be blessed with health and happiness.; [a.] New Ashford, MA

GROVER JR., JOSEPH EDWARD
[b.] October 28, 1964, Pittsburgh, PA; [p.] Gloria Williams; [ed.] High School; [occ.] Janitor; [memb.] Softball Association; [hon.] Softball Awards High School Awards Honor Roll; [oth. writ.] Poetry; [pers.] To enjoy writing poetry and my autobiography; [a.] Pittsburgh, PA

GUILMETTE, MARIE
[pen.] Gina Marie Sinclair; [b.] April 11, 1953, Brooklyn, NY; [p.] Edith and Vincent Gallope; [ch.] Mark James; [ed.] High School - Newfield HS, Selden, NY Suffolk County Community College - Selden, NY, Associates Degree; [occ.] Office Manager; [memb.] Sons of Italy Andrea Doria Lodge #2201; [hon.] Secretary of the Year 1971, Incentive Awards IRS 1976; [pers.] Life is a circle that never ends...; [a.] Selden, NY

GULDEN, K. A.
[pen.] Kenneth Kage; [b.] October 9, 1955, Fort Dix, NJ; [ed.] Vestal Central High, Nyack College; [occ.] President - Investment; [oth. writ.] Essential Connection (novel), several poems and short stories; [pers.] Too much of life is spent hurting. Words, when received, can help. I hope mine will.; [a.] Frederick, MD

GUNTER, MAMIE
[b.] February 2, 1916, Gladstone; [p.] Clifford and Mattie Burks; [m.] Thomas Gunter deceased, August 22, 1938; [ch.] Aline Richard and Kathy; [ed.] 7th Grade

GUTIERREZ, VERA ELNORA
[pen.] VEG; [b.] February 2, 1948, Evansville, TN; [p.] Noel Valentine and Mamie Elnora Knight; [m.] Jimmy Santiago V. Gutierrez, May 11, 1973; [ch.] Jason, Veronica, Valentina, Viola and Joseph; [ed.] 1967-68 North High School Evansville IN, Lockyear's Business College; [occ.] Grandmother and S.T.H.E.; [memb.] American Kennel Club, PTA, RCI, LDS Church, BBSI; [hon.] 18 Month LDS Employment Service Mission, 2 yr NSISD, San Antonio S.A.T. Executive Committee, PTA Awards, Eagle Scout, Mother genealogy rewards that inspired the DNA eyes poem; [pers.] "The choices we make are the truths we live, right or wrong, no one has walked the moments of time on our foot steps." -- VEG This is an honor and reward, right this moment in time!; [a.] San Antonio, TX

GWALTNEY, DEALIA M.
[b.] June 7, 1944, Agusta, GA; [ch.] Michelle, Michael, Eboni; [ed.] Stony Brook University - MSW; [occ.] Administrator: Queens Boro Services Office - Queens - N.Y.; [memb.] N.A.F.E. - AARP; [hon.] Woman of Year, New York Governor's Advisory Council on Developmental Disabilities; [pers.] In my writings I strive to share the beauty of God and nature, and question the unequal treatment of mankind to one another.; [a.] Queens Village, NY

HAACK, MR. MEYEL H.
[b.] June 11, 1918, Fern, IA; [p.] Miner and Gertrude Haack; [m.] Mary Louise Haack (Deceased), August 4, 1945; [ch.] Six; [ed.] Butler University 2 years, University of Iowa 2 years; [occ.] Citrus Grove Owner; [hon.] Purple Heart - 1994; [oth. writ.] Miner and His Boy, Take Two Hit Right. To the published later.; [pers.] To love

is to live only a life live for others worth living by Albert Einstein my wife, before then death, received 14 community service awards etc. she lived to be kind.; [a.] Groveland, FL

HAGER, CHRISTOPHER E.
[pen.] I am I; [b.] June 3, 1965, Daylestown, PA; [p.] Robert and Sandra Hager; [ch.] Alyssa Lynn Hager; [oth. writ.] A poem for every experience I have and every feeling I experience.; [pers.] I am, therefore, I write. For those who will to know me, I am love. For all others, I am war. Who am I?; [a.] Plumsteadville, PA

HAGOPIAN, GLORIA ELIAS
[b.] December 2, 1934, Fresno, CA; [p.] Paul and Elvira Pascuzzi; [m.] Vern Glen Hagopian, January 31, 1954; [ch.] Kirk Alexander, Kari Stephanie, Keve Victoria Hagopian; [ed.] All completed 1-12 and some college.; [occ.] Special Education Assistant with Autistic Students in (S.H.); [hon.] Positive Teaching Workshop of Special Education, Certificate of Award for...Excellence and Service to Children

HAIGHT, BRAD
[b.] January 8, 1971, Kalamazoo, MI; [p.] Clarence Haight, Deb Havens; [occ.] Filmmaker; [memb.] Chicago Filmmakers; [oth. writ.] Maxwell's Frontline, Dead in Michigan, Cassanova '94 (in progress); [pers.] The personal foundations of my work attempt to express the common emotions an individual is subjected to when gaining a higher level of understanding about themselves and the world around them.; [a.] Chicago, IL

HALE, BRENDA KAY
[b.] July 29, 1980, San Antonio, TX; [p.] Betty and Leroy Blankenship; [ed.] Devine High School, Devine, TX; [occ.] Student in Devine High School; [memb.] Planetary Society, and National Honor Society; [hon.] Editor's Choice Award for poem, "Exile", and various academic awards.; [oth. writ.] Poems published in two other anthologies: "Child of Darkness" and "Exile".; [pers.] I try to evoke strong emotions in readers because I want them to remember my writing and I want them to remember me. Most of all, I want them to know, peace, love, and hope can cure our world.; [a.] Devine, TX

HALL, AUDREY ARRINGTON
[pen.] Audrey Celeste; [b.] May 12, 1960, Danbury, NC; [p.] Hilda Rogers; [m.] Greg G. Hall, July 4, 1978; [ch.] Theadore Charles and Kerry Virginia; [ed.] Francisco Elementary School, North Stokes High School; [occ.] housewife, substitute Teacher; [oth. writ.] Writing is a passtime that I enjoy. I can also put my feelings on paper.; [pers.] This poem was written about my daughter, who is truly a gift from God. My children are a very important part of my life. I have always loved all types of poetry.; [a.] Westfield, NC

HALL, JULIA BETH
[b.] June 20, 1967, Montgomery County, NC; [p.] Eugene and Virginia Burroughs; [m.] John David Hall, April 24, 1988; [ed.] Mt. Gilead Elementary School, Highland Middle School, West Montgomery High School; [occ.] Secretary at Gilead Home Supply (Hardware Store); [memb.] Pee Dee Presbyterian Church, Deca Club in High School, French

Club in High School, Beta Club in Middle School; [hon.] A whorrie Patriots Chapter of the American Revolution - History Essay Contest 1977-1978, (Growing up in Colonial Times) Topic NC Deca District Runner Up 1985, Food Marketing Series, Comprehensive Occupational Exam; [oth. writ.] Essay - Growing up in Colonial Times - a few poems.; [pers.] Try to do your best in everything you do but always know it doesn't have to be perfect because nothing in life usually is.; [a.] Mount Gilead, NC

HALLBERG, CLARANORE KREY
[pen.] Clara Krey Hallberg; [b.] May 17, 1929, Falls City, NE; [p.] Peter and Esther Krey; [m.] Harold Hallberg (Deceased), August 10, 1952; [ch.] Five, 3 biological, 2 adopted from Korea; [ed.] H.S. and Nurses Training I am a registered Nurse and worked in Nursing 45 yrs. I have been widowed for 22 years.; [occ.] Nursing part time child care part time; [memb.] Lutheran Church; [oth. writ.] One book published "Thorns Among The Roses" (Autobiography) many poems, some published.; [pers.] True happiness is found in losing oneself in giving help and love to others. True peace is found in Jesus Christ, and the salvation he procured.; [a.] Omaha, NE

HAMLET, KATHY
[b.] April 26, 1956, Dearborn, MI; [p.] Dolores Vasconcelles and William McIvor; [ed.] Charlotte High, Edison Community College, Academy of Health Sciences (accredited through Baylor University); [occ.] Secretary - Free-lance writer; [memb.] Disabled American Veterans; [hon.] National Honor Society (High School), Phi Theta Kappa, Dean's List (College); [oth. writ.] Several poems published in greeting cards, local papers and contests. Articles in local newspapers.; [pers.] I write to educate, illustrate, or motivate to expand one's insight just for enlightenment. A delight it is to demonstrate and create, on demand, a verse that's light just for entertainment.; [a.] Orlando, FL

HANNA, KELLY
[pen.] Kelly Hanna, Clair Booth; [b.] March 16, 1959, San Diego, CA; [p.] Donald Long, Carol Long; [m.] Divorced - Jaime Hanna, July 8, 1978; [ed.] Patrick Henry High School - graduated, 1976 (early) went to work for father after grad., to learn trade of Construction/Office work.; [occ.] Disabled, I owned/operated a fax/copier shop as well as a blueprint shop.; [memb.] Copier/Fax Tech. Repair Association, worked with Cease Stalking Now, Inc, against Domestic Violence/Violent Crimes, Catholic Church - Comdex; [hon.] National Library of Poetry; [oth. writ.] In process of writing a novel, soon to be released. Poem - "Watching Me".; [pers.] I am very dedicated in helping victims of violent crimes, stalking, D.V., as I know that more enforced laws could bring more peace to all! In fact this is what started me to do poetry, and to write a novel, to try and help others through what I had lived.; [a.] Las Vegas, NV

HANNON, SUZANNE F.
[pen.] S. Hannon; [b.] November 2, 1966, Lebanon, PA; [p.] Francis A. and Patricia G. Hannon; [ch.] Brent T. Gates, Patrick J. Gates; [oth. writ.] Personal collection only; [pers.] Expression transcends from my spiritual self through my positive writings. My pen and my mind embrace one another to bring dreams, thoughts, and romance alive.; [a.] Shermans Dale, PA

HANSON, PATTY
[b.] April 26, 1937, Ventura, CA; [p.] Henrietta and Jesse Hollingsworth; [m.] Marvin L. Hanson, May 4, 1957; [ch.] Tammi Skiba and Lori Hanson; [ed.] Ventura Senior High School and Ventura College; [occ.] Retired Teachers Aide; [memb.] International Society of Poets, Ventura Community Orchestra, Ojai Summer Band; [hon.] Honorary Service Award from the California Congress of Parents and Teachers, Plaque for International Poet of Merit, 3 Editors choice certificates and $50 prize as semi-finalist at the 1995 Convention of International Society of Poets in Washington, DC; [oth. writ.] Articles and poems for several Metaphysical Newsletters including "Reflections", 3 poems published by the National Library of Poetry; [pers.] Poetry is the gift that gives each reader an opportunity to receive what they need at that moment, to lift their spirits, give them joy, let them cry, or just be entertained, by a lovely idea.; [a.] Ojai, CA

HARCHOL, VIRGINIA BUDDIE
[b.] September 17, 1932, Youngstown, OH; [p.] Michael Buddie, Anna Buddie; [m.] Richard Alpaugh Harchol, August 7, 1954; [ch.] Katherine Ann, Amy Lee, Richard Michael; [ed.] Poland High, Ohio Wesleyan University, Irvine Valley College; [occ.] Homemaker; [memb.] Irvine Art League, Costa Mesa Art League, Performing Arts Center Guild; [hon.] Valedictorian, Phi Beta Kappa, Blue Ribbon - Orange County Fair (Glass Sculpture) Honorable mention art Awards; [pers.] I like to open my mind to knowledge, whimsey, humor, love, and divine inspiration. Any resulting output enriches my life, and, I hope, the lives of others.; [a.] Irvine, CA

HARDEN, KATHERINE VAUGHN
[b.] May 1, 1956, Shreveport, LA; [p.] Alice Mae Jackson and Cornelious Vaughn; [m.] Revonne Harden Sr., April 5, 1993; [ch.] Alonzo Vaughn Johnson; [ed.] DeSoto High School, Mansfield, LA, Southern University (B.A.), Baton Rouge, LA Louisiana State University (M.A.) Baton Rouge, LA; [occ.] Speech-Language Pathologist, Palm Beach County Schools, Florida; [memb.] American Speech, Language, Hearing Association, School Advisory Council, Hilltop Missionary Baptist Church (Sunday School Teacher), Alpha Chi, Alpha Kappa Mu Honor Society; [hon.] Outstanding Young Women of America Award, 1988, Appreciation Award for Inclusive Education Workshop, 1995; [oth. writ.] Two poems published in Palm Beach County's Writing Works II, 1995 Summer Institute; [pers.] I have always been impressed with an author's ability to create "art" through the use of rhyme and rhythm. Lyric poetry has been my greatest influence.; [a.] Lake Park, FL

HARDY, PATRICK
[b.] November 19, 1977, Fremont, CA; [p.] Kathe Hardy; [ed.] Graduate Tanalpais High School entering University of Colorado Boulder 8/96; [occ.] Student; [hon.] Honor Roll '93-'96; [a.] Millvalley, CA

HARHIGH, DR. GEORGE H.
[b.] April 21, 1937, PA; [p.] Helen, Harry (D); [m.] Sherry; [ch.] Six; [ed.] College and Medical School; [occ.] Physician; [memb.] Fellow, American Academy Of Family Physicians, International Society of Poets; [oth. writ.] Random thoughts and poetry with several published.; [pers.] Have achieved many accolades in my life but none pleases me more than being the son of immigrant parents.; [a.] Camp Hill, PA

HARPER, DERRICK L.
[pen.] DeLeon; [b.] January 4, 1955, Mobile, AL; [p.] Ivory L. and Bettye Jean; [m.] Gaynell Joyce-Harper; [ch.] Nicole, Erica, Jasenn, Knykeda; [ed.] Life; [occ.] Singer, Songwriter, poet, writer of short stories; [memb.] Off Beat Register of Entertainers, New Orleans, Louisiana; [hon.] My family and my children, and the gift from God to be able to say so.; [oth. writ.] The Elders, It's Only A Little Thunder and Lightning, The Mental Me, No P.D., Instrument of Death, A Husbands Prayer, Once Upon A Time, Anecdotes and such Introspect, At The Sound of the Bell; [pers.] I write what my experience has taught me, what my mind conceives, and what my heart says. Always remembering, good sense is not always common, but common sense is always good.; [a.] Metairie, LA

HARPER, JESSICA G
[b.] July 2, 1971, Odessa, TX; [p.] Mr. and Mrs. Joe A. Gomez; [m.] Larry P. Harper, March 6, 1992; [ch.] One on the way; [ed.] High School Graduate, Odessa High School; [occ.] Pharmacy Technician; [oth. writ.] I have many other poems. My first poem was written in the year 1987. I basically like to write poems to put my feelings down on paper, it makes me feel better.; [a.] Eunice, NM

HARPER, MARGUERITE
[b.] May 5, 1938, Rock Mount, NC; [p.] Margaret Hynes; [ch.] Six; [ed.] High school GED Air and Travel, Beauty Culture. 1 yr Community College; [occ.] Health Field; [memb.] United Science of Mind Church NYC, Slim Seekers Weight Support Workshop NJ; [oth. writ.] Poems submitted to my church paper United Science of Mind Center of New York City; [pers.] After starting in religious science, I started to keep a journal. The writings in the journal soon developed into poetry and inner feelings.; [a.] Paterson, NJ

HARPER, VERNE J.
[b.] October 8, 1952, Greeley, CO; [ch.] Shanda, Jeremy, Weston, Skyler; [ed.] Attending Kilgore College, Kilgore, Texas and The University of Texas at Tyler, Tyler, Texas English Major; [occ.] Oil and Gas Landman; [memb.] Phi Beta Kappa; [oth. writ.] "An Angry White Male" a collection of short stories and poems (1995) working on another collection entitled "Friends, Lovers and the Way of Life" "Truths Talented Teacher" published in "Oil Patch Review"; [pers.] Writing is my art form. Through writing I try to capture the essence of an event, including its emotional element so that my reader can recreative it and experience it themselves.; [a.] Longview, TX

HARRIS, CHRISTINE PARRISH
[pen.] Chris; [b.] October 27, 1943, Chapel Hill, NC; [p.] Date and Lovie Stroud Parrish; [ch.] Darren Kareem Harris; [ed.] Lincoln High School, Chapel Hill, N.C., County of Orange; [memb.] Markham Chapel Baptist Church; [oth. writ.] Many other writings not released at present.; [pers.] I strive to reflect God in my writing. I have been greatly influenced by having him in my life.; [a.] Hillsborough, NC

HARRIS, JAMES LEON
[b.] April 18, 1946, Union, SC; [p.] Elizabeth Harris and Golden Bookman; [m.] Sandra J. Jennings-Harris, October 14, 1989; [ch.] Jamie J. Harris; [ed.] University of Illinois, Dean's List, Wilson Junior College, Hyde Park High School, Wadsworth Elementary School; [occ.] Account Representative for Harris and Harris Ltd.; [memb.] Sunday School Superintendent at St. Phillips A.M.E. Church, Distributor With Starlight International; [oth. writ.] Short stories: "The Black Plague", "Real is what you feel when you feel for real"; [pers.] I seek to convey a positive message of hope and regeneration to African-Americans to inspire our self-empowerment and self-determination to return to our respectful status in the world; [a.] Chicago, IL

HARRIS, KATHRYN EMILIE
[pen.] Kathryn Emilie Harris; [b.] January 15, 1979, Portland, OR; [p.] Lawrence and Judith Harris; [ed.] Glencoe High School - I will graduate in 1997; [occ.] Full time student at Glencoe; [memb.] 4-H Equestrian Dog and Vet Science, Drama Club; [hon.] Honor roll; [pers.] We may be just a "black dot" in a crowd, but even stars appear to be just a white dot in the sky. Like a diamond in a hillside, sometimes treasure awaits discovery.; [a.] Hillsboro, OR

HART, LEE EAGLE
[pen.] Lee Eagle; [b.] September 25, 1942, Alamosa, CO; [p.] Omar and Bertha Eagle (Deceased); [m.] Ivan Hart (Deceased), January 28, 1962; [ch.] Three - Alan, Rod, Michelle; [ed.] High School, two years Community College, New York; [occ.] Writer of Poems and Nonfiction Books; [memb.] Heartland Writers Guide; [hon.] Drama - Journalism High School 1957-1961; [oth. writ.] Pride without end non-fiction aprox, 70,000 words medical self help, seeking publication, dead beat, nonfiction, 50,000 woods, not completed.; [pers.] As I traveled with my husband in his career with the National Park Service for twenty five years I wrote and produced plays for the various park recreational clubs, my work is intended to enhance quality of life in a world of change.; [a.] Percy, IL

HART, MARGARET ANNE
[pen.] Margaret Anne Hart; [b.] June 21, 1934, Warrick Cy, IN; [p.] Dr. and Mrs. Quincy L. Hart; [m.] Divorced 11 yrs.; [ed.] B.S. Nursing - University of Evansville, H.S. Diploma from Lynnville High School, Lynnville, Indiana. 32 Credit hrs. (of 50) completed toward M.S. degree Retired RN; [occ.] Support group leader, facilitator of support group formation founder Ind. Chapt of Nat. Martan Foundation Val. teaching, counselling; [memb.] Member of National Morfan Foundation since 1987; [hon.] Dean's List, Through poetry, I attempt to show people how heroes and beautiful they are.; [oth. writ.] This poem is one of a collection (un-published) titled "Lemon Trees and Rainbows 1980 One other selection was published in graduate school newsletter, "One In Being". Fondest dream: publication of LT and R in toto.; [pers.] I believe that "At any given moment, most people are doing the very best that they are capable of". I also believe that we are related intimately to each other. Also, it is of primary importance as to why a person does what he does, rather than what he does. Motivation, purpose is the key to base judgements on.; [a.] Evansville, IN

HARTFIELD, ALTA
[b.] September 12, 1933, San Antonio, TX; [p.] William and Louia Dibrell; [m.] John Hartfield, January 8, 1993 (2nd); [ch.] Byron, Keith, Kara Hilderbrand; [ed.] 2 1/2 yrs. College St. Philip's U. of Denver and St. Mary's; [occ.] Retired (Civil Service); [memb.] Episcopal Church, Daughters of the King, Senior Volunteer Services; [hon.] Volunteer service awards and D.O.K. plaque; [oth. writ.] Resting Place, published by Vantage Press. Poems and articles by Church bulletins and local newspapers; [pers.] Hate lies and ignorance does not linger at the residence of real love, truth and common sense. (Original); [a.] La Vernia, TX

HARVEY, DELORES DEANE
[pen.] "Babe"; [b.] September 13, 1933, East Chicago, IN; [p.] Darrell E. Hill, Goldie Pearl Jones; [m.] John R. Harvey, April 15, 1951; [ch.] James, Jay, Jennifer, Jeffrey; [ed.] H.S. Lafayette, Indiana; [occ.] Housewife; [memb.] Fun Club of Macomb, Illinois, Funtimers Club, Gals Pizza Group; [oth. writ.] Recent published poems: "Bye Winter", "Asleep", "Forever", "The Mouse: The Tale of two Houses," "Moving Madness," "Noise," "Sweet Memories," "The Bunny that Was," "Carefree Days," "Gone," "Spring of '96", and "A Better Place".; [pers.] To make this world a better place, this should be our aim. There's more to life than getting rich . . . or simply growing fame, like loving one another and building hope for all. Nothing's more important than answering God's call.; [a.] Macomb, IL

HARVEY, NOEL E.
[pen.] Noel E. Harvey; [b.] September 14, 1934, Indianapolis, IN; [p.] Pearl A. Harvey, Roy S. Harvey; [m.] Barbara J. Harvey, August 21, 1976; [ch.] Son - Rich A. Harvey, four stepchildren; [ed.] Ben Davis High School Correspondence Courses in Accounting and Supervision; [occ.] Retired from U.S. Postal Service; [oth. writ.] Why Do I? A book that has been sent to the Library of Congress. Copy pending, has not been published.; [pers.] I enjoy writing humorous poetry, articles and books that make fun of myself.; [a.] Amo, IN

HATCHER, TAMARAH F.
[b.] June 28, 1979, Bay Medical; [p.] Lamar and Debby Hatcher; [ed.] Eleventh grade; [oth. writ.] An article for "The Bay County Voice"; [pers.] Life's a city full of strange streets, and death's the marketplace where each one meets. W. Shakespeare.; [a.] Blountstown, FL

HAWKEYE, MYKE
[pen.] Alexander G. Hawke; [b.] November 29, 1965, Fort Knox, KY; [p.] Kenneth Pierce and Patricia Angelo; [m.] Divorced; [ch.] Anthony - 11, Nicholas - 9; [ed.] B.S. U. of NY - Biology, 12 years U.S. Army, Special Forces Medic, Linguist Communication, Intelligence; [occ.] Manager of Medical Co, Freelance - writer, photographer, humanitarian; [memb.] Padi-Scuba, Fugakukai-Aikido, Greenberet - Sport Parachute Club, Special Forces Assoc.; [hon.] Cadburry Award - Writing School; [oth. writ.] Various short stories, poems, songs.; [pers.] "There is no reward."; [a.] Houston, TX

HAWTHORNE, DORIS HAYES
[b.] August 22, 1938, Inverness, MS; [p.] Davis and Lela Hayes; [m.] Joseph C. Hawthorne Sr. (De-

ceased), June 1, 1959; [ch.] J. Conrad, Jr., Anthony, Derek, Paul, Brian; [ed.] B.S. Chemistry; [occ.] Computer Training Instructor; [oth. writ.] Several poems written to family members, friends. "About Life" was written to my husband in 1982. Article written for local magazine. Several poems written for sorority including one put to music.; [pers.] "Share that which truly brings you peace, it may bring peace to others."; [a.] Orlando, FL

HAYASHI, RALPH
[b.] January 24, 1938, Hilo, HI; [p.] Ralph M. Hayashi, Haru Muraki Hayashi; [ch.] Sheri Lei Ritter, Tim A, and Chris M.; [ed.] Roosevelt High, University of Hawaii, Oregon State University, B.S. Sci., and B.S.C.E.; [occ.] Professional Engineer - Civil and Structural; [memb.] American Society of Civil Engineers, Structural Engineers Association of Hawaii; [oth. writ.] Published papers in technical journals; [pers.] Poetry reflects one's intimate feelings, and through poetry these feelings will last forever.; [a.] Kula, Maui, HI

HAYDEN, DAVID
[pen.] Elmo Fetus; [b.] March 27, 1945, Riverside, CA; [p.] Deceased; [m.] Esther Regina Hayden, May 23, 1992; [ed.] High School dropout A.A. B.A. with honors in Political Science, USTIC Hon Discharge CPL E-4; [occ.] Carpenter; [memb.] CSAA; [hon.] Founder: Whale Aid (Hawaii), Hawaiian Outrigger Canoe Coach; [oth. writ.] Novel: One Paddle, One Sun. Book: Rx America, several hundred songs and poems.; [pers.] Can't wait for the revolution.; [a.] Burlingame, CA

HAYES, PAULETTE
[b.] January 10, 1954, Manila, AR; [p.] Willis and Pauline Hollis; [m.] Donald Keith Hayes, March 4, 1978; [ch.] Candace, Kelly and Seth; [ed.] High School (12th Grade Graduate); [occ.] Secretary; [memb.] UPC Ladies Auxiliary; [oth. writ.] "The Gift" published by Sparrowgrass Poetry Forum. Publishing date August of "1996".; [pers.] It is the memories of the past, the love of the present, and hopes for the future that inspire the soul of a writer.; [a.] Greenville, MS

HAYMORE, VIRGINIA
[b.] September 2, 1980; [p.] Charmaine Latham and Albert Latham; [ed.] High School Jr. Yr., Streamwood High School; [occ.] McDonald's Cashier; [oth. writ.] Africa, That Special Friend, When...., Twist in Fate, When the Time Comes, The Coldness of my Soul, That Thoughtful Time, Our Passion Never Lies, A Taste of Our Heat, The Hidden Truth, etc.; [pers.] I strive to understand life as it is. And to show my work of art that is in my soul.; [a.] Streamwood, IL

HEALEY, DEBORAH L.
[pen.] Deb; [b.] May 8, 1986, Santa Fe, NM; [p.] James and Marjorie Healey; [ed.] She is in the 5th grade in Even's Elementary School in Alabama; [occ.] Student; [hon.] Poem is put into the Anthology of Poetry by Young Americans; [pers.] She wants to write some more poems, when she thinks of a good subject; [a.] Alamosa, CO

HEBERT, SHERYL
[b.] July 24, 1962, Houma, LA; [p.] Divorced, Leonard Ledet and Elsie Rice; [m.] Mark Anthony Hebert, June 7, 1980; [ch.] Corey Paul, Paul Anthony, James Christopher Hebert

HEISER, LORNA DELEE PUNCHES
[pen.] Lorna Delee (Punches) Heiser; [b.] December 9, 1936, Clinton, MA; [p.] Kenneth V. Punches, Elizabeth Hamilton; [m.] Divorced; [ch.] Sherryl 6/28/55, Jodi 9/25/57, C. Troy 1/23/65, Darcy 3/23/69; [ed.] Clinton H.S., Clint, MA, Riverside Junior College, CA Assoc. Deg., College, Ext. courses, AMA Seminars, Business, In-house trng. programs State and Private related.; [occ.] Retired Legal Administrator and Business owner; [memb.] Past Member 4 Chambers of Commerce, Past State Sec. Wn. Assn. for Social Welfare, Mbr. Bd. of Directors of WHEAT, Volunteer, Pierce Co. Crisis Clinic, Copyrighted 1st Self Divorce, Owner Self Divorce Services, Inc., AARP, Gov.'s Planning Committee for Mental Health and Retardation, Church Press Sec., Mbr. Olympia School Board; [hon.] Many through work experience monetary and other - meaningless compared to writing a poem related to an incident of happiness or tragedy which touches the soul and brings warmth and comfort or delight to the recipient.; [oth. writ.] Numerous editorials on issues, 1960's, Editor/Photo. of "Vocational Rehabilitation Outlook" bimonthly Wn. State Publication; [pers.] Necessity and survival breed stability through hard work and tenacity. Hidden creativity creeps through life to soothe such an active mind. Disability/retirement from hand to mouth existence, however rewarding financially and egotistically, finally allows your fragmented, lurking beauty to be enabled to shine through and gain freedom.; [a.] Tacoma, WA

HELTON, SHERRY
[pen.] Sherry Love; [b.] March 28, 1961, Ohio; [p.] Janice Lee (Mom); [m.] Dwayne Neal Helton, August 7, 1983; [ch.] Johnathon Dwayne Neal Helton; [ed.] Lake Brantley High School; [occ.] Homemaker/Author; [memb.] International Society of Poets; [hon.] Responsible Pet Owner Award, Orange County Florida, Editor's Choice Award 1995 and 1996; [oth. writ.] Poetry: "A Wedding Invitation," "Truck Driving Guitar Man," "Checkmate," "The Stars and The Moon," "Christine," "Satisfied Man," "Memory of Our Father," "The Man In the Bottle," "The Games That People Play"; [pers.] The words on paper are actually true-to-life experiences of mine, and hopefully there are lessons to be learned from each and every one that I may grow from.; [a.] Orlando, FL

HENDERSON, DARLENE ADAMSON
[pen.] "Dee"; [b.] September 4, 1956, Gary, IN; [p.] Vernon and Dollie Adamson; [m.] Booker T. Henderson II, June 12, 1976; [ch.] Dar Nieshia, Binika, Jamarr, Jasmine; [ed.] Bachelor of Science in Management from Calumet College of St. Joseph, and Masters in Education (M.ED) from Cambridge College; [occ.] Teacher of Kennedy King School with Gary School Corp; [memb.] Gary Educators for Christ "Gary Reading Council" "Merrillville" Multi Cultural Committee, and Northern Indiana Church of Encouragement; [hon.] Many Merits and Job Princeton Earth Physics Project at Purdue University; [oth. writ.]

I have written many inspirational poems of encouragement and poems of different occasions of life. I am presently writing an autobiography and document of several Pauline Epistles of the Bible.; [pers.] I have been divinely inspired to write poems and other literature by God and His son Jesus Christ through whom all blessings flow.; [a.] Merrillville, IN

HENK, LYNN E.
[b.] March 25, 1945, Evanston, IL; [p.] Anne and Walter Seidel; [m.] Charles W. Henk, March 14, 1970; [ch.] Roy (Deceased); [ed.] Evanstone Township High School, Evanston, IL: Parsons College, Fairfield, IA, Evanston Business College, Evanston, IL; [occ.] Clerk for Lions Clubs International, Oak Brook, IL; [memb.] International Society of Poets, Business and Professional, Women's Club of Evanston; [hon.] Paul Harris Fellow from The Rotary Foundation for Rotary International, several Editor's Choice Awards for poems from The National Library of Poetry; [oth. writ.] "Love In America" in U.S. in Clover '76, "A Holy Wish" in Our 20th Century's Greatest Poems and in The Space Between, "It's In The Stars" in The Coming of Dawn, "To My Son Roy" in After The Storm, "Memories Of My Time Up At The Cottage" in Best Poems of 1995, "A Sailor's Observation" in Mists of Enchantment, "Nature's Fireworks" in Windows of the Soul, "A Tribute to "Windows Of The Soul" in Best Poems of the '90s "Goal In Life" in Best Poems of 1996; [pers.] I like to think that life brings us what is good, and that we must make the best of it.; [a.] Cicero, IL

HENSLEY, KARI GAYLE
[b.] April 17, 1986, Knoxville, TN; [p.] Mr. and Mrs. David M. Hensley; [ed.] 5th grade Rush Strong School; [occ.] Student; [hon.] Honor Roll Gold Car Rally, Pre-teen Tennessee Finalist and Recognition Program Creativity Recognition of Accomplishment Accelerated Reader Award, Computer Achievement Award; [oth. writ.] Public readings of my work Windweed, Halloween, Just Me, Dandelion; [pers.] I enjoy writing about nature and history.; [a.] Strawberry Plains, TN

HER, SHEILA M.
[pen.] Peo Her; [b.] January 27, 1985, Long Beach, CA; [p.] Sam Her and Catherine Her; [ed.] 5th grade; [occ.] Baby sitting after school; [memb.] Fox Kids Club, Burger King Kids Club, and Cheer leader at my school; [hon.] Writer Hall of Fame, Honor roll, at my school, Good Student Award in math and spelling, Super Scientist Award, certificate of achievement in D.A.R.E. program. And Jog-A-Thon Outstanding Participation Award, and first place writing contest award; [oth. writ.] First place writing contest at my school, "My Hero"; [pers.] Writing poems and stories is my passion. When I grow up I want to be a famous writer and a super model.; [a.] Fresco, CA

HERD, THERESA DIMARCO
[b.] July 23, 1953, Coatesville, PA; [p.] Martha E. DiMarco, Late G. George M. DiMarco Sr.; [m.] Robert J. Herd, June 16, 1985; [ch.] No children of our own but love all children; [ed.] Graduated Downingtown Senior High School Class of 1972, Downingtown, PA; [occ.] Housewife; [pers.] Most of my poems are things that I remember about my childhood. They were such happy days.; [a.] Parkesburg, PA

HERINGTON, ANDREA
[b.] April 21, 1971, Mountain View, CA; [p.] Carl and Doris Herington; [ed.] St. Francis High School, Long Beach State, Fresno State Nursing Program - BSN.; [occ.] Registered Nurse, Huntington Memorial Hospital, Pasadena, CA; [memb.] Sigma Theta Tau International Honor Society of Nursing; [hon.] Dean's List, Sigma Theta Tau; [oth. writ.] Poems in high school paper, Editor on H.S. paper, poems at sister's wedding, and grandfather's, friend's memorials.; [pers.] I use writing as a way to express myself on paper. I like to touch people through my writing.; [a.] Los Altos, CA

HERNANDEZ, DIANE
[b.] March 3, 1978, Hialeah, FL; [p.] Rosmira and Rodolfo Hernandez; [ed.] North Blade Elementary School Perry Middle School Ely High School American School about to attend College.; [occ.] Secretary for a Golf Accessories Manufacturer.; [memb.] Light to the Nations Church Treasurer and Member.; [hon.] Spelling Bee champion, varsity swimming letter, Science ACE award and all around best student in 8th grade science class, Presidential Award Academic Fitness, 10th Grade English Award, Literary Fair 3rd place winner. Many other awards.; [oth. writ.] Several poems, presently working on my first book. One poem published in literary magazine of Ely High School.; [pers.] I strive to portray life in a realistic sense through the use of the imaginary in my writings. I've been inspired by non-traditional, experimental poets, such as Whitman.; [a.] Miramar, FL

HERNANDEZ, JOSE
[b.] August 22, 1976, Los Angeles, CA; [p.] Manuel and Maria Casas; [ed.] Woodlake Union High School; [pers.] Poetry, to me, are words arranged in a way that is pleasing to the mind and to express a certain feeling, to make it understood. My favorite writers are Emily Dickinson, T.S. Eliot and Colette.; [a.] Woodlake, CA

HERRING, JAMES MICHAEL
[pen.] Jim Michaels; [b.] January 16, 1970, Allentown; [p.] David and Donna Herring; [m.] Deana Herring, March 25, 1996; [ch.] Chris and Jean; [ed.] Whitehall - Coplay High School; [occ.] Restaurant Manager; [oth. writ.] No current writings - first publication.; [pers.] I try to make my audience say "Whoa!" about hardships of today's society.; [a.] Coplay, PA

HESTING, VINCENT SHANE
[pen.] White Tornado, Bear Oaks; [b.] July 27, 1967, Smith Center, KS; [p.] Paul and Ruby Hesting; [ed.] White Rock High 1986, Emporia State University (BS 1990), Emporia State University (MS Pending 1997); [occ.] Kansas Wildlife and Parks Research Fisheries Aide and Private Naturalist; [hon.] Dean's list, ESU Honor Roll, Kansas Master Angler, Magna Cum Laude 1990, Four Consecutive Certificates of Appreciation from Division of Biological Sciences, Emporia State University 1986-1990; [oth. writ.] Original news releases published by local newspapers, currently finishing MS thesis titled Abiotic Correlates of Fish Assemblage Structure in Melvern Reservoir, U.S.A., Poem, "Upon Mornings Dew," published by National Library of Poetry in Spirit of the Age (1996); [pers.] I try to interpret the wild and civilized

worlds I live in and how humans and wildlife perceive their lives on earth. Much of my writing is influenced by biology text, music, and what I see, hear, and listen to along old dirt roads, the roads of the will. "Will" is dedicated to my brother, Mat Hesting, who showed a young Shane Hesting the potential benefits available to the soul, hidden within ponds, creeks, and fields.; [a.] Burr Oak, KS

HEUER, ALAN
[b.] June 13, 1958, Munich, Germany; [p.] William Heuer, Jane Heuer; [m.] Kay Hazelip Heuer - Deceased (January 24, 1994), June 18, 1988; [ch.] Jackson and Gemma; [ed.] Bachelor of Arts, University of Wyoming, Master of Music, Brooklyn College Conservatory of Music; [occ.] Computer Consultant; [hon.] Graduated with honors, Cum Laude, Finalist International Clarinet Competition, Small Works Invitational - Blue Mountain Art Gallery - NYC; [oth. writ.] Working on an autobiographical fiction.; [pers.] I never really thought to write until life, death and love reached out and grabbed me by the throat. I really had little choice.; [a.] San Jose, CA

HEYSER, ELIZABETH
[pen.] E. A. Heyser; [b.] October 23, 1940, Conshonocken, PA; [p.] John Rowe, Colette Rowe; [m.] Samuel W. Heyser, November 17, 1962; [ch.] Susan Colette - Linda Marie; [ed.] Archbishop Kennedy High; [occ.] National Membership Director for American Bridal Association in Collegeville, PA; [memb.] Visitation B.V.M. Sodality Sacred Heart Mission League; [hon.] Forensic League; [oth. writ.] Many poems published in local newspapers. Articles written for the American Bridal Association.; [pers.] Knowing my writing brings pleasure to someone and encourages them to see life from a different point of view is the catalyst that makes me want to continue, and hope the link of poetic friendship will never be erased.; [a.] Eagleville, PA

HIGGINS, CHARLOTTE M.
[b.] September 20, 1915, Blanton, TX; [p.] J. E. Montgomery; [m.] Hallie C. Jordan Montgomery, September 16, 1933; [ch.] Eight; [ed.] 10th H. School. I believe in one God; [occ.] House wife; [memb.] Calvary Baptist Church; [hon.] I have 3 Awards from World of Poetry Edited by Eddie Low Cole; [oth. writ.] I have an album my grand daughter typed of my long hand.; [pers.] I am a direct descendent of Daniel Boone, my grandmother Clara T. Boone Jordan was a published poet who went to Baylor when it was Waco, U.

HILL, APRIL
[pen.] April Hill; [b.] February 6, 1980, Anaheim, CA; [p.] Sandra and Ronny Hill; [ed.] Presently Jr. in High School; [memb.] Chorale; [hon.] Chorale Award; [oth. writ.] Various poems; [pers.] My poetry is based on personal conflicts and/or events. I'm influenced by life. I write what I feel at the time.; [a.] White Water, CA

HILL, JOHN
[pen.] John Hill; [b.] June 27, 1932, Memphis, TN; [p.] John Hill Sr. and Edna Hill; [m.] Sandra Sue Hill, February 14, 1993; [ch.] Four: Russell Scott Hill, Stuart Kelley Hill, Tonia Sue Hill, Angela Jacobs; [ed.] Piano - 4 years, Medicine 8 yrs MD., English

Literature 2 yrs; [occ.] Physician; [memb.] AMA, Oklahoma State Med Society, Pittsburg County Med Society, Fellow American Academy of Pediatrics, Fellow American Society of Clinical Pathology, American Academy of Family Practice; [hon.] AMA, CME Award, Certificate of Achievement US Army, Dean's List, Invention of Olympic Bili Lite; [oth. writ.] Hyperbilirabinemia of the Newborn, Pediatric Audiodigest, Photo Therapy of Jaunduid Newborn, Chicago - AAP; [pers.] To me, creativity through art and science is a minute expression of the celestial mind of God and is all we leave behind that lasts forever.; [a.] Millerton, OK

HILLIGOSS, JOHN M.
[pen.] Mountain John; [b.] April 27, 1949, Bartlesville, OK; [p.] Mrs. R. G. Hilligoss; [ed.] Bachelor of Music Education Pittsburg State University Pittsburg Kansas; [occ.] Professional Poet, Musical and Troubador and Story Teller; [hon.] Five albums and one music video; [oth. writ.] Mountain John Poetry Collection #1 (Library of Congress) 5 albums (Music and Poetry), 1 music video (Mountain John Publishing) BMI.; [pers.] People should follow their dreams.; [a.] Champion, PA

HILLS, SARA ELIZABETH
[b.] July 24, 1960, Chicago, IL; [p.] Robert and Bernice Martinez; [m.] Steven Hills, June 15, 1985; [ch.] Samantha Ellen, Kyle Christian; [ed.] AA Degree in Sociology, graduate of Riverside Community College 1991; [occ.] Crisis Counselor (volunteer) at "Help Line" in Riverside; [pers.] This is my first poem ever put on paper. I have many thoughts running through my head from personal life experiences. This inspiration came from my daughter's homework.; [a.] Riverside, CA

HINDS, MICHAEL
[b.] September 22, 1980, Claremore, OK; [p.] Diana Hinds; [occ.] D.J. at Mid-City Skate Center, Claremore, OK; [oth. writ.] Many other unpublished poems; [pers.] Let your dreams carry you through life, don't let reality depress you.; [a.] Claremore, OK

HITT, MARY JO
[b.] June 10, 1981, Warrenton, VA; [p.] Mary Imhoff and Shirley Hitt; [ed.] Sophomore at Jefferson Cty High School; [memb.] Future Business Leaders of America, St. Thomas Evangelical Lutheran Church; [hon.] Excellence in English Award, Straight Honor Roll; [a.] Harpers Ferry, WV

HODGE, KATRINA
[b.] August 18, 1964, Corning, NY; [p.] Naia and Richard Hodge; [ch.] Noel Francis; [ed.] (GED) From the University of Texas, a degree in Auto cad Drafting from ATI Career Training Center; [occ.] Care Giver of the Disabled; [pers.] The format of my poem was based on actual knowledge. My child inspired this poem, for he is the Autistic child.; [a.] Caddo, TX

HOFF, JILL A.
[pen.] J. A. Hoff, Jill A. Hoff; [b.] July 25, 1973, York, PA; [p.] Timothy and Joanna Hoff; [ed.] Dover Area High School, Penn State University, University of Idaho; [occ.] Wildlife Biologist; [memb.] Wolf Education and Research, Center, University of Idaho's Student Chapter of the Wildlife Society; [hon.] Isaac Walton League Schol-

arship, Who's Who in America's Junior Colleges, Dean's List (University of Idaho); [oth. writ.] Plenty of other writings, but I haven't had any published.; [pers.] "Be Aware of Wonder" - Robert Fulghum, My influences derive from early and more modern surrealists. William Blake, Edgar Allen Poe, Jim Morrison.; [a.] Moscow, ID

HOFFMAN, DIANNA
[b.] July 10, 1943, Moline, IL; [p.] Floyd and Elizabeth Donner; [m.] Nelon Hoffman, January 20, 1990; [ch.] 2 from previous marriage; [ed.] Bachelor of Science in Business from California State University, Long Beach, CA; [occ.] Run my own company, Monad Internat'l and Pacific Guardian

HOFFMANN, LEIF BIRGER
[b.] March 21, 1975, Gelsem Kirchen, Germany; [p.] Hoffmann Erma-Luise and Rolf; [ed.] Stadtischess Gymnasium Henten, School exchange wits the comprehensive school on Banchory, Scotland, language classe: in Vichy, France, and on Malta, Semester of I. ernational Relations and Business English at Clackamas Community College; [occ.] Student of European Studies at Osmabruck University; [hon.] Several times member of the student body and Vice-President, DELF (Diplomas of French) from the French Cultural Ministry, Honor of Award as youngest participant of the Ruhrqebiet History Contest; [oth. writ.] "Hier ist es ein Cibchenanders" - Documentary about Russian immigrants of German descent in Herten, History Zeche Schlagel E Eisen, Co-author of documentary film about Auschwitz; [pers.] "But whosoever shall smite thee on thy right cheek, turn to him the other also." Mt. 5:39; [a.] Herten, Germany

HOLLIER, ANTHONY DAVID
[b.] July 31, 1981, Lafayette, LA; [p.] Vickie Hollier Lukaszeski and David Hollier (Deceased), Joseph Lukaszeski; [ed.] 8 yrs. Breaux Bridge Junior High School; [hon.] 2nd place in Young Author's contest in St. Martin Parish for the poem, "Dear Dad", National Torrance Test Creative Scholar; [pers.] I write just to write. I wrote this poem for extra points for my Language teacher, Mary Anthony and Art teacher, Deidre Robertson; [a.] Breaux Bridge, LA

HOLLON, DAN
[b.] May 30, 1957, Middletown, OH; [p.] James and Ada Hollon; [ch.] Crystal Hollon; [ed.] Miami University Oxford, Ohio; [occ.] Carpenter; [oth. writ.] I have a collection of material that I have penned. To date this is the first and hopefully not the last that will be published.; [pers.] Most of my poems are inspired by real life situations. Started writing in 1986 after a tragic accident killed my sister Regina Hollon, who was in every sense of the word a poet. This is dedicated to Regina.; [a.] Monroe, OH

HOLMAN, RENE
[pen.] Rene Holman; [b.] September 26, 1950, Milwaukee, WI; [p.] Ralph and Genevieve Monson; [m.] Michael B. Holman, August 27, 1972; [ch.] Shawn Michael and Jesse Allen Holman; [ed.] Custer High School; [occ.] Housewife, Mother, School Volunteer, active in Ministry; [memb.] Member of Gonzalez Congregation of Jehovah's witnesses; [hon.] Have re-

ceived many school volunteer Awards through the years; [oth. writ.] Many songs and poems, but none published; [pers.] Writing is a great therapy for whatever ails you and for expressing one's self. Mankind is indeed blessed, when properly using pen and paper.; [a.] Fantonment, FL

HOLMES, LINDA
[b.] November 26, 1959, Fall River, MA; [p.] Lee and Gene Lynch; [m.] Phil Holmes, January 12, 1985; [ed.] B.A. Elementary Education from the University of Central Florida; [occ.] First grade teacher, Palm lake Elementary, Orlando, Fl; [hon.] Teacher of the year 1992 -93 school year, Kappa Delta Pi, Education Honor Society, graduated Magan Cum Laude; [a.] Howey in the Hills, FL

HOLTGREWE, ANDREA M.
[b.] May 26, 1973, Decatur, IL; [p.] Ron and Judy Holtgrewe; [ed.] University of Nebraska-Lincoln, Lincoln Southeast High School; [occ.] Elementary School Teacher in Lincoln, NE; [memb.] Daughters of Union Veterans of the Civil War, Grace Lutheran Church, National Education Association; [hon.] Junior Youth Orchestra, Lincoln Youth Symphony, University Orchestra, NMEA Piano Competition (superior rating), Senior Soloist Finalist on Violin, University Dean's List; [oth. writ.] Unpublished short stories and other poetry. Unpublished children's book More Than Meets The Eye.; [pers.] I write to try to understand life and to motivate myself to reach my goals. I have been inspired by S. King, R. Bradbury, and M. L'Engle.; [a.] Lincoln, NE

HOLZINGER, MARY
[b.] May 1, 1962, Clifton Forge, VA; [p.] Paul and Martha Boucher; [m.] Ronald R. Holzinger, March 29, 1983; [ch.] Coral and Kera; [occ.] V.S. Coast Guard - Civil Service; [hon.] Department of Transportation's Award for Excellence, Department of Transportation's Award For Customer Service (Team Award); [oth. writ.] I write a lot of poetry - but this will be the first one ever published.; [pers.] As my parents told me, "Life can only be what you want it to be." I've been blessed with parents who hold a lot of knowledge and love and it is them who I gain a lot of strength from.; [a.] Petaluma, CA

HOMMA, MARY
[b.] September 9, 1956, Salt Lake City, UT; [p.] Stacey Robb Reed Sr., Elsie Reed; [m.] Michael M. Homma, May 2, 1986; [ch.] Merlaine, Myles, Mark, Matthew, Miko, Mikie; [pers.] I love to put the emotions of day-to-day life and the trials, tribulations, joys, heartaches, etc. of family, friends, peers and/or myself into poetic form. It relaxes me and makes the recipient "feel" what I write.; [a.] Broken Arrow, OK

HORTON, SHARAH T.
[b.] January 10, 1972, Livingston, NJ; [p.] Clarence Horton and Viola Horton; [ed.] Bachelor of Arts in Loyola University Philosophy. Currently seeking a Masters of Public Administration University of New Orleans; [occ.] Administrative Assistant - Farnet Hart Design Graphics Studio, Inc New Orleans Louisiana; [memb.] Delta Chi Omega Sorority Alumni, Art Directions and Designers Association New Orleans, American Diabetes As-

sociation, Juvenile Diabetes Foundation; [oth. writ.] Several short stories and poems for pleasure and sharing.; [pers.] I have always believed that human emotions, especially love, happiness and friendship are the greatest inspirations for writing and the creative arts.; [a.] New Orleans, LA

HOUCK, RYAN CRAIG
[pen.] Harvester of Sorrow; [b.] June 28, 1978, Webster, TX; [p.] Robert C. Houck, Vivian C. Muskovits; [ed.] High School Graduate; [oth. writ.] I have other writings but none have been published yet.; [pers.] This is clearly not my best writing. My best writing comes from my heart. I simply close my eyes and let my pen and heart take over.; [a.] League City, TX

HOULE, BRIAN F.
[b.] September 30, 1957, Sea, WA; [p.] Ronald James Houle, Darlene Louise Abraham; [m.] Rosalba Dominguez Lira, June 10, 1990; [ch.] Rose Eileen and Gariel; [ed.] H.S.; [occ.] Self-emp.; [oth. writ.] "The Amen," "Coops Flesh is The Wheat, His Blood the Wine," "Eat and Drink Truth"; [pers.] Onward to eternity! The earth itself is but a grain of sand upon the shore of the Heavenly Father's ever-expanding kingdom.; [a.] La Vergne, TN

HOUSTON, BILLIE
[pen.] Barri Bryan; [b.] November 24, 1927, Lehman, TX; [p.] Carl and Lucille Yeary; [m.] M. H. Houston, June 2, 1943; [ch.] Carlene, Michael, Robert; [ed.] AA-San Antonio College, BA-UTSA - MA-UTSA six teacher certifications; [occ.] Writer; [memb.] Austin Writer's League Romance Writer's of America, San Antonio Romance Authors (SARA); [hon.] Editor's Choice Awards '94, '95 and '96. Editor's Challenge award '95 and '96 2nd place in rhymed poetry by-Liners award. 3rd place Brazos writers short story contest - 1st place Stone Flower Quarterly '96 contest; [oth. writ.] Novels, poetry, anthology, essays, short stories; [a.] Von Ormy, TX

HOWARD, NIKKI JEAN
[pen.] Nikki Howard; [b.] September 20, 1980, Kinston, NC; [p.] Linda and Danny Howard; [ed.] 10th grade High School Student; [occ.] Student; [hon.] Trident Academy S.C. - Poem Writing; [pers.] Am dyslexic, love to read and write, education - South Lenior HS, NC Trident Academy SC parents Linda and Danny Howard Brother Greg Howard, Music - Saxophone, Piano, Voice.; [a.] Kinston, NC

HOWE JR., RALPH S.
[pen.] R. S. Howe Jr.; [b.] March 8, 1926, New Britain, CT; [m.] Nancy F. Howe, May 16, 1953; [ch.] Jonathan, Timothy and Elizabeth; [ed.] B.S. Yale U., R.P.I. Management Development; [occ.] Retired-former Vice Pres. of Fafnir Bearing Co.; [memb.] Corporator - New Britain General Hospital and New Britain Boys and Girls Club, Chairman - Board of Trustees First Church of Christ - New Britain, Former Chairman - Mooreland Hill School Board of Trustees; [hon.] 18 issued a U.S. patents which are in my name as inventor. This may explain some creativity - invention is part art part science in my view.; [oth. writ.] Several technical articles in trade magazines.; [pers.] In my view a short poem provides a unique opportunity for the

author to present forcefully and succinctly to the reader his/her inner feelings based on experience and observation.; [a.] New Britain, CT

HOWELL, SHANEE
[b.] May 14, 1982, Baltimore, MD; [p.] Victor Howell and Tonette Howell; [ed.] Graduated from Amelia County Middle School. Attending 9th Grade at Amelia County High School in the Fall.; [hon.] I won the grand prize in the Richmond Braves Essay Contest (a computer). I won a trophy for 3rd place with my debate speech.; [pers.] Writing comes naturally to me. My experiences and my imagination help me to write stories and poems. I love writing. Writing is my life.; [a.] Amelia, VA

HOY, CHAD
[pen.] Chad Hoy; [b.] July 20, 1972, Pottsville, PA; [p.] Carl and Carol Hoy; [ed.] Tri-Valley High School, Penn College of Technology, 2 years - Print Media and Broadcast Media; [occ.] Hershey Park; [hon.] 1989 Schuylkill Co., Writers Award, 1st place; [oth. writ.] Evil - Winner of Schuylkill County Award; [pers.] I enjoy reading and writing since early childhood. Words are a great source of learning and relaxation.; [a.] Valley View, PA

HOYNE, JAMES J.
[b.] January 22, 1960, Manhasset, NY; [p.] Evelyn Hoyne; [m.] DeeAnn, June 29, 1996; [ch.] Rhiannon, Kyle and Torri; [ed.] 4 yrs College B.S., 4 yrs Medical School, 3 yrs Residency; [occ.] Family Physician; [oth. writ.] Five other poems.; [pers.] Pursue excellence, embrace diversity, seek integrity, love or courage, conscious and sacrifice, and love with all your heart.; [a.] Roseburg, OR

HUBER, JANET L.
[b.] July 22, 1947, Lancaster, PA; [p.] Daniel and Esther Shenk; [m.] Robert L. Huber, April 8, 1978; [ch.] Jennifer L. Huber; [ed.] High School graduate; [occ.] Secretary/State Farm Insurance for 27 years; [memb.] Central Manor Church of God of Washington Boro, PA and serve on the Women's Ministry Committee; [hon.] I had submitted this poem in April 1991, to the World of Poetry Sacramento, California. It was a free contest and I received Honorable Mention, I'm thrilled that you want to print it, I think it is worth sharing with the world.; [pers.] This poem came about as a result of a poetry contest our office held on Valentine's Day, 1991, however, due to disinterest, it never came about. These words came to me one night when I could not sleep because of struggling with issues. It expresses my faith in God and His Son, Jesus.; [a.] Lancaster, PA

HUGHES, CONSTANCE
[b.] May 9, 1922, Saint Louis, MO; [p.] Lenna M. and Emmanuel Peden; [m.] John J. Hughes, January 14, 1945; [ch.] Carole Evelyn and John Joseph; [ed.] High School; [occ.] Retired; [oth. writ.] Too many to list; [pers.] It was never my intention to profit from my writings. It was only a means of expression.; [a.] Ferguson, MO

HULBERT, FRANK A.
[b.] October 7, 1941, Oklahoma City, OK; [p.] William P. and Mavis C. Hulbert Jr.; [m.] Brenda Ann (Flowers) Hulbert, July 15, 1961; [ch.] Frank

Angus Jr. and Arthur Harold; [ed.] Waco High, attended Tex. A. and M., Career NCO, USAF, Ret.; [occ.] Cattle Rancher; [memb.] Parks Southern Baptist Church, American Radio Relay League, Life Member National Rifle Assoc., American Legion; [oth. writ.] Local news articles; [pers.] Study hard, work hard, pray hard and enjoy God's blessings. Remember, "The world doesn't owe you a living".; [a.] Parks, AR

HUNTER, DEANNE R.
[pen.] De; [b.] January 7, 1965, Elkhart, IN; [p.] Richard Stewart, Val Simon; [m.] Paul M. Hunter, September 3, 1993; [ch.] 1 Great Dane - Lady and 5 cats - Hayes, Buttwheat, Steven, Bodhi and Kodhi; [ed.] Graduate of: Northridge High School Middlebury, IN; [occ.] Production Employee - hope to become Professional Writer; [oth. writ.] I have written many poems that cover a wide range of topics and emotions. I have written one children's short story. And I am currently working on a psychological thriller that I hope to make my first published book.; [pers.] I acquired my love for poetry and writing from my father. He spent time reading poetry and books to me when I was a child. I am especially fond of Native American poetry and culture.; [a.] Lawton, MI

HUNTLEY, TINA
[b.] May 10, 1960, Newton, KS; [p.] Lydia Owens; [ed.] 3 yrs. College for Computer Design; [occ.] Motorola Inc.; [memb.] American Heart Assoc., Motorola ERT; [oth. writ.] Publications in Local Women's Magazines, Windows of the Soul, Best of 96'; [pers.] I love writing poetry. It gives happiness to others and gives me great satisfaction. I write of life's experiences and feelings from within.; [a.] Chandler, AZ

HURLBURT, JAMES H.
[b.] June 4, 1918, Boston, MA; [p.] Deceased: Mary Charlotte/Melbourne Hurlburt; [m.] Alice C. Hurlburt, April 15, 1944; [ch.] Geraldine, Dennis, Robert Hurlburt; [ed.] Dorchester High School Graduate. Some junior College/Southwestern Jr. College, San Diego Area - Creative Writing and Art Classes with Art Show Displays; [occ.] Retired - from U.S. Navy 24 years/as CPO and 17 years from San Diego City School District; [memb.] Sea 'n Air Golf Club, (Men's) North Island Naval Air Station-Coronado CA; [hon.] Navy Unit Commendation (Retrieval of Lost Hydrogen Bomb at Palomares Bay, Spain); [oth. writ.] Technical articles in National Publications. Editor of Shipboard Publication Cruise books and other, US - Navy Wide.; [pers.] I sincerely look for the good things in life and in people. What little I can do to help this along gives me some satisfaction.; [a.] National City, CA

HUSS, BILL
[m.] Marlene; [ch.] Matthew Charlyn, Damon; [ed.] University of Southern California; [occ.] Writer; [pers.] We are awash in words, in books, magazines, newspapers, radio, television and movies. Some of us should take the responsibility of trying to write with significance.; [a.] Los Angeles, CA

HUTCHESON, JANET R. K., M.D.
[b.] February 21, 1934, New York City; [p.] Ida and John Kauderer; [m.] Robert H. Hutcheson, Jr (Divorced 1974), Eugene Streicher, August 9,

1979; [ch.] Jonathan E. Hutcheson; [ed.] BA -- Barnard College, 1955, MD -- University of Tennessee, 1959, Residency Radiology, Vanderbilt University, 1961-1965; [occ.] Retired radiologist; [oth. writ.] Published in professional journals, letter to the Washington Post, Dr. Gridlock; [pers.] I love the Romantic poets, especially Keats.; [a.] Bethesda, MD

HUTCHINS, ROBERT HAROLD
[pen.] Zarathustra; [b.] August 30, 1941, Decora, IA; [p.] Eugene, Irene Hutchins; [m.] Buneti (1962), Ellen (1970); [ch.] Trina (33); [ed.] Algona A.S. 1959 Amer Inst of Bus. 1960-1961 Russian U of Ind Cosaer BA Germani Schiller Cob, Heidelburg from St. Paris, Ph MAST U of Heidelburg, Ga MP Act Iowa St. V.; [occ.] Iowa Notary Germanlinguist-Tea/Translate; [memb.] Amer. Sec. Notaries VFM - Amer. Translators Assn. (Assoc.) - Church of Christ 95-96 International Society of Poetry; [hon.] 1980 Iowa Gov's Volunteer Award 90's 1980-81 Alaskan Pipeline Trans were Gernam Technical of Fischer Control Ints. Marshall Tran, Ia, Floyd Hartdoom Co., Mark Hinzelman Tech Libr.; [oth. writ.] Heidelburg Castles, Break Up of Soviet Union - 1968, MPA at Iowa State Univ. It DSM Church of Christ HEJS Noah - 'Be Ready!' Political Hilarious screaming satire; [pers.] Give and it will be given to you again. Jesus Lord gives and serves out of love, give of your talents, time, knowledge and resources. Jesus Is Lord and coming soon.; [a.] Des Moines, IA

ILIC, JULIE
[b.] December 18, 1957, San Jose, CA; [m.] Milisav Ilic, August 8, 1993; [hon.] Honorable Mention 1996- Aesthetics of Archetypes for Carl Cherry Center of the Arts (Carmel, CA); [oth. writ.] "The Painful Dance," "The Bondage of Love," "The Pain of Joy," "Abstraction," "Changes," where published on an internet poetry journal.; [pers.] I love to express myself through poetry about the affairs of the heart, pain, joy and hope.; [a.] Marina, CA

INKS, JACQUELINE
[b.] August 24, 1953, Washington, PA; [p.] Grace Davis, William Dombreck; [m.] Durward A. Inks, July 3, 1994; [ch.] Brice and Brent Hostutler; [ed.] Trinity High, Edinboro, CCAC; [occ.] R. A. Fogg Sales, Artist; [memb.] Blackhorse Trail Artists; [hon.] Different Drummer Cover Design 1989; [oth. writ.] Patriots, Arizona Christmas Edition; [a.] Gibbon Glade, PA

ISENMAN, PATRICIA
[b.] September 3, 1952, Missouri; [p.] Mr. and Mrs. Walter Weiler Jr.; [m.] Charles Isenman, June 13, 1970; [ch.] Brian, Greg, Thomas, Christina, Barb; [ed.] Farmington, High, Farmington, MO, Attended MAC for a while, very deep Christian Ed., Some Nursing; [occ.] Disabled physically-still can write!; [oth. writ.] Started writing when I was 14. Altogether I've written close to 1,500 poems, lyrics and short stories.; [pers.] God gives us many talents, if we do not use them we will not receive anymore. I thank God for all the talents He's given me and for my wonderful family.; [a.] Sainte Genevieve, MO

IWIG, LISA J.
[b.] August 14, 1969, Denver, CO; [m.] Steven C. Iwig, November 7, 1992; [ch.] Jacob Thomas; [ed.] North Valley High; [pers.] Wherever you go, there you are.; [a.] San Diego, CA

IWIN, KENNETH COLE
[b.] April 18, 1979, Birmingham, AL; [p.] Ken and LuAnne Iwin; [ed.] Currently a Junior at Carbon Hill High School; [occ.] Student; [hon.] Named All-American Scholar by The United States Achievement Academy; [a.] Nauvoo, AL

JACKSON, BARBARA BENICE MILES
[pen.] B. Miles Jackson; [b.] June 24, 1948, Fort Worth, TX; [p.] C. B. Miles and Maybelle Dugan Miles; [m.] Divorce; [ch.] Tracy D. Jackson; [ed.] I.M. Ferrell - Class of 1966; [occ.] Head Start - Day Care Association Ft. Worth and Tauant County; [memb.] Cater Metropolitan CME church; [hon.] State Employee of the year for 1990, (State of Tex. Dept. of Human Services) - Usher of the Year (Carter Metropolitan); [oth. writ.] Poetry - Atmospheric Conditions, Go Your Way, Ancient of Day, Silent Voices, A Sign, Void of Time, Be Sure, Answer, Keep, Times, Changing Times, Listen and See, The House On Southcrest, Verses - Death Comes at God's Will; [pers.] In Great times of sorrow and sadness - look up and know.; [a.] Forth Worth, TX

JACKSON, J. J.
[b.] February 18, 1944, So. Carolina; [ch.] Crystal and Mesheba; [ed.] B.A. English, 1978, Univ. Massachusetts/Boston; [occ.] Former high school teacher now owner/manager of auto repair shop.; [pers.] I always try to be fair and to acknowledge everyone I meet as an equal human being.; [a.] Santa Paula, CA

JACKSON, PAULA RAMONA
[pen.] Paula, Paula Jackson; [p.] Robert and Mary Jackson; [ed.] M.S.W. in Human Services; [occ.] Family Crisis Intervention Specialist; [memb.] Cancer Society, NAACP, National Association for the Education of Young Children, Christian Awareness; [hon.] Leaders Of Tomorrow All Hearts Association, Black Heritage Leadership, Sisters of the Struggle; [oth. writ.] 1) If God Was A Woman, 2) Thru The Eyes Of The Struggle, 3) Me And 'Eggbutt', 4) Ain't Your Mama On The Pancake Box?, 5) Leavin' Home; [pers.] I try to reflect the innermost feelings of people in struggle. I especially relate to and express feelings of the African American Woman.; [a.] Temple Hills, MD

JACKSON, PENELOPE DAVIDSON
[pen.] Penelope Davidson Jackson; [b.] November 7, 1969, Hamilton, OH; [p.] Lois J. Clark and James E. Davidson; [m.] Barry Lynn Jackson, September 1, 1995; [ch.] Lauren Marie Craig; [ed.] My Grandfather, Alden "Red" Davidson, was the teacher who taught me the most. The woods was my favorite "classroom."; [occ.] As I strive, to become a writer and photographer, there can be no room for a "typical" occupation.; [oth. writ.] At this time, I am working on a "Dog Care" book I have a collection of poetry that makes statements and tells stories. Articles are also in the works.; [pers.] When "one's" life is based on conveniences and the short cuts to success, one can lose the valuable experiences that can only be learned on the long road....; [a.] Sunman, IN

JACKSON, SALLY A.
[b.] May 8, 1929, New York City; [ch.] Paula Murray-Walter and Andrew W. Murray; [ed.] William Cullen Bryant H.S., courses Suffolk Community College, continuing education courses chosen for variety and inspiration.; [occ.] Retired School of Dental Medicine, State University, Stony Brook, NY, presently writing poetry, Oil Painting major endeavors; [memb.] Taught Sunday School, Girl Scout Leader (retired), Member of the National Library of Poetry, International Society of Poets; [hon.] Several poems published in local newspaper. Original poem published by the National Library of Poetry, "Beyond the Stars" anthology, 1995. Inclusion in Best poems of 1996, anthology from the International Society of Poets. Both poems selected for the "Sound of Poetry" tape. Editor's Choice Award, 1995. Guest Poetry Reader since being published in NLP and ISP; [pers.] Themes relating to love, life and nature built around the philosophy of Kahil Gibran have been a major influence. My observations and testimonies reflect my enthusiasm and excitement with living. Many years ago I wrote "Vision is not only the camera in one's eye - but the reflector of one's heart." When the poet writes is when one is invited into his soul. I am elated, honored and privileged that you like my poetry enough to publish it. My poetry is dedicated to my loving family who have always been a treasure of inspiration, and my gratefulness to NLP and ISP for making all this possible.; [a.] Long Island, NY

JACKSON, SHARON E.
[b.] November 30, 1943, Ohio; [p.] John and Edna Clouston; [m.] Carl A. Jackson, November 30, 1990; [ch.] Five; [ed.] High School/Business/College Courses; [occ.] Writer; [hon.] Compassionate Friends (Leader of Mesa/Tempe Chapter for 5 years); [oth. writ.] "Help Yourself...Love, Mom" publisher: Rainbow Books, Inc. Highland City, Florida. Self-help for young adults, single or married. From devising a budget, to Mom's favorite recipes, to making friends and setting goals, this practical guide has all the advice you used to groan over as a teen, but becomes invaluable as an adult.; [pers.] Never give up on yourself or your dreams. Life holds untraveled dreams, bridges to cross, friends to be made, blessings to receive, a 'difference to make,' and rainbows to build. Patience and persistence pay!; [a.] Mesa, AZ

JACKSON, THOMAS
[pen.] Thomas Jackson; [b.] April 30, 1976, Worcester, MA; [p.] Paul and Linda Jackson; [ed.] Worcester Voke Trade H.S. Culinary Arts; [occ.] Freshman Culinary Arts Degree Program - New Hampshire College; [hon.] Student of the Month Teresa Picknic Mem. Alumni Award I.B.P.O. Scholarship; [oth. writ.] 67 songs - such as "Lady", "Intended Love", "Simple Boy", "Loneliness", "Running Alone", all not published.; [pers.] I saw this beautiful girl in my H.S. Freshman Class and her name was Michelle. Everything about her influenced this poem. Her eyes, the way she moves, the way she was so kind. I needed to put into words how I felt about this special girl named Michelle.; [a.] Worcester, MA

JACKSON, VERTA
[b.] September 8, 1928, Carbondale, IL; [p.] Floyd Jones, Lucy Jones; [m.] Allen V. Jackson (Deceased 1988), January 25, 1947; [ch.] Sandra Aileene,

Duane Allen; [ed.] Carbondale High Courses John A. Jr.; [occ.] Retired Clerk Cashier, volunteer Carbondale Hospital; [memb.] First Baptist Church Hospital Aux.; [hon.] 1,000 hours Hospital Vol.; [pers.] 1989 had a near death experience with Lymphomo (cancer). Started writing poetry, forced to retire (Illness). God's true gifts are life and love for others.; [a.] Carterville, IL

JAHELKA, ANNETTE J.
[b.] July 1, 1940, Brooklyn, NY; [p.] Frank Zanfardino, Filomena Zanfardino; [m.] Raymond J. Jahelka, April 29, 1961; [ch.] Joseph Raymond Jahelka, Renee Ann Jahelka; [ed.] New Utrecht H.S.

JAMES, RAY ALLAN
[pen.] Jones; [b.] May 31, 1958, Wichita Falls, TX; [p.] Ray H. James and Betty Lile; [ed.] B.S. Mgmt/ Minor in PSY, January 26, 1990, (Univ. of Maryland), Heidelberg W. Germany, Assoc. Arts Degree, 1987 (Univ. Of Maryland); [occ.] Owner Operator (FFE), Psychic - (PRN); [memb.] President's Health SPA, Copyright Protected with Lib. of Congress - "The Do's and Don'ts of Numerology," and Democratic Nat. Committee, and Dem. Senatorial Committee; [hon.] Rated top 2% of all poets 1993, 1994, 1995, 1996. The Editor's Choice Award. Distinguished Poet Awards, Outstanding Poet of 94, 95, and 96, Best Poem of the 90's; [oth. writ.] Lyrics to "The Wild, Wild West," "You're All I Got," "Looking For Love," "My Eye's On You," and "Our Heavenly Father.", The I American Dream, Vision I, II, III,; [pers.] Singers like Garth Brooks, George Strait, Dolly Parton, and Paul Overstreet are the type of stars that could "make my day." They are welcome to record with me.; [a.] Wichita Falls, TX

JANDREAU, DIANA
[b.] March 4, 1966, Huntington, WV; [p.] Jack Estep, Erma Estep; [m.] John A. Jandreau, March 4, 1985; [ch.] Jacqueline, Johnny, Loriann, Tony; [ed.] Rose State College; [occ.] Office Clerk, Warehouse Market, Oklahoma City; [hon.] Rose State College President's Honor Roll; [pers.] Never be afraid to show your feelings.; [a.] Del City, OK

JANSSENS, JACQUELYNNE J.
[pen.] Jackie Salley, JJ, Jackie Janssens; [b.] February 28, 1970, La Mesa, CA; [p.] Rick and Debbe Salley; [m.] Dan R. Janssens, July 4, 1992; [ed.] Central Valley High School, Shasta Jr. College; [occ.] Self Employed; [pers.] "Time to Sleep" was written for my grandfather who was ill with cancer several months before he passed away. In those months, a special bond was formed between him, my mom and the rest of my family. Together we learned that death and dying was not something to fear or to be disgusted by, that it would actually be a sweet and beautiful experience. Also, someday, perhaps sooner than later, we will all be given our "Time to Sleep." So for now we must live each day of our life as if it was the last one. This poem was written for "Grangree," from my mom's heart, through my words, to your ears.; [a.] Redding, CA

JARAMILLO, JAMIE G.
[b.] April 6, 1976, Denver, CO; [memb.] World CARP Academy/The Holy Spirit Association for the Unification of World Christianity/Volunteers of America; [pers.] In order to give true love, you must first realize what true love is.

JASMER, LUCILLE BUHR
[pen.] Lucille Buhr Jasmer; [b.] March 4, 1947, Mt. Angel, OR; [p.] Henry Buhr, Rose Buhr; [m.] July 6, 1968; [ch.] Lynn Patrick, Henry Allan Jasmer; [ed.] Gervais High School; [occ.] Housewife; [hon.] C'ber of the year; [oth. writ.] I keep diaries. Wrote for the Lebanon express newspapers. Wrote club, city newspapers a poem was published in newspapers; [pers.] I enjoy writing. It brings the innermost out of myself. To be able to share it with others, makes the words come alive more.; [a.] Salem, OR

JAUS, KIMBERLY A.
[b.] May 30, 1983, Pomerado Hosp.; [p.] Gary and Aida Jaus; [ed.] Through seventh grade, still continuing; [occ.] Student; [memb.] Clairemont Lutheran Church and Youth Choir; [hon.] Two silver medals won in figure skating events.; [oth. writ.] Year poem, The Tiniest Sound; [pers.] "It feels totally natural, writing poetry. It is a lot of fun!"; [a.] Poway, CA

JENKINS, LISA BETH
[b.] February 1, 1955, Angola, IN; [p.] Alva L. Chaney (Deceased); [m.] Norma E. Chaney, Divorced; [ch.] Megan Elizabeth age 7; [ed.] Leo High School, Leo, IN; [oth. writ.] Book called Treasures of the Spirit, several poems published in local newspaper.; [pers.] Reflecting the sentiment of Saint Paul in 2nd Corinthians, I lovingly share my poetry with my readers as written not with ink, but with the Spirit of the living God.; [a.] Angola, IN

JENKINS, SHARON KAY
[b.] May 2, 1947, Oklahoma City, OK; [p.] C. L. Johnny, Betty Jean Duncan; [m.] Jack Dempsey Jenkins, April 3, 1965; [ch.] Jack Darryl, Chad Allan Jenkins; [ed.] Pryor High, Oklahoma State Board of Cosmetology, Medication Administration Technician, Sunday School Teacher Special Ed.; [occ.] Housewife, mother, hairdresser; [memb.] Windsor Hills Baptist Church; [hon.] "Most Pleasing Personality" 10th grade class of 62-63 High School T and I Sweetheart Attendant Class of 62-63 "Miss Pryor Contest" 1963; [oth. writ.] A couple of poems not published; [pers.] My writing is soul inspiring, faith in God, love for others, life and truth, wanting to give "Glory To God" and comfort to others, brings joy into my life.; [a.] Oklahoma City, OK

JENNETT, SHIRLEY L.
[b.] January 14, 1933, Sandpoint, ID; [p.] Alvin, Gwendolyn Gehrke; [m.] Joseph E. Jennett (Deceased), February 15, 1970; [ch.] Pamela Jean, David LeRoy, Michael Jon, and Lisa Diane; [ed.] Central Valley High School; [occ.] Retired Human Resources Manager; [oth. writ.] One poem published in military base paper and also in various church bulletins.; [pers.] I've always enjoyed reading and collecting poetry. I started writing when my husband was in Vietnam - from loneliness and my deep faith in God!; [a.] Veradale, WA

JENNINGS, BRENDAN
[pen.] Jennings; [b.] September 11, 1979, Ft. Stewart, GA; [p.] Patricia Furlong, Thomas Jennings; [ed.] Junior at Highland Regional High School, Graduating in 1997, a summer course at Hussian School of Art in Phila., PA; [occ.] Salesperson at Sater's School of Music; [memb.] High-

land Writing Club, Amnesty International; [hon.] Winner of Highland's 95-96 Photography Contest, Published Artist; [oth. writ.] Blue Tunnel, Soar and Bleed and You Shouldn't Have. Also several untitled works that will probably never see the light of day; [pers.] Anger, rage, and a good vocabulary can make anyone seem like a good writer. I think that those with a true gift will either become legendary or go through life completely unnoticed.; [a.] Erial, NJ

JENNINGS, SCOTT
[b.] March 17, 1977, S.F.; [p.] Brian Jennings, Betty Kurke; [ed.] High School, starting college; [memb.] Lacrosse Foundation; [hon.] Various Sports and Academic Awards i.e., Golden State Exams in Science and History; [pers.] If you're gonna do the job do it right.; [a.] Mill Valley, CA

JOHNSON, ALICIA LYNN
[b.] October 26, 1980, Shawnee, OK; [p.] Bruce and Elaine Johnson; [m.] Zachariah Whitaker (Soon to be); [ed.] I went to Kemper Military School of Boonville, MO., for 2 years; [occ.] Studying; [memb.] Nicoma Park, Baptist Church; [hon.] In elementary school I won at least a poetry contest or a drawing contest. I won 1st place at 2 local spelling Bees. I was on the Dean's List at Military School; [oth. writ.] This is actually the first National Poetry contest I've entered.; [pers.] I always try to reflect my most inner thoughts in what I write.; [a.] Oklahoma City, OK

JOHNSON, ELAINE VIOLA
[b.] July 1, 1958, Minot, ND; [p.] Viola Zablotney; [ed.] High School - 3 1/2 years college in Psychology and Social Work, and Business; [occ.] Own business; [memb.] Disabled American Veterans Salvation Army Church; [hon.] Five year volunteer work for the Veterans Administration, (have gotten Certificates every year.); [oth. writ.] Have written a lot of poetry, but never published in a book. Newsletters and news papers only.; [pers.] The biggest gift is to love ourselves and each other; if you've learned that, you've found God.; [a.] Lubbock, TX

JOHNSON, GREGORY E.
[pen.] G. E. Johnson; [b.] July 30, 1957, Falconer, NY; [p.] Rennie and Veronica Johnson; [m.] Kim E. Johnson, September 9, 1978; [ch.] Sarah E. Johnson, Krista M. Johnson; [ed.] Graduate of Washingtonville H.S., Washingtonville, NY; [occ.] Motor Equipment Operator for the Town of Goshen, NY; [oth. writ.] Many various love and relationship poems. Inspirational prayers.; [pers.] Love is a bond that should never be broken, for true love is a virtue only God can take control of.; [a.] Chester, NY

JOHNSON, LARNITA
[pen.] Alexus Waters; [b.] December 25, 1977, Jackson, MS; [p.] Mr. Percy Johnson, Mrs. Rosie P. Johnson; [ed.] Just graduated from High School getting ready to start College in the fall.; [hon.] Creative Writings Awards, Science Awards; [oth. writ.] I have written several other poems and a few fables; [pers.] I have been influenced by my mother, father, and siblings Antonio, Percy, Venessa, and Marcus. I write best when around family.; [a.] Jackson, MS

JOHNSON, LOIS BERYL
[b.] January 20, 1940, Cloquet; [occ.] Housewife; [hon.] Award of Merit certificate - For poem Do People Have Hearts Any More - Nov. 1988, Golden Poet Award in Appreciation - same poem, 1989, through World of Poetry; [oth. writ.] You already have my poem, The Rapist And His Victims. Here's One More; [pers.] I have been writing poetry since about age 11, I had a teacher tell me I could have been a poet. I love writing poetry. I believe a person should write what you feel is true and right from your heart. My inspiration is the Lord.; [a.] Cloquet, MN

JOHNSON, LYNETTE J.
[b.] May 18, 1958, Youngstown, OH; [p.] Harold Johnson Sr. and Gracie Johnson; [ed.] South High School, Ohio State University, Cleveland State University; [oth. writ.] Several poems, some published in local newspapers. A novel in process. A play in process.; [pers.] Ignorance limits growth, education opens the door to the world!; [a.] Maple Heights, OH

JOHNSON, ROBERT GORDON
[b.] June 22, 1951, British Guiana; [ch.] Richard, Rachel; [occ.] Surgeon; [pers.] I wish to record the human heart in conflict with itself. All thoughts, every struggle, each joy that we experience have been lived by others before us. Just as we read to know we are not alone, so we write to leave behind sign posts for our children.; [a.] San Antonio, TX

JOHNSON, TIA MARIE
[b.] January 30, 1965, PA; [p.] John and Phyllis Burek; [m.] Steven Johnson, January 6, 1984; [ch.] Amy Nicole, Molly Ann, William David; [ed.] Wheaton High School, Montgomery College; [occ.] Child Care provider; [pers.] I find that there is beauty in the simple tasks of everyday living.

JOHNSON, TINA CHARLENE
[b.] July 2, 1954, Burlington, IN; [p.] Don Hardy and Iris Harbour; [m.] Willie Johnson, May 5, 1989; [ed.] GED, 11 years Caprock High School; [occ.] Clean Up at - I.B.P. Iowa Beef Packers; [hon.] 4 HR. when young for 4 years, Speech and Choir played 3 chair flute church choir; [oth. writ.] Poems short children stories, short adult stories, comedy; [pers.] I try to look at the world thru kids' eyes and do the best I can. To keep God in my heart, and faith.; [a.] Amarillo, TX

JOHNSON II, MICHAEL
[pen.] Michael Johnson II; [b.] January 12, 1974, Paw Paw, MI; [p.] Michael Johnson, Myrtle Johnson; [m.] Melanie Johnson, July 1, 1995; [ch.] Two Cats - Karina, Maggie; [ed.] Byron Center and Bloomingdale Elementary, Byron Center and Decatur High; [occ.] Insulation - Commercial and Industrial; [oth. writ.] "Unlock", "In Your Place", "Questions Answered?", "Alone Stands The Willow", not published.; [pers.] Every day there are obstacles to overcome, and mistakes to be made. This is part of life, but always remember: A world without mistakes is like a classroom with no teacher.; [a.] Paw Paw, MI

JOHNSTON, JOSEPH A.
[pen.] "Joe"; [b.] August 16, 1934, Birmingham, AL; [p.] J. P. and Lyberyl Johnston; [m.] Marlorie,

February 11, 1956; [ch.] Sharon Lynn; [ed.] Associate Degree - Arts several military courses at AFIT (Air Force Institute of Technology) Dayton, OH; [occ.] Energy Manager of Little Rock AFB, AR; [memb.] 3rd Degree Mason, Base Chapel Member; [hon.] Various merit type within the military - served 21 years in the USAF. As civil servant have received step increase awards and monetary awards for work achievements; [oth. writ.] Several short stories and poems - non published. Periodic articles in Base paper to encourage people to conserve energy. I write to please others and myself.; [pers.] But natural resources are limited, let's all save some for tomorrow - especially for our grandchildren - they deserve a quality of life too.; [a.] Jacksonville, AR

JOHNSTON, SARAH JO
[b.] November 13, 1962, Binghamton, NY; [p.] Joseph and Jane Peone; [m.] Ted Johnston, August 13, 1994; [ch.] Alexander Bailey, Austin Theodore; [ed.] Currently finishing up AAS in Accounting at Cayuga Community College; [occ.] Work for Ted at his Machine Shop doing Bookkeeping and Accounting; [oth. writ.] This was my first attempt at having any of my work published! What a great incentive to keep at it!!; [pers.] I strive to be a fair and tolerant person and most importantly to raise my sons as such. I have been equally influenced by Robert Frost and W. H. Auden.; [a.] Auburn, NY

JONES, ELIZABETH
[pen.] James R. Branch and Henry Eaddy; [b.] December 23, 1955, Newsoms, VA; [p.] Janus and Allie Branch; [m.] (Fiance) Henry Eaddy; [ch.] Arnita S. Clementine Everette; [ed.] Currently attending Union County College, Cranford, NJ; [occ.] Secretary for Salvation Army; [pers.] I tell stories of nature and yesteryear. People need to feel the presence of their surroundings and the sweet years gone.; [a.] Elizabeth Jones, NJ

JONES, ENOLA MARIE
[pen.] Baby Stevenson; [b.] September 10, 1936, Beaumont, TX; [p.] Mary and Albert Stevenson; [ch.] Robert Phyllis, Larry, Michael and Katrina; [ed.] Charlton-Pollard High, Lincoln Business College, Urban League (Secreterial Science); [occ.] Executive Secretary; [memb.] Mother's Board-Morning Star C.O.G.I.C., Bible Band, President ADA, AARP, SCC; [hon.] President's Club 1984 Olympics (LA) Volunteer; [oth. writ.] Poems not published written for special occasions.; [pers.] All poems are written by the inspiration of God, who is the head of my life.; [a.] Los Angeles, CA

JONES, ERVIE C.
[b.] July 15, 1915, Trail, OK; [p.] Eura and General Jones; [m.] Murray, May 4, 1939; [ch.] Two Boys; [ed.] Business University; [occ.] Retired; [memb.] Masonic Lodge

JONES, FLORENCE M.
[pen.] Florencia; [b.] April 11, 1939, West Columbia, TX; [p.] Isaiah and Lu Ethel McNeil; [m.] Waldo D. Jones, May 29; [ch.] Roderick, Wanda and Erna; [ed.] Prairie View A.and M., University BS (Cum Laude) 1961, MEU same University, 1968 Othori Rill University, University of Houston and St. Thomas University; [occ.] Piano Instructor, Writer, Storyteller; [memb.] Life

Memperi Texas Retired Teachers Association, Distinguished Life Member/The International Society of Poets, National Women of Achievement, Tejas Storytelling Association, Oak Meallows; [hon.] Church of God, Several Editor's Choice Awards/The National Library of Poetry, Gold Cup (Music), Letters of Recognition for Outstanding Achievement in Ed./Pres. Bill Clinton, Gov. Ann Richards and Bush; [oth. writ.] Science pop up book, gifted and talented program, poems published in several National Library of Poetry anthologies and Sparrowgrass Poetry Foreign.; [pers.] The inspiration to write this poem originated from real teaching experiences, the mind is like the wind, and it soars when appropriate force is present. I believe we need to "spray" knowledge liberally as professionals.; [a.] Houston, TX

JONES, JACK R.
[b.] September 17, 1921, San Francisco, CA; [m.] Edith B. Jones, September 10, 1946; [ch.] Joyce Marie Jones; [ed.] College Graduate plus post graduate studies at various Universities; [occ.] Retired Safety Engineer; [memb.] American Society of Safety Engineers, National Association of Retired Federal Employees; [oth. writ.] Many rhymes or doggerel - none published — written for personal pleasure and amusement of family and friends.; [a.] Renton, WA

JONES, KAY
[b.] July 28, 1947, Cairo, IL; [p.] Helen M. Newcomb, Burley D. Watson Sr.; [m.] Ralph Jones, October 18, 1985; [ch.] Three sons; [ed.] Woodruff High, IL Central Jr. College; [occ.] Semi Truck Owner, Jones Trucking; [memb.] Truckstop Ministries, Cystic Fibrosis Assoc., Feed the Children, American Christian Trucking/Wheels Alive; [oth. writ.] Children's stories; [pers.] Communication, a kind word, a friendly gesture, a sunshine smile that will bring a rainbow into one's daily life is what we should be sharing. I love the beauty of life.; [a.] Hermitage, MO

JONES, MICHAEL D.
[b.] February 17, 1942, Crowell, TX; [p.] George and Bertha Jones; [m.] Frances A. Jones; [ch.] 7 Children; [ed.] 7th Grade; [occ.] Own my own company; [memb.] Member of God's Family. First Baptists Church, Houton International Society of Poets.; [oth. writ.] Other publications by the National Library of Poetry.; [pers.] God is the captain of my soul, with His hand He leads me. Without Him, nothing that is, would be.; [a.] Houston, TX

JONES, PAUL
[pen.] P. Harry Jones; [b.] April 25, 1960, Newark, NJ; [p.] Richard Jones, Nancy Jones; [ch.] Jennifer, Savanna, Dillon, Dakota; [ed.] North Pocono High School, Johnson School of Technology; [occ.] Electrical Designer; [pers.] Remember we are what we are not so much by choice but rather by design.; [a.] Chinchilla, PA

JONES, REBECCA L.
[pen.] Becky L. Jones; [b.] April 25, 1981, Hillsdale, IL; [p.] Alice Jones; [ed.] Lemont High School Sophomore; [occ.] Receptionist; [hon.] Cheerleading trophies for Lemont Hornets.; [oth. writ.] Broken Hearted, Why, Obsession, poems I like to write in my spare time; [pers.] In my poems I want people to see that you don't have to show off to be great. Just act like yourself and you'll be fantastic.; [a.] Lemont, IL

JONES, WILLIAM H.
[pen.] William Henry Jones, W.H. Jones Captain J, Bill Jones; [b.] April 1, 1924, Black Diamond, WA; [p.] Helenor Jones - Father (Deceased); [m.] Barbara A. Jones, May 17, 1960; [ch.] Robert, Jeffrey Jones, Denise Lynn Williams; [ed.] B.A. San Diego State Naval School of Hospital Administration; [occ.] Captain, U.S. Navy (Ret); [memb.] Federal Health Care Executives Institute Alumni Assn., Fleet Reserve Association, Distinguished Member International Society of Poets; [hon.] Legion of Merit (Navy) Numerous Service Medals and awards, Graduated with honors 5 Military schools, Advanced from Apprentice Seaman to Captain during Naval Career. Editor's Choice 1995, Editor's Choice Award 1996 (5); [oth. writ.] The National Library of Poetry, Beyond the Stars - Fall 1995, Best Poems of 1996 - Summer 1996, Spirit of the Age - Summer 1996, A Muse to Follow - Summer 1996, A Tapestry of Thought - Summer 1996, Where Dawn Lingers - Summer 1996, Through the Hourglass - Fall 1996, Across the Universe - Fall 1996, Best Poems of the 90's - Fall 1996. Sparrowgrass Poetry Forum, Inc. Treasured Poems of America - April 1996, Poetic Voices of America - June 1996, Treasured Poems of America - August 1996, Poetic Voices of America - October 1996, Treasured Poems of America - Winter 1996. Oroville Mercury Register, Oroville, Ca. Poetry Corner - September 28, 1995, News Reporter, San Marcos, Ca., Over the Transom - June 13, 1996; [pers.] I believe in personal achievement, inspiring others to fulfill their dreams, at peace with self and others, all with a sense of humor, dedication and perspective.; [a.] Lake San Marcos, CA

JOON, BRIAN A.
[b.] August 1, 1969, Orlando, FL; [p.] Adrian and Barbara Joon; [ed.] A.S. Degree - Video Arts and Sciences (Orando College) High school grad. (Winter Park High School); [occ.] Production Assistant - ZFX Productions; [memb.] Orlando Chess Club Member; [oth. writ.] Mostly songs - lead vocalist for the band, "Saccharin Black."; [pers.] I believe that compassion is the highest emotion a human being can feel, if that exists within the soul, then everything falls into perspective.; [a.] Orlando, FL

JORDAN, PAULA
[pen.] Jordan Davis; [b.] December 22, 1970, Kenton, OH; [p.] Paul and Billie Jordan; [ed.] Ohio State University, Columbus State Comm. College - A.A. in Law Enforcement-Corrections; [occ.] Correctional Program Specialist; [hon.] Dean's List; [oth. writ.] Personal Book of Poems, nothing ever published before; [pers.] I write about the real things in my life.; [a.] Richwood, OH

JOY, JIM
[b.] May 25, 1955; [ed.] BS Zoology, Colorado State University; [occ.] Zoo Consultant; [memb.] AAM, AZA, AABGA; [oth. writ.] Professional Journals, Newspaper Columns.; [pers.] War and Racism are evil.; [a.] Washington, DC

JUANATAS, ADELAIDA G.
[pen.] "Morning Star"; [b.] February 14, 1931, Pozorrubio, Pangasinan, Philippines; [p.] Eliseo Garcia and Sofia Rituaco; [m.] Teodorico O. Juanatas, November 19, 1955; [ch.] Six (Two Girls, Four Boys); [ed.] Bachelor of Science in Elem. Educ, Master of Arts in School Administration, retired Elem. School (Principal in the Philippines); [occ.] Plain Housewife; [memb.] Phil. Public School Teachers Association, Epicuyean Club, Manaoag District Teachers Association, Life in the Spirit Club, Fil-Am Vets Assoc. of Hawaii; [hon.] 1st Honors - Elem. graduate Manaoag Central School Pangasinan Phil., Valedictorian - High School Manaoag Nat. High School Pangasinan Philippines, Cum Laude - Phil. Normal University Manila, Philippines; [oth. writ.] 1. Operetta - Phil, Journal of Education, Oct, 1954, 2. May His Tribe Increase! PPSTA Magazine, Phil., 3. Articles to The Call High School Newspaper Philippines; [pers.] "Don't build your happiness upon the unhappiness of other people".; [a.] Honolulu, HI

JULIANO, ANN LOUISE F.
[b.] Brooklyn, NY; [p.] Florie Juliano and Rosaria Juliano; [m.] Fiancee: Aldo Gerenini; [ed.] LaFayette High School, GDA Computers, Institute of Children's Literature; [occ.] American Museum of Natural History, St. Finbar Church, Ellis Island Foundation, Inc., National Rifle Association; [memb.] Secretarial Studies, American History; [pers.] For my poems, I strive to reach inner feelings and emotions. I write. I believe my true love is writing (short stories) for children and teenagers.; [a.] Brooklyn, NY

JUST, MELISSA R.
[pen.] Melissa St. Cloud; [b.] November 16, 1968, Tennessee; [m.] Jimmy T. Just; [pers.] I grew up in Laredo, TX, where it was a high school teacher who encouraged me to pursue a career in journalism. I later moved to Georgia where I have written a few poems and short stories under various pen names I'm currently working on my first novel.; [a.] Martinez, GA

KAHN, SHEILA INA
[b.] June 11, 1948, New Brunswick, NJ; [p.] Ruth and Frank Kahn; [ed.] University of California, Santa Barbara, B.A. History, Calif. State Univ., Northridge (Teaching Credentials); [occ.] Reading Specialist, Santa Ana Unified School District; [memb.] University of California, Santa Barbara Alumni: Assoc. Santa Ana Educators Assoc. California Teachers Assoc.; [hon.] University of California, Santa Barbara Dean's List; [pers.] "Everyday is Special" is dedicated to my mother, Ruth Kahn, a kind and gentle soul; [a.] Irvine, CA

KANES, DR. MELISSA P.
[b.] July 30, 1970, New York; [p.] Peter and Fotoula Kanes; [ed.] Grad Herricks High School 1988, Grad. Stony Brook University 5/92, BA English Literature, Minors: Women's Studies, Health and Society, Grad. New York Chiropractic College Dec. 1995 with a doctorate in Chiropractic.; [occ.] Doctor of Chiropractic; [memb.] Nat'l Organization for Women American Chiropractic Assoc., International Chiropractic Assoc., New York State Chiropractic Assoc., Pan Hellenic Professional Network; [hon.] Phi Chi Omega Chiropractic Honor Society, NYCC Dean's List (4/95, 8/95, 12/95), The Glow (my first book of poetry) published in December 1995; [oth. writ.] I've recently published a book of poetry (Dec. 1995) The Glow by Seaburn Publishing in Astoria, Queens. Several poems published in literary magazines.; [pers.] I strive to explore and evoke emotion in my writing.; [a.] Manhasset Hills, NY

KANEY, ERICH LYNN
[b.] February 6, 1966, Freeport, IL; [ed.] Forreston High School, graduate of Devry Institute of Technology; [occ.] Computer Coordinator/Electronics Technician; [memb.] Devry Alumni Association, National Rifle Association Rock County Rifle and Pistol Club, Biomedical Association of Wisconsin; [hon.] Presidents Lists, Dean's List; [pers.] When writing poetry I take the philosophy of William Blake, "when the doors of perception are cleaned, man will see things as they truly are, infinite." Hence, I write about things as they truly are.; [a.] Beloit, WI

KASTER, BEVERLEE A.
[b.] December 26, 1957, Lafayette, IN; [p.] Floyd and Nanay Kaster; [m.] Patrick D. McDonald, May 16, 1992; [ch.] Cody (2 1/2), Stepchildren: Ryan (19), Jake (16), Cari (14); [ed.] Education in Psychology Parkway North High School, Southeast Missouri State University; [occ.] Homemaker, previously for 13 yrs. Resource Librarian; [memb.] Member of Sigma Sigma Sigma Sorority; [pers.] I write my poetry with a spiritual influence of God and a deep emotion for those I love and those who have loved me.; [a.] Saint Charles, MO

KATSOS, MARIA
[pen.] Maria Katsos; [b.] August 8, 1974, Jersey City, NJ; [p.] Gloria and Bill Katsos; [ed.] Jefferson Township High School, Modeling School, Morris County College, and currently enrolled in a business college.; [oth. writ.] Little Kisses Fly By, In My Hand, A Walk in the Forest. I have too many.; [pers.] I have been writing since I was 9. And I'm really proud that some of my work will be seen. I thank all the people that actually gave me something to write about. Embrace Pain.; [a.] Lake Hopatcong, NJ

KATZ, RONALD JOSEPH
[b.] December 25, 1928, Cincinnati, OH; [p.] Walter and Maude Katz; [m.] September 18, 1948; [ch.] Kathleen, Patricia, Ronald II; [ed.] Taft Elem. - 23rd Dist. Hughs High - U. of Cinn.; [occ.] Recently retired from Hamilton County Juvenile Court; [memb.] American Legion #437 - Amer. Red Cross - National Parks Assoc., U.S. Holocaust Memorial Museum; [hon.] "Man of the Year" 1992, Hillcrest School - The Cincinnati Enquire - Man of the Week Award; [oth. writ.] "A Friend Of Mine, Named Herman" - a short story for Reader's Digest.; [pers.] I sometimes think my father was right. "Anything worth having in life is worth waiting and working for."; [a.] Cincinnati, OH

KATZENMAIER, JONATHAN N.
[pen.] Jon Katzenmaier; [b.] August 14, 1970, Kettering, OH; [p.] David and Maris Katzenmaier; [m.] Susan E. Forgy, December 28, 1996; [ed.] West Carrollton High, West Carrollton, Ohio; [occ.] Automotive Parts Salesman Nashville, TN; [memb.] United Way; [hon.] The Bowling Hall of Fame St. Louis, MO - Perfect 300 Game; [oth. writ.] Many personal, romantic poems. "Forever Love" is my first entrant of any sort. Starting to write some songs.; [pers.] All of my writing comes from the heart. I started writing approx. 1-2 years ago to show my love and appreciation for my fiance. She has taught me how to open up and show my true feelings.; [a.] Nashville, TN

KEHOE, DANIEL T.
[b.] May 13, 1951, Queens, NY; [p.] John and Lilian Kehoe; [m.] Patricia Kehoe, June 26, 1976; [ch.] Cailin and Danielle; [ed.] Associate in Business Management; [occ.] Ultrasonographer R.D.M.S.; [memb.] Society of Diagnostic Medical Sonographers S.D.M.S.

KENNEDY, CARMEN G.
[b.] February 6, 1977, Detroit, MI; [p.] Harry and Angela Kennedy; [ed.] Graduate 1995 - Renaissance High School, Detroit, Sophomore, University of Wisconsin - La Crosse; [occ.] College Student; [memb.] Women's Sports Foundation, Asian, Latina, African, Native American Women, American Assoc. of University Women; [hon.] Dean's List, Outstanding Multi-Cultural Student, 47 All Star, All City, All Region, All State Awards in Basketball, Volleyball, Track and Field, Coca Cola National Scholar; [oth. writ.] Numerous poems and essays and editorials.; [pers.] Conceive, Believe, Achieve; [a.] La Crosse, WI

KENSTIENS, SONJA
[b.] July 1, 1938, Virginia; [p.] Wonley and Nora Ward; [m.] Bill Kenstiens, December 11, 1970; [ch.] Thomas McGrath, Nishma McGrath; [ed.] Red Bluff High School, Shasto College; [occ.] Retired January 1996, Credit Manager for Medical Group Legal and Secretary; [memb.] Bethel Assembly of God Church; [hon.] My honors and awards are my two precious children.; [pers.] This poem was written for my daughter for her 31st birthday. A special gift from God.; [a.] Red Bluff, CA

KEOWN, SHERRY
[b.] July 9, 1960, Detroit; [p.] Charles and Helen Weiss; [m.] David, September 22, 1978; [memb.] Humane Society, ASPCA, World Wild Life Fund; [oth. writ.] God For A Day, Kingdom On The Sea, Shadows, Halloween. all through, "The National Library of Poetry." Old Kentucky Home, through "Famous Poets Society."; [pers.] The words should sound from the laps, like the sweet song of a Robin, welcoming the new day.; [a.] Warren, MA

KERMANE, BRUCE NASSIRI
[b.] March 16, ME; [p.] Ahmad and Maryam Nassiri; [m.] Yoko, 1992; [ed.] Degrees from: Ohio State University, Kent State University, University of Sussex, England; [occ.] College English Instructor; [memb.] Professional Language Org. and Associations, active religious membership; [hon.] Poetry and writing awards; [oth. writ.] Articles and commentaries; [pers.] The most common events and objects around us can be viewed in a poetic, uplifting, or moral light.; [a.] Huntington Beach, CA

KERSTEINS, SONYA
[m.] William Dean Kersteins; [ch.] Nishma Christina McGrath Callahan, Eugene Thomas McGrath.

KEYS, SUSIE
[pen.] Dee Keys; [b.] July 10, 1954, AR; [p.] Junior and Betty Younger; [m.] William Dee Keys, December 23, 1990; [ed.] Graduated from the 12th grade at Watts High in 1973; [occ.] House wife and baby sitter; [oth. writ.] 'Once Is Enough' which has not been published a controversial story about a trucker named Sam, his wife Mattie and a strange house guest named Shiloh.; [pers.] If you have love you have everything.; [a.] Fayetteville, AR

KHAN, TALAT
[pen.] Talat Khan and (Aarti Makhija) (Psuedoname); [b.] April 26, 1957, Pakistan; [p.] Alfred and Violet S. Khan; [ch.] Frederick Samuel, Raza, Rajesh Moses; [ed.] RN Diploma; [occ.] Writer and Neonatal ICU Nurse; [oth. writ.] Poem collection soon to come out, Passions and Emotions. Several poems published in newspaper which went nationwide and also in magazines and International publications. I also write articles and will publish a "Women's Magazine"; [pers.] I reflect on recovery after hurt, pain and sorrow. My goal is to reach out and touch lives. I am influenced by great poets and writers.; [a.] Houston, TX

KIDD, CHESTINA LEE
[b.] July 7, 1973, Somerset, KY; [p.] Roger and Vicki Kidd; [ed.] McCreary Central High, Berea College; [occ.] United States Navy Airman; [memb.] People Who Care; [hon.] Who's Who in America; [pers.] I always feel it's best to write what you know and what you feel because most people can tell if you have manufactured your emotions.; [a.] Whitley City, KY

KILDAY, CHRISTINE
[b.] May 24, 1979, McHenry, IL; [p.] Maribeth and Paul Kilday; [ed.] I am still currently in high school as an honor student at McHenry East Campus.; [hon.] I maintain above a 3.0 honor roll grade point average in school. I am also editor of the school newspaper.; [oth. writ.] Poems - "Love for an Eternity", "Color Burden", and "I Still Love You."; [pers.] I write from my heart, and I write only about subjects that are near and dear to me. My biggest influence in poetry is Robert Frost.; [a.] McHenry, IL

KILLEN, JULIE
[pen.] Julie Killen; [b.] March 27, 1959, Winter Haven, FL; [p.] Frank and Wanda Harris; [m.] Jerry "Bill" Killen, April 5, 1984; [ch.] Eric E. Cayson; [ed.] Winter Haven High; [occ.] Senior Secretary, Polk County Bo CC, Barton, FL; [oth. writ.] One poem published in local newspaper, The Lakeland Ledger.; [pers.] I try to always smile upon others with a giving heart.; [a.] Bartow, FL

KILLEN, PATRICK M.
[b.] October 2, 1979, Montclair, CA; [p.] Dale Killen, Kathy Killen; [ed.] Currently a junior at Clovis High School, Clovis, New Mexico; [memb.] United Nations Association; [hon.] Premier Prix Award for Group Dramatics at Festival Romanico, a foreign language competition; [oth. writ.] Weekly video review column in local newspaper, helped compile "New Mexico Blue Book" for New Mexico Secretary of State, also serial unpublished works; [pers.] Many of my works reflect the comparison of the developed world and the undeveloped world. I also enjoy writing suspense stories aside from my poems.; [a.] Clovis, NM

KILLION, DEBORAH L.
[b.] August 24, 1964, Pocahontas, AR; [p.] Dr. and Mrs. Grant Killion; [ed.] B.S. Communications, B.S.E. Education, pursuing M.S. in Counseling; [occ.] Teacher; [hon.] Community Service Award, National Piano Auditions Awards, Editor's Choice Award, Music Award; [oth. writ.] I have written over 400 poems and 5 short stories. I have had to published. I was influenced by the style of Edgar A.

Poe.; [pers.] I believe in "Seizing the day," and enjoying the important things in life. My dream is to meet David Soul Of TV's "Starsky And Hutch." Marcia Clark of the O.J. Simpson trial is my pen pal.; [a.] Pocahontas, AR

KING, JO HANNAH
[b.] April 19, 1923, Kremmling, CO; [p.] Jake and Nell Young; [m.] Herb F. King, July 20, 1952; [ch.] Kimberly Jo (King) Cantu; [ed.] Graduated: Steamboat Sp '95 Colo. Correspondence writing courses; [occ.] Retired (to painting and writing); [memb.] Writers Association Lawton, OK; [hon.] From Honorable Mention up to First in Oils and Watercolor. (None, until now in writing) Many poems published in Parnassus - Forest Park GA Denver Stull publisher. 1940's Poems in Grand Lake, Co. Pioneer; [oth. writ.] Big Blue Goal (Atlanta, GA, unknowns Marla's Maniquines (Dance) The Perfect Shopper Ntnl. Super Mkt. Shopper Hempsted, NY, Marry Me, Mr Murphy (Unknowns), Letters to Editor Lawton Constitution more than two dozen in the past 15 years.; [pers.] Inspiration: from observing and living life in all it's forms! But don't paint or write gloom and gush and pessimism. Write or paint joy.; [a.] Lawton, OK

KING, PATRICIA ANN
[b.] September 3, 1951, Atmore, AL; [p.] Henry and Maude Guymon, Lowell and Mae Baker; [m.] W. Duane King, February 17, 1993; [ch.] Raina and William Fisher; [ed.] Flomation High, Flomation, AL, Bethel College, McKenzie, TN; [occ.] Home Maker, Student; [memb.] United Methodist Womens Club, American Legion, Non-Commissioned Officer Assn (NCDA), Disabled American Veterans (DAV); [hon.] National Dean's List (95/96), Who's Who Among College Students (95/96), Several Awards and Decorations Throughout a successful 10 year Military Career: US Army (83-93); [oth. writ.] Personalized greeting cards, occasional articles in local troa chapter newsletters, implemented training program for subordinates working with me in an assignment in Germany.; [pers.] Be actively involved with your life, live it to its fullest. Face each day with a good attitude - you are in control and are responsible for how your life is.; [a.] Paris, TN

KING, ZOLA ANNELLA
[b.] March 5, 1935, Miami, FL; [p.] Mr. and Mrs. A. R. Goodwin; [m.] Divorced from Austin Travis King Jr., August 10, 1957; [ch.] Douglas, Lisa, Angela and Pamela; [ed.] Two years at Florida State U.; [occ.] Retired; [oth. writ.] 'My Autumn', 'The Scents Of America', 'The Flying Dutchman', 'The Old Photograph Album'; [pers.] I try to put in my writing precious moments of little things that make our world so beautiful and great really what my spirit moves me to write about when I feel inclined to express gratitude in writing.; [a.] Mesquite, TX

KIRK, KELLY
[b.] January 12, 1979, Voorhees, NJ; [p.] Michael Kirk, Nancy Kirk; [ed.] Overbrook Senior High School; [occ.] Student in high school; [memb.] Berlin Municipal Alliance, S.A.D.D., Interact Club; [hon.] Honor Roll, earned a varsity letter for high school winter track, spring track, and soccer.; [pers.] Petrarch's idea of "looking backward in order to see forward" is a piece of wisdom that helps me get through life. This is my first and hopefully not last poem to be published.; [a.] West Berlin, NJ

KISH, JANET M.
[b.] December 30, 1946, Chicago; [p.] Henry and Martha Gleim; [ch.] Michael and Michele Kish; [ed.] Bachelor of Science in Management, University of Wisconsin, Management School; [occ.] Manager - SMH Federal CR UN; [memb.] Phi Theta Kappa, Dean's List - National Credit Union Institute; [oth. writ.] This is the first of many I hope.; [pers.] I find a sense of comfort in my writing. I write from the heart.; [a.] Calumet City, IL

KISSACK, JOSEPHINE A.
[pen.] Josephine A. Kissack; [b.] June 6, 1919, Kimball, SD; [p.] Joseph and Alberta Waite; [m.] John W. Kissack, November 17, 1944; [ch.] Nancy Jo Cejudo - Marilyn Trione - John K. Kissack - Janienne Scialfa; [ed.] Four year College; [occ.] Housewife lifetime bookkeeping and banking; [memb.] United Methodist Church - extension club (lifetime) American Heart Assn., News Writing Assn., American Red Cross; [hon.] Many writing awards over the years; [oth. writ.] Plays and readings for clubs and schools.; [pers.] As the time I wrote this, and was grieving the loss of my beloved husband. I enjoy writing and on a happier note.; [a.] Whitewood, SD

KLEIN, CHARLES
[b.] June 1, 1962, Chillicothe, OH; [p.] Charles and Shirley Klein; [ch.] Kenneth, Charles, Bryan; [ed.] '80 graduate Midwest City High School; [pers.] Dedicated to my father who gave me knowledge, love, honesty and passion to live life to the fullest. God Bless.; [a.] Midwest City, OK

KLEMPNER, JACK A.
[pen.] Jack A. Klempner; [b.] January 20, 1919, Gary, IN; [p.] Abel H. and Helen A. Klempner; [m.] Bonnie Jeanne Klempner, July 28, 1979; [ed.] High School, three credits short of AA degree.; [occ.] Retired from Aerospace as Quality Engineer; [memb.] Elks, Founder of the California Carvers Guild, National Woodcarvers Assn. VP of National Carvers Museum; [hon.] Many firsts and seconds in Woodcarving competitions, in Scouting Leadership Silver Arrow, Bear Claw, Management Awards for Cost Savings; [oth. writ.] Technical Quality Control Manuels, Science Fiction short story.; [pers.] If you don't try, you don't gain because you get out of life what you put into it. Credit for my poetry must be given to a High School english teacher, Isabelle Swatts.; [a.] Long Beach, CA

KNOX, FANNING AMY C.
[b.] December 14, 1967, Abington, PA; [p.] Catherine M. and Joseph A. Knox Jr.; [m.] Michael Fanning Esq., July 18, 1992; [ch.] Madison Rae, Autumn Catherine; [pers.] Within us all there is a need to understand all of our feelings and a desire to be content. By writing, I would like to help people achieve that goal. I also look forward to writing children's books.; [a.] Andalusia, PA

KNOX, JOHN S.
[b.] July 9, 1967, Richmond, VA; [p.] Dr. George W. Knox and Mary R. Tjernlund; [m.] Brenda Lynn Knox, June 27, 1992; [ed.] Crescent Valley High School, Oregon State University; [occ.] Technical Illustrator; [oth. writ.] "Old You Hear The Train Whistle?" - The Student; [a.] Aloha, OR

KOERNIG, FELISSA
[b.] October 22, 1982, Williamsport, PA; [p.] Barbara Koernig, Robert Koernig; [ed.] Canton Elem. School, Canton High School; [occ.] Student; [memb.] Girl Scout, Student Council, Band, Chorus; [hon.] Presidents Education Award, Academic Achievement Award, 1991 Pennsylvania State Library Essay Award; [oth. writ.] Presently working on first novel entitled "A"; [pers.] As a young artist I am proud to have my first of many pieces published.; [a.] Roaring Branch, PA

KOLINOFSKY, SANDRA ANN
[b.] November 11, 1942, Erie, PA; [p.] Annabel and Newton Thornton; [m.] George E. Kolinofsky, February 1, 1992; [ch.] Teresa Anne Hill; [ed.] Cameron County High School (Emporium PA), American Management Assoc. (Phila. PA), Computer Ed. School (Paramus, NJ); [occ.] Retired Career Woman (Business/Administration); [memb.] Member of "The Friends of Reading - Berks Public Libraries" (Reading, PA), Member of "Publishers Marketing Assoc." (Hermosa Beach, CA); [oth. writ.] Author of "Serenity" an inspirational book written to help one obtain this desired state of mind and recuperate from stress.; [pers.] Grandmother of Anthony and Sarah Grace - my life has been touched by faith, courage, enthusiasm, zeal and resolution.; [a.] Birdsboro, PA

KORB, VONNA L.
[b.] June 28, 1934, Oil City, MI; [p.] Jame and Neva Mumy; [m.] Divorced; [ch.] Bruce 37, Brian 36, Bradley 30 and Brenda 29, and six grand children; [ed.] B.S. in Nursing; [occ.] Retired; [memb.] Member of Johnson Ferry, Baptist Church, Marietta, GA; [pers.] I believed in God, our Creator, Sustainer.

KOTZO, PATRICIA B.
[b.] Oct. 6, 1941, Norfolk, VA; [p.] Meredith and Isabell Barden; [m.] Peter B. Kotzo, Dec. 25, 1987; [ch.] Daryl Kevin and Mia Blythe; [ed.] Suffolk High School, Children's Institute of Literature; [occ.] Clerical, Free-lance Decorator, Craftsperson; [hon.] Award of Merit 1990 -- World of Poetry for "The Silent Plea"; [oth. writ.] Poem -- The Silent Plea, Newspaper Editorials; [pers.] I write about those I love, family and beloved pets, dreams fulfilled or lost. Helen Steiner Rice is the source of my inspiration.; [a.] York, PA

KRAUSE, ELIZABETH
[pen.] Elizabeth Baird; [b.] February 12, 1938, Upstate New York; [p.] Deceased; [m.] Divorced; [ch.] Victoria Elizabeth Sugden, Thomas Andrew Sugden; [ed.] Registered Nurse by Profession; [occ.] Writer of Poetry - Modeling Part Time - Private Duty Nursing, Past Interests - Wrote Stories and Plays as a Child of nine years old - sang with Oratorio Society for 15 years, current interests - Writing, preventative Medicine, Gourmet Cooking, Singing, Outdoor Sports and Interior Design; [oth. writ.] Currently writing a book to help people realize they are not alone in living their daily lives in abusive households and how this situation was handled by a middle aged married woman. Have poems published in "Voyage to Remember" and "The Voice Within" an "Best Poems of the '90's" and "Amidst the Splendor."; [pers.] My poetry continues to be a source of joy to me and hopefully, pleasurable to my readers. Won Editor's Choice Award for first poem written. Distinguished Member, International Society of Poets.; [a.] West Henrietta, NY

KRAUSE, JOANN
[b.] November 17, 1941, Malone, AL; [p.] Grady Calhoun and Marie Calhoun; [m.] Roland E. Krause, September 3, 1976; [ch.] Annette Marie, Karen Lee, Cheryl Bee, Carol Dee, Robert Steven, Tara Michelle, Victoria J. and David; [ed.] La Grange High School, La Grange, GA. Hutchinson Community College; [occ.] Owner/Mgr. Snack Shack, Inc., Hutchinson, KS

KROCKER, KRISTIN M.
[b.] April 10, 1980, Eau Claire; [p.] Robert and Charlene Krocker; [ed.] St. Pius Grade School, Aquinas Middle School, Aquinas High School; [occ.] High School Student; [memb.] Girl Scout of America, National Honor Society; [hon.] Girl Scout Silver and Gold Award, Student of the month; [pers.] Reading opens your mind to a world of imagination. Writing enables you open others' minds to a world of imagination.; [a.] Stoddard, WI

KROL, ANNA M
[b.] April 8, 1963, Ellwood City, PA; [p.] Frederick Faraoni and Alberta Faraoni; [m.] Joseph S. Krol Jr., August 26, 1989; [ed.] Lawrence County Vo-Tech Superior Training Services (Truck Driving School); [occ.] Housewife (Ex-truck Driver); [oth. writ.] Several never turned in for publication - only written for personal use.; [pers.] This poem came straight from my heart, and it reflects my personal feelings concerning the unsung heroes who drive trucks across this great nation of ours.; [a.] Ellwood, PA

KULYNYIS, MARCUS WILLIAM
[b.] July 31, 1982, Fort Worth, TX; [p.] Rev. William and Mary Kulynyis; [ed.] Alvarado Middle School; [memb.] Grace Family Church Alvarado, Texas; [pers.] I owe my creative mind to my English teachers who showed me that I have hidden talents.; [a.] Alvarado, TX

LAAKE, EDWARD J.
[pen.] EJL; [b.] July 26, 1955, Cincinnati, OH; [p.] Edward R. Laake and Margaret A. Laake; [m.] Gretchen M. Stricker, 1979; [ch.] Pokey, Kelly, Hedgecat, Hijo, Zoot; [ed.] St. Xavier HS - Cincinnati, Harvard College, Univ. of Cincinnati Law School; [occ.] Attorney; [memb.] ABA, State Bars of OH, SC, AL, GA, Quincy Goodtimes Alumni Assn., Sierra Club, Audubon, Nature Conservancy; [hon.] Fellowship to the United Nations UN Human Rights Division, Urban Morgan Institute of Human Rights Scholar; [oth. writ.] Poems, short stories; [pers.] Look up at the beauty of the stars and moon, feel the power of Ocean, dance in the forest, swim in the streams! A loved one's eyes hold the Universe. Come with me!; [a.] Lawrenceville, GA

LABINOV, MARK
[pen.] Mark LaBinov; [b.] August 5, 1956, Kiev, Ukraine; [p.] LaBinov Solomon D. and Nafa; [m.] Maria Svechkova, June 12, 1983; [ch.] Alexander; [ed.] Ph.D. Physical Chemistry N.S. Thermal Engineering Russia; [occ.] Engineer Prattle Whitney Co.; [memb.] ASME, AIP, USCF; [oth. writ.] Scientific papers - totally 27.; [pers.] Science and poetry are connected through love.; [a.] Palm Beach Gardens, FL

LABORE, PETER
[pen.] Peter Labore; [b.] April 4, 1976, Hartford, CT; [p.] Kay Feeney (Deceased); [ed.] Wethersfield High, 2 years at University of New Haven; [memb.] N.O.R.M.L., D.E.C.A., S.A.D.D., Safe Rides, Young Democrats; [oth. writ.] This is the first poem published, many other poems in my own private collection.; [pers.] We must realize Mother Nature's demise, or soon we will have to face the hand of falling skies. Also, "where does it say in the scriptures that a person can't get high and raise their consciousness?" -- Jerry Garcia.; [a.] Gallatin, TN

LAJEUNESSE, JAMES EDWARD
[pen.] Jim, L.J., Frenchy; [b.] August 22, 1946, Philadelphia, PA; [p.] Richard and Rose LaJeunesse; [m.] Filomena Moran LaJeunesse, April 10, 1983; [ch.] Sons - Tennyson, Daniel, s/s Harold; [ed.] St. Marys Grammer School, Phillipsburg Catholic H.S., Ranken Trade School, Community College Air Force, A/S Degree, Aircraft Powerplat Technology; [occ.] Diesel Mechanic; [memb.] KOA - Kampsites of America; [hon.] High School, School Spirit Award and Band Award, USAF - Maintenance Professional of the Year - 1983, Master Jet Engine Instruction Award, Instruction Month - August 1983; [oth. writ.] "The Case of the Broken Television".; [pers.] My writings are from real life experiences and from the heart. My wife and I have been baby-sitting a 20 month little girl since she was 1 week old. You can guess, I will have some life experiences to tell.; [a.] Tampa, FL

LALLEY, JULIA
[b.] August 25, 1921, Oneida, PA; [p.] Johanna and John Bybel; [m.] Joseph H. Lalley, October 14, 1946; [ch.] 3; [ed.] 10th Grade, GED, Cleric Typist School; [occ.] Housewife; [pers.] I believe of all the people in this universe of ours, we are all unique in our own way, whether, physically, mentally or spiritually; [a.] New Castle, PA

LANCE, CANDICE ACKERMAN
[pen.] Candice Ackerman Lance; [b.] January 17, 1949, Gt. Falls, MT; [p.] Martin B. and Inez C. Ackerman; [m.] David R. Lance, August 5, 1967; [ch.] Wendy Holtmann, Shawn Lance, Martin Lance; [ed.] H.S. and 2 yrs. at Deaconess School of Radiology in Mt.; [occ.] Director of Mammography; [memb.] ASRT American Society of Radiologic Technologists; [oth. writ.] Are registered with the Library of Congress; [pers.] I believe the Lord intends for me to share my poetry. I will write for as long as God inspires me.; [a.] Kennewick, WA

LANDRUM, LARRY
[pen.] Nitro; [b.] January 25, 1956, Lauderdale County Toomsuba, MS; [p.] Henry and Littie Landrum; [m.] Divorced; [ch.] Katrina, Lorenzon, Pamela and Brian Landrum; [ed.] Middleton attendance center - Southeast Lauderdale High, Meridian Jr. College - all in Lauderdale county Mississippi; [occ.] Disable; [memb.] Spring Hill Baptist Church High School Basketball Team, started High School track - mile run, mile relay, College Basketball Team, College Marketing Club; [hon.] Southeast Lauderdale High Basketball Team, College Basketball Scholarship - Meridian Jr. College. I was a very good pool player, card player, bowler, table tennis, checkers, dominos, just about any sport or recreation, I played and was good at. Outside

school, I played basketball and put together a basketball team - coached and have trophies.; [oth. writ.] Just started, have others but not published. I really don't know what to do. I never thought about it, until I entered your contest. I said, let's see where it takes me.; [pers.] Whenever someone tells you, you can't ask, why not? I'll try anything, If, you tell me, I can't. I'm disabled, but I reach for the sky, I don't give up. Don't quit!; [a.] Toomsuba, MS

LARGENT, AMANDA NICOLE
[b.] April 29, 1986, Gaithersburg, MD; [p.] Otis W. and Amanda S. Largent; [ed.] 4th Grade (still a student); [occ.] Student; [memb.] Hampstead Baptist Church; [hon.] Perfect Attendance, Hanover United Poster Contest; [oth. writ.] Math, Halloween, Siblings, Softball; [a.] Hanover, PA

LARLHAM, OLIVER J.
[pen.] Oliver J. Larlham; [b.] June 25, 1918, Greenwood Lake, NY; [p.] William and Della Larlham; [m.] Dorothy Lee, December 14, 1940; [ch.] Dottie, Lyonda, Shirley, Mark, David, John; [ed.] High School did well in English Literature; [occ.] Retired Boilermaker; [memb.] Jehovah's Witnesses; [oth. writ.] Children's Story in verse - "Sneezy, the Honey Bee" trying to get it published; [pers.] I have discovered that getting older is not a disadvantage, but an opportunity.; [a.] Dover, DE

LARRIEU, ROSETTA H.
[b.] February 9, 1942, Greenwell Springs, LA; [p.] Edgar and Rose Lee Hunt; [m.] Clifford Larrieu - Deceased, June 7, 1963; [ch.] Terri, Jeanne, Stephanie; [ed.] Chaneyville High, Dillard University and University of New Orleans, Touro Infirmary School of Nursing; [occ] Registered Nurse - Director of Nursing, Eden Park Community Health Ctr.; [memb.] Lamda Pi Alpha Nursing Sorority, St. Luke U.M.C., LA Coalition For Teen Pregnancy Prevention, Women's Council of B.R.; [oth. writ.] This is my first publishing effort. I create greeting cards and include my poetry in them mainly for family and friends.; [pers.] I love the written word, and enjoy writing poetry that is joyous, insightful, inspirational and even painful at times. I am a romantic. I voraciously read historical romance novels and poetry. My most favorite poet and poem is Edgar Allen Poe and "Annabelle Lee". I allow God to be the guiding force in my life.; [a.] Baton Rouge, LA

LARSON, IRENE MARY
[pen.] Irene Mary Larson; [b.] September 19, 1921, Lynd, MN; [p.] Andrea and Mary Larson

LARSON, VIVIAN
[pen.] Viv Larson; [b.] December 16, 1936, Chicago, IL; [ed.] Alivernia High, Mattatuck Com. College Asso. Degree Nursing; [occ.] R.N. San Gorgonio Memorial Hosp. Banning, CA; [memb.] Mountain Disaster Com. Calif., Calif. Asso. Nurses; [oth. writ.] Published 1st Book - June '96, "Communing, Openings into awareness". Stone Hill Press, Idyllwild, Calif.; [pers.] First "I discovered that poetry, for me is a special way of communing, second I had so much personal velling-up that I had to."; [a.] Idyllwild, CA

LAWSING, BROOKE EVAN
[b.] June 28, 1979, Bangor, ME; [p.] James Lawsing and Lisa Lawsing; [ed.] Entering Senior Year at

George Stevens Academy, Blue Hill, Maine; [occ.] High School student; [memb.] Amnesty International, French Club, Literacy Magazine "The Pomegranate", Ed., Yearbook Committee; [hon.] Honor Roll, 1993-1996, Poem "Rhythms" in National Poetry Society Anthology of High School Students, currently in "Who's Who in High School, Sports" for High School Track accomplishment; [oth. writ.] Published "All Before Seventeen" in April 1996, a collection of Twenty - two poetry and prose pieces.; [pers.] I think that when I write, I'm the most honest with myself. Sometimes, it's hard to live up to that everyday.; [a.] Castine, ME

LEADINGHAM, ED
[b.] June 10, 1977, Elmhurst, IL; [p.] Richard and Kathie; [ed.] Willowbrook High School, Adams State College - Currently a Sophomore; [occ.] Promotions Manager of College Radio Station - KASF and DJ; [memb.] Member of Quill and Scroll; [hon.] District 88's Best in 1994, Mike Bergen's Hero; [oth. writ.] "Lights out except for Willowbrook" - a journal about High School football team.; [pers.] "Live for the Moment."; [a.] Lombard, IL

LEBERMAN, ESTELLE R.
[b.] April 16, 1906, Philadelphia, PA; [p.] Harry Rose Rosenthal; [m.] Dr. Paul R. Leberman (Dec.), September 1, 1932; [ed.] Girl's High School Temple University; [occ.] Retired - 1973; [hon.] 1956 - Honor, Outstanding Adult, Educator PA; [pers.] Sun School Teacher Family Case Worker Phila. B. Ed. 1929 Teacher Kgn. Ad Teacher Supervisor Admin. Teacher Trainer Dept Ad. Ed - Ed of Foreign Born Camp Head Swim Head Coun. NY, PA Camps. When you are happy with what you do it isn't work.; [a.] Philadelphia, PA

LEDEUX, TENAYA DIANE CORNFLOWER
[b.] April 26, 1980, Hayward, CA; [p.] Deana E. Aspinall; [ed.] San Lorenzo High, currently enrolled in Independent Studies; [hon.] Honorable Mention in Spring 1995 Iliad Literary Awards Program, Honorable Mention in Winter 1996, Iliad Literary Awards Program, President's Award for Literary Excellence in the Anthology Achieving Excellence, Cader Publishing, LTD; [oth. writ.] I have two poems published by Cader Publishing "Right Now" and "Her".; [pers.] My first published poem was about a doomed world. When my niece was introduced to my life she opened my eyes to a beauty that is truly magic. You mean everything to me Lydia.; [a.] San Leandro, CA

LEE JR., JOHNNIE
[b.] January 13, 1969, Saginaw, MI; [p.] Johnnie Lee Sr. and Betty L. Lee; [ed.] Graduated at Saginaw High School 1987; [hon.] Awards in Music at Jones Elementary School on June 9, 1981; [oth. writ.] Poems and books published in local school writings competitions.; [pers.] Thanks to God, also to my mother for believing in me.; [a.] Saginaw, MI

LEGARE, VALERIE
[pen.] Hope Nelson (for short stories/novels); [b.] February 18, 1954, Danville, IL; [p.] Robert J. and Hope M.; [ch.] One twelve-year old daughter; [ed.] Associate degree LAIS Four-year electrician apprenticeship graduate Caterpillar Inc., Currently Industrial Technology/English majors; [occ.] Electrician-Mitsubishi Motors Freelance Technical Edi-

tor-McGraw-Hill; [memb.] United Methodist Church, Central Illinois Arts and Science Guild, Peoria Obedience Training Club, MMMA Joint Apprenticeship Committee; [oth. writ.] Several locally published newsletter articles, business documents and advertising.; [pers.] I gained from my parents my love of the arts: from my father, carefree artistry, and by my mother, disciplined creativity; [a.] Morton, IL

LEHMAN, RUTH SERVERNS
[pen.] Ruth Serverns Lehman; [b.] Lima, OH; [p.] Dr. Robert J. Lehman; [ch.] Three daughters one son; [ed.] Lima Central High School Bluffton College (Bl. Ohio) Ohio Northern University Taught Elementary Ed.; [occ.] Retired; [memb.] Ky. Opera Guild Bd. Chair. of Children's Free Art Classes Met. Opera Guild member Filson Historical Soc. Lou. Ky.; [oth. writ.] None ever entered for publication. I did win 1st prize in recent "Lancome" contest in connection with their new perfume called "Poeme"; [pers.] From 1st grade throughout my life to present, the English language, has been a passion, from diagraming sentences to creative writing. I always carry writing material.; [a.] Louisville, KY

LEJEUNE, JENNIFER
[b.] March 21, 1981, Lafayette, LA; [p.] John LeJeune, Judy Hebert; [ed.] Freshman at Acadiana High School; [occ.] Student/Athlete; [memb.] Family Life Christian Church; [hon.] Scholar Athlete Award 1994-1995, National Educational Development Test Award, Honor Student, Beta Pres.; [pers.] Love and courage will help any tough situation. (Written about Brennam Hebert, my brother, battling cancer).; [a.] Duson, LA

LEMIEUX, PAULA A.
[b.] August 30, 1947, Norwich, CT; [p.] Donald and Natalie Gorman; [m.] John W. Lemieux (Deceased 1993), June 11, 1966; [ch.] John Jr and Lisa Marie; [ed.] Working towards my degree in Psychology; [occ.] Medical Assistant; [pers.] All I am I owe to the people I love. They are my inspiration. I dedicate this poem to the memory of my husband John.

LEONE, MICHAEL W.
[b.] February 17, 1941, Grosse Ile, MI; [ed.] BA University of Michigan Ann Arbor

LESLIE SR., FREDDIE
[b.] April 4, 1950, New Orleans, LA; [p.] Henry Leslie, Lillie M. Leslie; [m.] Divorced; [ch.] Freddie Jr., Latina, Henry; [ed.] College of Alameda - Poetry Creative Writings - News Paper Production - Dickerson Warren Business College - Accounting; [occ.] Poet - Lyricist; [hon.] Alameda College Dean's List 1981, Dickerson - Warren, Business College Dean's List - 1987; [oth. writ.] Several poems published in College newspaper also journals.; [pers.] I write to enhance my spirituality and others writings is a gift from God.; [a.] Moreno Valley, CA

LETSCH, MELISSA
[b.] July 4, 1979, Warsaw, IN; [p.] David and Gloria Letsch; [ed.] Senior at Lakeland Christian Academy; [memb.] United States Achievement Academy; [hon.] American Scholastic; [pers.] Every man thinks his own personal hell is the worst, but there is one whose sufferings are unfathomable. He understands your hell, so share it with him.; [a.] Warsaw, IN

LEWELLYN, MARION
[b.] December 21, 1921, Addyston, OH; [occ.] Retired; [hon.] Salvation Army, 1995 Volunteer of Year Eagle Creek Corps; [oth. writ.] Restful Ground, The Beauty of Autumn Life, The Pilgrims Holiday and more.; [pers.] Sometimes poetry can bring happiness and encouragement to someone else.; [a.] Indianapolis, IN

LEWIS, CATHERINE M.
[pen.] Penelope Price; [b.] January 23, 1948, Chicago, IL; [ed.] Attending Judson College, Elgin, Ill. and Chicago of Massage Therapy; [occ.] Student; [memb.] Faith Lutheran Church, Rochelle, Ill. Member of Channel Choir; [oth. writ.] Several poems, essays, and short stories not yet published.; [pers.] My goal is to one day work with people who have suffered abuse as children or as adults. I hope to help as many as possible to walk out of the darkness of evil into the light of love.; [a.] Rockford, IL

LEWIS, JULIA B.
[b.] August 18, 1935, Stonewall Co., TX; [p.] Roy (Deceased) and Faye Sherrod; [m.] J. O. Lewis, February 29, 1968; [ch.] Jana Lyn Lock Raab (Deceased), Jayme Alan Lock; [ed.] Lubbock High School; [occ.] U.S. Attorney's Office; [hon.] Several from U.S. Attorney and law enforcement agencies; [oth. writ.] Numerous poems and prose for family and friends.; [pers.] "If Not For Spring" was written as a loving tribute to the memory of my daughter and as encouragement to my family. I believe talent is God-given and is best used as the communicator of caring for our fellowman.; [a.] Waco, TX

LEWIS, ROSE D.
[b.] August 4, 1958, Manhattan; [p.] Woyd and Bernice Lewis; [m.] Fiance (Douglas Fayton); [ch.] Tammy and Tanya, Michael, Isaac; [ed.] Norman Thomas High School, 1984-86 Bronx Community College, 181 St University Ave, 1991-92, State University of New York 1666 Bathgate Avenue; [occ.] Emergency Medical Technician; [memb.] Poet's Guild; [oth. writ.] When Will I See, Rainbow of Colors, Gaining Life, Turn From the Drink, Feeling Low; [pers.] I applaud The National Library of Poetry for giving a Novice Poet like myself a chance to share my poetry with others in Your Prestigious Books. Your inspiration will keep me writing. Thank - You; [a.] New York, NY

LEWIS, THURSTON JOHN
[b.] April 27, 1917, Le Flore Co, OK; [p.] William Terrell and Lethul Van Winkle Lewis; [ed.] BA Henderson State U. - English major Spanish - minor, Oklahoma University, Ouzchitz Baptist University; [occ.] Seafarer (retired); [memb.] Vice-Chair Board of Directors - Central Arkansas Development Council Pres - Arkadelphia Senior Adult Center, Pres - Arkadelphia Chapter #4441; [oth. writ.] Poems working on novel "Bright And Morning Star".; [pers.] Looking to Christ for all inspiration and good writing.; [a.] Arkadelphia, AR

LEWIS, WILLIAM PAUL
[pen.] Will; [b.] September 7, 1979, Urbana, IL; [p.] John W. Lewis Jr. and Connie L. Lewis; [ed.] High School 6 grades 9-11; [occ.] Lawn Service; [memb.] National Rifle Association Thespian, National Honor Society, United States Achievement Academy, Who's Who Among American

High School Students; [hon.] Best Actor 1995 Zanesville High School (ZHS) Drama out, Best Supporting Actor 1996, ZHS Drama Club, Eagle Scout; [oth. writ.] Various other poems and short stories.; [pers.] I would like to dedicate this publication of my poem to my mother who has always encouraged my writing and has supported me in this area.; [a.] Zanesville, OH

LIGGIN, MARY M.
[b.] December 3, 1936, Atkinson County, GE; [p.] Ben Merchant, Minnie Merchant (Both Deceased); [m.] O. Fred Liggin Jr., October 3, 1954; [ch.] O. Fred III, Richard Allen, Ben Wallis; [ed.] Albany High School; [occ.] Ret. Medical Secretary, Ret. Substitute School Teacher; [memb.] Northside Church of Christ recently retired from singing with sweet Adelines for 8 years; [oth. writ.] Several poems published in church magazines, one children's story (unpublished). Have written a special poem for each of my 3 sons and for my 9 grandchildren, close relatives and special friends.; [pers.] Writing especially poetry, is the language of the heart. Poetry and music serve to gladden one's soul. If anything I write brings pleasure to others, I consider it a "Bonus" and a gift from God.; [a.] Forth Walton Beach, FL

LINDBECK, CHRISTOPHER
[b.] January 28, 1959, Chicago, IL; [p.] John and Marilyn Lindbeck; [ch.] Elisa Raine Lindbeck; [ed.] Chantilly H.S., National University; [occ.] Military Officer (USMC); [memb.] Republican Party, The Retired Officers Association, The Camp Pendeton Mens Gold Assoc., The Mexican-American Golf Assoc., Society of Children's Book Writers and Illustrators; [hon.] Summa Cum Laude, M.S. Program; [pers.] Life is just one of a multitude of things that is shown upon us each day.; [a.] Vista, CA

LITTLEFIELD, EDITH M.
[b.] September 5, 1941, Smithers, WV; [p.] Alex and Muriel Mansour; [ch.] Eight; [ed.] Bates College, Boise State University, Phillips Junior College, Brigham Young University; [occ.] ESL Teacher; [memb.] TESOL; [hon.] President's List, Phillips Junior College, Dean's List, Boise State University; [pers.] Featured on Korean Nation-wide TV while teaching English there. Reader on home study lesson tapes franchised throughout South Korea.; [a.] Salt Lake City, UT

LLINAS, EDGAR
[b.] April 29, 1940, Bogota, Colombia; [p.] Pablo A. and Teresa; [m.] Dolores, January 3, 1970; [ch.] Pablo and Ellen; [ed.] B.S. 1968 M.A. 1970 Certif. of. Lat. Am. St. 1971 Ph.D 1927 (Education) 1977, Columbia University (New York City); [occ.] Prof. of Education, National U. of Mexico; [memb.] Latin American St. Ass., American Academy of Political and Soc. Sc. Mexican Philosophical Ass.; [hon.] Mexican National Researcher, Ford Foundation Fellow, Columbia University Scholarships.; [oth. writ.] Ramon Beteta and the Economic Modernization of the Mexican State 1996, Revolution Education and Mexicanidad, 1982, Latin American Education, problems and prospectives 1986.; [pers.] Only through love can we encounter faith.; [a.] Tucson, AZ

LOCKREY, BRIAN
[b.] April 28, 1963, Philadelphia, PA; [p.] William Lockrey, Elsa Lockrey; [m.] Fiancee - Kate Marie Toner, to be married October 12, 1996; [ed.] Saint John Neumann H.S. Phila. PA; [occ.] Export Logistics Manager, Paul Sustek Co. Aston, PA; [oth. writ.] I basically only write for leisure, "Church" is my first public writing.; [pers.] Personalities fascinate me, particularly those close to me, effectually inspiring my writing.; [a.] Glenside, PA

LOEB, JOHN D.
[pen.] J. David Loeb; [b.] November 25, 1938, Oklahoma; [p.] John and Barbara Loeb; [m.] Shirley, September 15, 1962; [ch.] Two; [ed.] BA/Ed; [occ.] (Train) Locomotive Engineer, Pres. Otter Creek Printing; [memb.] KS. Reading Assoc., KS. Authors Club, Night Writers, Society of Children's Book Writers and Illus., Brotherhood of Locomotive Engineers, AM. Quarter Horse Assoc.; [hon.] Won a local poetry contest; [oth. writ.] Three children's books 1. The Train Ride, 2. Jack Rabbit Jack, 3. The Pool on Otter Creek and several unpub. books and poems.; [pers.] It is a desire for children of all ages to see my books and poetry, with the realization of the opportunity they possess as future authors and artists.; [a.] Mulvane, KS

LOFTON IV, ANDREW J.
[pen.] My best friend Raoul Astin; [b.] March 11, 1981, Chicago, IL; [p.] Brenda and Andrew Lofton; [ed.] Edward Coles Elementary School, Hales Franciscan High School; [occ.] Young Minister and Straight "A" Student at Hales Franciscan High school; [memb.] Organ Donor, Maryland Avenue Baptist Church, Youth Minister 1 Choir Member etc; [hon.] Honor Society at Hales Franciscan Winner of Poetry contests; [oth. writ.] I Dream Of Peace, Music To My Ears, Realize, No Greater Love, A Love Like Me, All Within Me, etc. Published in school newspapers.; [pers.] I try to inspire everyone with my gift of poetry and look to God from which cometh my help, for it only comes from him which made heaven and earth.; [a.] Chicago, IL

LOPEZ, AMANDA
[b.] February 16, 1982, Bayler in Dallas; [p.] Charles Lopez, Tyra Garcia; [pers.] I loved to write poems ever since I was eight. I hoped to make career out of it.

LORRAINE, TERESA
[b.] March 31, 1957, Eldorado, KS; [p.] Beverly Anderson, Harold Wilks; [m.] Divorced; [ch.] Two Amanda Dawn (19), Patricia Lee (17); [ed.] Waitress; [pers.] I have 2 wonderful daughters and a granddaughter -- her name is a very dawn Plato.; [a.] Calumet, OK

LOSH, RICHARD C.
[b.] April 3, 1916, Manhattan, KS; [p.] Deceased; [m.] Deceased; [ed.] Bachelor of Arts, Univ. New. Mexico Juris Doctor, Boston Univ. (1947); [occ.] Retired/Former Lawyer, Adminis Law Judge, U.S. Dept/H&HS; [memb.] American Bar Assn. State Bar of New Mexico (Ret'd), American Legion, etc. Scribes; [oth. writ.] Non-fiction, Case and Comment, National Parliamentarian, Bar Journals, Poetry, Bristol-Banner Books.; [a.] Denver, CO

LOUDENBER, KELLY ANN
[b.] June 15, 1982, Indiana; [p.] Roger and Cindy Loudenber; [ed.] St. Mary's Elementary School and Griffith Jr. High; [memb.] AAU Basketball, Bullets Softball Travelling Team, Young Ladies Sodality; [oth. writ.] Several poems published in school newspaper.; [a.] Griffith, IN

LOUISE, TOMILA JOANNA C.
[b.] July 20, 1950, Orlando, FL; [ch.] A son and two daughters; [ed.] A.B. University of Findlay-Honors in Hist. 57 62 Master of Divinity - Boston Univ. Sch. of Theo, H. Sch-Liberty-Benton, Findlay, Ohio 49; [occ.] Store Clerk; [memb.] Elder, Retired, United Meth. Ch. of New England; [pers.] Most of my effort express an awe of God and or of God's creation, a questing in depth for understanding of life, a questioning of arrogant belief systems, admiration for other persons lives, and a general praise of and thanks for beauty and gifts to my life.; [a.] North Truro, MA

LUCAS, JANET M.
[pen.] Janet Stem; [b.] January 6, 1948, State College, PA; [p.] John H. and Stem-Margaret Stem; [m.] Ralph E. Lucas, May 22, 1965; [ch.] Patti A., Karen M., Ralph E. II; [ed.] Bald Eagle High Wingate, PA; [occ.] Domestic Cleaning Business and also work at Days Inn Lounge Milesburg, PA; [hon.] My honors were raising my children and my awards were watching them grow up into beautiful adults that I am very proud of; [oth. writ.] Received certificates for other poems.; [pers.] I like to write and most times my feelings and parts of my life are put into poems. It is my book of "Silent Thoughts.".; [a.] Milesburg, PA

LUCIA, PAUL
[b.] June 15, 1931, Springfield, MA; [p.] Peter and Maria Lucia; [m.] Divorced; [ch.] Randy, Renee, Robin, Richard; [ed.] Bob Jones Academy, Bob Jones Univ. Science Teacher; [occ.] Entrepreneur; [memb.] Family worship Center, Italian American Club, Chamber of Commerce; [oth. writ.] "When I Look At You", "Waiting For You" "Love The Way It Ought To Be," "The Beauty In You", "Trash Lady"; [pers.] I strive to express "What every woman wants to hear her man express." In a true loving relationship and recognize the self-esteem in each.; [a.] Macon, GA

LUCKIE, ANDREA ELIZABETH
[b.] July 11, 1967, Newman, GA; [p.] Carol and Randall Luckie; [m.] Stephen Randall Luckie, February 14, 1994; [ch.] Pamela Luckie; [ed.] West Georgia College Carroll Technical Institute; [occ.] Housewife/Student; [pers.] While Sarah Teasdale has been one of my favorite poets, my husband, for whom this poem was written, has been my greatest influence and inspiration. Love is everything, love of friends, love of family, love of life.; [a.] Newman, GA

LUEDTKE, RICHARD WAYNE
[b.] July 20, 1916, Clarkfield, MN; [p.] Henry and Gracel Luedtke; [m.] Francis D. Luedtke (Die August 1995), June 1, 1961; [ch.] 2 step children; [ed.] High-School at Tech. High - St. Cloud, MNN, 1936; [occ.] Retired from Meat cutting with the Big Boys A & P - Von's 1982, worked for Sambo's; [hon.] Went to Lowry Field to train for photography, 1943; [pers.] Served in Air Force 1939 - 1945, W. W.II was Department Head in the Photo Dept.; [a.] La Grange, CA

LUKACIK, STEFAN
[b.] July 26, 1929, Nizna Nad Oravou, Slovakia; [p.] Stefan Lukacik, Zuzana Lukacik-Kazmier; [ed.] VSE (University of Economics), Bratislava, Slovakia, FAMU (Film Faculty of Muse Arts Academy), Prague, Czech Republic; [occ.] Film Maker; [pers.] I help mankind to keep the right way in this Universe.; [a.] Hollywood, CA

LUNSETTER, HOWARD M.
[b.] February 10, 1938, Gatzke, MN; [p.] Melvin and Esther Lunsetter; [m.] Mary Ann Bernstein, July 9, 1959; [ch.] Alan, Kristi, Five Grandchildren; [ed.] Middle River High School grad. 1956; [occ.] Farmer-Welder at Polaris Industries; [memb.] United Lutheran Church American Legion Post 449, Rollis Township Board, Roscau Area Writers Workshop; [oth. writ.] Poems published locally newspapers, poems and articles published in "Good Old Days", articles pub. fur-fish-game have collection of Christian and Romantic Poems about ready for pub.; [pers.] A country life puts me in the midst of Gods beautiful creation and my writing is most influenced by this and the love and support of my wife of 38 yrs. I'm a romantic at heart.; [a.] Gatzke, MN

LUTTRELL, GEORGE MILTON
[pen.] G. Milton Luttrell; [b.] November 11, 1939, Brooksville, FL; [p.] Alfred Wilbur Luttrell, Lucy Webster Luttrell; [m.] Betty Albright Luttrell, December 27, 1961; [ch.] Daniel Thomas and David Thiel; [ed.] BS Florida State University 1961, Med University of Florida 1965; [occ.] Environmentalist and Contractor; [memb.] Tampa Bay Poetry Club, Wanderlust Chapt., Florida State Poets Association, International Society of Poets; [hon.] Semi-Finalist T.B.P.C.'s "Mid-Winter" Oral Poetry Competition 2-4-'96; [oth. writ.] Writing poetry book entitled: "Of Cigarettes, Silhouettes and Meteorites"; [pers.] If young people today can become self-actualizing and develop tolerance toward others, then we can be a stronger nation.; [a.] Saint Petersburg, FL

LYNCH, BONNIE A.
[b.] December 12, 1927, Slater, MO; [p.] Amos Brumble Sr. and Clara Brumble; [m.] Edward V. Lynch (Deceased), November 10, 1945; [ch.] Michael, Pamela, Jean, Mary, Cindy and Tricia; [ed.] Marshall High; [occ.] Retired Gift Shop Owner; [memb.] Catholic Daughters of America; [oth. writ.] I've never entered a contest before. Or published anything except for paying to have several poems published in an anthology in 1975.; [pers.] Writing is a means to express my thoughts, feelings, ideas and deeds and still remain a private person.; [a.] Salinas, CA

MACK, BERNARD
[pen.] Flav; [b.] Feb. 3, 1969, Orangeburg, SC; [p.] Mr. and Mrs. Herbert Mack; [ch.] Lianna Mack; [ed.] BA, Savannah State College, HS, Orangeburg Wilkinson; [occ.] Waiter/Comedian; [memb.] Naval Reserves; [hon.] Teacher of the Day, Several High awards for Football; [oth. writ.] Several articles for the Times and Democrate Newspaper in Orangeburg, SC; [pers.] I can change the world. I will change the world. I have changed the world.; [a.] Savannah, GA

MAGGARD, LISA
[b.] April 12, 1971, Springfield, MO; [p.] James D. and Kathryn R. Maggard; [m.] Divorced; [ed.] Currently pregnant (with first viable pregnancy); [ed.] El Dorado High School; [occ.] I am currently unemployed while pregnant, but I am in the banking industry by trade.; [hon.] Numerous creative writing awards during grade school; [oth. writ.] Several other poems however none of them published.; [pers.] I only write poems when something really deep is weighing on me heavily. My true feelings just seem to flow out of me into my writings. I enjoy being able to reflect back on my trying experiences to see what I was feeling then.; [a.] Pollock Pines, CA

MAGGIT, CLAUDETTE
[pen.] Candy Cole; [b.] March 28, 1945, Blytheville, AR; [p.] Thomas V. Cole and Hattie B. Cole; [ch.] Four; [ed.] Bowling Green State University Mt. Senario Medical Asstng. College Cleveland State University; [occ.] Administrative Asst./Case Manager/Faculty; [memb.] Charter Member Zeta Phi Beta sorority Psi Epsilon; [hon.] Virginia Jones Scholarship, O.M. Hoover Scholarship, That Girl, M's Bold; [oth. writ.] Two collections of my poems 'Chocolate Covered Candy,' 'Sweeter Than Candy', two plays all the kings horses and baby girl; [pers.] I have been greatly influenced by Niki Giovani, Sonya Sanchez. And I was fortunate to have worked with and been encouraged by my dear friend James Baldwin. Jimi held me up when others told me to sit down. I dedicate much of my spirit to his memory.; [a.] Cleveland, OH

MAHIR, CHRISTIN
[pen.] Nemo; [pers.] When the world explodes, when everything dies, when the stars burn out and the universe folds onto itself, when the end has passed and the beginning has yet to come, remember to laugh.; [a.] CA

MALOCHA, RACHEL
[pen.] Moonchild; [b.] November 28, 1974, Saginaw, MI; [p.] Alex and Babs Malocha; [occ.] Student of Life and Universal Mechanisms; [oth. writ.] None whatsoever; [pers.] Wake up to the eternal and experience bliss.; [a.] Saginaw, MI

MALONE, FRANZELLA
[b.] May 8, 1980, Birmingham, AL; [p.] Ms. Bonzola Malone; [ed.] Parker High School Junior; [occ.] Laundry Attendant; [memb.] National Honors Society, Who's Who, Kids F.A.C.E.; [hon.] Top 5%, Top 10%, Honor Roll; [oth. writ.] I have written over 100 poems. I also write screen plays or movies. I have written five movie plots.; [pers.] I love to write. It gives me freedom to escape the world. Dreams are my key to writing. I write mostly about what I don't see.; [a.] Birmingham, AL

MALOY, DELORES
[pen.] Dee Maloy; [b.] February 8, 1936, Dallas, TX; [p.] Both Deceased; [m.] Single (Widow); [ch.] (6) Five living; [ed.] 9th grade; [occ.] Retired, (disable) Nurse's Asst, Home Health Aide; [memb.] (FEMV) Families and Friends of Murdered Victims; [hon.] Home Health Aide, Nurse Asst, Mt. Sac College Walnut, Cal. (cert) Superior court Juror, (cert) state Cal. county of Los Angeles. Soul-

Winning Society, EOF Christian ctr. (cert.) School of Biblical Worship. (cert) Victorville, CA (cert); [pers.] In memory of my son Aubrey Maloy, who was a victim of violent crimes. Aug. 25, 1994. Putting in writing (poetry) a part of his life, hoping that it will bring grief under control, to those who have lost loved ones, and bring healing to others, as well as myself.; [a.] Victorville, CA

MANCHESTER, T. J. REYCKERT
[pen.] T.J.; [p.] Chester and Jeannie Reyckert; [m.] Hal Manchester, June 9, 1995; [occ.] Aviation Technician, American Airlines Sports Coach, Personal Trainer; [oth. writ.] Current project children's book "When I Get To Heaven" helping children and adults deal with death and dying, various poems, articles and songs throughout high school and college.; [pers.] Heaven's edge can only be seen through God's clouds and mechanical wings.; [a.] Tulsa, OK

MARBERRY, GEOFFREY B.
[b.] August 10, 1978, Birmingham, AL; [p.] Ray and Ruby Marberry; [ed.] Hewitt Trussville High School graduate 1996; [occ.] Student - attending Univ. of Al. B'Ham, AL.; [memb.] First Baptist Church of Center Point; [pers.] Love and peace can only be achieved by knowing Jesus Christ as your Lord and Saviour; [a.] Birmingham, AL

MARCEDA, ANTHONY F.
[b.] N.Y., NY; [p.] James D. Maceda, Melina Carrara Marceda; [ed.] The Cooper Union for the Advancement of Science and Art, N.Y.C. (4 yr Priv. Col.); [occ.] Civil Eng'r. (Structures Sp'lty), Art Learner/Craftor; [memb.] Amer. Society of Civil Engineers, member; [hon.] Chi-Epsilon Civ. Eng'g. Hon Fraternity Election; [oth. writ.] Poems, American heritage essay, developments (unpublished); [pers.] Poetry can wield a singing blade to a vast jungle wilderness in exploring, protecting, enjoying, receiving enlightenment, seeing beauty and adding a singular vitality to life. Great minds - puny by comparison - have submitted to the Lord.; [a.] Bronx, NY

MARCUZZI, CHRISTIAN
[b.] July 17, 1984, Phillipsburg, NJ; [ed.] Our Lady of Mount Virgin Elementary School; [occ.] Student; [oth. writ.] Various; [pers.] "If someone tells you, you can't do something don't take it to heart because you can do whatever you want to do. In America, there are no limits".; [a.] Middlesex, NJ

MARINO, JUANITA ROSALIE
[b.] January 16, 1978; [p.] Judge and Mrs. Ruche J. Marino; [ed.] I will be a senior next year at Destrehan High School and I am also a dance student at New Orleans Center for Creative Arts.; [hon.] 2nd Place Non Fiction winner in Young Authors Contest '96-chosen as Who's Who Among American High School Students; [pers.] My main desire in life is to always achieve success in all that I do!; [a.] Norco, LA

MARKS, RITA
[b.] May 31, 1953, San Mateo, CA; [p.] Joseph and Sarah Marks; [ch.] Lazet Howard and Tanesha Howard; [ed.] Canada College, Redwood City, CA AA Degree, College of Notre Dame, Belmont, CA - expect Computer Science degree in 1998.; [occ.]

Sr. Admin., Asst./Purchasing Agent at Sun Microsystems, Inc., Mountain View, CA.; [memb.] Member of Fremont Bible Fellowship Church in Fremont, CA.; [hon.] Dean's List - twice, American Business Women's Scholarship three times, Redwood City Citizen's Scholarship, Canada College Scholarship, Bay Area Urban League Scholarship.; [oth. writ.] Self, Rare Bird, Who Was That? The Love are all published. Unpublished poems are: The Mountain, What is Love, and various others.; [pers.] All the praise and honor go to God for providing me with the ability to write and share my poems with others. I write straight from the heart. I thank my daughters Lazet and Tanesha Howard for their love and support.; [a.] East Palo Alto, CA

MARSH, LESLEY-ANNE
[b.] December 22, 1982, Fairfax, VA; [p.] John and Maryann Marsh; [ed.] Fox Mill Elem, Ben Franklin Intermediate Schools; [occ.] Student, 8th grade; [memb.] National Junior Honor Society; [hon.] Reflections Awards of Fairfax Co, VA; [oth. writ.] 1996 Edition of Pearls and Diamonds; [pers.] My mind, my heart, and my spirit have all be influenced by my parents.; [a.] Herndon, VA

MARTIN, FREDERIC
[b.] March 12, 1927, Syracuse, NY; [p.] Beatrice and Harvey Martin; [m.] Shirley Bernard Martin, March 7, 1958; [ch.] Two sons and one daughter; [occ.] Retired; [pers.] My poetry are lyrical deliberations on a very exciting life in the fields of journalism and labor relations/arbitration. I also write poems of whimsy.

MARTIN, JEAN M.
[b.] September 2, 1958, Pittsfield, MA; [p.] John and Theresa Layden; [m.] David L. Martin, November 18, 1978; [ch.] Jennifer Michelle, Lindsey Kate; [ed.] St. Joseph Central High, McCann Tech.; [occ.] Visual Therapist; [a.] Housatonic, MA

MARTIN, JILL LOUSTALOT
[b.] August 8, 1946, Bakersfield, CA; [p.] Lois Stevenson, Frank Loustalot Jr.; [m.] Lloyd H. Martin, October 5, 1985; [occ.] Retired; [oth. writ.] What if...I say no! We have a secret (1982 Crown Summit)

MARTIN, WESLEY TRUETT
[pen.] Finn Cormic and Yawnwind Arberth; [b.] April 22, 1977, Fort Worth, TX; [p.] Tim and Frances Martin; [ed.] Richland High School Tarrant County Junior College; [occ.] Student; [hon.] National Honors Society (High School) Magna Cum Laude (High School) Texas Scholar (High School) Dean's List (College); [oth. writ.] Cyrum Woman (unpublished), Battle songs for the Curmic Dead (unpublished), American Bastard (unpublished), Suburban Realm (unpublished) The Beauty of Nothing (unpb), Peyote Child (ch); [pers.] Inside ourselves lies self truth, and inside self truth there lies the whisper of God. I am desolate, but I am not last.; [a.] Fort Worth, TX

MARTINO, GRACE J.
[pen.] "Amazing Grace"; [b.] December 24, 1924, Durham, NC; [p.] Deceased; [m.] Divorced; [ch.] Judy Fierro, John Martino, Rebecca Brunell, Pam Holmes; [ed.] 11th Grade had to quit to go to work I'm going to get my GED though was scheduled to

do that, but, I've broken so many bones lately, had much surgery but, I'll do it; [memb.] New Life Family Church council on aging; [hon.] Being honored in the semi-finals for my poem/above all else though, the highest and most precious honor I could ever receive, and did receive was when I received Jesus as my Lord and Savior, and became a (Born Again Christian); [oth. writ.] Many, many others in fact, I'm sending another one in on the 1st of January '96 although, none have been published as yet, I know that they will be!!!; [pers.] I always keep my eyes on the Lord and always aim to honor and please Him at all times!!! It is because of God, that I'm able to write as I do, and, for His blessings, I thank Him every day!!!; [a.] East Longmeadow, MA

MARTINEZ, BOB G.
[b.] June 7, 1949, Las Vegas, NM; [p.] Mrs. Mary Jane Martinez; [m.] Annette E. Martinez, February 10, 1973; [ch.] Lita Martinez (19 yrs); [ed.] Denver North High School 1968, School of "Hard Knocks" since then.; [occ.] Security Officer Denver Merchandise Mart; [memb.] Distinguished Member of ISP - NCP Columbine Poets of Colorado and Mile High Poetry Society; [hon.] Eleven Editor's Choice Awards (in 18 anthologies) Voted "Father of the Year" by wife and daughter; [oth. writ.] Personal journal of years between 1945 to 1994 called "My time to Rhyme" and a compilation of my poems called "Sidetracks"; [pers.] Life's poetic verbiage becomes one's lyrical heritage.; [a.] Denver, CO

MARTINEZ, ELIZABETH
[pen.] Elle; [b.] March 11, 1970, Newark, NJ; [p.] Eliezer and Carmen Martinez; [m.] Ricardo Rodriguez, March 7, 1995; [ch.] Ricky Rodriguez Jr.; [ed.] Barringer HS, Concord School of Hair Design and Newark Police Academy; [occ.] Newark Police Officer; [oth. writ.] Many other poems for Individuals whom were in need of positive deep thinking through poetry.; [pers.] Sometimes we need to be reminded how beautiful words can be. We get so caught up in our every day life, we don't realize. Through my poetry I like to reminded them and take them away; [a.] Newark, NJ

MARTINEZ, FAITH
[pen.] B. Elliott; [b.] September 18, 1962, San Diego, CA; [p.] Mr. and Mrs. Francis Edward Elliott; [m.] Gerardo Martinez, December 22; [ch.] Alicia, Jerry, Joshua, Heather and Samantha; [ed.] Graduate of the American Institute of Interior Design 1996, Fountain Hills AZ, graduate Norman High School, Norman, Oklahoma 1980; [occ.] Project Coordinator, Ferrara's Design Studio and Interior Designer, Phoenix, AZ; [memb.] Allied Member, ASID, Member Abundant Life, Assembly Of God Church, and Sunday School Teacher - 4, 5 and 6th grades, Phoenix, AZ; [hon.] Junior Classical League 1979-1980, National Convention Awards for Art Work and Educational Achievements; [oth. writ.] Poems and verses written in eighteen month period, following this piece.; [pers.] There is no greater encouragement than from those who love us, and there is no greater inspiration than from those we love . . .; [a.] Phoenix, AZ

MARTINEZ, LEONARD
[pen.] Wind Warrior; [b.] January 5, 1950, San Antonio, TX; [p.] Leonard and Olivia Martinez; [m.] Ginger Lynn Martinez, November 7, 1985; [ch.] Sabrina, Lindsay, Jamie, David, grandchildren: Travor Reid; [ed.] South San High School; [occ.] Machinist; [oth. writ.] Poems and Devotional Thoughts, published by Sovereign Grace Ministries; [pers.] In my quest for knowledge I have strived to keep my feet firmly on the ground and my eyes wide open.; [a.] Del City, OK

MARTINS, TAVITA
[pen.] Tavita Martins; [b.] November 10, 1947, Trujuillo, Peru; [p.] Jose Soto and Eloyza Flores De Soto; [m.] Alvaro Martins (from Portugal) My husband is a poet but his writings are all in Portuguese, December 7, 1975; [ch.] Diana (13), Daniel (12); [ed.] Bachelor's Degree in Philosophy at City College of City University of NY and other Business and Secretarial Studies in Private Institutions.; [occ.] Purchasing agent for Techint, Inc. an International Construction Corp. and Steel Industries.; [memb.] No special Membership only to the Congregational Community Church where we attend every Sunday and I teach Sunday School during School Months.; [hon.] Sorry no Awards!! Even though I feel I should get one for holding a very busy full time job plus a busy household with two kids.; [oth. writ.] I do not write professionally. Only upon request, like now. As the matter of fact how did you get my name to make me a participant in this contest? I am thankful that you did. I might write more later on when I have more time.; [pers.] Trying to understand why life has more misery than goodness. Injustice over powers justice. The readings I consider myself influenced by are the Bible, Ayn Rand, Shakespeare, Doestoyvesky, Victor Hugo, etc.; [a.] Floral Park, NY

MARY ANN
[b.] Wadesboro, NC; [m.] July 22, 1977; [ch.] Isaiah, Calvin, Gordon, Cortney, Jamie; [ed.] Finish High School; [occ.] Wampler Longacre, Harristeeter; [oth. writ.] Write songs, something going on.; [pers.] I need this poem to dedicated to the following peoples, my sons my 5 sons.; [a.] Monroe, NC

MASEMER, ANDREA
[pen.] Andi; [b.] August 4, 1982, Gettysburg; [p.] Rick and Vicki Masemer; [ed.] Littlestown Maple Ave. Middle School; [occ.] Student; [a.] Littlestown, PA

MASER, FREDERICK E.
[b.] February 26, 1968; [p.] Herman A. and Clara Krumm; [m.] Mary Louise Jorden Maser, December 25, 1957; [ed.] Univ. College, Schenectady NY. AB, Princeton University M.A., Princeton Theological Seminary Th.M.; [occ.] Retired; [memb.] Union League, Phila., Phita Beta Club, Phila. Phila Alpha Club, Phila.; [hon.] D.D. from Dickinson College, St. Georges Gold Medal Award, Good Hart Award and others; [oth. writ.] Numerous articles and newspapers, magazines and learned journals, Ed. of Journal of Joseph Pilmore, Dramatic Story of Early American Methodism, Life and Robert Strawbridge, Hist, of Methodist in Central Penna., and others of field of Meth. history.; [pers.] The one honor to be sought is to have one's name written in the Lamb's Book of Life.

MASON, ANGELIQUE
[b.] February 19, 1976, Alexandria, LA; [p.] Paul and Charlotte Mason; [ed.] Junior at Peru State College majoring in Elementary Education; [memb.] Historian of Association of Challenged and Enabled Students, Council for Exceptional Children Member

MASON JR., CLARENCE E.
[pen.] Mark McColl; [b.] November 12, 1918, B'gham, AL; [p.] Clarence and Kathryn; [m.] Anna H. Mason, August 15, 1949; [ch.] Frances Patricia Dando; [ed.] High school, junior college (military), I semester as college junior.; [occ.] Retired; [memb.] Earlier: ELKS, American Legion, Hotel Greeters of America, Optimist; [oth. writ.] Western novel: "Guns Along the Brazos" - a series of 4 volumes (not yet published); [pers.] "Never read your future from the tea leaves in someone else's cup!"

MASON JR., JAMES EARL
[pen.] "Frugal Mulch"; [b.] September 25, 1948, Michigan City, IN; [p.] James and Madeline Mason; [m.] Clara Marie Mason, October 14, 1995; [ch.] Carla Leake, Tammy Utpatel; [ed.] Graduate of St. Mary's High School - 1996 attended Indiana Vocational Technical College; [occ.] Mason Shoe Dealer; [memb.] American Legion; [hon.] National Dean's List; [oth. writ.] Songs "Eileen", "We Make It Home", "Is Love Everlasting?", "She's Been Down, and "Out Remem'bring", "She Lost A Feeling, But I Lost MY Touch"; [pers.] If you can't be good be better!; [a.] Michigan City, IN

MASSEY, FRANK
[b.] July 4, 1947, Camden, AR; [p.] Dock and Mildred Massey; [m.] Shirley, January 6, 1973; [ch.] 3 sons; [ed.] Hormaney Grave High School, Camden, AR/Ozarka Tec. College, Melbueran Ark; [occ.] Mechanic; [memb.] VFW; [pers.] It is the changing of men's heart's and mines. Not the changing of men's law's, that makes men equal.

MATHIS, SALLY
[b.] February 16, 1947, Raton, NM; [p.] Gene Anderson, Martha Anderson; [m.] Wayne L. Mathis, June 1, 1968; [ch.] Gene Ray Mathis, LeiAnne Mathis; [ed.] Wheaton Central High School, Moody Bible Institute, Chicago University of Texas at El Paso; [occ.] Domestic Engineer; [hon.] Numerous Canning Awards, Craft Awards; [pers.] To be successful in life does not mean how much you have. Rather, to be successful is to use what God has so graciously given you for his glory. That is success.; [a.] Rosenberg, TX

MATTHIAS, MRS. JENNIFER R.
[pen.] Jenny; [b.] April 23, 1963, St. Thomas; [p.] Joseph and Rocita Williams; [m.] Mr. Ricky Matthias, December 29, 1990; [ch.] Mister Dimitri Matthias; [ed.] Graduate Charlotte Amalie High School 1983 North Carolina A and T State University; [occ.] Physical Education Teacher at Wesleyan Academy; [memb.] St. Thomas - St. John Volleyball Association; [hon.] Most Valuable Player North Carolina A and T and several other Sport Awards and North Carolina A and T; [oth. writ.] I write only for pleasure. I also write poems for my school's programs and presentations.; [pers.] My writing

are very spiritual. I try to awknowledge God in each of my poems. Each poem I write reflects my desire to bring peace, unity and harmony among ourselves: Mankind; [a.] Charlotte Amalie, VI

MATTINA, MICHAEL
[b.] June 22, 1982, Saint Louis; [p.] Anthony Mattina, Helen Mattina; [ed.] St. Gabriel the Archangel, Oakville Junior High; [a.] Saint Louis, MO

MAXWELL, LOUISE
[b.] November 26, 1925, Meridian, MS; [p.] Leon and Ola Middlebrook; [m.] Frank Maxwell, April 2, 1948; [ch.] Darlinda Maxwell Baldinger, Frank Maxwell Jr.; [ed.] Meridian High, Mississippi State University for Women; [occ.] Retired owner of Maxwell's Restaurant, Vicksburg, MS; [memb.] Vicksburg Junior Auxiliary, Church of the Holy Trinity, Friends of the International Ballet Competition; [pers.] "Here's to Frankie" was submitted as a memorial. To my husband, Frank, who passed two months after his 72nd birthday. I love poetry for it is created from the music of one's soul.; [a.] Jackson, MS

MAYFIELD, KENA
[b.] April 9, 1978, Metropolitan Hospital, San Antonio; [p.] Theresa and Mark Mayfield; [ed.] Will be attending Our Lady of the Lake University in the Fall. Graduate from Smithson Valley High School, top 5% of class 1996; [occ.] Telephone Operator (Process orders for many companies); [memb.] NHS, Spanish Club, Literary Magazine, in college will be participating in International Cultural Society and a writer for school newsletter; [hon.] USAA American Academic Award, History and Government Award, Employee of the Month (October 1994), Sweepstakes Band 92-96, Best Drumline Award '92, Honor Roll, $3,000 per semester scholarship at Our Lady of the Lake University; [oth. writ.] For my Grandmother, I added another chapter to the noted poem. I am hoping to finish my first three novels by the end of college (next 4 years) to add to my thesis of numerous poems and stories.; [pers.] This poem was written for my Grandfather, who recently passed away. Three months later my Grandmother, and his wife of 50 years, left this world, as well. I've lost an entire generation, but this allows new life in my era of writing.; [a.] San Antonio, TX

MAYNARD, ANNA RUTH
[pen.] Alice May Scohfield; [b.] April 23, 1936, Richmond, VA; [p.] Flora Bell Johnson Cole and Ira C. Cole; [m.] Gaylow Franklin Maynard, June 1, 1961; [ch.] Milliant Ruth B. Darriel Lee, McVerginia, Gale H., Rhanda Annette, C. Patricia L. D. and Delieo R. M.; [ed.] Graduated from Haverly High, School in May of 1957, Ellis Grove Elementary School in Waverly Tenn.; [occ.] Homemaker, Mother, Grandmothers; [memb.] Trace Creek Baptist Church on the 11th day of April for the year of our Lord 1993. Pastor Charles E. Gibbs of New Johnsonville Tennessee; [hon.] Honorable mention of other poems "Springtime" in 1987, and I have written several songs. "Let Me Say I Love You" and Just Before The World Look Him Away"; [oth. writ.] A Book of poetry was published October 16, 1991 "My Testimony" is the title of the book. Was published by Vantage Press in New York, N.Y.; [pers.] I have been influenced and encour-

aged to use my talents for the Lord and to encouraged younger people to do the same. I play the guitar, whenever opportunity presents itself. I sing C and W.; [a.] Bakersfield, CA

MAZZINI, ANTHONY E.
[p.] Carmen and Erasmus Mazzini; [m.] Pamela, February 14, 1984; [ch.] Laura, Christine, Anthony; [ed.] Degre in Psychology, Roosevelt University, Chicago, 1977; [occ.] Psychiatric Social Worker, Columbia Chicago Lakeshore Hospital; [memb.] American Legion, IL; [hon.] Dr. Frist Humanitarian Award 1986; [oth. writ.] Fifty unpublished poems. A play, several monologs.; [pers.] After everything's been said and done love is still the universal hope and the mentor of us all.; [a.] Chicago, IL

MCANEAR, TERESA MARIE
[b.] September 7, 1963, Anchorage, AK; [p.] Charles and Ruth Moss; [m.] Larry Don McAnear, August 25, 1989; [ch.] Nathan Charles, Allison Marie, Don Ross, John Thomas; [ed.] Ingleside High School, Massey Business School; [occ.] Legal Secretary in Corpus Christi, Tx; [oth. writ.] Have written several other poems for friends and family (not published); [pers.] God inspires me to write my poems. This one in particular ("The Hardest Thing") was for my Dad.

MCBRIDE JR., LARRY L.
[b.] May 30, 1975, San Antonio, TX; [p.] Mr. and Mrs. Larry L. McBride Sr.; [ed.] Graduated High School in 94 and currently working on a degree in animal science and range management; [occ.] College Student; [memb.] Boy Scouts, San Antonio Livestock Tours Committee; [hon.] All Sports Trainer 92-94; [pers.] Don't let anyone control your destiny, be sure you're right then go ahead.; [a.] San Antonio, TX

MCCART, AMANDA
[b.] August 26, 1981, Atlanta, GA; [p.] Steve and Susan McCart; [ed.] Currently Attending Brook Wood High School Gwinnett County, GA; [oth. writ.] This is first submitted writing.

MCCLAIN, JAMES EDWARD
[b.] June 8, 1940, Wendell, NC; [p.] James and Dorothy McClain; [ed.] High School; [occ.] Security Guard; [memb.] Bronx Council of the Arts, Community Board #4 Church; [hon.] American Song Festival Quarter Finalist Winner 1982, Song: "Somebody - Somewhere" written by James McClain; [oth. writ.] Working on two fiction novels, books. Songwriter, creative writer.; [pers.] I would love to retire and earn money from my writing talents. That is my goal.; [a.] Bronx, NY

MCCLAIN, MARGARET
[b.] April 3, 1978, Cologne, Germany; [m.] Don McClain; [ch.] Three (Ages 26, 24, 4); [ed.] B.A., M.A.; [occ.] College Instructor; [memb.] Northeast Arkansas Council on Family Violence, AASAP (American Association of Student Assistance Personnel); [hon.] Winner of Little, Brown Writing Contest for Developmental Educators 1995; [oth. writ.] Reviews of for those still at sea. The life of Karol Wojtyla Freelance Text Book Reviewer, scholarly articles.; [pers.] I am a teacher by profession as well as by temperament. But I am also

a learner. Every positive and negative experience of my life has taught me something, and has made me who I am.; [a.] Jonesboro, AR

MCCLURE, THOMAS A.
[b.] February 24, 1942, Tarentum, PA; [p.] Ethel and Walter McClure; [m.] Darlene Rahner McClure, November 23, 1963; [ch.] Sheryl, Shawn, Brian; [ed.] BBA University of Montevallo, Montevallo, AL, AS Gen. Ed, AS Bus Admin, Calhoun Jr. College, Decatur, AL; [occ.] Chief, Air Defense Div (Civil Service) Electronics Instructor, Drake State; [memb.] AARP, Phi Theta and Kappa, United Church of Huntsville, First Cavalry Division Association; [hon.] Poem "The Old Man" to be published in "Memories of Tomorrow"; [oth. writ.] Just A Man, Hope, Happenstance, Pleasantly Old, The Old Man, Principles, Reflections, Looking at Good, God's Realm, Beans, The Night Before The Budget, Unseen Beauties, A Summer's Night, Evolution of Love; [pers.] Poetry is the Lyrical experience of life.; [a.] Huntsville, AL

MCCOLLOM, CASSIE MARIE
[b.] December 1, 1971, Glendale, AZ; [m.] Richard Sean McCollom, June 1, 1996; [ed.] Lee Sr. High School-Houston, TX, San Jacinto College-Pasadena, TX; [occ.] Occupational Health and Safety; [pers.] I rely on spontaneous thought to bring out my creativity. When it happens, I write it.

MCCORMICK, BARBARA A.
[pen.] Bad Mc; [b.] March 1, 1965, Providence, RI; [p.] Nicholas and Avis DiLorenzo; [m.] Robert J. McCormick, May 30, 1987; [ch.] Nichole 7, Jessica 5, Jackie 4; [ed.] GED, High School, CCR.I Comp. 1; [occ.] Poet, Mother of three; [hon.] Editors Choice Award 1995 for the Poem "Brassrail", Editors Choice Award 1996 for the poem "The Grind"; [oth. writ.] I have written a book called "A Breath of Rhyme" containing 250 poems.; [pers.] Savage the human beast empty, a world without peace, crime the prolific feast, a creation destined to cease.; [a.] Johnston, RI

MCDANIEL, SHARON R.
[b.] October 20, 1969, Delano, CA; [p.] Fred and Minnie Hendryx; [m.] Jeff McDaniel, February 16, 1992; [ch.] Aimee R. McDaniel; [ed.] Graduated from McFarland High School; [occ.] Used book store owner; [oth. writ.] This is my first published work.; [a.] McAlester, OK

MCELVEEN, LAURI
[b.] April 6, 1970, Florence, SC; [p.] Robert K. McElveen and Ann McElveen; [ed.] West Florence High School, Francis Marion College; [occ.] Manager of Finkleas Moules, Florence, SC; [oth. writ.] I mainly write poetry - that is my favorite. This, however, was the first one that been published.; [pers.] I have been influenced by simply reading some of the greats. Ernest Hemingway, F. Scott Fitzgerald and Edgar Allen Poe. This particular poem is about myself that I wrote in a time I felt utterly alone.; [a.] Florence, SC

MCGRADY, MARY DOROTHY HARVEY
[pen.] Dorothy McGrady; [b.] January 22, 1922, Portland, MA; [p.] Richard E. Harvey, Mary Elizabeth McCahill Harvey; [m.] Paul T. McGrady, October 30, 1943; [ch.] Kathleen M., David J.,

Paul, T.J.R., Richard H. William W.; [ed.] Deering High School grad attended Westbrook Jr College, Colorado University, Arizona Western College, NAU, and Art Work Shops and Symposiums.; [occ.] Housewife, Artist, attend AWC writing College.; [memb.] Past, volunteer, URK "Auxiliary" at St. Anthony's Hospital, Member of Christ the King Church, Eolu. Oblate of St. Benedict; [hon.] Won Scholarship to The Boston School of Fine Arts. I have exibited Art work in the East and West and received awards; [oth. writ.] Poetry published in the "Colorado Crossing" AWC A Navella "Red Aspen" 1996 Pub. AWC.; [pers.] To carve out a poem is hard work in which I find expression and truth, peace and joy.; [a.] Indian Hills, CO

MCINTIRE, NANCY SUE JOHNS
[pen.] Nancy Johns; [b.] March 26, 1945, Norfolk, VA; [p.] George and Nancy Johns; [m.] Fred A. McIntire; [ch.] 8; [ed.] 8th Grade then GED and 2 yrs. College for Nursing; [occ.] Manager; [hon.] All on Nursing; [oth. writ.] I have written a few articles and wrote songs with mother and sister with only the articles being published.; [pers.] This has been a dream from childhood and now a reality.; [a.] Poland Township, OH

MCKINNEY, EFFIE
[b.] Manning, SC; [p.] Hayes and Frances McKinney; [ed.] Manning Training High, Marygrove College, Specs Howard School of Broadcast Arts; [occ.] Customer Service Representative; [memb.] Word of Faith Int'l Christian Center; [oth. writ.] A gospel play, several poems, currently writing the first entry of a mystery series.; [pers.] I write what I feel, and strive to showcase slices of Life in America. Some of my influences are: James Weldon Johnson, The Barret-Browning's, Joyce Kilmer, Maya Angelou.; [a.] Detroit, MI

MCMAHON, JOHN J.
[pen.] John J. McMahon; [b.] August 2, 1932, Louisville, KY; [p.] Joseph D. Nancy V.; [m.] Barbara Elaine, September 7, 1958; [ch.] Rone F. McMahon; [ed.] Brown H.S., High Museum of Art, Atlanta GA; [occ.] Retired but continue to paint; [hon.] One Man Exhibitions Lecture at Hirchorn Museum of Art 1994; [oth. writ.] (I need a publisher!) working on a book (half finished) on my experiences in N.Y.C. 1957-1963 (Art Scene) and working for Willem De Kooning for 1963-1974 10 yrs. De Kooning considered greatest painter in America.; [pers.] Art is a gift and becomes a conviction and a way of life for me. Painting and writing are verbs and not nouns for me.; [a.] Atlanta, GA

MCNEIL, TOM
[pen.] Tom McNeil; [b.] December 29, 1980, Antigo, WI; [p.] Mr. and Mrs. Ronald McNeil; [ed.] I go to Antigo Senior High School and am going to be a sophomore; [memb.] Art Club, German Club, and Varsity Choir; [hon.] In seventh grade I entered a contest about what our new school meant to me and won for my grade. The piece went into the time capsule to be opened one hundred years from now.; [oth. writ.] In the Minds of Criminals, What the Antigo High School Means to Me; [a.] Antigo, WI

MCQUESTION JR., THOM C.
[b.] July 28, 1971, Toledo, OH; [ed.] High School graduate, Wylie H.S. (Class of '89); [occ.] Ware-house receiving clerk RCL/Lyryck Corp. (Founder of Barney and Wishbone); [oth. writ.] Scrapbook full of various poems and songs; [pers.] I write mostly of personal experiences or emotions. I find the more I write the more complex my writings become. If you have a talent . . . use it. It is one step closer to achieving your goals or dreams.; [a.] Allen, TX

MCWILLIAMS, JETTIE M.
[b.] May 5, 1928, Alabama; [p.] B. F. Manning and Susie A. Culpepper; [m.] Robert A. Crisp Jr. (Deceased 1961); [ch.] Jane R., Victoria A., Kathryn D. and Yvonne N.; [ed.] Berea College, A.B., Bluffton College, Post Bac., University of KY. M.A. and Ed.D.; [occ.] Professor Emeritus, Northern Arizona University, Arizona Licensed Psychologist; [memb.] American Psy. Assn., Az. Counselors Assn., Phi Delta Kappa; [hon.] Editor, College Paper, Member of Twenty Writers Club, Various Awards for Writing Prose, selected by Bluffton College for "Outstanding Alumnus of 1971," Haggin Fellow at U. of Ky., "Outstanding Woman of The Year 1974" Pi Lambda Theta Chapter at Tenn. Tech. U.; [oth. writ.] Several short stories published in local newspapers, numerous professional publications in Psy. Journals, author of Tennessee Stress Scale-R. Currently writing poetry and children's stories.; [pers.] My daughters, grandchildren, and students continue to inspire me.; [a.] Phoenix, AZ

MEDLIN, KELLI
[b.] December 26, 1963, Gastonia, NC; [p.] Bob and Barbara Van Pelt; [m.] John T. Medlin, February 9, 1990; [ch.] Jennifer Van Pelt and Ashley Brilke; [ed.] 1 to 12th grade, Beauty School; [occ.] CNA; [hon.] Several awards in sports, I broke records in high jump and most points in basketball; [oth. writ.] Several poems and 2 children books; [pers.] I have always loved to write when my children were little I always made up poems and stories for them. They are my whole inspiration.; [a.] Castle Rock, CO

MEINKOTH, MICHELLE
[b.] May 14, 1983, Scott AFB, IL; [p.] Richard and Colleen Meinkoth; [ed.] Emge Jr. High; [occ.] Student; [memb.] Emge Jr. High - Band, Chorus, Math Team, and Scholastic Team, 1st Flute in the Band plus, in the school's gifted class; [hon.] Honor Roll, Presidential Academic Fitness Award, 7 firsts in the State Solo and Ensemble Contest plus 1 first superior, on the flute, State Winner for Illinois in the 1995 Young Inventors and Creators Program in the Category of Poem; [pers.] I write when I am at emotional peaks. I write my thoughts as I am emotionally depressed, or in pure bliss. I want the world to feel as I feel, deep in my soul.; [a.] Belleville, IL

MEISCHEN, BETTY
[b.] June 30, 1948, Bellville, TX; [p.] Arthur James Smith II and Sibyl Cloyd Smith; [m.] Delbert L. Meischen, June 20, 1970; [ch.] Jeffrey Layne (25), Michael Scott (22), Rebecca Lynn (19); [ed.] Salutatorian Bellville High School, BA - University of Texas 1970 with Honors (Cum Laude); [occ.] Real Estate Agent; [memb.] Past Secretary on Board of Little Country Theatre Austin County Museum Assoc, ADPA (Alrcraft Owners and Pilots Assoc), International Bell Society; [hon.] President-Austin, County Geneablogical Assoc, Treasurer - Bellrlle PTO, Registrar - Mother Officer's Wives Club Board, Historian - Alpha Gamma Delta Sorority (UT); [oth. writ.] Historical Column for three years entitled "Our Roots" in The Texas Advocate newspaper Columnin "Texas Antiques," Magazine entitled "Postcards from the Past" and articles in other publications.; [pers.] "It is every person's duty to seek out the truth, to strive for the highest and best ideals, to learn from the lessons life teaches us and to understand the true meaning of the world love."; [a.] Bellville, TX

MELVILLE, RICHARD S.
[b.] August 31, 1915, Los Angeles, CA; [p.] Frederick and Georgina Melville; [m.] Dorothy Irene Melville, May 8, 1938; [ch.] Richard, Jr., Andrew J. and James S.; [ed.] Junior College; [occ.] Retired; [memb.] Presbyterian Church; [oth. writ.] Illustrated A-B-C Books for Each of Six (6) Grand children. Publishers not interested in the book, at least not now Oh - the Alphabet is presented as poetry.; [pers.] I am very fond of poetry, especially that with provocative thought, such as Kipling's "If", and Many Of Burns' poems; [a.] San Juan Capistrano, CA

MERCHANT JR., WALTER G.
[pen.] Walt; [b.] April 29, 1953, Claremont, NH; [p.] Phyllis Robinson; [m.] Janice M. Merchant, May 29, 1981; [ch.] Christy, Carie, Pamela, Bonnie, Walter; [ed.] AA Liberal Arts, Saint Leo College, BA Business Admin., Saint Leo College, MS Education, Old Dominion University; [occ.] Systems Analyst, Working on completion of teaching certification so I can teach Math and English in 4-8 grades; [memb.] Delta Sigma Epsilon; [hon.] Cum Laude; [oth. writ.] Several hundred poems, a few short stories, and a life full of notes. None submitted for publication.; [pers.] Settle for nothing short of your dreams, less is not more, by any means. Take the chance, dare to be real, dare for your dream, your dreams to be real.; [a.] Virginia Beach, VA

MERRILL, BERNADETTE RAE
[b.] April 5, 1955, Winner, SD; [p.] James F. and Lavonne M. Wann; [m.] Charles H. Merrill III, May 21, 1973 - Divorced '84; [ch.] Charles H. IV, Melissa Mae, Heather Rae, Danielle Annette Merrill; [ed.] Graduated 1973 from Rushville NE, High School, courses at RCC, Riverside, CA, Special Training in Law Enforcement Academy, Sacramento, CA; [occ.] Retired Correctional Officer; [memb.] Member of Bethel Christian Center. I also contribute to many local charities.; [oth. writ.] I wrote numerous poems for personal satisfaction, none published.; [pers.] I've been influenced by my loving and supportive family and by my deep love of God. I try to express these values in my writings.; [a.] Riverside, CA

MESSINA, PATTI
[pen.] Patti Messina; [b.] April 13, 1932, Bridgeport; [p.] Carl A. D. Louhy, Mae Alice Burns; [m.] Edward A. Messina, December 14, 1951; [ch.] Gail - 44 yrs., Eddy Jr. 41 yrs., Rick 35 yrs.; [ed.] High School Graduate with Honors; [occ.] Housewife - Caretaker and loving wife to my husband; [memb.] Mayors Citizens Public Safety Task Force, G.R.I.E.F., Gun Responsibility in every family

North End Association - Re-Cording Sec., Vetern's Affairs; [oth. writ.] Writings published in local newspapers, many many poems, writings through the years.; [pers.] I find great comfort and release of stress in my writings - also I have so much to say!!

METCALF, CRAIG A.
[b.] October 30, 1969, Greer, SC; [p.] Russell E. and Betty J. Metcalf; [ed.] Student of Greenville Technical College and pursuing a degree in Dietetics; [occ.] Volunteer with the American Red Cross, Greenville, SC Chapter; [memb.] Member of the International Food service Executive Association (I.F.S.E.A.), Vice-President of the Greenville Tech. Student Branch of I.F.S.E.A.; [hon.] President's List, Greenville, Technical College, Greenville Tech. Ambassador Program; [oth. writ.] None published but have written many over the years.; [pers.] It is hoped that "Nature of Peace" will help to establish a sense of tranquility in all who read it. I believe that Nature possess a beauty that has the power to heal the damages of daily stress in our lives.; [a.] Greenville, SC

METZGER, ORPHA JUNE
[b.] June 11, 1927, Garrett, IN; [p.] Grant and Mabel Holman; [m.] James A. Metzger, March 4, 1953; [ch.] Maria Church (RN), James Metzger (Engineer), Margaret (Physical Terapist), Timothy (Novel Computer Engineer); [ed.] Bowling Green State University, Peabody College for Teachers, Transylvania College of Bible; [occ.] Care giver to 99 yrs old mother (Alzheimer), retired State of Florida Health and Human Services Program Specialist; [memb.] Angelica Church; [hon.] Camp Fire Girls District Chairman, Ill. Councilmember, LA, "Rolls Royce" District Employee Award, FL; [pers.] Life is poetry in motion — my writings have been for personal and friendship expression of emotions of living.; [a.] Columbus, NC

MIDDLETON, WANDA LEE
[pen.] Cookie; [b.] March 13, 1958, Baltimore, MD; [p.] Mrs. Dorothy Witherspoon Middleton; [ed.] Attended Northwestern High School (grad. 1976), Community College of Baltimore, Major in Liberal Arts; [occ.] Dietary Aide, Restaurant Worker; [memb.] St. Luke's House Writer's Center, Liberty Church; [hon.] Service and Merit, Asbury Methodist Home Outstanding Teenager Church Award, 6th Grade Classroom Messenger Award; [oth. writ.] Sparrowgrass Poetry Forum, Inc., Cader Publishing; [pers.] Thanks to my mother, Mrs. Dorothy Middleton, love, Christianity, Family Support of her children Wanda, Ryan, Willie, Russell and grands. I strive to reflect the goodness of mankind in my inspirational writing.; [a.] Rockville, MD

MIDGETTE, MIKE
[pen.] Mike Midgette; [b.] Charleston, SC; [p.] Renata Stowasser, Patrick Midgette; [ed.] Industrial Skills Centre and Loop College; [occ.] Wood worker; [pers.] God is nature. We are all a part of nature. So we're all a part of God.; [a.] Chicago, IL

MIDWELL, JENNIFER K. SPRAGUE
[pen.] Sprague; [b.] June 26, 1973, Spokane, WA; [p.] Linda and Darry Sprague; [ch.] Sarah, Brittney, and Christopher; [ed.] Finish 10th Grade Graduated May 17, 1996 from NAC class (NAC is Certified Nursing Assistant); [occ.] NAC at Valleycrest Nursing Home; [hon.] Graduated as highest Student in NAC Class; [oth. writ.] Have lots more poetry but never tried to publish any of my poems 'til now.; [pers.] I have trouble speaking how I feel, so I say how I feel through poetry. I was and am now greatly influenced by my loving mother Linda Sprague.; [a.] Spokane, WA

MILES, ISLA
[b.] 1942, Utica, NY; [p.] Karl and Mary Stauss; [ch.] Maat Flynn; [ed.] Staples High School, Westport, CT, Lauralton Hall, Milford, CT; [occ.] Retired; [pers.] I like to share in life's magnificent adventure by writing.; [a.] West Henrietta, NY

MILLER, JUDITH KELVIN
[b.] June 12, 1944, Flushing, NY; [p.] Michael and Helen Kelvin; [m.] James G. Miller, April 23, 1966; [ch.] Douglas Ryan; [ed.] Clayton High, A.B. from Washington U. (St. Louis), M.S. from Univ. MO. St. Louis, Ph.D. from Washington U. (St. Louis); [occ.] Molecular Biologist; [oth. writ.] Research papers in Scientific Journals.; [a.] Clayton, MO

MILLER, MICHAEL
[pen.] Charl Rellim; [b.] September 25, 1972; [p.] Bill and Sonya Miller; [ed.] Presently enrolled at California State University San Marcos; [hon.] Black Belt in Okinawa, Gojyu-ryu Karate-Do, Scuba DiveMaster, both by age 20; [pers.] My poem is a reflection of the atmosphere that occurs when we turn our backs on the Judaeo-Christian ethics that our country was founded on.; [a.] San Diego, CA

MILLER, SHARON
[b.] April 25, 1957, Ft. Wayne, IN; [p.] David and Joyce Drayer; [m.] Christian G. Miller, October 2, 1982; [ed.] Woodlan High School Woodburn, IN., Medical Classes at IVTech Ft. Wayne, IN.; [occ.] Unit Clerk Parkview Mem. Hospital Ft. Wayne, IN.; [pers.] Only God can take the mists of a dream and make it a graspable reality.

MILLER, STAN
[b.] May 10, 1942, Sedalia, MO; [p.] Voggi H. and Kathryn Miller; [m.] Jackie Miller, August 24, 1962; [ch.] (4) Kathryn Jeanne, Alicia Renee, Kimberly Rae, Eric Aarnold; [ed.] Grantsburg Wisc. High School 1960, Bethel College 1964 B.A., U. of Wisc. Superior 1974 MST; [occ.] 10-12 Social Studies Instructor Luck Public Schools - Luck, Wisc.; [memb.] Trade Lake Baptist Church, Luck Northwest United Educators, NEA; [hon.] H.S. Football All-Conference 57, 58, 59 College F. Ball MUP - 1964 FB. Co. Capt. 1959 and 1964 State Entry Solo and Ensemble/Sax Quarter 1960; [oth. writ.] None published - but I do write narrations for our Church's Christmas and/or Easter presentations on occasion.; [pers.] I try to reflect on God's goodness, mercy and love in most of what I write for it is to Him that I owe all that I have and all that I am.; [a.] Luck, WI

MILLS, FLORENCE M.
[pen.] Poby; [b.] April 6, 1974, Saugus, MA; [p.] Davida L. McCoy, Gordon Mills; [m.] Joseph E. Payne, July 26, 1997; [ed.] Burlington High School, attended Franklin Pierce College, hope to go back in the Fall; [occ.] Nexus - Assistant House Manager of Mentally Challeniged Adults; [memb.] HAWC - Help for Abused Women and Children; [hon.] English Award (HS) Track and Field letter and Wings Award for Competition of HAWC, Student Advisory Board Membership Awards (HS); [oth. writ.] Several poems written but only one other published "Silence" in my High Magazine, "Collab." That was my first attempt "Forgive Me" is my second.; [pers.] I personally believe in the impossible dream. What one man/woman finds to be impossible I find it to be the stuff worth living for. My favorite poems are by Alice Walker.; [a.] Lynn, MA

MINGO, RACHEL R.
[b.] September 18, 1963, Eugene, OR; [p.] Imojean, Neil Anderson; [m.] Dennis J. Mingo; [ch.] Aaron James, Cierra Chantell; [occ.] Homemaker, Writer; [memb.] Karnak First Baptist Church; [oth. writ.] Series of Children's Christian Books, awaiting publication.; [pers.] My inspiration is to touch readers in a way that inspires their heart, soul and mind.

MITCHELL, ESTHER
[b.] April 3, 1978, Spokane, WA; [p.] Donald and Linda Mitchell; [ed.] Kaiserslautern American High School (9-10)/Punxsutawney Area High School (11-12), Institute of Children's Literature; [memb.] Society for Creative Anachronism, International Society of Poets; [hon.] Presidential Academic Fitness Award, National Junior Honor Society, National Honor Society, High Honor Roll, Editor's Choice Award; [oth. writ.] Poetry published locally and in National Library of Poetry Anthology "The Path Not Taken".; [a.] Punxsutawney, PA

MITCHELL, WAYNE LEON
[b.] March 28, 1966, Newark, OH; [p.] Lucille M. Mitchell; [ch.] Josiah Stephen Mitchell; [ed.] Oakwood Academy Huntsville, AL, Oakwood College Huntsville, AL Brookhaven High School Col, OH; [occ.] Office Support Clerk, Cardinal Health Inc. Dublin, OH; [hon.] There are no honors or award just any love for God.; [oth. writ.] I have written many other poems that gave yet to be published 1st book not published "Don't miss it"; [pers.] The only reason for my writing is because of God gift of love he has for mankind. When is a free will love (my prayer is asking "Please fill my ignorance with the knowledge of your understanding so that my decision does not conquer the purpose of you being my connoisseur".; [a.] Columbus, OH

MITCHUM, CASSANDRA
[b.] June 11, 1950, Greensboro, NC; [m.] Preston Mitchum Sr., December 17, 1973; [ch.] Preston Jr., Cynthia, Vanessa; [ed.] Evander Child's High, Monroe Business School; [memb.] New Jerusalem Temple Church, Bible Way World Wide; [hon.] Award of Merit Certificate November 15, 1990, Poem Love, Understanding, and Compassion, Award Golden Poet 1991; [oth. writ.] Book of poems - God's Divine Love (non-published), Working On My Manuscript "A Mother's Love" - 3 chapters completed. The poem is from my book of poems "God's Divine Love."; [a.] Adelphi, MD

MITTOO WALKER, DOROTHY ELAINE
[b.] Jamaica, West Indies; [p.] Joseph and Leila Mittoo; [m.] Kenneth Walker, December 17, 1955; [ch.] Jackie Patricia, Michelle, Karen, Richard, Carolyn and Saundra; [ed.] Registered Nurse, graduate of the University College Hospital of the West

Indies; [hon.] Won a Scholarship to St. Simons College, Jamaica, West Indies; [oth. writ.] "The Magical Fountain of Love," a book of poems dedicated to my son Jackie Mittoo who has left behind him so much of his musical talent.; [pers.] The thoughts are the most beautiful part of one, they reflect the true beauty that lies deep within my soul, a special beauty that you will find in each poem that I send to you.

MOBERLY, KELLY ANN
[pen.] Kelly Ann Moberly; [b.] January 21, 1972, Riverside; [p.] Don and Kathy Moberly (Married 29 years); [m.] Engaged to Shawn Poling; [ed.] Finished High School at John W. North High School; [occ.] Homemaker; [hon.] While I was 15 I did some runaway modeling at the pomona county fair.; [oth. writ.] Vow Set in Stone is one of the first 5 poems I've written. The poem is written about my beautiful engagement ring that Shawn gave me.; [a.] Riverside, CA

MOHAMED, SHAZEENA
[b.] February 7, 1982, Guyana; [p.] M. S. Mohamed, B. Z. Mohamed; [ed.] John Adams High School; [hon.] Graduation Day: June 18, 1996 awarded a medal for Foreign language; [oth. writ.] One poem published in the school journal of Virgil I. Grissom Junior High School 226; [pers.] I write about the things around me, that seem unfair to others. I also write about my experiences with others and about growing up; [a.] Queens, NY

MOIR, INGAR C.
[b.] November 2, 1974, Boston, MA; [p.] Merlene and Calvin Moir; [ed.] Boston Technical High, Boston MA, Northeastern University, Boston, MA; [occ.] Security; [hon.] National Honor Society; [oth. writ.] Personalize poems for individuals, unpublished collection of poems and short stories.; [pers.] My purpose in life is to live and learn. I have not lived long, but I've learned plenty.; [a.] Boston, MA

MOJICA JR., ALBERT
[b.] May 26, 1963, Los Angeles; [p.] Albert and Virginia Mojica; [ch.] G.E.D./Self Educated; [occ.] Maintenance Worker; [memb.] CSEA; [oth. writ.] Blessing In Disguise, The Price, Inner Thoughts, Plastic World; [pers.] "Paradise" was one of my first poems written in my early teens. And is a personal favorite of mine. I hope that you will enjoy it!; [a.] La Puente, CA

MOLEPSKE, TIMOTHY D.
[b.] February 23, 1975, North Platte, NE; [p.] Doug and Jan Molepske; [ed.] Attending Southwestern A/G University; [occ.] Student; [memb.] New Life Fellowship Church, Boy Scouts of America; [hon.] Eagle Scout; [pers.] Jesus Christ is the only way, truth, and life. No man comes to the father but through him.; [a.] Plano, TX

MONDT, TANDY JO BOWMAN
[b.] June 17, 1964, Amarillo, TX; [p.] Delano and Jo Etta Bowman; [ed.] Will complete my BA degree in Music History in May 1977 and will continue on to complete my Master's and Doctoral degrees.; [occ.] Student and Family Business: Rental Properties, Adult Faster Care and Mrytle Lake Resort; [memb.] Involved year round with special Olympics, different types of church works,

Choir Manager 2 yrs for the Bemidji Choir, Member of MENC; [hon.] Deans Lists 2 yrs , Travere Music quarted 2 yrs for the Madrigal Dinners, Minstrel for The Madrigal Dinner, Traveled Europe with the Bemidji Choir, Historian for MENC; [oth. writ.] Higher and Higher published in Treasured Poems of America Fall 1995, God shows His Love published in Treasured Poems of America Winter 1996. Easter and Christmas cantatas and Youth Skits; [pers.] "My heart overflows with a godly theme, I address my psalm to a king, my tongue is as the pen of a ready writer."; [a.] Bemidji, MN

MONHOLLEN, JACQUELINE
[pen.] Jacky; [b.] November 28, 1984, Dayton, OH; [p.] John Monhollen, Beth Howkins; [ed.] Germantown Elementary School; [memb.] S.A.I.L. Young Astronauts Club, Jr. Poms Band Basketball Softball Safety Patrol Swimteam; [hon.] Certificate of Mathematics skills Award of Merit-safety Patrol The Starfish Award Presidential Award for Educational Excellence; [pers.] I think that everything we're doing and learning now is preparation for the future. We all should have fun now and if we want to regret it later, that's too bad.; [a.] Germantown, OH

MONSOUR, UNIS
[b.] November 29, 1935, Cleveland, OH; [ed.] Ohio State University; [memb.] Eckankar; [pers.] Within this flaming globe of protracted conflict, much kindness have I met, but little understanding -- "Vulneratus Non Victus."

MONTANEZ, SUMMER
[b.] August 21, 1975, Monterey, CA; [p.] Joe Montanez, Darlene Estes; [ed.] Monterey High School, MPC College; [occ.] Public Relations; [oth. writ.] Poems published in local newspaper - The Herald, also local magazines.; [pers.] I have so many "words" to write, and once in a while a few will manage to be freed, releasing once again another piece of me.; [a.] Monterey, CA

MONTEAGUDO, MYRA J.
[b.] May 16, 1978, Quezon City, Philippines; [p.] Novito and Clarita Monteagudo; [ed.] St. Paul College of Pasig, Ramapo Sr. High School; [occ.] Student; [memb.] Students against Drunk Driving, Asian-America Cultural Enlightenments, Work-experience Program; [hon.] Certificate of Appreciation from O and E work-cooperation Experience Program; [oth. writ.] Never published screenplays, novels and poems.; [pers.] Writing is a silent form of communication. I do believe that writing is more powerful than any words spoken.; [a.] Spring Valley, NY

MONTOYA, KATHRYN NELSON
[b.] February 5, 1933, Vera, TX; [p.] James L. and Alma Nelson; [m.] 1. Curtis Kidwell, January 14, 1950, 2. Lee Montoya, July 1, 1981 1981 (Divorced); [ch.] 2 sons and 2 daughters; [ed.] BA fr: The University of New Mexico 1968, MA in Education fr: UNM 1976 Post Graduate work also at UNM; [occ.] Retired teacher of English; [memb.] Calvary Baptist Church, Longview, TX; [hon.] Who's Who Among America's Teachers 1992, Award of Merit from World of Poetry, 1990, Golden Poet 1991 from World of Poetry; [oth. writ.] Poems: "Primer", "Going Home", "The

Waterer", "Pulling Daisies", "News Story", "Shame Of A Nation", "Portrait", "The Swing", and others.; [pers.] My philosophy is brief: only a strong faith in God will see us through the storms of life and prepare us for eternity. This theme is seen in my work frequently. Writing poetry has been my joy in the late years of my life when I finally have time to write.; [a.] Longview, TX

MONTZ, KATHRYN
[b.] May 3, 1916, Whitley Co., IN; [p.] Irvin and Bessie (Miller) Bolinger; [m.] Lloyd E. Montz, March 21, 1937; [ch.] Judith (School Nurse), Lorraine (Teaches Nursing), Nelson (College), Acting various work, (Foster Son) now retired education; [ed.] A farmer's wife - High School, the depression, and after family gone, a writer's correspondence course; [occ.] Retired; [memb.] Church - Mission Circle, and Garden Club right now; [hon.] Few and far between. The main one perhaps is that because we gave her Dad a family, our foster granddaughter adopted 7 biracial children and gave them a family; [oth. writ.] "A Mothers Tears" in Wind In The Night Sky and various papers, in reflections, a poetry quarterly - also writing other than poetry in certain newspapers.; [pers.] Due to a farm accident when almost seven years of age, I learned early life isn't always a bowl of ice cream and toppings. That has helped me over many rough spots. I am rich with family and love.; [a.] Cherokee Village, AR

MOODY, KIT
[b.] August 27, 1955, Gouverneur, NY; [p.] Byron and Lillian Gale; [m.] Steve Moody, January 26, 1990; [ch.] Aaron, Amanda; [ed.] University of South Florida special Education Major Gouverneur, Elementary and High School; [occ.] Teacher-pre school Home Day Care Provider; [memb.] Pinellis County Licensee Day Care; [oth. writ.] Children poems, song lyrics working on first novel.; [a.] Palm Harbor, FL

MOORE, ADAM
[b.] December 22, 1980, Westfield, MA; [p.] Ann Bledget, Bruce Moore; [occ.] Student attending Lemon Bay High School; [hon.] Varsity Swimming Award; [pers.] Special thanks to my mother Ann, and my English teacher Mrs. K. Burgess.; [a.] Englewood, FL

MOORE, ARNETTA
[b.] April 26, 1926, McAlester, OK; [p.] Fannie Mae Tyson, Jim Tyson; [ch.] April Cheavers CoCo Moore; [ed.] L, Ouverture High School, Okla. A. and M. College, Univ. of Okla. Medical/Center, College of Marin; [occ.] Administrator, of Residential Care Home for Disabled Adults; [pers.] I enjoy giving the viewer, a chance to head or visualize what I feel in my heart. "A Lifetime of Experiences."; [a.] Santa Rosa, CA

MOORE, LAURA J. TANNOCK
[pen.] Cupcake, Pumpkin; [b.] March 19, 1965, Warwick, RI; [p.] Ronald M. and Evelyn A. Tannock; [m.] John Moore, May 14, 1989; [ed.] Warren High School graduate 1983, 1985 - Business, Secretarial graduate of Katharine Gibbs; [occ.] Vice President, Owner, Operator of SLY Video Inc., DBA CJ's; [oth. writ.] Short stories and plenty of poems; [pers.] I would like to dedicate these words namingly - Days Are Dim, Sunniness Lost Yet, Days Are Spent Loving You.

MOORE, LOWELL
[b.] September 30, 1918, Bloomfield, MO; [p.] Alonzo and Adeline Moore; [m.] Anny E. Moore, October 13, 1962; [ch.] Ralph J. Moore; [ed.] Aurora Mo. High School, Strayer College, Washington, D.C. (Grad.) William and Mary, Williamsburg, Va. (No Degree); [occ.] Retired - Personnel, U. S. Gov't., Real Estate Broker, and Manager, Williamsburg, Virginia; [memb.] Former Williamsburg, Va. Lions Club, Member of First Baptist Church, Washington, D.C.; [hon.] Awards of Merit received through employment in the Federal Service and my associations in the Real Estate business; [oth. writ.] Have written short stories, poems and writings of a political nature.; [pers.] My writings (I hope) reflect the basic goodness of man and the positive rather than the down-side of mankind as He struggles through an ever-changing Environment and Social changes.; [a.] Williamsburg, VA

MOORE, MARGARET
[pen.] Margaret RenFrow; [b.] July 11, 1936, Oklahoma; [p.] Alma W. Northrup, Alfred W. RenFrow; [ch.] Leslie, Dale, Kenny, Mary, Keith, Tommy, Harvey; [ed.] 12 years; [occ.] Project Compassion, Fort Smith Av.; [memb.] Valley View Church of Christ; [oth. writ.] Several songs; [pers.] I strive to show my love for family and nature that my mother gave me, in my writings I can express this love for the beauty of nature and people.; [a.] Greenwood, AR

MORGAN, BRIAN PETER
[pen.] Rrothechild, Vein; [b.] July 26, 1976, Wenatchee, WA; [p.] Bill Morgan, Sue Morgan; [ed.] Cle Elum-Roslyn High; [occ.] Student; [oth. writ.] Several unpublished collections of poetry.; [pers.] I do most of my writing at night because I find I think better and am more imaginative and honest, and I use blank paper, no lines, I find lines too constricting.; [a.] Cle Elum, WA

MORGAN, EUNICE CONDRY
[b.] January 23, 1943, Quincy, FL; [p.] Bessie and Jessie Condry; [m.] Ezzie L. Morgan, September 7, 1995; [ch.] Kenneth, Kareen and Theodore; [ed.] Quincy Educational Center; [occ.] Home Health Aide; [oth. writ.] Several published poems.; [pers.] The Lord inspired me to write these poems to be an inspiration to others.; [a.] Quincy, FL

MORGAN, IONE MYERS
[b.] January 22, 1898, Dayton, OH; [p.] C. William and Wilomena Myers; [m.] Gale O. Morgan (Deceased), August 4, 1940; [ed.] Holy Trinity - Primary grades, Steele High School, Miami Jacobs College; [occ.] Retired at this time, formerly, Legal Secretary and Court Reporter; [memb.] Emmanuel Catholic Church, Good Samaritan Hospital Volunteer Association, (currently serving my 24th year) Lambda Omega Sigma Sorority (now extinct); [hon.] Special Award Dinner from Good Samaritan Hospital and, jointly, Maria-Joseph Living Care Center (a beautiful place where I presently reside, in the Independent Living Section) for "Outstanding Volunteer Service" (their words, not mine.); [oth. writ.] Quite a few poems: Published only in Maria-Joseph and Good Samaritan literature, worthwhile reading and widely distributed.; [pers.] First of all, thank you, you've made me very happy. I love the beauty of

Nature, poetry, music. As a pianist, I enjoy most playing by ear, entertaining groups from time to time. I try to partake of all social and educational programs offered at the Center and the Hospital, also; [a.] Dayton, OH

MORGAN, JERRY P.
[b.] April 13, 1944, Oakland, CA; [p.] Phil Morgan, Jewel Macomber; [m.] Shari Morgan, December 19, 1976; [ch.] Jerry II, Laron, Bill, Frank, Jerrica; [ed.] Ft. Greely H.S., Oakland C.C., Southern Bible Coll., Summit Sch. of Theol, Rose St. Coll.; [occ.] Master Plumber, Ordained Minister/Pastor; [memb.] N.A. Ministerial Council, Lions Club, United Auto Workers Union, Church of God 7th day, Chairman - Church Board; [hon.] Largest Energy Savings Award - Gen. Mot. suggestion Dept, Dean's List, Short Story Competition - 2nd place, most School Spirit; [oth. writ.] Several articles pub. in local newspaper, poem and articles pub. in Bible Advocate Magazine, article pub. in Harvestfield Messenger Mag.; [pers.] "You'll go along way in life with a good attitude."; [a.] Del City, OK

MORRIS, MARIANNE
[b.] October 1, 1951, Indianapolis; [p.] Robert and Marita Schafer; [m.] Ernest R. Morris, May 19, 1972; [ch.] Karen, Jay, Lisa, Bonnie, Jacob; [ed.] Chartrand High School; [occ.] Legal Secretary, Bose McKinney and Evans (Attorneys at Law); [memb.] Sacred Heart Catholic Church, Knights of Columbus, Musi-gals and Ambassadors; [hon.] "Knights and Columbus Grand Knights Award" and "Family of the Month" Award; [oth. writ.] Several articles published in daily papers and local weekly papers, many poems on various subjects.; [pers.] My poem "This We Ask of You" was written upon the death of my beloved father. My time on earth will never be long enough to refuse someone in need.; [a.] Indianapolis, IN

MORRISON, GARY L.
[b.] December 12, 1941, Detroit, MI; [p.] John Morrison - Bertha Stephens; [m.] Gayle Morrison (Divorced), August 31, 1963; [ch.] Jennifer Roshan, Kevin Alexander; [ed.] Ed.D., University of Massachusetts, M.A., Yale University (Southeast Asia Studies), B.A., High Honors, University of California Santa Barbara, Newport Harbor High School (California); [occ.] Secretary-General, Hawaii Baha'i Community; [memb.] United Nations Association - Hawaii Friends of the East - West Center Pacific and Asian Affairs Council (PAAC) World Watch Institute, Honolulu Institute for the Healing of Racism; [hon.] Woodrow Wilson Fellow, University of California Regents Scholar, National Defense Foreign Language Fellow Fulbright-Hays Fellowship; [oth. writ.] More than 25 articles and reviews published in various journals including "Education for World Consciousness" presented at Shanghai Municipal Women's Federation First Seminar on Women's Issues, "Stewart Medeiros and the Umeke Tradition in Hawaii", and poems "Nightfall of Sylvia Plath" in windows of the Soul and "Corcovado" in Mirror of the Soul.; [pers.] Influenced by modern existentialist writers, personal recovery processes and the universal principles of the Baha'i faith, my writing attempts to illuminate and transform inner states of psychic pain, to bear witness to personal and societal trauma to arrive at soulful moments of oneness, unity and wholeness.; [a.] Kaneohe, HI

MORRISON, R. A.
[pen.] R. A. Morrison; [b.] August 21, 1927, Loveland, CO; [m.] Doris (Divorced), October 1950; [ch.] Four Boys; [ed.] Master of Business Adm., Century University (1988), BSME - Cal State San Luis Obispo, Calif. (1950); [occ.] Air Force Consultant in Thermophysics; [memb.] National Rifle Assoc., Belmont Shore Improvement Assoc. (Past President); [hon.] Holder of Sixty-seven letters of patent. Twenty-seven technical articles, Inventor of the Year Award.; [oth. writ.] "Salvage" about three accidental deaths? Around the same smooth operator. (Unpublished) "Meat Getter" Article in National Rifleman (Unpublished).; [pers.] Writing starts with being a reader and a student of life. Life the more you put into it, the more you get from it.; [a.] Belmont Shore, CA

MORROW SR., DAVID A.
[b.] February 27, 1951, Kansas City, MO; [p.] Mrs. Eddie Mae Cook; [m.] Ethel V. Morrow, June 30, 1991; [ch.] Two sons and one daughter; [ed.] Two years Kansas City Art Institute, 1 year Penn Valley Community. He obtained his high school diploma while in the United States Marine Corps. (Kemo) Honorable Discharge U.S.M.C. '71; [occ.] Consultant/Activity and Sales Rolox Ind.; [memb.] Christ Temple Church Kansas City, Kansas (Baptism); [hon.] Ask to paint portrait (started Negro Baseball Museum) Woody Smallwood for Negro Baseball Museum (Paid Commissioned), Certified Social Service Designee, Ask to speak at health occupation student of Missouri; [oth. writ.] Book form with illustrations "If The Devil Would Only Die"/Illustration By Self, "A Thank You To Life, Before Judgement Is Past, Criminal: Fish out of Water, Black Poetry Book, "If the Devil Would Only Die"-K.C. Public Library, "Seven Great Negro Ballplayers"-book near completion, Professional Brass Engraver, Professional Artist, Expert Chess Player, Public Relations for Armour Home; [pers.] Having grown up in a terrible social environment and a loving family I learned the hard way how precious life is and how we must work toward perfection.; [a.] Kansas City, MO

MORSE, GEORGETTE
[pen.] Georgette Morse; [b.] September 23, 1961, San Diego, CA; [p.] David Smith Wyckoff and Reba Nadine Ronsley; [m.] Riki Morse, August 22, 1987; [ch.] Ashley Nadine, Brooke Ann, John Paul; [ed.] Hargrave High School, San Jacinto College South - degree earned - AA Social Science, University of Houston - Clear Lake (enrolled); [occ.] Licensed Staff Representative State Farm Ins., Houston, TX; [memb.] Phi Theta Kappa: Alpha Gamma Zeta Chapter, Texas State Education Association - Secretary Clear Lake Chapter - University of Houston; [oth. writ.] This is my first published work. I have been compiling a book of my own poetry which I hope to have published.; [pers.] I have always loved to write. Rhyming is my favorite teaching source with my children. My poems deal with personal feelings and events in everyday family life. Poetry is my way of experiencing life whole heartedly.; [a.] Friendswood, TX

MORSE, MILDRED I.
[pen.] Mildred Chase, Mildred Strahl Morse; [b.] November 16, 1928, Dundee, IL; [p.] Russell Lowell Strahl, Opal McVay Strahl; [ch.] Leanna,

Steven, Mark, Timothy; [ed.] Ad in Nursing, BS Health Care Management; [occ.] Retired RN, Working Part-time in post anesthesia care unit; [memb.] International Society of Poets St. Matthias Episcopal Church, Whittier; [oth. writ.] Have had several poems published in anthologies. Wrote a family narrative in 1994. Write non-published articles for own pleasure or need.; [pers.] Most of my writing is done when the idea and the words come without trying. I write mainly to express my feelings and thoughts, and find it rewarding.; [a.] Whittier, CA

MORTIMER, JASON EVERETT
[pen.] Jem; [b.] July 30, 1973, Hillsboro, WI; [p.] Dennis Mortimer and Vicki Parrish; [hon.] THe National Library of Poetry - Lyrical Heritage; [oth. writ.] Many poems, 2 children books, and have recently finished an autobiography, all of which have yet to be published, children's, Books "Once Upon A Time" and "Wishes From Galore", Autobiography "Vicious Circles"; [pers.] The beauty of a poem is merely a reflection of whom it is written for. Though their are many great poets, I find my only true love is the Bible. No other book is filled with such beauty and livelihood.; [a.] Reedsburg, WI

MOSES, PHYLLI R.
[pen.] Phylli Moses; [b.] September 15, 1926, Burleson, TX; [p.] R. Forrest and Lottie Beth Rogus; [occ.] Writer; [memb.] Hospice Volunteer, Member Aviation Organization; [hon.] Many; [oth. writ.] Freelance writer specializing in Aviation History; [pers.] It is my goal to help others to discover their potential to lead rich and neverending lives.

MOYER, DAWN R.
[pen.] Dawn Ruth, Dawn R. Moyer; [b.] April 21, 1961, San Deigo, CA; [p.] Jack and Chic Ruth; [m.] Timothy J. Moyer, November 21, 1987; [ch.] Sophia - 4, Tinytim - 3; [ed.] High School, Emt, Bible School 1 yr., LPN, Mission Courses, Intercultural Relations, Foster Care and Related Issues; [occ.] Day Care Giver, Homemaker; [memb.] Wycliffe Assoc., Christian Collition, Calvary Church of Souderton; [oth. writ.] (None published) short stories, 2 Novels, lots of poetry and devotional journels. Published "I Was Waiting" Poem 1986 Leaflet used by Crisis Pregnancy Clinics in Charlotte, NC; [pers.] I am constantly captivated by the displays of nature. I learn profound truths by watching, observing, and catching those sudden revealing episodes displayed in our great world.; [a.] Dublin, PA

MOYNIHAN JR., JERRY
[b.] February 1, 1949, Point Fortin, Trinidad, W.I.; [p.] Dr. Jeremiah Moynihan and Maura Murphy; [ed.] Colorado Alpine College Steamboat Springs, Colorado Milton College, Milton Wisconsin 71, BA English/Art; [occ.] Delicatessen Clerk Publix, Tower Square, Gainesville, Florida; [memb.] Queen of Peace (Catholic Church), PAL (Police Athletic League); [hon.] Golden Poet Award, Sears Brand Central, Kenmore 65th Anniversary, short story contest, honorable mention; [oth. writ.] Poetry book "Desirer", short stories: A Hay Bailing Summer, Sophomores In the Snow, Commercial, Jennifer, Norwegian Baby; [pers.] Love and Peace; [a.] Gainesville, FL

MOYTA, REBECCA
[b.] March 18, 1982, Pittsburgh, PA; [p.] Virginia and Richard Moyta; [ed.] Going into 9th grade.; [occ.] Babysitting; [memb.] West Alleghany Band and West Alleghany Marching Band; [oth. writ.] None but I hope to publish other of my poems.; [pers.] I hope all poets regardless of age, publish their writings because there is no such thing as a bad poem.; [a.] Coraopolis, PA

MUDGETT, CHRISTOPHER C.
[b.] September 14, 1962, St. Paul, MN; [p.] Allen Curtis Mudgett and Delores Margret Mudgett; [m.] Julie Ann Mudgett, April 20, 1991; [ch.] Nick Charles, Christopher Clay, Dylan Rolland and Collin Ryan; [pers.] My passion for writing is exceeded only by my passion for family. That is true inspiration. It is clearly seen in all that I have to offer. And in all that I have to write.; [a.] Cannon Falls, MN

MUELLER, GLENN D.
[b.] April 16, 1961, Milwaukee, WI; [p.] David and Leslyn Mueller; [a.] Kenosha, WI

MULLALEY, BARBARA J.
[b.] August 6, 1961, Indio, CA; [p.] John and Patricia Mullaley; [ed.] West Roxbury High School; [occ.] Accounts Payable Clerk at Boston Gas Co.; [oth. writ.] All of my poems in High School were published by our School newspaper. I also have other extensive material not published yet.; [pers.] With love and support anything can be accomplished.; [a.] Hyde Park, MA

MULLIGAN, WILLIAM T.
[b.] November 20, 1916, New York City, NY; [p.] William and Elizabeth; [m.] Ruth, August 5, 1944; [ch.] Carol and Thomas; [ed.] NY State Agricultural and Technical Institute, Delhi, NY completed a course in Building Construction; [occ.] Retired; [memb.] The world at large; [hon.] Honorable and discharge from U.S. Army after WW II with accompanying awards.; [oth. writ.] 2,000 short verses and many individually complimentary acknowledgements.; [pers.] Similar to Rodin's Statue of the Thinker, eternally reflecting.; [a.] Fairport, NY

MULLINS, CASSIE
[b.] May 28, 1981; [p.] Cheryl Mullins and Rick Anderson; [ed.] Going into the 10th grade at Pocatello High School; [oth. writ.] Favorite's Poet - Swimming loves to watch movies and knows practically everything about the movies stars. Loves to read and write poems. [a.] Pocatello, ID

MULLINS, JEANNIE
[b.] January 26, 1961, Clintwood, VA; [p.] Jerry M. and Mary E. Stanley; [m.] Lowell Wayne Mullins, July 21, 1978; [ed.] Clintwood High School, Mt. Empire Comm. College (Currently); [occ.] Deputy Treasure - Dickenson County, Virginia; [a.] Clintwood, VA

MULLIS, LELIA C.
[b.] December 7, 1949, Catoosa Co, GA; [p.] Leland L. and Ruth D. Christie; [m.] Olen D. Mullis, February 2, 1991; [ch.] Mike Ewton, Lee Ewton, Heath Ewton; [ed.] Ed. D., University of GA, Ed.s., West Georgia College, M. Ed., Berry College B.S., University of TN at Chattanooga; [occ.] Assistant

Professor, State University of West Georgia; [memb.] Chattanooga Association for the Education of the Young Child, Georgia Association for the Education of the Young Child, National Association for the Education of the Young Child, Association for Supervision and Curriculum Development, International Reading Assoc.; [hon.] Who's Who in American Education, Who's Who in Emerging Leadership, Who's Who in America; [oth. writ.] Articles for "The Reading Teacher" and "Tennessee and Children" Manuscript for University Microfilms International.; [pers.] Poetry is a celebration of joy and Love to me. I write it because it bubbles up in my soul.; [a.] Hixson, TX

MUNT, JASON
[b.] December 9, 1977; [p.] Marvin Munt, Joan Munt; [ed.] Indus High, Rainy River Community College; [pers.] My poems are meant to show the dark, hypocritical side of society. I believe that we must see these things to truly enjoy the good things in life.; [a.] Littlefork, MN

MURLEY, MICHAEL D.
[b.] July 18, 1965, Garrett, IN; [p.] Richard Murley, Mary Ann Murley; [m.] Mellissa K. Murley, September 19; [ch.] Cody Michael, Allie Rachelle; [ed.] St. Joseph Elementary, Garret High; [occ.] Electrical Supervisor; [hon.] Eagle Scout; [pers.] I write what I feel, it starts in my heart, and comes out my hand. The most meaningful things in life is your "family and friends".; [a.] Garrett, IN

MURPHY, TROY W.
[b.] July 5, 1972, Kansas City, KS; [p.] George Murphy, Linda Jones; [ed.] F.L. Schlagle H.S.; [occ.] Student; [oth. writ.] Soulja, Drifter, Friend; [a.] Morrow, GA

MY, PHAN TAN
[pen.] Y-Yen; [b.] 1934, North Viet-Nam; [ed.] Graduated from RVN Military Academy, Course 13, 1956-1958, Graduated from 2 US Military Courses, Company and Battalion Level, at Fort Benning, GA 31905; [memb.] Of Association of Artists and Writers/Army of Republic of VN; [hon.] Honorary Citizen of Columbus City, Georgia, 1971; [oth. writ.] Wrote to military reviews and Cultural magazines of The Republic of Viet Nam before 1975.; [pers.] All people are friends over the four seas.; [a.] San Jose, CA

MYERS, MARGARET
[pen.] Margaret Myers; [b.] July 16, 1942, Indiana; [p.] Carl Williams, Dorthy Julin; [m.] Jerry Lee Myers, August 7, 1960; [ch.] Gregory Lee, Clint Eugene, Rhonda Ruth, Jerry Lee Jr., Sarah Lynn; [ed.] Fairmount High, Indiana University; [occ.] Housewife; [memb.] Church of the First Born; [oth. writ.] Mostly poems of the family or songs of the Lord.; [pers.] I strive to show through personal experiences the hand of God is my life. My inspiration for my writings have come from my Lord.; [a.] Gas City, IN

NADER, KATHRYN
[b.] August, 13, 1969, Elizabeth, NJ; [p.] Nancy Dice and John Murin; [ed.] B.A. - Eckerd College; [occ.] Elderhostel Coordinators, Eckerd College; [memb.] Amer. Diabetes Assoc., Women of the Moose 562, Lifelink of FL, Lakeview Presbyterian

Church Youth Group Director; [hon.] Phi Delta Kappa, Omicron Delta Kappa, Who's Who Among Students in American Junior Colleges, Who's Who Among Students in American Colleges and Universities, Dean's List, National Dean's List; [pers.] Despite the tone of the poem, God has been good to me. I'm divorced, I lost eyesight about 5 years ago — it was restored, my kidneys failed about 4 years ago — I've had a transplant. And I returned to college and graduated Cum Laude at 26. Life is good!; [a.] Saint Petersburg, FL

NADER, PERCILLA
[pen.] "Pat"; [p.] Deceased; [m.] Deceased; [ch.] Three girls, 10 grandchildren, 5 great grandchildren; [ed.] Iji School, Education BA - MA Language; [occ.] Retired School Teacher, Second Career Receptionist; [hon.] Silver Award (Poetry Golden Award) World of Poetry, Award of Merit Honorable Mention World of Poetry; [oth. writ.] Short stories Cathale Annals Poetry: World of Poetry; [pers.] My inspiration to write poetry is God's Creation so beautiful the flower blooming, birds singing, human being walking this earth.; [a.] Worcester, MA

NADILE, BETTY
[b.] March 9, 1933, Bellows Falls, VT; [p.] Paul and Edna Nenninger; [m.] Joseph Nadile, July 19, 1968; [ch.] Cynitha, Paul, Edna, Steven; [ed.] High School Graduated; [occ.] Retired from: Naper's Jewelry Factory, April 19, 1996; [memb.] ARRP; [oth. writ.] Wrote poems for friends - published in local paper.; [pers.] My children are all grown up, married and out of the house. I wrote this poem. To show my congratulations the way they all have turned out and show their values to life.; [a.] Meriden, CT

NAKPODIA, ARTHUR O.
[b.] April 20, 1962, Nigeria; [p.] Wilson Nakpodia, Mene Agnes Nakpodia; [ed.] Lagos Progressive School, Ibru College (High School), Bevlah Heights Bible College, Atlanta Urban League (Business School), North Metro Technical Institute; [occ.] Ordained Minister, Security/Crime Prevention Officer, soon to be a netware (Networking) Engineer; [memb.] United Christian Church, Ministerial Association, A Member of "The International Gospel Outreach Ministries"; [hon.] Best Word Processor; [oth. writ.] Books soon to be published are: Transitional Quotations and Short Poems, Transitional Poems, Heart-Cry Quotations and Short Poems; [pers.] "Determination to move forward cancels all backwardness." "You can be who you want to be by being what you want to be, by doing what you need to do to be who you want to be."; [a.] College Park, GA

NAQUIN, DEBBIE RAMSIER
[b.] June 5, 1961, San Antonio, TX; [p.] Edgar and Elsa Gates; [m.] Richard Naquin, April 25, 1992; [ch.] Kennedy Paige and Kansas Christian; [occ.] Director of Marketing; [pers.] My heavenly Father has greatly blessed me with heart-felt words to put down on paper the love I feel and felt for my beloved brother.

NASH, MICHAEL J.
[pen.] Michael John Nash; [b.] February 7, 1968, Springfield, VT; [p.] Roy Nash Sr., Betty Nash;

[ch.] Ashley Jean, Natasha Marie; [ed.] Fall Mountain Regional High School; [oth. writ.] I have written many poems. I hope to someday get published.; [pers.] I love to reflect courage strength and hope also beauty through my poetry.; [a.] Charlestown, NH

NAVARRO, DANIEL E.
[b.] April 3, 1962, Argentina; [ed.] Currently a Psychology Major at I.U.P.U.I in Indianapolis, IN; [occ.] Student, Secretary at Vencor Hospice of Indiana; [memb.] Former performing artist, dancer, visual artist and independent choreographer in N.Y.C; [hon.] Dean's List in College in all semesters; [oth. writ.] Writings in spanish published in writer's journals in Argentina.; [pers.] My writing in a poetic journal, a lyrical record of my journey in words.; [a.] Indianapolis, IN

NAYLOR, NANCY
[pen.] Pat Naylor; [b.] January 13, 1936, Coatesville, PA; [p.] Nellie Jackson, George Leslie; [m.] George Naylor, April 20, 1957; [ch.] Linda Lee, Leslie Ann, Susan Marie; [ed.] Scott High School - Coatesville; [occ.] Housewife; [memb.] Eastern Star, Four Seasons Club, Leloa United Methodist; [oth. writ.] Poem published in Apprise Magazine.; [pers.] I have written about 150 poems, all inspired by my faith in God. It is my hope only that those who read my poems are touched as I have been touched and blessed by God.; [a.] Leola, PA

NELSON, ELIA J.
[b.] April 11, 1980, Rochester, NY; [p.] D. Christian Nelson, Lois A. Nelson M.D.; [ed.] Maumee High School (grad. 6/97); [occ.] Student; [memb.] American Harp Society; [oth. writ.] Several articles for diocesan church newspaper, Church Life (Episcopal Diocese of Ohio); [a.] Maumee, OH

NELSON, NIKI ZOE
[pen.] "Zoe"; [b.] April 4, 1983, Evansville, IN; [p.] Jeffrey Eden and Denise A. Nelson; [ed.] Carmi White County Illinois Schools; [occ.] Student and Ballet Dancer with Evansville Dance Theatre; [hon.] National Honor Society, Citizenship Award, Science Award; [oth. writ.] Book of poetry called "Poems of Comedy and Tragedy".; [a.] Evansville, IN

NELSEN, NORMAN R.
[b.] December 13, 1936, Staten Island, NY; [p.] Bernhard and Gladys Nelsen; [m.] Divorced; [ch.] Ronald Keith Nelsen (deceased) and Katherine Elizabeth Nelsen; [ed.] Princeton University AB 1958 Woodrow Wilson of Publish and International Affairs; [occ.] Retired; [memb.] The Presbyterian Church, Basking Ridge, NJ, Scholarship Commitee, The International Society of Poets; [hon.] Phi Beta Kappa; [oth. writ.] "Revival? in Sea of Treasures, several poems published in the local weekly newspaper; [pers.] Often I write of the Unity and Diversity in what God has created and continues to create.; [a.] Basking Ridge, NJ

NESSETH, SHIRLEY J.
[b.] November 12, 1938, Minneapolis, MN; [p.] Mr. and Mrs. Olaf Kjome; [m.] William M. Nesseth, April 18, 1959; [ch.] Julie Lynn Estigoy, 3 grandchildren - Andrew William, Adam Robert, Alison Marie; [ed.] Graduate Spring Grove High School and Minnesota School of Business; [occ.] Secretary

(retired) and homemaker; [memb.] Zion Lutheran Church, Michigan Education Ass'n. (MEA) and National Education Ass'n. (NEA); [oth. writ.] Several poems written for and about people for special occasions.; [pers.] My poetry reflects my inner feelings about people, times, experiences and places. I have been greatly influenced by my small town, rural upbringing in a Christian family.; [a.] Clawson, MI

NETTLES, ANITA G.
[b.] February 21, 1962, Monroeville, AL; [p.] Fred Clausell, Clara Clausell; [m.] Dan Nettles Jr., November 1, 1982; [ch.] Kimberly Monique Nettles; [ed.] Monroe County High; [occ.] Occupational Therapy A.T.C. North Side, Atlanta, GA; [memb.] Bethel Baptist Church; [pers.] I have accomplished a goal in my life, that is being a writer. Writing is a part of my life. I thank God for that gift. Being able to achieve and have success that there is hope.; [a.] Atlanta, GA

NEVELS, BRENDA
[b.] February 23, 1952, Midland, MI; [p.] Norman and Maryjane Sauer; [m.] Waldon Nevels, October 26, 1973; [ch.] Heather, Josh, grandmother of one; [ed.] Saginaw Valley University, Central Mich. University; [occ.] Homemaker, Independent Business Rep.

NEVILLE, JR. JAMES BRYANT
[b.] October 24, 1963, Petersburg, VA; [p.] James B. Neville Sr., Gloria B. Neville; [ed.] Dinwiddie County Sr. High John Tyler Community College; [occ.] First Vice President, Bank of McKenney, McKenney, VA; [memb.] Elder, Bott Memorial Presbyterian Church, past President, DeWitt - Rocky Run Ruritan Club, National Spinal Cord Injury Association; [hon.] Phi Theta Kappa, graduated Summa Cum Laude with degrees in Computer Programming and in Accounting, 1993 Outstanding Citizen, Dinwiddie County Ruritans; [oth. writ.] "Only a Mother Would Know - The Darker Side of Disability", Accent on Living magazines, December, 1994; [pers.] Because of an auto accident in 1981 that left me partially paralyzed, I've come to appreciate what we take for granted each day. I think it's important to help others to see this too.; [a.] DeWitt, VA

NEVSHEMAL, JOHN
[b.] October 14, 1935, Milwaukee, WI; [p.] Beatrice and Anthony; [m.] Divorced; [ch.] Kristine, John, Martin, Michael, Joseph; [ed.] Marquette University BS and MS Degrees; [occ.] Engineer, Professor and Consultant; [memb.] Society Sigma XI, Sigma Phi Delta, International Society of Poets Stephen Ministry; [hon.] International Society of Poets; [oth. writ.] Short stories, plays; [pers.] I attempt to explore the inner being of the person. Especially life's relationships and the family as the fundamental unit of human existence.; [a.] Parker, CO

NEWMAN, JONELLE R.
[b.] September 22, 1979, Manhasset, NY; [p.] Serena Bordes; [ed.] A Senior at Spanish River High School in Boca Raton, Florida; [occ.] Student; [memb.] President of the Creative Writing Club, currently in AP English (College level); [hon.] Received a Certificate for the Florida Writes Writing Exam; [oth. writ.] A poem entitled "Thank You" is currently being published in the book: An

Anthology of poetry by Young Americans.; [pers.] Writing is my passion, it is a certainty for me. It is so much a part of me, for it is my soul.; [a.] Boca Raton, FL

NEWTON, RANDY
[b.] July 8, 1963, Dinuba, CA; [p.] Lincoln and Barbara Davis; [occ.] Truck Driver; [a.] Reedley, CA

NICHOLS, STEPHEN
[pen.] Stephen D. Nichols; [b.] December 31, 1966, Charlotte, NC; [p.] Judith Nichols, Stephen E. Nichols; [ed.] Currently working toward an English Degree at Central Piedmont Community College; [occ.] Switcher at a Local Trucking Company; [pers.] I hope my writings entertain, teach and are enjoyed by everyone who reads them.; [a.] Charlotte, NC

NICKERSON, EDMUND J.
[b.] August 30, 1996, Chatham, MA; [m.] Janice G. February 2, 1946; [ch.] Lynne F, Lois D, Lana M.; [ed.] Chatham High, University Ala.; [occ.] Retired (33 yrs. worked for Comelec Co.); [memb.] American Legion, VFW, Moose Lodge, X. Marine; [hon.] Purple heart wounded in action at Battle of Tarawa in Pacific; [oth. writ.] First attempt

NIECIECKI, DANIEL OISIN
[b.] September 25, 1979, Syracuse, NY; [p.] Florence and Casimir Nieciecki; [ed.] Thomas J. Corcoran High School; [occ.] High School Student; [memb.] Most Holy Rosary Church Choir; [hon.] High Honor Student; [oth. writ.] Poems published in local poetry anthology and presented at ancient order of Hibernians National Convention, also short fiction and a historical novella; [a.] Syracuse, NY

NIELD, SHERRY
[b.] October 18, 1969, Deer Park, WA; [p.] Lorri Williams; [m.] Larry Nield, April 2, 1988; [ch.] Two; [ed.] High School; [occ.] Homemaker; [oth. writ.] Personal poems; [pers.] This poem is dedicated in loving memory to my wonderful mother-in-law, Mary Nield who lost a battle to cancer. I love you Mom!; [a.] Greenacres, WA

NOEL, AMALIA
[pen.] Amalia Noel; [b.] September 29, 1945, San Antonio, TX; [p.] Cayetano and Juanita Valenzuela; [m.] Divorced, February 14, 1990; [ch.] Carol, Frank, May, Kathie and Andy; [ed.] High School Edgewood High EODE, Teacher Aide Training, Self Taught Artist, Nurse Aide; [occ.] Artist stay at home Handicap; [memb.] San Fernando Cathedral Church Member, Daughters of Mary, CYO (Catholic Youth Association); [hon.] I was always shy and kept way from the limelight. I lived a life as a Ghost, yet I lived. I'm just not afraid any more.; [oth. writ.] Started a book, but blindness in one eye made me stop. Love to write poetry some from life some from pain and loss. Very versatile.; [pers.] Edgar Allen lived life to die. I'm dying to live. He was my mentor. Darkness lives in all of us. It's just up to us to love every day we live. Life is really interesting and new everyday.; [a.] San Antonio, TX

NOEL, DANAE
[pen.] Marie; [b.] August 18, 1950, Detroit, MI; [m.] Engaged to be wed February, 1914; [ch.] 2 children, 2 grandchildren; [ed.] B.A. in Religious

Studies, M.A. Counseling Psychology; [occ.] Psychotherapist intenn MFCCI; [memb.] CAMFT; [hon.] Outstanding Honor Student in Honors Program; [oth. writ.] Master's Thesis on the Recall of Reincarnation; [pers.] Each day I try to become more aware of myself, others, and my environment. I believe love in what you do is the most essential ingredient in life.; [a.] Santa Rosa, CA

NOEL, KATHERINE
[b.] March 31, 1959, Baltimore, MD; [p.] Juanita and Ronald Noel, Paul Bouthner (Stepfather); [ed.] Patapsco Sr. High, Baltimore MD; [occ.] Controller; [pers.] Poem written for 11th grade English class assignment.; [a.] Hawthorne, NJ

NOISETTE, VIVIAN
[b.] August 29, 1943, Atlanta City, NJ; [p.] Francis Taylor, Mary Taylor; [m.] Benjamin Noisette, July 17, 1969; [ch.] Tony, Guy, Sabena, Maryam; [ed.] Essex Co. High School; [occ.] Homemaker, sketches, make and sell clothes; [pers.] I write my poems and short stories based on what some might think simple things that surround my way of life. I really and truly am influenced by my thoughts and the final finish of my poems or the short stories. I love Maya Angelou.; [a.] Atlanta City, NJ

NORMENDIN, JASON P.
[b.] July 7, 1976, Providence, RI; [p.] Dennis and Donna Normendin; [ed.] Graduated William E. Tolman High School, Pawtucket, R.I. June 13, 1994. Three semesters college with 2.0 GPA.; [occ.] Warehousing Clerk for local department store chain; [hon.] Editors Choice Award for 1994 and 1996; [oth. writ.] I have been included in four other "NLP" anthologies, including "East of the Sunrise", "Best Poems of 1996", "Best Poems of the 90's", and "Journey of the Mind".; [a.] Pawtucket, RI

NORRELL, GENEVA STOCKTON
[pen.] Geneva Stockton Norrell; [b.] July 18, 1928, Okolona, AR; [p.] Alfred and Gertie Stockton; [m.] John C. Norrell, December 16, 1978; [ch.] Charyl and Wade Williams (Father Deceased 1959); [ed.] Okolona High School C. and H. Modeling and Fashion Display, Hot Spring's, Arkansas, National Institute for Residence Exterior and Interior Design, Dallas, TX; [occ.] Retired - Custom Home Builder; [memb.] Wesleyan Service Guild, Baptist Church, American Cance Society; [hon.] National Homes, Poet Laureate Plaques; [oth. writ.] Poems and articles printed in various newspapers and magazines, poems written and read in public appearances for special occasions.; [pers.] I have no major educational degrees. My genealogy is undistinguished. What you read in my poems reflects what I have to say about God, Jesus, The Holy Spirit, my loved ones and friends. Also about the The Wonderful World God created for mankind to live in. May God get the glory for the words in rhyme that he places on my heart to write.; [a.] De Soto, TX

NORTHCUTT, VIRGINIA LEE
[pen.] Virginia Lee Northcutt; [b.] July 13, 1930, Covington, KY; [p.] Lulu Slaughter; [m.] October 7, 1949 divorced now; [ch.] Judy Northcutt, Ron Northcutt; [ed.] 1-12th year/North Light School Of Art/Enrolled now in "The Institute of Children's Literature." Correspondence course.; [occ.] Re-

tired due to open heart surgery. Aorta valve replacement.; [hon.] Diploma "The North Light School of Art" B+-1994; [pers.] My writing began when I retired early, because I had open heart surgery. I no longer could do the things, I did before. I needed something else to fulfill my life of giving and caring. I started writing poems, at this time, to share with others. God gave me a new talent. The poem, I wrote, in the garden. This is what the clouds looked to me.; [a.] Covington, KY

NOTAR, SUSAN
[b.] August 13, 1965, Chicago, IL; [m.] Andrew Morris Williams, August 28, 1993; [ed.] B.A. French 1987, University of Wisconsin - Madison, La Faculte de Lettres, Aix-en Provence France 1985-86; [occ.] Policy Specialist Child welfare issues, U.S. Dept. Health and Human Services; [memb.] The Writer's Center, Bethesda, Maryland; [pers.] I'm interested in making poetry less intimidating and more approachable. I lpve poems that have a strong emotional impact-that "hit you in the pit of your stomach."; [a.] Arlington, VA

NOVACEK, KIMBERLY
[b.] November 15, 1977, Minneapolis, MN; [p.] William and Karen Novacek; [ed.] Graduated from Kennedy High School; [memb.] Bloomington Athletic Association (Softball); [hon.] Distinguished Student Award, Honorable Mention in Kennedy High School art competition, Certificate of Special Congressional Recognition from Jim Ramstad; [oth. writ.] First poem published.; [pers.] My feelings and beliefs are expressed an honored in my poems.; [a.] Bloomington, MN

NUTTALL, BILLIE K.
[b.] February 26, 1915, Arkansas; [p.] Harry and Maggie King (Deceased); [m.] Vincent W. Nuttall (Deceased), July 10, 1933; [ch.] Alan Nuttall; [ed.] High School grad.; [occ.] Homemaker; [oth. writ.] Tribute to Mother, Old Swimming Hole, Yosemite, Anniversary Poem, Old Homestead, The Mountains, Faith, Childhood in the Sierras, Friendship, etc; [pers.] Poem book for my son.; [a.] Wilseyville, CA

OATES SR., JEROME
[b.] April 19, 1921, Evansville, IN; [p.] George and Georgia Mae Oates; [ch.] Jerome Jr. G.; [ed.] High School 1939; [occ.] Master Herbalist Proctologist; [pers.] I am not sure how I learned the things I know, but no one doubts I know them.; [a.] Chugiak, AK

ODLE, DAVID CHRISTOPHER
[b.] May 19, 1975, Bryan, TX; [p.] Bill and Donna Odle; [m.] Brandi Odle, August 3, 1996; [ed.] Three years of Community College, toward a degree in English and Music. Eastfield Community College Mesquite, Texas; [occ.] Convenience Store Clerk; [pers.] "My intention is to make people more socially and politically aware of the most precious resources being exploited every day."; [a.] Garland, TX

ODOM, VERNON DEMETRIUS
[pen.] Vern Odom Bearanther and Verron D. Odom; [b.] April 2, 1955, Los Angeles, CA; [p.] Leodell Vera Stark and Louis Odom; [ed.] Graduate of John Muir High, Pasadena CA., B.A. in Communications, Theology, Theatre from Biola University in La Mirada, CA; [occ.] Shift Supervisor for Tower

Book in Sacramento, CA, on Florin Rd; [memb.] Brotherhood of Light, Agape Fellowship; [hon.] Entertainer of the Year, Writer of the Year and Academic Honors of the Year from the ABC program in John Muir High; [oth. writ.] Three Books: Jimmy The Detective Boy, Speaking Words of Wisdom, and That Side Of The Moon Is Too Dark, Articles in the Comptom Sporting News; [pers.] Everything is created in this life, to contribute to life for the continuation of life. Writing poetry is my small way oF contributing to life for the continuation of life. My hope is that my poems will inspire others to contribute something constructive to humankind.; [a.] Sacramento, CA

OFFNER, RANDY
[b.] July 2, 1965, Champaign, IL; [p.] David and Hazel Offner; [m.] Dr. Jennifer Kruse Offner, June 19, 1993; [ed.] Urbana High School, Southern Illinois University Carbondale, Eastern Illinois University, Parkland Junior College; [occ.] House Husband; [memb.] The International Thespian Society; [hon.] Dean's List; [oth. writ.] Several short stories, as yet unpublished; [pers.] Empathy is my life blood. If I can put into words a feeling or experience that even just one other person can relate to and gain perspective from, I feel personal fulfilled as a writer.; [a.] Quincy, IL

OHLENKAMP-LAVERY, RENAMARIE
[pen.] Jacinna Marie; [b.] 1950's, Washington; [p.] Ronald and Saundra Ohlenkamp; [m.] John Oliver "Hansom"; [ch.] Justin Ryan and Jairus Micah; [ed.] Highline High, some college at Highline Com. Coll; [occ.] Housewife and owner of Jon Marche "2nd time around useful items"; [oth. writ.] Poetry: "Alone", "Daddy Mine", "Morning Dew", "Rainbows" currently in production as a trilogy with 3 sub titles; [pers.] I believe with family support the world becomes small. With God our universe becomes a ball. And I have both, thank you all; [a.] Graham, WA

OLENEACK, DENEENE
[b.] May 15, 1954, Grand Rapids; [p.] Richard and Adeline Huedepoll; [ch.] Tabatha Walker and Rebecca Kukla; [ed.] 12th grade; [occ.] Lead person at Thornapple Valley; [pers.] God gave me this poem as a gift for my oldest daughter that I gave to her at her sixth grade graduation.; [a.] Grand Rapids, MI

OLIVER, JOYCE
[b.] August 15, 1950, Fredericksburg, VI; [m.] William Oliver, November 21, 1974; [ch.] Cynthia and Rebecca; [ed.] Graduate of Spotsylvania, Senior High School - 1969, Spotsylvania, VA; [occ.] Rural Carrier Stafford Post Office, Stafford, VA; [a.] Fredericksburg, VI

OLSEN, SUSAN
[b.] December 9, 1974, Saint Louis, MO; [p.] Jerry and Joan Olsen; [ed.] Indiana University at Bloomington; [hon.] Dean's List; [pers.] "Too Many Oreons" was inspired by Lisa Lipsman - always and forever my friend.; [a.] Saint Louis, MO

OLVERA, MARGARET
[pen.] Alanis; [b.] September 16, 1976, Tahoka, TX; [p.] Julia and Wally Ramos; [ed.] High school graduate from O'Donnell High; [occ.] Currently serving for the US Army; [oth. writ.] Other poems

that I've written; [pers.] I write poetry based on feelings and life. This is how I show my feelings to others. I like writing poetry, and it makes me feel good after I finish a new poem.; [a.] O'Donnell, TX

ONDROVIC, JOHN EDWARD
[b.] May 2, 1968, Portsmouth, VA; [p.] John and Suzane; [ed.] A.A. Indian River Community College - 1989 BS - Major and Minor General Bus. Administration and Minor Economics 1992, BS - Major Finance 1995, Part/Time Student in Masters (MBA); [occ.] Business Admisnitration/Fulltime Financial Analyst; [oth. writ.] First attempt at Poetry; [pers.] You must live your life like there is no tomorrow, you must love with all your heart you must strive to succeed, and you must show compassion for all human beings.; [a.] Tampa, FL

O'NEILL, PATRICIA
[b.] May 18, 1954, Mojave, CA; [p.] Michael J. Pisciotta and Peggy Jane; [ch.] Francisco, Michael, Jose, Phillip; [occ.] Premium Acctg Manager; [oth. writ.] Various short stories and poems - none published, nor submitted for publishing.; [pers.] This poem was written, for me to express my growth, goals and desires. It is always my hope that my writings can help others to reach within themselves and tap into their innermost feelings.; [a.] Brooklyn, NY

ORLOFF, GREG
[pen.] George Iagles-George Trent; [b.] May 17, 1932, Taft, CA; [p.] Maurice Orloff and Marian Joy Orloff; [m.] Sandra Lee Orloff, July 19, 1964; [ch.] Tracy Michele Orloff - Scott Hale Orloff; [ed.] Army Language School - 1954-55 Russian Translator - U of California Berkeley 1957 American Graduate School of International mgt 1959.; [occ.] V.P Kelmore Investment Co.; [memb.] Founder - Society for Appreciation of F Scott Fitzgerald 1954 Board of Directors - Santa Monica Little League 1982-88. YMCA - 1983-87; [hon.] Who's Who in the West National Program Chairman - Association for Corporate Growth Editor Founder/Quagmire (Monthly Magazine); [oth. writ.] Anonymity Spring, Three From Fitzgerald (play); [pers.] The conditions of life are those of defeat - the redeeming things the deeper satisfactions are those that develop from struggle.; [a.] Santa Monica, CA

ORSOMARSO, MARGUERITE ROCCO
[pen.] Marguerite Angelica; [b.] New York, NY; [p.] Gilda and Benjamin Rocco; [m.] Dom Orsomarso, July 2, 1955; [ch.] Donald Frank, Gail Marie; [ed.] Mother Cabrini High School, Hunter College (B.A.) and Hunter College (M.A.) - grad. work at Cornell, Columbia Univ.; [occ.] Retired Teacher, Volunteer Worker, Writer (A vocation); [memb.] Christian Assembly Women's Club, Member of New York State Retired Teachers, Professional Women's League; [hon.] Iota-Tan Alpha, (Language Medal Award), Dean's List for 4 years, History Medal etc., previous poems published in church and local publications.; [oth. writ.] Several poems and writings published in church and local publications, other poem published in the "Anthology of Thoughts".; [pers.] My goal is to help each of us, in all states of life, circumstances, and in all areas of life, the greatness and wonder of God - The Creator!; [a.] East Islip, NY

ORVIS, DAVID L.
[b.] January 18, 1981, Baltimore, MD; [p.] Richard and Karen Orvis; [ed.] Mechanicsville Elementary, West Middle, Westminster High; [occ.] Sophomore - Westminster High School; [hon.] Presidential Academic Fitness Award (Elementary and Middle School); [oth. writ.] "War" - Poem; [a.] Westminster, MD

OSBORNE, JOSEPH D.
[b.] December 24, 1970, Wurzburg, Germany; [p.] David and Barbara Osborne; [ed.] Harrison High Pikes Peak Community College, University of Colorado at Colorado Springs (Currently Attending); [occ.] Security Guard, Colorado Springs Fine Arts Center; [memb.] American Heart Association International Society of Poets; [hon.] Dean's List; [oth. writ.] "Loyalty and Trust" published by The National Library of Poetry; [pers.] My writings reflect my beliefs concerning marriage, relationships, and women. I hope to send a message to women that there still are few men out there who are romantics at heart.; [a.] Colorado Springs, CO

OTUM, ANNE
[pen.] Anny O., Nenny O., U. G.; [b.] June 3, 1980, Nigeria; [p.] Mr. and Mrs. Otum; [ed.] Morehead High School; [memb.] FHA, PYF, Soccer Team; [oth. writ.] Poems: Peace, Love; [pers.] I write for fun. I write because of the way I feel about things. I don't write because of what people say, I write for me, myself and I. I also think others should too.; [a.] Eden, NC

OWENS, TINA
[pen.] Tina Hall; [b.] June 10, 1943, Marked Tree, AR; [p.] Earnest A. and Neta F. Loveland; [m.] Jerry W. Owens, March 26, 1990; [ch.] Rodney S. Hall and Rhonda S. Russell; [ed.] Central High School, Harrisburg, AR, Grad. May 21, 1961; [occ.] Disabled due to cancer.; [memb.] Traceland Baptist Church; [oth. writ.] A large collection of unpublished quotes, poems and songs, 1 song recorded and copy write, several poems published in newspapers, 1 poem hanging in vestibule at bear creek baptist church in Ozark Mtns., AR, also greeting cards all occasions!; [pers.] If my work can touch just one person's life then I have achieved my purpose in my writings.; [a.] Verona, MS

OWUSU-ADUENING PAUL
[pen.] Derick Slave; [b.] July 26, 1954, Boni (Ashanti); [p.] Akwasi Amoako-Ayaa (father), Mary Akua Bronya (mother); [ch.] Franklin, Fred and Fabian; [ed.] St. Mary's College (Takoradi) 1970-74 Specialist Trg. College (Winneba) 1978-81, University of Science and Technology (UST), Kumasi-Ghana, 1989-92; [occ.] Art Educator, Sculptor; [memb.] Distinguished Member of International Society of Poets; [oth. writ.] Several Poems published in Ghanaian Newspapers (The Mirror) and 'Step' magazine, articles published in 'The Pioneer' - themes political.; [pers.] Music feeds the soul poetry lightens its path. We need both, humanly speaking, if our lives could be on course, devoid of thirst or tumbles.; [a.] Gaithersburg, MD

PACINI, CHRISTOPHER
[b.] January 18, 1964, Chicago, IL; [m.] Kelly V. Pacini, September 19, 1992; [ed.] Bachelor of Science (B.S.), Masters of Education (M.Ed); [occ.] Software Trainer and Support Specialist; [memb.]

Senior Niles Center Volunteer; [hon.] Received Stipend for graduate school; [oth. writ.] "A Message of Simplicity" (journal), "The Father Within" (Fictional novel), "Collection of Poems" 1981-present.; [pers.] "Be and let be".; [a.] Des Plaines, IL

PACK, MARK A.
[b.] February 2, 1975, Jacksonville, NC; [p.] Nancy Amir, Wayne Pack; [ed.] One year of College; [pers.] I think one of the most important things in life, is to take time to notice the less important things in life. I believe this is a very important step to achieving happiness. Simply slowing down can do wonders.; [a.] Smyrna, GA

PADGETT, MIRANDA
[pen.] Randi Padgett; [b.] July 1, 1981, Ashland, OR; [p.] Gordon and Susan Padgett; [ed.] Sophomore at Ashland High School, Ashland, Oregon; [occ.] Student; [oth. writ.] "I Have My Own Beauty" published in Fringes, articles and poetry published by Scream Louder - White Zombie Fanzine.; [pers.] I feel my poem expresses hope for the new generation of artists. We are all artists in our own way.; [a.] Talent, OR

PAGE, VALERIE ELIZABETH
[b.] August 10, 1981, Los Angeles, CA; [p.] Lucius and Gwen Page; [ed.] Canfield Elementary School, Crescent Heights Elementary School, Brentwood Science Magnet, Los Angeles CES, 9th grade; [occ.] Student at Los Angeles CES; [memb.] Greater Page Temple, C.O.G.I.C., Youth Choir; [oth. writ.] Paradise, School House, and Alone.; [a.] Los Angeles, CA

PALINKAS, BRENDA
[b.] December 14, 1967; [p.] John and Louella McCachren; [m.] Divorced; [ed.] South High, then went to Willoughby Tech Center; [occ.] Prep Cook; [oth. writ.] I have other poems.; [pers.] I started writing poems when I was nine. Everything I write is the way that I feel.

PANEL, REBECCA
[pers.] This limerick was written for my baby daughter, before her birth. Upon learning the sex of my baby, against her father's wishes, I wrote this quickly to distract him from the naughty error of my ways. Welcome to earth, baby!

PAQUINGAN, MANUEL L.
[b.] December 21, 1925, Iligan City, Philippines; [p.] Vicente Paquingan and Leona Ladlad; [m.] Miriam Oliverio Paquingan, November 17, 1995; [ch.] Rey, Roy, Orlando and Rolando; [ed.] High School Graduate, Iligan School, Iligan City Philippines; [occ.] A pensioner as a retiree; [memb.] Senior Citizens; [oth. writ.] Several poems still on file, articles published in our church magazine, the Harbinger; [pers.] In my writings, I aim to make people happy, not for prizes for "What shall it profit a man, if he gains the whole world and losses his own soul?"; [a.] Iligan City, Philippines

PARAN, TEMUJIN
[pen.] Tim Paran; [b.] August 12, 1958, Philippines; [p.] Felino Z. and Norma D. Paran; [m.] Susan Grace Navarro-Paran, February 22, 1985; [ch.] Philip, Eleanor, Norman and Maggie; [ed.] Bachelors degree in Economics; [occ.] Records and Informations Manager for the City of Odessa,

Texas; [memb.] ARMA (Association of Records Managers and Administrators), International Repertory Philippines; [oth. writ.] Asian Migration to the US Comparative studies on Philippine Culture. Relocation: Is it a Solution to the Philippines Housing Problem.; [a.] Odessa, TX

PARDUE, ANITA M.
[b.] January 8, 1960, Palymra, NJ; [p.] John and Ruth Pardue; [ch.] Niece - Marissa Carin Pardue (my inspiration to write); [occ.] Child Care Worker; [mem.] Sea Girt Lanes Bowling League; [hon.] Girl Scout Bake Off; [pers.] The poem represents the forgotten children of the Holocaust. Children of today are still victims of atrocities such as violence, child abuse, drugs and pornography. It is very important to remember that our children are our most precious resource, they are tomorrow's future.; [a.] Manasquan, NJ

PARFAIT, MITCHELL A.
[pen.] Mr. Pitifull; [b.] June 27, 1966, Terrebone Hosp.; [p.] Geraldine Carrege; [ch.] Two; [ed.] 10th grade, Vote-Tech; [occ.] Tug Boat, Deckhand eng.; [oth. writ.] Yes I would love to see my poems publishee. Also I have lost more that I have written over the years, just didn't send to no one. So, thanks; [pers.] Just want to say that I'm very glad that my poem was picked out from so many talented poem writers.; [a.] Houma, LA

PARKER, CREDELLA MAE
[pen.] Della, Little Mae; [b.] May 29, 1971, Wash. DC; [p.] William Parker and Credella Parker; [ch.] Pari, Adrian, and Leonard; [ed.] One year of college at the Univ. of Md Eastern Shore, Princess Anne, Md; [occ.] Homemaker, single parent; [memb.] Sweetheart Court of The Groove PHI Groove Social Fellowship; [hon.] Leadership, Courage, Honor Roll, Service and Community Service with DC Service Corps; [pers.] My poetry is my way of opening up the world, to its extensive opportunities.; [a.] Washington, DC

PARKER, HAL
[b.] October 3, 1980, Ind., IN; [p.] Cindy Feeback, Harold Parker; [ed.] West Grove Elementary, Center Grove Middle School, Center Grove High School 9th Grade; [oth. writ.] Nothing published; [pers.] Care about everything you do; it will come out a lot better for you.; [a.] Greenwood, IN

PARKER, TOY LATARSHA
[b.] September 21, 1974, Roanoke Rapids, NC; [p.] Debra Parker, James Parker; [ed.] Weldon High School, North Carolina Agricultural and Technical State University; [occ.] Associate Producer for Fox 8 the Piedmont News channel in High Point, NC; [memb.] NAACP, Student Union Advisory Board, NACA (National Association of Campus Activities), National Association of Black Journalists; [hon.] Dean's List, Student Union Advisory Board - Member of the year, Student Government Association Student Achievement award, NCA and TSU Woman of the year nominee; [oth. writ.] Several poems published in local newspapers and other publications. Articles for the Register at NCA and TSU.; [pers.] Remember while you read, words travel fast: They can rush from your mind and reach beyond the depths of your heart to the center of your soul and return to the page all in the same breath.; [a.] Greensboro, NC

PARKS, PRUDENCE P.
[pen.] Prudence Parkes; [b.] July 3, 1975, Hawaiian Gardens, CA; [p.] Daniel and Teresa Parks; [ed.] Yavapai College, Grand Canyon University - Journalism Major, Sociology Minor; [occ.] Day Care Teacher, Prescott Valley, AZ; [memb.] Calvary Chapel; [oth. writ.] Poem "No Answer" published in anthology by the National Library of Poetry. Special articles for "The Payson Round Up."; [pers.] I want to thank my loving Savior - Jesus Christ cause without Him I would not have this ability. Thanks also to everyone who believed in me! "All great poetry gives the illusion of a view of life".; [a.] Prescott, AZ

PARSONS, VIRGINIA M.
[b.] July 15, 1916, Samaria, MI; [p.] Amos Green, Mary Green; [m.] Marshall B. Parsons Sr. (Deceased), August 8, 1940; [ch.] Kenneth Wayne, Douglas Claude, Marshall B. Parsons II, Wanda Carol, Diane Lynette, Virginia Kay; [ed.] Ypsilanti High, Michigan State, Normal College (now E.M.U.); [occ.] Homemaker; [memb.] Faith Baptist Church seasoned Saints Senior Group - Secretary, Women's Missionary Ministries Council; [hon.] Oratory Contest; [oth. writ.] Articles and poems in church papers and for a Bible Study. Many poems for Christmas and other special occasions.; [pers.] My greatest joy in writing is telling others of Jesus Christ's death, burial, and resurrection. Who, by shedding his blood, paid the price for all our sins, and we, believing in what he did for us, are assured of eternity in heaven with him.; [a.] Greenville, SC

PASCUAL, RHETT VALINO
[pen.] Mariano Valino; [b.] January 12, 1969, Manila, Philippines; [p.] Concordia Valino and Wilson Pascual; [ed.] Univ. of California, Berkeley, B.A., 1990, Univ. of California, Berkley, Ph.D. 1997; [occ.] Student; [memb.] Scientists of Color, Amer. Assoc. for Cancer Research; [hon.] Howard Hughes Medical Institute Pre-Doctoral Fellow, Dean's List.; [pers.] I dedicate my writings to my mother and father. Their courage sustains my existence.; [a.] Berkeley, CA

PATRICK, CLAUDIA
[pen.] Chelsea Trip; [b.] February 7, 1948, Kansas City, MO; [p.] Claude Patrick, Arlene Patrick; [ed.] Old Dominion University, B.S. Northeastern University, Boston Museum School; [occ.] E.S.L. Instructor, Y.W.C.A., Intercultural Service Center, Tulsa English Teacher, Thomas Edison High School, Summer, Tulsa, OK; [pers.] I have been especially influenced by the poetry of John Milton, Emily Dickinson, and Sylvia Plath. I try to express personal impressions of contemporary people and events.; [a.] Tulsa, OK

PATTEN, TERRI SUE
[b.] May 28, 1961, Phoenix, AZ; [p.] Chris and Tom Tucker; [m.] Mark Patten, December 2, 1988; [ch.] Anthony Edward, Shawn Michael; [ed.] Justin Casey, Halee Lynne, Apollo High, Deloux School of Beauty; [occ.] Mother and housewife; [memb.] Moreno Valley Lioness Club; [oth. writ.] My Teen Ager - My Son..., As you Wake unto this Day..., A letter to my Brother..., Anthony - I believe in you!, My Friend..., In Memory of Lynne, Missy... In memory of Missy; [pers.] This poem is dedicated to my close, personal friend of many years, Heidi Turner, to whom I wish much love and success in the years to come.

PATTERSON, JEWEL
[pen.] Jewel Patterson; [occ.] Home Maker; [hon.] Six poem published in National Library of Poetry, two Editors Choice Awrd for 1995, 1996, member of International Society of Poets, two letters from President Clinton I have written from him, about the tragedy of Oklo Bombing, and being our President; [pers.] I love to write, I think it is a God given talent and my way of expressing things that comes from my heart. Soon I hope to publish my work, so I can reach out to help people who are in need. I can write on any subject. I want to thank the National Library of Poetry from the bottom of my heart. Thank to all of you.; [a.] Brighton, TN

PAUL, JOY A. BOUDREAU
[b.] July 26 1966, Massachusetts; [p.] Irene and Paul Boudreau; [m.] Joseph P. Paul Jr., September 21, 1996; [ch.] Step - three boys - Mike, Joshua and Joey; [ed.] Attend Southbridge High School, and I would like to continue my Education by taking some Literature Classes; [occ.] Assembly Worker; [hon.] This is the 1st time I've ever had any Writings Published thank you - it's a Great Honor; [oth. writ.] Promises Of Love, which is a poem I wrote as my vows on our wedding day.; [pers.] I wish to someday write for greeting cards and have plaques made up and sold in stores. This is the hidden talent I never knew I had and along with craft work I do.; [a.] Southbridge, MA

PAYNE, JENNIFER CHRISTINE
[pen.] Jenn C.; [b.] July 19, 1983, Takoma Park, MD; [p.] William and Delores Payne; [ed.] I will be starting 8 grade in the fall, Hammond Middle school; [hon.] Chorus, Academic Achievement Outstanding Performance; [oth. writ.] Nature's Wonders and "Why Do We Have To Die"; [pers.] I write poetry to express my thoughts and feelings, I want to let everyone know what I'm feeling about things from my point of view; [a.] Laurel, MD

PEARSON, DONYA RENEE
[b.] September 8, 1979, Tampa, FL; [p.] Judy and Donald Pearson; [ed.] Presently enrolled in King High School, Senior 96-97; [occ.] Phone Operator for Lawyer's Trust Referral Service; [memb.] Interact (Secretary), Future Business Leaders of America (President), National Honor Society, Riverhills Church of God; [hon.] Who's Who in American High Schools, 1995 and 1996, National Merit Letter, Key Scholar; [oth. writ.] In the Box, The Valentine, The Song, Chaos, You Know the Answer, published in Literary magazines and newsletters.; [pers.] "Scatter Joy!" - Ralph Waldo Enderson. And here is my joy . . . my Lord, Jesus Christ.; [a.] Tampa, FL

PEARSON, KAREN LEAH
[pen.] Leah Pearson; [b.] February 1, 1974, Bremerton; [p.] Tom Pearson, Everlena Pearson; [ed.] Bremerton High; [occ.] Dietary Aide; [pers.] The person who inspired me to write this poem was H. HJ someone very close to me.; [a.] Bremerton, WA

PEASE, FREDRICK BRIAN
[pen.] Travis Miles; [b.] July 16, 1966, Grand Rapids, MI; [p.] Marcia Pease, Charles Pease (Deceased); [ed.] East Kentwood High, Grand Rapids Community College, Lawrence Tech Univ; [hon.] Dean's List, Grand Rapids Community

College; [oth. writ.] I have written many poems out of pure enjoyment and release over the past eight years.; [pers.] I only write poetry when I am inspired about something. It's as if I'm dictating through a higher power. Chaotic thoughts become harmonizing order!; [a.] Wyoming, MI

PEEPLES, ERIC LEE
[pen.] Eric Lee Peeples; [b.] April 4, 1985, Ponca City, OK; [p.] Rhonda and Billy Naden; [ed.] Entering 6th grade; [pers.] I was named Eric Lee Peeples because I have one E in my first name, two E's in my middle name, and three E's in my last name. I play a violin. I Love Lucy is my favorite T.V. entertainer of all time is Lucille Ball.; [a.] Ponca City, OK

PEEPLES, LINDA
[b.] March 22, 1945, Clarksdale; [p.] Mr. and Mrs. G. M. Ruth; [m.] Franklin R. Peeples (Deceased), March 3, 1964; [ch.] Carol Hawkins - 28, Scott Peeples 20; [ed.] Graduate Clarksdale-Coahoma County High School. Graduate Mississippi Delta Jr. College School of Nursing; [memb.] I love my church work. I am women on mission director. I love missions, both learning about missions and doing mission work. My husband was ill for twenty years. This poem was written while I sat and watched the disease slowly take charge of his life.; [pers.] This poem was written in honor of my late husband, Franklin Peeples. He was a diabetic amputee. He died May 28, 1994, after a long illness of diabetes.; [a.] Clarksdale, MS

PEGRAM, TIFFANY
[b.] June 20, 1987, Charlotte, NC; [p.] John and Holly Pegram; [ed.] A.G. Student at Merry Oaks Elem. A honor roll

PELKEY, MELINDA
[pen.] Melinda Pelkey; [b.] November 15, 1980, Pittsburg, PA; [p.] Mary and Keith Pelkey; [ed.] Hampton High School, not in College yet; [oth. writ.] 5 other poems, not published.; [pers.] Writing expresses your feelings, expectations and dreams that no one else knows about except for you.; [a.] Allison Park, PA

PENA, STEPHANIE
[b.] February 21, 1981, San Antonio, TX; [p.] Jose and Herminia Pena; [ed.] Sophomore at East Central High School; [hon.] President of the National Junior Honor Society, Class Vice-President, several U.I.L. Ready Writing Awards; [oth. writ.] I own a personal diary of poems and essays on various topics for school purposes.; [pers.] I write about my own personal experiences. I plan to carry out my writing at New York University and have a career in the journalism field.; [a.] San Antonio, TX

PEOPLES, STEFANI
[b.] October 28, 1986, Midwest City, OK; [p.] John and Janice Peoples; [ed.] 4th grade honor student at Sequoyah Elementary School Shawnee, OK

PERKINS, ANTHONY JAMES
[pen.] H.J.; [b.] August 19, 1978, Lubbock, TX; [p.] Willie and Tina Perkins; [occ.] Student at John Jay High School San Antonio, TX; [a.] San Antonio, TX

PERKINS, ELLEN J.
[pen.] Ellen Perkins; [b.] October 4, 1921, Rutherfordton, NC; [p.] Thomas and Carrie Justice; [m.] Guy C. Perkins (Deceased), June 18, 1948; [ch.] Three; [ed.] High School, Nurses Training; [occ.] Retired R.N.; [oth. writ.] "Triple Trouble", "Book"; [a.] Albion, ME

PETERMAN, RUTH M.
[b.] December 6, 1919, Lakeview, MI; [p.] Mr. and Mrs. Edwin Mills (Deceased); [m.] Lorston (Mike) Peterman, October 7, 1978; [ch.] One son Robert L. Adoms and one step daughter Cristi Hardy; [ed.] High School; [occ.] Retired; [oth. writ.] I have written about 75 poems beginning in High School up to the present time. I love to write. Most of them have more than 20 lines.; [pers.] I am very active in sports also. Pitched Softball - Retired from it at the age of 67 yrs.; [a.] Greenville, MI

PETERSON, DAVID A.
[b.] July 14, 1982, San Antonio, TX; [p.] Margaret James (Grandmother); [ed.] 7th Grade; [occ.] Student; [hon.] 1st Place in Literate and Visual arts, from all grades in my school, 1996; [a.] San Antonio, TX

PETROSINE, JOAN T.
[pen.] Joan T. Petrosine; [b.] November 6, 1934, Jonkers, NY; [p.] Marian (Manfredi) and Joseph Petrosine; [m.] Single; [ed.] NY State Teachers College; [occ.] Retired Sales Administrator; [memb.] Big Sister; [oth. writ.] A novel, "Family Corners" (unpublished); [pers.] The good fortune of being born to a normal, loving family fills life with adventures that a writer can passion in hope of helping others.; [a.] Yonkers, NY

PHELPS, ROSIE T.
[pen.] Rosie; [b.] Homerville, GA; [p.] Mr. and Mrs T. G. Tanner; [m.] Chuck Phelps, February 9, 1993; [ed.] 12th grade; [occ.] House wife; [oth. writ.] I have written thing all my life I've never taken the chance of anyone reading any of it.; [pers.] I feel that I've always been more able to write the things I feel in my heart more so than speaking to someone and my heart is a very private place. I'm grateful you listened thank you.; [a.] Merietta, GA

PHILLIPS, CINDY A.
[pen.] Cindy Phillips; [b.] May 21, 1968, Brooklyn, NY; [p.] Caroline Higgins; [ed.] Clarkstown South High School, Capri School of Hair Design, Rockland Community College's Course in Real Estate; [occ.] Licensed Cosmetologist, Licensed Real Estate Agent; [memb.] Big sister involved with big brothers/sisters; [hon.] Finalist in Miss Rockland County Pageant; [oth. writ.] Poems written to give as gifts for family and friends. A few used for weddings and many for special occasions.; [pers.] To be able to evoke emotion, any emotion, from another, is a special gift. To use words set to bring people closer together is talent given by God.; [a.] Garnerville, NY

PHILLIPS, NANCE A.
[b.] June 14, 1963, Geneva, NY; [p.] Dick and Jane Simmonds; [m.] Gregory Phillips, August 4, 1984; [ch.] Ryan age 9, Jason age 4; [ed.] Geneva High School, Continental School of Beauty Culture;

[occ.] Owner, Operator of Sandy Acres Hair Hut. (Beauty Shop); [memb.] Oaks Corners Presbyterian Church; [pers.] This poem truly came straight from my heart. I thank God everyday for my husband, my children and my parents. They are truly my life.; [a.] Geneva, NY

PIERCE, VADIS
[b.] December 21, 1919, Russell, AR; [p.] H. L. Williams, Myrtle Williams; [m.] Deceased (Otis Irvin); [ch.] Brancen, Harmon, Garrell, Gary, Myrtlevene; [ed.] 8th Grade; [occ.] Retired; [memb.] Church of God Unit Representative; [hon.] Certificate of Participation; [oth. writ.] I have many poems and songs for personal use.; [pers.] I've written a lot of religious poems, trying to uplift God. I've written poems about each of my children.; [a.] Parrish, FL

PIERI, SHIRLEY A.
[pen.] Shirley A. Pieri; [b.] March 28, 1970, New Brighton, PA; [p.] Charles and Shirley Rhodes; [m.] Russell A. Pieri, August 18, 1989; [ch.] Tiffany Ann; [ed.] Shady Grove Christian Academy; [occ.] Housewife/Mother; [pers.] This poem was written from the heart. I was diagnosed with two infertility diseases. Tiffany is only here by Gods Amazing Grace. I firmly believe God hears the cry of his children.; [a.] East Palestine, OH

PINDAR, MARIANNE GERALDINE
[pen.] Mimi; [b.] November 7, Hazleton, PA; [p.] Mr. and Mrs. John and Dorothy M. Pindar; [ed.] MBA - Wilkes College, BA - King's College, AA - Pennsylvania State University; [occ.] MG Enterprise, Owner; [memb.] American Marketing Association, American Association of Notaries, Pennsylvania Association of Notaries, Doris Day Animal League, United State Golf Association; [hon.] Phi Sigma Tau - Philosophy Honor Society, Parnassue Honor Society Bloomsburg Fair - numerous awards (photography, needle craft, ceramics and sewing); [oth. writ.] In progress. "Money" - published in: "Famous Poems of the Twentieth Century" by Famous Poets Society 1996.; [a.] Hazleton, PA

PIRROTTA, EVELYN H.
[pen.] Eve Giorno; [b.] November 6, 1963, Port Chester, NY; [p.] Hope Okeepe, Frank Giorno; [ch.] Rocco Pirrotta; [ed.] Corpus Christi Elementary; [occ.] Marketing/Underwriting Rep for Insurance Company; [memb.] Westchester Volunteer Committee; [oth. writ.] Several unpublished poems, drama/musical play "To the Top"; [pers.] "Don't Stand Still" was dedicated to Nicholas Egan 12/94.; [a.] Greenwich, CT

PLOUFFE, ANITA M.
[pen.] "Anita"; [b.] May 4, 1940, Amesbury, MA; [m.] Widow; [ch.] Donna, Teddy, Michael, Brenda; [ed.] Amesbury High School, Home Health Aide Course, Currently enrolled in "Long Ridge Writers Group" Home Study Exeter High School Adult Education Course. "Keyboarding"; [occ.] Retired; [memb.] Hampton Falls Baptist Church International Society of Poets, Exeter Area Assoc. for the Arts "Tops" Organization; [hon.] 2nd Place - Oil Painting - Deerfield Fair, Homemaker-Home Health Aide Service Award; [oth. writ.] Editor for Newsletter "The Homemakers Rag" for HHHA Agency

- 1980's Poem to be published this summer in anthology called "Spirit of the Age"; [pers.] The secret of peace within your heart is "Learning Forgiveness."; [a.] Exeter, NH

POHLER, LAJEAN
[pen.] Lajean; [b.] June 4, 1943, Crockett, TX; [m.] December 28, 1968; [ed.] Graduated from Harlandale High, San Antonio TX. Also went to Draughon's Business College-1963.; [occ.] Homemaker; [pers.] I write, from within, of things and/or people that touch me and bring me joy. It pleases me to share these things with others.; [a.] Canyon Lake, TX

POPPE, BRIAN
[pen.] Brian Poppe; [b.] September 2, 1966, Lady Smith, WI; [p.] Marian and Delbert Poppe; [m.] Wanda Poppe, August 5, 1993; [ch.] Jonathan, Amanda, Heather, Anthony; [ed.] Fredrick Weyerhaeuser High School; [occ.] U.S. Air Force, Minot, ND; [memb.] All Air Force Rugby Team, NRA, Special Olympic Coach; [oth. writ.] Special poems for my wife.; [pers.] This poem was inspired by my beautiful wife, who has stood by my side through thick and thin for seven years. I love you, Wanda.; [a.] Glenburn, ND

POSTEN, FAITH
[b.] February 11, 1980, Kingston, PA; [p.] Donna Posten; [ed.] Junior at Wyoming Valley West High School; [occ.] Student; [memb.] Church of Christ Uniting and Wilkes University Upward Bound; [oth. writ.] "Different Worlds" which was published in Church of Christ Uniting monthly courier.; [pers.] I have been extremely interested in poetry since when I was 9 years old when I read "I'm Nobody" by Emily Dickenson. I strive to be known as Emily Dickenson Jr.; [a.] Kingston, PA

POWELL, CAROL M.
[pen.] Sunflower Poet; [b.] January 19, 1945, Denver, CO; [p.] Clarence and Leota Wright; [m.] Tommy W. Powell, July 31, 1970; [ch.] Steven Walter and Elizabeth Ann; [ed.] Jefferson High Edgewater Colorado; [pers.] If I write my poems correctly, I will paint words of color on the canvas of your thoughts, so that you will see the painting as it is painted on my heart.; [a.] Belle Plaine, KS

POWELL, CAROLYN
[b.] April 23, 1982, Emporia, KS; [p.] Helen Williams and Erman Williams; [ed.] William Allen White Elementary, Lowther North Intermediate, and Emporia Middle School; [memb.] St. James Missionary Baptist Church Member; [hon.] National Baptist Rose Queen '95-'96, Kansas State Rose Queen for '95-'96; [oth. writ.] Several other poems that express myself.; [pers.] I'm yet only 14 but my heart has felt, my eyes have seen, and my mind has thought things you won't believe. Thank God for His love, grace and mercy.; [a.] Emporia, KS

POWELL, CRYSTAL
[b.] April 29, 1982, Douglas, GA; [p.] Larry and Lynn Powell; [ed.] 9th Grade Student at Telfair Co. High School, McRae, GA; [occ.] Student 9th Grade; [memb.] Science Club, Y-Club, 4-H Club; [hon.] Honor Roll; [pers.] I strive to show the beauty of nature through the written word. I also like to reflect on the many different emotions of all human kind.; [a.] Lumber City, GA

POWLEY, ELEANOR E.
[b.] March 5, 1934, Philadelphia, PA; [p.] Roland Lee Duckworth, Eva Matilda Wagner Duckworth; [m.] William Carroll Powley Jr., August 15, 1953; [ch.] William C. Powley III, Barbara Elaine Powley, Janice Lee Powley; [ed.] West Philadelphia High School (Phila., PA), Montgomery County Community College, Career Track Seminars, Workshops, Forums in the following: Stress Management, Self-Hypnosis Yoga Middle Eastern Arts, Poetry.; [occ.] Adult Eve School Instructor same as above. Education Stress Management Consultant; [oth. writ.] Memories Child, Destiny of Time, Tomorrow and Tomorrow, Memories, Memories are Roses, Immortality of an Artists; [pers.] In my writings I use imagery, as experience comes to us largely through our senses — the language of sense experience.; [a.] Houston, PA

PRETZER, RANDALL WINSTON
[b.] January 2, 1976, Nurenberg, West Germany; [p.] Randall E. and Roasalyn D. Pretzer; [ed.] Graduated from Flour Bluff High School in May 25, 1995; [occ.] Student, Del Mar College, Corpus Christi, TX; [pers.] Poetry means freedom.; [a.] Corpus Christi, TX

PRIDDY, NINAKI
[b.] January 29, 1981, Los Angeles, LA; [p.] Maria and Dalton Priddy; [ed.] A Student at Immaculate Heart H.S. Class of '99; [occ.] Student; [a.] NH, CA

PUGH, JIM
[pen.] Jim Pugh; [b.] July 25, 1936, Greensboro, NC; [p.] Joe and Erylne Pugh; [ch.] Stephen Pugh, Pamela Inveen; [ed.] Rivers High School Ringling School of Art and Design; [occ.] President, Marketing Firm (Automotive); [hon.] Executive of the year Automotive Service Councils of South Carolina, Tire Executive of the Year (Nomination) California Tire Association; [pers.] I have written poetry since Prep School but have never been published. I feel that poetry (a poem) should be understand by the reader.; [a.] San Francisco, CA

QUIGLEY, DANIEL J.
[b.] October 13, 1977, Royal Oak, MI; [p.] Daniel B. and Marie E. Quigley; [ed.] Thunderbird High School, Phoenix, AZ; [occ.] Student at Northern Arizona University as of this fall; [oth. writ.] Many other unpublished poems; [pers.] I attempt to touch upon the deepest nature of people's feelings through my writing. I also try to reflect a positive side, though it is often very dark, in the situations I write about.; [a.] Phoenix, AZ

QUINN, SANDRA L. DUNCAN
[b.] December 1, 1958, Arcata, CA; [p.] Louis and Eva Duncan; [m.] Glenn E. Quinn Jr., July 24, 1995; [ch.] David and Dena, Lara, Travis, Trameena Quinn; [occ.] Housewife; [a.] Trinidad, CA

RAASCH, NETTIE L.
[b.] November 3, 1946, Belzoni, MS; [p.] James Richardson and Frankie; [m.] James Raasch, March 27, 1989; [ch.] John L. Coleman and Lamar D. Coleman; [ed.] Lincoln High School, UW - Milwaukee, BS and MA; [occ.] Elementary Teacher, Robert M. LaFollette Elem. School; [memb.] Metropolitan Milwaukee Alliance of Black School Educators, Jolly Fabulous Clowns, Disabled Ameri-

can Veterans, N.A.A.C.P.; [hon.] North Lincoln Alumni (10 yrs.), Cheerleading Award, PTO's Outstanding Performance Award; [oth. writ.] My poems and essays have been enjoyed by friends, colleagues, and relatives. I have not had any of my writings published until now. What a wonderful opportunity!; [pers.] Poetry is a beautiful way to embrace God's beauty, truth, and love. My high school teacher, Mr. Dale Hagan, inspired me to write. I am grateful for his teaching excellence.; [a.] Milwaukee, WI

RADKE, CHRISTEL
[b.] January 1, 1945, Hannover, Germany; [p.] Anni and Bruno Hirschberg; [ch.] Audrey, Dion and Christina Maher; [ed.] Cal. State University Northridge, Northridge, California; [occ.] Writer; [pers.] I hope to create writings with emotional texture, shaped by intimacy and personal contact, permitting interpretation rather than the absolute, I want to find Woman's voice. I have been greatly influenced by feminist writers and my mentor professor Jan Ramjerdi.; [a.] Culver City, CA

RAHM, NANETTE L.
[b.] January 11, 1957, Durango, CO; [p.] Larry and Maxine Willinger; [m.] Steve W. Rahm, January 7, 1984; [ch.] Kenny R., Evan W., Sammie Jo; [ed.] Farmington High, Burlington High, San Juan College; [occ.] Secretary at Big a Well Service; [pers.] I've written a personal book of poems, they've been used at weddings, funerals and just been read. The girls at work talked me into sending in a poem. This one poem happens to be true. (Sad feelings).; [a.] Farmington, NM

RAICHEL JR., WALTER ANDREW
[b.] May 2, 1956, Stockton, CA; [p.] Walter and Marie Raichel Sr.; [m.] Robyn Allison, 1982; [ch.] Heather Marie; [ed.] Amos Alonzo Stagg High, San Joaquin Delta College, University of Pacific, Advance Security Institute; [occ.] Commissioner, San Joaquin County, Juvenile Justice Delinquency Prevention Comm.; [memb.] St. Bernadette's Church, Free Will Baptist Church, Community Blind Center, National Multiple Sclerosis Society, Delta Humane Society; [hon.] S.J.C. Delta College, University of Pacific, S.J.C. Sherriff's Dept., 11th Congressional Dist., Community Blind Center, S.J.C. Human Services Agency Children Shelter; [oth. writ.] Preserve Our Heritage, The Nine Promises Of A Good Citizen, Keep Them In School, Releasing The Bite, Happy Birth First President George Washington; [pers.] I will try to make our community a better place in which to live. In thought, expression and action, at home, at school and in all my contacts, I will avoid any group prejudice, based on class, race, or religion. I am very thankful for all of the good people that help me because I have flourished successfully.; [a.] Stockton, CA

RAINBOLT, KEN
[pen.] Ken Rainbolt; [b.] August 20, 1978, Elgin, IL; [p.] James Rainbolt, Mickey Rainbolt; [ed.] Schaumburg High School; [occ.] Student; [oth. writ.] Three notebooks of unpublished poems.; [pers.] In my writings I tend to use a lot of emotion. Music influences my writing so emotion is put forth to get my point across.; [a.] Schaumburg, IL

RAINES, BETTY L.
[b.] December 15, 1932, Lincoln City, IN; [p.] Ruby Mae and Arville W. Garman; [m.] Morris Lloyd Raines, January 6, 1951; [ch.] Cynthia Anne and Morris Lee Raines; [ed.] Rec'd a Sociology Academic Scholarship from Austin Peay State Univ. at Clarksville, TN; [occ.] Homemaker and free lance writer; [memb.] Tenn. and KY Society of Poets, Natl. Society of Published Poets; [hon.] Rec'd an Honorable Mention Award Certificate for "Searching" from Illiad Press, 1996; [oth. writ.] "God's Word", "I Am That I Am", "The Rich Man", "Tomorrow May Be Too Late", "Everything Is Needed".; [pers.] I am proud of the fact that Frances Cook, a signer of the Mayflower Compact, is a ancestor of mine, also that I was born in Lincoln State Park where Nancy Hanks is buried.; [a.] Atlanta, GA

RALEY, LINDA J.
[b.] May 23, 1943, Gainsville, TX; [p.] J. D. and Jean Bacon; [m.] Thomas Raley, June 9, 1961; [ch.] Four married sons; [ed.] High School and one year of college; [occ.] Office Manager - World Baptist Fellowship Mission Agency, Arlington, Texas; [hon.] None published; [oth. writ.] My husband and I have been in Church and Foreign Mission work for the past 25 years. Our ministry has taken us to two foreign countries and three states in the US. Our ministry now involves helping missionaries around the world.; [pers.]; [a.] Arlington, TX

RAMEY, LINDA
[pen.] His Handmaid; [b.] March 15, 1946, Columbus, OH; [p.] Juanita Moore (widow); [m.] William Ramey, February 27, 1971; [ch.] (4 adult), Kevin, Trena, Sheri, David; [ed.] Have been certified to Evangelize, as well as, being certified to teach evangelism. I've also completed other courses through a nationally known ministry.; [occ.] Homemaker, writer of Poetry, Grandmother of Seven and one with Jesus = 8; [oth. writ.] A book of Poems, "From Jesus To Me" unpublished. "The Gospel Truth" to be published in The Madison Christian Chronicle at MACI, July "96" issue, "Breath of Life" printed in the Newsletter at the First Assembly of God Church, in Indiana, appros. 1980/90.; [pers.] My deepest longing is, "That I may know Him" Christ Jesus. My prayer for you would be If Only you could see, the fellowship we have when I write The Words He has, "On Eagles Wings".; [a.] Pickerington, OH

RAMIREZ, CONSUELO TREVINO
[b.] Kingsville, TX; [p.] Consuelo Benavides Trevino, Jose R. Trevino - World War II Veteran; [m.] Jose Oscar Ramirez; [ch.] Jose Luis Ramirez; [ed.] Five years old Master of Science Degree in Elementary Education and Psychology and a minor in art; [occ.] Guidance Counselor at Laredo Independent School District, Alma A. Pierce Elementary School, Pre-Kinder, 5th grades; [memb.] Association of Texas Counselors and Border Association of Counselor; [hon.] Artist of the Months and 1st place (Scholarship) in the South Texas Art Contest as a High School Senior, Award for Exceeding Achievements as a Counselor; [oth. writ.] Short story for children: Teddy The Turtle and 30 poems for children. I made these poems into songs.; [pers.] My dream is to one day publish my story and songs so that the children can enjoy them and learn from their important educational messages.; [a.] Laredo, TX

RAMOS, CYNTHIA A. N.
[b.] January 18, 1946, Honolulu, HI; [p.] Joseph and Eleanor Demicola and Alexander and Edith Burgess; [m.] Joseph P. Y. Ramos, March 12, 1962 (Divorced January 3, '89); [ch.] Jennie, Joseph Jr., and Alexander; [occ.] UN Employed at the Moment

RANDOLPH, DEBORAH
[b.] June 9, 1948, Dayton, OH; [p.] Harvey Kindell, Lois Kindell, Jobe; [m.] Larry Randolph, Oct. 18, 1985; [ch.] Robert, Lisa, Heidi; [ed.] Fairmont East High School class of 1966, Kettering, OH; [occ.] Resident Care Tech., Lincoln Park Manor, Kettering, OH; [oth. writ.] I have started my own personal collection of my poetry. I had one poem published in our local paper inspired by the tragic murder of a four-year-old girl, also read on national TV. Another poem is being used at local funeral homes.; [a.] Dayton, OH

RASMUSSEN, GARY C.
[pen.] Ras; [b.] February 8, 1935, Salt Lake City, UT; [p.] Peter Carlyle and Thelma; [m.] Norma, June 1, 1956; [ch.] Debra, Lesa, Paul and Douglas, Grandchildren - Jennifer and Meagan; [ed.] High School, some Business School and the College of Hard Knocks; [ed.] Retired; [memb.] Sport Fan Clubs, Laborers Union; [hon.] Employee of the year 1985, Salesman of the year 1994; [oth. writ.] Short Articles; [pers.] My father awoke in me a love of music at a very early age. He also made me aware, the foundation for most music is poetry.; [a.] Beaverton, OR

RAWLS, BRANT
[b.] June 4, 1976, Bogalusa, LA; [p.] Marie Rawls; [ed.] High School Degree and Junior in College Eckerd College, St. Petersburg FL; [occ.] Student; [hon.] Special Talent Scholarship, School President - McEachern High, Government Officer Eckerd College, National Association of Campus Activities - Multicultural Coordinator, Residential Adviser; [oth. writ.] "I Told You" - song; [pers.] Respect, be yourself, love, we, enjoy, and prosper. Life is what you make it!.; [a.] Saint Petersburg, FL

RAY, ROBERT
[b.] November 15, 1987, Reno, NV; [p.] Karen Ray; [ed.] 2nd grade Lois Allen, Elementary School, Sun Valley, Nevada; [occ.] Student and Martial; [memb.] Larry Hall's Academy of Martial Arts; [hon.] Honor Roll Student; [oth. writ.] Several other poems honoring his sense and craft.; [pers.] Everyone has some talent, no matter how young they are. I'm very happy to be allowed to explore mine.

REAVES, BETTY JO
[pen.] B. J.; [b.] July 10, 1933, Florence, AL; [p.] Tom and Dona Robertson; [ch.] 5 -3 boys, 2 girls, 1 son deceased; [ed.] 12th graduated - Cosmetologist - C.N.A. Member Cancer Society started "Support Group" - "called" Hope, (Helping others prevail emotionally); [occ.] C.N.A.; [memb.] Cancer Society - 10 yrs. Hope Rescue Mission - 20 yrs.; [hon.] Awards in Cosmetologist - Color, Haircuts - Spritz; [oth. writ.] My son was killed by a drunk driver, so I wrote a book. "Dear Broken Heart" I am looking for someone to read and publish it. I have someone getting it ready to be published.; [pers.] I am in Indiana-Christian college now. I am studying - public speaking and counseling.; [a.] Mishawaka, IN

REDDICK, BLONDINE LOUISE
[b.] July 18, 1919, Newark, NJ; [p.] Pauline and Oscar Bohler; [m.] Donald M. Reddick, September 7, 1956; [ch.] Jon Joel Gibbons, Cheryl Gibbons, Douglas Reddick, Blondine C. Meagher; [ed.] Asbury Park H.S., Asbury Business College, N.I.A. (Newspaper Institute of America) College of Continued Education; [occ.] Homemaker, Writer, Poet, Author; [memb.] NIA, ISP, IWWG, FFWA, EIA; [hon.] International Society of Poets (ISP - Advisory Panel) numerous Editor's choice and Monetary Awards from ISP and National Library of Poetry. (EIA - Entertainer - Indi Association), Nashville TN. Best Poet of 1994 and Editor's Poet Award 1994, Female Platinum and Florida Golden Poet Awards 1995 Best South Coast Poet Lyricist of 1996, Female Artist of 1996 - by EIA, 4 time Attendee of Orlando Sentinel "Letter Writer's Forum"; [oth. writ.] Book, "A Month of Revelations in Modern Tokyo, Japan" short stories in "Top Ten Short Stories of 1993" and "Ten Top Short Stories of 1994". Poems recorded as songs on CD's for worldwide distribution - EIA short stories and poetry published by Drury's Press and Sparrowgrass Poetry Forum, Inc.; [pers.] I plan to leave my writings as a legacy for my children and grandchildren letting them know there can be good times even though faced with adversities.; [a.] Longwood, FL

REDDINGTON, THOMAS E.
[b.] August 10, 1938, Everett, MA; [m.] Loaetta A. (Gibson), April 17, 1965; [ed.] BSME Northeastern Univ. Boston, MA., MBA Univ. of Dallas; [occ.] Retired as President of Manuf. Company; [pers.] Poetry is the consequence of inspiration uniting with the deepest sensibilities of the human spirit.; [a.] Norman, OK

REED, JARVIS LEE
[b.] February 11, 1971, Jonesboro, AR; [p.] James and Rosalee Reed; [m.] Kelly (Hutchens) Reed, September 3, 1994; [ed.] Couch High School, Williams Baptist College; [occ.] Minister; [hon.] Dena's List, American FFA Degree; [oth. writ.] Several unpublished poems.; [pers.] The ultimate goal of my writing is to cause people to think about and to explore their own thoughts and feelings about the subjects addressed within that work.; [a.] O'Kean, AR

REED, ROBERT DAVID
[pen.] R——t R—d; [b.] January 13, 1972 (GenXer), New Haven, CT; [p.] David and Sherri Reed; [ed.] Mark T. Sheehan High School Class of '90, University of Connecticut '90/'91, University of Arizona Class of '95, Double BA: Philosophy and (Socio) Political Science; [occ.] Co-Founder/Operator of Arizona OffRoad Adventures, Inc. (Azora) - an Adventure/Travel Company. 1-800-689-Bike; [memb.] International Mountain Bike Association (IMBA); [oth. writ.] I am solely responsible for the promotion/writing aspect of AZORA, Inc. This includes advertisements, business letters and brochures. There have been two brochures published, each an adventurous and descriptive example of our services and experiences.; [pers.] I am a writer. I write about romance, experience, sex, adventure, politics, women, people, metaphysics, cynicism ethics, epistemology, nature, love, lust and like. Writing in the analogic/mataphoric is my trestle to the unknown - to other

levels of consciousness and communication. Through writing and expression, I transcend time and space, the here and now. I relate to Zen Buddhism but attach myself to no religion, for I am a philosopher - a realist, a psychoanalyst, an idealist, Western, Eastern - whatever inspires me at the moment. I despise the media and embrace literature - the classics: Aldus Huxley, Robert Herrick, famous quote to which I relate, it is this: "Is it so bad, then, to be misunderstood? Pythagoras was misunderstood, and Socrates, and Jesus, and Luther, and Copernicus, and Galileo, and Newton, and every pure and wise spirit that ever took flesh. To be great is to be misunderstood." — Emerson. Visualize was written as I researched and wrote a final paper for a class, 'Woman and the Law.' The subject-matter was teenage pregnancy, what can be done? I am looking for a literary/writing agent or merely a publisher for all types of work: Books, novels, poetry, short stories, adventure/travel photojournalism, business writing, advertising, etc. My abilities span a broad base, and I have a flexible schedule for work and travel.

REEDY, MILLIE
[b.] February 24, 1954, Pattsville, PA; [p.] Clarence and Helen Herndon; [m.] Michael Reedy, October 16, 1970; [ch.] Michael Reedy Jr.; [ed.] Pottsville Area High School, Schuylkill Business Institute and varied knowledge from the street; [occ.] Volunteer at Christian Mission for the hungry and homeless; [memb.] Phi Beta Lambda, Make-A-Wish-Foundation; [hon.] Deans List, Outstanding Achievement Award in Business; [oth. writ.] Several Poems and Short Stories (never published); [pers.] I try to reflect my innermost feelings and emotions about life and family into my writings.; [a.] Saint Petersburg, FL

REIFSNYDER, IDA HOPKINS
[pen.] I. Hopkins Reifsnyder; [b.] October 4, 1924; [m.] Deceased, October 26, 1946; [ch.] Phylis May and Susan Marie; [ed.] Amity High, Pottstown Hospital School of Nursing R.N., Morcavian Univ. Yale Theological Seminary, 2 years Graduate of Bangor Theological Seminary Member of Bethany U.C.C.; [occ.] Ministry, currently Intern, C.P.E. at York Hospital; [memb.] Bethany Unity Church Christ; [oth. writ.] Wrote prose presented at C.P.E. incorporated in manuscript I am writing. Also wrote manuscript called "Dear Mom" awaiting to be published and "Mimi's Treasure"; [pers.] I believe, sisters and brothers, we should allow the spirit to guide ourselves through life while striving to live and serve one another in love. Gal. 6

REMILLARD, DAVID M.
[pen.] 'Lil' David Remillard; [b.] May 22, 1968, Toledo, OH; [p.] Real Remillard, Suzanne Remillard; [ed.] Central Catholic High School, Owens Community College; [occ.] I have my own business providing the service of grocery shopping and preparing meals for the retired and elderly; [oth. writ.] I have written five notebooks, containing my poems and prose, that I wish to submit for publication in the near future.; [pers.] The inspiration to write comes from the deep feelings of my heart and soul. My goals are to share, arouse, and inspire those feelings within the reader.; [a.] Toledo, OH

REVILLA, BARBARA
[pen.] Enchantress; [b.] February 13, 1976, Hobart, OK; [p.] Terry Kitch, Judith Kitch; [ed.] J.P.

McCaskey High School, Pennsylvania School of Art and Design; [hon.] PSPA awards for art and poem in literacy magazines; [oth. writ.] Poem selected and published for Watermark Press, several poems published throughout school in literary magazines; [pers.] I want to open people's minds and hearts to the worlds within themselves and to the worlds within others.; [a.] Lancaster, PA

RHEAUME, CHRISTINE
[b.] December 19, 1875, Seattle, WA; [p.] Joanna Rheaume; [ed.] Thunderbird Adventist Academy Pima Community College; [memb.] Philadelphia Church of God; [hon.] Highschool honor roll Recognition of performance in writing award - Thunderbird Adventist Academy; [oth. writ.] I've written several articles for my highschool newspaper. And I write many poems for myself and friends to enjoy in my personal time; [pers.] Special friendships and day to day experiences are expressed throughout my poetry. These are the things that inspire me to write.; [a.] Tucson, AZ

RHYMSTETT, GEORGE EDWARD
[b.] April 13, 1958, Czechoslovakia; [ed.] Lab. Technician - Czechoslovakia; [hon.] Honorable Mention for a poem Crime for Iliad Press Certificate of Poetic Achievement by Amherst Society; [oth. writ.] Crime, Happiness, Winter, The First Man, Melodies of Melancholy, Demonic Whispers, The Ghost of Hamlet; [pers.] Never published in my native language, I learned English by self-study to become an English teacher. After a four-time refusal of the university, I came to America to catch my dream -- to become a writer. I feel very blessed, and thanks to America that I can be published in this wonderful language!; [a.] Clinton Township, MI

RICCI, LYNN
[b.] August 9, 1947, Yonkers, NY; [p.] Alfred Lavorgna, Evelyn Lavorgna; [m.] Mose Ricci, January 2, 1987; [occ.] Secretary, Foster Grandparent Program; [oth. writ.] Article on a close friend in area newspaper.; [pers.] I often put into writing my feelings as events, good and bad, happen to myself or others close to me. At my most emotional times I put my thoughts on paper.; [a.] North Babylon, NY

RICHART, LYNETT E.
[b.] November 30, 1961, Wurzburg, Germany; [p.] Joyce Olsen, Larry Olsen; [m.] Victor H. Richart, May 20, 1995; [ed.] Resurrection Christian Academy; [occ.] Oil Field Operations Technician, Prudhoe Boy, AK.; [pers.] An optimistic, romantic at heart, I try to see the best in any given situation and portray it to others.; [a.] Eagle River, AK

RICKARD, KEVIN ERIC
[b.] December 9, 1977, Hannibal; [p.] Mr. and Mrs. Don and Rose Rickard; [ed.] GED; [occ.] Dura Automotive; [hon.] Artistry contest in Oakwood Elementary, for drawing the new school logo.; [pers.] I wrote this poem on behalf of my girlfriend breaking up with me. Plus if I could stand the pain in my heart if we got back together again, and then she left me again.; [a.] New London, MO

RICKARDS, LINDA S.
[b.] December 3, 1964, Cherry Hill; [p.] Charles and Veronica Rickards; [pers.] I hope that what I

write will make the reader think differently about difficult times. It's those times we show our true selves and learn life's greatest lessons. Happiness comes in moments, not months or years. Learn to recognize these times.; [a.] Delran, NJ

RICKS, RUTH P.
[b.] September 28, 1920, Virginia; [p.] Katie and Joe Prince (Deceased); [m.] George E. Ricks, August 10, 1946; [ch.] Pat and Linda; [ed.] High School (went 12 yrs. - did not graduate); [occ.] Retired Hairdresser; [oth. writ.] Write and share, God's word, weekly, at local nursing homes.; [pers.] I enjoy any and everything pertaining to God's word, the Holy Bible!; [a.] Virginia Beach, VA

RIDOLFO, PAULA SUE
[pen.] Paula S. Teele; [b.] July 17, 1959, Columbus, OH; [ed.] Northland H.S. - Cols. State Comm. College and United State's Navy School of Training, Damnec, VA - specialized. Also Indenp. Hrs of World History Culture-Ged; [occ.] Writing and the Before Mentioned; [hon.] The Nat'l Honorary Medal of Defense Deseret Shield/Storm; [oth. writ.] Coming in the near future: Upon the Great Plains of Abraham another angel was so forged! (A Child's Book). Other poem's to come: My Dear Soul. My Dear Sweet Heart. There are no greater loves and from angel to arch angel; [pers.] I hope to one day see total peace, acceptance and caring for one another everywhere. I am certain that you, too, would appreciate this more so if you had walked where I have walked - seen what I have seen and know what I know - and experienced what all I have. There is no way you could not agree. The Emerald Coast

RIESTERER, SAMUEL
[b.] October 8, 1974, Stayton, OR; [p.] Ken and Carrol Riesterer; [ed.] The Lord's Bible School; [occ.] Watchman; [memb.] Portland Four Square Church; [pers.] Matthew 13:44; [a.] Portland, OR

RIGBY, PETER
[b.] January 27, 1938, Ranchi, India; [p.] Thomas and Rita Rigby; [m.] Zebiya K. Rigby, September 22, 1963; [ch.] Kimuli S. Abella (Daughter); [ed.] Ph.D. Cambridge, England; [occ.] University Professor, MOI University, Kenya; [memb.] African Stories Assoc., Society for African Philosophy in North America, American Anthropological Association; [oth. writ.] Cattle and Kinship among the Gogo: A Semi-Pastoral Society of Central Tanzania, Ithaca and London: Cornell University Press (1969). Persistent Pastoralists: Nomadic Societies in Transition, London: Zed Books (1985). Cattle, Capitalism, and Class: Maasai Transformations, Philadelphia: Temple University Press (1992). African Images: Racism and the End of Anthropology, Oxford: Berg Publishers (Fall 1995). Plus 70 articles in Eastern African studies.; [pers.] I believe African philosophy and literature can teach the world, particularly the West, a great deal, and has already done so.; [a.] Philadelphia, PA

RIGGS, STEPHEN
[b.] December 29, 1959, Louisville, KY; [p.] Nanc Inman, George Riggs; [ed.] BA Art -Spanish University of Louisville; [occ.] Teacher; [memb.] AFT - American Federation of Teachers; [hon.] Deans Scholar 1985-1987 Graduated Cum Laude; [oth. writ.] The Novel El Salvador - The Savior,

which contains the poems Relent, Boy, and End, All of which have been published by the National Library of Poetry. I have also had an editorial piece published about the rigors of being a teacher.; [pers.] I've always been a soul- searching type of person but certain burdens in life have made writing something very therapeutic for me. I suffer from bi-polar disorder and am HIV+ so writing helps ease these burdens.; [a.] Austin, TX

RINGROSE, LLOYD
[pen.] Lloyd Ringrose; [b.] March 19, 1965, Florida; [p.] Lloyd T. Ringrose, Eileen C. Ringrose (both Deceased); [ed.] A.S. Degree (two year degree) in Paralegalism, Nettleton Jr. College Sioux Falls S.D. - currently student Huran University Sioux Falls S.D. - Criminal Justice major.; [occ.] Security officer/ College student/State Legislative Candidate; [memb.] Republican Party; [hon.] Honor roll Nettleton Jr. College, Who's Who in the Republic Party; [oth. writ.] None published; [pers.] I am philosophically a conservative person. I believe all people are equal in the eyes of God. This poem is dedicated "in memory of Eileen C. Ringrose."; [a.] Sioux Falls, SD

RIORDAN, MICHAEL
[pen.] Michael Riordan; [b.] July 1, 1939, Manhattan, NY; [p.] Peter and Margaret; [m.] Jamie (Divorced), September 15, 1968; [ch.] Timothy, Tabatha, Thomas; [ed.] BA John Jay College; [occ.] Courier State Street Bank; [pers.] I can't believe my good fortune. Thank you from the bottom of my heart.

RIVERA, PATRICIA
[pen.] Patti Lane; [b.] February 20, 1933, Great Britain; [m.] Divorced; [ch.] One son, Aaron; [ed.] School of Life; [occ.] Retired; [hon.] Many Honorable Mentions, Community Service Award, Notable Jazz Singer in Europe for many years; [oth. writ.] Many writings, songs and poems, stories and experiences; [pers.] Be the best we can be, all life is connected, we are only links in the Chain, The Stronger the Link, the Stronger the Chain of Life, P.R.E. Rivera; [a.] Agana, GU

ROBERTS, CANDACY M.
[pen.] Pam C. M. Roberts; [b.] November 3, 1960, Little Rock, AR; [p.] Edna C. Roberts, Levell Payne; [ch.] Anthony L. Roberts, Niece Carolyn; [ed.] Fremont High, U.S. Army Police School; [occ.] Directory Asst. Operator, General Telephone So. Cal.; [memb.] Pentecostal, C.O.G.I.C.; [hon.] Various decorations while in U.S. Army Military Police; [oth. writ.] Poem. Those that were was published in the Ft. Belvoir Post paper. Several other poems waiting for publication.; [pers.] Some lives are ruled by destiny, some live a life of dreams, some are touched by dreams and make them come true.; [a.] Bellflower, CA

ROBERTS, DARRELL
[b.] September 28, 1972, Ottumwa, IA; [p.] Keith and Lorene Roberts; [ed.] University of Northern Iowa, Indian Hills Community College, Cardinal High School; [occ.] Student, Artist; [memb.] Cedar Valley Hospice, Hearts Center for the Arts, Cedar Aids Support System, Archaeological Institute of America, Askelon Excavations, Israel; [hon.] Art work displayed at student art shows; [oth. writ.] Several writings created while thinking about my

paintings; [pers.] I desire to learn and will continue my academic endeavor to achieve knowledge about myself and the world I live in.; [a.] Cedar Falls, IA

ROBERTSON, KRISTIE
[pen.] Kristie Robertson; [b.] July 7, 1970, Richmond, IN; [p.] Mary Keiffer and Bill Morehead; [m.] Thomas L. Robertson, October 2, 1993; [ch.] Chelsea - 3 and Tyler - 1; [ed.] Graduated H.S. 2 years of psychology training; [occ.] Deputy for the 107 (Family fraternal organization); [memb.] I.O.F. (Member); [hon.] I was a Sunday school teacher for ages. 2.5. years old and the biggest honor is just being a wife and mother.; [oth. writ.] Have written as long as I can remember 8 years old I write song's stories and poems. I have dozens of poems I didn't believe they were good but my husband told me to enter and just see. He believed in me; [pers.] My family is the most important thing in my life except for God, of course. I believe that if you write, it should come from your heart or it's just useless words on pretty paper.; [a.] Clinton, IN

ROBIDOUX, ANDREA B.
[pen.] Andrea Robidoux; [b.] May 5, 1980, Concord, NH; [p.] Richard and Therese Robidoux; [ed.] Attending Bishop Brady High School; [occ.] Student and write daily; [hon.] Outstanding Achievement awards in several fields, received the gold pin of excellence, have top (#1) GPA in my class (of '98); [oth. writ.] Have no previously published work although I am hoping to write for our local newspaper and publish my novel when completed.; [pers.] I write from the depths of my soul in hopes to express abstract human emotions felt deep within the heart that binds together all humanity.; [a.] Concord, NH

ROBINSON, NATHAN E.
[pen.] Nathan E. Robinson; [b.] June 21, 1966, Bakersfield, CA; [p.] James W. Robinson and Helen J. Robinson; [m.] Aline Robinson, May 14, 1994; [ch.] Cambrinette Lafaye Payne-Robinson; [ed.] Freemont Elementary School, Bakersfield CA, Emerson Jr. High School Bakersfield CA, Bakersfield High School, Bakersfield, CA, Warren Travis High School, Dallas, TX, Three Restaurant Management Diplomas; [occ.] Advance Telemarketing Center an "American Express Representative"; [memb.] First Baptist of Hamilton Park, Church in Richardson Texas; [hon.] Best "swing manager in the Dallas Region in 1989 June 4th; [oth. writ.] Anger, Mirror Method, Minute Man, Bouncing back, Check Yourself, Robinson Theory, Great Procrastinator Growing, etc. "Non Published"; [pers.] The works that I have put together are meant to be "Timeless Peaces of Art" I hope that my poem "success" has accomplished that!; [a.] Dallas, TX

RODGERS, KERRY
[b.] December 24, 1978, Canton, OH; [p.] Beverly L. Rodgers and Robert G. Rodgers; [ed.] Timken High School grade level 10th; [occ.] Full time Student; [pers.] Writing poetry comes naturally to me.; [a.] Canton, OH

RODRIGUEZ, RUBEN
[pen.] Hot Rod; [b.] December 8, 1956, San Antonio, TX; [occ.] Texas Department of Criminal Justice - Correctional Officer; [pers.] Life is but a flicker of time, we're here one moment and gone

the next. We need to learn to live life to the fullest and love with every breath we take. If we could all do that then we would never die! Because, love is eternal!!!; [a.] San Antonio, TX

ROGERS, CHANTELLE
[b.] December 30, 1974, Houston, TX; [ed.] Westfield High School, Saint Edwards University, UT Austin; [occ.] Student, UT Austin Major Elementary Education; [a.] Austin, TX

ROGERS, LESLIE
[pen.] Leslie Rogers; [b.] July 19, 1984, Dayton, OH; [p.] Alan and Sharon Rogers; [ed.] Saville Elementary, Mad River Middle School. Spinning Hills, Junior High Middle School; [memb.] Students Environmental Action, Peers Assisting Success in School, Soccer, Track; [hon.] Blue Ribbon School of Excellence at Mad River Middle School, Presidential awards for academics, Won an essay contest to go meet President Clinton to receive Blue Ribbon Award at Mad River Middle School; [oth. writ.] Poems about nature, God and the deep meanings of words.; [pers.] I feel strongly against racism.; [a.] Riverside, OH

ROMINE, BOB
[pen.] Bob Romine; [b.] November 27, 1951, Canton, IL; [p.] Jack and June; [m.] Sara, 1979; [ch.] Jason, Josh, Melissa, Robbie, Alicia.

ROOS, C. SHANNON
[b.] January 19, 1970, Pensacola, FL; [p.] Phi Roos, Rickey and Sue Sowell; [ed.] Andalusia High, Troy State University B.S. Degree Economics; [occ.] Manager Home Town Electronics Troy, AL also United States Marine Corps Reserve; [memb.] Phi Alpha Theta, Tau Kappa Epsilon, Pike County Chamber of Commerce, Marine Association, St. Martin's Catholic Church, Desert Storm Veteran; [hon.] TKE Leadership Award, Oxford University ESU travel Scholarship.; [oth. writ.] "An Apology" a poem published in 1987. Several articles published in University Newspaper.; [pers.] Much of my poetry centers on man's relationship with God and our effort to become close with Him. I also explore the darker side of man's action and how mankind is good in spite of his somewhat cynical nature.; [a.] Troy, AL

ROPER, MICHAEL K.
[b.] February 14, 1938, Oxnard, CA; [p.] Edgar Roped and Irene Roper; [m.] Diana Jacques Roper, January 24, 1981; [ch.] Daniel, Michael, David and Sean; [ed.] Santa Paula High, Ventura, J.C.; [occ.] Retired - designer/draftsman 30 years (Development - Housing and Commercial); [memb.] Camarillo, Baptist Church; [hon.] Several Letters of Accommodation from County District Attorneys Office for Diagrams of Murders and other cases where diagrams are used in court; [oth. writ.] 60 other poems, some are good and some are pretty good, none published yet.; [pers.] There is at times a certain amount of humor in the truth as in most everything else in life — God, our father, gave us a brain to make choices with and think with, not to sit on.; [a.] Camarillo, CA

ROSE, SIMONE
[b.] October 1, 1980, Jamaica, W.I.; [p.] Marlene Blake, Leroy Rose; [ed.] Junior at Cardinal Spellman High School; [a.] Bronx, NY

ROSEN, SUNNY
[pen.] Sunny Rosen; [b.] September 16, 1946, Michigan; [p.] Max and Merle Stone; [m.] Leonard Rosen (Deceased), August 9, 1967, Jerome Stenn, November 27 1980; [ch.] Mara and Alaina Stern; [ed.] 2 yrs College 1965-67, Mortgage Broker, Real Estate Broker 18 yrs. Old and New Testament Bible Student; [occ.] Consultant Real Estate Developer, Self - Employed, Private Investments; [memb.] Supporter for numerous charities, Alheimers Care Comm., St. Jude Hospital, Key Life Ministries, Children's Home Society, Shul of Bal Harbor, several ministries and Evangelical Missionaries; [oth. writ.] The Pain, Marriage Cira 80's, Childhood Garden, Death; [pers.] All roads lead to where you stand; [a.] Bal Harbor, FL

ROSS, JAMES D.
[pen.] Read with me; [b.] January 1, 1949, Reno, NV; [p.] Mr. and Miss Thelma Wallace Corey; [ed.] Graduated from Wooster High School in Reno in Special Education; [occ.] SSDI, I was a maintenance Supervisor; [memb.] Learning Disabilities Association of Nevada, Northern Nevada Center for Independent Living, Nevada Adult Learner's; [oth. writ.] Not at this time; [pers.] The Northern Nevada Literacy Council and the Truckee Meadows Community College Literacy thank you for helping me to read and write. There are 96.4 million people with literacy problem in the US an there are 27.8 million people with learning disabilities in the U.S. Full independence in reading this poem "Rain." "Rain" is for all of these people if I can do it so can you (Thank you.); [a.] Sparks, NV

ROSS, MELISSA
[b.] March 6, 1985, Ithaca, NY; [p.] Father Daniel Ross, Stepfather Kenneth Scharke, Mother Susan Scharke; [ed.] J.D. Floyd Elementary School, Spring Hill, Florida; [occ.] Student; [memb.] Junior Deputy League, Inc. Dolphin Cruisers; [hon.] Art Achievement Certificate, Citizenship Award, Chorus Award; [oth. writ.] My Cat, The Sunset, My Friends, Rockin Mop; [a.] Spring Hill, FL

ROSTON, ROBERT
[b.] New York City; [ed.] B.S. Degree, Niagara University, (1980) Post grad. Philosophy and Literature; [occ.] Paralegal, story-teller; [hon.] Ockerman Award for Academic Excellence in the field of Labor Relations; [oth. writ.] Children's Stories, unpublished (Mr. Tibbs and Roberto, Adventures of a dog and his boy.); [pers.] Teach the children through art, literature and a good story.; [a.] Dannemora, NY

ROUND, PAULINE M.
[b.] Yakima, WA; [p.] George B. and Mabel L. Woolsey; [m.] William M. Round, November 16, 1963; [ch.] Pamela M. Round; [ed.] King's High, Seattle, B.S. Seattle Pacific College (Now University), B.S. in Nursing U. of WA, Seattle, R.N. (WA State, in active); [occ.] Piano Instructor; [hon.] Salutatorian, King's High, Scholarship Seattle Pacific College, Musical Achievement Award Evangelical Free Church; [oth. writ.] Many gospel song lyrics. Lyrics to one song recorded by Nashville. Several poems published and/or read publicly. Several non-published essays. 31 small books of Aphorisms (non-published).; [pers.] I have had a life long and respect for God the Father, His Son, His approaching Millennium, people, fine arts, the natural world, and true Science.; [a.] Tacoma, WA

ROW, STACI L.
[pen.] S.L. Row or S. Ogden Row; [b.] April 27, 1970, KY; [m.] Brad, 1992; [ch.] Lindsey and Haley; [ed.] School of Life; [occ.] Mother, wife and Office Manager, writer; [memb.] Harvest Fellowship Church; [oth. writ.] Several writing published in local newspapers and local poetry contests.; [pers.] I believe everything good comes from God and faith in Him is the best weapon you can have.; [a.] Jacksonville, AR

ROWSE, LYNDA D.
[b.] June 16, 1969, Boston, MA; [p.] Dale and Laurei MacLean; [m.] Jeffrey T. Rowse, October 30, 1994; [pers.] I am enchanted by the love, support, and devotion of my husband. He has brought out the beauty and magic in my heart. True love is always out there, looking for its soul mate. When you find it, you will know, just as I have.

RUANO, NICOLE ANN
[pen.] Nicole Ruano; [b.] July 23, 1981, Hayward, CA; [p.] Mom - Sarah Neklason, Step Father - Wayne Badding, Father - Mike Ruano; [ed.] Attend Jackson County High School (JCCHS) currently in 10th grade; [memb.] Beta Club and Symphonic and Marching Band; [hon.] GPA: 91.08 Class Rank: 25/341; [oth. writ.] Poems (2) published in 8th grade poetry class book write many other, unpublished poems.; [pers.] I try and be the best I can be but sometimes all I have to do is be me.; [a.] Jefferson, GA

RUCKER II, LONNIE DWEEN
[pen.] Lonnie Rucker, Dween, L. D. Rucker; [b.] June 23, 1977, Meridian, MS; [p.] Paige Hechler, Lonnie Rucker; [ed.] Millington Central High School; [hon.] Dean's List; [pers.] My writings are inspired by love and the lack thereof, and my search for true love. I credit my beginnings in poetry to Somar Presson.; [a.] Memphis, TN

RUCKSTUHL, CHARLES EMIL
[b.] April 21, 1918, New York City; [p.] Charles Emil Ruckstuhl (Sr.), M. Madeline Paltenghi; [m.] Muriel Moison Ruckstuhl, July 8, 1950; [ch.] Linda M. (Deceased); [ed.] Phillips Exeter Academy, 1938, Mass. Inst. of Technology, 1942; [occ.] Semi-retired consultant; [memb.] 32 Degree Mason, American Radio Relay League; [hon.] O.S.R.D. 1945; [oth. writ.] Exeter Review (Summer 1994), Fantastic Florida (1996), Groton Landmark; [pers.] I am just starting a writing career at age 78. Nonfiction and poetry, especially biographies, including mine as a starter. I have a world of experiences to relate.); [a.] Groton, MA

RUDD, SHAWN OSBORNE
[b.] November 28, 1972, Nashville, TN; [p.] Thomas Golden, Kathryn Carter - Golden; [ed.] Indian River Community College, University of West Florida; [occ.] Shift Supervisor/Trainer, Chilis Grill and Bar, Vero Beach, FL; [hon.] Dean's List, Gitenstein Music Scholarship, Indian Community College Music Scholarship; [oth. writ.] Several personal anthology, currently writing a children's poetry anthology.; [pers.] Have faith in God.; [a.] Vero Beach, FL

RUNNELS, WILLIAM JOSEPH
[pen.] Gray Wolf; [b.] July 13, 1946, Houma, LA; [p.] Cecile Runnels; [m.] Rosemarie Runnels, April 23, 1988; [ch.] Gina Marcel, Beau and William

Runnels Jr.; [occ.] Disabled American Veteran; [oth. writ.] We Are The Future - World of Poetry - April 12, 1990; [pers.] Suffering from P.T.S.D., from Combat, recovering Alcoholic, Love for God and Nature.; [a.] Houma, LA

RUOTOLO, CHRISTINA LYNN
[pen.] Christina Ruotolo; [b.] March 14, 1978, Burlington, NC; [p.] Nicholas and Linda Ruotolo; [ed.] Blessed Sacrament Catholic School K-7th Grade, Turrentine Middle 8th Grade, Williams High School 9th-12th Grade; [occ.] Bookkeeper, Teach Gymnastics; [memb.] SADD Club 1996, (WHS), Students Against Drunk Driving Environmental Club 1995, Honors Dance 1996, Blessed Sacrament Catholic Church 1978-1996; [hon.] 1st and 2nd Place in Photography (Color Pictures) (1996); [oth. writ.] Several poems were published in local magazine (Alamance News). Had poem read at school for a prom-promise assembly.; [pers.] Through writing I express my deepest feelings. I have been influenced by my 9th grade teacher Mrs. Mac and Emily Dickinson, and Robert Frost who are great of examples poets.; [a.] Burlington, NC

RUSSELL, DOREASE
[pen.] Dottie; [b.] April 14, 1953, Miss; [p.] Allie D. and George Braxton; [m.] Lonnie R. Russell, March 29, 1991; [ch.] Roshon LaVale, Natasha, Joe II; [ed.] High School Graduate, Chic University of Cosmetology, Kalamazoo Valley Community College; [occ.] Oxnard #636 Dept of Motor Vehicle Field Rep; [memb.] Oxnard Curren Elementary School PTA (president), Oxnard School District; [hon.] Curren Elementary Cheerleader Coach for three years, In Oxnard, CA - Also commended for my courteous and Professional manner in dealing with the public at the Dept of Motor Vehicle from the Deputy Director at State of California, D.M.V; [oth. writ.] Children poetry stories, singer-song writer published in Local Newspaper Star Free Press Oxnard, CA and Kalamazoo, Mich. Cable Access Channel.; [pers.] All my hopes, dreams and ambitions are to continue my quest in the art of writing, original, creative unique poetic childrens' stories, short novels and lyrics for songs. With feelings - that will touch the hearts, mind and souls of children and adults in all walks of life. My mind is a vessel to guide me in the direction of note worthy. My favorite childrens' author is Dr. Seuss.; [a.] Oxnard, CA

RYK, MARY ANN
[pen.] Mary Ann Ryk; [b.] December 12, 1943, Chicago, FL; [p.] Mr. Anthony Mishur, Helen (Dankowskil Mishur); [m.] Jan Ryk, April 20, 1963; [ch.] Laurens, Julie, Joseph, Jon, Anthony-Jacques, Adrian; [ed.] St. Gerald's Grammar School, Oaklawn-Reavis High School, Burbank-De Paul University, SNL-1989; [occ.] Retired Chaplain-Consultant Bethlehem Woods Ret. Liu. CTE-La Grange Pk., IL; [memb.] Hinsdale Music Club- St. Mary Of Gostyn Choir-Downers Grove. Poetry Society of America (1994-1996); [hon.] 2 Poems published in Anthologies, "Invisible" - "The Coming of Dawn", "Invitation" - "Whispers in the Wind" (?); [oth. writ.] Poetry of the Soul-Vol. I (Life), Poetry of the Soul-Vol. II (Love and Friendship), Poetry of the Soul-Vol. III (Storms and Rainbows) are illustrated and published by Mary A. Ryk.; [pers.] "I feel my poetry is the gift of a

Loving God who uses me as an instrument to sing His song." My poetry reaches into the depth of a person and touches the common threads of existence that connect us all.; [a.] Downers Grove, IL

RYNG, NEL
[pen.] Nel Ryng; [b.] September 27, 1933, Boston, MA; [p.] William and Nellie MacMillan; [ch.] Linda Donna, Edward, David Lori, John; [ed.] Norton High School 1952; [occ.] Retired; [hon.] Honorable Mention in a similar poetry contest; [oth. writ.] Psycho-spiritual autobiography in process.; [pers.] The romantic poets have influenced my poetry and writings in style and expression.; [a.] Attleboro, MA

SADLER, NORMAN J.
[pen.] Gordon Wain Wright; [b.] October 7, 1962, Janesville, WI; [p.] Rudy and Mary Wuksinich; [ed.] High School Diploma, Craig High School, One - year Diploma in Child Care Services, Blackhawk Tech. Asso. Degree in Visual Communications Milwankee Area Tech. College; [occ.] Retail Clerk; [oth. writ.] The Breathless Orgasm (Published) "Prozac Poems and other Things." (Published); [pers.] The way I see the world that I live in is written in my poems. Mary Shelley is my favorite author. She touches me.; [a.] Janeswill, WI

SAILSMAN, LORNA
[b.] Kingston, Jamaica; [p.] Lushington and Maude Sailsman; [ed.] Bachelor's Degree in Psychology, Rutgers University pursuing Masters in English Lit.; [occ.] Social Worker

SALOW, CINDY
[pen.] Cindy Salow; [b.] January 2, 1955, Earlville, IA; [p.] Clarence Salow and Iris McElmeel; [m.] David Sage, July 5, 1984; [ch.] Daughters: Lea, Jessie and Annie, Son: Jason, Grandson: Dillon; [ed.] Maquoketa Valley High School, Kirkwood Community College; [occ.] Paralegal; [memb.] Associate Member of the Academy of American Poets; [oth. writ.] Angel Poetry and other thoughts on Earth and Spirit; [pers.] My poems are about everyday life on Earth and the never ending task of dealing with it.; [a.] Delhi, IA

SAMPSON, MURTHLENE A.
[b.] March 18, 1974, Guyana, South America; [p.] Albertha Pollard and McCowan Sampson; [ed.] Borough of Manhattan Community College, Erasmus Hall High School; [occ.] Student; [memb.] Church Youth Director; [hon.] Certificate for poem writing in high school and best outstanding leader counselor in summer youth camp day care; [oth. writ.] Songs for demo packages, articles, and poems that was published in high school newspaper; [pers.] My hopes and aspirations are to obtain an ultimate goal as a notorious writer, relate to the experiences of others and bless the hearts of millions in my writing. I've indulged my swaying on fictional and non-fictional poems or poets.; [a.] Brooklyn, NY

SANBORN, KIMBERLEE R. J.
[pen.] Kim, Krys; [b.] March 25, 1995, Bangor, ME; [p.] Robert and Roxanne S. Yarrow; [m.] Gary Sanborn, Divorced; [ed.] Assoc. Degree Nursing; [occ.] R.N. Supervisor; [oth. writ.] What is a Rock, Each Step of the Way, Engagement Poem to my Young Sister, I write about nature though not complete at present.; [pers.] You can turn anything bad into some good in this world today. Look deeper.

SANDIKKIRAN, DENIZ
[pen.] Deniz Sand; [b.] Istanbul, Turkey; [p.] Orhan and Gale Sandikkiran; [m.] Pasi Iumanen, July 6, 1991; [ed.] Oglethorpe University, Atlanta, Academy for Paralegal Studies, Inc. (Oglethorpe), Janier College, Montreal, Sir Winston Churchill High School, Montreal; [occ.] Paralegal/Student; [memb.] Optimists International; [pers.] Do not fear to have grand dreams. The courage to dream is the first step to its realization. [a.] Suwanee, GA

SANDOVAL, DOMINIQUE MARIE
[b.] April 10, 1983, San Jose, CA; [p.] Robert Ray Sandoval, Rosary Ann Sandoval; [ed.] O.B. Whaley Elementary, Ley Va Jr. High; [pers.] I am 13 and have been writing poems for two years. My favorite author is Lurlene McDaniel. Most of my writing is based on my life experiences.; [a.] Stockton, CA

SAVAGE, ASHLEY
[b.] July 15, 1984, Amarillo, TX; [p.] Scott Savage; [m.] Connie Savage; [ed.] At time poem was Written Ashley was an eleven year old, sixth grade Student at Austin Middle School; [memb.] Student Council; [hon.] A - B Honor Roll; [oth. writ.] No other published.; [pers.] Ashley's goal is the become a Neonatal Intensive Care Nurse. "Why Them?" Was written as a class project and dedicated to the Neonatal Intensive Care Unit at North West Texas Hospital.; [a.] Amarillo, TX

SCARBEARY, GARY
[b.] October 16, 1950, Bloomington, IL; [p.] Daniel and Maxine Ralston-Scarbeary; [ed.] University High; [occ.] Int'l Logistics Coordinator; [oth. writ.] One poem published in A Tapestry of Thoughts of National Library of Poetry.; [pers.] Life is filled with words and words can be filled with life. It's both a joy and a profound experience to have words shape me and I them.; [a.] Bloomington, IL

SCHAFER, VIVIAN
[b.] March 31, 1924, Peshtigo, WI; [p.] Leonard Conjurski, Elsie Conjurski; [m.] John A. Ramsay (Div.), Paul Schafer (Deceased), June 15, 1946, May 31, 1975; [ch.] Bonnie Jean, John Scot; [ed.] Menominee High, Michigan; [occ.] Retired Secretary, now taking my Piano Playing Poodle to perform at schools, clubs, retirement and nursing homes and parties; [memb.] 1. United Methodist Church, 2. Audubon Society, 3. Rotary Club, 4. Rotary Club (Paul Harris Fellow), 5. Senior Center, 6. AARP; [hon.] First place in all events Brunswick Mesa Arizona Club 55 Senior Bowling Tournament 1982; [a.] Moses Lake, WA

SCHALIT, ROBERT E.
[b.] November 19, 1954, Albany, NY; [p.] Samuel Schalit, Anna Schalit; [m.] Margaret Foye Schalit, August 26, 1989; [ed.] B.A. English Literature, State University of New York at Binghamton, Albany High School; [occ.] Creative Director, D.J. Moore Advertising, Albany, NY; [memb.] Past President, Creative Club of Albany. Am a member and supporter of many environmental, animal rights and charitable organizations; [hon.] Phi Beta Kappa, numerous Advertising Awards; [oth. writ.] Poetry, advertising writings including prints ads, brochures, television, radio, jingles, outdoor, videos.; [pers.] This poems is dedicated to my father, Samuel Schalit, a research chemist who committed suicide in 1972.; [a.] Schenectady, NY

SCHENKS, JACQUELINE R.
[b.] June 5, 1956, Moorhead, MS; [p.] Robert and Vejetta Rowland; [ch.] Christopher and Crystal Schenks; [occ.] Cosmetologist; [pers.] I'm dedicating this poem with love, to my brothers and sisters. They mean more to me than all the riches in the world, because the love we have is solid gold.; [a.] Milton, FL

SCHLICKER, KARON F.
[b.] November 4, 1945, Rupert, ID; [p.] Mr. and Mrs. David S. Johnson; [m.] Lawrence E. Schlicker, November 18, 1961; [ed.] High School - GED; [occ.] Housewife; [memb.] Corner Stone Church, Moses Lake, WA; [oth. writ.] Approximately 250 poems unpublished; [pers.] Any talent I have has been given to me by God for his use.; [a.] Moses Lake, WA

SCHMIDT, ARLENE
[b.] October 20, 1938, Saint Louis; [p.] Thomas L. Floyd, Catherine Floyd; [ch.] Catherine Anna Schmidt; [ed.] Meramec Elementary, Hadley High School John 'O' Fallon High; [occ.] Dosmistic Engineer; [memb.] Casondelet -Markham Memorial Presbyterian Church; [pers.] It is an honor to have my poem published for the very first time. I hope my poem brings you joy, as it did me to share it with you.; [a.] St. Louis, MO

SCHMIDT, JEFFREY
[pen.] Genius Coyote; [b.] January 8, 1932, Alhambra, CA; [p.] Mr. and Mrs. Alvin Schmidt; [m.] Elizabeth, April 20, 1963; [ch.] Blair Schmidt, Ryan Schmidt; [ed.] BA, Chico State Schmidt 2 years Graduate Work, Chico; [occ.] Retired Parole Officer; [oth. writ.] Articles for union paper.; [pers.] Only recently I came to realize that many of my grandmothers adages came from early American poetry. Now, in the computer age, I see this as the thin thread of tradition that links us with the past. This is unfortunate. I would like to see modern poetry continue this legacy.; [a.] Kelso, WA

SCHMIDT, JENNIFER L.
[b.] February 19, 1986, Portland, OR; [p.] Gary and Melinda; [ed.] Gause Elementary School 4th grade; [occ.] Student; [memb.] Rangers Baseball Team; [hon.] Reading, Math, Building a Pioneer Wagon; [oth. writ.] Several poems including 'Death', 'The Tear', 'What's Life About'. and 'Flowers In The Garden'. A book of my own poems with illustrations.; [pers.] I live in Washougal, WA and have been writing poems for three years. My interests include writing poems, drawing, reading, camping and fishing. One of my favorite poems is called 'Passover' by Myra Cohn Livingston.; [a.] Washougal, WA

SCHNEIDER, CHARLOTTE
[b.] December 1970, Denver, CO; [p.] Alan Schneider, Daryle Schneider; [ed.] Community College of Aurora, Metropolitan State College; [occ.] Accounting Clerk, Biochemistry Student; [memb.] Phi Theta Kappa; [pers.] Life is like a recipe -- different ingredients mix together to make a better results.; [a.] Denver, CO

SCHNEIDER, KATIE
[b.] July 23, 1981, Frankfort, KY; [p.] Carolide and Mike Schneider; [ed.] St. John Neumann High School Sophomore (Entering); [occ.] Student; [memb.] Student Council, Key Club, Astronomy Club, Year Book Club, Running Club; [hon.] Second academic honors, several MVP's basketball, soccer, track, cross country, several Best Defensive Player - basketball, several Hot Shot Champ - basketball, several Free Throw Champ - basketball; [oth. writ.] Story published in a school poetry story book, during 2nd grade, I write often when I have something to say or when I'm stressed out or bored.; [pers.] My writings usually are written about others or my feelings. Writing comes from within me and it is difficult for me to explain. I started writing during 2nd grade, but before then I would sit with my grandmother and we would make poems together.; [a.] Naples, FL

SCHNEIDER, TIFFANY
[pen.] Tiffany Schneider; [b.] September 3, 1976, San Francisco, CA; [ed.] Currently on undergraduate; [oth. writ.] Currently writing poetry in the hope to publish it within the next couple of years.; [pers.] My dream is to inspire peace in the world and sensuality in people's personal lives.; [a.] San Francisco, CA

SCHREMP, FAITH M.
[pen.] Faythimes; [b.] May 15, 1921, Pickerel, WI; [p.] Vic and Bess Iames; [m.] Lester "Butch" Schremp, September 19, 1942; [ch.] Four, 3 girls and 1 boy, 11 grandchildren, 3 greats, 2 coming; [ed.] Some College and Scales of Life Experience; [occ.] Writer; [memb.] International Women's Writing Guild, National Writer's Club, Wisconsin Regional Writers and Antegs Writer's Club Member, International Society of Poets, 1995, Danae Lifetime Membership Award, 1950 by International Clover Poetry Assn, Washington DC, Marquis Who's Who in Entertainment 1992/3, Who's Who in American Women 1993/4; [oth. writ.] Novel, "The Last Switcherer," novel "Smalltown Wife and Mom", 1992 cookbook "Grani's Good Grub" 1992, Poetry, "Mom are we there yet?" 1994, numerous short stories and poems in papers and magazines; [pers.] "Life is short -- enjoy," (Let me leave some footprints in the sands of my life.)

SCHUCHART, RYAN PATRICK
[b.] October 26, 1975, San Antonio, TX; [p.] Wayne Schuchart, Shavawa Carlson; [ed.] Jourdanton High, University of Texas at Austin, University of Texas at San Antonio; [occ.] Student at the University of Texas at Austin; [memb.] National Honor Society, Business Professionals of America, Science/History Club, Drama Club, Texas Educational Theatre Association; [hon.] English Honor Award, Creative Writing Award for young writers; [oth. writ.] Poems, short stories, children's books, all unpublished.; [pers.] Thanks to Robert Chaney, Susan Ratliff, and Fran Hawener for giving me the support and courage to do what I love - write!.; [a.] Pleasanton, TX

SCHULTZ, BECKY
[b.] February 9, 1973, Ashland, PA; [p.] James and Daisy Hoffman; [m.] David L. Schultz, May 28, 1994; [ed.] North Schuylkill Jr. Sr. High; [occ.] Store Clerk; [hon.] Honor Society graduate; [oth. writ.] Two poems printed in my high school newspaper; [pers.] I am an aspiring artist. I'm just putting my foot in the door now.; [a.] Locustdale, PA

SCHULTZ, MARIE M.
[pen.] Marie Seitz Schultz; [b.] May 24, 1933, Essex, MD; [p.] George and Lillian Seitz; [m.] Arthur (Dutch) Schultz, December 15, 1952; [ch.] Brian K. and Michael S. Schultz; [ed.] Our Lady of Mount Carmel Elementary School, Baltimore, MD. Saint Michael's Business High School Baltimore, MD and Yavapai College Chino Valley, AZ; [occ.] Housewife and Writer; [memb.] Professional Writers of Prescott, Sedona Writer's Group; [oth. writ.] Short story (The Red Suitcase) published by American Literary Press, Inc.; [pers.] The poem "My True Love" was written for my parents who are now deceased.; [a.] Chino Valley, AZ

SCHUMM, AGNES B.
[b.] June 27, 1925, Clyde, NY; [p.] Albert Borau, Wilhelmina Borau; [m.] Harold E. Schumm, June 13, 1953; [ch.] Carol Piper, David Schumm; [ed.] Clyde Central School; [occ.] Watercolor artist, Homemaker; [memb.] Central New York Watercolor Soc., Onondaga Art Guild, Trinity Lutheran Church; [hon.] Numerous awards for my Watercolor Art, Award of Excellence for photography in Symposium "The World And It's People" NY World's Fair, 1964-5; [oth. writ.] This is my first literary offering.; [pers.] Through my painting and writing I hope to re-inforce that which is uplifting to the human spirit.; [a.] Syracuse, NY

SCOTT, ZAC
[pen.] Perro Grande; [b.] February 19, 1987, Fayettville, AR; [p.] Rusty Scott, Karen Gandy; [ed.] Still in High School at Smackover High School; [occ.] Mower of yards; [memb.] FTA, Spanish Club; [hon.] 1st place for innovative achievement for AGATE student competition, Top GPA of class 3 straight years; [oth. writ.] Several poems and short stories.; [pers.] My English teacher told me to write a poem about a favorite hobby or thing I do so I did, bass fishing. That's what you have to do.; [a.] Smackover, AR

SCOVEL, EVELYN GIBBS
[pen.] Gibbs Scovel; [b.] June 27, 1934, Gastonia, NC; [p.] Mr. and Mrs. Hubert Franklin Gibbs; [m.] Jackson Scovel, July 3, 1996; [ch.] Evelyn Christine Creasy Johnson; [ed.] Some College; [occ.] Artist, Painting Sculptor, Ceramic; [memb.] Brought of Norfolk chapter of NSDAR, Regents Club, Regent of Borough of Norfolk, Chapter of NSDAR, 6 yrs study at Orsolya Academy of Fine Arts; [oth. writ.] Many more poems, this is my first attempts to be published I hope to try again.; [pers.] We all could make a difference.; [a.] Norfolk, VA

SEARS, ANN SNELSON
[b.] January 5, 1961, Washington, DC; [p.] Thomas P. and Nina B. Snelson; [m.] Dennis Sears, June 12, 1982; [ch.] Parker Thomas; [ed.] Charleston High School, West Virginia University; [memb.] P.E.T.A - People for the Ethical Treatment of Animals, Clear water Marine Aquarium and Human Society of Pinellas; [hon.] D.A.R. - Daughters of the American Revolution essay winner, English honor student. Copy editor of Charleston High Yearbook; [oth. writ.] The Rose - poem published in 1995 Famous Poems of Today Anthology.; [pers.] I try to look for the good in the world and appreciate the beauty of it and try to preserve these treasures of beauty, such as dolphins and endangered species for my son Parker and the other children of the world.; [a.] Largo, FL

SEDILLO, RAFAEL R.
[pen.] Ramon; [b.] July 14, 1931, Colorado; [p.] Daniel and Jesusita; [ch.] Three; [ed.] B.S. Elect. Engr. B.S. Bus. Admin. Univ. of Colorado; [occ.] Retired Part-time Bus. Consultant; [pers.] I strive to make the real world happenings beautiful, rhythmic and pleasant reading, as well as, nice to recite with pleasure to the listener's ear.; [a.] San Jose, CA

SEEFELDT, DEBBY
[b.] April 3, 1958, Seattle, WA; [p.] Jimmy and Mary Jane Johnson; [m.] Gilbert G. Seefeldt, May 2, 1992; [ch.] Casey Kiann Lewis; [ed.] Immaculate High School, Highline Comm College, Univ. of Washington; [occ.] Interior Designer, Harris Office Interiors Yakema, WA; [memb.] W.A.R.M. - Washington Adoptees Rights Movement; [hon.] Phi Theta Kappa, Jr. College Honor Society; [oth. writ.] Many thousands but none published.; [pers.] I write from the heart in good times and bad. It's great therapy.; [a.] Yakima, WA

SEIB, CAROLYN E.
[b.] July 22, 1975, Honolulu, HI; [ed.] Attending Lamar University Beaumont, TX; [occ.] Editorial Assistant for Beaumont Enterprise Newspaper

SELMAN, CODY
[b.] April 1, 1985, Asheville, NC; [p.] Rick and Jade Selman; [ed.] 6th North Buncombe Middle School, Weaverville North Carolina; [occ.] Student; [hon.] Honor roll student 3rd, 4th, 5th, Awards Academic Achievement Fitness Star in gym, Athlete (basketball, baseball); [oth. writ.] Short stories; [pers.] In my free time I like to write short stories and draw illustrations for them. I also like shooting hoops.; [a.] Alexander, NC

SENIOR-POMEROY, IRENE
[b.] Detroit, MI; [p.] Deceased; [m.] Deceased, April 28, 1985; [ch.] Kenneth; [ed.] B.S. Hunter College - CUNY, M.A. J.C. Columbia University, M.Ed T.C. Columbia University, Doctoral Candidate 1984-1986; [occ.] Freelance Writer (Former Asst. Professor at Univ. of Nevada); [memb.] Sigma Theta Tau International Honor Society of Nursing, American Red Cross Volunteer AIDS Educator, American Nurses Association, International Women's Writing Guild (IWWG); [hon.] Community Service, dedication and time (NAACP 1993); [oth. writ.] (In publication) Up Sometimes, Sometimes Down, Laugh On, AIDS Booklet, (KAKM-AK) 2 1/2 hr. T.V. sows on Dance, (Reviewer) Times Herald Tribune, Middletown, NY; [pers.] I believe that sharing one's feelings through writing can be healing and uplifting. The style and point of view from which one writes is critical in preserving our folkways. Reading takes one where most cannot go.; [a.] Reno, NV

SENSENIG, JENNIFER
[b.] December 11, 1984, Columbus, OH; [p.] Scott Sensenig, Dominica Scibilia; [ed.] Hasbrouck Heights Elementary; [occ.] Student; [memb.] Girl Scouts of America, YMCA; [hon.] Selected for American Heart Association's Jump Rope for Heart demonstration team, Allied Signal Co. Teterboro, NJ Essay Contest Winner, Public Service Electric and Gas Company's Poster Contest Winner, Invention was selected to participate in New Jersey's Student Inventions through Educa-

tion Northern Region Exposition; [oth. writ.] "The Black Cat" published in "Amidst the Splendor"; [pers.] I write for the enjoyment of others.; [a.] Hasbrouck Heights, NJ

SESSOMS, LILLIA HINTON
[b.] August 24, 1953, Perquimans County, NC; [p.] Ellis and Essie Hinton; [m.] Calvin Andre Sessoms; [ch.] Trequita Darnee, Ashley Drane; [ed.] Perquimans Co. High, Elizabeth City State University; [occ.] Inventory Manager, U.S. Coast Guard, ARSC, Elizabeth City, NC; [memb.] NAACP, Elizabeth City Chamber of Commerce LDI Board member, U.S. Coast Guard Culture Heritage Awareness Committee, Poole's Grove Baptist Church; [hon.] 1996 graduated of Elizabeth City, NC Chamber of Commerce Leadership Development Institute Program, reciepent of 1992 Fifth Coast Guard District Black History Month Achievement Award, 1992 Chairperson U.S. Coast Guard Support Center Black History Committee; [oth. writ.] Numerous poems will be published in local newspapers.; [pers.] America must continue to fight to stamp out discrimination against its minorities and women and we must protect our most precious resource - our children greatly influenced by poet Maya Angelou.; [a.] Belvidere, NC

SHAFER, CAROLYN
[b.] February 12, 1924, Norwood, MA; [p.] Dr. and Mrs. Herbert Gurnea; [m.] James F. Shafer (Deceased), February 18, 1945; [ch.] James, Jr., Julie, Joseph, Mary, Daniel, Grace, Paul, Thomas, Ruth, Richard; [ed.] B.A. Arizona State University, M.S. East Texas State University; [occ.] Retired; [memb.] Bethel Christian Church, AARP, International Society of Poets, Tri-County Poetry Society of Texas; [hon.] National Honor Society, Magna Cum Laude from Arizona State University, International Poet of Merit Award from ISP, 3rd place award from "Tomorrow Never Knows", Semifinalist at 1995 ISP Convention; [oth. writ.] Religious publications, Spring '96 Poets Corner, poems published in National Library of Poetry Anthologies Tomorrow Never Knows, The Rainbow's End, Best Poems of 1996, The Voice Within.; [pers.] I am not limited as to subject matter: Everyday life, World events, things near and far however I must have the God-given inspiration that vitalizes the written word.; [a.] Athens, TX

SHAFFER, RICHARD M.
[b.] October 2, 1909, Masonville, WV; [p.] William C. and Tabitha (Sites) Shaffer; [m.] Virginia Woodruff (Deceased - April 14, 1941), Nellie Frasch, June 10, 1965; [ch.] Karen Engle, Linda Toledo and Rick Shaffer; [ed.] College Degree (all); [occ.] Retired; [memb.] Bethlehem Lutheran Church; [hon.] Trivial; [oth. writ.] A few poems in local Newspapers, and a few poems in Anthologies.; [pers.] This may sound mundane. I have found that money will not take care of you if you do not take care of it.; [a.] Middletown, OH

SHAHAYDA, JOSEPH JOHN
[pen.] Little Bubba Fish; [b.] April 12, 1967, Johnstown, PA; [p.] Karen and Alex Shahayda; [m.] Divorced; [ch.] Tara Sue Shahayda (Adams) Daughter; [ed.] 12th grade graduate; [occ.] Self employed/starving writer; [memb.] Catholic Holy Name Society; [hon.] Several certificates of Ap-

preciation (from the Holy Name Society) also a certificate for publishing an article for the younger kids in the news paper!; [oth. writ.] Numerous others poems!; [pers.] To love . . . is to accept and honor the love in return . . . no matter who it is!; [a.] Huntingdon, PA

SHAHPAR, M. S.
[pen.] Shahpar; [b.] April 22, 1933, Iran; [p.] Mir-Soltan; [m.] Atta, 1968; [ch.] Ms. Shahpar; [ed.] P.H.D.'s Persian Literature, Philosophy and Economy; [occ.] Chief Economist Advisor Indonesian, Rural and Urban Economy Development Institute; [memb.] Pen Club; [hon.] Role of Honour, President Reagan Gold Medal, Mehdi Mahboubian Foundation, N.Y.; [oth. writ.] Reflection Of Thoughts "Poetry Book" London 1981.; [pers.] True love is an art, real art is a reflection of love.; [a.] Santa Monica, CA

SHAPIRO, DARA
[pen.] Claudia Ambrosine; [b.] September 5, 1979, E. Meadow, NY; [p.] Nelson Shapiro; [ed.] John F. Kennedy High School; [occ.] Student; [memb.] World Wildlife Fund, North American Federation of Temple Youth; [hon.] National Honor Society; [oth. writ.] Various unpublished works.; [pers.] The world is a smoke-filled room. I am but an ash, yet I am constantly trying to build the ashtray around me, through my work.; [a.] Merrick, NY

SHAPIRO, JULIE
[pen.] Julie Shapiro; [b.] July 16, 1973, Johnson City, NY; [p.] Mary Bennett; [ed.] H.S. one year of College Marathon Academy and Cazenovia College; [memb.] Member of Marathon Fire Dept and Emergency Squad volunteer; [hon.] Honor roll four consecutive years in H.S., 3rd place in NYS Poetry contest '88 or '89.; [oth. writ.] "I Miss You" '89 published on a Thresh hold of a dream. Past '94, majority written for my boyfriend.; [pers.] If you have a dream, pursue it! Don't let anyone cut you down! People can be supportive. That is why I love my boyfriend.; [a.] Marathon, NY

SHAY, ANTHONY FRANCIS
[b.] April 2, 1968, La Crosse, WI; [p.] Patrick S. Shay, Lou Ann Shay; [m.] Jacqueline Lynn McGarvey-Shay, August 7, 1993; [ed.] Viterbo College; [pers.] "Unrequited Love" dedicated to M. Lange and my '95 renaissance.; [a.] Westby, WI

SHELDON, JOI
[b.] February 4, 1980, San Angelo, TX; [p.] Joseph'n Sheldon, Darylene Sheldon; [ed.] Junior at Wall High School, Wall, TX; [memb.] FHA and student council officer, Varsity cheerleader, basketball track church youth group and choir (first United Methodist Church of San Angelo), N.H.S.; [hon.] Recognized by the Duke University Talent Identification Program for distinction in mathematics and verbal. Selected for entry into the Texas Academy of Mathematics and Science at the University of North Texas. 1st in District in Headline writing, 4th in Regional in Headline writing; [a.] San Angelo, TX

SHELL, SHERMAINE
[pen.] S. Shell, Shairee; [b.] September 21, 1957, Rockford, IL; [ch.] Heather Cory, Kimberly Rae, Shaun Matthew; [ed.] First and foremost... I am a mom; [hon.] Member of Phi Theta Kappa Society;

[pers.] True magic is of the mind. One must first, look inside to find it, tap into it then utilize it. In this way - anything is possible.; [a.] Wintersville, OH

SHEPARD, SARAH G. SAWYER
[b.] October 28, 1919, New Bedford, MA; [p.] Mary F., Martin Frederick Sawyer; [m.] Walter Owen Shepard, October 28, 1939; [ch.] Brenda, Walter O. Jr., Faith Ann; [ed.] New Bedford Vocational High School, Diaman Vocational School of Nursing; [occ.] Retired Nurse, Artist; [memb.] Pat President and Member of St. Luke's Hospital Retirees, Bierstadt Art Society, International Society of Poets; [hon.] Thanks Badge Award as a Girl Scout Leader, Official Citation from Mass. State Senate for Distinguish Service for St Luke Retirees. At least 4 Art Awards for Paintings, Editor's Choice Awards 1994 and 1995 National Library of Poetry; [oth. writ.] Unpublished Family Cookbook, Quiet Place, Snow, Angry Storm all published National Library of Poetry; [pers.] My writings come from an extremely personal encounter with Chronic pain. Pain has made me very much aware of the feelings of other persons. Thru writing I hope to help those who suffer, cope with their pain and to know they are not alone.; [a.] New Bedford, MA

SHER, DARREN GRANT
[b.] March 26, 1980, Reno, NV; [p.] Charlene and Geoffrey Sher; [ed.] High School; [occ.] Musician and Student; [hon.] Musical Achievement Award in Canada; [oth. writ.] Vast Collection of individual/ original poetry.; [pers.] A quote by Joseph Campbell...."As you go the way of life, you will see a great chasm. Jump. It is not as wide as you think"; [a.] San Rafael, CA

SHERMAN, ARTHUR M.
[b.] July 2, 1963, Bronx, NY; [p.] Mr. and Mrs. Arthur S. Sherman; [ed.] High School Graduate 1982, Piscataway High School; [occ.] Driver; [memb.] Local Assembly of God Church; [oth. writ.] Several other poems already copyrighted, and yet to be published, Lord-Willing!; [pers.] Whatever I do, I want to work at it, with all my heart, giving Glory to God, as working for the Lord Jesus Christ, not for men!; [a.] Piscataway, NJ

SHIRAGA, GINA S.
[b.] December 27, 1974, Fresno, CA; [occ.] Student - University of Oregon; [a.] Eugene, OR

SIAS, VICKI
[b.] July 4, 1952, Berea, OH; [p.] Frank and Maxine Martin; [ch.] Kristi - 17, Dustin - 10; [ed.] High School - Midpark in Middleburg Hts., Ohio, Oral Roberts University - Tulsa Oklahoma; [occ.] Homemaker; [oth. writ.] Approximately 30 or more inspirational poems.; [pers.] I've written many poems, personal as well as general. Each one has been different and unique. Yet each reaching out to accomplish one special purpose - to inspire, encourage and uplift the hearts of all who have read them.; [a.] Geneva, OH

SIEGEL, DAVID
[b.] July 22, 1978, Plainview, NY; [p.] Bonnie L. Siegel, Mark P. Siegel; [ed.] Diamond Bar High School, The University of Arizona; [occ.] Student; [memb.] Comedy Sports LA, International Thespian Society; [hon.] National English Teacher's

Association if America Promising Young Writer Award, Numerous Theatrical Awards; [oth. writ.] Numerous poems, several plays.; [pers.] If only we could see how truly beautiful we are, what a paradise we could make of this world.; [a.] Diamond Bar, CA

SILBAUGH, NILA JO
[b.] December 11, 1930, Ill.; [p.] Ray and Mildred Ping; [m.] Ivan J. Silbaugh, February 9, 1951; [ch.] Two grown, five grandchildren; [ed.] B.S. from University of Wisconsin LA Crosse, WI, Element. Ed.; [occ.] Housewife; [memb.] Federated Women's Clge "Clio Club", Black River Memorial Hospital Aux., Sons of Norway, United Methodist Church Choir; [hon.] Prepared and chaired an Art Fair for Clio Club which received nat. recognition for charity through the Arts-furnished ??? of hosp., proposed and chaired re-building a Swinging Bridge at Park - club received award for community improvement, prepared and chaired 1st Doll House show furnished children's library, Inducted into Kappa Delta Pi Nat. Honor Soc. in Ed.; [oth. writ.] Come with Me (Penny Creek) Part I, Come with Me (Penny Creek) Part II, My Grandmother's Yard, Lilac Sunday, Proclamation, The Chaplain, Hope, Prayer for My Beloved, Salvation (none published non submitted) and others; [pers.] I have always loved poetry, my mother instilled it in me as a toddler and I have always been able to memorize and recite, I've been writing for about twenty years, many upon request for special occasions and religion and nature.; [a.] Black River Falls, WI

SILVERMAN, JUDE T.
[pen.] J. Silvs; [b.] September 11, 1970, Ridgway, PA; [p.] Dr. and Mrs. Larry Silverman; [ed.] Bachelor of Arts (English), Roanoke College (Salem, VA), Cicero - North Syracuse H.S., (Cicero, NY); [occ.] U.S. Postal Employee; [memb.] Catholic Charities; [pers.] "Aim at nothing and you will hit it." My motivation and inspiration come from life's experiences.; [a.] Roanoke, VA

SIMMONS, SHELTON
[b.] March 20, 1986, Columbia, SC; [p.] Cynthia Simmons (Deceased)

SIMOS, MARK ANTHONY
[b.] March 7, 1976, New Haven, CT; [ed.] St. Edwards, attending Rollins College; [oth. writ.] Poem in National Magazine; [pers.] My greatest goal in life and in writing it to be true to myself.; [a.] Vero Beach, FL

SIMPSON, SCOTT E.
[b.] July 30, 1947, Akron, OH; [p.] William G. and Viola K. Simpson; [m.] Mary Ann Simpson, August 16, 1970; [ch.] John, Gus and Bryan; [ed.] One year College: Idaho State University - Pocatello, ID; [occ.] Transportation Supervisor with Chicago based "TIX Company"; [oth. writ.] Currently compiling a collection of poetry for a book.; [pers.] I believe that people should appreciate people of different backgrounds and beliefs. Tolerance is the key to the future while divisiveness merely keeps us stuck in the past.; [a.] Upland, CA

SINGH, SOROJINI DEVI
[b.] December 25, 1979, Georgetown, Guyana; [p.] Tilak Singh, Toolawattee Singh; [ed.] Brentwood High School (Sonderling); [hon.] Honor Society

after school activities; [oth. writ.] "The Cheetah" for the Freshman Center Wet Feet.; [pers.] My Mom always say "Sweet Rewards come after bitter Struggle."; [a.] Brentwood, NY

SISSOM, RUTH
[b.] March 14, 1932, Marlette, MI; [p.] Norman and Merle Landon; [m.] Cecil Sissom (Deceased); [ch.] Carol, Janet and Paul; [ed.] Marlette High School, Registered Nursing Degree - Saginaw General School of Nursing; [occ.] Writer and Speaker; [hon.] Graduated Cum Laude, Aleda Lutz Nursing Award for Outstanding Achievement Clinically and Academically, American Hospital Association Leader Award for Diabetic Education program selected from 300 entries as one of Ten Nationwide for patient education excellence; [oth. writ.] Published Books: "Instantly A Widow", "Moving Beyond Grief"; [pers.] I strive to use my writing to embrace others who are hurting with hope and encouragement for the Bible and my experience to show that life's hurts can be transformed by God into gifts for ourselves and others. This poem was originally written for Patrick J. Livingwood, D. C.; [a.] Ypsilanti, MI

SLAVEY, KATRINA M.
[b.] May 1, 1965, Livingston, NJ; [p.] Herman and Elizabeth Van De Vaarst; [m.] Robert D. Slavey, April 16, 1993; [ed.] Associate Degree in Occupational Sciences; [occ.] Medical Staff Coordinator Charter Westbrook BHS, Richmond, VA; [oth. writ.] Non published; [pers.] Embrace the joys of life and the love of family and friends for all too often, these pleasures are too short.; [a.] West Point, VA

SMALLS, DAVID J.
[b.] November 5, 1927, Wilson, NC; [p.] Willie Smalls, Essie Smalls; [m.] Virginia L. Smalls, August 10, 1949; [ch.] Rosalyn, David, Roy, Ronald; [ed.] Saint Joseph's Univ - MBA (Eve) 1981-1982, Saint Joseph's Univ - BS (Eve), Acct, 1971-1981, Comm Col of Phila, Real Estate, 1985-86; [occ.] Retired; [memb.] Democratic Committee Man, President, Civic Association, St. Joseph's Univ Alpha Zeta, Member of Fed Bus Association, Member of Nat'l Freed Day Assoc.; [hon.] The Dean's List - St Joseph Univ, Alpha Sigma Lambda Honor Soc, Certificate of award, IRS; [oth. writ.] 420th Sup Co's Odyssey to Ft. Bragg, 1983, The Passing Of A Buddha 1991; [pers.] I have tried to be a role model for all of my children and their friends.; [a.] Philadelphia, PA

SMALLWOOD, VIVIAN
[pen.] Vivian Johnson; [b.] February 19, 1971, Austin, TX; [p.] Rita Walker, Don Johnson; [m.] Thomas Dray; [ch.] Micheal, Steven, Austin; [ed.] Jessamine Co. High; [occ.] Housewife; [memb.] PTA; [hon.] Cheerleading Little League; [oth. writ.] Lost and Found Mother, My Boys (Not published); [pers.] If you work at your dreams they can come true.; [a.] Nicholasville, KY

SMITH, ANASTASIA M.
[b.] August 23, 1967, Philadelphia, PA; [p.] David and Charlotte Kriley; [m.] Kerlin R. Smith, October 9, 1994; [ch.] Sara Elizabeth, Wyleden Sterling; [ed.] Marian High School, Art Institute of Philadelphia, Lehigh County Community College;

[occ.] Mother, Free Lance Artist, Pre-School Teacher, Face Painter; [memb.] American Heart Association Marketing Committee, Our Lady of the Valley School; [oth. writ.] My 1994 "Cabin Fever" Poem, "My Death"; [pers.] "I write as much as I can, as fast as I can, before I forget it!"; [a.] Summit Hill, PA

SMITH, CARRIE B.
[b.] May 2, 1915; [p.] Dan Paden, Sarah Paden; [m.] Robert Smith (Deceased), May 15, 1945; [ch.] Reginald Brooks (son); [ed.] 2 yrs College Practical Nurse; [occ.] (Retired) Cash Clerk Navy Dept.; [memb.] Foundry U.M. Church, National Council Sr. Citz. A.A.R.P., United Methodist Women, Foundry Church Community Mission; [hon.] Presidential Sports Award, Outstanding Community Award, Sewing and Modeling Award, Senior Olympics Award, Service Award, Black History; [oth. writ.] Several other poems. Not published; [pers.] My goal is to be a successful writer; [a.] Washington, DC

SMITH, DEBORAH M.
[b.] July 23, 1949, Washington, DC; [p.] George and Sally Tindley; [m.] Donnie N. Smith, September 5, 1970; [ch.] Detoria, Nicole, Donnita, Evony Smith; [ed.] D.C. Public Schools, Dorethea B. Lane Secretarial Sch.; [pers.] I would like to thank the National Library of Poetry for giving me the incentive to send in one of my poems.; [a.] Washington, DC

SMITH, DONALD
[b.] December 16, 1953, Denver, CO; [p.] Orville and Georgia Smith; [m.] Leslie Jean (Carder) Smith, February 18, 1978; [ch.] Donald Smith II; [ed.] John F. Kennedy High Denver, Co; [occ.] Painter; [memb.] Sheridan Optimist Club, Sheridan City Council, Mayor Proten Sheridan School Pest #2 Accountibilty Committee; [oth. writ.] Many writings on most subject all are unpublished.; [pers.] I am very open in my poems as there are my feelings at the time there are written. In putting my feelings in words I can better reflect my world around me.; [a.] Sheridan Lake, CO

SMITH, E. CAROLE
[pen.] E. Carole Smith; [b.] September 12, 1946, Newburgh, NY; [p.] The Late Pearl Mae and Ormond J. Sarvis; [m.] Earl W. Smith Sr., February 23, 1973; [ed.] Newburg Free Academy, Schenectady County Community College (SCC); [occ.] Switchboard Operator, Schenectady County Community College; [memb.] Disabled Students Advisory Committee, Academic Affairs Committee (SCCC); [hon.] Dean's List, Three Awards for Excellence in Poetry (1990-95) from Schenectady County Community College Rhythms magazine - published on campus; [oth. writ.] Twenty six pages of poems as handout on the subject of self-esteem during Public Speaking engagements. Articles in published in the Restaurateur of New York's Capital Region; [pers.] Having conquered the affects of being raised in an alcoholic environment, I write to encourage others that are still struggling. Along the way, I incorporate positive experiences of daily life; [a.] Rotterdam Junction, NY

SMITH, ELMER
[b.] February 20, 1923, Monongahela, PA; [p.] Rachel and Elmer Smith; [m.] Anna Pauline (Vogel) Smith, August 15, 1952; [ch.] Bruce E., Brian W., Brent R.; [ed.] Monongahela High, University of Pittsburgh Capital University (Col. Ohio) Graduate School BGSU; [occ.] Retired - Teacher for 33 years; [oth. writ.] Several poems written for Christmas cards. The poems were converted into acrostics; [a.] Norwalk, OH

SMITH, IRENE M.
[b.] April 12, 1956, Newark, NJ; [p.] Hedwig and Hoyle Smith; [ch.] Erica Smith; [ed.] Girl's Vocational High-Newark, NJ, North Ward Educational/Cultural Ctr. Newark, NJ (Business Course); [occ.] Office Manager for an Orthopaedic Surgeon; [memb.] P.E.T.A., I.F.A.W., Humane Society; [hon.] Elementary and High School Awards for Creative Writing, Short Stories, Poetry. Book Club Secretary; [oth. writ.] Poems for myself and friends. Make/sell decorative mirrors for a Gallery. Crafts on consignment to boutique.; [pers.] I believe we are either part of the problem or part of the cure. I hope my work is part of being the cure. Influenced by my own strong feelings are: Injustices or sadness or happiness.; [a.] West Orange, NJ

SMITH, JEANNE MARIE
[b.] October 3, 1937, Washington, D.C.; [p.] Raymond L. Trego, Irma M. Raum; [ch.] Debra, Sallie, Patrick, Brendan, Karen; grandchildren: Brian, Mason, Steven, Thomas; [occ.] Forty Years service with the Federal Government and in private industry; [memb.] St. Bernard's Catholic Church, Riverdale, MD, volunteer work tutoring elementary school children, working with homeless, visiting the sick in hospitals and visiting shut-ins; [oth. writ.] Poem, "Faith," was written for Mr. Charles Murray, of St. Bernard's Catholic Church; [pers.] Hobbies include art, music, poetry and photography. Recreational interests include swimming, bowling and theatre.

SMITH, JONI
[pen.] Becki Coombs; [b.] December 5, 1955, Valdosta, GA; [p.] Ann Blake; [m.] Gary Smith, February 14, 1995; [ch.] Charity Faidley 21, Brandy Moore 16; [ed.] Valdosta High School - American College; [occ.] Tech Group Tempe, Quality Auditor; [pers.] I strive to become a famous novelist someday.

SMITH, KATHY ANNETTE FREEMAN
[b.] August 7, 1951, Portales, NM; [p.] Paul and Betsy Freeman; [m.] Charles Larry Smith, October 16, 1969; [ch.] Kara - 24, Kalith - 20, Ryan - 17; [ed.] BS, Eastern New Mexico Univ., Portales, NM, MS Reading Education, Eastern New Mexico University; [occ.] English Instructor, Clovis High School, Clovis, NM; [memb.] National Education Association, National Forensics League, Delta Kappa Gamma, High Plains Writing group, National Council of Teachers of English; [hon.] Outstanding student in Reading Education 1995, Who's Who Among American Teacher; [oth. writ.] None published; [a.] Portales, NM

SMITH, LINDA L.
[b.] October 24, 1953, Paris, TN; [p.] W. W. Chandler and E. M. Chandler; [m.] Reese D. Smith, October 25, 1981; [ch.] David Charles, Michelle

Christin, Corwin Daniel; [ed.] SNVTC High, 2 years vocational; [occ.] Lighting Rep. in Salt Lake City; [oth. writ.] Written several items and currently working on a children's book.; [pers.] I like to write comforting word and inspiration. Also, like to write for children.

SMITH, LORI ANN GANSNER
[b.] February 1, 1967, Hillsboro, IL; [p.] Carl and Patsy Gansner; [m.] Edward John Smith, August 25, 1990; [ch.] Grady Lee Vollintine and Keith Edward Smith; [ed.] Hillsboro High School, Hillsboro, Illinois; [occ.] Housewife; [hon.] My greatest honor is my family and the love we all have for one another.; [oth. writ.] This is the first poem I ever sent in.; [pers.] This poem was written and will be read in a short time. But, the words of love for my family will be everlasting and true.; [a.] Mesquite, TX

SMITH, QUENTIN
[b.] February 25, 1977, Dallas, TX; [p.] Greg and Vicki Smith; [ed.] Currently Studying at the Dallas Art Institute; [occ.] Sales Associate; [pers.] I would like to thank my family for their love and their time. I would also like to thank Lori Sickel, my inspiration.; [a.] Kansas City, MO

SMITH, VIRGINIA M.
[pen.] Gini Moon; [b.] June 30, 1940, Stamford, NY; [p.] Rupert F. and Beatrice V. Sandberg; [m.] James P. Smith, June 20, 1959; [ch.] Lise Harrington, Kathleen Ferguson, Janice Semprini; [ed.] Nyack High School; [occ.] Hypnotherapist, Hypnotherapy Trainor, Reiki Practitioner; [memb.] National Guild of Hypnotists, National Society of Clinical Hypnotherapists, National Association of Transpersonal Hypnotherapists; [hon.] Member of year 1992 of National Guild of Hypnotists; [pers.] I write from my heart. I want to share my feelings with others, whether it be pain or great joy.; [a.] West Yarmouth, MA

SNEED, LORETTA JANETTE
[pen.] Jan Sneed; [b.] April 8, 1933, Fort Worth, TX; [p.] Bernice M. Short; [m.] Robert O. Sneed (Deceased), August 20 1976; [ch.] Michael, Jim, Tommy, John, Trisha Sneed, Larry Hermance, Kirk Sneed; [ed.] Univ. of Ark. 1954-55 33 1/2 hrs.; [occ.] Retired; [memb.] Past Beta Sigma Phi Pres. of Dallas City Council, Rebekah Lodge #176, Pres. Ladies Auxiliary Mart VFW #10426 (current); [hon.] Women of the Year Beta Sigma Phi, Pledge National Honor Society U of A; [oth. writ.] Articles for Hospice, Contributor Waco Tribune-Herald, poems published in Gospel Times; [pers.] I strive to reflect my love of God and of mankind.; [a.] Crawford, TX

SNYDER, AUDRA
[b.] April 28, 1971, Tacoma, WA; [p.] Raymond L. and Janice M. Snyder Sr.; [ed.] Rainier High, Clover Park Tech. College for Photography, Nisqually Tribal Center for Business Management.; [occ.] Housekeeper at a Motel; [hon.] Perfect attendance, honorable mention on a self-portrait, Keyboarding Award of Excellent.; [oth. writ.] I have wrote several poems, but none have been published.; [pers.] In life there are a lot of things to strive for. My hardest has been recognition. I get my ideas for my poetry from how I perceive life and life itself.; [a.] Rainier, WA

SOLINGER, TRACI
[b.] September 1, 1972, Yo., OH; [p.] Ronald and Georgina Solinger; [ed.] Pursuing a Degree in Professional Writing and Editing

SOLIZ, ALICIA
[pen.] Alicia Soliz; [b.] August 11, 1978, Berkeley, CA; [p.] Rolando Soliz, Sally Soliz; [ed.] Clark High School; [occ.] Student; [hon.] National Honor Society; [pers.] "Everything is possible for Him who believes." Mark 9:23; [a.] San Antonio, TX

SOLTERMANN, JOHANNES E.
[b.] March 8, 1957, Austria; [m.] May 24, 1993; [ed.] University of Graz, Austria, University of Wien, Austria, Degree: Cand. Med., Minneapolis Technical College, Degree: NAR; [occ.] Sculptor in wood, writer (poems, prose articles), musical (60 plus songs registered), jobs for money to survive.; [hon.] The honor of being soul in a free (inner) world.; [oth. writ.] Articles and poem for Austrian Newspaper "Sud-Ost-Ragespost". Founder, Editor and Author of "Die Wespe", A Journal for Literature and Art, Austria 1976. 4 Articles for "The Edge", A Minnesota Monthly Magazine 22,500 copies, 5 poems with Quill Books, Texas.; [pers.] True art has to be healing. Either through shock or through gentle touch. It has to reflect truth. Truth is love. Love can destroy if you stand in its way, or it can carry you into highest heavens, if you are ready.; [a.] Minneapolis, MN

SOMICH, MICHAEL DAVID
[b.] June 15, 1975, Cleveland, OH; [p.] Marsha and Alex Somich; [m.] Melissa Marie Sharp; [ed.] North Olmsted High School, Hocking College; [occ.] Landscaper; [memb.] Wildlife Forever, The National and Ubon Society; [hon.] Dean's List; [pers.] Be kind to mother earth. She is there to protect, feed and love us. Enjoy all her beauty she has to offer.; [a.] Pedro, OH

SONDOTA, TEDDY
[pen.] T. Bear, Sol Bianca; [b.] April 3, 1976, Masindi, Uganda; [p.] Eddie, Lucy; [ed.] Richardson High School (Richardson, TX), University of North Texas (Denton); [occ.] Student, Athlete at said University; [memb.] UNT Track Team (Decathlete); [hon.] Dean's List, Honors Roll, Richardson High School Hall of Fame; [oth. writ.] How Now Brown Cow, My Own Private Inferno, Beyond The Black Rose, To Each His Own, Once A Rose, Destination, About This Girl, Two, I Sat On The Moon One Day, Throw Away; [pers.] "...Not by wisdom do poets write poetry, but by a sort of genius and inspiration, they are like diviners or sooth sayers who also say many fine things, but do not understand the meaning of them..." Plato.; [a.] Denton, TX

SONIA, MR. BRETT D.
[pen.] Brett Sonia; [b.] June 12, 1968, Gloucester, MA; [p.] Robert A. Sonia, Shiela Sonia; [m.] Jill R. A. Sonia, June 11, 1996; [ch.] Heather A. Sonia; [ed.] North Shore Comm. College Bev., MA, Eng. Lit North Eastern Univ. Bost., MA, Spec thanks to: My wife and family and Ronnie Schriber who had faith in me; [occ.] Tractor Trailer Driver, Cullerny Arts Chef for 16 yrs.; [memb.] North Amercan Native Amercn's Assoc., supporter "Cherokee Nation", Sierra Club, Nat Wildlife Foun-

dation, Nrth Amercn Fishing Foundation, as well as the Nrth Amercn Hunting Foundation; [hon.] Publisher and Editor Salem Corr Facility Newsletter, Several Article in Boston Herald; [oth. writ.] "America's Lost Children", An in depth study of drugs and the homeless. "Fall Of The Planet Gibraltar" - Sci-Fi, "Occupation Of The Colonies", "The War Lance", "A Sudden Darkness" coming soon.; [pers.] I am truly saddened at how we treat this planet and each other, when will we learn to get along? When the air is unbreathable? When the Earth is uninhabitable? By then it will be too late for humanity try to remember this is the only planet!; [a.] Dunedin, FL

SOSTRE, GLORIA
[pen.] Gloria Sostre; [b.] April 4, 1934, Puerto Rico; [p.] Carmelo and Juana; [m.] Miguel A. Sostre Sr., August 30, 1958; [ch.] Jose Miguel, Miguel (Jr.) and Gloria; [ed.] Bachelor Degree Secretarial Sciences, Certificate Fiction Writer (Connecticut), Certificate Interpreter/Translator (Spanish-English) Clark University - Worcester, MA; [occ.] Interpreter/Translator and Notary Public in the State of Mass.; [memb.] World Vision Countertop Partner, North Shore Animal League Member; [hon.] High Honor - High School, Certificate of Appreciation (World Vision) and other charitable organizations.; [oth. writ.] Bilingual articles, poems and essays published in local newspapers in New York.; [pers.] I was born in love with nature and nature is God.; [a.] Worcester, MA

SPAGNOLA, OLIVIA
[pen.] Olivia Spagnola; [b.] October 10, 1913, Philadelphia, PA; [p.] Thomas and Olivia Gorman; [m.] Thomas Spagnola, July 25, 1932; [ch.] Carole, Taylor, Thomas Spagnola; [ed.] University of PA - 2 years, 4 years of Seminars Helant Seashore House Hospital Atlantic City, NJ; [occ.] Retired - 39 years occupational Therapy Children's Seashore House Atlantic City N.J., Workers with - Handicupped children - in occupational therapy; [memb.] President of two Parent Teachers. Association Brighton Ave. Atlantic City, NJ, Ventnor or City - P.T.A. Chair mon of March of Divines President of Ventnor Women's 1st Little Leaque/Hobb-Writing Poetry, Chairman of Boy Scouts Ventnor City - New Jersey. Daughter - graduate of A girl 57 years Columbia University - New Son - Grad from - 41 result York City Seton Hall - South Orange, NJ, Widow - Married 50 years widowed - 13 years - officer and volunteer of Ventnor City, NJ; [a.] Ventnor, NJ

SPARKMAN, LILLIE M.
[pen.] Lillie M. Sparkman; [b.] February 11, 1923, Stillwell, OK; [p.] John and Angie Black; [m.] Buford Sparkman; [ch.] Five children; [occ.] Retired; [oth. writ.] "You Grief is His to Bear", "God's Tender Rose Buds", "Lovely Spring", "My Prayer For You", "Autumn Splendor", "Should We Question His Purpose", "Sister"; [pers.] I am a 73 year grandmother. I have been writing poetry since I was a teenager for my own pleasure. But it has also been my way of expressing sympathy to friends and family during their times of need.; [a.] Arlington, TX

SPARKS, GWENDOLYN SUE
[b.] May 12, 1935, Middletown, NY; [p.] Charles G. Peroz - Pearl T. Peroz; [m.] Harry D. Sparks, January 16, 1955; [ch.] Linda Marie, Glenn Allan

and Christopher Todd; [ed.] Middletown High School, Semester 5 at Orange County Community College; [occ.] Savings Counselor First Federal Savings of Middletown, Mdtn., N.Y.; [memb.] Circleville Presbyterian Church; [hon.] Dean's List at O.C.C.C.; [oth. writ.] I have had poems published in school newspapers, have written several poems for bank functions (Retirement Dinners); [pers.] I thank God for the gift of nature and relationships with others which have served to inspire my writings...; [a.] Middletown, NY

SPAULDING, TINA M.
[pen.] Tina M. Spaulding; [b.] September 2, 1962, Oswego, NY; [p.] Rick Spaulding and Susan Pilon; [m.] Divorced; [ch.] Brandon and Matthew Shaw; [ed.] Graduated: Medical Assisting Red Cross CPR and FA Certification, Aids Awareness and Child Abuse reporting and recognition certification; [occ.] Medical Assistant/Cashier; [oth. writ.] I have written poems since the age of twelve; [pers.] I would like to become a freelance writer for a greeting card company.

SPEARS, MARILYN ELLEN
[b.] December 16, 1923, Eggertsville, NY; [p.] Alexander Moor, Alice Moor; [m.] Deceased - Stanley Spears, November 26, 1954; [ch.] David Raymond, Steven Arlen; [occ.] Inspirational Writing; [oth. writ.] Inspirational short articles - book in progress. Title release on publication.; [pers.] Expressing the positive life — keeping my dreams while opening the hearts and minds of the reader.; [a.] West Covina, CA

SPENCER, GLADYS E.
[b.] April 2, 1923, PG County, Groom, MD; [m.] Widow; [ch.] Donald A. Patricia, Cynthia M. and Paul E.; [ed.] High School - Fredrick Douglas High - Prince George's County - Upper Marlboro, MD; [occ.] Continue to work part time at St. Mary's since retiring in 1988 after 25 years.; [memb.] For the past 18 yrs. I have been a member of St. Mary of the Assumption Traditional Choir. I have recently become a member of Prince.; [hon.] George's Choral Society Award of Merit in Scouting year 1975. Award of appreciation from scouting 1976; [oth. writ.] Many poems in a variety of categories I have written. "The view from my window," is the only one I have submitted.; [pers.] I try to capture and express the beauty of everyday surroundings and put them into writing. I also try to relate to the feelings of individuals when I write.; [a.] Upper Marlboro, MD

SPINK, JENNIFER
[b.] June 30, 1979, WA; [p.] Donna and David Haswell; [m.] Thomas Spink Jr., October 3, 1996; [ch.] Caitlin Renae Spink; [ed.] Traverse City Senior High School; [occ.] Student; [oth. writ.] Mixed Emotions, Pheasant Ridge and When You Love Someone (all published); [pers.] When I write, I lose myself in it. Sometimes it's as though the pen has a mind of its own!; [a.] Traverse City, MI

SPROUT, AURELLE PURDY
[b.] April 23, 1943, Coraopolis, PA; [p.] Robert and Elsie Purdy; [ed.] Undergrad: B.S. Degree Art Education, Penn State Univ./Graduate: M.Ed. Degree, Dance, Temple University, Art, San Francisco State Univ.; [occ.] Art Teacher, Dance

Specialist - Montgomery Twp. Middle School, Skillman, NJ, National Art Education Association; [memb.] Art Educators of New Jersey, National Education Association; [hon.] Graduate assistantship in dance from Temple U - 1978-80, mini grant in art teaching 1995-96; [pers.] I believe in the arts as a way of life. It's focus for me. I love to interrelate the arts and love nature as inspiration.; [a.] Lambertville, NJ

STAHL, CAROLINE E.
[b.] June 21, 1942, Belleville, NJ; [p.] William and Dorothy Sayre; [m.] John Stahl Jr., September 8, 1962; [ch.] Nancy, John III, Judy and Amy; [ed.] Belleville High School; [occ.] Circulation Supervisor, Belleville Library; [memb.] NJALA; [oth. writ.] Poetry published in mother's day book of poetry for Belleville Library.; [pers.] I use my poetry as a way of expressing my inner most feelings.; [a.] Belleville, NJ

STANLEY, EDWARD A.
[pen.] Blake Edwards; [b.] December 5, 1955, Memphis, TN; [p.] Ronald and Barbara Stanley; [m.] Naomi Stanley, 1980; [ch.] Barbara, Kenneth, Stall, Kevin (Deceased); [ed.] Public Schools completed in Armed Forces; [occ.] Writer; [oth. writ.] Autobiography, (No title as yet) help in others cope with loss and grieving of child; [pers.] Yesterday is the past, tomorrow is the future, today is the present. Your children are your present from God. So please love them with all you heart, as you never know when God will take them back.; [a.] Woonsocket, RI

STANLEY, TERRY
[pen.] Zebra; [b.] October 29, 1933, San Francisco, CA; [p.] Wm. - Rita O'Halre; [m.] Deceased, December 24, 1956; [ch.] Charles, Nancine, Tammy; [occ.] Prop. MGMT; [oth. writ.] Children's Stories poems. I published.; [pers.] Success is not forever, failure is not fatal.; [a.] Oceanside, CA

STANTON, CHRIS
[pen.] Hatton, Gareth; [b.] October 1, Leicester, England; [p.] Derek Stanton, Audrey Stanton; [m.] Lynn Stanton, September 23, 1978; [ch.] Megan, Claire; [ed.] Alderman Newton's Boys' School Leicester, England University of Kent at Canterbury England; [occ.] Owner of Eddie's Market, Pasadena California; [memb.] British and Dominion Cricket Club, Anaheim California; [hon.] B.A. (Hons) Sociology University of Kent at Canterbury England; [oth. writ.] A single bundle of poems wrapped with thick brown paper and tied with old string, waiting to be published.; [pers.] Writing poetry is a need, almost an obsession. I find myself often dwelling on the feminine power of nature and man's desperate attempts to control her.; [a.] Pasadena, CA

STEHLIK, DANIEL A.
[pen.] Blue River Valley Cowboy; [b.] June 12, 1955; [p.] Leonard and Jan Stehlik; [ed.] University of Nebraska; [occ.] Farming, Teaching; [memb.] Bethlehem Lutheran Church, Crete Young Farmers Education Association, Saline County Farm Bureau Federation; [pers.] Agriculture and Education are the foundations of all other human advances.; [a.] Dorchester, NE

STEINBERG, ALLEN
[pen.] Allen Steinberg; [b.] May 9, 1979, Buffalo, NY; [p.] Leah and Jerome Steinberg; [ed.] Sweet Home School Dis., Currently at Sweet Home Senior High; [occ.] Student; [memb.] USY, Sweet Home Football Team; [hon.] Scholarships to go to is real, Merit Role Scholar, Chosen to be in Who's Who Among America's High School Students; [pers.] Life was meant to be lived!; [a.] Williamsville, NY

STEINKRAUS, CHRISTOPHER GENE
[b.] October 1, 1974, Anaheim, CA; [p.] Ron Steinkraus, Vicki Fink; [ed.] Sierra High School; [occ.] Trail Shot Fire fighter, USDA Forest Service; [pers.] I write poems as a way to talk about things that most people don't talk about. I believe that God is coming soon and hope my writings will change people's minds toward a better eternity.; [a.] Prather, CA

STEM JR., JOHN WINSTON
[b.] November 2, 1975, Baltimore, MD; [p.] John and Sandra Stem; [ed.] Carroll Christian Schools, Washington Bible College; [occ.] Student; [memb.] American Christian Honors Society; [hon.] Summa Cum Laude, Dean's List; [pers.] This poem concerns man's attempt to avoid being convicted by God or others by holding up a mask. This mask may deceive other people and the one it shields, but not God. God still sees each person a guilty sinner in need of a Savior -- Jesus Christ (John 3:16-17).; [a.] Woodbine, MD

STESSIN, ALEXANDER M.
[b.] September 26, 1978, Moscow, Russia; [p.] Michael Stessin, Marina Vitis; [ed.] Niskaguna H.S.; [occ.] Student; [hon.] National Merit Scholarship Winner; [pers.] My goal is to achieve a resonance between the stylistic elegance of verse and the emotional/intellectual value of the content. My inspirations include 20th century Russian poetry, French surrealism, the films of Andrei Tarkovsky, magic realism and infinite love for my parents.; [a.] Schenectady, NY

STEVENS, SHARON
[pen.] Sharon Stevens; [b.] July 2, 1946, Louisville, KY; [p.] Mr. and Mrs. Charles R. Boman; [ch.] Derek Young and Cory Stevens; [ed.] Hairdress, EMT, Student of Institute of Children's Literature; [occ.] Hair Dresser-writer; [memb.] Southeast Christian Church President of Angels Incorporated Certified Care Minister of Southeast Christian Church; [oth. writ.] 2 Books - "The Angels and The Lamb", "The Costs of Silence", some articles in "The Entertainer Magazine" and "Inside Louisville Newspaper" (Neither existent any longer); [pers.] It intrigues me to capture feelings through words and pass to others as pleasant experiences.; [a.] Louisville, KY

STEWARD, LINDA
[pen.] Tynitha Savannah; [b.] August 10, Cleveland, OH; [p.] Elizabeth and James; [ch.] Andrew Howard Samuels and Bobby Steward; [ed.] 1 Year of College also received a Certificate Diploma as a Medical Receptionist from Laural medical and Dental School Phoenix Ariz.; [occ.] Receptionist at a Ohio Nursing Home; [oth. writ.] Song call Listen Love was accepted by Grand Central Station I won Award in "1978" I also written 2 other poems

and 5 other songs that I haven't shown to the public or company for viewing but they have been copyright.; [pers.] This poem dedicated those who enjoy the sounds of the water, being with someone or even alone, walk alone the beach at dawn and feeling the relaxation to be near and seeing the view of the wave in water and it seems to clear your mind.; [a.] Shaker Heights, OH

STIGLIANO, JAMI
[b.] March 31, 1979, Shakopee, MN; [p.] Paul and Billie Stigliano; [ed.] Robinson High School; [occ.] Student, Art Center Volunteer; [memb.] Int'l Order of Rainbow for Girls, Meadowbrook Baptist Church, Future Educators, Quill and Scroll, National Honor Society, Senior Cotillion, UIL, One Act Play; [hon.] Drill Team Lieutenant 2 yrs, Captain Sr. Yr, All-American Drill Team, Most Spirited, Director's Award, 2nd Place District Ready Writing 95-96, Regionals - 5th Place 95-96 Vaportraits Business Mgr., Zone One Act Play "All Star Cast"; [oth. writ.] School Paper: Poems, Editorials, Feature Writing, School Yr Book Copy, PTA Newsletter Article; [pers.] EMail at Nikistig@aol.com; [a.] Waco, TX

STINESPRING, DOLORES
[pen.] Stinespring Dolores; [b.] March 20, Shinnston, WV; [p.] James and Anna Satterfield; [m.] William Christopher Stinespring; [ch.] Three; [ed.] University of Louisville, KY West VA University; [occ.] Retired - Social Worker Medical Assistant; [memb.] Stonewall Jackson Civil Club Woman is Club of Clarksbury Waldomare Ass. W.R.A.P., Harrison Co Historical Ass., Shinnston Historical Ass. Toastmasters, Int. Club 2885; [hon.] Celebrate Women Award from W.Va. Woman/Commission 3rd Place Award, World of Poetry Winner - R.W.A.P., Poetry Listed in Personalities of the South Past President of 8 organizations have lived in 9 States; [oth. writ.] Several poems "Time" - "Remembering" - "Autumn" - "Winter."; [pers.] Actress - Staring in Mame, A Little Night Music and Wednesday, etc. Tribute to Chautangan Performance of Mary Todd Lincoln and Women who went West on the wagon trains.; [a.] Shinnston, WV

STOCKERT, MARGIE J.
[b.] June 27, 1944, Independence, KS; [p.] George and Pauline Dodds; [m.] Elliott, August 6, 1977; [occ.] Mediator; [memb.] Beta Sigma Phi; [oth. writ.] Published several poems in "United Poets".; [pers.] I write for pleasure and inspiration. My love of poetry started with my grandmother, Anna Wilson when I was six years old.; [a.] Lees Summit, MO

STOOKEY, TAMMY LEE
[pen.] Tammy Lee Stookey; [b.] July 14, 1959, Dayton, OH; [p.] Ann and Alvin Stookey; [ed.] Fairview High School; [occ.] Trayline Worker Good Samaritan Hospital; [pers.] I write about the things that come from deep within my heart and soul, and it is reflected then upon me in my poetry! Also I have been influenced by Miona Lee Solomon and by my parents.; [a.] Dayton, OH

STORK, TAMI LOUISE
[pen.] Sam Stork; [b.] February 15, 1964, Denver, CO; [p.] Don and Shirlee Stork; [ed.] Englewood High School, Community College of Aurora Colorado. I am working toward a degree in early

childhood Education.; [occ.] I am currently looking for work while attending college.; [pers.] I try to let all the people in my life that I love know how much I love them and I find it easiest to do so in writing. My mother and father were my idols growing up, as is Kathy Finley now.; [a.] Aurora, CO

STORY, BARBARA
[b.] October 11, 1941, Sterling, CO; [p.] Hazel A. Timmons and Earl H. Timmons; [ed.] Glendale High, Glendale, Ari. Cosmetology, Mt. View, Calif., Nursing (L.V.N.) Southwestern-Leadership Courses (U.S.A.R.); [occ.] I work in restorative nursing as a R.N.A./C.N.A.; [memb.] I am a member of the United States Army Reserves since 31, May 1975; [hon.] Commander's Special Recognition Award, several Letters of Outstanding Performances. Southwest Asia Service Medal W/1-Bronze Service Star/Kuwait Liberation Medal/Army Components Achievement Medal 2nd OLC several Arcomw Olc and Meritorous achievements, overseas ribbons.; [oth. writ.] This is my first.; [pers.] Set your sights high and finish your goals. "I can do all things through Christ who strengthens me." Phil 4:13; [a.] Lakeside, CA

STOTLER, MARIE ELENA
[pen.] Marie; [b.] May 17, 1948, Coatesville, PA; [p.] Joseph Gavrish; [m.] Richard A. Stotler, September 9, 1972; [ed.] High School; [occ.] Housewife and Bee Skep (Hive) Weaver (Article enclosed); [memb.] Chester County Historical Society, Chadds Ford Historical Society (Board Member); [hon.] Watercolors - 3 first place, Original Counted Cross Stitch Colonial Samplers - 4 first place, Bee Skep - Early American Life Maga 1995 - Best in U.S. in this Craft (Card-over); [oth. writ.] I have written several poems and now writing a novel and a book on bee keeping with my own illustrations.; [pers.] I love what I do, and the life God has chosen for me, and want to share it with the world.; [a.] Malvern, PA

STOWERS, BARBARA FAITH
[b.] December 8, 1979, Agana, Guam; [p.] Robert and Diana Stowers Jr.; [ed.] 11 Grade of High School at Center High School; [occ.] Student; [a.] Elverta, CA

STRAIN, HEATHER K.
[b.] April 28, 1987, Phoenix, AZ; [p.] Terry and Janet Strain; [ed.] Sept. 1996, entering 4th Grade, Eagle Ridge Elementary; [occ.] Student; [memb.] Deer Valley Performing Dance Group - Performing since the age of 4 four the City of Phoenix Functions; [hon.] 1st and 2nd place in Dance Competitions for Tap and Jazz Dances; [a.] Phoenix, AZ

STROBEL, SUE A.
[m.] Yes; [ch.] Daughter/Son, 2 Grandsons; [ed.] Bank Loan Assistant; [oth. writ.] I've been writing for some 30 years however, this is my second attempt at a contest and second publishing.; [pers.] Most of my poetry paints a picture that enables the reader to envision the subject matter.

STRUPP, ANN C.
[b.] March 13, 1940, Rigby, ID; [p.] Wayne Chivers and Norma Chivers; [m.] Glen Strupp, May 15, 1981; [ch.] Darwin Wayne, David Joe, Holly Ann; [ed.] Rigby High School; [occ.] Office Man-

ager, Farm Bureau Insurance - 19 years; [memb.] Presently Serving on Rigby City Council, Director on Jefferson Co. Historical and TV Museum. Parade Chairperson for Ten years for Jefferson County Stampede Parade. One in Idaho's Largest; [hon.] Community Service Award 1988, Centennial award 1990, State of Idaho; [oth. writ.] Most of my poems have been on funeral programs.; [pers.] I write poems for those friends and family that need understanding and try to touch their lives with kindness and love.; [a.] Rigby, ID

STRYKER, SALLY
[b.] December 21, 1972, Stamford, CT; [p.] Betsey and Derek Stryker; [ed.] Mount Tabor High School, University of North Carolina at Chapel Hill; [occ.] Freelance Writer; [oth. writ.] Have had several articles published in 3 different newspaper publications — ranging from the arts to community features.

STUART, JULIE ANN
[b.] March 14, 1958, Salem, OR; [p.] Doris and Gary Kuebler; [m.] Deceased; [ch.] Tessa, Cassie and Chad; [ed.] MSSW Holistic Medical Science, Clayton School; [occ.] Writer, Brain Dominance Self Awareness Counselor; [memb.] American Holistic College, Noetic Sciences, N.S.W.A.; [oth. writ.] Where Do I Go, Mighty Warrior, Sorrow, Life Goes On, Lost, I Must Say Good-Bye; [pers.] My writing gives the reader a visual concept of my soul. Enduring the loss of my true love.; [a.] Dagsboro, DE

STUTLER, DELLA L.
[b.] February 10, 1931, Burnside, KY; [p.] James and Dolly Hall; [m.] Joseph H. Stutler, January 24, 1976; [ch.] Theresa, Kathy, Janis; [ed.] High school/Scarlet Oaks Career Development, University of Cincinnati (part time); [occ.] Retired (Senior Sales Associate) work part-time Evans, Inc. of Chicago; [memb.] Springdale Church of the Nazarene; [hon.] Awarded 4th place in a major valentine poem contest. Promoted by a major radio station who received 1000 entries from 12 states. Many poems published in church magazines and newsletters.; [oth. writ.] Family/friends for special occasion - any subject.; [pers.] Influenced by all nature, especially during early Spring and Autumm. Describing nature at peace in its habitat.; [a.] Cincinnati, OH

SULLIVAN, ANN M.
[pen.] Montarayan Star; [b.] March 31, 1963, Long Island, NY; [p.] James G. Sullivan (Deceased) and Ann C. Sullivan; [occ.] Advertising Account Executive; [hon.] New York State Honor Graduate in Business; [oth. writ.] A vast collection of other poems and lyrics, currently unpublished.; [pers.] The only thing that lasts forever is forever itself. Confronting the end, eternity blinks and inspires me to continuously write about it.; [a.] Huntington, NY

SULLIVAN, JUNE
[b.] December 17, 1957, Crailsheim, Germany; [p.] Fred and Helen Dail; [m.] Robin; [ch.] Jason, Tyson, Byrun, (Twins) Bryce and Kristopher; [ed.] Clover Park High, Knapp College; [occ.] Vice Pres. of College Educational Program; [memb.] American Heart Ass., Humane Society, Cancer Research; [pers.] Life is only as long as a single breath.; [a.] University Place, WA

SUMMERS, TREVOR
[b.] June 20, 1977, Chester, PA; [p.] Steven and Carol Summers; [ed.] H.S. Diploma - Garnet Valley H.S.; [occ.] Student; [pers.] "Let us then try what love will do." Wm. Penn

SUN, MICHAEL
[pen.] Asian Invasion, Dolomike; [b.] September 9, 1978, Spartansburg, SC; [p.] Jackie Chen, Joseph Sun; [ed.] Tamalpais High, UC Davis, UC Berkeley; [occ.] Freelance Comedy Writer, Marine Biologist; [memb.] Tiburon Player's Club, Chamber of Commerce, Landmarks Society, The Art Row Merchant's Club, Main Street Association; [hon.] Tiburon Chamber of Commerce Businessman of the Year, Fred Astaire, Court Jester, Best New Comedic Talent; [oth. writ.] A book of rhymes, a collection of several poems called the Magical Mystery Anthology of Poetry.; [pers.] I strive for outstanding achievement in the field of excellence. My favorite poets include Edgar Allen Poe, Samuel Coleridge, and Lord Tennyson.; [a.] Mill Valley, CA

SUTTON, OZO
[b.] October 13, 1911, Atlanta, GA; [p.] Deceased; [m.] Deceased; [ch.] 1 daughter living; [ed.] High School; [occ.] Retired; [oth. writ.] 2 books published 1 copy writed - not published 1 not copy writed or published

SWANIER, MRS. ANNA PIERNAS
[b.] May 27, 1925, Pass Christian, MS; [p.] Mr. and Mrs. Jules Piernas Sr.; [m.] Herman B. Swanier (Deceased), November 30, 1946; [ch.] Five; [ed.] Completed High School; [occ.] Retired (was Microphone Clerk - SA Water Board); [memb.] Thrifty Matrons Saving and Pleasure Club Ladies of Auxiliary of Knight of Peter Claver. Altar Society and Sodality; [hon.] Woman of the Year, My Parish St. Joan of ARC Outstanding Mother of Carrollton Community Queen of the Ladies of St. Peter Claver; [oth. writ.] Attribute to my deceased parents, attribute to: My 104 year old fellow senior citizen, a tribute to our choir directress.; [pers.] I sincerely hope I can write poems that will give others pleasure in reading.

SWEAT, REBECCA A.
[b.] January 16, 1958, Tampa, FL; [p.] Albert and Jeannie LeDuc; [m.] Richard Sweat, June 18, 1976; [ch.] Richard, Joseph, Tonya; [ed.] Florida State University; [occ.] Family Support Team, Big Bend Hospice; [memb.] Phi Sigma Pi Honors Member (Service Chairman), St. Elizabeth Seton Catholic Church lector, Sopchoppy th of July Committee; [hon.] Big Bend Hospice, Volunteer of the month, Phi Sigma Pi Honors; [oth. writ.] High School paper.; [pers.] Express yourself, so others may not overlook the beauty in thee. Inspired by my friend James Waters and my sister Cheryl Long. Both are writers of poetry.; [a.] Sopchoppy, FL

SYKULA, RICHARD
[b.] July 21, 1939, Poland; [p.] Junina and Stavisian; [m.] Wanda Sykula, March 9, 1987; [ch.] Robert and Richard Jr.; [ed.] Steel Construction College - Certified Construction Inspector. Certified Ship's Besher.; [occ.] Disabled totally.; [memb.] The National Humane Education Society. Society Honours. 1995; [hon.] Found Benefactor of the Tallgrass, Prairie National Preserve National Parks

Trust, 1994. Trust Honour 1995; [oth. writ.] Poems - Lyrical Heritage, Short Biografical Profile available.; [pers.] Citizen and Honorable Nobility Stockens of the Principality of the Huff River Province, Queensland, Australia. Honorable Citizen of the USA, Poland and Honorable Resident in Paris, France.; [a.] Brooklyn, NY

SZABO, EVA
[b.] January 14, 1929, Budapest, Hungary; [p.] Magdalen and E. Szollosy; [m.] Joseph Szabo, September 25, 1948; [ch.] Thomas Fitzroy, Szabo; [ed.] Sacre Coeur, (High School) Univ. of Budapest Architectural School; [occ.] Retired; [memb.] Friend of the Newton free library Hungarian Society of Mass. Officer Brandeis National Womens Committee; [pers.] Tread softly, but follow your instinct without compromise; [a.] Newton, MA

TAFE, JENNIFER L.
[b.] November 29, 1976, Ft. Walton Beach, FL; [p.] Walters and Kim Tafe; [ed.] Bitburg American High School, Studying Communication and English at East Carolina University; [hon.] Dean's List; [a.] Greenville, NC

TALLMAN, EVELYN
[b.] November 13, 1922, S. Westerlo, NY; [p.] Mrs. Hazel F. Mabie; [m.] Deceased, January 23, 1940; [ch.] One; [ed.] Greenville Central High School, National Baking School 825 Diverse Parkway, Chicago, IL; [occ.] Retired and write; [memb.] Social Service with Albany County Social Security Benefits; [oth. writ.] Wild of Poetry, 701 Dixieanne Ave., Sacramento, California

TANNER, ELIZABETH
[pen.] Flaming Star Rising; [b.] October 26, 1951, Dallas, TX; [p.] Lorene and E. H. Fowler; [m.] Joseph A. Tanner, August 21, 1993; [ch.] 2 Boys, 1 girl; [occ.] Healer-Teacher of Healing; [hon.] Reiki Master; [oth. writ.] This is my first time to enter anything, I have written many poems, but only my friends have read them so far. I have written poetry since I was 12.; [pers.] I am that I am.; [a.] Pasadena, TX

TAYLOR, CANDAS C.
[b.] January 18, 1980, Washington, DC; [p.] Manuel and Harriet Taylor; [ed.] Greater Mt. Zion Day Care, M.E. Gibbs Elementary School, Holy Comforter St. Cyprian, Charles W. Eliot J.H.S., School W/O Walls, S.H.S.; [occ.] Executive Assistant at Taylor System Solutions.; [memb.] National Geographic Society, B'nai B'rith Klutznick Museum, Who's Who Among American High School Students, etc.; [hon.] Honored in the 30th Annual Edition of Who's Who Among American High School Student, Honor Roll for the 4-Semester Term, Certificate of Appreciation from The Department of Administrative Services and the D.C. Commission on the Arts and Humanities etc.; [oth. writ.] Stereo Type a poem in the Fall 1994, Edition of the B'nai B'rith Klutznick Jewish Museum Newsletter, Combination Winds, Wonder (a short story), war etc.; [pers.] Always write what you feel, no censoring and no holding back. Let the words become you, and let your thoughts consume you. That is, to me, what a true writer is.; [a.] Washington, DC

TAYLOR, JULIA T.
[pen.] J. T. Taylor; [b.] October 17, 1936, Virginia; [p.] Eunice and Edmund Thompson; [m.] Rawleigh W. D. Taylor Jr., March 7, 1986; [ch.] Eunice, Lynn, and Robin (all daughters); [ed.] High School, some college; [occ.] Retired Nurse; [memb.] Local P.C. Users Group; [oth. writ.] The Land of Pooze, Whisperings, Memories of Growing Up; [pers.] The poem, "Searching" was written by me and is to be included with my forth-coming book "Whisperings".; [a.] Colonial Beach, VA

TAYLOR, MAUREEN
[pen.] Red; [b.] 9 January 1941, England; [ch.] Four; [ed.] Degree in Business Admin and Personel; [occ.] Work for Health Care Co. in Dallas; [memb.] Jewish; [oth. writ.] First born son writer-songwriter-singer (World Renowned) Classical Rock.; [pers.] World travelers mending Somalia, East Africa. My experience in life thought me many things. One being, we come here but once. The powers of the human mind never cease to amaze me.

TEAFORD, BECKY ELAINE
[pen.] Rebecca Laine; [b.] February 7, 1978, Danville, VA; [p.] Mike and Janie Teaford; [ed.] Gretna High School, attending Central Virginia Community College; [occ.] Student; [memb.] Springfield Baptist Church; [hon.] 2nd place poetry Peidmont Area Reading Council Young Author's Contest 1995, 3rd place Poetry Peidmont Area Reading Council Young Author's 1996; [oth. writ.] Several unpublished short stories.; [a.] Gretna, VA

TERRY, ANGLECIA
[pen.] Anglecia M. Terry (Angel); [b.] January 3, 1957; [p.] William P. Terry Jr. and Annie L. (Wright) Terry; [ch.] Ashante M. Malone and unborn Son; [ed.] West Side Sr. High, Indiana University and South Holland College; [occ.] Certifi Occupational Therapist Ass.; [memb.] Clark Road Missionary Baptist Church, Occupational Therapist Assoc.; [hon.] A Christian and Mother; [pers.] Within every person, there is good and the desire to do better. I was greatly influenced by my mother, Annie, and the elders in my childhood. Surroundings.; [a.] Gary, IN

TESTA, SOPHIE T.
[b.] May 3, 1928, Newark, NJ; [p.] Caterina and Matthew Nastasi; [m.] Leonard A. Testa, July 2, 1950; [ch.] Richard, Therese, Joseph, Leonard, Roy, Dean; [ed.] High school grad; [occ.] Retired bookkeeper Midlantic Nat'l Bank in Bloomfield N.J.; [memb.] General Assembly and Church of the First Born (Newark, N.J.), (Non-denominational) Born Again Hallelujah!!! 573 Springfield Ave - Newark N.J. 07103; [oth. writ.] Second book of poetry titled "Awesome God" (First book titled) "It Is Finished"; [pers.] All my poems are Holy Spirit inspired, and we can do all things through Jesus Christ.; [a.] Bloomfield, NJ

THERIAULT, ANN MARIE MCGOVERN
[pen.] "Ree", Ann Marie McGovern; [b.] April 20, 1958, Waltham, MA; [p.] Doris M. Leger and Francis J. McGovern; [m.] David J. Theriault, June 15, 1991; [ch.] Scott Munger, Sean Munger, Garbrielle Theriault; [ed.] Waltham High Class of 1976, Blaine Hair School 1986; [occ.] Hair Stylist for busy childrens hair salon. Free lance; [memb.]

South Side Seven; [oth. writ.] Several short stories articles and poems. I enjoy writing about life experiences.; [pers.] If you just believe, anything is possible.; [a.] Natick, MA

THOMAS, BARBARA M.
[pen.] Ann Thomas; [b.] April 3, 1942

THOMAS, CURTIS DOUGLAS
[b.] November 23, 1948, Wythe County, VA; [p.] Mr. and Mrs. Arthur P. Thomas; [m.] Sandra Layne Thomas; [ed.] B.S. in Business Administration, Virginia Poly Technic Institute and State University, Blacksburg, Virginia; [oth. writ.] None published, have been writing detailed investigative reports for criminal courts for twenty-five years.; [pers.] I write from the inspiration of things that interest me. I never labor to compose.; [a.] Max Meadows, VA

THOMAS, REBECCA
[pen.] Becky; [b.] June 18, 1925, Fayetteville, NC; [p.] Leroy and Fannie Thomas; [m.] Lawrence Thomas; [ch.] Three; [ed.] "Child Development Specialist"; [occ.] Retired at age 68 yrs.; [hon.] Just gratitude for writing why I chose to work at severely retard children. The children are helped developmentally and to see; [oth. writ.] None other than "Why I Chose To Work And Severe To Mildly Retarded Children".; [pers.] The progress in these children lets me know I have helped somebody learn to live a life according to their developmental level.; [a.] Philadelphia, PA

THOMPSON, ALAN RICHARD
[b.] April 23, 1930, Springfield, MA; [p.] Henry and Louise Thompson; [ed.] 2 years West New Engl Col.; [occ.] Survival Ctr: Food Closet Coordinator (4 hrs. a day); [oth. writ.] Poems: Doubt Believes, Eternal Measure, Triangle, Beset, Liking, Mill River Bridge, House of Willows and Pines Homely Chair; [a.] Amherst, MA

THOMPSON, JARED A.
[b.] September 14, 1983, Binghamton, NY; [p.] Gary and Ellen Thompson; [ed.] Northwest Cabarrus Middle School, Brookside Elementary; [occ.] Student; [pers.] I would like to dedicate my first published poem to my grandmother, Roseanne De Silva, who died January 21, 1995. I love you, Grandma.; [a.] Kannapolis, NC

THOMPSON, TERESA
[b.] November 8, 1952, Chicago, IL; [m.] Divorced; [ch.] Leslie Nicole Thompson age 17; [ed.] 1 1/2 year College - Dekalb College, Clarkston, GA; [occ.] X-Ray Technologist, Atlanta, GA; [pers.] Even when survival is the victor whether touched by heights of joy or depths of horror, life is never the same.; [a.] Ellenwood, GA

THRASH, STEVE
[pen.] Ronald Thrash; [b.] December 23, 1963, Purcell, OK; [p.] Casey and Kaye Thrash, and Jerry Sampson; [m.] Donald K. Thrash, March 8, 1996; [ch.] Carrie, Crystal and Kayla; [ed.] Purcell High School, Oklahoma City Community College, University of Oklahoma; [occ.] Student, Freelance writer, Farmer; [memb.] Iron Chapel Freewill Baptist Church - Washington, OK; [hon.] "Windmill, 1994" given me in honor of my poem "The

Potter", various other recognition of my poetry writings. Articles for the "Purcell Register" and the "Pioneer" newspapers; [oth. writ.] "The Potter" (poem published by University of Oklahoma Press "Windmill" publication 1994), articles for school newspaper, church articles in local paper, Misc. other articles in local newspaper.; [pers.] The peace of Christ Jesus, my wife, family and friends are my source of inspiration. There is much goodness left in this world and I will continue to search for and write about it.; [a.] Washington, OK

TILLMAN, NIKKOLE JESSICA
[pen.] Rebekah Heinz, Francesca Blake, Nikkolette; [b.] July 8, 1979, Bridgeton, NJ; [p.] G. Charles and P. A. Tillman; [ed.] Downe Twp. Elementary School, Bridgeton High School (Senior Year '96-'97); [occ.] Student, Aspiring Writer and English Ed./Journalism Major; [memb.] Future Educators of Am. (Co-Pres.), Student Government (Rep.) HOSA (State Pres. and Chptr. Pres.); [hon.] National Honor Society, Honors Student, Who's Who Among American High School Students; [oth. writ.] Short Story "The Zonule", (Francesca Blake), "Hope" (Nikkolette), "Death" (Rebekah Heinz) Will be published in 96-97 School Literary Magazine, I write for the school paper "The Echo".; [pers.] All of my writings (excluding newspaper) are influenced by my daily life and all of the wonderful people who I admire and respect. They inspire me so much. I thank God for all of my talents and achievements.; [a.] Newport, NJ

TINTO, WILMA JEAN
[b.] January 15, 1959, Santa Monica, CA; [p.] Anthony Joseph and Sue Neill Tinto; [occ.] Assistant Vice-President, Branch Manager for Universal Bank, Woodland Hills, California; [pers.] This poem was written and dedicated to my late father, Anthony J. Tinto Sr., who passed away on 06/10/95, who has been the one "true inspiration" in my life.; [a.] Van Nuys, CA

TIPTON, SETH
[b.] March 30, 1976, San Luis Obispo, CA; [p.] Isaac Tipton, Silvana Lupetti; [ed.] San Luis Obispo High School CA; [occ.] Student at Butte College CA; [hon.] 2nd Place in the San Luis Obispo County Congressional Art Contest, Honorable mention for a short story in the San Luis Obispo County writing contest.; [pers.] On an earth insulted by Cynics my fight, as a writer, is to reveal creation's beauty and underrated simplicity.; [a.] Chico, CA

TITUS, WILLIAM L.
[b.] October 14, 1945, Hammond, IN; [p.] Hersel W. and Mary E. Titus; [m.] Beverly J. Titus, July 31, 1970; [ch.] Lamont, Micheal, Philip, Angel, Susan, Mickey; [ed.] T. F. North High School; [occ.] Administrative Supervisor; [pers.] I write about life and everything it means to me.; [a.] Hammond, IN

TOBELMANN, LISA M.
[pen.] L. M. Tobelmann; [b.] November 10, 1978, Schenectady, NY; [p.] Rev. Charles J. Tobelmann and Linda C. Tobelmann; [ed.] Westfield High School (1996); [occ.] Student (First year at Houghton College); [memb.] Evangel Baptist Church, National Honor Society, Spanish Honor Society, Spanish Club, French Club, Art Club, Who's Who Among American High School Students (94-95, 95-96); [hon.] Student of the Month

(1/93), Dartmouth College Book Award (95), 7th place 1995 National Spanish Exam, President's Education Award's Program, New Jersey Garden State Scholar, Westfield High School Trigonometry/Algebra 3 Award; [oth. writ.] "Courage" - 1995 Anthology of New Jersey Young Poets, poems for church publication, poems for school literary magazines (Westfield High School).; [pers.] My writing is deeply personal in that it stems from intense feelings of both agony and joy that I experience. My love for creation is one of my most consistent inspirations.; [a.] Westfield, NJ

TOBY, BRIAN LEE
[b.] April 26, 1972, Seneca, KS; [p.] Robert E. and Jeannette Toby; [m.] Denise L. Bieling, February '97; [ed.] Graduated Nemaha Valley High School and Kansas State University, Bachelor of Science in Parks and Recreation Administration - May '95; [occ.] Corporate Recreation Specialist for Shawnee County Parks and Recreation; [memb.] Kansas Recreation and Parks Association (KRPA); [pers.] My family and friends inspire me the most and I want to thank all of them. I encourage everyone to at least try it, no matter what it is because you won't regret trying.; [a.] Topeka, KS

TOLSON, FRANCES E.
[b.] September 15, 1913, Licking Co; [p.] H.H. and Mary Hoover; [m.] Melvin L. Tolson (Deceased January 18, 1994), November 8, 1953; [ch.] One Stepdaughter deceased, four grandchildren, four great grandchildren; [ed.] Newark High School, Bachelor's Ohio State Un., Master's Art Education Kent State; [occ.] Retired Un. Art Teacher; [memb.] State Retired Teachers, Carroll Co. Retired Teachers, Carroll County Commission for the Advancement of the Arts; [hon.] Who's Who in American Education, Who's Who in the Arts 1971-1972; [oth. writ.] Christian Life Letters, The Lookout, Free Press Standard, World of Poetry Christian Evangelist; [pers.] I try to put feelings and images into words.; [a.] Carrollton, OH

TORRY, RAMON
[pen.] R. Torry; [b.] April 16, 1964, Ft. Eustis, VA; [p.] Rebbeca and Robert Torry; [m.] Mary A. G. Torry, July 20, 1991; [ch.] California Marie Torry; [ed.] Lincoln University MO, Langston University OK, Southwest High School MO, Soldan High MO; [occ.] Operations Officer: Captain, United States Army; [hon.] Various Military Decorations, and Ribbons; [pers.] Through constancy, dedication and hard work there is nothing you cannot achieve.; [a.] Rancho Corona, CA

TOSADO, DIANA M.
[b.] September 5, 1969, Bridgeport, CT; [p.] Barton Birch, Barbara Annecharico Birch; [pers.] Make resolutions today, for tomorrow may never come.; [a.] Stratford, CT

TOULOUSE, STEPHEN
[b.] August 6, 1972, Houston, TX; [p.] Kim and Ted Leverson; [ed.] Double Major English/Philosophy, 2.5 years, Southwest Texas State University; [occ.] Engineer, Microsoft Corp.; [pers.] My writings serve as snapshots of a mood or thought process. Sometimes not even I know what they mean, but I can tell you what I was thinking when I wrote them.; [a.] Irving, TX

TOWNSEND, BEVERLY J.
[b.] May 27, 1943, Waco, TX; [p.] Irene and Mac Glenn; [m.] Was married for 30 years; [ch.] Two sons and one daughter - all grown; [oth. writ.] Have been writing for years, just never sent any of them out until now. Some of poems I have sent to some Record Co. What I write comes from my own life and my heart.

TOWNSEND, COLLEEN PISI
[pen.] Maiden Narue; [b.] February 14, 1942, Sacramento, CA; [p.] Franklin and Dorothy Pisi; [occ.] Writing; [oth. writ.] C.W.P.; [pers.] I love writing poetry. I put down on paper what I have seen and felt through life. I know that everyone can find a fragment of themselves in what they read. I hope what I wrote will put a bit of daylight in your life.; [a.] Jamestown, CA

TOZZI, EZIO M.
[b.] November 8, 1929, Voorheesville, NY; [p.] Michael and Quinta Tozzi; [m.] Monica Tozzi, February 2, 1952; [ch.] Michael, Ross, Mario, Mark; [ed.] 12 years plus 1 year College Equivalent (GED), Ravena - Coeymans High School Military Inteligence Schools; [occ.] Retired Former Military and Postal Service (Hon); [hon.] Honor Society (High School) Military: Bronze Star, Joint Service Commendation, Army Commendation Medal; [oth. writ.] Positive Attitude! Positive Journey! Positive Life! (Between the raindrops). The Sunshine of Your Friendship (Best poems of 1996), A Sermon in Each Blade of Grass (The Path Not Taken) 4, Take My Hand Lord! (Carvings in Stone), Eternity is Ours (Best poems of the 90's); [pers.] Whatever talents we possess, are gifts from our creator, utilize your gift of life to love, honor and serve. Be mindful that the highway to Heaven begins here on Earth.; [a.] Odenton, MD

TRAP HAGAN, ALLAN W.
[pen.] Allan W. Trap Hagan; [b.] December 31, 1936, Urbana, IL; [p.] Woodrow and Elsie Trap Hagan; [ch.] Ann Marie Trap Hagan; [ed.] High School; [occ.] Electronics Factory Worker; [memb.] International Society of Poets, Distinguished Member; [hon.] Editor's Choice Award National Library of Poetry 1996; [oth. writ.] Anthologies: Shadows and light, Portraits of Life, Best Poems of 1990's, Lyrical Heritage; [pers.] I believe that a poem should be a condensed book.; [a.] South Bend, IN

TRAVER, GREGG
[b.] May 1, 1963, Waterbury, CT; [p.] Floyd and Katherine Traver; [ed.] B.S. Geography 24 credits towards M.S. Education; [occ.] Proofreader (for five national publications), Electroplaters; [memb.] United Way; [hon.] B.S. Degree; [oth. writ.] Unpublished; [pers.] God is alive and well. Have faith!; [a.] Naugatuck, CT

TRAVERS JR., WILLIAM T.
[pen.] Tom Travers; [b.] September 9, 1955, Wilmington, DE; [p.] Elizabeth V. and William T. Travers Sr.; [m.] Linda T. Travers, July 6, 1985; [ch.] Rhett J. Travers; [ed.] NBS School of Broadcasting, Philadelphia, PA, University of Delaware, Newark, DE, Brandywine High School, Wilmington, DE; [occ.] Disc Jockey and Sales Consultant; [oth. writ.] Wrote weekly column in local entertain-

ment magazine, editorials published in local newspaper, wrote and copy for print, TV and radio.; [pers.] Always be faithful and caring to your spouse and children, and never trust anybody who says, "Let's have lunch and let me pick your brain."; [a.] Newark, DE

TRAVISANO, RICHARD
[b.] June 11, 1939, Waterbury, CT; [ed.] BA - University of Connecticut, MA and PhD-University of Minnesota; [occ.] Sociologist; [memb.] Midwest Sociological Society, Society for the Study of Symbolic Interaction Eastern Sociological Society Modern Poetry Association; [oth. writ.] Articles in sociological journals and books, memoirs of growing up Italian, recipes and poems in local and national publications.; [pers.] I feel that rhythm is as important in blank verse as it is in traditional forms (or, for that matter, as it is in music). This because matter likes to dance and, as Robert Frost put it, "The aim was song."; [a.] Wakefield, RI

TRIPLITT, LOIS M.
[pen.] Lois Smith Triplitt; [b.] April 9, 1917, Bay City, MI; [p.] John C. and Edith E. Smith; [m.] Irvion Darrel Triplitt, May 27, 1950; [ed.] H.S., B.S., M.S. - '44-46, during WW2 I served as an Hospital Recreation Worker in the So. Pacific on the tiny island of Saipan, below Japan; [occ.] I'm a retired Nursing Education Consultant for Calif.; [oth. writ.] Poems: Survivors, My Cuckoo Clock, Fickle Mirror, I'd Know You In The Dark, Premonition, Endless Puzzle.; [pers.] I am fascinated by mystery, beauty, friendship, love, intuition, wisdom, wit, conflict, and music - I strive to write on uncommon topics - or common topics - with my unique slant.; [a.] Rocklin, CA

TROOP, CLARENCE TRUMAN
[pen.] Truman Troop; [b.] January 8, 1918, Oklahoma City, OK; [p.] P. G. Troop, Relda B. Troop; [m.] Mildred Estes Troop, March 28, 1997; [ch.] Peter, Mary, Ann Foster; [ed.] Oklahoma State University; [occ.] Retired; [memb.] Masonic Lodge #244; [oth. writ.] "Concrete Has A Human Relation Problem", Concrete, is concrete, is concrete; [pers.] Life at best is tedious, but fulfilling our dream is our life's desire.; [a.] Citrus Heights, CA

TRUITT, MAURINE I.
[pen.] Maurine I. Truitt; [b.] 1910, Idaho; [m.] Gerald L. Truitt, 1929; [ch.] Three; [ed.] High School; [occ.] Retired age 86; [pers.] I try to have an unusual ending or humor in the ending of my poems!; [a.] Baldwin Park, CA

TUCKER, QUENNIE A.
[b.] May 24, 1925, Trigg Co, KY; [p.] Nay and Flossie Armstrong - deceased; [m.] E. Clayton Tucker - deceased, September 6, 1947; [ch.] One Daughter; [ed.] High School plus 1 Year Sec. Tr. or Commercial College - Same thing.; [occ.] House Wife - When I worked it was always in an office.; [memb.] The only membership card that I have is WIBC - National Bowling Membership, Actually it is Women's International Bowling Congress; [hon.] I won first place in the Cultural Arts Division of the State Homemakers Convention in 1995, in Louisville KY, for one of my poems. One that I have not submitted to you; [oth. writ.] I have

lyrics that I think would make good Gospel Songs, however I have never submitted any of them to anyone to set to music; [pers.] I write just for enjoyment and sometimes when I am feeling down. Some of my poems have been written for fun, for others, and a few just to get my feelings on paper. I try to be optimistic in my outlook in life. I also try to see the fun side of life, as you can tell from my poem; [a.] Crofton, KY

TUCKER, SUE RICHARDSON
[pen.] Susan; [p.] Sam and Sarah Richardson; [m.] John R. Tucker, June 30, 1984; [ed.] Bethlehem Industrial Academy, Alabama State University, York College, City of New York, University of Pennsylvania (ICS), Master Art; [occ.] Retired; [memb.] St. Luke Baptist Church, St. Luke Deaconess Board, St. Luke Economic Development, St. Luke Missionary Society, Telephone Pioneers of America; [hon.] Outstanding Performance from AT&T, Outstanding Award as Family Historian from President Bill Clinton, Outstanding Performance from the Dale Carnegie Institute; [oth. writ.] Poems published: St. Luke Gazette, monthly books published, "How To Control Blood Sugar", "Fast Food, Killer of the Nation"; [pers.] I strive for the betterment of family, personal and spiritual values, in my writings. I have been gratefully influenced by the poet Maya Angelou.; [a.] Jamaica Estates, NY

TURNBULL, JOSHUA
[b.] November 17, 1982, Kokomo, IN; [p.] Edward Turnbull, Jerry Handy; [ed.] Hale Area Middle School; [occ.] Student; [pers.] I thank God for my gift of writing and I give him all the credit; [a.] Hale, MI

TURNER, CYNTHIA L.
[pen.] C. L. Turner; [b.] February 5, 1959, Danville, VA; [p.] Russell Keck, Ethel Keck; [m.] Burl Turner, May 20, 1984; [ed.] Ashbrook High, Cleveland Community College, Limestone College; [occ.] GED Instructor, Cleveland Community College, Shelby, NC; [memb.] The Gamma Beta Phi Society, National Teacher's Association, Animal Legal Defense Fund, ASPCA, The Humane Society of the U.S., World Wildlife Fund; [hon.] Who's Who in American Jr. Colleges, Dean's List, Presidents Lists, Student Marshall, Founders Scholarship, Endowed Scholarship, All-American Scholar, Magna Cum Laude; [oth. writ.] A collection of poems on various subjects, poem published in "Words From The Heart" entitled "Season of Change."; [pers.] I write what I feel most strongly about. Writing is a great release, and it gives a greater understanding to your emotions and the world around you. I plan to write short stories as well as poetry in the future.; [a.] Shelby, NC

TURNER, JANE
[b.] April 19, 1962, Carshalton, England; [p.] John and Roelie Stiff; [m.] Currently Separated; [ch.] Lauren age 6; [ed.] Coombre Girls School, Surrey, England; [occ.] Housewife; [memb.] Amateur Dramatic Group (England); [hon.] Nominated and Won Best Actress in Theatre Production "Wives Play", June 1994 (England); [oth. writ.] Poems published in School Magazines, Ghost Story, published in Local Newspaper, have also written poems and stories for children, "The Magic Penny", currently lodged with publisher.; [pers.] I have always had a vivid imagination. When a poem or

story comes into my mind I usually write it within one or two hours - and I need little adjustment once an idea has "flowed"!; [a.] Westlake Village, CA

TURNER, TAMARA
[pen.] Tammy Lee; [b.] August 24, 1981, Wharton, TX; [p.] Bruce and Pam Turner; [ed.] Junior at Wharton High School; [memb.] Drama Club, R.O.T.C.; [hon.] Who's Who Among American High School Students, R.O.T.C. Scholastic Achievement Ribbon, Junior National Honor Society, Duke Talent Search State Recognition; [pers.] In my poems, I write whatever comes into my head.; [a.] Wharton, TX

TUSQUELLAS, K. M.
[pen.] Ann O'Neamus; [b.] December 10, 1966, France; [occ.] House Stable; [pers.] Words only come to life through the reader's eyes, but they are born from a writer's turbulent mind in love with a restless pen.

TYLER, MICHAEL B.
[b.] October 26, 1978, Baltimore, MD; [p.] Jayne Ann Tyler/Leroy Albert Tyler; [ed.] Archbishop Curley H.S.; [occ.] Deli Man; [hon.] To believe, my parents, brother, and sister my Tuli; [oth. writ.] Over 300 other poems and essays. Selected poems in process or being published.; [pers.] My poetry tries to portray from my eyes. If I am able to serve one person to help themselves to solve life's enigma then they have read my poetry and understood it. Thanks be to God.; [a.] Baltimore, MI

TYLER, NICOLE RENE
[pen.] Nickey; [b.] December 12, 1983, Saint Louis, MO; [p.] Michael and Barbara Tyler; [hon.] June 7, 1996 Conduct Award, Twillman Elementary School-1996 Miss Missouri, American Pre-Teen Pageant-Reading Circle Certificate June 1996 Twillman School-Student Council Award June 1996 Twillman School-Most Talented Award June 1996 Twillman School; [oth. writ.] "I Did Not Die"-"Where Is The Love"-"Cherish The Day", "Everyone Has Something They Can Do"; [pers.] I have learned in writing poetry, it helps me to express my true feelings and emotions, I enjoy writing.; [a.] Saint Louis, MO

UNDERHILL, ROBBIN TAYLOR
[b.] April 30, 1961, Michigan; [p.] Claude and Helen Taylor; [m.] Terry Underhill, August 5, 1988; [ch.] Nathan, Tessa Shy and Arista; [occ.] House wife and mother of four; [hon.] I consider being a mother and wife my biggest honor and reward.; [pers.] My family is my love, life and my inspiration, and for me there is nothing greater than being loved by them.; [a.] Murray, KY

UNDERWOOD, JEROME B.
[b.] March 30, 1976, Bristow, OK; [p.] Diane Brooks; [ed.] Richland Northeast High, South Carolina; [occ.] Office Clerk; [pers.] More people should pick up a pen and write.; [a.] Bristow, OK

UNDERWOOD, RITA
[b.] July 2, 1951, Kingsville, TX; [p.] Vivian Foley and The Late R. E. Meeker Jr.; [m.] John Underwood, June 4, 1977; [ch.] 3 cats and 2 dogs, Kemo, Snowkitty, Samantha, Tramp and Lady; [ed.] Calallen High School, Corpus Christi, TX,

attended Harding University Searcy, AR, Rose State Coll. - Midwest City, OK - graduated August 1991 with AAS; [occ.] Registered Respiratory Therapist - Vencare - a subdivision of Vencor long term sub acute hospital; [memb.] American Association for Respiratory Care (AARC), National Board for Respiratory Care (NBRC) South Main Church of Christ of Weatherford, TX; [pers.] "I Found an Old Christmas Card" was written to help heal the memory that a friend and co-worker chose to end her life. May 1987 I lost a friend and two weeks later my father died - this poem helped to heal a memory.; [a.] Weatherford, TX

VALENCIA, CELIA VERONICA
[pen.] Vero, Veronica; [b.] May 24, 1982, Concord, CA; [p.] Gloria and Carlos Valencia; [ed.] St. Catherine's School of Sienna Elementary and Carondelet High School; [memb.] National Soccer Academy, Walnut Creek Soccer Club, Martinez Community Swim Team and Martinez Softball Team; [hon.] Publication Awards Honor Roll/Principal's List, Service Award; [oth. writ.] This is my first piece of writing to be published.; [pers.] My note is to keep trying, even when things are going wrong, and to do your best. Be all you can be and always try to make wise choices.; [a.] Martinez, CA

VALENTINE, DAVID
[pen.] Paris Collins; [b.] May 7, 1980, Van Wert; [p.] Jan and Lloyd Valentine; [ed.] So far a cheep one at Van Wert High School; [occ.] Burden on Society (a joke); [memb.] None, there's nothing that interesting in this town; [oth. writ.] Eddie's Never and Nothing, Second Civilization and some other poems (All not published); [pers.] I have been influenced by Music and Movies. In statement, odd things, odd people. The unknown, unthought of heroes, (Jim Carrol, Sex Pistols.); [a.] Van Wert, OH

VALLADAO, MAGGIE
[b.] October 11, 1980, Berwyn; [p.] Mark and Jacqueline Valladao; [ed.] Schafer, St. Alexander's Willowbrook High School (Sophomore at Willowbrook); [occ.] Volunteer Aide for swim lessons at Jefferson Pool; [oth. writ.] Published in High School paper "The Skyline".; [pers.] My writing is influenced from my own personal experiences ranging from my family to school or just everyday life. Writing is the best way for me to express myself, deal with my problems and hopefully help others.; [a.] Villa Park, IL

VAN ALSTINE, EURSULA BRYANT
[b.] July 30, 1936, Norfolk, VA; [p.] Celithia and Arthur Bryant; [m.] Cyle Van Alstine, December 25, 1975; [ch.] Steven John, Clifford Matthew; [ed.] Maury High School, William and Mary College, Illinois Univ.; [occ.] Teacher, Instructor, Counselor, Artist; [hon.] I had my own TV and Radio call in show.; [oth. writ.] Several poems and writings in booklets distributed in self help.; [pers.] My inspiration for my poems has been through the writings of Gibran. I believe in the "Fatherhood of God and the Brotherhood of Man" - love makes the difference in one's life, so inspires my poems.; [a.] McHenry, IL

VAN DER LINDEN VOOREN, MERCEDES
[pen.] Mercedes Moor; [b.] August 1, 1907, Amsterdam; [p.] Roelof Van Der Linden Vooren,

Klazina Brouwer; [ed.] Atheneum, Amsterdam, London School of Jazz; [occ.] Song writer, singer; [oth. writ.] Non-published, registered latin/jazz/pop songs.; [pers.] Many of us know what it feels like to be a victim of society. Eventually, the way we feel, we can change by altering our perceptions. The way we dream can change the world. There's always the possibility of a dream coming true. Isn't that what makes life interesting?; [a.] Hollywood, CA

VAN PHAM, TIEN
[b.] June 8, 1970, Ho Nai, Vietnam; [p.] Yen Viet Pham, Phuong Thi Vu; [ed.] Parkview High School, Southwest Missouri State University (B.A.); [hon.] George Washington Carver Award; [oth. writ.] Have several poems published in Vietnamese magazines and newspaper.; [pers.] All are for the love of God and humankind.; [a.] Springfield, MO

VAN SHULTZ, KURT
[pen.] Christian; [b.] December 22, 1970, Elyria; [p.] Carole Van Shultz; [ed.] Rocky River High School; [occ.] Server; [memb.] Calvary Chapel (Cleveland); [oth. writ.] Currently writing of Book of Poems "Introducing The Disappearing Kurt Van Shultz; [pers.] "If I am the influence, what good am I to God..."; [a.] Cleveland, OH

VAN VALKENBURGH, INA C.
[pen.] Catskill Mountains, NY; [ed.] High School - Olean High, Olean NY, Arts Schools - Art Institute of Buffalo, Buffalo, NY, Ringling School of Art Sarasota, FL, Art institute of Pittsburgh, Pittsburgh, PA; [occ.] Retired from career as Graphic Artist; [memb.] International Society of Poets; [hon.] Critical Acclaim from professionals in the state of Florida Educational System. "Quill Books" - Poetry Publishers National Library of Poetry; [pers.] I have been writing poetry since the late 1960's. Have shown art work locally since that time. My poetry and art are "Expressionist" in content and technique. Eclectic if you will, from past and present personal experience, thoughts and "in depth" feelings. An essay of my life. And an empathy and compassion with and for fellow humans.; [a.] Tampa, FL

VANBUSKIRK, DONNA L.
[pen.] Mrs. V.; [b.] June 16, 1942, Columbus, OH; [p.] Thomas and Luella Edwards; [m.] Terry VanBuskirk, June 25, 1960; [ch.] Two - Dawn Lynn and Diana Lynn; [ed.] High School - Child Care Training Realestate Sales and Management; [occ.] Home day care provider. Owner (with husband) of T. and D. Architectural Supply; [oth. writ.] I wrote a book. But it's never been published; [pers.] I try to treat all people with respect. It's not the size of your bank account, or the beauty you behold that makes you special or a friend of mine. It's the person inside when you are stripped of these things.; [a.] Andrews, IN

VANCOUR, ALICE CLEMONS BEYER
[ch.] Mitch, Ethel, JoAnne, Judy, Lester, Carl-Denise; [occ.] Retired; [memb.] International Society of Poets A.A.R.P.; [hon.] Editors Choice Award poem "Home", Merit of Award Certificate Poem "Its Almost Over," Editor Choice Award poem "Be Happy", Editors Choice Award poem "Two Pine Trees"; [oth. writ.] Poem "Bed of Life" published summer 95 arcadias poetry anthology poem "Dog

Sledding With Lester" published in best poem of the 90 National Library of Poetry - poem - "When Your Down And Feeling Blue" published in famous poems of today 95.; [pers.] Poem "Alive in Ninety-Five" published fall 96 edition Treasured Poems of America (poem "Ah!!! Spring Fever" published - winter 97 Treasured Poems of America, also poem "Hey Doc. How Come" and "Bruce" and "Castle") tape of poem "Visions."; [a.] Copenhagen, NY

VANDE-ZANDE, MARIE THERESA
[b.] July 21, 1952, Appleton; [p.] Eugene and Mary Jacobs; [m.] Mitchell Paul Vande-Zande, December 3, 1971; [ch.] Andrea and Steven; [ed.] Xavier High School and City College of Cosmetology; [occ.] Clerical Office/Bookkeeper; [hon.] National Honor Society, Music Achievement Award, High Scholastic Award; [oth. writ.] Portfolio of similar other poems; [pers.] I found that through my writing I was able to reflect upon and express many inner emotions. My poems have touched my inner self and hopefully will touch others.; [a.] Kaukauna, WI

VANDENEINDE, KRIS D.
[b.] May 23, 1979, Aurora, CO; [p.] Kevin Fox and Michelle Fox; [ed.] Hinkley High School, T.H. Pickens Technical Center; [occ.] Electrician, Aurora Public School District; [oth. writ.] "Wild Beauties" my first published poem, by the "Anthology of Poetry by Young Americans" 1994 Edition.; [pers.] This poem was inspired by and dedicated to Julie Oldenkamp, the one true love that I will forevermore cherish within my heart.; [a.] Aurora, CO

VAUGHAN, ALISA MAY
[pen.] Alisa May Vaughan; [b.] October 9, 1981, Troy, ID; [p.] Terry and Alice Vaughan; [ed.] McGhee Elementary, Sacajawea Junior High, Sophomore Lewiston Senior High; [memb.] The Beta Club - (Vice President); [hon.] Presidential Academic Award, Honor Roll, 2nd Place in School Writing Contest; [oth. writ.] Short story published in the Idaho - Statesman.; [pers.] I can do all things through Christ who strengtheneth me. Philippians 4:13.; [a.] Lewiston, ID

VAUGHAN, SHANNON E.
[b.] July 25, 1973, Bremerton, WA; [p.] Virgil and Kathy Claycamp; [m.] Michael A. Vaughan, February 4, 1995; [ed.] Stateline Christian School, Austin Community College, Allied Health Careers; [occ.] Housewife, Freelance Writer; [oth. writ.] Poems for church bulletins, special occasions, will be published in 1996 Edition of Who's Who in New Poet's (currently submitting more work to various magazines and publications); [pers.] I can't imagine having more fun than I am right now! Writing is a personal hobby, a challenge that I can see myself pursuing for the rest of my life. I strive to, in some way, give back what has been given to me.; [a.] Comfort, TX

VEGA, NORMA
[b.] April 17, 1932, Havana, Cuba; [p.] Carlos Valdes, Ines Valdes; [m.] Amador Vega, May 31, 1952; [ch.] Vilma - Jon; [ed.] High School The Apostolado Catholic School Havana - Cuba; [occ.] Housewife; [oth. writ.] This is my first poem in the English language but I have many more in Spanish (never published).; [pers.] I started writing since I was 14 yrs. old and my poems reflect the way I feel.; [a.] Miami, FL

VELIS, DIANA LIEN
[pen.] Diana Lien Velis; [b.] October 17, 1945, Logan, UT; [p.] Mr. and Mrs. Gerard A. Lien; [m.] Nickolas Alexander Velis, February 14, 1971; [ch.] Brian, William, Motes, Kari, Diana Motes, Georgia Maria Velis, Panagiota Kristina Velis, Alexandra Nicole Velis; [ed.] 1st year College, Utah State University, 30 years in the Food Service Industry - a real education!!; [occ.] Chef at a Private Club (Zippers); [memb.] Sons of Norway Jolis Daughters IOJD; [hon.] The only honors and awards I have come from traveling and studying french, and watching people - Especially my children; [oth. writ.] My other writings have been personal stories and poems - some that I have illustrated also.; [pers.] I love to write and meditate about the inequities and agonies of life. If seems that a Mystical attitude is required to comprehend its meaning and obtain peace.; [a.] Ogden, UT

VESSEY, CARRIE
[pen.] Sharon Jensen; [b.] January 11, 1968, CO; [m.] Mike, August 23, 1986; [ch.] 4 children, 3 boys, 1 girl; [ed.] Santa Rita High School - Tucson, AZ; [occ.] Medical Transcriptionist; [pers.] Creative writing was one of my favorite classes in high school - through my poems I am able to express my deepest emotions.

VEST, KEVIN WARREN
[b.] May 3, 1960, Montgomery Region; [p.] Mr. and Mrs. Warren Vest; [m.] Regina L. Vest, August 29, 1982; [ch.] Evonna Leigh Vest and Megan Leann; [ed.] Graduated in 1978 from Floyd High School; [occ.] Mixing Room Operator at Wolverine Gasket of Blacksburg; [memb.] Belonged to Triangle Bass Masters Radford, Virginia; [pers.] This poem was written after a boating accident in October of 95. I lost a Dear Friend in this accident. It was a hard thing on everyone involved but this is how I expressed my feelings.; [a.] Floyd County, VA

VETZEL JR., ALFRED LEON
[b.] October 6, 1938, Lakeland, FL; [m.] Bobbie Dallas Vetzel Jr., September 18, 1959; [ch.] Rhonda Yevette Gilmore, Gwendolyn Ruth Vaughan; [ed.] High School and Two Years of College; [occ.] Weight Master and Dispatcher; [hon.] Dean's List in College, and Officer of the Year while working for the Seminole Dept. of Law Enforcement; [oth. writ.] Six poems published in anthologies. A collection of poems, "Musing In Rhyme", some were written for a therapeutic endeavor, some for protest, and others from a recollection of personal experiences.; [pers.] I enjoy writing poems and find that I am often able to vent frustration in regard to national and world events which are beyond my control. I can only hope some of these poems contain a worthwhile statement.; [a.] Westville, FL

VICARO, TRACY
[b.] August 10, 1968, Belleville, NJ; [p.] Sharon Vicaro; [m.] John Vicaro, October 9, 1993; [ch.] Jennifer Rose; [ed.] Belleville High; [occ.] Artist; [pers.] These words came solely from my heart for my husband, who now keeps me warm and safe at night. My great influence was my Grandmother Rose Werner who believed in me and let me believe in myself with a little help from my mom and brothers.; [a.] Port Richey, FL

VILELLA, JESSICA ANN
[b.] December 11, 1985, Mt. Pleasant, PA; [p.] Paul and Carole Vilella; [ed.] Completed 4th grade at Conn Area Catholic School Connellsville PA; [oth. writ.] "My Birthday" is being printed by the Anthology Poetry of N.C.; [a.] Connellsville, PA

VINSKI, EDWARD J.
[b.] December 25, 1969, Southampton, NY; [p.] Edward and Kathleen Vinski; [ed.] BA - Providence College, MS - St. John's University, currently studying for Ph.D in School Psychology at City U. of New York; [occ.] Applied behavior specialist student; [memb.] American Psychological Association, American Psychological Society, National Association of School Psychologists; [hon.] National Dean's List; [oth. writ.] Several unpublished poems, stories and essays as well as a number of scientific research projects.; [pers.] I have been greatly influenced by the writings of C. S. Lewis. As a result, much of my writing contains a strong religious and meditational flavor. Other influences: Thomas Moore, Albert Camus.; [a.] Bridgehampton, NY

VINSONHALER, JASON D.
[pen.] Jason D. Lamar; [b.] July 26, 1978, Astoria, OR; [p.] Mary Vinsonhaler and Larry D. Vinsonhaler.

VOEGELE, AMBER ROSE
[pen.] Amber Rose; [b.] December 18, 1977, Circle, MT; [p.] Sandy and Layne Voegele; [ed.] High school, will be attending college at the University of Montana, Davidson Honors College.; [occ.] Student, employed currently at a telephone company.; [memb.] Columbia House; [hon.] Voice of Democracy Speech Winner, Hugh O'Brian Youth Leader, National Honor Society Vice President, Who's Who, All-American Scholar Recipient; [oth. writ.] I took an advanced composition class this year and completed a five page story, a ten page story, an illustrated children's story, and a hundred page story. I also keep journals of poetry.; [pers.] I intend to live my life simply. I only want to be happy and free. I love life.; [a.] Circle, MT

WADLOW, RICKY G.
[b.] February 21, 1957, St. Louis, MO; [p.] Arlis Wadlow, Jacquelyn Wadlow; [ch.] Stacy A. Wadlow; [ed.] 2 years collegiate study; [occ.] Truck driver with Schneider National Carriers; [memb.] VFW, American Legion, American Traders Assoc.; [hon.] Class President, Combined Insurance School, Chicago, IL; [oth. writ.] Currently working on my first book, titled "Go Ahead And Tell, Or Live Through Hell." First hand look about living a double standard life as a gay individual.; [pers.] Striving to eliminate "homophobia" in today's society.; [a.] Evansville, IN

WAGNER, DORIS W.
[pen.] Doris W. Wagner; [b.] February 16, 1926, Carroll Co., MD; [p.] John Earl and Pearl E. Walkling; [m.] George Everett Wagner, October 20, 1979, (2nd marriage); [ch.] 8 (From 1st Marriage); [ed.] Registered Nurse -graduated from St. Agnes Hospital School of Nursing 1946, Emphasis on Literature and Art in high School. Non-credit courses in various subjects.; [occ.] Now partly retired from Nursing (Specially in Geriatrics), part-time Assistant Accountant; [memb.] Humane Society of Carroll Co. (President of Board) American Assoc. of Retired Persons; [hon.] Plaques and Certificates through years of home health Nursing.; [oth. writ.] Several essays related to enchantment of well-being of the aged. Thoughts on my own life in relation to children, grandchildren, friends, some written poetically.; [pers.] Life-time interest in literature with emphasis on history and biographies of early Americans and Native Americans. Avid fox hunter and horse woman until unable to ride due to physical limitation. "Do something interesting each day."; [a.] Mount Airy, MD

WAGNER, TINA M.
[pen.] Maybow Knupko; [b.] April 13, 1980, Toledo; [p.] Dave and Shirley Wagner; [ed.] Greenwood Elementary, Jefferson Junior High, and attending Whitmer High School; [occ.] Student; [memb.] Whitmer Track, and Cross Country, French Club and honorary. Also Future Teachers of America Club; [hon.] Many school Athletic and Academic Awards in school; [oth. writ.] Several unpublished poems.; [pers.] Thanks to my family, and my friends for their support. Especially Shannon Best, Maggie Flath, Lisa and Laura Grudzinski, and Carrie Dunnigan. Friends influence me.; [a.] Toledo, OH

WAGNER, WANDA J.
[b.] March 8, 1977, Meyersdale, PA; [p.] Ray and Stella Patton; [m.] Christian Wagner, May 18, 1996; [ed.] Somerset Sr. High; [occ.] Fast Food Worker; [pers.] I would like to express that all of my writings are either something I have experienced or something that I have seen in my life.; [a.] Hooversville, PA

WAKEFIELD, LANA MARIE
[pen.] Lana Lights, Lana Banana, Short Stuff; [b.] August 17, 1963, Ogden Weber, UT; [p.] Dennis and Louise Wakefield, October 17, 1962; [ed.] Quincy Elem. 1970-1975, Burch Creek Elem. 1975-76, (Towndown), South Ogden Jr. High 1976-1978, Bonniville High 1978-1981, graduated in 1981 at age of 16, 4 years of Seminary of the LDS Church; [occ.] Food service at McKay Dee Hospital for 15 years, January 25, 1997; [memb.] Member of the Church of Jesus Christ of Latter Day Saints. Held a calling as Relief Society's Nursery Teacher for 15 years (10 mon. after I got my job); [hon.] In my 5 year reunion, I got an award for the person to change the least. Other than that nothing else; [oth. writ.] "The Baby in Me" was written as an assignment, and published in the yearbook 1983-84., Cloud 9, Time, Life, I Want To Be A Pioneer, The Holy Temple, The Salt Lake Temple, plus 25-30 others Temple Square year around, unfinished "My Life With the Savior" (Based on the original 12 apostles), unfinished, and 5 others. My first poem was in English Class in my senior year. I threw it away when class began. My teacher read it, liked it and asked me if I wrote it. I said "No," because I was afraid of being laughed at or ridiculed. I wrote short stories and poems after I graduated from high school. For 6 years I was afraid of showing my work, or sharing it. I am into Utah History, Photography. I love my job and hope to go on an LD's Mission in 1997 or 1998 if things go well. I have other family members on my both parents' sides who wrote poetry. The 1st book will be my memorial to them. Graduated with one story written; [a.] South Ogden, UT

WAKEMAN, GEORGIA L.
[b.] December 29, 1947, Arlington, VA; [p.] George E. Gheen, Dorothy L. Scohlock; [m.] Neil D. Wakeman, August 29, 1966; [ch.] Tracy W. Cook, Dana S. Sewell; [ed.] Washington Lee High School; [occ.] Have own business; [pers.] I dedicate this poem to my very loving in-Laws, (Walter and Lessie Wakeman), and to my ninth grade teacher (Mrs. Duncan) who believed in me.

WALDROP, DONALD
[pen.] Donald Waldrop; [b.] April 11, 1952, Memphis, TN; [p.] William C. Waldrop, Anna Waldrop; [m.] Donna Patricia Waldrop, December 3, 1988; [ch.] Thomas Jay, William Carson; [ed.] Paxton Community High, Parkland College Champaign, IL, Community College of the Air Force, Gunter, AL (AS); [occ.] U.S. Government Safety Manager; [memb.] Loyal Order of Moose, Boat U.S. Association; [hon.] 1993 Safety Award International Safety, Manager of the Year.; [oth. writ.] Several poems relating Midwest and specific areas of Illinois nd Indiana.; [pers.] Thru my many travels in different countries and people, I see how the same we all are as one great humankind.!; [a.] Heverlee, Belgium

WALENTA, NATHAN M.
[b.] September 12, 1978, Lincoln, NE; [p.] Robert and Marlene Walenta; [ed.] Crete High School - entering my senior year of High School; [occ.] Professional Boxer; [pers.] Always be yourself, just ignore what people think, if you like yourself that's all that matters; [a.] Crete, NE

WALKUSH, DEBRA ANGELINE
[b.] May 7, 1974, Garland, TX; [p.] Barb and Tom Walkush; [occ.] Sculpture and Painting Student, Wayne State University; [pers.] I am a servant to the divine muse and what you would get if you introduced E. E. Cummings to Emily Dickinson and then asked to see Charlotte Perkins Gilman.; [a.] Troy, MI

WALSH, PHYLLIS N.
[b.] October 7, 1928, California; [m.] Walter R. Walsh, March 5, 1972; [ed.] Boulder High, Delta College, San Joaquin School of Nursing; [occ.] Retired; [a.] Lakeside, OR

WALSH, SUSAN A. L.
[pen.] Suzy Q., Mother to many, Sue; [b.] February 20, 1960, Ontario County, NY; [p.] Thomas G. West Sr., Gloria A. Spencer; [m.] William G. Walsh, September 27, 1980; [ch.] Shawn, Shannon, Independent: Sahra and Kris, fostered many more; [ed.] Bloomfield Elem. School, Bloomfield Central School, both in East Bloomfield, NY; [occ.] Presently - Housewife, birth mother, independent and foster mother, Financial Manager, Partner S and W Sharpening and Refinishing, owner of Sue's Huggables (Kennels), Poetry writer; [memb.] Distinguished member of International Society or Poets, Foster Parent Ass. (Ontario County, NY), R.O.C.O.S.H. (Roch. Council on Occupational Safety and Health); [hon.] Jr. High, Poetry Piece - "They Dress So Drab", publicators in, Shadows and Light intitled "Children", "No Time To Die" published in the best poems of the 90's and editor's choice award by National Library of Poetry for "Children" publication "Puppy Love" in lyrical heritage; [oth. writ.] "Children", "No Time To Die", "Mirrored Blanket", "Betrayal In A Child", "Her Final Gift To Me", "Lay Upon My Back", "He Feared She'd Say No", "Remembrance of Rebbecca" and others on our children and feelings in thought; [pers.] I write from the heart, family, hardships, strengths within, fears, all that makes me, who I am, including pets. I use the reflection in these, not just in poetry but the children and future choke, in options, sometimes we need to bleed to feel and see.; [a.] Canandaigua, NY

WALTERS, MICHELLE
[b.] May 11, 1985, Saint Croix, VI; [p.] Claudette Walters; [ed.] Two years at the Seventh Day Adventist School, 4 years at the Ricardo Richards Elementary; [occ.] Student going on to the 7th grade, 11 years old; [hon.] All year honor student; [pers.] I aim to maintain the talent of other poetry that has left a deep mark in my life.; [a.] Saint Croix, VI

WALTON, MR. JAMIE L.
[b.] July 9, 1973, Salem, OH; [p.] Jack and Judy Walton; [m.] Linette S. Walton, July 20, 1991; [ed.] Lisbon David Anderson High, Kent State University; [occ.] Student - Aerospace, Engineering Technology; [memb.] Columbia Church Of The Nazarene; [a.] Salem, OH

WARD, GWENN
[b.] September 27, 1947, San Francisco; [p.] Bob and Erlene; [m.] Glenn, October 8, 1983; [ed.] College educated; [occ.] Horse Trainer; [pers.] Horse crazed -- earning a living doing what I've always loved — the horsey world. Married to a Horseshoer (convenient) fulfilled a childhood dream. Awake every morning to the sound of eager, hungry, happy horses.; [a.] Lakeport, CA

WARD, RICHARD J.
[b.] November 7, 1921, Beverly, MA; [p.] Ralph and Margaret Ward; [m.] Cecilia Butler Ward, September 1, 1951; [ch.] Timothy, Richard Jr., Mary Eliz., Christopher; [ed.] Harvard College BS, Michigan Uni. MA, Ph.D.; [occ.] Chancellor Professor Emeritus and Consultant, Writer; [memb.] Association for Social Economics as Dean of a College, American Assembly of Collegiate Schools of Business; [hon.] Distinguished Service Cititaton, U.S. Foreign Aid Mission, Jordan, Outstanding Service Award, Univ. of Mass. Dartmouth, Governors Citation, Community Service, Chancellor Professorship, Marquis Who's Who for 20 years; [oth. writ.] Economic Principles Sadlier Co, 1967, Development Problems of the 1970, Dunedon Press, 1973, The Palestine State, Kenmkat Press, 1978, others. Numerous Journal Articles.; [pers.] Have written poetry since a young man, simply for my own satisfaction and respite from economics and administrative duties.; [a.] Dartmouth, MA

WARN, L. MILA
[b.] March 23, 1913, Portland, OR; [p.] Harold and Rena Warn; [ed.] Elementary (Evegorn Heights School), High School (Grant High School - Graduated 1931), College (University of Oregon Graduated 1937); [occ.] Retired - Volunteer Tutor in two High Schools - Madison and Cleveland; [memb.] AARP (Am Assoc. Retired Person National Preliminaries), OREA (Oregon Retired Teacher Assoc.); [hon.] Only Nat'l Library of Poetry for poem ("Christian Woman") and Published of a poem called "Words" in the Portland Salvation Army Bulletin in Jan. 1996; [oth. writ.] Just poetry; [pers.] I have always written poetry all my life. It is my gift during outstanding careers in Portland, New York and Los Angeles. I worked at Meier Frank.; [a.] Portland, OR

WARREN, BARBARA E. SCRUGGS
[b.] May 13, 1959, Little Rock, AR; [p.] Helen F. King-Scruggs, Mary Lee Wimpy; [ch.] Beau and Lexie; [ed.] Graduated from Silverton Union High School, in Silverton, OR; [memb.] Rebekka's Lodge Reservist - U.S. Navy; [pers.] "Life is a challenge, learn from all that you can. Remember to be positive, have faith and always believe in God, and yourself."; [a.] Coburg, OR

WASHINGTON, AMELIA ROLAND
[pen.] Amelia Roland Washington; [b.] November 22, 1950, Meridian, MS; [p.] Curtis and Ruth Roland; [m.] G. Gregory Washington, June 21, 1986; [ch.] Paula and Emileigh; [ed.] Harris High, Meridian Community College, Antioch University; [occ.] Home maker and Artist former Nursing Administrator; [memb.] Many Christian and Civic memberships; [hon.] Many Christian, Civic and Former Employment related honors and awards; [oth. writ.] Poetry manuscript "Death Throes of a Fallen Angel" presently working on a collection of Christian poems "The Deceitfulness of Riches".; [pers.] Many of my poems reflect the twists and turns that life's paths may take, and the raw Emotions evoked by search for one's own destiny. My favorite poets are Maya Angelou and T.S. Eliot; [a.] Stillwater, OK

WASHINGTON, SABINA TAYLOR
[b.] July 28, 1954, Wash., DC; [p.] William and Lucy Washington; [ch.] Jose Washington; [ed.] Anacostia Senior High Washington DC, attended George Wash. Univ. for Dramatic Arts, opportunity presented itself due to writing ability in English; [occ.] Professional Child Care Provider; [memb.] Member of Bethel Apostolic Tabernacle Church, under the leadership of Dr. Robert L. Etheridge, Ft Worth Texas; [pers.] I strive to reflect the love of Jesus in my writing, to all mankind!; [a.] Justin, TX

WATERS, NORA CATHERINE
[pen.] Catherine Waters; [b.] June 2, 1940, Eureka, CA; [p.] Cedric A. and Charlotte B. Heighs; [m.] James M. Waters, June 24, 1994; [ch.] Cris Jay Gwin and David Allen Gwin; [ed.] Contra Costa College; [occ.] Self-employed; [oth. writ.] Various poems and short stories. I am working on my autobiography.; [pers.] I have been greatly influenced by Helen Steiner Rice and only hope to be as inspirational to society as she was.; [a.] Austin, TX

WATESKI, CAROL J.
[pen.] Unicorn; [b.] August 10, 1952, La Crosse, WI; [p.] Robert and Lorraine Scholberg; [m.] Robert J. Wateski, December 24, 1982; [ch.] Christopher, Cliff, and Nicholas; [a.] La Crosse, WI

WATKINS, CHRISTINE I.
[pen.] Christina Watkins; [b.] December 29, 1945, London, Ontario, Canada; [p.] Angus and Sheila McLachlin; [m.] David H. Watkins, September 9, 1967; [ch.] Jennifer, James, Jillian; [ed.] Alma

College, B.A., Laurentian University M. Div., Emmanuel College of Victoria University, Toronto; [occ.] Spiritual Director/Companion Teacher, Volunteer, Wife, Mother of young adults.; [memb.] Columbine Poets, Foothills Poets; [oth. writ.] Several poems published in Canadian theological journals, newsletters, etc.; [pers.] Compassion, silence, stories, poetry and music open hearts.; [a.] Englewood, CO

WATSON, THOMAS O.
[pen.] Tow; [b.] February 9, 1946, Charleston, WV; [p.] Carl Watson, Elaine Watson; [ed.] De Vry Institute of Technology, (Dean List); [occ.] Senior Computer Operator, County of Los Angeles Fire Department; [hon.] Vice-President of High School Student Body. Dunbar High School; [pers.] "Look for the good in a person. The bad can easily be found." Poem to be dedicated to - Le Non Norris Austin, Christ Solano, Lauren Solano.; [a.] La Puente, CA

WEAVER, MAXIE TAYLOR
[b.] January 8, 1948, Pt. Arthur, TX; [p.] Mary Lou Taylor and Lester L. Taylor; [m.] Dennis Clifton Weaver (Deceased), September 18, 1971; [ch.] Dennis Colt Weaver; [ed.] Tyler Junior College, Stephen F. Austin University; [occ.] Associate Clinical Psychologist I/Licensed Social Worker - University of Texas Medical Branch, Psychiatric Facility at rusk, Texas; [memb.] Phi Theta Kappa (Nat'l. Honor Fraternity of the American Two yr. College), Texas Sigma Chapter of Alpha Chi, (Nat'l. College Honor Scholarship Society), Nat'l. Assoc. of Social Workers, Alpha Delta Mu (SFA Social Work Honor Society); [hon.] Cumb Laude Graduate of Tyler Junior College, Cum Laude Graduate of Stephen F. Austin University; [oth. writ.] Sunshine and Shadows, Annual Rings, Autumn's mistress, Lifes Perpetual Calendar, In Awe of a Magnolia Grandiflora, Innocence Betrayed.; [pers.] "Life is not the candle, nor the wick. It's the burning!"; [a.] Whitehouse, TX

WEAVER, TAMI SUE
[b.] June 4, 1962, Lehighton, PA; [p.] George Strohl, Margaret (Eisenhower) Strohl; [m.] Larry D. Weaver, March 13, 1988; [ch.] Larry D. Weaver Jr.; [ed.] Lehighton High School, Continuing Education related to present job in Geriatrics; [occ.] Activities Assistant at Gnaden Huetten Convalescent and Rehabilitation Center; [memb.] Trinity Evangelical Lutheran Church, V.F.W., Salesian Missions; [oth. writ.] Poems published in local newspapers, Girl Scout Magazine, and personalized greeting cards for friends and co-workers.; [pers.] I enjoy writing poetry on many different subjects - poems about people, feelings, nature, and all aspects of life.; [a.] Nesquehoning, PA

WEBB, CHRISTOPHER
[pen.] Christopher Webb; [b.] November 19, 1973, Elmhurst, IL; [p.] Bernard and Ada; [ed.] Immaculate Conception H.S., Univ. of Wissc.-Milw. 2 yrs. Milwaukee School of Eng. 2 yrs. (no degree yet); [occ.] Student; [pers.] I enjoy writing poetry because of the sheer beauty of it.; [a.] Elmhurst, IL

WEBB, MOLLY
[b.] May 18, 1961, Dayton, OH; [p.] Jem Hilda Glaser and Gary Barb Cornell; [m.] Jeff Webb, May 17, 1986; [ch.] Samantha Webb, Maxwell Webb; [ed.] Montgomery County J.V.S. Cosmetology Trotwood Madison High School, Sinclair College; [occ.] Child Care/Freelance Writer; [memb.] Southbrook Church; [oth. writ.] (Children's Book) My Aunt Gail; [pers.] I have always felt that deep down in my heart, writing for the sheer joy of writing, is not something you start out of boredom. It is something that is felt in your heart. Writing is the best format to express my personal feelings.; [a.] Springboro, OH

WEBBER, MARK N.
[b.] August 3, 1969, Hillsboro, OR; [p.] Suzanne C. Webber, Terry L. Webber; [m.] Michelle L. Webber, March 27, 1993; [ch.] Brittnee Lisabeth Webber, Morgan Nicholas Webber; [ed.] B.S. (Computer Applications Management) at University of Portland in Portland, Oregon; [occ.] Computer Analyst; [hon.] 1986 Oregon 4A State Champion in Cross Country, 1995 Total Quality Management Champ Morse Bros. Inc.; [pers.] Success comes from knowing how far a person's "will" can take them. However, without parents that plant the seed, success will remain a dream.; [a.] Canby, OR

WEBBER, SANDRA
[pen.] Sandra Webber; [b.] January 11, 1949, Dayton, OH; [m.] Ed Webber, July 2, 1970; [ch.] Tammy Merrill, T.J. Webber; [ed.] Nurse (LPN)/Two years of study in writing for children. Institute of Children's Literature; [occ.] Nurse in an urgent care clinic.; [oth. writ.] Outbound, (news paper for physician' assistants) Sport Aviation for Kids.; [pers.] This poem was written for a friend of mine who lost her two month old baby to a long, distressing illness. We all felt her pain. I wrote this to help see through her pain.; [a.] Battle Ground, WA

WEBER, PAUL
[b.] March 24, 1947, Portland, OR; [p.] Harvey Weber and Shirley Weber; [ed.] Clackamas High School - University of Portland; [occ.] Branch Manager of Power Transmission products distributor; [pers.] One should strive to put the needs of all life, be it human, animal or plant, ahead of their own. When we all do this we will all be taken care of.

WEBER, RONI
[pen.] Shortfellow; [b.] February 25, 1943, Scheffield, ND; [p.] Jerome and Emma Schoch; [m.] Tony Weber, September 19, 1991; [ed.] High School graduate of Good Council Academy, Mankato, Minn., Associate degree of Nursing obtained at Dichinson State University, Dichinson, ND; [occ.] Registered Nurse - just completed 31 yrs. of nursing on Med/Surg., Husband - professional accordionist and band leader.; [oth. writ.] My own personal notebook of poems.; [pers.] This poem came from my heart after the loss of my dear Pomeranian puppy — she was speaking to me in my sorrow.; [a.] Dickinson, ND

WEDDLE, RICHARD A.
[pen.] Richard Weddle, Richard W., Rich W.; [b.] October 21, 1955, El Paso, TX; [p.] William Joseph and Andrewana Claire; [ch.] Lauren and Ryan; [ed.] AB in Biological Sciences, 1976 MD, 1981; [occ.] Physician; [memb.] ASGE, ACG, AGA, Smithsonian, Indianapolis Zoo, Planetary Society, AOPA, EAA, YMCA, CCFA; [oth. writ.] Numerous essays and poems published in a national 12-step recovery program bulletin.; [pers.] I pray for God's will in my life. God's will for me is not always clear. I know this will include removing in recovery, being the best father I can, and caring for others within loving relationships.; [a.] Bloomington, IN

WEIR, SHANNA
[b.] October 24, 1974, Mineral Wells; [p.] Gene and La Jean Graham; [m.] Ronald Weir, June 30, 1994; [ch.] Brittani and Jarin; [ed.] Denver City High, New Mexico Junior College; [occ.] Housewife; [memb.] National Honor Society; [hon.] Who's Who Among American High School Students; [oth. writ.] Essay won contest in Lubbock Avalanche Journal. Poems displayed in local Arts Festival.; [pers.] This poem was written for my Uncle Bill. I gave it to him the night before he went in the hospital to have a brain tumor removed. I'm glad I let him know how I feel because it was the last time I saw him alive.; [a.] Denver City, TX

WEISENT, CHARLIE
[pen.] Chee-Chee D'Argo; [b.] January 16, 1978, Canton; [p.] Rosemary and Kenneth Weisent; [ed.] McKinley Sri High School; [occ.] Stocker; [oth. writ.] A play I wrote (called "The Cloak") was performed in front of an audience by the drama class of McKinley.; [pers.] I believe that, to write, you have to open yourself to the pain — good or bad. Only in truth can you like that you wrote. The aspects of naturalism have greatly affected the style I write in.; [a.] Canton, OH

WEITZEL, SUSAN ROTH
[pen.] Adrian Hart; [b.] April 19, 1948, Findlay, OH; [p.] Vern and Ellen Hart; [m.] Wm. Weitzel, September 5, 1987; [ch.] Stephanie; [ed.] High School graduate and Nursing School; [occ.] Nurse; [memb.] International Society of Poets and Poet Guild; [hon.] Editors choice award - "Daughter"; [oth. writ.] Other poems published in National Library of Poetry and Poets Guild

WELBORN, PHIL
[pen.] Phil Easy Welborn; [b.] October 8, 1952, High Point; [p.] Dale and Nora Welborn; [m.] Divorced; [ch.] Two; [ed.] 12 Grade High School; [occ.] Heat and A.C. Contractor and Maintenance at G.T.T.C. College; [oth. writ.] Lady Glow, Lady's In The Know, Beautiful Ease, 'Bleed For Years After Years', "Application Dedication, A Curse", and etc.; [pers.] Like my daddy and granddaddy, fast on a greasy working man, and to some ladies a man of poetry and roses, I thank God for my breath everyday and ability to work.; [a.] High Point, NC

WELCH, DANIEL CLAY
[pen.] Danny; [b.] April 2, 1961, Oklahoma City; [p.] Henry and Mary Welch; [m.] Divorced - Kathy L. (LeMaster), June 9, 1989 - March 31, 1995, Divorced; [ch.] Daniel, Zachary; [ed.] Choctaw High School; [occ.] Clerk/Manager; [memb.] Lethal Hands Registry #831085; [oth. writ.] "Dad" published in The National Library of Poetry's "A View From The Edge".; [pers.] In my poetry and my art, I express all my feelings and turmoil. If we could teach younger generations to do things (on paper or canvass) instead of expression of violence, we would have more productive kids and less criminally minded kids.; [a.] Choctaw, OK

WELLS, PAULA
[b.] April 23, 1955, Flint, MI; [p.] Wallace Lloyd, Bertha Lloyd; [m.] Herbert E. Wells II, December 16, 1977; [ch.] Todd Brall, Chaz Cannoy; [oth. writ.] Yes, but have never had any published.; [pers.] I would like to add that in writing that poem, it gave me an inner peace after the death of my brother.; [a.] Flint, MI

WELTER, PAULA JO
[pen.] Paula's Prose; [b.] February 12, 1959, Xenia, OH; [p.] William and Shirley Kailey; [m.] Herb Welter, March 9, 1985; [ch.] Andrew McQuoid, Laura Jo, Hannah Lynn; [ed.] Rosemount High, Indian Hills Co. College; [occ.] Home maker, LPN; [memb.] Seward Area Christian Home schoolers (member), Lincoln Christian Fellowship (member), Neighbor Hood Watch (Member); [hon.] Good Conduct Medal U.S.A.F., Honorably Discharged U.S.A.F.; [pers.] In my writings I focus on relationships and the greatness of the Lord.; [a.] Lincoln, NE

WESSEL, PATRICIA A.
[pen.] Patricia Fanning Avery Bawcum Wessel; [b.] May 11, 1942, Weehawken, NJ; [p.] James J. and Elizabeth C. Fanning Sr.; [m.] James R. Wessel, March 1989; [ch.] Jayson Keith Bawcum (my son), Deborah K. O'Mara (my daughter); [ed.] In 1960 I graduated from St. Mary's High School in Alb. NM, from 1960 to 1961 I attended the University of New Mexico in Alb. NM, and attended Technical Vocational Institute in Albuquerque, NM; [occ.] Retired Administrative Secretary; [memb.] International Society of Poets, The National Authors Registry, The International Society of Authors and Artist, Songwriters Club of America (A different point of view on an idea.); [hon.] 4th place in Our Captured Moments, thru Creative Arts and Science Ent., Honorable Mention, "Inspirations" and Crossings, Iliad Press, Accomplishment, Creative Arts and Science, Ent., The National Library of Poetry Editor's Choice Award in (A Tapestry of thoughts), etc.; [oth. writ.] Poems in JMW Publishing sparrow grass Poetry Forum, Inc., World Art Publishing, the Amherst Society Iliad Press, The Best New Poems of 1995, and The Best New Poems of 1996 thru Poet's Guild, Quill Books, The National Library of Poetry in "A Tapestry of Thoughts," Carvings in Stone, Reflections of Yesterday, Lyrical Heritage, Field of Gold, etc.; [pers.] It is my objective in writing poetry to bring a subject to which there will be encouragement and hope and perhaps a new. I thoroughly enjoy both reading and writing poetry. It is my desire to write my poetry in a way that will be very clear to the reader. The reader will notice my poetry is like a short story. For people who do not enjoy poetry or are unable to read due to loss of sight or any other reason, I put my poetry on tape so they may hear the words if they are unable to see. I, myself, learn so much from other people's poetry.; [a.] Albuquerque, NM

WESTBERRY, SETH MICHAEL
[b.] May 25, 1978, Corry, PA; [p.] W. Steven and Bonnie L. Westberry; [ed.] James Buchanan High School; [occ.] Student at Liberty University Majoring in Communications: Media Graphic Production

WESTBROOK, CHRISTAL MAGHIELSE
[b.] August 5, 1951, Wyandotte, MI; [p.] Dorothy M. Maghielse, Chris E. Maghielse; [m.] James G. Westbrook, July 27, 1976; [ch.] Cindy Matey; [ed.] Junior at Black Hills State University H.S. - Theodore Roosevelt High - Wyandote Mich, Elementary - Lutheran Schools; [occ.] Student - College Psychology - Indian Studies; [memb.] American Legion Aux, Women's Veterans; [hon.] Dean's List; [oth. writ.] Book CC "A Guide to Cleaning Shells", 1980's several articles on seashells in "The Sundial Ed" of newspaper "The Keynote" Marathon, Florida article in book "Marathon Heart of Florida" keep about my story.; [pers.] I am a self-taught Malacologist and recently decided to further my education in Psychology and Native American studies. My philosophy is to help others when and where I can and to do God's will as much as possible.; [a.] Nisland, SD

WHALEN, EVE K.
[pen.] "Vera Joyce" (Long ago); [b.] May 15, 1913, Hartford, CT; [p.] Edward and Marie Kuehn; [m.] Frank D. Whalen, October 1, 1940; [ch.] Dick and Curtis Whalen; [ed.] William H. Hall High School Seminars, Geo. Washington U. and U. of Chicago as Dir. Public Relations and Vols. Alexandria Hospital; [occ.] Housewife; [memb.] Alexandria Hospital Foundation, Honorary Member Jr. Assoc. Hosp. and Health Vol. Directors, Price of Peace Lutheran Church, many others when I was a Navy wife and worked in the hospital.; [hon.] Teenage Vol. Program, Rec'd National Award by American Hosp. Assoc. JAHA Honorary Member VA Assoc. Hosp. and Health Dirs. of Vol. I organized the First State Organization and was elected first President.; [oth. writ.] Alexandria Hospital Patient Handbook placed second in VA Hospital Assoc., many other poems, some printed in Church newsletter.; [pers.] I am an ex-Navy wife, was a Pearl Harbor when Japanese attacked. Started a book on my experiences there. I have made 2 moves in 22 years of Navy life. Was on Guam when the last two Japanese visited at night when my husband was away.; [a.] Annandale VA

WHALEN, RITA
[b.] August 28, 1957, Syracuse, NY; [p.] Frank and Carmela Russo; [m.] Michael Stephen Whalen, August 22, 1981; [ch.] Shawn Michael Whalen, Kristine Marie Whalen; [ed.] Assumption Catholic Academy, Contemporary School of Beauty, Onondaga Community College; [occ.] Homemaker and mother; [memb.] Parent Teachers Associations, Le Moyne Girls Softball Committee; [a.] Syracuse, NY

WHALEN, WILLIAM
[pen.] Wil Whalen; [b.] March 28, 1988, Norman, OK; [p.] Susan and Tom Whalen; [ed.] Monte Cassino School, Truman Elementary, All Saints School; [occ.] Hard working 3rd grader; [memb.] Boy Scouts of America: Bear Cub. The Bombers: Intramural Basketball; [hon.] Wolf badge, 3rd place in the Science Fair, 1st place in the district pine wood derby; [oth. writ.] The Trap Book, a collaborative interpretation of the nativity story, other unpublished poems and short stories.; [a.] Norman, OK

WHEAT JR., ALONZO
[pen.] On a Qwest; [b.] September 5, 1974, Cleveland, OH; [p.] Alonzo Wheat, Zeola Wheat; [m.] Single; [ed.] McIntosh High; [occ.] College Student, Barber-Scotia College, Concord, NC; [pers.] Dedicated to Zeola, Alonzo, Renee, Regina, the entire Davis tribe, Jameena and Vanessa. I love you all and I thank God for blessing me with you in my life.; [a.] Concord, NC

WHITE, ANGELA PHELPS
[b.] December 16, 1960, Washington, DC; [p.] James Phelps and Ruby Phelps; [m.] Theodore White Jr., May 6, 1989; [ch.] Taylor White; [ed.] Parkdale Senior High, University of Dayton, University of Dayton School of Law; [occ.] Magistrate - General Division Franklin County Common Pleas Court; [memb.] Order of Eastern State, PHA, League of Women Voters Bar Association. Columbus Bar Association; [pers.] You can be all that you want to be. Never let someone else determine your potential.; [a.] Blocklick, OH

WHITE, CHRIS
[p.] Joy and Jim White; [ed.] Going to be a senior in High School; [occ.] Student; [hon.] Honor roll; [oth. writ.] No other poems published; [pers.] From my thoughts I write these poems as a gift to you, may you give them power through the reading.; [a.] Carmicheal, CA

WHITE, MICHELLE
[pen.] Shel and Spanky; [b.] June 12, 1974, Concord, NH; [p.] Linda White, Theodore White; [m.] Engaged - Andrew Simoneau; [ch.] Tazz T.A.L, Dustin G.C. (Simoneau); [occ.] Mother; [hon.] Writing and reading (school); [oth. writ.] Many - none published; [pers.] My poems are written for family and friends. All are dedicated to my father.; [a.] Laconia, NH

WHITE, MR. DARYL E.
[b.] November 3, 1958, Meridian, MS; [p.] Mr. William M. White and Mrs. Katie R. White; [ed.] Graduated Demopolis High School - 1977, U.S. Navy 1977-1985, Travels through the Orient and Southern Europe; [occ.] Paperwork, James River Corp.; [memb.] United Paperworkers International Union, National Rifle Association, International Society of Poet's; [hon.] The National Library of Poetry's, "Editor's Choice Award", 1996; [oth. writ.] Published in a previous National Library of Poetry Anthology.; [a.] Demopolis, AL

WHITMIRE, BONITA
[pen.] Pulaski D. Ethridge; [b.] August 8, 1959, Baltimore, MD; [p.] John and Eva Lee Whitmire; [ed.] Southside High School 1976, Greenville Technical College 1979, University of South Carolina 1987; [occ.] Communications; [memb.] Pleasantburg Lions Club, Edwards Rd Baptist Church, Chancel Choir, Girl Scouts 68-73; [hon.] Melvin Jones Fellow 1992, 1st Woman President of Pleasantburg Lions 94-96, Zone Chairman Zone 6, 32-A 1995-96, Region Chairman, Region 0 32A 1996-97; [oth. writ.] Glimpses Of Grove, Palmetto Lion, Reedy River Review, East Of The Sunrise, Best Poems Of 1996, A Tapestry Of Thoughts, Where Dawn Lingers, A Muse To Follow, Carvings In Stone; [pers.] When I write poems it seems to flow from me with no apparent control. It seems to be free flowing from my mind and soul.; [a.] Greenville, SC

WHITNEY, KATHERINE M.
[b.] April 2, 1961, West Branch, MI; [p.] Katherine Awrey and Thomas Awrey; [ch.] Tonya Lynn, Wayne Lee, Nicholas Michael; [ed.] Ogemaw Heights High School 2 1/2 years Apprenticeship for Plumbing and Heating; [occ.] Apprentice in Plumbing and Heating; [memb.] American Business Women's Association Girl Scout Leader; [oth. writ.] Several articles published concerning our children in local newspaper.; [pers.] I have been writing short stories and poems for years. I have kept a journal for my children since I was nine years old. Some day they will be able to enjoy life's trials and changes.

WHITTENBERG, DANIELLE A.
[b.] August 28, 1980, Miami, FL; [p.] John Whittenberg, Brenda Whittenberg; [ed.] Florida A and M Developmental Research School, Tallavana Christian School; [occ.] Student (High School Junior); [memb.] Girl Scouts 1985 - Present, Jr ROTC 1994-1996 FBLA 1994-1996, North Florida String Institute, FAMU DRS Marching Band and Symphonic Band; [hon.] Girl Scouts Silver Award, Superior Award in State Band Competition (Flute) 1st Place 1995-96 Science Fair, Cadet Lt. JROTC; [oth. writ.] Unpublished poems; [pers.] I strive to express my inner feelings through the power of the written word; [a.] Tallahassee, FL

WILCOX, KRISTIN
[pen.] Kris Wilcox; [b.] October 27, 1982, Hudson, NC; [p.] Deena and Marc Suddeth; [ed.] Hudson Middle School, 8th grade; [memb.] Michael Jackson Fan Club, Janet Jackson Fan Club; [hon.] 4 Awards of National Fitness, 6 President Physical Fitness Awards, and 3rd place in Science Fair; [oth. writ.] Alone that was published in A Voyage To Remember.; [pers.] My influence of my writings is I love to read poetry and when I hear music like Michael Jackson writings in his music thought I read more poetry like Robert Frost is my favorite poet. I would like to thank Kim Bolick and Keith Locke for being so kind, and being there for me.; [a.] Hudson, NC

WILEMAN, WALLACE K.
[pen.] Wallace K. Wileman; [b.] April 3, 1919, Chicago, IL; [p.] Deceased; [m.] Deceased; [ch.] John Wileman - Cecil Alexiades; [ed.] Degree Mechanical Engineering Columbia University - Buffalo, N.Y. 1952, Degree in Business Administration Y.M.C.A. College 1970 Chicago, Illinois; [occ.] Writer - Teacher; [memb.] National Association of Power Engineers, National Institute of Uniform Licensing for Power Engineers; [hon.] National Engineer of the Year-1985, Hall of Fame-Personalities of America - Contributions to Physical Plant Improvement; [oth. writ.] Author - This is Your Life - Start Living It, author - Creative Problem-Solving, author - Universal Vision, author - Energy Conservation, author - Engineers Role in Safety; [pers.] Life is not something to be endured. It is to be lived abundantly - every person should be limitless, living with the "Inner Source" of accomplishment.; [a.] Chicago, IL

WILENS, MARTIN B.
[b.] May 8, 1934, Chicago, IL; [p.] Sally Wilens (91), Irving (Deceased); [ch.] Herbert, Susan, Douglas and Bonnie; [ed.] Bachelor of Science (B.C.E.) Civil and Nuclear Engineering Cornell Univ., Ithaca NY, NASD Broker Dealer 1980-83; [occ.] V.P. Corporate Finance Euclid Systems Corp. Fairfax, VA; [memb.] Member - Boston Stock Exchange 1980-83, Member of 1953-54, Ivy League Championship Basketball Team, Major Letters (3) Basketball, Baseball, Track; [hon.] Superior Performance Award, Nuclear Ship Savannah Program, U.S. Atomic Energy Commission, (Deputy Mgr.) Shared Presidential Award with Naval Patrol, Forces in So. Vietnam for work in analysis of VC Networks in Mekong Delta and Countering Effectiveness of VC Distribution Network; [oth. writ.] Center for Naval Analyses Report. Counter Insurgency Warfare in the Mekong Delta (So. Vietnam).; [pers.] Depend only upon what your brain tells you your eyes have seen. Think for yourself, Grandchildren -- Benjamin 13, Michael 4, Nicole 2.; [a.] Bethesda, MD

WILKIN, MICHELLE
[b.] February 1, 1978, Englewood, CO; [p.] Joan and Gary Wilkin; [ed.] Going to be attending the University of Northern Colorado in the fall. Recently graduated from Highlands Ranch H.S.; [occ.] College Student; [a.] Littleton, CO

WILLARD, BERNICE
[pen.] Muffin; [b.] October 21, 1965, Longs, SC; [p.] Shirley Ward and Florrie Gore; [m.] Ralph C. Willard Sr., September 19, 1984; [ch.] Shiba, Ralph Jr., Cleya and Shirl and stepdaughter Nosha; [ed.] Secretary at Horry - Georgetown Technical College, Graduated at Loris High School; [occ.] Sales and Church Coordinator and Typist; [memb.] S.C. Notary Public Freemont Missionary Baptist Church; [hon.] Dean's List, have an unpublished Children's Book I've written; [oth. writ.] Children's Book.; [pers.] This is dedicated to my brothers Lee Grant, Antonio and Anthony also to my church. I'm hoping that one day I'll be as lucky with an adult novel and a children's book that I've also written.; [a.] Longs, SC

WILLIAMS, ALFREDA D.
[b.] May 30, 1958, Dawson, GA; [p.] Johnny Daniels, Freddie Will Daniels; [m.] Rev. Wadis Williams, June 20, 1981; [ch.] Ashley Michelle, Jonathan Wadis, Joshua Jerome; [ed.] Albany High School, Valdosta State College, Albany State College; [occ.] Second grade Teacher-Radium Springs Elem. School; [memb.] AMVETS, World Vision, American Lung Association, Church of the Living Word, Committee Youth, Mercer Grove Baptist Church, Youth Committee, Mt. Grove Baptist Church - Youth Committee; [hon.] In School Teacher of The Year 1991-92, Parents Volunteer Awards; [oth. writ.] Short Stories not published, yet!; [pers.] I have a strong belief in the fact that with Christ all things are possible.; [a.] Albany, GA

WILLIAMS, BARBARA ANN
[b.] June 9, 1960, Worcester, MA; [p.] Warren and Barbara Williams; [ed.] BS in Health Education, Diploma in Nursing at Worcester City Hospital SON; [occ.] Registered Nurse; [memb.] ARN (American Rehab in Nursing) Wesley United Methodist Church Worc. MA.; [hon.] Member of my 1980 College Basketball National Championship team the "Lancers"; [pers.] My heart has directed my mind, body and soul to write. Love is my theme, to continue to write poetry and share "truth with the world". Thank you, Mom and Dad.; [a.] Worcester, MA

WILLIAMS, DONALD
[pen.] M. D. Williams, Len Williams; [b.] July 19, 1969, Pittsburgh, PA; [p.] Deborah Williams, John Walker; [m.] Cartina Williams, August 24, 1989; [ch.] Sarah Williams; [ed.] College Student; [occ.] State Contractor; [memb.] H.B.O. Education Committee

WILLIAMS, MAXINE E.
[b.] January 18, 1964, Suffolk, VA; [p.] Artis Lee Thorne and Bernice Brickhouse; [m.] Lawrence G. Williams, March 15, 1985; [ch.] Timothy, Lauren and Lawrence II; [ed.] I.C. Norcom High School and Kee Business College; [occ.] Travel Accounting Clerk, AAA Leigh Valley, Allentown, PA; [pers.] I enjoy writing from life experiences and I think life has a lot of valuable lessons to teach us if we listen with our hearts.; [a.] Allentown, PA

WILLIAMS, SHANA L.
[b.] April 7, 1972, Bridgeton, NJ; [p.] Hannah Williams, Eugene Coleson; [ed.] Seton Hall University, South Orange, NJ; [occ.] Track and Field Athlete; [memb.] Kappa Delta Pi; [hon.] Dean's List, Kappa Delta Pi, Community Service Award, U.S.A. 1996, Olympian in Track and Field; [pers.] Continue to glorify the Lord and put him first in your life and whatever you ask will be given unto you -- Praise God.; [a.] Eugene, OR

WILLIAMS, THELMA P.
[b.] September 29, 1934, Hunt, AR; [p.] Dan Parker, Anna Parker; [m.] J. C. McClelland - Deceased, February 12, 1951; [ch.] Ricky Charles, Paula Ann, Donna Gail, William Frank; [ed.] Ozark High School Ozark-Ark Molers Barder College, Tacoma Wash. Art Instruction Schools Minneapolis Minn; [occ.] Retired; [pers.] I strongly believe in the Golden Rule; [a.] Ozark, AR

WILLIAMS, VAN ALICE
[b.] September 16, 1952, Tchula, MS; [p.] Ed Williams Sr. and Carrie Williams; [ed.] Master Degree in Special Education; [occ.] Teacher; [memb.] Eta Phi Beta Sorority, Inc. Delta Hambda Chapter Tchula, MS; [hon.] Mississippi Education Ass., National Education Association - Holmes County Schools, Mileston Elementary school Junior Girl School Troop 235 Leader; [oth. writ.] Mileston Elementary School Alma Mater, Dr. Martin Luther King, Jr. Lighting Ceremony; [pers.] Believe in God and yourself. God never fails.; [a.] Tchula, MS

WILLIAMS III, SAINT C.
[pen.] Saint; [b.] March 7, 1967, Green Cove Springs, FL; [p.] Lillie B. Williams; [ed.] Clay High, Bethune-Cookman College; [pers.] I hope to spark love between men, women, and the world.; [a.] Green Cove Springs, FL

WILLINGHAM, SHIRL
[b.] Center, TX; [p.] R. B. Fausett Jr., Fleta Fausett; [m.] Ray Willingham, January 10, 1962; [ch.] Roxann and Wendi Willingham; [ed.] Center High - Deanza College; [occ.] Real Estate Broker; [hon.] Best all around high school sophomore/Campbell Beautification; [oth. writ.] Poetry included in "Elementary Journey" and "Fun Library" unpublished.; [pers.] I like to show the magical and fun side of life in my poetry.; [a.] San Jose, CA

WILLIS, LORISA F.
[b.] September 21, 1963, Bergton, VA; [p.] Eugene and Naomi Hostetter; [m.] Robert A. Willis, July 11, 1992; [pers.] This poem was written during a time of recovery from deep hurt and confusion. I was separated from my husband and being hospitalized at a psychiatric hospital. It was one of my first times allowed outside and I was noticing birds flying. The title is based on a scripture which says every good gift is from God, revealing how active He is in our lives. I find scripture a reliable source of truth, a record I have no reason to repeat as inspired by our Creator.; [a.] Olney, MD

WILLIS, M. A.
[pen.] A. C. Dennison; [b.] February 3, 1944, Saint Louis, MO; [p.] Claude and Norma Willis; [ed.] Cleveland H.S., N.E. MO., State U. - B.S. in Ed./B.A./M.A., U. of North Texas - Ph.D.; [occ.] International Consultant; [memb.] Phi Alpha Theta, Pi Sigma Alpha, World Wildlife Fund, The Humane Soc. of the U.S.; [hon.] Teaching Assistantship, Teaching Fellowship, Who's Who; [oth. writ.] Unpublished collections - "To be Forgotten In Name" and "One Clear Call For Me."; [pers.] Influenced by life's relentless march of time, and inspired by my Mother's courage and unselfish kindness.; [a.] Saint Louis, MO

WILLIS, TREVELL
[b.] December 10, 1983, Detroit; [p.] Belinda Willis; [ed.] Thurgood Marshall Elementary 6/96 Graduated 6th grade - will attend Hally Magnet Middle School 9/96; [hon.] 3rd place trophy for "Young Black Male" Honor roll trophy and several certificates for 6th grade; [oth. writ.] First time; [pers.] I want other males (black, white, etc.) young males to see the importance of staying away from drugs and to stay in school; [a.] Detroit, MI

WILSON, MICHELE RENEE
[pen.] Girlie; [b.] June 11, 1969, Pawnee, OK; [p.] Nita Snake and Francis L. Wilson; [m.] Divorced; [ch.] Three: Gary Houston III, Deja L. Wilson, Fabian M. Blankenship; [ed.] Cushing schools finished sophomore year; [oth. writ.] I had several others, but I can remember one title only and it was "In God's Kingdom". But, it and others were lost and have never been found.; [a.] Cushing, OK

WILSON, NEIDRA S.
[b.] June 29, 1986, Atlanta, GA; [p.] Brenda and Raymond Johnson; [ed.] Mimosa Elementary, Crabapple Middle School; [occ.] Student; [hon.] Honor roll student at Crabapple Middle School, 1st place ribbons at school's olympics for 50m dash and 4x100 co-ed; [pers.] I'm honored to know that my poem has been published in a book. I thank my mother and father for being there for me. And for you young writers like myself you can do anything if you put your mind to it.; [a.] Roswell, GA

WINBERRY, RHONDA
[b.] August 19, 1959, Saint Louis, MO; [ed.] Cahokia Senior High, Institute of Children's Literature; [pers.] My writing is inspired from life itself. I strive to reach others through words that may speak for all.; [a.] Blue Eye, MO

WINDEN, TRICIA
[b.] December 4, 1979, Illinois; [p.] Wes and Karen Winden; [ed.] Capital High School - Junior; [occ.]

Working for my Horse Trainer; [memb.] Capital High Cadettes (Half-Time Entertainment), NRHA (National Keining Horse Association); [a.] Helena, MT

WINN, SANDY
[b.] February 11, 1953, Danville, VA; [p.] Ruby B. Grubbs and The Late Henry Thomas Grubbs; [m.] Richard G. Winn Jr., June 17, 1995; [occ.] State Filings Supervisor, Virginia Professional Underwriters, Inc.; [memb.] West End Community Church of the Nazarene, Board Member, Society of State Filers; [pers.] My writing comes from the heart and my influences a fellow author and friend. "Everything is possible for him who believes" Mark 9:23 NIV.; [a.] Richmond, VA

WINTERS, SUSAN
[b.] February 15, 1940, Clayton, NJ; [p.] Frank and Adele Dennis; [m.] Divorced; [ch.] Frank - died in Army, Melanie; [ed.] B.S. Springfield College, Springfield Mass; [occ.] Physical Education, Health, Parenting Teacher - soon retired; [oth. writ.] I have been writing for myself as a way of expression since high school. It seems like a lot of my poems "just come" to me. Very seldom do I ever change a word once I've written it down.; [pers.] My son, Frank who was a U.S. Army Ranger was killed in a training accident in 1987. Since that time I can get a thought and just write down my feelings. I have no way to vent - so I use the written word.; [a.] West Palm Beach, FL

WISNIEWSKI, KAREN
[pen.] Caryn Morgan; [ed.] Northeast Wisc Tech College - registered nurse training. LaSalle University - law classes, writer's digest school.; [occ.] Ad Representative - Nightingale Newsletter, Freelance Writer, Medical/legal Consultant; [memb.] National Writers Association, American Medical Writer's Association, Bay Area Humane Society, Women's Humane Society, ASPCA; [hon.] Veteran's Administration - Performance Award; [oth. writ.] Several poems published in various anthologies. Book of poetry. Several nursing reference books nearing completion; [pers.] My goal as a writer is to enlighten those in the medical field regarding changes in nursing and health care.; [a.] Green Bay, WI

WOOD, HAROLD WM.
[b.] July 9, 1905, Prague, OK; [p.] S. A. Wood, Melvina C. Wood; [m.] Eva Carol Wood, July 3, 1938; [ch.] Evelyn Carol Winkel, Harold Wm. Wood Jr.; [ed.] B.S. Oregon State University DVM, Texas AM University, Master Travel Certificate; [occ.] Retired Veterinarian, World Wide Travel and Lecturer; [memb.] AVMA, CVMA, SCVMA, Masonic Lodge; [hon.] AVMA, Honor Roll CVMA and SCVMA Life Memberships; [oth. writ.] Local newspaper by lines, Scientific Papers in every county off Oregon. Article Sunday Oregonian (Portand), How to train and raise labador rertivers (co-author) poetry in long beach poetry club my autobiography, numerous poems and short stories (published and unpublished).; [pers.] Creative writing is my companion day and night comfort. Poetry is like a bubbling stream singing through eternity.

WOOD, JOHN C.
[pen.] J.C.W.; [b.] April 1, 1926, Gettysburg, PA; [p.] Esther Anna and William Wallace Wood; [m.]

Ruth L. Wood, December 1949; [ch.] John Jr. (deceased), Robert Hunter, Peter Gregory, Ellen Wallace; [ed.] Curtis High School, S.I., NY Yale University, BS Columbia College of Physicians and Surgeons, University of Pennsylvania; [occ.] Hospital of Physician - cardiologist - recently, retired; [memb.] American College of Cardiology, American College of Physicians, The College of Physicians of Philadelphia; [hon.] AOA - National Medical Honor Society; [oth. writ.] Technical - Medical publications, submission and publication of essays, poetry a recent and limited phenomenon; [pers.] The practice of medicine has always been a blend of art and science, to the extent that either component is discarded, it is diminished.; [a.] Yardley, PA

WOOD, TAMIE CHRISTINE
[pen.] T. Christine Wood; [b.] October 30, 1960, Milan, OH; [p.] Mr. and Mrs. Ray A. Stiert; [m.] Daniel Brian Wood, November 6, 1981; [ch.] Erin Elizabeth (10 yrs.), Bryan Nicholas (7); [ed.] Milan Elementary School, Berlin Milan Middle School, Edison High School Milani Ohio, Home of Thomas A. Edison; [occ.] Housewife, Educator, Floral Designer, Mother of two; [oth. writ.] I have written two manuscripts, Grandmothers Special Drawer: A Christmas Story, Clay Marbles in a Jar and a poem, Being The Littlest Is The Worst all currently unpublished at this time; [pers.] I enjoy writing about things I know, connecting the past which today's children and learning it's readers with a feel good feeling. I am inspired by my historical past and my present life and love of my children and husband.; [a.] Monroeville, OH

WOZNY, JOEL
[b.] June 5, 1981, Park Ridge; [p.] Mark Wozny and Jan Wozny; [ed.] O.L.V. Our Lady of Victory Elementary School, Weber High School; [occ.] Student; [oth. writ.] Personal writings and ideas.; [a.] Chicago, IL

WRITHT, DOROTHY
[b.] December 10, 1925, Lima, OH; [p.] Ted and Bertha Hollingsworth; [m.] Ted L. Wright (Deceased), April 18, 1949; [ch.] Kip, Tim, Teresa, Lorrie, Jack; [ed.] Lima South High (1943), Lima Memorial Hospital School of Nursing (1947), Worked as R.N. for 45 years.; [occ.] Retired; [memb.] American Nurses Assoc., Michigan Nurses Assoc.; [oth. writ.] None published as yet -- poetry, essays, children's stores.; [pers.] This poem was written to inspire compassion in Nursing Assistants and co-workers when I worked at a Nursing Home in 1993 and 1994.; [a.] Celina, OH

WRIGHT, MARGOT E.
[pen.] Margot; [b.] May 10, 1945, Berkeley, CA; [m.] Terry L. Wright, August 17, 1973; [ch.] Rick, Marla and Ron (Twins), Tera, Ryan; [ed.] Campbell High, American Institute of Banking, University of Calif, L.A. con't ed, Medical Ed. Group Learning Systems, Kings River Comm. College; [occ.] Surgical Asst - Drs Jonker, Northrop and Van Wagenen - Oral Maxillo Facial Surgeons; [memb.] Mother of Twins Club, EMT for Madera, Fresno, and Kings County. I'm one of Jehovah's Witnesses teaching bible laws, truth and principles, educating people to be better mothers, fathers, sons and daughters, brothers or sisters, to live in peace and harmony as

productive individuals in society; [oth. writ.] "Looking Forward to a Rosebud", "Survivors of Abused Ones", "Diary of an Unborn Child", "The Greatest Gift," "A Special Friend" "Turbulent Sea", "Beholding", etc.; [pers.] I care about people and continue to strive to bring a touch of happiness and hope to those I have the opportunity to converse with even if it's only an up building thought.; [a.] Oakhurst, CA

WRIGHT, TIFFANY
[b.] October 16, 1974, North Plainfield, NJ; [p.] Mr. and Mrs. Charles O. Wright; [ed.] Gettysburg College (grad. 1997); [memb.] Alpha Phi Omega; [hon.] Dean's List; [oth. writ.] Two articles published in the Gettysburg Times; [pers.] Not every person involved in your life is meant to be permanent. But each and every being you connect with, whether for a brief moment or for a lifetime, offers some learning or love, or both. Treasure every soul you meet and the experiences you have.; [a.] Gettysburg, PA

WRIGHT, W. PAUL F.
[b.] October 14, 1982, Sheridan, WY; [p.] Frank and Becky Wright; [ed.] Completed 7th grade in January, 1996; [occ.] Student; [memb.] 93-94 Florida Odyssey of Mind (2nd Place team, state level); [hon.] C.T.Y. Talent Search: Seventh Grade, Johns Hopkins Univ. - State Award (PA), in Mathematics and Verbal on S.A.T., College Board Test, Misc., School Achievement Awards; [pers.] The fact that a peacemaker is not safe, is partially what provoked me to write the poem.; [a.] Littlestown, PA

WYMER, AMANDA
[b.] December 30, 1973, Michigan; [p.] Greg and Kathy Wymer; [ed.] Evanston High, Central Wyoming College; [hon.] Student of the week, Central Wyoming College, Dean's List; [oth. writ.] Many more poems, several short stories.; [a.] Evanston, WY

XING, LU YANG
[b.] April 19, 1982, Beijing, China; [p.] Wendy Xiasfeng He, T. K. Tian; [ed.] Just graduated from Bowditch Middle School, Foster City, California; [hon.] High Honors, Presidential Academic Award; [pers.] Born and lived in China for nine years, I came to America in September of 1991. Over the past five years. I learned many valuable things from my parents, teachers and friends. But the most important people must have been my grand parents. They are the ones who encouraged me to write. They taught me about life.; [a.] Foster City, CA

YANEZ, CHRISTOPHER
[pen.] Sunday Driver; [b.] January 14, 1970, Los Angeles; [p.] Mother - Mary Yanez; [m.] My imaginary Girlfriend; [ed.] High School Graduate, now attending College; [occ.] Student/Worker; [memb.] The Contemporary Art Museum, Downtown, Los Angeles; [hon.] I'm still alive; [oth. writ.] Penners, Poems as Gifts, and various Poetry Pamphlets in the Silverlake area.; [pers.] Ink on paper lives forever.; [a.] Los Angeles, CA

YANG, HU
[b.] May 5, 1960, Yunnan, P.R., China; [p.] Dehva Yang, Rurui Xing; [m.] Qiongbo Zheng, February 14, 1990; [ch.] Shelley Zheng Yang, William Zheng Yang; [ed.] Yunnan Normal University,

B.A., University of North Texas, MBA; [occ.] Computer Analyst and Programming in Client/server Technology; [hon.] Dean's List in College; [oth. writ.] Some poems and prose published in Chinese. Currently I am writing a book in English about my experiences in America.; [pers.] Progress every day!; [a.] Marietta, GA

YARBER, LORA RENEE
[b.] May 12, 1967, Fort Oglethorpe, CA; [p.] George Hanvey, Chris and Judy Lehman; [m.] Steve Yarber, April 28, 1985; [ch.] Brandy Lynn, Heather Lea; [occ.] YMCA Preschool Teacher; [memb.] Lighthouse Baptist Church, McBrien PTA, International Society of Poets; [hon.] Editor's Choice Award from National Library of Poetry; [oth. writ.] "What's in Your Hands" published in "The Rainbow's End", "I Am a Prayer" in "The Best Poems of the '90's"; [pers.] Trading Places is a child's poem from a "child's heart" (Luke 18:17); [a.] Chattanooga, TN

YARNUTOSKI, EILEEN
[pen.] Eileen Raymond; [b.] January 20, 1946, Queens, NY; [p.] John and WiniFred Sich; [m.] Raymond Yarnutoski, January 29, 1966; [ed.] Scotch Plains - Fanwood H.S., New Jersey Franklin Beauty School, Elizabeth N.J., Pasco-Hernando College, New Port Richey, Florida; [occ.] Novelist; [oth. writ.] Poetry in MoBius (College Press), Like Father, Like Son (Novel) Northwest publishers, Desperate Measures (Novel) Commonwealth publishers, Mule Train, Guardian Son, Like Mother, Like Daughter - Novels pending; [pers.] "Any dream can be attained successfully if one can learn to dedicate themselves to remain focused while waiting...; [a.] New Port Richey, FL

YOUNGER, ROBERT H.
[b.] July 17, 1957, Chehalis, WA; [p.] Gene and Rose Younger; [m.] Charlene, October 7, 1978; [ch.] David, Daniel, Jenny, Angela; [ed.] Clackamas High School - 75; [occ.] Truck Driver; [memb.] National Historic Trucks, Brooks Ore.; [hon.] 1994 Oregon State straight Truck Champion, 7th Place Finish National Truck Driving Championships; [oth. writ.] Personal poems for family and friends.; [pers.] Faith and Family are our gifts from God. Never take them for granted.; [a.] Saint Helens, OR

YOUNIE, JUSTIN
[b.] April 11, 1975, Hawarden, IA; [p.] Richard and Vicki Younie; [ed.] Graduated in 1993 from West Sioux High School in Hawarden at the of his death, he was a sophomore at the University of South Dakota, Vermillion, SD; [hon.] Graduated from high school with honors.; [pers.] Justin wrote this poem in a Creative Writing course that he was taking in college a couple of months before he was murdered on Jan. 14, 1995. Above all things in life, Justin treasured friendship the most.; [a.] Hawarden, IA

ZAKRZEWSKA, MAGDALENA
[pen.] Maggie Z; [b.] August 28, 1978, Slupsk, Poland; [p.] Bogdan and Danuta Zakrzewska; [occ.] Student; [hon.] Outstanding Achievement in Honors Civics. Principals Honor Roll; [oth. writ.] Several poems have been published in local newspapers, I try to express my emotions in the shortest type of poem called Haiku; [pers.] I have been greatly influenced by the polish author living

in California - Czeslaw Milosz. My writings often reflect the idea of existentialism in which each person is alone and completely responsible for their own actions.; [a.] Turlock, CA

ZAMORA, LETICIA
[b.] May 3, 1969, Weslaco, TX; [p.] Alfredo Zepeda, Ana Zepeda; [m.] Dorian Zamora, September 13, 1989; [ch.] Dorian Von Andrew, Dillon Skylar; [ed.] 1988 Graduate of Harlingen High School; [occ.] Homemaker and proud mother of two; [a.] Mercedes, TX

ZAPKO, MARY CLAIRE
[b.] January 25, 1952, Pittston, PA; [p.] Rose O'Brien; [m.] George Zapko; [ch.] Gina and Russell; [ed.] Pittstown Area, HS, H&R Block, WB VoTech Nursing, WB Computer Program; [occ.] Nurse; [memb.] Women of the Moose, St. Miachel's Church; [hon.] Perfect Attendance Nursing School, Award for Volunteer with Hospice St. John (Cancer); [oth. writ.] Chili Recipe published in Hospice, St. John's Cookbook.; [pers.] Life is what you make it. Never give up. There is always hope. Enjoy every day, tomorrow may be your last.; [a.] Pittston, PA

ZARELKA, JESSICA ANEZKA
[pen.] Anezka; [b.] August 21, 1981; [p.] John and Cheryl Zarelka; [ed.] Currently attending the Hockaday School of Dallas as a freshman; [occ.] Student; [memb.] Iliad press, the Wexford Poetry Society, The Poetry Society of Texas; [hon.] Consistant participant and winner in the Poetry Society of Texas for the past 4 years. Published work the Iliad press's the Wexford Poetry Society in the past year.; [oth. writ.] Your Love, I love the way the sky looked last night; [pers.] If you're going to walk on ice you might as well dance. The philosophy of one generation is the common sense of the next.; [a.] Frisco, TX

ZENGEL, JOHN JACOB
[b.] June 8, 1975, Flemington, NJ; [p.] John Zengel, Sandra Zengel; [ed.] Phillipsburg High, Bucknell University; [occ.] Chemical Engineering Research, Student; [memb.] American Institute of Chemical Engineers, Bucknell Jazz and Rock Ensemble; [hon.] Eagle Scout; [pers.] I write about my own feelings and thoughts from the heart in an attempt to reveal my shadowed creative side. Inspired by the love of Megan.; [a.] Phillipsburg, NJ

ZURAWSKI, KAREN D.
[pen.] Firehawk; [b.] February 2, 1953, Liberty, NY; [ed.] BA English Literature and Secondary Education, continuing education in Computer Sciences. Lifetime independent studies of philosophy and sociology; [occ.] Author, Artist, Philosopher; [oth. writ.] Poetry, articles and short stories for a variety of local journals spanning many years. Present projects included a collaborative book of prose, poetry art, a short book of philosophy and self-healing book.; [pers.] Life in all its forms is a many-faceted experience. My work illumines details of humanity and nature from my experience. I believe this sharing from every artist and every voice - helps us as a people to grow on old foundations new blooms and fresh fruit for the future.; [a.] Santa Fe, NM

INDEX
OF POETS

Index

Fitzmayer, Mandy 193
Flanagan, Dennis T. 317
Flanigan, James F. 258
Flax, Scott G. 466
Fleming, Bill 20
Fleming, Martin 81
Fleming, Sharon 350
Fletcher, Anthony 220
Fletcher, C. Theresa 406
Fletcher, Cheryl Ann 212
Fletcher, De 247
Fletcher, France 276
Flohr, Elizabeth 3
Fogt, L. L. 315
Foisy, Anna Marie 396
Fontan, Lysette 108
Forcum, Matt 23
Forczek, Kirsten E. 374
Ford, Shirley Ann 366
Forney, Gary 227
Fornis, Sarah R. 187
Fort, Rebekka 267
Forte, Denise 423
Fortin, Michelle 33
Foschini, Renee 476
Fossen, Sandra 9
Foster, Ashley 121
Foster, Burke 119
Foster, Frank 462
Foster, Joseph R. 20
Foster, Kathy 351
Foster, Kevin Dean 387
Foster, Louise 103
Foster, Rosie C. 236
Fowlkes, Susan 71
Fox, Carrie 227
Fox, Jocelyn L. 426
Fox, Mary 225
Frank, Michael C. 461
Frant, Dimitri 407
Frantz, Jeannette 164
Frazier, Nyata C. 400
Freel, Brian 247
Frees, Nancy J. 469
Freimuth, Linda 276
Freudig, Helen T. 31
Fritter, Paul R. 389
Fritts, Jerel 37
Fritz, Jessica 208
Fritz, Steven R. 129
Frix, Scarlett 248
Fronek, Roger Lee 42
Fuerte, Dr. Victor Haim L. 416
Funk, Robert 85
Furfaro, Novella C. 425
Fuss, Cindi M. 251

G

G., J. Jenny 249
Gabinski, Dennis 409
Gable, Eugene L. 361
Gadsden, Vertella S. 308
Gair, Kevin 385
Gale, Elizabeth 404
Gale, Everett Edwin 302
Galiatsatos, Sharon 122
Galindo, Maria E. 460
Galka, Irena 202
Gallaway, Dawn 287
Gallegos, Dave J. 89

Gallegos, Mark 383
Galo, Mary Ellen 467
Galvez, Romana 474
Gambill, Sharon B. 350
Gambrell, Beth J. 347
Gammill, Michael 132
Gancheff, D. 229
Ganley, Tom 48
Ganshert, Alan L. 54
Garbarini, Stephanie 25
Garcia, Julia P. 389
Garcia, Ricky A. 377
Gardner, Douglas 260
Gardner, Marian E. 278
Gardner, Susan Doleen 459
Gargano, George G. 469
Garibotto, Carlos 486
Garland, Jeremy C. 5
Garland, Megan 284
Garner, Sylvia 123
Garnham, Harry L. 366
Garrett, Florence L. 412
Garrett, Valerie A. 446
Garrity, Wendy L. 137
Garvey, Nichole 281
Gasca, Rose M. 70
Gaskin, Teresa 391
Gates, John R. 370
Gates, Natasha E. 181
Gates, Nettie 262
Gates, Tamara A. 69
Gatti, Mark Lazarus 238
Gaudet, Felicity 104
Gauthier, Janet L. 194
Gauthier, Todd 441
Gaydosh, Donna C. 363
Gayles-White, Lela 147
Gazarek, Maggie 222
Geanangel, Debbie 200
Gebhart, Jenna Dee 363
Gee, Amanda 365
Gee, Christel 224
Geertz, Dora 224
Geise, Carol Ann 303
Gelletly, Sarah 124
Gemienhardt, Olive 281
Gendreau, Elizabeth 179
Gensur, Christopher 291
Gentner, Art 343
George, Erin 366
Gerard, Rose E. 79
Gerber, Bonni 75
Gerke, Julie Anne 382
Gerkin, John G. 361
Germino, Thomas 498
Gess, Charlie E. 361
Gessing, Patricia 408
Ghattas, Christopher 133
Ghazzoul, Seandee M. 245
Giangiulio, Nancy DiMaio 68
Gibbs, Frederick W. P. 362
Gibel, Gladys M. 309
Gibson, Chrissy 278
Gibson, Opal 126
Giessman, Carrie L. 252
Gifford, Margaret R. 28
Gilbert, Josephine C. 106
Giles, Catrice 256
Gill, Allison Dawn 273
Gillette, Christopher D. 489
Gilliam, Jessica 201

Gilrane, Thomas R. 363
Girvin, Michael S. 102
Giuliani, Frances Beall 311
Glaser, Philip John 243
Glasgow, Karl E. IV 121
Glass, Alice C. 203
Glass, Robert J. 208
Glass, Ruth McMahon 393
Glaude, Annette 284
Glazewski, Nita L. 379
Glenn, Jim 443
Glessner, Stacy Rae 261
Glover, Jennifer 234
Goad, Robin James 241
Gobel, Shana Marie 327
Goddard, Pat 448
Goff, Daria 246
Goldsberry, Vickie L. 394
Golub, Barry 76
Gomez, Diane L. 224
Gonnerman, Kurt 49
Gonski, John 354
Gonzales, Lily K. 269
Gonzalez, Alex 170
Gonzalez, Alfredo J. 386
Gonzalez, Amelia 244
Gonzalez, Brant 79
Gonzalez, Gabrielle 31
Gonzalez, Gail A. 32
Gonzalez, Simeon 151
Gonzalez, Tamar 498
Good, Kevin W. 78
Goode, Nancy L. 357
Goodman, Angie 150
Goodman, Mary 355
Goodwin, Adam Russell 457
Goralski, Ronald J. 341
Gordillo, Felix, Jr. 445
Gordon, Miles 4
Gordy, Charlie L. 298
Gorman, Amber 228
Gornick, Ira 491
Gorski, Geralyn 455
Gortemoller, Elizabeth J. 452
Gosch, William Jerome Jr. 285
Gosselin, Danielle 17
Gotsch, John Michael 244
Gould, Nathan 112
Goulet, Margaret 9
Graalfs, Jefferson 287
Gracey, Eirene 246
Grader, Jan 1951-1994 397
Graf, Christopher 44
Gragg, Jeffrey P. 257
Graham, Timothy H. 276
Graliker, Mary 13
Granati, Jacqueline 449
Grant, Jamilah A. 299
Grantham, Hannelore 11
Graves, Hazel 497
Graves, Jane 473
Gray, Brad 375
Gray, Deanna 95
Gray, Helen 168
Gray, Paula B. 150
Gray, Stephen H. 36
Gray, Terra 124
Grayson, Arzo Jr. 154
Graziosi, Toni 225
Green, Beatrice C. 428
Green, Bernetta 166

Green, Beryl 454
Green, James F. 266
Green, Lois J. 492
Green, Louis F. 54
Green, Louis Freeland 76
Green, R. 99
Green, Stacie 477
Greenan, Kathleen Meehan 454
Greenberg, Frank 98
Greene, Daniel 232
Greene, Fred 114
Greene, Laura 393
Greene, Marcy B. 37
Greenough, Lavina M. 150
Greenwald, Saul 426
Gregg, Bernice K. 26
Gregory, Allison 125
Gregory, Kimberly S. 452
Greiner, Kendra Leyn 319
Gremillion, Sadie C. 254
Griffin, Barbara K. 463
Griffin, Deanna 85
Griffin, Genevieve R. 469
Griffin, Marion E. 262
Griffin, R. J. 257
Griffith, Greg E. 358
Griffith, Shirley 4
Griffiths, Lisa Marie 69
Griggs, Fred 189
Grigsby, Jeffery 100
Grimme Bunner, Susann R. 105
Grinley, Pamela 237
Groesbeck, John W. 223
Grogan, Calvin K. 230
Groh, LeAnna W. 96
Gross-Haley, Erma 211
Grosso, Edmond V. 337
Grover, Joseph Edward Jr. 126
Groves, Cheryl 259
Grunzke, Andrew Lawrence 206
Grzymkowski, Larry A. 243
Guidoux, Nita 129
Guillermo, J. Cap 204
Gulin, Iain 388
Gulmette, Marie L. 277
Gunter, Danita 6
Guntes, Mamie 15
Guthrie, Scott J. 208
Gutierrez, Pedro 70
Gutierrez, Vera E. 198
Guyer, Ruth C. 469
Gwaltney, Dealia 80

H

Haack, Meyel H. 384
Haapala, Mark 233
Haarmann, Landry 220
Hachman, Leah R. 454
Hager, Christopher 454
Haggerty, LaRee 288
Haggerty, Mark W. 403
Hagopian, Gloria 27
Haight, Brad 241
Halden, Lisa Dawn 424
Hale, Brenda Kay 287
Hale, Dana L. 456
Hall, Audrey A. 493
Hall, Constance 489
Hall, Gabriela 451
Hall, Gary 280

Sustarich, Michelle 344
Sutton, Ozo A. 112
Swan, Everret H. 298
Swanier, Anna P. 134
Swansey, Louise Magill 432
Swatling, Carol-Ann 373
Sweat, Rebecca 466
Sweeney, Donna M. 421
Sweigart, Jean R. 8
Sweitzer, Dorothy I. 106
Swies, Angel 358
Swinbank, Hannah 376
Syed, Adnan Hafeez 143
Sykes, Patricia S. 432
Szabo, Eva 324
Szczerbowski, Brian G. 504

T

Tabb, Leonard 144
Taber, Jennifer L. 12
Tadsen, Kim 479
Tafe, Jennifer L. 126
Taffee, June 226
Taladay, Stacy 79
Talas, Ronnie 496
Tallman, Evelyn T. 332
Tallman, Miki 132
Tarin, Carolyn 204
Tassi, John Jr. 225
Taubenberger, Susanna G. 450
Taufer, Jed R 348
Tay, Amy 484
Taylor, Candas 353
Taylor, Judy L. 393
Taylor, Julia T. 353
Taylor, Leslie G. 422
Taylor, Lora 262
Taylor, Maureen 410
Taylor, Norma S. 120
Taylor, Sheryl R. 433
Taylor, Susan 220
Teaford, Becky 385
Tejeda, Maria 238
Tenedine, Carolyn 9
Tenney, Nicole M. 297
Terrebonne, Holly B. 172
Terry, Anglecia 295
Terwilliger, Charlotte 15
Tesch, Jack 294
Testa, Sophie 351
Tetrault, Martin 220
Tetro, Harold M. 209
Thayer, Bruce 101
Thiele, Kathryn 433
Thielman, Dorothy E. 200
Thomas, Barbara M. 326
Thomas, Christina M. 210
Thomas, Curtis D. 213
Thomas, Daniel 304
Thomas, Effie Louise 226
Thomas, Gregory Owen 107
Thomas, Hillary 464
Thomas, Jarod 51
Thomas, Kathy 449
Thomas Mantenuti, Carol 13
Thomas, Rachel 44
Thomas, Rebecca D. 38
Thomason, Norman 206
Thompson, Alan R. 215
Thompson, Carol L. 59

Thompson, Cindy Lee 357
Thompson, Cliff C. 272
Thompson, Jared 21
Thompson, Matt DP 461
Thompson, Michael Corey 430
Thompson, Rebecca 434
Thompson, T. Don 257
Thompson, Teresa 353
Thompson, Theodore 277
Thompson, Timothy T. 77
Thompson, William D. 499
Thompson-Rodriques,
        Mary Ellen 334
Thorpe-Wamser, Denise 19
Thrash, Donna K. 49
Thrash, Steve 109
Throndsen, Amy 60
thrush, robbin 362
Tickle-Golden, Linda 140
Tiess, Timothy 494
Tillman, Nikkole J. 228
Timberlake, Amy 98
Tindle, Merletta Ann 76
Tinto, Wilma Jean 320
Titus, William L. 437
Tobelmann, Lisa M. 95
Toby, B. L. 359
Tolan, Meredith R. 85
Tolson, Frances E. 8
Tompkins, Holly 368
Tomsik, Sarah 229
Tonkovic, Denise L. 118
Tonnesen, Sonja 17
Torres, Cindy 121
Torry, R. 371
Tosado, Diana M. 45
Toulouse, Stephen James 91
Tousley, Leslie 434
Townsend, Beverly 8
Tozzi, Ezio M. 452
Tracey, Bridget M. 34
Tran, Christine 77
Tran, Nathan 291
Trap Hagan, Allan W. 297
Trapp, Charlotte A. 91
Traub, Amy 62
Travagline, Lawrence E. 400
Traver, Gregg W. 285
Travers, Reginald W. 301
Travers, William T. Jr. 147
Travisano, Richard 120
Trebilcox, Robert D. 222
Trendle, Mary 220
Trent, Anthony 81
Tringali, Linda 74
Trinh, Nga Tuyet 446
Triplitt, Lois Smith 444
Tripp, Lucille 57
Trogdon, Molly 128
Troop, Truman 434
Trotter, John R. IV 310
True, Jennifer 447
Truitt, Maurine I. 260
Truong, Lily 178
Tsai, Lenore 221
Tubman, Kris 367
Tucker, Quennie 313
Tucker, Sue R. 412
Tuffly, Bart 214
Turnbull, Joshua David 434
Turner, Cynthia L. 483

Turner, Erna Parpard 327
Turner, Jane 55
Turner, Jennifer 309
Turner, Tamara 377
Turner, Thomas Lee 149
Turrill, Wanda J. 28
Tuttle, Barbara 349
Tuttle, Lindsey 230
Tuttle, Regan 282
Twigg, Emmie 139
Twitchell, Margaret 126
Tyler, Daniel Swift 61
Tyler, Mike 45
Tyler, Nicole René 204
Tyson, Keshia 264

U

Ubelhor, Heather 489
Ullrich, F. Katherine 118
Ulrich, Rachel 273
Underhill, Robbin Taylor 353
Underwood, Jerome B. 230
Underwood, Rita K. 427
Unterreiner, Ronald J. 480
Uriegas, Julia A. 289

V

Valadez, Jazmenda 416
Valdon, Shari J. 91
Valencia, Celia Veronica 490
Valentine, David 387
Valentini, Debbie 314
Valentini, Sabrina 140
Valerio, Barbara 56
Valim, Sarah 423
Valko, Haley M. 214
Valladao, Maggie 65
Vallejo, Raul 155
Valora, Frank E. 297
Van Arsdale, Vicki L. 464
Van Cour, Alice Clemons 365
Van Creef, Frank 124
Van Heel, Kimberly 60
Van Pham, Tien 59
Van Rader, Joseph 202
Van Slyke, G. Edward Jr. 498
Van Valkenburgh, Ina 312
Van Williams, Alice 287
Vanbuskirk, Donna L. 414
Vance, Ethelmae 353
Vande Zande, Marie T. 150
Vanden Einde, Kris 210
Vander Wagen, Robert C. 353
VanTine, John E. 105
Vasquez, Elizabeth 408
Vasquez, Julio 294
Vaughan, Alisa 358
Vaughan, Virginia Davis 17
Vaughn, Helen E. 265
Vaughn-Harden, Katherine 280
Vaught, John 74
Vega, Norma 48
Vegter, Jocelyn 258
Velazquez, Liz 52
Velez, Fausto Art 219
Velis, Diana Lien 447
Vest, Kevin W. 342
Vetzel, Alfred L. Jr. 350
Vicaro, Tracy 78
Videlock, Seymour 241

Vilella, Jessica 24
Villegas, Leti 12
Villines, J. Everett 150
Vinski, Edward J. 200
Vinsonhaler, Jason D. 362
Vit, Ivano 148
Vitori, Jennifer 341
Vitrano, Andrea 202
Vivian, Paul 139
Viviano, Mark G. 403
Voegele, Amber Rose 257
Voelker, Ethel L. 163
Volak, April 235
Volodzko, David Josef 376
Von Shultz, Kurt 440
Vozel, Kara N. 116

W

Wadlow, Ricky G. 435
Wagner, Betty M. 247
Wagner, Doris W. 57
Wagner, Nonnie 422
Wagner, Tina Marie 435
Wagner, Wanda J. 252
Waide, Edwina 310
Wake, Ann Marie Frank 443
Wakefield, Lana 298
Wakeman, Georgia L. 273
Walden, Angela L. 237
Walden, C. T. 299
Waldrep, Amy 215
Waldrop, Donald R. 416
Waldrop, Sharon 58
Walencewicz, Pamela 326
Walenta, Nathan M. 50
Wales, Alexander H. 378
Walker, Christina 20
Walker, Frank 4
Walker, Jeanne 26
Walker, Tim 490
Walkush, Debra Angeline 292
Wall, John Duddy 25
Wallin, Kelli M. 435
Wallin, Richard L. 495
Walls, Rose 435
Walsh, Herb 157
Walsh, Phyllis N. 322
Walsh, Susan A. L. 435
Walter, Ethel K. 353
Walters, Dorman L. Jr. 21
Walters, Michelle 145
Walters, Shelly Dawn 42
Walther, Dawna 24
Walton, Jamie L. 143
Walton, Kathy D. 321
Walulak, Tina 289
Walz, Carina 401
Wander, Marguerite 505
Ward, Angelene 493
Ward, Gwenn 151
Ward McClement, Ruth 112
Ward, Richard J. 477
Ward, Sarah Collins 30
Ward, Susan Epps 155
Wardrup, David A. Jr. 52
Warfel, Joann S. 245
Wargo, Paul 245
Warn, L. Mila 370
Warner, Carolyn M. 155
Warren, Anne M. 322